NAKED AND
UNASHAMED

Bob,
May your financial life
continue to bloom & blossom
as you run your race with
patience.

Eureka Young

NAKED AND
UNASHAMED

Ten Money Conversations
Every Couple Must Have

Ericka Young

Publishing, composition, and design managed by Niche Pressworks

www.nichepressworks.com

ISBN Print: 978-1-946533-00-5
ISBN Digital: 978-1-946533-01-2

Praise For NAKED AND UNASHAMED

I have had the chance to witness firsthand what happens when a person grabs a hold of the sound financial principles that Ericka shares in Naked and Unashamed. She has helped so many people in our church get out of debt, save money, and live like no one else. In her book, Ericka has masterfully explained how our faith, fears and family history have affected the way we see money today. Having known Ericka for many years now, she doesn't just teach these principles, she has lived these principles. You can hear and feel her passion for seeing people walk in real financial freedom all throughout her book! This is definitely a must read and a keeper for your personal library.

> Sean Moore, Senior Pastor, Faith Christian Center,
> Phoenix, Arizona

Naked and Unashamed changes everything when it comes to money conversations in marriage. As a licensed counselor, I've seen countless couples struggle to tackle financial challenges. But this book makes it easy, providing a step-by-step guide to help couples take the masks off and create the financial future they desire. If you're married, do yourself a favor and read every page of this book.

> Nicole Elam, Couples Coach and Founder of
> www.BadtoBetterGoodtoGreat.com

As I was reading *Naked and Unashamed* I thought to myself: This book needs to be mandatory reading for all couples going through premarital counseling.

v

Following the advice Ericka gives in the book will ensure that couples have a solid financial footing as they begin their lives together as husband and wife and will save them from heartache, disappointment and financial stress. It will also help couples who have already encountered financial problems to communicate openly, address their issues and get into a more secure financial position. I highly recommend *Naked and Unashamed*.

Rosie Brock, Author of *Hope Infusion: The Stabilizing Force in an Unstable World*

Early on in marriage you realize a big part of marriage is learning how to communicate. *Naked and Unashamed* is the book I wish I had in the early years when I struggled to understand and express my money fears. The 10 conversations in this book would have helped us get on the same page much sooner and possibly avoid some of the many mistakes we made along the way.

Kendra Tillman, Event Host and Author of *You Are Stronger Than You Think: Lessons of Endurance in the Race of Faith*

Dedication

To my husband, Chris, who has made the ups and downs of creating a life we truly love worth it.

To our daughters, Faith and Olivia. You are the reason we have embarked upon this journey of financial freedom. Your presence has given us the purpose and passion to accomplish far more financially, than we ever thought possible. May you both experience the prosperity God desires for you as well.

Acknowledgements

Birthing a book is no small endeavor. It literally took an army of people to finally gets this book in your hands. As a result, there are many people to thank.

First of all, without my Lord and Savior Jesus Christ, there would be no story to tell. Thank you for setting me free of all bondage and giving me the courage to share my journey with others, so we can all experience the life you desire us to live.

Thanks to my amazing husband, Chris. You've been so patient, encouraging, and understanding during this season. It wasn't easy but it was worth it. I'm so glad we get to create a financial future we can enjoy together. I love you!

Thank you Nicole Gebhardt and Crystal Yeagy, for helping me get this project finished. This book would never have gotten to print or be something people want to read, without you both!

Thanks to all the people who helped me edit, rework, and eventually complete this work – Christine Simmons, Elisha Martin, Holly Kile, Rosie Brock, and Nicole Elam, and Emily Schmitz.

Kendra, you've been my biggest cheerleader throughout my entire business journey. Without you, I know for certain, I would not have gone into business. Thank you for believing in me and making sure I didn't quit.

Table of Contents

Introduction

Imagine a life where you and your spouse are on the same page financially. You have dreams and goals that you are reaching every year, and you get to enjoy the journey along the way. That's what we expected when we said, "I do," right?

What you may not realize is that your past relationship with money has affected your present situation. And, your present habits with money are determining your future. Most of the time, we're not even aware that this is going on. So many people end up at the age of sixty-five, thinking about retiring, but have no funds because they didn't make a plan ahead of time. Your story doesn't have to end this way.

Naked and Unashamed is all about coming clean financially, so you can create the future you desire together, as a couple. Think about this: on average, we get married before we turn thirty, most of us retire around sixty-six, and, you can expect to live to be about eighty years old. This means that you will spend fifty years with your spouse, and nearly twenty-five of those years will be in retirement. That is way too many years to suffer from debt, financial stress or tension, and still not have accumulated any money.

It is very possible you have tried all kinds of things to fix your financial mess. Budgets seem to be the one thing everyone runs to when trying to make their finances work. Every financial professional (myself included) will tell you to create a written game plan, and, yes, that normally includes a budget. However, if a budget was all you needed to get and stay out of debt, then everyone would have one, and you would see financially successful people all over the place. Here's the deal...

1

The budget will only work, if you work the budget.

Most people don't work the budget. They don't revisit it regularly to implement what it says. In addition to that, the budget is simply one tool. Granted, it is a tool I love because I'm a nerd with spreadsheets, but nonetheless, the budget doesn't tell the entire story. It's one tool of several that you will need. But what's the real reason you aren't making financial progress? This book will show you that there is more involved in your financial picture, than you've been led to believe.

When you said "I Do!", you committed to a lot of things, like staying "for richer or poorer". Many brides and grooms don't really believe they will ever have to endure the latter, yet "richer" doesn't just happen. We can get so caught up in the moment and details of the wedding, that we don't stop to think about the actual marriage. It takes work, discipline, and unity in a relationship to reach your financial goals. As you conquer these goals, you get closer and grow stronger as a team. If you follow the principles described in this book, you will be well on your way to having the financial future you both desire, and that you imagined on your wedding day.

In the Beginning

"I'm not good with numbers."

"If I just made more money, I could get my finances in order."

"I don't have enough time."

Well-meaning couples, families and individuals have shared these sentiments time and again in my coaching practice. Let's face it, it's easy to justify not handling money prudently. Believe me, I've done it too! We tend to sweep things under the rug and believe that love will conquer all.

Love can't conquer misbehavior with money and it sure won't pay the bills.

Yes, sometimes life is hard. We do have emergency situations that cause drama in our financial life. Nothing and no one is perfect. However, the above statements are the excuses that wage war against our ability to succeed with money.

I wish there was a magic wand to make your finances work out, in an instant. While I don't have a magic wand, you do. Your magic wand is disguised as a thing called work. Any financially successful person will tell you that it takes diligence, patience, and a lot of hard work to create the financial picture you desire. They'll also tell you, it's worth it.

In order to find true healing in our financial lives, we must take a look at what God initially intended for us to have in our relationships and, subsequently, with our money. Going back to the very beginning brings perspective.

Therefore a man shall leave his father and mother and be joined to his wife, and they shall become one flesh. And they were both naked, the man and his wife, and were not ashamed. - Genesis 2:24, 25 NKJV

Adam needed companionship. Therefore, God created a woman to meet that need for a partner. She was his perfect help, friend and partner. When they were introduced, they were *Naked and Unashamed.*

Think about this in terms of today's environment. We have so many life experiences that prevent us from truly being naked and unashamed with our partner, especially with money. Being naked requires that we reveal our flaws, which takes courage, trust, and vulnerability. We have made mistakes in the past, which we bring into our current relationship. We have our own dysfunctional upbringings that cause our world view to be distorted. And because we work so hard in our careers to produce this money, we can be protective, selfish, and independent when it comes to sharing this piece of our lives.

My goal with this book is to recover what has been lost. God created us to be naked and unashamed with our partner in all areas of our lives – including money. He wants us to see each other for who we really are, without hidden agendas, smoke screens, or loads of baggage. When we shed the layers that are holding us back, we create an interdependence with one another. It's time we are finally able to say we're one with our spouses in our money.

Dream Again

When was the last time you allowed yourself to dream about a future that wasn't limited by debt? When we're suffocating with the worry and stress that debt brings, dreams are one of the first casualties.

I have dreams of vacationing around the world. I want to set my feet on every continent and experience for myself the way other cultures live.

I can imagine spending weeks in different places around the globe before I take my last breath. And I want to share all of that with my husband, Chris. We love to travel. We want the freedom to do that without financial worries. Taking our family around the world, whenever we want, sounds like freedom to me.

What are your dreams for you and your family? What would a lifestyle without financial challenges look like for you?

Obviously, the kind of lifestyle I described takes money, time and good health. The kind of traveling I enjoy, requires me to be healthy and strong enough to climb mountains, ride horses, and zip line without fear of dying from exhaustion, or having a heart attack. I also don't want to wait until I'm in my "golden years" to travel the world. This is my motivation for living financially free. Take a moment to ponder your motivation for living a financially free life, and what that could look like.

Do you want to live on the mission field without worrying about financial support?

Can you imagine having the ability to take care of aging parents or a child with a disability?

Do you have a desire to start your own business?

Is it in your heart to give to charitable organizations, or community work, etc.?

When you're strapped with debt, overcome with payments and suffocating from working so hard, you can't even think about this kind of freedom. Your time, effort, and energy all go towards paying the bills, raising a family, or simply just surviving. You can break this cycle.

It is this passion for debt-freedom that stirred up my desire to help others. I started Tailor-Made Budgets, my budget coaching firm, in 2005, with a simple mission of giving dreams a place to flourish. In nearly twelve years, I have personally worked with over 300 families in getting them free of financial bondage, and paying off over $2.5 million in debt!!

I learned from personal experience, and have seen it time and time again with the families I've helped, that once you are free of payments, you can literally do anything with your income.

Let's Be Naked and Unashamed!

In *Naked and Unashamed*, we will discuss many topics that will help a struggling marriage. However, it is not designed to take the place of professional help.

I am not a marriage counselor, nor do I profess to have all the relationship answers you may need. If you have marital issues that go beyond the scope of money, I highly encourage you to seek professional advice, from a trained marriage counselor. Financial issues can show up in many ways. You can have a breakdown of trust, lack of leadership or vision, mismanagement of funds, chronic overspending, etc. All of these things can stem from deeper issues or cause them to show up.

Throughout this book I will reference the "Team Couple". A healthy married couple is one that is a good team. You balance each other out and complement each other well. Where one partner is weak, the other might be strong. Nope, they aren't perfect, but they are working (or at least willing to work) together, and that's the key. The Team Couple will greatly benefit from taking their finances more seriously and creating a game plan that works.

In *Naked and Unashamed,* we will discover how your money past is affecting your money present and your money future.

It's time to shed light on your current state of financial affairs so you can wake up and do something about it.

You need a road map to create the kind of future you desire and deserve.

According to a survey conducted by credit scoring company, Fair Isaac & Company or FICO, financial responsibility beats out sex in sustaining a marriage relationship. As a matter of fact, respondents to this survey said financial responsibility was twice as important as sexual compatibility!

Maybe this information is just what you need to get your spouse on board with the household finances. Take the pen, paper, and calculator to the bedroom and see if these two areas jump up on your list of important things in a satisfying marriage!

Decide today that the two of you will form a team in the area of finances. After all, you plan to live together forever! Sit down and talk money immediately. This book will help you do just that. Discuss how certain behaviors make you feel, and listen attentively to each other. You may not work everything out in one session, but keep the dialogue open and improvements will come.

At the very least, decide on one thing you will agree to work on where your finances are concerned. Give it time, and see what your teamwork will do in that one area.

Look at your marriage as a dynamic team, embarking on a journey in life that no one else can take. It was designed specifically for just the two of you.

Keep God at the Center

Let me establish something up front: I'm a believer. The way in which I see life, includes pursuing God's purpose for it. Therefore, this book is biblically based. You will see scripture and biblical principles throughout. By no means am I a trained minister; but what God has shared with me, I am sharing with you.

If you keep God at the center of your relationship, and look to Him for wisdom and direction as you communicate about money, this entire process will go much smoother. His ways are perfect and will produce the best results. As you read, slow down enough to listen for His leading. Pray over your next moves, both alone and together as a Team Couple. Then, give Him praise and glory when your financial life is a beautiful picture to behold.

Keep in mind that just because you invite God in, doesn't guarantee everything will magically fall into line, and work out. However, He made and created you both. He knows you intimately, and wants you to know each other intimately as well. God knows what's best for your relationship and, when you pray, it changes you. Developing a heart for God's desires comes from prayer, spending time in God's Word and ultimately, making decisions that He will be pleased with.

Get the Most From This Book

Naked and Unashamed has three sections. In the first section, you will find clarity regarding your financial foundations. You will dive in and explore your past experiences with money. This begins with your childhood and progresses to where you are today. Unraveling your upbringing, messaging, and previous financial decisions will shed light on how and why, you operate the way you do now.

The goal is for you to see clearly how your money past is affecting you today. Sharing this clarity will also help your spouse understand you in a deeper and more connected way.

The second section helps you get clear about where you are financially, at this point. This is the most challenging part but, you must face where you are today, in order to create the future you desire. We are developing a road map to your best future, and you must locate yourself, so you can begin appropriately.

In this section, you will experience a financial reality check. This is best done individually, and then shared with your spouse. There is no judgement, only information. Together, you will develop a plan to get out of any financial quicksand, and move closer to your dream future.

The third, and final section allows you to dream again. As children we were sure that we could do and be anything we wanted. It seems that somewhere between dancing in ballet slippers and wearing firemen hats we "woke up."

Our lofty visions of fun careers, lots of money, and no worries got interrupted with reality. We had to begin paying the bills, taking care of kids, and pleasing the boss. When the day-to-day life took over, we stopped dreaming about our future. We began to doubt our ability to succeed financially, and simply stopped trying. Treading water is not where any of us wants to be; it is time to awaken your dreams again.

Your best financial future is calling for you to take action today.

It is possible to enjoy life today, and also be financially secure when you reach retirement.

Get to Talking

This book is designed to get you talking. Lifestyle website YourTango.com polled 100 mental health professionals, and discovered that 65% of couples cited communication breakdown as the leading cause for divorce. You must have a discussion - especially about your finances.

In this book you will have ten money conversations. You can read them in order, or pick one conversation at a time to focus on. Make time now, and consider this an investment in the future of your relationship.

You may need to get a sitter for the kids, meet somewhere outside the home, or it might even take getting away for the weekend.

I highly recommend lots of chocolate, music, candles, etc., to set a relaxing stage for communication. Whatever it takes to have focused time, effort, and energy, do it.

"Till death do us part" doesn't just happen on its own- you have to work for it. These are the conversations that will help you work through the financial aspects of a functional, healthy relationship.

If your spouse is reluctant, find out where the hesitation is coming from. Finances are very personal. There are a lot of emotions such as guilt, shame, and embarrassment that cause us to hide or retreat. These emotions are real, but they don't have to hold you back from having the kind of relationship you want: one that takes you from where you are now financially, to where you really want to be.

Sometimes, taking positive action or one step forward, towards progress is all that's needed. Make sure to clear the air with your spouse first. Discuss why gaining control over your finances is important to you, and gently lead the conversation to healing. Create a safe place for your spouse to share his/her feelings. Let your spouse know that you are committed to being a team with money.

Every "Naked Conversation" will have "Get Real" questions for you to privately answer yourself. You may want to journal your responses or take some personal reflection time to gain your own clarity. There is no reason to hide.

If you can't be real with yourself, you definitely can't be real with your spouse.

There are also "Get Naked" questions that you answer with your spouse. Allow yourselves to be vulnerable. Take the masks off and share your hearts with each other. You've each made the choice to spend the rest of your lives together, now it's time to bare it all and allow each other into the deepest parts of your heart. This may feel uncomfortable at first, but it takes time for financial intimacy to develop. Getting naked during these conversations might be fun but it may distract you, so keep your clothes on, and save that for later!

Now you have a choice to make. You can continue down the path of debt, mismanagement, and lack of good communication with your spouse, or you can take the challenge this book offers.

Get talking, get into action and subsequently get free of financial bondage. You can be on the same page with your spouse. You can also experience the comfort and security of a partnership that produces financial fruit.

It is possible to finally exhale, because you know that everything is going to be ok. This book will show you how to cultivate the "I Do!" you desire today, and create the picture you envisioned on your wedding day.

Are you ready?

Section 1: Your Money Past

"Those unable to catalog the past are doomed to repeat it."
Lemony Snicket, The End

We must uncover, deal with, and catalog our past money connections. This helps us to understand why we do what we do today. It also gives us the freedom to release the past and move forward, unchained.

"Many of the things I shared with you, I've never even spoken out loud about to anyone (such as some of the past experiences and how it formed my behaviors toward life and money). I felt intense anxiety for a very long time, about whether or not I would be able to achieve most of my important financial goals. These feelings began to subside and fade away little-by-little, during the course of our call. Now I feel as though I would like to totally take the reins and dig into it as fully and completely as possible."

— Christy

Naked Conversation 1:
Uncover and Make Peace With Your Money Past

Just take it off! Don't you feel so much more relaxed and comfortable without clothes on? It is freeing to let go of skinny jeans, ties, cumbersome belts, and itchy bras. When you get that private moment to just shed everything, you relax in places you didn't know were pent up and, you get some fresh air and cool off. This is the time to let it all hang out, no one will judge you, no one is looking. You get to be free.

Getting naked with your money will require you to shed the extra clothing that you hide behind. We make ourselves look good with great clothes, new rides, and professional jobs. Meanwhile, we hide behind the truth of who we really are. If we're being honest, the truth is ugly. Our past isn't always a pretty sight. Maybe you need to face a few unpleasant times in your life. At some point, we've all wished that *Groundhog Day* would give us a do over for real.

I'm going to ask you to be courageous here; let go of the armor that hides imperfections, and just be your true self. Then accept these imperfections so they don't continue to cause shame, guilt and remorse. You are capable of taking this important step, and you are ready.

Take a look at your past childhood experiences with money, so you can uncover what lies beneath the surface – the good, the bad, and the ugly.

Whether you know it or not, you are a product of your money past. You make decisions today, based on what happened in the past. Your fears around money are rooted in what you witnessed as a child. Even the tiniest fragment of a conversation from many years ago, can shape how we think, feel, and ultimately, the actions we take.

It's time to go deeper, gain clarity, and break free of any chains that hold you back. You don't have to be a prisoner of your past any longer. Once you understand the money beliefs that are holding you back, you can proactively make changes today that will affect your money future.

Here's my story...

Single Mom on a Mission

My mom was a busy professional, and from my childlike perspective she seemed to make a good living. She valued education and earned both her bachelor's and master's degrees. She was a very committed and respected state employee and counselor for forty years. During all of this, my mom raised me and my sister by herself. She was truly a rock star. My sister and I didn't want for anything. We lived in the suburbs and went to good schools, took dance classes, played instruments, and I was a cheerleader for all four years of high school. None of that was cheap! Paying for it all couldn't have been easy for her.

I remember when she paid the bills, and how much stress it caused her to balance the checkbook. Sometimes she would say, "Wait until payday," when I asked for something. I honestly wished there was something I could do to take the stress away. Sometimes, I'd cook and clean (unasked!) to compensate. I did well in school and tried to make sure she had no reason to stress about anything else. In truth, I was scared that we wouldn't have enough. As a result, today I over analyze the numbers to make sure there is always enough. But, I've had to learn to trust God with money matters too, because life doesn't always fit in my tidy, little spreadsheet.

Sadly, I do remember how I treated my mother when I didn't get what I wanted all the time. (Yes, sometimes I was a brat!) From my mom, I learned that hard work and sacrifice produce fruit. Now, I think about the sacrifices she had to make, and how challenging those days must have been for her, and I am so grateful for my mother and the example she set.

These experiences have shaped who I am today. Because we didn't want our kids to struggle with money and debt, my husband and I determined that we would change our family tree. I have changed my career path to become a financial coach, and help others get free of debt so they can live life on their terms. Proactive money management is now both my professional mission, and personal passion.

Grandpa Had the Cash!

It can be easy to focus on the challenging parts of our lives and not see the good that we've experienced. As you reflect on your own past experiences don't miss the lessons that have had a positive impact on you as well.

My grandfather was an assistant pastor of Second Baptist Church in Detroit for many years. Looking back, I don't believe he made lots of money, but as a child, I thought he was rich. I admired him because he always had cash.

One day, my mom's car died and we needed a reliable source of transportation so, my grandfather took us to a car dealership. When my mom decided what she wanted and the car salesman shared the price, my grandfather pulled out $6,000 in cash! I couldn't believe he had that much money! He lived simply, dressed in suits and a hat every day, but he had a generous heart.

Today, when I use cash it makes me feel secure, in control, and able to be a blessing, just like Grandpa. Cash in hand is finite, and I learned that lesson early on. My husband and I live our lives with cash, and no debt. Thanks, in part, to the example from my Grandpa.

Watch Your Mouth!

The lessons we learn growing up don't only include what we see, but also the things we hear.

Have you ever heard your mother say, "Watch your mouth?" We all have, and we knew that what had come out was not something that she wanted to hear. Sometimes, the roles are reversed. Our parents, and other influential people in our lives, can make or break us with words. They have a lasting impact that we may not notice at the moment. Think about the following phrases. Have you heard them? Or, said them yourself?

"Wait until payday."

"We can't afford it."

"Money doesn't grow on trees."

"I don't make enough money."

"I'm broke."

We've all heard those statements. Maybe we've even said those things. At the time, we probably didn't understand the damaging effects of negative messaging. But words are powerful, they can even change what we feel we are capable of doing.

I've worked with countless clients who come into my office and talk about their past relationships with money. They've told me all the reasons why they're in their present financial state. Then I ask them what they heard from their parents as they were growing up. Every single time, I can link a negative money statement to a behavior that my clients now have.

If you were told to wait until payday, you may have gotten used to paycheck to paycheck living as an adult. If your parents felt like they never made enough money, you may believe that you will never make enough either. These beliefs can ultimately hinder your earning potential. All of the messages we received as children, stay with us throughout our entire lives. It takes a lot of work and some reprogramming, to begin believing something different.

Say It Again

If we are going to highlight the problem, let's create a solution. Not only do you need to understand what you currently say, you also need to change it to something that is empowering.

If you say something over and over again, it takes on a life of its own and you begin to believe it. Others hear it and get on the bandwagon with you too.

Here are a few ways we can alter our words to make a more powerful and encouraging statement:

"Wait until payday…" becomes "Let's put that in the next budget."

"We can't afford it," becomes "That is not a high priority right now."

"I don't have the money," turns into "Maybe not today, but one day…"

"Money doesn't grow on trees," can be "There is enough money to go around and I'm earning more and more each day."

"I don't make enough money," becomes "I have all the money I need."

"I'm broke," could be "My present financial state is improving day by day."

If some of the above statements resonate with you, fantastic. If not, take some time and find mantras that really speak to you. Think about what you want to see in your future and begin to say it out loud. Then say it over and over again. One of our mantras was "We are changing our family tree." It was easy to remember and could be applied to different areas of our life, including our finances. It gave us a purpose for getting out of debt, saving money, and managing our money so that our family tree was truly impacted.

Learn, Forgive, and Let Go

Take some time to reflect on your life with money including both the good and bad experiences. Identify critical moments that changed the way you thought about money, and how they have affected your choices and responses today. Get clear about how God is involved, and how He has spoken to your heart about what is possible. This is your motivation. It fuels your determination and, subsequently drives you to action.

The past is a great teacher if we allow it to be. We can learn from the not so great teachers and the great ones, alike. You can quickly identify the unhealthy habits and messages that were lived out in front of you and the ones that you can build upon. Give yourself the opportunity to distinguish these and respect the lessons to be learned. We can't change the past, but we can be free of any negative power it has had over our lives up to this point.

There are times when experiences with money have hurt us and caused us pain. As you ponder your past money memories, allow your heart to heal. Someone may have stolen from you. Perhaps, you grew up very poor, and blamed your parents. It is entirely possible that your past experiences around money have paralyzed you, and this conversation, even with yourself, is difficult.

Be kind and compassionate to one another, forgiving each other, just as in Christ God forgave you. - Ephesians 4:32 NIV

We are in need of God's forgiveness for all the things we've done wrong with money. Therefore, let us begin with forgiving others for their part in our past negative money experiences. Healing begins with you and it starts in your heart. For the most part, our parents, teachers, and influential adults have done the best they could in our development. Now it's your turn: you know better and now, you have the opportunity to do better.

Getting free of your past also involves letting go. You will never be able to erase the memories from your past, but you can let them go. Don't allow ties to unhealthy relationships to remain. Choose to do things differently from the negative examples you had. Make a commitment with yourself, your spouse, and God that you will learn, forgive, and then let go of the bondage that past money experiences have had on you.

Let go of the feelings that hold you back, and use these experiences to catapult you to new levels. Maybe, just maybe your money story is the reminder you needed to get to where you've always wanted to be. Use it for your purposes and pray that you are able to release any connections that keep you from financial success. Then you will be able to see the direction you need to go.

Get Real

Let's start by uncovering your personal money past. Review the following questions, and answer them thoughtfully. Get a journal and write down everything that comes to mind. Give yourself the opportunity to release all that you've held back before. You may want to talk it out verbally or record yourself and listen to what comes up. Either way, don't hold back. This is the time for reflection and healing, as you discover what has led you to who you are today with your money.

What were you taught about money?

As a child or young adult, what ideas did your parents and other influencers teach you about money? Think about the messages that surrounded money transactions, such as grocery or clothes shopping. Think about how purchases of all kinds were treated. Consider what you were taught about banking habits, if anything. Try to recall the messages that were shared with you about how you needed to "treat" money.

How did your parents behave with money?

We already know that our parents have great influence as to how we behave as adults. Sometimes, we grow up to be exactly like them, and sometimes, we're the exact opposite. Money influence is no different.

Did your parents have open conversations about money around you, or was it a "hush-hush" subject? Did you ever watch them or hear them talk about balancing the checkbook or paying the bills? Did your family have a budget, and did you know what that budget entailed? Did your parents spend freely, or were they extremely frugal? Did you have nice, brand new things or was the focus on finding used items, or items that could be repurposed?

What do you wish you knew as a child about managing money?

Have you ever thought, *I sure wish they had spent more time talking to me about balancing a checkbook?* Those types of thoughts come up often, as we experience financial struggles. Identifying those "I wish…" and "I wonder if…" thoughts can't change the past, but it can provide us insights on how we can shift for our future. What do you wish you knew as a child about managing money? Hindsight is always 20/20. Identifying these thoughts, can help you shift to thoughts like, *Because I didn't learn this as a child, I am now going to fill that gap as an adult.* You can create new conversations with your own children, even if your parents didn't have them with you.

Who did you admire, and why?

I always love asking this question because at first, many people wonder what this has to do with their money past. It's easy. As a child, your admiration is so pure. It's about seeing people that have things or possess qualities that you want.

It's important to see that the innocence of childhood doesn't recognize this as jealousy, but rather as a mechanism for learning about a different way of life that you want for yourself. If you saw the neighbor who always had a brand new car, and admired them for that, it's not that you were a jealous 9-year-old. It's simply that you recognized a lifestyle that you would like to have someday.

Part of this exercise is about recognizing the people you admired. But as you do so, I also want you to let go of any shame or guilt you feel (or felt) about that admiration. Getting clear about why you admired these people, will give understanding to your actions today.

What is the most challenging financial experience you have faced?

Every successful person has had financial challenges, so it's a very normal occurrence. While it may be painful to discuss for some of us, if we truly want to create a stress-free and debt-free financial future, we have to acknowledge our past challenges.

First, we need to acknowledge them so that we learn what got us there. Then, we need to acknowledge that they are in the past. These challenges are over, and we don't have to revisit them again as long as we make the right choices. Describe the situation in detail and how you felt. Begin to link these experiences to your beliefs and behaviors now.

Get Naked

And they overcame him by the blood of the Lamb, and by the word of their testimony; and they loved not their lives unto the death. - Revelations 12:11 KJV

There is freedom in sharing your story; not only for you, but for those you share it with. Dysfunctional money dynamics are present in every family, and affect you to this day. You may have witnessed theft, eviction, layoffs, simple mismanagement of funds or some other form of financial challenges. Whatever was present for you then, affects how you behave with money today.

If your spouse has an understanding of your money past, it will help them to be sensitive to your needs. Sit down and have a conversation with your spouse, your children, or whomever is in your life that needs to be aware of your past challenges.

Review the Get Real questions and determine what your loved one needs to know. Communicate that this is a safe space – there is no judgement or condemnation, only information. You need to be heard and understood. These are your ground rules.

It is important for you to release this information with someone who cares about you and/or who is affected by the choices you have made financially. Don't allow this information to remain a secret. Think of this exercise as the catalyst to your freedom and an opportunity to help others get free too.

Naked Conversation 2
Grow Up Financially and Understand Your Money Story

Potty training stinks! I remember potty training my oldest daughter, Faith. I thought I was going to lose it! I mean, she really gave me a run for my money. She would pee in the toilet only when she wanted to, take off her undies at any given time, laugh when it was time to go and soil her beautiful dress instead. I'm not the only parent who has experienced this, right? Potty training is not for the faint of heart. You must be mentally ready, but also willing to let your kids go at their own pace.

Eventually, my daughter got the hang of it. I could tell her that it was time to put her "big girl pants" on, and put the training pants away. This is the first big accomplishment in a toddler's young life. They are excited and you are nervous. What if she has an accident? What if she forgets? What will people say if her pants are wet? No one can make them do it. They actually have to want to go potty themselves for any of this to work. The same is true of adults – we have to put on our "big girl (or big boy) pants"…

Our parents have trained and molded us. But when we leave the house, go to college, and get a job, everything falls on our shoulders. We will make a mess of some things but, it is up to us to truly put on our big girl (or big boy) pants and take on the responsibility we are now ready for.

Lots of things can change when you grow up, get a job, and live on your own. For some reason, society expects us to have it all together right out of college.

The holy grail is to graduate college and get a job - as if simply making money is good enough.

Once you have a good job, then you should be able to have a nice car, a nice home, and quit asking mom and dad for money. The unfortunate truth is that this scenario is rare. Student loans, high unemployment, less than expected salaries, and lack of financial education, turn these expectations on their side. It is time to explore the next phase of your money past.

No Place To Hide

Do not judge others, and you will not be judged. For you will be treated as you treat others. The standard you use in judging is the standard by which you will be judged. And why worry about the speck in your friend's eye when you have a log in your own. – Matthew 7:1-3 NLT

Sometimes that verse is challenging to live out every day. It is even more challenging to stop yourself from the temptation of judging others. Chris and I learned early on in our relationship, what "no judgement" really meant.

In pre-marital counseling, we were told to pull our individual credit reports and bring them to the next meeting. I thought we were going to look at them and discuss what was there together. Instead, the minister took the credit reports and handed mine to Chris and Chris' to me. He allowed us to decide if we would look at the reports together, or separately. Either way, I was shocked, scared, and I really felt naked.

Chris was going to know what I did right, and wrong with money, before he came into my life. I was concerned he would have second thoughts about our future together. Seriously! What would he think of me? It made me feel vulnerable. And, yes, I was ashamed! There were late payments, a charge off, and lots of debt on my credit report. That was not something I wanted to share. Actually, at the time, I wished the minister had a magic wand that would make it all go away!

Then I thought, *I have his credit report in my hand. Whoa!* I began to think, *What if he has something less than stellar on his report? How much debt did he have? What if his credit score was less than mine?* All of these thoughts rolled through my head. It was nerve-wracking. The good news is that when I looked up at Chris, he appeared to feel the same way I did. We were both in shock; our nakedness revealed.

I went home as fast as I could, sat in a quiet spot, and opened Chris' credit report. It showed where he lived in the past, his current credit accounts, how often he was late, and when he last applied for credit. It honestly felt better to sit alone and read his credit report, so I could process everything.

Sharing credit reports brings up lots of good discussion. I had more questions than answers when we finally talked about it. I wanted to know more. The funny part about this exercise was that our credit reports mirrored each other's pretty well. We had similar student loan debt, the same amount of credit cards, and not many late payments on them. I had one derogatory entry on mine that needed explanation, and of course, I told him the truth even though it was painful.

It felt like I was in confession, but when our conversation was over, I felt clean and free. Now he knows, there is no place to hide and, we can work through this together.

Starting Out Together

When Chris and I got married, we moved to Arizona. God led us the entire way. I had a very good job opportunity, and we had family as well as a church home there. It seemed like the perfect way to start our relationship. Perfect except that we didn't have any money! Our friends and family gave us money and gift cards at our wedding, but that didn't last very long. It was a month before I started my job and another month before Chris started his. Needless to say, things were tight.

For two months we lived very simply. We didn't have much furniture, we actually sat on the floor on pillows made by my gracious great-aunt, and watched TV until we could, over time, buy a couch and settle in.

After we'd been in Arizona for six months, my mother and sister came to visit. We had a great time showing them around town and giving them a taste of our new world. The last day they were with us, however, was strange. It was time to take them to the airport and I wasn't feeling up to it. As a matter of fact, I was "sick as a dog." We said our goodbyes and Chris took them to the airport.

After a few days of vomiting, I went to the doctor. When asked if I had a taken a pregnancy test, I laughed. Hysterically, actually. *How could I be pregnant?* I took the pill every day. Well, I think I did, anyway. I went home and took a pregnancy test. Twice. And fell on the floor in tears.

Yes, I was pregnant! *What in the world?* We could barely take care of ourselves, let alone someone else! This was crazy! Thank God for my good man, he said "We are going to be good parents." That is not what I wanted to hear, but I will never forget those words. I wanted this to be a joke or to wake up from a bad dream. *Somebody, help me!*

Consider this our wake up call. We knew our finances weren't perfect and we had limited funds to handle it, but with a child on the way, we had to get our act together. Thankfully, God provided everything we needed. We had a baby shower, and though we had only been in Arizona for fourteen months, we didn't have to pay for any baby items. All our friends and family made sure we had everything we needed.

When our beautiful baby girl was born, we had finally settled into the idea of parenthood. Of course, that didn't mean we knew what we were doing, but we accepted it. And for the most part, while I was on maternity leave, there were no financial issues. However, the "crap hit the fan" when our car died. Think about this: we had a brand new baby, a new home 2000 miles away from our parents, our savings account had very little in it, and our checking account had only the money we needed to pay bills and eat, while I was on maternity leave. We did not have the money to resurrect this car.

So, what do you do when you can't fix your car but you need transportation? You buy another car, of course! Surely a newer car for $18,000 is better than a paid for car that needed $1,000 in repairs. But that is what you do when you have no solid financial foundation and no money: you go into debt. Our options were limited and we were scared, broke, and full of post-partum emotions. Sadly, this is normal for so many people.

Dave Ramsey literally saved our life. Chris heard him on the radio and instantly became a fan. He came home and told me all about his plan. I was receptive, although reluctant. Chris took my credit cards away from me. It's funny how an engineer with no money has lunch with co-workers and it goes on the credit card. Chris put a stop to that. We got on a budget and decided that we were going to change our family tree together.

We added up all our debt, which amounted to $80,000 at that time, and we shut down all extra spending. This journey wasn't easy. We had many bumps in the road like job loss, deaths in the family and, of course, another baby. But, we were determined to get and stay out of debt so we could give our kids a better start than we had.

Share Your Story

Our experiences shape the way we see life and create a personal story. No one else will fully understand why I do what I do because they haven't lived my story. It's up to me to be exactly who God created me to be, and to give others the space to understand me better. You have that same opportunity. Mutual understanding will reduce conflict, help you gain awareness, and garner respect.

When you are married, baring it all makes you one. Taking all the layers off and getting naked allows you to share the most vulnerable parts of yourself. Only your spouse sees this side of you and, you need the same intimacy with your finances. There are many financial conversations that you will never have with anyone other than your spouse.

You may need to write out your story like I did, and share it or allow your spouse to read it. Sometimes, it's easier to write the words than to say them out loud. Allow the clarity and openness to happen organically.

Give yourselves enough time to actively listen and respond. You don't want to be rushed during this time. It may be good to schedule the time so you aren't distracted. Take your 1st step as a Team Couple and share your stories with each other.

Get Real

- What did you expect to do with your money when you first got a job?

- What really happened once you began to receive your paychecks?

- What did it feel like to pay the bills? Did you automatically know what to do? Were you taught how to manage the bills?

- How old were you when you made your first big money mistake and what was it?

Once you understand your spouse's money past and vice versa, then you can work through anything together. If you don't understand each other's stories, you will continually fight about your differences. The point is not to do everything exactly the same. After all, you are two different people. The goal is mutual understanding and interdependence, so you can work through anything together.

Get Naked

- What were you afraid of sharing about your finances when you met your spouse?

- What financial behaviors have changed since you met?

- Discuss what you'd like to see happen in your finances as a team.

- Create a family mission statement or mantra that speaks to how you want to live your life.

Come Clean With Your Honey

Have you ever been so dirty that you thought you would never get clean? My husband and I recently went on a couples trip to Costa Rica. Yes, it was amazing! We couldn't wait to drive ATVs through the jungle. We covered our faces with scarves, our eyes with goggles, and our hair with more scarves and helmets. I thought I was completely covered. Boy was I wrong! We rode at 40+ miles/hour through the tropical rain forest for hours. We saw thousand-year-old trees. We listened to howling monkeys and drove away as fast as we could! The experience was completely exhilarating!

When we arrived back to the starting area and took off our scarves, helmets, and goggles, I looked several shades darker. My clothes were filthy, and I'm pretty sure there was a bug stuck to my eyelid. Of course, the 1st thing I did was take a shower in the hotel room. But for the rest of the week, whenever I showered, I found more dirt in my ears, nose, hair and other places you don't want to hear about. How could I have been this dirty?

Sometimes you don't know where the dirt is hiding; you can't get into all the hidden crevices. But you do your best to get clean when things get dirty. Getting clean financially can be a huge hurdle to overcome.

Let's be honest: no one wants every dirty, little, secret revealed. We fear judgement, and imagine the worst. We wonder, *What will they think of me?* We may even assume those we love will lose respect for us.

According to a Money/CNN survey, "71 percent of those polled owned up to one kind of money secret or another. We want people to see us as we wish we were rather than as we fear we are."[1]

Here's the deal: if we continue to put on a façade, who are we really? If we're hiding behind some mysterious persona, no one will know who we really are. And one day, you may forget to put the mask on.

Financial secrets are dangerous, they can last a long time. They are hurtful and may involve money other people worked hard to earn. The last thing you want to do is keep a secret that will affect someone else. So, it is imperative that you come clean.

Just Tell the Truth

While I know it is best to tell the truth and nothing but the truth before marriage, that is not always going to happen. My husband and I had great pre-marital counsel, that led us to reveal the financial part of our lives to one another. If you have that, fantastic. If you didn't or you're like most couples I've encountered, you've been married a while before this conversation takes place. You have made some mistakes. You hid the shopping bags in the car, applied for that credit card without your spouse knowing or, you gave a family member money and didn't "fill in" your other half.

Whatever is on your heart right now needs to be said. That dirty little secret tugging at your heart must be confessed. This small infraction could be just the thing keeping you farther from your spouse than you would like to be.

---

[1] Scott Medintz, Money Magazine Article "The Lies We Tell" http://money.cnn.com/2005/03/09/magazine/magpl_secrets_0504/ (March, 2005)

You Can't Love Both

It is easy to go to work all day and give it your all, then come home and have nothing for the people you love. In a sense, you are giving your time, attention, resources, and love to someone or something else.

For the love of money is a root of all kinds of evil, for which some have strayed from the faith in their greediness, and pierced themselves through with many sorrows. - I Timothy 6:10 NKJV

Many people misquote this scripture and say, "Money is the root of all kinds of evil". When read in its entirety, the verse truly states that *"the love of money"* is the root of all kinds of evil. This needs to be noted because money isn't inherently bad or evil. Technically, it is what we do with money that can be perceived as bad, or evil.

A brick can build a beautiful home for a family to live in. Or, if thrown, it can be a weapon used to destroy. What you do with money will determine its future path. That is your responsibility and your choice.

It is possible to chase after money with everything you have and not realize the impact caused in other areas of your life. Imagine looking for the next big business idea and buying into it every time. Many people sacrifice time with their families to chase the golden ticket of more money. It is important to get your priorities in line, so that your money is used wisely, and to not allow the thrill of the chase to become the goal.

When one partner has a misplaced priority of money, the signs are clear. They are controlling where the money is concerned, and won't share details with their spouse about what is happening. This partner spends enormous amounts of time trying to figure things out on their own. Hiding important details about how things are being taken care of is a normal occurrence. They don't trust their spouse to participate in any way. These unhealthy behaviors lead to all kinds of marital problems.

If you find yourself in this position, it's time to come clean and possibly seek marital help. When you share everything with your spouse, the rest of your financial journey together will be significantly easier.

Washed Clean

On the surface, Tracy seemed to have it all. She had been married to a hard-working man for many years, had two boys who did well in school, and her career was taking off. She came into my office with some financial questions, but left with something she didn't expect.

As Tracy began to describe her household financial situation, there were small nuggets of information hidden in the dialogue. For starters, her husband wasn't present. Did he support her coming for help? Was he also concerned about their finances? Her reply was sadly typical, he didn't know she was there. As a matter of fact, he also didn't know about the $25,000 in debt she had charged! This is a classic case of financial infidelity.

Intentionally hiding money related secrets from your spouse is financial infidelity.

Tracy had been keeping a secret from her husband the size of Mount Everest and she was looking for an accomplice!

Don't look at her with shame. You may have done it too. You see, she was embarrassed that they weren't making ends meet. She handled paying the bills and things were getting out of control. As her boys grew up, their activities, clothing, and household needs exploded, and she began using credit cards to fill the gap. She figured that as long as everything got paid, she was in control. Tracy reasoned that if she just took care of it and didn't bother her husband with it, then everything would be ok.

One day, she tried to use the credit card and it was declined. Her "luck" had run out and so had the money. She searched for help in desperation. She needed a way out. Tracy's biggest fear was that she wouldn't be able to pay the bills, her husband would find out the big hairy secret, and he would leave her.

Tracy wondered if there was hope for her; there is always hope. If you want freedom badly enough, you will do whatever it takes to get it. However, it may involve coming clean. Conquering financial infidelity begins with coming clean. Tracy's 1st assignment was to talk to her husband. She needed clarity about their financial picture and she needed to share it with him. She immediately began to cry and said she couldn't. Sometimes, the hardest things to do are the very actions needed to break free.

Her problem was not her debt, it was her deception.

Work on the solution could not begin until she had this conversation with her husband, and he came with her to the next appointment.

Weeks went by, but when she finally called to share an update, she was ecstatic! The conversation with her husband had gone much better than she expected. He was not pleased, to say the least. But he didn't throw stones, like she had expected. As a matter of fact, prior to her disclosure, he had been wondering how everything got paid. You see, he already suspected there was more to the story, but he didn't investigate. He allowed this deception to continue just as much as she did. However, they were finally on the road to becoming a Team Couple. He covered her sin with forgiveness and washed her clean by moving forward.

Once they were clear about where they were, they could do something about it and together, we created a plan that worked for them.

Now it's your turn, think about all the times you told partial truths. Remember when you allowed your spouse to think one way and didn't correct it? Take a moment to come clean.

Get Real

- Have you ever hidden shopping bags, opened a credit card, or overspent when you had agreed not to do those things?

- Are there hidden accounts that need to be shared?

- What things have you allowed your spouse to believe that simply aren't true?

Get Naked

- Have you controlled the finances in your home without help from your spouse?

- Discuss how you can move closer to becoming a Team Couple by coming clean.

- Share the secrets that only you know, but that could impact your spouse.

- Give your spouse access to all accounts even if his/her name isn't on them.

Section 2: Your Money Present

The best preparation for the future is the present well-tended. - George MacDonald

Facing your current financial situation may seem daunting and it may look ugly. But if you never take the cover off, you will not experience the freedom and future you desire. Deal with it today so tomorrow is bright.

"With Ericka's help, I have taken my finances from disorganized and messy to very organized and manageable. She has truly been a Godsend in my life. In 10 months, I have paid off over $13,000 in debt! I've been trying for a long time and made no progress. I have become more aware of my spending habits and have modified the ones causing the most problems. Small changes, have already led to big results... not to mention the significant reduction in stress I was feeling due to my finances. As a single mother, this means so much to the future I will be able to offer my son and myself."

Live The Life I've Imagined - Debt Free 2018! — Sonya

Naked Conversation 4
Turn the Lights On With A Reality Check

Have you ever gotten dressed in the dark and thought you looked nice, only to discover the horrible mess you put together once out in public? When those lights come on – you can't help but notice your hair is a "hot mess", it's really time to hit the gym, or you have two different colored shoes on. And, yes, that has happened more than once to a few friends of mine!

Sometimes, we don't know what our blind spots are until someone else reveals them to us. That is what this reality check is designed to do. Your financial reality check is like looking in the mirror with the bright lights on. It shows you exactly where you are and what your financial life is projecting.

Face today's money situation with clarity. We are going to see everything for what it is and not sugarcoat it. We like to make our finances look pretty. We move credit card debt to home equity lines of credit so that we get a tax break, we tell ourselves that student loans are "good debt", and we use credit cards for the points and say it is a good deal.

It's time to face the facts, turn the lights ON! Debt is debt, and you must add it up so you can get rid of it all. The amount of cash you have on hand is real, and you need to know how much you have. There will be a day when you no longer want to work, and you need to save some money so you can retire.

Eyes Wide Open

Your reality check involves gathering some important information. Let's keep it simple and limited to the following three elements:

- Typical monthly spending by category

- Current financial statement or net worth

- Official credit report and score

You may already be sweating just thinking about facing this. Rest assured, you will feel better when it is all completed, and I'll be with you all the way.

Monthly Spending

Thomas J. Stanley, Ph.D. and William D. Danko, Ph.D. have done a fantastic job of researching, analyzing, and presenting the habits of today's American millionaires in their book *The Millionaire Next Door*. One of the questions they ask the reader is: "Do you know how much your family spends each year for food, clothing, and shelter?"[2] According to their research, about two-thirds of the millionaires surveyed could answer yes to this question. Some may wonder why anyone with that kind of money would care about how much they spent in any given category.

These millionaires understood and controlled their spending before they had any wealth. Tabulating, or adding up all expenses, helps control consumption. Often you will see areas of improvement instantly when it's laid out in front of you. You will make better spending decisions because you know where your

---

[2] Thomas J. Stanley, PH.D. and William D. Danko, PH.D., *The Millionaire Next Door pg. 42* (MJF Books, 1996)

income goes. You'll be able to easily see if your financial goals are being met as well.

Add up all of your expenses for one month. Get all bank and credit card) statements for the entire household and add up all expenses by category. It is important to have groceries, dining out, clothing, entertainment, household, etc., all totaled up separately. It is also important that you don't leave out any statements on accounts with which you spend money.

An easy way to do this is by using a software tool like Quicken`, Mint`, or EveryDollar. These tools allow you to keep track of all your spending by category and know precisely how much is available in your checking account.

Make sure to do this for a "normal" month. If you went on vacation or had some other abnormal events occur in a given month, pick a different month. You want to get a feel for what happens with your money most of the time. Anomalies will occur, but for this exercise we don't want that information to skew the results.

You need to evaluate what you are looking at, and then make decisions about what to do next. It may be shocking to face the reality. Many times, there is a distinct difference between what you think you spend and what you actually spend. Now that you know the truth, you can do something about it.

Financial Statement

Your net worth is the value of all the assets less any debts against them. Your net worth number is calculated on a financial statement.

Download your own financial statement at
www.nakedandunashamedbook.com/resources

Create one worksheet for each Team Couple. To calculate yours, first estimate the total value of the items you possess for the entire household.

If you have credit card debt, you'll need to add that under liabilities only because there is no asset associated with it. Next, you subtract the debt or amounts owed on these items from the value. Finally, you total up all the values and see what you truly own today, your net worth. This can be particularly scary for some people. No one wants to see negative numbers because of your debt load. You also don't want to see small numbers in the positive because you feel like you haven't done enough.

Here's the deal: If you don't look at this, you won't learn how to improve it. And, everyone has to start somewhere. Your "somewhere" may just be on that net worth worksheet. This worksheet is important when applying for mortgages, reviewing with your financial planner, and possibly uncovering tax savings opportunities.

Credit Report and Score

No part of our financial lives brings more anxiety than our credit report and FICO® Score. It is a measure of our responsibility with money up to this point. Your credit score affects interest rates on any kind of loan. Sometimes auto, home, and rental insurance companies will check your score for rate quotes. And nowadays, you may need a clearance for work that includes a credit check. This is definitely an area to stay on top of.

Check your credit report and score annually. For free access to your credit report, go to www.annualcreditreport.com and www.creditkarma.com if you want your free credit score. You can also go to the three individual credit reporting agencies (Equifax®, TransUnion®, Experian™).

As you pay off debt, it could take three to six months for updates to occur on your report, so be patient. Each of these agencies could show slightly different credit scores and slightly different information on your report, so be sure to review all three.

Your credit score results from an equation made up of several factors. Check out the following chart:

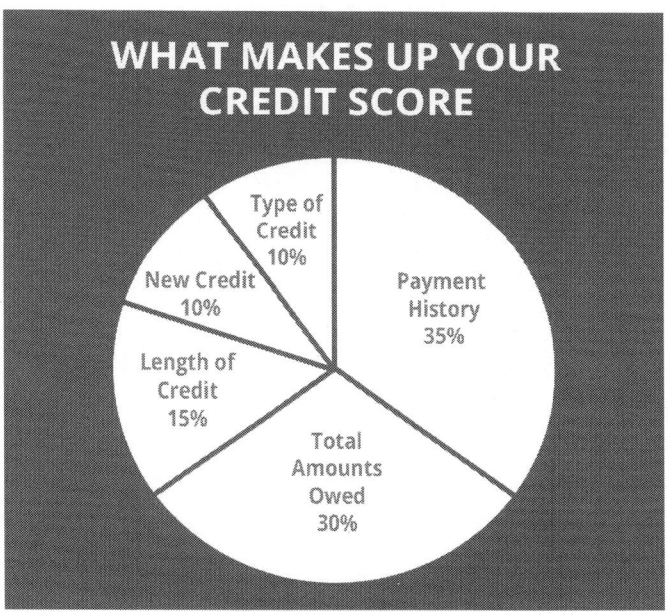

As you can see, the majority of your credit score is impacted by the total amount of debt owed and your payment history. Eliminating your debt and paying all your bills on time, are the best ways to improve your credit. Having credit for long periods of time, not applying for new credit too often, and keeping a mixture of different types of debt (credit cards, auto loans, student loans, mortgages, etc.) all contribute to your score as well, but in smaller ways.

When you apply for credit, lenders are evaluating a three-digit number, resulting from all of the shown factors applied in an equation. This number ranges from 300-850. The higher this number is the better. Check out the thermometer below from www.creditcovered.org, which shows the benefits of a high credit score.

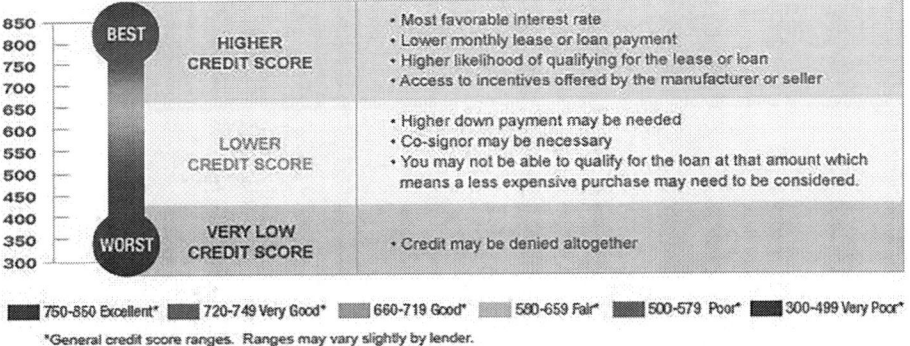

850 BEST

HIGHER CREDIT SCORE
- Most favorable interest rate
- Lower monthly lease or loan payment
- Higher likelihood of qualifying for the lease or loan
- Access to incentives offered by the manufacturer or seller

LOWER CREDIT SCORE
- Higher down payment may be needed
- Co-signor may be necessary
- You may not be able to qualify for the loan at that amount which means a less expensive purchase may need to be considered.

WORST VERY LOW CREDIT SCORE
- Credit may be denied altogether

■ 750-850 Excellent*   ■ 720-749 Very Good*   ■ 660-719 Good*   ■ 580-659 Fair*   ■ 500-579 Poor*   ■ 300-499 Very Poor*
*General credit score ranges. Ranges may vary slightly by lender.

Keep your score in perspective. In order to maintain a high score, you have to use and keep lots of different kinds of debt. This is dangerous because at some point we all make mistakes and this isn't what we want long-term. Don't allow a low score to get you discouraged. This is one measure of your financial health and you can do something about it. Use the credit score factors to strategically improve your score over time. And believe it or not, if you eventually have no debt at all, including a mortgage, there will be nothing to calculate your score. Having cash will then give you the opportunity to buy whatever you want.

Your credit will not affect your spouse's unless both of your names are on the credit account. It is important that both spouses are aware of any debt present in the relationship, but it isn't necessary that both names are on every single credit account.

Now is a good time to get your credit score and report to check for errors as well. Once you have reviewed your report, you need to share it with your spouse. Just like Chris and I did when we were in pre-marital counseling, exchange the report with one another. Do not judge, just be aware. Discuss any areas of concern and begin to make a plan to improve those areas.

Check Your Habits

Goals shape priorities

Priorities shape plans

Plans shape behaviors

Behaviors lead to financial success

We teach our children to say no to drugs because we know the negative effects of drug use. Some of those negative effects can include physical injuries, violence, internal damage, risk of diseases, addiction, stress, depression, legal issues, damaged relationships, and financial pressures. It's clear that we would do whatever was needed to help deter our children from going down a path that could expose them to any of those consequences.

Have you ever stopped to think about the negative effects of poor financial habits? Poor spending can lead to stress, depression, legal issues, financial pressures and more.

The bottom line is that we need to treat our financial habits with care. We need to have respect for our budget and our goals. In addition, we must make sure to cultivate good habits that bring us closer to those goals. If we don't, there could be terrible consequences. If your spending habits are endangering your future, you need to make changes, starting today.

Your current money habits include those behaviors that you do on a regular and consistent basis. They have subsequently led you to where you are today with money. We all have habits that aren't serving us well, so not all of these habits are good ones. But everyone has strong points too. It is time to get clear on what you are doing well and what you could improve upon as a Team Couple. In order to start building healthy habits, we need to see what habits you already have in place. In other words, we're taking your financial pulse.

I have created a Healthy Habits Checklist for you to complete individually.

Download the Healthy Habits Checklist at www.nakedandunashamedbook.com/resources

---

Next, go through each item on the list and put a checkmark in the box next to the ones that apply to you right now. This process is simple, but it's challenging to face. It requires you to take a good look at what is and isn't working in your life, financially speaking. This exercise is not meant to bring you shame or make you feel bad. It's simply meant to figure out your starting point. Just answer honestly and quickly so you don't overthink it. Take the time to ponder your responses so you gain clarity about your current money habits and where you can improve.

Shared Goals

Before you begin to clean up your financial life, you need vision and concrete goals. Good financial communication between couples begins with shared goals. There are things you want to accomplish individually, either personally or in your career, and there are things you want achieve as a team. Goals are the glue that make budgeting, debt reduction, and saving money worth doing. Think about where you want to go together and find commonality. The Team Couple is on the same page in the same book.

Can two people walk together without agreeing on the direction? - Amos 3:3 NLV

Imagine you and your spouse are in a potato sack race. You each have one leg in the sack and one leg outside the sack. How difficult would it be if you try to go east and your spouse wants to go west. It simply won't work!

My husband and I wanted to change our family tree. We were committed to giving our kids a bright and financially stress-free future. We didn't want to hold them back with debt, loans, and the payments that come with it. Therefore, our shared goal was to have enough money saved to get them through college and be able to fund our own retirement. If we didn't take care of our retirement, then we'd better hope our girls want to take care of us! I didn't want to chance our relationship because we didn't prepare adequately.

Many people set goals at the top of each calendar year. However, just as many find themselves "falling off the wagon" within the first two months. Here are three smart strategies to help you be successful with goal setting:

1. **Be clear and specific.** It's easy to say, "I'm going to save money," or "I'm going to get out of debt." But, if you don't make this goal measurable, then it's not only difficult to achieve, it's easy to quit. Create SMART (Specific, Measurable, Attainable, Reasonable, and Time-Bound) goals for your financial life.

2. **Write your goals down.** Goals that aren't written down are just a thought - they aren't a commitment. Write them down and put them where you will see them every day. This will ensure you are reminded of the goal, which will help you stick to it and get into action.

Download your Goals Worksheet at
www.nakedandunashamedbook.com/resources

3. **Share the goal with someone to hold you accountable.** One of the best ways to achieve a goal is to share it with someone so they know what you are working towards. This person can hold you accountable to reaching your achievements, but they can also be a huge help when you feel stuck or frustrated. Not sure if a friend is the right way to go here? This is where financial coaching comes into play. A financial coach is not only an expert, he/she is also a neutral source of accountability and inspiration.

Goals are the glue that keep your financial plan in place. All of the work you do to get organized, make improvements, and stay on target financially is for a specific goal. Sharing goals with your spouse helps you both remain committed and excited about what you are doing. The goals are your reminder that something bigger and better is coming, so stay the course!

Take Baby Steps

It may seem like a daunting task to tackle your financial situation head on. Many times you don't know where to begin or even how to get there. Start with Baby Steps. These steps were originally developed by Dave Ramsey. The baby steps will help you clarify your own shared goals and what you need to work on right now. Taking a lead from Dave Ramsey's original Baby Steps, I have added step 1.

Baby Steps

1. Get ALL "well-being" bills current (food, clothing, shelter, transportation).

2. Set aside $1,000 to start an Emergency Fund.

3. Pay off all debt using the Debt Snowball (except the house).

4. Set aside 3-6 months of expenses in savings to complete the Emergency Fund.

5. Invest 15% of household income into Roth IRAs and pre-tax retirement.

6. Start college funds for children.

7. Pay off home mortgage early.

8. Build wealth and give! Invest in mutual funds and real estate.

Let's break this down. You want to get current on your basic living expenses within a month. Taking longer than that will cause frustration. Next, sell some stuff or cut out extras to get your $1,000 emergency fund quickly. Having these funds set aside will allow you to relax tremendously and bring you peace. Then, get out of debt. Don't allow this phase to take longer than 2-3 years, if possible. Your motivation and determination to finish will be strained if getting out of debt goes on forever.

It took me and my husband five years to get out of nearly $100,000 in debt, on just over $67,000 starting income. If we had made some different choices, it would have taken less time. Once your debt is gone, save all you can each month to create a solid emergency fund of 3-6 months of expenses. This phase won't take long now that the debt payments are gone. Additionally, saving for retirement and college will be easier since the cash is freed up.

Paying off your home will take some time, seven years is common, but don't allow any lifestyle adjustments to derail your total freedom. Give yourself the opportunity to have some fun with money and enjoy it, but balance that goal with keeping a long-term focus. Building wealth and giving is the fun part! During this time, your dreams begin to come true, financially speaking. Everyone completes these goals at different paces so don't think you aren't doing well if it is taking longer than you'd like, or if someone else did it faster. Just keep moving forward together.

Get Real

- What are your daily/monthly habits that show up on your bank statement? Is this what you expected?

- Is your money going where you want it to go?

- What surprised you about your spending?

Get Naked

- What is your financial sore spot right now as shown on your credit reports?

- Discuss together what you want to improve.

- Set a date to review your progress.

- Create goals around what you want your net worth, credit score and bank accounts to look like.

- What new habits with money will you work on as a team?

Don't Mimic the Joneses: They Are Broke

Take a look down your street or get on Facebook for five minutes. What do you see? Do you see friends with expensive cars and designer clothing, or neighbors with swimming pools, lavishly furnished homes, etc.? Or are you the one living in the lap of luxury? We have all heard of the Joneses, but who are those people anyway? Think about this question and be honest with yourself: Are you the Joneses, or are you trying to be like them? Both positions could be equally damaging to your financial future, depending on the way you look at it.

Who Are These People Anyway?

The Joneses in America today, are the people who appear to have everything. They have the look, the house, and all the stuff that goes with it. But is it worth the price they paid?

Buying things you can't afford, to impress people who aren't paying the bills, is a slippery slope to financial instability.

Would you believe that 70% of Americans live from paycheck to paycheck? This means that if Mr. Jones missed one paycheck, he would be in a world of hurt. The Joneses haven't saved any money for a rainy day. Here is the debt load for a typical American family who uses debt of any kind. This a picture of the Joneses financial life.

Type of Debt	Average Household Amount
Credit Cards	$15,762
Auto Loans	$27,142
Student Loans	$48,172
Total Debt	**$91,076**

NerdWallet's 2015 American Household Credit Card Debt Study[3]

Debt has become so socially acceptable that the average American family has nearly twice the average household income ($53,000) tied up in debt! The Joneses can't get ahead financially or save any money, because they are strapped with debt and payments. Is that who you envy? Is that who you want to be like? I'm sure your answer is "NO".

On the flip side, are the people who desire to have what they see the Joneses have. For some, it's not enough to keep up with the Joneses. Nowadays, everyone wants to BE the Joneses. Of course, it looks tempting, fun, and stress-free but the reality is that "normal" in America is full of hassles that none of us want to deal with. Why waste your life desiring what your neighbor has?

Measuring yourself against what someone else has is a sorry gauge of your own potential.

God has so much in store for us that we cannot even imagine it all. Don't spend your life trying to make someone else's story your own.

---

[3] Erin El Issa, 2015 American Household Credit Card Debt Study,
    https://www.nerdwallet.com/blog/average-credit-card-debt-household/ (Q4 2015)

Mow Your Own Lawn

Your financial situation is a lot like a lawn. Paying attention to your own lawn will get your focus in the right place and off of what the Joneses are doing. The questions you need to answer are: "Do you have a lawn that is well-manicured?" or "Is your lawn a hot mess?"

Just drive around your neighborhood a bit. You will have different and very distinctive reactions to a lawn that is well-cared for versus one that is overgrown with weeds. The lawn which is well-manicured features green grass that is trimmed nicely with healthy and shapely shrubs. You may also see colorful, weed-free flower beds and a driveway or sidewalk that is edged and free from debris.

This is the house that you want to come home to, and you want to enter to see more. There is something about this house that draws you in, and makes you take notice.

On the other hand, think about the opposite - the lawn that is a "hot mess." The brown grass looks like you need to wade through it, the flowerbeds are overgrown with weeds or they're nonexistent and there are leaves covering the driveway, and bits of trash scattered on the sidewalks.

When you step in front of this house, you feel overwhelmed with the work that needs to be done. You have a feeling that it's probably more of the same mess when you walk in the door. Things just feel very chaotic. You definitely don't want this house next door to yours.

Similarly, if you have a money situation that is a hot mess, you may:

- Feel overwhelmed by a stack of debts that need your attention (weeds).

- Have overdue bills with late fees (overgrown grass).

- Have a checkbook that is in desperate need of balancing (sidewalk full of debris).

Here's the deal: that well-manicured lawn takes time. You need to have a lawn mower, tools, fertilizer, water, plants, experience, time, and vision. The other option is to hire someone with all that stuff and give it time to mature and develop. That beautiful lawn didn't happen overnight and the same is true for your money. You need some tools like a budget, debt reduction plan, or account tracking tool. You will need to take the time to learn how to get a well-manicured financial picture, or hire someone to help you.

It's NOT a Dirty Word!

In order to be successful with your new shared goals and personal financial focus you need tools. One in particular is a budget. But, many people are afraid of that word. It causes them to cringe, feel pain, perspire, and yes, sometimes cry! Doing a budget won't allow you to fake it. It shows you the truth of what you can spend, and we don't like that. Hear me loud and clear - "Budget" is just a word. Our own personal experiences have caused us to see it as a negative. We have given it a negative connotation because it didn't work for us or we didn't work it at all. Let's look at the real definition:

Budget: an estimate, often itemized, of expected income and expense for a given period in the future (www.dictionary.com).

In my terms, it is simply a plan! Budget is not a dirty word!! I would even venture to say that it can become your trusted friend in planning your finances, if you allow it to do so. Understanding the power that lies in creating a written game-plan with our money helped me and my husband stay focused on our goal of debt-freedom. This can be the case for you too.

So, how do you go from viewing budget as negative, to seeing it as a tool to get you where you want to be in life?

When you create your own plan for your monthly expenses, you are in control. You have decided what is going to happen and are taking steps to see it to completion. This is your plan not someone else's. Release yourself from any restrictions, and get rid of the notion that your budget is bondage. Embrace the fact that it can be your financial pathway to success.

If it makes you feel better, call it something different - a spending plan, cash flow statement, or monthly financial strategy. Whatever name gets you in the mood to take action, that's what you need to call it.

From month to month, sit down with your spouse and decide how your money will be spent before it reaches your hands. This is what it looks like to be intentional with your money. That simple proactive step keeps you in the driver's seat and in control of your spending. Each month of the year is different and requires changes to your plan. If something during the month takes you off course, then you know how to adjust and get back on course with a plan. It doesn't need to be over- complicated, but a written game plan for your money will help you get to your goals faster than if you didn't use one at all.

...Write the vision; make it plain on tablets, so he may run who reads it. - Habakkuk 2:2 ESV

The budget is your vision, and every spending decision you make daily is you, walking or running that vision out.

Every financial expert will tell you to budget. They will even give you templates. You can go online right now and find hundreds of examples of budgets.

Download your budget template at
www.nakedandunashamedbook.com/resources

However, this book is about more than just the mechanics, you need to know how to make it happen in real life. Keep the following tips in mind, as you and your spouse put your own plan together, they will help you succeed with budgeting:

Budgeting tips:

1. *Write it out early.* Before the money is in your hands or in your account, you need a plan. This way, you already know how the money will be spent and aren't tempted to do something different.

2. *Make it zero-based.* Spend every dollar on paper. If you have funds left over, find a place to put them (i.e., debt, savings, etc.). If money doesn't have a home it will find its way to the department store. If the budget is negative then reduce spending so that it balances.

3. *Look at it regularly.* Print the budget out or set a consistent time to review what the plan is telling you to do. If you don't, you will inevitably fall off the wagon.

4. *Create some wiggle room.* Always add in miscellaneous money for things you don't know are coming. It doesn't need to be a lot but, if you don't have it the budget will feel tight.

5. *Put some fun in the budget.* Make sure to be realistic about activities you want to participate in. Think about kids' sports, school involvement, and seasonal needs.

6. *Create a spending plan.* Break the budget down by the dates you get paid. This will help you pay your bills on time and still be able to feed your family. Make sure that you see how much is coming in and going out each time

you get paid. You may need to change some due dates on your bills so your spending plan flows properly.

7. ***Make it realistic.*** The 1ˢᵗ few times you create a budget you may miss some categories. Over time, it will be easier to predict what needs to be changed. Do not undercut categories if you will break the budget in those areas to spend that money anyway. Adjust it to make sure you have everything you need.

8. ***You need pocket change.*** It's a good idea to decide how much money each spouse needs as pocket change. List a lump sum that does not have to be itemized. Neither one of you should feel that you must explain your $2 gas station runs after work. Just build in some pocket change that each of you is free to spend as you like.

9. ***Commit together.*** As a Team Couple, make sure both parties are ready to stay on budget. Review the budget together and hold each other accountable to what it says. Remember that it is your plan. You can change it together, if you agree that it needs to be changed.

10. ***Use cash.*** For discretionary categories like groceries, dining out, clothing, etc. using cash will help you stay on target, keep your limits in mind and avoid buying items you don't need.

Be careful not to try and create the perfect budget. There is no perfect budget. However, we can create healthy boundaries that protect us from our own spending habits. When you are aware of your upper limits, you are less likely to overspend. But, we are imperfect people, attempting to manage our financial lives the best way we can. The challenge is that life doesn't always fit in our nice and neat boxes, although, I sure wish it would! The budget is a guide and plan. When things change, you change the plan. The Team Couple will work to compromise, stay within their income limits, and discuss the daily expenses along the way. Always pay your needs first, keep your goals in mind next, and then add in wants that fit within your income.

As I mentioned earlier, *The Millionaire Next Door* is one of my favorite books. In the studies by Stanley and Danko, what did they find that is surprising yet profound?

> *"They became millionaires by budgeting and controlling expenses, and they maintain their affluent status the same way."*[4]
>
> *AND*
>
> *"More than half of all millionaires budget."*

So you want to get out of debt, manage your finances, and basically live a financially free life? Do what today's millionaires did and still do: budget. Many of the wealthy individuals studied were first generation rich, and therefore, did not qualify as recipients of inheritance or trust funds. They were hard-working Americans just like you and me.

You Need Cushion

Good budgeting can end paycheck to paycheck living, but only if you take the next step. Margin bridges the gap between you and life. This margin creates space, so that you aren't living too close to the edge and constantly looking at the calendar, to see when you have another paycheck. If you have cushion in a few places, it reduces stress and gives you the opportunity to be successful with budgeting.

Create a cushion for 4 reasons:

---

[4] Thomas J. Stanley, PH.D. and William D. Danko, PH.D., The Millionaire Next Door pg. 40 (MJF Books, 1996)

1. **A buffer in your checking accounts.** Give yourself room to breathe, a cushion helps you do that. The amount is different for everyone. To determine how much cushion you need, imagine that all your bills are paid for the month, you have groceries in your fridge, gas in your car, and some cash in hand. When you review your checking account balance, how much money do you want to see that doesn't have to be spent on anything? At what point will you get uncomfortable if you go beneath that dollar amount? This should be your cushion amount. If it is $100, then you can probably keep that in the account right away. If your number is $1,000, then you may need to save it up over time to get there. Either way, this cushion provides peace of mind, so you aren't checking your bank account every day.

2. **For emergencies.** Money in savings helps you to weather life's "oh no's!" The money here is only for emergencies like loss of income, major medical, auto accidents, or last minute family emergencies, like funerals. While you are in debt, start with $1,000 in this account. If your mortgage payment is more than $1,500 per month, your family size is five or greater, or there are medical concerns in the home you may want to keep $2,000 in the account. If your household income is less than $40,000 annually, then you may want to begin with $500 and save more over time. No matter what, get this baby emergency fund in place inside of sixty days! Do not delay! Sell something, reduce expenses, or get a 2nd job. Your sleep at night will improve greatly by having this money on hand. As an added bonus, your need to run up your credit cards reduces greatly as well.

3. **For small unplanned expenses.** Things don't always go as planned. I love to budget. It gives me great pleasure to see my account balance, all monies spoken for, and every need met. However, we simply cannot think of everything. Sometimes our kids get sick and need a doctor's visit along with prescriptions. Sometimes, school supplies cost more than we anticipated. When life happens, we need a safe place to fall. Miscellaneous money in the budget provides a cushion to make room for the unexpected

small things that life brings. Make sure you always put that in your plan so you aren't caught off guard.

4. **For non-monthly expenses.** Some expenses can catch up to us and surprise us year after year. Do you ever get that bill in the mail to renew your license plates and feel like you've just been hit by a truck? Or maybe like me, you forgot about the home owner's association dues until January came and Christmas festivities left you slim on cash. The secret to managing your non-monthly expenses (and eliminating the surprise) is to budget for it each month, so that over the years' time, you have accounted for the entire bill. If your auto registration is $240, it's a whole lot easier to save $20 each month, than to scramble for the $240 in one month. Non-monthly expenses could also include large purchases such as cars, household furniture, major car repairs, vacations, planned medical expenses, appliances, etc. Basically, if you don't need it right away and the total amount you must spend won't fit into your monthly budget, then you can begin a regular savings for it until the amount you need is available in cash.

Maintaining a cushion in all of these areas will ensure you are successful with your budget and ultimately your goals.

Get Real

- Be honest. Are you the Joneses or are you trying to be the Joneses?

- What have you been faking? How will you decide to change so that you win financially?

- What does your financial lawn look like?

- What goals do you want to achieve financially in one or two years?

Get Naked

- Decide on the kind of lifestyle that works for both of you. Be clear about what you will and won't do with money, no matter what you see happening in other households.

- Has budgeting worked for you in the past? If not, what stopped you from succeeding?

- Create a household budget with your spouse.

- What financial cushions do you need to establish?

Naked Conversation 6
Get Out of Debt!

"Buy Now, Pay Later" has become the American financial mantra. We have truly taken this phrase and run with it. Sometimes this becomes… "buy now and pay *a lot more, much later*". We are a nation of consumers who love stuff, but don't want to pay for it right away. We use it up, eat it quick, or drive it to death before we ever finish paying for it!

We've all done it. We have put lunch on a credit card, and carried a balance that costs us 20% interest, on meals we ate months ago. We've taken vacations on credit and the remnants, or debt, of our trip lasts for years. We've bought new "reliable" vehicles and spent more than five years to pay for them, while their value plummeted to half the purchase price, or less. This mentality and spending pattern has trickled into every area of our way of life. Our government sets the same standard. Our children only repeat what they see us do. We must change! It can begin with you.

Remember the Joneses? They had $91,000 in debt. Let's break down what their payments look like. Check out the following chart of the Joneses debt load with additional information.

Type of Debt	Debt	Minimum Payment	Interest Rate	Total Interest	Years in Debt
Credit Cards	$15,762	$250	18%	$20,294	12
Auto Loans	$27,142	$515	4.99%	$3,559	5
Student Loans	$48,172	$400	6%	$12,463	10
Total Debt	**$91,076**	**$1,165**		**$36,316**	

Listen, it's time to get and stay out of debt. Who wants to be the average American, making monthly payments of $1,165, but still end up paying $36,316 in interest over 12 years? No one wants that, we need a new mantra.

Buy Now, Pay Now

In order to see the future we truly desire to have, we must change the behavior that got us here. There is no microwave method to getting out of this mess. Only sound, practical strategies that will last a lifetime - these are the tools you need to be free. Believe me, once you are out of debt completely, you won't want to return to payments that follow you around like a pet.

75% of Forbes 400 wealthiest people surveyed said,
"The #1 key to building wealth is to be debt free."

When my husband and I totaled our debt, and the shocking $80k number came quickly into view, we didn't know what to do. Instead of stopping the bleeding right away, our debt load instead rose to nearly $100k before we quit using the banks to buy what we desired. Sadly, we were a picture of the average American household very early on. Do not allow this to be said of you. Commit right now that you will stop using debt. If the item is good enough to buy today, it is certainly worth waiting until you have the cash. Repeat this over and over to yourself:

Sacrifice is giving up something good for something better.

The "something better" for most of us is a life of financial freedom. Everyone defines financial freedom uniquely for themselves. But I'm sure nobody wants a life of payments without a clear end in view.

Steps Out of Debt

Debt robs you of your choices, and makes you feel guilty for wanting to live well. The giant backpack full of debt weighs you down when there is a mountain of bills to pay.

For many people, seeing no way out of debt holds them back from ever getting where they really want to be. The first meeting I have with potential clients is a Debt-Free Strategy Session. This is the time for us to get to know one another, find out what is going on in their finances right now, and determine how I can help. It is my goal that you walk away with tips and tools that will improve your financial life right away, whether we work together or not.

Let's make your path to freedom clear. Here are the steps out of debt which I share with potential clients that will make a difference for you as well:

1. **Save some money quickly** – You need this so that when emergencies strike, you don't go into debt trying to manage them.

2. **Quit borrowing money** – You can't get out of debt and borrow more money at the same time.

3. **Budget** – You will find extra cash to put towards debt by doing this. Staying within your income limitations creates healthy boundaries too.

4. **Use CASH** – Studies have shown that by using cash you will spend 12-18% less than if you used any type of card (credit or debit).

5. **Sell something** – We all have too much stuff. Someone may be able to use those items that are simply taking up space in your home. Use craigslist.com, ebay.com, or just have a garage sale! More money in your pocket leads to more peace.

6. **Increase your income** – Start a side business or get an extra job. Extra money means more money towards debt. If someone owes you money can you change the terms and increase their payments? If you always get a tax refund, it might be time to adjust your withholdings so you get more in your paycheck today.

Finally, keep your head up! Times are good if you see what is present. Opportunities are all around if you just pay attention. Your next career may be around the corner or your next business idea may sprout wings right in front of you. If you just see beyond your current circumstances, you just might be able to see exactly what can make the difference in your own situation.

Give Me a Date!

As of this writing, I have run five half marathons, having just completed my last one several weeks ago (in the pouring rain)! Running has become a good way to clear my head, listen to music or podcasts, and keep in shape at the same time.

When I train for a race, typically, there are a certain number of miles that I need to run each week. To be fully prepared for the race, I have to practice just like with any sport. A half marathon is 13.1 miles and let me tell you… there is no way I'm running that far without training. I need mile markers along the way as well, to let me know I'm making progress. I use my running app to tell me "good job, keep going" or "four miles completed." I need to be able to tell my legs, "only one more mile to go." If I just go running without knowledge of how far I'm going, I may never reach my training goals.

Your finances are the same way, you need mile markers along the way to ensure you are making progress. It is encouraging to be certain that your journey to debt-freedom will last only two years. Wouldn't it be nice to know for a fact that you are halfway there? Breaking down your big goal into bite sized chunks, allows the process to go smoother and for you to celebrate along the way. That is what a Debt-Free Date does for you. If you know when the finish line will occur, then you can plan for it. The Debt-Free Date will also create anticipation for the couple who is a true team. Here's how you find your own Debt-Free Date.

First begin with the Debt Snowball created by Dave Ramsey. This is a tool used to organize your current debts. It provides you with a plan to pay off debts in an efficient and organized manner. Correctly utilizing the Debt Snowball will facilitate how, and when your creditors will be paid in full. Here's how you do it.

1. List your consumer debts (student loans, car notes, credit cards, and personal loans) from the smallest to largest total balance. Record the current balance, the minimum monthly payment, and your proposed monthly payment for each debt. The proposed monthly payment includes any extra funds you have found in your budget, to attack the debt.

2. Start with your smallest debt. Pay it off as quickly as possible. Then take the money you were paying on that monthly payment, and roll it into the next listed payment. Keep rolling the minimum payments until you get to your last debt.

3. Throughout this process, continue paying all your creditors. While you are paying extra on one debt, pay the minimum monthly payment for all your other remaining debts. This will keep you current on all of your bills.

4. Divide the balance for each debt by the proposed monthly payment. This is the total number of months it will take to pay off that one debt.

5. Calculate your Debt-Free Date by adding up the number of months it will take for you to pay off all your debt.

Your Debt-Free Date is your motivation to keep moving forward. Once you know how long it will take you to pay off all your consumer debt, it will be easier to push past the resistance.

Download your Debt Snowball worksheet at www.nakedandunashamedbook.com/resources

---

Get Back Up

You already know I'm a runner but it took a while to get here. In June of 2011, I could barely run a mile without stopping. Today, I have run thousands of miles in training for many races. Not once during all of this running did I ever fall down. Until one spring day while training for a 10k.

I had only run about 0.7 miles, and planned on running four total, when somehow the ground reached up and grabbed me. Or maybe it was the size 10 boats attached to the bottom of my legs! Surely there was something on the ground that I had tripped over. Regardless, I suddenly found myself heading for the ground at 5+ miles/hour.

I landed on the ground and slid forward for a split second. It was at this moment that I had a huge decision to make - *Do I lie there for a minute, or get right back up and act like nothing ever happened?* There was pain in my elbow and hip (I'm no spring chicken!), grass was all over my clothing, and I was probably bleeding.

Then I remembered what real estate mogul Barbara Corcoran of Shark Tank said. "Successful people fail well. They can take a hit and jump back up." So I got back up, brushed off my pants quickly and finished that four mile run. It's all in how you get back up. When I got home and took my shower, there was blood and an open wound on my elbow, which would probably scab, bruise and take a long time to heal. But I felt good about finishing what I had started.

Now I ask you, have you fallen down? Are your finances a hot mess? Do you feel like you've been beaten up with debt? If so, I encourage you to get back up and keep moving forward.

Just because you are reading this book and now have the tools to gain success with your money and your honey, doesn't mean you won't ever fall down, financially speaking.

We all have a decision to make. Will we get back up when things go wrong? I knew how many miles I needed to run. I knew that I couldn't make it up later in the day. I knew that each step I took would bring me closer to my goal. I also knew walking home would mean defeat. I pushed through and so can you. Now get back up!

You may need a coach on your team for accountability and direction. A game plan for success makes your path clear. Right now though, push through the pain and rough spots so that you can see and cross your Debt-Free finish line.

My fall taught me that it doesn't matter what I encounter. I am a fighter. You are a fighter too. Your goals are worth fighting for. Your dreams can become a reality. Your money can produce a lifetime of fruit for you. Now is the time to make it happen.

Get Real

- Revisit your credit report. Capture all of your debts on one paper to get clarity about what you owe.

- Think about how quickly you'd like to get out of debt.

- What is one thing you can do now to show your spouse how bad you want debt-freedom?

- What would you do with your monthly payments if you were debt-free?

Get Naked

- Create your debt snowball with your spouse. All debt on one spreadsheet is best, so you see everything in one place and you are working together as a team to get free.

- Calculate your Debt-Free Date. Total up the number of months it will take to pay off all your debt.

- Discuss what you will do as a team to accelerate your progress. Do you need to sell some things, get a 2nd job, or reduce other spending in your budget?

Naked Conversation 7
Set Healthy Boundaries

My husband and I have two kids and a king size bed, but it's never been big enough. When my girls were little and had a bad dream, they would run to our room, crying. Snuggling up with mom and dad felt safe. When the girls shared a room, one would wake up the other and our bed would fill up quickly. They felt no danger in the bed with us. No monsters could get to them when Mom and Dad were protecting them underneath the covers.

Sometimes it was nice to have them close and snuggle together. But in the morning I might have a foot at my head or an elbow in my rib. Even when they were two and six years old, that king size bed wasn't big enough. When you are married, your bed is made for only two, no matter how big it is. Your financial decisions are made for only two as well.

Just Between Us

There are lots of financial decisions that we keep between us. We've decided that our families don't need to know how much money we make, what is in our bank accounts or how much we pay for large items.

We have an understanding that there is a limit to how much of our personal financial lives we share with friends. Some things are just none of their business. Not only that, it's nice to know these important facts of our life are things just between us. These are the secrets it's ok to keep.

We've even discussed the standards that our family will live by. It is critical that you set the stage for what you will and won't do. If these healthy boundaries aren't established, you can fall into adult peer pressure by trying to be the Joneses, as I mentioned earlier.

No Strings Attached

The Team Couple not only needs to create money standards but also healthy boundaries around giving money to others. There can be a lot of temptation to ask relatives for money or to loan it out when an emergency arises. Typically, these loans are interest free and can be accessed without a run of your credit. That is tempting to take advantage of. But what are you truly doing when money is exchanged between you and someone you love?

The rich rule over the poor, and the borrower is slave to the lender. - Proverbs 22:7 NIV

Here are some reasons why it is never a good idea to borrow from relatives and friends:

1. You are creating a slave/master relationship between the parties involved. A slave is owned by the master until his/her debt is paid. We want to call our father, "Dad" not "Master", so let your dad keep his money.

2. Each time you see the person who lent you money, you will think about the debt owed, and that causes anxiety between you. Thanksgiving dinner doesn't taste the same when money matters are on your mind or your creditor is sitting next to you.

3. It is easier to miss payments because you believe that your relatives or friends won't hound you like credit card companies do. At least you will

make it a priority to pay the credit card companies back. Typically, when money is loaned to relatives it is not considered as important or urgent.

4.   The benefactors of the loan will think they now have a right to ask questions about your spending habits. They believe the right to that information has been bought with your loaned money. And... if you have nosey relatives and friends, your financial business could spread throughout the family tree. No loan is worth the trouble and embarrassment that could bring.

The best way to handle difficult financial situations is to handle them yourselves. This breeds responsibility, self-confidence, strength and character. When you've successfully gone through a tough time, but managed to do it all on your own, you feel like you can take on the world.

Early in our marriage, three of our family members passed away in the same year. My family was hurting. I lived in Arizona and desperately needed to get home to Michigan and be with my family for a funeral service. But, we had no money for plane tickets. A friend of ours heard about our loss and wanted to help. He gave us two buddy passes for the airline he worked for, so we only had to pay taxes for the flight. That saved us! It was the difference between paying $100 total or $1,000 for two last minute plane tickets with money we didn't have. The alternative? Not going at all.

Being creative and flexible saved us the embarrassment of asking family or friends for money. You need to have something saved, so that emergencies like this don't turn into stressful financial situations.

When my husband and I climbed out of the mountain of debt we had, we did it without the financial help of anyone. No one paid our bills. As a result, we knew that we could tackle any financial setback that came our way, including job loss, career changes, family emergencies, etc., without leaning on anyone. Our relationship grew stronger and we felt empowered! Don't you want the same feeling?

Now turn the tables around. What if a friend or relative is asking you for money? How are you going to handle that situation? The above concerns still apply. And when you loan someone money you enable the overspending. If the behaviors that got them into this situation are not dealt with, then more debt will still be incurred. This does not help the borrower, but it can hurt them tremendously.

Let's not enable our loved ones or allow ourselves to be enabled. If you truly want to help someone financially, just give them the money with no strings attached. Just give it up. A gift is better than debt any day. Let's tackle the real problem systematically and change the behaviors that caused us to need extra money in the first place. That is true empowerment!

To Sign or Not to Sign?

Many couples choose to help out family by co-signing for loans. Maybe it's a daughter who is just starting out with a new job, and doesn't have the cash to get a new car. Maybe it's a brother who has been unwise with money, and needs a house to live in but his credit is shot.

In these circumstances, we are tempted to co-sign on a loan or document, ensuring that our loved one can "get ahead", financially speaking. What this really does is obligate you to pay if they default on the loan or agreement. The bank is saying that they don't trust your loved one with the debt, so they need a co-signer.

Simply put, if the banks don't trust someone to pay the debt, neither should you. According to the Federal Trade Commission (FTC), 75% of all defaulting loans with co-signers are eventually paid by the co-signer, and not the original borrower.

If Sally doesn't pay her car payment every month, and the car is repossessed or auctioned off, the bank will come after you for the difference of what is owed and what it sold for at auction if you co-signed for her loan! If your brother is late on his mortgage, the lender may not actually call you, but your credit will show late pays. This can also affect your debt-to-income ratio because you are liable for another debt even if the item isn't yours!

It's poor judgment to guarantee another person's debt or put up security for a friend. - Proverbs 17:18 NLT

The best way for a Team Couple to respond to any requests for co-signing is an emphatic "No!" As mentioned previously, give money with no expectation that it will be returned, if someone needs help in this way. With no strings attached or long-term credit obligations owed by those close to you, you are keeping both your relationship, as well as your credit in a healthy position.

Do You Give Until It Hurts?

I have been working with people for more than eleven years on budgeting, getting out of debt, and managing money. Hundreds of people have sat at my desk, or called me on the phone, to get free of their financial challenges. I have seen the good, bad, and ugly.

What surprises me most is that there's a common thread with many of my clients; they are, by nature, givers. When a relative is in a tight spot, they dig in their purse and write checks for hundreds of dollars. When adult children lose a job, they are right there to help pick up the financial pieces. It is in their make-up to give, even if it hurts.

This blesses my socks off because that kind of character is rare. Giving is sacrificial and selfless. You think more of others than you do yourself. However, this becomes a problem when your own personal situation is negatively affected by your outward generosity.

There is no reason for you to go into debt, not pay a bill or skip meals to help someone else. Derailing your own budget, financial plan, or future only causes more financial stress down the line.

Envision the way you will feel when you can give without worrying about the financial ramifications. Imagine being debt-free and paying someone else's debt off. Picture yourself helping someone else get financially fit because you have done it yourself. Giving is so much sweeter when you don't feel guilt or regret afterwards.

The next time you feel the urge to give, and you don't know where the money will come from, answer the following questions for yourself:

1. Is this the best way I can help them?

2. Is now the time for me to help in this way?

3. Is my motive right for giving?

4. How much is appropriate for me to spend if I decide to?

If you are blessed with the spirit of giving, don't lose heart! Others wish they could have your kind of freedom and generosity. Create your plan of freedom and give to yourself this time. Give yourself the gift of debt-freedom first. Establishing this healthy boundary will benefit you and others.

If you are living paycheck to paycheck, growing a savings account is a present you give to your future self. If you simply don't have any money to give to others but desire to do so, think of ways to be a blessing that don't involve money. Giving your time, listening ear, effort and energy will also be rewarded.

Here are a few ways you can say no without feeling guilty afterwards:

"It's not in the budget right now to give you ___. Here's how I can help..."

"We are focused on getting out of debt. I hope you understand that comes first."

"I really wish I could help you but now isn't a good time. Would you like to talk about your options with me and find another way to solve this problem?"

The key is that you can help without giving and be honest about where you are. People respect that, even if it doesn't help them financially. Be true to yourself and your plan so you don't take two steps backward for other people.

It's Not Yours Anyway

"Bring the whole tithe into the storehouse, so that there may be food in My house, and test Me now in this," says the LORD of hosts, "if I will not open for you the windows of heaven and pour out for you a blessing until it overflows." - Malachi 3:10 NASB

We have to discuss tithing in a Naked Conversation about giving money. Let's begin with the Merriam-Webster definition:

Tithe - to pay or give a tenth part of, especially for the support of the church. (dictionary.com)

Simply put, tithing is giving 10% of your income to your local church. Anything above the tenth is offering. That is your generosity.

I am always in support of tithing. As a matter of fact, Chris and I tithed our way out of debt. We made sure to give God his 10% before we did anything else with our money. God honors the tithe and will show you how to live on the 90%. He will add his "super" to your "natural" and give you a supernatural result of provision. Sadly however, some people are in situations where they cannot tithe, due to where they are with their finances. Laura was in that position.

Laura came into my office with a lot of debt, modest income and a heart to be a tither. She felt like she could make ends meet and still give to her local church, but she didn't know for sure. Looking over her income and expenses, there was a car note, expensive house payment, and credit card debt. She made $50,000 every year but her debt load totaled more than $30,000. She really felt God pressing on her heart to be a tither and give the tenth but she didn't know what to do.

Her debt was keeping her from giving to her local church. She had put priorities on "stuff" up to that point, and didn't think about what it would take to pay the debt off each month. First, her house payment was more than 35% of her household take-home pay and suffocating her ability to maintain the home.

Second, her car note of $450/month was way more than she needed to spend on a vehicle. Finally, her debt was climbing because she couldn't keep up with her payments. Her budget was upside down. She was paying her bills, making purchases, then thinking about how to tithe. The tithe is 1st, and when you are in debt you have to turn your budget upside down to see how you can make tithing a top priority. Sometimes, doing that is a process and doesn't happen overnight. Here's the catch: don't begin tithing immediately if you aren't going to be able to pay all of your necessary bills or if it will limit your ability to put food on the table. That is not wise.

We devised a plan for Laura to sell her vehicle and purchase one with cash within the next year. Then she decided to get a part-time job on the weekends to pay off her credit card debt over the next 2 years. Laura also decided to be faithful to God by paying 5% of her income to her church, until she got completely out of debt. She needed to learn how to be faithful with a little, until she could give more.

For Laura, simply having a plan to get where she needed to be created peace in her heart. She also realized that just because she couldn't give 10%, didn't mean she couldn't give something faithfully.

Tithing is a heart issue between you and God. Understand that all the money you earn comes from Him. He gave you the gifts and talents to create that income, therefore, true stewardship involves giving some back. If you are a believer, you understand that the money is not yours anyway!

The church is a business. It operates on the tithes and offerings of its parishioners. How can you expect the lights to stay on, your kids to have toys in children's church and your pastor to keep food on his own table, if you don't give? Nobody else is funding the church.

But also know that no one should make you feel bad because you can't give the entire 10% right now. Actually, no one really has to know besides God. If your budget is upside down like Laura's was, and you are having a hard time just paying your basic living expenses, your responsibility is to get your finances in order. Creating healthy financial boundaries now, will prepare you to give more at the proper time.

According to healthresearchfunding.com, 8 out of 10 tithers have zero credit card debt.[5]

This could be just the motivation you need to get free of your debt once and for all. For now, give your time, prayer, etc., to your church and be faithful until your finances allow you to be a tither.

---

[5] "21 Fascinating Tithing Statistics", http://healthresearchfunding.org/21-tithing -statistics/ (October, 2014)

Team Couples especially need to be on the same page with tithing. I've typically seen one spouse wanting to tithe, while the other spouse is not quite ready. Here's the deal, as long as you both have discussed and agreed to your commitment, that is what matters.

Get Real

- Have you loaned money to someone in the past? How did that turn out?

- Has anyone loaned you money? Did you pay it back in full?

- Are you a co-signer on someone's account? It may be time to have a conversation with that person to see if you can get your name removed.

- Has someone co-signed for you? If so, think about how fast you can pay off that debt or change the terms so his/her name is removed.

- How do you personally feel about tithing or giving, in general?

Get Naked

- Get clear on what standards you will set with your household finances. Make a list of possible guidelines so you are clear on what you will and will not take part in (no credit cards, etc.)

- Decide on the dollar amount of financial help you will give to friends or family if asked. The amount can change as time goes on, but it is good to have an upper limit given your current financial situation.

- Be sure to set aside money for a rainy day. You never want to be in a position where you have to lean on someone else in the event of an emergency.

- As a Team Couple, will you tithe or give a portion of your income? Decide on what that amount is and be faithful. God will show you how to make the rest work.

Section 3: Your Money Future

"The reason most people never reach their goals is that they don't define them, or ever seriously consider them as believable or achievable. Winners can tell you where they are going, what they plan to do along the way, and who will be sharing the adventure with them." — Denis Waitley

Your future is as bright as you make it. It's time to dream again. Think about what the perfect picture of your finances looks like and make it happen.

"My Fiancé and I hired Ericka to help with our wedding budget and plan our financial life ahead as husband and wife. Ericka helped us set financial goals, track them and even held me responsible for my spending! She was amazing at making everything so specific to our goals and lifestyle. She is a wonderful financial expert and even makes saving and budgeting fun. We have benefited tremendously by following her guidelines. We look forward to working with her again in the future as life's financial demands change."

— Jason and Linsley

Naked Conversation 8
Get Into Agreement

As a child, you played follow the leader, right? Whatever the leader said to do, you had to follow. It was a game of order and silliness, at the same time. If you had a good leader, you would enjoy doing whatever they told you to do. It was easy to follow the directions, if you knew you would end up laughing and having a good time.

The same is true for your money. Many times in a relationship there is a person who is naturally suited to handle money matters. This person enjoys balancing the bank account. He or she may be very organized and wants to ensure all the bills are paid. Following this natural financial leader is easy. It is also possible one spouse has a hard time with numbers. Getting burned in the past around money, can put a damper on trying to get your financial life in order today. So many people shy away from the actual work of budgeting, paying bills, and balancing the accounts. Although this is understandable, somebody's got to do it!

When you are a Team Couple, both spouses are Chief Financial Officers of their home, each sharing the workload. But, there usually is one who takes the reigns and runs with them. It's time to get on top of your finances, get into agreement, understand your roles, and learn how to run with them.

It Takes Two

If you haven't already figured it out, marriage is a partnership. You want the best for each other and your future. You should also want the best for your finances because it creates a more solid future together.

A few years ago, Jerry called to discuss his finances. It was clear he was frustrated and at his wits end. He was intent on getting an appointment quickly, and didn't want to waste any time. It is best if both spouses are involved in gaining clarity about their money. With this knowledge, he quickly shared that his wife was reluctant and may not want to come at all.

I quickly realized that what Jerry wanted was an accountability partner for his wife. He wanted me to work with *her* to get her financial habits in order. Jerry was a saver and his wife was a spender, and these two worlds were colliding. He was unable to save all that he wanted and she wasn't able to spend all the money she wanted. Neither were happy and they were fighting.

Jerry talked about his budget worksheets and how perfect they were. He then noted how unorganized his wife was with money. He clearly didn't trust her with any of the financial responsibilities, so she had none.

Can you identify the nerd and the free spirit in this scenario? The nerd of the relationship loves the numbers, budgeting, spreadsheets, and in general, all things finance. The free spirit wants to have fun without having to worry about the money. The misconceived notion is that if two nerds get together they will not have any problems with money. That couldn't be farther from the truth, no two people always see eye to eye. Therefore, you must capitalize on each person's strengths.

Jerry needed to have a heart-to-heart conversation with his wife. He had to understand why she avoided budgeting money and yet loved to spend. He also needed to help her find the hidden natural talents she possessed that would help the family financially.

Every person in the family is necessary and what they each bring to the table is vitally important.

If a nerd doesn't have a free spirit in his/her life, they may never have any fun. If a free spirit doesn't have a nerd in his/her life, they may never have any money. Embrace your differences and make sure to find a way for each spouse to play a role in the finances.

Don't try to do this money thing all by yourself – you need each other. Your spouse brings unique perspectives, balance, and insight. When you see things one way, your spouse can shed light in a way you hadn't been able to visualize. Remember, you are a Team Couple.

Are You Compatible?

Some experts lead you to believe that you can be financially compatible and that you should find this information out before marriage. First, let's start with Ericka's definition:

Financial Compatibility – Ability to financially exist together without trouble or conflict.

One might think that being financially compatible requires that both parties are the same in the way they handle money matters. Even if both partners are big time savers without any debt, it is absolutely impossible to exist without any conflict! When you are in a healthy loving relationship, you can conquer any financial challenge as long as both parties are willing to work on it.

If one of you doesn't enjoy working with numbers, make sure you have a plan for the spouse who does to take the lead on that. If one of you is a spender, then put up healthy boundaries, (like using cash) so that you don't overspend unnecessarily. If you are both having trouble seeing how to create the future you desire, then hire someone (a coach or financial planner) who can help you define your future vision, and create a plan to help you get there.

Marriage is work, and that includes the financial part. Being financially compatible, where you balance each other out and all the responsibilities work together well, is fantastic. But let's face it. If you are already married, you cannot go find another partner just because your husband or wife doesn't want to create a budget.

Now, if there are toxic behaviors that are coming in between you and financial success, like chronic over drafting, unwillingness to have open, honest communication, or blatant mismanagement of funds, then there is more to this story. As I mentioned in the beginning, in these cases, you may need marital counsel; these behaviors often go beyond just money.

Let's revisit the Team Couple. This is the couple who are willing to explore each other's strengths with money and take responsibility for using them. If they don't have the answers, they are willing to find them. The Team Couple works on compatibility regularly.

If you aren't yet married, it is easier for you to ask questions that reveal to you how a person has handled their money. Then you can make decisions, prior to marriage, about what you will tolerate and what you won't. However, I don't recommend you end a relationship simply because you don't always see eye to eye on these matters. My husband and I don't always see eye to eye. We do however share the same values and are confident that our paths lead in the same direction. Different perspectives should be welcomed, listened to and considered. This is how you preserve a good relationship, no matter what the subject is.

Take Inventory of Your Strengths

Getting on top of your finances requires work. It is important to take an inventory of what each person is good at, it will help determine the roles you each will play. Then, sort through what you enjoy doing.

Here are the financial tasks that need to be done in every household:

- Creating and maintaining a monthly budget and spending plan

- Paying the bills (including setting up and monitoring automatic payments)

- Balancing the checking account so you know exactly how much money is in the account from day to day

- Clipping coupons and/or saving money

- Looking for deals on insurances, maintenance, repairs, etc.

- Arranging service calls

- Scheduling meetings with financial professionals like a CPA, financial planner, attorney, etc.

- Updating financial documents

In my house, I'm sure you aren't surprised that I am the budgeter. I need to know that everything is going to balance and that we have enough money to live on. I also enjoy paying the bills and can exhale once I know that everything is paid, and the checking account is balanced.

My husband has a different role, he loves to get the cash out of the account, and put it in envelopes. He is also great at scheduling service for repairs and wants to be involved in all of those details.

Explore what you each are good at, what you are interested in, and what you enjoy, then divide up these responsibilities. Think about what you haven't yet taken care of, and make sure one of you is the leader in that area. This way, you know what to expect when situations arise.

Keep in mind, these roles can change at any time. Don't feel like once you take on a role that you must do it for the rest of your life. There have been a few times that I was burnt out with budgeting and just didn't want to look at it. Since I'm married to a good man, he took over and gave me a much needed break. That is what being a Team Couple is all about. The point is to share the load. If you do that then everything will still get accomplished.

Sometimes You Need Headlines

If you are in a position where one spouse is doing most of the work, you are not alone. It is easy for one person to take over. The problem lies when you leave your spouse in the dark.

This is where you need good headlines. Headlines are all the important nuggets of the budget, bank accounts, and large decisions. Maybe you don't have time to sit together and do the budget. Or one spouse is out of town and you can't meet together to get the bills paid. In these cases, one of you needs to do the actual work and give headlines to the other spouse.

Here is a list of what you share with your spouse to keep them informed and up to date:

- Budget highlights for the month, and explanations for any items out of the norm

- Checking account balance after bills are paid

- Emergency fund balance

96

- Upcoming decisions that need to be made
- Overall progress towards goals
- How to access all accounts

This will help both of you stay on the same page. It is vital that Team Couples take fifteen minutes, at least once a week to discuss these areas. That way, neither one of you are surprised if anything changes. It is helpful to decide on a specific day and time that you will always connect on the money. Having a weekly or bi-weekly appointment ensures that you are taking your finances seriously and doing it consistently.

Become One

It has been long debated whether couples should keep their money in one account. By observing my clients, I have noticed that if you have established yourself and been on your own for a while, it is difficult to imagine putting all your money together in one account. You have been independent for some time and have gotten used to managing everything yourself. Usually, there is some reservation with divulging the intricacies of your spending habits with someone else.

Conversely, if you are starting out in life and beginning your careers, it may seem easier to combine accounts and use just one. Either way, a large part of remaining open and honest about your finances revolves around the bank account. There can be no secrets at all. You can look online immediately and see the debits on your account. That can be scary.

Managing your finances with one account builds accountability and trust. In addition, it forces you to communicate regularly about what is happening with the money. How can you be one in everything else but get selfish about the money in your account? How can you say you are playing on the same team if you don't know all the plays? If you feel you cannot keep the same account, I suggest you take baby steps toward it.

Here's how...

1. Discuss why you are hesitant, clear up misconceptions between you, and keep an open mind.

2. Map out what it would need to look like for you to share an account.

3. Determine your time frame for making the transition complete.

4. If you must keep separate accounts, do it only for gift giving to each other or miscellaneous spending, up to a dollar amount you both agree upon. You can also use cash to avoid separate accounts. Have an agreed upon limit on gift giving amounts, so no one is upset or in the dark about how much was spent.

5. Decide on the banking institution you will use.

6. Put both names on all checking and savings accounts. In the event of an emergency, you both must have access to all funds the household has available.

7. Go to your employer and change your direct deposit.

8. Decide on who will manage each account on a regular basis.

In addition to keeping one household account, Team Couples must talk about all purchases over a certain dollar amount. If I spend over $100, I call my husband to either let him know or ask if it is ok. I just don't feel comfortable otherwise. It is simply an agreement that we've made.

Let's be clear here, having a spending limit is not about controlling one another. It is simply a clean way to control the money, monitor your behaviors, and allow each partner to know what to expect. Remember, no surprises.

This is also a good time to discuss the boundaries and standards that you will live by. Decide what you will stand for, and what you will not. It may be important that you not use credit cards at all. For others, tithing will be your "no matter what" category. Savings could be a major priority for some couples. The key is to hold each other accountable for what you desire as a team, and make it happen together.

Get Real

- What can you do personally to be more financially compatible with your spouse?

- What parts of the financial management do you enjoy or want to lead in?

- How are your accounts set up? Do you need to add your spouse to any account so he/she has access to it?

Get Naked

- In what areas of your finances are you not behaving as one?

- What day and time each week will you discuss your household finances?

- Do you use only one household account? If not, what steps will you take to get there?

Naked Conversation 9
Create a Financial Vision

The Ford® Motor Company motto "Built to Last" is powerful when you think about it. Can't you imagine the steel branding symbolized by each vehicle's ability to outlast its competition in areas of durability? The marketing team hit a home run on that one! We need that kind of confidence in our financial plan and our ability to finish strong, when we simply don't feel like it.

There are times when life hits you with blows, and you need to regroup and chart a new path. There will be moments when you wonder why you are doing all this work. You may also feel like everything is simply taking too long. Stay the course, keep moving forward, and dig deep. In order to get where you want and need to be financially, it will take stamina.

Define Financial Independence

All the work you have done with your honey thus far, has led you to this place. You have uncovered your past and found ways to make peace with it. Next, you got honest with yourself about where you are today. Now we must create a vision for your future. This is all about where you want to go as a Team Couple.

And you shall remember the LORD your God, for it is He who gives you power to get wealth, that He may establish His covenant which He swore to your fathers, as it is this day. – Deuteronomy 8:18 NKJV

God gives you the power to get wealth because he actually wants you to have it! Meditate on that for a moment. He desires for you to be wealthy, have lots of money and enjoy it! He also gives you the power, knowledge, and skills needed to acquire it! But how do you define financial independence or true wealth? Is it being able to live comfortably, without having to work for someone else? Is it doing whatever you want financially, at any point in life? Is it being debt-free or not having to think about where the next paycheck is coming from? Financial independence can be all of the above.

I'm looking forward to a financially stress-free life when I am living on the interest of my money.

Simply put, you can quit your job and eat tomorrow. And you don't have to live like a pauper to keep up this lifestyle for the rest of your days. The best we can do to prepare for a financially stress-free life is to save now. If you have all the money needed to care for yourself until you die, then there is no stress attached to living every day. So, how do we get there?

One major contributor to the average American's inability to save for their twilight years is car payments.

The typical American car payment is $374! If you invested that amount at 12% interest for 30 years you would have $1,300,000 dollars!!

Can you live off the interest of one million dollars? I'll bet you could! As described in *The Millionaire Next Door*, 81% of millionaires purchase their vehicles, they don't lease.[6] They also spend about $25,000 on their vehicles, which is less than 1% of their net worth. We can learn something from them.

---

[6] Thomas J. Stanley, PH.D. and William D. Danko, PH.D., The Millionaire Next Door pg. 112 (MJF Books, 1996)

They don't use a lot of their cash on vehicles and they pay cash for them. Don't allow yourself to get sucked into the media's picture of wealth, you only see the picture they want you to see. Define wealth for yourself and go after it.

Think about this: do you frequent Starbucks for coffee at $4 each visit? If you do that each week day, it amounts to $80/month. Over 30 years at 12% interest it grows to $280,000!

You see, it isn't that we cannot save for the future. It's the choices we make today, that shape our tomorrow. What is holding you back from your "financial independence"? If it isn't the car or the latte, what is it? Are you supporting your grown children? Are you dining out several times a week? Do you spend more than is necessary for clothing? Believe me, we all have our area of weakness. One of the keys to financial success is knowing your personal weakness, and setting healthy boundaries today, that will ensure a stress-free future.

Becoming a millionaire is a rite of passage that many people want to achieve. It is a large number and sounds so important. Imagine you have $1,000,000. Woo-hoo!!! You have arrived! By the way, let's be clear that a millionaire has $1,000,000 as a total of all assets, less any debts.

But can you live on the interest of that money for the rest of your life? Here's how you can find out:

Let's say that you are able to make about 5% interest on your money routinely, and that you have this $1,000,000 in retirement assets available to you penalty-free when you reach age 59-½. The interest rate may go up and down a bit, but on average that is reasonable to assume for income generation.

$1,000,000 X .05 = $50,000 per year or $4,166 each month

The big question is… can you live off that income every month? If you follow the baby steps and have no debt, including no mortgage, your monthly expenses need to remain beneath $4,166 each month. The average household income in

2014, was $53,657, so many people are living off that income. As you think about all the ways you can enjoy life, take care of your health and keep up with all normal expenses, you must decide if this is enough. I recommend you do a retirement budget before you need it. That way, you will really understand what it takes to live financially free for yourself.

Let's take this one step further. What if you are twenty-five years old and reading this book? All you need to do is save $100 every month until age sixty-five and you will be a millionaire. Because of compound interest you will only have invested $48,000 total! The rest is interest upon interest! If you are forty-five, you need to save $1,000/month to reach that goal. Yes, you will invest $240,000 of your own money, but again, the interest is $760,000!! You simply cannot beat compound interest, no matter when you begin to save. If you are within ten years of retirement, you really need to work on paying off your home. Having no house payment is critical to being able to live stress-free in retirement.

What Is Your Number?

Back in the 80s and 90s pension plans were shifting. New companies were forming but they weren't offering pensions as retirement income. At the same time, many companies still offering pensions began to realize that the money may run out. Baby boomers (those born between 1946 and 1964) took over the workforce. Retirees were living longer than the pension calculators estimated, therefore companies began to scale back on projected incomes offered to employees.

You may say, "what in the world does this have to do with me?" I'm glad you asked! The baby boomers relied much more heavily on pensions and social security to fund their retirement, largely because companies routinely made pensions available to them. Generations that followed do not have the same retirement security that our baby boomer parents or grandparents had. Pension plans are not offered to many new workers and social security is being drawn on heavily by today's retirees. I do not believe that the current generation will have zero social security benefits. I do, however, think that the amount will change greatly from those statements you currently get in the mail (25% less is my guess).

You simply can't allow social security to fund the goals and dreams you have for the future. It is time you took matters into your own hands, to the best of your ability. Your enjoyment and fulfillment in retirement is largely based upon what you put into it today. And by that, I mean you must save for your own dreams and not rely upon anyone else to make your dreams come true. Everything you have worked on with your spouse in this book has been leading up to this moment. Finally, it can all make sense.

Best-selling author of the book *Retire Inspired*, Chris Hogan, wisely notes that retirement is not an age, it's a financial number.[7] You need to know yours. This number is the amount of money that will allow you a financially stress-free retirement in which, you are living on the interest from the money you have saved. You can go to www.chrishogan360.com to find your number. Basically, if you invest for your retirement in tax-favored retirement accounts, and save enough that you can live on the interest from your money, that is your "Retire Inspired Quotient" or R:IQ as Chris Hogan puts it. This number, not age, defines when you can retire and how much you can do once you get there.

It Doesn't Need to be Complicated

Now that you know what you are investing for, why it is so important, and the number you need to reach, it is time to understand how to get the job done. Let's be clear, I am not a financial planner. My focus is helping families build a

---

[7] Chris Hogan, *Retire Inspired* (Ramsey Press, The Lampo Group, Inc. 2016)

solid foundation so they can be consistent, long-term investors and reach their future goals and dreams.

Sometimes financial planners have a hard time translating financial jargon into common terms many of us can understand. This leads to confusion and discourages potential new investors from even taking the 1st step. But, it doesn't have to be complicated.

Long-term savings is for goals that are at least five years away. You could be planning for retirement, kids college education, a home down payment, etc. No matter what the long-term savings is for, the general rule should be that you save it in mutual funds, only if you know you won't need the money for at least five years. The reason behind this is volatility in the stock market.

Over long periods of time the stock market is a great way to save for future endeavors, as you could see 10%, 12% or more in returns. But if you need your money in a relatively short period of time, you don't want to pull funds out of the market during a potential down period.

Be sure about what you are saving for so your end is clear. When you have a purpose and reason for savings, it is much easier to reach the goal. Once you are out of debt and have an emergency fund, it is time to invest for retirement. Here's where you do it...

1. If your company has a 401k plan or similar plan (403b, etc.) invest up to the match the company is giving you. Sometimes this amounts to a dollar for dollar match up to 6% or more. This is free money! There is no other place you can earn a 100% return guaranteed, so make sure you start here. Plus every dollar you invest is pre-tax until you take withdrawals at age 59-½.

2. Invest in a Roth IRA outside of your company with a good financial planner. The after-tax dollars you invest here grow tax free. Currently, the annual maximum is $5,500 ($6,500 for those over age 50). This can change yearly, so double check it often and make sure your household income still

qualifies to take advantage of it. You will be happy to take distributions at retirement that you don't have to pay taxes on. A Roth IRA is always a good deal.

3. Finally, if you still aren't investing 15% of your income, it is time to go back to the company plan and increase your contributions. Today's annual maximum personal contribution is $18,000 ($24,000 for those over 50) and is also subject to change, so be sure to check the limits annually.

If your company 401k plan has a Roth IRA option, definitely take advantage of that. You will be able to invest up to the company match (any matching contributions go into the regular 401k portion) with the after-tax dollars.

The goal with these investment options, is to reach 15% of your total pay (between both spouses) that you're saving for retirement. Make sure to total up how much you are both contributing, so you know you are on track. If you aren't at a place where you can invest the entire 15%, increase it yearly when you get raises until you reach that number.

Start where you are and keep moving forward. Many people don't even begin investing because they can't start with a large amount. Be faithful and consistent with what you have today, and over time you will get where you really want to be.

The final piece of the puzzle includes knowing how to invest your funds. The approach is simple. Invest in four types of mutual funds: growth, growth and income, aggressive growth, and international. Put 25% of your money into mutual funds that fall into each of these categories.

There has been a shift recently to age-based funds that typically get more conservative as you get older. This type of investing assumes your risk tolerance goes down as you age. I consider this is a lazy way of investing. It may work for you, but it could also be too conservative. You give up some control by investing this way. Be careful and do your research when choosing how to invest your money.

My largest piece of advice for investing is to ask a lot of questions. After all, your future is at stake. Never invest in something you don't fully understand. You have the basics of what to do and how to do it and now, you must proactively make it happen. As a Team Couple, look for an investing advisor who will teach you, and make sure you are clear on what you are investing in. Both spouses must be a part of this process and have a voice in all conversations.

The Heart of a Teacher

Throughout life, we all need advisors that can help us make sound decisions and progress through the Baby Steps. When selecting tax advisors, financial planners, lawyers, insurance and real estate agents, coaches, etc., we must be very selective. It is critical to your success that these people embody the heart of a teacher. Anyone giving you advice or counsel should be knowledgeable about the subject matter, sensitive to your needs, non-judgmental, wise, and a good listener.

Always seek out an expert in the field. Be careful about choosing your advisors based upon relationship. Just because the financial planner is your uncle, doesn't mean he is knowledgeable and shares your vision.

Where no counsel is, the people fall: but in the multitude of counselors there is safety. - Proverbs 11:14 KJV

When you surround yourself with knowledgeable people who have your best interest at heart, you are better prepared to make good decisions. You will feel safe because you are at peace in your decision-making, and you know that wise people are only a phone call away.

Many professionals offer a free consultation before you make the decision to work with them. During this session, you should be able to walk away with some needed information and a short to do list. He or she has listened to your needs and provided a brief lesson on the issue at hand. You should feel encouraged and motivated to take any necessary action. If the professional you are looking to hire fits this bill, then you know you have one with the heart of a teacher.

No Excuse Is Good Enough

Several times a year my family and I take time to go back home to Michigan. Our parents are there, and it's always great to see family. On one of these trips, I spent some of my stay with my father in Detroit. He was a most gracious host who cooked breakfast for me and my girls each morning. We enjoyed omelets, pancakes, bacon, grits, etc. Yes, my father could have been a chef.

One morning he woke me early to go for a run at the nearby high school track. My father enjoys running to keep in shape and has definitely been my inspiration for running. As a matter of fact, he's finished two marathons, both when he was over the age of forty-five. My daughters watched a movie with him one of the evenings we were there. I even got to relax while getting a back massage from my dad. He can put you to sleep on the massage table!

What may come as a surprise to you is that my dad is legally blind and has hearing loss. Although technically, he is considered handicapped, he has never made excuses for those challenges or allowed them to keep him from being a great example for others to follow. He has persevered when others thought he should quit or slow down. He has employed his creative juices to survive, and even thrive, while facing his unique circumstances.

My father may not be able to function exactly as the rest of us who have complete vision, but he has carved out his niche in this world. He uses his hands to relieve pain, encourage relaxation, and improve circulation through massage therapy. He's been in business now for over twenty-five years. He has also committed himself to healthy eating and exercise, because that is his part in living a long and full life. No, he didn't say, "Woe is me." He looked inside and said, "Wow is me!"

It is time to use your unique gifts and talents to capitalize on the opportunities that lie ahead. Now is the time to get a handle on your financial situation, so that you are prepared to weather any storm that may come. Maybe you need to get your business off the ground. Maybe you need to ask for a raise at work. Or now could be the time to get out and expand your network, so you can begin to see new options.

It's time to dream again! Somewhere between our childhood and getting a job, we stopped dreaming. We used to believe we could conquer the world, that nothing could stop us! What happened? Many will say that we woke up and found those dreams hard to achieve. Ask yourself the question,

What needs to change within me so that my dreams can become a reality?

My own reflections let me see that every good coach has a coach herself. I hired Monica when I was at a low point in my business. I had just moved across the country from Arizona to Indiana, I was rebuilding my client base and trying to understand my new territory. The new clients were coming very slowly and my income was low. I was frustrated after six months with very few results. Believe it or not, I even considered closing my business and getting a job. Monica analyzed my business and gave me a few strategies to employ right away.

One of the 1st things she told me to do involved writing a dream budget. She told me that I was great at making any amount of money work to accomplish a specific goal, whether for myself or my clients, but she asked me what I would do in my own life, if there were more money than the budget even needed? I mean, I had never asked myself that question. Don't we always think the budget won't have enough? How are you supposed to act if there were actually more than enough? She told me to write down what more than enough would look like in my house. Wow, was that eye opening!

In order to get me to dream again, she told me to write down everything I really wanted. She asked me what I would do, if money was no object. As a result, I created my dream budget. Now I ask you:

What services do you want around your home (landscaping, housekeeping, nanny, etc.)?

What needs to happen so your home is comfortable for you and your guests?

Do you enjoy travel and visiting new places?

Are there activities you'd like to participate in on a regular basis?

What do your kids want that you haven't been able to provide?

Do you have dreams of paying off your home?

Are there philanthropic opportunities you'd like to capitalize on?

Is it in your heart to give, be a tither, or donate to specific causes on a regular basis?

How do you want to dress and present yourself to the world?

Are there personal care services you'd like every month (massage, manicure, pedicure, etc.)?

Are there educational goals you'd like to pursue? Special classes you'd like to take? Or a new skill you'd like to learn?

Take a moment to write down all of the things you'd like to have and do. Go back to the budget you previously created a few Naked Conversations ago. Add in amounts for each line item that you wish had money in it.

When I did this exercise, I wrote in funds for a housekeeper, money to save for a newer car, a landscaper, vacations, regular massages, increased funds for retirement and giving, and money to pay off my house early. It was fun to write in amounts that put a smile on my face.

Think about what will bring you true joy and not just collect dust in your home and put those goals in your budget. Total up the new amount. This is your "goal" or "dream" budget. This is what you are striving for.

The thief cometh not, but for to steal, and to kill, and to destroy: I am come that they might have life, and that they might have it more abundantly. – John 10:10 KJV

God wants you to live a full and abundant life that includes all these things. Now it is up to you to create the income this requires. Think about what it would take to make this a reality. Your gifts and talents will make room for you. Expand your thinking, take the shackles off and begin to say that it will happen. Then create a plan to make it work.

As I worked with my coach over the following year, my revenue nearly doubled. A year later, I had the best month ever in nine years of doing business! In addition, my husband and I purchased a "new to us" $30,000 vehicle, put 50% down, and paid it off in eight months! That vehicle was one of the things on my dream budget!

Sometimes life gets so busy that we don't sit down to make our dreams a true reality. If you want change in your financial life badly enough, you won't make excuses for why it can't happen. No excuse is good enough! My father had plenty of excuses he could have employed too. Instead he tapped into his creativity, God-given gifts, and determination to become a role model, not only for me, but for everyone who crosses paths with him. You can do it too!

Get Real

- What is holding you back from the future you desire?

- What one change can you make personally that will positively affect your household bottom line?

- What do you desire now in life that you currently don't have because of financial pressures?

Get Naked

- As a Team Couple get clear about how much you are currently contributing to any retirement accounts. Discuss when you can increase it to try and reach 15% and by how much.

- Get your retirement IQ from www.chrishogan360.com.

- What shifts do you need to make in your retirement planning?

- Do you have professionals that you both trust to help where necessary?

- Create your dream budget with all the goals you want to achieve at your next level.

Naked Conversation 10
Teach Your Kids

I debated for days over whether to write a chapter on how couples discuss money and kids. Originally, it didn't seem to fit with all the other money conversations that this book laid out. Then I began to see all the faces of my clients, most of whom have children, and would do anything for them. Children cost us an arm and a leg, mine included!

It dawned on me that the reason people get, and stay in debt is because of their deep desire to provide a wonderful life for these babies. We sacrifice a lot for them, and it can cost us deeply. I explained early in the book how my mother sacrificed to make sure my sister and I had all we needed and more. It cost her hundreds every month just to keep us in dance lessons, cheerleading, and tennis as well as to live in a good school district. No doubt, I'm grateful and I wouldn't be who I am today without those experiences. But sometimes I wonder how scaling back would have more positively affected my mother's financial future.

Chris and I had our kids early in our relationship. We justified our car purchases because we wanted our girls to be safe. We remained in debt longer than we would have liked, because we had child care costs that took priority. Even now, we find ourselves wanting to do so much for them, that we really have to make it a priority to keep our retirement goals at the top of our minds.

In this chapter, we will explore some of the important conversations couples need to have concerning, or even with their children. Be level-headed and as objective as possible. Be honest with yourself about how your children, or those that you will have in the future, change the way you manage and grow your money. Real talk… it isn't easy.

Just Say No!

John and Patty came into my office for a Debt-Free Strategy session. They were referred to me by their daughter, whom I worked with as well. This couple was in their late fifties and ready to retire soon. The debt load they carried was overwhelming, and they simply couldn't see a way out. At the time they had about $100,000 in debt, but that was not all.

John and Patty had lived in the same house for their entire thirty-five-year marriage. So, of course, I thought the home was paid for. They paid it off alright. Unfortunately, a few years prior to our meeting they refinanced their home to "get rid of" or consolidate all the debt they had at that time.

When you consolidate your debt or take out a home equity line of credit to pay off your debt, you are only moving the debt around. People do this to make their debt look prettier and get a tax break but, you still have to pay it. The story gets better. Remember John and Patty came into my office with $100,000 in debt. Well, they mortgaged their debt and racked up more because the credit cards were clean. This was heartbreaking to hear, and they were embarrassed about what had happened to their financial lives.

As we talked, it became clear that their two adult daughters meant the world to them. They went on vacations together, John helped them with house repairs, Patty watched the grandkids for them and they even went so far as to purchase vehicles for them. This was no doubt a close family. But the way they showed love for their daughters was putting a burden on their finances, and left them with thousands in credit card debt.

The good news is that they were ready to finally break this cycle of spending. They wanted to retire without debt in tow and wanted to relax, and enjoy their family. It was time to do something different. John and Patty witnessed their daughter's financial transformation as a client of mine and wanted to experience that as well.

As a result of our work together, John and Patty have paid off $175,000 in debt in 5 years, cars included! We got them on a budget and debt reduction plan immediately. Both decided to work in addition to living on their pension funds which gave them the income they needed to attack the debt quickly.

One of the hardest things for them to do was tell their grown children, "No," when it was necessary. They worked on that and it is still a process. Sometimes when you have to say no to one thing there is a bigger yes behind it. For John and Patty, the bigger yes included a trip to Hawaii for their 40th anniversary. They saved and spent cash, so that the vacation didn't follow them home, and they had a wonderful time.

Spending so much time and money on others caused them to put themselves last. Our work together became about more than just the debt reduction, it was also about them taking care of themselves for once.

Today, John is fully retired and Patty only has a few months left to work. They are able to live on their pensions and social security comfortably, but only because there is no debt in the picture. The beauty of this story is that it has ended well. But it could have been a very different story if they hadn't opened their eyes to the situation. Children are a blessing from the Lord. Just don't allow their presence to keep you from the future you desire.

Let's Have a Baby!

Starting a family is one of the happiest times in a couple's life. It's been said that children are like your heart walking outside your body. That is the perfect description of what having a child does to you. Nothing can describe or compare to the experience of child-rearing. This is why we have to be so careful about the financial aspect. Our brains can go completely out the window when our hearts are walking around in this world!

According to the latest annual report, "The Cost of Raising A Child", from the U.S. Department of Agriculture, it takes $245,340 to raise a child from birth to age 18![8] That is a staggering number, and it doesn't even include college costs!

Having said that, don't wait for that perfect moment to have kids because there is no perfect moment. If you want children, have them. Just be as rational as possible and go into it with your eyes wide open. No doubt, kids are a joy and I wouldn't trade mine for any amount of money.

The first thing the Team Couple needs to discuss is the impact of having a baby. This includes child care costs, deciding if both parents will work, and determining the number of children you both want. It is important to count the cost, where possible, and consider how many kids you can feasibly take care of, and raise to be responsible adults.

It is not uncommon for parents to sacrifice everything so their kids can go to the best day care, preschool, and then primary school. While this may seem like the right thing to do at the time, it can quickly wreak havoc on your other financial plans and future goals.

---

[8] Release No. 0179.14, https://www.usda.gov/wps/portal/usda/usdahome?contentidonly=true&contentid=2014/08/0179.xml (August, 2014)

Many of my clients come into my office having already given their children the world, and they're wondering how they got into so much debt. People wonder if they will ever be able to quit working at retirement age, just like John and Patty. It is wise to balance what you do for your kids, while keeping in mind your future plans.

If you give them everything and don't save anything for your retirement, you better hope those kids want to take care of you when your working years are over!

Put on your parachute first, as the flight attendants say before takeoff! That is why the baby steps require you to save for your retirement prior to saving for college funding.

The bottom line is to embrace the budget during the years when you are raising your children. Write down all the costs associated with diapers, formula, health care, child care, etc., while they are young. Think about this as much as possible before having more children too.

Train Them Up

Train up a child in the way he should go: and when he is old, he will not depart from it. The rich ruleth over the poor and the borrower is slave to the lender. - Proverbs 22:6,7 KJV

It's no coincidence that these verses are one right after the other. As we train our children, we must include lessons on money. Let them know early on, what debt does to your future and how to avoid it. Teach them to respect what money can bring, while giving them opportunities to manage it themselves. Personal responsibility grows and develops with practice. You don't want their

1st interaction with money to be when they get a job. It's too late then. Teach them while they are under your roof and are able to practice the skills needed to succeed.

One of the most powerful impacts that you can make is teaching your children how to manage money when they are old enough to understand these concepts. During preschool years, they can learn about giving, saving and spending. Give them small chores to do like cleaning their rooms, making their beds, and putting toys away.

Learning about work and reward early on, will give them an appreciation for having a job and earning money later. You want them to understand the old saying "money doesn't grow on trees". The only way to do this is to show them the opportunities that allow them to earn money.

Gratitude comes from giving. When your child is able to part with money for a good cause, it helps them see that money isn't just for them, and that they have enough to give away. What a powerful lesson for a five-year-old to learn!

Finally, we must teach our children to save. The reason it is so hard to save money as an adult is because we learned its importance too late in life. Get your kids in the habit of saving when they're young so that it's second nature when it really matters.

As children get older, they must understand the difference between a need and a want. If a child can comprehend that a need is something necessary for survival (food, clothing, shelter, transportation etc.), they will gain perspective when the wants rise up.

Kids ask for a million things during one outing to the store, and we want to give them all of it. But when you are on a budget, getting out of debt, or simply want to save for your own future, income limitations dictate that you can't buy the entire store.

Every child must understand the difference between a need and a want. As parents, we make sure they have all their needs met, then we decide on the wants that make sense. Involving the kids in this process will also help them with decision-making skills.

When our kids become teenagers, it's vital that the previously mentioned skills are ingrained. They will experience peer pressure on all ends. They want to look good with the latest clothing and accessories. In addition, to have well rounded students, after-school activities, church involvement and social events become much more important. None of this is free.

As a Team Couple, it is critical that you discuss what is best in your individual household. Make sure you reiterate your household values, standards, and expectations concerning money. It would also be a valuable exercise to show your teenager a budget, so they understand where all the household money goes.

Sharing any struggles with debt in an effort to deter them, may also be a strategy you employ once they can grasp these concepts. When you set a good example you have done your job. Your kids will see how you handle money and what matters to you, then it begins to matter to them also.

Launch Them Out

The most expensive part of raising children involves sending them to college. As of this writing, a moderate in-state 4-year undergraduate degree program, including room and board, will cost a family $96,422. Out of state tuition or a private university could reach twice that amount. No other financial decision or conversation between a couple is more important than where to send their child to college. Student loans have the potential to cripple your retirement plans or derail the good start in life you want your child to have.

According to the 2014 U.S. Census, millennials ages 25 to 32, report median annual earnings for full-time working college-degree holders are $17,500 greater than for those with high school diplomas only.[9]

Many parents include college planning in what they want to provide for their children for this reason. This is a part of giving your child more opportunities to succeed in life. And as I always tell my kids, you are going to college so you don't end up living in my basement for the rest of your life!

What parents need to understand is that college is a privilege and not a right. You do not have to provide all the means for your children to go to college, you just need to show them the way, and why it is so important.

If you are able to afford the costs of college without derailing your financial future, fantastic! But if paying for their college education will put a damper on your personal savings and future planning, then you must think of other ways to help your kids succeed, or adjust how much you contribute. Simply put, your kids can get student loans for college but, you can't get loans for retirement. It isn't ideal but it is an option.

Here are some things to consider when helping your child to launch out, go to college and eventually leave the nest for good:

- Invest in your child early, good grades in high school are critical to gaining access to scholarships and entry to a school of choice. Think about how much cheaper tutoring is versus college tuition.

- A well-rounded student is much more likely to get noticed by college admissions officers, than one without any extracurricular involvement. Encourage your student early to volunteer, join clubs, take up an

---

[9] The Rising Cost of Not Going to College", http://www.pewsocialtrends.org /2014/02/11/the-rising-cost-of-not-going-to-college/ (February, 2014)

instrument, or play a sport. Learning to balance education and fun early on, will serve them well for the rest of their lives.

- If your child isn't interested in a 4-year degree or his/her grades aren't great, consider vocational education or a community college, so they can develop further and save money on the 1st two years of prerequisites.

- Consider having your student work while going to school and be responsible for certain expenses. Not only does this develop character, it also allows them to have some stake in the game.

- Applying for scholarships should be a priority. During your child's junior and senior years, a good part-time job is seeking scholarships. Where else will your child be able to earn upwards of $100,000 in college fees paid for by someone else in a 4-year time period? Nowhere! And many scholarships go unclaimed.

- Save early. The education savings programs are different for each state but can be beneficial to you and your student. For instance, the state of Indiana has a 529 program, that allows anyone to open an education account for a child, and you can contribute up to $5,000 per year. Not only can you choose the investments for the account but, you also get a state *tax credit* for 20% of what you deposit in that calendar year. **This means that an Indiana family will pay $1,000 less in state taxes for saving $5,000 for a student's education.**

One of the most important conversations parents can have with their children involve expectations. Discuss ahead of time, how much you are willing and able to pay early, so there are no surprises when the bills come due.

Get Real With Your Spouse

- If you don't have kids, discuss how many you each want and when you'd like to have them.

- If you already have children, determine the age appropriate conversations about money so that you have a basis for the future.

- Discuss how much you'd like to contribute to college education, so you are on the same page before you talk with your kids.

Get Real With Your Kids

- Discuss needs vs. wants. Make sure your kids understand the difference and how your family handles both at the appropriate ages.

- Help your child find ways to earn money so they can give, save, and spend.

- Set expectations for spending categories that involve your children like clothing. Let them know the healthy boundaries ahead of time so there is no confusion when money is spent.

- It is never too early to discuss college. Talk to your children about their options and why it is important before they need to know.

Conclusion

Congratulations! Finishing this book is a huge step towards financial freedom and now it is time to get into action.

So you see, faith by itself isn't enough. Unless it produces good deeds, it is dead and useless. – James 2:17 NLT

Don't just read this book, say it's nice and never apply the principles you've learned. Give yourself the opportunity to win with money. Commit to having the tough conversations with your spouse. Remember your story so you and your spouse can relate to why you do certain things. Don't glorify these mistakes. Learn from them so you can find freedom from the traps they've already created. There is hope and you can find it together.

Show your children that it is possible to make a difference in your family tree. Put into place some boundaries that will help your family now, and far into the future. Don't you deserve a life of freedom, instead of a life of payments? This is the kind of legacy that lasts for generations. Long after your car has died, your clothes are worn, and all the stuff you accumulated is no longer worth anything, you will have something that money can't buy- peace of mind!

Don't succumb to mediocrity, anybody can do that. It takes a true Team Couple to create lasting change where other people take notice. You will grow closer together and develop intimacy in your relationship that you never thought possible. Getting vulnerable with money will ultimately affect many other areas of your life, if you continue to get Naked and Unashamed.

Your future is calling you to take action! Put your thoughts on paper, count the cost, and take small steps every day, to see them come alive. We are better, more balanced, and complete people when we make room for the life we truly want.

There are brilliant ideas, inventions, businesses, books, etc., to be developed inside you, that no one else can create quite like you would. Your piece of the puzzle is vital to the world, or God wouldn't have given you the passion for it in the first place. Someone else needs you to make your dream a reality! Getting your financial house in order gives these dreams a place to flourish.

You absolutely can create a future of your choosing. Yes, it will require work and commitment on your part, but it can be done.

"Never get so busy making a living that you forget to make a life!"

This is the quote on the wall of my office. It reminds me and my clients that we need balance, not just money. Money doesn't buy happiness and chasing happiness is a futile pursuit. We must dig deep and find a joy and peace, which no money can buy. Work to fulfill your calling and don't forget that you were put on this earth for a purpose. Making, managing, and growing your money will help you fulfill that purpose.

Hopefully you have resonated with my personal story and it encourages you to get more clarity on your own. This process will help you to be aware when past behaviors creep up. You will finally know why they are there and what to do about it. The journey to debt freedom, and your eventual complete financial freedom doesn't have to be drudgery or about deprivation. You can enjoy the journey with a good game plan that works. Together you and your spouse can create the future that matters to you and is a blessing to others.

Conclusion

Thank you for allowing me to be a part of that journey.

To Your Financial Success!

Ericka Young

Client Testimonials

"When the student is ready, the teacher appears."

Thanks SO much for your time today! We are so excited and already feel better knowing that we are putting time and effort into a strategy with our money. You exceeded our expectations and we are so glad to have found you. We are looking forward to the next few months working with you.

— Kevin and Michelle

My budgeting and debt reduction are going well! I will be done with all my credit card debt ($8200) at the end of July! I will then start working on aggressively paying down my car payment which I think has me slated to be done within a year and a half and I'm motivated to get it done quicker than that. I'm so happy I engaged you at the beginning of the year and I already feel so much more financially free from where I started! I'm very motivated to stay on the right track. Oh and I'm very happy to report per Credit Karma I've now reached a 750 credit score!

Thanks for all you have done to help me!!

— Brynn

Thank you so much for getting us started on this journey. We were one of those people who lived paycheck to paycheck and had no idea where our money was going. The truth is, we were afraid to take a real look at our financial situation and preferred to stay in the dark. Ericka's strategies and direct approach laid everything out for us so we could see how much money was coming in and where it was all going. Her system makes our finances easy to track and now there's a light at the end of the tunnel. Now we're on a clear path to pay off our debts and a big weight has been lifted off our shoulders. We look forward to learning more through her great newsletter and other communications. A big thank you! We found your services very valuable.

— Ron and Diana

When I started working with Ericka I thought, I didn't know if I should be paying for this since I'd already gone through Financial Peace University. I started out owing over $54,000 in debt. Since working with Ericka I've paid off $11,000 and bought a car for $12,000 cash. Ericka helps guide but she listens to what I feel is important and assists me right where I am in the moment. There's more to it than just getting out of debt, although that is one of my goals. Ericka has encouraged me to enjoy life along the journey of being free from debt. She has given me ideas about increasing business revenue for a company that I recently started as well. I told someone recently that I can't imagine my life without Ericka as my coach.

— LaKendra

If anyone needs financial advice or peace in their life, then they need look no further than Ericka Young. This outstanding woman has literally changed lives, including ours. My husband and I were in debt straight out of college and, since taking a course facilitated by Ericka, we were inspired to make life changes that drastically improved our financial status. Ericka's passion about educating and helping her community to be better stewards over their finances, is awesome. We've now worked with Ericka in many different capacities and she has always proved to be very reliable and professional with a zest for promoting financial peace. We have absolutely NO hesitation to recommend her services if you are looking to get out and STAY OUT of debt! Your life will never be the same! Ours sure isn't!

— Patrick and Mariah

We finally have a plan in place!! We will definitely be more aware of what we are spending and where the money is going. It is more work but worth it for sure! In just six months of using Tailor-Made Budgets, Ericka has helped us pay off two loans that we have been wanting to payoff for the past 3 years. All while paying off unexpected medical and car repair bills in cash from our emergency fund! Ericka is awesome!! She is so easy to work with and to understand as well. Ericka has given us good suggestions we will be implementing right away!

— Gabriel and Sara

I wanted to thank you again for your help last year. That was really a humble "re-start" for me and your insights lead me to the Dave Ramsey's work that I now use as a guide for my financial success. 2012 ended up as a breakthrough year for me and my future is bright.

— Jeff

I wanted to take a moment and say thank you. You were such an encouragement to my husband and me at our last budget meeting. Facing financial reality is tough, but your easy going and positive attitude have really helped us to take positive steps forward. You did a great job in the role of "sounding board" and counselor for us. It was so helpful to discuss these difficult and emotional financial decisions in a safe and comfortable environment. After our meeting, we both decided to move forward with our business ideas. We have a renewed hope that our financial situation can be improved.

— Conrad and Carlie

Ericka is deeply passionate about helping people. She immediately has people at ease when discussing money matters with a real compassion for what people are dealing with in their finances. Thank you Ericka for your fine coaching and the clarity you provided for me regarding my personal finances and budget!

— Cindy

Ericka is a terrific budget adviser who can relate to an individual's needs and specialize a budget that fits that individual perfectly. We had excellent results with Ericka's service and came away with results and knowledge beyond what we expected to receive. We have recommended Ericka and will continue to do so.

— Tim and Penny

My wife and I have worked with Ericka for budget consulting for about 2 years. In that time, she has helped us and other friends and family members to reduce debt and change the way we manage our finances. She has a passion for what she does, and the clients that she works with. She has a unique skill of being very easy to work with, but can also be assertive in her coaching style. I will continue to refer friends and family to Ericka, and highly recommend her to others.

— Gil and Kim

Ericka is outstanding as a coach. She helped me to focus not on the problem but on solutions. She also has insight, and could point out areas and the roots of the problems that were causing me to be stuck. Ericka has a passion and understanding that makes the difference.

— Linda

Ericka has given us HOPE that we can one day be debt free. She has been most helpful in looking at our overall picture and giving her recommendations for living on a budget. Our only regret is that we did not seek her out sooner, but are so thankful for her expertise. We know she is an answer to our prayers for someone who has our best interest in her heart.

— Ken and Donna

In November 2010 I took the Dave Ramsey Financial Peace University course through my church. I understood the concept of the course and so desperately desired to be debt free, however I was overwhelmed by the budgeting portion of the course. I looked on the Dave Ramsey website and found Tailor-Made Budgets and Ericka Young. After viewing Ericka's video on her website I instantly knew she had the positive energy I needed to tackle the budgeting task. After meeting with Ericka for three months, she made budgeting a simple and easy task for me. Additionally, after applying Ericka's budgeting tips I was able to pay off approximately $6,500 in debt and increase my savings to $1,500!! All in just three months!! I am no longer overwhelmed by budgeting and actually look forward to planning out my expenditures each paycheck! Thank you Ericka, I couldn't have done it without you and thanks to your expertise I am on the road to being debt-free by the end of the year!"

— Stacey

We are pleased to highly recommend Ericka Young! We have consistently hired Ericka since 2006 not only for personal financial coaching, but also, to financial consulting for our business. She is an expert in her field, provides exemplary value, and exercises uncompromised integrity. Ericka is a 'must have' in life in order to reach financial freedom and achieve life goals.

— Aaron and Trish

I signed up with Ericka for financial coaching because I had come off a bankruptcy and I started repeating old money habits. I had to change my ways and knew I needed help. Ericka turned me around! During the time I worked with her, I got on a budget and started planning. I used to live paycheck to paycheck, biting my nails the day before payday, waiting for my next check. Now, I have saved an emergency fund, can buy a car in cash, and have a new perspective on living within my means. I used to feel like I would never get out of the black hole of my finances; but Ericka made my budget so easy, it was hard not to follow it! Now I look forward to all the things I can do with my life.

— Patricia

Before Ericka we were stressed out and feeling hopeless. We learned the difference between wants and needs. We had relied on want now and pay later. My spouse is happier and much more peaceful. We have paid off $175,000 in debt and feel the relief of that weight. We now have a plan for where all our money goes and is to be spent. We work together for the most part and occasionally, we have slip ups, but we are still working on changing our thinking and behaviors. This will take years as it took years to develop our old negative ways of thinking and behaving. Our savings has increased and saved us during emergencies several times.

My vision for the future is to pay off the rest of our debt and be able to live on our pensions. We do not want to worry about debt and have to struggle with a fixed income.

We have learned to not use credit cards, have a budget and plan ahead. If we don't have the money, then we don't buy it. We save and plan for it. We also learned to be on the same page about money. We plan ahead for annual, quarterly, and monthly expenses. We are working on not giving so much money to our children. We learned about setting goals and how to attain them with accountability.

A financial coach is a must. The cost is an investment in your future. Be honest and be willing to change your habits. It will be hard work but it's worth it. Ericka is very positive and hopeful. We still make mistakes and feel a little defeated by life and circumstances at times. But we always know that we can be hopeful and reset and keep going. We learned to never give up. Ericka never gives up. She keeps us on track and forces us to look at our money monthly. Ericka is tough but we love her!!

— Bill and Glinda

I decided to seek financial coaching because I had a desire to get out of debt. I also was close to retirement age and wanted to prepare a plan for the time I'll be transitioning from full time work to building my own business in retirement. I wanted accountability in the process.

I learned that you can get into debt quickly and easily, but it takes much longer and a plan to get out. I've paid close to $6,200 off so far and am on track to eliminate the balance by the end of 2017. I have my emergency savings set aside and have set up an additional savings account for non-monthly expenses so I have funds available when they come up. I've also been able to set funds aside for special giving and benevolence needs, something that's very important to me.

I would tell anyone who had a question about working with a financial coach to consider it seriously, even if only for the accountability. I know I can spend my money any way I choose, even outside the budget. But knowing that I'm going to meet with Ericka monthly and she's going to ask me questions, makes me think hard about the financial decisions I make and the way I spend my money.

I see a light at the end of the debt tunnel and I'm looking forward to also paying off my mortgage and second mortgage once my other debts are paid. I will be able to live comfortably on a reduced income in retirement once all my indebtedness is gone. I'll also have money to give and to travel as opportunities arise.

Ericka has become an accountability partner in my plan for debt elimination. Her encouragement and genuine excitement as I reach each goal has made this process so much more enjoyable.

— Rosie

No one ever taught me how to manage money. My parents never talked about it. In college, I racked up student loan and credit card debt. I went on to become a teacher, and while not making much money, I managed to purchase a home. I earned a master's degree, and went on to add more graduate work so I could add to my teaching certifications. As the Great Recession became greater, gas prices rose, my variable rate mortgage adjusted higher and higher, and credit card minimum payments grew, I found myself stuck—frozen solid. I was completely stuck. I was living off credit cards and sheer luck. Payments escalated, and I didn't know what to pay or whom to pay next. Debt collectors called day and night, even on holidays.

Around this time, my grandmother passed away. I could barely see through the grief, let alone be able to deal with all this mounting debt. So, I just shut down. I quit opening the mail, paying bills, actively trying to deal with my finances (actively trying to deal with life, actually).

One night I was opening the mail, and I learned that my home was about to be in foreclosure. I was at the bottom, and I knew I needed help. I defaulted to what I knew: education. If I didn't know how to do something myself, I would find someone who could teach me how to manage my money. At the urging of my father, I searched the internet to find someone to teach me to budget. I found Ericka Young.

My financial situation changed exponentially during the time Ericka coached me. By budgeting and thinking ahead, I was able to pay down in excess of $24,000 of debt. I had and maintained an emergency fund that was only used for emergencies. Going through this process gave me hope. It afforded me a hope that next month, next year, or the next decade would be better. I controlled my money for the first time rather than my money controlling me.

— Cheryl

About the Author

Ericka Young is the president and founder of Tailor-Made Budgets. After college, Ericka took an expected path in her degreed field of engineering. During this time, Ericka and her husband Chris carried loads of debt that included student loans, car payments, credit cards, and a mortgage. They were doing the things that all young couples do, but along with that came added stress.

It was during this time that Ericka and her husband discovered Dave Ramsey's program. Within 5 years, following the program, Ericka and Chris climbed their way out of nearly $100,000 in debt. As a result of their success and seven years of working as an engineer, Ericka realized that her true passion was not in the technical field of engineering, but in helping others gain control over their money through financial coaching.

Her love for numbers and data crunching translated easily into analyzing financial information. She became a certified financial coach by Dave Ramsey's Lampo Group and is now a recognized financial expert, helping people significantly improve their finances, family and their future.

Ericka currently teaches her message of debt freedom through her e-newsletters, personal coaching, group programs, workshops and speaking engagements. When she's not helping others attain financial freedom, you might see her running through her neighborhood, traveling to interesting destinations, or spending time with her husband Chris, and daughters Faith and Olivia.

Next Steps

Becoming a Team Couple doesn't happen overnight. It is probably daunting to figure out how to apply all of these principles and determine how to move forward given your personal situation.

I want to invite you to take the next very important step with me right there beside you. It is time for you and your spouse to create a debt-free, stress-free life together.

With that in mind, join me on this journey by participating in the Naked Conversations Program. I created this program especially for you to be able to take all of the principles you've learned in this book and apply them specifically to your life. Let's keep the momentum and make your goals a reality as quickly as possible.

If you're ready to make the leap, I'm ready to help you get there. We've talked a lot in this book about working together, having a plan with accountability and now it's time to put that in action....TOGETHER.

To learn more and accept this invitation, visit me online at **www.nakedandunashamed.com/nakedconversations**

Made in the USA
Charleston, SC
31 January 2017

About This Study Guide

The purpose of this Study Guide is to provide you with an effective tool for finding problem material related to the topic you are studying in the textbook. The Learning Chart found in each chapter aligns the topics covered in the chapter with example problems (which are found in the textbook), review questions, multiple choice questions, exercises, and assignment problems so that you can easily find either the commentary or problem material related to a particular tax issue. In each chapter of the textbook, after various topic discussions, we have provided a list of review questions, multiple choice questions, and/or exercises that relate to the topics discussed. The intent of providing this list is to help you pause to take some time to practice what you have just learned.

This Study Guide also contains the questions and solutions to the following problem material for each chapter:

- Review Questions
- Multiple Choice Questions
- Exercises

Also provided in this Study Guide are the Assignment Problem questions. The solutions to the Assignment Problems are not provided, as many instructors use them for hand-in assignments for grading.

Also provided in this Study Guide following the above specific chapter materials are Comprehensive Case Problems. These cases, with solutions, integrate topics from multiple chapters in the textbook. Each case includes a notation of the relevant chapters from the textbook to which the case relates. At the beginning of the Comprehensive Case Problems chapter, we have provided an index for each problem and listed the chapters that relate to that specific problem.

Note that the Study Guide materials related to Chapter 20 of the textbook, Goods and Services Tax (GST)/Harmonized Sales Tax (HST), are incorporated in various chapters throughout the Study Guide. These problems are highlighted with the following note:

> *Authors' Note: The following problem includes GST/HST implications. Students should review Chapter 20 of the textbook, Goods and Services Tax (GST)/Harmonized Sales Tax (HST), before attempting this problem.*

Students should review Chapter 20 of the textbook before attempting these Study Guide materials.

Study Notes: Space has been provided in the Study Guide for you to write your own notes.

References

References are provided in the outer margin of the text beside the paragraphs to which they pertain. These references are to the following sources:

1. ITA refers to the sections of the *Income Tax Act* to be discussed in the chapter;

2. ITR refers to the *Income Tax Regulations* which are also found in the volume containing the Act;

3. ETA refers to sections of the *Excise Tax Act* in which provisions of the Goods and Services Tax (GST)/Harmonized Sales Tax (HST) can be found;

4. IT, IC, and ATR refer, respectively, to Interpretation Bulletins, Information Circulars, and Advance Tax Rulings, and are available on the CRA's website;

5. ITTN refers to Income Tax Technical News releases that are published by the CRA intermittently to provide current technical interpretations.

6. *Folios* refers to *Income Tax Folios* which are being published by the CRA in chapters by topic to update and replace ITs and ITTNs.

7. Cda–U.S. TT refers to the *Canada–United States Income Tax Convention (1980)*.

An explanation of these references is provided in Chapter 1 of the textbook. References to sections of th Act are provided for exercises and assignment problems. It should also be understood that in the course of thei use within the paragraph of the text, all references preceded by such specific terms as "section", "subsecton", "paragraph", "subparagraph", etc., without any indication of the pertinent statute, refer to the provisions othe *Income Tax Act*. Similarly, the provisions of the *Income Tax Regulations* are preceded by the term "Regulabn" without specifying the relevant legislation. In the margin, these references are preceded by "ITA" and "IR", respectively.

References to the *Excise Tax Act* are usually confined to the GST/HST part of a chapter and are specifially indicated as being to that legislation. References in the margin are preceded by "ETA". An attempt has been mde to integrate GST/HST with relevant transactions discussed under the *Income Tax Act* in the chapters where tbse transactions are discussed.

Acronyms

An alphabetical list of acronyms used in the book appears in the first section of this Study Guide, immediatly following the Table of Contents. The list provides the meaning of the acronym and paragraph references where tie term is used in the textbook.

Review Questions

A set of review questions is provided in this Study Guide for Chapters 2 to 19. These short-answer questios attempt to review key points made in the text or points that are not integrated into the example problems, multipe choice questions, exercises, or assignment problems in this Study Guide. Discussion notes on the review questiois are provided in the Study Guide.

Multiple Choice Questions

Since multiple choice questions are common in professional examinations and can be very helpful in learning specific provisions of the Act, this Study Guide provides six or seven such questions covering the material in each chapter, starting with Chapter 2, for a total of over 100 questions. Annotated solutions are provided in the Study Guide to enhance learning through self-study.

Exercises

Exercises have been provided for each chapter in this Study Guide. These usually consist of short problems to highlight particular areas of the chapter. They are designed to be fairly narrow in scope, to provide the student with an opportunity to apply the material in the chapter to a specific problem situation. Solutions to these exercises have been provided in the Study Guide.

Assignment Problems

Assignment problems are provided for each chapter of the textbook in this Study Guide. These problems are designed to have the student apply the material discussed in each chapter of the textbook to an actual fact or problem situation. While these problems focus on the key elements of the chapter in much the same way that the solved example problems in the commentary do, the problems are not identical in their coverage or presentation. As a result, it will be necessary for the student to read the assignment problems very carefully in preparing a solution. Solutions to these problems are not available.

Assignment Problems are identified as either Type 1, 2 or 3. Type 1 problems will only deal with issues from that specific chapter. Type 2 problems will be "cumulative" and will deal with issues from that specific chapter along with issues that would have been addressed in a previous chapter. Type 3 problems will be extended "case"-type problems, intended for the more advanced student. These will be used primarily to help students identify tax issues.

Selected assignment problems in Chapters 13 to 18 require students to apply the Problem Solving Process For Tax described on page xxv. For each problem of this type, students must assess the situation involving a taxpayer described in the problem, identify the tax issues relevant to the taxpayer, analyze the issues using both qualitative and quantitative analysis, and use the analysis to provide advice and make recommendations. These problems introduce students to a case analysis approach to solving problems. The approach encourages the development of issue identification and analysis skills.

Integrated Cases

Integrated cases are provided in a dedicated section at the end of this Study Guide. These comprehensive cases are designed to develop integration skills. To solve these problems, students must integrate and apply knowledge from multiple chapters. For instance, students may be required to integrate personal tax knowledge from Chapter 3 related to employees and employment income with corporate tax knowledge from Chapter 13 related to owner-manager compensation decisions of the corporate employer. Solutions to these cases are provided for self-study purposes. These cases are designed for the more advanced tax-elective course.

Suggested Approach to Assignment Problems

The authors suggest the following approach to the use of these materials. First, the students should identify the issue in an assignment problem that they need to research. The Problem Solving Process for Tax described on page xxv may be helpful to students in identifying issues in a problem even where a problem does not specifically request the use of the process.

Once the issue(s) are identified, students can then scan the headings of the relevant chapter(s) and use them to look for the topics that relate to that issue. Once the relevant parts of the chapter are identified, students should read the commentary, including any referenced material such as sections of the Act or Regulations and CRA publications. Reviewing any example problems to see how the provisions work will also help develop understanding.

The solutions provided for the example problems within each chapter demonstrate the approach that can be taken for the type of assignment problem under consideration. The solutions can also be used as a check of the students understanding as well as a means of providing further interpretation and explanation of the material covered. The exercises at the end of the chapter can be used in a similar manner.

When reviewing material for examination or other purposes, the multiple choice questions at the end of each chapter can be attempted to test understanding. The solutions in the Study Guide can then be checked. When studying for a cumulative midterm or final exam, the integrated cases can provide good review of topics covered in multiple chapters.

Learning Outcomes

To be a successful tax adviser it is not enough to develop strong technical competencies through studying the textbook and the Act. You need to understand the purpose behind the rules so you can explain to others why your tax plan does not violate either the provision as it is written or purpose behind the provision. You also need to be able to apply your knowledge of the technical material to a fact situation and blend a number of complex provisions into a comprehensive plan to accomplish the goals and objectives of your client or employer. The development of problem solving and decision making skills are critical.

A conscientious effort to complete the work and, particularly, to prepare the problems and apply what has been read is essential to a good understanding of this material. Practicing the ability to identify tax issues and apply knowledge of the legislation through both qualitative and supporting quantitative analysis is critical to success. Consideration of the tax profile of the client and the clients needs, objectives, and risk tolerance is important when developing a plan and recommendations for the client.

The authors have attempted to meet the challenge of presenting the material by setting out the work that must be done and by explaining, as best they can, the major provisions of the legislation. The Problem Solving Process For Tax on page xxv can assist student skill development. The approach mirrors that used by experienced tax professionals to analyze clients complex transactions in a logical, efficient, and effective manner. The challenge of learning how to use this process and applying the material is, of course, left to the student.

Robert E. Beam
Stanley N. Laiken
James J. Barnett
Nathalie Johnstone
Devan Mescall
Julie Robson

May 2018

Table of Contents

Acronyms

Acronym	Meaning	¶
A		
AB	Active business	12,140
ABI	Active business income	12,100
ABIL	Allowable business investment loss	7,510
ACB	Adjusted cost base	7,050.20; 8,015
ACL	Allowable capital loss	7,025
AII	Aggregate investment income	12,335
AOC	Acquisition of control	11,090
ART	Additional refundable tax	12,335
ATR	Advance Tax Ruling	1,630.30
B		
BFTC	Business foreign tax credit	10,475; 11,335
Boot (expression)	Non-share/non-partnership interest consideration	16,050
C		
CCA	Capital cost allowance	5,005
CCPC	Canadian-controlled private corporation	11,212
CCB	Canada child benefit	10,530
CDA	Capital dividend account	15,050
CDSB	Canada disability savings bond	9,030.50
CDSG	Canada disability savings grant	9,030.40
CESG	Canada education savings grant	9,025.20
CFA	Controlled foreign affiliate	19,545
CG	Capital gain	7,020
CGD	Capital gains deduction	13,360
CGE	Capital gains exemption	13,360
CL	Capital loss	7,025
CLB	Canada learning bond	9,025.30
CNIL	Cumulative net investment loss	13,380
CRA	Canada Revenue Agency	1,030.10
CUP	Comparable uncontrolled price	19,410
D		
DBP	Defined benefit pension plan	9,320
DPSP	Deferred profit sharing plan	9,340
DTC	Dividend tax credit	6,040
E		
ETA	*Excise Tax Act*	
F		
FAPI	foreign accrual property income	19,545
FCA	Federal Court of Appeal	1,420.50
FMV	Fair market value	16,170
FTC	Foreign tax credit	10,490; 11,335

Acronym	Meaning	¶

G

GIS	Guaranteed income supplement	10,120
GRIP	General-rate income pool	12,040
GST	Goods and Services Tax	1,700

H

HBP	Home buyers' plan	9,355.10
HST	Harmonized Sales Tax	1,700

I

IC	Information Circulars	1,630.30
IT	Interpretation Bulletins	1,630.30
ITA	*Income Tax Act*	1,020
ITAR	Income Tax Application Rules	1,620.40
ITC	Investment Tax Credit	11,340
ITC	Input Tax Credit	1,770
ITR	Income Tax Regulations	1,620.60

L

LLP	Lifelong learning plan	9,355.20
LLP	Limited liability partnership	18,015
LOCP	Lower of cost or proceeds	5,025.20
LPP	Listed personal property	7,015.30
LSC	Legal stated capital	15,035

M

M&P	Manufacturing and processing	11,910
MPP	Money-purchase pension plan	9,330

N

NBFTC	Non-business foreign tax credit	10,490; 11,330
NCL	Net capital loss	10,040; 11,075
N-CL	Non-capital loss	10,035; 11,065

O

OAS	Old Age Security	9,005.10

P

PA	Pension adjustment	9,350.30
PE	Permanent establishment	11,260
PI	Partnership interest	18,060
POD	Proceeds of disposition	7,020
PRE	Principal residence exemption	7,115
PSB	Personal services business	12,155
PSBI	Personal services business income	12,155
PUC	Paid-up capital	15,025
PUP	Personal-use property	7,105

Q

QSBCS	Qualifying small business corporation shares	13,340
QROC	Qualifying return of capital election	19,530.10

R

RDSP	Registered disability saving plan	9,030
RDTOH	Refundable dividend tax on hand	12,345
REOP	Reasonable expectation of profit	4,237
RESP	Registered education savings plan	9,025
RRIF	Registered retirement income fund	9,360.30
RRSP	Registered retirement savings plan	9,300

Acronym	Meaning	¶
S		
SBC	Small business corporation	13,345
SBD	Small business deduction	12,140
SCC	Supreme Court of Canada	1,420.60
SIB	Specified investment business	12,150
SIBI	Specified investment business income	12,150
T		
T1	Personal income tax return	
T2	Corporate income tax return	
T3	Income tax return for a trust	
TIEA	Tax Information Exchange Agreement	19,530
TCG	Taxable capital gain	7,005
TFSA	Tax-free savings account	9,120
TOP	Tax otherwise payable	11,330; 11,335
TOSI	Tax On Split Income	6,150; 13,100
TPM	Transactional profit method	19,410
TTM	Traditional transaction method	19,410
TV	Tax value	16,010
U		
UCC	Undepreciated capital cost	5,015

Reading the *Income Tax Act*[1]

Reading the *Income Tax Act* is often avoided by students, because they are intimidated by the volume of words and the apparent complexity of the expression of the provisions. Keeping in mind a few simple principles and procedures of statutory interpretation and applying them in your reading of a provision will address the intimidation successfully. For an overview of the development of some of the principles of statutory interpretation in the common law as they pertain to the *Income Tax Act* (the Act), refer to ¶1,500 of the textbook. This section will take a "how to" approach that should prove helpful in reading the Act. It is broken down into four sections, each framed as a question:

How do I find something?

How do I read the legislation?

What am I missing?

Am I reading the provision correctly?

HOW DO I FIND SOMETHING?

Before you can interpret a provision of the Act, you need to be able to find it in the Act. In practice, a client will present you with a set of facts, whether complete or incomplete, and you will have to search for the provision or provisions that might apply. Here are some procedures that you should follow to find a provision:

1. Know how the Act is structured in order to recognize where something is most likely to be found.

a. Parts (particularly Part I), Divisions, Subdivisions

— For example, if the facts suggest that you are dealing with an employee and you need to determine whether an amount must be included in income, you should know that the most likely place to find a provision that would deal with that issue is in Part I, Division B, Subdivision a, subsection 6(1), which contains a number of paragraphs listing possible inclusions. After subsection 6(1), subsection 6(2) to 6(23) are what might be termed "amplification" rules, which provide clarification for a rule in subsection 6(1) or a formula for a calculation of an inclusion, rather than a new inclusion rule.

— On the other hand, if the facts of a situation require a determination of whether an amount is deductible from business income, you should know that you should look in Part I, Division B, Subdivision b, subsection 20(1) to see if the expenditure is specifically listed there. Then, if the expenditure is not listed in subsection 20(1), look in subsection 18(1) to see if it is prohibited as a current-year deduction. If it is neither prohibited nor specifically allowed, then it might be allowed on the general principle that it was incurred to earn income. This possibility may have to be researched in court decisions or other interpretations.

---

[1] The materials in this section of the note have benefited from reference to materials prepared as their course notes by Chasmar and by Laiken, as listed in the References section.

b. Know where to find the definition sections for each Division or Subdivision and for the Act and note the wording used to indicate the scope of a definition or where in the Act the definitions are applicable. For example, see

— S.248(1): Note that the opening words, often referred to as the preamble, are "in this Act", indicating that the definition is applicable to the use of the word or term anywhere in the Act. Some terms listed in subsection 248(1) will refer you to another definitions section. For example, the term "adjusted cost base" is listed in subsection 248(1), but you are referred to section 54 for the definition to be used throughout the Act.

— S.54: Here the preamble used is "in this subdivision", indicating that these definitions are applicable to the use of the word or term only in Part I, Division B, Subdivision c, pertains to taxable capital gains and allowable capital losses.

— S.74.4(1): The preamble for this definitions provision is "in this section", thereby limiting the scope of the use of these definitions to section 74.4 pertaining to transfers and loans to corporations.

2. **Look in the alphabetical Topical Index** compiled by the editors of the edition of the Act that you are using. If the word or term is used anywhere in the Act or the Regulations, it may be listed there with a provision reference.

3. **Look in the Detailed Table of Sections List** provided immediately before the provisions of the Act. Scanning the headings in that list in the area of the Act that you are searching may help you determine a provision that is applicable. For example, if you are searching in subsection 6(1) for a possible inclusion, looking down the list of headings of the paragraphs of subsection 6(1) may identify quickly an appropriate provision.

4. **Look at the "Related Sections" and other notes** at the end of subsections and paragraphs to see if there are any other provisions or issues to consider.

HOW DO I READ THE LEGISLATION?

Having found a provision or provisions that might apply to the facts that you are trying to analyze, the next step is to read the provision to determine if it actually does apply and what it does.

1. Does this provision apply?

a. Identify the start and end of the sentence.

— Note that, typically, each subsection of the Act is one sentence. Subsection 6(1), pertaining to amounts to be included in income from an office or employment, extends through several pages of paragraphs, each of which ends with a semicolon, until paragraph 6(1)(*l*), which ends with a period, indicating the end of subsection 6(1). On the other hand, subsection 6(1.1), pertaining to parking cost, is a much shorter subsection and, hence, a sentence of only a few lines.

b. Identify the components of the provision. There will usually be four components, as follows:

i. To whom, i.e., an individual, a corporation, a partnership or a trust, does the provision apply?

— For example, the preamble to subsection 6(1) indicates that the provision applies to "a taxpayer" who has income from an office or employment. It can be determined from the definition of "office" and "employment" in subsection 248(1) that only an individual can hold these positions.

— To keep the specific facts of your situation straight, insert the names of persons in your fact situation into the provision that describes those persons.

ii. What is the transaction, activity or event to which the provision applies, and what are the conditions for that provision to apply?

— Continuing with the use of subsection 6(1) as an example, the taxpayer must receive or enjoy one or more amounts or benefits listed in the paragraphs of subsection 6(1). Each of those paragraphs contains conditions on or a description of what must be included and some contain exceptions to the inclusion rule. For example, paragraph 6(1)(*b*) requires the inclusion of "all amounts received . . . as an allowance". This condition is followed by 11 subparagraphs describing exceptions, each with its own descriptions or conditions.

— To understand the basics of a provision, on the first read, you might ignore any exceptions. However, on subsequent reading, it is important to see if any of the exceptions apply to your fact situation.

iii. What are the consequences of the provision, if it applies, to the person who is involved in the transaction, activity or event?

— Under subsection 6(1), the taxpayer/employee must include in his or her income from an office or employment any amount determined to meet the inclusion conditions in one or more of the paragraphs of subsection 6(1).

— Other consequences may involve:

— charging a person with the responsibility to pay tax (e.g., subsection 2(1) — "an income tax shall be paid"),

— charging someone with the responsibility to withhold tax (e.g., section 153 — "every person paying . . ."),

— permitting a deduction (e.g., subsection 8(1) — "there may be deducted . . ."),

— denying a deduction (e.g., subsection 18(1) — "no deduction shall be made . . ."),

— changing the nature of income or a deduction (e.g., subsection 55(2) — where a taxable dividend is deemed not to be a taxable dividend, but to be proceeds of disposition of shares or a gain of the dividend recipient),

— changing the timing of income or a deduction (e.g., subsection 73(1), which defers an unrealized capital gain on the transfer of a capital property to a spouse or common-law partner), or

— changing the person who pays the tax on income (e.g., subsection 74.1(1), which attributes income on property owned by a spouse or common-law partner to the spouse who originally owned and transferred the property to the owner-spouse).

iv. What is the timeframe over which the provision applies?

— Under subsection 6(1), the inclusion in "the income of a taxpayer" is "for a taxation year" in which the amount is received or the benefit is enjoyed, as specified in one or more of the paragraphs of subsection 6(1).

— Under subsection 156(1), individuals must pay quarterly instalments, under specified conditions, on the 15th day of March, June, September and December, i.e., the last month in each calendar quarter.

— Under subsection 165(1), a deadline is established for filing a notice of objection in respect of an assessment.

c. Determine the meaning of the key words used in the provision by following some established principles of interpreting a statute.

  i. Grammar, including punctuation, sentence structure, and the ordinary sense of words are important in determining the meaning of words, phrases, clauses and sentences in a provision.

   — For example, the following question might be asked about the application of paragraph 20(1)(*n*): does the paragraph apply on a sale of land held as inventory?

   — The question revolves around whether the exception (within the commas in the provision) applies to the whole provision, meaning that the reserve does not apply on the sale of land held as inventory or whether that exception applies to the two-year payment requirement, such that the two-year requirement does not apply to a reserve on the sale of the land held as inventory.

   — A reasonable interpretation would suggest that the exception, following the "and" between the two conditions, should apply only to the second condition involving the two-year requirement.

  ii. What is the intention of Parliament for or the policy purpose of this provision?

   — Look at the explanatory notes that accompany the introduction of a provision or published practitioner or government commentary to determine why Parliament legislated a provision and used the words that it did.

   — Paragraph 56(1)(*n*) requires the inclusion in a student/taxpayer's income of amounts received in respect of scholarships and similar awards. Within that paragraph is an exception, often referred to as a "carve-out" that would except from the treatment of amounts as scholarships "amounts received in the course of or by virtue of *an office or employment*" [italics added]. Did Parliament intend the reference to "an office or employment" to be to that of the student/taxpayer or to that of anyone else's office or employment? The carve-out was legislated to counteract the situation in the Supreme Court of Canada decision in *Savage* (83 DTC 5409) involving an employee who received a prize for achievement, personally. Apparently, Parliament's intent in legislating the exception was to make the prize employment income of the recipient as an employee and, therefore, not subject to paragraph 56(1)(*n*). For example, where an employer offers a scholarship to the child of an employee, is it the employment of the parent that should result in the exception being applied? Would it be reasonable to interpret "an office or employment" in this general way?

   — It is important to test the reasonableness of the result of your interpretation by comparing that result to your understanding of the purpose of the provision that you are interpreting.

  iii. Are any of the words or terms used in the provision defined in the *Income Tax Act?*

   — A definition contained in the Act overrides the ordinary meaning of a word or term.

    — Check the "Related Sections" note at the end of a subsection or paragraph.

    — Be careful to note the scope of the definition by the use of words like: "in this Act", "in this subdivision", or "in this subsection".

— Some terms used for different purposes in the Act are defined differently for a particular purpose.

— For example, the term "earned income" is defined in subsection 63(3) for the purposes of the child care expense deduction in subsection 63(1). That definition is limited to section 63. The definition reflects the type of income that the government is attempting to encourage by providing a deduction for child care expenses, i.e., employment, business and student income.

— The same term, "earned income", is defined differently in subsection 146(1) only for the purposes of section 146, pertaining to the deduction for contributions to Registered Retirement Savings Plans (RRSPs). This definition reflects the type of income that the government is attempting to encourage as the base for tax-assisted retirement savings, i.e., income that requires a certain amount of activity to generate, rather than passive investment income.

iv. Are there words used in the Act that are not defined in the Act but that derive meaning from the way in which they are used?

— Distinguish between the words "means" and "includes".

— Note how the definition of the term "capital property" in section 54 uses the word "means", indicating that this definition is comprehensive and nothing more can be considered. Note also that this definition applies to the use of the term in Subdivision c of Division B in Part I of the Act.

— On the other hand, the definition of the term "personal-use property" in section 54 uses the word "includes", suggesting that use of the term is not limited to the property specifically listed in the definition.

— Both words, "means" and "includes", can be used in the same definition, as found in the definition of the word "office" in subsection 248(1).

— Note the use of the expression "for greater certainty".

— For example, this expression is used in paragraph 256(1.2)(*b*) to expand the meaning of the concept of "control", as used in subsection 256(1), among other provisions in section 256, pertaining to associated corporations.

— A deeming rule is often used to change the ordinary meaning of a term under specified facts or conditions.

— For example, subsection 250(1) "deems" a person, who may not ordinarily be considered to be a full-year resident of Canada based on the facts, to be deemed to be a resident of Canada for a full year. One condition for that deeming rule to apply is set out in paragraph 250(1)(*b*), where the person "was, at any time in the year, a member of the Canadian Forces". That person may not have been physically present in Canada at any time in the year but is deemed to be a full-year resident.

— Distinguish between the use of the words "may" and "shall".

— Where a provision uses the word "shall", the rule is mandatory. For example, subsection 6(1) begins by stating that "there shall be included . . .".

— Where a provision uses the word "may", the rule is permissive. For example, subsection 20(1), pertaining to deductions from business or property income, indicates that "there may be deducted" specified amounts listed in the subsection. Hence, a deduction for capital cost allowance or a reserve is permissive and need not be taken to the maximum allowed or at all.

— Note the use of the words "notwithstanding" and "except".

— For example, "notwithstanding" is used in subsection 20(1) to allow certain deductions specified in the subsection despite the fact that certain paragraphs in subsection 18(1) may prohibit their deduction, by stating that "no deduction shall be made" for in respect of specified expenditures. As a specific example, paragraph 18(1)(*b*) prohibits the deduction of "an outlay or loss or replacement of capital property" or "an allowance in respect of depreciation". However, paragraph 20(1)(*a*) provides for the deduction of capital cost allowance, which represents all or part of the capital cost of a property.

— Note that paragraph 18(1)(*b*) also provides an exception to its prohibition, by the use of the words "except as expressly permitted in this Part". Paragraph 20(1)(*a*) provides for such express permission for capital cost allowance.

— Note the use of the words "and" and "or", which are often used to separate conditions in a provision. Usually, these words are used between the second-last and last conditions in a list of more than two. However, they may be inserted between each condition in a list of more than two, as is the case in paragraph 256(1)(*c*), pertaining to a rule determining associated corporations, where "and" is inserted twice to join three conditions.

— Where the word "and" is used, each one of the conditions in the list must be satisfied for the provision to apply. Hence, if one condition in the list is not satisfied, then the provision does not apply.

— Where the word "or" is used, only one of the conditions in the list must be satisfied for the provision to apply. See for example, paragraph 256(1)(*b*) pertaining to a rule determining associated corporations.

— If a requirement or condition is stated in the negative, the use of the word "or" may have the same effect as the use of the word "and" in a positive statement of the requirement. For example, look at paragraph 8(1)(*f*) pertaining to the deduction of sales expenses by an employee. There are three conditions in subparagraphs (v), (vi) and (vii), joined by the word "or". However, these conditions are preceded, in the midamble (i.e., in the middle of the paragraph), by the words "to the extent that those amounts were not . . .." This means that none of the three conditions can be satisfied by the facts if the deduction provision is to apply with the effect that the word "or" after the negative statement has the same effect as the word "and" following a positive statement.

— Consider the use of limiting terms and their effect on the meaning of words.

— Note the use of the phrase "for the purposes of" in subsection 6(2). This subsection provides a formula for calculating a reasonable standby charge for the purposes of the inclusion specified in paragraph 6(1)(*e*).

— Also, note the use of the phrase "subject to" in subsection 9(2), pertaining to a loss from business or property. The rule in subsection 9(2) is subject to the rule in section 31 which limits the loss otherwise determined by subsection 9(2) in the case of certain farming losses.

— The word "prescribed" is used throughout the Act to signal the existence of a Regulation that must be considered or a form that must be filed in complying with the provision of the Act. The word is defined in subsection 248(1).

— Look at the use of the phrase "prescribed by regulation" in paragraph 110.1(8)(*e*), pertaining to the deduction of certain donations by a corporation. The notes to that provision contain a section for "Related Regulations", which specifies the particular regulation that is prescribed.

— For an example of the use of "prescribed form", look at subsection 8(6.1), pertaining to the deduction for an eligible tool of an employee tradesperson. Paragraph (*c*) of that provision requires certification in prescribed form. The notes to that provision contain a "Forms" section which indicates that the prescribed form is T2200.

— The word "Idem" is often seen as the heading (in bold type) of a provision. It is the Latin word meaning "the same", as in the same heading.

— Look at the heading for subsection 13(2), pertaining to recapture of capital cost allowance claimed on certain passenger vehicles. This provision follows subsection 13(1) pertaining to recapture, generally, so subsection 13(2) is headed "Idem" to denote that it deals with more on recapture.

v. Can the meaning of general words used in the Act be determined by inference following an established rule of interpretation?

— Class words: where a general word, such as the word "similar", follows a list of particular or specific words (i.e., words of a class of words), the general word is to take its meaning from the context of the specific words.

— For example, see the definition of "eligible capital expenditure" in subsection 14(5). Subparagraph (*f*)(iii) lists "a share, bond, debenture, mortgage, hypothecary claim, note, bill or *other similar property*" [italics added]. A "similar" property would have to fit in the same class as the properties specifically listed.

— As another example, consider the definition of "listed personal property" in section 54. Paragraph (*a*) lists "print, etching, drawing, painting, sculpture, or *other similar work of art*" [italics added]. A "similar work of art" would have to fit the same class as the listed types of art. Would a poster be similar to a print?

vi. Are there words used in the Act that may derive their meaning from other legislation?

— Some legal terms used in the Act may derive their meaning from other Canadian statutes.

— For example, the word "corporation", by itself, is not defined in the Act. Reference to a corporate law, like the *Canada Business Corporations Act*, may be necessary.

— Similarly, the term "legal stated capital" may be defined in corporate law.

— A dictionary of legal terms can be consulted for a consolidation of these definitions.

vii. What is the role of the *Interpretation Act* in interpreting undefined words or terms used in the *Income Tax Act*?

— This legislation was enacted to provide a source of defined words or terms used in all federal statutes and regulations, including the *Income Tax Act*.

— Section 16 of the *Interpretation Act* indicates that words used in a Regulation are to be given the same meaning as the same words used in the Act to which the Regulation relates.

— Section 26 indicates that when a deadline falls on a "holiday", the deadline is considered to fall on the next day that is not a holiday.

— For example, if the 60-day RRSP deadline, which is usually March 1 in years other than a leap year, falls on a holiday, the deadline is moved to the next business day. The word "holiday" is defined in section 35, the general definitions section of the *Interpretation Act*, to include Sunday.

viii. What is the role of the courts in determining the meaning of words used in the *Income Tax Act*?

— The courts have considered and continue to consider the meaning of words and terms used in the Act.

— The meaning of the word "profit" has been considered by the courts over a period of years. In the process, the reliance on accounting principles in the determination of profit has been established.

— The basis of the meaning of the word "control", used in the context of legal control, as in provisions pertaining to acquisition of control in subsection 111(4), was established many years ago by the Exchequer Court of Canada, the intermediate-level court at the time. The same meaning of the word "control" is used in section 256, pertaining to associated corporations, but the concept has been broadened to include "control in fact", as described in subsection 256(5.1), applicable to the use of that phrase anywhere in the Act.

— In determining the meaning of a word not defined in the Act, the courts have often attempted to ascertain the ordinary meaning of a word in the context in which it is used in the Act.

— In this process of determining the ordinary meaning of a word, the courts have often consulted a standard dictionary. If you are trying to determine the meaning of a word used in the Act, but not defined in the Act or other relevant legislation and not considered in the same context by a court, you could do the same. It is best to consult a Canadian edition of a standard dictionary which is more likely to provide an appropriate meaning in the Canadian context.

— The courts attempt to determine the conventional, normal or everyday meaning or usage of a word or term. In the process, the courts follow the presumption that Parliament used words of ordinary or common usage and the more common meaning of the word is used.

WHAT AM I MISSING?

1. Consider the consequences of one provision on another.

— For example, consider the impact of your determination of proceeds of disposition of property for a vendor on the ACB of the purchaser and the impact of the relationship between the parties on both proceeds and cost.

— Look for related provisions and regulations in the notes to the provision you are attempting to interpret.

2. Look for the existence of and consider the applicability of an anti-avoidance rule that is specific to the provision and/or consider the applicability of the general anti-avoidance rule (GAAR).

AM I READING THE PROVISION CORRECTLY?

Look for other sources to confirm your interpretation, such as:

— court decisions for the judicial position in common law

— CRA publications, including Interpretation Bulletins (ITs), Information Circulars (ICs), technical interpretations, etc. and their replacements in *Tax Folios* (these do not have the force of law unless they can be shown to have a basis in law, but they can be instructive in helping to understand the CRA's views and administrative position)

— articles in technical publications of the Canadian Tax Foundation, such as the *Canadian Tax Journal* and *Conference Reports*, while not the law, provide views of professionals in the field

EXHIBIT: SUMMARY OF READING THE *INCOME TAX ACT*

How do I find something?

1. Know how the Act is structured in order to recognize where something is most likely to be found.

a. Parts (particularly Part I), Divisions, Subdivisions

b. Know where to find the definition sections for each Division or Subdivision and for the Act, and note the wording used to indicate the scope of a definition or where in the Act the definitions are applicable

2. Look in the alphabetical Topical Index compiled by the editors of the edition of the Act that you are using. If the word or term is used anywhere in the Act or the Regulations, it may be listed there with a provision reference.

3. Look in the Sectional List provided immediately before the provisions of the Act. Scanning the headings in that list in the area of the Act that you are searching may help you determine a provision that is applicable.

4. Look at the "Related Sections" and other notes at the end of subsections and paragraphs to see if there are any other provisions or issues to consider.

How do I read the legislation?

1. Does this provision apply?

a. Identify the start and end of the sentence.

b. Identify the components of the provision. There will usually be four components, as follows:

i. To whom, i.e., an individual, a corporation, a partnership or a trust, does the provision apply?

ii. What is the transaction, activity or event to which the provision applies, and what are the conditions for that provision to apply?

iii. What are the consequences of the provision, if it applies, to the person who is involved in the transaction, activity or event?

iv. What is the timeframe over which the provision applies?

c. Determine the meaning of the key words used in the provision by following some established principles of interpreting a statute.

  i. Grammar, including punctuation, sentence structure and the ordinary sense of words are important in determining the meaning of words, phrases, clauses and sentences in a provision.

  ii. What is the intention of Parliament for or the policy purpose of this provision?

  iii. Are any of the words or terms used in the provision defined in the *Income Tax Act*?

  iv. Are there words used in the Act that are not defined in the Act but that derive meaning from the way in which they are used?

  v. Can the meaning of general words used in the Act be determined by inference following an established rule of interpretation?

  vi. Are there words used in the Act that may derive their meaning from other legislation?

  vii. What is the role of the *Interpretation Act* in interpreting undefined words or terms used in the *Income Tax Act*?

  viii. What is the role of the courts in determining the meaning of words used in the *Income Tax Act*?

What am I missing?

1. Consider the consequences of one provision on another.

2. Look for the existence of and consider the applicability of an anti-avoidance rule that is specific to the provision and/or consider the applicability of the general anti-avoidance rule (GAAR).

Am I reading the provision correctly?

Look for other sources to confirm your interpretation.

REFERENCES

Chasmar, Hugh. *TAX 616, Statutory Interpretation, Course Notes*, MTax Program, School of Accounting and Finance, University of Waterloo.

Laiken, Stanley N. *ACC 604, Statutory Interpretation, Course Notes*, Master of Accounting Program, School of Accounting and Finance, University of Waterloo.

Problem-Solving Process for Tax
A Case Analysis Framework

Introduction

During the Fall 2012 and Winter 2013 terms, Jim Barnett and Julie Timmermans (Centre for Teaching Excellence at the University of Waterloo) spent time identifying topics in the University of Waterloo's undergraduate tax program that students found challenging (bottlenecks). Information gathered from students and faculty was used to develop and prioritize a list of topics that presented the greatest barriers.

Students rated a list of potential bottlenecks in terms of their perceived level of importance and their perceived level of understanding. The topic that was rated as the most important and least understood was being able to identify tax-related issues in a non-directed fact situation.

We worked with tax faculty and tax practitioners to "decode" this bottleneck that is, to construct a series of steps that experts in the field would use to identify tax issues. By following these steps, you will be able to develop your skills faster and more completely than if you are left to figure out these steps on your own.

Decoding the Bottleneck

In the following four steps — assess the situation, identify tax issues, analyze the issues, and provide advice or recommendations — we will address this "decoding" in detail.

Assess the Situation:	1.	Draw a diagram identifying all stakeholders e.g. corporate org chart
	2.	Identify the relationships among the stakeholders e.g. related, affiliated, associated, connected
	3.	Identify the profile of each stakeholder e.g. tax features, risk profile
		a. Individuals, corporations, partnerships, etc.
	4.	Fully understand the decision maker and their objectives
		a. What objectives have they specifically mentioned and what is the purpose behind these objectives?
		b. What have they specifically asked you to do?
	5.	Identify the relevant past transaction/events or planned future transactions/events and create a timeline.
Identify the Issues:	1.	Identify all of the major tax issues and any non-tax issues.
		a. Stated issues and required, unstated issues, priorities, options.
		b. Define the issues
	2.	Identify missing information or assumptions made.
Analyze the Issues:	1.	Identify and perform the qualitative analysis of the transactions and plans including an analysis of the applicable provisions of the Act.
	2.	Identify and complete the supporting quantitative analysis of the transactions and plans using an appropriate analysis format.
	3.	Identify risks including missing information, assumptions and uncertain research positions.
	4.	Reach a conclusion on each issue.
	5.	Evaluate the strengths/weaknesses/risks of your conclusions.
Advise/Recommend:	1.	Advise the decision maker, integrating your conclusions on each of the issues with their objectives, giving priority to the most important issues.

Tax-Related Issues[1]

What do we mean when we use the term "tax-related issue"? A tax-related issue is something that might have positive or negative implications that needs further analysis. Issues may relate to opportunities that can be taken advantage of or penalties to be avoided. They may be tax specific or related to financial accounting, finance, ethics, governance, business or personal matters that relate to the tax matters under consideration.

Tax is often transaction-based. The purpose of identifying transactions and events as part of the "Assess the Situation" section is to help identify tax-related issues relevant to past or future transactions or events.

Identify these issues as you "assess the situation". Issues may be identified early or near the end but never stop looking for them. Issues that are identified can be addressed but those that are not identified represent a potential threat either as an opportunity missed or a penalty incurred; neither option is desirable.

We have decoded this bottleneck by setting out steps organized under four main headings. In this section we will describe in some detail our approach and provide an example of how to apply it.

Assess the Situation

In this first section, the goal is to find out all the information you can, to "establish the facts". You want to know about the parties involved and their relationships to each other and the details of their actual or planned transactions.

1. Draw a diagram identifying all stakeholders e.g. corporate org chart

Start by drawing a diagram indicating all of the parties involved, their relationships to each other, and, if there is a transaction involved, the ownership of the assets both before and after. Relationships include parent-child, brother-sister, employer-employee and shareholder-corporation.

2. Identify the relationships among the stakeholders e.g. related, affiliated, associated, connected

Relationships need to be identified. Are the parties involved related or affiliated? If the shareholder is a corporation, are they connected or associated? Is the relationship one or more of employer/employee, corporation/shareholder, partnership/partner or trust/beneficiary?

The tax consequences of transactions are often determined by the relationships between or among the stakeholders. Therefore it is important to identify the tax relationships early.

For example, related persons do not deal at arm's-length, so related-party transactions that are not at fair market value will be adjusted, usually with negative tax consequences.

3. Identify the profile of each stakeholder e.g. tax features, risk profile

A tax profile is just an organized way of gathering all the information you need on your client. Not all of it will be directly related to the particular situation you are analyzing but sometimes it is difficult to determine this in advance. It is best to gather too much information than not enough.

Individual

For individuals, you should know their age, significant relationships and, if possible, their estate plans.

Trust

If the client is a trust then determine whether the person who set up the trust was alive at the time (*inter vivos* trust) or whether the trust was established under someone's will on death (testamentary trust).

Corporation

Identifying the type of corporation is crucial for determining how the income earned in the corporation is taxed. The main classifications are Canadian-controlled private corporation (CCPC) or public corporation.

Within the CCPC category, consider whether the company meets the conditions to be a small business corporation (SBC), which is important for purposes of the capital gains exemption and the allowable business investment loss provisions.

---

[1] Barnett, J., & Timmermans, J. (2013)

Assets and liabilities of each client

The tax value of each asset is important information. For each significant asset, identify the adjusted cost base (ACB), fair market value (FMV), undepreciated capital cost (UCC) or other tax attribute.

Debt plays a key role in financial planning. For any debt, identify the amount outstanding and the terms such as repayment terms and restrictive covenants.

Amount and type of income being earned by each taxpayer

It is very common for different types of income to be taxed in different ways for both individuals and corporations. As a result, it is important to identify the types of income being earned by the different types of taxpayers identified above. The following is a list to consider:

Individuals

Types of income

— Employment

— Business — Canadian or foreign

— Property — Canadian or foreign

— Dividends from Canadian corporations — eligible dividends and non-eligible dividends

— Dividends from foreign corporations and tax withheld at source

— Taxable capital gains and allowable capital losses, including whether QSBC shares or other types of capital property were disposed of

— Income (loss) vs. capital gain (capital loss)

— Other income or deductions

— Net or non-capital losses from other years

— Available capital gains deduction

— Personal tax — graduated tax rates, marginal tax rate, credits applicable

Corporation

Types of income

— Active business income — Canadian and foreign

— Personal service business

— Aggregate investment income — Canadian and foreign property income, net taxable capital gains

— Dividends from Canadian-connected and non-connected corporations

— Dividends from foreign corporations and tax withheld at source

— Income (loss) vs. capital gain (capital loss)

— Net or non-capital losses from other years

— Corporate tax — basic tax rate, provincial abatement, small business deduction, general rate reduction, foreign tax credit, additional refundable tax, Part IV tax, refundable Part I tax, dividend refund, ITCs

Shareholders

It is important to have detailed information on shareholders, particularly, shareholders of closely-held private corporations. This section applies to all shareholders regardless of whether they are individuals, corporations, trusts or partnerships.

Details of shareholdings includes such information as number of shares owned, what they paid for the shares (ACB), what the voting rights of the shares are and what the paid-up capital (PUC) is.

It should also be determined whether the shareholder has any financial or other influence that, if exercised, could result in control (*de facto*) of the corporation.

The details of a shareholder agreement are also very important.

Has the shareholder ever reported an allowable business investment loss (ABIL) or claimed a capital gain deduction?

Liability for tax

Are the parties Canadian residents and, therefore, subject to tax on their world-wide income or are they foreign residents and taxed in Canada, in some fashion, on their Canadian-source income?

Tax risk profile

Before making any recommendation to a client, it is important to understand their risk tolerance, particularly, as it relates to tax. Some taxpayers want to pay the least amount of tax and are willing to accept some risk of reassessment in order to do this. Others want to minimize any risk of reassessment.

You also need to assess your own risk tolerance as a professional advisor. There may be some transactions that you are not comfortable supporting because of the risk involved.

Risk is not simply the risk of reassessment and potential interest and penalties; it also involves risk to reputation and relationships. A significant reassessment could damage your reputation in the community as well as the relationship between the taxpayer and the professional advisor.

4. Fully understand the decision maker and their objectives

a. What objectives have they specifically mentioned and what is the purpose behind these objectives?

b. What have they specifically asked you to do?

It is important to know who your client is, what "business" they are in and what their short and longer-term goals are. With this understanding it may be possible to find a more tax efficient way for them to achieve their objectives. It is also helpful to understand what they don't want to do or what their tax risk tolerance is (see below) as this may put some limits on what you might recommend.

Identifying the decision-maker's objectives helps you prioritize issues of most importance. It will also help in devising recommendations. Advice and recommendations should meet the client's needs and requests.

5. Identify the relevant past transaction/events or planned future transactions/events and create a timeline.

Virtually all transactions or events have tax consequences. Create a timeline to identify all those that are completed or proposed. Also, large transactions may be made up of a series of smaller transactions, so identify each component. Do not just consider financial transactions. Events such as marriage and death have significant tax implications as well. Here are some things to consider.

Identify all of the completed or planned transactions or events such as a sale, purchase, loan given or received, gift given or received and benefit given or received.

Draw one or more diagrams showing the transactions or events and all of the parties involved. You may need to draw multiple diagrams if there is a series of transactions. This will help you identify each of the components involved in each of the transactions.

Draw a timeline identifying dates of the completed or planned transactions or events. The order of transactions or when they occurred or will occur is often an important detail.

Identify the taxpayer's purpose for the transaction. Examples include business expansion, creditor proofing, income splitting, loss utilization and estate planning. Understanding the purpose may help you identify problems or alternatives.

Identify the Issues

1. Identify all of the major tax issues and any non-tax issues.

Now that you have gathered the information, you need to condense it into specific issues and determine the issues in light of the taxpayer's objectives, the transactions involved and the level of risk. At this point you don't need to have all the issues resolved, just identified.

Remember what we mean when we use the term "tax-related issue". It is something that might have positive or negative implications that require further analysis. Issues may relate to opportunities that can be taken advantage of or penalties to be avoided. They may be tax specific or related to financial accounting, finance, ethics, governance, business or personal matters that relate to the tax matters under consideration.

a. Stated issues and required, unstated issues, priorities, options

Identify all of the issues that are supported by the facts (tax, accounting, finance, ethical, governance, business, personal, etc.). Identify compliance (completed transactions) vs. planning (proposed transactions) issues.

Often issues are stated in a case but not all of the implications are identified. For example, a transaction may be proposed but all of the tax issues resulting from the transaction are not identified for you.

Use judgement to prioritize and group the issues in terms of importance to your role and importance to the client's objectives. Considerations include urgency, materiality and risk.

b. Define the issues.

Be able to explain why these issues are relevant to your client.

2. Identify missing information or assumptions made

It is important to identify any information that you think is missing by looking for gaps in the tax profile or missing information about a transaction or event. Clearly identify this information and list any assumptions you are making.

Analyze the Issues

Now that you have gathered all the information, the next step is to analyze the transactions or events to determine the tax consequences.

1. Identify and perform the qualitative analysis of the transactions and plans including an analysis of the applicable provisions of the Act

For each issue, identify the provisions of the Act that might apply and determine whether the conditions of each provision are met.

Determine whether any anti-avoidance or other special provisions apply. This is especially relevant where there are transactions among related or affiliated parties, e.g., stop loss rules.

Clearly communicate the application of the provision to the relevant issue and its actual or potential implications.

2. Identify and complete the supporting quantitative analysis of the transactions and plans using an appropriate analysis format

All transactions have more than one party involved. They may be individuals or corporations or partnerships or trusts. The transaction may, for example, be that of vendor/purchaser, donor/recipient or estate/beneficiary. Since all transactions will have an impact on income it is important to identify the income effect on each of the parties involved either now or in the future.

All transactions have more than one party involved. They may be individuals or corporations or partnerships or trusts. The transaction may, for example, be that of vendor/purchaser, donor/recipient or estate/beneficiary. Since all transactions will have an impact on income it is important to identify the income effect on each of the parties involved either now or in the future.

When doing this analysis make sure you use the format that is appropriate to the issue. As part of your study you should make sure you identify and understand the analysis applicable to each type of transaction or event.

Any quantitative analysis should be referred to and its relevance explained as part of the qualitative analysis of each issue.

3. Identify risks including missing information, assumptions and uncertain research positions

Missing information, assumptions and uncertain tax positions all pose risks to the conclusion you reach. Be sure to identify these risks.

4. Reach a conclusion on each issue

For each issue identified, reach a conclusion.

5. Evaluate the strengths/weaknesses/risks of your conclusions

At this point, assess whether you, and your client, are willing to live with the conclusion given the risks involved.

Advise/Recommend

1. Advise the decision maker, integrating your conclusions on each of the issues with their objectives, giving priority to the most important issues

Sometimes a conclusion can be reached on an issue independent from conclusions reached on other issues. These conclusions can be considered when making recommendations to the client. However, in other situations your conclusion on one issue will impact your conclusion on another. In this case, it is necessary to consider the objectives and priorities of the client to determine which issue/conclusion takes priority. It may be necessary to perform additional analysis with respect to an issue because of the impact of a conclusion on a related issue.

There are also times when a client's objectives cannot be met without negative tax consequences. This doesn't mean they should not be met it just means that the client needs to assess the costs vs. the benefits. Advising the client provides the opportunity to integrate all of your knowledge, analysis, and conclusions to provide useful practical recommendations that can be implemented by the client to meet their stated and unstated objectives.

Exhibit

Summary of Problem Solving Process for Tax

Assess the Situation:	1.	Draw a diagram identifying all stakeholders e.g., corporate org chart
	2.	Identify the relationships among the stakeholders e.g., related, affiliated, associated, connected
	3.	Identify the profile of each stakeholder e.g., tax features, risk profile
		a. Individuals, corporations, partnerships, etc.
	4.	Fully understand the decision maker and their objectives
		a. What objectives have they specifically mentioned and what is the purpose behind these objectives?
		b. What have they specifically asked you to do?
	5.	Identify the relevant past transactions/events or planned future transactions/events and create a timeline.
Identify the Issues:	1.	Identify all of the major tax issues and any non-tax issues.
		a. Stated issues and required, unstated issues, priorities, options.
		b. Define the issues
	2.	Identify missing information or assumptions made.
Analyze the Issues:	1.	Identify and perform the qualitative analysis of the transactions and plans including an analysis of the applicable provisions of the Act.
	2.	Identify and complete the supporting quantitative analysis of the transactions and plans using an appropriate analysis format.
	3.	Identify risks including missing information, assumptions, and uncertain research positions.
	4.	Reach a conclusion on each issue.
	5.	Evaluate the strengths/weaknesses/risks of your conclusions.
Advise/Recommend:	1.	Advise the decision maker, integrating your conclusions on each of the issues with their objectives, giving priority to the most important issues.

Exhibit

Summary of Problem Solving Process for Tax

Assess the Situation	1. Draw a diagram identifying all stakeholders e.g., corporate org chart
	2. Identify the relationships among the stakeholders – e.g., related, affiliated, associated, connected
	3. Identify the profile of each stakeholder e.g. tax features - risk profile – individuals, corporations, partnerships, etc.
	4. Fully understand the decision maker and their objectives
	a. What objectives have they specifically identified and what is the purpose behind those objectives
	b. What have they specifically asked you to do?
	5. Identify the relevant past transactions/events or planned future transactions/calls and create a timeline
Identify the Issues	1. Identify all of the relevant tax issues and any non-tax issues
	a. Stated issues and required/implied issues: priorities, options
	b. Define the issues
	2. Identify missing information or missing instructions
Analyze the Issues	1. Identify and perform the qualitative analysis of the transactions and plan including an analysis of the applicable provisions of the Act
	2. Identify and compute the supporting quantitative analysis of the transactions and plans using an appropriate analysis format
	3. Identify risks including missing information, assumptions and necessary research positions
	4. Reach a conclusion on each issue
	5. Evaluate the strengths/weaknesses/risks of your conclusions
Advise/recommend	1. Advise the decision maker, integrating your conclusions on each of the range with their potential, giving priority to the most important issues

Chapter 1

Introduction

Learning Goals

Know, Understand and Explain

By the end of this chapter you will know, understand and be able to explain:

- The different roles that professional accountants and lawyers may play in providing tax services.
- The principles that make good tax policy.
- How the perspective on income differs among economic analysis, financial reporting, and the *Income Tax Act*.
- How tax policy is created in Canada.
- The appeals process in the Canadian tax system.
- Strategies for interpreting the *Income Tax Act*.
- How to reference the *Income Tax Act*.
- The common sources of tax rules and sources for interpretation in the Canadian tax system.

Apply

By the end of this chapter you will be able to apply your knowledge and understanding to:

- Assess the attributes of prospective tax policies.

Exercises

¶1,850 in the Study Guide

Assignment Problems

¶1,875 in the Study Guide

CHAPTER 1 — LEARNING CHART

Problem Descriptions

Exercises

1	Identify sections of the Act
2	Determine income, taxable income and basic federal tax
3	Identify components of 212(1)

Assignment Problems

1	Identify section of the Act
2	Determine income using ordering rules
3	Identify and define words/terms found in section 2

Study Notes

¶1,850 EXERCISES

Exercise 1

ITA: 8, 15, 20, 38, 69, 81, 108, 150

For each of the following items, identify the appropriate provision of the Act which deals with the item listed. Be as specific as possible in citing the reference to the Act, i.e., Part, Division, Subdivision, Section, Subsection, etc. Use of the Sectional List at the beginning of the Wolters Kluwer edition of the CANADIAN INCOME TAX ACT and/or the Topical Index at the end of the book may be helpful.

(A) Definition of "taxable capital gain".

(B) Deduction for certain annual professional membership dues paid by an employee.

(C) Taxability of payments received as income from property acquired as personal injury award.

(D) Deductibility of an expense based on its magnitude.

(E) Definition of a "parent" under the Act.

(F) Definition of an *"inter vivos"* trust.

(G) Deadline for filing of a tax return for a deceased person.

(H) Taxability of a benefit received from a corporation by a shareholder.

(I) Transaction price in a non-arm's length disposition of property.

(J) Deductibility of fees for investment advice.

Exercise 2

ITA: Divisions B and C

Mr. Malcolm Miller has provided you with a list of various sources of income, losses, deductions, and credits for the purpose of determining his basic federal tax.

Income (net):

Business income	$10,000
Property income	3,000
Retiring allowance from a former employer	20,000
Employment income from new employer	60,000
Taxable capital gains (net of allowable capital losses)	20,000

Deduction and Losses:

Rental property loss	4,000

Carry forward Losses and Tax Credits:

Canada Pension Plan contributions tax credit	389
Non-capital losses from a previous year	4,000
Tuition tax credits transfer from son	80
Net capital losses from a previous year	5,000
Basic personal and spousal tax credits	3,542
Employment Insurance premiums tax credit	129
Tuition tax credit for night course on computer applications	68
Charitable gifts tax credit	550
Canada employment tax credit	179

— *REQUIRED*

(A) Determine the income, taxable income and basic federal tax based on the above correct information using the ordering rules in sections 3, 111.1, and 118.92. Assume that federal tax before credits is $18,424 in 2017.

(B) Cross-reference each amount to the appropriate section of the Act.

Exercise 3

ITA: 212(1)

Identify the following components of subsection 212(1):

(A) the person who is the subject of the provision,

(B) the activity, event, or condition that must be met for the provision to apply,

(C) the consequences of the activity or event to the person who is the subject of the provision, and

(D) the time frame for the application of the provision.

¶1,875   ASSIGNMENT PROBLEMS

Type 1 Problems

Problem 1

Identify the provision of the Act which deals with each of the following items. Be as specific as possible in citing the reference to the Act (Part, Division, Subdivision, Section, Subsection, etc.). Use of the sectional list at the beginning of the Wolters Kluwer edition of the Act and/or the topical index at the end of the book may be helpful.

(A) Definition of a "person".

(B) Tax credit for donation made by a Canadian resident individual to a Canadian university.

(C) Definition of "balance-due day".

(D) Taxability of group term life insurance premiums paid by an employer on behalf of an employee.

(E) Definition of "capital dividend".

(F) Computation of income tax instalments for individuals.

(G) Definition of a "qualified small business corporation share".

(H) Prescribed requirement to file an information return for a corporation paying a dividend.

(I) Definition of a "testamentary trust".

(J) The calculation of a benefit associated with an interest-free loan from an employer to an employee.

(K) Definition of a "disposition" of non-depreciable capital property.

(L) Limitation on deduction of RRSP administration fees.

(M) General limitation on the amount of deductible expenses.

(N) Deduction from taxable income for taxable dividends that were received by a Canadian corporation.

(O) Tax payable on excess contributions to an RRSP.

Problem 2

ITA: 245; Division B, C

Ms. Irene Vanburg had a tumultuous year. She broke her engagement early in the year and quit her job. She moved to a resort area to take a waitress job and to start up a fitness instruction business. She has had the following items correctly calculated and classified as either inclusions, deductions or tax credits for the purposes of determining her taxable income and federal tax.

Income (net):

Employment Insurance benefits	$ 600
Employment income	32,600
Property income	775
Rental property income	975
Taxable capital gain (net of allowable capital losses)	100
Retiring allowance from previous employer	800

Deductions and Losses:

Business loss	(275)

Deductions, Losses, and Tax Credits:

Charitable gifts tax credit	26
Child care expenses	1,800
Canada Pension Plan contributions tax credits on employment earnings	216
Medical expenses tax credit	9

Moving expenses 1,700

Non-capital losses from previous year 600

Personal tax credit 1,771

Employment Insurance premiums tax credit 81

Canada employment credit 179

Irene has asked you to determine the income, taxable income, and basic federal tax based on the above correct information using the ordering rules in sections 3, 111.1, and 118.92. Assume federal tax before credits is $4,721 in the year.

For your files you should cross-reference each amount to the appropriate section of the Act.

Problem 3　　　　　　　　　　　　　　　　　　　　　　　　　　　　　ITA: 2

Many words and terms used in the Act have very specific interpretations. Awareness of these interpretations is fundamental to understanding the scheme and application of the Act. These interpretations come from various sources. The primary source is statutory definition; that is, the term is explicitly defined in the Act. Common law principles also determine interpretations for terms. Many court cases have centred on the interpretation of specific words or phrases which were not explicitly defined in the statute. Once such terms are interpreted by the Courts, that interpretation becomes standard for that term. If a term is neither defined in the statute, nor the subject of a common law definition, the word or term must be assigned the meaning provided by everyday language. The definition is often that which can be found in a common dictionary.

Division A of Part I of the Act outlines who is liable for tax. This Division is a fundamental building block for the Act as it defines to whom the Act will apply. Therefore, it is essential that the terms used in this Division are clearly understood.

You have been asked to identify and define those words and terms found in section 2 of the Act, in the order of their use, which you believe require definition. Indicate the references in the Act to the source of the definition for those words or terms which you have so identified.

You have also been asked to identify the following components of subsection 2(3):

(i) the person who is the subject of the provision,

(ii) the activity, event, or condition that must be met for the provision to apply,

(iii) the consequences of the activity or event to the person who is the subject of the provision, and

(iv) the time frame for the application of the provision.

CHAPTER 1 — SOLUTIONS TO EXERCISES

Exercise 1

The following summary is discussed in more detail below:

Case	Topic	Part	Division	Subdivision	Provision
(A)	Taxable capital gain	I	B	c	paragraph 38(*a*)
(B)	Membership dues	I	B	a	subparagraph 8(1)(*i*)(i)
(C)	Personal injury award	I	B	g	paragraph 81(1)(*g*.1)
(D)	Expense limit	I	B	f	section 67
(E)	Parent	XVII	—	—	subsection 252(2)
(F)	*Inter vivos* trust	I	B	k	subsection 108(1)
(G)	Filing deadline	I	I	—	paragraph 150(1)(*b*)
(H)	Shareholder benefit	I	B	b	subsection 15(1)
(I)	Non-arm's length	I	B	f	paragraph 69(1)(*b*)
(J)	Investment fees	I	B	b	paragraph 20(1)(*bb*)

(A) Part I, Division B, Subdivision c, paragraph 38(*a*): — Most definitions applicable to the Taxable Capital Gains and Allowable Capital Losses subdivision of Part I, Division B are found in section 54. However, this definition is set out at the beginning of Subdivision c. Definitions of terms used throughout the Act are found in subsection 248(1). If a term is not specifically defined in subsection 248(1) or in a section elsewhere in the Act, judicial precedents should be consulted for the meaning of the word.

(B) Part I, Division B, Subdivision a, subparagraph 8(1)(*i*)(i): — Employment income and deductions are set out in sections 5 to 8 of Part I, Division B, Subdivision a of the Act. All deductions from this source appear in section 8 with the major list of deductions occurring in subsection 8(1) and further explanation or restriction of these deductions appearing in subsections 8(2) to 8(11).

(C) Part I, Division B, Subdivision g, paragraph 81(1)(*g*.1): — Income from property acquired as personal injury award is one in a limited list of items found in section 81 which are not included in computing income.

(D) Part I, Division B, Subdivision f, section 67: — Inclusions and deductions in the computation of income are generally found in Part I, Division B, Subdivisions a, b, c, d or e. In this case, however, the rule is found in Subdivision f dealing with general rules relating to the computation of income from all sources.

(E) Part XVII, subsection 252(2): — The word "parent" appears throughout the Act, so the definition is most likely to be in Part XVII on "Interpretation."

(F) Part I, Division B, Subdivision k, subsection 108(1): — Trusts and their beneficiaries are dealt with in Subdivision k of Part I, Division B. The definitions section for this subdivision is section 108.

(G) Part I, Division I, paragraph 150(1)(*b*): This is a procedural matter generally handled in Division I of Part I of the Act dealing with Returns, Assessments, Payment and Appeals.

(H) Part I, Division B, Subdivision b, subsection 15(1): — A benefit received by a shareholder, if it is to be taxed, would likely be income from property which is handled in Subdivision b of Division B of Part I. Inclusions from that source are generally listed in sections 12 to 17.

(I) Part I, Division B, Subdivision f, paragraph 69(1)(*b*): — This provision can be found in the set of general rules pertaining to the computation of income in Subdivision f of Division B of Part I because it affects the computation of income from a variety of sources.

(J) Part I, Division B, Subdivision b, paragraph 20(1)(*bb*): — Investments provide income from property and deductions from such income are generally listed in subsection 20(1).

Exercise 2

DIVISION B

Par. 3(a)	*Subdivision a*			
	Sec. 5, 6, 7, 8	Employment income		$ 60,000
	Subdivision b			
	Sec. 9	Business income	$ 10,000	
	Sec. 9	Property income	3,000	13,000
	Subdivision d			
	Par. 56(1)(a)	Retiring allowance		20,000
		Total par. 3(a) income		$ 93,000
Par. 3(b)	*Subdivision c*			
	Par. 38	Taxable capital gain (net of allowable capital loss)		20,000
				$113,000
Par. 3(d)	*Subdivision b*			
	Ssec. 9(2):	Rental property loss		(4,000)

Division B income			$109,000
Par. 111(1)(a)	Non-capital loss	$ 4,000	
Par. 111(1)(b)	Net capital loss	5,000	(9,000)
Taxable income			$100,000

Federal tax after credits

Tax before credits			$ 18,424
Sec. 118(1)	Personal credits		(3,542)
Sec. 118(10)	Canada employment credit		(179)
Sec. 118.7	CPP contributions credit		(389)
Sec. 118.7	EI premium credit		(129)
Sec. 118.5	Tuition credit		(68)
Sec. 118.6	Tuition credit transfer		(80)
Sec. 118.1	Charitable donation credit		(550)
Basic federal tax			$ 13,487

Exercise 3

Subsection 212(1) is a "charging provision" because it charges someone with the responsibility for paying a tax.

The components of subsection 212(1) are as follows.

(A) the person who is the subject of the provision

- "every non-resident person"

(B) the activity, event or condition that must be met for the provision to apply

- "on every amount that a person resident in Canada pays or credits or is deemed by Part I to pay or credit to the non-resident person as . . ." [followed by paragraphs (a) to (w) that list types of payments, such as a management fee, interest, rent, etc.]

(C) the consequences of the activity or event to the person who is the subject of the provision

- "*shall* pay an income tax at 25% on every amount . . ."

- note the use of the word "shall", indicating a mandatory payment

- note that the 25% rate can be reduced by a tax treaty which overrides the Canadian *Income Tax Act*

(D) the time frame for the application of the provision

- in the year that the amount is paid or credited is implied

Chapter 2

Liability for Tax

Learning Goals

Know, Understand and Explain

By the end of this chapter you will know, understand and be able to explain:

- The definition of person under the Act.
- Factors used to determine the residency status of a person under the Act.
- The tax liability for resident and non-resident persons.
- The effects of an existing international tax treaty on the tax liability of a person.

Apply

By the end of this chapter you will be able to apply your knowledge and understanding to:

- Determine the residency status of an individual, including the status of a part-year resident in a year of transition.
- Determine the residency status of a corporation.
- Advise clients and employers on the tax implications of the determined residency status.

Review Questions
¶2,800 in the Study Guide

Multiple Choice Questions
¶2,825 in the Study Guide

Exercises
¶2,850 in the Study Guide

Assignment Problems
¶2,875 in the Study Guide

CHAPTER 2

CHAPTER 2 — LEARNING CHART

Problem Descriptions

Textbook Example Problems

2-1	Resident vs. non-resident — individual
2-2	Resident vs. non-resident — corporation

Multiple Choice Questions

1	Corporate residence
2	Individual residency
3	Canadian income of non-resident
4	Canadian income of part-year resident
5	Individual residency
6	HST

Exercises

1	Individual residency — multi-part
2	Individual residency — case
3	Corporate residency — multi-part
4	Canadian income of non-resident
5	Individual residency
6	Corporate residency
7	Ceasing residency

Assignment Problems

1	Individual residency — multi-part
2	Individual residency — case
3	Individual residency — case
4	Individual residency — case
5	Corporate residency — multi-part
6	Corporate residency — case
7	Corporate residency — case
8	Corporate residency — case
9	Transfer to France
10	Move to Chile
11	Individual residency

Study Notes

CHAPTER 2

¶2,800   REVIEW QUESTIONS

(1) Canadian citizens pay tax in Canada on their world income. Comment.

(2) If a non-resident vacations in Canada for 180 days during the year, then he or she will be considered a Canadian resident for the full year. Comment.

(3) If an individual sells his or her house and then leaves the country, the person will be considered to be a non-resident. Comment.

(4) Assume that an individual resided in Buffalo and carried on a proprietorship business in St. Catharines. How would he or she pay tax on the business income earned in Canada?

(5) An individual who moves to Canada on March 31 of the year will be considered resident in Canada throughout the year since he or she was resident here for more than 183 days. Comment.

(6) Since a corporation is an artificial legal entity, it does not "reside" anywhere in the sense that an individual does. Comment on how the residency of a corporation is determined.

(7) A company was incorporated in Canada on November 30, 1965, but has been carrying on business in Bermuda since that date and all of the officers and directors have always been resident there. Comment on the company's tax liability in Canada.

(8) A company was incorporated in Canada on November 30, 1964, but has been carrying on business in Bermuda since that date and all of the officers and directors have always been resident there. In the years from incorporation to 1971 the company actively solicited orders in Canada by telephone. It stopped this activity in Canada at the end of 1971. Comment on the company's tax liability to Canada.

(9) A Canadian executive is transferred to the U.S. with his company on a five-year contract. He and his family sell all their Canadian assets and move to the U.S. in December of the year. Due to the lower personal income tax rates in the U.S., he has the Canadian company defer the payment of the bonus of $100,000 that he earned in Canada in the year until the next year when he is resident in the U.S. Comment on whether the executive will be taxed in Canada on this bonus.

(10) If a U.S. corporation has an employee located in Canada who is selling goods on behalf of the employer, then would the U.S. company be taxable in Canada?

(11) If a U.S. corporation has an agent located in Canada who is selling goods on behalf of the U.S. company, then would the U.S. company be taxable in Canada?

(12) If a person is resident in Canada, can that same person also be resident in the U.S.?

(13) If a Canadian corporation is carrying on business in the U.S. through a permanent establishment in the U.S., will the Canadian company be considered resident in the U.S. and be subject to tax in the U.S. on the total corporate income?

(14) Mr. Smith is an independent consultant who provides his services wherever he can get the work. He has been asked by a U.S. company to go to the U.S. to consult with them. He thinks that he will have to spend 25 days travelling to their many locations in the U.S. over the next year and that he will earn $50,000 for his efforts. His lawyer has told him that he will be taxed in the U.S. on this business income. What do you think?

¶2,825   MULTIPLE CHOICE QUESTIONS

Question 1

X Ltd. is a corporation which has always been managed by the *same* Board of Directors. The Board of Directors has always met where the directors reside. Based on these facts, X Ltd. will NOT be resident in Canada for income tax purposes if X Ltd. was:

(A) incorporated in Canada in 1968 and its directors are all U.S. residents;

(B) incorporated in the U.S. in 1970 and its directors are all U.S. residents;

(C) incorporated in the U.S. in 1968 and its directors are all Canadian residents;

(D) incorporated in Canada in 1964 and its directors are all Canadian residents.

Question 2

Joe is legally separated from his wife and has two adult children who live with his wife and are not dependent on him for support. Joe is leaving Canada to take a job in Germany on June 30 of this year. He plans to stay in Germany indefinitely and has purchased a home there. Which one of the following things is the most important for Joe to do to help ensure that he is not a resident of Canada for Canadian income tax purposes after he leaves?

(A) Take his wife and children with him to Germany.

(B) Give up his Canadian citizenship.

(C) Sell his Canadian home or rent it under a long-term lease.

(D) Put all his household furniture and personal effects into storage in Canada.

Question 3

Mr. Ng is *not* a resident of Canada. In the year, he had worldwide income of $200,000, including $50,000 of employment income earned in Canada (from director's fees) and $10,000 of interest on Government of Canada bonds.

What amount of taxable income must Mr. Ng report on his Canadian personal income tax return for the year?

(A) $10,000

(B) $50,000

(C) $60,000

(D) $200,000

Question 4

Jay ceased to be a resident of Canada on April 30 of the year and moved to New Zealand on that date. During the first four months of the year, he earned $25,000 of employment income in Canada and $1,000 of interest income from his bank accounts in Canada. While living in New Zealand during the remainder of the year, he earned $30,000 (Cdn. $) of employment income in New Zealand and received $2,000 of interest income from his Canadian bank accounts.

What amount of taxable income must Jay report on his **Canadian** personal income tax return for the year?

(A) $58,000

(B) $56,000

(C) $26,000

(D) Nil

Question 5

In which of the following situations is the person considered a non-resident of Canada for Canadian income tax purposes in the year in question?

(A) James Hill, a 25-year-old engineer living in Ottawa, accepted a six-month transfer to an office in London, England for the period July 1 to December 31, of the year in question. He returned to Canada in the following year. James is not married and has always lived at his parents' house in Ottawa.

(B) Judy Gordon, a financial analyst, lives in a house she owns in London, England. She had lived in Toronto all her life, until she started a minimum three-year contract with CS Services Inc., which started in July of the year in question. Judy is single and terminated the lease on her apartment in Toronto before moving her belongings to England when her position started in July.

(C) ERT Limited was incorporated in Canada in 1987 and, until recently, its manufacturing plant was located in Ontario. In June of the year in question, it moved all of its operations, including the manufacturing plant, to Mexico.

(D) Doug Stewart, a member of the Canadian Armed Forces, has been stationed in Germany for the last 5 years, including the year in question. Doug was born in Canada and lived in Canada prior to moving to Germany.

Question 6

Authors' Note: The following problem includes GST/HST implications. Students should review Chapter 20 of the textbook, "Goods and Services Tax (GST)/Harmonized Sales Tax (HST)", before attempting this problem.

CART Ltd. is registered for HST purposes. The following is a summary of the transactions for CART Ltd. for the month of December:

Account	*Amount (Net of HST)*
Sales (Taxable at 13%)	$250,000
Exports	100,000
Purchase of supplies from a registrant	(30,000)
Salaries	(70,000)
Interest Expense	(20,000)
	$230,000

The HST that has to be remitted in respect of the above transaction is:

(A) $19,500

(B) $26,000

(C) $28,600

(D) $39,000

¶2,850   EXERCISES

Exercise 1

ITA: 2, 114, 115, 250(1)

Determine the form of residence, if any, for each of the following individuals.

(A) Alpha had lived all of his life in Vancouver until this year when he left with his family on August 27 to live in Los Angeles.

(B) Beta is a Canadian citizen who has lived in the United States with his family for the past nine years.

(C) Gamma lives in Niagara Falls, New York, but works Monday to Friday from 9:00 a.m. to 5:00 p.m. in an office in Niagara Falls, Ontario.

(D) Delta had lived all of his life in Dallas, Texas. He moved with his family to Calgary, Alberta, early this year to take a job with Dome Petroleum. He moved back to Dallas in the summer of this year. While in Canada he invested in the shares of a private corporation operating in Calgary. These shares were later sold during the year after he left Calgary.

(E) Epsilon was born in Philadelphia. He is now 10 years old and has never been to Canada but his mother has been consul in the Canadian Consulate there for the past 12 years.

(F) Mu is a German citizen who is married to a member of the Canadian forces stationed in Germany. She has been to Canada only for brief visits when her husband was on leave.

Exercise 2

ITA: 2, 114, 250; Income Tax Folio S5-F1-C1

The following is a summary of the statement of fact of the situation.

- Mr. O. MacDonald was about 58 years old in the year under assessment.

- He was at all material times an American citizen.

- He is a sea captain and sails tankers around the world. His employer is the Cities Services Corporation of New York and the ships bear United States registry. He is paid in United States currency from New York for the last 12 years he has been Master of the "S.S. Cities Services, Norfolk".

- Prior to six years ago, Mr. MacDonald and his wife had always lived in the United States. Until then, they owned a house in Massachusetts. In June, six years ago, they moved, with their furniture, to Fredericton, NB. Mrs. MacDonald rented a house in her name to live nearer their two youngest sons, who were attending a boarding school in Saint John, N.B. Their two oldest children were married and another was attending the Springfield (Mass.) College. Upon moving, they sold their nine-room house in the United States.

- About 15 months after their move to Fredericton, Mr. and Mrs. MacDonald purchased a house in Fredericton which was registered in joint tenancy in both their names. On the advice of an American lawyer, Mr. and Mrs. MacDonald tried to purchase a house in Canada within the year in order to avoid the American capital gains tax; unfortunately, they jointly bought this house two months too late and had to pay the tax.

- Prior to the purchase of the house Mr. and Mrs. MacDonald lived in the rented premises in Fredericton.

- Mr. MacDonald filed a T1 Income Tax Return for the taxation year immediately prior to the year under assessment on which he stated, "the above taxpayer and his family are American citizens and are merely residents of Canada. He is a U.S. ship captain and is employed full-time by a U.S. company".

- Mr. MacDonald paid a small amount of Canadian income tax for that previous taxation year after using his foreign tax credit.

- The routine into which Mr. and Mrs. MacDonald have settled over the past years is as follows: The appellant receives his orders to sail from New York. He may be gone months at a time. He may dock at U.S. ports such as Galveston, Texas, or San Francisco.

- After Mrs. MacDonald moved to Fredericton, Mr. MacDonald retained two rooms in his sister's house in Stoneham, Mass., U.S.A. He gave his sister's number as his telephone number in the United States.

- At all material times, the appellant:

  — worked for a U.S. company;

  — was paid in U.S. currency;

  — was a member of the First Baptist Church at Wakefield, Mass.;

  — had two children living in the United States;

  — had a bank account or accounts in the United States;

  — had investments, including stocks and bonds, in the United States;

  — had a pension plan with a U.S. company;

  — intended and still intends to retire in Florida;

  — banked his pay at the First National Bank in Malden, Mass. and enough to maintain his wife and children was sent to her. The rest stayed in the United States where he still retains a chequing account in Malden.

- The appellant, during 1964:

  — had a joint bank account in Fredericton with his wife;

  — had a family phone number in his wife's name;

  — neither applied for nor received family allowance for his children;

  — neither was employed nor carried on business in Canada;

  — never belonged to a church or club in Fredericton;

  — was never a member of a Canadian union;

  — had no Canadian investments;

  — owned a car jointly with his wife with a New Brunswick registry.

- The appellant's sole connections with Canada during 1964 were:

  — his wife lived in Fredericton with one son;

  — he visited Fredericton for a total of 166 days at the following times in the year:

January 3 to February 22	51 days
June 1 to August 7	68 days
November 14 to December 31	47 days
	166 days

- In about a year and a half after the year under assessment the house in Fredericton was sold and Mr. and Mrs. MacDonald moved back to the United States.

- As already mentioned, during the year under assessment, her husband lived 166 days in Fredericton and spent the rest of the time at sea. While away, his pay cheques were sent directly from the New York office to a bank in Malden, Mass., and his wife received monthly cheques for living expenditures in Canada. During his vacation, his pay cheques were deposited in a joint bank account in Fredericton. His trips usually lasted three to four months, and six months when bound for foreign ports. When he was unable to come home, his wife would visit him in New York or at his sister's home in Massachusetts. Mr. MacDonald contended that, in the year under assessment, he resided with his sister and could be reached there at any time, but did not enjoy the exclusive right to the use of rooms and furniture; during that period, his wife stayed there with him for three or four weeks.

— REQUIRED

Prepare an analysis of the residence issue. Evaluate in detail the alternatives in the residence issue as they relate to this fact situation for the year under assessment. Discuss each possible degree of residence and its tax consequences. Weigh the relevance of the facts you consider and come to a conclusion on the case.

Exercise 3

ITA: 2, 250(4)

Determine the form of residence, if any, for each of the following corporations.

(A) Inch Incorporated was incorporated in 1982 in North Dakota. However, its directors are all residents of Saskatchewan where all meetings of the board of directors have been held since incorporation.

(B) Foot Limited was incorporated in Manitoba in 1972. However, it is managed in Japan where all directors' and shareholders' meetings have been held since incorporation.

(C) Yard Incorporated was incorporated in Ohio in 1967, but until five years ago all of the directors' meetings were held in Ontario and the president of the company was a resident of Ontario. However, five years ago the president moved to Ohio and from then on all directors' meetings have been held there.

(D) Mile Limited was incorporated in Nova Scotia in 1964 where all directors' meetings were held until 1971 when the directors moved to Boston where they met regularly.

Exercise 4

ITA: 2(3)

Samson Industries Inc. is a small American company located in Minneapolis, Minnesota. Samson sells various items by mail-order, mostly advertising trinkets such as pens, telephone diaries, post-it notes, and similar items, to Canadian businesses. Last year was the first year they did this and profits on its Canadian sales amounted to $76,000. The principals of Samson are worried about their liability for Canadian income tax and have come to you for advice. Advise Samson on their Canadian tax liability. Include an explanation of your rationale.

Exercise 5

The taxpayer was a resident of Canada since birth. He departed from Vancouver in December 2014 and travelled to Australia, where he arrived December 22, 2014. He applied for, and was granted, permanent resident status in Australia at that time. He enrolled in the Masters of Law program at the University of Sydney in 2016 and graduated in March 2018.

After completing the law program, he returned to Canada on June 30, 2017, arriving in Vancouver on that date. He then travelled to Toronto, where his parents resided, before returning to Halifax which is where he attended undergraduate law school and now practises law. He had his belongings shipped back from Australia to Halifax after his arrival in Halifax.

When he left for Australia, he sold nearly all of his belongings to help finance the trip. He did not own any real property in Canada (i.e., real estate), or keep any residence or bank account in Canada while he was away, as he did not then know when or if he was ever going to return. He did not carry on any business in Canada while he was in Australia.

In September 2017, he commenced a nine-month articling period with a law firm in Halifax. During that period he considered himself to be looking over prospects in Canada, until June 2018 when he accepted full-time employment in the office of the Crown Attorney in Halifax. He remains in that position to the current date. In 2017, he was physically present in Canada for 185 days.

Evaluate, in detail, the alternatives in the residence issue for 2017 as they relate to this fact situation. Present your answer by discussing each possible degree of residence and its tax consequences, and by stating your conclusions on the case after appropriately weighing the significance of the facts considered.

Exercise 6

The taxpayer company was incorporated in the Bahama Islands in 1967 as a subsidiary of S Ltd., a public Ontario company. Two other subsidiaries of S Ltd. were engaged in the business of casualty and property insurance in Canada and were experiencing difficulty in complying with Canadian and Ontario government regulations requiring insurance companies to limit their premiums to twice their capital and surplus. To solve this problem, the taxpayer company was incorporated to engage in the reinsurance business. Originally the taxpayer company had five Bahamian directors and four Canadian directors. However, by September, 1969, all the Canadian directors had resigned with the exception of one who subsequently became a Bahamian resident. All meetings of the taxpayer were held in the Bahamas where its books, minutes and shareholders' registry were kept and where all corporate housekeeping

CHAPTER 2

activities were carried out. The taxpayer's income had not previously been earned in Canada, but was new income which came from new business, and legitimate business reasons existed for its incorporation, i.e., the Canadian subsidiaries did not have to increase their capital.

The office, the books, the majority of the directors, the solicitor and the auditor of the taxpayer and the bank accounts were in the Bahamas. The Board meetings, the reports to various government departments, the investment of funds, and the deposits in the bank were all carried out in the Bahamas.

During the year in question, the taxpayer entered into treaties or contracts of reinsurance with the Canadian insurance companies whereby it assumed certain portions of the risks on insurance contracts in consideration of the receipt of certain portions of the premiums. The contracts were in a standard form used by arm's length companies engaged in the reinsurance business.

Evaluate in detail the alternatives in the residence issue. Determine whether the company was resident in Canada during any year after incorporation in 1967 and provide support for your conclusion.

Exercise 7

Your client, Dundas Valley Machinery Ltd. ("Dundas Valley"), has asked you to advise Mr. Fern Flaming on his income tax position for this year. Mr. Flaming was born in Moosonee 55 years ago, was educated in Sudbury and has lived and worked in Canada all of his life. Until mid-April of this year, he had been executive vice-president of Dundas Valley, earning an annual salary of $80,000 and a bonus based on the profitability of the corporation that amounted to $8,000 to April 15 of this year.

Effective April 15 of this year, Mr. Flaming was promoted to president of the corporation's wholly owned subsidiary in Mexico. He now earns an annual salary of $100,000 and is eligible for a bonus of $30,000 from April 15 of this year. He also receives a living allowance of $3,000 per month and a travel allowance of $1,200 per month. All of these amounts are paid by the Mexican corporation, including moving costs for his family and household effects, which amount to $29,000. No definite term was placed on his contract with the Mexican subsidiary. He is generally regarded as the leading candidate for the office of president of Dundas Valley when the incumbent retires within the next several years.

Mr. Flaming left Canada on April 15 of this year to take up his new position in Mexico. At that time his two minor children were still in high school. As a result, his wife and the two children stayed in Canada until June 30, when school was over and when the sale of the Dundas house closed. The Flamings did not sell their cottage in Huntsville, but they did enter into a long-term contract with a realtor to have the cottage rented during the ski season and the summer vacation period, except for the first two weeks in August when they intended to vacation there with their family. The Dundas home was and the Huntsville cottage is owned by Mr. Flaming. The Flaming's two married children, of course, remained in Canada.

Mr. Flaming rented an unfurnished house that was smaller than his Dundas house in Mexico. He rented some basic furniture for the short period to July of this year, when his furniture from Dundas was moved. The Flamings left some of the furnishings from their Dundas home, including, some valuable paintings and pieces of sculpture, with their married children for their use. Title to this property was not formally changed, but the Flamings had listed this property in their wills as being transferable to these children on death.

Mr. Flaming maintained his portfolio of investments in Canada with the Canadian broker that he had always used. He did this because of his lack of familiarity with other financial markets. He also decided to maintain his accumulated pension credits with Dundas Valley, rather than transfer them to the Mexican corporation's pension plan. However, he did join the Mexican company's plan for services after April 15 of this year. He closed all of his bank accounts, except for one necessary for the running of the Dundas household until June 30 of this year, at which time this account was also closed. He had funds transferred to that remaining account for the use of his wife and children. He terminated his Canadian health and car insurance and his business and social club memberships, effective April 15 of this year. He sold one car on April 10 of this year and the other on June 25 of this year, but he kept his Canadian driver's licence in force.

The Flamings and their unmarried children spent about two weeks in Canada during the Christmas period visiting with the married children in addition to their two-week vacation in Canada in August.

— *REQUIRED*

Summarize, in point form, Mr. Flaming's tax situation for this year and the Canadian income tax implications.

¶2,875 ASSIGNMENT PROBLEMS

Type 1 Problems

Problem 1

Identify the criteria you will use to determine residency for individuals and the steps you will use to apply them.

For each of the following individuals, apply your criteria and determine and explain their residency status for tax purposes. Where there is a change in resident status in a year, explain how the individual will be taxed in that year and the next.

(a) Anthony entered Canada on March 1 of this year, and worked as a domestic on a southern Saskatchewan ranch for the remainder of the year. On December 15 of this year, Anthony's wife moved to Canada with their three children and all of their belongings. They plan to stay permanently in Canada.

(b) Lubie is a U.S. citizen who has lived in Detroit her entire life. For the last 10 years she has been a full-time employee in Windsor, so she commutes across the border every day. She has also traded large volumes of shares and bonds in her own stock account at a broker in Windsor.

(c) Ephran, a computer programmer with Xion Corporation in Toronto, accepted a long-term transfer to Silicon Valley, California. He committed to stay for at least five years. On May 1 of this year, he flew to California and began work on the same day. Most of his belongings remained in Toronto until July 30 of this year. His common-law spouse waited until this day, when the house was sold, the bank accounts were closed, and her contract with the Toronto Public School Board was fulfilled.

(d) Julia, a citizen of the United States, moved with her parents in August two years ago to Edmonton, Alberta. From September 1 two years ago to April 30 of last year, she attended the University of Alberta after transferring credits from her U.S. university. Her parents moved to Edmonton as a result of a job transfer. On May 1 of last year, she accepted an employment position as a mountain bike guide in Colorado and resided there until August 30 of last year. Then, she returned to Edmonton to complete her commerce degree. On June 1 of this year, Julia began full-time employment with a public accounting firm in Edmonton.

(e) Helen Huang has lived in Florida for many years and is a U.S. citizen. All her children also live in Florida. While she enjoys Florida during the winter months, she prefers the relatively cooler weather in Toronto during the other months of the year. As a result, she owns a condo along Queen's Quay in downtown Toronto. Last year, she travelled back and forth between Florida and Toronto fairly often, and when she checked her calendar she found that she had stayed in Toronto on 205 nights. Her children would sometimes come up for short visits.

Problem 2

ITA: 2, 114, 250; Income Tax Folio S5-F1-C1

The client was born and raised in Canada. After obtaining his MBA in 2003, he began working as a consultant. In July 2017, the corporation of which he was a major shareholder entered into a contract with a Canadian Crown corporation to furnish consulting advice in Nigeria. Services were to commence July 15, 2017 and end January 14, 2019. A daily rate of fees was set, but total billings were not to exceed a specified maximum. The contract also provided for moving, travel and living expenses for the client and his dependants up to a specified maximum.

All fees and expenses were paid to the client's corporation in Toronto. He continued to be a shareholder, director and officer of the corporation and he remained very interested in its activities. The corporation paid the client and was instructed to deposit these payments in the client's Canadian bank account which he continued to maintain for this purpose and for the operation of the rental property that he owned. He felt that the Canadian bank account was necessary because of foreign exchange difficulties that he might otherwise encounter. He instructed the corporation not to withhold any income taxes on these payments because he intended to give up his Canadian residence status to establish an international consulting business abroad upon termination of the Nigerian contract.

Since the client had little time before leaving for Nigeria, he quickly rented the unit that he had been occupying in a duplex that he owned, on a month-to-month basis. He intended to sell the property when the market would provide him with a reasonable profit. He arranged to have his corporation manage the renting of this property for a fee which he paid to the corporation.

He stored his major furnishings and winter clothing in Canada. His smaller household and personal effects were shipped to Nigeria. He sold his car, cancelled his auto insurance and a gasoline company credit card and obtained an international driver's licence. He retained credit cards such as American Express, Visa and MasterCard, as well as his RRSP accounts. Under the contract he was also required to maintain his provincial health insurance coverage.

When he left Canada for Nigeria, he was accompanied by his friend, Martha, who had been a part of his life for over a year before their departure. She had obtained leave from her university program of studies for the fall 2017 term. The couple took up residence in a hotel suite that was converted into an apartment at the Holiday Inn in Lagos, Nigeria. No conventional living quarters were available, because of the housing market. During his stay in Nigeria, the client obtained a Nigerian driver's licence and maintained two bank accounts and two cars. He joined sports, dining and social clubs in Lagos. He was provided with an office by the Nigerian government and he carried business cards which identified him as a consultant with that government. He promoted the consulting business of his Toronto corporation actively in Nigeria in the hope of establishing the business abroad, but he did not generate sufficient business to stay in Nigeria beyond the period of the existing contract. He did not seek to extend his visa or pay any form of tax on his income in Nigeria.

Martha returned to Canada for the winter 2018 term, and then returned to Nigeria for the summer of 2018, but returned again to Canada in September 2018 to begin a new program.

By December 2018 the client had billed the limit under the contract. He vacated his apartment, sold his cars, packed up his possessions, including some artwork, textiles and other souvenirs that he had acquired, and returned to Canada.

Prepare a memo for the tax person in your firm who will advise the client on the income tax consequences of these facts. Evaluate in detail the alternatives in the residence issue as they relate to this fact situation. Discuss each possible degree of residence and its tax consequences. State your conclusions on the case after weighing the significance of the facts considered.

Problem 3

ITA: 2, 114, 250; Income
Tax Folio S5-F1-C1

The client is an electronic engineer. He was born in Erith, England, on July 7, 1977. During the relevant times the client held a valid passport for the United Kingdom of Great Britain and Northern Ireland. The passport declares him a British subject with a residence in the United Kingdom with the right of abode therein. The passport was issued on September 26, 2012 for a 10-year period.

Prior to the client's second marriage in 2016, his parents maintained a bedroom for him in Kent, England.

In 2016, the client married Cathy, a Canadian citizen residing in Canada who had no income of her own and was wholly dependent on the client. She has always resided continuously in Canada.

In June of 2016, a house near Apsley, Ontario, was purchased by Cathy with money supplied by the client. In September of 2017, Cathy borrowed money by way of a mortgage. The client guaranteed the mortgage which has an affidavit attached dated September 13, 2017 where he swore that he was not then a non-resident of Canada. For a purchase of property in Ontario, he would otherwise have had to pay a 20% non-resident land transfer tax.

During the three-year period at issue in this case, 2016 to 2018, the client regularly returned to Canada when he was not working. Each time the client entered Canada, his passport was stamped by Immigration Canada with the majority of the entries setting out a date upon which he must leave Canada. The authorized period of stay varied from five days to 45 days. On some of the stamps the word "visitor" was written in by an immigration official. Throughout the three-year period, the client was employed full-time by a non-resident corporation and all work was performed outside Canada on an oil rig at sea. All income was deposited directly into a Canadian bank.

The client indicated that he was charged in Provincial Court for failure to file an income tax return for 2016 and was acquitted (likely on the basis that he was not required to file in Canada for that year).

During the three-year period (2016 to 2018), the client indicated or claimed that he:

(a) never filed a tax return or paid income tax anywhere;

(b) was not allowed to work in Canada;

(c) was given a fixed date to leave Canada on entry (i.e., not allowed to stay in Canada);

(d) could not join OHIP, pay EI, maintain an RRSP or join a pension plan;

(e) was out of the country more than 183 days per year;

(f) had no desire to work in Canada;

(g) had a residence in Britain in the home of his mother and father;

(h) held a mortgage in Britain on his first wife's house;

(i) could not live a normal life in Canada as he had to leave every 27 days; and

(j) had a bank account with the Royal Bank of Canada both in Canada and the Caribbean.

In 2017, the client purchased a car in Canada. In 2018, the client:

(a) obtained a Canadian driver's licence;

(b) obtained a Canadian visa; and

(c) became a landed immigrant in Canada.

Prepare a memo for the tax person in your firm who will advise the client on the income tax consequences of these facts. Evaluate in detail the alternatives in the residence issue as they relate to this fact situation for the period in question. Discuss each degree of residence and its tax consequences as it applies to this fact situation. Note that in this case, residence under the common law principle could only result from a "fresh start" at a point in time in the period in question. Therefore, part-year residence would depend on there being a period of non-residence prior to a "fresh start", if any.

State your conclusion on this case after appropriately weighing the significance of the facts considered. Your conclusion should indicate whether the client became a resident at any point in the period or remained a non-resident throughout the period. If you conclude that he became a resident, indicate the point in time when the "fresh start" was made.

Problem 4

ITA: 2, 114, 250; Income Tax Folio S5-F1-C1

The client is a mechanical engineer, born and educated in England. The client was married in England in 1990 and he and his wife, Dawn, had three sons born in 1991, 1993, and 1998. In 1996, the client and his wife and family moved to Canada where he immediately commenced employment with Imperial Oil in Sarnia, Ontario. With Imperial Oil and/or its parent corporation, Exxon Corporation, the client and his family moved to various locations throughout Canada until 2012. In 2012, while residing and working in Edmonton, Alberta, the client was offered the position as deputy manager of the Exxon refinery at Port Dickson in Malaysia. He accepted the position because it presented the opportunity to likely become manager of this same refinery within a three-year period.

At the time of his acceptance of the above position, the client and his wife were experiencing marriage difficulties. As a result of these difficulties, it was mutually agreed that the client would go to Malaysia on his own. His wife and youngest son remained in the family home in Edmonton. His older sons were living on their own by this time.

The client and his employer undertook the following steps in preparation for his move from Canada:

● his employer obtained a work permit for him in Malaysia;

● he sold his car;

● he cancelled his provincial health plan;

● his employer obtained private health insurance for him;

● he closed all of his existing bank accounts at Royal Bank;

● he opened a savings account at the Bank of Nova Scotia because this bank had a branch in Kuala Lumpur, the capital of Malaysia;

● he allowed his membership in the Edmonton Petroleum Club to lapse; and

● he allowed his participation in the Model Guided Plane Association to lapse.

The client moved to Malaysia in the last few days of September 2012. He stayed in a hotel in Malaysia for the first few weeks and then moved into a company-provided home. His employer charged him with a monthly rent of $1,000 for his use of this house. He took the following items with him from Canada to Malaysia:

● all of his clothes and personal effects; and

● an airplane kit for model guided planes and a radio control transmitter for his hobby of model guided planes.

¶2,875

CHAPTER 2

Once in Malaysia, the client undertook to establish Port Dickson as his home. To this end, he:

● purchased a car;

● obtained a Malaysian driver's licence;

● joined the Port Dickson yacht club which was, in fact, a social/recreational club;

● joined the petroleum club at Kuala Lumpur;

● opened a chequing account at the Bank of Nova Scotia in Kuala Lumpur;

● opened a chequing account at the Standard Chartered Bank at Port Dickson;

● acquired two Malaysian credit cards;

● became a patient at a Port Dickson medical clinic and, as well, made regular visits to a dentist in Port Dickson; and

● joined the Port Dickson Golf Club in 2013.

In accordance with Exxon corporate policy, the client remained on the payroll and in the pension plan of the Canadian subsidiary. His monthly pay was deposited into his Edmonton bank account. There was no income tax withheld at source on the client's salary because the Canadian subsidiary knew that he was working full-time outside of Canada. The total cost of his salary and related benefits (including pension) were charged by the Canadian subsidiary to Exxon Corporation International.

The client made only two visits to Canada during the period from 2012 through 2016. He visited for 14 days in 2013 and 14 days again in 2014. On each of these visits, he stayed in the family home in Edmonton. During the same period, the client's spouse made eight visits to him in Malaysia. She made no visits after January 2015, but prior to that time, the length of her visits ranged from 19 days to 32 days. On each of these visits, she stayed with the client in his Malaysian home. The client and his wife remained married throughout the relevant period.

The client maintained the following Canadian investments while he was residing in Malaysia:

● his 50% interest in the family home in Edmonton;

● a 50% investment in a rental property which his wife purchased after his move to Malaysia, because she thought it would be a good investment;

● his RRSP;

● his company savings plan; and

● a few personal shares in Canadian public companies.

He did maintain his memberships in the Canadian Society of Mechanical Engineers and the Association of Professional Engineers and Geologists of Alberta.

The client became manager of the Port Dickson plant in 2016 and eventually retired from Exxon in the summer of 2017 under the terms of an early retirement package. Upon retirement from Exxon, the client returned to Edmonton to the family home. In late 2017 the client started seeking employment in Malaysia and in January 2018 he and his wife went to Malaysia hoping that he would find employment and they would both live there. His wife returned to Canada in February 2018 and he moved on to Thailand where he stayed through July 2018 (working for the 12-month period from August 2018 through July 2019). When the Thailand employment ended, the client returned to Canada. He and his wife then worked out a plan of separation.

Prepare a memo for the tax person in your firm who will advise the client on the income tax consequences of these facts. Evaluate in detail the alternatives in the residence issue as they relate to this fact situation for the period October 1, 2012 through the summer of 2019. Discuss each possible degree of residence and its tax consequences. State your conclusions on this case after weighing the relevance of the facts you have considered.

Problem 5

ITA: 2, 250(1)

For each of the following corporations, determine and explain the type of residency, for tax purposes for this year.

(a) ABI, incorporated in Montreal, Quebec, in 1980, carries on a clothing manufacturing business in Hong Kong. All directors' meetings and staff meetings are held in Hawaii, United States, each year.

(b) Nickel Company, incorporated in the Bahamas in 1966, operates a mining business in Northern Ontario. All profits are paid out as dividends directly into a Swiss bank account. All books and records are maintained in the president's office in Ontario. The company directors all live in Toronto and meet monthly for their directors' meeting.

(c) Saffron Ltd. is a 40% subsidiary of a Canadian corporation located in Houston, Texas. The products manufactured by Saffron are sold directly to the Canadian market. No revenues are earned from U.S. sales.

Problem 6

ITA: 2, 250, 253

Far Eastern Airlines is a company incorporated in Korea in 1974. Its general manager and other active officers of the company are resident in Korea and have their offices there. The directors and corporate officers of the company live in Korea as well.

During the year in question, its sole business was operating an international airline which had no landing rights in Canada. However, in that year it had raised capital on the Canadian market for its international operations by selling an issue of its stock through an investment dealer in Vancouver. The vice-president–finance of the company, who believed the stock issue would sell better in Canada, travelled from the head office in Korea to Vancouver to instruct the investment dealer.

The stock issue was highly successful and the proceeds of the issue were accumulated in a bank account in Vancouver. During the several months in the year in question when these funds were being accumulated, the company became aware of an opportunity to purchase a vast quantity of aviation fuel at a very low price. A purchasing agent was dispatched from the head office in Korea to Canada to complete the purchase using some of the funds accumulated from the stock issue. The fuel was stored in Canada temporarily in rented facilities pending shipment to San Francisco, where it could be used by aircraft landing there. Subsequently, the company was unable to make suitable arrangements for shipment. The fuel was sold to a Canadian buyer at a considerable profit. All contracts involved in the purchase and sale transactions were drawn up by a Canadian lawyer under the direction of the purchasing agent who operated from a hotel room in Vancouver during the period of the transactions.

Prepare a memo for the tax person in your firm who will advise Far Eastern Airlines on the income tax consequences of these facts. Evaluate in detail the alternatives in the residence issue as they relate to this fact situation. Discuss each possible degree of residence and its tax consequences. State your conclusions on the case after considering the relevant international tax agreement and after appropriately weighing the significance of the facts considered.

Problem 7

ITA: 2, 250, 253

Wong Computer Games Inc. (WCG) was incorporated in the state of Illinois in the last decade. The founding shareholder, Mr. Andrew Wong, is an inventor of computer simulation models. His products include a wide variety of computer games as well as some programs which have industrial applications.

Mr. Wong is the controlling shareholder of WCG. His brother owns a minority interest, as does Walter Bends, a long-time associate of Mr. Wong, who often collaborates in the development of new products. All three shareholders are resident in Chicago. In addition to Mr. Wong, the WCG Board of Directors includes George Wolf, who represents the Chicago law firm, which advises WCG, and Tony Aster who represents First National Bank of Chicago, which provides most of the financing for WCG's operations. The Board meets approximately every six months to review financial results, discuss product development and decide on strategic initiatives. The meetings are usually held in the boardroom of George Wolf's law firm.

Two years ago, Mr. Wong achieved an industry breakthrough when he developed his latest game, SuperPilot. SuperPilot is a computer game in which the operator attempts to safely land a disabled airliner. SuperPilot provided special effects which were far beyond those available in any other commercially available product. Although other WCG products were only available in the U.S. market, Wong was convinced that SuperPilot would be a global success. To ensure the competitive advantage would be maintained, Wong Computer Games Inc. took the required legal steps to ensure copyright and patent protection of the program in a variety of countries, including Canada.

By last year, SuperPilot was doing very well in the U.S. market and WCG began to launch the product in other markets. Walter Bends was assigned responsibility for the Canadian market and took a short-term lease on a Toronto apartment in March of last year. WCG established a bank account with a Toronto branch of a Canadian bank. This account was to be used by Bends for promotional expenses and other incidentals. All other expenses, including Bends' salary, continued to be paid from Chicago.

Bends attended a number of Canadian trade shows, exhibiting the SuperPilot program. Prospective purchasers were provided with SuperPilot game cartridges as a promotional item. Bends was given the authority to sign supply contracts which would permit the purchaser a one-month supply of cartridges. At the end of the one month, if the distributor was still interested, a longer-term supply contract would be required. Bends was not permitted, however, to sign any of these long-term agreements without receiving prior approval from the WCG Board. All game cartridges, including promotional cartridges, were supplied from Chicago. If the product began to sell well in Canada, the WCG Board had discussed establishing a Canadian warehouse.

By January of this year, it became obvious that SuperPilot was not going to be a Canadian success. No distributors had requested a long-term supply contract and only one, Pete's Gaming Emporium, had agreed to stock the product for one month. At the end of the month, sales had been so slow that Pete's was not interested in continuing the relationship. Bends returned to Chicago, the bank account was closed, and WCG refocused its marketing efforts on the U.S. market.

Prepare a memo for the tax person in your firm who will advise WCG on the income tax consequences of these facts. Evaluate in detail the alternatives in the residence issue as they relate to this fact situation during last year and this year. Discuss each possible degree of residence and its tax consequences. State your conclusions on the case after appropriately weighing the significance of the facts considered.

Problem 8

ITA: 2, 250, 253

Capitol Life Insurance Company ("Capitol") was incorporated in the U.S.A. in the state of Colorado at the turn of the century. Its head office had always been in Denver, Colorado. Capitol was a subsidiary of Providence Capitol Corporation which in turn was a subsidiary of Gulf & Western Industries Inc. ("Gulf"). Gulf owned approximately 600 subsidiaries, 240 of which were in turn owned by Associates Corporation of North America ("Associates"). Six of these latter corporations were Canadian companies.

Capitol was in the business of writing individual and group life and health insurance policies. Capitol also wrote creditor's group life and health insurance policies for the 240 finance companies which were part of the Gulf group of companies. Under a creditor's group insurance policy, Capitol would pay to the finance company, upon the death or disability of the borrower, the outstanding amount of the loan in the case of death or the required instalment payments in the case of disability. The costs of the insurance were effectively passed on to the borrower, either as a separate charge or as a higher interest rate.

About 25 years ago, Capitol planned to expand into Canada and obtained licences in nearly every province and obtained federal registration under the *Foreign Insurance Companies Act* ("FICA"). The FICA registration required that Capitol name a chief agent in Canada and that he be given a power of attorney. Capitol was also required to make deposits with the insurance superintendent and maintain assets in Canada. Two bank accounts were opened in Canada. The planned expansion into Canada was cancelled. However, the licences and registration were maintained. This required that Canadian representatives and agents be retained as locations for the licensing authorities to serve legal notices. All reports to the licensing authorities and all inquiries of the licensing authorities were to be passed through the Canadian chief agent. The reports to the licensing authorities were prepared in Denver and all inquiries were passed on to Denver by the chief agent. The chief agent was required to maintain copies of records required by the superintendent of insurance. None of Capitol's representatives or agents ever solicited insurance or were expected or authorized to do any business.

The chief agent countersigned the cheques on Capitol's general bank account on the requirement of the insurance superintendent. He had no means to verify the legitimacy of the cheques; as all books and records were maintained in Denver where the cheques were prepared. The agent later deposited the premiums received in an effort to streamline the former procedure of having the premiums sent to Denver and then sent back to Canada through the bank for deposit into the Canadian general account to meet licensing requirements. All investments were administered and managed in Denver.

Capitol did not have anyone in Canada who solicited insurance business, collected premiums, processed or paid claims, administered investments or countersigned any claim cheques. Capitol had five group insurance contracts under which the lives of Canadian residents were insured. These policies were all issued to affiliated companies without solicitation in Canada. Two of these policies were creditor's group insurance policies with Associates. They were each drafted in accordance with Denver law and signed in Denver by the president of Associates, who was a resident of Indiana. Associates was shown as the insured company and paid all premiums. On the insistence of the Canadian insurance authorities, the wording of the agreements was amended to reflect "a premium collection fee". The original agreement provided for a retroactive adjustment of premiums based upon past claim experience. Capitol and Associates continued to administer, interpret and apply the agreement in the same manner as the original agreement. Blank insurance certificates were also required to be issued so that they could be provided to borrowers whose loans were insured as a way of informing them of the terms of the coverage. The coverage took place independently of the issuance of a certificate to an individual. These certificates listed the Canadian head office of Capitol as being in Don Mills, Ontario, as required by the federal insurance superintendent. This office was never used as a head office. The federal insurance superintendent also required the issuance of a brochure for the information of the Canadian borrowers whose lives and health were insured.

The income that Capitol received from the Canadian insurance and investments represented a very small proportion of its total revenue. Canadian operations were not kept separately from U.S. operations, no Denver personnel were charged with Canadian operations, and there were no special Canadian claim forms or procedures. The only separation of Canadian business from U.S. operations to be found in the accounts of Capitol was to comply with the Canadian insurance authorities. All corporate meetings as well as all levels of management took place in the U.S.A.

Prepare a memo for the tax person in your firm who will advise Capitol on the income tax consequences of these facts. Evaluate in detail the alternatives in the residence issue as they relate to this fact situation. Discuss each possible degree of residence and its tax consequences. State your conclusions on this case after weighing the relevance of the facts you have considered.

Problem 9

Sally has just come to you for advice on a possible job transfer to Paris, France. She is currently working for a large private corporation located in St. Catharines, Ontario. It is now April and the president of the company has asked Sally, who is the company's computer network expert, to move to Paris for at least two years. Her time there may extend beyond two years, but that will depend on the success of the project she will be working on.

Sally is married to Harry and they have two daughters, ages six and eight. The company wants Sally to be in Paris and working by May 15, so she will have to leave by May 10 to get there and settled in time. She is planning to rent a furnished apartment when she arrives. Her children are in school and won't be done until the end of June. Harry has his own career as a school teacher and is willing to take an unpaid leave of absence for two years, but he can't leave until the end of June or middle of July at the earliest.

Sally and Harry enjoy golf and have recently joined a fairly exclusive club in the St. Catharines area, after an eight-year waiting period and after paying a large initiation fee. They do not wish to give up this membership. Their home is located just outside the city on 20 acres and they are very reluctant to sell it, as they would not be able to replace it on their return.

Both Sally and Harry grew up in the St. Catharines area and their families still live there. Sally's parents and Harry's parents are retired.

Sally and Harry both want to move to Paris, and they have come to you for tax advice on whether they could be considered non-residents of Canada, or what, if anything, they could do to achieve this result.

Problem 10

The plaintiff, Jennifer Marken, is a 21-year-old Canadian citizen and has always lived and worked in Regina except for the last two years. During these two years, she obtained a position as an English teacher for a local school in Osorno, Chile. Originally, the two-year contract could have been extended into a permanent position at Jennifer's option. However, at the end of the two-year period Jennifer's brother became suddenly ill and she opted to return to Regina and complete her education degree.

She is scheduled to appear in court next week to claim that she was a non-resident of Canada during the two-year period and, therefore, should not be liable for Canadian tax. Both the CRA and Jennifer's counsel agree on the following facts:

- Jennifer is a Canadian citizen and all of her direct family resides in Saskatchewan.

- Jennifer's fiancé visited her five times during the two-year period and lived in Chile during his summer vacations. He plans to complete his accounting designation with a Canadian firm in Saskatchewan.

- All of Jennifer's income during the two-year period ending in January of this year was paid by the Chilean school.

- Upon departing for Chile, Jennifer put all of her furniture in storage and leased her car to her younger sister on a month-to-month basis. Her household belongings were shipped to Chile.

- While in Chile, she maintained her provincial health care policy, her Canadian savings account and a Canadian American Express card. She cancelled her Canadian chequing account, and her Canadian Visa card.

- Before leaving, she cancelled all of her club memberships and abdicated her position as the honourary chair of the Beta Gamma Phi sorority.

- While in Chile she made no attempt to learn the Spanish language and did not join any Chilean organizations. She rented a one-bedroom apartment from another Canadian living in Osorno.

- Over the two-year period, Jennifer visited Canada each Christmas, at Easter, and for the marriage of her best friend. Her total number of days in Canada over the two-year period amounted to 50 days.

Jennifer's litigation counsel would like your advice on the income tax options for the two-year period during which Jennifer worked in Chile. Provide your perspective on the facts that support each place of residence and the tax consequences they entail. Weigh the relevance of the facts and conclude on the likely outcome in this situation.

Problem 11

The taxpayer came to Canada in 1977. He stayed in Canada until 1987. Prior to 1987 the taxpayer studied engineering and obtained an engineering degree. He also married. In 1987 the taxpayer went to England for post-graduate studies; he returned to Canada with his wife and two children in 1989. For three years he worked as an engineer in Canada. In 1992 he moved to the United States with his family. He remained there continuously until 2012 when he became a naturalized U.S. citizen. Also in 2012, following the loss of his job in the United States, he returned to Canada to take a new job. The new job lasted for two years. During 2013 and 2014 the taxpayer remained in Canada, working as a self-employed consultant. In 2015 he moved back to the United States. There he worked as an employee for six months. Thereafter, he practiced his profession on a self-employed basis working for various companies in the United States which required his services. He practiced his profession from an office in his home. An apartment was occupied by the taxpayer under a lease entered into in 2013 and renewed yearly thereafter.

When the taxpayer returned to Canada in 2012 he bought a house in Mount Albert, Ontario. A few months later, after the necessary domestic arrangements had been made, the taxpayer's wife and children joined him, and the family lived in the house at Mount Albert. Marital difficulties arose. The taxpayer's wife and children remained behind in Mount Albert when the taxpayer returned to the United States in 2015. The taxpayer visited Canada rather infrequently after 2015. With two exceptions, his post-2015 visits to this country were for the purpose of seeing his children, and were made three or four times a year. Although during those visits he stayed in the Mount Albert home, he appears to have stayed as a visitor only and not a person whose home it was. During the post-2015 period, the taxpayer made monthly payments to his wife for her support and that of the children.

The two exceptional post-2015 visits were made in order to fulfill a contract made by the taxpayer with a company that needed the services of an engineer who had expertise in U.S. military specifications. The first such visit, in June and July 2018, lasted for thirty-two days. The second, in August of that year, lasted for sixteen days.

In 2018, the taxpayer held what he said was non-resident membership in the Ontario Association of Professional Engineers. He also held membership in the Engineering Institute of Canada and the Canadian Society of Mechanical Engineers. The taxpayer maintained a bank account in Newmarket, Ontario. He mistakenly filed a 2018 tax return with the Canada Revenue Agency, indicating that he resided in Mount Albert.

Evaluate, in detail, the alternatives to the residence issue for the taxpayer in 2018. Provide support for your conclusions.

CHAPTER 2 —
DISCUSSION NOTES FOR REVIEW QUESTIONS

(1) Canadian individuals are taxed based on residency and not their citizenship. Canadian residents are taxed on their world income.   ITA: 2(1)

(2) He or she will be deemed to be a resident only if he or she sojourned in Canada for 183 or more days during the year.   ITA: 250(1)

(3) You need to look at other factors to determine where they have a "continuing state of relationship", such as family and social ties and other personal property. The Income Tax Folio categorizes the type of facts that can be used to establish residential ties.   Income Tax Folio S5-F1-C1 — Determining an Individual's Residence Status

(4) He or she would be considered to be a non-resident of Canada throughout the year. However, since he or she carried on business in Canada during the year while a non-resident, he or she would be taxable in Canada on his or her Canadian business profits for the year.   ITA: 2(3)

(5) If he or she is establishing a "fresh start" in Canada on March 31 then he or she becomes resident on that date and is taxed in Canada on his or her world income from that date. The sojourning rules would not apply since they only apply to non-residents who are in Canada on a temporary basis.

(6) The residency of a corporation is either determined by the common law test of "central management and control", or a corporation is deemed to be a Canadian resident if it is incorporated in Canada after April 26, 1965, or it meets the tests outlined in the Act if it was incorporated before that date.   ITA: 250(4)

(7) A corporation is deemed to be resident in Canada if it was incorporated in Canada after April 26, 1965. Reference to the tax treaty would be the next step but Canada does not have a tax treaty with Bermuda. Therefore, it would be resident in Canada and taxable in Canada on its world income.   ITA: 250(4)(a)

(8) Any company which was incorporated in Canada before April 27, 1965 and which carried on business in Canada in any year after that date is deemed to be resident in Canada. An extended meaning of carrying on business includes soliciting orders in Canada. The facts fit the meaning because of the continuity of the order solicitation over a period of years. Therefore, the company would be resident in Canada and taxable in Canada on its world income.   ITA: 250(4)(a)
ITA: 253(b)

(9) Subsection 2(3) refers to "employed in Canada in the year or a previous year". Therefore, section 115 of Division D requires the income from an office or employment to be taxed in Canada.   ITA: 115(2)(c)

(10) The U.S. company is soliciting orders in Canada and, therefore, is carrying on business in Canada. The corporation is, thus, taxable in Canada on the profits related to these sales.   ITA: 2(3), 115, 253

(11) Under the extended meaning of carrying on business, the U.S. company would be a non-resident carrying on business in Canada and liable for tax on its earning in Canada. However, under the Canada–U.S. tax treaty, the U.S. company would probably not be taxable in Canada because its profits are not earned from a permanent establishment in Canada.   ITA: 253

(12) Yes, a person can be a resident of more than one country since residency is determined under the laws of each country. Article IV of the Canada–U.S. tax treaty provides rules for resolving who collects the tax where a person is a resident of both the United States and Canada.

(13) Under Article VII of the Canada–U.S. tax treaty, it will only be subject to tax on the income attributable to that permanent establishment.

(14) Article XIV of the Canada–U.S. tax treaty will cause him to be taxed in the United States only if he has a "fixed base regularly available to him" in the United States Therefore, he will only pay tax in Canada on this income.

CHAPTER 2 — SOLUTIONS TO MULTIPLE CHOICE QUESTIONS

Question 1

(B) is correct. Since X Ltd. is not incorporated in Canada, it is not deemed to be resident in Canada. Since the directors are not resident in Canada, X Ltd. is not resident in Canada under the common law "central management and control" rule.

ITA: 250(4)

(A) is incorrect because X Ltd. is deemed to be resident.

ITA: 250(4)(*a*)

(C) is incorrect because X Ltd. is resident under the common law "central management and control" rule.

(D) is incorrect because X Ltd. is deemed to be resident; the common law "central management and control" rule would also apply.

ITA: 250(4)(*c*)

Question 2

(C) is correct. Generally, the CRA will consider the individual not to have severed residential ties within Canada if he has a dwelling available for occupancy.

Income Tax Folio S5-F1-C1 — Determining an Individual's Residence Status

(A) is incorrect, because taking his wife and children with him to Germany is not feasible, since the couple is legally separated and the children are not dependent on him for support.

Income Tax Folio S5-F1-C1 — Determining an Individual's Residence Status

(B) is incorrect, because giving up Canadian citizenship has little relevance in determining residency.

(D) is incorrect. Although putting all his household furniture and personal effects into storage in Canada is a residential tie, the tie is a weaker one than that cited in (C).

Income Tax Folio S5-F1-C1 — Determining an Individual's Residence Status

Question 3

(B) is correct. Only the $50,000 of employment income earned in Canada would be reported on Mr. Ng's Canadian personal income tax return for the year.

ITA: 2(3), 115

(A) is incorrect. The $10,000 interest, earned by the non-resident, is not taxable under either Part I (ssec. 2(3)) or Part XIII (ssec. 212(3), "fully exempt interest").

(C) is incorrect for the same reason as (A).

(D) is incorrect, because only residents of Canada are subject to Canadian income tax on their worldwide income.

ITA: 2(1)

Question 4

(C) is correct. Because Jay ceased to be a resident of Canada on April 30 of the year, only his worldwide income during the first four months of the year ($26,000 = $25,000 + $1,000) is subject to tax in Canada under Part I and would be reported on his Canadian personal income tax return for the year.

ITA: 2(1), 114

(A) includes income earned while not a resident of Canada: $58,000 = $25,000 + $1,000 + $30,000 + $2,000. The $30,000 of employment income earned in New Zealand and the $2,000 of Canadian interest earned from May 1 to December 31 of the year are not subject to Part I tax because Jay is not resident in Canada at that time. The $2,000 of Canadian interest is exempt from withholding tax under Part XIII.

ITA: 2(1), 114

(B) includes the salary earned in New Zealand: $56,000 = $25,000 + $1,000 + $30,000. As in (A), above, the $30,000 of employment income earned in New Zealand is not subject to tax in Canada.

(D) excludes the worldwide income earned while Jay was a resident in Canada. As discussed in (A), above, this would be reported on his Canadian personal income tax return for the year.

ITA: 2(1), 114

Question 5

(B) is correct. Judy is a non-resident. She seems to have severed her residential ties to Canada (moving her belongings) and established new ties to London, England (buying a house).

(A) is incorrect. James is still a resident of Canada. There is no indication that James has severed his residential ties to Canada or established ties to London, England.

(C) is incorrect. Since ERT Limited was incorporated in Canada after April 26, 1965, it is deemed to be a resident of Canada. ITA: 250(4)(*a*)

(D) is incorrect. Doug is deemed to be a resident of Canada because he is a member of the Canadian armed forces. ITA: 250(1)(*b*)

Question 6

(C) is correct.

Sales (taxable at 13%)	$250,000
Purchase of supplies from a registrant	(30,000)
	$220,000 × 13% = $28,600.

(A) incorrectly takes a deduction for salaries which is an exempt supply: $250,000 – $30,000 – $70,000 = $150,000. $150,000 × 13% = $19,500.

(B) incorrectly takes a deduction for interest expense: $250,000 – $30,000 – $20,000 = $200,000. $200,000 × 13% = $26,000.

(D) incorrectly includes exports (which are zero-rated) and takes a deduction for interest expense (an exempt supply): $250,000 + $100,000 – $30,000 – $20,000 = $300,000. $300,000 × 13% = $39,000.

CHAPTER 2

CHAPTER 2 — SOLUTIONS TO EXERCISES

Exercise 1

(A) Alpha is a part-year resident of Canada in the year. He would be a resident until August 27 of the year when he appears to have made a "clean break" with Canada. While in Canada he would not have been sojourning, so the deeming rule would not apply.

ITA: 250(1)(a)

(B) Beta has no residential ties with Canada. Citizenship is not a determining factor in establishing such ties.

(C) Gamma is a non-resident of Canada and is taxable only on employment income earned in Canada.

ITA: 2(3)(a), 115(1)(a)(i)

(D) Delta is either a part-year resident of Canada or a non-resident employed in Canada, depending on the facts of his stay in Canada. He is also taxable under paragraph 2(3)(c) because the shares are taxable Canadian property.

ITA: 115(1)(b)(iv)

(E) Epsilon is deemed a resident of Canada because of his relationship to his mother.

ITA: 250(1)(c)(i), 250(1)(f)

(F) Mu is not deemed to be a resident of Canada by any of the deeming rules. She has never been resident in Canada. Therefore, she is not a resident of Canada.

ITA: 250(1)

Exercise 2

[See: *MacDonald v. M.N.R.*, 68 DTC 433 (T.A.B.).]

(A) The resident option → taxed in Canada on worldwide income for full year:

ITA: 2(1)

Criterion: residence is a question of fact dependent on the degree of permanency in the relationship between a person and a place;

Evidence:

(i) factors indicating this relationship between the appellant and Canada,

1. he sold his house in the United States and paid an American capital gains tax for not buying another residence,

2. his wife, upon arriving in Canada, rented premises pending the purchase of a house,

3. she and the children, whom the appellant was supporting to the extent of $600 per month, stayed in Canada all year-round,

4. he stayed in Canada when he was off-duty to the extent of 166 out of 180 days in 1964,

— full-time presence is not necessary,

5. other non-determining factors,

— joint account in Canada where pay cheques were deposited during his vacations,

— joint ownership of a car with New Brunswick registry,

— citizenship irrelevant;

(ii) factors detracting from a relationship with Canada,

1. a few rooms, without exclusive use, made available for him at his sister's house in the United States,

— not a permanent abode,

— an individual can have more than one residence,

2. U.S. citizen and previously and subsequently resided in the United States with a stated intention to return,

— but only 1964 in question on the facts,

— stated intention must be supported by behavioural facts,

— worked for a U.S. company and paid in U.S. currency,

> — but not determining because a Canadian resident can be involved in such a situation, providing employment services abroad for a non-Canadian company,
>
> — memberships and investments including bank accounts, securities and pension plan in United States,
>
> > — factors may indicate U.S. residence, but not determining and also possible for a person resident in Canada,
>
> — no Canadian memberships or investments and no application for family allowances,
>
> > — not determining factors and also possible of a Canadian resident,
>
> — children living in United States,
>
> > — married and apparently not dependent,
>
> — phone in wife's name in Canada,
>
> > — a factor, but hardly determining,
>
> — neither employed in Canada nor carrying on business in Canada,
>
> > — not necessary condition for full-time residence.

(This list of factors is longer but there is more substance for full-time residence.)

(B) The deemed resident option → taxed in Canada on worldwide income for full year: ITA: 2(1)

Criterion: the condition of sojourning an aggregate of 183 days or more; ITA: 250(1)

Evidence: his total stay in Canada in the year was only for 166 days; therefore, the condition is not met.

(C) The part-year resident option → taxed in Canada on worldwide income for part of the year ITA: 2(1), 114, 118.91
resident in Canada with deductions applicable to the period of part-year residence and non-refundable tax credits either prorated for or applicable to the period of part-year residence (as long as not resident in Canada during some other part of the year);

Criterion: clean break or fresh start during 1964;

Evidence: neither occurred.

(D) The non-resident option → taxed in Canada on income earned in Canada: ITA: 2(3)

Criteria: employed in Canada, carried on business in Canada or disposed of taxable Canadian property in the year;

Evidence: none of these conditions occurred in the year. ITA: 2(3)

(E) Conclusion: if the taxpayer is to be found a resident it must be as a full-time resident:

> — the major factors indicate a relationship with Canada which would warrant a conclusion of such resident status.

Exercise 3

(A) Inch Incorporated is resident in Canada by virtue of the common law principle of central ITA: 250(4)
management and control. The corporation cannot be deemed resident in Canada because it was not incorporated in Canada.

(B) Foot Limited is deemed resident in Canada because it was incorporated in Canada after ITA: 250(4)(a)
April 26, 1965.

(C) Yard Incorporated is not resident this year by virtue of the common law principle of central management and control. Furthermore, the corporation cannot be deemed resident in Canada because it was not incorporated in Canada.

(D) Mile Limited is resident in Canada. The corporation was incorporated in Canada before ITA: 250(4)(c)
April 27, 1965 and after that time it was resident by virtue of the central management and control rule.

CHAPTER 2

Exercise 4

Canada levies tax on non-residents who carry on business in Canada. Carrying on business in Canada is distinguishable from carrying on business with Canada. While Samson solicits sales from Canadians, it does not have a permanent establishment in Canada, nor does it employ a Canadian salesperson or agent. Given these facts, Samson is not liable for Canadian income taxes on the $76,000 profit originating from within Canada.

ITA: 2(3)

Exercise 5

Warren K. Zimmer v. The Minister of National Revenue, (TRB) 81 DTC 550

A. Resident — tax on worldwide income for 2017.

— requires a continuing state of relationship with Canada based on facts

— past history in Canada: born, raised, and educated in Canada

— return to Canada after completion of studies in Australia

— absence just an extraordinary event in his life (to get degree)

— parents live in Canada

— permanent resident status in Australia does not in and by itself mean that the individual is a non-resident of Canada [IT Folio S5-F1-C1 paragraph 1.21]

— only sold belongings in Canada to help finance trip to Australia

B. Deemed resident — same consequences as above.

— requires sojourning (temporary stay) in Canada for a total of 183 days or more during 2017

— physically present in Canada for 185 days

— but not sojourning for that full period

— may have sojourned from arrival in Canada on June 30, 2017 to time of visiting with parents in Toronto and to time of taking articling position in Halifax

— but sojourning in Canada stopped when

— he began the articling job in Halifax in September 2017

— his belongings arrived in Halifax and he established a permanent home

— sojourning did not stop in 2017 when he took the position in the Crown Attorneys Office, because he had established a permanent home before that time

— with respect to sojourning, there was no difference between his employment as an articling law student and his employment as a lawyer

— the only difference was professional status which does not affect sojourning.

C. Part-year resident — tax on worldwide income for the part of 2017 that he was resident.

— requires a "fresh start" in Canada

— would require facts suggesting that previous ties with Canada had been severed in 2014 and that new ties were established in 2017

— he did not leave a dwelling place in Canada available for his occupation [IT Folio S5-F1-C1, par. 1.12]

— his parents' home would not qualify since he was not living at home prior to leaving Canada in 2013

— he did not leave spouse and dependants in Canada

— he did not leave any personal property or social ties

— he sold nearly all of his belongings to finance the trip to Australia, and the remainder he must have taken with him

— he did not keep a bank account in Canada while in Australia.

D. Non-resident employed in Canada in 2017 — tax only on employment income in Canada

— he was at least employed in Canada in 2017 from September of that year, while articling with a law firm in Halifax

— he held permanent residence status in Australia since 2014.

E. Conclusion

— he was a part-year resident in 2017

— his previous ties to Canada had been severed in 2014

— the remaining ties indicated were not strong enough to conclude that he remained resident in Canada for tax purposes while in Australia

— he established residence in September 2017 (at the latest) when he took the job in Halifax and had his belongings shipped

— his would be enough to argue against being merely a non-resident employed in Canada during 2017.

Exercise 6

(See *Victoria Insurance v. MNR*, 77 DTC 320)

— Resident by common law principle: taxed in Canada on worldwide income

— central management and control in Canada

— subsidiary of Canadian company

— but

— all directors Bahamian or resident in Bahamas

— all meeting held in the Bahamas

— books, minutes, and shareholders registry kept in Bahamas

— all corporate housekeeping activities carried on in Bahamas

— office, solicitor, auditor, and bank accounts in Bahamas

— reports to governments and investment of funds carried on in the Bahamas

— deemed full-time resident by ssec. 250(4): taxed in Canada on worldwide income

— requires incorporation in Canada

— incorporated in Bahamas

— non-resident carrying on business in Canada: taxed on business income in Canada

— not carrying on business in Canada

— income came from new business not earned in Canada

— conclusion

— central management and control not exercised by Canadian parent which was the taxpayer's only connection with Canada

— corporation is not resident in Canada

Exercise 7

A. Resident in Canada

(1) Must establish a continuing state of relationship with Canada

— evidence

— past history in Canada: born and educated in Canada, always lived there

— expectation that he might return as president of the Canadian company at some time in the future

— wife and minor children did not leave with him and had a car, furnished house, and bank account available to them

— retained the cottage and rented it out

— rented house in Mexico; did not buy

— left some home furnishings — valuable paintings and sculptures — with married children

— maintained investment portfolio in Canada

— maintained pension in Canada

— maintained Canadian driver's licence

— returned during August and December

(2) Income tax consequences if resident in Canada throughout the year

— would pay Canadian tax on worldwide income, which would consist of:

Canadian salary to April 15 ($80,000 × $^{3.5}/_{12}$)	$ 23,333
Canadian bonus	$ 8,000
Mexico salary ($100,000 × $^{8.5}/_{12}$)	$ 70,833
Mexico bonus	$ 30,000
Living allowance (8.5 × $3,000)	$ 25,550
	$ 157,666

— the travel allowance would not be included by virtue of spar. 6(1)(b)(v), since he could be expected to negotiate contracts as president, as long as the allowance is reasonable when compared to his actual travel expenditures.

— the moving costs paid by the Mexican company would not be a taxable benefit.

B. Deemed resident in Canada by virtue of par. 250(1)(a)

— in this case, must show that he was sojourning in Canada for 183 days or more resulting in the same tax consequences as full-time resident

— until April 15, he was not sojourning (i.e., not visiting)

— after that date, he was sojourning, but not for 183 days or more (about 30 days)

— therefore, par. 250(1)(a) not applicable in this case

C. Part-year resident in Canada

(1) Must establish a clean break from Canada in the year

— evidence

— he took a position with a Mexican company this year

— he left Canada in April for an indefinite period

— his wife and unmarried children followed him to Mexico as soon as practical; their stay in Canada to June 30 was merely to complete the school year

— Dundas home sold

— had a permanent home in Mexico

— most household effects moved to Mexico

— property that remained in Canada effectively given to married children

— cottage rented for most of the year and not available for his use

— closed bank accounts and terminated insurance and club memberships

(2) Income tax consequences

— Section 114 will apply because there was a period after April 15 in which he was not employed in Canada and not carrying on business in Canada

— taxed in Canada on worldwide income while resident in Canada to April 15 of $31,333 (i.e., $23,333 + $8,000)

— tax liability on sale of taxable Canadian property after April 15

— non-refundable tax credits pro-rated on a reasonable basis

— deemed disposition of all property immediately before he became a non-resident on April 15 except:

— pension rights

— taxable Canadian property which would include:

— home in Ottawa and cottage (i.e., real property)

— therefore, investment portfolio and listed personal property (paintings and sculpture) would be subject to deemed disposition rules

— can elect to be deemed to have disposed of taxable Canadian property, as well

— the gain on the sale of the home on June 30 would be taxable in Canada, subject to principal residence exemption

CHAPTER 2

Chapter 3

Employment Income

Learning Goals

Know, Understand and Explain

By the end of this chapter you will know, understand and be able to explain:

- The basic provisions of the *Income Tax Act* (the Act) that relate to employment income.
- The factors that distinguish an employee from a self-employed individual.
- What amounts must be included in employment income.
- How employment deductions are calculated.
- The special rules relating to the expenses of a commission sales person.

Apply

By the end of this chapter you will be able to apply:

- Your knowledge and understanding to calculate net employment income to real-life situations.

Review Questions
¶3,800 in the Study Guide

Multiple Choice Questions
¶3,825 in the Study Guide

Exercises
¶3,850 in the Study Guide

Assignment Problems
¶3,875 in the Study Guide

CHAPTER 3

CHAPTER 3 — LEARNING CHART

Problem Descriptions

Textbook Example Problems

3-1	Employed vs. self-employed — case
3-2	Employee loan
3-3	Employee stock option
3-4	Employee stock option
3-5	Employee stock option
3-6	Standby charge and operating benefit — employer owned — employment kilometres < 50%
3-7	Standby charge and operating benefit — employer owned — employment kilometres > 50%
3-8	Standby charge and operating benefit — employer leased — employment kilometres < 50%
3-9	Standby charge and operating benefit — employer leased — employment kilometres > 50%
3-10	Deductible automobile expenses — employee owned car
3-11	Deductible automobile lease expense — employee leased car
3-12	Deductible automobile expenses — employee leased car
3-13	Comprehensive example — employment income and expenses

Multiple Choice Questions

1	Standby charge, operating benefit
2	Car allowance
3	Home office expenses
4	Employee loan
5	Employee stock option — public
6	Commission expenses & limitation

Exercises

1	Employed vs. self-employed
2	Employed vs. self-employed
3	Taxable benefits
4	Legal expenses — deductibility
5	Employee discount
6	Moving expense reimbursement
7	Employee benefits — employer payments
8	Employee stock option — CCPC
9	Standby charge, operating benefit
10	Home office expenses
11	Personal meals while travelling
12	Employment income — comprehensive calculation
13	Employment income — implications of components of a compensation offer
14	Employee vs. independent contractor
15	Employment income — expenses of a salesperson

Problem Descriptions

Assignment Problems

1	Auto benefits — company owned vs. company leased
2	Stock option — comparing CCPC to public company
3	Employee benefits — multi-part
4	Employee benefits — multi-part
5	Employee loans, car expenses
6	Commission expenses & limitation
7	Employee travel expenses
8	HST rebate
9	Employed vs. self-employed — Chow
10	Offer of employment — compensation options
11	Calculate employment income — benefits, stock option
12	Compensation alternatives — salary, bonus, benefits or stock option
13	Compensation alternatives — forgivable loan, stock option
14	Auto benefits — company owned vs. leased
15	Car allowance vs. reimbursement
16	Payment on termination
17	Calculate employment income — benefits
18	Calculate employment income — expenses
19	Calculate employment income — benefits, expenses, stock option
20	Calculate employment income — travel expenses
21	Calculate employment income — comprehensive benefits
22	Calculate employment income — comprehensive expenses
23	Calculate employment income — comprehensive benefits, auto expenses
24	HST Rebate
25	Calculate employment income — comprehensive benefits, auto expenses
26	HST Rebate
27	Employed vs. self-employed
28	Employed vs. self-employed
29	Employed vs. self-employed, resident
30	Employed vs. self-employed, resident
31	Employment income comprehensive calculation
32	Employee vs. independent contractor
33	Employment income — comparison under two alternative employment offers

CHAPTER 3

Study Notes

¶3,800   REVIEW QUESTIONS

(1) The best way to calculate employment income is to follow the format used on the personal tax return. Comment on the accuracy of this statement.

(2) It does not matter whether an individual is employed or self-employed since he or she can claim the same expenses under either category as long as the expense was incurred to earn income. Comment on the accuracy of this statement.

(3) If an individual fails any one of the tests which are used to determine employed versus self-employed status then the individual is employed. Comment.

(4) When determining whether a person is employed or self-employed, one of the subtests used in the economic reality or entrepreneur test is the "control test". What does this test involve?

(5) When determining whether a person is employed or self-employed, one of the tests used is the "integration or organization test". What does this test involve?

(6) When determining whether a person is employed or self-employed, one of the tests used is the "specific result test". What does this test involve?

(7) If a bonus cheque is received by an employee, Ms. Davis, on December 15 of this year and she chooses not to cash her cheque until January 5 of next year, then she will be able to defer the tax on the bonus until the next year since individuals are taxed on the cash basis. Comment.

(8) A bonus is payable to an employee, Mr. Lee, on December 15 of this year and he decides that he wants to be taxed on the income in the following year instead of this year. He can ask his employer to defer the payment of this bonus until next year to accomplish his goal. Comment.

(9) Employees are taxed on income from their employer to the extent that it is a gross payment before withholding tax or a taxable benefit. The employer can deduct, as an expense, the full amount of the gross payments before withholding tax and taxable benefits that are reported on the employee's T4. Comment.

(10) To maximize the after-tax income from a disability insurance policy to a disabled employee, the employer should not pay *any* of the premium for the coverage. Comment.

(11) On June 2 of this year, Opco loaned $10,000 to an employee and did not charge interest. The employee repaid the loan on June 30 of the same year. How many days are included for purposes of determining the deemed interest benefit?

(12) Explain the differences between a reimbursement and an allowance.

(13) Opco bought a new car for its president that cost the company $40,000 plus $5,200 for HST. How much is the standby charge for this car for a full year assuming it is driven 40% for business purposes?

(14) What are the five conditions that must be met before a sales/negotiating person can deduct expenses?

(15) What are the four conditions that must be met by an employee, who is not a sales/negotiating person, in order to allow him or her to deduct travelling expenses other than car expenses?

(16) Mr. Wang is a part-time lecturer at the University of Waterloo. He lives in a location in Toronto which is 105 kilometres away from the university. The rest of the time he has a tax consulting practice which he operates out of his home. The university pays him $0.40 per kilometre to travel to and from the university. He is issued a T4 at the end of the year for his teaching income on the basis that he is a part-time employee. How is the travel allowance of $0.40 per kilometre treated for tax purposes?

(17) Guidelines for the deductibility of expenses related to work space in the home for employees are included in subsection 8(13). Under paragraph (*a*) of this provision the expenses are allowed if one of two conditions are met. In these conditions, the words "principally" and "exclusively" are used. What do these words mean for tax purposes?

(18) Ms. Smith has come to you to ask your tax advice. She has just had a large bonus paid to her on December 31 and wants to defer some of it until next year. She is arguing that since the CRA's portion was not sent to the Receiver General until January 15 she should be able to defer that portion until the next year on the basis that it was not received until January 15 when it was sent to the CRA. What do you think?

¶3,825   MULTIPLE CHOICE QUESTIONS

Question 1

This year, Bob's employer provided him with an employer-owned automobile costing $34,500 (including HST) for 12 months. His kilometres for personal use were 15,000 out of a total of 20,000 kilometres. Operating costs paid by his employer during this year were $3,600 (including HST). Which one of the following statements is TRUE for this year?

(A) Bob's minimum standby charge is $8,280.

(B) Bob's minimum operating cost benefit is $2,700.

(C) Bob's minimum operating cost benefit is $3,600.

(D) Bob can elect to use ½ of his standby charge as his operating cost benefit.

Question 2

This year, Mary earned a $50,000 annual salary as a computer repair person and received a total yearly car allowance of $3,500. The car allowance was paid to her monthly and was not based on the number of kilometres that she drove. Her employment-related expenses (all reasonable) were:

Automobile expenses (gas, parking, CCA)	$3,000
Entertainment	2,000

What is Mary's minimum employment income for the year?

(A) $53,500

(B) $50,500

(C) $49,500

(D) $49,000

Question 3

Susanne Denholm is employed as a provincial payroll tax auditor and is required by contract to maintain an office in her home. Susanne works at home most of the time and has been provided with a laptop computer and a fireproof audit bag for her files. She has not been provided with any reimbursement or allowance in connection with her home office, which occupies 10% of the square footage of her home. She incurred the following costs to maintain her entire home this year:

Telephone (general line)	$ 600*
House insurance	2,000
Property taxes	4,000
Heat, hydro & maintenance	5,000
Mortgage interest	24,000

* Susanne estimates that she used her telephone 50% for employment purposes during the year.

What is the maximum amount that Susanne can claim for the costs she has incurred in respect of her home office?

(A) $500

(B) $1,100

(C) $1,400

(D) $3,800

Question 4

On April 1, 2015, E Ltd. made a loan of $100,000 to Mr. Walker, a new employee of the corporation, to assist him in purchasing a residence when he moved from Quebec to commence employment in British Columbia. The loan bears interest at 2%, which is to be paid monthly. The principal of the loan is to be repaid in full on April 1, 2024. The prescribed interest rate on April 1, 2015 was 4%. Assuming that the prescribed interest rate throughout 2018 was 3% and only the interest owing on the loan is paid each month, which one of the following amounts represents the increase in Mr. Walker's employment income in 2018 due to the loan.

(A) $1,000

(B) $2,000

(C) $3,000

(D) $4,000

Question 5

Tanya, an employee of a Canadian public company, received an option to purchase 1,000 common shares of her employer at $30 per share in April 2017, when the shares were worth $19 per share. In December 2018, when the fair market value was $40 per share, she exercised her options. In January 2019, she sold all the shares for $48 per share. Tanya wants to know what employee benefit she will have to report on her tax return. She wants to pay the lowest amount of taxes possible.

(A) $5,000

(B) $18,000

(C) $14,000

(D) $10,000

Question 6

Tim began employment as a commissioned salesman in July of this year and received a base salary of $60,000 and $5,000 in commissions based on sales for the year. During the year, Tim worked away from the office negotiating sales contracts. Tim is required to pay his own travelling expenses and his employer has signed a T2200 form certifying that requirement and certifying that no reimbursements are paid for any expenses Tim incurs to earn commissions. Tim incurred the following work-related costs from July through December of this year and all expenses are reasonable:

Meals and entertainment for potential customers $14,000	
Automobile costs (90% of the following amounts were for employment purposes based on kilometres driven):	
Fuel	4,000
Insurance	750
Repairs	2,250
Leasing costs for a car costing $20,000 ($500 per month)	3,000

What is the maximum deduction Tim may claim for employment expenses for the year?

(A) $5,000

(B) $9,000

(C) $14,000

(D) $16,000

¶3,850   EXERCISES

Exercise 1

Isaac v. M.N.R., 70 DTC
1285 (T.A.B.)

The taxpayer is a qualified registered nurse, is entitled to use the traditional letters "R.N." after her name and, in answering the questions contained in her income tax return, described herself as a "private duty" nurse both in the space provided for employed persons and in the space provided for persons in business or practising a profession. Thus, in trying to answer all the official questions on her return, the taxpayer indicated, on the one hand, that she was employed "as a private duty nurse" by the Canadian Forces Hospital at Halifax and, on the other hand, that she was in business of practising her profession "as a private duty nurse" in connection with the same hospital. The basic issue to be decided is, briefly, what was the taxpayer's correct status vis-à-vis the Canadian Forces Hospital, Halifax in the taxation year in question.

The taxpayer launched the present appeal by Notice of Appeal in which she alleged (in effect) as follows: that in the relevant taxation year she was employed by the Canadian Forces Hospital, Halifax, on a day-to-day basis terminable on 24 hours' notice; that the usual so-called fringe benefits made available to and enjoyed by the regular full-time army nursing sisters such as holidays, sick pay, retirement plan, and so on, were not made available to her as a private duty nurse; that the regional surgeon's office in Halifax classified her as a "self-employed R.N."; that in her previous return she claimed and was permitted to deduct from her income expenses of a similar type to those disallowed in the taxation year now under appeal; and that several of her fellow private duty nurses employed at the Canadian Forces Base, Halifax, were employed on the same basis as she was and had claimed expenses of a similar type to those disallowed in this appeal (i.e., the type of expenses one would associate with a private duty nurse). The CRA stated that, in making the assessment now in dispute, he had acted upon the following assumptions of fact — that the taxpayer is a registered nurse and was employed by the Department of National Defence at the Canadian Forces Hospital and Base, Halifax, during the taxation year, that in the course of carrying out her engagement as a general duty nurse the taxpayer was subject to supervision and discipline by the hospital authorities, and that of the expenses allegedly incurred by the taxpayer only the amount claimed as "R.N. fees" and the amount being her contribution to the Canada Pension Plan were permitted under the Act.

The taxpayer testified, in effect, as follows: that she is a registered nurse; that in the relevant taxation year she was living in Halifax and was employed at the Canadian Forces Hospital (Stadacona Hospital), "not as a staff nurse but more or less as a private duty nurse, though my times were made up ahead of time" (the correct interpretation to be placed on the word "employed" in this appeal appears to be the key to the solution); that private duty nurses are allowed to claim as deductions from income certain expenses such as laundry, uniforms, travelling expenses, and so on; that the only difference between herself and a private duty nurse is that the hospital deducted her Canada Pension Plan contributions from the per diem amounts payable to her; that she acted as a private duty nurse at Stadacona Hospital for about five years, after which she moved from Halifax to Charlottetown and became associated with the Charlottetown Hospital as a relief nurse; that she is presently working under exactly the same conditions under which she carried on at the Canadian Forces Hospital, Halifax, i.e., "If I don't work, I don't get paid, I have no benefits or holidays. I get private duty wages (these amounted to $15 per day in Halifax and now amount to $20 per day). My time is made up. If they get full-time nurses they can let me go"; that she and other private duty nurses were hired by Stadacona Hospital (on a day-to-day basis) to fill in while the hospital "didn't have enough service nurses"; and that in the year before she was replaced the said hospital "did get a large supply of military nurses in and we were all cut down" (i.e., a number of private duty nurses were simply laid off which was easy to do because they were working on a day-to-day basis). The Hospital supplied all equipment and supplies used by the taxpayer. The Hospital hired and fired all nursing assistants and other support staff who assisted the taxpayer in the performance of her duties. The taxpayer could request the Hospital to hire additional support staff but she personally did not hire them.

The taxpayer also testified, in effect, as follows: that her time sheet in the Canadian Forces Hospital, Halifax, was made out a week in advance; that the said hospital's authority to hire civilian nurses to meet its requirements was only valid while there was a shortage of military nurses; that, as they became available, the civilian nurses were replaced; that the hospital asserted its right to dismiss civilian nurses on 24 hours' notice — "we were told that when we went there to work"; that she, herself, was not replaced by a military nurse in the taxation year, now under appeal, but later her shifts were cut down and she was eventually replaced; that she was, of course, obliged to follow hospital regulations with regard to the administration of drugs, medications, and so on, as she would be in any recognized hospital; that, when she was working at the Canadian Forces Hospital, Halifax, she was told which patients to look after; and that she did not sign any form of contract with the above hospital when she started to work there.

— *REQUIRED*

Is the taxpayer in this case employed or self-employed? In presenting your answer, discuss the tests that are applied by the courts in this type of situation and consider how the facts relate to these tests.

Exercise 2

Due to the poor economy, Davies Ltd., an architectural firm, has instituted a freeze in hiring. However, the company wants to engage the services of a specific architect, Anne Capwell, to manage the completion of a specific project over a two-year period. Following negotiations between the parties, a consulting contract was signed. Ms. Capwell will be paid $4,000 per month to work at least 14 days per month (i.e., between three and four days per week) for a two-year period. The agreement stipulates that Davies Ltd. will provide Ms. Capwell with an office and pay for underground parking at Davies Ltd. Ms. Capwell has other architectural work and she estimates that she derives approximately 30% of her consulting income from other sources.

ITA: 248(1); Wiebe Door Services Ltd. v. M.N.R., 87 DTC 5025 (F.C.A.)

— *REQUIRED*

Express your opinion as to whether Ms. Capwell is considered an employee or an independent contractor.

Exercise 3

ITA: 6(1)(a); Income Tax Folio S2-F3-C2

William Winter works for an extremely generous employer, Benjamin's Ltd., which paid the following amounts on behalf of William:

(a) Registered pension plan contributions (defined benefit)	$1,000
(b) Provincial employer health tax	600
(c) Extended health care premiums — Sun Life	250
(d) Drug plan premiums — Mutual of Omaha	150
(e) Tuition fee for a basket weaving course offered by a local high school	75
(f) Non-cash Christmas gift which the company did expense for tax purposes	65
(g) Subsidized lunches at company cafeteria:	
Fair market value	640
Actual cost	420
Amount paid by William	200
(h) Membership fees in Exclusive Private Club for his personal use	800
(i) Financial counselling — ABC Investment Counselling Ltd.	1,000

— *REQUIRED*

Comment on whether these amounts are taxable.

Exercise 4

ITA: 6, 8

Subdivision a — Income or loss from an office or employment, outlines the basic rules, inclusions and deductions when computing net income from employment.

— *REQUIRED*

Explain when legal expenses are deductible in computing income from employment. Identify your references and outline any related sections, other resources and other relevant information.

Exercise 5

ITA: 6(1)(*a*); Income Tax Folio S2-F3-C2

Melanie Hughes, a division supervisor for Eli's Ltd., a large department store chain, receives a 35% discount on all merchandise purchased through Eli's Ltd. This discount is available to all executives above assistant department heads. Melanie calculated that the discount saved her $6,000 this year.

— *REQUIRED*

Discuss whether there is a benefit.

Exercise 6

ITA: 6(1)(*a*); Income Tax Folio S2-F3-C2

John Scott, an employee of Kelly Ltd., lives in Burlington and commutes by GO Train to Toronto where Kelly Ltd. is located. John, who is bored by reading, decides to move to Toronto, about 50 kilometres closer to his work, in order to cut down his travelling time. Kelly Ltd. reimburses him for the following amounts:

Moving van costs	$2,500
Reimbursement of actual loss suffered in selling the house	5,000
	$7,500

— *REQUIRED*

Discuss whether there is a benefit.

Exercise 7

ITA: 6(1)(*a*), 6(1)(*f*)

Tanya Sims, who is chairperson of her union's negotiating team, has approached you concerning the management's offer in connection with fringe benefits. The company proposes to pay one-half of the premiums of the following plans:

(a) group term life insurance;

(b) extended health care — a private plan;

(c) dental care — a private plan;

(d) an accident and sickness income protection plan — a private group plan covering up to 50% of the wages.

All of these plans have premiums which are approximately the same. The company at present does not contribute to any of these plans.

— *REQUIRED*

Discuss the tax implications of the company's proposal.

Exercise 8

ITA: 7; IT-113R4

Katrina Knorr was granted, in year one, an option to purchase 50,000 common shares at $1 per share from her employer, Michael Ltd., a Canadian-controlled private corporation. The shares had an estimated fair market value at this date of $1.50. However, according to the agreement, Katrina could not exercise her option until her fourth employment year. Katrina did exercise her entire option in year five; the fair market value of the shares at that time was $3. Katrina sold all the shares in year six, at $6 per share.

— *REQUIRED*

Discuss the tax implications of the above transactions.

Exercise 9

ITA: 6(1)(e), 6(1)(k), 6(2)

Ms. Singh has full use of an employer-owned Mustang GTS purchased for her use in mid-December of last year. It is now January. The original cost to the employer of this classic is $20,000, including HST. Other details of the car for the coming year are as follows:

Capital cost allowance to be claimed by employer	$4,792
Operating costs for the year paid by the employer, including HST and insurance ($600)	$3,500
Personal-use kilometres	12,000
Number of months available	12
Reimbursement to employer for personal use at 15 cents per kilometre	$1,800

— REQUIRED

Compute the taxable standby charge and operating cost benefits, if the business-use kilometres are:

(a) 10,000

(b) 20,000

Exercise 10

ITA: 8(1)(i), 8(13); IT-352R2

Calvin Cheng, who is employed and lives in Calgary, takes a considerable amount of office work home and, therefore, has built and furnished an office in his fully paid home. On this year's tax return, he claimed the following expenses in respect of his office which represents approximately ⅛ of the home.

Estimated rental value for office space	$1,000
Maintenance — ⅛	250
Taxes — ⅛	200
Insurance — ⅛	80
	$1,530

— REQUIRED

Discuss whether Calvin's course of action was correct.

Exercise 11

ITA: 8(4), 67.1(1)

The deduction for meals under paragraph 8(1)(f) — (sales expenses), is restricted to those incurred while entertaining a client or a customer or a prospective client or customer.

— REQUIRED

Determine the condition(s) under which personal meals consumed by an employee while travelling on business are allowable. Are there any restrictions if a deduction is allowed?

Exercise 12

Susie Sellem is a top real estate salesperson employed by Sellem, Sellem and Fast Limited, a Canadian-controlled private corporation located in Burlington, Ontario.

Susie has provided you with the following details of her remuneration for the year ended December 31, 2018.

Gross commission before payroll deductions		$126,000
Less:		
Income taxes withheld at source	$44,617	
Canada Pension Plan contribution	2,594	
Employment Insurance contribution	858	
Registered pension plan contribution (money purchase; current service)	6,750	
Group term life insurance premium	300	
Group accident income protection plan premium	250	
United Way payroll deduction (registered charity)	360	(55,729)
Net commission after payroll deductions		$ 70,271

Susie indicated to you that her employer paid the following amounts on her
   behalf during 2018:

Registered pension plan contribution (money-purchase)	$ 6,750
Group term life insurance premiums	700
Group accident income protection plan premium	250
Employer health tax	2,520
Dental plan premium paid to Manulife Financial	1,440
Extended health care premium paid to Blue Cross	960
Membership in Cedar Springs Fitness & Racquet Club	1,800

The fitness club membership gives Susie access to a formal dining room, which she uses on a regular basis to entertain clients. She also takes clients out to special events at the club over the course of the year. Susie and her employer are in agreement that her membership at this club is primarily for the employer's benefit as Susie would not otherwise have purchased this membership on her own.

Susie has provided you with the following additional information related to her employment during 2018.

(1) Susie received a sales incentive prize for being the top salesperson for the first quarter of the year. She received an all-expenses-paid trip for two to Nassau, Bahamas. She took her husband. The value of the prize was $4,000 which represented $1,000 related to airline tickets and $3,000 related to accommodation and expenses in the Bahamas. The value of the airline tickets was before HST @ 13%. There was no HST payable on the Bahamian accommodation charges.

(2) Susie received a $40,000 interest-free loan from Sellem, Sellem and Fast Limited on January 4, 2018. The loan was to aid her in the purchase of an automobile required for employment purposes. Assume that the prescribed interest rate was 4% for all of 2018. The purchase of the automobile took place on January 4, 2018 as described in (4) below.

(3) Susie received monthly allowances as follows:
   (a) $450 a month for her automobile expenses and
   (b) $300 a month to cover the costs she incurred in travelling out of town to meet clients and entertaining clients.

(4) Susie incurred the following automobile related expenses during 2018 (including HST where applicable). She drove her automobile 95% for employment purposes during 2018.

(a) Purchase price of a new vehicle acquired January 4, 2018	$41,400
(b) Gas and oil	2,500
(c) Maintenance	1,300
(d) Insurance	1,600
(e) Licence	90

(5) Susie incurred travel and entertainment related expenses during 2018 (including HST where applicable) as follows:

(a) Meals for meetings with out-of-town clients (she was out of town for more than 12 hours on all occasions)	2,400
(b) Accommodation for meetings with out-of-town clients	4,200
(c) Hamilton Symphony Orchestra tickets for entertaining	900

(6) Susie maintains an office in her home as required under her employment contract. This workspace is her only available office. Susie estimates that approximately 10% of the total square footage of her home is occupied by her home office. She has provided the following TOTAL expense amounts (including HST where applicable) for expenditures made during 2018 related to her home.

(a) Mortgage interest	8,000
(b) Property taxes	5,300
(c) House insurance	600
(d) Repairs and maintenance	450
(e) Repainting office only	300
(f) Office supplies consumed in the course of employment	200

— *REQUIRED*

(A) Determine Susie Sellem's employment income for tax purposes for 2018. Ignore the effects of a leap year in your answer.

(B) Indicate briefly why you did not use any of the above information in your response.

Exercise 13

Rae Bob is currently the director of human resources for a relatively small region of Strikebusters Ltd. (SL), located in Windsor, Ontario. She is seriously considering accepting a promotion to the position of director of human resources for the company's largest office, located in London, Ontario.

SL has agreed to help her finance the purchase of a new home and relocate her family to London.

She has a letter from SL outlining her new job responsibilities and her compensation package, should she choose to accept the promotion. The compensation package is attractive but she is uncertain of the tax consequences. She has asked you to advise her.

In addition to an annual salary of $125,000, SL has offered the following to Rae if she accepts the promotion:

1. Rae is to receive a lump-sum payment of $20,000 on January 1 of this year coinciding with the effective date of her promotion. This payment is to compensate Rae and her family for the emotional upheaval and inconvenience associated with moving to a new city.
2. Rae will be a member of the company's defined benefit registered pension plan. Membership in the plan is limited to the London office key executives. This year, Rae and SL will each be required to contribute $10,000 to the plan.
3. SL will pay 100% of the premiums for extended health coverage, a dental plan and group term life insurance coverage of $125,000.
4. SL will provide Rae with a monthly car allowance of $600. She expects her actual costs of operating the car (personal and employment combined) to be $600 per month.
5. SL will loan Rae $150,000 to help finance a new house in London. The loan will bear interest at 2% per annum payable no later than 30 days after the end of the year.
6. SL will loan Rae $20,000, interest-free, to help her finance the purchase of a new car. Rae expects to purchase a $40,000 car, including HST @ 13%. Her job responsibilities require her to provide her own car. Her responsibilities are such that she expects that 95% of the usage of the car will be in carrying out her duties of employment.
7. Rae is concerned about selling her Windsor home as house prices in Windsor have fallen significantly. SL has offered to reimburse Rae for any loss she incurs on the sale of her Windsor home, as well as for the cost of hiring a moving company to pack and move her furniture and personal effects from her Windsor home and unpack them in her London home. All other costs incurred by her, related to the move, will be reimbursed also.
8. Rae will be permitted to participate in the company's stock option plan. She will be permitted to purchase 500 non-voting, fully participating common shares of SL over the next five years, with a stipulation that she cannot purchase more than 200 shares in any one calendar year. The option price will be $18 per share. The shares are currently valued at $21 per share and are expected to increase in value.

The following additional information has been provided:

(a) SL is a Canadian-controlled private corporation;
(b) the distance between Windsor and London is greater than 40 kilometres; and
(c) the prescribed rate of interest is 4% for the first two quarter of this year and will increase to 5% for each of the last two quarters. All loans were issued on January 1 of this year.

— REQUIRED

Comment on the tax implications of each item in the compensation package.

Exercise 14

Mr. Macher, a film director of repute, entered into a verbal agreement with Shlock Films Ltd., a production company, to provide his talent and energy in the direction of commercials. There was no specific term to the agreement, but Mr. Macher agreed not to direct commercials for other production houses.

The director was responsible for finding clients to create business. He was reimbursed for certain expenses such as lunches with clients and promotion. Prior to production of a commercial, he would be involved in discussions with the clients on planning the commercials and these discussions would take place in various offices including those of the production company and the clients or in restaurants. During the production phase, the director was in charge of the talent and the crew. This phase could take place in a studio or on location anywhere. At the post-production stage, the director was responsible to put the commercial together by directing the work of editors and sound engineers. In general, the director had artistic control over the commercial, while the production company provided the finances and had an input on decisions such as overtime shooting. The director selected the talent and could hire his own assistants. The production company provided and paid for the equipment, such as cameras and lights, and the individuals who worked on the film, such as editors, camera crew, sound crew, lighting crew and assistant script writers.

Mr. Macher was paid $905 every two weeks or $22,000 for a year as a retainer or guarantee for his services. He was also paid $850 per shooting day. He was not paid for re-shooting if he made an error. To be paid, he had to invoice the production company. He reimbursed the production company for its share of the premium for the medical plan in which he participated. He had no specified hours of work. He had no profit-sharing arrangement and no ownership rights in the commercials he made.

The CRA disallowed Mr. Macher's unreimbursed expenses incurred in the work he did on the basis that he was not self-employed.

— *REQUIRED*

As a judge of the Tax Court of Canada, discuss and evaluate the positions of Mr. Macher and of the CRA.

Exercise 15

June is a salesperson who earned a total of $40,000 in the current year, including $5,000 in commissions. She was required to travel in her job and was required to pay her own expenses, which consisted of the following annual amounts (including HST when applicable):

(a) entertainment of clients (incurred in equal monthly amounts), including golf membership dues of $600 . . . . $3,700
(b) home office expenses (including an allocated portion based on square footage of the home office of mortgage interest of $700 and municipal taxes of $250)   3,500
(c) car operating expenses   4,900
(d) interest paid on bank loan to purchase car (12 months of payments)   1,500
(e) convention dues (excluding meals and entertainment)   700
(f) meals expense (incurred in equal monthly amounts) while travelling (away from the metropolitan area of her employer for more than two days at a time)   1,000

She owns her own car which she uses for employment purposes. The capital cost allowance available on the car for the year is $4,000 before reduction for employment use. The car was driven a total of 28,000 kilometres during the year, of which 18,000 kilometres were driven in the course of her employment.

— *REQUIRED*

Calculate June's minimum employment income under the following independent assumptions:

1. She received no kilometre allowance for the use of her automobile in carrying out her duties of employment.
2. She received an allowance of $0.35 per kilometre plus a yearly allowance of $1,200. She received both allowances for the use of her car in carrying out her duties of employment. The allowances were in addition to her $40,000 income.

Ignore the effects of a leap year in your answer.

¶3,875   ASSIGNMENT PROBLEMS

Type 1 Problems

Problem 1

You have come out of a meeting with Lisa, one of your personal tax clients. She is about to start a job with a public company and, as part of the compensation package, she is offered the use of a company car. She is given the choice between two options and she wants your opinion on which she should choose. The make, model, and year of the car are the same in both cases. She expects to drive about 24,000 km per year. However, she is not sure how many personal versus business kilometres she will be driving. She expects it will be either 60% business or 40% business. Assume that she is in the 41% combined (federal and provincial) marginal tax bracket. She has asked you to analyze the options below to determine which option minimizes her taxes payable on the automobile benefit.

Option 1: The company will provide a company-owned automobile that costs $35,000 (before HST of 13%). The company will cover the insurance and operating costs which will cost $8,000 per year.

Option 2: The company will provide a company-leased automobile that costs $750 per month (before HST of 13%). The company will cover the insurance and operating costs which will cost $8,000 per year.

Problem 2

You have been asked for advice on employee stock options by two different clients.

(a) Omer is part of the management team of a Canadian public company and is eligible for the employee stock option plan. A few years ago he received an option on 1,000 shares. The current price of the shares is $35, and he is optimistic that it will go up. The option requires him to pay the option price of $30 (the value at the time the option was granted) for the shares at the time he exercises his option. He plans to sell these shares when they reach $45.

He has asked you to tell him the amount of income he will have to report and when he must report as a result of exercising the option and buying the shares for $30.

(b) Hilda is part of the management team of a Canadian-controlled private company and is eligible for the employee stock option plan. A few years ago she received an option on 1,000 shares. The current price of the shares is $35, and she is optimistic that it will go up. The option requires her to pay the option price of $30 (the value at the time the option was granted) for the shares at the time she exercises her option. She plans to sell these shares when they reach $45.

She has asked you to tell her the amount of income she will have to report and when she must report as a result of exercising the option and buying the shares for $30.

Problem 3

Rishma, a good friend from your university days, has just left your office. She remembered that you have specialized in tax and has come to you for advice on an offer of employment that she has received. Motion Tech Inc., a public company, has offered her the position of VP of Human Resources. Motion Tech has a year end of November 30th. Her start date is one month from now.

ITA: 5(1); 6(1)(*a*), (*b*); 8(1)(*m*); 62; 118.2(2)(*q*); Income Tax Folio S2-F3-C2

She has made the following list of items that are included in the package and would like your advice on the tax consequences of each:

1. A salary of $90,000 per year, payable by direct deposit on the last day of each month.

2. A bonus payable based on the year-end results of the company. The bonus would be up to $10,000.

3. Motion Tech has a defined contribution registered pension plan where Rishma and the company each contribute 6% of her salary.

4. Since she will have to move to Waterloo to take up this position, the company will pay her an allowance of $15,000 to cover her moving expenses.

CHAPTER 3

5. Motion Tech will cover the annual dues for a fitness club up to a cost of $2,000 per year.

6. The company will pay for Rishma to have her personal tax return prepared at a cost of up to $1,000.

7. The company provides a group health plan administered by Manulife, including glasses. Rishma will pay about $200 per month and the company will pay about $800 per month.

Problem 4

You are working in the finance department at Auto Supply Inc. during your co-op work term. The CFO knows you have just taken a tax course and has asked you to do some research for him. The company is looking at possible employee benefit options and would like you to write a memo explaining whether each of the following would be considered taxable benefits of the employees.

1. Free parking.

2. Wedding or birthday gifts of up to $200.

3. All-expense paid holiday won as part of a sales contest.

4. The employee uses frequent flyer points for a personal trip. These points were earned as a result of business trips.

5. The company provides an employee discount of 24% on products sold by Auto Supply.

6. The company pays to provide financial counselling for all vice presidents, including the preparation of their personal tax returns.

7. The company will pay for annual professional dues for employees. For example, accountants and lawyers.

Problem 5

ITA: 6(9), 8(1)(*j*), 80.4, 80.5

Leonard Lewis, an employee of BGE Ltd., received the following loans on January 1 of this year from his employer:

6% . . . . . $15,000 loan to purchase a car to be used primarily for employment purposes,

4% . . . . . $100,000 loan to purchase a home, and

7% . . . . . $10,000 loan to consolidate his other debts.

Leonard does not receive a mileage allowance and is specifically required by his contract to pay his car expenses. According to Leonard's travel log, he used the car for employment purposes, for 27,000 kilometres out of a total of 45,000 kilometres.

Assume that the prescribed rates for this year were:

1st Quarter — 7%	3rd Quarter — 8%
2nd Quarter — 6%	4th Quarter — 7%

Leonard paid the interest on these loans on January 15 of the following year.

Compute the interest benefit and any deduction for interest. Ignore the effects of any leap year.

Problem 6

ITA: 8(1)(*f*), 8(1)(*i*), 8(4)

Reille travels extensively with Biotech Corporation to market new pharmaceuticals throughout Canada. He is paid a base salary of $2,200 per month plus a 2% commission on gross sales. Reille was required to incur the following expenses to earn $24,000 in commission income:

Hotel and airfare	$18,000
Out of town meals	4,000
Entertainment meals	2,500
Professional dues	250
Notebook computer	3,900
Total	**$28,650**

Compute employment expenses deductible under section 8 of the Act.

Problem 7

ITA: 6(1)(*b*), 13(7)(*g*), 67.2; IT-522R

Ms. Irvine, who is employed by Susan's Super Ltd., travels extensively across Canada in her role as an internal auditor. According to the terms of her contract, she receives an accommodation allowance of $10,000 per year.

The contract states that she must use her own automobile and pay for all travelling expenses. Ms. Irvine acquired a new car, on January 5, 2018, for $32,000 plus HST at 13%. Her kilometres for business purposes were 15,000 out of a total of 21,000 kilometres.

During the year, Ms. Irvine paid the following amounts, all of which are reasonable in the circumstances and which are supported by receipts:

(a) accommodation, including meals of $4,500 (including HST)	$12,000
(b) total car expenses: gas (including HST)	1,500
maintenance (including HST)	500
insurance	1,200
licences	90
interest on bank loan	4,000

Ms. Irvine calculated her capital cost allowance to be:

$$(\tfrac{1}{2} \times 30\% \times \$32,000) = \$4,800$$

Ms. Irvine also filed the prescribed form (T2200) which her employer had signed. Assume that the employment use of the car is reasonable in the circumstances.

Discuss the tax consequences of the allowance and related expenses plus the deductibility of the car expenses. Ignore the effects of any leap year or any potential HST rebate implications.

Problem 8

ITA: 6(8); ETA: 253(1)

Authors' Note: The following problem includes GST/HST implications. Students should review Chapter 20 of the textbook, Goods and Services Tax (GST)/Harmonized Sales Tax (HST), before attempting this problem.

Based on the facts and solution for Problem 7 determine the potential HST rebate and income tax consequences upon receipt of this amount.

Problem 9

ITA: 248(1); *Wiebe Door Services Ltd. v. M.N.R.*, 87 DTC 5025 (F.C.A.)

Harry Chow, the owner of Chow Installation and Repair Ltd. ("Chow") has come to you for advice, but first he describes his business. Chow is in the business of installing and repairing overhead doors. Chow maintains a list of qualified installers and repair-persons and contacts them as work becomes available. Chow informed these workers that they would be considered to be running their own business, so no withholding of income tax, EI or CPP is made. Workers are paid by the job and work mostly on their own. If the person contacted refuses the assignment, Chow will call the next person on the list. The person who agrees to the job goes directly to the job site; he or she does not report to Chow's work place, except to pick up a door or parts.

Chow supplies the doors and the parts used in the repair or installation. Each worker maintains his or her own truck and tools. Chow, however, owns specialized racks made for transporting the doors and a special drill which can be used on cement. These items are available to any worker who requires them.

CHAPTER 3

Chow guarantees all work for one year. Under the terms of the agreement between Chow and the workers, if a guarantee has to be honoured, the worker will be responsible to fix any defects. If any parts are required to correct the defect, the worker has to pay for them.

Harry then asks you the question he wants advice on, "What is the risk that his installers will be considered employees for tax purposes?" He has heard that some other businesses are being reassessed and are facing significant liability for withholding taxes and he wants your advice on what his risk of reassessment is. You have agreed to meet with Harry again in one week and provide him with advice on this issue. As you think about how you will approach this assignment, you decide that you need to determine whether the workers should be considered employees of Chow or independent contractors. To do this you will need to consider the tests that are applied by the courts to this type of situation, and relate the facts of this case to those tests.

Problem 10

ITA: 5, 6(1)(*a*), 6(1)(*b*), 80.4; Income Tax Folio S2-F3-C2

Miriam, the sole tax adviser of a financial planning firm, is contemplating an offer to become Director of Taxation of Neil Manufacturing Limited (NML) of Dundas, Ontario. The offered compensation package would include the following:

- a salary of $132,000 per year, payable monthly;

- a one-time flat allowance of $25,000, payable on acceptance of the position, to help move her and her family to Dundas;

- a company contribution of 6% of her salary to a defined benefit registered pension plan;

- company payment of the premiums for extended health coverage and a dental plan provided by Star Insurance;

- company payment, valued at $900, for the preparation of her tax return by the company's accountants;

- company payment, valued at $2,500, for her membership in the Dundas Valley Golf and Curling Club;

- a company loan of $200,000 to help finance the purchase of a new home in Dundas. The loan will bear interest at 2% per year payable monthly and will be made on May 1 of this year, the closing date on the purchase of the home.

Miriam does not deal with many employment-related tax issues and recognizes the need for a corroborating opinion on the tax consequences of this compensation package. She has asked you to comment on the income tax consequences for employment income of each item in the compensation package. Assume that the prescribed rate of interest for employee loans is 1% throughout the year. Ignore any effects of a leap year.

Problem 11

ITA: 5, 6(1)(*a*), 6(1)(*b*), 80.4; Income Tax Folio S2-F3-C2

Erin is an employee of TD-ROM, Inc., a public company. In 2018, her compensation package was as follows:

Gross salary	$59,000
Less: Payroll deductions	
Employee contribution to a registered pension plan	(3,000)
Charitable donations — United Way	(55)
Canadian Pension Plan contributions	(2,594)
Employment Insurance contributions	(858)
Net pay received	$52,493
Non-cash perks	
Employer contribution to a registered pension plan	$ 3,500
Private dental plan valued at	$ 800
Mandatory employer-paid provincial health tax	$ 450
Reimbursement of moving expenses for relocating from Edmonton	$ 900
Club membership (for company promotion)	$ 1,800
Supplier's prize for outstanding employee sales — Hawaii golf trip valued at	$ 6,000
Bonus declared but not paid	$ 2,000
Hard hat and safety glasses	$ 450

The company states that club memberships should be used for business promotion.

TD-ROM also offered Erin a stock option to purchase 1,000 corporate shares at $12 a share. On June 4, 2018, she exercised the option. As of December 31, 2018, Erin had not disposed of the shares.

February 1, 2011, Fair market value — Grant date	$11
June 4, 2018, Fair market value — Exercise date	$19
December 31, 2018, Fair market value	$16

Erin has asked you to calculate her income from employment for income tax purposes.

Problem 12

ITA: 5, 6, 7

Three senior executives are renewing their employment contracts with Global Consulting Ltd., a public corporation. The corporation has provided each of them with the following alternative compensation plans for 2018 in addition to the $145,000 base salary each receives:

(a) A cash raise of $5,000 in 2018.

(b) A bonus of $5,500 payable in 2019.

(c) Use of the company condominium in Hawaii for two weeks, valued at $3,000.

(d) A stock option arrangement to purchase 1,000 shares of Global Consulting, a public company, in December 2018, when the fair market value of the shares is $5, and the option price would be $3.50 per share. Management anticipates the share price in December 2019 will be $6.50.

The senior executives have asked you to analyze the various alternatives and provide a recommendation. You agreed to assume a marginal tax rate of 45%.

Problem 13

ITA: 6, 110(1)(*d*)

Craig Hunt is the general manager of the local professional hockey team, the Vancouver Golden Seals Ltd. (a Canadian public corporation). Assume that today's date is November 15, 2018. Craig has obtained approval from the owner of the hockey club to offer a contract to a 27-year-old free agent player who is available to the highest bidder. In addition to an offer of a $300,000 signing bonus and a $750,000 annual salary, Craig is authorized to offer the following two items as additional compensation:

(a) an interest-free employee loan of $100,000 that will eventually be forgiven by the hockey club; and

(b) a stock option to buy 100,000 common shares of Vancouver Golden Seals Ltd. Assume that on the grant date, the fair market value of the common shares is $10 per share, and that the exercise price will be $10 per share.

Craig has asked for your advice on the following:

(a) Assuming the player will exercise all shares when the FMV is $15.00 per share and then sell the shares immediately on the open market, outline the income tax consequences with respect to the stock option and explain how this will affect the player's net income for tax purposes.

(b) From the player's perspective, what, if any, are the consequences of the signing bonus and the proposed employee loan that will be forgiven in the final contract year?

(c) Assuming instead that the loan will not be forgiven, calculate the deemed interest benefit of the loan for the 2018 and 2019 taxation years. Assume the prescribed rate of interest on the loan is 6%. Ignore the effects of any leap year.

CHAPTER 3

Problem 14

ITA: 6(1)(*a*), 6(1)(*e*), 6(1)(*e*.1), 6(1)(*k*), 6(2), 6(2.2)

Your best friend, Mitch, was at a sales conference recently. During one of the breaks, he entered into a conversation with one of the other attendees, Darly, regarding the perks provided by their respective employers. In both cases, the employer provides a car. However, Darly commented on the significant tax advantage available to her since her employer leased the car instead of buying the car. Mitch was able to obtain all of the information from Darly regarding her car.

Mitch has come to you for some "free" tax advice. He has asked you to compare the tax position he is in currently with the employer-owned car to the position that Darly is in with the leased car.

Mitch

Capital cost of the car including HST	$38,772
Capital cost allowance claimed by the employer	6,375
Operating costs paid by the employer (including HST)	4,250
Kilometres (as calculated from Mitch's log):	
Employment	8,000
Personal	10,000
Amount reimbursed to the company for the personal use at 14 cents per kilometre	$ 1,400

Darly

Lease cost including $1,650 of insurance and HST	$12,450
Operating costs paid by the employer (including HST)	2,975
Kilometres (as calculated from Darly's log):	
Employment	23,000
Personal	9,000
Amount reimbursed to the company for the personal use at 9 cents per kilometre	$ 810

Mitch wants you to calculate the minimum car benefit that would be included in employment income for 2018 for both him and Darly.

Problem 15

ITA: 8(1)(*h*.1)

Crowchild Pipelines Corporation has offered Bing Lee a base salary of $65,000. Bing must choose one of the following compensation packages for the use of his personal automobile.

(a) To receive a reasonable car allowance of $6,000 per year to compensate for the operating expenses and the depreciation of his Jeep, used to drive to remote work sites. The allowance is based on the kilometres to and from the remote location, multiplied by the number of workdays.

(b) To submit receipts for all of his operating expenses for full reimbursement. Bing estimates that his total operating expenses are $4,000 annually. However, this amount does not cover the wear and tear on his car. Bing will use his car approximately 65% of the time for employment and he will be able to claim capital cost allowance (tax depreciation) equal to $3,000.

Bing has a marginal tax rate of 45%. He has asked you to determine, with explanation, whether he would be indifferent to the choice between these two compensation packages?

Problem 16

ITA: 5, 6(3)

Chrisa had been an employee of David Hardware, a hardware product distributor, for 15 years. Chrisa sold the David hardware products directly to hardware stores. She was a salesperson and she was paid 100% by commission. Chrisa was personally responsible for all of her business expenses. Expenses, for example, for office supplies, stamps, telephone, parking, entertainment, promotion and samples, were supported by receipts and she deducted them.

During the years that Chrisa was employed by David, she sold products and developed the hardware market in her geographic area. One of the ways in which she developed the market was by "renting" floor space in various stores to display the David products. However, no receipts were received from the various stores, because in many ways the money was considered a "tip" by the managers of the hardware stores. Chrisa did not deduct these expenses. Through this process, Chrisa had significantly increased David's sales in her sales region and she had developed a loyal following in the hardware business.

At the time of Chrisa's departure from David, David paid $15,000 to Chrisa. The conditions of the agreement surrounding the $15,000 payment were as follows:

- David was "buying back" Chrisa's sales territory;

- Chrisa agreed not to enter a similar business to that of David's business, in David's distribution area, for a period of three years; and

- David and Chrisa agreed that the $15,000 would constitute a reimbursement of capital invested by Chrisa (i.e., the amounts she had paid to the stores for the rental of floor space for David products).

Chrisa has asked you to explain the income tax implications of the receipt of the $15,000.

Problem 17

ITA: 5, 6(1), 7, 8(1)

The following information relates to Leonard, a middle-management accountant, not engaged in negotiating contracts, of a public corporation, Peter Productions Ltd. which is located in Ontario.

(A) Salary — gross		$ 80,000
Payroll deductions:		
Income taxes	$23,412	
Registered pension plan (money purchase; see (B) below)	5,500	
Canada Pension Plan contributions	2,594	
Employment Insurance contributions	858	
Charitable donations	350	
Employee's portion of benefit plans (see (B), below)	800	(33,514)
		$ 46,486

(B) The company paid the following additional matching amounts on behalf of Leonard (an equal amount was withheld from salary as the employee's contribution, as shown in (A) above):

Registered pension plan	$5,500
Dental plan — Sun Life Co.	175
Group income protection — Royal Insurance Co.	225
Extended health care — Liberty Mutual	150
Group term life insurance — General Insurance Co.	250

The group term life coverage for Leonard was $300,000.

(C) Selected additional information concerning Leonard's receipts, disbursements, and other benefits:

(i) Trip to Europe from one of Peter Productions Ltd.'s clients in appreciation of Leonard's services (including HST) .... $ 6,000

(ii) Periodic payments received from Royal Insurance under the group income protection plan during a three-month illness. This plan had been in existence since 2006 and Leonard's share of the premium since that date was $2,300 12,000

(iii) Peter Productions Ltd. paid Leonard's annual membership fee in a golf club ... 2,100

(iv) Early in 2018, Leonard was granted an option to purchase 1,000 of the company's shares for $2 per share. At that time the shares were trading on the market at $3 per share. Later in the year, Leonard exercised the option and acquired 1,000 shares when they were trading at $4.50 per share. In December 2018, he needed cash, so he sold the 1,000 shares for $5 each.

(v) Leonard paid the following amounts during the year:

Annual membership fee of a professional accounting body (including HST)	800
Registered retirement savings plan	3,500

Leonard has asked you to calculate his employment income for 2018. For your files you also should document why you omitted any of the items mentioned above.

Problem 18

ITA: 5(1), 6(4), 8(1)(*f*), 8(1)(*j*); Income Tax Folio S2-F3-C2

On September 1, Maria Battelio, a Calgary resident, commenced work as an investment dealer with Top Investments Corporation. Prior to September, Maria was a fourth-year commerce student at the University of Alberta. Maria's contract of employment required that she use her own car and incur the necessary expenses to earn commission income. Maria purchased her car on September 1 for $21,000. Top Investments Corporation lent her the $21,000 for the car and she agreed to repay them $7,000 annually, without interest, on December 31 of each year. Assume that Maria's deductible capital cost allowance (net of personal use) on her automobile is $2,000.

Total distance travelled from September 1 to December 31	
Total kilometres driven	12,500
Personal kilometres driven	5,000
Maria received the following net pay in the year:	
Gross salary	$ 4,000
Commissions	18,000
Bonus	300
Employment Insurance contributions	(359)
Canadian Pension Plan contributions	(916)
Charitable donations	(280)
Income tax withheld at source	(4,200)
Net pay	$16,545
To earn commission income, Maria incurred the following:	
Meals and entertainment	$ 2,300
Client promotion materials	1,500
Gasoline and operating expenses	1,600
Total	$ 5,400

Top Investment paid for the airfare and accommodation for Maria and her spouse to attend a conference in New York. The trip cost $800 for each person attending the conference. The company also pays premiums of $400 per employee for group life insurance with coverage of $100,000. Assume a 7% prescribed rate of interest on the employee loan.

Maria would like you to calculate her income from employment. Ignore the effects of any leap year.

Problem 19

ITA: 5(1), 6(1)(*a*), 7(1), 8(1)(*f*), 8(1)(*i*)

Susanna Sculley, a marketing representative with MBI Technology Inc. (a public company), provided the following information relating to her current year's personal income tax return. Susanna's cumulative pay at year end revealed the following:

Gross pay	
Base salary	$42,000
Gross commissions	23,500
Daycare subsidy program	1,200
Deductions from gross pay	
Employment Insurance contributions	(858)
Canadian Pension Plan contributions	(2,594)
Union dues	(280)
Income tax paid	(19,800)
Net pay	$43,168
Expenses to earn commission income	
Meals and entertainment	2,300
Hotel and travel incidentals	1,780
Airfare	1,800
Total	$ 5,880

MBI also granted Susanna a stock option, which she exercised in April of the current year. The following information relates to the stock option:

Number of shares for options exercised	1,000
Fair market value — grant date	$1.50
Option price	$1.80
Fair market value — exercise date	$2.50

Susanna's employer did not reimburse her, or provide her with an allowance for the expenses incurred to earn commission income. However, MBI did expect her to take clients out for lunch and travel when necessary.

Susanna would like you to calculate her income from employment for the current year.

Problem 20

ITA: 5, 6, 7, 8

Sylvanna Chapelle, a national sales manager at Merche Tools Ltd. in Peterborough, Ontario, presented the following information for the current taxation year.

1) Gross salary		$48,000
Bonus based on sales		40,000
Less payroll deductions:		
Employee contribution to a Registered Pension Plan	(4,000)	
Charitable donations — Heart Foundation	(150)	
Canada Pension Plan contributions	(2,594)	
Employment Insurance contributions	(858)	
Net salary		$80,398

According to Sylvanna's contract of employment, she must travel to Vancouver, Edmonton, Calgary, and Regina to oversee operations in western Canada. Sylvanna must pay for travelling and promotional expenses. The company does not provide her with a travelling allowance. Instead, Sylvanna receives a bonus based on a percentage of western Canada sales. Syvanna's travelling expenses were as follows:

2) Meals while travelling out of town (45 days)	$ 1,500	
Accommodation	5,200	
Airfare	7,800	
Taxi	500	

3) Client promotion costs:		
Company logo shirts and golf balls	700	
Client meals and entertainment	2,200	
Holiday gifts for prospective clients	3,500	
Annual golf membership	1,800	

4) Sylvanna's employment contract also required her to travel to the Oshawa manufacturing plant and four other warehouse outlets in Southern Ontario. The corporation provided her with a new four-door van last year. The cost of the van, including HST of 13%, was $36,000. The company also paid $2,400 for 100% of the operating cost. Sylvanna used the vehicle for the full calendar year for both employment and weekend pleasure. Personal kilometres driven totalled 9,900 and total kilometres driven is 18,000.

5) Merche Tools also paid out the following amounts:		
Tax return preparation for Sylvanna	$ 350	
Life insurance premium	150	

Sylvanna would like you to calculate her income from employment for income tax purposes for the current year.

Problem 21

ITA: 5, 6; Income Tax
Folio S2-F3-C2

Anita Lee, Vice-President of Gary Inc., has asked for your assistance concerning the tax implications of certain amounts and benefits she received from her employer during 2018.

Salary, gross		$ 90,000
Payroll deductions:		
Income taxes	$36,000	
Canada Pension Plan premiums	2,594	
Employment Insurance premiums	858	
Group accident disability insurance premiums	110	(39,562)
Net pay		$ 50,438

Additional Information

(1) In November 2018, Anita was in a skiing accident and was unable to work for four weeks. During this period she received disability payments totalling $1,600 from Paris Life Insurance Ltd. Half of the disability insurance premiums were paid by Gary Inc. and half by Anita (see payroll deduction above). Anita has paid a total of $350 in disability insurance premiums since she commenced employment at Gary Inc. in 2015.

(2) In 2018, Gary Inc. paid $424 (including HST) for the preparation of Anita's 2017 income tax return and $530 (including HST) for Anita to see a financial planning consultant regarding retirement planning.

(3) Anita is taking courses towards her M.B.A. degree on a part-time basis during the evening. She is taking the courses on her initiative and for her own benefit. During 2018, Gary Inc. paid for the tuition for these M.B.A. courses which amounted to $1,000. Gary Inc. also paid $400 in tuition for Anita to attend a two-day computer workshop on company time to learn about the new software system that the company had just installed.

(4) Director's fees of $2,000 were received by Anita from Clint's Hi-Tech Ltd., a company owned by Anita's spouse.

(5) Birthday gift of $200 cash was received and was expensed by Gary Inc.

(6) Anita received an employee loan of $8,000 on January 15, 2018, at 1% interest to purchase a notebook computer for personal use. The interest was payable on each anniversary date of the loan, and Anita paid the interest owing on the loan on the due date in 2019. Assume that the prescribed interest rates applicable to employee loans for 2018 are: first quarter, 2%; second quarter, 1%; third quarter, 3%; fourth quarter, 1%.

(7) For 12 months, Gary Inc. paid Anita a monthly gas allowance of $250 regardless of the number of kilometres she drove. In addition, she was provided with a company-owned automobile costing $38,500 (including HST) at the beginning of January. Anita's kilometres for personal use were 16,000 out of a total of 25,000 kilometres. Operating costs paid (excluding gas) by Gary Inc. during 2018 amounted to $2,920, including insurance of $600 and HST.

(8) Anita and her spouse Clint were provided with Gary Inc.'s condo in the Bahamas for a one-week holiday during the winter. Excluding HST considerations, such accommodation during this peak period would have cost them $500 as opposed to the $100 actually paid by Anita.

(9) Anita used her frequent-flyer points accumulated as a result of her business trips (which had been paid by Gary Inc.) for her holiday in the Bahamas. She saved $800, plus $104 of HST, by using the frequent-flyer points.

(10) Anita bought merchandise from Gary Inc. during the year and saved $180 (excluding HST of $23) using its 30% employee discount, which is available to all employees. Gary Inc.'s mark-up is 100%.

Anita would like you to calculate her employment income for 2018. For your file you also should document the basis for your decision to include an item or not, i.e., whether it is based on the Act or on the CRA's administrative position. You decide to ignore the impact of any leap year.

Anita also wants you to recalculate her employment income assuming that the company did not provide her with a car as she used her own car instead. In this case the company would continue to pay for the operating costs of Anita's car.

Problem 22

ITA: 5, 6, 7, 8, 67.1, 67.2,
67.3; IT-352R2

Robby Beamon has recently been appointed vice-president of sales and marketing for Lori's Unpublished Books Limited, a public company. Robby has come to you for advice regarding the tax implications of his new position. During your meeting you were able to determine the following information:

Remuneration for the year:

Salary — gross		$84,800
Less: Canada Pension Plan contributions	$2,594	
Employment Insurance contributions	858	
Disability insurance premiums	600	4,000
		$80,748
Bonus based on company sales		34,000
Allowances for the year (paid monthly):		
meals, accommodation and air travel		13,000
car		6,300
entertainment		2,000
Moving allowance		15,000

Robby has summarized the following expenses related to his employment:

Gas and oil — automobile	$ 3,900
Painting (office only)	100
Licences — automobile	100
Meals (consumed while travelling away for more than 12 hours)	7,000
House insurance	800
Accommodation (while travelling on company business)	10,000
Interest expense — car loan	3,600
General maintenance (house)	300
Car insurance	1,900
Hydro	700
Air travel	4,200
Car maintenance	1,000
Supplies	700
Fuel (house)	1,200
Property taxes	4,500
Mortgage interest	24,000
Salary (to wife, including payroll taxes and employer contributions)	15,000

Lori's Unpublished Books Limited requires Robby to provide an automobile in order to carry out his duties of employment. Robby is responsible for his travelling expenses. On March 17, 2018, he acquired a new car for $46,000, including HST at 15%, financing part of the acquisition through a bank loan arranged for the same date. The capital cost allowance rate in the first year is effectively 15%. He estimates that he will drive 38,000 kilometres in the course of his employment. He expects his total kilometres to the end of the year to be 45,000. The car and the employment use are reasonable for his position and his work requirements.

Robby's contract also requires that he maintain an office in his home, since no other office is provided. He is responsible for all costs related to the operation of the office. He does not receive an allowance or reimbursement related to any of these costs. Robby has estimated that the office occupies approximately 15% of his home. This estimate is based on square footage. Robby estimates that if he had to rent a comparable amount of space he would have to pay $850 per month plus utilities.

(A) Robby would like you to calculate his employment income for 2018, assuming that all expenses are reasonable in the circumstances and will be documented. Ignore consideration of the HST rebate.

¶3,875

(B) Robby would also like you to recalculate his deductible expenses assuming the following:

ITA: 8(1)

- the car was leased instead of purchased on March 17, 2018.

- monthly lease payments are $1,100 including HST at 15%.

- manufacturer's list price is $48,500 excluding HST.

Problem 23

ITA: 5, 6, 7, 8, 67.2, 67.3;
Income Tax Folio
S2-F3-C2

Anita Flare is a skilled tool and die worker. She has been working for Car Parts Inc., a large manufacturer of parts for the automobile industry for over 10 years. Car Parts Inc. is a Canadian-controlled private corporation. Anita has become their "Jane on the Spot" as far as diagnosing and quickly retooling machinery that breaks down or needs to be updated to run a short order. Anita is single and she rents a home in north Toronto. Because Anita is required to travel for 75% of the year, Car Parts Inc. actually pays the $1,200 monthly rent on Anita's home in Toronto. Anita reimburses the company for 25% of this amount ($300 per month) through payroll deduction as set out below.

The head office of Car Parts Inc. is located in north Toronto. The company, however, has plants that are located throughout Ontario and Quebec, wherever there are large automobile manufacturing operations to be supplied with parts. When a plant requires emergency retooling or repair Anita is sent out to that location to supervise and organize the work. As stated above, this involves about 75% of Anita's total employment hours for any given year. She stays at a particular location for a period of days or weeks depending on the nature of the job involved. She is never at a site for less than 36 hours. For the balance of the year, Anita works at the head office in the research department.

Anita's final 2018 pay stub showed the following totals for the year.

Gross salary	$115,000
Payroll deductions:	
Income tax withheld	$44,200
Canada Pension Plan contributions	2,594
Employment Insurance premiums paid	858
Contributions to company group RRSP	1,750
RPP contributions on account of current service	5,000
Union dues to Canadian Union of Automobile Workers (HST exempt)	800
Group accident income protection insurance premiums (matched by company)	240
Monthly rent reimbursement (as described above)	3,600

In discussion with Anita you determined that the company also provides the following fringe benefits.

Payment of board and lodging costs at special work sites as required — at cost to company	$18,000
Bonus based on company profits for the year above budgeted targets	12,500
Provision of safety boots and company uniform consisting of five shirts and five matching pairs of pants; the shirt is embroidered with her name on the front pocket and has the company name on the back	450
Registered pension plan contributions to defined benefit plan	6,750
Monthly allowance of $150 to cover personal phone calls, laundry costs and other incidentals while travelling. (She estimates that she spends $100 per month.)	1,800
Fitness club membership dues to a club with locations across Ontario (including HST); Anita feels that it is important to her productivity to remain in top physical shape as her work can be physically demanding	805

Anita was injured on the job early in the year and received total payments of $11,500 out of the company group income protection plan for 2 months while she was recuperating. She had not previously received any payments under this plan and has paid total premiums of $2,880 into the plan since she began employment 12 years ago (this includes all of the year 2018 premiums paid through December 2018).

Due to her extensive travel, Anita's employer requires her to have an automobile for employment purposes. Anita has provided you with the following details of her automobile expenses.

	Owned car[1]	Leased car
Leasing costs[2]	n/a	$3,680
Gasoline and oil (including HST)	$2,880	1,440
Insurance	1,333	667
Maintenance (including HST)	400	240
Licence	90	30
CCA	1,207	n/a

NOTES:

[1] She owned an automobile until August 31, 2018, at which time she disposed of that vehicle and began leasing a new one. Assume that there are no tax consequences to Anita of the disposition of the automobile other than the fact that she can claim CCA in 2018 on this vehicle, as set out above, since it was a luxury vehicle.

Anita received an automobile loan to purchase the owned automobile. She received the loan on April 1, 2013, for $40,000, but has been making principal repayments annually on April 1 each year. She made the last principal repayment of $8,000 on April 1, 2018. There was no interest payable on the loan. Assume that the prescribed interest rate for employee loans was 1% for all of 2018.

During 2018, Anita drove the owned car a total of 40,000 kilometres, of which 35,000 kilometres were employment related.

[2] Anita leased the car as of September 1, 2018, at a cost of $920 a month that includes HST. The lease is for a three-year period that will expire August 31, 2021. At the time that she leased the car, the manufacturer's list price on the vehicle was $55,000 excluding all taxes.

During 2018, Anita drove the leased car a total of 20,000 kilometres, of which 18,000 kilometres were employment related.

Anita would like you to calculate her income from employment for 2018. Ignore the effects of any leap year.

For your files you should reference your findings to the appropriate section of the Act or CRA publication. Also you should indicate why you did not include any of the above amounts in your answer with the appropriate cross-reference.

Problem 24

ITA: 6(8); ETA: 253(1)

Authors' Note: The following problem includes GST/HST implications. Students should review Chapter 20 of the textbook, Goods and Services Tax (GST)/Harmonized Sales Tax (HST), before attempting this problem.

Based on the facts and solution for Problem 23, determine the potential HST rebate and income tax consequences upon receipt of this amount.

Problem 25

ITA: Subdiv. a of Div. B, 67.1, 67.3; Income Tax Folio S2-F3-C2

Mr. Ned Newell is employed by Snoopy-Snacks Ltd. (a Canadian-controlled private corporation). As of February 15, 2018, Ned was promoted to vice-president sales due to his hard work negotiating puppy snack contracts on behalf of the company. This promotion required Ned to relocate from the Toronto office of Snoopy-Snacks Ltd. to its Victoria, British Columbia office.

Ned has provided you with the following information regarding his 2018 income and expenses. He requests your assistance in determining his 2018 employment income for tax purposes.

Payroll details:		
Gross salary		$125,000
Less:		
Income taxes	$45,000	
Canada Pension Plan contributions	2,594	
Employment Insurance contributions	858	
Registered pension plan contributions: defined benefit	6,750	
Group income protection premiums paid	120	
Group term life insurance premiums paid	180	55,502
		$ 69,498

CHAPTER 3

Employer-paid amounts and fringe benefits paid by Snoopy-Snacks Ltd.:

Dental plan premiums — paid to Star Insurance Company	$ 245
Group term life insurance premiums	90
B.C. provincial health care premiums	640
Group income protection premiums	400
Monthly allowance to cover travel and automobile expenses (based on a flat monthly amount of $400 for travel and $400 for auto)	9,600
Travelling expenses for Ned and his wife to Bermuda for a sales conference. Ned's time was spent attending the conference but his wife was on vacation the entire time. No HST was payable on the trip since it was outside of Canada. One-half of the expenses related to Ned and one-half to his wife.	2,800
A birthday gift (a watch) received while in Ontario (including HST). Snoopy-Snacks Ltd. deducted the cost of this gift as a business expense.	150
Outside financial counselling fees (including HST). The counselling firm indicated that 80% of its fees relate to counselling for future retirement while the remaining 20% of its fees relate to tax preparation.	2,568

Other Information:

1. Snoopy-Snacks Ltd. provided Ned with some assistance that relates to his move from Toronto to Victoria. The details of that assistance are set out below.

a) Ned purchased a new home in Victoria just prior to his move. However, he could not take possession of that home until April 30, 2018. Snoopy-Snacks Ltd. paid Ned's rent for a Victoria apartment for the months of February through April 2018. The rent paid was $1,200 per month.

b) Ned and Snoopy-Snacks Ltd. agreed that he would receive reimbursement from Snoopy-Snacks Ltd. for one-half of the loss realized by him on the sale of his Toronto home. Ned received $16,500 as a result of this agreement.

c) Ned received an allowance of $15,000 to cover his moving expenses.

In addition to the above, Ned's employer agreed to reimburse him an amount equal to one-quarter of his annual mortgage interest payment for the first five years of his mortgage on his new Victoria home. This was intended to compensate for higher real estate prices in Victoria. For 2018, Ned received $2,000 under the terms of this agreement.

2. Ned had unlimited use of the company's private swimming pool. All management level employees are permitted to utilize this pool. The local private swimming pool charges annual fees of $1,800 per year before HST.

3. Ned had the following expenditures during 2018.

Automobile operating expenditures:

Lease payments for 12 months ($850 a month including HST of 12%)	$10,200
(lease commenced July 1, 2016 for a period of three years; deducted lease costs for 2016 were $4,585)	
Gasoline and oil	1,300
Insurance	1,050
Maintenance	180
Licence	120

Travelling expenditures:

Meals (consumed while out of metropolitan area for greater than 12 hours)	7,200
Accommodation	12,000

During 2018, Ned travelled a total of 36,000 kilometres, of which 22,500 kilometres were employment-related. The manufacturer's list price on his automobile was $33,000 before HST.

Ned would like you to calculate his employment income for tax purposes for 2018, cross-reference your answer to the appropriate sections of the Act and/or Income Tax Folios, and for your files you should indicate why you did not include any of the above amounts in your answer with the appropriate cross-reference.

Problem 26

ITA: 6(8)

Authors' Note: The following problem includes GST/HST implications. Students should review Chapter 20 of the textbook, Goods and Services Tax (GST)/Harmonized Sales Tax (HST), before attempting this problem.

Consider the fact situation presented in Problem 25. Ned would also like you to compute the potential HST rebate in 2019 and the income tax consequences upon receipt of the HST rebate. While B.C. has both PST and GST, assume an HST rate of 12% for this purpose.

Problem 27

Sandra Rae has worked in the investment business in Calgary for 12 years and is a salaried plus commissioned employee. Recently, however, Sandra has wished for more independence in her career. The alternative of starting her own mutual fund company is neither feasible nor cost effective. A recent offer from a new investment corporation has drawn her attention.

Sandra decided to enter into a contract arrangement with Global Investments Inc. According to the agreement, a license costing $10,000 would give her the right to use the Global name on her letterheads, business cards, and any promotional materials. Sandra could also participate in selling any Global Investment product. The arrangement is peculiar. According to the agreement, Sandra is required to execute a minimum of $750,000 in sales each year before her contract can be renewed for another year. Although Global Investments has an office in Calgary, the agreement stipulates that Sandra use her own office, supplies, computer, printer, fax, telephone, and automobile. The agreement also stipulates that Sandra not work for any other investment firm, nor act as her own agent. Although Sandra will execute transactions, closing a sale requires the signature of the client, herself and a vice-president of Global Investments. Upon the close of a sale, Sandra submits an invoice to Global Investments earning her a management fee equal to 4% of gross sales.

Sandra converted her guest bedroom into a full-time and sole-purpose home office. She will not be reimbursed for any expenses incurred for setup, travelling or office expenses. She is also required to carry professional liability insurance. On the other hand, Global Investments will provide the expertise, research, promotion, and ordering materials. Last week, Global Investments placed an announcement in the newspaper introducing five new sales associates, including Sandra.

How does this new venture affect her computation of net income?

Problem 28

Betina Harty, a well-known Vancouver artist, signed a contract with the University of Calgary to beautify the campus. Betina spent all of the year in completing the beautification. During that time, she enhanced the campus with her own artwork and pieces bought at local auctions.

The University restricted Betina's choice of art to Canadian artists. As well, the University controlled the colour schemes and the types of art selected (e.g., paintings, sculptures, or murals) for the various locations on campus. However, within these requirements, Betina was permitted to exercise artistic discretion over the actual pieces chosen. This gave her a great degree of latitude over the beautification of the campus.

She could produce the art herself, purchase another artist's work and focus on any theme she desired. Betina worked at her own studio and used her own tools for her own productions. If the University did not like the art she produced or bought, she was not reimbursed costs and had to sell the art on the open market. Over the year, Betina channelled all of her energy into the University's beautification and did not produce art for any outside clients.

How should Betina's income from this contract be treated?

CHAPTER 3

Type 2 Problems

Problem 29

The taxpayer, Sherry Cane, is an unmarried research analyst and senior executive for TSE Consultants in Toronto. In January 2016, TSE entered into a contract with the Iraq government, for $390,000, requiring that Ms. Cane be in Iraq from March 2016 to October 2017 to examine the long-term energy issues facing OPEC countries. TSE terminated Ms. Cane's employment and engaged her as an independent subcontractor to perform this task.

Sherry gave up her office downtown, terminated her condominium lease, moved out, and stored her furniture and personal effects at her mother's house. Further, she shipped her clothing and books to Iraq. She retained her Canadian bank account so TSE could deposit the monthly contract income of $12,000 directly into her Canadian bank account. They did not withhold any income taxes. Similarly, in Iraq, no taxes were payable, and the government provided Ms. Cane with suitable living quarters, meals, and a part-time domestic for housekeeping. Since she intended to visit her boyfriend, Shawn, and family in Canada, she retained her Visa card and Ontario Health Care. Ms. Cane wanted to retain non-residency status for obvious reasons.

While in Iraq, Ms. Cane carried her business card with the TSE logo and promoted herself as a TSE representative. Shawn, an English professor from Queen's University, spent one six-month term on sabbatical at the University of Iraq. The letters mailed to the Canadian company from Iraq, however, indicated that she wanted to come home. She also noted that the cultural differences and political uncertainties were extreme. Ms. Cane returned home on October 17, 2017, married Shawn and purchased a lovely home in Waterloo, Ontario, with her savings.

It is now October 29, 2018, and Sherry Cane is sitting in your office as you read the following Notice of Reassessment from the CRA:

> We have completed our review of your personal returns of income for the taxation years 2016 and 2017. Based on our findings, you are a resident of Canada for tax purposes. Thus, we have adjusted your computation of net income to include the receipts of income from TSE, plus a portion of the personal benefits received during your temporary stay in Iraq.

Determine whether a Notice of Objection should be filed.

Problem 30

Claire Jordan, a registered dental hygienist, would like to file a Notice of Objection with the CRA for taxation years 2015 and 2016. The CRA has reassessed Claire as a resident in Canada for 2015 and as an employee for 2015 and 2016. Claire describes herself as an independent self-employed dental hygienist. For the past two years, Claire was employed by the Canadian Forces Dental Unit to work on a day-to-day basis. Generally, the Mobile Dental Unit contracts for her, in advance, depending on the regional demand for dental cleaning and examinations.

In 2015, Claire contracted with the Canadian Forces Mobile Dental Unit to temporarily work at a Canadian Forces base in Saudi Arabia. The terms of the contract specified that she would work on a day-to-day basis depending on the demand for dental services over the next two years. Economically, the contract was very worthwhile because her room and board were provided by the government and her pay each day was $340. Despite the risk of no work, the pay she received was earned tax-free because she considered herself as a non-resident during her absence. Prior to leaving Canada, Claire sold her condominium and car and stored her furniture at her parents' home. She also cancelled her membership at the YWCA in New Brunswick and put her engagement on hold for an indefinite period. Her plan was to stay away for the full two years, assuming that all went as planned. Unfortunately, after 12 months, the Mobile Dental Unit ceased operations and Claire was scheduled to return to Canada. The Department of Finance had severely reduced the budget for National Defence. Claire was happy to return home on January 1, 2016. She married three months after her return and resumed her work with the Mobile Dental Unit in Moncton, New Brunswick.

Claire's compensation package with the mobile dental unit differs from other employees of the Canadian Forces. Other employees are assistants and support staff who are paid on a monthly basis with fringe benefits. Claire does not receive any benefits or holidays. In Canada she is paid on a day-to-day basis ($280 per day with no deductions for EI, CPP, or tax). All dental clinics are headed by a dentist who is professionally responsible for overseeing the work of both contract and salaried dental hygienists and dental assistants. The Canadian Dental Association does not permit dental hygienists to administer anaesthetic or work without supervision. The clinic provides all of Claire's tools, supplies, and support staff. If a workday is not more than 60% booked, patients are rescheduled to another day and Claire does not work. It is not unusual for the contract dental hygienists to be temporarily laid off. This does create problems because the contract specifies that Claire must be available to work at least four days per week (so she cannot work elsewhere). This has not bothered Claire because she has claimed all of her laundry, uniforms, shoes, and travelling expenses as a deduction against her self-employed business earnings. Travelling expenses are justifiable because the mobile unit moves to various remote locations outside of Moncton.

Advise Claire on the filing of a Notice of Objection in respect of 2015 and 2016. How would you treat the various expenses incurred by Claire Jordan in each of the taxation years?

Problem 31

The following information for 2018 has been presented to you by Paula Promoter, the new vice-president of marketing for a public Canadian oil company, Overpriced Petroleum Limited. Paula, who is 52 years old and now lives in Calgary, travels extensively across Canada. Paula, whose duties involve the negotiating of contracts, began her employment with Overpriced Petroleum on January 1, 2018.

Receipts and Fringe Benefits — 2018

Salary — net of payroll deductions		$ 50,450
Director fees		5,000
Receipt of an amount, not to compete, from former employer		50,000
Termination payment from former employer		8,000
Travel allowance (Note (1) below):		
Accommodation and meals @ $200 per day for 150 days		30,000
Car operating cost allowance @ 45¢ per kilometre plus $10 per day of travelling for business travel only (9,000 kilometres) for 150 days		5,550
Income protection receipts received from Regal Assurance (Note (2) below)		15,000

Benefits paid by the corporation:

Registered pension plan	$ 4,000	
Extended health care — Liberty Mutual	2,125	
Group income protection premiums — Regal Assurance (Note (2) below)	1,050	
Membership fee in Petroleum Club (membership required by all employees)		
— initiation fee	1,000	
— annual fee	2,500	
Moving costs (Note (3) below)	42,000	
Group term life insurance (coverage is $300,000)	600	
Loans by company (Note (4) below)	160,000	$213,275
		$377,275

Payroll deductions and selected disbursements — 2018

Payroll deductions:

Income taxes withheld	$ 41,001	
Registered pension plan (defined benefit) — current contribution	4,000	
Canada Pension Plan contributions	2,594	
Employment insurance contributions	858	
Group income protection premiums (Note (2))	1,050	$ 49,403

Purchased 2,000 common shares on July 1, 2018 under a stock option plan at a price of $25 per share. Fair market value of shares at the date of purchase was $35. Fair market value of the shares was $25 per share on the date when the option was granted		50,000
Legal fees paid in connection with the collection of the $50,000 non-competition receipt from her previous employer		5,000

Notes and Additional Information:

(1) Paula's actual travelling and car expenses, which she is required to pay according to the terms of her employment contract, are as follows:

Meals	$11,250
Accommodation	23,750
Travel costs (other than car see below) reimbursed by company	6,000

Car expenses (9,000 kilometres for business purposes out of total kilometres of 16,000):

Gasoline	$1,700
Maintenance	800
Auto accident costs while on a business trip	1,600
Insurance	1,800
Licence	90
Interest paid on car loan (see Note (4), below)	300
	$6,290

(2) The company paid 50% of the premium to Regal Assurance re income protection payment. During 2018, Paula received $15,000 in periodic payments in respect of an eight-week illness.

(3) Although Paula started to work for Overpriced Petroleum on January 1, 2018, her family did not move to Calgary from Toronto until February 28, 2018. The company paid for all the moving costs of $12,000, an actual loss on the sale of Paula's Toronto home of $25,000 and a disruption allowance of $5,000.

(4) Paula obtained two loans from the company as part of her employment contract:

(a) Loan of $150,000, dated July 1, 2018, to acquire a new home in Calgary. The loan bears annual interest at 2% and is repayable over a 25-year period in equal annual instalments on the anniversary date of July 1. Interest is payable on the same date.

(b) Loan of $10,000, dated January 1, 2018, to assist in the acquisition of a car acquired in early January 2018 for $35,000 (excluding GST; no PST in Alberta) to be used in connection with her duties of employment. The loan bears annual interest at 3%, and is repayable over the next three years in equal annual instalments. Interest is payable December 31 each year. Paula paid the interest for 2018 on time on December 31, 2018.

(NOTE: For simplicity you may assume that the prescribed interest rate is a constant 4% for all quarters.)

Determine Paula Promoter's employment income for 2018 in accordance with Subdivision a of Division B. Ignore the effects of a leap year in your answer.

Indicate why you have excluded any of the above amounts from your answer.

Problem 32

The taxpayer, Mr. Jayem Gee, a lawyer, had agreed to the following yearly contract in the three years at issue:

- The contract is between the firm of Perry and Mason hereinafter called "the firm" and Mr. Jayem Gee hereinafter called "the lawyer".

- The firm retains the services of the lawyer for the year _____, from January 1 to December 31, and the lawyer agrees to provide his services exclusively to the firm for the aforementioned period.

- The lawyer will receive, for his services, fees representing 2.1% of the gross income of the firm, excluding work in progress, all as established by the firm's accountants.

- This percentage has been set with reference to the number of lawyers practicing in the firm as of January 1, _____.

- Any change in the number of professionals practising in the firm will give rise to a revision in the fee percentage.

- The lawyer will receive, as an advance on fees, the sum of $1,450 in each two-week period and any adjustment will be made at the conclusion of the firm's fiscal year.

- In consideration of the fact that the lawyer is receiving fees, no withholdings of income tax, or deductions in respect of pension plans, health insurance, or others will be made by the firm, and the lawyer will be personally responsible for making any payments required by the government authority in respect of these items.

There were seven or eight other lawyers in the same position with the firm as Mr. Gee, and there were about nine other lawyers who were senior. Mr. Gee had no capital investment in the firm and had no ownership claim to client accounts. All expenditures necessary for the proper operation of the firm such as support staff wages and office expenses were borne by the firm. The firm was responsible for billing clients for services that had been provided and for the collection of the billings for all lawyers including the senior lawyers.

In Mr. Gee's opinion, his relations with clients, his work habits and how he organized his work, whether with respect to keeping track of files or the place or method chosen for carrying out his responsibilities were similar to those of the senior lawyers. On the other hand, he indicated that there were differences in responsibilities in that, for example, the senior lawyers periodically examined his work. The senior lawyers, both individually and as a group, exercised greater control of the conduct of business in the firm. The lawyers in the firm were largely specialized in various areas of law, and as far as possible, every lawyer was free to follow his own direction, as long as he adhered to the general policy of the firm and his work appeared to be to the benefit of the firm. There was no evidence that the senior lawyers assigned legal files to the junior lawyers more than to themselves, or that the clientele or account books of the two groups were differently constituted. Mr. Gee did not pay personally for any insurance premium or expenses relating to his professional responsibility, being covered by liability insurance taken out by the firm.

Mr. Gee further submitted that he did not receive orders or instructions from the firm on how to carry out his duties. He decided on his own the number of hours he would devote to his profession and no set timetable was imposed on him. He was in charge of the steps to be taken to carry out instructions from his clients.

If for any reason Mr. Gee could not carry out a particular task, the firm selected someone to replace him according to which of the other lawyers in the firm were available and what their areas of expertise were. The selection also took into account the client's preference.

Mr. Gee considered himself to be a partner of the firm, earning income from the business of the firm, while the CRA considered him to be an employee of the firm. At issue was the deductibility of about $20,000 of expenses over the three years in question.

Is Mr. Gee, in this situation, an employee or a partner (i.e., self-employed)? In presenting your answer, discuss the tests that are applied by the courts in this type of situation and consider how the facts relate to these tests by discussing both points of view on each issue. Be sure to state a conclusion based on your evaluation of the facts in this manner. (Do not reach a conclusion first and use only those facts or arguments which support your conclusion.)

Problem 33

Graham Grepzer has come to you in connection with two offers of employment as a salesperson from two rival dry-goods manufacturing companies. Neither company has an office in Graham's present location of Beamsville, Ontario, and he would be required to operate from the basement of his home. Graham indicates that his estimated cash expenses including HST @ 13% would be:

Travel outside of Beamsville			
Meals (equal monthly amounts)		$3,200	
Accommodation		5,000	$8,200
Total car operating costs (Note (1))			
Gas and Oil		$2,200	
Maintenance		800	
		3,000	
Insurance (if car owned)		1,300	$4,300
Office expenses — 20% of total space (Note (2))			
Mortgage interest	20% × $19,000	$3,800	
House insurance	20% × 800	160	
Municipal taxes	20% × 2,500	500	
Utilities	20% × 1,000	200	
Interest on bank loan (Note (3))		500	$5,160
Entertainment expenses including golf club membership of $1,100 (equal monthly amounts)			$4,000
Telephone — long-distance calls			$1,000
Office supplies			$ 500

Assume that all these expenses are reasonable in the circumstances.

Notes:

(1) These amounts are the total car expenses. He estimates that his total kilometres will be 30,000 of which 24,000 will be for business purposes.

(2) The home was purchased ten years ago for $150,000.

CHAPTER 3

(3) The interest on the bank loan is for the acquisition of $5,400 of office equipment.

Offer 1

Employer Alpha's remuneration package would consist of a salary of $58,000 plus estimated commissions of $12,000. Employer Alpha would also pay for a private dental and drug plan ($700/yr) and a contribution to a defined-benefit registered pension plan at 6% of gross salary and commissions but exclusive of other fringe benefits ($4,200/yr). Graham would be required to contribute an equal amount to the pension plan.

Graham would be required to use his own car and pay for all of the expenses. However, the company would pay him a flat allowance of $450 per month for his 24,000 business kilometres. Graham has indicated that he would have to acquire a new car with an estimated cost of $19,000, including HST, which would be financed fully through a bank loan at 10%.

Offer 2

Employer Beta's remuneration package would consist of a straight salary of $70,000. Employer Beta would also pay for income protection premiums ($500/yr). A leased company car would be provided which would cost his employer $6,300 per annum including $1,100 for insurance, but excluding HST. Employer Beta would pay him a monthly travel allowance of $1,500 and the annual club dues ($1,100) at the local golf course for entertaining corporate clients. However, Graham would have to directly pay all of his expenses. In addition, the company would contribute to a money-purchase registered pension plan, 6% of Graham's gross salary exclusive of other fringe benefits; Graham would contribute an identical amount.

Compute Graham's employment income for tax purposes for 2018 under the two proposals given the assumption that these amounts are for a full calendar year. Ignore any effects of a leap year.

Explain why you excluded any of the above information from your calculations.

CHAPTER 3 —
DISCUSSION NOTES FOR REVIEW QUESTIONS

(1) The personal tax return (T1 General) does not include RPP contributions, union and professional dues and other paragraph 8(1)(*i*) deductions in the calculation of employment income. These are included under the heading "Net Income" in the personal tax return. It would be misleading to use the personal tax return format for this specific purpose, because certain deductions are limited to the amount of employment income in the year, such as the home office expense deduction.

(2) An employee can only deduct those expenses that are specifically allowed under section 8 whereas a self-employed individual may deduct all expenses incurred to earn business and property income as permitted by Subdivision b. Both the employee and the self-employed individual are subject to the reasonableness test.   ITA: 67

(3) No one test is conclusive in itself. All tests should be considered together before a conclusion is reached.

(4) The control subtest in the economic reality or entrepreneur test determines whether one person is in a position to order or require not only what is to be done but how it is to be done. Where such control, by the business over the individual, does exist, an employer–employee relationship is implied.

(5) The integration or organization test examines the degree of economic dependence of the individual on the organization. Where the individual is financially dependent on the organization, then an employer-employee relationship is implied.

(6) The specific result test looks at the expected results of the work performed. An employee–employer relationship usually contemplates the employee putting his or her personal services at the disposal of his or her employer during a given period of time without reference to a specified result and, generally, envisages the accomplishment of work on an ongoing basis. On the other hand, where a party agrees that certain specified work will be done for the other, it may be inferred that an independent contractor relationship exists.

(7) The Act uses the word "received" to determine the timing of the taxation of employment income. In this case, she will be considered to have received her bonus in the year she received the cheque. Just because she chose not to cash the cheque does not change the timing of when she received the payment.   ITA: 5

(8) The Act uses the word "received" to determine the timing of the taxation of employment income. The voluntary deferment of an unconditional right to receive the bonus is not an acceptable method of deferring income.   ITA: 5
Blenkarn v. M.N.R., 63 DTC 581 (T.A.B.)

(9) Employers cannot deduct all of the taxable benefits reported on the employee's T4. Items such as deemed interest benefits and standby charges for automobiles are not deductible to the employer since they are not expenses that are incurred for the purpose of earning income.   ITA: 80.4

(10) If the employer makes *any* of the premium payments then the benefit payments received will likely be taxable.   ITA: 6(1)(*f*); IT-428

(11) The CRA follows normal commercial practice such that the first day of the contract is counted and the last day is excluded for purposes of determining the number of days of interest. In this case the number of days from June 2 to June 29 inclusive will be used to determine the benefit, that is, 28 days.

(12) A reimbursement is a payment by an employer to an employee for expenses of the employer which have been paid by the employee and which are substantiated by receipts. This is normally accomplished by submitting an expense report. An allowance is a fixed amount which is paid to an employee in excess of his or her salary without the requirement that the employee be accountable for the amount expended.   IT-522R, pars. 40, 50

CHAPTER 3

(13) The standby charge is calculated as follows:

$$\frac{20,004}{20,004} \times 2\% \times 12 \times (\$40,000 + \$5,200) = \$10,848.$$

(14) The five conditions that a salesperson must meet in order to be able to deduct expenses are: ITA: 8(1)(*f*)

   (a) he or she must be employed in the year in connection with the selling of property or negotiating of contracts for his or her employer;

   (b) under the terms of his or her contract of employment he or she must be required to pay his or her own expenses;

   (c) he or she must be ordinarily required to carry on his or her duties away from his or her employer's place of business;

   (d) he or she is remunerated in whole or in part by commissions or other similar amounts fixed by reference to the volume of the sales made or the contracts negotiated; and

   (e) he or she was not in receipt of a reasonable allowance for travelling expenses in respect of the taxation year that was not included in computing his or her income.   ITA: 6(1)(*b*)(v)

(15) The four conditions that must be met to allow an employee to deduct travelling expenses, other than car expenses, are: ITA: 8(1)(*h*)

   (a) he or she is ordinarily required to carry on his or her duties away from his or her employer's place of business or in different places;

   (b) under his or her employment contract, he or she is required to pay the travelling expenses incurred by him or her in the performance of his or her duties;

   (c) he or she was not in receipt of a reasonable allowance for travelling expenses that was not included in computing his or her income; and   ITA: 6(1)(*b*)(v), 6(1)(*b*)(vi), 6(1)(*b*)(vii)

   (d) he or she did not claim any deduction for railway company employees, salespersons, or transport company employees.   ITA: 8(1)(*e*), 8(1)(*f*), 8(1)(*g*)

(16) There is nothing in paragraph 6(1)(*b*) that would exclude this allowance from income. However, another rule would apply to cause this receipt to be exempt from tax. In order to be exempt under this provision, the allowance must meet the following tests: ITA: 81(3.1)

   (a) he must deal at arm's length with his employer;

   (b) he must have other employment or business income (not necessary in this case, since he is employed as a professor or teacher at a designated educational institution);

   (c) the amount received must be reasonable and must relate only to travel to and from part-time employment; and

   (d) the part-time location must be at least 80 km away from both the employee's ordinary place of residence and his principal place of employment or business.

(17) Neither word is defined in the Act. However, an Interpretation Bulletin interprets the word "principally" as more than 50%. Therefore, as long as the employment-use of the workspace is its main or chief purpose, the test is met. "Exclusively" is not defined in the tax law, so reference is made to other sources. *Webster's English Dictionary* defines "exclusively" as "to the exclusion of all others" which is a much more onerous test.   IT-352R2, par. 2

(18) The Act deems that taxes withheld have been received at the time the bonus was paid. Therefore, even though the company still had the government's portion of the bonus, tax cannot be deferred on it. In addition, if the amount withheld in respect of the tax was not deemed to have been received by Ms. Smith, then she would not have received credit for the payment of this tax on her personal tax return.   ITA: 153(3)

CHAPTER 3 — SOLUTIONS TO MULTIPLE CHOICE QUESTIONS

Question 1

(A) is correct: $12 \times 2\% \times \$34,500 = \$8,280$.

ITA: 6(2)

(B) and (C) are wrong because the operating cost benefit is computed as:

ITA: 6(1)(*k*); ITR: 7305.1

Part (B) incorrectly computes the operating cost benefit as: $15,000/20,000 \times \$3,600 = \$2,700$.

Part (C) incorrectly uses the employer paid operating costs instead of 15,000 personal use kilometres x 0.26 = \$3,900.

(D) is wrong because he does not have more than 50% employment use.

ITA: 6(1)(*k*)(iv)

Question 2

(B) is correct: \$50,000 salary + \$3,500 allowance – \$3,000 automobile expenses = \$50,500. The car allowance is taxable because it is not based solely on kilometres driven. Since the car allowance is taxable, the automobile expenses can be deducted. The entertainment expenses are not deductible because she has no commission income.

ITA: 6(1)(*b*)(x), 8(1)(*f*), 8(1)(*h*.1)(iii)

(A) incorrectly excludes a deduction for automobile expenses: \$53,500 = \$50,000 salary + \$3,500 allowance. The automobile expenses are deductible because the allowance is included in income.

ITA: 8(1)(*h*.1)
ITA: 6(1)(*b*)

(C) incorrectly includes a deduction for entertainment expenses: \$49,500 = \$50,000 salary + \$3,500 allowance – \$3,000 automobile expenses – \$1,000 entertainment expenses. The entertainment expenses (50% × \$2,000) are not deductible because she has no commission income or income from negotiating contracts.

ITA: 8(1)(*f*)

(D) incorrectly excludes the car allowance and the deduction for automobile expenses and incorrectly includes a deduction for entertainment expenses: \$49,000 = \$50,000 salary – \$1,000 entertainment expenses.

Question 3

(A) is correct. Susanne Denholm can claim home office expenses because she is required by contract to maintain an office in her home and she works principally in her home (i.e., "most of the time"). The \$500 correct amount of deductible home office expenses is calculated as follows:

ITA: 8(1)(*i*)(iii), 8(13)(*a*)(i)

Heat, hydro & maintenance: $\$5,000 \times 10\% = \$500$

Subsection 8(13) allows deductions under paragraphs 8(1)(*f*) or 8(1)(*i*). Since Susanne does not have any commission income, she can only deduct items under paragraph 8(1)(*i*). The distinction between (*f*) and (*i*) is that under (*f*) the expenses are fixed in nature and under (*i*) they are variable in nature (like supplies deductible under (*i*)). Since the only expenses that are variable with use are the heat, hydro, and maintenance, they are the only ones deductible. The mortgage interest is not deductible under either (*f*) or (*i*), since the only interest that is deductible as an employment expense is for automobiles and aircraft.

ITA: 8(1)(*f*), 8(2)

(B) incorrectly includes a deduction for property taxes and insurance: \$1,100 = \$500 + \$200 insurance + \$400 property taxes. The insurance (10% × \$2,000) and property taxes (10% × \$4,000) are not considered to be supplies. However, if Susanne had commission income, 10% of her insurance and property taxes would be deductible.

IT-352R2, par. 6
ITA: 8(1)(*i*)(iii)
ITA: 8(1)(*f*)

(C) incorrectly includes deductions for insurance, property taxes and the general telephone line: \$1,400 = \$500 + \$200 insurance + \$400 property taxes + \$300 general telephone line. The insurance, property taxes and the cost of the general telephone line (50% × \$600) are not deductible. If Susanne had commission income, the cost of the general telephone line would still not be deductible — only long-distance calls would be deductible.

IT-352R2, pars. 6, 10(a)
ITA: 8(1)(*i*)(iii)

CHAPTER 3

(D) incorrectly includes insurance, property taxes, the general telephone line and mortgage interest: $3,800 = $500 + $200 insurance + $400 property taxes + $300 general telephone + $2,400 mortgage interest. The insurance, property taxes, the cost of the general telephone line and mortgage interest (10% × $24,000) are not considered to be supplies. If Susanne had commission income, the mortgage interest would still not be deductible since the Act limits interest expense of an employee to interest on automobiles and planes.

IT-352R2

ITA: 8(1)(*i*)(iii)
ITA: 8(1)(*j*)

Question 4

(A) is correct. The loan qualifies as a home relocation loan. The benefit is computed using the lower of the prescribed interest rate at the time of the loan (4%) and the prescribed interest rate during the year (3%). Therefore the employment benefit is $1,000 (3% × $100,000 – 2% × $100,000 interest paid).

ITA: 6(9), 80.4(1), 80.4(4)

(B) incorrectly computes the employment benefit using 4%: $2,000 = 4% × $100,000 – 2% × $100,000.

(C) incorrectly ignores the 2% interest paid in the computation of the interest benefit: $3,000 = 3% × $100,000.

(D) incorrectly computes the employment benefit using 4% rather than 3%. The 2% interest paid is not deducted: 4% × $100,000.

Question 5

(D) is correct. The stock option benefit is ($40 – $30) × 1,000 shares = $10,000.

(A) incorrectly subtracts a deduction (½ × $10,000) in computing the benefit ($10,000 – $5,000). This deduction is a Division C deduction.

ITA: 110(1)(*d*)

(B) incorrectly computes the benefit based on the sales price of $48,000 ($48,000 – $30,000 = $18,000) rather than the price of the stock at the time of purchase.

(C) incorrectly includes the taxable capital gain in the employee benefit (($48,000 – $40,000) × ½ + ($40,000 – $30,000) = $14,000).

Question 6

(B) is correct.

Meals and entertainment (50% × $14,000)	$ 7,000
Driving costs (90% × $10,000)	9,000
Expenses eligible for deduction	$16,000

ITA: 8(1)(*f*)

Tim can either claim a deduction for these amounts to the extent of his commission income ($5,000) or he can claim a deduction for his automobile costs ($9,000) alone, without the commission limitation. The maximum deduction is therefore $9,000.

ITA: 8(1)(*f*)
8(1)(*h*.1)

(A) is incorrect because it is the commission-limited amount.

ITA: 8(1)(*f*)

(C) is incorrect because it is the full meals and entertainment amount ($14,000) and ignores the $5,000 commission limitation.

ITA: 67.1

(D) is incorrect because it represents the expenses eligible as a salesperson ($16,000) but ignores the $5,000 commission limitation.

ITA: 8(1)(*f*)

CHAPTER 3 — SOLUTIONS TO EXERCISES

Exercise 1

[See: *Isaac v. M.N.R.*, 70 DTC 1285 (T.A.B.)]

Although the test had not been articulated at the time of this case, the courts are now starting with a consideration of whether there is a mutual understanding or common intention between the parties regarding their relationship. That is best reflected in a contract between the parties, but in many cases, such as this one, no written contract is in evidence. In this situation, the courts have looked at how the parties treat each other. In the case, it appears that the hospital is treating the nurse as a non-military independent contractor by paying her a fixed rate with none of the usual employee benefits. The nurse has, at least, accepted that for about five years. However, the same facts might be used to suggest that the relationship between the parties was that of an employer/part-time employee.

The following tests are applied to support the determination of the objective intention of the parties as to whether R.N. should be regarded as an employee or an independent contractor.

Economic Reality or Entrepreneur Test

In applying the control subtest, the question is whether Canadian Forces Hospital, Halifax controlled not only what was done by R.N. but how it was done. In this case the Hospital exercised control over R.N. in connection with dividing up the patients to be cared for among the available nurses and imposing routine rules and regulations with regard to the administration of drugs and other medications. On the other hand, the Hospital did not exercise any control over the method in which R.N. did her work, which requires special knowledge, skill, and judgment. Accordingly, it does not appear that the Hospital exercised sufficient control to conclude that R.N. was an employee on the basis of this test alone.

However, the application of the other subtests is particularly revealing. R.N. does not run the risk of financing the equipment, supplying other assistants necessary to carry out her duties in the Hospital or seeking out clients. R.N. used the equipment and supplies furnished by the Hospital. She neither hired nor fired any of the nursing assistants who worked under her. She could only request that the Hospital hire additional staff to assist her. The clients were patients of the Hospital. R.N. was not in a position to substitute the services of another nurse if she was unable to perform her duties. All this evidence tends to establish that from an economic reality point of view R.N. was an employee, but this test may not be definitive in this case.

Integration or Organization Test

The Hospital deducted Canada Pension Plan contributions from her pay as they did with the nurses who were employed full-time by the Hospital. R.N. appeared to be economically dependent on the hospital, although she was not precluded from offering her services elsewhere. R.N. was subject to co-ordinational control of the hospital in terms of where to perform her services and when to do so. On the other hand, R.N. was not eligible for the regular benefits of a full-time nurse such as holidays, sick pay, retirement plan, etc. She was hired on a day-to-day basis at a *per diem* rate of pay. Her services could be terminated on 24 hours notice if full-time nurses became available. On the weight of the evidence it can be argued that R.N. is an employee of the Hospital based on the integration test.

Specific Result Test

On the one hand, it was R.N.'s personal services that were at the disposal of the Hospital. Her work was done on a continuous day-to-day basis without there being any limited or specified amount of work that she had, by contract, to accomplish. She could not substitute another person to perform her duties if she was unable to do so. On the other hand, R.N. was not a full-time nurse for any specified period of time. Her time was made up on a weekly basis in advance. She could be laid off on 24 hours notice. On balance, it appears that the evidence leads to the conclusion that, by applying the specific result test, R.N. was an employee. This conclusion is consistent with that for the integration or organization test.

Conclusion

The application of the control subtest of the economic reality or entrepreneur test leads to the conclusion that R.N was not an employee of the Hospital. The application of the other subtests of the economic reality test, the integration test and the specific result test leads to the inference that R.N. was an employee of the Hospital. Thus, there is evidence to support the determination of an employment relationship. (Your own conclusion after weighing all of these tests.)

CHAPTER 3

Exercise 2

The courts generally rely on three tests to support a determination of the objective intention of the parties as to their relationship as either independent contractor or employment. In this case, a contract was negotiated that could be interpreted as establishing an independent contractor relationship. However, a contract can be written to be self-serving to both parties. Hence the need to apply the three tests to help determine the status of Ms. Capwell in relation to the architectural firm of Davies Ltd.

ITA: 248(1); Wiebe Door Services Ltd. v. M.N.R., 87 DTC 5025 (F.C.A.)

(1) Economic Reality or Entrepreneur Test

(a) Control Test

The first subtest examines the day-to-day time commitment that is expected of an individual and the accountability of the individual to the corporation. In this instance, Ms. Capwell must work at least 14 days a month on the project (but the specific days appear flexible); however, she appears to be able to work under her own direction and on other projects on her days off. It does not seem to be conclusive as to whether or not Ms. Capwell is an employee given this test, but the evidence supports that she would be an independent contractor given the circumstances.

(b) Ownership of Tools

It is not clear, but Ms. Capwell appears to provide her own car, equipment, and technical expertise. We might also conclude that since she is working on the premises, many of her expenses, such as supplies and her place of work, will be covered by Davies Ltd. This test appears to support contractor status.

(c) Chance of Profit, Risk of Loss

This subtest assesses whether the individual incurs her own business risk, legal liability, and expenses. In this case, she is getting paid a flat fee of $4,000 per month, which we must assume is directly related to billable hours of work. She estimates that 30% of her contracting revenues will come from other sources, which is not entirely insignificant. This test is also not conclusive, and depending on the details, could go either way.

(2) Integration or Organization Test

This test determines whether or not the individual is economically dependent on the payer organization and is an integral part of the corporation. In this case, Ms. Capwell is not completely dependent on Davies for all of her income, but she retains an office on the premises and also receives some employee benefits in the form of underground parking. However, it's possible that the nature of the work demands she attend the company's offices. This test is inconclusive, but depending on the circumstances, slightly favours her being viewed as an employee.

(3) Specific Results Test

As the name suggests, the object of this test is to determine whether the individual's services were acquired to complete a specific task. In this case, there is no doubt that Ms. Capwell was taken on to complete a specific project, after which the contract will be fulfilled. Given this, she would appear to be an independent contractor.

Conclusion

The tests would seem to support independent contractor status, principally because of the signed contract agreeing to a flat fee for one specific project suggesting a mutual understanding or common intention to enter an independent contractor relationship.

The results of the tests do not always provide us with a definitive answer as to whether or not an individual should be viewed as an employee. However, they can help guide us to make that determination. In this case, the facts lead toward the independent contractor conclusion. Given that the contract was drafted for a specific project, and that Ms. Capwell seems to be working independently, the courts would probably allow the designation of independent contractor status.

Exercise 3

(A) Specifically exempted.

ITA: 6(1)(a)

(B) Exempted; provincial employer health tax.

ITA: 6(1)(a)

(C) and (D) Exempted, since the premium was paid to a private medical plan.

ITA: 6(1)(a)

(E) Taxable. The Income Tax Folio only exempts tuition fees where the course is primarily for the benefit of the employer.

ITA: 6(1)(a), Income Tax Folio S2-F3-C2

(F) Normally, taxable, but since the payment meets the conditions, namely that the Christmas gift is under $500 and is not cash or near cash, the CRA's position is that the gift is not a taxable benefit.

ITA: 6(1)(*a*)

(G) Partly taxable: The CRA takes the position that there will be no benefit if William had reimbursed the company the actual cost ($420). Since William did not completely reimburse the company for the actual costs, then the benefit would be calculated by taking the difference between the actual costs ($420) and the amount paid by William ($200) for a taxable benefit of $220.

ITA: 6(1)(*a*); Income Tax Folio S2-F3-C2

(H) Taxable, but the CRA takes the position that the amount would not be taxable if the membership was principally for the employer's advantage rather than the employee's.

ITA: 6(1)(*a*); Income Tax Folio S2-F3-C2

(I) Taxable unless the financial counselling was in respect of re-employment or retirement.

ITA: 6(1)(*a*), 6(1)(*a*)(iv)(B)

Exercise 4

Paragraph 8(1)(*b*) allows for the deduction of legal expenses against employment income in the year, on account of legal expenses incurred by the taxpayer to collect or establish a right to salary or wages owed to the taxpayer that, if received by the taxpayer, would be required by this subdivision to be included in computing the taxpayer's employment income.

ITA: 6, 8

Paragraph 6(1)(*j*) requires any reimbursement to either be included in income or reduce the expense being claimed.

Legal expenses may also be deductible for other purposes such as to earn income from business or property or as another deduction [ITA 60(*o*), (*o*.1)], but only those expenses specifically listed in section 8 can be deducted from employment income [ITA 8(2)].

Other resources — IT-99R5, Legal and Accounting Fees; CRA Guide T4044, Employment Expenses

Exercise 5

The $6,000 merchandise discount is a taxable benefit. Administrative practice reflected in the Income Tax Folio does exempt discounts on merchandise, but they must be offered to all employees and not to just select groups. If there was an overall discount of 10% to all employees, it would seem reasonable in the circumstances to include only 25% in income; however, the Income Tax Folio is silent on this point.

Income Tax Folio S2-F3-C2

Exercise 6

None of the $7,500 is a taxable benefit. The exclusion for an eligible housing loss applies because the loss was incurred in an eligible relocation. This conclusion is supported by a 2012 Tax Court of Canada decision.

ITA: 6(1)(*a*), 6(19), 6(20), 248(1) "eligible relocation"; *Wunderlich v. The Queen*, 2012 TCC 539; Income Tax Folio S2-F3-C2

Note that on the sale of the house, the loss cannot be greater than the actual loss to the employee, calculated as the amount by which the cost of the house exceeds the net selling price received. A reimbursement of actual moving costs is not a taxable benefit.

Income Tax Folio S2-F3-C2

Exercise 7

Premiums paid:

(A) Group term life insurance premiums paid by an employer are a taxable benefit.

ITA: 6(1)(*a*), 6(4)

(B) and (C) The extended health care and dental care plans are private medical plans; hence, the premiums paid by the employer are not employment income.

ITA: 6(1)(*a*)

(D) Since the sickness or accident income protection plan is a group plan, premiums paid by the employer are exempt from employment income.

ITA: 6(1)(*a*)

Conclusion:

The following rearrangement would result in a lower tax cost:

(A) Company should pay for 100% of the extended health care and dental plan.

(B) Employees should pay the provincial medical plan premiums since company payments would be taxable benefits.

(C) Employees should consider paying the sickness or accident income protection premium themselves.

CHAPTER 3

When an employer pays *any* portion of the premium for this type of plan, amounts that are paid out of the plan are taxable as employment income, less the employee's contribution to date. Conversely, if the employee pays all of the premiums, none of the amounts paid out of the plan are taxable. Since this particular plan has benefits of only 50% of the wages, the employee would be in a relatively poor cash position. The imposition of tax, even though at a lower rate, would certainly result in extreme hardship if the illness is prolonged.

ITA: 6(1)(*f*)

Exercise 8

Year 1 — No tax effect.

Year 4 — No tax effect.

Year 5 — No tax effect, since the employer is a Canadian-controlled private corporation.

Year 6 — Must take into employment income under Division B the following:

ITA: 7(1.1)

$$50,000 \text{ shares} \times (\$3 - \$1) = \underline{\$100,000}$$

— Will have a capital gain of
$$50,000 \text{ shares} \times (\$6 - \$3) = \underline{\$150,000}$$

— May be eligible for the capital gains deduction for qualifying small business corporation shares.

ITA: 110.6(1), 248(1)

— Since Katrina sold these shares within two years after the date of acquisition, she is not entitled to a deduction of one half of the subsection 7(1.1) inclusion. She is also not entitled to a general deduction since the exercise price of $1.00 was less than fair market value ($1.50) at the date the option was granted.

ITA: 110(1)(*d*), 110(1)(*d*.1)

Exercise 9

(a) Car benefit if business-use kilometres are 10,000

Standby charge		
$\dfrac{20,004 \text{ km}^{(1)}}{20,004 \text{ km}} \times [2\% \times (\$20,000 \times 12)] = \ldots\ldots\ldots\ldots\ldots\ldots\ldots\ldots$	\$4,800	
Operating costs$^{(2)}$ (12,000 km × \$0.26) ·	3,120	\$7,920
Less: amount reimbursed		1,800
Total car benefit if business-use kilometres are 10,000		\$6,120

ITA: 6(1)(*e*), 6(2)

ITA: 6(1)(*k*)(v)

(b) Car benefit if business-use kilometres are 20,000

Standby charge		
$\dfrac{12,000 \text{ km}^{(3)}}{20,004 \text{ km}} \times [2\% \times (\$20,000 \times 12)] = \ldots\ldots\ldots\ldots\ldots\ldots\ldots\ldots$	\$2,879	
Operating costs$^{(4)}$ (50% × \$2,879) =	1,440	\$4,319
Less: amount reimbursed		1,800
Total car benefit if business-use kilometres are 20,000		\$2,519

ITA: 6(1)(*e*), 6(2)

ITA: 6(1)(*k*)(v)

NOTES

$^{(1)}$ The employee does not qualify for the standby charge reduction since the car is not used more than 50% in the performance of employment duties when the business use is only 15,000 km. Therefore, in this outcome, the value of A in the formula (i.e., 12,000 km) is deemed equal to the value of B in the formula (i.e., 1,667 × 12 rounded).

$^{(2)}$ The election method is not available to the employee, since the car is not used more than 50% for business.

ITA: 6(1)(*k*)(iv)

(3) When the business-use kilometres is 20,000, the employee qualifies for the standby charge reduction and the numerator becomes the lesser of (a) 12,000 km, and (b) 1,667 km × 12 months.

(4) The operating benefit election at 50% of the standby charge is the same as $0.26 × 12,000 km = $3,120. The election method is available since employment kilometres comprise more than 50% of the total.

Exercise 10

The Act would appear to deny any deduction in respect of Calvin's workspace in the home. In order for Calvin to avoid the restrictions, one of two conditions must be met, neither of which appear to be adhered to. The first alternative condition is that the work place in the home must be where the individual principally performs the employment duties. The second alternative condition is even more stringent, namely, that the work place must be used exclusively for employment income purposes and that the work place must be used on a regular and continuous basis as a meeting place for employment-connected persons.

ITA: 8(13)

If Calvin had met one of the conditions, then he would be able to deduct some of the expenses indicated as long as he met the conditions of paragraph 8(1)(*i*). First Calvin must have a contract with his employer indicating that he must pay for office rent and supplies and the employer completes and signs a T2200. However, of the expenses indicated, only the maintenance expense, including fuel, electricity, light bulbs, cleaning materials and minor repairs, on a prorated basis will be permitted. The imputed rent of $1,000 is not deductible; this position was confirmed in the *Thompson* case by the Federal Court–Trial Division.

ITA: 8(13)

IT-352R2, par. 2, 3
89 DTC 5439 (F.C.T.D.)

Exercise 11

Since the question refers to meal expenses for employees, you need to refer to subsection 8(4). A deduction for personal meals consumed while travelling is only allowed where the employee is away from the municipality/metropolitan area for a minimum of 12 hours. All meal costs, regardless of their nature and purpose, are also restricted by subsection 67.1(1) to 50% of the actual cost. However, long-haul truck drivers can deduct 80%.

ITA: 8(4), 67.1(1)

Exercise 12

Part (A)

Commission income	$126,000	sec. 5
Group term life insurance premiums paid by employer	700	ssec. 6(4)
Sales incentive prize ($4,000 + $130 → HST on $1,000 only)	4,130	par. 6(1)(*a*) ssec. 6(9)
Imputed interest benefit on automobile loan ($40,000 x .04 x 362/365)	1,587	ssec. 80.4(1)
Monthly automobile allowance (not based on km driven for employment)	5,400	spar. 6(1)(*b*)(x)
Monthly travel allowance (unreasonably low when compared to actual in Note 2, below)	3,600	spar. 6(1)(*b*)(v)
Less:		
Registered pension plan contributions made by Susie Sellem	(6,750)	par. 8(1)(*m*)
Home office deductible under 8(1)(*i*):		
Repairs and maintenance ($450 x 10%)	(45)	par. 8(1)(*i*)
Repainting	(300)	par. 8(1)(*i*)
Office supplies	(200)	par. 8(1)(*i*)
Interest and CCA on automobile deductible under 8(1)(*j*) (Note 1)	(6,338)	par. 8(1)(*j*)

Expenses limited to commission income under par. 8(1)(*f*):			
Automobile operating expenses (Note 2)	$ 5,216		
Travel expenses (Note 3)	5,400		
Entertainment (50% x $900)	450		
Home office property taxes ($5,300 x 10%)	530		
Home office house insurance ($600 x 10%)	60		
Limited to commission of $126,000 (fully deductible)	$11,656	(11,656)	par. 8(1)(*f*)
Employment income		$116,128	

Notes to Solution

1. CCA on new vehicle ($30,000 x 1.13 x 30% x ½)................ $ 5,085
    Interest benefit deemed to be interest paid (see below)   1,587
                                                                        ─────────
                                                                           6,672
                                                                         x 95%
                                                                        ─────────
    Employment use .... $ 6,338
                                                                        ═════════

2. Gas and oil   2,500
    Maintenance   1,300
    Insurance   1,600
    Licence   90
                                                                        ─────────
    Subtotal .... $ 5,490
    Employment use ....   x 95%
                                                                        ─────────
    Deductible amount .... $ 5,216
                                                                        ═════════

3. Meals (50% x $2,400) .... $ 1,200
    Accommodation   4,200
                                                                        ─────────
    Deductible amount .... $ 5,400
                                                                        ═════════

Note: The deductible interest on the automobile is the lesser of:
        (i) interest paid in the year (in this case deemed paid by 80.5) $ 1,587
        (ii) $300 x 362/30 $ 3,620

Part (B) Omitted Items

1. Income taxes withheld at source are not deductible by virtue of ssec. 8(2).

2. Canada Pension Plan contributions and Employment Insurance contributions are not deductible by virtue of ssec. 8(2) but are eligible for deduction as tax credits in computing taxes payable.

3. Group term life insurance premiums and group accident income protection plan premiums paid by Susie Sellem are not deductible by her by virtue of ssec. 8(2).

4. United Way donation made via payroll deduction is not deductible in computing income from employment by virtue of ssec. 8(2) but will be eligible for a tax credit in computing taxes payable.

5. Registered pension plan contributions, dental plan premium and extended health care premium paid by employer are not a taxable benefit to Susie by virtue of subpar. 6(1)(a)(i) of the Act.

6. Employer contributions under the group accident insurance plan are not a taxable benefit to the employee [6(1)(a)].

7. Employer health tax paid by employer is not a taxable benefit because it is a payroll tax required to be paid by the employer. This is confirmed in Income Tax Folio S2-F3-C2, Benefits and Allowances Received from Employment.

8. The membership in the fitness club is not considered a taxable benefit by virtue of Income Tax Folio S2-F3-C2, Benefits and Allowances Received from Employment based on the assertion by Susie and her employer that it is principally to the employer's benefit for her to maintain membership in this club.

9. Mortgage interest on home office is a capital expenditure and is denied by virtue of subpar. 8(1)(f)(v), since par. 8(1)(j) only allows interest expense for automobiles and aircraft.

Exercise 13

(a)   The $125,000 salary will be included in income for tax purposes in the year of receipt (ssec. 5(1)).

(b)   The $20,000 lump-sum payment will be included in employment income for this year (ssec. 6(3)).

(c)　The $10,000 contributed by SL to the RPP will not be included in income for tax purposes. It is specifically excepted (par. 6(1)(a)). Rae is entitled to deduct the $10,000 contribution she is required to make to the RPP in computing her employment income for tax purposes par. 8(1)(m) and 147.2(4)(a)).

(d)　The benefit derived from SL's contributions to extended health care and the dental plan is not included in income for tax purposes. The benefit derived from an employer's contribution to private health plans is specifically excepted (par. 6(1)(a)).

(e)　The premium for group life insurance coverage paid by SL is included in employment income for tax purposes (ssec. 6(4)).

(f)　Since the car allowance is not based solely on the number of kilometres for which the motor vehicle is used in connection with employment, it is deemed not to be a reasonable amount (spar. 6(1)(b)(x)) and, therefore, is included in employment income for tax purposes (spar. 6(1)(b)(vii.1)). She will be entitled to claim a deduction for her actual car expenses (par. 8(1)(h), (h.1)).

(g)　Rae will have an annual benefit with respect to the housing loan and the car loan included in her employment income for tax purposes (ssec. 6(9)) computed as follows:

par. 80.4(1)(a):	housing loan $150,000 x .04 x 365/365	$ 6,000
	car loan $20,000 x (.04 x 181/365 + .05 x 184/365)	901
		$ 6,901
par. 80.4(1)(c):	interest paid for the year, not later than 30 days after the end of the year, $150,000 @ 2%	(3,000)
		$ 3,901

Note:　The prescribed rate of interest used to calculate the benefit on the housing loan in each quarter of this year is less than or equal to the prescribed rate in effect at the time the loan was made (ssec. 80.4(4)).

Rae will be entitled to a home relocation loan deduction of $1,000 in computing her taxable income. The deduction is computed as follows:

par. 110(1)(j):　　the least of:

　　　　(i)　$6,000 - $3,000 = $3,000

　　　　(ii)　$25,000 x (.04 x 365/365) = $1,000

　　　　(iii)　$3,901

Rae can claim as a travelling expense deduction, 95% of the aggregate of her automobile expenses (par. 8(1)(h.1)) and interest and CCA (par. 8(1)(j)). The imputed interest benefit on the car loan, $901, and any interest paid on any additional loan incurred by her to purchase the car, will be included, but the total interest is restricted to a maximum of $300 per month (sec. 67.2).

The deduction for capital cost allowance on the car for this year would be computed as follows:

　　　　$30,000 (1 + .13) x 30% x ½ x 95% = $4,831

The reimbursement of Rae's loss on the sale of her Windsor home is a taxable benefit to the extent of one-half of the amount in excess of $15,000 [par. 6(1)(a), ssec. 6(20)]. The reimbursement by SL of any other expenses related to her move, as listed, is not a taxable benefit [Income Tax Folio S2-F3-C2, Benefits and Allowances Received from Employment].

(h)　As SL is a CCPC, Rae will have no income inclusion with respect to the stock option until the year in which she disposes of the shares. At that time, the difference between the fair market value (FMV) at the time she exercised the option and the option price of $18 will be included in her income as employment income (ssec. 7(1.1)). Half of the difference between the selling price of the shares and the shares' FMV at the time of exercising the option will be included in her income as a taxable capital gain. Providing she holds the shares for two years from the date of exercising the option, she will be entitled to an employee stock option deduction in computing her taxable income equal to ½ of the benefit included in employment income (par. 110(1)(d.1)). If she does not hold the shares for two years after exercising the option, she will not be entitled to the par. 110(1)(d.1) deduction nor will she be entitled to the par. 110(1)(d) deduction as the FMV of the shares at the time the option was granted exceeded the option price.

CHAPTER 3

Exercise 14

1. Economic Realty Test: the economic nature of the relationship

    (a) Control — whether someone is in a position to determine not only what is to be done but also how it is to be done

    — arguments supporting employment

    — as producer, the production company exerted financial control

    — arguments supporting self-employment

    — the director was not subject to detailed control over his work since he had the final artistic say;no one set out how he was to do his work

    — he had to find the work

    — he had no specific hours of work

    — in this situation, it would be difficult to exercise control over the manner of doing the work because of the professional or skilled nature of the work, whether it is performed by an employee or an independent contractor

    (b) Ownership of the Tools

    — arguments for employment

    — the production company provided the equipment and the personnel to work with

    — arguments for self-employment

    — the director provided the professional skills

    (c) Chance for Profit

    — arguments for employment

    — no profit-sharing arrangement

    — no ownership rights to the product

    — arguments for self-employment

    — the payments for shooting days were dependent on the amount of work he obtained

    (d) Risk of Loss

    — arguments for employment

    — he was reimbursed for certain expenses

    — he did not pay for those who worked with him

    — he received a fixed amount every two weeks

    — arguments for self-employment

    — he could have hired assistants

    — his fee for shooting days was dependent on how much work he got

    — he was not paid for re-shooting if he made the error

2. Integration Test: whether the individual is economically dependent on that organization

    — arguments supporting employment

    — the director worked on commercials for only one production company as part of his agreement

    — arguments supporting self-employment

    — the director used facilities not only of the production company, but also of clients and others

    — he had to invoice the production company to be paid

    — he reimbursed the production company for its share of the medical plan premium

3. Specific Result Test: whether personal service were put at the disposal of someone for an indefinite period of time without reference to a specific result

    — arguments for employment

    — the agreement was for an indefinite period of service

    — no specific amount of work was to be completed; the verbal contract was not specific as to the work to be completed

    — arguments for self-employment

    — he could hire assistants; he did not have to do all of the work personally

    — he had complete control over the manner of doing the work to produce commercials

Exercise 15

1. Minimum employment income — June received no kilometre allowance:

			Applicable Provisions
Salary and commissions		$40,000	sec. 5
Deductions:			
Entertainment [Note 1]			par. 18(1)(*l*)
(50% of ($3,700 - $600))	$1,550		par. 8(1)(*f*) ssec. 67.1(1)
Home office: municipal taxes [Note 2]	250		par. 8(1)(*f*)
Car operating expenses			
(18/28 km x $4,900)	3,150		par. 8(1)(*f*)
Meal expenses			par. 8(1)(*f*)
(50% of $1,000)	500		ssec. 8(4)
	$5,450		ssec. 67.1(1)
Deductions not in excess of commission [Note 3]	5,000		
	$35,000		par. 8(1)(*f*)
Less: Deductions not limited to commission income:			
Home office [Note 2]	$3,500		par. 8(1)(*i*)
Less: interest & municipal taxes	950	2,550	
CCA on car [Note 4]			
(18/28 km x $4,000)		2,571	par. 8(1)(*j*)
Interest on car [Note 5]			
(18/28 km x $1,500)		964	par. 8(1)(*j*)
Employment income		$28,915	

June can apply for an HST rebate when she files her tax return for the year. The HST rebate will be received in the year she files her return and is calculated as:

13/113 x the sum of:

(a) deductible expenses			
entertainment	$1,550		
car operating expenses	3,150		
meal expenses	500		
	$5,200		
deduction limited		$ 5,000	
home office expenses			
($3,500 - $700 - $250)		2,550	$ 7,550
(b) CCA			2,571
			$10,121
13/113 thereof			$ 1,164

In the year she receives the HST rebate, the following income tax adjustments would be required:

Par. 6(8)(c) employment income inclusion

$$\frac{\$\ 7,550}{\$10,121} \times \$1,164 = \underline{\$868}$$

Par. 6(8)(d) capital cost reduction

$$\frac{\$\ 2,571}{\$10,121} \times \$1,164 = \underline{\$296}$$

Notes:

(1)   The golf club membership dues are specifically denied as a deduction by par. 18(1)(*l*) and spar. 8(1)(*f*)(vi). Paragraph 67.1(1) limits the deduction for entertainment expenses to 50% of that which would otherwise be deductible.

(2) Outlays on account of capital are not deductible except for interest and CCA on a car used in the course of employment. Interest on account of the home mortgage is not deductible. Municipal taxes are deductible because June is claiming expenses under par. 8(1)(*f*) of the Act. Municipal taxes are not deductible under par. 8(1)(*i*).

(3) Paragraph 8(1)(*f*) limits the deduction for expenses claimed there under to the commission earned.

(4) Paragraph 8(1)(*f*) does not restrict the deductions under par. 8(1)(*i*) or par. 8(1)(*j*) (i.e., interest and CCA on the car, office-in-home expenses) to commission income.

(5) Interest expense deducted is limited to $300 for each 30-day period in the year that the loan was outstanding. This is $300 x 365/30 = $3,650 for the year. This is greater than the actual interest paid so the actual interest paid is deducted.

(6) By virtue of ssec. 8(2), convention expenses may not be deducted from employment income since they are not listed in ssec. 8(1).

2. Minimum employment income — June received an allowance of $0.35 per kilometre plus a yearly allowance of $1,200:

Although the combined package of the two allowances may be reasonable in the circumstances, spar. 6(1)(*b*)(x) deems the allowances not to be a reasonable amount since the motor vehicle allowances received were not based solely on the kilometres. Hence, both allowances are taxable under spar. 6(1)(*b*)(v). June would have to include the allowances in income, but could deduct all of the automobile expenses. Her minimum employment income would be as follows:

Employment income as calculated above:		$28,915
Add:		
$0.35 x 18,000 km	$6,300	
yearly allowance	1,200	7,500
		$36,415

The HST rebate computations would remain the same as option 1.

Chapter 4

Income from Business: General Concepts and Rules

Learning Goals

Know, Understand and Explain

By the end of this chapter you will know, understand and be able to explain:

- The basic provisions of the *Income Tax Act* (the Act) that relate to the calculation of business income.
- The criteria for determining whether a gain is one of capital or business income.
- The underlying distinction between business income and property income.
- The rules outlining amounts to be deducted from business income for tax purposes.

Apply

By the end of this chapter you will be able to apply your knowledge and understanding to:

- Start with accounting income and make the necessary adjustments to arrive at business income for tax purposes.

Analyze

By the end of this chapter you will be able to analyze:

- Different sources of income and determine whether it should be treated as capital or business income.
- A situation and determine whether reasonable expectation of profit exists.

Review Questions
¶4,800 in the Study Guide

Multiple Choice Questions
¶4,825 in the Study Guide

Exercises
¶4,850 in the Study Guide

Assignment Problems
¶4,875 in the Study Guide

CHAPTER 4 — LEARNING CHART

Problem Descriptions

Textbook Example Problems

4-1	Income vs. capital
4-2	Valuation of inventory
4-3	Amortization included in cost of inventory
4-4	Reserve for services not provided
4-5	Reserve for proceeds not yet due
4-6	Schedule 1 reconciliation
4-7	Sales person's expenses

Multiple Choice Questions

1	Business & property deductions
2	Business & property deductions
3	Business & property deductions
4	Business & property — legal and accounting fees
5	Income vs. capital gain
6	Business & property deductions

Exercises

1	Employee benefits — employer/employee implications
2	Income vs. capital
3	Automobile options
4	Contract termination payment
5	Income vs. capital
6	Inventory valuation
7	*Income Tax Act* references
8	Recreational facilities
9	Home office expenses
10	Deductibility of expenses
11	Bond discount
12	Schedule 1 reconciliation
13	Income reserve
14	Schedule 1 reconciliation — HST

Assignment Problems

1	Independent issues — deductibility of expenses
2	Home office
3	Sale of assets including accounts receivable
4	Debt forgiveness
5	Income vs. capital
6	Four independent issues
7	Reasonable expectation of profit
8	Schedule 1 reconciliation
9	Schedule 1 reconciliation
10	Schedule 1 reconciliation
11	Schedule 1 reconciliation

Problem Descriptions

12	Income from business
13	Schedule 1 reconciliation
14	Income from business with home office
15	Schedule 1 reconciliation — comprehensive
16	Income from business with home office
17	Schedule 1 reconciliation
18	GST/HST implications
19	Income vs. capital, soft costs
20	Company automobile — impact on employer
21	Stock option — impact on employer
22	Employee benefits — impact on employer
23	Employee benefits — impact on employer
24	Employed vs. self-employed
25	Sales expenses of employee or self-employed
26	New job offer — employee & employer
27	Reassessment, employee compensation
28	Accounts receivable and warranty claims
29	Business start-up costs
30	Business income and expenses — implications to payor and recipient

Study Notes

¶4,800   REVIEW QUESTIONS

(1) Mr. Fritz is a commissioned real estate client of yours. He has just bought and sold a piece of land in a "quick flip" transaction. What kind of income might this be to him: employment, business, property or capital gain?

(2) Does the Act require that the "profit" from a business be calculated in accordance with generally accepted accounting principles?

(3) Opco Ltd. is in the business of manufacturing equipment under contract for other manufacturers. One of its customers failed to live up to its contract and would not take delivery of or pay for its order. Opco took the customer to court and was awarded the amount of $100,000 as damages. Can this amount be treated as a non-taxable capital receipt by Opco?

(4) Aco Ltd. and Xco Ltd. entered into an agreement to manufacture a new product for the next 20 years. This represented 80% of Aco's business. After five years it was decided that the two parties could not work together so Xco paid Aco $500,000 to terminate the agreement. Is the receipt of this amount by Aco considered to be business income?

(5) Donald Corleone owns an illegal gambling house. He has made significant "profits" on this activity, but has not reported the income since he believes it is not taxable. Is he correct?

(6) Opco Ltd. took advantage of a program offered by the government and hired two employees whose wages were partially offset by a government subsidy. The owner felt that since he was really just getting some of his tax dollars back through this subsidy, the amount received would not be taxable. What do you think?

(7) As long as an expenditure was made for the purpose of earning income from a business or property then it is deductible. Is this statement true? Comment.   ITA: 18

(8) One of your clients is having some short-term cash flow problems and cannot pay his year-end tax liability. He decides that he will defer his payment to the Receiver General instead of trying to get another short-term bank loan. He reasons that in either case the interest will be deductible. Comment.

(9) Subsection 18(1) lists those items that are prohibited from being deducted because of the nature of the expenditure. If an expense passes those tests, will it be deductible?

(10) A client had to replace the roof on its factory at a cost of $100,000. The client deducted the cost of the roof on the basis that it was simply replacing the previous roof with a new one of the same quality. Is the cost deductible?

(11) Is the portion of the airline ticket that represents the meal subject to the 50% limitation on meal expenses?

(12) Will a company that offers a warranty with its product be able to deduct a reserve?   ITA: 20(1)(*m.*1)

¶4,825   MULTIPLE CHOICE QUESTIONS

Question 1

Which one of the following items is NOT deductible in computing the income of a corporation under Division B of the Act?

(A) Amounts paid for landscaping business premises.

(B) Interest on money borrowed to finance the purchase of a factory for use in its business.

(C) The premium on a $100,000 term life insurance policy on an employee if the beneficiary of the policy is the employee's family.

(D) Interest and penalties on late income tax payments.

Question 2

Which one of the following amounts is DEDUCTIBLE in computing the income of a corporation under Division B of the Act?

(A) $11,000 of accrued legal fees for a pending law suit. The accrual is an estimate because no work has been done to date by the lawyers.

(B) $4,000 of donations to registered charities made for no business reason.

(C) $15,000 spent on three social events in the taxation year for all employees at a particular location.

(D) $1,500 for golf club membership dues for employees.

Question 3

Which one of the following amounts is DEDUCTIBLE in computing income of a corporation under Division B of the Act?

(A) $5,000 of donations to federal political parties.

(B) $44,000 in accrued bonuses unpaid 7 months after year end. The amounts were legal liabilities at year end.

(C) A $10,000 increase in the financial accounting reserve for warranty expenses.

(D) The $2,000 cost of tickets for meals and entertainment at a gala fund-raising event for a registered charity.

Question 4

XYZ Ltd.'s current financial statement shows a deduction for $20,000 of legal and accounting expenses. This amount consists of the following items:

- $5,000 of legal expenses related to the purchase of an investment in shares;

- $5,000 of legal expenses incurred to dispute a tax assessment;

- $5,000 of legal expenses related to the issuance of debt; and

- $5,000 of accounting fees related to the preparation of a prospectus regarding the issuance of shares.

What amount is deductible under Division B of the Act?

(A) $7,000

(B) $8,000

(C) $15,000

(D) $5,000

Question 5

Ten years ago, Sam, a real estate agent, purchased a piece of land for $50,000. His intention at that time was to build a rental building on the land and use it to earn rental income, which he did four years ago. In the current year, he sold the land and building for $100,000 and $80,000 respectively after receiving an unsolicited offer.

Based on the facts, which one of the following statements is true?

(A) The CRA may argue that the gain on the sale of the land is a capital gain, because Sam is a real estate agent.

(B) The CRA may argue that the gain on the sale of the land is business income, because of the 10-year holding period of the land.

(C) The CRA may argue that the gain on the sale of the land is business income because of the unsolicited offer for sale.

(D) The gain on the sale of the land will likely be treated as a capital gain for income tax purposes.

Question 6

Which of the following amounts is DEDUCTIBLE in computing the income of a corporation under Division B of the Act?

(A) $13,000 of legal fees to defend a lawsuit brought by a customer.

(B) Accounting loss on the sale of a capital property.

(C) The principal amount of a mortgage on a company's warehouse.

(D) The personal and living expenses of the shareholder who works very hard in the business and is not paid a salary.

¶4,850 EXERCISES

Exercise 1

ITA: 9, 11, 18, 20

Each of the following employee perks were provided to a senior executive of IPL Engineering Services:

Value of university tuition fees for the employee's child (age 21)	$ 2,800
Out-of-town meals for a three-day management seminar	150
Entertainment meals for clients (reimbursement)	1,500
Professional dues to Civil Engineering Society	250
Notebook computer provided for employment use	3,500
Membership to Centre Health Club (client promotion)	1,400
Interest-free loan for the purchase of company stock	40,000
Premiums paid for group term life insurance	150
Reimbursement for engineering systems software	2,000

Assumptions:

(a) Prescribed rate of interest throughout the year is 1%.

(b) The senior executive takes the notebook computer home to complete IPL assignments and memos. Personal use is minimal.

— *REQUIRED*

For each of the above, *discuss and quantify* the income tax implications to the employer and to the employee.

Exercise 2

ITA: 9; IT-218R

The taxpayer corporation, Singh Enterprises Ltd., purchased a property consisting of some eight separate residential apartment buildings. When purchased, the property was ready for profit-producing operation and immediate arrangements were made for such operations.

The principal shareholder of the corporation, Sam Singh, was an individual with a long history of trading in real estate in many different countries. He fully expected that the property would increase in value in the future.

About 11 months after the purchase of the property, circumstances dictated a change in the investments of the corporation and the property was sold for a substantial profit.

— *REQUIRED*

Determine whether the profit realized by the sale of the property was income from a business or a capital gain.

Exercise 3

ITA: 9, 11, 18, 20

Samuel, an employee of the Fish Company, needs a vehicle to complete his employment duties. Samuel generally drives approximately 10,000 kilometres for personal reasons. His manager estimates that Samuel will need to drive 7,000 kilometres to complete employment duties. Samuel estimates that his total operating expenses will be $2,500. The corporation offered Samuel three alternatives:

(a) Twelve months use of a leased vehicle plus a reimbursement for 100% of the total operating expense. The leased vehicle costs the corporation $400 per month (including HST).

(b) The same vehicle can be purchased for a total cost (including 13% HST) of $22,000 and Samuel would be reimbursed for the total operating expense.

(c) Samuel provides his own vehicle and is reimbursed 55 cents for each of the first 5,000 kilometres and 49 cents for the balance of employment kilometres.

— *REQUIRED*

Assess the tax impacts for each alternative for both the employee and the employer for the current tax year.

Exercise 4

ITA: 9

Cars Limited had a franchise for the distribution in Saskatchewan of Belchfire automobiles made in Argentina. The business had grown rapidly in its 10 years of existence. However, soon after the expansion of its facilities, Argentina Motor Industries terminated the distribution agreement and voluntarily agreed to pay Cars Limited $225,000.

— REQUIRED

What are the tax implications to Cars Limited?

Exercise 5

Alta Management Corporation (AMC) purchased three parcels of land in July of this year at an estate auction. Immediately after, the purchase plans were in place for the development of the properties into community shopping plazas. As a result of an unsolicited offer, two parcels of land were resold for an immediate and substantial gain. The third parcel of land sat vacant for three months while the corporation waited for the development and building permits from City Hall. The city would not approve the project because of several complaints from local residents. Consequently, the property was listed for sale with a realtor, Charles Roonie. Charles is also the major shareholder of Alta Management Corporation. The sale took place, with a substantial profit, six months after the purchase of the land.

Presently, the corporation holds two other pieces of undeveloped land, which it intends to develop if the economy improves. It also manages several apartment blocks and one shopping centre. The corporation often sells property when it becomes unfeasible to develop. For this reason the company always ensures that any real estate purchased has good resale value.

— REQUIRED

What type of income was earned from the disposition of each real estate property? Provide reasons for your answer, and consider all factors that the courts may consider in substantiating the intent of the taxpayer.

Exercise 6

ITA: 10

Holey Mufflers Limited operates a fast-service repair shop. At the end of its fiscal year its inventory records showed the following:

Item	Number	Actual cost	FIFO cost	Replacement cost	Net realization value
Mufflers	64	$17.50	$16.25	$18.40	$15.50
Tailpipes	157	4.75	4.25	5.00	4.50
Exhaust systems	39	16.25	16.30	17.00	15.50
Shock absorbers	256	19.45	18.85	20.50	19.75
Brackets	932	1.40	1.35	1.50	1.30
Clamps	1,746	.65	.70	.75	.80

— REQUIRED

ITA: 10(2.1)

What values could be used for the total inventory for tax purposes? (Assume that the method of valuing inventory could change with permission.)

Exercise 7

ITA: 18(1)(*a*), 18(1)(*b*), 18(1)(*c*), 18(1)(*e*), 18(1)(*h*), 67, 248(1)

The Act restricts the deduction of certain expenses incurred. In general, the following limitations determine the deductibility of expenses from a business:

(a) Income earning purpose test

(b) Capital test

(c) Exempt income test

(d) Reserve test

(e) Personal expense test

(f) Reasonableness test

— REQUIRED

Cite the appropriate references for the above tests in specific provisions of the Act, including up to three related sections, ITs (primary) or Income Tax Folios, or ICs from the footnotes to those provisions in the Act.

CHAPTER 4

Exercise 8

ITA: 18(1)(*l*)

Advice Limited, a consulting firm in Calgary, owns a small lodge in the Banff area. The lodge is used throughout the year for the purposes of entertaining clients.

— *REQUIRED*

(A) Comment on the deductibility of maintenance costs in respect of the lodge.

(B) Reconsider the deductibility of these costs if the property is rented during the week to the public and used to entertain clients only on the weekends.

Exercise 9

ITA: 18(12)

Amina and Karim are married and work together as self-employed management consultants. They both work full-time on various projects in a 500-square-foot office located in their home. The total square footage of their home (bedrooms, kitchen, living room, and dining room) is 2,000 square feet. Amina teaches one evening course at the university each week. She earned $70,000 in consulting income and Karim earned $65,000. Other expenses, as listed below, were also incurred:

Expenses:	
Supplies and materials	$ 1,800
Computer and software lease	2,300
Total	$ 4,100

Total home overhead costs incurred during the year:	
Mortgage interest	$16,000
Utilities, water, and electricity	2,400
Property taxes	2,200
House cleaning	2,400
Home insurance	600
Total	$23,600

— *REQUIRED*

Advise Amina and Karim on the deductibility of their home office expenses.

Exercise 10

ITA: 17, 20(1)

Mr. M. Black is the controller with responsibility for tax compliance of International Widget Manufacturing Limited based in Calgary. He has called to ask your advice, as the company's accountant, on various matters pertaining to the company's 2018 tax return. He has asked you the following questions.

(A) On March 1, 2019, the company paid $234,000 for the benefit of 30 employees to a defined benefit registered pension plan. Of the $234,000 paid, $129,000 represents an adjustment required as a result of an actuarial valuation; the remainder was based on a current service contribution equal to 6% of each employee's wages for 2017. What is the total amount that can be deducted for tax purposes in 2018?

(B) The company paid $15,000 representation costs to obtain a special licence from the State of Montana to sell its widgets in the state. This amount was written off in the financial accounts but added back and amortized over a 20-year period in calculating income for tax purposes. How should this item be treated?

(C) The amount of $1,500 spent to connect gas lines on conversion from oil to gas in the Toronto plant was added to the cost of the building for financial accounting purposes and depreciated with the building. How should the amount be treated for tax purposes?

(D) The president's wife is employed full-time as his secretary and paid $7,000 per month. Is this amount deductible and if not, how much is deductible?

— *REQUIRED*

Provide brief answers to the questions posed by the controller.

Exercise 11

ITA: 20(1)(*f*)

In August 2013, Steel Blind Manufacturing Co. Ltd., a venetian blind manufacturer, issued a series of bonds at $956.71 per $1,000 par value. The issue matured in August 2018 and was redeemed at that time at par value. It bears a coupon rate of 4% to yield 5% to maturity.

— REQUIRED

How much of the bond discount can be deducted and in what year can it be deducted?

Exercise 12

ITA: 9–12, 18–20

The following information concerning the financial statements of Incredible Incubators Incorporated for its fiscal year ended September 30, 2018 has been presented to you in order to prepare tax returns.

(a)	Net income after tax per financial statements	$150,000
(b)	Provision for income taxes — current	25,000
	— future	130,000
(c)	Amortization expense	40,000
(d)	Reserve for doubtful debts — deducted in 2017	10,000
	deducted in 2018	15,000
(e)	Interest on income taxes paid after due date	2,500
(f)	Bond interest expense (including annual discount amortization of $7,500 re bonds issued this year)	39,500
(g)	Landscaping costs re factory premises — debited to land account	12,000

— REQUIRED

Using the foregoing information, compute income for tax purposes for Incredible Incubators for their fiscal year ended September 30, 2018. [Ignore capital cost allowance in respect of depreciable capital property.]

Exercise 13

ITA: 9, 12(1)(*e*)(ii), 20(1)(*n*), 20(8)(*b*)

Quickturn Land Limited bought for cash 25 acres of land at a cost of $107,500 during the year. About two months later the land was sold to a developer for $250,000 consisting of a $110,000 down payment in cash and a note without interest due in one year for the balance. A real estate commission of $12,500 was paid. The company often engages in this type of transaction.

— REQUIRED

Compute the minimum net income for the company in the year of sale and the next year in respect of this transaction.

Exercise 14

ETA: 123(1), 169(1), Schedule V, Part VII

Authors' Note: The following problem includes GST/HST implications. Students should review Chapter 20 of the textbook, Goods and Services Tax (GST)/Harmonized Sales Tax (HST), before attempting this problem.

Reconsider the facts of Exercise 12.

— REQUIRED

Outline the proper HST treatment by the corporation of the items presented.

CHAPTER 4

¶4,875 ASSIGNMENT PROBLEMS

Type 1 Problems

Problem 1

You are a co-op student working in the accounting department at Crystal Enterprises Inc. and have been asked to help with the year-end tax provision. You have gone through the detailed accounts that make up the company's income statement and have made a list of items for which you have questions.

When you took them to your boss, he asked you to determine whether the accounting treatment and the tax treatment are the same, and, if they are not, what they should do.

(1) The company made charitable donations of $15,000 in the year.

(2) While looking at the accounts receivable you noticed that they had set up an allowance for doubtful accounts for $120,000, calculated, based on their past history, as 60% of the accounts receivable that have been outstanding more than 60 days.

(3) You also noticed that they wrote off bad debts of $15,000 during the year.

(4) They included in revenue $10,000 received from a customer for goods to be delivered about two months after the year end. This is not a material amount so no adjustment was made at year end to account for this as deferred revenue.

(5) You noticed that the professional fees showed legal and accounting fees of $25,000 related to the re-financing of the company's long-term debt.

(6) In miscellaneous expenses you saw that some application software of $12,000 was expensed, as was $30,000 for landscaping the grounds around their office building.

(7) The company expensed a total of $55,000 on meals and entertainment, including $18,000 for a summer picnic for all employees.

(8) They also expensed the cost of club dues for senior executives amounting to $8,000. This covered the dues for the Westmount Golf Club, the Board of Trade, and the Downtown Racquet Club.

(9) The company expensed the costs of maintaining a small lodge located in the Muskoka area of Ontario north of Toronto and used throughout the year for the purposes of entertaining clients.

(10) You know from experience that the company pays $0.60 per kilometre as the mileage rate for the use of employee-owned cars. You noticed that some of the employees are travelling a lot, with two employees driving 6,000 km in the year.

Problem 2

Victoria carries on a retail business as a sole proprietor in a commercial plaza. All the floor space is used for displays or storage so she set aside one room (estimated to be 15% of the floor space) in her house to look after the administration. She has asked you to explain what expenses she will be able to deduct related to this space.

Problem 3

ITA: 22

Mr. Flint has arranged to sell substantially all of the assets of his proprietorship business, including accounts receivable valued at $36,000, to Mr. Small who will continue the proprietorship business. At the end of last year, Mr. Flint had deducted a reserve for doubtful debts of $6,500. The face value of the accounts being sold is $45,000.

What are the tax implications to both Mr. Flint and Mr. Small of using section 22 on the sale of accounts receivable?

Problem 4

ITA: 80(2)

Carson Manufacturing Inc. (Carson) is under financial stress. As a result of plummeting sales and increasing costs, it has been losing money and has now run out of cash. Last year, one of its biggest suppliers, Scott Distribution Inc. (Scott), loaned it $300,000, on commercial terms, to support them and guarantee a supply of product to them. They are expecting that they will have to sell their land and building next year to pay off some debts, including the bank. At the current time they have non-capital losses of $120,000 and net capital losses of $30,000.

The land and building have the following values:

	Land	Building
Fair market value	$1,900,000	$1,100,000
Cost	1,500,000	900,000
UCC		700,000

At this point it appears unlikely that Carson will be able to repay the loan, since all of their assets have been pledged to the bank as security. As a result of recent discussions, Scott has agreed to forgive the loan. Now, Carson wants to know what the impact of this forgiveness will be on Carson.

Problem 5

ITA: 9; IT-218R

A piece of land was purchased by Yacov Corporation Ltd. for the purpose of constructing a high-rise residential building. Plans were made for the development of the property, surveys were made and the land was stripped and excavated in preparation for construction. Subsequent to this work on the land, it was determined that the location was not suitable for the intended purpose, due to heavy truck traffic in the area. As a result, the property was listed for sale with the realtor who acted in the original purchase. The sale at a substantial profit took place approximately six months from the purchase.

The corporation had been newly formed when the above land was purchased. At about the same time, another piece of land was purchased and was developed into a commercial/industrial plaza which the corporation continues to own as a rental property. The principal shareholder of the corporation, Jake Yacov, owns and operates an electrical contracting business.

The Articles of Incorporation of the corporation contain the following statement of objects:

. . . to purchase, lease, acquire, hold, manage, develop, operate, pledge and mortgage, either absolutely as owner or by way of collateral security or otherwise, alone or jointly with others and either as principal or agent, property, real or personal, and assets generally of any and every kind of description.

No mention is made of the purchase and sale of land as a business activity.

Write a memo for the Yacov Corporation Ltd.'s file evaluating the issue of whether the sale of the land should be treated as a receipt of income or capital gain for tax purposes. Arrive at a conclusion consistent with your analysis of the facts, but indicate the basis for any areas of potential opposition to your conclusion.

Problem 6

ITA: 6(1)(a)

Comment on the income tax consequences for each of the following independent situations:

(a) Dan, a construction contractor, entered into a verbal agreement with his friend, Mike, last year. Dan agreed to oversee a small renovation to Mike's house in exchange for Mike's painting services.

(b) Yoko's company won a $100,000 lawsuit against a competitor for patent infringement.

(c) Isaac Corporation, a local observatory, hired Cornell for the summer. For each hour that Cornell worked, Isaac received $5 an hour from the government as part of a student employment grant. Cornell's total compensation is $10 per hour.

(d) Jessy works part-time as the residential manager in an apartment block. In exchange for the management and cleaning services she offers, she receives free rent in a two bedroom apartment. Jessy uses her own supplies and equipment. One bedroom is used as an office for carrying out her duties and meeting existing and potential tenants.

Problem 7

ITA: 18(1)(a), 18(1)(h), 248(1)

Cameron Chase purchased 200 acres of property about 30 years ago in the eastern Ontario area between Peterborough and Ottawa, as a holiday property for himself and his family. About two years later, it became their principal residence. He worked in Ottawa, both at that time and in the subsequent years; initially he commuted between the property and his Ottawa job on a daily basis. About 10 years later, he began living in Ottawa during the week and commuting home to the property only on weekends. When the property was first purchased, there was an old brick house on it which was not suitable as a residence for the family. A new house (referred to by Cameron as the D.V.A. house) was built; the family moved into it. It is clear that the family's lifestyle was such as to enjoy the rural location.

CHAPTER 4

About 14 years ago (i.e., 15 years after the purchase of the property), Cameron decided to turn part of the property into a campground; eight serviced campsites and approximately twelve unserviced sites were created for this purpose. There was as well room for at least 10 other unserviced campsites more or less immediately available and potential for expansion to a much larger number (e.g., 100). Outhouses were built; a trout pond constructed; and the requisite service roads installed. The tax treatment of the expenses incurred with respect to this construction is not part of the dispute in this case.

After these initiatives had been taken, about a year or so later, Cameron sought the advice of a consultant with the Ontario Ministry of Tourism, a Mr. Bingham. The advice sought was with respect to the possibility of developing the campground and obtaining a business loan for this purpose. Cameron had applied around that time for a loan and was turned down in September of that year.

Cameron's consultations with Mr. Bingham at that time led to suggestions for the development of the campsite through the construction of additional facilities: additional serviced sites; proper toilets; laundry facilities; a store on the property; a swimming pool; an activities building which might be used by the campers in bad weather. Cameron's accountant, Mr. McCoy, prepared projections as to the proposed profitability of the venture if the proposed development took place. These projections showed losses in the first year of operations (about 12 years ago) but a profit thereafter. The projections were based on information given to Mr. McCoy by Cameron and they envisaged the obtaining of a $500,000 loan. Cameron applied to the Eastern Ontario Development Corporation, in the third year of operations, for a loan ($80,000, not $500,000). Mr. Bingham was asked to evaluate the loan application from the Department of Tourism's point of view. He was asked to consider: whether Cameron had the management capability to effect and operate the proposed development; whether there would be any negative effects on competitors in the area if the development took place; whether Cameron's marketing plans looked reasonable. Mr. Bingham's evaluation did not involve any financial analysis of the application. Mr. Bingham recommended that the loan application go forward for the next step, evaluation by the Eastern Ontario Development Corporation. Cameron was unable to obtain the loan, because the Eastern Ontario Development Corporation's funds are new money for new projects.

Cameron purchased a "pre-fab" house for $70,000 which was constructed across the road from the D.V.A. house. The family moved into that house eight years ago. Cameron indicated that he had decided to proceed with the plans for the development of the campsite by turning the D.V.A. house into the general activities building envisaged in the projected development. He planned to add laundry facilities, toilets, etc., thereto. The first year after moving in, Cameron rented the D.V.A. house to his daughter for $100 per month. This was not sufficient to cover the mortgage costs of the property. In May of that year, Cameron had a massive heart attack. He was incapacitated until at least September of that year. Cameron continued to charge the mortgage expenses of the property as a business expense.

The profit and loss record of Cameron's business never showed a profit from the first 10 years of its operation. Losses ranged from about $24,000 to $73,000, but have decreased somewhat in the last two years.

The gross income for the campground itself for the six years was minimal.

In the last five years, the campground income was reported in a combined fashion with that received from the cottage and farmhouse property; therefore, it cannot be separately identified. The record is sketchy with respect to the renting of the cottage, the farmhouse, and the D.V.A. house. That which exists does not show a vigorous and concerted effort to run a business. The D.V.A. house, as well as being rented to the taxpayer's daughter for $100 per month five years ago, was rented during a few of the winter months in the next year to some loggers and for approximately six months in that year to some miners who were prospecting in the area.

Camp Chase was listed in a Government of Ontario camping brochure published for the second season and Cameron had had some calling cards made with Camp Chase, the address, a map and rates listed thereon. No expenses for advertising of the Camp were included in his tax returns for the period of operations to date.

Determine whether expenses incurred by Cameron during the two peak loss taxation years (five and four years ago) are business expenses that are deductible for tax purposes.

Problem 8

TalkTech Inc. is a manufacturer and wholesaler of cellular communication products. TalkTech Inc's customers are retailers who promote TalkTech Inc.'s products to the general public. TalkTech Inc. has an October 31 year end. You are conducting a review of TalkTech Inc's year-end accounting records for its 2018 fiscal year and have been provided with the following information.

ITA: 12(1), 18(1), 20(1); IT-442R

TalkTech Inc. has the following recorded reserves:

Account	Opening	Additions	Subtractions	Closing
Warranty reserve	$35,000	$10,000	$17,500	$27,500
Allowance for doubtful accounts	32,000	7,500	5,000	34,500

TalkTech Inc. provides a one-year warranty on most of its products. The warranty is for defects in workmanship or component parts. This warranty is provided as part of the purchase price of TalkTech Inc.'s products. TalkTech Inc. honours its own warranties. The 2018 addition of $10,000 represents a standard percentage of sales made in the 2018 fiscal period. The 2018 subtraction of $17,500 represents an amount actually paid to honour warranties.

The addition of $7,500 to the allowance for doubtful accounts is a result of the application of TalkTech Inc.'s annual year-end aging analysis. In conversation with the controller of TalkTech Inc. you determine that this $7,500 increase in the allowance for doubtful accounts was computed by applying the company's historical collection percentages to the aged accounts receivable balances. Also, during its 2018 fiscal period, TalkTech Inc. wrote off $5,000 (the subtraction noted above) of amounts previously expensed and included in the opening allowance for doubtful accounts. TalkTech Inc. also ended up collecting $1,500 of previously written-off bad debts.

In an attempt to attract a particular retail customer, TalkTech Inc. provided this new customer with an incentive to make a large initial purchase of its products. On April 1, 2018, TalkTech Inc. sold $300,000 worth of cellular phones to CellBlock Limited. TalkTech agreed to the following payment terms in an attempt to entice CellBlock Limited to make the purchase:

● $100,000 due and payable May 1, 2018; and

● $50,000 due and payable January 1 each year starting January 1, 2019 through January 1, 2022.

The cost of the goods sold under this contract was $180,000. The delivery date for the cellular phones sold under this contract was May 1, 2018.

One of TalkTech's customers, Phones'N'Things, was experiencing financial trouble. As a result, TalkTech Inc. had agreed to make shipments only if payments were received well in advance of the anticipated shipping dates. Under the terms of this agreement, TalkTech Inc. received $40,000 from Phones'N'Things on September 30, 2018. This payment was an advance payment for a shipment of new technology cellular phones which TalkTech Inc. expected to be shipping to customers commencing February 1, 2019. In the event that TalkTech Inc. was unable to honour its contract with Phones'N'Things, a full refund of the $40,000 was payable.

You agree to prepare a schedule showing the effect of the above information on income for tax purposes of TalkTech Inc. for the year ended October 31, 2018. You will also determine any adjustments that would be necessary to reconcile accounting income and income for tax purposes for the year.

In addition, you agree to analyze the tax consequences if the $5,000 subtraction in the allowance for doubtful accounts in 2018 included an account receivable of $800 which was written off only because it has been outstanding for more than 180 days. In fact, it has been outstanding for one year and is part of the opening allowance of $32,000. This $800 could still be collected and there has been no serious attempt to collect it. The remainder of that customer's account is current and further sales have been made to that customer.

CHAPTER 4

Problem 9

Jordana is self-employed in the T-shirt distribution business. The following is Jordana's income statement, for the calendar year ending December 31.

Statement of Income
For the year ended December 31

Gross revenue		$60,000
Cost of goods sold		(10,000)
Gross profit		50,000
Expenses:		
Accounting and legal	$2,000	
Advertising	800	
Golf dues	3,000	
Reasonable estimated bad debt expense	2,000	
Business, taxes, and licenses	1,000	
Amortization expense	8,000	
Cycle Safety Program	1,200	
Interest	7,800	
Meals and entertainment	4,000	
Rent and lease	2,200	
Office rent	1,000	
Salaries and wages — staff	6,000	(39,000)
Net income per financial statements		$11,000

Notes:

(a) Legal fees include $500 of accrued fees for a pending lawsuit against Jordana for the sale of distasteful T-shirts.

(b) Accounting fees include the purchase of a $1,200 computerized cash register.

(c) Interest expense includes $3,000 paid to the CRA for late instalment interest.

(d) The Cycle Safety Program cost was for Jordana, who is an active environmentalist and rides her bicycle to work every day.

(e) Included in the cost of goods sold is $3,200 incurred for the purchase of shelving and lighting.

(f) Due to the nature of the transaction, the sale of Disney rights were not included in the financial statements. Jordana actively trades rights for T-shirt logos. Net proceeds from the sale of the Disney rights were $15,000, and the cost of the logo rights was $6,800.

Jordana has asked you to calculate her income from a business for tax purposes, before CCA, for the calendar year ending December 31.

Problem 10

Source Renovations Ltd. specializes in home renovations and interior design in the Montreal area. Most of the construction and finish carpentry work is subcontracted to self-employed contractors. The following information relates to the corporation's net income for the year ended July 31.

Sales revenue		$4,100,000
Direct contracting expenses		3,750,000
Gross profit		350,000
General and administrative expenses:		
Salary to Ginny (president)	110,000	
Salary to spouse (accounting)	50,000	
Meals and entertainment (Note a)	12,200	
Advertising expenses (Note b)	4,900	
Travelling expense (Note c)	19,500	
Interest and bank charges (Note d)	18,000	
Amortization (Note e)	8,000	
Office expenses	6,000	
Total expenses		228,600
Net operating profit		$ 121,400

Other:

Gain on sale of real estate (Note f)	$ 55,000
Sale of design contracts (Note g)	19,000
Net income	$ 195,400

Ginny informed you that there was one unrecorded receivable of $14,500 for a renovation project completed on July 30.

Notes:

(a) Meals and entertainment includes:

Club dues	$ 1,800
Promotional meals and season hockey tickets	10,400
Total	$12,200

(b) Advertising expenses include:

Charitable donations	$2,200
Community promotion	650
Local advertising and mail outs	2,050
Total	$4,900

(c) Travelling expense includes both air travel and travel reimbursement to employees for business travel. The company's policy is to reimburse employees 55 cents per kilometre for the business use of their automobiles. The employees drove less than 5,000 kilometres.

(d) Interest and bank charges include:

Interest expense — operations	$ 9,400
Penalty interest for late filing prior year's corporate tax	8,100
Bank charges	500
Total	$18,000

(e) The company uses the straight-line method of amortization. The maximum capital cost allowance that may be claimed is $8,900.

(f) During the year, the company purchased two homes. After Ginny redecorated, the corporation sold the homes for a profit. The corporation has sold six homes in the last two years using the same strategy.

(g) The sale of design contracts resulted from Ginny's desire to downscale her involvement in commercial design. The gain on sale is net of all costs and expenses and is considered to be a capital gain.

(h) The salary to Ginny's spouse is considered reasonable because he spends most of his working day administering her business.

The controller of Source Renovation Ltd. has asked you to calculate the company's income from a business for tax purposes.

Problem 11

ITA: 18, 19, 20, 67.1(1), 78(4)

Duncan Ltd. is a Canadian-controlled private corporation owned by Mr. William Duncan. Mr. Duncan purchased all shares of Duncan Ltd. on July 1 of the prior year for $500,000 in an arm's length transaction. Duncan Ltd. manufactures fabrics and will continue with its June 30 year end. The following is Duncan Ltd.'s income statement for the period of July 1 to June 30 of the current year.

Duncan Ltd.
Statement of Income
For the period July 1 to June 30

Gross revenue		$6,000,000
Cost of goods sold		(4,000,000)
Gross profit		2,000,000
Expenses:		
Accounting and legal	$ 60,000	
Advertising	100,000	
Personal expense of Mr. Duncan	30,000	
Bad debts	20,000	
Business taxes and licenses	10,000	
Amortization	80,000	
Interest	90,000	
Meals and entertainment	40,000	
Rent and lease	220,000	
Office	10,000	
Salaries and wages	600,000	(1,260,000)
Net income per financial statements		$ 740,000

Notes:

(a) Legal fees include $15,000 of estimated fees for a threatened lawsuit against the company.

(b) Advertising expenses include a $10,000 payment to a television station in the United States for commercials promoting the company's products to the Vancouver market.

(c) Interest expense includes $5,000 of interest paid to the CRA for late instalments.

(d) Capital cost allowance deductible under paragraph 20(1)(a) is $14,210.

(e) On July 31 in the current fiscal year, Duncan Ltd. paid $30,000 to an agent for services to raise financing. The amount is included in the advertising expense.

(f) An $80,000 bonus is included in salary and wages. The amount will be paid on January 15, next year.

(g) Included in the cost of goods sold is $50,000 incurred for the purpose of earning exempt income.

(h) On January 1 of the current year, Duncan Ltd. paid $100,000 to one of its tenants to cancel a rental lease agreement because Duncan Ltd. required the space for its own business operations. The amount has been included in the rent expense figure. The lease of property commenced on January 1 and had five years remaining at that time.

Mr. Duncan has asked you to calculate the company's income from a business for tax purposes for the year ended June 30.

Problem 12

ITA: 9, 12(1), 18(1)

A senior tax partner in your office has requested that you meet with Mr. Jehangir Dauwalla, a new client, to assist in preparing his personal income tax return. During your initial client meeting, you obtained the following information about Mr. Dauwalla's new business, which he started on June 1. The proprietorship provides hot air balloon rides and weekend leisure trips. His accounting is prepared on the cash basis.

Up and Away
Cash Flow Statement from Proprietorship
June 1 to December 31

Cash receipts (Note a)		$27,220
Cash disbursements:		
Advertising (Note b)	$ 2,200	
Charitable donations	380	
Equipment rental	3,450	
Liability insurance	2,860	
Licences (Note c)	680	
Salary paid to Jehangir	14,750	
Supplies	3,870	
Telephone — Long distance	610	(28,800)
Cash outflow		($1,580)

Notes:

(a) Payments received from customers in January for all December flights and outstanding accounts receivable total $4,650 and are not included above.

(b) Advertising includes $462 of meals and entertainment expenses relating to promoting business with clients.

(c) Licences expense includes $460 for golf memberships for Jehangir and his spouse. He has met several potential new customers through the club and feels that this cost should be deductible. The remaining amount was for business licensing.

(d) In September, Jehangir won a new car through a minor hockey association ticket raffle. The prize had an estimated fair market value of $12,500.

Jehangir has asked you to calculate his income from a business for tax purposes.

Problem 13

ITA: 18(1)(a), 18(1)(b), 18(1)(l), 18(1)(n), 67.1

Marty started a self-employed bakery business in a North Bay warehouse on March 1, and he has selected a fiscal year end of December 31. His business includes the baking and delivery of muffins and bagels to various coffee shops throughout the city.

Ma Bagels
Statement of Income
For the period March 1 to December 31

Gross revenue	$340,000
Cost of goods sold	(190,000)
Gross profit	$150,000

¶4,875

Expenses:

Accounting amortization (Note a)	$4,000	
Repairs and maintenance	2,800	
Annual tennis club dues	2,500	
Uncollectible bad debts (Note b)	4,200	
Political donations	1,000	
Charitable donations	8,000	
Hotel and travel	7,800	
Meals and entertainment (Note c)	3,400	
Building rent	12,000	
Salary to spouse (Note d)	40,000	(85,700)
Net income		$ 64,300

Notes:

(a) On March 1, Marty purchased a large gas oven, a computerized blender, and a used van for his business. Marty only used the van for deliveries. Assume the deductible CCA on this equipment is $2,400.

(b) Uncollectible bad debts are from Jo Jo's coffee shop. The owner has declared bankruptcy and the business closed on September 15.

(c) Meals and entertainment expenses were incurred in the attempt to gain new business with several coffee shops.

(d) Diane, Marty's spouse, worked full-time for Marty overseeing hiring, orders and delivery of all goods.

Marty has asked you to calculate his income from a business for tax purposes for the calendar year ending December 31.

Problem 14

ITA: 9, 18, 20(1)(*l*)

Traci works evenings and weekends as a computer consultant. Weekdays she is employed full-time as a network administrator with Jimac Distributors Ltd., a Canadian-controlled private corporation. Traci has an office organized for her consulting business in her four-room condominium where she takes care of paperwork as well as the assembly and repair of computers. This room is the smallest in the condominium taking up only 50 m^2 of the 400 m^2 total space. The following information was provided by Traci.

Receipts for condo fees	$1,800
Mortgage interest	5,250
Receipts for utilities (light, heat, water)	800
Telephone bills	600
Deductible CCA on computer equipment used for diagnostic purposes	1,500

The telephone is used personally and for business. Long distance bills for business total $250. All consulting revenues are deposited into her personal account but she keeps a record in her consulting journal. All payments for supplies are paid out of her personal bank account. She provided you with the following information from her cheque book.

Money received for consulting services	$35,000
Cheques issued:	
CompWorld for parts	18,000
Computer Association	50
Savoir Faire cocktail party for clients	300
Future Shop for a television and DVD player	200
Straw Warehouse for living room furniture	5,500
Computer World magazine subscription	80

Notes:

(a) By looking at Traci's last year's tax return, you notice she claimed a reserve of $500 for amounts not collected. This year, $1,200 is outstanding on doubtful customers' accounts. Traci's records indicate that she was unable to collect $300 for two jobs completed last year.

(b) At the beginning of the year, Traci had $1,500 worth of parts. At the end of the year, she held an inventory of SIMMS that had dropped drastically in price; while the original cost was $2,000, the replacement cost is only $1,200.

(c) Traci often travels to a customer's place of business to provide training, installation, and Home Page design services. Traci uses her own car and charges the customer an extra $50 (included in consulting services) for the on-site service. Assume that Traci's capital cost allowance is $600. Traci kept track of her receipts and the kilometres she drove during the calendar year.

Total kilometres driven	15,000
Kilometres for business	4,500
Gas and oil	$ 1,500
Repairs (tires and muffler)	$ 350

Traci would like you to calculate her income from business for tax purposes.

Problem 15

ITA: 18, 19, 20(1), 147.2(1)

You have been assigned to the audit team for B.B. JAMS Ltd., one of your significant clients. Below is the income statement prepared by the company's accountant for the December 31, 2018 year end.

B.B. JAMS LIMITED
INCOME STATEMENT

FOR THE YEAR ENDED DECEMBER 31, 2018

Sales	$147,840,000
Cost of sales (Note (1))	(119,859,000)
Gross profit	$ 27,981,000
General and administrative expenses (Notes (2)–(7))	(12,374,000)
Selling expenses (Note (8))	(9,311,000)
Income from operations	$ 6,296,000
Other income (Notes (9)–(10))	16,000
Net income before income taxes	$ 6,312,000
Provision for income taxes	(2,528,000)
Net income	$ 3,784,000

Notes:

Through various discussions with the accountant, you have been able to determine that the following information has been recorded in the financial statements:

(1) JAMS had a number of items of inventory that did not sell well in the current year. For accounting purposes, the accountant has recorded a reserve for inventory obsolescence. The reserve was calculated based on the carrying value of any inventory item that had not had a sale in the last 180 days. The reserve at year end was $1,285,000.

(2) JAMS provides insurance for employees and paid the following amounts to Nat Insurance Company during the year:

$2,000,000 insurance policy on the life of the president included in insurance expense ($300 per month)	$ 3,600
$1,000,000 insurance policy on the life of the vice-president — marketing included in insurance expense	2,000
Group term life insurance for employees included in salaries and benefits ($37,000 × 12 months)	444,000
Total	$449,600

JAMS is the beneficiary of the policies on the president and vice-president. On June 1, 2018, JAMS renegotiated its bank debt, and due to the ever increasing responsibilities of the president, the bank required the insurance policy on the life of the president as part of the collateral for the loan. The premiums on the policy are equal to the net cost of pure insurance for the policy.

(3) An analysis of the professional fees for 2018 revealed the following expenses:

Legal and accounting fees related to the issuance of shares	$29,300
Legal fees related to amending the articles of incorporation	2,300
Costs incurred regarding the renegotiating of the bank loans	46,100
Costs incurred to defend the company against a wrongful dismissal charge	59,600
Costs related to the structuring of an agreement for the purchase of equipment from a foreign company	38,700
Appraisal costs to determine value of the equipment for the bank	5,100

(4) During the year, there were substantial repairs completed to the outside of the building. After the repairs some of the landscaping had to be redone. The total costs were $139,000. Of this, $23,500 relates to the landscaping costs. The entire $139,000 was included in general and administrative expenses.

(5) A review of the other expense accounts included in general and administrative expenses showed the following:

Amortization	$4,560,000
Interest on late payment of municipal taxes	900
Severance payments to four managers*	245,000
Loss from theft by accounting clerk	4,500
Donations to various registered charities	57,000

* All of the amounts were paid in the year.

(6) The salaries and benefits account shows contributions for certain employees to the company's registered pension plan. The contributions were not actually made until March 31, 2019. The pension plan is a defined contribution (money purchase) plan. The company matches the employees' contributions on a dollar for dollar basis.

	Registered pension plan	Employment compensation
President	$13,360	$250,000
Vice-president	10,250	150,000
Accountant	5,400	70,000

(7) In early November 2018, JAMS announced an early retirement package that was made available to employees over the age of 60. In order to provide employees with the time required to assess the offer, the deadline for accepting the package has been set at February 15, 2019. While no formal replies were received as of December 31, 2018, the personnel manager anticipates a high acceptance rate. She expects that the costs associated with the packages will be $672,000. This cost has been accrued in the 2018 financial statements.

(8) The following information was taken from the various selling expense accounts:

Cost of sponsoring presentations at a local theatre company	$15,000
Hockey game tickets given to customers	8,000
Meals and entertainment costs of salespeople	109,500
Staff holiday party and summer barbecue	43,800
Cost of sponsoring local little league teams	5,000
Memberships for salespeople at local golf courses	12,700

(9) The other income includes a loss on the sale of various fixed assets of $35,900.

(10) During the year, the company had cash on hand for a short period of time due to the timing of certain contract payments. The funds earned interest income of $10,400 while they were held.

Other Information:

(11) The accountant has calculated that JAMS is entitled to claim capital cost allowance of $5,835,000 in 2018. You have confirmed that this calculation is correct.

(12) In reviewing the income tax assessments, you noted that JAMS had been charged interest of $4,900 on the late payment of instalments. You discussed this with the accountant and determined that the interest was recorded in the income tax expense account.

Based on the information that you have obtained, your manager has asked you to calculate the income from business for tax purposes for JAMS for December 31, 2018. He also wants you to show all calculations whether or not they seem relevant to the final answer and comment on all items omitted from the calculation.

Problem 16

On February 1, 2019, Wynn, a recent commerce graduate, began a self-employed, unincorporated coffee business, Chino's & Beano's Unlimited. Wynn would like assistance preparing his 2018 tax return. He has prepared a brief, unaudited statement of income.

ITA: 12(1)(a)(ii),
18(1)(a), 18(1)(b),
18(1)(h), 18(1)(l),
20(1)(b)

Chino's & Beano's Unlimited
Statement of Income
For the year ended December 31, 2018

Sales revenue		$95,000
Less: Provision for returns	$1,200	
Cost of goods sold	22,000	23,200
Gross profit		$71,800
Expenses:		
Travel — meals	$1,500	
Travel — accommodation	2,000	
Travel — total operating expenses — car	2,350	
Sales manager's convention	600	
Salaries paid to staff	30,000	
Health club dues	2,200	
Child care and housekeeping expenses (nanny — single parent)	12,000	
Home office expenses (Note e)	1,400	
Telephone bills	350	
Office supplies	1,700	
Entertainment — drinks and meals	1,800	
Private dental plan — for staff members	2,400	
Restaurant structural renovation costs	21,200	
Straight-line amortization	3,800	
Total expenses		83,300
Business loss before tax		($11,500)

Wynn also supplied the following additional information:

(a) Wynn used his personal automobile for all his business travel. The $2,350 represents his total expenses for the 12-month period. His travel log included business mileage of 14,400 kilometres; the total number of kilometres driven during the 12-month period totalled 18,000 kilometres.

(b) Wynn would like to deduct all of his nanny expenses against his income since the expenses were incurred to earn income.

(c) There are no unrecorded revenues. However, Wynn feels that $380 of his accounts receivable balance is uncollectible because the customers recently declared bankruptcy. Wynn did not provide for this bad debt expense in his financial statements.

(d) The structural renovation of the coffee shop included new walls, flooring, an office for Wynn, and a kitchen.

(e) To ease the burden of being a single parent, Wynn set up a home office. Wynn uses the office to complete his administrative work in the evenings. The home office expenses relate to a proportion of heat, light and power.

Wynn would like you to calculate her net income from a business for tax purposes, ignoring CCA.

CHAPTER 4

Problem 17

ITA: 9–12, 18–20, 37, 67.1, 78, 147

The *unaudited* income statement for Lomas & Sons Limited, a Canadian-controlled private corporation, for its year ended December 31, 2018 shows the following:

Sales		$ 795,000
Cost of sales	$350,000	
General and administrative expenses	225,000	
Research and development expenditures	65,000	(640,000)
Operating income		$ 155,000
Other income		20,000
Net income before taxes		$ 175,000
Provision for income taxes:		
— current	$ 27,000	
— future	25,000	(52,000)
Net income after income taxes		$ 123,000

The information in the following notes has already been reflected in the above income statement.

(1) Payment made by company on April 1, 2019, to a defined contribution (money purchase) registered pension plan for the president of the company in respect of current employment service, allocated to 2018 expenses by the company's accountant; in addition, the president had $7,500 withheld from his compensation of $74,000 for the RPP .... $ 7,000

(2) Increase in warranty reserve on company's product (net of expense incurred; based on self-insurance warranty program) 16,000

(3) Amortization expense recorded in the financial statements 30,000

(4) Landscaping costs re: factory premises 2,500

(5) Interest on bank loan obtained for the purpose of purchasing common shares in Advanco Ltd., a dividend-paying Canadian corporation 6,300

(6) Legal costs of arranging an agreement among shareholders 8,500

(7) Legal and accounting fees related to issue of shares 12,700

(8) Interest on municipal real estate taxes paid late in error 1,000

(9) Golf club membership fees 2,200

(10) Donation to United Way 3,000

(11) Meals and entertainment for clients 4,000

(12) Appraisal fees to determine selling price of fixed assets 6,200

(13) Premium on term insurance on life of president with the corporation as beneficiary; policy was not required to be assigned as collateral for corporate borrowing from the bank 2,800

(14) Management bonuses ($20,000 of the bonuses expensed in 2018, and shown as "Bonus Payable" on the Balance Sheet as at December 31, 2018 has not been paid at the time of filing the corporate tax return on June 30, 2019) ... 40,000

(15) Amortization of bond discount on bonds issued in 2013 3,400

(16) Interest and penalties on income tax assessments, expensed for accounting purposes 1,250

(17) Items included in the financial accounting statements in arriving at the net profit:

Amount paid by an insurance company on its business interruption insurance to compensate for loss of profits when company was closed down for a month during the year because of a fire 26,800

Dividends received 1,700

Volume rebates and discounts on purchases 16,000

Your manager has asked you to compute the income from business or property for tax purposes, ignoring tax deductions in respect of depreciable capital or eligible capital property for Lomas and Sons Limited in respect of its 2018 fiscal year. In addition, she wants you to comment on all items not included in your derivation of income from business or property.

Problem 18

ETA: 123(1), 161, 164, 169(1), 170(1)(*a*), 232, 236, Sched. V, Part VII

Authors' Note: The following problem includes GST/HST implications. Students should review Chapter 20 of the textbook, Goods and Services Tax (GST)/Harmonized Sales Tax (HST), before attempting this problem.

Reconsider the facts of Problem 19 and:

(A) Outline the general HST requirements applicable in this corporate situation.

(B) Indicate which of the items listed in the additional information notes represent costs incurred for:

1. taxable supplies, eligible for an ITC, and

2. exempt supplies, not eligible for an ITC.

(C) Comment on the appropriate HST treatment of the other items listed in the additional information notes and on the income statement.

Problem 19

Ryan Holeman, the president of Nine Iron Ltd., has come to your office seeking a second opinion. Nine Iron Ltd. carries on a mini golf and retail business in southern Manitoba. The CRA has reassessed Nine Iron Ltd. for the following transactions that occurred during last year:

(a) Eighteen months earlier, the company purchased two acres of land just outside of Winnipeg with the intention of possibly developing a second retail outlet. Ryan did not have firm plans when he purchased the land. At the time, he thought he could either develop the property into a mini golf and retail outlet or build a gas station with an overnight park for recreation vehicles. Unfortunately, a significant lender backed down and the company was forced to sell the land. Luckily, as Ryan had speculated, the land was sold for a profit of $90,000. The new owner plans to develop an overnight park for recreation vehicles.

(b) Nine Iron Ltd. immediately purchased a smaller plot of land within walking distance. The company is planning to build a second mini golf and retail outlet location next year. During the year, the company expensed interest and property taxes of $26,000 relating to the vacant land. The company also expensed $7,000 in architect's fees, and legal and surveying costs for the development of the amusement park. The CRA reassessed Nine Iron Ltd. for $26,000 plus $3,500 in interest charges, claiming that Nine Iron Ltd. purchased the first plot of land with the intention of trading for profit. The CRA is also disallowing the expenses incurred on the second plot.

Advise Ryan on the income tax issues that Nine Iron Ltd. must address with respect to the above transactions.

Type 2 Problems

Problem 20

Lisa has come to see you again. She came to see you last week [Chapter 3 — Problem 1] about her decision to accept a company-owned or a company-leased car. Now she wants to make sure that she understands the company's position before she makes her decision. She would like you to explain the impact on the company's income for tax purposes of leasing or owning the car.

Problem 21

You have again been asked for advice on employee stock options by two different clients [Chapter 3 — Problem 2].

(a) Omer wants you to explain the impact of the stock option on his employer.

(b) Hilda wants you to explain the impact of the stock option on her employer.

Problem 22

Rishma has left your office again. She came to see you last week [Chapter 3 — Problem 3] about her offer of employment from Motion Tech. Based on your advice to her, she has again met with the company. Now she wants to make sure she understands the company's position before she makes her decision. She would like you to explain the impact of the list of items in her offer on Motion Tech's income for tax purposes.

CHAPTER 4

¶4,875

Problem 23

The CFO for Auto Supply Inc. has asked you to explain to him the impact of the possible employee benefits you considered in Chapter 3 — Problem 4 on the company's income for tax purposes.

Problem 24

ITA: Subdivisions a and b

Coco Hardy is an apprentice with Sepp, a design house in Toronto. In her spare time, during some evenings and on weekends, she operates a sewing service for clothing manufacturers. She has set aside a spare room in her apartment where she keeps her equipment and materials and performs her services. This room occupies approximately 20% of her apartment. She sews for many of the same companies that deal with her employer, Sepp. The demands of her employment with Sepp will continue to prohibit her from expanding her sewing services. Consequently, she has not advertised for additional sewing work. Her sewing billings average approximately $600 per month.

She and the manufacturers mutually agree upon what type of sewing is to be done in order to meet the manufacturers' production deadlines. Her hourly rates are determined by the type of sewing required for a particular manufacturer. At the end of each month, she will issue a bill to the manufacturers bearing her name, home address, and home telephone number. Her clients pay her the gross amount on the invoice which does not include HST.

Ms. Hardy has incurred some direct sewing expenses and has allocated some of her other costs to her sewing services in respect of the past year as follows:

Direct expenses:			
Sewing supplies			$ 2,890
Meals and entertainment for manufacturers			500
Sewing machine repairs			425
Long distance telephone calls to manufacturers			710
Delivery of finished product			1,500
Total direct expenses			$ 6,025
Allocated costs:			
Rent ($1,000 per month)		$12,000	
Utilities		2,100	
Insurance		400	
		$14,500	
Allocation to sewing room		× 20%	$ 2,900
Capital cost allowance:			
Sewing room furniture		$ 450	
Sewing machine		325	
Automobile for deliveries		1,200	$ 1,975
Total allocated costs			$ 4,875
Total			$10,900

Coco has asked you to analyze the facts and determine whether she is earning employment income or business income from her sewing service.

She also wants you to calculate her income as business income and again as employment income and comment on whether the listed expenses and allocated costs are deductible for income tax purposes under each alternative.

Problem 25

ITA: 8(1)(f), 8(1)(h), 8(1)(h.1), 8(1)(i), 8(1)(j), 8(3), 8(4), 18–20

Mr. Peter Rajagopal, who is a salesman in Regina, Saskatchewan, has incurred the following expenses in connection with his employment in 2018. He was not reimbursed and did not receive an allowance in respect of any of these expenses. Peter has a Form T2200, signed by his employer, attesting to all of these expenses.

(1) Peter uses one room in his home exclusively as a home office. He uses his home office most days and evenings to do paperwork and make phone calls and his home office computer is connected to his employer's computer system. He visits his office at his employer's premises approximately once a week and spends the remainder of the time on the road, making sales calls throughout Western Canada.

(2) The following expenses relate to Peter's home office which occupies 10% of the square footage of his house:

Utilities	$ 3,100
Mortgage interest	12,000
House insurance	1,150
Municipal taxes	3,050
Maintenance and repairs	2,700
Total	$22,000
10% thereof	$2,200
Capital cost allowance on computer equipment	1,035
Rental of photocopier	1,200
Office supplies	750
Cellular phone charges (used for employment-related calls only)	700
Long distance calls related to business	1,000

(3) Peter also has the following promotional expenses:

Meals (with clients in Regina, Peter's meals)	$2,000
Client's meals	$2,100
Theatre tickets	1,200
Promotional gifts	1,300
Country club membership	3,200

(4) Peter paid the following automobile expenses:

Gas and oil	$2,000
Insurance	1,100
Licence	90
Repairs	800
Parking (employment related)	320

Peter purchased the car that he uses for employment purposes on August 1, 2017 for $50,000 plus $2,500 GST and $2,500 PST. Peter did not claim CCA on the car in 2017; therefore, the capital cost allowance rate for the car is 30% in 2018. The car was driven a total of 40,000 kilometres in 2018; 32,000 of the kilometres driven related to Peter's employment use.

(5) Peter also incurred the following travel expenses (while away at least 12 hours):

Airfare	$ 4,520
Meals and accommodation (including $2,400 for meals)	4,960
Registration fees for convention in Vancouver to increase product knowledge	800
Out-of-town entertainment	3,200

(6) Interest on bank loan:

— to buy the computer equipment for the home office in (1) above	$ 320
— to buy the car in (4) above	800

(7) Peter's remuneration from employment is as follows:

Salary	$40,000
Bonus based on company sales	35,000

(8) Saskatchewan has GST of 5% and PST of 5%.

Peter has asked you to calculate his income and expenses assuming he is an employee and assuming he is self-employed. You have agreed to do this and present him with the results with two columns; one for each option and one showing the differences, if any.

Problem 26

Valerie Borg is a vice-president of Program Management with an equipment leasing company in Calgary. Recently, Valerie was approached by a large public company, Key Equipment Finance Limited ("Key"), which is based in Toronto, about the possibility of joining their firm. Valerie has always been looking for opportunities for career advancement and Toronto is an ideal city for relocation.

Valerie is in the process of negotiating her compensation package. She has just received a letter outlining a proposed package from Key. The package looks very attractive, but she would like to know the tax impact on various items outlined in the letter. Valerie is also interested in knowing the tax implications of the compensation package to her future employer. She believes that if she knows the cost to the employer, she will be in a better position to negotiate.

ITA: 5(1), 6(1)(a), (b), (c), (e), (g), (k), 6(2), 7(1), 7(8), 6(9), 80.4(1), 110(1)(d); Income Tax Folio S2-F3-C2

CHAPTER 4

1. An annual salary of $150,000 and bonus, tied to the company's financial performance. Calculation of the bonus is based on the firm's December year-end results, with payment to occur on June 30.

2. Key offers to loan Valerie $200,000, interest-free, to help finance a new house. In addition, Key will reimburse all of her moving costs.

3. Key will pay the premium for Valerie to join its group term life insurance plan. Key will pay the premiums for a private health plan, a dental plan, and a drug plan. The company's insurance company is Green Shield.

4. Valerie is required to travel to Europe on a regular basis. Company policy permits a spouse to accompany its executives for these trips. Valerie's husband, Matt, is a freelance writer working from home. He is very excited about going to Europe with Valerie. The main purpose of the trips will be for Valerie to oversee the company's global operations. Her husband will spend his time visiting local museums. Key will pay a portion of the travelling expenses related to Matt.

5. Key will provide a BMW to Valerie. Valerie expects to drive the car 30% for business and 70% for her personal use. Valerie will receive a company credit card to be used to pay for gas and maintenance of the car. Key will pay a monthly lease of $850, including HST. Valerie will drive the car approximately 20,000 kilometres per year.

6. Key recently installed a fitness club in its building. All employees are encouraged to use the club free of charge. The club also offers free personal training. The equivalent value for similar facilities at a private club would be $1,100 per year, including applicable taxes.

7. Key pays for counselling services related to the physical health of its employees. Valerie will be covered by this service.

8. Valerie will participate in Key's defined contribution (i.e., money purchase) registered pension plan. The company will match Valerie's contributions to the plan, which are not to exceed 50% of the maximum deductible amount.

9. Key owns a yacht and it is made available to all of its executives. This offer is extended to Valerie. She can have it free for one week each year.

Valerie would like you to explain the tax implications of the compensation package to both herself and Key.

She would also like you to describe the tax-related issues to be considered when designing an employee compensation package.

Type 3 Problems

Problem 27

Samara, the president of Eden Prospects Ltd., has come to your office for a second opinion. Eden Prospects is a national marketing firm specializing in the development and implementation of marketing plans for partners in practices of law, accounting, medicine and dentistry. Samara is on the premises daily, carrying out her duties as president and a senior adviser to clients. The CRA recently reassessed Eden Prospect's 2017 taxation year and is requesting that an additional $140,000 in taxes and $28,000 in interest and penalty charges be paid immediately for the following transactions.

(a) In December 2017, the company declared a bonus of $280,000 to Samara and several senior vice-presidents. The amount was paid in September 2018.

(b) In 2017, the corporation provided three senior executives with an interest-free loan of $240,000 for the purchase of shares of Eden Prospects Ltd. The company borrowed the funds from the bank and incurred $20,000 in interest charges. The executives began repayment in 2019. No amount was shown by Eden Prospects as a taxable benefit for these employees.

(c) The corporation pays Samara a nominal salary to act as president. Samara provides her senior advisory services to Eden Prospects through a proprietorship, Sole Trust. Every month, Samara prepares an invoice on behalf of the proprietorship for services rendered to Eden Prospects. Prospects is Sole Trust's only client. The CRA imposed a large penalty on Eden Prospects for not treating Samara as an employee and remitting Canada Pension Plan, Employment Insurance and withholding taxes.

(d) In 2017, the corporation rented a fishing lodge to carry out group think sessions with three of their most senior clients. The purpose of the sessions was to provide a comfortable setting for the company's largest clients to share marketing ideas. The sessions also helped Eden Prospects to become closer to their clients — especially while fishing and golfing. The corporation was denied a deduction for the rent of the lodge, although it was allowed 50% of the meals, entertainment and green fees.

Advise Samara by preparing a memo on the various income tax issues that both Samara and Eden Prospects must address with respect to the above transactions.

Problem 28

London City Electronics Inc. has been a client of yours since it started in business five years ago. Isabelle Joy, the founder, has been very successful with her main product, which is a valve that measures and controls the flow of liquids. It is now the middle of March and you have just started your review engagement field work for the company's December year end when Isabelle asks you to come into her office to talk to her.

The first thing you do is congratulate her on the good year she had last year. Her sales, gross profit, and net income are all up substantially over the previous year. You are surprised when she starts to complain about the poor results so far this year. She indicates that her customers are just now starting to stretch their payments because they are facing increased competition from imports. In fact, one of her customers has given London City Electronics some of its products in exchange for the amount it owed.

To compound this problem, Isabelle has had some quality control problems in her manufacturing process and she has been receiving a large number of warranty claims. Sometimes she is able to repair the valve before there is significant cost to the customer, but in some cases the customer has had financial losses as a result of the faulty valve.

Isabelle would like your advice on the tax implications of her situation.

Problem 29

Jordana Fluge and Noa Gold were finally able to hold the grand opening for their medical supply import business. It had been an expensive party, but both Jordana and Noa felt that their suppliers, customers, and new employees had appreciated it.

It seemed like a long time ago that they got the idea and started to develop their plans. In fact, the idea had been introduced to them 12 months ago during a trip they took to California to look for business opportunities. Once they returned, they began to do their own research. They had one of the local universities do some market research for them to see whether their idea was viable. The research supported their idea of importing medical supplies from a large U.S. supplier to compete against other importers for the Canadian market.

Six months ago, the U.S. supplier put them in touch with their local importer, Beam Inc., whose owner wanted to retire. Since that time, they have been busy negotiating with Mr. Beam and the supplier, finding their own leased warehouse space (Beam Inc.'s space was too small), visiting customers, setting up the office and modern control systems and assessing the employees of Beam Inc. Even before the opening, they had spent $25,000 of their own money on expenses such as:

- their initial travel costs to California (July, last year);

- market research (September, last year);

- negotiating the operating line of credit (May, this year);

- leasehold improvements, equipment (May, this year);

- travel and entertainment expenses (January to June, this year); and

- legal and accounting costs for the incorporation (June, this year).

But now it is all coming together. Jordana is going to provide the initial capital, including the personal guarantee to the supplier and the bank, and Noa is going to manage the business. They have bought the inventory, customer lists, accounts receivable, and equipment from Beam Inc. Their initial lease is for five years with two, five-year renewal options.

Advise Jordana and Noa on the tax implications of the issues raised by this situation. Assume that they incorporated a company in June, but they have not used it in any way yet, and that it is now July when they are asking for your advice.

Problem 30

The following analysis of certain expense accounts and related additional information was discovered during the December 31, 2018 year-end audit in the month of April 2019 for Meshigoneh Distributors Limited, a Canadian-controlled private company, owned 100% by I.M. Meshigoneh.

Employee remuneration:

Salaries	$ 125,000
Commissions accrued but not paid until Jan. 2019	10,000
Bonuses (Note (1))	50,000
Christmas presents to employees (Note (2))	2,000
	$ 187,000

Fee for loan guarantee provided by Meshigoneh's spouse (Note (3))	$ 8,000

Bond discount: (Note (4))

Amortization on new bonds	$ 20,000
Paid on redemption of old bonds	40,000
	$ 60,000

Costs of issuing new bonds: (Note (4))

Legal	$ 5,000
Accountingp	2,00
Printing	500
	$ 7,500

Depreciation and amortization: (Note (5))

Building (capital cost, $1,000,000)	$ 33,333
Automobile (capital cost, $35,000, excluding HST)	8,500
	$ 41,833

Advertising: (Note (6))	$ 50,000

Notes:

(1)   The 2018 bonuses had not been paid by the date of the audit.

(2)   The company gave each employee a $100 gift certificate.

(3)   The 2018 fee had not been paid by the date of the audit. The 2017 fee of $10,000 and 2016 fee of $7,500 had not been paid either.

(4)   During 2018, the company redeemed its outstanding 10% bonds, face value $100 each (10,000 units) for $970,000. In order to acquire a new building, the company had issued these bonds in 2010 for $930,000 to yield 12% to maturity. The company issued new 13% bonds at the request of its creditors under the threat of a bankruptcy action. The bond issue was for the same face value amount $1,000,000; however, the company only received $980,000.

(5)   For book purposes, the company is depreciating and amortizing the aforementioned capital assets on a straight-line basis:

Building	30 years
Automobile	5 years
Organization expense	10 years

The automobile was purchased February 1, 2018 and was used by the president, I.M. Meshigoneh, for business use (8,000 kilometres) and for personal use (13,000 kilometres). The organization expense was incurred in 2010 when the company was formed.

(6)   The $50,000 represents full payment for a series of advertisements in a local newspaper for the 2018-2019 Fall/Winter season of which only 60% have appeared by December 31, 2018.

Discuss, in point form, the tax implications for each of the above transactions with appropriate references to the *Income Tax Act* or Interpretation Bulletins/Income Tax Folios from the viewpoint of:

(A)   Meshigoneh Distributors Limited, and

(B)   the recipients of these payments and/or benefits, if applicable.

CHAPTER 4 —
DISCUSSION NOTES FOR REVIEW QUESTIONS

(1) This type of transaction is commonly referred to as an "adventure in the nature of trade" and would result in business income, if the facts of the situation indicate that it has the "badges of trade". One of the indicators that a transaction is an adventure in the nature of trade is that the taxpayer has specialized knowledge in respect of the transaction. Mr. Fritz is a real estate salesperson and, hence, on the surface appears to meet this test. Since "business" is defined to include "an adventure in the nature of trade", this transaction would be classified as business income.

ITA: 248(1)

(2) There is no requirement in the Act to use GAAP for tax purposes. The courts have, on occasion, rejected conformity between income for accounting and tax purposes, particularly in cases where GAAP is at variance with the court's concept of ordinary commercial trading and business principles and practices or common law principles. However, GAAP profits are usually used as the starting point for the calculation of net income for tax purposes.

(3) No. Since the performance of this contract would have been income to Opco if the customer had completed it, the damages received would also be treated as business income.

(4) The agreement was of such importance to Aco Ltd. that it would constitute a large part of the company's total business structure. As a result, the receipt may be treated as a capital transaction on the sale of class 14.1 property with no cost base. Thus, 50% of the receipt is included in business income. (See Chapter 5.)

(5) No. Income from illegal activities is taxable. Subsection 9(1) does not impose conditions on how the profit is earned. See Income Tax Folio S3-F9-C1 for the CRA's position. See, also, the cases listed in the text on this issue.

Income Tax Folio
S3-F9-C1

(6) The subsidy is taxable as if it were an expense reduction to Opco. Refer to the CRA's position.

IT-273R2

(7) There are a number of limitations that restrict the deductibility of expenses even though they may have been incurred to earn income. Expenditures that are not deductible include:

ITA: 18

- capital outlay or loss;

ITA: 18(1)(b)

- use of recreational facilities and club dues;

ITA: 18(1)(l)

- political contributions; and

ITA: 18(1)(n)

- limitations on interest and property taxes.

ITA: 18(2), 18(3.1)

(8) A provision specifically prohibits the deduction of any amount paid or payable under the Act. As a result, the interest paid to the Receiver General will not be deductible.

ITA: 18(1)(t)

(9) Not necessarily. The Act also places a limitation on the amount of an outlay or expense. It can only be deducted to the extent that it is "reasonable in the circumstances".

ITA: 67

(10) If the replacement of the roof served to restore it to its original condition then the cost should be fully deductible in the year incurred. If the replacement roof was superior to the old roof, the cost could be considered capital in nature. This would result in an addition to the undepreciated capital cost pool. Then, the cost would be deductible over a number of years. An Income Tax Folio comments on the issue of income versus capital expenditures.

Income Tax Folio
S3-F4-C1

(11) No. Airplane, train, or bus fares are specifically excluded from the 50% limitation.

ITA: 67.1(4)(a)

(12) The reserve is only allowed if the company is the manufacturer of the product and pays an arm's length party to take over the obligations of the warranty for the company.

ITA: 20(1)(m.1)

CHAPTER 4

CHAPTER 4 — SOLUTIONS TO MULTIPLE CHOICE QUESTIONS

Question 1

(D) is correct. A deduction for interest and penalties on late income tax payments is denied.   ITA: 18(1)(*t*)

(A) is a deductible item. A deduction for amounts paid for landscaping business premises is allowed.   ITA: 20(1)(*aa*)

(B) is a deductible item. A deduction for interest on money borrowed to finance the purchase of a factory for use in its business is allowed.   ITA: 20(1)(*c*)

(C) is a deductible item. If the beneficiary of a $100,000 term life insurance policy on an employee is the employee's family, the cost of the insurance premium is part of the cost of the employee's remuneration package. As such, it is not denied as it is incurred for the purpose of earning income.   ITA: 18(1)(*a*)

Question 2

(C) is correct. The entire $15,000 spent on three social events for all employees at a particular location is deductible as long as the number of events does not exceed six.   ITA: 67.1(2)(*f*)

(A) The deduction for $11,000 of accrued legal fees for a pending law suit is not allowed, because it is a contingent liability. There is no legal liability to pay this amount.   ITA: 18(1)(*e*)

(B) The deduction for $4,000 of donations to registered charities is denied because it is not incurred for the purpose of earning income. The donations would be deductible in the computation of taxable income.   ITA: 18(1)(*a*), 110.1(1)(*a*)

(D) The deduction of $1,500 for golf club membership dues for employees is denied.   ITA: 18(1)(*l*)

Question 3

(D) is correct, because the Act provides an exception to the 50% rule for the cost of meals and entertainment relating to a fund-raising event the primary purpose of which is to benefit a registered charity.   ITA: 67.1(2)(*b*)

(A) is incorrect since donations to political parties are not deductible. The federal political donation would be eligible for a tax credit.   ITA: 18(1)(*n*), 127(3)

(B) is incorrect, because accrued bonuses are not deductible if they are unpaid 180 days after year end.   ITA: 78(4)

(C) is incorrect, because the deduction for a financial accounting reserve for warranty expenses is denied.   ITA: 18(1)(*e*)

Question 4

(A) is the correct answer. The $7,000 deduction is computed as follows:

Legal expenses related to the purchase of an investment in shares	$ 0	ITA: 18(1)(*b*)
Legal expenses incurred to dispute a tax assessment	5,000	ITA: 60(*o*)
Legal expenses related to the issuance of debt (⅕)	1,000	ITA: 20(1)(*e*)
Accounting fees in connection with the preparation of a prospectus (⅕)	1,000	ITA: 20(1)(*e*)
	$ 7,000	

(B) incorrectly deducts $1,000 for the legal expenses related to the purchase of an investment in shares: $8,000 = $1,000 + $1,000 + $5,000 + $1,000.

(C) incorrectly deducts all of the legal expenses related to the issuance of debt and the accounting fees in connection with the preparation of a prospectus but none of the legal fees for the tax dispute: $15,000 = $5,000 + $5,000 + $5,000.

(D) incorrectly deducts only the $5,000 legal expenses related to disputing the tax assessment.

Question 5

(D) is correct. Most of the facts support capital gains treatment: the nature of the asset (real estate), its use and intended use (rental), the 10-year holding period and the unsolicited offer for sale. As a result, the gain on the sale of the land will likely be treated as a capital gain for income tax purposes.

(A) is incorrect. Because Sam is a real estate agent, the CRA may argue that the gain on the sale of the land is business income (not a capital gain).

(B) is incorrect. The fact that the land has been held for 10 years supports capital gains treatment, not business income treatment.

(C) is incorrect. The unsolicited offer for sale supports capital gains treatment, not business income treatment.

Question 6

(A) is correct. Legal fees to defend a lawsuit brought by a customer would be deductible.   ITA: 18(1)(*a*)

(B) and (C) are incorrect because these items (accounting loss on the sale of capital property and the principal amount of a mortgage) are on account of capital and therefore not deductible.   ITA: 18(1)(*b*)

(D) is incorrect because personal and living expenses are not deductible.   ITA: 18(1)(*h*)

CHAPTER 4

CHAPTER 4 — SOLUTIONS TO EXERCISES

Exercise 1

Employee Perk	Employee Taxable Benefit	Employer Impact	
Tuition fees for the child of employee	$2,800 not a taxable benefit and jurisprudence supports an exempt scholarship for the child.	Deductible as compensation expense	ITA: 9, 11, 18, 20
Out-of-town meals	Not taxable to employee	50% deductible for employment duties	
Entertainment for clients	Not taxable to employee	50% deductible for employment duties	
Professional dues	Not taxable to employee	Deductible for employment duties	
Notebook computer for employment	Not taxable to employee	Deductible CCA for employment duties	
Membership for health club	Not taxable if employment-related	Not deductible for company	
Interest-free loan	$40,000 is subject to an imputed interest taxable benefit of $400 (deductible by the executive as was used to invest in company shares)	No impact on employer	
Life insurance premiums	$150 taxable benefit	Deductible as compensation expense	
Reimbursement for supplies	Not taxable to employee	Deductible CCA for employment duties	

Exercise 2

[See *Hiwako Investments Limited v. The Queen*, 78 DTC 6281 (F.C.A.)]

The intention of the taxpayer corporation in this case can only be inferred from the facts of the case. The nature of the asset involved in the transaction is of prime importance in this case. It was an income-producing asset that would have been regarded as a fixed capital asset had it been held longer. Normally, the increase in value on the sale of a capital asset is taxed as a capital gain. The gain represents an enhancement of value by realizing a security in the same sense that a growth stock may be sold for a gain that is regarded as a capital gain. Thus, the prospect of an increase in value does not, by itself, characterize the gain as income from business.

The nature of the activity surrounding the transaction could characterize it as an adventure in the nature of trade. However, it could be argued that an income-producing property was purchased as an investment and circumstances changed such that the investment had to be sold. This would not necessarily be regarded as a gain made in an operation of business in carrying out a scheme for profit-making.

The Court indicated that the concept of "secondary intention" does no more than refer to a practical approach for determining certain questions that arise in connection with "trading cases". If property is acquired where there is no business or the purchaser has not considered how he or she will use it, then the sale may be regarded as an adventure in the nature of trade, supporting a secondary intention to sell at a profit. However, where the property in question is an active, profit-producing property, it may be more difficult to conceive of its having been held as a speculation in the sense of an adventure in the nature of trade.

The fact that the principal shareholder of the corporation had a long history of trading in real estate does not necessarily mean that his intention in the transaction at hand was to trade. That fact could be outweighed by the income-producing capital nature of the particular property in question.

The Court held that the gain was not income from a business, based on the foregoing reasons. However, some believe that the arguments for business income are stronger in this case and that the decision in this case should be limited to its specific facts.

Exercise 3

(a) If the company leased the vehicle and provided it for Samuel, the company would be able to deduct the cost of the lease as a business expense limited by the formula in section 67.3. Samuel would have a taxable benefit that would consist of:

ITA: 9, 11, 18, 20, 67.2, 67.3

Standby charge	($400 × 12 × ⅔) =	$3,200
Operating cost benefit	(10,000 × $0.26) =	2,600
Taxable benefit		$5,800

(b) If the company purchased the vehicle, it would claim capital cost allowance using the CCA rate of 30%, limited to a capital cost of $30,000. Interest on funds borrowed would be limited by section 67.2, thus receiving a tax reduction. This option requires the company to lay out cash and the company should do an analysis of which of the first two options is better for it for the period of time the automobile is needed.

Samuel would have a taxable benefit that would consist of:

Standby charge	2% × $22,000 × 12 =	$5,280
Operating cost benefit	10,000 × $0.26 =	2,600
Taxable benefit		$7,880

(c) The allowance would cost the company $3,730, calculated as follows:

$0.55 × 5,000 km =	$2,750
$0.49 × 2,000 km =	980
Total	$3,730

This amount would be deductible as an expense for the employer as it is tied to the CRA's automobile expense deduction limits.

Samuel's operating costs incurred for business purposes = $1,029 ($2,500 × 7,000/17,000) plus depreciation. Samuel would be receiving $3,730 per year, which implies $2,701 ($3,730 – $1,029) for depreciation.

Exercise 4

The $225,000 would be considered a capital receipt based on the

62 DTC 1148 (Ex. Ct.)

Parsons-Steiner Limited v. M.N.R. case.

The following paraphrased excerpt from that case will help explain the conclusion:

> On the whole therefore having regard to the importance of the franchise to Cars' business, the length of time the relationship had subsisted, the extent to which the appellant's business was affected by its loss both in decreased sales and by reason of its inability to replace it with anything equivalent, and the fact that from that time the appellant was in fact out of business, leads to a conclusion that this was a capital transaction. The payment in question was to replace "a capital asset of an enduring nature". It was one which Cars had built up over the years and which on the termination of the franchise they were obliged to relinquish. The payment received in respect of its loss was accordingly a capital receipt.

Exercise 5

Various factors must be examined in the determination of whether the dispositions should be considered income from a business or a capital gain.

ITA: 248(1)

Primary intention

The stated primary intention was to develop the properties into shopping plazas, thus, to earn income from these properties. However, this intention must be supported by objectively observable behavioural factors.

CHAPTER 4

Behavioural factors

Relationship of the transaction to the taxpayer's business

AMC's main business appears to be the development and management of revenue properties. It also frequently engages in the sale of undeveloped properties. The fact that these transactions are closely related to AMC's main business and the fact that its major shareholder is a realtor and, therefore, heavily involved in buying and selling land, points to treatment of the sales as income from a business.

AMC often sells property when it is not feasible to develop and, as such, purchases land with good resale value. This focus on good resale value indicates an underlying intention of selling property for a gain. This indicates a treatment of the dispositions as business income.

Number and frequency of transactions

Transactions of buying and selling undeveloped land are frequently entered into as it is AMC's business to develop land. This frequency indicates treatment as income from a business.

Conclusion

It could be argued that AMC's primary intention was to hold the third parcel of land to develop it and earn income from it; therefore, its sale should be treated as a capital gain. But because of the likely secondary intention of earning a profit on its sale, the frequency of this type of transaction, and the closeness to AMC's primary business, it is likely the court would consider all the dispositions as income from a business. The court could say that AMC held onto the third parcel for six months only in order to get the best price and therefore to make a substantial profit.

Exercise 6

Since actual cost is known it must be used. Therefore, an assumption about cost is not appropriate. Market value is probably best reflected in net realization value for this inventory. The following calculation of inventory values could be used:

Item	Actual cost	Reg. 1801 Market	Ssec. 10(1) Each item at lower of cost or market
Mufflers	$1,120.00	$ 992.00	$ 992.00
Tailpipes	745.75	706.50	706.50
Exhaust system	633.75	604.50	604.50
Shock absorbers	4,979.20	5,056.00	4,979.20
Brackets	1,304.80	1,211.60	1,211.60
Clamps	1,134.90	1,396.80	1,134.90
Total		$9,967.40	$9,628.70

Either the $9,967.40 value can be used or the $9,628.70 value can be used. However, the ending valuation method used in a particular year must be the same as that used for the end of the preceding year.

ITR: 1801
ITA: 10(1), 10(2.1)

Exercise 7

(a) The *income-earning purpose test* is found in paragraph 18(1)(a) — the "general limitation" re: an outlay or expense made or incurred for the purpose of gaining or producing income from the business or property. Students can list any of the following related sections, ITs or ICs in their answer:

ITA: 18(1)(a), 18(1)(b), 18(1)(c), 18(1)(e), 18(1)(h), 67, 248(1)

Related sections: subsections 20(1), 20(16); subsection 21(1); subsection 26(2); section 30

ITs: IT-99R5; Income Tax Folio: S3-F9-C1; IT-211R; IT-261R; IT-357R2; IT-364; IT-467R2; IT-475; IT-487; IT-521R

ICs: IC 77-11; IC 88-2

(b) The *capital test* is found in paragraph 18(1)(*b*) — no deduction is allowed for an outlay, loss, or replacement of capital, a payment on account of capital or an allowance in respect of depreciation, obsolescence or depletion except as expressly permitted by this Part.

Related sections: subsection 14(5); subsections 20(1), (10), (16); subsection 24(1); subsection 26(2); section 30

ITs: IT-187; IT-467R2; IT-475

ICs: none

(c) The *exempt income test* is found in paragraph 18(1)(*c*) — limits an outlay or expense to the extent it may reasonable be regarded as having been made or incurred for the purpose of gaining or producing exempt income.

Related sections: none

ITs: IT-467R2

ICs: none

(d) The *reserve test* is found in paragraph 18(1)(*e*) — no deduction for an amount as, or on account of, a reserve, a contingent liability or amount or a sinking fund except as expressly permitted by this Part.

Related sections: none

ITs: IT-321R (archived); IT-467R2

ICs: none

(e) The *personal expenses test* is found in paragraph 18(1)(*h*) — no deduction for personal or living expenses of the taxpayer, other than travel expenses incurred by the taxpayer while away from home in the course of carrying on the taxpayer's business.

Related sections: subsections 20(1), (16); subsection 248(1) "personal or living expenses"

ITs: no primary ITs

ICs: none

(f) The *reasonableness test* is found in section 67, which states no deduction is allowed for an outlay or expense in respect of which any amount is otherwise deductible under this Act, except to the extent that it was reasonable in the circumstances.

Related sections: subsection 8(9); subsection 248(1) "amount"

ITs: no primary ITs

ICs: none

Exercise 8

(A) The deduction of these costs are prohibited, notwithstanding the argument that the lodge was used to produce income from client business.

ITA: 18(1)(*l*)

(B) The deduction of costs are allowed if they were incurred in the ordinary course of the company's business of providing the property for rent. The facts of this case *may* fit this exception.

ITA: 18(1)(*l*)

Exercise 9

First, it must be determined whether any expense incurred may be deducted in respect of the home office. To make this determination, the specific conditions outlined in subsection 18(12) are that:

ITA: 18(12)

(i) the office is the principal place of business; or

(ii) it is used exclusively for the purpose of earning business income and is used on a regular and continuous basis for meeting clients, customers, or patients in respect to the business.

Since Karim performs only consulting work, the home office qualifies under condition (i). Although Amina teaches in addition to consulting, it is only part-time and her principal business is consulting. Therefore, she also qualifies under condition (i). Amina and Karim are carrying on separate self-employed businesses. Since they also live together, the home office expenses would be split on an agreed basis. Assuming that the split was agreed at 50%, both taxpayers would be permitted to deduct 50% of the eligible home office expenses. Eligible home office expense is equal to 500/2,000 square feet times the total home office costs. Supplies, materials, and software would be considered business expenses, not home office expenses. Therefore, Amina and Karim may **each** deduct the following as their 50% share of the expenses:

CHAPTER 4

Home office expense (subsection 18(12))	$23,600 × 25% × 50% =	$2,950
Supplies and materials	$1,800 × 50% =	900
Computer and software lease	$2,300 × 50% =	1,150
Total		$5,000

Exercise 10

(A) — contribution may be made within 120 days of the end of 2018,

— an employer contribution to a defined benefit RPP is deductible where it is made on the recommendation of an actuary in whose opinion the contribution is required so that the plan will have sufficient assets to provide benefits in accordance with its terms as registered,

— in this case, both the current service contribution and the lump-sum amount based on an actuarial valuation would be deductible in 2018 if they are in accordance with the plan.

(B) A full deduction of an amount paid in the year is permitted — or a taxpayer may elect to write it off in equal amounts over the 10-year period beginning in the current year.

ITA: 20(1)(*cc*)
ITA: 20(9)

(C) The deduction of the full amount of utilities connection costs is permitted. Since the taxpayer does not own the gas lines but the utilities company does, the amount is not eligible for capital cost allowance.

ITA: 20(1)(*ee*)

(D) Salary of an owner-employee's spouse is an allowable deduction to a corporation as long as it is reasonable in the circumstances. While $7,000 per month for full-time secretarial work is probably not reasonable, some lesser, reasonable amount would be deductible in this case. The amount in excess of a reasonable amount will not be deductible to the corporation, but will be included in the recipient's income from employment.

Exercise 11

Only ½ of the discount of $43.29 may be deducted because the bond was issued at less than 97% even though within the ⁴/₃ × 4% or 5.33% yield range.

ITA: 20(1)(*f*)

Given that the discount is paid effectively on maturity when the principal amount is repaid, then ½ of the $43.29 or $21.65 is deductible in 2017.

Exercise 12

Net income per financial statements		$150,000
Add: Items deducted in financial statements but not deductible for tax purposes:		
Provision for income taxes — current	25,000	*ITA: 18(1)(e)*
— future	130,000	
Amortization expense	40,000	*ITA: 18(1)(b)*
Non-deductible interest — re interest on late		
taxes	2,500	*ITA: 18(1)(t)*
Bond discount	7,500	*ITA: 18(1)(b), (e)*
Reserve for doubtful debts	10,000	*ITA: 12(1)(d)*
	$365,000	
Deduct: Items not deducted in financial statements but deductible for tax purposes:		
Landscaping costs.	$12,000	*ITA: 20(1)(aa)*
Reserve for doubtful debts	15,000	(27,000)
		ITA: 12(1)(l)
Net Income for tax purposes before CCA	$338,000	

Exercise 13

This transaction would likely involve a receipt of income because the intention is likely to make a profit on the purchase and sale of land. This would be substantiated by the frequency of transactions in land or, at least, the indication of an adventure in the nature of trade. During the year of sale the following income would be computed:

Revenue from the sale of land		$250,000
Less: cost of land	$107,500	
real estate commission	12,500	120,000
Income from the sale of land		$130,000
Less: reserve for amount not due until later year*		
$\dfrac{\$130,000}{\$250,000} \times (\$250,000 - \$110,000)$		72,800
Income after reserve		$ 57,200

ITA: 9
ITA: 20(1)(*n*)

* The reserve is not available, unless the sale occurred within 36 months of the end of the year in which a reserve is to be taken.

ITA: 20(8)(*b*)

Note that the minimum two-year repayment period does not apply on the sale of land which qualifies for the reserve. In the next year, the reserve of $72,800 would be taken into income.

ITA: 12(1)(*e*)(ii), 20(1)(*n*)(ii)

Exercise 14

Authors' Note: The following problem includes GST/HST implications. Students should review Chapter 20 of the textbook, Goods and Services Tax (GST)/Harmonized Sales Tax (HST), before attempting this problem.

Since the corporation is carrying on business, it is engaged in a commercial activity. Therefore, the corporation is required to register and collect HST on its supplies, i.e., sales of goods, which are "taxable supplies." As a registrant, the corporation is entitled to a full input tax credit (ITC) in respect of HST paid or payable on goods and services that it purchases exclusively for use in its commercial activity. If HST collected or collectible on its sales exceeds its ITCs, the corporation must remit the difference. On the other hand, if ITCs exceed HST collected or collectible, a refund of the excess is available.

ETA: 123(1)

ETA: 169(1)

The following is the appropriate HST treatment of the items listed:

(a) Net income per financial statements would have been increased by HST charged which is included in revenue and reduced by HST paid or payable which is included in costs. HST charged net of ITCs from HST paid or payable must be remitted.

(b) There are no HST implications for the provision for income taxes.

(c) HST paid on the purchase of depreciable property provides an ITC, as discussed in Chapter 5. When the cost of the asset is subsequently written off through depreciation or capital cost allowance, there are no further HST implications.

Landscaping goods and services would involve payment of GST/HST on taxable supplies and, hence, would give rise to an ITC.

The following costs would not involve the payment of HST, since they are for exempt supplies:

(a) interest paid on income tax due results from a financial service,

(b) bond interest also results from a financial service, and

(c) similarly, the reserve for doubtful debts has by itself no GST/HST implication as it is not a supply. This is different from the bad debt expense incurred when an account receivable is actually written off. In such cases, the registrant is entitled to recover the GST/HST portion of the write-off.

Chapter 5

The Capital Cost Allowance System for Depreciable Property, Including Intangibles

Learning Goals

Know, Understand and Explain

By the end of this chapter you will know, understand and be able to explain:

- The basic provisions of the *Income Tax Act* (the Act) that relate to depreciable property, including intangibles.

- The similiarities and differences between the accounting and tax deductions as they relate to depreciable and capital property.

- That capital cost allowance amounts are the tax equivalent of accounting amortization/depreciation for capital, including intangible, property.

- How to classify commonly purchased assets given the information and circumstances.

- The tax implications of asset disposal as it relates to depreciable, including intangible, property.

Apply

By the end of this chapter you will be able to apply your knowledge and understanding to:

- Correctly calculate capital cost allowance amounts that replace accounting deductions.

- Advise taxpayers on the tax implications of the purchase and sale of these assets.

Review Questions
¶5,800 in the Study Guide

Multiple Choice Questions
¶5,825 in the Study Guide

Exercises
¶5,850 in the Study Guide

Assignment Problems
¶5,875 in the Study Guide

CHAPTER 5 — LEARNING CHART

Problem Descriptions

Textbook Example Problems

5-1	Tax shield
5-2	Half-year rule
5-3	Disposal of depreciable assets
5-4	Short fiscal year
5-5	Additions and disposals over five years
5-6	Replacement property

Multiple Choice Questions

1	Luxury vehicle CCA
2	Leasehold improvements
3	Intangible Assets
4	Leasehold improvements
5	CCA
6	Patent options

Exercises

1	Choice of CCA class
2	Luxury automobile CCA
3	Sale of luxury automobile
4	CCA schedule
5	Rental property CCA
6	CCA calculations
7	CCA schedule
8	Personal CCA on automobile
9	Sale of intangible capital property
10	Purchase and sale of intangible capital property
11	Purchase and sale of goodwill
12	CCA calculations

Assignment Problems

1	Purchase and sale of assets
2	Leasehold improvements
3	Luxury automobile
4	Goodwill
5	Short fiscal year
6	Available for use
7	Asset disposition
8	CCA schedule
9	CCA on change of use
10	Intangible asset transactions
11	Intangible asset transactions
12	Five independent issues
13	CCA schedule

Problem Descriptions

14	Class 12 assets and half-year rule
15	Schedule 1 reconciliation and CCA schedule
16	Insurance and damages receipts
17	Purchase and sale of assets
18	Deductible expenses and employee benefits
19	Schedule 1 reconciliation and CCA

Study Notes

¶5,800   REVIEW QUESTIONS

(1) In the year of acquisition only one-half of the capital cost of an asset is added to the CCA class. Comment.

(2) If an asset is sold for less than the UCC balance in the class then there will be a terminal loss that can be used to reduce income. Comment.

(3) The "cost amount" of depreciable property is the original cost of the asset. Comment.

(4) The "capital cost" of depreciable property is the original cost of the asset before any CCA is claimed. Comment.

(5) The half-year rule applies to all property acquired in all CCA classes. Comment.

(6) The half-year rule is designed to take into account the period of ownership during the year and the fact that not all assets are purchased at the beginning of the year. Comment.

(7) CCA can be claimed in the year that title and the incidence of ownership are acquired by the taxpayer. Comment.

(8) Once a CCA claim has been made a taxpayer cannot go back and change the amount of the prior year's claim. Comment.

(9) When the fiscal period of a business is less than 365 days then the CCA must be prorated for the number of days in the fiscal year. Comment.

(10) Once an asset has been disposed of, then no CCA can be claimed on that asset. Comment.

(11) A client bought a new piece of equipment that cost her $50,000. Because of the nature of the asset she has received a government grant of $15,000 to help pay for it. She thinks she can only depreciate $35,000. Comment.

(12) It has cost a client $20,000 in legal fees to obtain a patent on some new equipment. Given his profitability, he is unhappy that he can only depreciate these costs as a Class 14 asset over the 20-year life of the patent but his controller says that he does not have any choice. Comment.

(13) Mrs. Smith has incorporated her company to carry on a retail business. As part of the start-up costs she has paid $800 to have the company incorporated and $10,000 to obtain the indefinite-life franchise that she wanted. Each of these expenditures is a Class 14.1 intangible depreciable property and since they are different they each go into a separate Class 14.1 pool. Comment.

(14) Mr. Fin has come to tell you that he has decided to wind up his business and retire. He is in the process of selling all of his assets but he cannot find one buyer who will continue the business and pay him something for goodwill. He is disappointed since he has a balance of $15,000 in his Class 14.1 that cannot be used. Comment.

¶5,825 MULTIPLE CHOICE QUESTIONS

Question 1

Authors Note: The following question includes GST/HST implications. Students should review Chapter 20 of the textbook, "Goods and Services Tax (GST)/Harmonized Sales Tax (HST)", before attempting this problem.

X Ltd. purchased a $50,000 passenger vehicle in 2018. What is the maximum amount that X Ltd. may claim as capital cost allowance for the vehicle in 2018, ignoring HST and GST?

(A) $7,500

(B) $9,000

(C) $4,500

(D) $4,725

Question 2

R Ltd. owns a restaurant business which it carries on in rented premises. R Ltd. redecorated and renovated in 2018 and made $80,000 of leasehold improvements. The lease expires on December 31, 2022 (five years) and has two successive renewal options of three years each. Assuming that R Ltd. has a December 31 year end, what is the maximum CCA that R Ltd. can claim in 2018 in respect of these improvements?

(A) $5,000

(B) $8,000

(C) $10,000

(D) $16,000

Question 3

In the year, ABC Ltd. purchased goodwill relating to a business for $100,000. Assuming ABC Limited has no other depreciable property, what is the maximum write-off that ABC Ltd. can claim for this goodwill in the year?

(A) $2,500

(B) $5,000

(C) $7,000

(D) $5,250

Question 4

On January 1, 2016, ABC Ltd. signed a five-year lease for retail space for a store. The lease expires on December 31, 2020, and has two successive renewal options for three years each, In 2018, ABC Ltd. made $60,000 of leasehold improvements to this space. Assuming that ABC Ltd. has a December 31 year end, what is the maximum capital cost allowance claim that ABC Ltd. can make in 2018 in respect of these improvements?

(A) $3,750

(B) $5,000

(C) $6,000

(D) $7,500

Question 5

During the year, Swiss Restaurants purchased the following assets for its restaurant and catering business:

Moulds for fancy chocolate items ($300 each)	$ 1,200
An accounting program (computer software)	600
Linens for tables in the restaurants	400
Cutlery, dishes, and kitchen utensils costing less than $500 each	15,000

What is the maximum CCA claim for these assets?

(A) $8,600

(B) $16,300

(C) $16,900

(D) $17,200

Question 6

The new controller of a pharmaceutical company has asked you how the legal costs to obtain a 20-year patent on a new drug are treated for tax purposes. Which one of the following options is not available?

(A) include in Class 14

(B) include in Class 44

(C) deduct in the year incurred

(D) include in Class 14.1

¶5,850   EXERCISES

Exercise 1

ITA: 14(5), 20(1)(a);
ITR: 1100

Businesses in two plazas operating on either side of a very busy city street decided to pool their promotional efforts. They also decided to build an overpass so that customers could avoid crossing the street when shopping at the plazas. The overpass was constructed at a cost of $150,000 after appropriate arrangements were made with the city because the footings to the overpass had to be placed on city property. These arrangements did not include a leasehold interest in the city property.

— REQUIRED

In what class of assets can the overpass be placed for capital cost allowance?

Exercise 2

ITA: 13(7); ITR: 7307(1)

Harrison Chen, an insurance salesperson, acquired a luxury antique sports car in 2018 for a capital cost of $42,000. The car will be used 40% of the time in performing his duties of employment.

— REQUIRED

Compute Harrison's estimated CCA in his first and second year of owning the car (ignore HST).

Exercise 3

ITA: 20(16.1), 21(1);
ITR: 1100(2.5), 1100(6)

Scott is a commission salesman who has been claiming capital cost allowance on his automobile under paragraph 8(1)(j). The automobile was purchased for $38,000 (including 13% HST) in October 2016. The undepreciated capital cost of his automobile at January 1, 2018, was $20,170. In 2018, he sold the automobile for $12,000. Scott does 75% of his driving for employment purposes out of 16,000 kilometres of total driving.

— REQUIRED

(A) What are the tax consequences in 2018 to Scott on the sale of the old car?

(B) What are the tax consequences in 2018 if Scott buys a new car in October 2018 for $36,000 including HST (13%)? His net commission income after deducting cash expenses for 2018 is $3,000.

Exercise 4

ITA: 20(1)(a); ITR: 1100;
Sched. II, III

The following balances were found in the various classes of depreciable assets on the books of Wasting Assets Ltd., as at January 1, 2018:

Class 1 (see (1) below)	$120,000
Class 8	75,000
Class 10 (truck for transportation of goods)	40,000
Class 13 (see (2) below)	42,000
Class 14 (see (3) below)	54,400

Additional information and transactions during 2018:

(1) The Class 1 undepreciated capital cost represents two buildings costing $100,000 each. One building was sold for $150,000 during 2018.

(2) The Class 13 balance relates to a long-term lease on a warehouse for 30 years with an option to renew for a further 20 years. The original cost of the leasehold improvements in 2002, when the lease was entered into, was $50,000.

(3) Class 14 consists of a patent for 20 years costing $68,000 on January 1, 2014. (Ignore the effects of the leap years in the period.)

(4) Purchases during the year:

Manufacturing equipment	$50,000
Office equipment	10,000

— *REQUIRED*

Prepare a schedule showing the maximum capital cost allowance deductions for tax purposes in 2018.

Exercise 5

ITA: 13

Liam O'Neille acquired an apartment building a few years ago for $240,000. The cost of the entire property was allocated as follows:

Land	$80,000
Building	$160,000

The UCC of the building as of the beginning of this year was $144,500, and the net rental income for last year was $4,800. Liam turned 65 years old this year and decided to begin his retirement by selling his apartment building. He received $280,000, $100,000 of which was allocated to the land and $180,000 to the building.

— *REQUIRED*

Calculate the maximum capital cost allowance that may be claimed in the current year, and compute the undepreciated capital cost, recapture, or terminal loss.

Exercise 6

ITA: 20(1)

The following are independent situations:

(a) Gimcrack Inc. purchases its sole asset, costing $100,000, on February 15. The company has a February 28 year end. The asset purchased is a Class 8 asset.

— *REQUIRED*

Calculate the capital cost allowance that may be claimed in the taxation year under the following independent scenarios.

    (i) Fiscal period is 365 days.

    (ii) Fiscal period is 90 days.

(b) RSI Ltd. sells computers and has a December 31 year end. RSI Ltd. leased a warehouse this year for ten years with a renewal option of two years and a second renewal option of three years. Leasehold improvements of $25,000 were made to the warehouse during the year. RSI has no other leasehold improvement assets.

— *REQUIRED*

Calculate the maximum amount of CCA that may be claimed in this, the first taxation year.

(c) Constabulary Ltd. acquired franchise rights for the amount of $25,000 to operate a doughnut and coffee shop. The franchise is valid for a period of 15 years commencing March 1. Constabulary Ltd.'s year end is July 31.

— *REQUIRED*

What CCA or other deduction is Constabulary Ltd. allowed this year?

Exercise 7

ITA: 20(1)

Mr. E. Presley has been operating an automobile repair business since 2004. The fiscal period of the corporation ends on September 30. The business owns the following assets:

(a) A frame building used as a garage was acquired in 2008. The capital cost of the building in 2008 was $250,000. The UCC of this Class 1 asset was $208,985 as of the last year end. During the current year, renovations were made to the garage in the amount of $20,000.

(b) A warehouse adjacent to the frame building was leased. The lease has a term of five years with five options for renewal of five years each. The lease period commences April 15. The cost of leasehold improvements was $70,000.

(c) Computer equipment was acquired on April 15, 2015. The UCC at October 1, 2017 is $40,000. The equipment was used to perform analysis for repairs.

(d) Two trucks were acquired in a previous fiscal period. The UCC as of the last year end for these Class 10 assets was $25,000. One of the trucks was sold this year for gross proceeds of $10,000. The capital cost of the truck was $15,000. Selling costs incurred to sell the truck were $1,000.

(e) The rights to a licence to sell special racing car parts was purchased for $30,000. The licence is valid for a period of 15 years commencing June 1 this year.

— *REQUIRED*

Compute CCA for Mr. Presley's automobile repair business for the taxation year ended September 30, 2018. Ignore the leap year effects.

Exercise 8

ITA: 13(7)(*d*)

Steven purchased a car in 2016 for $14,600. His business use of the car during 250 days each year based on mileage of 16,000 kilometres in total and the fair market values of the car in each of the years to the present were as follows:

	Business use	Fair market value
2016	85%	$14,600
2017	80%	12,200
2018	90%	9,800

— *REQUIRED*

Compute the maximum capital cost allowance that can be claimed.

Exercise 9

ITA: 13(1), 20(1)(*a*)

Ms. Glutton sold her unincorporated grocery business in 2021 and received $45,000 for goodwill. The business had a December 31 year end. The grocery store had been purchased on January 2, 2018 with a payment of $10,800 for goodwill at that time

— *REQUIRED*

Compute the effect of the 2021 sale on Ms. Glutton's income. Assume that maximum deductions for amortization have been made in previous years.

Exercise 10

ITA: 20(1)(*a*)

ITA: 13(1), 20(1)(*a*)

Buylo Ltd., which has been in the same business, except as noted below, since 2018, made the following purchases and sales throughout the period 2018 to 2024.

Jan. 1, 2018	Purchased goodwill at $40,000.
June 1, 2020	Purchased a government licence with an indefinite life for $50,000.
Mar. 1, 2021	Purchased a trademark for $20,000.
Nov. 1, 2022	Purchased goodwill for $50,000.
Sept. 7, 2023	Sold goodwill for $100,000.
Aug. 3, 2024	Sold all of the remaining assets of the business to a competitor for $500,000 of which $150,000 could be attributed to the licence and $200,000 to the trademark.

— REQUIRED

Calculate the effect of these transactions on income for the 2018 to 2025 taxation years, assuming   ITA: 13(1), 20(1)(a)
the company always took the maximum tax amortization deductions each year for its fiscal years ending
December 31. Calculate the amount of UCC balance as at January 1, 2025.

Exercise 11
ITA: 13(1), 20(1)(a)

Chalupshka Inc. has carried on business from the beginning of its 2018 taxation year. In that year, it
purchased a store and paid $5,000 for goodwill. In 2020, the store was sold and $6,500 was received for
the goodwill. Also, in 2020, Chalupshka Inc. purchased another store and paid $4,450 for goodwill. Then,
in 2021, Chalupshka Inc. ceased to carry on business and sold the business with no part of the proceeds
attributed to goodwill which had a nil fair market value.

— REQUIRED

Calculate the income effects of these transactions for each of the years in question, assuming that
Chalupshka Inc. claimed the maximum CCA each year.

Exercise 12

Golden Horseshoe Manufacturing Ltd., incorporated in Ontario in 1975, manufactures widgets in a
small community just north of Toronto. The following balances are reflected in the company's books of
account and tax records as at January 1, 2018. The controller has asked us to prepare a schedule for tax
purposes to reflect the corporation's capital asset transactions and to calculate the maximum capital
cost allowance for 2018 and the UCC balances on January 1, 2019. (Note: Ignore the effect of the ssec.
13(4) election on the sale of the building).

| | Book records | | | Tax records | |
Type of asset	Rate of write-off	Cost	Book Value	Class	Balance Jan. 1, 2017
Brick building	20 yr.	$160,000	$24,000	3	$70,000
Equipment					
— office	10 yr	10,000	4,000	8	6,000
— manufacturing	5 yr.	65,000	28,000	43	27,000
Trucks (for transportation of goods) . . .	5 yr.	30,000	12,000	10	13,000
Leasehold improvements (Note (1)) . . .	13 yr.	24,000	21,176	13	19,500
Patent (Note (2))	17.5 yr	29,000	26,500	44	25,375
Intangibles	Indefinite	Nil	Nil	14.1	Nil

NOTES:

(1) The leasehold improvement represents an improvement to a leased warehouse in downtown
Toronto on January 1, 2016, costing $24,000. The lease is for three years with two successive options to
renew of five years each.

(2) The patent was purchased on June 30, 2016 at a cost of $29,000. The originator of the patent
had registered the patent on January 1, 2014.

(3) During 2018 the company made the following expenditures:

(a) Purchased a newly built brick building in Hamilton, Ontario for total cost of $350,000,
including land costing $100,000. The building is used 95% for the manufacturing operations.

(b) Additional expenditures concerning the building:

Paved parking lot	$ 5,000
Landscaping	4,000
Utilities service connection	1,000

(c) Further renovations to leased warehouse (see Note (1), above) of $9,000 on January 1, 2018.

(d) Equipment purchased in 2018:

Computer hardware and systems software	$10,000
Manufacturing	25,000
Office	2,000
Small tools (costing less than $500 each)	6,000

(e) Purchased a 5-year licence to manufacture a related product line from a foreign manufacturer on April 1, 2018 at a cost of $12,000.

(f) Legal fees, paid on October 1, 2018 in reorganizing the capital structure of the company, cost $11,000.

(4) During 2018 the company disposed of the following assets:

	Proceeds (net)	Capital cost
Building (brick)	$300,000	$160,000
Office equipment	1,000	1,500
Manufacturing equipment (class 43)	5,000	8,000

¶5,875 ASSIGNMENT PROBLEMS

Type 1 Problems

Problem 1

Memorandum
Acme Inc.

To:	Staff Accountant
From:	Controller
Date:	Month xx, Year xx
Subject:	CCA Calculations and Adjustments

We are in the process of completing the corporate tax return and we have come to the fixed asset section, where we have identified three things that I would like you to do.

(1) Calculate the maximum CCA that can be claimed, as well as any other income inclusions or deductions.

(2) Calculate the ending UCC balance in each class.

(3) Identify adjustments you will need to make to reconcile accounting income and income for tax purposes.

The following is the information in our files:

Acme Inc. has been in business for a number of years. The following are the balances in its CCA classes at the end of its last fiscal year:

Class		Note	Rate	Balance
1	Single building (NRB)	1	6%	$ 225,000
8	Multiple assets	2	20%	30,000
10	Multiple assets	3	30%	20,000
10.1	Passenger vehicle	4	30%	13,000

During the year Acme had the following transactions:

(1) It sold its building and moved into rented space. It received proceeds of $250,000 for the building which had an original cost of $275,000 and a net book value of $180,000.

(2) It sold a class 8 asset for $3,000 which had an original cost of $6,500 and a net book value of $3,600.

(3) It bought a class 10 asset for $6,000. It also sold a class 10 asset for $8,000 which had an original cost of $7,000 and a net book value of $5,500.

(4) It sold the class 10.1 asset for $15,000 which had an original cost of $45,000 and a net book value of $35,000.

Problem 2

Memorandum
Acme Inc.

To:	Staff Accountant
From:	Controller
Date:	Month xx, Year xx
Subject:	Leasing Issues

When we moved out of our building we rented a building. To make it work for us we had to make leasehold improvements costing $250,000. Our lease has a term of five years with a five-year renewal period. I would like you to determine what is included in leasehold improvements, how much we can deduct for the leasehold improvements, and what lease terms would have been ideal to maximize the tax deduction.

Problem 3

Memorandum

To: Accounting Associate
From: Tax Manager
Date: Month xx, Year xx
Subject: Seaforth Consulting Inc.

The Controller at Seaforth Consulting Inc., our client, has reached out to us with some questions about the tax treatment of some capital transactions. She has asked us to provide her with detailed notes on how to treat them on the company's tax return for its year ended August 31, 2018 and how to report it on the 2018 T4 for Judy Wall, the corporation's president.

Seaforth, a Canadian-controlled private corporation, provides a car for its president. In its 2014 fiscal year it purchased a new car for her use costing $45,000 plus HST. On December 31, 2017 they replaced this car; they sold the old one for $25,000 and bought a new one for $50,000 plus 13% HST.

The NBV of the car purchased in 2014 was $27,000 at the time of sale. The corporation has claimed maximum CCA each year.

Please report to me the impact of these transactions on the company and on Judy.

Problem 4

Memorandum

To: Accounting Associate
From: Tax Manager
Date: Month xx, Year xx
Subject: Green Proprietorship

Our client, Ms. Green, has asked us to determine the impact of some transactions involving the purchase and sale of goodwill projected over the next few years.

Effective January 1, 2018, she purchased a health food store. As part of the purchase price she paid $20,000 for goodwill. She plans to build up the customer base, and in 2023 she expects to sell the store. As part of the selling price, she expects to receive $30,000 for goodwill.

Ms. Green operates the store as a proprietorship, with a December 31st year end and intends to claim the maximum CCA deduction.

In addition to considering the impact on income of the projected sale of goodwill in 2023 for $30,000, consider the impact if Ms. Green sold the goodwill in 2023 for:

(a) $20,000; and

(b) $10,000.

Assume that the legislation in this area remains unchanged in the period under consideration.

Problem 5

Memorandum

To: Accounting Associate
From: Tax Manager
Date: Month xx, Year xx
Subject: Farthing Proprietorship

Our client, Vicky Farthing, has decided to purchase, personally, a used building in 2018 to be used in her new proprietorship business, which is considered to have started with preliminary work on May 1, 2018 and will have a December 31 year end. As part of her planning, she would like to know what CCA deduction she can take on the purchase of the building if it becomes available for use on September 30th. The cost of the building is $350,000.

Would there be a difference if she incorporated her business on May 1, 2018 and had the corporation buy the building to be available for use on September 30th? The corporation's year end would be December 31.

¶5,875

Problem 6

Memorandum

To: Accounting Associate
From: Tax Manager
Date: Month xx, Year xx
Subject: Huang Manufacturing Inc.

Huang Manufacturing Inc. has been in business for many years with a December 31st year end. Our audit staff has become aware that, in 2018, the company bought a new manufacturing machine at a cost of $500,000 plus HST. They received the machine on November 30th, but it took some time for them to install it, so it wasn't ready to be used until January 15, 2019.

We need to determine the maximum CCA that can be claimed in 2018 and 2019 related to this machine.

Problem 7

ITA: 13, 20(16)

Memorandum

To: Accounting Associate
From: Tax Manager
Date: Month xx, Year xx
Subject: Silvia Fields

business income not employment

Our client, Silvia Fields, is the self-employed operator of a VIP delivery service. Three years ago, Silvia purchased her only asset, a van, for a cost of $24,000. The van has been used 100% for business deliveries since it was purchased. The UCC balance in Class 10 at the beginning of this year is $14,280. On March 1, Silvia sold the van for $10,300 and leased a new van for $400 a month.

Please draft the contents of a letter to Sylvia explaining the income tax implications of the disposition of the van.

Problem 8

ITA: 13(1), 13(2), 20(1)(a), 20(16.1); ITR: 1100(1), 1100(2.5), 1100 (3), 1101(5p), 1103(2h), 7307(1)(b); Sch. II, III

On March 1, 2018, Jennifer Lobo incorporated Lobo Enterprises Inc. (LEI)) with a December 31 year end. The corporation purchased the licence to manufacture the computer software version of the latest trivia game, "Tax is a Microcosm of Life on DVD". LEI acquired the following assets:

Manufacturing equipment	$20,000
Tools (each costing under $500)	16,000
Dies and moulds	8,000
Computer equipment and systems software	12,000
Photocopier	6,000
Office furnishings	15,000
Customer lists (expected to be used indefinitely)	4,000
Delivery van	28,000
TV commercial video tape	22,000
Chairs and tables (for the employee eating area)	2,500
Automobile (for use by sales manager)	38,000
Licence to manufacture, based on patented information, "Tax is a Microcosm of Life on DVD" for three years ending February 28, 2021	30,000
Made improvements on the building that LEI leased on March 1, 2018; the lease was for three years with two successive options to renew of three years and four years	9,000

During 2019, LEI made the following disposals:

Sold the photocopier	(4,000)
Sold the automobile	(23,000)
Sold the TV commercial video tape	(18,000)
Sold some of the tools (costing less than $500 each)	(5,000)

You have been asked to prepare a schedule to show the maximum capital cost allowance for the fiscal years ended December 31, 2018 and December 31, 2019, ignoring HST considerations. For file documentation, where choices are available, state the reasons for your decision. Ignore the effects, if any, of a leap year.

Problem 9

ITA: 13(7)

Memorandum

To: Accounting Associate
From: Tax Manager
Date: Month xx, Year xx
Subject: Sale of Residence

On June 1, 2018, a residential property owned by an individual was sold for fair market value of $305,000. The property originally cost $280,000. On January 20, 2016, it was converted into a rental property. At that time the property had a fair market value of $320,000.

I would like you to research the following question. If the building was the only asset in Class 1, which has a 4% capital cost allowance rate, how much capital cost allowance may be deducted for the years 2015 through 2017, inclusive? [Note that where an individual has income from property, the taxation year for that income is the full calendar year, i.e., there cannot be a short taxation year for that income.]

Problem 10

ITA: 13, 20(1)(a)

Sharp is a musician. In 2018, he purchased the name of a popular local band that stopped performing earlier that year. The cost of the name was $16,000. Also in 2018, he purchased for $5,000 an indefinite-life licence from the city which allowed him to perform on a street corner on Saturday afternoons. In 2019, Sharp found that he wanted to spend more time in the studio, so he sold the street corner licence for $6,000. In 2021, Sharp decided to break up his band and pursue a career as an accountant. He sold the band name for $20,000.

Sharp has not yet filed his tax return for 2021. The year end of the business is December 31.

You have been asked to prepare a schedule calculating the balance of the CCA account on January 1, 2021 and calculating the impact on income for 2021. Assume that the legislation remained unchanged throughout the period described.

Problem 11

ITA: 13, 20(1)(a), 20(1)(cc); IT-206R

Con-Glo Corporation has been involved in various food services businesses since its incorporation in 2018. Con-Glo has a December 31 year end. You have been asked by the controller to examine the transactions involving various intangible assets due to an impending sale of the business. The controller wants to ensure that he understands the implications on the sale in 2023. You have been provided with the following information.

Shortly after the business was incorporated, Con-Glo developed, on its own, a property that it owned into its first family restaurant. In 2018, after operating this business for a number of years and ensuring that it was profitable, another restaurant was purchased. The purchase included goodwill in the amount of $68,000. The second restaurant had more of a roadhouse atmosphere. The business had obtained an unlimited life liquor licence. The value of the licence at the time of the purchase was $15,850, and this amount was allocated to the licence in the purchase agreement.

Con-Glo operated the two restaurants until 2019 when it purchased a fast food franchise. The franchise was for an undefined number of years and cost $103,000. Also in 2019, it was determined that the original family restaurant would be more successful if it obtained a liquor licence. In order to obtain the licence a presentation had to be made to the liquor licensing board. Con-Glo paid $29,000 in legal fees related to the presentation to the board.

The fast food restaurant, while successful, was too much of a drain on the time of the owners of Con-Glo and was sold in 2022. The value of the franchise agreement was determined to be $110,000.

In 2023, the second restaurant was sold. Con-Glo received $80,000 for the goodwill and $60,000 for the liquor licence.

Due to health problems of the owner's wife, Con-Glo is also considering a sale of the balance of their restaurants in 2024. The selling price will include $250,000 for goodwill.

The controller has asked you to prepare a schedule calculating the UCC balance for the intangible asset transactions as of January 1, 2025, and determine the impact of the above transactions on income for 2018 through 2024. Assume that the company took the maximum tax write-offs that it was entitled to each year. (Hint: consider paragraph 20(1)(cc).) Assume also that Con-Glo was deemed to be in the same business in respect of its restaurant and fast food business as per IT-206R and that the legislation remained unchanged from 2018 to 2025.

Problem 12

ITA: 20(1), 20(16)

For each of the following independent situations identify the deduction for CCA, amortization, or other amount.

(a) Janice Martin was an employee of Bayshore Ltd. She was required to use her car in her employment duties and at the end of last year the UCC of her car (Class 10) was $3,500. She left Bayshore during this year and began working for Executive Search Service, where she was not required to use her car. Janice sold her car this year for $3,200.

(b) Ramesh acquired a residential rental building on September 1 this year at a cost of $75,000. His net rental income for the four months is $2,000. He wants to claim the maximum CCA.

(c) In a prior year, William acquired two residential rental buildings at a cost of $60,000 each. He has sold one for $90,000. The opening UCC of each building was $45,000. Ignore any capital gain.

(d) Colin bought a piece of land that he is renting to a farmer for pasturing his cows. The land cost $35,000 and Colin received $1,500 in rent. Is Colin restricted on the CCA he is allowed?

(e) Randi sold her residential rental property last year for $100,000. The allocation was $75,000 for the building and $25,000 for the land. Her legal fees for selling the property were $2,000. What are her proceeds of disposition for the building?

Problem 13

ITA: 13, 20(1)(*a*);
ITR: 1100; Sched. II, III

Jon's Auto Parts Ltd., which manufactures small equipment, was incorporated in 1993 and had the following balances in its records concerning its capital assets as at January 1, 2018.

	Amortization		CCA	
Type of asset	*Straight-line*	*Book value*	*Class*	*UCC*
Land	Nil	$102,000		
Building	40 years	900,000	1	$568,000
Equipment	5 years	163,000	8	39,000
Rolling stock — trucks, etc. (for transportation of goods)	3 years	306,000	10	170,000
Leasehold improvements (see note (1), below)	life of lease	113,000	13	165,000
Licences	5 years	70,000	14	87,393
Intangibles	indefinite	Nil	14.1	Nil

Additional Information

(1) The Class 13 assets consist of:

— Improvements to a leased warehouse costing $100,000 in 2017. The remaining length of the lease in 2017 was six years with two successive options of four years.

— Improvements to a leased office space for head office downtown, costing $81,600 in 2016. The remaining length of the lease was five years with an option to renew for an additional one year.

(2) The licences were purchased to start on April 22, 2016, at a cost of $110,500 and had a life of five years.

(3) During 2018, the company had the following capital transactions:

Additions:　　　　　　　　　　　　　　　10%.　　　　　　1 300 000
— Purchased, in June, a new concrete manufacturing building costing $1,625,000, including $325,000 for land. Take out land
— Additional expenditures re the building:
　Paved parking lot for employees . . . . $ 97,000 Class 17
　Erected a steel fence around an outside storage area . . . . 65,000 Class 6
— Further renovations to leased office space, costing . . . . 51,000 Class 13
— Purchased equipment:
　Office equipment . . . . $ 47,000 Class 8
　Manufacturing equipment . . . . 255,000 Class 53
　Radio communication equipment . . . . 60,000 Class 8

— Purchased a distributing licence on March 1, 2018, for five years from a foreign ~~Class 14~~
  manufacturing company of a related product line, cost: $240,000.
— Paid $34,500 in legal fees in reorganizing the capital structure. ~~Class 14.1~~
  ~~Can't deduct $3000~~

Disposals:

	Cost	Book value	Proceeds	
Equipment — office	$ 16,250	$ 4,225	$ 1,950	~~Class 8~~
Brick building in Cl. 1 (excluding land)	1,400,000	900,000	568,000	

You have been asked to prepare a schedule for tax purposes to reflect the above transactions and
calculate the maximum write-off for tax purposes. (Ignore the effects of the replacement property rules
in subsection 13(4) and the effects of leap years.)

Problem 14

ITR: 1100(2)

Both cutlery and word processing software are included in Class 12. Determine, by specific
reference to the *Income Tax Regulations*, whether the half-year rule applies to these two items.

Type 2 Problems

Problem 15

ITA: 13, 14, 18–20;
ITR: 1100; Sched. II, III

The controller of Choleva Products Limited has provided you with the following draft income
statement as well as some notes that she made during the preparation of this statement.

Choleva Products Limited

STATEMENT OF INCOME
For the year ended December 31, 2018

Sales		$ 8,300,000
Cost of goods sold (Note (1))		(6,800,000)
Gross profit		$ 1,500,000
Commission income		70,000
		$ 1,570,000
Administrative and marketing expenses (Note (2))	$500,000	
Amortization (Note (3))	80,000	
Interest on long-term debt (Note (4))	70,000	
Interest on bank indebtedness	120,000	(770,000)
		$ 800,000
Gain on disposal of property, plant and equipment (Note (3))		40,000
Net income before income taxes		$ 840,000
Provision for income taxes		(400,000)
Net income after income taxes		$ 440,000

Notes Prepared by Controller:

(1) The cost of goods sold expense includes the following amounts:

(a) A $9,000 loss from a theft by a warehouse employee;

(b) A $15,000 reserve for future decline in the value of inventory because of new products
expected to be introduced by the competitor. There was no such reserve in 2017.

(2) Administration and marketing expenses include:

(a) An $11,000 increase in the reserve for warranty expenses;

(b) $4,000 of donations to registered charities;

(c) $1,500 for golf club membership dues for the Vice-President of Sales and $2,000 for meals and entertainment expenses at the golf club. The Vice-President of Sales uses the club to generate sales;

(d) $85,000 in accrued bonuses, including $62,000 paid to employees on May 31, 2019, and $23,000 paid to employees on June 30, 2019;

(e) A $15,000 year-end party for all employees;

(f) $8,000 of financing fees incurred in connection with the mortgage of the corporation's new plant, including legal fees of $6,000 and an appraisal fee of $2,000;

(g) $5,000 of legal fees in connection with the purchase of shares of another company; and

(h) $300 for an upgrade of word processing software.

(3) The fixed asset section of the controller's working papers indicate the following:

(a) The undepreciated capital cost balances at January 1, 2018 were as follows:

Class 1	$200,000
Class 8	60,000
Class 10	80,000
Class 13	37,500
Class 14.1	Nil

(b) Gain on disposal of property of plant and equipment consists of the profit on the sale of the corporation's only Class 1 asset (proceeds: $180,000; original cost in 1994: $300,000). The land on which the building was situated was also sold for its fair market value which was equal to its cost in 1994.

(c) During 2018, the corporation made the following purchases:

- A new office building was purchased in October for $700,000. The cost of the related land was $400,000. It cost $20,000 to pave part of the land for use as a parking lot;

- New office furniture was purchased for $25,000. This purchase replaced office furniture which was sold for its $4,000 net book value (original cost: $10,000);

- An unlimited life franchise was purchased for $100,000;

- A 10-year licence to use patented information (expiring June 30, 2028) was purchased on July 1 for $20,000; and

- Improvements on its leased head office premises which were rented in 2016 for four years with two successive options to renew for five years and five years. Improvements had originally been made in 2016 in the amount of $45,000. Additional improvements were made in 2018 at a cost of $28,000.

(d) During the year, the corporation sold some small tools (each costing less than $500) for their net book value of $500.

(4) Interest on long-term debt includes:

(a) Bond discount amortization in the amount of $2,000;

(b) $18,000 of interest on bonds issued to buy shares in another company; and

(c) $50,000 of interest on the mortgage on the new plant.

You have been asked to calculate the corporation's minimum income from business or property for the year ended December 31, 2018. Assume that all expenses are reasonable in the circumstances. For file documentation purposes, you have been asked to support your treatment of each item listed above with a reason or a section reference. Ignore the effects of leap years.

Type 3 Problems

Problem 16

RBL Proprietorship was heavily damaged during a recent street riot. The mobs broke in, set fire to the store, and physically assaulted the owner, Larry. Fortunately the business was insured, and the owner received the following amounts without delay:

Personal injury damage award	$ 50,000
Insurance receipts — business interruption	80,000
Insurance receipts for delivery truck destroyed	30,000
Insurance receipts for leaseholds destroyed by fire	15,000
Total	$175,000

The undepreciated capital cost in Class 10 is $15,000 and in Class 13, $10,000. The original cost of the truck was $35,000 and the original cost of the leaseholds was $20,000.

Larry does not understand why the damages are not treated as an expense for tax purposes. RBL plans to replace the truck immediately. The damage to the leaseholds, however, presents a challenge because the cost to repair the damage far exceeds the insurance compensation. RBL is considering relocating its business to a safer location. The company will then be able to change its image to suit a new clientele. The architect estimates that the leasehold improvements could be completed in 12 months. The total cost for the move would be as follows:

Moving costs	$ 12,000
Business interruption	48,000
Leasehold improvements	60,000
Lease cancellation penalty	4,400
Total	$124,400

Larry would like your advice on the tax implications of his plans.

Problem 17

Dundas Printing Inc. has been in business for the past 20 years. It has only been in the past three years that Bill Peach has taken over the operations from his father (who founded the company and is now retired). As a result of his new-found management freedom and changes in the marketplace, Bill has decided to expand his operations.

One of the printing presses he needed to buy would have been too expensive if he had bought it new, so he found a used press at half the price. The drawback is that it will take some time to get the press into production, since it needs some repairs to put it into workable condition. However, Bill feels that this is still a good buy since it will meet his needs for the next five years, by which time new technology will probably make it obsolete and he will be forced to buy a new machine.

Before his retirement, Bill's father drove a car that the company had purchased for his use at a cost of $45,000. The car was given to Bill for his use on his father's retirement. Bill has now decided that he is going to trade in this car for a car that he always wanted — a sports car that is going to cost $65,000 less the trade-in value of $25,000 for the old car. Bill promises to take you for a ride when it is delivered.

In order to increase his market share, Bill bought all of the assets of one of his competitors. This not only gave him access to some important customers, it also allowed him to acquire some specialized equipment and skilled operators. The vendor had wanted to sell Bill the shares of his company, but Bill had convinced the vendor to sell him the assets, instead, including goodwill of $40,000.

Bill would like your advice on the tax implications of his plans.

Problem 18

Kingston Carpets Inc. ("Kingston") has been operating a retail carpet business out of the same location for the past 18 years. It has been very successful in gaining business from the local developers, who use Kingston almost exclusively to provide their flooring. In addition, Kingston is used extensively by the area insurance adjusters for carpet replaced due to fire and other damages. This business did not come to Kingston overnight. The owners, Andy and Sue Greene, have always spent much of their time promoting their business to these markets.

Both Andy and Sue are avid golfers. They each belong to a different golf club, in order to be members at the clubs where most of their customers play. They find that golf is an activity that has paid off, since they have conducted a significant amount of business through their contacts at the golf clubs. They will often use these clubs for lunch and dinner meetings with customers, as well as for the company's seasonal holiday party.

Last year, the company bought a building across the street from its original retail store. The previous owner had been leasing out the building and had not spent much money on repairs over the last five years. As a result, while Kingston paid a relatively low price for the property, it has had to spend a considerable amount on repairs over the past year. Prior to this purchase, Kingston had been leasing its space.

To maintain their image of success, Sue and Andy both drive expensive cars and often entertain customers at their cottage or on their boat. This approach seems to work, and their customers are always asking when the next outing will be.

Besides treating their customers well, Sue and Andy also treat their employees well. All employees belong to the group benefit plan that provides extended health care, dental, life insurance, and disability coverage. Because of the low coverage from the company's group life and disability insurance, Andy and Sue have had the company take out individual policies on both of them. The beneficiary on the life insurance policies is the company, and on the disability policies the beneficiaries are Andy and Sue.

One of their valued employees was recently divorced and during the divorce her family home was sold. In order to keep her concentrating on business, Andy and Sue had the company loan her enough to buy a house. The loan was secured by the house and no interest was charged. At that time, the company did not have enough cash to make this loan so it had to borrow the funds at prime plus $\frac{1}{2}$%.

In addition to all of this, Andy and Sue have been actively involved in a number of charitable and political activities and have made donations to both. Even these activities have turned into business opportunities. Last year, they gave a donation to a local charity and shortly thereafter they received an order for the new carpet that was to go in the charity's offices.

Advise Sue and Andy on the tax implications of their situation and that of Kingston Carpets.

Problem 19

The controller of Martinez Power Tool Corporation Ltd. has reached out to us, requesting that we calculate the minimum income from business or property of the company for the year ended December 31, 2018 under the provisions of the *Income Tax Act*. She would like us to indicate, briefly, the reasons for making any necessary adjustments to financial accounting profits. She would, also, like us to indicate reasons for not considering an item in our computation, so that all items are accounted for in our work.

The corporation has carried on business in Canada since its incorporation under the *Canada Business Corporations Act* in 1974. Its net income for the year ended December 31, 2018, as determined under generally accepted accounting principles, is as follows:

Martinez Power Tool Corporation Limited
INCOME STATEMENT
For the Year ended December 31, 2018

Sales		$8,500,000
Cost of goods sold:		
Inventory, January 1, 2018	$ 800,000	
Purchases	7,000,000	
	$7,800,000	
Inventory, December 31, 2018	600,000	
Cost of goods sold		(7,200,000)
Gross profit		$1,300,000
Selling expenses	$ 500,000	
General and administrative expenses	100,000	(600,000)
		$ 700,000
Other income		60,000
		$ 760,000
Provision for income taxes		(300,000)
Net income		$ 460,000

Included in this summary of the financial results of Martinez Power Tool Corporation Ltd. are the following details:

(1) Closing inventory was written down, for a possible future impairment of fair market value below cost, by $40,000 in 2018 and $25,000 in 2017.

(2) Selling expenses include:

Meals and entertainment	$11,500
Golf club memberships	10,000
Utilities service connection	1,000
Charitable donations	5,000
Bonus declared but unpaid	20,000

(3) General and administrative expenses include:

Provincial payroll taxes	$ 1,000
Depreciation	29,000

(4) Other income includes:

Gain on disposal of truck (proceeds of $10,000; net book value of $7,500)	2,500
Interest income	3,000
Dividends from taxable Canadian corporations	1,500
Volume rebates	2,000

(5) The truck sold during the year had an original cost of $15,000. A replacement truck was purchased in the year at a cost of $20,000.

(6) The corporation has operated from leased premises since 2016 when it spent $30,000 on infrastructure during the first year of a five-year lease with two three-year renewal options. During 2018, improvements were made to the premises at a cost of $6,000.

(7) In 2018, the corporation purchased goodwill for $36,000 and an indefinite-term licence for $20,000. The corporation had not purchased any intangible assets prior to 2018.

The 2017 T2 Schedule 8 prepared by the corporation indicates that at December 31, 2017, the corporation had the following undepreciated capital cost balances:

Office equipment	$43,000
Trucks	64,000
Leasehold improvements	24,375

The bonus remained unpaid on May 15, 2019 when the 2018 corporate tax return was being prepared.

CHAPTER 5 —
DISCUSSION NOTES FOR REVIEW QUESTIONS

(1) This statement is not correct. The full amount of the capital cost is added to the CCA class. The half-year rule makes a separate adjustment for purposes of calculating CCA in the year of acquisition, to take into consideration the fact that the asset has not been owned for a full year.

ITR: 1100(2)

(2) A terminal loss is allowed only when the asset sold is the last asset in the class. Otherwise, the proceeds are credited to the UCC of the class under the definition of "undepreciated capital cost" and CCA is claimed on the remaining balance.

ITA: 13(21), 20(16)

(3) "Cost amount" reflects the tax value of an asset at a particular moment in time. With respect to depreciable property, cost amount is that proportion of the UCC that the capital cost of the asset is of the capital cost of all the assets in the class. Capital cost is not defined, but as used here, it means the laid-down cost which includes the actual cost plus all costs of preparing the asset for use.

ITA: 248(1) "cost amount"

ITA: 13(21)

(4) The "capital cost" is the amount that is added to the CCA class when the asset is first acquired [item A in the definition of "undepreciated capital cost"]. See (3) above for a broadly worded definition.

ITA: 13(21)

(5) Certain exceptions to the half-year rule are found in the Regulations. However, regulations for leaseholds and for classes like Classes 24, 27, and 29 provide their own version of the half-year rule.

ITR: 1100(2)
ITR: 1100(1)(*b*),
1100(1)(*t*), 1100(1)(*ta*)

(6) The half-year rule is a simple, arbitrary adjustment that is made to reflect a period of ownership during the year. It is a simpler alternative to prorating CCA for the number of days the asset is owned during the year.

(7) Normally, the statement is true. However, the "available-for-use" rules do not allow CCA to be claimed until the asset is available for use by the taxpayer.

ITA: 13(26)–(32)

(8) An Information Circular provides the CRA's position on when the CCA claim for prior years can be changed. If the change results in a lower taxable income for the year, it must be requested within the normal time limits for appeals (see Chapter 14). If the change does not result in a lower taxable income, as, for example, the case of a loss year, the change will be allowed.

IC 84-1, par. 9, 10

(9) A regulation provides for this daily proration in the case of the short taxation year of, for example, an incorporated business, as might occur, for example, in the start-up year of a corporation.

ITR: 1100(3)

(10) Normally, this statement is true. However, a regulation allows a CCA claim equal to one-half the normal CCA in the year of disposition, as compensation for the inability to claim a terminal loss on the disposal of a Class 10.1 automobile. To qualify, the taxpayer must have sold an auto that was in Class 10.1 and that was owned by him or her at the end of the preceding year.

ITR: 1100(2.5)

(11) Your client is correct. The Act reduces the capital cost of depreciable property for grants, subsidies, forgivable loans, deductions from tax, investment allowances or other assistance received on the acquisition of the property. CCA should only be claimed on actual or net cost.

ITA: 13(7.1)

(12) There are four choices available for the legal costs of obtaining the patent:

    (a) deduct them as expenses of representation;

    (b) deduct the costs equally over 10 years;

    (c) capitalize them in Class 14 by an election not to include them in Class 44 and depreciate them over the life of the patent; or

    (d) capitalize the costs in Class 44 and depreciate them at a 25% declining-balance rate.

ITA: 20(1)(cc)

ITA: 20(9)

ITR: 1103(2h)

Any deduction under paragraph 20(1)(*cc*) or subsection 20(9) is subject to recapture.

ITA: 13(12); IT-99R5

(13) There is only one Class 14.1 for all intangible depreciable property for each business. Since Mrs. Smith is only carrying on one business within her corporation, the additions to the company's Class 14.1 in the year will be $10,000. The $800 of incorporation expenses are deductible, since they are not in excess of $3,000.

ITA: 20(1)(b)

(14) He is able to deduct the full Class 14.1 balance as a terminal loss from business in the year that he ceased to carry on business. Since he is ceasing his business and he is unable to find a buyer to purchase the goodwill, he will be deemed to have disposed of his goodwill for proceeds of zero.

ITA: 20(16)

CHAPTER 5 — SOLUTIONS TO MULTIPLE CHOICE QUESTIONS

CHAPTER 5

Question 1

Authors' Note: The following solution includes GST/HST implications. Students should review Chapter 20 of the textbook, "Goods and Services Tax (GST)/Harmonized Sales Tax (HST)", before attempting this problem.

ITA: 13(7)(*g*); ITR: 7307(1)

(C) is correct. The maximum CCA is: ½ × 30% × $30,000 = $4,500.

(A) incorrectly uses the $50,000 cost of the vehicle to compute CCA: ½ × 30% × $50,000 = $7,500.

(B) incorrectly ignores the half-year rule: 30% × $30,000 = $9,000.

(D) incorrectly includes GST in the calculation ($30,000 x 1.05)x ½ x 30%.

Question 2

(A) is correct. $10,000 is the lesser of ⅕ × $80,000 = $16,000 and $80,000/8 = $10,000. For 2017, the year the cost was incurred, the maximum CCA = 50% of $10,000 = $5,000.

ITR: 1100(1)(*b*), Sch. III

(B) is incorrect. It is 50% of ⅕ × $80,000. Five years is the minimum amount of time leaseholds can be depreciated. A taxpayer must calculate the two amounts and depreciate the leasehold the lower of the two amounts of depreciation. In the year of acquisition, the half-year rule must then be applied to the lower of the two amounts.

(C) is incorrect because the $10,000 figure does not take into account the 50% rule.

ITR: 1100(1)(*b*)

(D) is incorrect for the reasons outlined for (B) and (C) combined.

Question 3

(A) is correct. The maximum CCA claim in Class 14.1 is: $100,000 × 5% × ½ = $2,500.

(B) is incorrect: $100,000 × 5% = $5,000. The half-year rule applies for purposes of additions to Class 14.1.

(C) is incorrect: 7% × $100,000 = $7,000. The Class 14.1 rate is 5% and it is subject to the half-year rule.

(D)is incorrect: 75% x $100,000 x 7% = $5,250. The full cost of $100,000 is added to Class 14.1 with its 5% rate, subject to the half-year rule.

Question 4

(B) is correct because the remaining lease term in 2018 is three years and the first renewal period is three years. The maximum CCA claim is $5,000, calculated as follows:

Lesser of: (i)   ⅕ × $60,000   = $12,000
           (ii) $60,000/(3 + 3)   = $10,000

For 2018, the year the cost was incurred, the maximum CCA is: 50% of $10,000 = $5,000.

ITR: 1100(1)(*b*)

(A) is incorrect, because it uses the initial 5-year term of the lease in the calculation in place of the remaining lease term of three years: $60,000/(5 + 3) = $7,500 × 50% = $3,750.

(C) is incorrect, because the greater ($12,000), as opposed to the lesser ($10,000), of the two amounts calculated has been used: $6,000 = 50% × $12,000.

(D) is incorrect, because it uses the initial 5-year term of the lease in the calculation in place of the remaining lease term of three years and ignores the 50% rule in Regulation 1100(1)(*b*): $60,000/(5 + 3) = $7,500.

Question 5

ITR: 1100(2)

(B) is correct. Under the Regulations, dies and moulds and software are not excepted from the half net-amount rule, but the other Class 12 items are: linens are listed in paragraph (*g*), cutlery and dishes are listed in paragraph (*b*) and kitchen utensils costing less than $500 are listed in paragraph (*c*). ½ ($1,200 + $600) + $15,000 + $400 = $16,300.

(A) is incorrect because it uses the half-year rule on all Class 12 assets: ½ ($1,200 + $600 + $15,000 + $400) = $8,600.

(C) is incorrect because it ignores the half-year rule on the dies and moulds: $1,200 + (½ × $600) + $15,000 + $400 = $16,900.

(D) is incorrect because it ignores the half-year rule on the dies and moulds and software: $1,200 + $600 + $15,000 + $400 = $17,200.

Question 6

(D) is not available, since the property is not intangible property with an indefinite life.

(A), (B), and (C) are all options for the treatment of patent costs.

CHAPTER 5 — SOLUTIONS TO EXERCISES

Exercise 1

The overpass is not eligible for capital cost allowance, since the owners have no title to the land on which the footings are placed and capital cost allowance cannot be claimed on assets that are not owned (see *Saskatoon Community Broadcasting Co. Ltd. v. M.N.R.*). The cost of the overpass qualifies as an eligible capital expenditure.

58 DTC 491 (T.A.B.)

Exercise 2

Harrison's automobile is defined as a passenger vehicle for CCA purposes. Passenger vehicles with a cost in excess of $30,000 (2018 amount) must be placed into a separate CCA class, Class 10.1. The depreciation rate for class 10.1 assets is 30%. However, CCA may only be taken on the deemed capital cost of the vehicle up to a maximum of $30,000 (paragraph 13(7)(*a*) and ITR 7307(1)). Harrison's maximum CCA claim for the first and second year of owning the car would be calculated as follows:

ITA: 13(7); ITR: 7307(1)

Year 1

Capital cost of additions	$30,000
Less CCA (30,000 × 30% × 50%*)	4,500
UCC, end of year 1	$25,500

* Half-year rule applied.

Business use CCA (CCA × usage %) = $4,500 × 40% = $1,800

Year 2

UCC, Beginning of Year 2	$25,500
Less CCA @ 30%	7,650
UCC, end of Year 2	$17,850

Business use CCA (CCA × usage %) = $7,650 × 40% = $3,060

Exercise 3

No terminal loss can be deducted for an automobile in Class 10.1. The special "half-year rule" to compute capital cost allowance in the year of disposition applies to Class 10.1.

ITA: 20(16.1); ITR: 1100(2.5)

(A)	Class 10.1		
	Jan. 1/18	UCC (Class 10.1)	$ 20,170
	2018	CCA (1/2 × .30 × $20,170)	(3,026)[1]
		Proceeds of disposition	(12,000)
		Balance in the Pool	$ 5,145
		Terminal loss denied	Nil
(B)	Class 10.1		
	2018	Purchase ($36,000) max.	$ 33,900[2]
	Dec. 31/18	UCC before adjustment	$ 33,900
		One-half of net amount (1/2 × $33,900)	(16,950)
		UCC before CCA	$ 16,950
		CCA @ 30% of $16,950	(5,085)[3]
		Add: 1/2 net amount	16,950
	Jan. 1/19	UCC	$ 28,815

—NOTES TO SOLUTION

[1] Note that 75% of $3,026 or $2,270 is the deduction based on business use.

[2] Limited to $30,000 plus HST (13%) or $33,900, since it was acquired after 2000.

[3] Note that 75% of $5,085 or $3,814 is deductible, since CCA claimed is not subject to the limitation on sales/negotiating person's expenses.

ITA: 8(1)(*f*), 8(1)(*j*)

Exercise 4

	Cl. 1: 4%	Cl. 8: 20%	Cl. 10: 30%	Cl. 13: S.L.	Cl. 14: S.L.	Cl. 53: 50%
Jan. 1/18						
UCC	$120,000	$75,000	$40,000	$42,000	$54,400	Nil
2018 Purchases:						
— mfg. equip.						$50,000
— off. equip.		10,000				
Disposals:						
— building (LOCP)	(100,000)[1]					
Dec. 31/18						
UCC before adjustment	$ 20,000	$85,000	$40,000	$42,000	$54,400	$50,000
1/2 net amount	Nil	(5,000)	Nil	Nil	N/A	(25,000)
UCC before CCA	$ 20,000	$80,000	$40,000	$42,000	$54,400	$25,000
CCA.	(800)	(16,000)	(12,000)	(1,250)[2]	(3,400)[3]	(12,500)
1/2 net amount	Nil	5,000	Nil	Nil	N/A	25,000
Jan. 1/19						
UCC	$ 19,200	$69,000	$28,000	$40,750	$51,000	$37,500

—NOTES TO SOLUTION

[1] Capital gain on disposition of building of $50,000.

[2] Lesser of: (a) 1/5 of $50,000 . . . . $10,000

(b) $50,000/40 (max.) . . . . $ 1,250 }$1,250

— not reduced by 1/2 because not first year of ownership.

[3] $\dfrac{\$68,000}{(20 \times 365)} \times 365 = \$3,400$

Exercise 5

The proceeds from the sale of Liam's building are greater than the UCC of the building. This would indicate that, although Liam claimed CCA in previous years, the market value of the building did not decline. Accordingly, CCA claimed in previous years must be recaptured and added to income for tax purposes in the current year. Liam must report recaptured CCA of $15,500, calculated as follows:

ITA: 13

Class 1 — 4%		
UCC, beginning of year		$144,500
Less disposition at lesser of:		
Capital cost	$160,000	
Net proceeds	$180,000	160,000
UCC Balance		(15,500)
Recaptured CCA		(15,500)
UCC Balance after accounting for recapture		Nil

Note that no CCA may be claimed in the year of the disposition since the UCC balance in the class after recapture is nil.

Exercise 6

(a)(i) $100,000 × 20% × ½ = $10,000

ITA: 20(1)

(ii) $100,000 × 20% × ½ × (90/365) = $2,466

In (ii), CCA is prorated because the taxation year is less than 365 days.

(b) Leasehold improvements — CCA is lesser of

(1) $25,000 × ⅕ × ½ = $2,500

(2) $25,000 × 1/12 × ½ = $1,042

(Twelve years is the denominator; this includes the initial lease term and the first renewal period.)

(c) The franchise is for a limited term, hence it is a Class 14 asset. The CCA on Class 14 assets is computed on a straight-line basis over the remaining life of the asset. The half-year rule does not apply to Class 14. CCA allowed to July 31 (153 days) is:

$25,000 × 1/15 × (153/365) = $699

Exercise 7

ITA: 20(1)

(a)	**Class 1 — Building** ($208,895 + ½ ($20,000)) × 4%		$ 8,756
(b)	**Class 13 — Leasehold Improvements** Lesser of:		
	(i) 1/10 × ½ × 70,000	$3,500	
	(ii) ⅕ × ½ × 70,000	$7,000	
	CCA for the year		$ 3,500
(c)	**Class 50 — Computer Equipment** UCC, beginning of year CCA 40,000 × 55%		$40,000 (22,000)
	UCC, end of year		$18,000
(d)	**Class 10 — Trucks** UCC, beginning of year Less dispositions ($10,000 – $1,000)		$25,000 (9,000)
			$16,000
	CCA 30%		4,800
	UCC, end of year		$11,200
(e)	**Class 14 — Licence** $30,000 × 1/15 × (122*/365)		$ 668

* Number of days from June 1 to September 30.

Exercise 8

The business use rules could be applied as follows:

		Cl. 10: 30%	Business deduction of CCA
2016	Purchase...............	$14,600	
Dec. 31, 2016	UCC	$14,600	
	CCA @ 30% of ½ × $14,600	(2,190)	85% of $2,190 = $1,862
Dec. 31, 2017	UCC	$12,410	
	CCA @ 30%	(3,723)	80% of $3,723 = $2,978
Dec. 31, 2018	UCC	$ 8,687	
	CCA @ 30%	(2,606)	[80% + ½ (90% – 80%)][1] of $2,606 = $2,215
Jan. 1, 2019	UCC	$ 6,081	

— NOTES TO SOLUTION

(1) An increase in use for business represents an addition to the class which is subject to the half-year rule. In practice, the CCA may be computed simply as 90% of $2,606 or $2,345. ITA: 13(7)(*g*)

Exercise 9

The Class 14.1 balance would be affected as follows:

Year	Opening UCC Balance	Additions (Dispositions)	Par. 20(1)(a) CCA Deduction[1]	Ssec. 13(1) Business Income Inclusion	Closing UCC Balance
2018	-	$10,800	$270[2]		$10,530
2019	10,530	—	527		10,003
2020	10,003	—	500		9,503
2021	9,503	(10,800)	—	$ 1,297	—
Total			$1,297		

2021 Opening balance	$ 9,503
Sale (LOCP)	(10,800)
Negative UCC balance	(1,297)
Recapture to business income	1,297
Closing UCC balance	Nil

Proceeds ($45,800) in excess of capital cost ($10,800) is a capital gain of $34,200.

— NOTES TO SOLUTION

(1) 5% of declining balance with half-year rule applied in 2018. ITA: 20(1)(*a*)

(2) $10,800 x 5% x ½.

Exercise 10

Class 14.1: 5%

Jan. 1/18	Purchase of goodwill		$ 40,000
Dec. 31/18	CCA @ 5% × ½		(1,000)
Jan. 1/19	UCC		$ 39,000
Dec. 31/19	CCA @ 5%		(1,950)
Jan. 1/20	UCC		$ 37,050
June 1/20	Purchase of licence		50,000
Dec. 31/20	UCC		$ 87,050
	CCA @ 5% of ($37,050 + ½ × $50,000)		(3,103)
Jan. 1/21	UCC		$ 83,947
Mar. 1/21	Purchase of trademark		20,000
Dec. 31/21	UCC		$ 103,947
	CCA @ 5% of ($83,947 + ½ × $20,000)		(4,697)
Jan. 1/22	UCC		$ 99,250
Nov. 1/22	Purchase of goodwill		50,000
Dec. 31/22	UCC		$ 149,250
	CCA @ 5% of ($99,250 + ½ × $50,000)		(6,213)
Jan. 1/23	UCC		$ 143,037
Sept. 7/23	Sale of goodwill (LOCP: $40,000 + $50,000 < $100,000[1])		(90,000)
Dec. 31/23	UCC		$ 53,037
	CCA @ 5%		(2,652)
Jan. 1/24	UCC		$ 50,385
Aug. 3/24	Sale of license (LOCP: $50,000 < $150,000)[1]		(50,000)
	Sale of trademark (LOCP: $20,000 < $200,000[1])		(20,000)
Dec. 31/24	UCC		$ (19,615)
	Recapture to business income		19,615
Jan. 1/25	UCC		Nil

— NOTES TO SOLUTION

[1] Proceeds – Cost = Capital gain, half taxable

Exercise 11

Class 14.1 (5%)

2018	UCC at the beginning of the year	$	Nil
	Add: purchase during the year		(5,000)
	UCC before adjustment	$	5,000
	Deduct: ½-year amount on excess purchases-disposals		(2,500)
	UCC before CCA	$	2,500
	Deduct: CCA @ 5%		(125)
	Add: ½-year amount		2,500
2019	UCC at the beginning of the year	$	4,875
	Deduct: CCA @ 5%		(244)
2020	UCC at the beginning of the year	$	4,631
	Add: purchase during the year		4,450
	Deduct: disposition (LOCP)[1]		(5,000)
	UCC before adjustment	$	4,081
	Deduct: ½-year amount on excess purchases-disposals		(Nil)
	UCC before CCA	$	4,081
	Deduct: CCA @ 5%		(204)
	Add: ½-year amount		Nil
2021	UCC at the beginning of the year	$	3,877
	Deduct: disposition (LOCP)		(Nil)
	UCC at the end of the year	$	3,877
	Terminal loss (positive balance but no assets)		(3,877)
	UCC balance after terminal loss		Nil

— NOTES TO SOLUTION

(1) Taxable capital gain = 1/2($6,500 − $5,000) must also be included in income.

Exercise 12

Schedule to Reflect 2018 Capital Write-Offs and Balance in Tax Accounts

	Cl. 1 (separate)	Cl. 3	Cl. 8	Cl. 10	Cl. 12	Cl. 13	Cl. 14
	10%	5%	20%	30%	100%		
UCC Jan. 1, 2018	Nil	$70,000	$6,000	$13,000	Nil	$19,500	—
Additions							
Bldg.	$250,000	—	—	—	—	—	—
Leaseholds	—	—	—	—	—	$9,000	—
Office equip.	—	—	$2,000	—	—	—	—
Jigs etc.	—	—	—	—	$6,000	—	—
Licence	—	—	—	—	—	—	$12,000
Disposals							
Bldg.	—	(160,000)	—	—	—	—	—
Office equip.	—	—	(1,000)	—	—	—	—
Net	$250,000	$(90,000)	$7,000	$13,000	$6,000	$28,500	$12,000
Less: 1/2 of net additions	125,000	—	500	0	n/a[1]	n/a[1]	—
UCC after net adj.	$125,000	$(90,000)	$6,500	$13,000	$6,000	$28,500	$12,000
Recapture	—	90,000					
CCA — 2018	(12,500)	Nil	(1,300)	(3,900)	(6,000)	(3,750)[3]	(1,808)[3]
1/2 of net additions	125,000	—	500	n/a	n/a	n/a	n/a
UCC Jan. 1, 2019	$237,500 (B)	Nil (B)	$5,700 (B)	$9,100	Nil	$24,750	$10,192

	Class 14.1	Class 17	Class 43	Class 44
	5%	8%	30%	25%
UCC Jan. 1, 2018	Nil	Nil	$27,000	$25,375
Additions				
Parking lot	—	$5,000	—	—
Legal fees	$11,000	—	—	—
Disposals	—	Nil	—	—
Manufacturing equip.	—	—	(5,000)	—
Net	$11,000	$5,000	$22,000	$25,375
Less: 1/2 of net additions	(5,500)	2,500	n/a	Nil
UCC	$5,500	$2,500	$22,000	$25,375
CCA — 2018	(275)	(200)	(6,600)	(6,344)
1/2 of net additions	5,500	2,500	n/a	Nil
UCC Jan. 1, 2019	$10,725	$4,800	$15,400	$19,031

	Cl. 50	Class 53
	55%	50%
UCC Jan. 1, 2018	Nil	Nil
Additions		
Computer hardware/software	$10,000	
Manufacturing equipment		$25,000
Disposals	0	Nil
Net	$10,000	$25,000
Less: 1/2 of net additions	5,000	12,500
UCC after net adj.	$5,000	$12,500
Recapture	—	
CCA — 2018	(2,750)	(6,250)
1/2 of net amount	5,000	12,500
UCC Jan. 1, 2019	$7,250	$18,750

Other Transactions:

— landscaping fully deductible [par. 20(1)(*aa*)]

— utility service connection fully deductible [par. 20(1)(*ee*)].

—NOTES TO SOLUTION

[1] The half-net-amount rule does not apply to parts of Class 12 plus Classes 13, 14, and certain other classes, although only half of the maximum CCA in Class 13 is allowed in the first year of a leasehold improvement.

[2] Class 13: Leaseholds
2016: Lesser of

(a) $\dfrac{\$24,000}{5} = \$4,800$

(b) $\dfrac{\$24,000}{3+5} = \$3,000$

$\left.\rule{0pt}{40pt}\right\}$ $\$3,000$

plus
2018: Lesser of

(a) $\dfrac{\$9,000}{5} = \$1,800$

(b) $\dfrac{\$9,000}{1+5} = \$1,500$

$\left.\rule{0pt}{40pt}\right\}$ $\$1,500 \times 50\% \rightarrow \underline{\$750} = \underline{\$3,750}$

[3] Class 14:

$\dfrac{\$12,000}{1,825 \text{ days}} \times 275 = \underline{\$1,808}$

Chapter 6

Income from Property

Learning Goals

Know, Understand and Explain

By the end of this chapter you will know, understand and be able to explain:

- The basic provisions of the *Income Tax Act* (the Act) that relate to property income and attribution rules.
- The rules relating to the inclusion of interest income for corporations, trusts and individuals.
- The difference between eligible and ineligible dividends and its effects on the taxation of an individual.
- The distinction between property and business income.
- The purpose of integration and how it affects the overall tax paid on income earned in a corporation.

Apply

By the end of this chapter you will be able to apply your knowledge and understanding to:

- Correctly determine the amount of interest and dividends that must be included in income.
- Correctly determine the eligible expenses that may be deducted against property income.
- Advise taxpayers on the tax implications of a non-arm's length transaction as it relates to income splitting.
- Advise taxpayers on tax planning techniques to maximize deductions and minimize overall tax.

Review Questions
¶6,800 in the Study Guide

Multiple Choice Questions
¶6,825 in the Study Guide

Exercises
¶6,850 in the Study Guide

Assignment Problems
¶6,875 in the Study Guide

CHAPTER 6 — LEARNING CHART

Problem Descriptions

Textbook Example Problems

6-1	Reporting interest income
6-2	Reporting interest income
6-3	Interest income
6-4	Damages received
6-5	Dividends — public company
6-6	Attribution — spouse
6-7	Attribution — child
6-8	Carrying charges on land
6-9	Rental property CCA

Multiple Choice Questions

1	Dividends — CCPC
2	Rental property CCA
3	Attribution
4	Deductible expenses
5	Dividends — CCPC, public
6	Kiddie tax

Exercises

1	Interest income
2	Attribution — spouse
3	Carrying charges on land
4	Rental property CCA
5	Rental property disposal
6	Interest expense
7	Rental property
8	Rental property during construction
9	Business or property income expenditures
10	Non-arm's length transactions

Assignment Problems

1	Attribution — spouse, children
2	Dividends — eligible, other, foreign
3	Sale with earn out
4	Interest vs. dividend and attribution
5	Expenses of vacant land
6	Income from rental properties
7	Construction costs
8	GST/HST
9	Property income and employee loan
10	Attribution
11	Property income
12	Interest expense
13	Interest expense
14	Business and property income, attribution

Study Notes

CHAPTER 6

¶6,800   REVIEW QUESTIONS

(1) Billy has come to you to tell you that he has found a great way of generating income of which only one-half is taxable as a capital gain. He buys a bond that pays interest annually and he holds it until just before the payment date and then he sells it, including the accrued interest, at a gain. Comment.

(2) Mr. Simpson owns an unincorporated business. In recognition of his wife's considerable contribution of her time and skills to the business he gives her a one-half share of the business income. Comment.

(3) Mr. Smith has guaranteed a bank loan that his wife has taken out to buy shares in a corporation carrying on a business that she is starting. He is concerned about the attribution rules. Comment.

(4) Opco Inc. recently borrowed $300,000 to buy 30 acres of industrial land. The corporation has constructed a building, shipping and receiving areas and parking for employees on this property using up 20 acres. The remaining 10 acres is available for future needs. Is all of the interest on the $300,000 loan deductible?

(5) Rent Co. Ltd. is a corporation in the residential rental business. Because of some recent purchases, its financing costs are high and it is operating at a break-even before CCA this year. However, in the prior three years it made a profit. Can the corporation claim CCA to create a loss this year to carry back to the prior years, using the carryover rules in Division C, to offset income in those years?

(6) Ms. Campbell has bought some gold as a protection against inflation. However, she did not have the cash to make the purchase so she borrowed from the bank to buy the gold. This is the first time that she has done this and she plans to hold the gold for some time. She is repaying the loan over three years. Will she be able to deduct all or some of her interest expense? Explain.

(7) You have been told of a court case where a taxpayer borrowed money initially to purchase a home, because some of the funds that he was to receive from Iran had not arrived when expected. When the funds at last arrived, interest rates had risen above that rate he was paying on his house mortgage. He then chose to invest his money at these higher interest rates instead of paying off the mortgage. He deducted the interest portion of his mortgage payments on his tax return. Comment.

(8) A client is in the process of selling his house and buying a bigger one. However, the real estate market has slowed down and in order to sell his existing house he is going to have to take back a mortgage for $100,000 at 5% for a five-year term. Since he does not have any extra cash, he is going to have to borrow that $100,000 from you in order to buy his new house. Is the interest going to be deductible on his mortgage? If not, how might he restructure the transaction to make it deductible?

(9) You have just interviewed a new client and have discovered that she borrowed to buy shares in a private corporation five years ago. The loan is still outstanding but the corporation has since gone bankrupt. Is the interest she is paying on the loan still deductible?

¶6,825 MULTIPLE CHOICE QUESTIONS

Question 1

Max is planning to invest in preferred shares of a friend's Canadian-controlled private corporation, which are paying a $12,000 dividend per year from income taxable at the low corporate rate. Assuming that Max is in the top federal tax bracket (33%) and that the provincial tax on income rate in his province is 17%, how much income tax will Max pay on this income? Also assume that the combined federal and provincial dividend tax credit is equal to the dividend gross-up.

(A) $2,674

(B) $5,040

(C) $6,960

(D) $6,000

Question 2

Wendy Jang owns three rental buildings (all three properties are residential). All of the buildings are in Class 1:

	Property		
	1	*2*	*3*
Original cost	$120,000	$ 80,000	$150,000
UCC at Jan. 1	100,000	75,000	150,000
Rental revenue for the year	58,000	22,000	20,000
Expenses for the year:			
Interest	20,000	10,000	8,000
Property taxes	13,000	6,000	11,000
Other	17,000	4,000	1,000

What is the maximum CCA that Wendy Jang can claim on the rental properties for the year?

(A) $13,000

(B) $10,000

(C) $7,000

(D) $6,500

Question 3

In the year, Mr. P made the following loans and gifts to family members to split income with his family members. Which one of the loans and/or gifts will result in income being attributed to Mr. P?

(A) A gift of $100,000 to his son, Peter, age 21. Peter invested the money in a term deposit and earned $3,000 of interest income.

(B) An interest-free loan of $100,000 to his mother-in-law, Mabel, age 81. Mabel invested the money in mutual funds and earned $12,000 of dividend income.

(C) An interest-free loan of $100,000 to his daughter, Daphne, age 28. Daphne bought a cottage and used it for personal use.

(D) A gift of $100,000 to his wife, Debbie. Debbie put the money in her non-interest bearing chequing account and paid all the family's household expenses from the account. She then used $100,000 of her own money to invest in the stock market and earned $10,000 of dividend income.

Question 4

Which of the following items is DEDUCTIBLE by Canadian taxpayers in the computation of income from business or property in Subdivision b of Division B of the Act?

(A) Commissions paid on the purchase of an investment in common shares.

(B) The premium paid on a $100,000 term life insurance policy on the taxpayer's life which is required as collateral for a $100,000 bank loan used to purchase a $100,000 investment in common shares.

(C) Interest expenses on a loan to invest in a registered retirement savings plan.

(D) Commissions paid on the sale of an investment in common shares.

Question 5

During the year, Mike received two cheques, one in the amount of C$20,000, the other in the amount of C$8,500. The $20,000 cheque was a dividend from business income taxed at the low corporate rate of a Canadian-controlled private corporation. The $8,500 cheque was a dividend from a foreign corporation, net of the $1,500 of foreign tax withheld by the foreign country from the dividend payment. Which of the following amounts must Mike include in his income for Canadian income tax purposes in respect of these two dividend cheques?

(A) $20,000

(B) $28,500

(C) $30,000

(D) $33,200

Question 6

Ron Bordessa is 18 years of age. He inherited shares of Royal Roads Ltd., a private corporation, on his grandfather's death three years ago. Which of the following statements is true?

(A) Any dividend that Ron receives on these shares will be subject to the tax on split income.

(B) The tax on split income does not apply to any dividends on these shares because they were inherited.

(C) Any capital gains that Ron realizes on the disposition of these shares to an arm's length person, will be subject to the tax on split income.

(D) The tax on split income does not apply to any dividend on these shares because Ron has reached the age of 18.

¶6,850   EXERCISES

Exercise 1

ITA: 12(1)(c), 12(4), 12(11)

What would be the *first* year in which the taxpayer would have to include interest in income in each of the following cases and to which years would that interest relate?

(A) A corporation with a June 30 year end buys a bond that pays interest semi-annually on March 31 and September 30 from its previous owner on January 1, 2018.

(B) An individual buys a compounding GIC on November 1, 2018.

(C) An individual buys a zero coupon bond, issued on January 1, 2018, in 2018.

(D) On June 1, 2018, an individual buys a $1,000 bond paying $40 interest by cheque each May 31 and November 30. The bond was issued on December 1, 2017.

Exercise 2

ITA: 74.1, 74.5

(A) A husband wants his wife to have a $1,000 bond that he owns paying interest at 7%. What are the consequences to the couple during the year if:

(i) he gives the bond to her without receiving any financial consideration from her in return?

(ii) he sells the bond to her for $1,000 plus accrued interest to the date of sale in return for cash?

(iii) he sells the bond to her for $1,000 plus accrued interest to the date of sale in return for a demand note which she signs payable to him without interest?

(iv) he cashes the bond lending the proceeds to her in return for a promissory note which she signs payable to him without interest but with a definite repayment period and she uses the funds from the loan to buy a similar bond?

(B) Would any of the above answers change for the current year if he undertook the same transactions with a trust set up in favour of a child aged 15 instead of his wife?

(C) Would any of the above answers change if he undertook the same transactions with a child aged 20?

Exercise 3

ITA: 18(2)

A downtown hotel bought a vacant lot adjacent to the hotel building. Comment on the deductibility of property taxes and interest paid on funds borrowed to buy the property if:

(i) the property is used as a parking lot for hotel guests;

(ii) the property was bought for potential gains on future sale but in the meantime it is being used as a public parking lot generating net revenues before the taxes and interest of 75% of the expenditures for taxes and interest;

(iii) the property was bought for future expansion of the hotel and in the meantime is being used under the same condition as in (ii) above.

Exercise 4

ITR: 1100

Mr. Provident is a salaried employee who invests in small residential rental properties. He bought Property 1 last year and at the beginning of this year the undepreciated capital cost balances for that property were as follows:

Class 1 — brick building $148,000

Class 8 — furniture and fixtures   25,000

This year he bought Property 2 for $150,000 including land valued at $12,500. The net income before capital cost allowance for each property this year was:

Property 1 . . . . $ 9,270

Property 2   3,750

— *REQUIRED*

Compute the maximum capital cost allowance on these rental properties for the current year.

Exercise 5

ITA: 20(1)(*a*); ITR: 1100, 1101(1ac)

Ms. Alimeag owns two residential rental properties. One produced rental revenue of $13,500 and had allowable expenses (excluding capital cost allowance) of $11,250. The other had rental revenue of $22,500 and expenses of $18,750. Data on the two Class 1 buildings are as follows:

	Property A	Property B
Capital cost	$360,000	$600,000
UCC, January 1	$330,000	$480,000

During the year, Property A was sold for net proceeds of $336,000.

— *REQUIRED*

(A) What is the effect of the above information on the income of Ms. Alimeag for the year?

(B) Can an election be made under subsection 13(4) if Property A is replaced by the end of the next year?

Exercise 6

ITA: 20(1)(*c*)

Nadi borrowed $140,000 at an 5.5% annual interest rate from a local financial institution to finance the following investments.

	Cost
Common shares of a public corporation paying no dividends	$20,000
Gold bullion (treated as capital)	25,000
Corporate bond (yield is 6% *per annum*)	20,000
Preferred shares (4% annual dividend) purchased in RRSP . . .	10,000
Common shares (2% annual dividend) in spouse's name	30,000
Paintings from well-known galleries	15,000
Guaranteed Investment Certificate paying interest at 6% *per annum*	20,000
Total cost	$140,000

— *REQUIRED*

Assuming that the investments were held for the full calendar year, determine the deductibility of interest expense for each investment.

Exercise 7

ITR: 1100(11), 1101(1ac)

Capital cost allowance, recapture, and terminal loss all form part of the net income calculation for rental properties. There are two special rules that apply only to rental properties that serve to limit the treatment of capital cost allowance.

One of the special rules stipulates that each rental property having a cost of $50,000 or more must be held in a separate capital cost allowance class.

— REQUIRED

Determine the second special rule.

Exercise 8

You have just been to your physician, Dr. Do Good, for your annual physical. During your visit, he told you about his latest investment. On April 1, 2018, he purchased an old Victorian home at what he is sure was the bottom of the real estate market. He paid $300,000 for the home and figures 50% is attributable to the value of the land and the other 50% to the building. After putting a first mortgage of $200,000 on the property at 10% and paying cash for the remainder, he hired the best architect in the city to renovate the house as a triplex. The renovations began April 1 and were completed by October 31. The first tenant moved in on November 1. The renovations were expensive and as he could not persuade the bank to take a second mortgage on the property, he placed a 10%, $150,000 mortgage [representing the full cost of the renovations] on his principal residence on May 1, 2018 in order to finance the renovations.

Dr. Do Good is delighted with his investment: the renovations are beautiful, all three units are rented and he will be able to write off a large loss on the property against his income from his medical practice. His brother-in-law, the real estate agent who sold him the house, has prepared a draft of his 2018 taxable income calculation (Exhibit I) and Dr. Do Good would like you to have a look at it.

— REQUIRED

Review Dr. Do Good's 2018 draft taxable income calculation and make any corrections that are necessary. Explain any changes you make to the return.

Ignore the effects of a leap year in your answer.

EXHIBIT I
Draft of Dr. Do Good's 2018 Personal Tax Return

Practice income		$400,000
Rental income		
Rental revenue	2 months	$12,000
Mortgage interest	$200,000 @ 10% x 275/365	$15,068
	(April 1 to December 31)	
Mortgage interest		
–principal residence	$150,000 @ 10% x 245/365	$10,068
	(May 1 to December 31)	
Property taxes 9 months		$4,000
Insurance	9 months	$1,500
	7 months (paid by tenants since Novem-	
Utilities	ber 1)	$1,400
Advertising		$500
Repairs and maintenance		
Replace carpet		$5,000
Repair roof		$3,000
Painting		$2,000
Capital cost allowance, Note 1		$14,500
		$57,036
		$(45,036)
Taxable income		$354,964

Note 1

Capital cost allowance

Cost of building purchased	$150,000
Renovations	$150,000
Less: repairs and maintenance included in renovations	$(10,000)
	290,000
CCA rate (Class 3)	×5%
CCA claimed	$14,500

Exercise 9

Mr. Radical, a relatively new client, has decided to quit his present employment and to start up a computer consulting business. After discussing with him the various forms of business organization, Mr. Radical has decided on a corporate structure, Dude Ltd., with its first year ending June 30, 2019, but only being eight months long.

You have been asked to draft a memorandum to Mr. Radical explaining the tax implications of the following specific transactions relating to the corporation and its shareholders.

(a) Costs related to incorporation of the new company

Legal fees	$2,200
Accounting fees	$1,100
Government fees	$660
	$3,960

(b) Both Mr. and Mrs. Radical will be common shareholders of the corporation. Mr. Radical will acquire 80% of the shares and Mrs. Radical will acquire 20%. However, since Mrs. Radical does not have adequate funds, Mr. Radical will lend her the necessary funds evidenced by promissory note with specific repayments and a rate of interest at 7%.

(c) The corporation will have to establish a line of credit with the bank. For this purpose, financial statements and business plans were developed for him at a cost of $6,700.

(d) Dude Ltd. acquired the following assets on November 1, 2018, for use in the business:

General office equipment	$17,000
Computer hardware	$12,000
Customer lists	$15,000
A 5-year licence to market some U.S. software	$27,000

(e) Dude Ltd. will lease its premises. The following facts relate to the leased quarters:

(1) Lease terms are five years with two seven-year renewal options at an annual cost of $14,000;

(2) First 12 months rent paid on November 1, 2018;

(3) Renovations to the leased property = $23,000.

(f) Dude Ltd. intends to buy a 1966 Rambler convertible from Mr. Radical's brother-in-law, Stan. The car will be used exclusively for business purposes and will bear the corporate logo. The car was personal-use property of Mr. Radical's brother-in-law.

Cost of car to Dude Ltd.	$15,000
Cost of car to Mr. Radical's brother-in-law (including all major expenditures)	$2,500
Estimated FMV at date of sale	$19,000

(g) Dude Ltd. obtained a long-term contract to provide computer consulting services to a large public corporation with an annual fee of $45,000 payable in advance. The first annual fee was received on November 1, 2018.

— *REQUIRED*

Draft a memorandum to Mr. Radical, as president of Dude Ltd., explaining the income tax implications of the above proposed transactions.

Ignore the effects of a leap year in your answer.

Exercise 10

Robin is an extremely wealthy lawyer who wants to lower his taxes without losing control over his wealth. On January 1, 2014, he decided to make an interest-free loan of $75,000 to his 25-year-old daughter, Faith. Immediately, Faith used the money to purchase 750 shares of Hiflier Public Co., which paid dividends of $7,500 in 2018. Faith had no other income in 2018.

— *REQUIRED*

What are the tax consequences to Robin and Faith for 2018?

¶6,875 ASSIGNMENT PROBLEMS

Type 1 Problems

Problem 1

Donna is married to Don and they have two children, Danielle, age 25, and Susan, age 15. Donna earns $250,000 annually while Don earns $100,000. Danielle works full time and earns $30,000 annually while Susan is still in high school and doesn't have any income. Donna has been looking for ways to pay less tax and a friend of hers has suggested that she take advantage of the lower tax brackets of her husband and children. With $100,000 of extra cash in her bank account she is considering the following options and would like your advice as her accountant. Assume the following combined tax rates:

Donna	53%
Don	41%
Danielle	25%
Susan	—

(1) Loan the $100,000 to her husband at 0% interest. He would invest it in a bond earning 3%.

(2) Give the $100,000 to her husband. He would invest it in a bond earning 3%.

(3) Loan the $100,000 to her 15-year-old daughter at 0% interest. She would invest it in a bond earning 3%.

(4) Give the $100,000 to her 15-year-old daughter. She would invest it in a bond earning 3%.

(5) Loan the $100,000 to her 25-year-old daughter at 0% interest. She would invest it in a bond earning 3%.

(6) Give the $100,000 to her 25-year-old daughter. She would invest it in a bond earning 3%.

Problem 2

Victor is confused, so he has come to you for advice. He has heard that not all dividends are treated the same, so he would like you to explain how the following are taxed to decide where he should invest his money. Victor is in the top tax bracket, which is 53%.

Assume the following:

(1) $1,000 of dividends from Canadian public companies.

(2) $1,000 of dividends from Canadian private companies earning active business income taxed at the low rate.

(3) $900 of dividends from foreign public companies. $100 was deducted at source and remitted to the foreign government.

- Dividends from public companies: the dividend tax credit is equal to $6/11$ (federal) and $6/11$ (provincial) of the gross-up.

- Dividends from Canadian private companies earning active business income taxed at the low rate: the dividend tax credit is equal to $8/11$ (federal) and $3/11$ (provincial) of the gross-up.

Problem 3

ITA: 12(1)(g); IT-462

The Country Pie is a highly recognized baker of quality pies in Beamsville, Ontario. The current proprietor, Rudolph Strudel, started the business about 20 years ago with an initial purchase of equipment of $150,000 and built up the name of the company by closely supervising the pie production process. Many have said that it is this attention and his recipes that have made the business a success. Rudolph has decided to sell his business and move to the coast to get away from the pressures of running a business. An offer has been made for the assets of The Country Pie by Big Food Corporation Ltd. ("BFC"). There was a meeting of the minds as to the value of the fixed assets of The Country Pie. However, there was considerable dispute as to the value of The Country Pie name in generating pie sales after a purchase by BFC. Consequently, it is proposed that the full proceeds be determined in part by future sales.

The BFC offer is for $50,000 cash; $60,000 to be paid on the basis of sales over the next three years with any balance of the $60,000 remaining at the end of the third year payable at that time; and 25% of gross sales in the next five years. As part of the agreement, Rudolph would provide consulting services to BFC as needed during the next three years.

Rudolph would like you to explain the income tax implications of the proposal from BFC.

Problem 4

ITA: 12(1)(c), 12(1)(j), 74.1, 74.5, 82(1); IT-510, IT-511R

Mr. Wiser is contemplating investing in two different mutual funds. His investment options are set out below.

Amount	Mutual Fund	Distribution
$200,000	International Income Fund	Annual interest of 4.0%
$200,000	Canadian Dividend Fund	Annual dividend of 3.0%

Mr. Wiser contemplates holding both mutual funds for the same period of time — from purchase to December 31, 2020. Mr. Wiser is in the top federal income tax bracket (33%). Mr. Wiser's provincial tax on income rate is 20%. Assume that the combined federal and provincial dividend tax credit is equal to the dividend gross-up. Assume that the Canadian Dividend Fund receives and distributes dividends from Canadian-resident public corporations.

Mr. Wiser would like you to advise him on the following:

(A) Based on the above information, which mutual fund should he prefer?

(B) Can he achieve any advantage by purchasing the above mutual fund in the name of his 8-year-old daughter who has no other source of income?

(C) His spouse has no source of income. Can he achieve any advantage by lending $200,000 to his spouse and having her purchase a rental property earning $16,000 per year? The $200,000 loan would be evidenced by a promissory note repayable in four equal annual instalments on each of December 31, 2017 to 2020 and bearing interest at the prescribed rate of 1%.

Problem 5

ITA: 18(2)–(3)

Furniture Focus Limited provides competitive prices to consumers by using a no-frills approach to displaying its product in large stores surrounded by ample parking. Furniture Focus Limited has excess land that is not currently used in its business. This vacant land is rented to the adjacent automobile dealer who stores new cars on it.

For the year ended December 31, 2018, Furniture Focus Limited had the following operating expenses:

Sales	$35,000,000
Cost of goods sold	(20,000,000)
Gross profit	$15,000,000
Selling expenses	(5,000,000)
General and administrative expenses	(2,000,000)
	$ 8,000,000
Other income	50,000
Net income	$ 8,050,000

The general and administrative expenses include $30,000 of interest and $5,000 of property taxes on the vacant land rented to the automobile dealer. There are no other expenses connected with this land. Other income includes $10,000 of rental income paid by the automobile dealer.

Determine the income tax consequences of the various payments related to the vacant land.

Problem 6

ITA: 20(1)(a); ITR: 1100(11), 1101(1ac); Sched. II

Sara Shimizu is the owner of two rental properties, 509 Brunswick Avenue and 356 Spadina Road. These properties were purchased six years ago for $525,000 and $600,000, respectively. In 2018, 509 Brunswick Avenue was sold for $550,000. A reasonable allocation of this amount is considered to be 75% to the building and 25% to the land. The following income and expenses were incurred in renting out the two properties in 2018:

Rental	$ 60,000
Interest on mortgage	(40,000)
Operating costs	(15,000)
Promotion costs for sale of property	(5,000)
Net income	0

There are no meal or entertainment expenses included in the $5,000 of sales promotion costs. At December 31, 2017, the undepreciated capital cost of 509 Brunswick Avenue was $383,500 and that of 356 Spadina Road was $400,000.

Sara has asked you to determine her income from the property, assuming she wishes to report the least amount possible for tax purposes in 2018.

Problem 7

ITA: 18, 20

It is early January 2018 and the president of BDC Distributing Limited, a client of your firm, called recently to discuss the tax implications regarding the construction of a new building. BDC has been growing rapidly and needs new warehouse space. They have been unable to locate any suitable space in the existing buildings in town and, therefore, have decided that their only option is to build their own building. They have identified the site and have estimated the costs of the project. These projected costs (and dates of completion) are as follows:

The land that has been identified will be purchased on February 15, 2018, for $405,000. There is no significant site preparation required so construction of the building can commence immediately. The cost of the building is estimated to be $1,348,000 plus the costs noted below. It is anticipated that BDC will be able to occupy the building on October 31, 2018.

BDC currently has an architect finalizing the drawings for the building. The architect fees, which will all be paid in 2018, will amount to $7,200. There will also be fees of $2,100 for an engineer to examine the drawings.

BDC has arranged for the financing required for the project. The project will be financed with a mortgage of $875,000 and $1,000,000 of preferred shares issued on January 15, 2018. Interest on the mortgage is payable semi-annually on July 15 and January 15 at a rate of 8% *per annum*. The preferred shares pay dividends of 5% *per annum*, payable semi-annually on July 15 and January 15. There will be a number of costs incurred in order to issue the debt and shares. These costs are legal and accounting fees of $18,450, commissions of $58,300 and registration fees of $1,800 for amending the articles of incorporation to allow the issuance of the preferred shares. BDC had previously deducted $3,000 for its original incorporation costs.

The balance of the costs related to the building are summarized below:

Building insurance from April 15, 2018 @ $450 per month	$ 3,825
Property taxes from February 15, 2018 @ $770 per month	8,085
Soil testing to determine location of footings for building	1,825
Relocation expenses	34,100
Utilities service connections estimated to be completed on May 20, 2018	3,800
Mortgage insurance premium from March 1, 2018 of $325 per month	3,250
Maintenance from October 31, 2018	2,500
Utilities from October 31, 2018	6,300
Landscaping	15,500

The president would like you to advise him of the impact of the proposed transactions on their December 31, 2018 income tax return. Ignore the effects of a leap year.

Problem 8

ETA: 123(1), Sch. V, Parts VI, VII

Authors' Note: The following problem includes GST/HST implications. Students should review Chapter 20 of the textbook, Goods and Services Tax (GST)/Harmonized Sales Tax (HST), before attempting this problem.

Reconsider the facts of Problem 7. Assume that HST was paid at 13%, where applicable, in addition to the amounts shown.

The president of BDC Distributing Limited has asked you to calculate the HST consequences of the transactions presented.

Problem 9

ITA: 20(1)(c), 80.4(1)

Tim Markus, Vice President of Phone Lines, earned $92,000 in salary last year. In addition to his salary, he also received low-interest loans from his employer. Tim's interest rate on these loans is 0% and he owed $160,000 throughout last year. Tim used the loan to purchase a rental property (see Schedule 1). Assume a prescribed interest rate of 2% for the entire year. Five years ago, Tim invested in some common shares of a foreign corporation. He receives $18,000 in dividends (net of $2,000 with-holding tax) annually from this corporation. Last year, he also received taxable eligible dividends of $30,000 from his investment in a Canadian public company which is resident in Canada. Tim also owns $100,000 worth of 5% bonds.

Schedule 1:

Rental revenue	$16,400
Maintenance expenses	5,500
Utilities on rental units . . .	8,200
CCA — half-year rule	3,200

Tim has asked you to calculate his income for tax purposes for last year.

Problem 10

ITA: 12(1)(j), 74.1

The following are independent situations:

(a) Tony Lee gave $50,000 to his wife, Shannon, for the acquisition of shares of a Canadian company on the Toronto Stock Exchange. During the year, an eligible dividend of $5,000 cash was paid on the shares owned by Mrs. Lee.

(b) At the beginning of the year in which her daughter Carey turned 18 in December, Ellen gifted $25,000 directly to Carey. Carey invested the $25,000 in an income-bearing investment that paid her interest of $2,500 during the year. In addition to the $2,500, Carey also earned another $7,500 in interest income from monies received from her mother previously.

What are the tax consequences for the above situations?

Problem 11

ITA: Subdivision b

John Ingles has provided you with the following information related to his various investment holdings as of December 31, 2018.

Interest earned on joint bank account with his spouse (spouse contributes equally).	$ 2,000
Interest earned on his investment account (not joint) with his investment broker	800
Interest earned on 2017 personal income tax assessment	450
Interest on short-term investments:	
$20,000 term deposit taken out November 30, 2018 (interest at maturity in six months)	
Accrued interest from December 1 to December 31, 2018	85
$200,000 GIC purchased November 1, 2017 (interest payable at maturity on October 31, 2020)	
Accrued interest from November 1, 2017 to October 31, 2018	16,000
Accrued interest from January 1, 2018 to December 31, 2018	16,214
Government of Canada Treasury Bills purchased for $9,009 on January 3, 2018	
Amount received on maturity on December 31, 2017	10,000
Cash dividends received from investment in common shares of Canadian resident public corporations	24,000

Cash dividends received from common shares in US corporations (net of $3,000
   of foreign withholding taxes; all in Canadian dollars)   17,000
Rental details from operation of two separate rental properties:

	Property 1	Property 2
Gross rental revenue	$ 30,000	$ 46,000
Utilities	5,000	8,000
Property taxes	2,400	3,500
Repairs	1,500	4,800
Mortgage interest	20,000	32,000
Opening UCC	$368,209	$520,225

Interest expenses paid during 2018:

Interest on bank line of credit used for investing in shares described above	$50,000
Interest on loan to acquire an automobile for his daughter for her 18th birthday	3,200
Interest on a parcel of vacant land (purchased in 2013, the land does not generate any income)	10,000

Based on the above, John has asked you to calculate his income for the year. He would also like you to comment on the income tax implications of items not included in your calculations.

Problem 12

ITA: 18(2), 20(1)(c), 74.1

Your client, Ashley, has come to you for some advice on computing her net income from property.

(a) In February, Ashley sold all her investments and paid off her personal residence mortgage. On March 1, she borrowed $90,000 to reacquire many of the same investments she previously held. Many of the common shares purchased do not carry dividend rights. Her spouse has insisted that 50% of the investments be placed in his name.

(b) On April 15, Ashley purchased a government bond that pays annual interest of 2.5%. When the bond was purchased, Ashley paid accrued interest of $262.50 to the previous owner of the bonds.

(c) On June 1, Ashley borrowed $450,000 to purchase the vacant land next to her apartment block. The land is used as a parking lot and she collected monthly revenues of $2,500. She plans improvements that will double her income from the lot. Ashley's only expenses were $45,500 for interest and property taxes.

Ashley has asked you to explain the income tax implications of each item above.

Problem 13

ITA: 18(1), 20(1)(c);
IT-533

Funds are borrowed by an individual from a financial institution at a 7% *per annum* interest rate to purchase the following unrelated investments:

(a) gold coins on which gains or losses will be treated as capital gains or losses;

(b) an RRSP portfolio of investments yielding 8% in interest;

(c) a five-year GIC paying interest at 4% *per annum*;

(d) common shares of a Canadian-resident public corporation paying no dividends;

(e) preferred shares of a Canadian-resident public corporation paying 5% dividends;

(f) preferred shares of a U.S. corporation paying 6% dividends;

(g) Mindy owns 1,000 shares of International Inc., a corporation listed on the TSX, for which she paid cash. Mindy also owns the condominium she lives in that is financed with borrowed money. Mindy is planning to sell the 1,000 shares of International Inc. and use the proceeds from the sale to pay off the mortgage on the condominium. She will then borrow money to buy another 1,000 shares of International Inc.;

(h) lottery tickets which yielded $75,000 in winnings which were reinvested in short-term securities yielding 2%; and

(i) common shares of a Canadian-resident public corporation paying dividends of 6%; later in the year the shares were sold at a small gain to repay a 8% second mortgage on a principal residence.

Determine the deductibility of the interest expense in each of these unrelated cases.

Type 2 Problems

Problem 14

Trent Zalinski recently retired as a football player with the Saskatchewan Roughriders. In the current year, he received his salary of $150,000 from the team and is eligible for a CFL pension in 15 years. He and his wife Mary have settled in Weyburn, Saskatchewan, where he runs a small sporting goods store as a proprietorship. He has provided you with the following additional information.

(a) His net income from the store for the fiscal year ended December 31 was $35,000. Next year he is hoping to double that. Mary works in the store about 35 hours a week and is paid $6 per hour. This is already included as an expense in determining the $35,000.

(b) Trent's other current-year receipts are: fees received from endorsement of a brand of football equipment, $30,000; eligible dividends from Canadian public corporations, $7,200; dividends from foreign public corporations, (net of $750 withholding tax) $6,750; interest from Canadian bank, $3,000.

(c) Trent also had the following expenses: cycling trip to Cypress Hills Provincial Park with family, $2,200; interest on bank loan to acquire public company shares, $4,050.

(d) In May of the previous year, Trent purchased a five-year GIC in Mary's name. The interest rate was 6%, and it was for $10,000. None of the interest is receivable until maturity in five years.

Trent has asked you to calculate his income for tax purposes. In addition, he wants you to provide any basic tax planning advice that might be appropriate.

CHAPTER 6

CHAPTER 6 —
DISCUSSION NOTES FOR REVIEW QUESTIONS

(1) The principal would be separated from the accrued interest and cause the interest to be included in Billy's income as interest income. The purchaser can deduct the same amount that the vendor included in income.

ITA: 20(14)(*a*)
ITA: 20(14)(*b*)

(2) Attribution would not appear to apply to cause any income allocated to Mrs. Simpson to be reallocated to her husband since there is no attribution of business income. (It should be noted that, if she is not actively involved in the business, then she will not be a specified member of the partnership and the income from the partnership will be deemed to be income from property.)

ITA: 74.1(1)

ITA: 248(1), 96(1.8)

(3) Although the corporation is carrying on a business, Mrs. Smith is not. She will be earning property income (i.e., dividends on the shares), so the exception to the attribution rules for business income does not apply. Attribution as a result of guarantees would only cause the attribution rules to apply if the loan was not at commercial rates. If the bank is charging commercial interest rates, then the attribution rules will not apply.

ITA: 74.5(7)
ITA: 74.5(1)

(4) The interest on the 10 acres would be capitalized since it is not used in business and there is no revenue from the land.

ITA: 18(2)

(5) CCA cannot be claimed to create or increase a loss on rental property. However, those loss limitation rules do not apply to a corporation whose principal business was the leasing, rental, development or sale, or any combination thereof, of real property owned by it. In this case, Rent Co. will be able to claim CCA to create or increase a loss.

ITR: 1100(11)–(14)

(6) No interest is deductible if Ms. Campbell is considered to realize a capital gain on the sale of the gold. Since capital gains are not income from business or property, she does not meet the requirements and cannot deduct the interest. Also, there is no provision that would allow her to capitalize the interest to the cost of the gold. On the other hand, if the gain on the sale of the gold is considered to be income from business or property, the interest would be deductible. Note that the CRA would allow her to choose income treatment for these transactions.

ITA: 9(3)
ITA: 20(1)(*c*)
ITA: 53
IT-346R, par. 8

(7) In the *Attaie* case, the Federal Court–Trial Division agreed that the interest expense was deductible. However, the Federal Court of Appeal reversed this decision and decided that the interest was not deductible, since there was not a direct link between the borrowed funds and the income from property.

87 DTC 5411 (F.C.T.D.)
90 DTC 6413 (F.C.A.)

(8) Under the proposed plan, the interest would not be deductible since the money is not being used to earn income. However, if your client were to borrow from the bank the $100,000 needed to loan to the purchaser in order to complete the sale of his existing house, then at least the interest would be deductible up to 5%. The purchaser would then be in a position to pay the full purchase price for the new residence.

(9) Since the corporation that your client invested in has gone out of business, there is no longer a possibility of earning income from business or property. However, the amount of the lost capital would be deemed to continue to be borrowed for the purpose of earning income and, hence, would allow the interest in this case to continue to be deductible. Refer to Income Tax Folio S3-F6-C1, paragraph 1.41.

ITA: 20.1(1)

CHAPTER 6 — SOLUTIONS TO MULTIPLE CHOICE QUESTIONS

Question 1

(B) is correct. The calculation is as follows:

Grossed up dividend ($12,000 × 1.16)	$13,920
Combined tax rate	× 50%
	$ 6,960
Dividend tax credit	(1,920)
Net tax	$ 5,040

(A) incorrectly ignores provincial tax: $13,920 × 33% – $1,920 = $2,674.

(C) incorrectly ignores the dividend tax credit:

$$\$13,920 \times 50\% = \$6,960$$

(D) incorrectly ignores the gross-up and the dividend tax credit: $12,000 × 50% = $6,000.

Question 2

(B) is the correct answer. The calculation is as follows:

	Property			
	1	*2*	*3*	*Total*
UCC at Jan. 1st	$100,000	$75,000	$150,000	
Rental revenue for the year	$ 58,000	$22,000	$ 20,000	
Expenses for the year	50,000	20,000	20,000	
Income before CCA	$ 8,000	$ 2,000	(Nil)	$10,000
CCA: 4% × UCC	$ 4,000	$ 3,000	$ 6,000	$13,000
Maximum CCA [Reg. 1100(11)]				$10,000

(A) is incorrect. $13,000 is the CCA calculation ignoring the rental property restriction. **ITR: 1100(11)**

(C) is incorrect. $7,000 is the maximum CCA calculation on the first two buildings only. This calculation ignores the fact that the CCA on the third property can be claimed against the net rental income on the first two properties.

(D) is incorrect. It is one-half of the $13,000 calculated in (A) above.

Question 3

(B) is the correct answer. The $12,000 of dividend income will be attributed to Mr. P. Mabel and Mr. P are related and it can reasonably be considered that one of the main reasons for making the loan was to reduce tax. **ITA: 56(4.1)**

(A) is incorrect. The $3,000 of interest income will not be attributed. Peter is not under 18 years of age and, therefore, attribution does not apply. If it had been a loan, instead of a gift, subsection 56(4.1) would apply and may attribute the income. **ITA: 74.1(2)**

(C) is incorrect. Even though an interest-free loan was made to which attribution would apply, there is no property income from the cottage to attribute. **ITA: 56(4.1)**

(D) is incorrect. Even though a gift was made to a spouse to which attribution would apply, there is no property income from the chequing account to attribute. **ITA: 74.1(1)**

CHAPTER 6

Question 4

(B) is correct. The premium paid on a $100,000 term life insurance policy on the taxpayer's life which is required as collateral for a $100,000 bank loan used to purchase a $100,000 investment in common shares is deductible.   ITA: 20(1)(*e*.2)

(A) is incorrect because commissions paid on the purchase of an investment in common shares are capitalized as part of the cost of the shares.   ITA: 18(1)(*b*)

(C) is incorrect because the Act does not allow a deduction for interest expense on a loan to invest in a registered retirement savings plan.   ITA: 18(11)(*b*)

(D) is incorrect because commissions paid on the sale of an investment in common shares are a selling cost deducted in computing the capital gain on the sale of the shares. One-half of a capital gain is a taxable capital gain which is computed under Subdivision c of Division B of Part I of the Act, whereas income from business or property is computed under Subdivision b.

Question 5

(D) is correct: $20,000 × 1.16 + $8,500 + $1,500 tax withheld = $33,200.   ITA: 82(1)

(A) is incorrect because it ignores the gross-up on the dividend and the foreign income: $20,000.

(B) is incorrect because it ignores the gross-up on the dividend and the foreign tax withheld: $20,000 + $8,500 = $28,500.

(C) is incorrect because it ignores the gross-up on the dividend: $20,000 + $8,500 + $1,500 = $30,000.   ITA: 120.4 "split income"

Question 6

(D) is correct.

(A) is incorrect because the tax on split income only applies to taxpayers under age 18 throughout the year. Since Ron is 18, the tax on split income will not apply.   ITA: 120.4 "specified individual"

(B) is incorrect because the only exemption regarding inherited shares is for shares inherited from a parent. If Ron had been under 18 at any time in the year, the tax on split income would have applied to dividends received on the shares.   ITA: 120.4 "excluded amount"

(C) is incorrect because the tax on split income does not apply to capital gains on a disposition to an arm's length person.   ITA: 120.4 "split income"

CHAPTER 6 — SOLUTIONS TO EXERCISES

Exercise 1

(A) In its June 30, 2018 taxation year, the corporation would be required to include in income the interest received March 31, 2018 for the period October 1, 2017 to March 31, 2018 plus interest accrued from April 1 to June 30, 2018. Accrued interest from October 1, 2017 to January 1, 2018 (the period prior to acquisition), which was purchased with the bond, would give rise to a deduction.

ITA: 12(3), 20(14)

(B) The Act would require accrued interest from November 1, 2018 to October 31, 2019 to be included in income in 2019.

ITA: 12(4)

(C) The anniversary day would be December 31, 2018. Accrued interest from the date of purchase to December 31, 2018 would be included in 2018 income.

(D) The $80 received each year would be included in income. On November 30, 2018, there will be an anniversary day, but all of the interest accrued to that day will have been included in income as interest received in the year.

ITA: 12(1)(c)

Exercise 2

(A) (i) The Act would attribute the income on the bond to him even though she is legally entitled to receive it, since a gift is considered to be a transfer and is not a fair market value exchange which would be exempt.

ITA: 74.1(1), 74.5(1)

(ii) Since a sale is also considered to be a transfer, attribution would apply except that, in this case, the transfer would be exempt because it was for fair market value consideration, as long as they elect jointly not to have the rollover apply.

ITA: 74.1(1), 74.5(1)(a), 73(1)

(iii) This situation still involves a sale directly between husband and wife and is, therefore, a transfer subject to the attribution of income. A non-interest bearing demand note would not qualify for the exception because a commercial rate of interest was not charged.

ITA: 74.1(1), 74.5(1)(b)

(iv) The loan of funds would result in attribution, because the exception would not apply since a commercial rate of interest was not charged on the loan.

ITA: 74.1(1), 74.5(2)

(B) If the loan was to a non-arm's length minor or a niece or nephew who is also a minor, then attribution would apply to transfers or loans by means of a trust to or for the benefit of a minor in the same way as spousal attribution applied in part (A), above. However, there are special rules pertaining to transfers or loans to a trust which will be discussed in Chapter 18.

ITA: 74.1(2)
ITA: 74.1(1)

(C) Attribution of income does not apply to a transfer involving an individual who is 18 or older. However, another provision might apply to transactions (iii) and (iv) involving loans. The key condition for this rule to apply is that one of the main reasons for the loan was to reduce or avoid tax on income from property or substituted property. A loan bearing a commercial rate of interest would be exempt from attribution.

ITA: 74.1(2)
ITA: 56(4.1)

Exercise 3

(i) The deductibility of carrying charges is not limited because the land is being used in the course of the hotel business.

ITA: 18(2)

(ii) The Act will limit the deductibility of carrying charges to 75% of their total (i.e., to the amount of the net revenues) so as not to create a loss by their deduction, unless the land is owned by a corporation whose principal purpose is the rental of real property (i.e., land and building) owned by it. This is not the principal purpose of a hotel corporation.

ITA: 18(2)(e)

ITA: 18(2)(f)

(iii) The deductibility of carrying charges may be limited in the same manner as in (ii), above, until the property is used in the business.

ITA: 18(2)

CHAPTER 6

Exercise 4

	Class 1: 4%	Class 1: 4%	Class 8: 20%	Total
	Building 1	Building 2[1]		
UCC, January 1	$148,000	—	$25,000	
Purchases	—	$137,500	—	
UCC, December 31	$148,000	$137,500	$25,000	
CCA..............	5,920	2,750[2]	4,350[3]	$13,020
UCC, January 1	$142,080	$134,750	$20,650	

— *NOTES TO SOLUTION*

[1] Separate class for rental building costing $50,000 or more.   ITR: 1101(1ac)

[2] 4% of [$137,500 – ($\frac{1}{2}$ × $137,500)].

[3]

Net rental income before CCA ($9,270 + 3,750)	$13,020
CCA on rental building and leasing properties (i.e., furniture and fixtures) limited to $13,020 [$13,020 – ($5,920 + $2,750) = $4,350]	(13,020)
Net income from rental properties...........................	Nil

Note that where less than maximum capital cost allowance is taken, the less than maximum amount should be taken in classes with relatively higher CCA rates, so that the UCC carried forward to the following year is eligible for CCA at the higher rate in that subsequent year.

Exercise 5

(A)

	Property A	Property B	Total
UCC, January 1	$330,000	$480,000	
Disposal	(336,000)	—	
UCC, December 31	$ (6,000)	$480,000	
Recapture	6,000	—	
CCA @ 4% (Class 1) — see below	—	(12,000)	
UCC forward	Nil	$468,000	
Revenue	$ 13,500	$ 22,500	$36,000
Recapture	6,000	—	6,000
Expenses before CCA	(11,250)	(18,750)	(30,000)
Net	$ 8,250	$ 3,750	$12,000
CCA (4% of $480,000 = $19,200; limited to net above)			(12,000)
Net income from property			Nil

(B)   The rule to defer recapture applies on a voluntary disposition of a "former business property". A   ITA: 13(4), 248(1)
rental property is excluded from the definition and, hence, the deferral rule does not apply.

Exercise 6

Interest expense is deductible if there is a reasonable expectation of earning income from property.   ITA: 20(1)(c)

Investment	Not deductible	Deductible
Common shares		$20,000[1]
Gold bullion	$25,000[2]	
Corporate bond		20,000[3]
Preferred shares (RRSP)	10,000[4]	
Common shares		30,000[5]
Paintings	15,000[6]	
GICs		20,000[5]
Total	**$50,000**	**$90,000**

Deductible interest = $90,000 × 5.5% = $4,950

— NOTES TO SOLUTION

[1] As there is an expectation of dividend income on common shares, the interest is deductible.

[2] As capital treatment has been chosen for gains/losses on the gold bullion, the interest is not deductible.

[3] The corporate bond is income-producing and the associated interest would be deductible.

[4] The preferred shares were purchased in an RRSP; deduction of interest is disallowed.

[5] The associated interest on the common shares and GICs would be deductible, as there is the expectation of earning property income.

[6] The paintings from well-known galleries would be considered an investment for earning future capital gains and, therefore, the associated interest would not be deductible.

Exercise 7

Since the rule relates to capital cost allowance, Regulations Part XI, Capital Cost Allowances, would be a starting point. More specifically, ITR 1101(1ac) deals with the separate classes rule related to rental properties having a cost of at least $50,000.   ITR: 1100(11), 1101(1ac)

The other special rule is ITR 1100(11), which states that capital cost allowance on rental properties can only be deducted to the extent that it does not create or increase a net loss from all rental properties combined. Note that Interpretation Bulletin IT-195R4, Rental Property — Capital Cost Allowance Restrictions, provides further details.

Exercise 8

			Notes
Practice income		$400,000	
Rental income			
Rental revenue	$12,000		
Mortgage interest	3,342		1
Mortgage interest - PR	2,507		2
Property taxes	887		1
Insurance	333		1
Utilities	—		3
Advertising	500		4
Repairs and maintenance	—		5
CCA	4,431		6
	12,000		
Net rental income		—	
Taxable income		$400,000	

Notes:

1. Costs which are attributable to the period of renovation and relate to the renovation or the ownership of the land must be capitalized to the building [ssec. 18(3.1)].

	Total 275 days	Renovation Period 214 days	Rental Period 61 days
Mortgage interest	$15,068	$11,726	$ 3,342
Property taxes	4,000	3,113	887
Insurance	1,500	1,167	333

2. In general, the interest on the mortgage on Dr. Do Good's principal residence will be deductible against the rental income since the mortgage was used to earn rental income and not for personal purposes.

   Applying ssec. 18(3.1) as outlined above:

	Total 245 days	Renovation Period 184 days	Rental Period 61 days
Mortgage interest	$10,068	$ 7,561	$ 2,507

3. Applying ssec. 18(3.1), the full amount of utilities will be capitalized since it relates to the renovation during the renovation period.

4. The advertising expense does not relate to the renovation of the building or the ownership of the land during that period of time, and, therefore, is fully deductible.

5. The repairs and maintenance are likely of a capital nature. In any event, ssec. 18(3.1) will require them to be capitalized to the building since they relate to the renovation.

6. Capital cost allowance:

   The property is available for use since construction was complete on October 31.

Cost of building purchased	$150,000
Renovations [includes R&M — see Note 1 in problem]	150,000
Less: R&M	(-)
Add items capitalized:	
Mortgage interest	11,726
Mortgage interest — PR	7,561
Property taxes	3,113
Insurance	1,167
Utilities	1,400
Advertising	—
	324,967
Less: 50% of addition	(162,483)
	162,484
CCA rate (Class 1)	4%
	$ 6,499

   The CCA claim is restricted to the net rental income before CCA, i.e., CCA cannot be used to create or increase a loss. There is no proration of CCA for short fiscal periods since it is property income calculated on a calendar year.

Alternatively, $4,431 of soft costs could be deducted in accordance with ssec. 20(29) instead of the CCA. The soft costs deducted under ssec. 20(29) would not increase the capital cost of the building.

Exercise 9

(a) The incorporation costs greater than $3,000 will be included in class 14.1. The first $3,000 will be expensed in the year incurred. The remaining balance of of $960 can be written-off at the rate of 5% declining balance at the discretion of the taxpayer.

(b) The loan would avoid the attribution rules for income and capital gains only if:

   (i) the proposed 7% rate of interest is not less than the lesser of the prescribed rate or a commercial rate; and

   (ii) the interest is actually paid by January 30 each and every year (sec. 74.5).

(c) Although these expenses appear to be capital expenditures, a write-off at the straight-line rate of 20% per year is permitted but prorated on a daily basis of $^{242}/_{365}$ for 2019 taxation year.

(d) The office equipment, computer and licence are depreciable property subject to the capital cost allowance rules, whereas the customer lists are eligible capital property and subject to the rules described in part (a).

	Class	Maximum Rate	Method of Write-off
Office Equipment	8	20%	declining balance
Computer	50	55%	declining balance
Licence	14	20%	straight-line over 5 years

The office equipment and computer capital cost allowance would be restricted to $\frac{1}{2}$ of normal CCA pursuant to the net amount rule (reg. 1100(2)).

The capital cost allowance is prorated to 242 days by virtue of reg. 1100(3) for Classes 8 and 50, and reg. 1100(1)(*c*) for Class 14.

(e) Rental payment of $14,000 has a prepaid component as at June 30, 2019 of $4,718. Therefore, only $9,282 will be an expense for the 2019 taxation year (sec. 18(9)).

Renovations are leasehold improvements in Class 13 and are written off on the straight-line basis over the lesser of 5 years or 12 years.

Lesser of   (i) $\dfrac{\$23,000}{5} = \$4,600$

               (ii) $\dfrac{\$23,000}{12} = \$1,917$

For the 2019 taxation year, only 50% of the normal CCA can be claimed, prorated on the number of days in the 2019 taxation year (242).

(f) On the assumption that the fair market value is $19,000, the selling price will be deemed to be $19,000, the fair market value at the date of sale. Mr. Radical's brother-in-law is not dealing at arm's length with Dude Ltd. (ssec. 69(1)), since Mr. Radical is related to Dude Ltd. (spar. 251(2)(*b*)(iii)). Thus, Stan will have a taxable capital gain of $8,250, being $\frac{1}{2} \times$ ($19,000 – $2,500).

The adjusted cost base of the car will be $15,000, not the deemed proceeds of disposition and, hence, there may be some double taxation on the eventual disposition of the car by Dude Ltd. (par. 69(1)(*b*))

The capital cost to Dude Ltd. will be the original capital cost of $2,500 plus capital gain inclusion of $8,250 (spar. 13(7)(*e*)(ii)).

CHAPTER 6

The car should be in Class 10 - 30% for capital cost allowance purposes and will be subject to the net amount rate (½ year rule) since the car was not depreciable property to Mr. Radical's brother-in-law (reg. 1100(2.2)(*f*)). The CCA will have to be prorated for a short taxation year of 242 days.

(g) The $45,000 payment will be composed of two parts: income of $30,000 (⅔ × $45,000) and prepaid services received of $15,000 (⅓ × $45,000). Both amounts are income for tax purposes (par. 12(1)(*a*)). However, a reserve may be claimed to reflect the services which will be rendered after the year end (par. 20(1)(*m*)).

Exercise 10

Subsection 56(4.1) will apply to deem the dividend income of $7,500 received by Faith to be Robin's income and not Faith's income for tax purposes. Robin loaned money directly to his daughter, a non-arm's length party, with one of the main reasons being to reduce tax.

Chapter 7

Capital Gains: Personal

Learning Goals

Know, Understand and Explain

By the end of this chapter you will know, understand and be able to explain:

- The different types of capital gains a taxpayer can incur on the sale of capital property.
- The special provisions for the taxation of capital gains as they relate to the different types of capital property.
- The meaning of a capital gain, taxable capital gain, capital loss, and allowable capital loss.
- The circumstances in which an individual can claim the principal residence exemption.
- The tax implications on the death of a taxpayer.
- The tax implications on ceasing or establishing residency in Canada.

Apply

By the end of this chapter you will be able to apply your knowledge and understanding to:

- Classify capital property into three different categories: personal use, listed personal, and other capital property.
- Correctly determine the tax implications of non-arm's length transfers.
- Correctly determine the adjusted cost base and the proceeds of disposition on the disposition of a capital property under various circumstances.
- Minimize the tax implications of disposing of more than one principal residence.
- Apply your knowledge to advise a client or employer on the tax implications on the death of a taxpayer and plan to meet the client's needs.
- Apply your knowledge to advise a client or employer on the tax implications of ceasing or establishing residency in Canada.

Review Questions
¶7,800 in the Study Guide

Multiple Choice Questions
¶7,825 in the Study Guide

Exercises
¶7,850 in the Study Guide

Assignment Problems
¶7,875 in the Study Guide

CHAPTER 7 — LEARNING CHART

Problem Descriptions

Textbook Example Problems

7-1	Sale of mutual funds
7-2	Personal-use and listed personal property
7-3	Principal residence
7-4	Change in use of principal residence
7-5	Principal residence — transfer between spouses
7-6	Share transactions
7-7	Share transactions — open market and stock option
7-8	Stock dividends
7-9	Superficial loss
7-10	Share transactions
7-11	Options
7-12	Capital gains deferral
7-13	Allowable business investment loss
7-14	Allowable business investment loss

Multiple Choice Questions

1	Personal-use property
2	Principal residence
3	Change in use of principal residence
4	Stock dividend
5	Personal-use and listed personal property
6	Transactions with child
7	Transactions with spouse
8	Transactions with spouse and child
9	Death of a taxpayer
10	Becoming non-resident

Exercises

1	Principal residence
2	Principal residence
3	Change in use of principal residence
4	Personal-use and listed personal property
5	Share transactions
6	Share transactions
7	Listed personal property
8	Stock dividends
9	Arm's length
10	Non-arm's length transaction
11	Transactions with spouse
12	Becoming a resident
13	Sale of shares

CHAPTER 7

Problem Descriptions

14	Non-arm's length transactions
15	Superficial loss
16	Non-arm's length transactions

Assignment Problems

1	Stock transactions
2	Stock option — capital gain
3	Sale of mutual fund
4	Death of a taxpayer
5	Becoming resident and non-resident
6	Non-arm's length transactions, attribution
7	Non-arm's length transactions, attribution
8	Allowable business investment loss
9	Transfer of property on divorce
10	Related, affiliated, arm's length
11	Personal-use and listed personal property
12	Principal residence
13	LPP loss and ABIL
14	Option
15	Allowable business investment loss
16	Principal residence with change in use
17	Stock transactions
18	Stock transactions
19	Death of a taxpayer
20	Going non-resident
21	Non-arm's length purchase of rental property
22	CCPC stock option with attribution
23	Comprehensive
24	Going non-resident
25	Asset sale
26	Case

Study Notes

¶7,800   REVIEW QUESTIONS

(1) A client invested in a rental property some years ago and paid $10,000 as a down payment and $150,000 was in the form of a mortgage. Recently, the vacancy rate has climbed and the value of the property has fallen. She thinks that she will just walk away from the property and let the mortgage company take over the property. What will her proceeds of disposition be?

(2) As a result of a reorganization in a company in which Mr. Smith is a shareholder, he has just had a return of some of the corporation's capital. As a result, the adjusted cost base of his shares has become negative. This does not bother him since he has been told that as long as he continues to own the shares he will not have to recognize this built-in capital gain. Comment.

(3) Mr. Chan has come to you with a problem. He owns the family cottage and his wife owns the house in town. Both housing units were purchased within the last 30 years. They are thinking of selling both of these properties and moving to another province. He thought they could each claim the principal residence exemption to avoid any tax but someone has told him that they can only claim one of the residences. In general terms can you explain the rules to him?

(4) Ms. Starra bought a cottage property on a lake that has since become polluted. As a result, the value of the property has declined and she has sold it, since no one wants to go there anymore. She realized a loss on the sale and wants to claim the loss on her personal return. Can she do it?

(5) What is the "$1,000 rule" as it relates to personal-use property? Does the same rule apply to listed personal property?

(6) Mr. Davids has come to you to have his personal tax return done. He sold some shares of a public corporation that he has owned for some years and wants help in minimizing his tax on the transaction. One point that is confusing him is the stock dividend that he received this year. He does not know how to treat the dividend for tax purposes. Please help him.

(7) Under Divisions B and C, what happens when the capital losses exceed the capital gains in any one year?

(8) If you were to win a Mazda MX5 in a lottery, what would the cost base be to you given that you might want to sell it to buy a car more fitting (boring) for an accountant?

(9) Ms. Dempster has had her company buy her a car and register it in her name. The CRA discovered this and has assessed her with a shareholder benefit for $35,000, the value of the car. Ms. Dempster is going to have to sell the car to pay the tax liability. What will her cost base be on the car?

ITA: 15(1)

(10) On July 1 of this year, John Smith died leaving his wife and four children in financial difficulty. In order to earn extra income Mrs. Smith painted the basement, put carpet down, and then rented it to students. Comment on the tax issues.

(11) On July 1 nine years ago, Ms. Marr was transferred with her family to Victoria from Toronto by her employer, a large public company. She was sure that the value of her Toronto house would go up significantly so she kept it and rented a house in Victoria. It was this year that the same employer moved Ms. Marr and her family back to Toronto, at which time they moved back into their house. However, they found that the neighbourhood had changed significantly so they decided to sell the house and buy in another location. Discuss how much of the principal residence exemption she can claim on the sale of the Toronto home.

(12) Last year Ms. Milne inherited $5 million from her uncle's estate and is now appalled by the amount of tax that she has to pay on her interest income. She has always liked the Cayman Islands and has decided to move there permanently in order to avoid Canadian tax. Her only assets are $5 million of term deposits but she has heard that there is a lot of tax to pay on leaving the country. What do you think?

(13) Mr. Shiloh was transferred to Canada by his employer four years ago and is now being transferred back to the U.S. At the time he entered Canada he held shares in his U.S. employer which are listed on the TSX Stock Exchange. He still owns all these shares and is unhappy about all the tax he is going to have to pay on the deemed disposition. Advise him.

ITA: 128.1(4)

(14) Ms. Green has been told that a good way to create a capital gain is to buy shares on the stock market and then sell someone an option to buy the shares at a price slightly higher than the current market price. Her understanding is that the proceeds on the sale of the option is a capital gain. What advice can you give her?

(15) Mrs. Garland has been going south for many years and usually keeps some U.S. currency handy in case she needs it. This year, because of some unusual fluctuations in the Canadian dollar, she realized an exchange loss on her U.S. dollar transactions of $2,500. How will this be treated for tax purposes?

(16) Mr. Oats is a farmer who is fortunate enough to have farm land close to the city. Because of the prime location he has been approached to sell the land, but he is reluctant to do so since he wants to farm for the next five years. However, he is willing to sell someone an option to buy the land in five years at what he thinks is a generous price. He is to receive $50,000 for granting this option. He thinks he can defer the gain on granting the option until the year of sale by reducing the ACB of his land by $50,000. What do you think?

(17) Mr. Rollins bought a convertible debenture two years ago for $10,000 and is now in the process of converting it into common shares of the company. The debenture is convertible into 1,000 common shares. At the time of the conversion the common shares are worth $20 each. What are the tax effects of the disposition of the debenture and the acquisition of the shares?

(18) Mrs. Gleba owns 20 acres of land that have an appraised value of $100,000. She is considering selling the land to a friend for $50,000 in order to have the friend living closer to her. The two individuals are not related. What tax issues would you discuss with her?

(19) Scott was 25 years old when his father Bill gave him shares in Bell Canada as a gift. Bill had paid $1,000 for them 10 years ago and they were worth $5,000 at the time of the gift. Scott has come to you to find out how much tax he will have to pay. Discuss the tax implications to Scott and Bill of the gift.

CHAPTER 7

¶7,825   MULTIPLE CHOICE QUESTIONS

Question 1

During the year, Mina sold the following personal assets, all of which she had acquired within the last 10 years:

	Cost	Proceeds
Automobile	$20,000	$18,000
Boat	600	1,500
Painting	600	1,300
Jewellery	1,400	200

Her capital gain for the year from these dispositions is:

(A) $900

(B) $800

(C) $500

(D) $400

Question 2

Amanda sold her cottage for $130,000 in May 2018. The cottage cost her $50,000 in 2011 and qualifies as a principal residence. The only other principal residence that Amanda has owned during her lifetime was her Toronto home, which she owned from 2009 to 2017. Even though she sold it for $200,000 more than it cost, she did not report the gain on her 2017 tax return because it was her principal residence. What is the minimum taxable capital gain that Amanda must report on her 2018 tax return in respect of the sale of the cottage?

(A) $80,000

(B) $25,000

(C) $30,000

(D) $50,000

Question 3

Gary Chin purchased his first and only principal residence in 2001 for $350,000. The residence was in Toronto, and when he was transferred to Windsor because of a promotion to managing partner in 2012, he rented the residence. The residence was worth $550,000 in 2012 and he elected to be deemed not to have changed the use of the residence. Gary rented an apartment in Windsor with the expectation of moving back into his Toronto residence on retirement. On January 1, 2018, Gary received an unsolicited offer of $850,000 for the Toronto residence and sold it. Which of the following is a true statement?

ITA: 45(2)

(A) There is no taxable capital gain to report in 2012 or 2018 in respect of the principal residence.

(B) There is no capital gain to report in 2012 in respect of the principal residence. The taxable capital gain is $13,889 in 2018 in respect of the principal residence.

(C) The taxable capital gain is $100,000 in 2012 and $150,000 in 2018 in respect of the principal residence.

(D) The taxable capital gain is $250,000 in 2018 in respect of the principal residence.

Question 4

A Canadian resident individual received a stock dividend from a public corporation of one share. The dividend is a taxable dividend. The stock dividend resulted in an increase in the paid-up capital of $4 for each share issued but the fair market value of each share is $10. Which of the following statements is correct about the stock dividend received?

(A) The cost of the stock is deemed to be $4 and the individual's net income increases by $4.

(B) The cost of the stock is deemed to be $4 and the individual's net income increases by $5.52.

(C) The cost of the stock is deemed to be $10 and the individual's net income increases by $10.

(D) The cost of the stock is deemed to be $10 and the individual's net income is deemed to be $13.80.

Question 5

Donna Jailal has provided you with the following information in connection with her income tax return for the year:

Capital Gains:

Shares	$1,600
Personal-use property	700
Listed personal property	500

Capital Losses:

Shares	$ 820
Personal-use property	1,000
Listed personal property	140
Listed personal property losses from the previous year	100

What is the minimum net taxable capital gain that she must report as Division B income for the year?

(A) $370

(B) $740

(C) $870

(D) $920

Question 6

On December 31 of this year, Ms. Y gave her 6-year-old child some common shares of a public corporation with an adjusted cost base of $900,000 and a fair market value of $1,000,000. Which one of the following statements is TRUE?

(A) The attribution rule will apply to attribute to Ms. Y any future dividends received by her child on the shares. This attribution will continue until the year in which the child becomes 18 years old.

(B) The attribution rule will apply to attribute to Ms. Y any future dividends received by her child on the shares as well as any capital gains or losses if her child sells the shares. This attribution will continue until the year in which the child turns 18 years of age.

(C) Ms. Y will report no gain or loss on the transfer of property this year because it is a gift.

(D) Ms. Y will report a $100,000 taxable capital gain on the gift this year.

Question 7

Ms. Y sells a stock (adjusted cost base $900,000) to her husband for $800,000 cash (the fair market value of the stock) and elects out of the interspousal rollover. Which one of the following statements is TRUE?

ITA: 73(1)

(A) Ms. Y will report an allowable capital loss of $50,000 which she can only deduct against taxable capital gains.

(B) Ms. Y does not have a capital loss because transfers to a spouse are made for proceeds equal to adjusted cost base.

(C) Ms. Y does not have a capital loss because of the superficial loss rules.

(D) The attribution rule will apply to attribute to Ms. Y any future dividends received by her husband on the shares as well as any capital gains or losses if her husband sells the shares.

Question 8

Mike purchased 100 shares of Pubco (a taxable Canadian corporation and public company) in 2015 for $3.11 per share plus $39 in commissions. In 2016, Mike purchased another 100 shares of Pubco for $4 per share plus a brokerage commission of $50. On March 1, 2018, when the shares were worth $6 per share, Mike gifted half the Pubco shares to his 8-year-old son and half to his wife (no special elections were filed). What is the amount of the taxable capital gain that Mike must report in 2018?

(A) $100

(B) $122

(C) $200

(D) $400

Question 9

Mr. Smith died on June 30 of this year and left his entire estate to his son, Mark. His executor has provided you with a list of assets and their fair market value at the date of death.

List of Assets	Cost	Fair Market Value
Toronto home (sole principal residence during past 23 years)	$300,000	$840,000
Rental property in London, Ontario		
— Land	50,000	100,000
— Building (UCC: $2,000)	25,000	35,000
Mutual fund units	12,000	60,000
Shares of a public companies	90,000	100,000

What is the amount that must be included in Mr. Smith's Division B income for the year of death?

(A) $59,000

(B) $70,500

(C) $82,000

(D) $352,000

Question 10

Mr. T ceased to be a resident of Canada on September 1, 2018. At that date, he owned the following assets:

	Year acquired	Cost	Fair market value Sept. 1, 2018
Rental real estate in Canada	2002	$50,000	$100,000
Registered retirement savings plan	2010	60,000	80,000
Painting	2013	6,000	10,000
Shares of a public corporation (listed) resident in Canada (owns less than 1%)	2014	10,000	40,000

Which one of the following amounts represents Mr. T's minimum taxable capital gain on the above assets for 2018?

(A) $15,000

(B) $17,000

(C) $27,000

(D) $42,000

¶7,850   EXERCISES

Exercise 1

ITA: 40(2)(*b*), 54

Ms. Amin has come to you for advice on the tax consequences of the disposition of the following two residences in 2018:

Residence	Date of purchase	Cost	Selling price
Regina home	2007	$400,000	$517,500
Cottage	2012	250,000	375,000

— *REQUIRED*

Compute the minimum amount of taxable capital gains.

Exercise 2

ITA: 40(2)(*b*)

Peter Patel has only two residences which he wishes to dispose of in 2018. The following facts relate to those residences:

	Date purchased	Cost	Real estate commission	Estimated selling price
City home	2003	$180,000	$12,000	$247,000
Cottage	2008	90,000	6,000	164,000

— *REQUIRED*

Determine how Peter must designate residences in order to achieve the minimum capital gain.

Exercise 3

ITA: 40(2)(*b*), 45, 54, 54.1

Howard Bauer, who presently lives in Vancouver, is considering moving to Montreal. Although Howard intends to purchase a home in Montreal, he does not want to sell his fully-paid Vancouver home in case he decides to return some time in the future. Howard would rent his Vancouver home which cost him $50,000 in 2003 and now has a fair market value of $350,000.

— *REQUIRED*

Discuss the tax implications concerning Howard's Vancouver home if:

(A) Howard is self-employed; or

(B) Howard is employed.

Exercise 4

ITA: 41, 54

Karl Kim disposed of the following assets in 2018, all of which were bought within the last nine years:

	Sale price	Cost	Selling cost
Painting	$2,000	$ 300	$100
Antique clock	1,200	250	20
Outboard motor	750	500	15
Gold coin	600	1,000	10

— *REQUIRED*

Determine Karl's net taxable capital gain for the year.

Exercise 5

ITA: 53(1)(f), 54

Ivan Bedard purchased the following shares of Solid Investments Ltd.:

March 1, 2017	100 shares @ $30 including brokerage
June 1, 2018.	150 shares @ $35 including brokerage
January 10, 2019	200 shares @ $26 including brokerage

On December 15, 2018, Ivan sold 200 shares @ $25 less brokerage of $75.

— REQUIRED

(A) Determine Ivan's taxable capital gain or allowable capital loss on his December 15, 2018 disposition.

(B) Compute the adjusted cost base of the shares on hand on January 10, 2019.

Exercise 6

ITA: 47(1)

Regan San Juan participated in the following stock transactions to December 31, 2018:

Date	Description	Share price	Number of shares	Broker fees
Jan. 1/12	Hi Growth Co. — purchased	$3.00	1,000	$70
Jun. 5/13	Hi Growth Co. — purchased	2.80	3,000	90
Aug. 5/14	Hi Growth Co. — purchased	3.80	1,500	70
Dec. 3/15	Hi Growth Co. — purchased	5.10	1,000	120
May 1/15	Hi Growth Co. — sold	7.50	3,000	420
Nov. 8/16	Hi Growth Co. — purchased	5.75	1,000	130
Jan. 9/17	Hi Growth Co. — sold	8.40	1,500	240
Jan. 10/12	Hi Risk Co. — purchased	0.25	20,000	200
Jan. 14/12	Hi Risk Co. — purchased	0.80	4,000	75
May 20/18	Hi Risk Co. — sold	0.30	24,000	150

— REQUIRED

(a) Compute Regan's adjusted cost base for the shares of Hi Growth Co. that he still holds at the end of 2018.

(b) Compute Regan's 2018 taxable capital gain or allowable capital loss on the disposal of the Hi Risk Co. shares.

Exercise 7

ITA: 3, 5, 6, 7, 8, 9

Fong currently earns $23,000 income from employment and $10,000 from operating a part-time coffee bar business. In 2009, Fong inherited an antique painting. At that time the heirloom was worth $9,000. Today, the painting is apparently worth $29,000.

— REQUIRED

What would Fong's income for tax purposes be if he sold the painting and realized a capital gain?

Exercise 8

ITA: 53(2)

Miriam Franklin decided to purchase shares in Strippit Limited, a public company, listed on the Canadian Venture Exchange. Miriam purchased 1,000 shares at $35 per share plus brokerage of $500 on December 10, 2008.

Miriam received the following dividends during the intervening years:

February 1, 2011 . . . . .   A stock dividend of 5% with a paid-up capital of $10 per share.
April 10, 2013 . . . .   A stock dividend of 10% with a paid-up capital of $10 per share.
August 1, 2015 . . . .   A stock dividend of 20% with a paid-up capital of $10 per share.

— *REQUIRED*

Determine the adjusted cost base of Miriam's shares as at December 31, 2018.

Exercise 9

ITA: 251

Which of the following individuals are not at arm's length with Ms. Gamma:

(A) her brother's wife?

(B) her niece?

(C) her husband from whom she is legally separated?

(D) an unrelated person?

Exercise 10

James Meadows is not at arm's length with his son Hayden. James wants Hayden to have a painting that cost him $1,200 and now has a fair market value of $1,500. What are the consequences under the non-arm's length transfer rules to James and Hayden if:

ITA: 69(1)

(A) he sells the painting to him for $2,000?

(B) he sells the painting to him for $1,200?

(C) he gives the painting to him without any financial consideration?

Exercise 11

ITA: 73, 74.1, 74.2, 74.5;
IT-511R

Alice Verwey is considering the following courses of action in transferring assets to her spouse this year:

(A) gifting to her husband shares with a fair market value of $15,000 and an adjusted cost base of $12,000;

(B) selling to her husband shares with a fair market value of $15,000 and an adjusted cost base of $12,000 for cash of $15,000. An election out of the interspousal rollover was made;

ITA: 73(1)

(C) selling to her husband shares with a fair market value of $15,000 and an adjusted cost base of $12,000 for a $15,000 non-interest bearing promissory note with a definite repayment period;

(D) gifting to her husband $15,000 such that he purchases the shares on the open market; and

(E) lending her husband $15,000 evidenced by a non-interest bearing promissory note with a definite repayment period such that he purchases the shares on the open market.

— *REQUIRED*

Discuss the tax implications arising from the above transactions and any subsequent disposition by the spouse.

Exercise 12

ITA: 128.1(4), 115

Mr. Emerson, a United States citizen, entered Canada on June 1, 2013, and became resident in Canada for tax purposes. Mr. Emerson had a capital asset A which he brought with him upon his entry to Canada. The cost of the asset was $2,000 and the fair market value was $5,000 at the time of entry. In 2014, Mr. Emerson purchased another capital property B for $10,000. Mr. Emerson is considering returning to the United States on a permanent basis in 2018. He estimates that the two properties will have fair market values of $12,000 for A and $20,000 for B.

— REQUIRED

Discuss the tax consequences of Mr. Emerson's pending departure from Canada.

Exercise 13

Mr. I.M. Smart has come to you for some tax advice concerning the sale of his shares of XYZ Ltd., a public corporation, to his wife, a friend, and to his 10-year-old son by means of a trust. As consideration for the shares, he accepted a non-interest bearing demand note.

	Date of sale	No. of shares	Selling price	FMV at date of sale
Wife	Jan. 1, 2018	500	$35	$60
Friend	Mar. 1, 2018	500	55	55
Son	Apr. 1, 2018	500	40	70

Mr. Smarts records show the following information concerning the shares:

Purchases

2010	500 shares @ $10
2011	300 shares @ $15
2012	100 shares @ $20
2013	500 shares @ $30

Dividends Received

2010–2018	—	June 30th each year; a cash dividend of approximately 10% of fair market value.
2014	—	10% stock dividend which resulted in an increase in the paid-up capital of $5 per share.

Additional Information:

(1) Mr. Smart does not wish to elect to use subsection 73(1).

(2) Mr. Smart's spouse and child (by means of a trust) plan to invest the dividend income on these shares in five-year compounding 8% Guaranteed Investment Certificates.

— REQUIRED

(A) Explain the tax implications of the above transactions, supported by all your computations.

(B) If Mr. Smart had consulted you prior to these transactions, what advice would you give him to avoid the adverse tax consequence in part (A), if any?

Exercise 14

Sandi Senseless completed the following transactions during 2018:

(1) She gifted her husband 1,000 Bell Canada shares. The fair market value at the time of the transfer was $65 per share, and her adjusted cost base was $40 per share.

(2) She sold to her fifteen-year-old child a valuable painting that had a fair market value of $125,000 for $1,000. Sandi had inherited the painting from her father, at which time the painting had an appraised value of $40,000. Her son intends to sell this painting five years hence to finance his university education.

(3) She loaned her husband $190,000 through a non-interest-bearing note. Her husband acquired a farm with these funds and operated the farm successfully in 2018, making a substantial profit. However, in 2019 he sold the farm for $310,000.

— *REQUIRED*

Discuss the income tax implications.

Exercise 15

Your client, Mr. Y, has unused capital losses forward of $30,000. In January 2018, he sold his mutual fund investments and immediately repurchased them in order to trigger a $50,000 capital gain. Since that time, the mutual funds have declined in value so that he has an accrued loss of $10,000. Mr. Y plans to sell his mutual fund holdings in August 2018 and immediately repurchase them in order to trigger a $10,000 capital loss.

— *REQUIRED*

Comment on Mr. Ys plan.

Exercise 16

Mr. S has non-capital losses that are about to expire. Therefore, he gifted his investment portfolio to his wife. He will elect in his 2018 tax return not to have subsection 73(1) (transfer to spouse at adjusted cost base) apply to the transfer so that the transfer is at fair market value and the capital gain will be realized. He also feels that this will help him income split since he plans to have his wife claim all future income and capital gains from investments.

— *REQUIRED*

Comment on Mr. S's income splitting plan and provide any suggestions that might be necessary to make the plan successful.

¶7,875   ASSIGNMENT PROBLEMS

Type 1 Problems

Problem 1

During the year Rachael had the following transactions in common shares of Carnegie Inc., a Canadian public company. She would like you, as her tax adviser, to explain the tax consequences to her of each of the following transactions:

Date	Transaction	Price/Share	Number of Shares	Broker Fees	Notes
Jan 15/18	Purchase	$35	1,000	$700	
Feb 20/18	Purchase	37	200	150	
April 5/18	Stock dividend — 10%		120		1
Sept 16/18	Stock split		1,320		2
Nov 30/18	Sold	17	100	75	
Dec 12/18	Purchase	13	200	125	

Notes:

(1) The April 5, 2018 stock dividend resulted in an increase in paid-up capital of $30 per share.

(2) The stock split gave Rachael one share for every share she held at the time.

(3) On December 15th she received a cash dividend of $10 per share.

Problem 2

This is a continuation of Assignment Problem 2 in Chapter 3. The following two situations are not related. Once again, you have been asked for advice on employee stock options by two different clients.

(1) Omer is part of the management team of a Canadian public company and is eligible for the employee stock option plan. A few years ago he received an option on 1,000 shares. The option required him to pay the option price of $30 (the value at the time the option was granted) for the shares at the time he exercises his option.

Omer exercised the option three years ago when the shares were worth $35 and is now selling the shares for $45. He has asked you to tell him the amount of income he will have to report.

(2) Hilda is part of the management team of a Canadian-controlled private company and is eligible for the employee stock option plan. A few years ago she received an option on 1,000 shares. The option required her to pay the option price of $30 (the value at the time the option was granted) for the shares at the time she exercises her option.

Hilda exercised the option three years ago when the shares were worth $35 and is now selling the shares for $45. She has asked you to tell her the amount of income she will have to report.

Problem 3

ITA: 53

Ivy Jackson invested $2,000 on April 1, 2017, in Growth Mutual Fund sold by a major financial institution. Her investment purchased 72.788 units of the fund. On December 31, 2017, the fund allocated $96.37 of capital gains to her account. As a result, the $96.37 was reinvested in the fund to purchase 3.774 units at the market value of $25.535 per unit.

On June 30, 2018, she sold 25 of her units for a total of $718.

Ivy has asked you to calculate the effects of these events on her income for tax purposes in 2017 and 2018.

Problem 4

Brandon died on March 15, 2018. His estate is not complicated, as most of his assets were bank deposits. However, he did have 1,000 shares in a public company at the time of his death. Of these, he left 500 to his surviving spouse and 500 to his daughter. The executor would like your advice on the tax consequences to the estate and the beneficiaries of these bequests.

The shares have a fair market value at the time of death of $50 per share. Brandon's adjusted cost base at the time of his death was $20 per share.

Problem 5

The following two situations are not related:

(1) Stella moved to Canada from Greece early this year to work for a financial institution in Toronto. Her family moved with her and they bought a house in Oakville. At the time of her move, she owned shares of a public company listed on the New York Stock Exchange. These shares had a fair market value of $40,000 at the time she became a resident. She originally paid $25,000 for the shares. They are now worth $50,000.

Stella is now considering selling these shares and has asked you to advise her on the Canadian tax consequences.

(2) Harry moved to England from Canada early this year to work for a financial institution in Oxford. His family moved with him and they bought a house near Oxford. At the time of his move, he owned shares of a public company listed on the New York Stock Exchange. These shares had a fair market value of $40,000 at the time he ceased to be a resident. He originally paid $25,000 for the shares. They are now worth $50,000.

Harry is now considering selling these shares and has asked you to advise him on the Canadian tax consequences.

Problem 6

Donna has 1,000 shares in a Canadian public company that are worth $100,000 and pay a dividend of $5,000 each year. Her adjusted cost base on these shares is $70,000. She is already in the top tax bracket. For estate planning purposes she is proposing the following options, but she would like your advice as her personal tax planner before she makes a decision.

Options considered:

(1) Give the shares to her husband.

(2) Give the shares to her 15-year-old daughter.

(3) Give the shares to her 25-year-old daughter.

Problem 7

Katie has Canadian public company shares that are worth $50,000 and pay a dividend of $2,500 each year. Her adjusted cost base on these shares is $35,000. She is already in the top tax bracket. She would like your advice on the following proposed transactions:

Sell the shares to her husband

(1) Sell the shares to him for cash of $50,000

(2) Sell the shares to him for a non-interest bearing note of $50,000

(3) Sell the shares to him for cash of $40,000.

Sell the shares to her 25-year-old daughter

(1) Sell the shares to her for cash of $50,000

(2) Sell the shares to her for a non-interest bearing note of $50,000

(3) Sell the shares to her for cash of $40,000.

Problem 8

Ten years ago, Mr. Chu invested in Able Inc., a Canadian private company which is a "small business corporation". He invested $100,000 in common shares and made an unsecured loan of $60,000 with an interest rate of 5%. He has been receiving interest on this loan until recently. He has just found out that due to the bankruptcy of a significant customer and the loss of the related accounts receivable, Able Inc. is also in significant financial difficulty. Mr. Chu has come to you for tax advice.

(1) At this point, can Mr. Chu claim a loss on either the loan or the shares without disposing of the shares or debt?

(2) He has someone who is interested in buying the shares for $10,000 and the debt for $6,000. What are the tax consequences if he does this?

Problem 9

Sally and Harry have ended their 15-year marriage and are now living apart. They have sold their house and divided the proceeds, but they don't necessarily want to sell some shares that Sally owns. However, they have agreed that Sally needs to transfer 50% of her shares to Harry as part of the equalization payment.

Sally's shares have a fair market value of $40,000 and an adjusted cost base of $25,000.

They would like you to explain the tax consequences of this transfer.

Problem 10

Mr. and Mrs. Grand are married with one child, Noah, who is 16 years old. Mr. Grand owns his own business, which he operates out of a company called Father Inc. He owns all the shares. Mrs. Grand owns her own business, which she operates out of a company called Mother Inc. She owns all the shares of this company.

Identify, with reference to the Act, who is:

— Related

— Affiliated

— Arm's length

Problem 11

ITA: 41, 46

Mr. Adam Lamb sold the following assets this year, all of which were purchased within the last 10 years:

	Cost	Proceeds
Oil painting	$2,500	$ 500
Canoe	700	500
Rare coin	1,300	500
Bible produced in 1635	800	5,000
Antique car	15,000	10,000
Antique chair	300	1,200
Antique table	1,500	2,000

Mr. Adam Lamb has an unclaimed capital loss on listed personal property of $1,200 arising three years ago.

Mr. Lamb would like you to calculate his net taxable capital gain for this year.

Problem 12

ITA: 40(2)(*b*), 54

Mr. Doug Hart, who lives in Ontario, is contemplating moving to Switzerland. He came to you to discuss the tax consequences of disposing of his residences, as indicated below, in April 2018. He is single and ordinarily inhabits each of the residences for several months each year. He has never used his principal residence exemption since purchasing these properties.

The following information relates to the proposed 2018 dispositions.

Residence	Date of purchase	Cost	Selling price
Toronto home	2011	$160,000	$240,000
Farm in Quebec	2013	100,000	148,000
Condominium in Florida	2016	150,000	186,000

— REQUIRED

Mr. Hart has asked you to calculate the minimum amount of taxable capital gains that he will have to report in 2018.

Problem 13

ITA: 3, 41

Dave Stieb reported the following information for tax purposes:

	2016	2017	2018
Business income	$ 60,000	$ 65,000	$70,000
Property income	2,000	3,000	(1,000)
Capital gains:*			
Listed personal property	5,000	(7,000)	3,000
Personal-use property	(2,000)	5,000	4,000
Other	(8,000)**	6,000	(16,000)

    * Brackets indicate capital loss.
    ** Includes a $4,000 business investment loss.

Your manager has asked you to calculate the income under Division B for each year *after* making the necessary amendments to the returns of other years. (Deal with each item line-by-line across the years, rather than computing income one year at a time.) Assume that no capital gains deduction was ever claimed.

Problem 14

ITA: 49

Doctor Wright, a general practitioner, has decided to move into a larger office. On July 1, 2017, he paid $5,000 to Devalued Properties Ltd., a developer, for a one-year option to purchase a residential building which he would use for business. On February 1, 2018, Dr. Wright sold his option to another medical practitioner, Dr. Holmes, for $2,000. On May 1, 2018, Dr. Holmes exercised the option and paid $100,000 for the building.

You have been asked to explain the tax implications in the above situation for Doctors Wright and Holmes and for Devalued Properties Ltd.

Problem 15

ITA: 3, 39, 41

Simon has the following sources of income and losses for tax purposes:

	2017	2018
Employment income	$25,000	$30,000
Property income	10,000	(4,000)
Business income — other	8,000	(9,000)
Capital gains (capital losses):		
— Listed personal property (Note 1)	4,000	(1,500)
— Personal-use property	8,000	(1,000)
— Shares — Canadian-controlled private corporation (Note 2)	(6,000)	(2,000)
— Public corporation	(12,000)	9,000

Additional Information

(1) Simon has a capital loss from listed personal property of $1,000 carried forward from 2014.

(2) These losses qualify as business investment losses. No capital gains deduction has ever been claimed.

Simon has asked you to calculate his Division B income for 2017 and 2018. (Deal with each item line-by-line across the years, rather than computing income one year at a time.)

Problem 16

ITA: 40(2)(*b*), 45(2), 54

Ms. Andrews purchased a home in Waterloo in 2008 at a cost of $86,000. She lived in the home until January 29, 2011, at which time she moved to Vancouver and rented a home in Vancouver. At the time of the move, Ms. Andrew's Waterloo residence had risen in value to $230,000. Expecting that real estate prices would continue to rise, Ms. Andrews chose to retain ownership of her Waterloo home and rented it to a third party.

In June 2017, Ms. Andrews decided she missed living in Waterloo and chose to return. She returned to Waterloo where she took up residence in her Waterloo home. At the time, the Waterloo residence had a fair market value of $294,000. In March 2018, Ms. Andrews decided she was tired of living in the city. She sold her Waterloo home for $284,000 and moved to the countryside.

Prior to filing her 2018 personal tax return, Ms. Andrews has requested your advice in minimizing the capital gains she must report on the sale of her home.

Ms. Andrews has asked you to calculate the minimum capital gain that she will have to report on the sale of her home under the following circumstances:

(A) assuming that she elects to be deemed not to have changed the use, and

ITA: 45(2)

(B) assuming that the election is not made.

Problem 17

ITA: 47, 53

Sherman Schleuter likes to invest in the stock market for the long term. While some of his investments have been failures, some have been very successful. Generally, he has been very fortunate in buying certain stocks at a relatively low price and selling them at their peak. One such stock is Headed For the Sky Corporation, a public corporation. Sherman has provided the following trade information related to this investment:

Nov. 8, 2011	Purchased 1,000 shares at initial offering price of $5.
Apr. 15, 2012	Purchased 2,000 shares at price of $3.50.
June 6, 2013	Sold 500 shares at $2.75, incurred brokerage commission of $50.
July 2, 2013	Purchased 2,000 shares at $4.
Apr. 30, 2014	Received a stock dividend of 10% of shares held; stock dividend increased corporation's paid-up capital by $.50/share.
June 20, 2015	Two-for-one stock split.
Nov. 8, 2016	Purchased 2,000 shares at $6.
Jan. 12, 2017	Received a stock dividend of 10% of shares held; stock dividend increased corporation's paid-up capital by $1/share.
Nov. 5, 2018	Sold 10,000 shares for $7.50/share, incurred brokerage commission of $650.

Sherman has asked you to calculate the taxable capital gain or allowable capital loss on the above transactions.

Problem 18

ITA: 52; 53

Ms. Plant decided to purchase shares in Schvantz Ltd., a public company. She purchased 800 shares at $25 per share plus brokerage of $690 on May 24, 2004.

The following additional transactions took place:

June 30, 2005	— Purchased 500 shares of Shtupp Metals Ltd., a public company, at $35 plus brokerage of $600.
Aug. 20, 2005	— Purchased 1,100 additional shares of Schvantz Ltd. at $30 plus brokerage of $940.
Aug. 27, 2007	— Sold 900 shares of Schvantz Ltd. at $24.50 per share plus brokerage fee of $760.

Sept. 20, 2007	— Purchased 600 additional shares of Schvantz Ltd. at $19.50 plus brokerage of $400.
Oct. 31, 2007	— Sold 200 shares of Shtupp Metals Ltd. at $32 per share plus brokerage fee of $220.
June 9, 2009	— Sold 250 shares of Schvantz Ltd. at $32 per share plus brokerage fee of $275.
May 24, 2011	— Received a 10% stock dividend from Shtupp Metals Ltd. (i.e., 30 shares) of which $20 per share issued was credited to paid-up capital.
June 30, 2013	— Sold 150 shares of Shtupp Metals Ltd. at $36.50 per share plus brokerage fee of $165.
Aug. 20, 2015	— Received 10% stock dividend from Schvantz Ltd. of which $20 per share issued was credited to paid-up capital.
Dec. 28, 2018	— Sold 350 shares of Schvantz Ltd. at $29 per share plus brokerage fee of $355, settlement date January 4, 2019.

Ms. Plant has asked you to calculate the taxable capital gain or allowable capital loss for each of the above sales.

Problem 19

ITA: 13(7)(*e*), 70(5)(*a*), 70(5)(*b*), 70(5)(*c*), 70(6)(*d*), 70(6)(*e*); ITR: 1100(2)(*h*), 1102(14)(*d*)

On July 31 of the current year, Mary McArthur passed away after a lengthy illness. Mary was survived by her husband and one adult child, Margaret. Both her husband and daughter are residents of Canada. Information related to Mary's assets as at her date of death, is set out below.

Description	Capital Cost/ACB	UCC	Fair market value	Beneficiary
Rental property — Toronto, Ontario				
Land	$40,000	n/a	$ 100,000	Spouse
Building (Class 3)	55,000	$15,000	145,000	Spouse
Rental property — Stratford, Ontario				
Land	25,000	n/a	45,000	Daughter
Building (Class 1)	65,000	42,000	93,000	Daughter
CBV shares (see Note below)		n/a	1,000,000	Spouse
View Canada shares (see Note below)		n/a	150,000	Daughter

Note:

Mary inherited these shares from her father upon his death a few years ago. Her father had an adjusted cost base of $250,000 in the CBV shares. The fair market value of the CBV shares on the date of his death was $500,000. Her father had an adjusted cost base of $150,000 in the View Canada shares. The fair market value of the View Canada shares on the date of his death was $180,000.

The executor for the estate has asked you to calculate the minimum income and/or taxable capital gains to be reported by Mary McArthur in her final return in respect of the above-noted assets. Ignore any available elections.

The executor has also asked you to determine the cost amounts of the above assets to the respective beneficiaries.

Problem 20

ITA: 3, 41

In Billy's attempt to sever all business and personal ties with Canada before beginning long-term and permanent employment in Beijing, he sold all his personal assets and most of his investments.

Description	Sale proceeds	Cost	Disposition costs
Personal residence	$475,000	$125,000	$3,600
Household furniture	20,000	35,000	800
Skis, bicycle, and skates	750	1,200	0
Rights to season tickets	4,000	3,500	0
Paintings	2,400	1,900	120
Chevrolet	3,600	12,000	350
Fishing lodge	45,000	31,000	4,500
Business loan — private	0	8,000	0
ABC shares (public co.)	46,000	20,000	200

Additional Information:

- All years available for a principal residence designation were used to exempt the gain on the personal residence, leaving no years available to designate the fishing lodge.
- The business loan was made to a Canadian-controlled private company, which is now in receivership.
- Billy has never claimed a capital gains exemption.

Billy has told you that his employment income is $48,000 and asked you to calculate his income for tax purposes.

Type 2 Problems

Problem 21

ITA: 13(7)(e)

On October 1, Roxanne acquired her brother's West Vancouver condominium rental property for $600,000 (ignore any land portion). Her brother has owned it for five years and had a capital gain of $250,000 on selling it to Roxanne. He will include 50% of that in his income. Roxanne believes she can earn net rental income of $9,000 annually, and ¼ of that amount for the final quarter of this year.

Roxanne has asked you to calculate the maximum CCA that she may claim in this first taxation year.

Problem 22

ITA: 7, 69, 73, 74.1, 74.2, 74.5, 56(4.1), 110(1)(d)

During 2017, Madame Martel exercised a stock option that she held in her employer (a CCPC). It is now November 2018. She is currently contemplating a number of scenarios in terms of the shares she received under the 2017 stock option exercise. She has asked you to explain the tax consequences of her actual and contemplated transactions.

The details of the stock option exercised during 2017 are as follows.

Number of shares purchased	Exercise price	Fair market value of shares at exercise date	Fair market value of shares at grant date
6,000	$20	$35	$20

The current fair market value of a share is $42.

Madame Martel is married and has two children (ages 21 and 15). She is expecting large dividends to be paid on the above shares in December 2018 and each December on an ongoing basis. She also expects that the shares will increase in value quite considerably over the near future. As a result, she is looking for a means of splitting income with her immediate family. She is proposing the following scenarios in terms of distributing these shares amongst her immediate family:

(1) gift the shares to her spouse and children (⅓ to her spouse and ⅓ to each child);

(2) sell the shares to her spouse and children (⅓ to her spouse and ⅓ to each child) for cash proceeds of $20 per share; or

(3) sell the shares to her spouse and children (⅓ to her spouse and ⅓ to each child) in exchange for a note payable of $42 per share.

The note payable described in (3), above, will be payable over five years with no interest. Since the note pays no interest and is repayable over future years, the estimated present value of the note is $25 per share.

Madame Martel has asked you to prepare a memorandum explaining the income tax consequences of her completed and proposed transactions.

Problem 23

ITA: Division B, Subdivisions a, b, c

Mr. Richmond, a new client, has invested in rental properties, principal residences and other capital property with inheritance monies and other liquid cash. He provides you with the following information with respect to his 2018 taxation year.

Mr. Richmond is employed by Wealth Inc., a Canadian-controlled private corporation, and received the following income and benefits:

(1) Salary (net)		$ 49, 835
Payroll deduction:		
Income taxes	$15,013	
CPP	2,594	
EI	858	
Registered pension plan (defined benefit: current service)	3,700	22,165
		$ 72,000

(2) Mr. Richmond paid professional fees of $500 to the Professional Engineers of Ontario.

(3) Mr. Richmond sold two lots of his stock options. He provides you with the following:

1st lot — 450 shares sold on March 15, 2018, for $26.50 per share. These shares were purchased in February 2011 for $8 at which time the shares were valued at $10.50.

2nd lot — 600 shares sold on December 5, 2018, for $25 per share. These shares were purchased on April 12, 2018, for $15 at which time the shares were valued at $21. The fair market value at the date of grant was $17.

(4) Mr. Richmond received an interest-free loan of $9,000 on March 12, 2018, to enable him to purchase shares of Wealth Inc. The loan was outstanding until the shares were sold on December 5, at which time the loan was repaid. Assume that the prescribed rate throughout the year was 7%.

In addition, during 2018, Mr. Richmond received the following income from various sources including certain capital dispositions.

(A) Mr. Richmond sold the following assets:

	Cost	Proceeds
Antique foot stool	$1,100	$ 900
Painting	950	1,500
Stamp collection	250	850

(B) During 2018, Mr. Richmond sold his two residences, in order to purchase a larger home in an expensive suburb. The following facts relate to these two residences:

	Date purchased	Cost	Commission	Proceeds
City home	2009	$95,000	$21,000	$350,000
Cottage	2004	15,500	12,000	200,000

(C) In addition to his residences, Mr. Richmond owns two rental properties. The following information pertains to these two properties:

	Wealthier St.	Richmount St.
Cost of land	$70,000	$100,000
Cost of building	$55,000	$ 80,000
UCC — January 1, 2018, Class 1	$39,000	$ 65,000

	Wealthier St.	*Richmount St.*
Rental revenue in 2018	$18,000	$ 7,600
Expenses:		
Taxes (property)	$ 2,100	$ 1,800
Other expenses	4,300	6,100
Mortgage interest	3,600	Nil
	$10,000	$ 7,900

The Richmount St. rental property was sold in November for proceeds of $250,000 less $9,000 of selling costs. Of the proceeds, $140,000 was for the land.

Mr. Richmond purchased the Wealthier St. rental property by placing a mortgage on his home. His monthly payments are $450 per month, of which $300 per month represents interest.

(D) Mr. Richmond gifted his wife $10,000 in June 2018 to allow her to invest in the stock market. Mrs. Richmond decided to be a cautious investor for the first while; as a result, she invested the $10,000 in Treasury Bills which earned $600 from June to December 2018.

(E) In addition, Mr. Richmond decided to provide his younger brother, who is 22, with a non-interest bearing loan of $5,000 to allow him to complete his Masters in Marine Biology. Mr. Richmond's brother paid his tuition fees with the funds.

(F) Mr. Richmond gifted $8,500 to each of his twin children, Dolly and Camp, aged 15. Both children placed their monies in high interest-bearing savings accounts each receiving interest of $1,050 in 2018.

(G) Mr. Richmond received dividends from the following investments:

Wealth Inc. — a Canadian-controlled private corporation (from income
taxed at the low corporate rate)   800

(H) Mr. Richmond owns units in Dumark Mutual Fund. He received a T3 slip from Dumark Mutual Fund indicating the following income amounts allocated to his account and reinvested in 2017:

Capital gains	$1,200
Actual amount of dividends	362
Taxable amount of dividends	500

Mr. Richmond had invested $20,000 in the Dumark Fund in 2017. This resulted in the purchase of 1,640.824 units of the fund. In 2017, income of $46.31 was allocated to his account and reinvested. The reinvestment resulted in the purchase of 3.845 units at the market value of $12.044 per unit. The 2018 income allocation resulted, on reinvestment of the $1,544.97, in the purchase of 119.358 units at the market value of $12.944 per unit. Late in 2018, after the income allocation, Mr. Richmond sold 1,000 units for a total of $12,881.

(I) Mr. Richmond sold a $100,000 Government of Canada bond for $115,327. This bond paid interest semi-annually at an interest rate which was much higher than current interest rates. The proceeds received of $115,327 included accrued interest of $5,327. Mr. Richmond had purchased the bonds on the open market for $98,000.

(J) In 2015, Mr. Richmond loaned $120,000 to his brother-in-law's company which was a small business corporation. The loan paid interest at commercial rates, but no interest was received in 2018 because the company went into receivership. As an unsecured creditor, Mr. Richmond received 10 cents on the dollar ($12,000) in 2018 in full payment of this loan.

(K) Mr. Richmond has a listed personal property loss, carried forward from 2012, of $500.

Mr. Richmond has asked you to calculate his Division B income according to the ordering rules in section 3 for 2018. Assume that he claimed $60,000 of his capital gains exemption in prior years. Ignore the effects of any leap year.

Problem 24

Theresa Vert is considering emigration to the United States. She has approached you to estimate the income tax consequences on her holdings of taxable capital property. Her plan is to dispose of all the real estate holdings and retain her investments in stocks and bonds. Theresa and her husband currently live in a downtown townhouse which was purchased in 1996 for a cost of $130,000. The estimated value is now $320,000. Theresa also inherited a cottage in 1997 (estimated fair market value was $55,000). The value of the cottage is now approximately $270,000.

In 1993, Theresa purchased a rental property for $105,000 of which $25,000 was allocated to the land. There is no mortgage on the property. The land and the building have a fair market value of $150,000 and $100,000, respectively. Legal costs at the time of purchase totalled $3,000 and the estimated cost of disposal is $20,000. The UCC on the building is $30,000.

Theresa also has the following investments:

- Common shares of Canadian publicly traded companies. These shares were purchased on October 19, 1997, at a cost of $140,000 and have current value of $190,000.

- A $100,000 10-year Province of Alberta 12% bond, due in five years, with interest payable annually on June 30. The bond has a current value equal to $110,000.

- A Steinway grand piano purchased at an auction for $8,000. Theresa can sell this to her piano teacher for $10,000.

Advise Theresa on the various income tax consequences of emigrating and the tax treatment of her holdings.

Problem 25

Tony is 59 years of age. Tony established and, for 34 years, successfully maintained Tony's Future Hardware, a proprietorship in a small city. The business has a December 31 year end. Tony has come to you for tax advice on how to best structure the sale of all the assets, what after-tax cash from the sale would be retained by him, and when he would pay the tax on the sale.

Tony, a hard-working man, is looking forward to retirement. Fortunately for Tony, a large hardware store chain, Nailem Inc. (which was looking to expand), offered on August 31, 2018, to purchase all of the business assets from Tony. Nailem has stated that it is only interested in the purchase of the assets of an existing hardware store business, not the shares of an incorporated hardware store business. Nailem Inc. is willing to pay the following fair market values for all the listed assets.

	Net Book Value	Fair Market Value
Accounts receivable (net of allowance for doubtful accounts of $2,000)	$ 18,000	$ 17,000
Inventory	35,000	48,000
Furniture & equipment (Class 8 UCC – $10,000; cost – $15,000)	11,000	11,000
Computer equipment (Class 50 UCC – $8,000; cost – $18,000)	10,000	7,000
Land (cost – $20,000)	20,000	140,000
Building (Class 3 UCC – $6,000; cost – $30,000)	6,000	260,000
Trade payables	(10,000)	(10,000)

Nailem proposes to buy Tony's business for $663,000 cash, net of the trade payables of $10,000. This price includes $190,000 for the internally generated goodwill produced by Tony. The closing date is scheduled for September 30, 2018, if Tony accepts Nailem's offer.

Tony is taxed at a combined federal and provincial marginal rate of 46% (ignore any possible effects of the alternative minimum tax). He estimates that the taxable income from the business from January 1, 2018 to September 30, 2018 will be approximately $40,000. He has never previously had any capital gains or losses and has had no investment losses. He is willing to accept the offer if the after-tax cash from the sale is at least $500,000.

CHAPTER 7 —
DISCUSSION NOTES FOR REVIEW QUESTIONS

(1) "Proceeds of disposition" is defined to include the principal amount of the mortgage that is owed to the mortgage company. This transaction may trigger recaptured CCA or a terminal loss.

ITA: 13(1), 13(21.1), 20(16), 54 "proceeds of disposition" (h)

(2) Whenever the adjusted cost base becomes negative there will be an immediate capital gain. The only exception to this rule is for a partnership interest in a general partnership (but not a limited partnership).

ITA: 40(3)

(3) The principal residence exemption is restricted to one residence per family unit. The rules provide the framework for deciding which residence should be claimed for which years in order to maximize the exemption. Mr. Chan and his wife must choose one residence or the other for the exemption.

ITA: 54 "principal residence" (c)
ITA: 40(2)(b)

(4) The cottage is considered to be "personal-use property" (PUP). Any loss on the disposal of PUP cannot be deducted. The losses are considered to arise as a result of normal personal use over time.

ITA: 40(2)(g)(iii), 54

(5) For the purpose of calculating the capital gain or loss on any disposal of PUP the taxpayer's cost is deemed to be the greater of the adjusted cost base of the property and $1,000. Similarly, the taxpayer's proceeds of disposition are deemed to be the greater of actual proceeds and $1,000. Listed personal property (LPP) is defined to be a subset of PUP; therefore, the $1,000 rule also applies to LPP.

ITA: 46(1)
ITA: 54

(6) The dividend should be grossed up and the grossed-up amount included in income. The amount of the dividend before the gross-up will increase the cost base of the shares and effectively reduces the capital gain or increase the capital loss when the shares are sold.

ITA: 53(2)

(7) The result of the taxable capital gains minus the allowable capital losses cannot be negative. Any negative amount is a "net capital loss" that can be carried back three years or forward indefinitely.

ITA: 3(b) of Div. B; 111(1)(b), 111(8) of Div. C

(8) You would be deemed to have acquired the prize at a cost equal to its fair market value at the time you received it.

ITA: 52(4)

(9) The car has a cost base equal to the $35,000 benefit included in her income as a shareholder benefit.

ITA: 15(1), 52(1)

(10) If Mrs. Smith did not make any structural changes to the house, then there will not be any change in use. The house will still remain her principal residence. She will have to declare the rental income and can deduct the expenses that relate to it.

Income Tax Folio S1-F3-C2 — Principal Residence

(11) Since she was moved by her employer nine years ago and was still employed by that employer when she moved back this year, the Act modifies paragraph (d) of the definition of "principal residence" to allow her to continue to claim her house as her principal residence for more than the 4 years generally allowed on a normal change in use under the definition. All years qualify since she was still resident in Canada, as required. She still has to make the election not to have a change in use in the year they moved. As a result, on the sale of the house, she will be able to claim the full principal residence exemption.

ITA: 45(2), 54, 54.1
ITA: 40(2)(b)

(12) The Act causes a deemed disposition on all her property other than certain property and certain items that are subject to withholding tax. In this case the term deposits will be deemed to be disposed of, but since there is no capital gain, there would not be any tax.

ITA: 128.1(4)

(13) Mr. Shiloh will be excepted from the deemed disposition rules on the shares of his U.S. employer since he was in Canada less than 60 months in the past 10 years.

ITA: 128.1(4)

(14) The Act generally treats the sale of this option as a disposition with the cost base being nil. Therefore, the capital gain will be equal to the proceeds and will be taxed in the year the option is sold.

ITA: 49(1)

CHAPTER 7

(15) The loss on foreign currency is a capital loss. However, as an individual, she must deduct $200 from the loss in arriving at her capital loss. In this case her capital loss is $2,300.

ITA: 39(2)(b)

(16) On the granting of an option there is a disposition and the ACB is deemed to be nil. He does not have the alternative of reducing the cost base.

ITA: 49(1)

(17) A rollover on the exchange of the common shares for the debentures is provided as long as the debenture had the conversion feature built into its terms and no consideration other than shares (i.e., cash) was received. The shares will have a cost base of $10 each, so the accrued gain of $10 per share will be deferred until the common shares are sold.

ITA: 51

(18) If a person sells something to someone with whom he or she does not deal at arm's length then the proceeds will be deemed to be the fair market value. Related parties do not deal at arm's length, but in this case the two are not related. However, it is a question of fact whether persons not related to each other are dealing at arm's length. In this case there is no evidence of hard bargaining and the transaction is obviously not at fair market value. Therefore, it would be unlikely that they would be considered to be dealing at arm's length and the proceeds would likely be deemed to be $100,000. Her friend will have a cost base equal to what she paid for the land of $50,000. As a result there will be double taxation.

ITA: 69, 251, 251(1)(c)

(19) At the time of the gift, Bill will be deemed to have sold the shares at their fair market value. Scott will be deemed to have received the shares at a cost to him equal to the fair market value at the time of the gift. Since the shares were a gift, the attribution rules applicable to an income-splitting loan will not apply.

ITA: 69(1)(b), 69(1)(c)

ITA: 56(4.1)

CHAPTER 7 — SOLUTIONS TO MULTIPLE CHOICE QUESTIONS

Question 1

(C) is correct. The loss on the automobile is not allowed since it is personal-use property (PUP). The $1,000 rule means that the gain on the boat (which is PUP) is $500, the gain on the painting (which is listed personal property (LPP)) is $300, and the loss on the jewellery (which is LPP) is $400. Since the deductible portion of the $400 LPP loss is limited to the LPP gain in the year ($300), the capital gain is: $500 + $300 – $300 = $500. The $100 LPP loss can be carried over against LPP gains.

ITA: 2, 41(1), 46(1), 54

(A) is incorrect, because it ignores the $1,000 rule and computes the gain on the boat (PUP) as $900, the gain on the painting (LPP) as $700, and the loss on the jewellery (LPP) as $1,200. The LPP gain is then offset by a portion of the LPP loss, leaving the $900 gain.

(B) is incorrect, because it does not subtract the deductible portion of the LPP loss from the LPP gain: $500 + $300 = $800.

(D) is incorrect, because it deducts the full LPP loss ($400) against all the gains: $500 + $300 – $400 = $400.

Question 2

(B) is the correct answer. Since Amanda had no capital gain on her house, she must have designated it as her principal residence for all but one of the years 2009 to 2017. She therefore has two years to designate in respect of the cottage: one of the years not used on the house (say, 2017) plus 2018. Since she owned the cottage eight years (2011 to 2018), the principal residence exemption for the cottage is: $^3/_8 \times \$80,000 = \$30,000$ (3 = 2 years designated + "one-plus rule"). Therefore, Amanda's taxable capital gain is $25,000 ($^1/_2 \times$ ($80,000 – $30,000 principal residence exemption)).

(A) is incorrect, because $80,000 is the capital gain before the exemption.

(C) is incorrect, because it uses $^2/_8 \times \$80,000 = \$20,000$ as the principal residence exemption: $^1/_2 \times$ ($80,000 – $20,000) = $30,000.

(D) is incorrect, because $50,000 is the capital gain, not the taxable capital gain.

Question 3

(B) is correct. Because Gary made the election to be deemed not to have changed the use in respect of the property, there is deemed to be no change in use in 2012. The only disposition occurs in 2018 on the date of sale. The Act allows Gary to designate the property as his principal residence for up to four years where the election was made. The gain on the property is $500,000 ($850,000 – $350,000) and the total years of ownership were 18 (2001 to 2018) and the maximum number of years that can be designated is 16 (2001 to 2012 plus 4). Therefore, the principal residence exemption is [(16 + 1)/18] × $500,000 or $472,222. The capital gain is therefore $27,778 ($500,000 – $472,222) and the taxable capital gain is $13,889 ($^1/_2 \times$ $27,778).

ITA: 45(2)

ITA: 54

ITA: 45(2)

(A) is incorrect because there is a taxable capital gain to report in 2018 because not all years of ownership qualify as years eligible for a principal residence. The extension of the four-year rule does not apply, because Gary did not move back into the residence before it was sold.

ITA: 54.1

(C) incorrectly calculates taxable capital gains of $50,000 in 2012 [$^1/_2$ ($550,000 – $350,000)] and 2018 [$^1/_2$ ($850,000 – $550,000)]. The timing is wrong because there is no deemed disposition in 2012 because of the election. The amount is also wrong because 12 years (2001 – 2012) can be designated in respect of the residence.

ITA: 45(2)

(D) correctly calculates the gain in 2018 as $500,000 without claiming any principal residence exemption, resulting in a taxable capital gain of $250,000 ($^1/_2 \times$ $500,000).

CHAPTER 7

Question 4

(B) is correct. The amount of the dividend is $4, the increase in the paid-up capital, and this is also   ITA: 82(1)
the cost of the shares (ssec. 53(3)). However, the individual's net income would increase by $5.52, since
it is a taxable dividend: $4 × 1.38 gross-up = $5.52.

(A) is incorrect because although $4 is the amount of the dividend, the amount included in net
income is the grossed-up dividend (1.38 × $4 = $5.52).

(C) is incorrect because the amount of the dividend is not based on the $10 fair market value of the
share.

(D) is also incorrect because the amount of the dividend is not based on the $10 fair market value
of the share and the amount included in income is the increase in paid-up capital grossed up by 1.38,
not the fair market value grossed up by 1.38.

Question 5

(C) is correct.

Shares		$1,600
Personal-use property		700
Listed personal property	$500	
Listed personal property	(140)	
Listed personal property losses of prior year	(100)	260
Shares		(820)
Personal-use property		Nil
Capital gain		$1,740
Taxable capital gain (½)		$ 870

(A) is incorrect because it deducts the $1,000 personal-use property loss: ½ ($1,740 – 1,000) = $370.

(B) is incorrect because it deducts the $1,000 personal-use property loss and does not multiply by
the ½ fraction: ($1,740 – $1,000) = $740.

(D) is incorrect because it does not deduct the listed personal property loss of other years: ½ ×
($1,740 + $100) = $920.

Question 6

(A) is correct.   ITA: 74.1(2)

(B) is incorrect, because capital gains or losses do not attribute on loans or gifts to minors.

(C) is incorrect, because there will be a capital gain on the gift.   ITA: 69

(D) is incorrect. $100,000 is the capital gain. The taxable capital gain is:

      ½ × $100,000 = $50,000.

Question 7

(C) is correct. There is a superficial loss because Ms. Y has incurred a loss and an affiliated person   ITA: 40(2)(*g*), 54
(Mr. Y) acquired the shares within 30 days of the disposition.

(A) is incorrect, because it ignores the superficial loss rule and computes the loss as ½ × ($800,000
– $900,000).

(B) is not correct, because Ms. Y elected out of the interspousal rollover.   ITA: 73(1)

(D) is not correct. There is no attribution because she elected out of the subsection 73(1) rollover   ITA: 74.5
and received fair market value consideration (i.e., $800,000 cash).

Question 8

(A) is correct since only the gift to the son will result in a taxable capital gain.

The ACB of Mike's stock is:

$100 \times \$3.11$ plus \$39 commission (incl. sec. 7 benefit)	\$350	
$100 \times \$4$ plus \$50 commission	450	
$\underline{200}$	$\underline{\$800}$ = \$4 ACB per share.	ITA: 47, 53(1)(*i*)

His taxable capital gain on the gift to his son is: $\frac{1}{2}$ ($6 – $4) $\times$ 100 = $100.

There is no taxable capital gain on the gift to his wife, because the transfer occurs at his $4 ACB since no special election was filed.   ITA: 73(1)

(B) incorrectly excluded brokerage commissions from the ACB of his shares as: $\frac{1}{2}$ ($6 – $711/200) $\times$ 100 = $122.

(C) incorrectly computes a taxable capital gain on the gift to Mike's wife: $\frac{1}{2}$ ($6 – $4) $\times$ 200 shares = $200.

(D) is incorrect, because it incorrectly computes a capital gain on the gift to his wife and does not apply the $\frac{1}{2}$ fraction to compute the taxable portion of the gain: ($6 – $4) $\times$ 200 = $400.

Question 9

(C) is correct. The calculation is as follows:

	Division B income
Toronto home (no capital gain; principal residence)	—
Rental property in London, Ontario	
— Land: $\frac{1}{2}$ ($100K – 50K)	$25,000
— Building: recapture = $25K – $2K	23,000
Taxable capital gain = $\frac{1}{2}$ ($35K – $25K)	5,000
Mutual fund units: $\frac{1}{2}$ ($60K – $12K)	24,000
Shares of a public company: $\frac{1}{2}$ ($100K – $90K)	5,000
	$82,000

(A) incorrectly ignores recapture: $82,000 – $23,000 = $59,000.

(B) incorrectly multiplies the recapture by the $\frac{1}{2}$ taxable capital gains fraction: $25,000 + $\frac{1}{2}$ $\times$ $23,000 + $5,000 + $24,000 + $5,000 = $70,500.

(D) incorrectly includes a capital gain on the principal residence: $82,000 + $\frac{1}{2}$ $\times$ ($840,000 – $300,000) = $352,000.

CHAPTER 7

Question 10

(B) is correct, because the taxable capital gain is computed as follows: listed shares of a public corporation resident in Canada (= ½ × ($40,000 – $10,000) = $15,000) + painting (= ½ ($10,000 – $6,000) = $2,000) = $17,000.

The rental real estate in Canada and the registered retirement savings plan are specifically exempted from the deemed disposition rules.   ITA: 128.1(4)

(A) incorrectly excludes the taxable capital gain on the painting.

(C) incorrectly includes ½ of the gain on the RRSP ($10,000).

(D) incorrectly includes a $25,000 taxable capital gain on the rental real estate in Canada.

CHAPTER 7 — SOLUTIONS TO EXERCISES

Exercise 1

Step 1: Determine gain per year of ownership

	Regina home		Cottage	
Par. 40(2)(*b*) gain				
P of D		$ 517,500		$ 375,000
ACB		(400,000)		(250,000)
Gain		$ 117,500		$ 125,000
Gain per year	$\dfrac{\$117,500}{12 \text{ years}} =$	$ 9,792	$\dfrac{\$125,000}{7 \text{ years}} =$	$ 17,857

Step 2: Assignment of no-option years

In the five taxation years 2007 to 2011, Ms. Amin owned only the Regina home. Therefore, there is no option in those years but to designate the city home as her principal residence.

Step 3: Gain determined under paragraph 40(2)(*b*)

The gain per year of ownership for the cottage ($17,857) exceeds that for the city home ($9,792). If all seven years are assigned to the cottage, however, one year will be wasted. Hence, the city home should be designated for one of the years 2012 to 2018.

	Regina home	Cottage
Gain	$ 117,500	$ 125,000
Exemption	(68,542)[(1)]	(125,000)[(2)]
Capital gain	$ 48,958	Nil
Taxable capital gain	$ 24,479	Nil

— NOTES TO SOLUTION

(1) $\dfrac{1 + 5 + 1}{12} \times \$117,500 = \$68,542$; years designated — 2007–2011 and one of 2012–2018

(2) $\dfrac{1 + 6}{7} \times \$125,000 = \$125,000$; years designated — all but one of 2012–2018

Exercise 2

Step 1: Determine gain per year of ownership

	City home		Cottage	
P of D		$ 247,000		$ 164,000	ITA: 40(2)(*b*)
ACB	$ 180,000		$ 90,000		
SC	12,000	(192,000)	6,000	(96,000)	
Gain		$ 55,000		$ 68,000	
Gain per year	$\dfrac{\$55,000}{16 \text{ years}} =$	$ 3,438	$\dfrac{\$68,000}{11 \text{ years}} =$	$ 6,182	

Step 2: Assignment of no-option years

In the five taxation years 2003 to 2007, Peter owned only the city home. Therefore, there is no option in those years but to designate the city home as his principal residence.

Step 3: Gain determined ITA: 40(2)(*b*)

The gain per year of ownership for the cottage ($6,182) exceeds that for the city home ($3,438). If all 11 years are assigned to the cottage, however, one year will be wasted. Hence, the city home should be designated for one of the years 2008 to 2018.

CHAPTER 7

	City home	*Cottage*
Gain	$ 55,000	$ 68,000
Exemption	(24,063)[(1)]	(68,000)[(2)]
Capital gain	$ 30,937	Nil

— NOTES TO SOLUTION

[(1)] $\dfrac{1 + 5 + 1}{16} \times \$55,000 = \$24,063$; years designated — 2003–2007 and one of 2008–2018

[(2)] $\dfrac{1 + 10}{11} \times \$68,000 = \$68,000$; years designated — all but one of 2008–2018

Exercise 3

When Howard rents his home, he is deemed to have changed the use of the home and a capital gain may be triggered. However, Howard can designate the home with the appropriate number of years and should not be taxed on the gain. Under this course of action, Howard would now have a rental property from which he must declare the income less all his expenses. However, a rental loss could not be generated with capital cost allowance on the home and equipment therein.

ITA: 45(1)

ITR: 1100(15))

Alternatively, Howard could elect to defer the gain until he either sells the home or rescinds his election. Note that the CRA normally permits a retroactive election at the time of sale. In this situation, Howard would not be allowed to claim any capital cost allowance on the home or the election to be deemed not to have changed the use would be invalid.

ITA: 45(2)
Income Tax Folio S1-F3-C2 — Principal Residence
ITA: 45(2)

The election would permit Howard to designate his Vancouver home as his principal residence for at least four extra years depending upon whether he is self-employed or employed.

ITA: 45(2)

(A) Self-employed

Paragraph (*d*) in the definition of a "principal residence" permits Howard to designate his Vancouver home as his principal residence for four years, while it is being rented, if he elects to be deemed not to have changed the use according to paragraphs (*b*) and (*d*) of the definition.

ITA: 54
ITA: 45(2)

Howard might consider rescinding his election after the fourth year. This course of action would enable Howard to claim capital cost allowance after the fourth year subject to the loss restrictions discussed above.

(B) Employed

The Act waives the four-year restriction discussed above if Howard (or his wife) has moved at least 40 km closer to his new work location. Howard then can designate his Vancouver home as his principal residence during all the rental years if:

ITA: 54.1

(i) Howard subsequently resumes ordinary habitation of his home while employed with the same employer; or

(ii) Howard subsequently resumes ordinary habitation of his home within one year from the end of the year in which he terminates employment with that employer; or

(iii) Howard dies.

Note that "ordinarily inhabited" means any time during the year according to the CRA, but Howard cannot temporarily move back in order to qualify for this exemption.

Income Tax Folio S1-F3-C2 — Principal Residence

Exercise 4

	Painting		Antique clock		Outboard motor		Gold coin	
P of D		$2,000		$1,200		$1,000		$1,000
ACB	$1,000		$1,000		$1,000		$1,000	
SC	100	(1,100)	20	(1,020)	15	(1,015)	10	(1,010)
CG (CL)		$ 900		$ 180		$ (15)		$ (10)

Net taxable capital gain:

LPP — Painting......................	$ 900	
— Gold coin	(10)[1]	
	$ 890	
— ½		$ 445
PUP — Antique clock (½ × $180)		90
		$ 535

—NOTE TO SOLUTION

[1] Listed personal property losses, whether current or carried-over, are applied at the full capital gain (capital loss) amount.

Exercise 5

(A)

P of D 200 shares @ $25		$5,000
ACB 200 shares @ $33[1]		$6,600
SC	75	(6,675)
CL[2] (Superficial loss of $1,675)		Nil

(B) Adjusted cost base of shares

50 shares @ $33	=	$1,650
200 shares @ $26	=	5,200
superficial loss		1,675
		$8,525 ÷ 250 shares = $34.10

—NOTES TO SOLUTION

[1]
100 shares @ $30	=	$3,000
150 shares @ $35	=	5,250
		$8,250 ÷ 250 shares = $33

[2] Since Ivan acquired additional shares of Solid Investments within the 30-day period.

CHAPTER 7

Exercise 6

(a) For identical properties, the weighted "moving average" basis is to be used to calculate the ACB   ITA: 47(1)
of each individual property (subsection 47(1)).

High Growth Co.

Date	Shares Purchased	Share Price	Adjusted Cost Base	ACB/Share
Jan. 1/12	1,000	$3.00	$ 3,070	$3.07
Jun. 5/13	3,000	2.80	8,490	
	4,000		11,560	2.89
Aug. 5/13	1,500	3.80	5,770	
	5,500		17,330	3.15
Dec. 3/14	1,000	5.10	5,220	
	6,500		22,550	3.47
May 1/15	(3,000)	3.47	(10,410)	
Nov. 8/16	1,000	5.75	5,880	
	4,500		18,020	4.00
Jan. 9/17	(1,500)	4.00	(6,000)	
	3,000		$12,020	4.00

Note: The disposition of shares has no effect on the moving average cost.

(b)

HIGH RISK CO. ACB:

Jan. 10/12	(20,000 × $0.25) + $200 =		$5,200
Jan. 14/12	(4,000 × $0.80) + $75 =		$3,275
Totals	24,000 shares		$8,475
May 20/17	Proceeds	$7,200	
	ACB	(8,475)	
	Broker fees	(150)	
	Capital loss	$(1,425)	
	Allowable capital loss	$(712.50)	

Exercise 7

ITA: 3, 5, 6, 7, 8, 9

		With Sale
Paragraph 3(*a*)	Sources of income	
Sections 5–8	Employment income	$23,000
Section 9	Business income	10,000
Paragraph 3(*b*)	Taxable capital gains	
	Sale of antique painting	
	(.50 × (29,000 – 9,000))	10,000
Section 3	Net income for tax purposes	$43,000

Exercise 8

Adjusted cost base:	
1,000 shares @ $35	$35,000
brokerage	500
2011 — stock dividend — 50 shares (5% × 1,000) × $10	500
2013 — stock dividend — 105 shares (10% × 1,050) × $10	1,050
2015 — stock dividend — 231 shares (20% × 1,155) × $10	2,310
	$39,360

Shares (1000 + 50 + 105 + 231) = 1,386
ACB per share: $39,360 ÷ 1,386 = $28.40

Exercise 9

(A) Since they are related by marriage, they are not at arm's length. ITA: 251(2)(*a*), 251(6)(*b*)

(B) Since they are not considered to be related by blood, they are at arm's length. ITA: 251(6)(*a*)

(C) Since they are still legally married, they are not at arm's length.

(D) The facts of a situation can determine that two unrelated persons are not at arm's length. ITA: 251(1)(*b*)

Exercise 10

	James (seller or transferor)	Hayden (purchaser or transferee)
(A) sale at $2,000	has proceeds of $2,000 and, hence, a capital gain of $800 (i.e., $2,000 − $1,200)	deemed [par. 69(1)(*a*)] to have acquired at $1,500 resulting in potential double-counting of $500 gain
(B) sale at $1,200	deemed [par. 69(1)(*b*)] to have proceeds of $1,500 and, hence, a capital gain of $300	acquired at $1,200 resulting in potential double-counting of $300 gain
(C) gift	deemed [par. 69(1)(*b*)] to have proceeds of $1,500	deemed [par. 69(1)(*c*)] to have acquired at $1,500

Exercise 11

(A) (i) Since a gift is a transfer, the interspousal rollover would automatically deem that Alice's proceeds of disposition are equal to her adjusted cost base ($12,000), resulting in no capital gain. ITA: 73

(ii) Alice would be subject to the income attribution rules on any dividends from the shares, because a gift would not meet the exception, since the fair market value of the property transferred exceeded the fair market value of the consideration received and an election out of the interspousal rollover was not made. ITA: 74.1, 74.5(1)(*a*)

ITA: 73(1)

(iii) Alice would also be subject to capital gains attribution for the same reason as discussed in part (A)(ii), above. There would be full capital gains attribution on all substituted property. ITA: 74.2; IT-511R, par. 27

(B) (i) Since Alice does elect out of the interspousal rollover, the non-arm's length transfer rule, with which the transaction conforms, will apply, since the cash consideration ($15,000) was equal to the fair market value of the property transferred. A capital gain of $3,000 would be triggered. ITA: 73(1)
ITA: 69(1)(*b*)(ii)

(ii) There would be no income or capital gains attribution, because Alice has conformed with the attribution rule exception. The fair market value of the property transferred did not exceed the fair market value of the consideration received and an election out of the interspousal rollover was made. ITA: 74.5(1)(*a*)

ITA: 73(1)

(C) (i) Unless Alice elects not to have the provisions of the interspousal rollover apply, there will be no capital gain triggered on the transfer to her husband. ITA: 73

(ii) Although Alice has received consideration (debt) with a face value ($15,000) equal to the fair market value of the property transferred, the interest rate must be at least equal to the pre-scribed rate at the time or a commercial rate. In addition, the Act requires that Alice elect out of the interspousal rollover. Therefore, Alice will be subject to both income and capital gains attribution. ITA: 74.5(1)(*b*)(i)

74.5(1)(*c*)

(D) The result would be the same as in (A), above, since the shares would be considered substituted property for a transfer of cash for no consideration.

(E) The result would be the same as in (C), above, since the shares would be considered substituted property.

Exercise 12

Capital property A

(A) If Mr. Emerson departs prior to June 1, 2018, there will be no capital gain on the capital asset   ITA: 128.1(4)
which he brought from the U.S. by virtue of the 60-month short-term exemption.

(B) If he departs subsequent to June 1, 2018, there will be a taxable capital gain on ½ of the excess
of the proceeds of disposition ($12,000) over the fair market value at the time of entry ($5,000), namely,
$3,500.

Capital property B

(A) First, it is necessary to determine whether the capital property acquired in Canada is exempt   ITA: 2(3)
from immediate departure tax but will be taxed on its ultimate disposition.

(B) If the property is not exempted then the taxpayer will be taxed at the time of exit from Canada.

Exercise 13

(A)(i) Transfer to wife

Capital gains

Since Mr. Smart does not wish to elect out of subsection 73(1), his proceeds of disposition are
deemed to be equal to his adjusted cost base (i.e., $17.66 per share as calculated below) and hence there
is no capital gain or loss. Mr. Smart's adjusted cost base becomes his wife's adjusted cost base.

P. of D. — deemed (500 shares @ $17.66)	$ 8,830
ACB (500 shares @ $17.66[(1)])	$ 8,830
	Nil

Mr. Smart has transferred property (shares) to his wife and, therefore, ssec. 74.1(1) will require
him to include in his income any dividend income received on the shares. Also, subsection 74.2(1) will
require him to include in computing his income any subsequent capital gain or loss on the shares.
Income realized on previously attributed income from property is exempt from the attribution rules. The
entire gain on substituted property acquired will be attributed.

The above attribution will not apply if the transfer is at fair market value and if Mr. Smart receives
consideration equal to the fair market value of the property received [par. 74.5(1)(a)]. However, in this
case, the transaction is at less than fair market value ($35 < $60). In addition, par. 74.5(1)(b) exempts
the transfer where consideration received includes indebtedness with an interest rate equal to the lesser
of the prescribed rate or a commercial rate. Finally, in order for a capital transaction between spouses to
be exempt from the attribution rules, par. 74.5(1)(c) requires the transferor spouse to elect not to have
ssec. 73(1) apply.

Dividend income

The proposed five-year GIC acquired with the dividend income is an investment contract and will
require an annual accrual income inclusion [ssec. 12(4)]. Since this income is in respect of previously
attributed income, the amounts will not be attributed back to Mr. Smart.

(ii) Transfer to friend

Capital gains

The taxable capital gain to Mr. Smart is determined as follows:

P. of D. (500 shares @ $55)	$27,500
ACB (500 shares at $17.66)	$ 8,830
Capital gain	$18,670
Taxable capital gain (½ × $18,670)	$ 9,335

Dividend income

There is no attribution of dividend income back to Mr. Smart as the transferee is not a spouse or
non-arm's length person, niece or nephew under 18 years old.

(iii) Transfer to son

Capital gains

Taxable capital gain to Mr. Smart is determined as follows:

P. of D. ($500 at $70)*	$ 35,000
ACB (500 shares at $17.66)	$ (8,830)
Capital gain	$ 26,170
Taxable capital gain (½ × $26,170)	$ 13,085

    * The proceeds are deemed to be fair market value [par. 69(1)(b)].

Son's adjusted cost base is the amount paid, since sec. 69 is only a one-sided adjustment.

The interest on the GICs is income on income and is not attributed back to Mr. Smart.

Dividend income

Dividend income on the shares will be attributed back to Mr. Smart until the son reaches 18 [ssec. 74.1(2)]. The sale is not exempt, because fair market value consideration was not received [ssec. 74.5(1)]. Note, however, that if the son were to realize a capital gain or capital loss on his ultimate sale of the shares while he was under 18 years of age, the capital gain or capital loss would not be attributed back to Mr. Smart since there is no provision similar to sec. 74.2 in respect of minors.

(B) Advice:

The mistake was transferring shares to a trust for the son at less than fair market value. The problem is that the son has a low adjusted cost base (the actual price paid $40) while the father's proceeds were high (equal to the fair market value of $70 [spar. 69(1)(b)(i)]). There is the potential for double taxation when the son eventually sells the shares.

The best alternative probably would have been to sell some of the shares at fair market value (in order to receive the same $35,000 of proceeds) and to gift the rest, which would have resulted in proceeds and adjusted cost base being equal to the fair market value [spar. 69(1)(b)(ii) and par. 69(1)(c)]. Attribution could have been avoided on the non-gifted shares by ensuring that any debt consideration received bore a rate of interest equal to the lesser of:

  (a) the prescribed rate, or

  (b) an arm's length commercial rate at the time the loan was made.

—*NOTE TO SOLUTION*

		#		
(1)	2010	500	500 shares at $10	$ 5,000
	2011	300	300 shares at $15	4,500
	2012	100	100 shares @ $20	2,000
	2013	500	500 shares @ $30	15,000
		1,400		
	2014	140	stock dividend (140 shares @ $5)	700
		1,540		$27,200

    $27,200 / 1,540 = $17.66

Exercise 14

(1) The tax consequences depend upon whether Sandi elects not to have sec. 73 apply.

(a) Assuming no election (sec. 73 apply).

   — Sandi is deemed to have sold the Bell Canada shares for proceeds of disposition equal to her ACB ($1,000 × 40). Hence, no capital gain is triggered. Her husband's ACB is equal to her ACB.

   — Any dividends received by her husband on the Bell Canada shares will attribute back to Sandi, since the transfer was not at fair market value (sec. 74.1 and 74.5).

   — If and when her husband sells the shares, there will be attribution of the capital gain calculated on his ACB of $40.

— There will be no attribution of income on previously attributed amounts of income. However, capital gains earned on attributed capital gains are attributable (IT-511).

(b) Assuming she elects not to have sec. 73 apply.

— Sandi's proceeds of disposition will be deemed to be the FMV (10,000 shares x $65) resulting in capital gain of $25,000 (spar. 69(1)(*b*)(ii)).

— The husband's ACB will equal the deemed proceeds of $65,000 (par. 69(1)(*c*)).

— Attribution of both income and capital gains as discussed above will continue since Sandi did not receive consideration equal to the fair market value.

2. The sale of the painting to her son for $1,000 will have the following tax consequences:

— Sandi will be deemed to have sold the painting to her son at the FMV ($125,000), triggering a taxable capital gain of $42,500 [($125,000 – $40,000) × ½] (par. 69(1)(*a*)).

— Her son's ACB will be $1,000 (the amount paid for the painting). This will very likely trigger a capital gain in five years when the son sells the painting to finance his university education. The capital gain could be as much as $124,000 plus any further increase in value after the date of transfer. Hence, the capital gain of $124,000 may be taxed twice. In this case, a gift of the property would have been better, because the son's ACB would be deemed to be $125,000 (par. 69(1)(*c*)).

— There will be no attribution of income on substituted property for the child as long as the proceeds of disposition are received after he becomes 18 years of age.

— There will be no attribution of capital gains in respect of the son no matter when he disposes of the painting.

3. Loan to husband

— No attribution of income, since the loaned funds were used to produce business income, not property income.

— Attribution will apply to the taxable capital gain of $60,000, since the loan did not bear a rate of interest equal to the lesser of the quarterly prescribed rate or a commercial rate at the time the loan was made.

Exercise 15

— The $10,000 loss will be denied as a superficial loss since he will have repurchased the mutual funds within 30 days of the disposition that triggered the loss, assuming that he owns the mutual funds at the end of the 30-day period.

— The $50,000 gain will not be denied since there are no superficial gain rules.

Exercise 16

— Mr. S's current income splitting plan will not work since the attribution rules will apply and any future income and capital gains or losses will be attributed back to him.

— The attribution rules would not apply if all of the following conditions were met:

(a) Mrs. S paid fair market value consideration for the investment portfolio instead of receiving it as a gift;

(b) if the fair market value consideration in (a) included a loan then interest must be charged on the loan at a rate equal to or greater than the lesser of the prescribed rate of interest at the time of the transfer and the current arm's length rate and the interest must be paid each year within 30 days after the end of the year; and

(c) Mr. S must elect not to have the provisions of subsection 73(1) apply (he was planning to do this anyway to trigger the capital gain).

If the current prescribed rate is relatively low, you might suggest that Mr. S transfer the investment portfolio to Mrs. S and receive a note for the fair market value of the portfolio bearing interest at the prescribed rate, which must be paid in the year or within 30 days after the end of the year. In this manner, any future capital gains and income will be included in Mrs. S's income, she will have a deduction for the interest paid and Mr. S will have income of the interest received from Mrs. S.

Chapter 8

Capital Gains: Business Related

Learning Goals

Know, Understand and Explain

By the end of this chapter you will know, understand and be able to explain:

- The tax implications of selling a property through instalment payments and the options available to minimize tax.

- The tax implications of a bad debt as it relates to the disposition of a capital property.

- The deferral available when a property is replaced within the eligible time frame for both involuntary and voluntary disposition.

- The rules related to the disposition of land and building where a terminal loss occurs as a result of the sale.

Apply

By the end of this chapter you will be able to apply your knowledge and understanding to:

- Conclude whether the nature of a transaction is business income or capital gain by applying accepted behavioural factors to case facts.

- Correctly calculate the capital gains reserve that may be claimed in a given period.

- Determine the adjusted cost base of a depreciable asset, including any allowable adjustments and for non-arm's length situations.

- Correctly calculate the deferral amount and the cost base of the new property under the replacement property rules for both capital gains and recapture.

- Correctly calculate the reallocation of proceeds of disposition between the land and building when a terminal loss occurs on the building as a result of the sale.

- Correctly determine the tax implication when a capital property has a deemed disposition as a result of a change in use.

- Apply your knowledge to specific circumstances to minimize the current tax paid by the client on the disposition of a capital property.

Review Questions
¶8,800 in the Study Guide

Multiple Choice Questions
¶8,825 in the Study Guide

Exercises
¶8,850 in the Study Guide

Assignment Problems
¶8,875 in the Study Guide

CHAPTER 8 — LEARNING CHART

Problem Descriptions

Textbook Example Problems

8-1	Capital gains reserve
8-2	Recapture — Involuntary Disposition
8-3	Replacement property
8-4	Replacement property
8-5	Replacement property
8-6	Disposal of building with terminal loss
8-7	Disposition of depreciable property
8-8	Election on change in use
8-9	Foreign exchange gains and losses
8-10	Schedule 1 reconciliation

Multiple Choice Questions

1	Capital gain reserve
2	Replacement property
3	Income vs. capital
4	Replacement property
5	Disposal of building with terminal loss

Exercises

1	Replacement property
2	Sale of accounts receivable
3	Sale of building with terminal loss
4	Inherited property
5	Replacement property
6	Income vs. capital
7	Sale of a business; replacement property
8	Income vs. capital

Assignment Problems

1	Sale of land and building, reserve
2	Dividend in kind
3	Foreign exchange
4	Income vs. capital
5	Reserves if income or capital
6	Replacement property
7	Replacement property
8	Sale of building with terminal loss
9	Sale of building with terminal loss
10	Replacement property
11	Schedule 1 with capital transactions
12	Replacement property
13	Sale of land with apple trees
14	Income vs. capital
15	Sale of a business; replacement property

CHAPTER 8

Study Notes

¶8,800   REVIEW QUESTIONS

(1) Tom, Dick, and Harry formed a partnership in order to invest in a tract of land just outside a large urban area. Five years later, the partnership sold the property making a large profit. According to the partnership agreement, profits from this venture were to be split equally. Discuss whether this is an income or a capital receipt.

(2) Rachel is a real estate salesperson who invests her spare cash in "good land buys" which she occasionally finds. This year Rachel sold one of these properties and realized a large profit. Is this an income or a capital receipt?

(3) Winston White, an accountant, uses his spare time and cash to trade in low-cost mining shares listed on a Canadian stock exchange. Winston made a large profit this year on his stock market transactions. Is this profit income or capital gain?

(4) Diana purchased some land to erect a shopping centre which she intended to sell. However, zoning bylaws could not be changed and Diana sold the property at a large profit. Is this profit income or a capital gain?

(5) Doug spends his Saturday afternoons at the race track. This year Doug was extremely fortunate and his net winnings were $15,000. How will these winnings be taxed?

(6) Mr. Cole bought six acres of lake-front property 15 years ago for $24,000. This year, he sold the three acres that are not on the lake to a neighbour who wanted the woodlot. His proceeds on the three acres sold are $30,000. Discuss what the cost base of the three acres sold would be.

(7) Two years ago, Mr. Bosma had 20 acres of his farm expropriated by the city for industrial land. Because he disputed their value, the proceeds were not finally decided until this year. How soon does he have to replace the land in order to defer the tax on the capital gain realized on the sale of the land?

(8) Opco Ltd. had a large piece of equipment destroyed by fire with the insurance proceeds being paid and the machine replaced in the same year. Can the replacement property rules be applied?

(9) Mrs. Smith owns 100% of Holdco Inc., which in turn owns 100% of Opco Inc. Holdco owns the building which is used by Opco in its active business and rents it to Opco under a five-year lease. Mrs. Smith wants to sell the building and buy a bigger one for the same purpose, but she has been told that the building is considered to be a rental property and, therefore, does not qualify for the replacement property rules since it is not a "former business property". She has asked for your comments.   ITA: 248(1)

(10) Mr. Carr bought and operated a parking lot for the past 10 years. He has now decided that it is time to do something different. However, instead of selling the parking lot he wants to rezone the property and develop and sell condominium apartments. On July 1 of last year, he applied for rezoning and on December 1 of last year, he received the zoning change and a building permit. By October 31 of this year, he had completed construction and sold the units. What kind of income would he have to report and when?

(11) Last year Ms. Chung sold some land that was capital property and realized a capital gain of $150,000. As part of the proceeds she took back a note for $100,000 at 12% which unfortunately was unsecured. This year she realized that the note will become a bad debt, but since she has not disposed of the note she does not think that it can be used for tax purposes. What is your advice to her? What would be the result if the land that was sold was personal-use property?

CHAPTER 8

¶8,825   MULTIPLE CHOICE QUESTIONS

Question 1

On April 1 of this year, X Ltd., with a December 31 year end, sold a parcel of land, a capital property with an adjusted cost base of $100,000, for $600,000. The $600,000 proceeds were payable in the form of a mortgage, with principal payments of $90,000 due every six months, starting on October 1 of this year. What is the minimum taxable capital gain that X Ltd. must report in the current year?

(A) $100,000

(B) $50,000

(C) $75,000

(D) $37,500

Question 2

Mega Ltd., which has a May 31 year end, had its land and building expropriated on June 30, 2018, and received $1 million of compensation from the government for the expropriation. Which one of the following is the deadline for Mega Ltd. to replace the property with another property costing at least $1 million in order to defer the entire recapture and capital gain on the disposition of the expropriated property?

(A) On or before May 31, 2020.

(B) On or before June 30, 2020.

(C) On or before December 31, 2020.

(D) On or before May 31, 2021.

Question 3

Steve is the proprietor of a sporting goods retail business. By chance, he discovered on the Internet a used motor boat for sale for $4,000 — a bargain price. He purchased the motor boat and immediately sold it for a profit of $3,000. He did not use the boat. Which of the following best describes the tax treatment of this transaction?

(A) The motor boat purchase is an investment, and the sale results in a taxable capital gain.

(B) The motor boat purchase is an investment, and the sale results in property income.

(C) The motor boat purchase is an adventure or concern in the nature of trade, and the sale results in business income.

(D) The motor boat purchase is an adventure or concern in the nature of trade, and the sale results in a taxable capital gain.

Question 4

Frames Inc. had a warehouse where it stored its inventory of picture frames, but a fire destroyed the Class 1 building in September 2017. The original cost of the building was $800,000 and the UCC value at the time was $540,000. The insurance company decided the building was a write-off and paid Frames Inc. $850,000 for the building in October 2018. Frames Inc. paid $950,000 to construct a new building by November 2018. What is the UCC of the building before CCA to Frames Inc. for its taxation year ended December 31, 2018, assuming they wish to minimize tax?

(A) $640,000

(B) $690,000

(C) $950,000

(D) $900,000

Question 5

Gloria owned a non-residential building, purchased in 2012, the original cost of which was $400,000, plus $150,000 for the cost of land. The UCC value of the building was $360,000, and the land and building were sold for $750,000 in 2018. The split the taxpayer used between land and building was $300,000 for building and $450,000 for land. Assuming that Gloria wishes to minimize her taxes, what are the tax implications regarding the sale?

(A) A capital gain of $300,000 and a terminal loss of $60,000.

(B) A capital gain of $240,000 and a terminal loss of nil.

(C) A capital gain of $150,000 and a terminal loss of $60,000.

(D) A capital gain of $120,000 and a terminal loss of nil.

¶8,850   EXERCISES

Exercise 1

ITA: 13(4), 44

Tax Processing Ltd.'s computer was completely destroyed in a fire in 2016. The insurance company has been disputing the claim. In the meantime, the company is renting computer time until the claim is settled. The following facts relate to the destroyed computer:

Capital cost	$50,000
UCC immediately before the fire — Class 10	17,150

During 2018, the insurance company paid $60,000 in respect of the claim. The company continued to rent computer time for another 24 months, and in 2020 it purchased a new-generation computer for $70,000.

— *REQUIRED*

Indicate the tax consequences for Tax Processing Ltd. for the above years.

Exercise 2

ITA: 20(1)(*l*), 20(1)(*p*), 22, 38, 39, 50

Mr. Flint has arranged to sell substantially all of the assets of his proprietorship business, including accounts receivable valued at $36,000, to Mr. Small, who will continue the proprietorship business. At the end of last year, Mr. Flint had deducted a reserve for doubtful debts of $6,500. The face value of the accounts being sold is $45,000.

What are the tax implications to both Mr. Flint and Mr. Small of not using section 22 on the sale of accounts receivable?

Exercise 3

ITA: 13(21.1)

Sienna Research Inc. has one last building to dispose of in its liquidation process. Higher Peaks Ltd. has agreed to purchase the building for $1.28 million. The president of Sienna would like to maximize the after-tax profits of the disposition by creating a terminal loss on the building. He bragged about how the terminal loss on the building would nicely reduce the capital gain on the land. He drafted a sales contract allocating the total proceeds as follows:

Land	$ 895,000
Building	385,000
Total	$1,280,000

The capital cost of the land and building was as follows:

Land	$345,000
Building	520,000
Total	$865,000

The UCC of the building (last asset in Class 1) is $438,700.

— *REQUIRED*

The president would like you to confirm the tax implications of this disposition.

Exercise 4

ITA: 40(1)(*a*)

Mary Jane inherited a parcel of land from her father in 1995 when she inherited his proprietorship business assets. The land was used as a customer parking lot for the proprietorship business. She sold the land in 2018 for $200,000. Her father paid $30,000 for the land and the value in 1995 was $60,000. The purchaser paid 50,000 cash, with the remaining $150,000 plus interest due in 2020. Mary Jane has calculated her capital gain as $140,000.

— REQUIRED

Determine if Mary Jane's calculation of her capital gain is correct. Indicate if she has any other alternatives for reporting the gain. Your answer should be supported with appropriate references to the Act.

Exercise 5

ITA: 13(4)

Windswept Storage Ltd. had a brick warehouse that was completely destroyed by a tornado early in its 2017 fiscal year ended December 31. The building had cost $300,000 and its Class 3 undepreciated capital cost at the time of its destruction was $221,000. Agreement was reached on the insurance claim later in 2017 when the company received only $295,000. A new brick building was fully constructed by August 2018 for $400,000.

— REQUIRED

Trace the effects of these events on the balance of the undepreciated capital cost from 2017 through to the beginning balance for 2019, assuming that the proper election is made.

ITA: 13(4)

Exercise 6

The appellant company was incorporated in 1951 with broad charter powers to engage in the real estate business. The objects of the company included the power to buy, sell, subdivide and dispose of properties. Over a period covering about fifteen years, the company purchased various properties in the Toronto area, holding some as investments and reselling others. To the date of the case, the company had sold 12 properties. Two were sold at large profits because good offers were received. The appellants two principal shareholders had a history of extensive dealing in real estate.

In three purchases during a four-year period, the appellant assembled a parcel of land in a Toronto suburb with the intention of erecting buildings on the property for rental purposes. This would be done if the surrounding area developed to the extent that rental of the planned buildings was viable. The property was resold at a substantial profit nine years later. It had been listed for sale with a real estate corporation, wholly owned by the president of the appellant, and had remained undeveloped from the time of purchase to the time of sale.

When the Minister taxed the profit as income, the appellant contended that its profit was a capital accretion from the realization of an investment.

— REQUIRED

Analyze the facts of this case thoroughly by considering all of the factors that have been developed by the courts to determine whether the receipt involved in the sale of the property was one of income or capital. Draw a reasoned conclusion from your analysis.

Exercise 7

On March 1, 2018, Mr. Sole Proprietor sold for cash his printing shop, located in downtown Oakville, to a competitor, as indicated below:

	Cost	UCC Jan. 1, 2018	Cash proceeds
Accounts receivable net (see Note (1), below)	$ 12,000	—	$ 8,000
Inventory	20,000	—	17,000
Land	20,000	—	75,000
Building — Class 3	60,000	$47,000	200,000
Equipment — Class 8	30,000	8,850	10,000
Goodwill	—	—	50,000

CHAPTER 8

Additional information concerning the sale of business:

(1) The accounts receivable cost is net of a $2,000 allowance for doubtful accounts which was claimed at the end of the preceding year.

(2) Mr. Proprietor has been in the same business since 1992 and has a fiscal year ending December 31.

During February 2019, Mr. Proprietor purchased the following capital property and other assets in order to start a new printing business in Northern Ontario:

Land	$ 90,000
Building (new)	135,000
Equipment — Class 43	50,000
Inventory	25,000

— REQUIRED

(A) Compute the minimum amount of income Mr. Proprietor must include in his 2018 tax return from the sale of the printing business, assuming he does not elect under sec. 44, par. 13(4)(*d*), and sec. 22.

(B) Compute the minimum amounts of income Mr. Sole Proprietor must include in his 2018 return if he elects under sec. 44 par. 13(4)(*d*), and sec. 22. Also, compute the undepreciated capital cost on January 1, 2020 of the new building.

(C) Give a brief explanation to Mr. Sole Proprietor as to why the use of these elections is advantageous.

Exercise 8

In 2014 Hi-Tech Limited's computer research facility was substantially destroyed by fire. They were fortunate in obtaining rental space from which to operate while searching for a suitable building to purchase. They located a building on 10 acres of land in a suburban area for sale, but were reluctant to acquire so much excess land. The vendor indicated that he would only consider offers for the entire property. However, after several additional months of searching they acquired this property for $1,750,000. (The appraisal indicated that the building had a value of $1,250,000 and the land had a value of $500,000.)

After obtaining the property, Hi-Tech decided that they would move their head office to a new building to be constructed adjacent to the research facility when the lease in their downtown office tower expired in 2018. Hi-Tech's financial position deteriorated substantially and management concluded in 2018 that the commencement of construction of the new head office would be too great a financial drain. Shortly thereafter, a developer approached Hi-Tech and suggested a joint venture to construct an exclusive community of homes on the excess acreage.

The joint venture agreement provided that Hi-Tech would receive 20% of the proceeds from the sale of the 20 homes, to a maximum of $500,000. All homes were constructed and sold by the end of 2018 and Hi-Tech received $500,000.

— REQUIRED

Discuss the alternative methods of treating the gain on the sale of the five acres of land and recommend the position that Hi-Tech should take when filing their 2018 income tax return.

¶8,875   ASSIGNMENT PROBLEMS

Type 1 Problems

Problem 1

Lev has owned his commercial property for many years, but he has now decided to sell it. The potential purchaser does not have enough cash to pay the full price of $775,000, so he is asking Lev to accept cash of $475,000 and a note payable of $300,000 with interest at 5% for the balance. The note would be repayable in equal annual amounts of $150,000 on the anniversary of the original closing. Lev has come to you for your advice on the tax consequences of this proposal.

	Cost	UCC	Proceeds	Proposed Consideration Cash	Note
Land...............	$100,000		$550,000		
Building	200,000	$155,000	225,000		
	$300,000		$775,000	$475,000	$300,000

Problem 2

Adele owns 100% of Active Inc. The company owns a small piece of land that she would like to now own personally. It has been proposed that she declare a "dividend in kind" where instead of paying cash as a dividend the company will transfer the land to her name. The land is currently worth $100,000 and has an adjusted cost base of $45,000. Adele would like to understand the tax implications of this proposal.

Problem 3

When he was vacationing in Florida this year, Joe Raymer sold, for US$10,000, an asset used in his proprietorship business in Ottawa, which he purchased four years ago for C$4,000. Joe was paid in U.S. dollars. At the time of the sale, US$1 bought C$1.28. When Joe returned, he converted the U.S. currency to Canadian dollars and received C$13,500.

ITA: 39(2)

Joe has asked you to calculate the taxable capital gain or allowable capital loss, if any, arising on the above transactions.

Problem 4

Schillaci v. M.N.R., 92 DTC 1648 (T.C.C.)

Jean-Luc, the taxpayer in this case, was experienced in retail real estate, having originally been employed by a fast-food chain of restaurants. His duties were to locate, acquire and open restaurants on behalf of his employer. He acquired extensive knowledge in packaging sites for retail operations.

Two years ago, Jean-Luc began to work as an employee for Jorge, a successful builder of homes and condominiums, real estate developer for investment of rental apartments and retail plazas, and trust company owner. Jean-Luc was employed on a salary and bonus basis. At the time, Jean-Luc was also a licensed real estate broker and owned a brokerage firm.

Jean-Luc's first project for Jorge involved developing a retail complex in Toronto. He was instrumental in obtaining two anchor tenants as well as two others. This was a successful venture.

His second venture involved a strip plaza in London, Ontario. By the time Jean-Luc and Jorge were prepared to purchase the property, most of the pre-development work had been completed and two nationally recognized restaurant chains had signed letters of intent and/or offers to lease. These two tenants represented 60% of the rentable area of the plaza. With those tenants in place, other tenants were prepared to rent because of the traffic which would be generated by the presence of the two popular fast-food restaurants. As a result, financing the project would not be a problem.

All of the leases which were negotiated were of the "net-net" type — the landlord being responsible only for its financing costs. The tenants were responsible for all other costs and expenses involved with the plaza, in addition to their own businesses.

CHAPTER 8

A partnership of Jorge (74%), Jean-Luc (24%), and Shloimie (2%), the long-time accountant for Jorge, was established to own the plaza. Neither Jean-Luc nor Shloimie paid for his respective interest in the partnership. Jean-Luc considered this to be a long-term project that would provide income for his children's future. Jorge and Shloimie regarded the project as an opportunity to acquire and own an income-producing property with very little investment, since most of the funds were provided by debt financing.

City planning and zoning for the plaza was approved and most of the financing was in place. Last year, about a year after the purchase by the partnership, the building was completed to the point where the tenants took possession. Shortly thereafter, the tenants completed their respective areas and were in operation and paying rent. Temporary financing was in place and permanent financing was being negotiated pending a drop in interest rates at the time.

This year, Jorge began to have financial difficulties and his assets were liquidated by his creditors. Since his creditors did not have security on the plaza project, Jorge was in a position to sell that asset in an orderly manner. Although Jorge controlled the partnership, he received Jean-Luc's consent to sell the property. Jean-Luc's share of the gain on the sale was about $157,000.

Jean-Luc filed his tax return for this year showing the gain as a capital gain.

A CRA assessor has called to indicate that she is considering a reassessment of the income in question as income from a business, an adventure in the nature of trade, or from a profit-making undertaking or concern.

As Jean-Luc's tax adviser, evaluate the fact situation and recommend a course of action.

Problem 5

ITA: 20(1)(n), 20(8), 40;
IT-152R3

Len Jamal bought a parcel of land in 1998. It was his intention that he would relocate his proprietorship business to the land some day. However, the city continued to delay issuing permits to landowners in the area and eventually Len purchased another property to relocate his proprietorship business to. He held onto the land for a number of years but has now decided that he needs the cash and will sell the property. The details related to his purchase of the land are set out below.

Purchase Price: $4,000; Purchase Date: May 21, 1998

Len has received an offer from an acquaintance to purchase the land. The payment terms are set out below and are considered to represent fair market value.

Purchase Price: $160,000; Purchase Date: October 1, 2018

Payment terms: $40,000 down payment on purchase date; $20,000 payable on January 1 each year for the period January 1, 2019 through January 1, 2024 inclusive. Interest: Interest is payable at 6% annually on the unpaid balance.

Len is uncertain as to whether the disposition is on account of capital or income.

You have been asked to compare the income tax consequences to Len of this sale if the sale is on account of capital and, alternatively, if it is on account of income. Do not calculate the interest income. Ignore the consequences and calculation of the interest income.

Problem 6

ITA: 13(4)

Elaine Barblaik owns an apartment building which she holds for rental income. In November 2017, Elaine settled with municipal authorities on expropriation proceeds for the property including the building. The agreed expropriation proceeds for the building and the separate sale proceeds for the appliances and fixtures are indicated in the following data:

	Expropriated building Cl. 1	Sold appliances & fixtures
Cost	$406,000	$26,000
UCC January 1, 2017	188,500	7,250
Proceeds	362,500	2,600

Since negotiations had been prolonged, Elaine was able to anticipate the approximate date of settlement and, as a result, she was able to replace in 2018 the assets expropriated.

Replacement cost for the building and the cost of new appliances and fixtures were as follows:

Building	$1,276,000
Appliances and fixtures	46,400

Elaine would like you to calculate the undepreciated capital cost for both assets through to the opening balance on January 1, 2019 assuming no further additions are made to either class of assets.

Problem 7

ITA: 13(4), 44

During its year ended December 31, 2018, Power Boat Corporation Ltd. sold its retailing facilities in Kingston. As the sale occurred in December, business activity was at a low. New facilities were purchased in February 2019 in Parry Sound on the shores of Georgian Bay. The corporation sold its Kingston land and building for $300,000 and $200,000, respectively. This land and building had a cost in 2001 of $50,000 and $100,000, respectively. At the end of 2017, the building had an undepreciated capital cost of $55,000 for income tax purposes. In Parry Sound, the corporation purchased land and building for $75,000 and $350,000, respectively.

You have been asked to do the following:

(A) Prepare two calculations of the income tax consequences of the above move, one without an election for additional deferral and one with this election. ITA: 44(6)

(B) If the property disposed of by the corporation in 2018 had been an apartment building held for rental purposes and producing income from property:

(i) what would the tax consequences of a sale of the property have been after a replacement of the property with another apartment complex in 2019?

(ii) what would the tax consequences on an expropriation have been after a replacement of the property with another apartment complex in 2019?

Problem 8

ITA: 13(21.1)

Pidgeon Dock Ltd. (PD) sold a property in its year ended January 31, 2018. The details are as follows:

	Proceeds	Cost	UCC
Building	$300,000	$400,000	$350,000
Land	$175,000	$100,000	N/A

The building was the last remaining asset in Class 3. PD prepared its corporate tax return based on the proceeds of disposition shown above. The CRA is now auditing PD.

PD has asked you to identify and calculate any adjustment the CRA will make to their 2018 income tax return.

CHAPTER 8

Problem 9

ITA: 13(21.1)

Johnny Wong had purchased a dilapidated apartment block, The Empress, 20 years ago for $220,000. At the time, the purchase price had been allocated $80,000 to the land and $140,000 to the building. The Empress is the only building Johnny owns and is considered a Class 3 asset for CCA purposes. To date, Johnny has claimed CCA of $37,000.

High Towers has acquired all the lots in the same block as Johnny's building, except for The Empress. Johnny realized that as the last hold-out he was in an enviable negotiating position with High Towers. High Towers was desperate to gain ownership of The Empress and tear it down. After receiving ever-escalating offers, Johnny agreed to accept High Towers' offer of $1,000,000.

Johnny has been asked for your advice regarding the allocation of the purchase price between the land and building.

Type 2 Problems

Problem 10

ITA: 13(4), 44

On March 1, 2017, Raymond Fan, a sole proprietor, sold his garden supply store in downtown Toronto to a competitor because of declining sales caused by competition from large suburban hardware and grocery stores. The following information relates to the sale of the business:

	Proceeds	Cost	UCC Jan. 1, 2017
Accounts receivable	$ 6,000	$10,000	—
Land	120,000	65,000	—
Building — Class 1	170,000	62,000	$28,000
Equipment — Class 8	3,000	1,200	300
— Class 10	4,000	12,000	800
Inventory	5,200	7,000	—
Goodwill	52,000	—	—

Raymond's business year end coincided with the calendar year. Raymond has been in the same business since 1999. As of December 31, 2016, there was a balance in the allowance for doubtful accounts for tax purposes of $1,300.

Subsequent to the sale of the business, Raymond worked for his brother, Kevin, who owned a shoe store. However, Raymond became bored and when a garden supply store on a busy highway north of Toronto came on the market in late November 2018, he immediately bought it. The following information relates to his purchase of assets of the new business:

Land	$105,000
Building (built and used before 2007)	220,000
Equipment — Class 8	9,000
— Class 10	11,000
Goodwill	Nil

Raymond has asked for your help and you have decided to do the following:

(A) Compute the minimum amount Raymond must include on his 2017 tax return in respect of the sale of the business, before any election is made to defer capital gains and recapture.

ITA: 13(4), 44

(B) Show the effect on Raymond's 2017 (amended) and 2018 tax returns if he elects to defer capital gains and recapture after purchasing the new business, but does not elect for additional deferral.

ITA: 13(4), 44
ITA: 44(6)

(C) Discuss whether Raymond should have elected for additional deferral.

(D) If the above situation had been an involuntary disposition instead of a voluntary disposition, how would your answer under part (B) differ?

ITA: Subdivisions b and c;
ETA: 123(1), 169(1),
170(1)(*a*), 174, 231, 236

Problem 11

PITA Co. Ltd. is a nutritional consulting firm that advises manufacturers and distributors on consumers' dietary needs and preferences. For its year ended December 31, 2018, it reported net income before taxes of $900,000 for financial statement purposes. This amount included a gain on the disposition of land held as capital property of $50,000 and of a building (not the only one in the class) of $95,000. The corporation also realized an accounting loss of $20,000 on securities and of $10,000 on a trademark. These assets were acquired for the following amounts:

land . . . . $120,000 in 2007

building . . . . . .   100,000 in 2007 (UCC of the class is $125,000)

securities . . . . .   50,000 in 2016

trademark. . . . .   80,000 in 2015 (assume Class 14.1 existed prior to 2017)

The proceeds of disposition of these assets were as follows:

land $150,000

building 120,000

securities   30,000

trademark.   75,000

The corporation has reported accounting amortization of $80,000 and wishes to claim the maximum available capital cost allowance of $100,000. During 2018, the corporation also made payments in respect of interest on unpaid income taxes ($1,500), charitable donations ($10,000), and an annual employee dinner-dance in December 2018 ($14,000). During 2018, the corporation established that an unsecured $5,000 note receivable in respect of the sale (as capital property) of a parcel of land in the prior year had become a bad debt. This was not reflected in the financial statements.

PITA has asked you to do the following:

(A) Prepare a reconciliation between net income for financial statement purposes and net income for income tax purposes for the year ended December 31, 2018. Support your reconciliation with references to the *Income Tax Act*.

(B) Discuss in general terms the treatment of these items by the corporation for purposes of the HST.

Type 3 Problems

Problem 12

Sudbury Processing Inc. has had some tough times. In December 2017, just before its December 31st year end, there was a fire in its processing plant which destroyed the building and most of the contents. Tom Haskett, the owner, had to move fast to get back in operation before he lost customers to the competition.

Tom owns all the shares of Sud Holdings Inc. ("Holdings"). Holdings owns all the shares of Sudbury Processing Inc. ("Processing"), which is the operating company. Holdings also owns the land, building, and equipment used by Processing (the ones destroyed by fire).

In order to get back into business, Tom had Processing lease a new building until he could make arrangements for a new permanent home. He had some delay in making any new arrangements, because he and the insurance company had a difference of opinion on the replacement value of the building and equipment that were destroyed. They eventually agreed in March 2018, and Holdings received the cheque shortly thereafter for the building, equipment, and some repairs. However, the delay meant Tom had to make alternate arrangements for acquiring new equipment, so Processing entered into an equipment lease with an option to buy it at the end of the five-year term. Luckily, Processing had business interruption insurance, which paid it $10,000 per month for four months until it was up and running again.

In July 2018, Tom made the final decision on a new factory. He decided not to build at the old location. Instead, that land is being sold and new property is being bought with the intention of constructing a new building in the next couple of years. On the sale of the existing land, the purchaser wants a warranty that there are no environmental problems as a result of the fire. Holdings and the purchaser agreed that if there were any problems, then Holdings would pay $20,000 of the purchase price back. Rather than purchase the new parcel of land at this time, Tom has had Holdings buy an option to acquire the land at any time in the next two years for an agreed-upon price.

Advise Tom on the tax implications of Sudbury's situation.

Problem 13

Mac Tosh is 66 years old and was a self-employed apple farmer in Kelowna. Since his children did not want to take over his farming business, he sold the farm (which qualifies for the lifetime capital gains deduction) to a real estate developer for $450,000. The developer sold the crop in late August, cleared the land and began the development of a 50-unit condominium complex.

Mac Tosh paid $10,000 for the land in 1983 and planted 500 apple trees with a cost base of $2,000. He was saddened by the attitude of the developer, as the farm had been his pride and joy. Since Mac never used insecticides or fertilizers, he could earn a premium on the sale of the "organic" apples. Mac had the land appraised at $400,000 by two independent appraisers. The appraisal values were supported by the price of a piece of raw land which had recently sold in a nearby community. To compensate Mac Tosh for all his hard work over the years as well as for the current crop, the developer agreed to pay an additional $50,000 over the appraised land value. Mac Tosh's annual revenues from his apple harvest were approximately $15,000. Mac was pleased with this additional offer because it was very similar to the offer he received the previous year for his entire farm and crop from a neighbouring farmer. Mac has not had any other dispositions of capital property, and has no other sources of earned income.

Just last week, Mac received a letter from the CRA requesting further details on the sale of his farm. He was requested to submit appraisals and a statement regarding the reason behind his tax treatment of the disposition. Mac reported the entire disposition as a capital gain and offset the gain by utilizing the necessary capital gains deduction. Mac did not have any cumulative net investment losses.

Mac can't understand why the CRA wants this information. He thought that he had considered all income tax implications of the disposition of the farm. He even read a professional tax planning book. How should Mac have reported the transaction?

Problem 14

Four young couples from Dundas frequently socialized together on Saturday evenings. They were recently married with young children and, thus, often spent the evening enjoying good conversation at the home of one of the couples.

During a discussion on one such Saturday evening, they decided to pool their funds together for investment purposes. They all came from lower to middle income families and all believed that the way to be successful and to be prepared for unforeseen tough times was to own land. Their dream was to own a rental property. None of them, individually, had the ability to save the down payment required for such an acquisition. Thus they decided that each Saturday night they met, each couple would put $25 into a fund which would be invested in interest bearing securities until the fund was large enough to make a down payment on a rental property. Thus the Dundas social and investment club ("the club") was formed.

Over the next three years they discussed various rental properties that came onto the market, but all required a larger down payment than the club could afford.

In 1999, the club finally agreed to buy a 30-acre piece of farm land near Copetown for $120,000. The purchase of the property had been recommended to the club by a friend of one of the members. They trusted her recommendation as she was a real estate agent and had made a lot of money from buying and reselling land. The club had sufficient funds to pay the down payment required of $12,000. The location of the land was such that it would be suitable for development of rental producing properties in the future.

One of the members of the club was a young lawyer and thus was able to save the club some money by preparing the legal documents herself. She prepared the following four agreements:

(1) An agreement of purchase and sale for the property.

(2) A rental agreement with a farmer, whereunder the farmer could use the land to grow crops and would pay as rent ⅓ of the proceeds from the crops annually. The agreement could

be terminated by either party with six months notice. (The rent received by the club was about $3,000 per year on average).

(3) An agreement among the couples in the group to the effect that if the group, for whatever reasons (no longer friends, divorce, etc.) decided to break up, the members had to continue making their weekly contribution until the property was paid for. None of them could withdraw their equity until such time as the property was sold.

(4) An agreement which stated: "In the event of a *bona fide* offer being received by any member of the club for the purchased land, such offer shall be communicated to the entire group, and no sale shall be made without the consent of the entire group. In the event that some of the members wish to sell and others do not, those not wishing to sell have the right to purchase the proportionate interest of the others wishing to sell at the proportionate share of the offered price."

Over the years, many offers were received to sell the property even though it was never advertised for sale. None of the offers were accepted. In fact, the club never even made a counter-offer.

In 2008, a railroad approached the club about purchasing two acres of the land. The club refused. In early 2008 the railroad expropriated two acres of the land giving the club $65,000.

In 2011, the club received an offer to sell the remaining land for $1,080,000. They refused as they still believed the land was a good investment and that it was still appreciating in value.

In 2013, the railroad expropriated a further eight acres of the land paying the club $350,000.

In 2018, the Village of Copetown informed the club of their wish to purchase 14 acres of the land for a new roadway. It was the opinion of the club that they should stay on good terms with the village. If the club decided to develop the land, they would need the co-operation of the village in obtaining approval for zoning changes, etc. The land was still zoned for farm use only. Thus the club advised the village they would co-operate in view of the village's need for the land, but that they would prefer to exchange land with the village, rather than sell the land to them. The village considered this but determined that it did not have any land suitable for such an exchange. Thus, three months later, the 14 acres were sold to the village for $700,000.

Discuss whether the sale of the land in 2018 was an income receipt or a capital receipt. Fully support your conclusion.

Problem 15

Joe Shmaltz had come to you for some tax advice concerning the potential sale and relocation of his computer service business, a sole proprietorship under the name of Joe's Computer Service. Joe had inherited the present site of his business from his father in 2007. He has received an offer to sell the present land and building for an excellent price. Joe has investigated other properties in the area and believes he can acquire a suitable site which is now being rented until October 2019. Joe cannot resume his business operations until this date and intends to sell all his present business assets. He will then acquire the necessary assets to resume business under the present name.

The following list of assets will be sold in September 2018:

	Estimated Proceeds	ACB	UCC Jan. 1, 2018
Accounts receivable	$ 9,600	$12,000	n/a
Land	720,000	180,000	n/a
Building — Class 3	420,000	120,000	$54,000
Equipment — Class 8	12,000	60,000	24,000
Inventory	14,400	15,600	n/a

Additional Information:

(1) The accounts receivable will be sold to a factoring agent.

(2) There is a balance in the allowance for doubtful accounts of $960.

(3) The cost of land and building reflects the fair market value at the date of his father's death.

(4) The equipment will be sold to another computer service business.

(5) The present business, Joe's Computer Service, has a December 31 year-end. Joe will retain this year end when he resumes business in November 2019.

(6) Joe will acquire the new land and building for $575,000 and $360,000, respectively.

Indicate the tax consequences of the sale of the present business assets and acquisition of the new real property supported by your computations.

CHAPTER 8 —
DISCUSSION NOTES FOR REVIEW QUESTIONS

(1) The transaction will probably be an income receipt. The partnership appears to have been set up specifically to buy and hold the land. The partnership agreement seems to confirm that their primary intention was to make a profit, since the agreement specifically states how the income is to be split. If, after five years, they still have done nothing to develop the land to earn rental or other income, then it would appear to be a speculation gain and, therefore, income.

(2) The transaction will probably be an income receipt. Rachel has used her specialized knowledge, derived from her normal occupation, to make the large profit. This factor, combined with her trading history, would weigh heavily in favour of income treatment.

(3) Normally, stock market transactions are treated as capital gains or losses. However, his intention seems to be to make a profit in trading shares, thereby indicating an income receipt. He may elect to have these transactions treated as capital gains. However, Winston should be careful that the CRA does not subsequently deem him to be a "trader" and thereby revoke his election.

ITA: 39(4), 39(5)

(4) The transaction would probably be an income receipt. Her primary intention is to develop the shopping centre for sale which would be an income transaction. Therefore, the sale of the land prior to development would also be an income transaction.

(5) Capital receipt (not taxable). Doug's $15,000 net winnings should not be treated as income because his actions are more in the nature of a hobby, not making a profit. If this was his business, the profits would be taxable and any losses would be deductible.

Income Tax Folio: S3-F9-C1 Lottery Winnings, Miscellaneous Receipts and Income (Losses) from Crime

(6) One way to approach this question is to assume that the cost was allocated equally to each acre. Therefore, the cost of the three acres sold would be ½ of the original cost of the six acres or $12,000. However, the CRA, in applying the law, may consider that $12,000 is too high an amount to be "reasonably regarded as attributable to that part," since the lake-front portion would usually be more valuable than the non-lake-front property assuming that access is still available to both parcels. This, then, becomes a valuation issue.

ITA: 43

(7) He has to replace the land before the end of the second taxation year after the initial year. If they finally agreed to the price in 2018 then he has until December 31, 2020 to replace the property. The initial year is the year that the "amount has become receivable as proceeds of disposition", i.e., 2018 in this case.

ITA: 44(1)(c)

ITA: 44(1), 44(2)

(8) Yes. In order for these rules to apply the destroyed equipment must be either property that was stolen, destroyed or expropriated or a "former business property". The definition of former business property only refers to real property which has a common law definition of "land and building". Equipment is not included in that definition. However, if the property is stolen, destroyed or expropriated, it only has to meet the definition of "property". In this case the equipment meets this definition and the replacement property rules can apply. Of course, any potential recapture would be offset, by the normal rules, because the purchase of the new machine was made in the year of loss.

ITA: 248(1) "former business property"

(9) Under the definition of "former business property" the advice she received was incorrect. This building qualifies as a former business property, since it is rented to a related corporation and is used in the related corporation's business.

ITA: 248(1) "former business property", 251

CHAPTER 8

(10) A change in use does not include a transfer of property from one income-producing use to another. In this case the property is being transferred from earning property income to earning business income. As a result there is no income to report on July 1 of last year when zoning was applied for. However, when the property is eventually sold an assessment will need to be done at July 1 of last year since the increase in value up to that point will be a capital gain and any profit after that date will be business income from the sale of the condominiums.

ITA: 13(7), 45(1); IT-218R

(11) Ms. Chung can elect to have disposed of her note when it is established to have become uncollectible. This will result in a capital loss equal to $100,000 and the note will then have a cost equal to nil. All or some of this loss can then be carried back under Division C to be applied against the previous capital gain. If the original property disposed of was personal-use property then the debt would have been "personal-use property". Then the Act allows a capital loss only to the extent of the capital gain on the original disposition.

ITA: 50(1), 54 "personal-use property"

ITA: 50(2)

CHAPTER 8 — SOLUTIONS TO MULTIPLE CHOICE QUESTIONS

Question 1

(B) is correct. The gain is: $600,000 – $100,000 = $500,000. The maximum 2018 reserve is computed using the lesser of the percentage of proceeds payable after the end of the year ($510,000/$600,000 or 85%, in this case) and four fifths (⅘). Since the lesser amount is four fifths, the reserve is $400,000 (⅘ × $500,000) and the capital gain is therefore $100,000 ($500,000 – $400,000). The minimum taxable capital gain is therefore $50,000 (½).

ITA: 40(1)(*a*)

(A) is incorrect, because the capital gain must be multiplied by ½ to compute the taxable capital gain.

(C) is incorrect, because it uses the 85% figure to compute the reserve and does not multiply the result by ½: $500,000 – 85% × $500,000 = $75,000.

(D) is incorrect, because it uses the 85% figure to compute the reserve: $75,000 × ½.

Question 2

(D) is the correct answer. Since the expropriation is an involuntary disposition, the property must be replaced by the later of two taxation years from the end of the taxation year in which the disposition took place or 24 months from the end of the taxation year in which the disposition took place. Since the relevant taxation year was May 31, 2019, the two-year deadline is May 31, 2021.

ITA: 44(1)(*c*)

(A) incorrectly uses the one-year deadline which is applicable for voluntary dispositions.

(B) incorrectly uses two years from the disposition date as the deadline.

(C) incorrectly uses two years from the end of the calendar year of the disposition as the deadline.

Question 3

(C) is correct

It can be concluded from the facts that Steve's primary intention was to purchase the boat and sell it for a profit. He bought the boat and immediately sold it for a profit the way a person in the boat-sales trade would act. He did not use the boat personally or rent it out for use as a capital asset. The transaction was, in some sense, related to his sporting goods retailing business which would give Steve some insight into the purchase and sale of a boat in this way. Profit from an adventure in the nature of trade is considered to be business income.

(A) incorrectly includes the profit as a taxable capital gain, rather than business income.

(B) incorrectly includes the income as income from property, rather than income from business.

(D) incorrectly includes the profit as a taxable capital gain, rather than business income from an adventure in the nature of trade.

Question 4

(A) is correct

Involuntary disposition: They replaced within the time limit.

Replacement cost	$950,000
Deferred capital gain	(50,000)
Capital cost	$900,000
Deferred recapture	(260,000)
UCC before CCA	$640,000

(B) incorrectly ignores the deferred capital gain.

(C) incorrectly ignores all deferrals.

(D) incorrectly ignores the deferred recapture.

CHAPTER 8

Question 5

(B) is correct

Result	Land	Building	Total
Proceeds	$390,000	$ 360,000	$750,000
Capital cost	$150,000		
UCC		360,000	
Capital gain	$240,000		
Terminal loss		$ 0	

Subsection 13(21.1) would disallow the terminal loss by making the proceeds on the building equal to the UCC with the remaining proceeds allocated to the land.

(A) incorrectly ignores the reallocation of proceeds.

(C) incorrectly ignores the reallocation of proceeds and calculates the taxable capital gain, rather than the capital gain, as required.

(D) incorrectly calculates the taxable capital gain, rather than the required capital gain.

CHAPTER 8 — SOLUTIONS TO EXERCISES

Exercise 1

(A) During the years prior to the settling of the claim, Tax Processing Ltd. is deemed to own the ITA: 44(2) destroyed asset. Hence the company can continue to take capital cost allowance.

		Class 10: 30%
UCC before the fire		$17,150
CCA — 2016	$ 5,145	
CCA — 2017	3,602	(8,747)
UCC before proceeds received		$ 8,403

Note that the available-for-use rules do not apply when the asset has been used by the taxpayer. ITA: 13(27)(*a*)

(B) In the second year after the fire (2018) when the company received the proceeds, the company would be deemed to have sold the computer for $60,000 with the following tax consequences:

Taxable capital gain:

P of D	$60,000
ACB	(50,000)
CG	$10,000
TCG (½ × $10,000)	$ 5,000

Recapture:

UCC before proceeds received		$ 8,403
Less the lesser of:		
(i) Capital cost	$50,000	
		(50,000)
(ii) P of D	$60,000	
Recapture		$41,597

(C) In the year of purchase of the new computer (2020), which is within the 24-month time limit for an involuntary disposition, Tax Processing Ltd. would file an amended return for the 2018 year in which the taxable capital gain and recapture were recognized.

Taxable capital gain:

½ of the lesser of:

(i) capital gain (see above) $10,000

(ii) P of D $60,000

     less replacement cost   70,000   Nil   = Nil

ACB of new computer in 2020: ($70,000 – $10,000) = $60,000   *ITA: 44(1)(f)*

Recapture: *ITA: 13(4)*

                                                                Class 10: 30%

UCC before proceeds received (see above calculation) . . . . $ 8,403

Less deemed disposal: *ITA: 13(4)(c)*

    lesser of (i) cost ($50,000)

               (ii) P of D ($60,000) $50,000

Less the lesser of:

    (i) the recapture

        ($8,403 – $50,000) $41,597

    (ii) replacement cost   70,000   41,597   8,403

UCC after proceeds received, Dec. 31, 2018 . . . .   Nil

                                                                Class 50: 55%

2020 addition:

    Capital cost of replacement property $70,000

    Less reduction for deferred gain   10,000   *ITA: 44(1)(f)*

    Deemed capital cost $60,000

    Less reduction for deferred recapture   41,597   *ITA: 13(4)(d)*

UCC before CCA $18,403

    CCA (55% of ½ × $18,403) . . . .   (5,061)

UCC after CCA $13,342

Exercise 2

If section 22 is not used, Mr. Flint must still include in income last year's reserve of $6,500. However, the loss of $9,000 will be regarded as a capital loss which is only fractionally deductible and can be offset only against taxable capital gains. Since Mr. Small has not included any amount as income in respect of these accounts receivable, he will not be allowed a deduction for a reserve or for bad debts because the conditions of the reserve for doubtful debts or the bad debt expense rules will not be met. If Mr. Small collects more than the $36,000 fair market value, the excess will be a capital gain and, if he collects less than $36,000, the difference will be a capital loss.   *ITA: 20(1)(l), 20(1)(p)*

Exercise 3

Sienna Research Inc. has what, at first, appears to be a terminal loss on the building and a capital gain on the land. When this occurs, subsection 13(21.1) reallocates the proceeds so that the terminal loss is reduced by the capital gain on the land.   *ITA: 13(21.1)*

Without adjustment	Land	Building	Total
Proceeds per contract	$ 895,000	$ 385,000	$ 1,280,000
ACB, UCC	345,000	438,700	
Capital gain, terminal loss	550,000	(53,700)	

With subsection 13(21.1) adjustment	Land	Building	Total
Adjusted proceeds	$ 841,300	$ 438,700	$ 1,280,000
ACB, UCC	345,000	438,700	
Capital gain, terminal loss or recapture	$ 496,300	Nil	

There are no tax implications on the disposition of the building. Even though the deemed proceeds are less than the capital cost of the building, a capital loss can never arise on the disposition of depreciable property.

Exercise 4

Property received as an inheritance has an ACB equal to the FMV when acquired. In this case, the ACB is $60,000.

ITA: 40(1)(*a*), 69(1)(*c*)

Mary Jane has correctly calculated her capital gain. However, she only received $50,000 of the proceeds in 2018 and the balance is not due until 2020. Therefore, she can consider claiming a reserve under subparagraph 40(1)(*a*)(iii), calculated as the lessor of the following two amounts:

i) $\dfrac{\text{Amount not due}}{\text{Proceeds}} \times \text{capital gain} = \dfrac{\$150,000}{\$200,000} \times \$140,000 = \$105,000$

OR

ii) $\frac{4}{5}$ of the gain = $\frac{4}{5} \times \$140,000 = \$112,000$

The minimum capital gain that must be reported is $140,000 – $105,000 = $35,000

Mary Jane can claim a reserve of $105,000. This reserve will then be included in income in 2019 and a reserve calculated based on proceeds not yet due. Mary Jane must file Form T2017 with her 2018 income tax return.

Exercise 5

Cl. 3: 5%

Jan. 1, 2017	UCC	$ 221,000
	Disposal[1]	
	lesser of:	
	(a) capital cost $300,000	
	(b) proceeds $295,000	(295,000)
Dec. 31, 2017	UCC	$ (74,000)
	Recapture	74,000
Jan. 1, 2018	UCC	Nil
Aug. 2018	File an amended return for 2017 as follows:	ITA: 13(4)
Jan. 1, 2017	UCC	$ 221,000
	Deemed proceeds	ITA: 13(4)(*c*)
	lesser of:	
	(a) capital cost $300,000	
	(b) proceeds ...... $295,000 → $295,000	
	reduced by lesser of:	
	(a) recapture	
	($295K – $221K) $ 74,000 → $ 74,000	
	(b) replacement cost $400,000	$(221,000)
Dec. 31, 2017	UCC	Nil

	Recapture	Nil	
Jan. 1, 2018	UCC	Nil	

Cl. 1-NRB: 6%[2]

2018	Purchase of new building	$400,000	
	Less: reduction above	74,000	$ 326,000	ITA: 13(4)(c)
Dec. 31, 2018	UCC		$ 326,000
	CCA @ 6% of [$326,000 – (½ × $326,000)]		(9,780)
Jan. 1, 2019	UCC		$ 316,220

— *NOTES TO SOLUTION*

[1] The CRA appears to require that even if a replacement property is purchased before the tax return for the year of disposition must be filed (i.e., within six months of the taxation year end), the recapture must be reported in the year of disposition. The taxpayer can request a reassessment if and when the replacement is purchased within the specified time limits. In lieu of paying tax initially on the recapture, the CRA will take acceptable security until the final determination of tax is made.

IT-259R3, par. 3

[2] Note how the rules allow for a replacement with an asset of another class.

ITA: 13(4)

Exercise 6

Manru Realty Limited v. M.N.R., 72 DTC 6415

— Intention: must be established by reference to facts classified by behavioural factors below

(a) primary: to erect buildings on the property for rental purposes, thereby using the land as a capital asset

(b) secondary: to purchase and sell land at a profit

— if the area developed, the land would be built on; if not developed, then it would have been sold, providing a suitable profit opportunity presented itself.

— Behavioural factors used to classify facts on intention

(a) Relationship to the taxpayer's business

— the appellant's two principal shareholders had a history of extensive dealing in real estate

(b) Nature of the activity surrounding the transaction

— the sale of the land did not result from an unsolicited offer, reflecting an intention to trade

— the land was listed for sale by a real estate corporation

— but there was no evidence that the appellant took any concrete steps to develop or build on the land at any time

(c) Nature of the asset

— circulating or working capital since it was handled like inventory

— the land was bought as raw land and it was sold as such

— no income was generated by the use of the land as a productive asset

(d) Number and frequency of transaction

— to the date of the case this company had sold 12 properties

(e) Corporate objects

— included the power to buy, sell, subdivide and dispose of properties thereby encompassing the transaction at hand.

— Conclusion

— the evidence would suggest a trading intention on the part of the appellant at the time the property in question was purchased.

Exercise 7

(A) Division B Income Arising from Sale of Business Assets

Accounts receivable — opening reserve [par. 12(1)(d)]	$ 2,000
— capital loss (($8,000 – $14,000) × ½)	(3,000)
Inventory [sec. 23] ($17,000 – $20,000)	(3,000)
Land (($75,000 – $20,000) × ½)	27,500
Building — taxable capital gain (($200,000 – $60,000) × ½)	70,000
— recapture ($47,000 – $60,000)	13,000
Equipment — Class 8 recapture ($8,850 – $10,000)	1,150
Goodwill (50% × $50,000)	25,000
	$132,650

(B) Division B Income Arising from Sale of Business Assets

Accounts receivable — opening reserve [par. 12(1)(d)]	$ 2,000
— business loss ($8,000 – $14,000) [sec. 22]	(6,000)
Inventory [sec. 23] ($17,000 – $20,000)	(3,000)
Land[(1)]	Nil
Building — taxable capital gain[(2)] (½ × $50,000)	25,000
— recapture[(3)]	Nil
Equipment — Class 8 recapture ($8,850 – $10,000)	1,150
Goodwill — taxable capital gain (50% × $50,000)	25,000
	$ 44,150

(C) The ssec. 44(1) election combined with the ssec. 44(6) election permits a deferral of capital gain in respect of the land and the building. However, with the building, the potential future capital cost allowance claim is accordingly reduced by the $75,000 capital gain deferral and the $13,000 recapture deferral.

The sec. 22 election has advantages to both Mr. Sole Proprietor and the purchaser. First, the otherwise allowable capital loss of $3,000 is converted to a full $6,000 business loss for Mr. Proprietor. Without the sec. 22 election, the purchaser is denied a reserve or future bad debt write-offs under ssec. 20(1) since he has not included in income an amount in respect of these receivables. Section 22 permits these deductions if the $6,000 loss is included in the purchaser's income.

CHAPTER 8

— NOTES TO SOLUTION

			No ssec. 44(6)	*Ssec. 44(6)*
(1) Land — lesser of	(a)	P. of D. — actual	$ 75,000	$ 75,000
		Plus ssec. 44(6) election	Nil	15,000
		Deemed P. of D.	$ 75,000	$ 90,000
		ACB	(20,000)	(20,000)
		C.G.	$ 55,000	$ 70,000
	(b)	Deemed P. of D.	$ 75,000	$ 90,000
		Replacement cost	(90,000)	(90,000)
		Excess, if any	Nil	Nil
		Reported gain	Nil	Nil
		Deferred gain	$ 55,000	$ 70,000
		ACB of replacement	$ 35,000	$ 20,000
(2) Building — lesser of	(a)	P. of D. — actual	$200,000	$200,000
		Less ssec. 44(6) election	Nil	(15,000)
		Deemed P. of D.	$200,000	$185,000
		ACB	(60,000)	(60,000)
		C.G. [cls.44(1)(e)(i)(B)]	$140,000	$125,000
	(b)	P. of D. — deemed	$200,000	$185,000
		Replacement cost	(135,000)	(135,000)
		Excess, if any [cls. 44(1)(e)(i)(B)]	$ 65,000	$ 50,000
		Reported gain	$ 65,000	$ 50,000
		Deferred gain	$ 75,000	$ 75,000
		ACB of replacement	$ 60,000	$ 60,000

		Building Cl. 3: 5%
(3) UCC prior to disposal		$ 47,000
Less par. 13(4)(c) deemed disposal — lesser of:		
(a) cost — $60,000	$ 60,000	
(b) P. of D. — $200,000*		
Less — the lesser of		
(a) Recapture ($60,000 credit to class — $47,000 UCC)	13,000	
(b) Replacement — $135,000		47,000
UCC December 31, 2018		Nil

Reported recapture		Nil
Deferred recapture		$ 13,000

		*Building Cl. 1: 6%***
Replacement cost	$135,000	
Less: par. 44(1)(*f*) ($125,000 – $50,000) with ssec. 44(6) (deferred gain)	(75,000)	
par. 13(4)(*c*) reduction (deferred recapture)	(13,000)	$ 47,000
Less: ½ of net amount		(23,500)
UCC, December 31, 2019		$ 23,500
CCA (i.e., 6% of $23,500)		(1,410)
½ of net amount		23,500
UCC, January 1, 2020		$ 45,590

* Note that the deemed proceeds arising from ssec. 44(6) are not applicable for the purposes of section 13.

** The new building can be put into Class 1 and is eligible for the 6% CCA rate available to non-residential buildings in this class.

Exercise 8

— The courts have attempted to assess the intention of the taxpayer at the time of the purchase in this type of case:

(a) primary: did the taxpayer enter the transaction to make a business profit?

(b) secondary: did the taxpayer know at the time of the purchase that there was a profitable "escape hatch" if the primary intention to hold the property as a capital asset did not work out?

— Since intention is a state of mind, the courts must be presented with evidence of intention from the taxpayer's whole course of conduct, i.e., actual behaviour, before, during, and after the particular transaction in question (See IT-218R):

(a) relationship of the transaction to the taxpayer's business

— if a taxpayer's regular business is associated with land (i.e., a builder or a real estate agent), it will be considered a business transaction (in the absence of evidence to the contrary)

— Hi-Tech is not in the real estate business

— they have no known expertise in real estate

— however, they entered a joint venture with a developer

(b) organization or activity associated with trade

— if a sale of property is the result of an active campaign to sell it rather than the result of something unanticipated at the time of purchase, (e.g., expropriation, sudden need of money, frustration of original intention), the profits will be considered business income from an adventure in the nature of trade:

— unsolicited offer by developer

— sold because financial position deteriorated

CHAPTER 8

       — however, in the joint venture with the developer, an organized effort was put into the sale of the excess land

(c)   nature of the asset

     — the nature of some assets is such that they can only be considered as either inventory or fixed assets

     — land can fall into either category, but when an organized effort is made to put a property into a more marketable condition (e.g., laying sewers, building roads, preparing a plan of subdivision), it indicates inventory for a business of selling properties.

       — Hi-Tech was forced to buy the new property, including the excess land, as a result of the fire

       — another suitable property could not be located

       — the vendor would not sell the building without also selling all 10 acres of land

       — Hi-Tech planned to construct an office building on the land, i.e., fixed asset

         — however, no evidence of plans for the building was offered

(d)   number and frequency of transactions

     — a history of extensive buying and selling of similar properties or of quick turnover of properties may be taken as evidence indicating that a taxpayer is carrying on a business of dealing in real estate

       — Hi-Tech had no prior land transactions

(e)   corporate objects or articles

     — if the transaction belonged to a class of profit-making operations contemplated by the objects, then in the absence of any evidence to the contrary, the profit would be one arising from the business of the taxpayer

       — not definitive and no evidence in this case

— Recommendation

     — recommend that they file their 2018 return on the basis that the gain is a capital gain

     — company should be warned of the possibility of reassessment

Chapter 9

Other Sources of Income and Deductions in Computing Income

Learning Goals

Know, Understand and Explain

By the end of this chapter you will know, understand and be able to explain:

- The basic provisions of the *Income Tax Act* that relate to income and other deductions.
- How pension income is taxed.
- How to calculate the taxable portion of an annuity.
- How contributions and withdrawals from RESP and RDSP programs affect the calculation of net income for tax purposes.
- The benefits of contributing to an RESP or RDSP.
- The difference in tax treatment for spousal support and child support.
- The difference between an RRSP contribution and a contribution to spousal RRSP and when it may benefit a taxpayer.
- The taxation of contributions and withdrawals into Registered Savings Plans.
- The different tax treatments for contributions and withdrawals for TFSAs, RRSPs and RESPs.
- The tax impacts of transitioning RSPs into retirement income.
- When moving expenses are deductible and when they are not.

Apply

By the end of this chapter you will be able to apply your knowledge and understanding to:

- Calculate deductible moving expenses.
- Calculate deductible child care expenses.
- Calculate disability support deductions.
- Split pension and CPP income to minimize tax payable.
- Calculate the RRSP contribution limit for a taxpayer.

Review Questions
¶9,800 in the Study Guide

Multiple Choice Questions
¶9,825 in the Study Guide

Exercises
¶9,850 in the Study Guide

Assignment Problems
¶9,875 in the Study Guide

CHAPTER 9 — LEARNING CHART

Problem Descriptions

Textbook Example Problems

9-1	Moving expenses
9-2	Child care expenses
9-3	Disability support deduction
9-4	RRSP contribution
9-5	Spousal RRSP withdrawal
9-6	Home Buyers' Plan
9-7	Retiring allowance

Multiple Choice Questions

1	Retiring allowance
2	RRSP contribution
3	Child care deduction
4	Moving expenses
5	Earned income
6	Moving expenses

Exercises

1	Definition of "earned income"
2	RRSP deduction
3	Investing in or outside of an RRSP
4	Spousal RRSP withdrawals
5	Transfers between deferred plans
6	Moving expenses
7	RRSP deduction
8	Childcare deduction
9	Personal expenses
10	Earned Income
11	Earned Income \ Attribution
12	RRSP deduction
13	Transfers between spouses

Assignment Problems

1	Moving expenses
2	Child care expenses
3	Spousal support payments
4	Transfer of RRSP on divorce
5	RRSP
6	RRSP vs. TFSA
7	RRSP
8	Moving expenses
9	Child care expenses
10	Comprehensive
11	Calculate income, provide advice
12	Comprehensive
13	Comprehensive
14	Becoming a resident
15	Comprehensive
16	Reassessment
17	Retirement package

CHAPTER 9

Study Notes

¶9,800   REVIEW QUESTIONS

(1) Ms. Tang had been working for the same employer for the past 10 years and was tired of her job. She decided to quit and travel to Australia for a year. On leaving, her employer paid her a lump-sum amount of $15,000, since Ms. Tang had been a good employee of theirs and they were hoping she might come back to work for them when she returned to Canada. Ms. Tang had no intention of working for them again but was grateful for the payment. Comment on how this payment should be taxed.

(2) Mr. Everett has worked for the provincial government for the past 35 years and was now eligible for early retirement. As part of his retirement package he is entitled to a lump-sum payment for unused sick days in the amount of $20,000 and unused vacation days of $25,000. On retirement, he is going to receive a cheque for $45,000 as payment for the above amounts. How will this amount be taxed?

(3) Charles and Dee Bowan have decided to end their 12-year marriage. As part of their written separation agreement, they agree that Charles will pay Dee $3,000 per month for her personal support and maintenance, including $1,200 per month for the mortgage on the house that Dee will be living in. The original principal amount of the mortgage is $120,000. What limitations, if any, will Charles encounter when deciding the deductibility of the payments related to the mortgage?

(4) Mark and Ann have agreed to a separation agreement that requires Ann to pay $2,000 per month to Mark as an allowance for his maintenance. Initially, this payment will consist of $1,500 paid to Mark directly and $500 paid to the financial institution that holds the mortgage on his condominium. Mark may change this arrangement at any time to have the full $2,000 paid to him directly. Comment on the deductibility of these payments.

(5) Sam Sider reached an agreement with his employer to pay for his education and living expenses while he returned to university. The agreement was that, if he returned to work for his employer when he graduated, there would be no repayment of the amounts he received. If he did not return to work for his employer, the payments he received would have to be repaid in full. How would this be treated for tax purposes?

(6) Mrs. Smith, a 75-year-old widow, has applied for and received the Guaranteed Income Supplement. This payment is based on the fact that her income is below a certain threshold amount. She has asked you to tell her how this is treated for tax purposes.

(7) Mr. Singh, a consultant, did some work for ACME Corporation with the agreed-upon fee being $15,000. When the time came for the billing to be done, Mr. Singh sent an invoice to ACME with instructions that the cheque be made payable to his wife. What would your comments be to Mr. Singh and his wife on this arrangement?

(8) How do you determine how much of the employer's contributions to a defined benefit pension plan are deductible?

(9) Joe is confused. He is trying to understand the pension rules and he cannot understand why the limit on a money purchase pension plan is based on 18% of this year's income while the limit for an RRSP is based on last year's income. Explain this difference to him.

(10) Jennifer wanted to withdraw $20,000 from her RRSP in January in order to buy a new car. She had spent a long time accumulating this amount, but felt that it was more important to buy a car now than accumulate for retirement later. How can she minimize the tax that is withheld on the $20,000 taken out of the plan?

(11) Mr. McDonald, a widower, has died and now his executor has come in to administer the will. His only assets on his death were an RRSP worth $150,000 and his house and other personal assets worth $150,000. Both of his children were grown up so he thought that his was a simple estate. He left the RRSPs to his daughter, Kim, and the residue to his son, Jim. Is there likely to be any conflict between the beneficiaries?

(12) Joan had worked for the same employer for 15 years. Two years ago she was fired. She took legal action against her former employer on the basis that it was wrongful dismissal. This year she won her case and was awarded $40,000. She then paid her legal fees of $8,000 and contributed $32,000 to her RRSP as a retiring allowance. She is glad the case has been settled since she has not worked since her dismissal. What would you show on her personal tax return for the year based on this information?

ITA: 60(*j*.1)

¶9,825   MULTIPLE CHOICE QUESTIONS

Question 1

Max retired in 2018 and received a $100,000 retiring allowance. Max worked for his employer for the past 18 years. He never belonged to a registered pension plan or a deferred profit sharing plan during any of those years. What is the maximum amount of retiring allowance that Max can shelter from tax by transferring it to his RRSP?

(A) Nil

(B) $27,000

(C) $63,000

(D) $100,000

Question 2

Ms. Assad wants to know the maximum RRSP contribution she can make in 2018 or in the first 60 days of 2019 that will be fully deductible on her 2018 tax return. The following information was taken from Ms. Assad's 2017 tax return:

Income from employment	$44,000
RPP contributions deducted in arriving at employment income	1,000
Moving expenses	300
Taxable spousal support received	3,600
Pension income	6,000
Real estate rental income	1,400

The pension adjustment reported by Ms. Assad's employer for 2017 was $4,000. Ms. Assad also has a $1,000 unused RRSP deduction limit room which has carried forward from 2017.

What is the maximum RRSP contribution that Ms. Assad can make in 2018 or in the first 60 days of 2019 and deduct fully on her 2018 tax return?

(A) $4,920

(B) $5,000

(C) $6,000

(D) $17,000

Question 3

Meg and James Rashev were both employed full-time during the year. The Rashevs have four children: Joanne (age 17), Susie (age 14), and Sarah and Kelly (4-year-old twins). The Rashevs employed a nanny to look after their children and paid her $15,000 for the year. In addition, during July, Susie went to overnight camp for two weeks at a cost of $250 per week. The Rashevs' family income is summarized below:

	Meg	James
Salary & taxable benefits	$ 46,000	
Employment expenses [sec. 8]	(2,800)	
Business income:		
Revenues		$ 50,000
Expenses deductible for tax purposes		(32,000)
Interest income	800	1,500

Which one of the following represents the maximum child care deduction that can be claimed by the Rashevs in the year?

(A) James can claim a deduction of $12,000.

(B) Meg can claim a deduction of $15,250.

(C) James can claim a deduction of $21,000.

(D) James can claim a deduction of $15,500.

Question 4

Ms. Chiu moved from Toronto to Vancouver to start a new job. She earned $40,000 from her Toronto job and $50,000 from her Vancouver job in the year of the move. Ms. Chiu incurred the following costs of moving all of which can be substantiated by receipts:

Moving van to transport household effects	$ 5,000
Travelling costs — self, spouse and two children	3,000
Legal fees — Vancouver house	900
Legal fees — Toronto house	1,100
Loss on sale of Toronto house	25,000
Costs while waiting for Vancouver house — Hotel (20 days × $100)	2,000
Meals (20 days × $45)	900
House hunting trip (prior to Vancouver move)	800

Travelling costs consist of three meals a day for four persons over five full days, gas and other car costs, and hotel for five nights at $100 per night. The distance moved between Toronto and Vancouver was 4,430 kilometres.

Which one of the following amounts represents the maximum amount that Ms. Chiu can deduct as moving expenses on her personal income tax return for the year of the move?

(A) $12,560

(B) $15,539

(C) $16,880

(D) $17,059

Question 5

Sahar's income for tax purposes for 2017 and 2018 is as follows:

	2020	2020
Salary	$100,000	$110,000
Taxable benefits under sections 6 and 7	8,000	8,000
Travel expenses under section 8	(3,000)	(2,000)
Registered pension plan contributions under s. 8	(4,200)	(4,200)
Business losses	(1,000)	(1,200)
Rental income (net of expenses and CCA)	3,200	3,600
Spousal support paid	(12,600)	(12,000)
Net income under Division B	$ 90,400	$102,200

Which of the following statements is correct?

(A) The earned income that should be used to calculate her child care expense deduction for 2018 is $110,000.

(B) The earned income that should be used to calculate her RRSP deduction for 2018 is $106,400.

(C) The earned income that should be used to calculate her child care expense deduction for 2018 is $102,200.

(D) The earned income that should be used to calculate her RRSP deduction for 2018 is $94,600.

Question 6

Natalie Doak moved 1,000 kilometres from Winnipeg, on March 1, 2018, to a new job and earned $40,000 in her new work location. Her employer reimbursed the costs of selling her old residence and purchasing her new residence. She did not receive any allowance or reimbursement in respect of the following expenses, all of which she paid in 2018:

Moving van	$ 2,600
Travelling costs to move Natalie and family (four persons in all)	900
Cost of cleaning house in new work location	100
Cost of painting and installing new carpets and windows	10,000
Cost of maintaining vacant former residence for three months until it was sold (mortgage interest and property taxes of $3,000 per month)	9,000
Cost of changing address on legal documents	100
House hunting trips for new residence	3,000
	$25,700

Travelling costs consist of three meals a day for four persons over three full days, gas and other car costs, and hotel for two nights at $100 per night.

What is the maximum amount Natalie can claim for moving expenses in 2018?

(A) $25,700

(B) $16,007

(C) $12,600

(D) $8,982

¶9,850   EXERCISES

Exercise 1

ITA: 63(3), 146(1)

Subsection 248(1) is one of the key definition sections found in the *Income Tax Act*. Definitions are also found elsewhere in the Act.

— *REQUIRED*

Find the section in the Act that contains the definition for "earned income" used in the calculation of the RRSP contribution limits.

Exercise 2

ITA: 60(*i*), 146(1), 146(5)

Don Bickle contributed $5,000 to a spousal RRSP on February 15, 2019. Don's income for tax purposes for 2017 is as follows:

Salary	$70,000
Taxable benefits	1,200
	$71,200
Less: Registered pension plan contributions — defined contribution	(2,800)
Employment income — Subdivision a	$68,400
Rental loss	(5,000)
Dividend income from taxable Canadian corporations grossed up	800
Interest income — Canada Savings Bonds	400
Division B income	$64,600

Don's employer reported a PA of $6,084 in respect of 2017.

— *REQUIRED*

Determine the maximum amount Don can deduct on his 2018 tax return in respect of his 2019 contribution to his spouse's RRSP and the amount, if any, that he can contribute and deduct in respect of his own RRSP.

Exercise 3

ITA: Division B

A taxable investment of $15,000 in bonds yields 4% per year before tax. The same investment can be acquired in a self-directed RRSP (tax sheltered). Assume that the yield is reinvested each year at the same 4% before tax. Further assume that the investment is held for 10 years, at which time the RRSP will be cashed in and taxes paid at 46%.

— *REQUIRED*

Which investment approach provides the best cash return?

Exercise 4

ITA: 146(1)

Douglas has been contributing $3,000 annually to a spousal RRSP for his wife, Donna, in each of the last six years, but not this year. The RRSP has grown to $30,000 and Donna has withdrawn $10,000 of the RRSP this year. The withholding tax was $2,000.

— *REQUIRED*

Describe the full income tax aspects and consequences of this RRSP withdrawal.

Exercise 5

ITA: 60(*i*), 60(*j*.1)

Ivan Reimer received the following amounts for 2018, the year of his retirement:

Employment income (see (1), below)	$ 7,000
Pension income:	
Lump-sum RPP payment from a defined benefit plan	100,000
Superannuation payments (eight monthly pension payments of $3,000)	24,000
Old Age Security pension	6,850
Canada Pension Plan	12,460
Retiring allowance	50,000
Interest income	8,000
	$208,310

Additional Information

(1) Ivan resigned his position on April 1, 2018. The employment income for tax purposes above includes a $300 contribution to his employer's RPP.

(2) On April 1, 2018, Ivan had his employer transfer directly the lump-sum payment from the RPP to his RRSP. In addition, Ivan's employer transferred $20,000 of his retiring allowance directly to his RRSP.

(3) Ivan has been employed by the same employer for 15 years.

(4) Ivan was 65 on October 31, 2017.

(5) Ivan's employer reported a PA for him of $700 in respect of 2017. Ivan's earned income for 2017 was $120,000.

— REQUIRED

Determine the tax consequences of the above transactions for 2018, supported by your computations.

Exercise 6

ITA: 62

Edwin Edwards was transferred from Vancouver to Montreal by his employer on October 1, 2018. The following expenses were incurred by Edwin:

Airfare for family	$ 1,300
Moving cost of furniture	1,000
Cost of disposing of Vancouver home	
— legal fees	500
— real estate commission	10,000
Cost of purchasing Montreal home	
— prepaid realty taxes	500
— legal fees	1,000
— Quebec transfer tax	300

Edwin's employment income for tax purposes earned in Montreal during 2018 was $7,000. Edwin's employer reimbursed Edwin for $5,000 of the moving expenses.

— REQUIRED

Calculate the amount that Edwin can deduct as moving expenses.

ITA: 62

Exercise 7

On July 1, 2017, Mr. Big Shot took early retirement because of job dissatisfaction. During the rest of 2017 and most of 2018, he was unemployed. However, on November 1, 2018 he obtained an employment position. His income for tax purposes for 2016 to 2018 was as follows:

	2016	*2017*	*2018*
Employment income	$ 65,000	$ 35,000	$ 12,500
Pension income	Nil	$ 22,500	$ 22,500
Dividends from taxable Canadian public corporations	$ 15,000	$ 13,500	$ 10,000
Interest income	$ 10,000	$ 6,250	$ 7,500
Rental loss	$ (2,500)	$ (3,750)	$ (6,000)

Mr. Big Shots pension adjustment for 2016 and 2017 was Nil.

On February 15, 2018 he contributed $18,000 to a spousal registered retirement savings plan (RRSP) of which he claimed $15,500 for 2017 and plans to claim $2,500 for 2018.

In November and December 2018, Mr. Big Shot contributed $600 to his new employer's defined-benefit, registered pension plan to which his employer also contributed, and $446 to the Canada Pension Plan.

On November 1, 2018, Mr. Big Shot received a reassessment notice in respect of his 2017 RRSP deduction reducing the amount claimed from $15,500 to $11,250.

— *REQUIRED*

(a) Determine whether the $11,250 reassessment amount is correct.

(b) Determine the deductible RRSP amount for 2018.

Exercise 8

Ms. Antibellum, a single parent, supports her three children, ages 3, 6, and 11, who live with her. Ms. Antibellum paid the following amounts in respect of care of the children during 2018:

Babysitting services — local independent person during her working days	$8,000
Babysitting during certain evenings and weekends	$1,200
Camp fees for 3 weeks for children ages 6 and 11	$2,700

Ms. Antibellum provides you with her sources of income for tax purposes:

Employment income	
Gross salary	$ 26,000
Stock option	$ 4,000
Low-interest loan benefit	$ 2,500
	$ 32,500
Registered pension plan contribution	$ (3,200)
	$ 29,300
Share of partnership income from a retail store	$ 7,000
Rental of a basement apartment	$ 9,000
Support payments received in respect of the children	$ 18,000
Interest income	$ 5,000
	$ 68,300

— *REQUIRED*

(i) Determine the maximum child care deduction for Ms. Antibellum for 2018. Show all parts of the calculation.

(ii) Explain why you excluded any of the above amounts in your calculation for (i), above.

Exercise 9

Spencer Stable owns 50% of the outstanding shares of Stable Estates Limited. His sister, Tracy, owns the other 50%. During the winter months, the company's construction activities are rather slow so Spencer uses this time to design new homes for the spring. At the beginning of January, to keep the company's largest subcontractor busy over the long winter months, he asked the subcontractor to build an addition to his ski chalet so that he can use it to entertain guests. The controller of Stable Estates Limited has expensed the $40,000 invoice from the subcontractor. Spencer had told the controller to treat the invoice as a business expense.

— *REQUIRED*

If the CRA were to discover this transaction during its audit, how would it reassess? Assume that HST @ a rate of 13% applies for 2017 in the province in which Spencer resides.

Exercise 10

Mrs. Worker, a computer consultant, did some work for Macrohard Inc. The agreed fee for her work was $12,000. Her husband is out of work; therefore, she invoiced Macrohard Inc. and asked that it make the cheque payable to her husband. Mrs. Worker plans to have the $12,000 reported on her husband's tax return.

— *REQUIRED*

Discuss how the CRA would treat this $12,000 item.

Exercise 11

Bob Carling is 75 years old. He has substantial assets and is trying to divest himself of some of them to reduce any taxes payable on his death. It is January 2018 and he was planning to do the following:

(1) Give his granddaughter, Janet, his 1,000 shares of Canadian Business Machines Ltd. These shares cost him $5,000 in 2000 and are now worth $45,000. Every December 15, the company pays a dividend of $1 per share. Janet is 17. Next year, she will be 18 and plans to sell about 100 shares to fund her university education.

(2) Sell 10,000 shares of Lower Down Group to his wife. Bob purchased these shares in 1998 for $1,000. They are now worth $52,000. His wife will give him $52,000 in cash. The corporation pays dividends of $2 per share each June 30.

(3) Transfer $50,000 cash to his 40-year-old daughter, Dianne. He is unsure whether he should give the money to her or lend it interest-free. She is a frugal woman and will put the money into a one-year investment that earns 7% interest.

— *REQUIRED*

For each of the above transactions, outline the tax implications to both Bob Carling and the recipient of the asset.

Exercise 12

George Cosmo has unused RRSP contribution room of $35,000 available for his 2018 taxation year. He decides that, during 2018, he will contribute $35,000 to his RRSP in the following manner:

He will transfer the following shares to his RRSP:

	FMV	ACB
ABC Public Company	$ 25,000	$ 10,000
XYZ Public Corporation	$ 10,000	$ 25,000
	$ 35,000	

— *REQUIRED*

What are the tax consequences to George resulting from the above action?

Exercise 13

Mr. Transfer would like guidance with his dilemma. He owns a house in Toronto, which is in his name. He purchased the house in 2005 for $70,000. The house is now worth $300,000. His wife owns a cottage on Lake Eugenia, which is in her name. She purchased the cottage in 2007 for $40,000. The cottage is now worth $150,000. Prior to 2005, neither Mr. nor Mrs. Transfer owned any properties. Mr. Transfer is being transferred to Vancouver, B.C. Therefore, he and his wife have decided to sell both the home and the cottage in December 2018.

— *REQUIRED*

In general terms, explain the rules to Mr. and Mrs. Transfer with respect to the tax implications arising from the disposal of the properties.

¶9,850

¶9,875 ASSIGNMENT PROBLEMS

Type 1 Problems

Problem 1

ITA: 62(3)

Diane Weber is employed as Personnel Director of B. Ltd., an international corporation. Diane was living in Vancouver at the beginning of last year, but B. Ltd. moved her to Hamilton effective December 1. Diane rented a three-bedroom townhouse in Vancouver but purchased a two-bedroom house in Hamilton on December 20. Diane has supplied you with the following information concerning her moving costs:

Air transportation for Diane	$3,000
Moving costs	3,100
Temporary living expenses (hotel and meals) in Hamilton for 20 days	2,500
Storage	1,250
Lease cancellation fee paid to Vancouver landlord	1,200
Legal fees to purchase new home	3,600
Property taxes paid from December 21–31	400
Moving allowance paid by B. Ltd.	4,000
Diane's net employment income in Hamilton December 1–31	5,600

What is the deductible amount of moving expenses that Diane can claim in her personal income tax return for the year of the move?

Problem 2

ITA: 63

Charles Hughes was a university student in full-time attendance for 30 weeks and worked as a salesman for the balance of the year. His wife, Cathy, was also employed. The Hughes have four children: Sharon 17, Shawn 14, Sally 6 and Stephen 4. Child care expenses for the year amounted to $200 per week for 52 weeks. Charles' and Cathy's receipts and withholdings are summarized below:

	Charles	*Cathy*
Gross salary	$23,000	$47,000
Taxable fringe benefits	850	4,000
Interest income	200	—
Scholarship	3,600	—
Student loan	2,500	—

Deductions from Charles' and Cathy's employment income were:

	Charles	*Cathy*
Income taxes withheld	$ 3,800	$13,700
RPP contributions	2,000	3,700

Calculate the child care expenses deduction allowed to Charles and Cathy for 2018.

Problem 3

ITA: 56(1)(*b*), 56.1, 60(*b*), 60.1

Uriah and Ursalla Underhill decided to terminate their marriage of 10 years. On June 1 Uriah moved out. From the period of June 1 to October 31, Uriah paid Ursalla $900 per month, made up of $200 for the support of herself and $700 for their two children. On November 1, Uriah and Ursalla signed a written separation agreement which confirmed the $900 a month payment. In addition the agreement provided that Uriah would pay the monthly mortgage payment of $400 on the home which is in Ursalla's name and all medical expenses for the children. During November and December Uriah made the appropriate payments as per the written agreement and paid $100 of dental bills in respect of the children.

Discuss the tax implications of the above facts for both Uriah and Ursalla.

Problem 4

Liz and Richard have ended their marriage and are now living apart. They have sold their house and divided the proceeds, but they now need to deal with Richard's RRSP. They have agreed that Richard needs to transfer $100,000 from his RRSP to Liz as part of the equalization payment.

They would like you to explain the tax consequences of this transfer.

Problem 5

ITA: 146(5)

Diana Capriati, a Canadian resident for income tax purposes, has the following income for 2016 and 2017:

	2016	2017
Income from employment		
Gross salary	$130,000	$135,000
Less contribution to employer's RPP	(1,500)	(3,000)
	128,500	132,000
Income from property		
Taxable dividends from Canadian public corporations	32,000	20,000
Gross-up (38%)	12,160	7,600
	44,160	27,600
Bank interest received	3,000	5,000
	47,160	32,600
Rental income — gross	25,000	30,000
Deductible rental expenses	(18,000)	(12,000)
	54,160	50,600
Other income		
Alimony payments received	10,000	10,000
Loss from business		
Share of loss from partnership	(30,000)	(20,000)
	$162,660	$172,600

Diana has asked you to determine the maximum RRSP contribution that she can deduct in 2018. Assume that Diana put $10,000 into her self-administered RRSP on February 12, 2019. Further, assume that Diana was an active member of the partnership and that her pension adjustment for 2016 and 2017 was $4,000 and $7,000, respectively. She did not make an RRSP contribution for 2017.

Problem 6

ITA: 146(1), 146.2

The following table provides information relating to three individuals who each plan to invest $4,500 per year, before tax, starting in 2018. Each individual's before-tax rate of return on a 10-year investment is 8%. Note that each has a different marginal tax rate today (Year 0). However, in 10 years, all are expected to have a marginal tax rate of 40%.

	Taxpayer		
	A	**B**	**C**
Earned income	$65,000	$45,000	$25,000
Marginal tax rate (Year 0)	45%	40%	27%
Marginal tax rate (Year 10) . . .	40%	40%	40%
Before-tax rate of return	8%	8%	8%

You have been asked to do the following:

(A) Compute the future value of the investment for each taxpayer assuming:

    (i) The individual does not contribute to an RRSP but invests the after-tax proceeds of the $4,500 earned income in a tax-free savings account (TFSA).

    (ii) The individual contributes to a self-directed RRSP and withdraws the amount in Year 10.

(B) Should each individual contribute to an RRSP or to a TFSA?

Problem 7

ITA: 60(*i*), 60(*j*.1), 146(5), 146(5.1), 146(8.2), 146(8.3), 147.3(4), 147.3(9)

Mr. Rui retired from his job with Wise and Foresighted Consulting Ltd. on February 28, 2018. Mr. Rui expects his 2018 income for tax purposes to be as follows:

Employment income	$ 7,000
Pension income:	
Monthly superannuation (10 months of $3,450)	34,500
Old Age Security	6,942
Canadian Pension Plan	12,100
Farming income	20,000
Income from rental of apartment	10,800
Royalty income from books written by Mr. Rui	14,200
Interest income	12,000
Total income	$117,542

Additional Information

(1) Mr. Rui's 2018 employment income is net of an RPP contribution of $300. His PA for 2018 is expected to be $600. *[handwritten: Pension Adjustment]*

(2) Mr. Rui will be 71 in February 2019. His wife is now 67.

(3) In 2018, Mrs. Rui withdrew $6,000 from her RRSP. Mr. Rui had made the following contributions to Mrs. Rui's RRSP: January 2018 — $2,000; April 2017 — $1,000; February 2016 — $1,000; December 2015 — $3,000. Mr. Rui did not deduct the January 2018 contribution in 2017.

(4) Mr. Rui's employer reported a PA for him of $7,000 in 2017. His earned income in 2017 was $66,000.

(5) Mr. Rui has unused RRSP deduction room from prior years of $5,000.

Mr. Rui has asked you to do the following:

(A) Determine the tax implications of Mrs. Rui's $6,000 RRSP withdrawal.

(B) Determine his maximum tax deductible RRSP contribution for 2018. What additional RRSP contribution should he make for 2018?

(C) What should he contribute to his RRSP for 2019?

(D) What additional planning steps would you advise him to take in connection with his RRSP in 2019?

Problem 8

ITA: 62; IT-178R3; Income Tax Folio S1-F3-C4

Sue and George Shaker lived in Halifax, Nova Scotia, while George completed his combined law and MBA degree at Dalhousie University. The Shakers purchased a home in Halifax when they first moved to Nova Scotia. Due to contracting mononucleosis in his second year of the program, George completed his degree in December 2018 rather than in the spring of 2018.

George excelled in the program and had numerous job offers. He finally accepted a job with NorthAm Co. in Toronto. In order to convince George to accept the job, NorthAm Co. offered to pay the Shakers an amount equal to any loss that they incurred on the sale of their Halifax home and provide them with a $10,000 moving allowance.

Sue has been working for an insurance company in Halifax while George has been attending school. Sue intends to find work in Toronto, but will be unable to continue working for the same insurance company.

George accepted the job with NorthAm Co. in September 2018. During October 2018, George and Sue flew to Toronto to look for a home. They spent a week in Toronto and on the fifth day managed to find and purchase a home with the purchase contract closing on December 15, 2018. The remaining two days were spent arranging for painting and cleaning of the new home. Their expenditures on that trip were: *[handwritten: Can you deduct house hunting cost?]*

Two Air Canada tickets (return Halifax to Toronto) . . . . $ 1,200   Can not deduct
Motel room, 7 days @ $75 per day   525
Meals, 7 days @ $50 per day   350
Car rental   350

George and Sue managed to sell their Halifax home. That sale closed on December 15, 2018. The statement of account from the lawyer (dated January 15, 2019) revealed the following expenses:

Real estate commission . . . . $7,000   fully reimbursed
Legal fees, old home   2,000
Legal fees, new home   2,500
Land transfer tax, new home   1,000

                                                     # 20000

The house in Halifax was sold for $140,000. The Shakers had originally paid $160,000 for the house. NorthAm Co. provided a cheque for $27,000 in February 2019 to reimburse them for the loss and the 20000 real estate commission. (NorthAm Co. did not include the legal costs when calculating the loss eligible for reimbursement.)   5500 (2000+2500+1000)

Subsequent to finalizing the sale of their Halifax home and George's completion of his exams, Sue and George packed up their car and drove to Toronto. The trip took 7 days due to a leisurely pace and some bad weather delays, and since their home was not ready when they arrived, they stayed in a nearby motel for 11 days.   Cannot exceed 15 days

The cost of trip and stay in motel was as follows:
                                        11-hotel
                                         7-driving
Meals, 18 days @ $100 (substantiated by receipts) $1,800
Motel room, 18 days @ $80   1,440
Gasoline (2,000 kilometres driven)   250

In late December, the Shakers paid a moving bill consisting of $5,000 for the actual move and $250 for storage. George received the $10,000 allowance for moving expenses in December 2018. He commenced work for NorthAm Co. in January 2019 at a salary of $80,000 per year. Sue commenced work for Toronto Insurance Co. in September 2019 at a salary of $85,000 per year.

Sue and George have asked you to calculate their allowable moving expenses for both 2018 and 2019 and discuss the tax treatment of the loss reimbursement. Assume that all expenditures made were reasonable and can be substantiated by receipts.

Problem 9   ITA: 63

Nina Diamond and Len Dirkfeld are married and have five children: Lindsay age 18, Trevor age 15, James age 7, Ben age 5, and Rebecca age 3. During 2018, they paid a nanny $250 per week for 50 weeks to look after their children while they worked. During July, they paid $3,000 ($1,500 each) for Trevor15 and 1James to go to an overnight summer camp for four weeks. In addition, they paid their child Lindsay18 $300 to babysit the other children at various times when they worked late.

Can use above 18

Len is a physician and has his own practice. Nina worked full-time as a computer consultant during the first eight months of the year. In September, she went back to university on a full-time basis for 13 weeks. On December 11, her courses were finished and she went back to work.

Nina and Len's incomes are summarized below:

	Nina	Len
Salary	$50,000	
Taxable benefits	3,000	
Employment expenses	(800)	
Employment income	$52,200	
Business income		$120,000
Interest income	2,000	3,000
Rental income		6,000
RRSP contribution	(5,000)	(10,000)
Net income under Division B	$49,200	$119,000

Nina and Len have asked you to calculate the maximum 2018 child care deductions they can claim.

They would also like to know how your answer would change if Nina went back to university for 13 *Changes to month* weeks on a <u>part-time basis</u> rather than a full-time basis. Assume Nina took a minimum of 12 hours of courses each month, but do not redo all the calculations.

Problem 10

ITA: 56(1)(*a*), 60(*b*), 60(*i*), 60(*j*.1), 60(*o*), 60.1, 62, 63, 146(1), 146(5), 146(8.2), 147.3

In late 2017, Dr. Elaine Matthews separated from her husband. She maintained full custody of the couple's only child, a seven-year-old girl. Since May 1, 2002, Dr. Matthews had been working as a public health consultant for the Oshawa region. Around the middle of 2018 she had chosen to take advantage of a severance package from the Oshawa region. She accepted a staff position at Joseph Brant Memorial Hospital in Burlington, Ontario and moved directly from Oshawa to Burlington on September 1, 2018. She sold the former family home in Oshawa on September 15, 2018. Her husband had rented an apartment in Oshawa in late July 2018.

Dr. Matthews has some experience preparing her own tax returns but she has been particularly busy in recent months. She started her 2018 return but quickly decided she simply did not have time to finish it. She requested your assistance in completing her return.

You met with Dr. Matthews to go over her tax information related to 2018 and determined that she had correctly calculated her income under Subdivisions a, b, and c of Division B to total $158,488. Included in this correct computation were the following items:

Salary (from former employer)	$ 96,000
Salary (from Joseph Brant Memorial Hospital)	60,000
Taxable benefits under section 6 of the *Income Tax Act*	1,743
Registered pension plan contributions (defined benefit plan)	(6,750)
Consulting income (reported as business income)	8,000
Interest income from investments	540
Taxable dividends from investments	1,250
Share of rental loss from childhood home inherited from her parents	(1,495)
Net taxable capital gains	4,800
Interest paid on investment loans	(2,400)
Loss from limited partnership investment (rental property)	(3,200)
	$158,488

She provided you with the following *additional details* relating to 2018:

Miscellaneous income

    Severance from former employer .... $ 41,538

Transfer of RPP accrued from former employer

    Her former employer made a direct transfer of her accumulated RPP bene-
    fits (within prescribed limits) to her RRSP; her former employer had
    made vested contributions for the years 2001 through 2018 .... $210,000

Spousal support

    Under the terms of her separation agreement signed in September 2018,
    Dr. Matthews paid the following amounts for support of her husband:

    Support ($500 a month for September–December) .... $ 2,000
    Rent on his new Oshawa apartment ($750 a month for
      September–December) 3,000

Moving expenses from Oshawa to Burlington

    Gas for house-hunting trips (four trips made during late August 2018) ... $ 40
    Selling costs of former Oshawa home (owned 100% by her; sold
      September 15, 2018):
    Real estate commissions .... $ 12,000
    Legal fees 1,050
    Costs of purchasing new Burlington home:
    Legal fees .... $ 850
    Land transfer tax 3,250

Costs of moving herself and her household effects:

Moving van to transport belongings	$ 600
Gas to drive herself and her daughter (120 km driven)	60
Hotel (2 nights while new home was being painted and cleaned; 2 × $100)	200
Meals (same two days as above 2 × $55)	110

You have determined that the distance from her new home to Joseph Brant Hospital is 3.5 kilometres. The distance from Joseph Brant Hospital to her former home was 115 kilometres.

Care of her daughter

Part-time nanny employed January 1–August 31	$ 8,976
YMCA overnight summer camp for two weeks in July while nanny was on vacation ($200 a week)	400
Fall term (September–December) tuition fees for private school (excluding before and after school daycare)	4,000
Before and after school daycare for September–December (provided on premises of private school)	720
Fall term (September–December) transportation to private school	1,200

Registered retirement savings plan contributions

Personal contributions through employment (March–December 2018)	10,000
Personal contributions through employment (January–February 2019)	4,000

Her 2017 earned income for RRSP purposes was $120,000; her employer had reported a pension adjustment on her 2017 T4 of $9,500; she had no unused RRSP contribution room at the start of 2018 and no undeducted balance of RRSP contributions

Legal fees paid

Legal representation during separation proceedings to establish requirements to make support payments	$ 1,600
Appeal of her 2016 income tax assessment (which she won)	1,200

You have been asked to complete the calculation of her income under Division B. Show all calculations whether or not they are necessary to the final answer. Explain briefly any items not used in your calculations.

Type 2 Problems

Problem 11

ITA: 5, 6, 8, 18, 56(1)

Sibbald Kay, age 30, earned $48,000 last year as a dental hygienist for Hi Care Dental Associates. During the year, Sibbald also received director's fees of $600, and incurred the following expenses:

Uniforms purchased for employment purposes	$480
Parking expenses ($80/month)	$960
Hygienist association fees	$280

Sibbald also earned interest income of $3,200 from holding a $50,000 cash balance in T-bills and paid $1,200 in interest expense relating to a loan for an RRSP contribution. Sibbald has not repaid this loan because she believes that saving is more important. Sibbald also has 600 shares of Battery Inc. in her self-directed RRSP. During the year, she sold 400 shares at $20 for a capital gain of $6,000. She withdrew the proceeds of disposition and purchased living room furniture.

Sibbald has asked you to calculate her income for tax purposes, and provide her with tax-planning opportunities for the upcoming years.

Problem 12

ITA: Subdivision b, 248(1)

Mariah Holt, a management consultant, provided you with the following statement for the year ended December 31.

Fees received (gross)	$145,000
Salaries and benefits expense	55,500
Liability insurance expense	5,000
Office expense	1,200
Office equipment	1,000
Automobile expenses	1,000

Interest expense (loan for business use)	10,500
Professional courses	1,400
Beginning undepreciated capital cost	
Automobile (Class 10.1)	20,000
Office equipment (Class 8)	30,500

For the year, Mariah drove her automobile 30,000 kilometres, of which 15,000 kilometres were driven for business purposes. Mariah and her sister purchased a commercial rental property on December 5. The cost of the property was as follows:

(1) land $950,000,

(2) building $500,000, and

(3) furnishings $3,000.

The rental income and expenses for the 26 days were as follows:

(1) rent $24,000,

(2) operating expenses $20,000, and

(3) interest expense $6,250.

Mariah, a single parent of two children aged three and five, paid $800 per month to a babysitter to care for the two children in her home. In January, Mariah had purchased her first home for $115,000, paid $2,400 for commissions and $1,900 to move 45 kilometres closer to her consulting office. She withdrew $20,000 from her RRSP under the Home Buyers' Plan.

Mariah has asked you to:

(a) Calculate her net income for the taxation year.

(b) Identify any area of her income that may be controversial, particularly with the CRA.

Problem 13

ITA: 5, 6, 8, 12, 20, 39, 40(2), 56, 60, 75, 146

Ms. Sui is an executive of a large public retail corporation, Clothes to You Ltd., situated in Dundas, Ontario. Ms. Sui is not married. However, she has two adopted children, ages 8 and 10, who reside with her.

Ms. Sui has provided you with the following information for 2018:

Clothes To You Ltd.:

Gross salary	$150,000
Commission income	30,000
Canada Pension Plan contributions	(2,480)
Employment Insurance premiums	(931)
Registered pension plan contributions (money purchase)	(6,000)
Income taxes deducted	(55,000)

(1) Clothes To You Ltd. provides Ms. Sui with an automobile. The annual lease cost of the car, including HST, is $18,400. Ms. Sui is reimbursed for her operating expenses when using the car for business. Clothes To You Ltd. also pays for any insurance, licence fees and repairs and maintenance related to the operation of the automobile. The operating expenses for the year totalled $6,200, including HST. She used the car 10,000 kilometres for pleasure and 30,000 kilometres for business. She is charged $200/month for the use of the car and operating costs.

(2) Ms. Sui received stock options in the year. She has the option to purchase 20,000 shares at $3.50/share. The value of the shares at the date of the issue of the option was $3.50/share. Ms. Sui has not yet exercised any of her options.

(3) Ms. Sui received a piece of artwork worth $750, including HST, from the company at Christmas time.

(4) Clothes To You Ltd. paid $1,300, including HST, for her membership in a fitness club. The corporation also paid Private Health Insurance premiums of $350.

Investment Receipts:

Interest income.	$1,100
Dividends received from Canadian-resident public corporations	7,500
Dividends from U.S. corporation — net of 15% withholding tax (in Cdn. $)	680

Other Items:

(1) Annuity payments under contract from Profound Life Assurance Co.
    The capital portion of the annuity was $650 . . . . $2,000

(2) Net proceeds on the sale of her house on March 15, 2018 —
    net of real estate commission of $12,000 . . . . $188,000

   The house cost $90,000 in 2005. She had previously sold her cottage in 2007, giving the cottage
   the maximum designation as a principal residence in order to have a nil taxable capital gain.

(3) At Christmas 2017, Ms. Sui gave each of her children a 6%, $2,000 five-year bond.

Expenditures/Losses:

(1) Investment counsellor's fees . . . . $ 1,100

(2) Interest on bank loan to purchase shares 850

(3) Registered retirement savings plan contribution 14,000

   Ms. Sui's earned income in 2017 was $170,000. The PA on her 2017 was $7,000.

(4) Ms. Sui incurred meals and entertainment expenses 8,300

(5) Rental loss (before CCA) 3,500

(6) Ms. Sui invested in a limited partnership tax shelter in 2018. The loss per form T5013 is $3,200.
    She invested $5,000 in the partnership units in early 2018.

Ms. Sui has asked you to calculate her income for tax purposes for 2018.

Problem 14

ITA: 63

Ed Sigmond was transferred from England to Ottawa by Pharmadyne Supplies Inc. on April 1, to
assume the permanent position as Vice President, Canadian operations. Ed was a permanent resident of
England prior to the move. His earnings for the year are as follows:

Gross salary — January 1 to March 30	$ 12,000
Income tax paid in England	(3,200)
Gross salary — April 1 to December 31	$ 62,000
Income tax withheld	(21,000)
CPP/EI withheld	(3,499)
Donations to United Way withheld	(400)

Ed's spouse, Laura, arrived in Ottawa on July 15, with three children (all seven years of age or
older). On August 1, she resumed her full-time studies at the University of Ottawa, where she was
awarded a $2,500 scholarship. In England, she had attended the University of Cambridge from January 1
to April 30. In England, Laura paid $1,000 per month for a nanny for the children. In Canada, she took
her children to the local daycare for $1,360 per month. The Sigmonds also incurred the following
moving expenses:

Airfare/lodging — house hunting in Ottawa	$3,500
Airfare — family move	7,000
Moving van fees	3,200
Legal fees and land transfer taxes on acquiring the Ottawa home	5,500
Meals and hotel expenses (12 days prior to employment)	3,800

Ed is having some problems in calculating his and Laura's income for Canadian tax purposes, and
has come to you for assistance. He has asked you to calculate his income for tax purposes.

Problem 15

ITA: Division B

Ms. King had a busy year in 2018. During the year, she formally separated from her husband and retained custody of her five-year-old daughter, Kelly. She also decided that she needed a fresh start in another city, so she quit her job in Belleville, Ontario, and got a new job in Windsor. Ms. King and her daughter moved to Windsor, Ontario, in November 2018. She has asked you to help her estimate her 2017-2018 income for tax purposes. In order to help you, she has prepared the following list of all the transactions which she thinks might be of interest to you.

(1) Her employment income from her employer in Belleville for the first 11 months of 2018 was $55,000. Her deductions at source included CPP/EI of $3,400 and income tax of $11,000.

Before she left the Belleville employer, a public company, she exercised a stock option that she had for 800 shares. When this option had originally been granted, the share price was $15. The exercise price of the option was $17. At the time she exercised the option, the market price was $25. She immediately sold these shares on the open market for $25.

(2) Her new employer in Windsor agreed to pay some of her moving expenses, but in order to simplify things, they were going to give her an allowance of $8,000. She was responsible, then, for her own expenses.

Her moving costs were as follows:

Moving company charges	$5,500
Gas for trip to Windsor at the time of the move (600 km driven)	75
Motel in Belleville for one night on the day of the move	75
Meals during the one-day move to Windsor	100
Lease cancellation charge in Belleville	200
	$5,950

She had made a trip to Windsor to look for an apartment for her and Kelly and she had incurred the following expenses:

Gas for trip to Windsor and return	$150
Motel costs in Windsor	150
Meals	75
	$375

(3) Her income from her new employer in Windsor during the month of December was $5,000.

(4) During the year she incurred the following expenses for the care of Kelly:

Food and clothing	$6,000
Babysitter costs while she was at work	3,000

(5) Ms. King incurred legal fees of $3,200 to establish her right, under the *Divorce Act*, to support payments in connection with the finalization of the separation agreement. She feels that this was well spent, since her lawyer was successful in getting her husband to pay child support to her for Kelly in the amount of $800 per month, starting in February 2018. So far, her husband has been making these payments on time.

She also had trouble with her 2016 tax return and had to pay her previous accountant $400 to deal with the CRA. It turns out that the CRA has correctly assessed her return.

(6) She is totally confused by the RRSP rules, so she wants you to tell her what the maximum amount is that she can contribute to her RRSP for 2018. She wants you to assume that she will make these payments within the time deadlines.

(7) Five years ago, Ms. King inherited some shares in a Canadian-resident public company, Facai Ltd., from her mother. She believed that the shares were capable of making money for her. She sold the shares in 2018, in order to put money into a mutual fund that a friend recommended. Her mother had paid $5,000 for these shares in 1990 and at the time of her mother's death, the shares were worth $60,000. Ms. King sold them for $180,000.

Ms. King received cash dividends from these shares during the year in the amount of $9,058.

(8) One of her good friends had been a battered wife, so Ms. King had donated $2,000 to the local registered charity which protects battered women.

(9) Ms. King gave you a copy of her 2017 tax return and it showed employment income of $55,000, child care expenses of $2,000 and taxable dividends of $10,000. She made the maximum RRSP contribution for 2017.

Ms. King has asked you to calculate her income for 2018. Explain why you omitted any amounts from your calculations. Show all calculations.

Problem 16

ITA: Division B

Cam Renaz, a self-employed geologist, is a single parent with full custody of his two daughters, Sharee and Susanna (ages 13 and 15). During the past year, Cam retained the full-time services of a nanny to care for them while he worked. Unfortunately, this was a difficult year in Cam's field and his earnings were low. To assist in financing his living expenses, he withdrew $12,000 from his RRSP. He also settled with his wife and she paid him $20,000 as a lump sum in exchange for being relieved of any liability for future alimony payments. To save even more money, Cam prepared his own income tax return, instead of using his accountant's services.

Below is a summary of Cam's income tax information:

Consulting income, net of expenses	$28,000
Car purchased — used 40% for business use	(18,000)
Nanny's salary ($1000/month)	(12,000)
RRSP withdrawals (gross)	12,000
Canadian dividends — cash amount (from CCPCs whose active business income is eligible for the small business deduction)	1,500

When Cam filed his income tax return, he deducted the nanny expense from his consulting income, and wrote off 40% of the cost of the car as business expense. He did not report the RRSP withdrawals because 20% tax was withheld at source.

When Cam received his notice of assessment from the CRA, he was shocked to see that he owed substantially more income tax. The following comments were made in his notice of assessment:

- Child care expenses are not deductible as a self-employed business expense and have been disallowed.

- Cannot deduct price of car as a business expense, and the item has been disallowed.

- Your dividend income has been increased by $270.

- Our records indicate that you withdrew $12,000 from your RRSP and received $20,000 from your ex-spouse for alimony; these amounts have been added to your income.

Cam does not understand why the CRA is assessing him this way. He particularly recalls his accountant telling him that the nanny expenses would be tax deductible.

Compute Cam's net income, considering the legislation, common law and administrative practice, and the correct income tax treatment of each of the items creating problems in Cam's income tax return.

Type 3 Problems

Problem 17

ITA: Division B

Myron Van Doulis, age 42, just left your office with his spouse, Jennifer Barnes. Over the past several years Myron, a former VP at TNS Communications, has been successfully promoted and now earns $220,000 annual salary. The couple worked assiduously for their social position; Myron encouraged his wife to learn bridge, tennis, and to work as a charitable member of the local community. Jennifer continues to pay her law society dues, hoping that someday she will return to her profession. Myron's treadmill was running at full-speed until last month when TNS was suddenly acquired by MIC International. Myron's life was in crisis when the president, accompanied by a security officer, guided him from his office with a $120,000 severance package. The presidents of TNS and MIC both agreed that Myron's work ethic and performance were less than marginal when compared with the performance of MIC's senior vice president.

While the couple's children (ages 8, 10, and 13) are in school, Jennifer has been secretly writing and working on the computer. Over the past five years, Jennifer has developed a few unique software packages for specialized legal services. Her software was tested and favourably accepted by a large international law firm. Jennifer now has a lucrative proposal from a leading software publishing company. Over the past month, Myron has had time to reflect, ponder, and examine his future needs.

Myron just finished reading the best-selling book, *Take Your Money and Run*. Given the ever-increasing debt load, Myron believes that the government will continue to raise his federal income tax rates. He also believes that the cost of health care and education will increase dramatically. The current market value of Myron's net assets are as follows:

Cash	$ 13,000
Treasury bills and bonds	120,000
Speculative stocks (cost $95,000)	4,000
RRSP: Securities	149,000
House (cost $210,000)	240,000
Bank loan for trading	(140,000)
Net assets	$386,000

Myron's most immediate concern is his severance pay. He has a few options. His marginal tax rate this year will be 50% and, in 20 years, when he retires, he estimates a marginal tax rate of 40%.

(a) In the details of Myron's severance package, MIC is willing to pay an $80,000 retirement allowance. Assume for the purposes of this case that all of the $80,000 may be contributed to his RRSP due to Myron's unused RRSP room. Myron can invest the $80,000 in the Province of British Columbia strip bonds with an annual yield to maturity (YTM) of 5%. MIC has also agreed to pay a cash settlement of $40,000. Currently, the annual GIC rate is 4%.

(b) Alternatively, MIC is willing to provide Myron with 12,000 shares of ITT, a Canadian public corporation, currently trading at $8, and a cash settlement of $40,000. The shares pay an annual 5% dividend; the company expects growth of about 4% per year. This assumes that the new vice president will improve the financial returns and reap greater rewards in the derivative marketplace.

Myron feels like escaping for a few years. He's thinking of selling his home and purchasing a yacht outfitted with communications technology. According to the book, *Take Your Money and Run*, he could sever all ties (for about two years), transfer his assets and severance to a tax haven, and incorporate offshore. The company could rent a home in Canada for the children while they complete their education. The technology on board would permit his wife to communicate with her publisher (although she insists that she would have to spend at least four months of the year in Canada, visiting the children). Further, Myron can continue his adventurous trading in the options and derivative markets. One last problem: the CRA has disallowed his business loss of $90,000 in last year's income tax return. His trading in the options market generated losses of $90,000, including commission expenses. The CRA has assessed the loss as a capital loss because, in the prior year, Myron had reported his $22,000 in profits from trading in the options market as a capital gain and not as business income.

Draft a report to Myron, detailing and quantifying where possible, the income tax position he faces. Include the financial quantification of the two retirement packages he has been offered. Assume the tax rate on dividends equals approximately 25%.

CHAPTER 9 —
DISCUSSION NOTES FOR REVIEW QUESTIONS

(1) The payment was made to Ms. Tang "upon or after retirement of a taxpayer from an office or employment in recognition of her long service" and as such should qualify as a retiring allowance and be included in income. An Interpretation Bulletin states that "the cessation of employment for any reason is considered as being retirement or loss of employment". Therefore, even though she quit, this amount should still qualify as a retiring allowance.

ITA: 56(1)(a)(ii), 248(1) "retiring allowance"

Income Tax Folio: S3-F9-C1 — Lottery Winnings, Miscellaneous Receipts, and Income (and Losses) from Crime

(2) The accumulated sick days will qualify as a "retiring allowance" and be taxed as such. However, the unused vacation days will not qualify under this definition, according to the Interpretation Bulletin, and will be taxed as employment income.

ITA: 6(3), 56(1)(a)(ii), 248(1) "retiring allowance"; IT-337R4 par. 5

(3) Since the $3,000 per month is contained in the written agreement and the $1,200 mortgage payment is part of the "allowance," the full amount should be deductible. However, the deductibility for the mortgage payment is limited to ⅕ of the original principal. In this case, ⅕ × $120,000 = $24,000. After 20 months ($24,000/$1,200), Charles will no longer be able to deduct the payments related to the mortgage and Dee will no longer have to take them into income.

ITA: 60.1(2)

(4) Under this agreement, the $500 in monthly fees paid to the financial institution will qualify as an allowance since Mark does have the discretion as to where the $500 is paid. In addition, this amount is part of the monthly spousal maintenance payment specified in the agreement.

(5) The loan would have to be included in employment income when received. Such amounts are not awards and are not subject to the rules for scholarships and research grants. As a result, neither the full exemption for scholarships nor research expenses are available as deductions. Any repayment of this repayable award is deductible provided the conditions of that paragraph are met.

ITA: 5(1), 6(3), 8(1)(n); Income Tax Folio S1-F2-C3 — Scholarships, Research Grants and Other Education Assistance

ITA: 56(1)(n), 56(1)(o)

(6) The Guaranteed Income Supplement would fall into the category of "social assistance payments" since it is based on an income test. As a result, the payments are included in net income, but there is a corresponding deduction to exclude it from taxable income. The effect of these two provisions is to raise Mrs. Smith's income to a point that no one can claim her as a dependant, but at the same time not to make Mrs. Smith taxable on this amount.

ITA: 56(1)(u), 110(1)(f)

(7) The $15,000 will be taxed in Mr. Singh's hands on an indirect payment and not in Mrs. Singh's hands.

ITA: 56(2)

(8) Defined benefit pension plans are approved by and registered with the CRA. Once the CRA has agreed to the terms of the plan, the amount that the company can deduct is determined by an actuary who certifies the amount that is necessary to fund the accruing benefits of the plan.

(9) The explanation is based on the fact that the two pension systems are integrated and the integration is based on how rich your pension plan is. The richness of your pension plan is determined by the Pension Adjustment calculation. For this system to work, the pension calculation has to come first. So, your maximum pension contribution is based on your current income. Then, early in the following year your pension adjustment (PA) is calculated. Finally, your RRSP limit is determined, based on your earned income and PA, both of which relate to the prior year.

(10) The Regulations set the withholding rates based on the amount of the withdrawal — 10% of the amount if it is $5,000 or less; 20% if the amount is between $5,000 and $15,000; and 30% if the amount exceeds $15,000. The rates are one-half of these amounts in Quebec. Based on this formula, the withholdings would be 30% of $20,000 or $6,000. Instead, if she were to withdraw four payments of $5,000, then the tax withheld would amount to only 10% of $20,000 or $2,000. In both cases the $20,000 withdrawn will have to be included in her income for the year and the same amount of ultimate tax will have to be paid. The tax will

ITR: 103(4), 103(6)

have to be funded from other sources to allow for the $20,000 to be spent for the car. Alternatively, the withdrawal will have to be increased for the amount of the tax to be paid. The necessary withdrawal would be $20,000/(1 − t), where t is her marginal tax rate.

(11) Since he left his RRSP to an adult child, the estate will have to pay tax on the basis that the full amount of the RRSP was included in income in the year of death. At a 50% tax rate, this will amount to $75,000 of tax which will come out of the residue or Jim's share of the estate. As a result, Kim will receive $150,000 of cash and Jim will receive the residue of the estate minus the $75,000 of tax and any other tax that may be payable. Mr. McDonald should have calculated the division of property based on the after-tax values to the estate.

(12) The following items would show up on her personal tax return:

(a) the $40,000 would be included in income as a retiring allowance; and

(b) the $8,000 of legal fees could be deducted.　　　　ITA: 60(*o.*1)

The $32,000 (net of legal fees) retiring allowance is not eligible for a deduction on contribution to the RRSP. As a result, she will have an overcontribution which will attract a penalty of 1% per month in the RRSP, unless she removes the overcontribution on a timely basis.

CHAPTER 9 — SOLUTIONS TO MULTIPLE CHOICE QUESTIONS

Question 1

(A) is the correct answer in this case, since no amount of the retiring allowance provides a deductible RRSP contribution.   ITA: 60(j.1)

(B), (C), and (D) incorrectly consider any amount of the retiring allowance to be deductible in this case when no amount is deductible.

Question 2

(C) is correct. The $6,000 is calculated as follows:

The lesser of:		
the 2018 RRSP dollar limit		$26,230
18% of earned income for 2017:		
Income from employment	$44,000	
RPP contributions	1,000	
Spousal support received	3,600	
Real estate rental income	1,400	
	$50,000 × 18%	$ 9,000
The lesser amount		$ 9,000
minus 2017 PA		(4,000)
add unused deduction room		1,000
		$ 6,000

(A) incorrectly uses $44,000 as earned income: 18% × $44,000 – $4,000 PA + $1,000 = $4,920.

(B) incorrectly excludes the unused deduction room: $9,000 – $4,000 = $5,000.

(D) incorrectly ignores the earned income calculation: $20,000 – $4,000 + $1,000 = $17,000.

Question 3

(A) is correct. The calculations are as follows:

	Meg	James	
Salary	$46,000		
Employment expenses	(2,800)		ITA: 8
Business income	—	$18,000	
Interest income	800	1,500	
Net income	$44,000	$19,500	
Earned income	$46,000	$18,000	ITA: 63

Since James has the lower net income ($19,500), he must claim the deduction, which is the least of:

(a) Eligible child care expenses: $15,000 + ($125 × 2 weeks) $15,250

(b) Eligible children:
$5,000 × 1 = $5,000
$8,000 × 2 = 16,000 . . . . $21,000

(c) ⅔ × James' earned income: ⅔ × $18,000 . . . . $12,000

Since Joanne is age 17, she is not an eligible child. The deduction for the overnight camp for Susie is restricted to $125 per week. ITA: 63(3)

(B) is incorrect, because Meg cannot claim the deduction, since she has the higher net income.

(C) and (D) are incorrect because they are not the least amount calculated in (A) above.

Question 4

(B) is correct and is calculated as follows:

Moving van to transport household effects		$ 5,000
Travelling cost — self, spouse and two children		
Meals — flat rate ($51 × 4 persons × 5 days)	$ 1,020	
Car — flat rate (4,430 kms × $0.555)	2,459	
Hotel ($100 × 5 nights)	500	3,979
Legal fees — Vancouver house		900
Legal fees — Toronto house		1,100
Costs while waiting for Vancouver house —		
Hotel (15 days (max.) × $100)		1,500
Meals (15 days (max.) × 4 persons × $51)		3,060
		$15,539

The mileage rate is determined by the province in which travel began.

(A) incorrectly excludes the legal fees on the houses and uses $3,000 as travel costs: $15,539 – $2,000 – $3,979 + $3,000 = $12,560.

(C) incorrectly includes all the hotel costs and the house hunting trip and uses $3,000 as travel costs: $15,539 + $1,520 + $800 – $3,979 + $3,000 = $16,880.

(D) incorrectly includes all the hotel costs: $15,539 + 1,520 = $17,059.

Question 5

(D) is correct. The earned income that should be used to calculate her RRSP deduction for 2018 is her 2017 earned income, which is: ITA: 146(1)

	2017	
Salary	$100,000	
Taxable benefits	8,000	ITA: 6, 7
Travel expenses	(3,000)	ITA: 8
Business losses	(1,000)	
Rental income (net of expenses and CCA)	3,200	
Spousal support paid	(12,600)	
2017 Earned income	$ 94,600	ITA: 146(1)

(A) and (C) are incorrect. The earned income that should be used to calculate her child care   ITA: 63(3)
expense deduction for 2018 is $118,000:

	2018
Salary	$110,000
Taxable benefits	8,000
Earned income	$118,000

ITA: 6, 7
ITA: 63(3)

(A) incorrectly includes 2018 salary only ($110,000).

(C) is the 2018 net income under Division B which includes amounts for travel expenses, RPP   ITA: 63(3)
contributions, business losses, rental income and spousal support which are not part of the earned
income calculation for the child care expense deduction.

(B) is Sahar's 2018 earned income for computing her 2019 RRSP deduction: ITA: 146(1)

	2018
Salary	$110,000
Taxable benefits	8,000
Travel expenses	(2,000)
Business losses	(1,200)
Rental income (net of expenses and CCA)	3,600
Spousal support paid	(12,000)
Net income under Division B	$106,400

ITA: 6, 7
ITA: 8

Question 6

(D) is correct. Deductible moving costs are: ITA: 62(3)

Moving van		$2,600
Travelling costs to move Natalie and family		
Meals — flat rate ($51 × 4 persons × 3 days)	$ 612	
Car — flat rate (1,000 kms × $0.47)	470	
Hotel ($100 × 2 nights)	200	1,282
Cost of maintaining vacant former residence (maximum amount)		5,000
Cost of changing address on legal documents		100
		$8,982

(A) $25,700 incorrectly includes all expenses listed, including only $900 for travelling costs.

(B) $16,007 incorrectly includes the actual cost of maintaining the former residence (an additional
$4,000) plus the $3,000 house hunting trip.

(C) $12,600 incorrectly includes all actual cost of maintaining the former residence (an additional
$4,000) and uses only $900 for travel.

CHAPTER 9 — SOLUTIONS TO EXERCISES

Exercise 1

The definition of "earned income" is found in two places in the Act, subsections 146(1) and 63(3). The definition found in subsection 63(3) relates to child care expenses. The definition of earned income contained in subsection 146(1) is used in the calculation of the RRSP contribution limit and is quite different from the definition contained in subsection 63(3). You will note that section 146, entitled "Registered Retirement Savings Plans", appears in Division G — Deferred and Other Special Income Arrangements.

ITA: 63(3), 146(1)

The definition of "earned income" pertaining to the child care expense deduction can be seen to reflect the economic activity that the government is encouraging when taxpayers incur child care expenses. These are limited to: employment, carrying on business (in an unincorporated form), or studying where student income like a net research grant is obtained.

The definition of "earned income" pertaining to an RRSP can be seen to reflect, conceptually, a source of income that requires some amount of active involvement in the earning process, rather than a passive source, like a passive investment in stocks or bonds earning dividends or interest.

Exercise 2

The maximum amount that Don is able to deduct in respect of a spousal RRSP is his annual contribution limit, less any contributions made to his own RRSP in respect of the year.

Don's annual contribution limit for 2018 is calculated as the lesser of 18% of his 2017 earned income (i.e., $11,916 as calculated below) and the RRSP dollar limit for 2018, which is $26,230, less the PA reported by his employer in respect of 2017 of $6,084.

Don's earned income for 2017 is calculated as:

ITA: 146(1)

Employment income — Subdivision a	$68,400	
Add: RPP contribution	2,800	$71,200
Rental loss		(5,000)
Earned income		$66,200
18% thereof		$11,916

Therefore, Don is able to deduct $5,832 (i.e., $11,916 – $6,084) of RRSP contributions in 2018. Since he has already contributed $5,000 to a spousal RRSP, he can either contribute $832 to his own RRSP, or an additional $832 to the spousal RRSP for 2018.

Exercise 3

To calculate the after-tax rate of return for the first investment alternative — the bond held outside of an RRSP — you must multiply the pre-tax rate of return by (1 – t). Therefore, the after-tax rate of return will be 2.216% (8% (1 – 0.46)), or $324. As the annual after-tax yield is reinvested at the same pre-tax 4%, the compounded yield is $3,574 (i.e., $15,000 $(1.0216)^{10}$ – $15,000).

Inside the RRSP, the 4% interest compounds unhindered by tax, and in 10 years the RRSP amount grows to $7,204 (i.e., $15,000 $(1.04)^{10}$ – $15,000); however, income taxes must be paid on withdrawal from the RRSP at 46% equaling $3,314 and yielding $3,890.

The RRSP approach produces the better after-tax yield, $3,890 versus $3,574 outside the RRSP.

Exercise 4

As this was a spousal RRSP, it is subject to the three-year rule. Douglas will be required to report $6,000 as his income. Under the three-year rule, Douglas's income is the lesser of (A) and (B).

ITA: 146(1)

(A) Spousal RRSP contributions, current year $0; preceding two taxation years $6,000.

(B) RRSP withdrawn $10,000.

Donna will report the remaining $4,000 of income ($10,000 – $6,000).

While income is reported by Douglas, the income tax withholding of $2,000 remains as a credit in Donna's tax return.

Exercise 5

Mr. Reimer is able to contribute $20,900 to an RRSP for 2018 [(lesser of 18% of his earned income from 2017 (i.e., 18% of $120,000 = $21,600 and $26,230) less his 2017 PA of $700]. He may make this annual contribution to either his own or a spousal RRSP, as long as the total of the contributions does not exceed $20,900. These contributions may be made in the year or within 60 days of December 31, 2018.

He does not have to include the lump-sum transfer from his RPP in his income nor does he get an offsetting deduction, as long as it is eligible to be transferred.

ITA: 147.3(4), 147.3(9)

Mr. Reimer is not allowed to transfer any amount in this case to his RRSPs in respect of his retiring allowance.

Exercise 6

Allowable moving expense deduction

(A) 2018

Travelling cost — air fare	$ 1,300	ITA: 62(3)(a)
Household effects — transporting	1,000	ITA: 62(3)(b)
Selling costs of Vancouver residence		ITA: 62(3)(e)
— legal fees	500	
— real estate commission	10,000	
Allowable purchase cost of Montreal residence		ITA: 62(3)(f)
— legal fees	1,000	
— Quebec transfer tax	300	
Total potential deductions	$14,100	
Less		
Amount paid by the employer not included income	$ 5,000	ITA: 62(1)(c)
	$ 9,100	
Deduction restricted to income from new work location — 2018	$ 7,000	ITA: 62(1)(f)

(B) 2019

Balance deductible from income from the new location only in 2019	2,100	ITA: 62(1)
	$ 9,100	

Exercise 7

(i) Amount deductible for 2017 would be the reassessed amount of $11,250 calculated as the least of:

    (a) $18,000 Contribution

    (b) $26,010 Limit

    (c) 18% × amount of 2016 earned income ($62,500)* = $11,250

*Earned income in 2016

Employment income	$ 65,000
Rental loss	$ (2,500)
	$ 62,500

Note that Mr. Big Shot's pension adjustment for 2016 was nil.

(ii) The amount deductible for 2018 would be $5,625 which is the least of:

    (a) $6,750 ($18,000 – $11,250) un-deducted contributions

    (b) $26,230 – Nil (PA for 2017) = $26,230 limit

    (c) 18% × amount of 2017 earned income ($31,250)* – Nil (PA for 2017) = $5,625

*Earned income in 2017

Employment income	$ 35,000
Rental loss	$ (3,750)
	$ 31,250

Mr. Big Shot has made excess contributions to his RRSP as of February 2018 in the amount of $18,000 – [2017 deduction] $11,250 – [2018 deduction] $5,625 = $1,125. Since this is below the allowable limit for excess contributions, no penalties will apply.

Exercise 8

(i) Least of:

    (i) qualifying amounts paid

    $8,000 + ($125 × 3 weeks) + ($200 × 3 weeks) = $8,875

    (ii) ($8,000 × 2 children) + ($5,000 × 1 child) = $21,000

    (iii) ⅔ × ($32,500 + $7,000) = $26,333

(ii) Babysitting of $1,200 excluded on the assumption that these expenditures were not for the purpose of earning income.

Registered pension plan contributions ignored since only income inclusions not deductions are included in "earned income" for this deduction.

The following sources of income are not included in "earned income" by virtue of the definition.

Rental of basement apartment	$ 9,000
Support payments	$ 18,000
Interest income	$ 5,000

Exercise 9

The CRA would assess Spencer Stable a shareholder benefit under ssec. 15(1) in the amount of $45,200, being the cost of the addition, including 13% HST. This income would be treated as income from property in the calendar year that the addition is built. Stable Estates Limited would also be reassessed to deny the deduction for the cost of the company of the subcontractor fees under par. 18(1)(*a*) since the expenses were not incurred to earn income. The expense would be considered to be a personal or living expense and denied under par. 18(1)(*h*). Penalties under ssec. 163(2) may be levied if the CRA considers the understatement of income to be as a result of gross negligence.

Under the *Excise Tax Act*, ssec. 172(2) would likely be applied to this transaction to deem Stable Estates Limited to have sold property for $40,000 and to have collected HST of $5,200. This amount would have to be remitted to the Receiver General.

Exercise 10

Subsection 56(4) would apply to cause the $12,000 to be taxed in Mrs. Worker's hands and not in Mr. Worker's hands. One should note that IT-440R2, paragraph 10, threatens to have the $12,000 taxed in both of their hands if there was a deliberate attempt to evade or avoid tax.

Exercise 11

(1) Gift of shares to granddaughter

Under par. 69(1)(*b*), Bob will be deemed to have disposed of his 1,000 shares of Canadian Business Machines Ltd. for their fair market value of $45,000 since he gifted these shares to a non-arm's length person for no proceeds. Therefore, on Bob's 2018 tax return, he will have to report a capital gain of $40,000 ($45,000 – $5,000). The taxable capital gain will be $20,000 ($40,000 × ½).

Pursuant to ssec. 74(2), the $1,000 dividend received in 2018 will be taxable in the hands of Bob and not Janet since Janet is a related minor and attribution applies.

Janet's ACB for the shares will be $45,000.

Next year, when Janet sells the shares, no attribution of the capital gain or loss applies. Capital gains and losses of minors are not attributable to the transferor. In addition, as Janet turns 18 next year, ssec. 74(2) will no longer apply to attribute the dividend income to Bob.

(2) Sale of shares to spouse

If Bob elects, in his 2018 tax return, to not have the provisions of ssec. 73(1) apply, then he will have to report a taxable gain of $25,500 (($52,000 – $1,000) × ½).

The adjusted cost base of the shares to his wife will be $52,000.

Since the conditions of ssec. 74.5(1) have been met, any future dividends and capital gains or losses on the sale of the shares will be taxed in the hands of his wife and will not be attributed to Bob.

Alternatively, if Bob does not elect out of ssec. 73(1), then Bob's deemed proceeds will be equal to the adjusted cost base of his shares or $1,000. Therefore, no capital gain arises on the disposition. Furthermore, the $20,000 dividends paid each June 30 will be attributed back to Bob pursuant to ssec. 74(1). Also, whenever his wife sells the shares to a third party, any capital gain or loss will be attributed back to Bob pursuant to ssec. 74.2(1).

Bob's wife will have an adjusted cost base of $1,000 for the shares even though she paid fair market value of $52,000 for them. Furthermore, as mentioned above, dividends and capital gains and losses will not be taxed in the hands of Bob's wife, but rather in Bob's hands.

Also, in the latter alternative, any income Bob earned on the $52,000 cash received will be attributed to his wife.

(3) Gift of cash or loan to adult child

The gifting of cash to an adult child will not cause a capital gain or loss to Bob. If Bob loans the funds to Dianne on an interest-free basis (rather than having gifted the money to her) and if it can reasonably be considered that one of the main reasons for Bob making the loan was to reduce or avoid taxes by causing Dianne to be taxed on the income from the investment instead of Bob, then ssec. 56(4.1) will attribute the interest earned on the loaned funds to Bob.

Assuming that ssec. 56(4.1) does not apply, Dianne will be taxed on the interest income generated by the $50,000.

Exercise 12

George will have an RRSP deduction available to him of $35,000. He can use this deduction against his 2018 total income or he may choose to carry some or all of it forward.

He will be deemed to have disposed of his shares at fair market value. This will cause a taxable capital gain of $7,500 (($25,000 – $10,000) × ½) on the ABC Public Company shares. The capital loss of $15,000 ($10,000 – $25,000) on the XYZ Public Corporation shares will be deemed to be nil by virtue of clause 40(2)(*g*)(iv)(B).

Exercise 13

The principal residence exemption is restricted to one principal residence designation per year per family by virtue of paragraph (*c*) of the definition of "principal residence" in section 54. The rules in par. 40(2)(*b*) and ssec. 40(6) provide the framework for deciding which residence should be claimed for which years in order to maximize the principal residence exemption.

It would appear that Mr. Transfer should elect on the house for 2005 to 2017 since the "1 plus" rule would allow the entire gain to be covered by the principal residence exemption. Mr. Transfer should elect on his property since the annual gain of $16,428 (see note) is greater than the annual gain of $9,166 on Mrs. Transfer's property. Mrs. Transfer could designate the cottage for the 2018 year, allowing (1 + 1) ÷ 12 of the gain to be exempt. The remainder of the gain would be treated as a capital gain.

Note:

	Mr. Transfer Toronto Home	Mrs. Transfer Lake Eugenia Cottage
Year of purchase	2004	2006
Fair market value	$ 300,000	$ 150,000
Cost	70,000	40,000
Gain	$ 230,000	$ 110,000
Years owned	14	12
Gain per year	$ 16,428	$ 9,166

Chapter 10

Computation of Taxable Income and Taxes Payable for Individuals

Learning Goals

Know, Understand and Explain

By the end of this chapter you will know, understand and be able to explain:

- The difference between net income for tax purposes and taxable income.

- Which deductions are used in the computation of net income for tax purposes and which deductions are used in the computation of taxable income.

- The difference between a tax credit and a tax deduction.

- The difference between a refundable and non-refundable tax credit.

- Non-refundable tax credits available to a taxpayer.

- Refundable tax credits available to a taxpayer.

- How computations of net income for tax purposes impact the calculation of refundable tax credits.

- The purpose of the minimum tax.

- Situations when minimum tax may apply.

Apply

By the end of this chapter you will be able to apply your knowledge and understanding to:

- Calculate the taxable income for an individual taxpayer.

- Calculate the tax owing for an individual taxpayer.

- Calculate tax credits for an individual taxpayer.

Review Questions
¶10,800 in the Study Guide

Multiple Choice Questions
¶10,825 in the Study Guide

Exercises
¶10,850 in the Study Guide

Assignment Problems
¶10,875 in the Study Guide

CHAPTER 10 — LEARNING CHART

Problem Descriptions

Textbook Example Problems

10-1	Employee stock option
10-2	Net capital losses
10-3	Deduction of loss carryovers
10-4	Deduction of loss carryovers
10-5	Personal tax credits for dependants
10-6	Medical tax credits
10-7	Medical tax credits for dependants
10-8	Transfer of education credits
10-9	Tax on Old Age Security
10-10	Transfer of credits to spouse
10-11	Taxable income and credits — ordering rules
10-12	Comprehensive
10-13	Comprehensive
10-14	Working income tax benefit
10-15	Minimum tax

Multiple Choice Questions

1	Employee stock option
2	Non-refundable credits
3	Transfer of tuition credits
4	Calculate taxable income and tax payable
5	Minimum tax

Exercises

1	Identify sources of income
2	Loss carryovers
3	Calculate income for tax purposes
4	Calculate income, taxable income, tax payable
5	Personal credits
6	Withdrawal from RPP
7	Transfer of credits to spouse
8	Transfer of dividends
9	Foreign and dividend tax credits
10	Minimum tax
11	Marginal tax rate
12	Minimum tax
13	Becoming resident in Canada
14	Calculate taxable income, personal credit base amount
15	Taxable income of an individual
16	Individual taxes payable
17	Individual taxes payable
18	Income, taxable income, taxes payable for an individual
19	Capital gains deduction, personal tax credits, donations — charitable and political
20	Capital gains deduction, personal tax credits, donations — charitable and political

Problem Descriptions

21   Sale of investments; attribution
22   Sale of investments; attribution

Assignment Problems

1   Dependent credit
2   Tuition credits
3   Exempt income, non-capital loss
4   Income and taxable income, ordering rules
5   Credits
6   Dependent credit
7   Credits — single parent, infirm child
8   Medical expenses
9   Dividend election
10   Credits for U.S. university
11   Credits for U.S. and Canadian universities
12   Tax payable, refundable GST credit and CCTB
13   Pension vs. dividends, OAS claw back
14   Minimum tax
15   Stock option — Division C deduction
16   Loss carryover
17   Allowable business investment loss
18   Marginal tax rates
19   Maximum eligible dividend without tax
20   Pension splitting
21   Income, ordering rules
22   Income and taxable income, ordering rules
23   Income and taxable income, ordering rules
24   Income and taxable income, ordering rules
25   Subdivision e deductions; taxable income for an individual; personal tax

CHAPTER 10

Study Notes

¶10,800   REVIEW QUESTIONS

(1) Ms. Gnu, a new client of yours, has brought in her tax information and is confused. In prior years, she has had some financial difficulties and has lost money in a number of her business ventures. As a result, she has some net capital and some non-capital losses. This year, she earned some income, but she does not know how to decide which losses to apply against this income. What advice do you have for her?

(2) Evan earns $150,000 of employment income and has come to you to talk about his investment income. He earns $10,000 of dividend income from a Canadian-resident public corporation in the year. He wants you to tell him what his marginal tax rate is on this dividend income.

(3) Phil earns $150,000 of employment income and has come to you to talk about his investment income. He earns $10,000 of interest income in the year. He wants you to tell him what his marginal tax rate is on this interest income.

(4) Karen earns $150,000 of employment income and has come to you to talk about her investment income. She realized a $10,000 capital gain in the year and wants you to tell her what her marginal tax rate is on this capital gain.

(5) Ms. Aarts is a painter who specializes in watercolours. In the artistic tradition, she does not make a great deal of money. In fact, she has never made over $20,000 of taxable income in any year. This year is no exception. She expects to have taxable income of $20,000 but she is also planning to donate one of her watercolours to a local charity to be used in one of their fundraising events. The value of the painting is $8,000 and her cost of the painting is $200. She has heard that there are special rules for artists making charitable donations of their work but she does not know if these rules will help her. She does not make any other donations. What is your advice?

(6) During the year Patricia had full-time employment income from employer A of $65,000 and from employer B of $60,000. Both employer A and employer B each deducted $2,594 from her salary for CPP. What impact will the CPP contributions for her employment income have on her personal tax return?

¶10,825   MULTIPLE CHOICE QUESTIONS

Question 1

Banbury Ltd. (BL) is a Canadian-controlled private corporation (CCPC). Brad King is one of BL's employees and deals at arm's length with BL. On April 30, 2015, Brad was granted an option to purchase 1,000 BL shares at $2 per share. Brad exercised the stock option on June 30, 2016, when the market price was $5 per share. In December 2018 Brad sold the shares for $7 each. The fair market value of the shares on April 30, 2015, was $2.50.

Which one of the following amounts represents the increase in Brad's taxable income resulting from the above transactions?

(A) $3,000 in 2016 and $1,000 in 2018

(B) $2,250 in 2016 and $1,000 in 2018

(C) $2,500 in 2018

(D) $4,000 in 2018

Question 2

Bob, a widower who is 65 years old, has correctly calculated his taxable income for 2018 as follows:

Employment income under Subdivision a	$10,000
Pension income (registered pension plan)	20,000
Old Age Security and Canada Pension Plans	10,000
Dividends from Canadian-resident public corporations (grossed up)	2,760
Interest income	5,000
	$47,760

What is the maximum amount (rounded to the nearest dollar) of federal income tax credits that Bob can claim on his 2018 tax return?

(A) $3,044

(B) $3,108

(C) $3,523

(D) $3,766

Question 3

In 2018, Shabir Hassam attended McGill University on a full-time basis for eight months, paying tuition fees of $3,900 for that period. In April 2018, Shabir moved back to Toronto to stay with his family and worked as a waiter. Shabir earned $10,500 in wages and $1,500 in tips during the summer. His moving costs were $200 to Toronto in April 2018 and $500 to Montreal in September 2018. Shabir also received a $1,500 scholarship from McGill in September 2018.

What is the maximum amount of federal personal income tax credits that Shabir can transfer to a parent in respect of his university education in 2018?

(A) $585

(B) $601

(C) $750

(D) $375

Question 4

Kyle, who is employed by a CCPC, had the following sources of income for the year:

Salary	$ 60,000
Dividends from Canadian-resident public corporation (amount received)	20,000
Employee stock option benefit	200,000
Capital gain	200,000

The stock option benefit relates to 50,000 shares that Kyle acquired under an employee stock option plan in January 2018 when the fair market value of the shares was $10 per share. Kyle paid $6 per share for the stock, which was the fair market value of each share at the time that the employee stock options were granted to him. He sold the stock when it was worth $14 per share.

Kyle's employer withheld $2,594 for CPP and $858 for EI.

Kyle is married and his wife works full-time, earning a salary of $95,000. Their three children attend university. Each child has transferred the $5,000 maximum amount of tuition credit to Kyle.

Based on this information, what is Kyle's federal Part I tax for the year under the regular rules, ignoring the minimum tax rules?

    (A) $65,786
    (B) $67,423
    (C) $69,931
    (D) $98,786

Question 5

Based on the information in Question 4, above, what is Kyle's minimum amount of federal tax for the year under minimum tax, after deducting minimum tax credits?   ITA: 127.53

    (A) $51,532
    (B) $49,282
    (C) $42,532
    (D) $33,532

CHAPTER 10

¶10,850   EXERCISES

Exercise 1

ITA: 3

Paragraph 3(*a*) of the *Income Tax Act* requires that all non-capital sources of income be included. It is necessary to disclose each source of income in the computation of net income for tax purposes. Consider the following:

(a) Dividend income from a CCPC.

(b) Loss from a sole proprietorship.

(c) Cashier's income from a grocery store.

(d) Commissions earned from sales with a real estate company.

(e) Research consulting fees.

(f) Rental income earned on a single dwelling.

(g) Bonus income.

(h) Gain on the sale of land by a real estate development company.

(i) Profit from the sale of shoes earned in an incorporated company.

(j) Employment insurance income.

(k) Dividend income earned from a foreign investment.

(l) Tips earned as a hair stylist.

— *REQUIRED*

Identify the source of income for each of the above.

Exercise 2

ITA: 3, 111

The following information has been provided by your client, Ms. Campbell.

	2016	2017	2018
Capital gains (CG)	$37,500	$50,000	$11,250
Capital losses (CL) (excluding BIL)	15,000	—	22,500
Business investment loss (BIL)	—	30,000	—

Additional Information

(1) The above capital gains do not include capital gains from qualified farm property or qualified small business corporation shares.

(2) Ms. Campbell had a $7,500 net capital loss which was realized in 2014.

(3) Ms. Campbell has not had a taxable capital gain prior to 2016.

(4) Ms. Campbell had a property loss of $7,000 in 2017 and property income of $1,000 and $2,000 for 2016 and 2018, respectively.

¶10,850

— REQUIRED

(A) Determine Ms. Campbell's income from the sources indicated for 2016 to 2018 according to the ordering rules in section 3.

(B) Determine Ms. Campbell's taxable income from the sources indicated for 2016 to 2018 according to the ordering rules in Division C after amending the returns.

Exercise 3

ITA: 3, 111

Consider the following two taxpayer situations.

Taxpayer	A	B
Gross salary	$45,000	$15,000
Interest income	2,000	
Self-employed income (assume for tax purposes)	5,000	
Loss from business		(18,000)
Charitable donations	(280)	
Income tax paid	(15,000)	(3,200)
Net cash flow	$36,720	($6,200)

— REQUIRED

Compute each taxpayer's net income for the year, utilizing the aggregating formula of section 3 of the *Income Tax Act*. Where necessary, compute the net capital loss or the non-capital loss.

Exercise 4

ITA: Divisions B and C

Mr. Ethan Benjamin has provided you with a list of various sources of income, losses, deductions, and credits for the purpose of determining his basic federal tax.

Inclusions:

His share of tax profit from a partnership business	$10,000
Canadian bank interest	3,000
Retiring allowance from a former employer	20,000
Gross salary from new employer	60,000
Director's fee	5,000
Taxable capital gains	20,000
Taxable benefits from employment	3,000
Rental income from a triplex	25,000

Deductions, Losses, and Tax Credits:

Mortgage interest on triplex	23,000
Canada Pension Plan contributions tax credit	389
Property taxes and insurance on triplex	4,500
Non-capital losses from a previous year	4,000
Allowable capital loss for this year	2,000
Net capital losses from a previous year	5,000
Maintenance costs for triplex	1,500
Contribution to employer's registered pension plan	4,000
Basic personal and spousal tax credits	3,543
Fees to a professional engineering society	300
Employment Insurance premiums tax credit	129
Tuition tax credit for night course on computer applications	68
Charitable gifts tax credit	550
Canada employment tax credit	179

— REQUIRED

(A) Determine the income, taxable income and basic federal tax based on the above correct information using the ordering rules in sections 3, 111.1, and 118.92.

(B) Cross-reference each amount to the appropriate section of the Act.

Exercise 5

ITA: 118, 122.6, 122.61; IT-513R

Dan, age 50, supported the following persons during 2018:

	Net income for tax purposes
Wife, Dolly, age 45	$3,000
Son, Don, age 24	3,800
Son, Dave, age 20, infirm and living with Dan and Dolly	3,200
Daughter, Doris, age 17	2,800
Son, Dan Jr., age 14	Nil
Mother, age 83, infirm and living with Dan and Dolly	7,000

Don is attending university; Dave has been unemployed most of the year; and Doris and Dan Jr. attend high school. Ages are given as of the end of 2018.

— REQUIRED

Determine Dan's total federal personal tax credits under section 118 for 2018.

Exercise 6

ITA: 8(1)(*m*), 56(1)(*a*), 118(3)

Sally was employed for a little under two years at the Banff Springs Hotel as a bellhop. When Sally resigned her position, she withdrew her total contributions of $800 from her employer's pension plan. Sally's contribution to this plan for her last year was $300.

— REQUIRED

Determine the tax consequences of the above situation.

Exercise 7

ITA: 118.8

Tina, age 72, has income for tax purposes from the following sources in 2018:

Pension income:		
Old Age Security pension	$7,040	
Canada Pension Plan	2,654	
Registered pension plan	350	$10,144
Investment income:		
Canadian bank interest		100
Total Division B income		$10,144

— REQUIRED

Determine the amount Tina can transfer to her husband Tom in 2018.

Exercise 8

ITA: 82(3)

Henry, a resident of your province, cannot decide whether it would be advisable to elect to include in his income, his wife's cash dividends of $900 received from Canadian-resident public corporations. This is her only income for 2018.

— REQUIRED

Determine whether Henry should elect under subsection 82(3) for 2018 assuming his federal marginal tax rate is 29%.

Exercise 9

ITA: 126(1)

The following selected information has been taken from the 2018 tax return of Adam, who is a bachelor:

Income — Division B	$156,800
Taxable income	150,800
Basic federal tax	31,707

Included in the Division B income was foreign interest of $1,500. Withholding tax of $225 had been deducted by the foreign government. This income is not subject to an international tax agreement.

Also included in the computation of Division B income were $300 of dividends received from Canadian-resident public corporations. Included in the computation of taxable income were deductions for net capital losses carried forward of $6,000.

ITA: 111(1)(*b*)

— *REQUIRED*

Determine the amount of the federal foreign tax credit that can be claimed.

Exercise 10

ITA: Division E, E.1

Compute the federal tax at the top bracket, under minimum tax and regular Part I tax for 2018 on $100 of:

(A) interest;

(B) cash dividends from Canadian-resident public corporation;

(C) capital gains.

Exercise 11

ITA: 117(2), 120

Marginal tax rates, or the tax rate applicable to the next dollar of income earned, are relevant to many decisions. Jacob earns $95,000.

— *REQUIRED*

Calculate Jacob's marginal tax rate using the federal and notional provincial rates provided in this chapter.

Exercise 12

ITA: Division E, E.1

The following is a correct calculation of Betty's Division E tax payable for 2018:

Employment income		$160,000
Dividends from Canadian-resident public corporation		30,000
Gross-up @ 38%		11,400
Loss created by resource property shelter		(103,200)
Net income for tax purposes and taxable income		$ 98,200

Tax on first	$ 93,209		$ 16,544
on next	4,992	@ 26%	1,298
	$ 98,200		$ 17,842

Less tax credits:		
Basic personal (15% × $11,809)	$1,771	
Employment Insurance premiums (max.) (15% × $858)	129	
CPP contributions (max.) (15% × $2,594)	389	
Dividend tax credit ($^6/_{11}$ × $11,400)	6,218	
Employment (15% of $1,195)	179	(8,686)
Division E tax		$ 9,156

— *REQUIRED*

Determine if Betty is subject to minimum tax in 2018.

¶10,850

Exercise 13

ITA: 63, 118

Mr. and Mrs. Ataila immigrated to Canada on May 1 (not a leap year). Mr. Ataila earned $12,400 in Argentina and $72,400 as a senior geologist in Canada. Mrs. Ataila is a homemaker, and mother of three children over the age of 6. Her child care expenses totalled $4,580 for the time she spent planning her entry into the workforce.

Mr. and Mrs. Ataila have approached you for assistance with their Canadian tax returns.

— *REQUIRED*

Discuss what you believe are the areas of their returns that they are most interested in.

Exercise 14

ITA: 63, 118

Pierino's wife died last year. Her income for the year was $28,000. Pierino has a 15-year-old dependent son, James. Pierino works for the Saskatoon Transit Commission and earns $65,000 yearly. He also has a part-time business operation on which he has a loss of $5,250. Pierino contributed $10,000 to his RRSP by transferring some shares in Public Co. Ltd. to his self-administered RRSP. The ACB of the shares was $6,000. He has $3,000 in net capital losses being carried forward.

— *REQUIRED*

Calculate Pierino's taxable income and the base amounts of his personal tax credits. Ignore any CPP and EI contributions.

Exercise 15

The following selected information has been taken from the tax records of Ms. Cheryl:

	2016	2017	2018
Employment income (loss)	$ 15,000	$ 20,000	$ 25,000
Rental income (loss)	$ 4,000	$ (2,000)	$ 2,000
Business income (loss)	$ (32,000)	$ 15,000	$ 14,000
Capital gains (capital losses):			
Listed personal property	$ 5,400	$ (7,000)	$ 3,600
Other personal-use property	$ 5,000	$ (3,000)	$ 2,000
Other	$ 6,000	$ 12,000	$ (7,600)
Other deductions:			
Spousal support paid	$ 9,000	$ 9,000	$ 9,000

Additional Information

(1) Losses carried forward from 2015:
   Non-capital losses arising in 2015 .... $ 42,000
   Net capital losses arising in 1999.............................. $ 23,000

(2) The 2018 capital loss of $7,600 includes a business investment loss of $3,000.

— *REQUIRED*

Determine the income for each of the above years according to section 3. Then determine the taxable income for each year in accordance with the ordering rules of Division C.

Exercise 16

Stewart Struggles, age 50, and his wife, age 45, provide you with the following information concerning their 2018 transactions. The Struggles are resident in your province for tax purposes.

	Mr. Struggles	Mrs. Struggles
Employment income received	$ 40,000	Nil
Business income (consulting)	$ 6,000	-
Canadian bond interest received	$ 750	$ 840
Dividends received from taxable Canadian public corporations	$ 200	$ 1,200
U.S. bond interest received, net of a 15% withholding tax	$ 425	-

	Mr. Struggles	Mrs. Struggles
Capital gains (losses):		
Personal-use property assets	$ 350	$ (200)
Listed personal property assets	$ (400)	-
Canadian securities	-	$ 500
	$ 47,325	$ 2,340

Additional Information

(1) Mrs. Struggles suffered a stroke in 2017 and was confined to bed throughout 2018. As a result, she was certified by a medical doctor as impaired.

(2) The Struggles have two children. Anne, age 17, was a full-time student at the University of British Columbia for eight months in 2018. Anne received the following income in 2018:

Employment income for tax purposes during summer in your province	
($81 for CPP and $85 for EI withheld)	$5,140
Interest income	$100
Scholarship	$3,300
	$8,540

Anne paid the following selected amounts in 2018:

Tuition fees, net of non-allowable items of $100	$6,100
Moving expenses to and from British Columbia ($750 to school, $400 home for summer)	$1,150
Rent paid while at university	$2,300

Their second child Tony, age 12, had no income in 2018.

(3) Mr. Struggles made a $420 donation to the Heart Fund (a registered charity) in 2018. This is consistent with prior years.

(4) Mr. Struggles has a 1999 net capital loss carry forward of $4,000.

— *REQUIRED*

Compute Stewart Struggle's lowest amount of basic federal income tax.

Exercise 17

Theresa Taxplan has the following sources of income and deductions for 2018. She is single with no dependants. She made $780 in charitable donations in 2018, which is consistent with prior years donation amounts.

Employment income for tax purposes*	$ 50,000
Grossed-up Canadian dividends**	$ 5,000
Taxable capital gains	$ 51,000
Foreign investment income***	$ 10,000
Loss on resource property shelter	$ (40,000)
RRSP contribution	$ (9,000)
Interest expense	$ (3,000)
Net and taxable incomes	$ 64,000

* Employment Insurance premiums of $858 and CPP contributions of $2,596 withheld.

** From Canadian-controlled private corporations; 16% dividend gross-up and 8/11 dividend tax credit.

*** $1,500 tax withheld thereon.

— *REQUIRED*

Calculate Theresa's federal income tax payable for 2018.

Exercise 18

The following is a summary of Mrs. Smith's income for 2017 and 2018.

	2017	2018
Employment income	$ 32,000	$ 18,000
Retiring allowance	Nil	$ 10,000
Interest income	$ 6,000	$ 6,000
Cash dividends from Canadian public corporations	Nil	$ 9,000
Canada Pension Plan received	Nil	$ 2,000
Old Age Security pension received	Nil	$ 3,120
	$ 38,000	$ 48,120

Mrs. Smith retired from Hudsons Bay Company on July 1, 2018, at age 65. She had been employed by The Bay as a merchandise buyer since July 30, 1994. She has never been a member of a pension plan. She had unused RRSP deduction room at the end of 2017 of $4,000. During 2018, she contributed $5,000 to her RRSP plan. In February 2019, she contributed $12,000 to a spousal RRSP. Mr. Smith retired two years ago and has an annual net income of $30,000.

— *REQUIRED*

Calculate Mrs. Smith's federal tax payable for 2018. She wishes to claim the maximum deductions and credits available to her to reduce her tax liability. Assume a combined CPP and EI credit of ($718 + $299) × 15% = $153.

Exercise 19

Mr. Black is a widower with five children, ages 22, 18, 16, 11, and 9. The 22-year-old attended Queen's University for eight months in 2018. The tuition fees were $5,000. The 22-year-old and the 18-year-old were the only children with income in 2018. They each had net income of $8,000.

— *REQUIRED*

With the information provided, compute the maximum federal non-refundable tax credits that may be claimed by Mr. Black in 2018. Show all your calculations.

Exercise 20

Mr. Green made the following contributions during 2018:

Cancer Society	$ 100
Church	$ 4,000
Liberal Party of Canada	$ 200
University of Waterloo	$ 1,000
United Way	$ 3,000
Conservative Party of Canada	$ 200

His net income for 2018 after deducting his $16,500 RRSP contribution was $132,000.

He makes similar charitable donations on an annual basis.

— *REQUIRED*

By what amount do the above contributions reduce Mr. Green's federal tax liability for 2018? Show all your calculations.

Exercise 21

During 2018, Lot Saluk sold his 500 shares of a small business corporation, Downer Ltd., for $2 per share. He had acquired these shares for $20 per share in 2016. Lot claimed capital gains deductions of $1,000 in 1992 and $2,000 in 1994 only. His only income for 2018 is interest income of $600 and employment income of $15,000.

— *REQUIRED*

Calculate Lot Saluk's taxable income for 2018 and show all calculations.

Exercise 22

Adam owns the following assets:

	FMV	UCC	UCC
Upper Public Corp. shares	$ 40,000	Nil	$ 50,000
Rental building	$900,000	$400,000	$500,000

— *REQUIRED*

For each of the following three scenarios, determine:

(a) the income tax consequences to Adam on the disposition in 2018;

(b) the income tax cost of the asset to the first acquirer; and

(c) the income tax consequences of the subsequent events.

Scenario #1: Adam sells the rental building to his daughter, age 23, for $850,000. She earns $6,000 rental income annually from the building. Later, she disposes of the building at a substantial gain.

Scenario #2: Adam sells the shares to his wife for $40,000 cash. She receives $4,000 in dividends on the shares and then sells them for $45,000.

Scenario #3: Adam gifts the shares to his 11-year-old nephew, and the nephew receives $4,000 in dividends.

CHAPTER 10

¶10,875   ASSIGNMENT PROBLEMS

Type 1 Problems

Problem 1

ITA: 118; IT-513R

Jack and Jill were married on December 1, 2018. Jill and her two children of a previous marriage moved into Jack's home. Jill's children are 14 and 16 and have no income.

Jack and Jill have the following income for tax purposes for 2018:

	Prior to the marriage	Subsequent to the marriage
Jack	$33,000	$3,000
Jill	9,800	800

You have been asked to:

(A) Determine the optimum personal tax credits under section 118 for both Jack and Jill for 2018.

(B) How would your answer change in 2019 if the income levels remain the same?

Problem 2

ITA: 118.6, 118.8, 118.9

Sammy, who was a resident of Canada and who attended the University of Alberta on a full-time basis for eight months during 2018, has employment income for tax purposes of $5,000. He paid tuition fees of $1,800 in 2018. Withheld from his income were $83 in Employment Insurance premiums and $74 in CPP contributions.

Determine the amount Sammy can transfer under section 118.8 or 118.9 to another qualified person.

List the potential persons to whom Sammy can transfer his tuition tax credits.

Problem 3

ITA: 2(2), 3, 111

Blake, a recent accounting program graduate, earned the following during the year:

Gross income from employment	$ 7,000
Provincial lottery winnings	2,500
Capital gain on ABC shares	1,200
Inheritance from grandmother	12,000
Interest income from inheritance	800

Blake has asked you to:

(a) Calculate his net income for tax purposes for the year.

(b) Calculate his taxable income for the year. Assume that Blake has a non-capital loss carryforward from last year of $3,000.

Problem 4

ITA: 3, 111

The following information has been provided by your client, Mr. Stanley Norman:

	2016	2017	2018
Employment income	$75,000	$80,000	$ 90,000
Property income (loss)	(4,000)	3,000	(6,000)
Capital gains (CG)	144,000	—	160,000
Capital losses (CL) (excluding BIL)	18,000	22,500	80,000
Business investment loss (BIL)	36,000	54,000	—

Additional Information

(1) The above capital gains do not include capital gains from qualified farm property or qualified small business corporation shares.

(2) Mr. Norman had a $21,000 net capital loss which was realized in 2013.

(3) Mr. Norman did not have a capital gain prior to 2016.

Dealing with each item line-by-line across the years, rather than one year at a time:

(A) determine Mr. Norman's income from the sources indicated for 2016 to 2018 according to the ordering rules in section 3, and

(B) determine Mr. Norman's taxable income from the sources indicated from 2016 to 2018 after amending the returns.

Problem 5

[handwritten: no age credit → possible spouse transfer]

ITA: 56(1)(*u*), 56(1)(*v*), 74.1(1), 110(1)(*f*), 118, 118.3, 118.6, 118.9, 122.6, 122.61

Mrs. Plant, <u>age 47</u>, <u>is married</u> and has three children: Amanda, age 24, Joan, age 17, and Courtney, age 16. Her own income for tax purposes of $60,000 includes employment income of $58,000.

Amanda has been certified as impaired by a medical doctor. Her only income is $7,000 from social assistance payments relating to her disability. She took a university course on a part-time basis for four months. Mrs. <u>Plant paid her tuition fees of $300.</u>

[handwritten: mother can use]

<u>Joan</u> attended a university on a full-time basis in another city for eight months, had employment income for tax purposes of $4,200 from a summer job while living at home and received a $2,500 scholarship. Mrs. <u>Plant paid Joan's tuition fees of $3,000</u> and Joan paid her own moving costs to and from the university which were $150 each way.

[handwritten: mother can use]

Courtney, who is attending high school, had employment income for tax purposes of $2,800 from summer employment and a part-time job. *[handwritten: nothing can be claimed by mother]*

Mr. Plant, age 50, has been certified as physically impaired and infirm as a result of a workplace accident. He has the following sources of income:

[handwritten: Div B Income: 5K + 0.1K = 5.1K]
[handwritten: TI = 150]

Worker's Compensation payment	$5,000
Cash dividends from shares of <u>Canadian-resident public corporations</u> *[handwritten: Eligible Dividends]* purchased with Mrs. Plant's savings .... *[handwritten: Not Mr. Plant's income; is Mrs. Plant]*	4,000
Bank account interest earned from reinvestment of dividend income	100

Mrs. Plant has asked you to calculate the non-refundable tax credits available to her for 2018. Compute Joan's taxable income to determine if any of her tuition credits will be available to Mrs. Plant. Prepare detailed calculations supporting your claim. All ages are given as of the end of 2018.

Problem 6

ITA: 118(4)

Angelina and Romeo are the divorced parents of Maria, who is 10 years old. Angelina and Romeo have joint custody and Maria lives every second month with the other. Both Angelina and Romeo have claimed Maria for the wholly dependent person (equivalent to spouse) tax credit.

Is the claim by Angelina and Romeo allowed?

Problem 7

ITA: 118, 118.2–118.9; IT-513R

Mrs. Jackson, age 66, separated from her husband on October 17, 2018. She started receiving <u>support payments</u> from Mr. Jackson of $2,500 per month in November 2018. All of the support payments made commencing in November 2018 are considered to be pursuant to the divorce settlement. Of the $2,500 monthly payment, $1,000 is for the support of their daughter, Rachel. (In 2018, Mr. Jackson earned a salary of $100,000 per year and also earned other investment income.) Mrs. Jackson has income of $26,200.

Their eldest daughter Rachel is <u>40</u> and <u>infirm</u> and lives with Mrs. Jackson since <u>she is severely mentally handicapped.</u> She has been <u>certified as impaired</u> by a medical doctor. A part-time attendant helps care for Rachel at a cost of $12,000 per year. Rachel has no income.

Mrs. Jackson would like to know what <u>tax credits related to her daughter Rachel</u> are available to her.

CHAPTER 10

Problem 8

ITA: 118.2

Mr. Jennings provides you with the following medical expenses and additional information for himself and members of his family who live with him, when he asks you to prepare his 2018 tax return.

Assume that you have correctly computed the incomes under Division B for 2018 as follows:

Mr. Jennings	$55,000
Mrs. Jennings	Nil
Son, age 19	8,000
Son, age 15	2,000
Daughter, age 14	1,800

Medical expenses for 2018:

February	Prescription drugs for daughter	$ 20
May	Doctor's bill paid for son, 15	15*
June	Chiropractor's bill for the past year	1150*
July	Glasses for Mr. and Mrs. Jennings	300
		$1,485

Medical expenses to March 31, 2019:

February	Orthodontist fee for daughter		$2,550
March	Expenses relating to older son's car accident:		
	Hospital	$1,500	
	Surgery	1,000	
	Drugs	200	2,700*

Additional expenses anticipated by May 31, 2019:

(a)	Additional medical bills from son's accident	$ 750*
(b)	Eyeglasses for his younger son and daughter ($225 each)	450
(c)	Dental bills (²/₃ for Mr. & Mrs. Jennings)	375
(d)	Chiropractor's bill for the past year	1,050

---

* Excess over provincial plan payments.

Discuss the tax implications of Mr. Jennings claiming the above medical expenses for each of 2018 and 2019. Assume that all income amounts for 2019 will be the same as those for 2018.

Problem 9

ITA: 82, 118, 118.8

Mr. and Mrs. Reid, ages 55 and 50, received the following income during 2018:

Mr. Reid:

Employment income (commission)	$15,000
Employment expenses	(13,000)
Investment income:	
Canadian interest	2,000
Dividends received (in Cdn. $):	
Canadian-resident public corporations	1,000
U.S. corporations (net of 15% withholding tax)	680

Mrs. Reid:

Employment income	54,000
Investment income:	
Canadian interest	1,000
Dividends received from Canadian-resident public corporations	2,000

Calculate Mrs. Reid's federal tax (ignoring the foreign tax credit) under the following situations:

(A) No election to include spousal dividends.

ITA: 82(3)

(B) With an election to include spousal dividends.

ITA: 82(3)

Problem 10

ITA: 118.5(1), 118.6; Income Tax Folio S1-F2-C2 — Tuition Tax Credit

Pamela is 38 years old and lives in Welland, Ontario. She commutes daily to Niagara University, in Niagara Falls, New York. She is completing a full-time Masters in Education that is 12 consecutive months in duration. Her tuition fees are the equivalent of C$20,000 per year.

Advise Pamela if she can claim the tuition fees on her personal income tax return.

Your answer should be supported with appropriate references to the Act.

Problem 11

ITA: 118.5; Income Tax Folio S1-F2-C2 — Tuition Tax Credit

Stuart presents to you the following information concerning tuition fees paid for 2016, 2017, and 2018:

2016	Harvard University, Masters in Business Administration, fall term	$15,000
2017	Harvard University, Masters in Business Administration, winter and fall terms	30,000
2018	Harvard University, Masters in Business Administration, winter term	15,000
	Re-read fee for failed course	300
	Make-up course at Harvard for failed course, July–August	3,000
	Income tax course at University of Toronto, fall term; the tuition fee of $500 was paid through a scholarship that Stuart received from his father's employer, Universal Exports Inc.	500
	Fitness course taken at a local secondary school in Ontario	35

Discuss the tax implications of the above tuition fee payments.

Problem 12

ITA: 117, 118, 121, 122.2, 122.5, 122.6–122.64, 180.1

Patty, a single parent of two children (ages nine and seven) works part-time as a clerk in a law office. She has provided you with the following information for 2018:

Income:	
Workers' Compensation payments	$ 9,000
Employment income (Subdivision a)	35,000
Cash dividend from Canadian-resident public corporations	480
University scholarship received	600
Expenses:	
Canada Pension Plan contributions	1,559
Employment Insurance contributions	581
Cost of subsidized day care for the children (three days a week)	2,400
University tuition paid for a three-month evening course	600

Patty receives the Workers' Compensation payment because of the accidental death of her husband two years ago. Her two minor children have no income.

Patty had $700 of tax withheld from her employment income and has paid no income tax instalments.

Based on the information above, compute Patty's total federal tax for 2018 and her tax refund or balance due.

Determine if Patty is eligible for the refundable goods and service tax credit. Explain.

Authors' Note: The previous problem includes GST/HST implications. Students should review Chapter 20 of the textbook, Goods and Services Tax (GST) / Harmonized Sales Tax (HST), before attempting this problem.

¶10,875

Problem 13

ITA: Division B, C, E

Clare and Alan, both age 70, widowers, and retired successful businesspeople, love to argue. The one fact that they agree upon is that they pay too much income tax. They both receive $7,040 of Old Age Security and $9,000 of Canada Pension Plan payments each year. Clare has $52,000 of income from a registered pension plan. Alan receives $52,000 in dividends from the active business income taxed at the low rate in his incorporated business, a CCPC, which is now managed by his son.

Determine which one of the two pays the most federal income tax for 2018.

ITA: 82(3)

Problem 14

ITA: Division E, E.1

Dawn, a client of yours, generally has employment income from her company and some investment income. In early 2018, you arranged Dawn's affairs such that she would crystallize her $500,000 capital gains exemption on qualified small business corporation shares. For 2018, her income is estimated as follows:

Employment income (CPP $1,931)	$ 42,500
Interest	12,800
Dividends from Canadian-resident public corporations	20,000
Gross-up @ 38%	7,600
Taxable capital gains	250,000
Interest expense	(10,000)
RRSP contribution	(14,500)
Capital gains deduction	(250,000)
Taxable income	$ 58,400

Calculate what effect, if any, minimum tax will have on Dawn's 2018 federal tax payable.

Type 2 Problems

Problem 15

Once again, you have been asked for advice on employee stock options by two different clients. This is a continuation of Assignment Problem 2 in Chapter 3 and Assignment Problem 2 in Chapter 7.

(1) Omer is part of the management team of a Canadian public company and is eligible for the employee stock option plan. A few years ago he received an option on 1,000 shares. The option requires him to pay the option price of $30 (the value at the time the option was granted) for the shares at the time he exercises his option.

Omer exercised the option three years ago when the shares were worth $35 and has sold the shares this year for $45. He has asked you to tell him the effect of this option on his taxable income for all the years.

(2) Hilda is part of the management team of a Canadian-controlled private company and is eligible for the employee stock option plan. A few years ago she received an option on 1,000 shares. The option requires her to pay the option price of $30 (the value at the time the option was granted) for the shares at the time she exercises her option.

Hilda exercised the option three years ago when the shares were worth $35 and has sold the shares this year for $45. She has asked you to tell her the effect of this option on her taxable income for all years.

Problem 16

Nate has come to you for tax advice for 2018. He has identified the following income for 2018 and would like you to calculate the effects of the above on his income, taxable income, and loss carry forward for the year.

Employment	$ 40,000
Lottery winnings	3,000
Stock option benefit	5,000
Division C deduction for stock option	(2,500)
Business	(60,000)
Taxable capital gain	15,000
Allowable capital loss	(20,000)
Inheritance from his grandmother	12,000
Dividends Cash	1,000
Gross-up	170

Problem 17

Natalia has the following income for 2018:

Employment	$ 40,000
Stock option benefit	5,000
Division C deduction for stock option	(2,500)
Business	(60,000)
Taxable capital gain	15,000
Allowable business investment loss	(20,000)
Dividends Cash	1,000
Gross-up	160

Calculate the effects of the above on Natalia's income, taxable income, and loss carry forward for the year.

Problem 18

The accounting firm you work for is preparing a booklet on personal tax, and the tax partner has asked you to prepare some of the material. She has asked you to calculate a generic marginal tax rate for individuals in the top tax bracket for each of the following types of income. Assume $10,000 of each type of income is earned.

Employment
Business
Interest
Eligible dividends
Other Canadian dividends
Capital gains

To be able to move this into the publication easily she has asked you to use the following format:

Tax Brackets	over
	$200,000
Tax Rates By Bracket	
Federal rate	33%
Provincial rate	17%
	50%

Federal + provincial dividend tax credit = gross up

Marginal Tax Rates	
Employment	%
Business	%
Interest	%
Eligible dividends	%
Other Canadian dividends	%
Capital gains	%

Problem 19

Peter and Shikha were at a party on the weekend where someone said that they earn a substantial amount a year in dividends and don't pay any tax. They want to know if this is true and, if it is, whether they can benefit from it.

You agreed to do some basic calculations to start the discussion.

You have decided that your assumptions will be:

— The individual's primary source of income is eligible dividends with a minor source of non-dividend income which could be used to absord excess tax credits from the dividends.

— They have federal personal tax credits of $1,771 and provincial personal tax credits of $1,181.

— For eligible dividends the provincial dividend tax credit is ⁵/₁₁.

— For non-eligible dividends the provincial dividend tax credit is ³/₁₁.

You will calculate the maximum they can earn without paying any net federal or provincial income tax. Also, do the same for non-eligible dividends as the primary source of income for the year.

Problem 20

Harry and Shia are married. Both are retired and over 65 years old. They have the following income in 2018:

	Harry	Shia
Company pension	$120,000	$ –
Canada Pension Plan	12,100	6,000
Old Age Security	7,040	7,040
Registered Retirement Income Fund		12,000

They have asked you to calculate the amount of federal tax they will pay on this income in 2018.

Part 1: Do not split pension income as allowed. Report it as shown above.

Part 2: Split pension income as allowed (refer to Ch. 9).

Hint: Only calculate the personal, married, age, and pension credits. Remember to calculate any tax on Old Age Security income.

Problem 21

ITA: 2(2), 3, 111

Jeffrey Lowe is an associate in a local law firm. He also has a number of sources of income from various investments and sideline businesses. Jeffrey has provided you with the following information for 2018:

Salary from law practice	$120,000
Business loss	(7,500)
Gross rents received from rental property	25,000
Operating expenses on rental property	(31,000)
Capital gain on sale of shares	10,000
Net interest income	9,000
Allowable capital loss (including allowable business investment loss of $6,000)	(11,000)
Contribution to RRSP	(1,000)
Share of net income from duplex rental property (owned by Jeffrey and his sister)	15,000
Net capital losses from 2012	(3,000)

Jeffrey has asked you to calculate his 2018 net income for tax purposes in accordance with the ordering rules in section 3 of the *Income Tax Act*.

¶10,875

Problem 22

ITA: Division B, C

The following tax information is extracted from Mrs. Hawkins' books and records:

Employment income (before effects of items below)	$72,000
Interest income	5,000
Capital gains (on securities)	9,900
Deductible carrying charges	1,000

The following balances are losses carried forward from December 31, 2017:

Non-capital loss arising — 2012	$24,000
— 2013	26,000
— 2016	28,000
Total non-capital losses	$78,000
Net capital loss arising in 2017	$12,000

During the latter part of 2018, Mrs. Hawkins moved from Montreal to Toronto to commence working for Leaves Co. Ltd. She received a $100,000 housing loan from Leaves Co. Ltd., which she used to help purchase a house in Toronto. Mrs. Hawkins received the interest-free loan on October 1, 2018.

Mrs. Hawkins previously worked for Les Habitants Co. Ltée (a public company). Prior to leaving Les Habitants Co. Ltée on April 15, Mrs. Hawkins exercised the stock option that she held in Les Habitants Co. Ltée. Mrs. Hawkins was able to purchase 2,000 listed common shares of Les Habitants Co. Ltée for $4 per share (the fair market value of the shares at the time the option was granted). The shares were trading at $10 per share at the time she exercised her option to purchase the shares.

Assume that the prescribed interest rate for the last quarter of 2018 is 1%.

Calculate Mrs. Hawkins' income and taxable income in 2018, in accordance with the ordering rules of Divisions B and C. Ignore any effects of any leap year.

Problem 23

ITA: 3, 111, 111.1

The following selected tax information has been taken from the books and records of your client, Mr. Weilman, who is 51 years old.

	2017	2018
Employment income	$ 47,000	$ 55,000
Other business income (loss)	(14,000)	(23,000)
Property income:		
Canadian interest	7,000	16,000
Rental income from real property (loss)	3,000	(4,000)
Capital gains (capital losses):*		
Listed personal property	6,000	20,250
Other personal-use property	2,000	(4,000)
Other capital property	6,000	(45,000)
Other deductions:		
RRSP	1,000	3,000
Support of former spouse	7,000	7,000

* The 2018 other capital property loss includes a business investment loss of $24,000.

The following balances are losses carried forward from December 31, 2016:

Non-capital loss arising in 2014	$33,000
Net capital loss arising in 2015	25,000
Listed personal property loss arising in 2014	5,000

Mr. Weilman was not a member of a registered pension plan and, hence, his pension adjustment for the relevant years was nil. His earned income for 2016 was $33,250.

Prepare a schedule for the calculation of income and taxable income for 2017 and 2018, in accordance with the ordering rules under Divisions B and C, after applying any loss carryforward and loss carryback provisions through an amended return. (Deal with each item line-by-line across the years, rather than computing income one year at a time.)

Problem 24

ITA: 245; Division B, C

Ms. Isabelle Cardin had a tumultuous year in 2018. She broke her engagement early in the year and quit her job. She moved to a resort area to take a waitress job and to start up a fitness instruction business. She has had the following items correctly calculated and classified as either inclusions, deductions or tax credits for the purposes of determining her taxable income and federal tax.

Inclusions:

Benefit received from Employment Insurance program	$	600
Board and lodging provided by employer during busy season of resort		8,000
Bonus from resort employer		500
Business revenue from fitness instruction fees		2,000
Gratuities as a waitress		12,100
Interest on Canada Savings Bonds		775
Rental revenue		6,000
Salary received as a waitress		12,000
Taxable capital gain		3,750
Retiring allowance from previous employer		800

Deductions, Losses, and Tax Credits:

Allowable capital loss	4,500
Capital cost allowance on fitness business equipment	1,300
Capital cost allowance on rental building	1,200
Charitable gifts tax credit	26
Child care expenses	1,800
Canada Pension Plan contributions tax credits on employment earnings	215
Medical expenses tax credit	9
Business expenses of earning fitness instruction fees	900
Expenses of objection to a tax assessment	65
Interest on funds borrowed to pay expenses of earning fitness instruction fees	75
Maintenance on rental property	1,100
Mortgage interest on rental property	2,500
Moving expenses	1,700
Non-capital losses from previous year	600
Personal tax credit	1,771
Property tax on rental property	1,000
Employment Insurance premiums tax credit	80
Union dues	100
Canada employment credit	179

You have been asked to:

(A) Determine the income, taxable income and basic federal tax based on the above correct information using the ordering rules in sections 3, 111.1, and 118.92.

(B) Cross-reference each amount to the appropriate section of the Act.

Problem 25

Mr. I.M. Leaving formally separated from his wife early in 2018. Custody of his four children, aged 18, 13, 12, and 11 at the end of 2018, was given to him as part of an agreement worked out with his wife in family court. To make a fresh start, effective March 31, 2018 he resigned his position in Toronto, where he had been employed by the same employer since November 1983, and took a position in Kanata near Ottawa. In previous years, he had always prepared his own tax return, but because of the extraordinary events of 2018, he was having some difficulty with the calculation of his income and taxes payable. He has come to you for help with these calculations, having already correctly calculated his income under Subdivision a, b, and c of Division B as follows:

Subdivision a

Salary (from both employers in 2018)		$75,000
Taxable group term life insurance premium paid by both employers	550	$75,550
Less:		
RPP — (both employers)		(5,100)	$70,450

Subdivision b

Business income: Share of partnership income (drawings of $4,000)			$ 8,500
Property income:			
Net rental loss from apartment building	$(4,500)		
Grossed-up dividends from taxable Canadian public corporations	1,250		
Canada Savings Bond interest	600		
	(2,650)		
Less: interest on loan to buy shares	250	(2,900)	$ 5,600

Subdivision c

Taxable capital gains net of allowable capital losses			
Sale of shares		$ 6,000	
Sale of cottage owned jointly with wife for past 5 years (after principal			
residence exemption)		5,000	
Sale of painting		500	11,500
Total			$87,550

Additional Information

Getting money Add on

(1) He had the following additional receipts during 2018:

A lump-sum payment out of the RPP of his former employer who had made vested contributions for the last 10 years (including 2018) transferred directly to his RRSP	$20,000
A retiring allowance for long service from his previous employer	60,000
	$80,000

(2) He made the following selected payments in respect of 2018:
RRSP contribution for 2018 (Assume earned income in 2017 was the same as for 2018 and his pension adjustment for 2017 was $5,000) $70,000

Legal fees:		
— representation in family court	$4,500	
— appealing a tax assessment, which he lost	1,250	5,750
Charitable donations (consistent with prior years)		$ 1,250
Maintenance payments for wife by virtue of agreement made pursuant to a court order.		
Total of monthly payments for her maintenance	$8,000	
Total of monthly payments directly to owner of her apartment	5,000	13,000
		$90,000

(3) Mr. Leaving had net capital losses of $11,466 in 1999, which he has not used.

(4) Mr. Leaving has never had a capital gain or loss before, nor has he ever claimed any of his capital gains exemption.

(5) Mr. Leaving had the following amounts withheld from his employment wages:

Canada pension plan premiums	$2,594
Employment insurance premiums	$ 858

(6) Mr. Leaving's oldest child, Scott, attends Queen's University and paid $64,000 in tuition fees for eight months of full-time attendance during 2018. Scott earned gross employment income of $2,500 during the summer. No deductions were taken from his pay.

(7) Mr. Leaving's other children do not have any income.

— REQUIRED

Complete the following calculations. Show all calculations whether or not they are necessary to the final answer.

(1) Calculate the Subdivision e deductions for Mr. Leaving.

(2) Calculate his taxable income and show all deductions to arrive at his taxable income.

(3) Calculate his federal taxes payable.

CHAPTER 10 —
DISCUSSION NOTES FOR REVIEW QUESTIONS

(1) There is no ordering that is required to be followed when choosing among the different kinds of losses, except that the oldest losses are always applied first. Generally, the rule of thumb is that the most restricted losses are claimed first. The factors that would have to be taken into account in making this decision are as follows:

ITA: 111(3)(*b*)

(a) Does she have the kind of income needed to offset the losses? She would need net taxable capital gains to offset net capital losses.

(b) Which losses are going to expire first? Net capital losses can be carried back three taxation years and forward indefinitely and non-capital losses can be carried back three taxation years and forward twenty taxation years.

(c) What is the likelihood that she will realize the type of income needed in future years to offset those losses she decides not to claim this year? If she uses up her non-capital losses this year and not her net capital losses, what is the likelihood that she will have a taxable capital gain in the future?

(2) His marginal tax rate on dividend income would be:

Cash dividend	$10,000
Gross-up 38%	3,800
Taxable dividend	$13,800
Federal tax @ 29%	$ 4,002
Dividend tax credit @ $6/11 \times \$3,800$	(2,073)
Basic federal tax	$ 1,929
Provincial tax @ 17% of $13,800	2,346
Provincial dividend tax credit @ $5/11 \times \$3,800$	(1,727)
Total tax	$ 2,548

His marginal tax rate on these dividends is $2,548/$10,000 = 25.48%.

(3) His marginal tax rate on interest income would be:

Interest earned	$10,000
Federal tax @ 29%	$ 2,900
Provincial tax @ 17% of $10,000	1,700
Total tax	$ 4,600

His marginal tax rate on this interest is $4,600/$10,000 = 46%.

(4) Her marginal tax rate on capital gains would be:

Capital gain	$10,000
Taxable capital gain (½)	$ 5,000
Federal tax @ 29%	$ 1,450
Provincial tax @ 17% of $5,000	850
Total tax	$ 2,300

Her marginal tax rate on this capital gain is $2,300/$10,000 = 23%.

(5) The Act allows an artist to designate the proceeds of the piece of art that is not established to be cultural property at anywhere between the cost and the fair market value, in this case between $200 and $8,000. Looking at the two alternatives: ITA: 118.1(7)

(a) if she designates $200 she will report no net income since her proceeds equal her cost. However, she will receive a donation receipt for $200 which is worth a federal credit of $200 × 15% = $30;

(b) if she designated $8,000 as the proceeds, she would report an additional $7,800 in income and pay an additional federal tax of $7,800 × 15% = $1,170. However, she will also receive a donation receipt for $8,000 which will generate a federal credit of $200 × 15% + $7,800 × 29% = $2,292. On a net basis she would have a net federal credit from this alternative of $2,292 − $1,170 = $1,122.

On a net basis, she would be further ahead to designate the full $8,000 as the proceeds. She would receive an incremental benefit of $1,092 (i.e., $1,122 − $30) plus the provincial tax effect.

If the work of art is a cultural gift, the Act deems the artist to have received proceeds of disposition equal to the cost. However, the legislation would entitle the artist to a credit based on the certified fair market value of the work. As a result, no income needs to be reported on the disposition and a credit based on the full value is available.   ITA: 118.1(7.1)   ITA: 118.1(1)

(6) Patricia will receive a personal credit of 15% times the maximum CPP contribution for the year of $2,594. The excess $2,594 will be refunded to her since it will be an overcontribution.   ITA: 118.7

CHAPTER 10 — SOLUTIONS TO MULTIPLE CHOICE QUESTIONS

Question 1

(C) is correct. Since BL is a CCPC and is at arm's length with Brad, the stock option benefit will be included in Brad's income in the year of sale (along with Brad's taxable capital gain). The stock option benefit is $3,000 (($5 – $2) × 1,000). Brad's taxable capital gain is $1,000 (½ × ($7 – $5) × 1,000). Since Brad held the shares for at least two years, he can claim a Division C deduction of $1,500 (½ × his $3,000 option benefit).   ITA: 7(1.1)   ITA: 110(1)(d.1)

(A) incorrectly includes the section 7 benefit in 2016 and ignores the deduction.

(B) incorrectly includes the employment benefit and the incorrectly calculated Division C deduction   (at ¼ of the $3,000 benefit) in 2016.   ITA: 7, 110(1)(d.1)

(D) incorrectly ignores the Division C deduction.   ITA: 110(1)(d.1)

Question 2

(C) is correct and is calculated as follows:

Basic	$11,809		ITA: 118(1)(c)
Age: $7,333 – 15% × ($47,760 – $36,976)	5,715		ITA: 118(2)
Pension	2,000		ITA: 118(3)
Employment	1,195		ITA: 8(10)
	$20,719 × 15% =	$3,108	
Dividend tax credit: ⁶⁄₁₁ × $760		415	ITA: 121
		$3,523	

(A) incorrectly ignores the pension credit and the employment credit: ($11,809 + $5,715) × 15% + $415 = $3,044.   ITA: 118(3), 118(10)

(B) incorrectly ignores the dividend tax credit: ($11,809 + $5,715 + $2,000 + $1,195) × 15% = $3,108.   ITA: 121

(D) incorrectly ignores the income restriction on the age credit: ($11,809 + $7,333 + $2,000 + $1,195) × 15% + $415 = $3,766.   ITA: 118(2)

Question 3

(A) is correct. Shabir's net income and taxable income is calculated as follows:

Scholarship income (exempt)	$ Nil
Employment income	12,000
Moving expenses:	
to McGill University (limited to scholarship income)	Nil
to Toronto	(200)
	$11,800

Since Shabir's income is less than $11,809, (personal tax credit) + $1,195 (employment credit) his   ITA: 118.9
entire tuition credit can be transferred.

Tuition fee	$3,900
	$3,900× 15% = $585

(C) incorrectly computes the credit base as the maximum ($5,000 × 15% = $750).

(B) incorrectly includes the scholarship in income and claims the full moving costs to McGill: $1,500 + $12,000 – $500 – $200 = $12,800. Since this income exceeds $11,809 ($12,800 – $11,809 = $991), then $4,009 ($5,000 – $991) can be transferred resulting in a credit of $601 to a parent.

(D) incorrectly imposes a $2,500 limit: $2,500 × .15 = $375.

Question 4

(A) is correct.

Salary	$ 60,000
Canadian dividends	20,000
Gross-up 38%	7,600
Stock option benefit	200,000
Taxable capital gain (½ × $200K)	100,000
Net income	$387,600
Stock option deduction (½ × $200K)	(100,000)
Taxable income	$287,600
Tax:	
first $205,842	$ 47,669
balance @ 33% of $81,758	26,980
Basic personal amount ($11,809 × 15%)	(1,771)
CPP (15% of $2,594)	(389)
EI (15% of $858)	(129)
Transfer of tuition credits (15% of $5,000 × 3)	(2,250)
Employment (15% of $1,195)	(179)
Dividend tax credit (⁶/₁₁ × $7,600)	(4,145)
Federal tax	$ 65,786

(B) incorrectly omits the gross-up on the dividend and the dividend tax credit: $65,786 – (33% × $7,600) + $4,145 = $67,423

(C) incorrectly omits the dividend tax credit: $65,786 + $4,145 = $69,931

(D) incorrectly omits the stock option deduction: $65,786 + 33% × $100,000 = $98,786

Question 5

(A) is correct.

Taxable income	$287,600
Add:	
30% of capital gain	60,000
³⁄₅ of the stock option deduction	60,000
Deduct:	
Gross-up on dividends	(7,600)
Adjusted taxable income	$400,000
Less: Basic exemption	$(40,000)
Net	$360,000
Minimum tax before minimum tax credit ($360,000 × 15%)	$ 54,000
Basic personal amount ($11,809 × 15%)	(1,771)
Employment ($1,195 × 15%)	(179)
CPP (15% of $2,594)	(389)
EI (15% of $858)	(129)
	$ 51,532

(B) incorrectly deducts the $2,250 transfer of tuition credits:
$51,532 – $2,250 = $49,282.

(C) incorrectly omits the adjustment to add back the stock option deduction:
$51,532 – 15% × $60,000 = $42,532.

(D) incorrectly omits the adjustment to add back the tax-free portion of the capital gain and the stock option deduction: $51,532 – 15% × $120,000 = $33,532.

CHAPTER 10 — SOLUTIONS TO EXERCISES

Exercise 1

(a) Property income

(b) Business income

(c) Employment income

(d) Employment income

(e) Business income

(f) Property income

(g) Employment income

(h) Business income

(i) Business income

(j) Other income

(k) Property income

(l) Employment income

ITA: 3

Exercise 2

	2016	*2017*	*2018*	
(A)				
Income from non-capital sources (≥0):				ITA: 3(*a*)
Property income	$ 1,000	Nil	$ 2,000	
Net taxable capital gains (≥0).				ITA: 3(*b*)
Taxable capital gains				
(see Schedule 1, Part (A), below)	$18,750	$25,000	$ 5,625	
Allowable capital losses	(7,500)	Nil	(11,250)	
	$11,250	$25,000	Nil	
Total income	$12,250	$25,000	$ 2,000	ITA: 3(*b*)
Losses from non-capital source and ABIL:				ITA: 3(*d*)
Property loss	Nil	$(7,000)	Nil	
ABIL	Nil	(15,000)	Nil	
Division B income	$12,250	$ 3,000	$ 2,000	ITA: 3(*e*)
(B) Deduct: Net capital losses (see Schedule 1,				
Part (B) below for maximum)	(441)	Nil	Nil	
Non-capital losses	Nil	Nil	Nil	
Taxable income (max. equal to personal tax credit base)	$11,809	$ 3,000	$ 2,000	

SCHEDULE 1

	2016	*2017*	*2018*	
(A) Net taxable capital gains				
Taxable capital gains (TCG)	$18,750	$ 25,000	$ 5,625	
Allowable capital losses (ACL)	(7,500)	—	(11,250)	
	$11,250	$ 25,000	$ (5,625)	
(B) Net capital losses				ITA: 111(1)(*b*), 111(1.1)(*a*), 111(8)(*a*)

	2016	*2017*	*2018*
Lesser of:			
(i) Net TCGs for the year	$11,250	$25,000	Nil
(ii) Total of adjusted net CLs	$ 7,500	$ 6,577	$6,524
Lesser amount	$7,500	$6,577	Nil

(C) Loss continuity schedule

	2016	2017	Total
Net CL	$ 7,500	$5,625	$13,125
Utilized in 2016	(441)	N/A	(441)
Available in 2019	$ 7,059	$5,625	$12,684

Note: Only $923 of the Net CL was claimed in 2016 to bring taxable income down to equal the personal credit of $11,809 for that year. No Net CL was claimed in 2017 or 2018 as income was below the personal credit level.

Exercise 3

Taxpayer computation of net income for tax purposes		**A**	**B**	ITA: 3, 111
Paragraph 3(*a*)				
Section 5	Employment income	$45,000	$15,000	
Section 12	Interest income	2,000		
Section 9	Net income from a business	5,000		
Paragraph (*d*)	Current-year business loss		(15,000)	
Net income for tax purposes		$52,000	0	
Non-capital loss carryforward				
Current business loss ($18,000) – loss utilized ($15,000) =			$(3,000)	

Charitable donations are a non-refundable tax credit and reduce taxes payable.

Exercise 4

DIVISION B

Par. 3(*a*)	*Subdivision a*			
	Sec. 5	Salary	$ 60,000	
	Par. 6(1)(*a*)	Taxable benefits	3,000	
	Par. 6(1)(*c*)	Director's fees	5,000	$ 68,000
	Less:			
	Par. 8(1)(*i*)	Professional engineering fees	$ 300	
	Par. 8(1)(*m*)	Registered pension plan contributions	4,000	4,300
				$ 63,700
	Subdivision b			
	Sec. 9	Business income — share of partnership tax profits	$ 10,000	
	Par. 12(1)(*c*)	Canadian bank interest	3,000	13,000
	Subdivision d			
	Par. 56(1)(*a*)	Retiring allowance		20,000
		Total par. 3(*a*) income		$ 96,700
Par. 3(*b*)	*Subdivision c*			
	Par. 38(*a*)	Taxable capital gain	$ 20,000	
	Par. 38(*b*)	Allowable capital loss	(2,000)	18,000
				$114,700
Par. 3(*d*)	*Subdivision b*			
	Ssec. 9(2):	Rental loss		
		Rental revenue	$ 25,000	
		Less: Expenses		
		Par. 20(1)(*c*) Mortgage interest	(23,000)	
		Par. 18(1)(*a*) Taxes and insurance	(4,500)	
		Par. 18(1)(*a*) Maintenance	(1,500)	(4,000)
Division B income				$110,700
Par. 111(1)(*a*)	Non-capital loss		$ 4,000	
Par. 111(1)(*b*)	Net capital loss		5,000	(9,000)
Taxable income				$101,700

Federal tax after credits

Tax on $93,208 .... $ 16,544

Tax on next $8,492 @ 26% 2,208

    Tax before credits .... $ 18,752

Sec. 118(1)	Personal credits	(3,543)
Sec. 118(10)	Canada employment credit	(179)
Sec. 118.7	CPP contributions credit	(389)
Sec. 118.7	EI premium credit	(129)
Sec. 118.5	Tuition credit	(68)
Sec. 118.1	Charitable donation credit	(550)

Basic federal tax .... $ 13,894

Exercise 5

(A) Personal tax credits   ITA: 118

Basic personal tax credit base	$11,809		ITA: 118(1)(a)
Dolly's tax credit base: $11,809 – $3,000	8,809		ITA: 118(1)(a)
Don:[1] over 18 years old and not infirm	Nil		ITA: 118(1)(d)
Dave: Canada caregiver credit base:[2]	6,986		ITA: 118(1)(d)
Mother: Canada caregiver credit base[3]	6,986		ITA: 118(1)(c.1)
Total tax credit base[4]	$34,590		
Total personal tax credits @ 15%	$ 5,189		

— NOTES TO SOLUTION

[1] Don's father may claim the transferred tuition fee credits, since Don's income tax will be completely offset by his basic personal tax credit.   ITA: 118.9(1)

[2] Because Dave is an adult child (18 and over), the base is $6,986.

[3] Base is $6,986.   ITA: 118(4)(d)

[4] An impairment tax credit of $1,235 ($8,235 × 15%) is also available in respect of the mother and son Dave, if their impairment is certified by a medical doctor.   ITA: 118.3(1)

Exercise 6

$300 contribution is an employment deduction.   ITA: 8(1)(m)

$800 is pension income.   ITA: 56(1)(a)

A pension credit is not available since the amount is not from a life annuity, as required in the definition of "qualified pension income".   ITA: 118(3), 118(7)

Exercise 7

Tax payable by Tina:

Division B income and taxable income		$10,144
Federal tax 15% of $10,144		$ 1,522
Less: basic personal tax credit	$1,771	
other tax credits (age ($1,084), pension (15% of $350))	1,137	(2,908)
Federal tax payable		Nil

CHAPTER 10

Transferable tax credits available:

Age credit (15% of $7,333)	$1,100
Pension credit (15% of $350)	53
Total credits available to Tina's husband	$1,153
Less: federal tax payable net of basic personal tax credit ($1,507 – $1,771)	—
	$1,153

Exercise 8

Income increased by grossed-up dividend ($900 × 1.38)			$1,242
Increase in federal tax @ 29% of $1,242			$ 360
Less increase in tax credits:			
Married credit with election [15% of ($11,809 – nil)]	$ 1,771		
Married credit without election [15% of ($11,809 – $1,242)]	(1,585)	$ 186	
Dividend tax credit (⁶/₁₁ × $342)		187	373
Net federal tax reduction			$ 13

ITA: 82(3)

Therefore, the election should be made in this case, although it is marginal.

ITA: 82(3)

Exercise 9

Federal foreign tax credit

lesser of:

$$\text{(i)} \quad \$225$$

$$\text{(ii)} \quad \frac{\$1,500}{\$156,800 - \$6,000} \times (\$31,707 + \$62^*) = \underline{\$316} \quad \left.\right\} \ \$225$$

---

* The dividend tax credit is equal to ⁶/₁₁ of the gross-up of $114 (i.e., 0.38 × $300).

Exercise 10

	Regular Part I Tax			Minimum Tax	
(A) $100 interest	($100 × .33)		$33	($100 × .15)	$15
(B) $100 cash dividend					
($138 grossed up)	$138 × .33	$46		($100 × .15)	$15
	DTC	(21)	$25		
(C) $100 capital gains ($50 taxable capital gains)	($50 × .33)		$17	($50 + $30) × .15	$12

Exercise 11

Jacob's marginal tax rate is 41% (26% + 15%) where the provincial marginal tax rate is assumed to be 15%.   ITA: 117(2), 120

Exercise 12

Taxable income		$ 98,200
Add: CCA loss on resource property shelter		103,200
		$201,400
Less: gross-up of dividends		(11,400)
Adjusted taxable income		$190,000
Less: Basic exemption		$(40,000)
Net		$150,000
Minimum tax before minimum tax credit (15% of $150,000)		$ 22,500
Less basic minimum tax credits:		
Basic personal (15% × $11,809)	$1,771	
Employment Insurance premiums	129	
CPP contributions	389	
Employment	179	2,468
Minimum amount		$ 20,032

Betty's Part I tax will be her minimum amount of $20,032 with $10,876 ($20,032 − $9,156) carried forward and applied to reduce tax payable in a subsequent year.

Exercise 13

Since Mr. and Mrs. Ataila were resident in Canada for 245 days, their non-refundable tax credits will be prorated by $^{245}/_{365}$. For Mr. Ataila this includes the basic personal tax amount of $11,809 and the spousal amount of $11,809, and the Canada Employment credit of $1,195. Mr. and Mrs. Ataila are considered residents of Canada only for the time since May 1, and will be taxed on their worldwide income. Any income earned during the four months prior to May 1 that they were non-resident will not be subject to tax in Canada.   ITA: 118, 63

The child care expenses are only deductible if Mrs. Ataila has earned income, is in attendance of full-time studies at an educational institution, or is mentally or physically unable to care for the children. If Mrs. Ataila attended full-time studies in order to obtain a job in the workforce, then her husband may claim the child care expenses.

CHAPTER 10

Exercise 14

Pierino's taxable income is:

ITA: 118, 63

Salary from Saskatoon Transit	$ 65,000	
Business farm loss	(5,250)	
Taxable capital gain	2,000	(50% ($10,000 – $6,000))
Total income	$ 61,750	
RRSP contribution	(10,000)	
Net income	$ 51,750	
Net capital losses forward	(2,000)	(maximum of taxable capital gains)
Taxable income	$ 49,750	
Personal tax credit base amounts		
Basic personal tax credit base	$ 11,809	
Canada employment credit	1,195	
Eligible dependant (ETM)	11,809	
	$ 24,813	

Exercise 15

		2016	*2017*	*2018*
Par. 3(*a*)	— Sum of all incomes from non-capital sources:			
	Employment income	$ 15,000	$ 20,000	$ 25,000
	Rental income	4,000	—	2,000
	Other business income	—	15,000	14,000
	Total par. 3(*a*)	$ 19,000	$ 35,000	$ 41,000
Par. 3(*b*)	— LPP	—	—	$ 1,000[1]
	— PUP	$ 2,500	—	1,000
	— Other	3,000	$ 6,000	(2,000)
	Total par. 3(*b*)	$ 5,500	$ 6,000	Nil
Par. 3(*a*) + par. 3(*b*)		$ 24,500	$ 41,000	$ 41,000
Par. 3(*c*)		(9,000)	(9,000)	(9,000)
Net		$ 15,500	$ 32,000	$ 32,000
Par. 3(*d*)	— ABIL	—	—	(1,500)[2]
	— Business loss	(32,000)	—	—
	— Rental loss	—	(2,000)	—
	Division B income	Nil	$ 30,000	$ 30,500
	Par. 111(1)(*b*) — net capital loss[3]	$ (5,500)	(6,000)	Nil
	Par. 111(1)(*a*) — non-capital loss[4]	—	(11,527)	(17,865)
		Nil	$ 12,473	12,635

— *NOTES TO SOLUTION*

(1) The 2017 listed personal property loss of $7,000 was applied to the listed personal property gains of 2016 ($5,400), leaving $1,600 to be applied to 2018 which resulted in a capital gain of $2,000 of which 1/2 was included in income.

(2) ABIL — $\frac{1}{2} \times$ BIL ($3,000) minus disallowed portion (nil) = $1,500

(3) Lesser of:

	2016	*2017*	*2018*
(i) Net TCGs for the year	$ 5,500	$ 6,000	Nil
(ii) Total adjusted net CLs*	$15,333	$ 9,833	$ 3,833
Lesser amount	$ 5,500	$ 6,000	Nil

* Net capital loss continuity schedule:

Unadjusted net CL from 1999	$23,000
Adjusted to 2016 inclusion rate (x $\frac{4}{3} \times \frac{1}{2}$)	$15,333
Utilized in 2016	(5,500)
Available in 2017	$ 9,833

Utilized in 2017	(6,000)
Available in 2018	$ 3,833
Realized in 2018 [$2,300 – ($1,000 + $1,000)]	300
Available for carryforward	$ 4,133

(4) Non-capital loss — 2015 . . . . $ 42,000

2016 Subsection 111(8) non-capital loss:

Business loss for the year (2016)	$32,000	
Add: net capital loss claimed	5,500	
Less par. 3(c)	(15,500)	
Non-capital loss for 2016 (carry forward to 2017)		22,000
2017 application* ($24,000 – $11,635 – 1,178)		(11,187)
Carried forward to 2018		$ 52,473
2018 application* ($30,500 – $11,809 – 1,195)		(17,496)
Balance		$ 35,317

* This amount leaves enough taxable income to be offset by the personal tax credit and the Canada employment amount

Exercise 16

Subsection 82(3) election decision	*With election*	*No election*
Mrs. Struggles income ($2,340 – $1,200)	$1,140	$2,340
Add: dividend gross-up (0.38 × $1,200)	—	456
Deduct: untaxed fraction of capital gain (½ × $500)	(250)	(250)
Add: non-deductible PUP loss	200	200
Division B and taxable income	$1,090	$2,746
Federal tax @ 15%	$ 164	$ 412
Less basic personal tax credit	1,771	1,771
Federal tax payable	Nil	Nil
Mr. Struggles married tax credit [eligible for family caregiver]:		
15% of [$13,991 – $1,090]	$1,935	
15% of [$13,991 – $2,746]		$1,687

In this particular case, the following will be the effects on Mr. Struggles tax of making ssec. 82(3) election:

Increase in taxable income by wifes grossed-up dividend (1.38 × $1,200)		$1,656
Increase in federal tax @ 20.5% of $1,656		$ 339
Less increase in tax credits:		
Married ($1,935 – $1,687)	$ 248	
Dividend tax credit (⁶⁄₁₁ × $456 (gross up))	249	497
Decrease in basic federal tax		$ 158

Therefore, the subsection 82(3) election should be made.

Mr. Struggles basic federal income tax:

Income:

Employment	$40,000
Consulting income	6,000
Canadian interest	750
Grossed-up dividends [1.38 × ($200 + $1,200)]	1,932
U.S. interest income ($425/.85)	500
Taxable capital gains (½ × $350)	175
Division B income	$49,357
Less: Net capital loss¹	(175)
Taxable income	$49,182
Federal tax: ($6,991) + (20.5% of ($49,182 – $46,605))	$ 7,519

Less tax credits:

Basic personal		$1,771
Spouse, 15% of [$11,809 – $1,090]		1,608
Spouse, Canada caregiver credit		327
Canada employment credit		179
Annes transfer[2]		750
Spousal transfer of unused credits		
Disability	$1,217	
Less: federal tax net of basic personal tax credit	Nil	1,217
Charitable gifts		
15% of first $200	$ 30	
29% of balance ($420 – $200)	64	94
		5,946
Dividend tax credit (6/11 × $532 (gross up))	290	6,236
Basic federal tax		$1,283

— *NOTES TO SOLUTION*

(1) Lesser of:

(i) Net taxable capital gains for the year (1/2 × $350)	$ 175	
(ii) Total of adjusted net capital losses ($4,000 × ½ × ⁴/₃)	$2,667	
Lesser amount		$ 175

(2) Annes income:

Employment income — Subdivision a		$5,140
Interest income		100
Scholarship (not taxable)		Nil
		$5,240
Less: Moving expenses (limited to $nil to school*, $400 returning for summer job)		400
Income (Division B) and taxable income		$4,840

Tuition credit transfer:

Lesser of: (a) $750		
(b) 15% × ($6,100) =	$ 915	$ 750
federal tax (15% × $4,840)	$ 726	
less: personal tax credit	(1,771)	
Canada employment credit	(1,794)	
CPP tax credit (15% × $81)	(12)	
EI tax credit (15% × $854)	(13)	Nil
		$ 750

* Scholarship income is not taxable

Exercise 17

(A)

Regular Part I tax on first $46,605		$ 6,991
on next 17,395 @ 20.5%		3,566
$64,000		$10,557
Less personal tax credits:		
Basic personal	$1,771	
Canada employment credit	179	
Employment Insurance premiums (15% of $858)	129	
CPP contributions (15% of $2,594)	389	
Charitable donations		
15% of $200	$ 30	
29% of ($780 – $200)	168	198
Dividend tax credit (8/11 × $690 (gross up))	502	3,168
Basic federal tax		$ 7,389

Less: foreign tax credit
    lesser of:
      (a) $1,500

      (b) $\dfrac{\$10,000}{\$64,000} \times (\$7,389 + \$502) = \$1,233$ 1,233*

                                               $ 6,156

* The unused foreign taxes paid of $1,500 – $1,233 can be claimed on a provincial tax return subject to a similar formula to the federal formula above and any balance still not claimed can potentially be claimed under ss. 20(11) as a deduction in computing income.

Exercise 18

Mrs. Smith's income as given in the question		$48,120
Dividend gross-up $9,000 × 0.38		3,420
RRSP deductions:		
Par. 60(j.1) Lesser of (i) the retiring allowance received $10,000		
(ii) $2,000 × 2 years = $4,000		(4,000)
Undeducted contributions = 12,000 + 5,000 – 4,000 = $13,000		
Par. 60(i) Least of (i) $26,230		
(ii) 18% × $32,000 = ...	$ 5,760	
Unused deduction room at end of 2017	4,000	
	$ 9,760	(9,760)
Net income		37,780
Division C deduction		0
Taxable income		$37,780
Federal tax $37,780 × 15%		$ 5,667
Non-refundable tax credits:		
Basic	$11,809	
Age $7,333 – 15% × ($37,780 – $36,976) =	7,212	
	19,021	
	× 15%	(2,853)
Canada employment credit		(179)
CPP & EI		(153)
Dividend tax credit ($^6/_{11}$ × $3,420 (gross up))		(1,865)
Federal tax payable		$ 617

Exercise 19

Federal non-refundable Tax Credits		
Basic		$11,809
Wholly dependent person [equivalent to spouse] for one child under age 18 with		
no income		11,809
Tuition fee amount transferred from 22-year-old*		5,000
		$28,618
		@15%
		$ 4,293
*Tuition fees paid	$5,000	
Child's taxable income	$ 8,000	
Less: basic amount	(11,809)	Nil
Tuition Fees available for transfer		$5,000
Maximum transferable		$5,000

Exercise 20

Charitable Donations
Cancer society . . . . $ 100
Church   4,000
University of Waterloo   1,000
United Way   3,000

	$8,100	200 @ 15%	$ 30
		7,900 @ 29%	2,291
			$2,321

Political Donations
Liberal Party of Canada . . . . $ 200
Conservative Party of Canada   200
                                                                                            $ 400

Credit equal to 75% of the first $400 . . . . $ 300

Exercise 21

Employment income	$ 15,000
Interest income	$ 600
	$ 15,600
Less: Allowable Business Investment Loss (par. 3(*d*))	$ 2,500
Taxable income for 2018	$ 13,100

Allowable business investment loss

Proceeds of disposition (500 × $2)	$ 1,000	
Adjusted cost base (500 × $20)	$10,000	
Business investment loss (par. 39(1)(*c*))	$ 9,000	
Less:		
Disallowed portion of BIL (ssec. 39(9))		
⁴⁄₃ × capital gains deduction claimed in 1991 (⁴⁄₃ × $1,000)		
+ ⁴⁄₃ × capital gains deduction claimed in 1993 (⁴⁄₃ × $2,000)	$(4,000)	
	$ 5,000	
multiplied by inclusion rate for 2018	×½	
Allowable business investment loss (par. 38(*c*))	$ 2,500	

Exercise 22

Scenario #1

(a) Subparagraph 69(1)(*b*)(i) will deem Adam's proceeds to be equal to the fair market value of the rental building, $900,000.

Adam will have recaptured depreciation of $100,000 (UCC of $400,000 less the lower of cost, $500,000, and proceeds, $900,000).

Adam will have a taxable capital gain of $200,000 (½ × $900,000 – $500,000)).

(b) The ACB of the asset to Adam's daughter will be the amount she paid for the building — $850,000 — since the Act does not make a corresponding adjustment to her ACB.

(c) There will be no attribution of annual rental income back to Adam under ssec. 74.1(2) because his daughter is over 18 years of age. When his daughter disposes of the building, the capital gain will not attribute back to Adam.

Scenario #2

(a) Since the sale is to a spouse, ssec. 73(1) will apply to deem Adam's proceeds of disposition to be equal to his cost of $50,000 so that no loss will arise on the disposition. If Adam elected out of ssec. 73(1) for proceeds of $40,000, the capital loss would be denied as a superficial loss under sec. 54.

(b) Adam's wife's ACB is also $50,000 due to ssec. 73(1). If Adam elects out of ssec. 73(1) the superficial loss of $10,000 is added to the adjusted cost base of $40,000 for a total of $50,000.

(c) The dividend received and the capital loss arising on the disposition of the shares by Adam's wife will be attributed back to Adam under provisions 74.1 and 74.2, respectively.

Section 74.5 exempts from the attribution rules income or capital gains arising from property transferred for proceeds equal to fair market value (i.e., $40,000 cash) provided that the transferor elects that ssec. 73(1) not apply.

Scenario #3

(a) Subparagraph 69(1)(*b*)(ii) provides that an *inter vivos* gift by Adam to any person results in deemed proceeds of disposition equal to the fair market value of the gift. Therefore, Adam will realize a capital loss of $10,000. The superficial loss definition in sec. 54 will not apply to deny the loss to Adam.

(b) The nephew's ACB is also the FMV of $40,000 by virtue of par. 69(1)(*c*).

(c) Subsection 74.1(2) attributes to Adam the income on the shares transferred to any related minor or niece or nephew (in this case the $4,000 dividend received by the nephew). However, there is no attribution of capital gains realized on property transferred to minors. The dividend attribution will cease in the year the nephew turns 18.

Chapter 11

Computation of Taxable Income and Tax After General Reductions for Corporations

Learning Goals

Know

By the end of this chapter you will know:

- The key components in the calculation of taxable income and tax payable for a corporation.

Understand and Explain

By the end of this chapter you will understand and be able to explain:

- Why the various items in Division C are deductible.
- How loss carryovers are restricted.
- How an acquisition of control impacts a corporation.
- Why the various taxes and tax reductions are part of the tax system.

Apply

By the end of this chapter you will be able to apply your knowledge and understanding to:

- Calculate taxable income including the carryover of losses.
- Calculate basic tax payable for a corporation.
- Calculate the tax consequences of an acquisition of control.

Review Questions
¶11,800 in the Study Guide

Multiple Choice Questions
¶11,825 in the Study Guide

Exercises
¶11,850 in the Study Guide

Assignment Problems
¶11,875 in the Study Guide

CHAPTER 11 — LEARNING CHART

Problem Descriptions

Textbook Example Problems

11-1	Calculate non-capital loss
11-2	Calculate taxable income and loss carryovers
11-3	Non and net capital losses
11-4	Acquisition of control
11-5	Acquisition of control
11-6	Acquisition of control
11-7	Calculate taxable income
11-8	Provincial abatement
11-9	Foreign tax credit
11-10	Investment tax credit
11-11	Investment tax credit

Multiple Choice Questions

1	Acquisition of control — year end
2	Acquisition of control — loss recognition
3	Acquisition of control — deemed CCA
4	Acquisition of control
5	Calculate taxable income
6	Calculate federal tax payable

Exercises

1	Calculate taxable income
2	Maximizing charitable donations
3	Calculate non-capital losses
4	Calculate net capital losses
5	Calculate net and non-capital losses
6	Calculate taxable income
7	Calculate taxable income
8	Acquisition of control
9	Business foreign tax credit
10	Calculate Part I tax — various sources of income
11	Investment tax credit
12	Acquisition of control
13	Federal Abatement & Permanent establishment
14	Acquisition of control

Assignment Problems

1	Taxable income
2	Permanent establishment
3	R&D
4	Income from business with SR&ED
5	Tax payable, ITC
6	Acquisition of control
7	Acquisition of control
8	Acquisition of control
9	Schedule 1 reconciliation and taxable income
10	Tax payable — provincial allocation
11	Tax payable
12	Tax payable

Problem Descriptions

13	Acquisition of loss company
14	Acquisition of control

Study Notes

Question 4

For its year ended December 31, 2017, its first year end since its incorporation, Lakehead Co. (Lakehead) reported the following income (losses) for tax purposes.

Business loss (retailer of widgets)	$ (20,000)
Capital loss	(6,000)

On January 1, 2018, Pacific Co. acquired control of Lakehead from an unrelated person and transferred its profitable gadget retailing business to Lakehead. For its year ending December 31, 2018, Lakehead is expected to have the following income/losses.

Business loss (widgets)	$ (3,000)
Business income (gadgets)	15,000
Taxable capital gain on sale of capital asset	6,000

Assuming widgets and gadgets are similar products, which one of the following statements is TRUE?

(A) For its year ending December 31, 2018, Lakehead will be able to deduct net capital losses of $3,000, provided the widget retailing business is carried on throughout the taxation year ended December 31, 2018 with a reasonable expectation of profit.

(B) For its year ending December 31, 2018, Lakehead will be able to deduct non-capital losses of $18,000 (maximum), provided the widget retailing business is carried on throughout the taxation year ended December 31, 2018, with a reasonable expectation of profit.

(C) For its year ending December 31, 2018, Lakehead will be able to deduct non-capital losses of $12,000 (maximum), provided the widget retailing business is carried on throughout the taxation year ended December 31, 2018, with a reasonable expectation of profit.

(D) For its year ending December 31, 2018, Lakehead will be able to deduct non-capital losses of $15,000 (maximum), provided the widget retailing business is carried on throughout the taxation year ended December 31, 2018, with a reasonable expectation of profit.

Question 5

During 2018, Curran Ltd, a public corporation, has net income for tax purposes of $600,000, including $100,000 of dividends from taxable Canadian corporations and $500,000 of retailing profits. It made $200,000 of charitable donations during the year. Income earned in a province was 90%.

What is Curran Ltd's taxable income for the year?

(A) $600,000

(B) $500,000

(C) $400,000

(D) $300,000

Question 6

Refer to the facts given in Question 5, above. What is Curran Ltd.'s federal tax payable for the year?

(A) $22,000

(B) $48,000

(C) $87,000

(D) $52,500

¶11,850   EXERCISES

Exercise 1

ITA: 110.1, 111

Generous Limited has income (loss) under Division B of $(7,350) in 2016 $22,050 in 2017, and $14,700 in 2018. During this period it made donations to registered charities of $2,625 in 2016, $4,700 in 2017, and $12,000 in 2018. It also made a donation of ecologically sensitive land valued at $19,700 to the Government of Canada in 2017. The company began operations in 2016.

— REQUIRED

Compute the corporation's taxable income for the years indicated.

Exercise 2

ITA: 110.1, 111

Determined Limited predicts, with reasonable accuracy, its income under Division B before capital cost allowances will be: $100,000 in 2016, $115,000 in 2017, and $132,250 in 2018. Capital cost allowances available are expected to be $200,000 in 2016, $170,000 in 2017, and $150,000 in 2018. It made charitable donations of $10,000 in 2012 and $11,500 in 2013, which it could not absorb before 2016.

— REQUIRED

How can the company maximize its charitable donation deduction while minimizing the taxes it pays in the period shown? (Hint: Take advantage of the loss carryover rules.)

Exercise 3

ITA: 111(8)

TPM Limited has computed the following income (loss) for the year ended December 31, 2018:

Loss from business	$(129,000)
Income from property including dividends of $10,750 received from taxable Canadian corporations	32,250
Capital gains	46,400
Capital losses	(12,000)
Business investment loss	(16,000)

The corporation has a net capital loss of $27,000 arising from 2012.

— REQUIRED

Compute the corporation's non-capital loss for the year.

Exercise 4

ITA: 111(8)

CLR Limited had a large allowable capital loss of $51,750 on one transaction during its current taxation year ended December 31. In addition, the following information pertains to its situation for the year:

Income from business	$155,250
Income from property	17,000
Taxable capital gain	4,700
Allowable business investment loss (not included in above allowable capital loss)	(8,300)

— REQUIRED

Compute the corporation's net capital loss for the year.

¶11,850

Exercise 5

ITA: 111(1), 111(1.1)

Abigail Corporation has income from business of $55,500 and a taxable capital gain of $37,000 in 2018. It also has the following losses:

Non-capital losses (expiring beyond 2018) . . . . $ 82,500
Net capital losses (2012) . . . . $ 40,000

— *REQUIRED*

How much of the above losses will be available for carryforward after this year?

Exercise 6

ITA: 3, 110.1–112

Reconsider the example problem of FT Limited in this chapter in ¶11,160. If $3,378 less capital cost allowance had been taken in 2017, all $23,000 of the inter-company dividends could have been deducted, pursuant to section 112, in 2017.

— *REQUIRED*

Recalculate the taxable income of the corporation for the years indicated after taking $7,900 less in capital cost allowance for Class 8 in 2017. Comment on whether the corporation is in a better tax position at the end of 2017 with respect to capital cost allowance and taxable income under this alternative.

Exercise 7

ITA: 110.1, 111, 112

Plego Limited, a Canadian corporation, had its net income under Division B computed as follows for the year ending December 31:

Par. 3(a)	Income from non-capital sources:		
	Income from business operations	$ 66,625	
	Income from foreign property	7,175	
	Dividends from taxable Canadian		
	corporations	12,300	
Par. 3(b)	Net taxable capital gains	30,750	
Income under Division B	$116,850	

During the year the corporation made charitable donations of $80,000. Its carryforward position from the previous year was as follows:

Charitable donations $10,250
Non-capital losses 61,500
Net capital losses (realized in 2012) 27,000

— *REQUIRED*

Compute the corporation's taxable income for the current year.

Exercise 8

ITA: 111(4), 111(5), 111(5.1), 249(4)

In 2015, a chain of bakeries, called Buscat Ltd., commenced operation. The industry is highly competitive and because of Mr. Buscat's lack of marketing skills, the corporation incurred losses in the first three taxation years of operations as follows:

Taxation year end	Non-capital losses (business)	Capital losses
Dec. 31, 2015	$60,000	$12,000
Dec. 31, 2016	45,000	8,000
Dec. 31, 2017	25,000	4,000

On July 1, 2018, Mr. Buscat decided to sell 75% of his common shares to Mr. Bran, owner of Buns Plus Ltd. Mr. Bran has been in the business of supplying bread dough, pastry dough and bun bags for 10 years and has been very successful. Buns Plus Ltd. has two divisions: a bakery and a coffee shop, which it intends to transfer to Buscat Ltd.

The following income tax data relates to Buscat Limited's operations from January 1, 2018 to June 30, 2018:

(a) Business loss (before inventory valuation) $10,000
(b) Allowable capital loss   2,000
(c) Property loss (assets sold in April)   5,500
(d) Assets at June 30, 2018:

	Cost/ACB	UCC	FMV
Inventory	$ 85,000	—	$ 65,000
Land	155,000	—	195,000
Building (Class 1: 4%)	65,000	$45,000	75,000
Bakery equipment	100,000	86,000	70,000

During the later part of the 2018 calendar year, the bakery/coffee shop of Buns Plus Ltd. was transferred to Buscat Ltd. For the six-month period ending on December 31, 2018, Buscat Limited had net income of $90,000 from all its businesses.

The net income earned was as follows:

Buscat bakery . . . . $(55,000)
Buns Plus bakery   130,000
Coffee shop   15,000
                                                                                                    $ 90,000

In the 2019 taxation year, Buscat Ltd. expects to earn $250,000, of which $65,000 will be from the original Buscat bakery business and $20,000 from the coffee shop business.

Prepare an analysis of the income tax implications of the acquisition of shares. In your analysis, consider the two election options from which an election choice is most likely to be made.

Exercise 9

ITA: 126

Exporter Limited is a Canadian public company carrying on a part of its business through an unincorporated branch in Japan. Its income from that business in Japan for the current taxation year ended December 31 was 54,025,200 yen. The corporation paid income tax instalments on that income during the year of 21,610,080 yen. During the year the exchange rate was 1 yen = C$0.01131.

During its current taxation year ended December 31, Exporter's income under Division B was $2.5 million excluding the income from Japan. During the year, the corporation received dividends of $100,000 from taxable Canadian corporations. This amount was included in the computation of Division B income. The corporation was also able to deduct $25,000 of its net capital losses carried forward. There was no foreign investment income during the year. Taxable income earned through a permanent establishment in Canada comprises 75% of total taxable income.

— REQUIRED

Compute the corporation's foreign business tax credit for the year.

¶11,850

Exercise 10

ITA: 110–112, 123, 124, 125.1, 126, 127

Maxprof Limited is a Canadian public company with the following income under Division B for its taxation year ended December 31, 2018:

Wholesaling income	$1,495,000
Foreign business profits (before $36,800 in taxes paid)	115,000
Dividends from taxable Canadian corporations	517,500
Dividends from foreign investments (before $25,875 in taxes withheld)	172,500
Canadian interest income (investment income)	345,000
Income under Division B	$2,645,000

During the year the company made donations of $69,000 to registered charities and $5,750 to federal political parties. It was carrying forward non-capital losses of $127,600. It is considered to earn 86% of its taxable income in Canada, as computed by the Regulation.

— *REQUIRED*

Compute the federal Part I tax payable for the year.

Exercise 11

ITA: 127

Consider the following data:

Qualified current expenditures eligible for investment tax credit . . .	$90,000
Taxable income before qualified current expenditures	$300,000
Federal tax rate after abatement and reduction	15%

— *REQUIRED*

Compute the amount of the investment tax credit that will be deductible for the year and the net federal Part I tax payable after the investment tax credit.

Exercise 12

Computer Rental Ltd., a computer rental business, commenced operations in 2016 with a December 31 year end. A highly competitive market and an unstable corporate sales force resulted in losses being incurred for 2016 and 2017 as follows:

	2016	*2017*
Non-capital/business losses	$75,000	$90,000
Net capital/allowable capital losses	40,000	80,000

On January 1, 2018, Processing Ltd., a company carrying on a work station rental business, purchased 55% of the shares of Computer Rental Ltd. The President and Vice-president of Computer Rental Ltd. were replaced by personnel from Processing Ltd. and extensive training programs, which had been highly successful in Processing Ltd., were given to the sales force of Computer Rental Ltd.

In June 2018, Processing Ltd. transferred a profitable division of its work station operation to Computer Rental Ltd. which continued to carry on the computer rental business.

At the time of the acquisition of the shares, Computer Rental Ltd. had the following assets:

	Cost	*UCC/CEC*	*FMV*
Marketable securities	$ 120,000	—	$ 70,000
Land	150,000	—	450,000
Building	600,000	$400,000	400,000
Furniture & fixtures	200,000	160,000	165,000
Computers	1,200,000	480,000	200,000

In 2018, Computer Rental Ltd. earned net income of $65,000, as follows:

Computer rental operations	$25,000
Work station rental operations	40,000
Total	$65,000

The computer rental operation was discontinued by Computer Rental Ltd. in 2019 as the work station rental operation was more profitable. No income was earned from the computer rental operation in 2019, but income of $85,000 was earned from the work station rental operation in that year.

— *REQUIRED*

(A) What are the income tax implications of the acquisition of shares of Computer Rental Ltd. by Processing Ltd. on the assumption that Processing Ltd. is confident that non-capital losses of Computer Rental Ltd. can be utilized in future years?

(B) To what extent are the non-capital losses of Computer Rental Ltd. deductible in the computation of its taxable income for 2018 and 2019? (Ignore the assumption in part (A)).

Exercise 13

Canco Inc. is a Canadian corporation with its head office in Ontario. Its factory premises and a warehouse are also located in Ontario. The company manufactures metal containers which are sold throughout Canada and the United States.

The company rents public warehouse space in Saskatoon, Saskatchewan and in Poughkeepsie, New York. The company has no employees at the warehouses. All goods are handled by warehouse personnel.

The company has a Canadian sales force responsible for all Canadian sales. A sales representative is employed in each province and reports to a sales manager in Ontario. Each sales representative operates from his home, and the companys name does not appear on the premises. The company does not reimburse the sales representatives for any portion of the costs of operating from their homes. All orders are submitted to head office for credit approval. Head office provides the appropriate warehouse with shipping instructions.

The company employs a sales representative in Poughkeepsie. This employee also operates from his home. His address and telephone number are listed in the Poughkeepsie phone book under the companys name. The company reimburses him for the cost of household expenses related to the use of his home office. The employee is authorized to accept orders on behalf of the company. He also arranges shipments.

In addition to taxable income of $300,000, Canco has provided the following information with respect to its fiscal year ended December 31:

Sales:

Saskatchewan warehouse	$ 3,000,000
Poughkeepsie warehouse	2,000,000
Ontario warehouse	5,000,000
Total	$10,000,000

The Saskatchewan warehouse makes shipments to all provinces west of Ontario. The Ontario warehouse sells to all other provinces and its sales also include $250,000 of shipments to a customer in Florida. The Poughkeepsie warehouse ships only within the U.S.

Salaries and wages:

Factory	$1,000,000
Sales	300,000
Administrative	200,000
Total	$1,500,000

All factory and administrative salaries are paid to employees in Ontario. The sales salaries include $20,000 to each of the 10 provincial sales representatives and $100,000 to the U.S. sales representative.

— *REQUIRED*

(A) Determine where Canco has permanent establishments by reference to the *Income Tax Act* and applicable Regulations. Where relevant, state your reasons for determining why Canco does not have a permanent establishment in a particular place.

(B) Based on your conclusion in (A), compute the taxable income allowable to each province and the United States, and the amount deductible under subsection 124(1) from corporate tax otherwise payable. Show all calculations.

Exercise 14

As the auditor of Mother Ltd. (Mother), you have been asked to draft a memorandum to the president to explain the future deductibility of loss carryovers of its wholly-owned subsidiary, Childco Ltd. (Childco). Mother acquired Childco on January 1, 2018, when Childco was experiencing financial difficulties. Childco manufactures paper products, whereas Mother is a wholesaler of office supplies and equipment. Both companies are Canadian-controlled private corporations and have December 31 year ends.

The loss carryovers of Childco are:

	Non-Capital Losses	Net Capital Losses
2013	$300,000	$ 50,000
2014	250,000	—
2015	200,000	—
2016	150,000	100,000
2017	50,000	—

On December 31, 2017, Childco had the following assets, which are still on hand:

	Cost or Capital Cost	UCC–Dec. 31 2017	FMV–Dec. 31, 2017
Land	$ 700,000	N/A	$1,000,000
Building	600,000	$ 500,000	400,000
Manufacturing Equipment	1,000,000	NIL	300,000
Patent (Cl. 14)	125,000	100,000	20,000

— *REQUIRED*

Draft a memorandum to the president explaining the deductibility and the amount of the loss carryovers which are available in the 2018 year.

¶11,875 ASSIGNMENT PROBLEMS

Type 1 Problems

Problem 1

ITA: 3, 110.1–112

The following data summarize the operations of Red Pocket Limited for the years of 2015 to 2018 ended September 30.

	2015	2016	2017	2018
Income (loss) from business	$54,000	$32,000	$(75,000)	$62,500
Dividend income — Taxable Canadian corpora-tions	42,500	22,500	18,000	10,500
Taxable capital gains	11,000	2,500	5,000	9,000
Allowable capital losses	2,000	4,500	3,500	—
Allowable business investment loss	3,750	—	—	—
Charitable donations	23,000	9,000	3,000	13,000

The corporation has a net capital loss balance of $9,000 which arose in 2012.

Compute the taxable income for Red Pocket Limited for the years indicated and show the amounts that are available for carryforward to 2019.

Problem 2

ITA: 124; ITR: 400

The taxpayer, whose head office was in Manitoba, manufactured and sold various fans. Local sales agencies were maintained in Ontario and in Quebec. At the Ontario agency, two qualified representatives handled business under the company name. They were authorized to sign quotations. Contracts could be made, terms of payment arranged and credit given without reference to the head office in Winnipeg. The company name was displayed for public visibility, was used on calling cards, and was listed in the telephone directory. The Ontario agency, occupying one-half of a building with warehouse facilities, maintained an inventory worth about $6,000. Orders for standard-sized fans were filled from stock-in-trade. Orders for large fans were filled from the head office in Winnipeg. The Quebec agency was substantially similar to that in Ontario.

You have been asked to determine whether or not the company has a "permanent establishment" in the provinces of Ontario and Quebec. In reaching a conclusion, you should compare this situation with the case of *M.N.R. v. Sunbeam* discussed in this chapter.

61 DTC 1053 (Ex. Ct.)

Problem 3

ITA: 37; ITR: 2900(2), 2900(3), 2903

Old Tech Inc. has been in business for many years. Recently, it has been significantly impacted by its competitors who are using technology to improve their products and take market share. As a result, this year, for the first time ever, they are expecting to record a loss for the year. Also, they have spent $150,000 in research to create new products that can compete effectively. These expenditures qualify as scientific research and experimental development for tax purposes. For accounting purposes this has been expensed. How should it be treated for tax purposes?

Problem 4

Joe's Widget Manufacturers Inc. (JWMI) is an established manufacturing company with a growing research and development (R&D) department. JWMI is a Canadian-controlled private corporation with no associated companies. The research part of the business is new and the company's accountant has no experience dealing with the tax implications of the expenditures in this area. He has correctly computed the company's net income for tax purposes before specific R&D related adjustments as $615,000 and would like your input on the impact of the transactions described below.

For the year ended December 31, 2018, the following R&D related expenditures were made.

Description	Amount
Purchase of lab machinery and lab equipment	$450,000
Purchase of a new building to house laboratory	120,000
Salaries of lab staff	100,000
Operating costs directly related to the lab	40,000

For financial accounting purposes, the salaries and operating costs, net of the investment tax credit below, have been expensed. The lab machinery, equipment and building are used 100% for R&D

activities. The lab machinery and equipment have been capitalized for accounting purposes and are being amortized over an eight-year period. Thus, amortization expense of $56,250 was recorded for accounting purposes on the lab machinery and equipment. Amortization expense was recorded on the building. Capital cost allowance for the lab machinery and equipment in Class 53 has been deducted in computing net income for tax purposes.

The company is eligible for investment tax credits at a rate of 15% and has correctly determined that they are eligible for investment tax credits at this rate on all of the above expenditures with the exception of capital expenditures. For accounting purposes, the company's accountant has netted the investment tax credits against the related expenditures as follows.

Expenditure	Gross amount	ITC	Amount recorded for accounting purposes
Lab machinery and equipment . . .	$450,000		$450,000
Building	120,000		120,000
Salaries of lab staff	100,000	15,000	85,000
Operating costs of lab	40,000	6,000	34,000

You have been asked to explain to JWMI's accountant what adjustments are necessary to compute income for tax purposes for the years ended December 31, 2018 and 2019.

Problem 5

ITA: 12(1)(*t*), 37, 127(5)–(11); ITR: 2900

Infotech is a public company in its first year of business in the information technology industry. It operates out of a plant in Ottawa, Ontario. In 2018, it incurred $2.2 million of SR&ED expenses which qualifies for deduction under subsection 37(1) of the Act.

Infotech's federal income tax rate after abatement is 15%. Its income before deducting the $2.2 million claim under section 37 is $3.2 million.

You have been asked to:

(A) Compute the maximum investment tax credit available to Infotech in 2018.

(B) Compute the company's net federal Part I tax payable after the investment tax credit, assuming a maximum section 37 deduction is claimed.

(C) Determine the amount, if any, of the investment tax credit carryover.

(D) Compute the company's deduction or income inclusion in the following year if no further SR&ED expenditures are made.

Problem 6

The president of Purchaser Inc. (Purchaser) is planning to have the company acquire all the shares of Target Inc. (Target) on September 1, 2018. He has asked you to calculate what losses will be available in Target after he acquires it and explain the future deductibility of those losses after the purchase. Target manufactures paper products, whereas Purchaser is a wholesaler of office supplies and equipment. Both companies are Canadian-controlled private corporations and have August 31 year ends.

The loss carryovers of Target are expected to be as follows:

	Non-Capital Losses	Net Capital Losses
2014	$300,000	$ 50,000
2015	250,000	—
2016	200,000	—
2017	150,000	100,000
2018	50,000	—

On August 31, 2018, Target will have the following assets which are still on hand:

	Cost or Capital Cost	UCC	FMV
Manufacturing Equipment	1,000,000	NIL	300,000

Problem 7

ITA: 111(4), 111(5), 111(5.1), 111(5.2)

All of the voting shares of Lofty Limited, a manufacturer of widgets, have been acquired by Holdco Ltd., an investment holding company. At the time of the acquisition on March 10, 2018, Lofty Limited had non-capital business losses of $600,000 generated in 2017. Lofty Limited also had $20,000 of net capital losses carried forward from 2012. As well, at the time of the acquisition, it was discovered that the balance of undepreciated capital cost in its Class 8 was $70,000 while the fair market value of the assets in that class was only $40,000. The UCC balance in Class 14.1 (being from the acquisition on January 5, 2018, of an exclusive customer list for $60,000) was $58,500 while the fair market value of the customer list was $63,000. The corporation's inventory had a cost of $630,000, while its market value was $680,000. The book value of the corporation's receivables was $240,000, while its realizable value was estimated at $225,000. The corporation's only non-depreciable capital property, land, had accrued gains of $56,000 over its cost of $200,000. Lofty Limited has a December 31 year end.

The corporation had business losses of $3,000 from January 1 to March 9, 2018. This amount includes the normal calculation of cost of goods sold.

The holding company will inject added capital and augment the management of Lofty Limited in an attempt to turn Lofty's widget manufacturing business around.

What are the tax implications of the acquisition of the shares of Lofty Limited by Holdco Ltd., assuming the maximum election under paragraph 111(4)(e) is made?

Determine the minimum amount of elected proceeds under paragraph 111(4)(e) to offset expiring losses, if the accrued gains on the land were $100,000 instead of the $56,000 and Lofty Limited had an additional loss arising from property of $10,000.

Type 2 Problems

Problem 8

On November 1, 2018, Chris purchased all the issued shares of Transtek Inc. from an acquaintance, Tom. Transtek carries on a transmission repair business and has done so since its incorporation on January 1, 2017. In addition to the transmission repair business, Transtek rents out a small building it owns. Neither the transmission repair business nor the rental endeavour has been successful.

When Chris purchased Transtek, his financial projections indicated that Transtek would have significant income within two years. Chris credited Transtek's failure to Tom's brash personality and laziness. Chris, on the other hand, has a strong work ethic and has many contacts in the automotive industry to refer work to him.

The values of the capital assets owned by Transtek at the time of purchase by Chris are as follows:

	Repair shop		Rental property	
	Land	Building	Land	Building
FMV	$140,000	$230,000	$70,000	$120,000
Cost/ACB	80,000	150,000	90,000	120,000
UCC	—	147,000	—	120,000

Chris selected June 30, 2019, as the first fiscal year end for Transtek after his purchase. The following is a schedule of Transtek's income (and losses) from its inception, January 1, 2017 through June 30, 2020.

Period	Transmission repair business	Rental income (loss)	Capital Loss
Jan. 1/2017–Dec. 31/2017	$ (40,000)	$(2,000)	$ (10,000)
Jan. 1/2018–Oct. 31/2018	(60,000)	(5,000)	—
Nov. 1/2019–June 30/2019	(25,000)	6,000	—
July 1/2020–June 30/2020	54,000	11,000	—

You have been asked to discuss the tax implications of the acquisition of Transtek Inc. on November 1, 2018, ignoring all possible elections/options.

In addition, you have been asked to determine the tax consequences of the acquisition of Transtek Inc. under the assumption that:

(i) the maximum amount of all elections/options is utilized; and

(ii) the partial amount of all elections/options is utilized so that only enough income is generated to offset most or all of the losses which would otherwise expire on the acquisition of control.

Problem 9

ITA: 9–20, 38–55, 110.1–112, 111(4), 111(5), 111(5.1), 249(4)

The controller of Video Madness Inc., a Canadian public corporation, has prepared the accounting income statement for the year ended April 30, 2018:

VIDEO MADNESS INC.

INCOME STATEMENT

FOR THE YEAR ENDED APRIL 30, 2018

Sales		$995,000
Cost of sales	$523,000	
Administrative expenses	185,000	(708,000)
Operating income		$287,000
Other income and expenses		55,000
		$342,000
Provision for income taxes		(102,000)
Net income		$240,000

Other Information

(1) Included in the calculation of "Administrative expenses":

    (a) Interest on late income tax payments .... $ 435

    (b) Amortization (maximum capital cost allowance of $149,500) 104,900

    (c) Club dues for the local Country Club 1,750

    (d) Federal political contributions 2,500

    (e) Donations to registered charities 22,500

    (f) Property tax with respect to vacant land not being used
        in the course of the business 3,000

    (g) Life insurance premium with respect to the president
        (the company is the beneficiary; not required for financing) 1,950

(2) Included in the calculation of "Other income and expenses":

    (a) Landscaping of ground around new premise 4,800

    (b) Fees paid with respect to the investigation of a suitable site for the
        company's manufacturing plant 5,500

    (c) Dividends received from taxable Canadian corporation 42,800

    (d) Gain from the sale of another piece of land, used in the business, sold
        for $200,000 in March (purchased for $73,800) 126,200

    (e) Loss on sale of investments held as capital property purchased for
        $85,000 and sold for $75,000 10,000

(3) Loss carryforwards from 2017 are:

    (a) Non-capital losses 73,800

    (b) Net capital losses (realized in 2012) 50,000

You have been asked to prepare a schedule reconciling the accounting net income to income for tax purposes and taxable income. Indicate the appropriate statutory reference for your inclusions or exclusions.

Problem 10

No SBD   No MAP   ITA: 123, 124, 126

Barltrop Limited is a Canadian public company involved in the software consulting business. Its controller provided you with the following information related to its 2018 taxation year ended December 31:

Income under Division B from consulting business including $100,000 earned in U.S. operations (before deducting $16,000 U.S. tax paid)	$264,000
Canadian investment royalty income	10,000
U.K. non-foreign affiliate dividend income (before $3,000 tax withheld)	20,000
Taxable dividend received from non-connected Canadian corporations	5,000
Taxable capital gains.	6,000
Charitable donations	100,000
Unused foreign tax credit in respect of U.S..	3,000
Net capital losses carried forward arising in 2012	8,000

Barltrop Limited has permanent establishments in the United States, British Columbia, and Alberta. Its gross revenues and salaries and wages data have been allocated as follows:

	British Columbia	Alberta	United States.
Gross revenues.	$3,000,000	$3,000,000	$4,000,000
Salaries and wages.	500,000	300,000	200,000

Assume that the British Columbia and Alberta corporation tax rates are both 10%. Also, assume that taxable income for British Columbia and Alberta is computed on the same basis as federal taxable income.

Gross revenues exclude income from property not used in connection with the principal business operation of the corporation.

Federal & provincial

You have been asked to calculate the total tax payable by the company for the 2018 taxation year, including provincial tax. Show all calculations.

Problem 11

ITA: 123, 124, 125.1, 126, 127(5)

Up, Up and Away Limited is a public corporation that distributes hot air balloons in the Province of New Brunswick. For the year ended September 30, 2018, its accounting income statement was as follows:

Sales	$1,225,000
Cost of sales and other expenses including CCA	(725,000)
Operating profit	$ 500,000
Other income	198,500
Net income before taxes	$ 698,500
Provision for taxes	(200,725)
Net income	$ 497,775

Selected Additional Information

(1) Other income includes:

Dividends from taxable Canadian corporation	$ 85,000
Canadian interest income	52,500
Foreign interest income, net of withholding taxes of $10,000	61,000

(2) Up, Up and Away Limited has a non-capital loss carryforward of $255,545.

(3) Donations to registered charities were $9,755 (deducted from accounting income).

You have been asked to calculate the total taxes payable for 2018 using an 11% provincial rate of tax.

Problem 12

ITA: 123, 124, 125.1, 126, 127(5)

Tecniquip Limited is a public corporation whose head office is located in Toronto, Ontario. The activities of the corporation are carried on through permanent establishments in the provinces of Ontario and Alberta.

For the year ended December 31, 2018, Tecniquip Limited obtained the following results:

Income from distribution operations in Ontario	$1,000,000
Income from distribution operations in Alberta	1,040,000
	$2,040,000
Canadian-source interest income (investment)	32,000
Taxable capital gain	10,000
Taxable dividends from taxable Canadian corporations	15,000
Net income under Division B	$2,097,000

In computing income from distribution, the corporation claimed a deduction of $150,000 under subsection 37(1) of the Act for SR&ED. No SR&ED expenditures are expected to be made in 2019.

During the year, the corporation made charitable donations totalling $50,000 and claimed non-capital losses of $60,000 and the net capital losses carried forward from 2013 of $6,000.

You have been asked to calculate the federal Part I tax payable. Show all calculations, whether or not necessary to your final answer.

Type 3 Problems

Problem 13

Ian King has operated a successful office supply wholesaling business, King Enterprises Inc., for many years. Last week, he called to tell you that he is interested in putting an offer in on the shares of a company that is in some financial difficulty, Royal Forms Inc. ("Royal").

Royal is in the business of producing custom, as well as standard, forms for business use. In fact, Royal is a supplier of King Enterprises. This company has been in business for the past eight years, but has been losing money for the past six years. Last year they sold the land and building they used in their operations in a depressed real estate market, in order to get some cash. Their big problem seems to be that they are undercapitalized.

Ian sees this purchase as a real opportunity for him to pick up a company at a bargain price, turn it around to profitability and, at the same time, reduce King Enterprises' tax liability with the losses. He would like you to prepare a report for him on the tax issues before he decides whether to make an offer.

Problem 14

Style Ltd., a retailer of ladies' fashion athletic shoes, commenced operations in 2016 with a December 31, year end. The market for athletic shoes is highly competitive and because of Style Ltd.'s lack of funds to spend on advertising and lack of good contracts in the industry, the corporation incurred losses in its first years of operations as follows:

	2016	*2017*
Non-capital losses	$175,000	$225,000
Net capital losses	Nil	Nil

On April 1, 2018, 80% of the shares of Style Ltd. were acquired by Pro Ltd. Pro Ltd. has been in the business of retailing ladies' fashion shoes for a number of years and has been very successful. A number of years ago, Pro Ltd. had the opportunity to acquire a warehousing operation, which it did. This has also been a very lucrative business. In 2017 alone, Pro Ltd.'s income from these two businesses was in excess of $1,000,000.

Pro Ltd. intends to inject additional capital and augment the management of Style Ltd. Pro Ltd. is certain that with its expertise, it will be able to turn Style Ltd.'s business around and make it profitable within 12 months.

CHAPTER 11

An interim financial statement was prepared for Style Ltd. for the period January 1, 2018 through March 31, 2018. From this, it was determined that Style Ltd. had incurred a business loss of $5,500 for the three months.

The values of the assets owned by Style Ltd. on March 31, 2018 were as follows:

	Cost	UCC	FMV
Land	$500,000	$ —	$700,000
Building	90,000	90,000	105,000
Store fixtures and equipment	30,000	26,000	23,000
Inventory	45,000	—	40,000
Market securities	9,000	—	3,000

On September 1, 2018, Pro Ltd. transferred its warehousing business division to Style Ltd., which also continued to carry on its retailing business.

At its year ending December 31, 2018, Style Ltd. had net income of $375,000, all of which was earned during the period April 1, 2018 to December 31, 2018. The income was derived from the following sources:

Warehousing business (September 1 through December 31)	$390,000
Retailing of ladies' athletic shoes (loss)	(20,000)
Taxable capital gain on marketable securities	5,000
	$375,000

Although the business of retailing ladies' athletic shoes was projected to earn a small profit for 2019, Style Ltd. discontinued the business as of February 28, 2019. The profit from retailing ladies' shoes for the 2 months of operation in 2019 was $7,000. The reason for discontinuing the business was to enable management to spend more time on the warehousing operation which was growing fast. In 2019, the warehousing operation was projected to generate income of $950,000.

— REQUIRED

(a) What are the income tax implications of the acquisition of shares of Style Ltd. by Pro Ltd.?

(b) To what extent are the losses of Style Ltd. deductible in 2018 and 2019?

CHAPTER 11 —
DISCUSSION NOTES FOR REVIEW QUESTIONS

(1) Charitable donations are tax credits only on personal tax returns. On corporate tax returns they are deductions under Division C. Donations up to 75% of net income plus 25% of the amount of a taxable capital gain and 25% of recapture in respect of gifts of capital property with appreciated value can be deducted in the year. If the charitable donations are in excess of this amount then the excess can be carried forward for five years.

ITA: 110.1

(2) Income can be increased in the current year by not claiming some of the optional deductions for tax purposes. For example, the deductions for the allowance for bad debts, CCA, CECA or scientific research and experimental development expenditures can be fore-gone in order to increase income. These deductions will be available in future years and will not be lost. Also, the CRA will allow the revision of some permissive deductions for prior years. In addition, the company could consider the sale of any redundant assets to generate income through recapture and/or capital gain.

IC 84-1

(3) Where there has been an acquisition of control, the corporation cannot carry over its net capital losses. To the extent that the corporation has *net* taxable capital gains in the year, it may take an optional deduction of net capital losses which may in turn increase the amount of non-capital losses. Accrued capital losses are deemed to be realized in the deemed year end immediately preceding the acquisition of control. However, there may be some relief because the corporation is allowed to trigger, on an elective basis, enough unrealized accrued capital gains to use up the net losses that are going to expire.

ITA: 111(4), 111(8)

(4) The first restriction is on the type of income against which the loss carryover can be deducted, and the second restriction is on the number of years a loss can be carried over.

Net Capital Losses: Applied against taxable capital gains only; carried back 3 years and forward indefinitely.

Non-capital Losses: Applied against all sources of income; carried back 3 years and forward 20 taxation years.

(5) The deemed year end applies whenever there is an acquisition of control even if the company acquired is not a loss company. Mr. Magee will not be able to claim a full year of CCA since CCA is prorated for a short fiscal year.

ITR: 1100(3)

(6) The three main objectives are:

(a) alleviate double taxation;

(b) prevent the avoidance of tax through the use of a corporation; and

(c) provide tax incentives to corporations.

See the text in ¶11,210 of Chapter 11 for details.

(7) The gross revenue from that sale will be attributed to Alberta since, even though the sale was handled from Ontario, the order was delivered to a province in which the company had a permanent establishment.

ITR: 402(4)(*a*)

(8) The theory is that the country where the income is earned has the first right to tax the income. Then, in order to prevent double taxation when Canada also taxes this income, a credit is given in Canada for the foreign taxes paid.

CHAPTER 11

(9) Investment income may be taxed in the foreign country even though there is no permanent establishment in that country. Canada assumes that this investment income, other than from real property, is earned through its permanent establishment in Canada and, therefore, considers this income to be earned in a province for purposes of section 124. Foreign business income, on the other hand, is assumed to be earned in a permanent establishment in the foreign country and, therefore, is not eligible for the federal abatement.

(10) Since Lossco does not have any net income or Canadian income tax, it cannot claim a foreign tax credit. No carryover is allowed for non-business income tax. However, the corporation can deduct the foreign taxes which will increase its loss for the year. This deduction will at least provide the benefit of the foreign taxes being carried forward as part of the non-capital losses.

ITA: 126(1)
ITA: 20(12)

CHAPTER 11 — SOLUTIONS TO MULTIPLE CHOICE QUESTIONS

Question 1

(B) is correct. Loss Co may select any date, within the 53-week period commencing February 1, 2018, as its new year end.　　ITA: 249(4)(*b*), 249(4)(*d*)

(A) is incorrect, as the taxation year is deemed to have ended immediately before control was acquired. Since control was acquired on February 1, 2018, the year is usually deemed to have ended January 31, 2018. (Technically, it is possible to have an acquisition of control occur at a specific time, say, 10 a.m. on February 1, in which case, the taxation year can be deemed to have ended on February 1 at 9:59 a.m. Usually, a time is not specified, in which case, the taxation year is deemed to end the day before.)　　ITA: 249(4)(*a*)

(C) is incorrect because the corporation is deemed not to have established a fiscal period yet. This being the case, the corporation is free to select any year end, within the 53-week limitation.　　ITA: 249(4)(*d*)

(D) is incorrect for the same reason as (C).

Question 2

(C) is correct. The ACB of the land is reduced from $200,000 to $140,000, its FMV. The $60,000 reduction is deemed to be a capital loss for the taxation year ended May 14, 2018.　　ITA: 111(4)(*c*), 111(4)(*d*)

(A) is incorrect as it includes the $25,000 accrued loss on the building which is depreciable property. Capital losses on depreciable assets are specifically disallowed.　　ITA: 111(4)(*c*)

(B) is incorrect as it includes the $20,000 accrued loss on the inventory which is not a capital property.

(D) is incorrect, because the $60,000 accrued loss on the land was reduced by the $10,000 accrued gain on the marketable securities. The recognition of the accrued gain on the marketable securities is not required. An election is available to recognize the accrued gain, if it is desirable.　　ITA: 111(4)(*e*)

Question 3

(C) is correct. The UCC of the Class 50 computer equipment is reduced by $5,000, from $38,000 to $33,000. The UCC of the Class 8 office furniture and equipment is reduced by $10,000, from $58,000 to $48,000. The total of the two reductions, $15,000, is deemed to have been claimed as CCA in the year ended March 31, 2018.　　ITA: 111(5.1)

(A) is incorrect as this amount adjusts the UCC of all the classes to the FMV of the classes. This amount includes an adjustment of $8,000 to increase the UCC of the Class 10 automobiles and the Class 12 assets to the FMV of the respective classes. The $8,000 is then subtracted from the $15,000 reduction calculated in (C). This is incorrect. The adjustment applies only to the classes where the UCC is higher than the FMV.　　ITA: 111(5.1)

(B) is incorrect as it includes only 72% of the adjustment calculated in (C).

(D) is incorrect for the same reason as (A). The difference between (A) and (D) is that in (D) the positive and negative adjustments have been totalled, whereas in (A) they have been netted.

Question 4

(D) is correct. For its year ending December 31, 2018, Lakehead Co. will be able to deduct non-capital losses of $15,000 (maximum), provided the widget retailing business is carried on throughout the taxation year ended December 31, 2018 with a reasonable expectation of profit.　　ITA: 111(5)(*a*)

(A) is incorrect as net capital losses incurred prior to the acquisition of control expire on the date control is acquired.　　ITA: 111(4)(*a*)

(B) is incorrect. Non-capital losses realized prior to an acquisition of control cannot be deducted against taxable capital gains incurred after the acquisition of control. Non-capital losses are only deductible against income from the business in which the losses were incurred and income from a similar products or services.　　ITA: 111(5)(*a*)

(C) is incorrect. The non-capital loss deduction has been limited to the income from a similar products or services net of the loss from the widget business. The netting of the widget business loss is not required.　　ITA: 111(5)(*a*)

CHAPTER 11

Question 5

(D) is correct.

Net income for tax purposes	$ 600,000
Canadian dividends	(100,000)
Charitable donations	(200,000) – not exceeding $450,000 (75% of net income)
	$ 300,000

ITA: 112

ITA: 110.1

(A) incorrectly makes no adjustments: $600,000.

(B) incorrectly omits the deduction for charitable donations: $600,000 – $100,000 = $500,000.

(C) incorrectly omits the section 112 deduction for Canadian dividends: $600,000 – $200,000 = $400,000.

Question 6

(B) is correct.

Taxable income as per the answer to Question 5	$300,000
Part I tax on taxable income	
Tax @ 38% on $300,000	$114,000
Deduct: Federal tax abatement (10% × 90% × $300,000)	(27,000)
	$ 87,000
Deduct: 13% rate reduction (13% of $300,000)	(39,000)
Total federal tax..	$ 48,000

(A) incorrectly applies the rate reduction to $500,000 of business income: $87,000 – 13% of $500,000 = $22,000.

(C) incorrectly omits the 13% rate reduction.

(D) incorrectly calculates the rate reduction as 11.5% × $300,000 rather than 13% × 300,000: $87,000 – 11.5% of $300,000 = $52,500.

CHAPTER 11 — SOLUTIONS TO EXERCISES

Exercise 1

	2016	2017	2018
Income under Division B	$(7,350)	$22,050	$14,700
Deduct: charitable donations limited by 75% of income above			
— carried forward	Nil	$ 2,625	Nil
— current	Nil	Nil 4,700 (7,325)	$11,025[1](11,025)
unlimited charitable donation			
— carried forward	Nil	—	$ 3,675
— current	Nil	Nil $14,725[2](14,725)	— (3,675)[3]
non-capital loss from 2016[4]	Nil	Nil	Nil
Taxable income	Nil	Nil	Nil

— *NOTES TO SOLUTION*

[1] Limited to 75% of $14,700 = $11,025; $975 is available to carry forward five years to 2023.

[2] If the donation of the land gave rise to a capital gain, the taxable portion would be included in the amount of income under Division B.

[3] $1,300 ($19,700 – $14,725 – $3,675) is available to carry forward four more years to 2022.

[4] $7,350 is available to carry forward 20 taxation years to 2036.

Exercise 2

	2016	2017	2018
Option A: Claiming maximum charitable donations			
Income before CCA	$ 100,000	$115,000	$132,250
CCA	(200,000)	(101,667)[1]	(116,917)
Income (loss) under Division B	$(100,000)	$ 13,333	$ 15,333
Charitable donations:			
— Carried forward	Nil	(10,000)[1]	(11,500)[1]
— Current	Nil	Nil	Nil
Non-capital loss carried forward from 2016	N/A	(3,333)	(3,833)[2]
Taxable income	Nil	Nil	Nil
Option B: Non-capital loss utilization			
Income before CCA	$100,000	$115,000	$132,250
CCA	(107,167)[3]	(86,333)	(132,250)
Income (loss) under Division B	$ (7,167)	$ 28,667	Nil
Charitable donations:			
— carried forward	Nil	(21,500)	Nil
— current	Nil	Nil	Nil
Non-capital loss carried forward from 2016	N/A	(7,167)[3]	Nil
Taxable income	Nil	Nil	Nil
Option C: Maximum donation and non-capital loss utilization			
Income before CCA	$100,000	$115,000	$132,250
CCA	(107,166)	(101,667)	(116,917)
Income (loss) under Division B	$ (7,166)	$ 13,333	$ 15,333
Charitable donations:			
— Carried forward	Nil	(10,000)[4]	(11,500)[4]
— Current	Nil	Nil	Nil
Non-capital loss carried forward from 2016	N/A	(3,333)	(3,833)
Taxable income	Nil	Nil	Nil

● *Summary*

	Options		
	A	B	C
Total donations claimed	$ 21,500	$ 21,500	$ 21,500
Total CCA claimed	418,584	325,750	325,750
Unclaimed non-capital loss	92,834	Nil	Nil

— NOTES TO SOLUTION

[1] CCA amount selected to provide sufficient Division B income for a deduction of charitable donations (maximum of 75% of Division B income). The 2012 charitable donations would, otherwise, expire after 2017.

[2] $92,834 of non-capital loss from 2016 remains.

[3] Determined by looking forward to 2017 and creating the maximum non-capital loss in 2016 that can be fully utilized in 2017.

[4] Uses the five-year carryforward of charitable donations to the maximum — i.e., the $11,500 donations of 2013 may be carried forward to 2018, as in Option A.

Exercise 3

Sum of: loss from business		$129,000
allowable business investment loss		8,000
dividends deductible under sec. 112		10,750
net capital loss deducted [$27,000 − $17,200 = $9,800 remaining]		17,200[1]
		$164,950
Less: income from property	$32,250	
net taxable capital gains [½ × ($46,400 − $12,000)]	17,200[1]	(49,450)
Non-capital loss for the year		$115,500

— NOTE TO SOLUTION

[1] The corporation may deduct the net capital loss from income even though it has no impact on the taxable income. However, the deduction is restricted to the net taxable capital gain for the year. Once deducted, the net capital loss can be included in the non-capital loss computation.

Exercise 4

Allowable capital loss (excluding ABIL)	$ 51,750
Less: taxable capital gain	(4,700)
Net	$ 47,050
Add: unutilized allowable business investment loss in respect of which the carryover period expires in the year (i.e., the 20th carryforward year)	Nil
Net capital loss for the year	$ 47,050

Exercise 5

	Option A[1]	Option B[1]
Income from business	$55,500	$55,500
Taxable capital gains	37,000	37,000
Income under Division B	$92,500	$92,500
Less: net capital losses	(37,000)[2]	(10,000)[2]
non-capital losses	(55,500)	(82,500)
Taxable income	Nil	Nil
Summary:		
Unutilized non-capital losses	$27,000	Nil
Unutilized net capital losses	3,000[2]	$30,000[2]

— NOTES TO SOLUTION

(1) In Option A, maximum net capital losses are claimed before non-capital losses. In Option B, maximum non-capital losses are claimed before net capital losses.

(2)

	Option A	Option B
2012 net capital loss	$40,000	$40,000
Utilized in 2018 (limited to TCG)	(37,000)	(10,000)
Available to carryforward	$ 3,000	$30,000

Exercise 6

	2017		2018	
Net income (loss) per financial accounting statements	$(53,000)		$126,000	
Add total of items not deductible for tax purposes	127,700		240,700	
	$ 74,700		$366,700	
Less CCA ($3,378 less in 2017)	51,700		51,316	
Income for tax purposes	$ 23,000		$315,384	
Inter-company dividends	$23,000		$23,000	
Charitable donations (max. 75% of income):				
Carried over	—		15,000	
Current	Nil		15,000	
Non-capital loss carryover	—	23,000	18,000	71,000
Taxable income		Nil		$244,384
Taxable income originally computed		Nil		$245,060

Conclusion:

This calculation produces better results. All of the inter-company dividends are fully deductible in 2017 with the reduction of the capital cost allowance by $3,378. Both options allowed, in total, an equal amount of non-capital losses and donations to be claimed over the two-year period. Although the original calculation enabled $2,702 (i.e., $55,078 + $50,640 − $51,700 − $51,316) more capital cost allowance to be claimed in total over the two years, the original calculation could not utilize $3,378 of the potential dividend deduction. This alternative increases the future CCA write-offs by $2,702 as shown below.

	Building *Class 1: 6%*	*Equipment* *Class 8: 20%*
Capital cost allowances were computed as follows:		
2018: UCC, January 1, 2018	$ 246,667	$ 182,578*
CCA (total deduction: $51,317)	(14,800)	(36,516)
2019: UCC, January 1, 2019	$ 231,867	$ 146,062
UCC originally computed	$ 231,867	$ 143,360

* $179,200 + $3,378.

Exercise 7

Division B income		$116,850
Less: charitable donations limited to 75% of $116,850 or $87,638		
— carried forward	$10,250	
— current	77,388[1]	(87,638)
dividends from taxable Canadian corporations		(12,300)
subtotal		$ 16,912
non-capital losses[2]		(16,912)
net capital losses[2] (not to exceed the taxable capital gains for the year)		(Nil)
Taxable income		Nil

— *NOTES TO SOLUTION*

[1] The balance of $2,612 in current charitable donations may be carried forward to the next five years.

[2] These carried-over losses may be claimed in a different sequence and in different amounts from that shown. For example, if there is little prospect of future capital gains, the corporation might make the following deductions:

subtotal	$16,912
net capital losses	(27,000)
non-capital losses	Nil
taxable income	Nil

The balance of the net capital losses may be carried forward indefinitely.

Net capital losses claimed are added to the non-capital loss balance carried forward.

Exercise 8

The data given in the problem statement can be summarized as follows:

carryforward losses	non-capital losses	net capital losses	expiration after deemed year-end
2015	$60,000	$6,000	
2016	45,000	4,000	
2017	25,000	2,000	
	$130,000	$12,000	→$12,000

current deemed year-end losses	from non-capital sources	allowable capital losses	
ACL		$2,000	→ 2,000
business—operations	$10,000		
—inventory	20,000		
—equipment terminal loss	16,000		
	$46,000		
property	$5,500		→ 5,500
			$19,500

potential elections	business income	taxable capital gain
recapture—building	$20,000	
TCG—land		$20,000
—building		5,000
		$25,000

The two election options to consider are the maximum election and the partial election.

(a) Maximum Election

If the maximum election is made, the $20,000 of recapture offsets the business loss, leaving $26,000 (i.e., $46,000 – $20,000) of net business loss. The $25,000 of taxable capital gain offsets the $19,500 of expiring losses, leaving $5,500 (i.e., $25,000 – $19,500) to offset the remaining $26,000 of business loss, leaving $20,500 of that business loss. As a result, the non-capital loss available for carry forward from June 30, 2018 is $150,500 (i.e., $20,500 + $130,000).

(b) Partial Election

If only a partial election is made to offset the $19,500 of expiring losses, the current business loss of $46,000 is not offset and, hence, is available to carry forward, along with the $130,000 of non-capital losses, from June 30, 2018 for a total of $176,000. If the election is made on the land, the ACB of the land can be increased without a tax cost.

(c) No Election

Note that if no election is made there is no income to offset the current business loss of $46,000 or the non-capital loss carryforward of $130,000. Therefore, the non-capital loss available to carry forward from June 30, 2018 is $176,000 (i.e., $46,000 + $130,000), which is the same as in the partial election, but there is no increase in any cost value.

Deemed Year end

Buscat Ltd. is deemed to have a taxation year ending June 30, 2018, immediately before the acquisition of control by Buns Plus Ltd. on July 1, 2018 [ssec. 249(4)]. Tax returns will have to be filed for this short taxation year (i.e., six months) and amounts such as CCA will have to be prorated. In addition, the short taxation year will cause the counting of a carryforward year for the non-capital losses from 2015, 2016, and 2017.

Loss from Non-Capital Sources

Losses from non-capital sources for the deemed taxation year ended June 30, 2018, before any elections and options are computed as follows:

CHAPTER 11

Loss from business			$ 10,000
Add: Inventory loss [ssec. 10(1)] ($85,000 – $65,000)			20,000
Bakery equipment — Deemed CCA ($86,000 – $70,000)			16,000
Total business losses			$ 46,000
Add: Property loss (will expire unless utilized by June 30, 2018)			5,500
Total losses from non-capital sources			$ 51,500

Maximum Election

Division B income and taxable income

Par. 3(a)	Income from non-capital sources			Nil
Par. 3(b)	Net taxable capital gains:			
	Election on land [($195,000 – $155,000) × ¹/₂]		$ 20,000	
	Election on building [($75,000 – $65,000) × ¹/₂]		5,000	
			$ 25,000	
	Less: Allowable capital loss		(2,000)	
Par. 3(c)	Sum of par. 3(a) plus par. 3(b) less any Subdivision e deductions (nil)			$ 23,000
Par. 3(d)	Property loss	$ 5,500		
	Business losses	46,000		
		$ 51,500		
	Less: Building recapture	(20,000)	31,500	
Sec. 3 income				Nil
Division C deductions:				
Net capital losses:	2015		$ 6,000	
	2016		4,000	
	2017		2,000	$ 12,000
Taxable income				Nil

Non-capital losses available for carryforward after acquisition of control:

Balance — July 1, 2018			
2015 non-CL		$ 60,000	
2016 non-CL		45,000	
2017 non-CL		25,000	$ 130,000
Non-CL from deemed taxation year before acquisition of control:			
Total par. 3(d) loss (see above calculation)		$ 31,500	
Add: Net capital loss deducted		12,000	
		$ 43,500	
Less: Par. 3(c) income above		(23,000)	20,500
Total non-capital losses			$ 150,500

The $150,500 loss carryforward balance must "reasonably be regarded as its loss from carrying on a business."

2015, 2016, and 2017 loss carryforwards from a business as stated in the question			$ 130,000
June 30, 2017 business loss net of recapture		$ 26,000	
Less portion of this loss used against par. 3(c) income*		(5,500)	20,500
			$ 150,500

* Par. 3(c) income			$ 23,000
Less:			
Property losses	$ 5,500		
Net capital losses restored as business losses	12,000	(17,500)	
		$ 5,500	

The non-capital losses will expire in 20 taxation years, including the deemed taxation year, from the year of the loss as follows, assuming that Buscat Ltd.'s fiscal year end after the acquisition of control returns to December 31.

2015 non-CL — on December 31, 2034

2016 non-CL — on December 31, 2035

2017 non-CL — on December 31, 2036

2018 deemed taxation year — on December 31, 2037

The adjusted cost base/capital cost of the properties which were deemed to be sold at their fair market values would be:

	Capital Cost	UCC	Adjusted Cost Base
Bakery Equipment	$100,000	$ 70,000	$100,000
Land	n/a	n/a	195,000
Building* (Class 1)	70,000	70,000	75,000

*65,000 + ½ ($75,000 – $65,000).

In order for these non-capital losses to be deductible in subsequent fiscal periods, two conditions in subparagraph 111(5)(*a*)(i) must be met:

(a) the bakery business which generated the loss must be carried on throughout the taxation year in which the non-capital loss is deducted; and

(b) the bakery business must be carried on for profit or with a reasonable expectation of profit.

It would appear that both conditions will be met, since the Buscat business is being carried on and Buns Plus expects that the Buscat bakery business will earn a profit of $65,000 in 2019.

If the conditions of subparagraph 111(5)(*a*)(i) are met, then the non-capital losses may be deducted from income of the bakery business that generated the loss plus the income from the sale of similar products or services. If it can be assumed that the bakery business, transferred to Buscat Ltd., sells similar products and/or services as the Buscat bakery business, then the maximum $90,000 of non-capital losses can be deducted on December 31, 2018 as follows:

Lesser of:

(a)	Net income for year		$ 90,000
(b)	Income from: the loss business	Nil	
	the sale of similar products	$130,000	$130,000

The remaining $60,500 ($150,500 – $90,000) of non-capital losses can be carried forward to 2019 subject to the deductibility tests discussed above.

Partial election

The minimum amount to be elected upon under paragraph 111(4)(*e*) (i.e., proceeds of disposition) should be an amount equal to two times the sum of:

(a) the allowable capital loss of $2,000 which is about to expire,

(b) the net capital losses of $12,000 which would otherwise expire, and

(c) the property loss of $5,500 which otherwise expires plus the adjusted cost base of the property to be elected upon.

If the land was chosen as the asset to trigger all of the taxable capital gain, then the deemed proceeds would be determined as:

[2 × ($2,000 + $5,500 + $12,000) + $155,000] or $194,000

The resulting taxable income computation would be:

Par. 3(a)	Non-capital sources of income			Nil
Par. 3(b)	Net taxable capital gain:			
	Land, $\frac{1}{2}$ ($194,000 – $155,000)	$ 19,500		
	Allowable capital loss	(2,000)	$ 17,500	
Par. 3(c)	Sum of par. 3(a) plus par. 3(b) less any Subdivision e deductions (nil)		$ 17,500	
Par. 3(d)	Property loss	$ 5,500		
	Business loss	46,000		
		$ 51,500		
	Less: Building recapture	Nil	51,500	
Sec. 3 income			Nil	
Division C				
Net capital loss			$ 12,000	
Taxable income			Nil	
Non-capital losses available for carryforward after the acquisition of control:				
Balance, July 1, 2018			$ 130,000	
Non-capital losses from the deemed taxation year ended June 30, 2016		$ 51,500		
Add: Net capital losses deducted above		12,000		
		$ 63,500		
Less: Par. 3(c) income above		(17,500)	46,000*	
Total non-capital losses			$ 176,000	

---

* Exactly equal to the business loss above.

Summary

The two alternatives presented above are summarized as follows for comparative purposes:

Taxable Income for the Deemed Taxation Year Ended June 30, 2018:

		Maximum election		Partial election	
Par. 3(a)	Income from non-capital sources (≥ 0)		Nil		Nil
Par. 3(b)	Net taxable capital gains (≥ 0):				
	Deemed taxable capital gains (elective):				
	land	$ 20,000		$ 19,500	
	building	5,000		Nil	
	Allowable capital loss	(2,000)	$ 23,000	(2,000)	$ 17,500
Par. 3(c)	Par. 3(a) + par. 3(b)		$ 23,000		$ 17,500
Par. 3(d)	Losses from non-capital sources and ABILs:				
	Loss from business	$ (46,000)		$ (46,000)	
	Recapture (elective): building	20,000		Nil	
	Loss from property	(5,500)	(31,500)	(5,500)	(51,500)
Division B income			Nil		Nil
Optional net capital loss deducted			(12,000)		(12,000)
Non-capital loss deducted			Nil		Nil
Taxable income			Nil		Nil

Non-Capital Losses Available for Carryforward at Deemed Taxation Year Ended June 30, 2018:

	Maximum election		Partial election	
Balance, Jan. 1, 2018		$ 130,000		$ 130,000
Non-capital loss — June. 30, 2018:				
Par. 3(d) losses — see above	$ 31,500		$ 51,500	
Add: net capital losses deducted	12,000		12,000	
	$ 43,500		$ 63,500	
Less: par. 3(c) income — see above	(23,000)	20,500	(17,500)	46,000
		$ 150,500		$ 176,000
Less: losses utilized at June 30, 2018	Nil		Nil	
losses not utilized but expired	Nil	Nil	Nil	Nil
Available for carryforward from June. 30, 2018		$ 150,500		$ 176,000
Net Capital Losses Available for Carryforward		Nil		Nil

The results of the above comparison of the two alternatives are further summarized as follows:

Options	(a)	(b)	Difference
Taxable income	0	0	0
Net capital loss deducted	$ 12,000	$ 12,000	0
Total non-capital losses available for carryforward	150,500	176,000	$ 25,500
ACB of land	195,000	194,000	(1,000)
UCC of building (Class 1: 4%)	70,000	45,000	(25,000)
ACB of building	75,000	65,000	(10,000)

Option (b) is better if the additional $25,500 of non-capital loss can be offset by income generated in the next 20 years. The resultant lower ACB of the land under this option is only relevant on a disposition. The lower UCC on the building only represents a loss of CCA at a 4% declining balance rate. On the other hand, if an additional $25,500 of income cannot be generated in the next 20 years (i.e., business losses continue), alternative (a) is better. Note that 20 years is a long time to sustain continued business losses without generating at least $25,000 of business income. It is unlikely that alternative (a) is better, unless the land and building will be sold in the near future.

Exercise 9

Income from Japan in Canadian dollars (54,025,200 yen × 0.01131)		$ 611,025
Total income under Division B ($2,500,000 + $611,025)		$3,111,025
Less: Dividends deductible under sec. 112	$100,000	
Net capital losses carried forward (adjusted to current year inclusion rate)	25,000	125,000
Taxable income		$2,986,025
Tax @ 38%		$1,134,690
Less: Federal tax abatement (10% of 75% of $2,986,025)		(223,982)
General tax reduction @ 13% of 2,986,025		(388,183)
Net tax		$ 522,525

Foreign Business Tax Deduction

Least of: (a) amount paid (21,610,080 yen × 0.01131) .... $ 244,410

(b) $\dfrac{\text{income from Japan}}{\text{Div. B income minus s. 112 ded. and net capital loss ded.}} \times \begin{array}{l}\text{tax otherwise}\\ \text{payable before}\\ \text{abatement minus}\\ \text{general rate reduction}\end{array}$

$= \dfrac{\$611,025}{\$3,111,025 - (\$100,000 + 25,000)} \times \begin{array}{l}(\$1,134,690 - \\ \$388,183)\end{array}$ .... $ 152,756

(c) Part I tax otherwise payable before abatement minus foreign non-business tax credit ($1,134,690 – $388,183 – nil) ...... $ 746,507

Therefore, the foreign tax deduction is $152,756.

Exercise 10

Income under Division B		$2,645,000
Less: Charitable donations	$ 69,000	
Taxable dividends deductible under sec. 112	517,500	
Non-capital losses	127,600	714,100
Taxable income		$1,930,900
Tax @ 38%		$ 733,742
Less: Federal tax abatement (10% of 86% of $1,930,900)		166,057
		$ 567,685
Less: Non-business foreign tax credit (see Schedule 1)	$ 25,676	
Business foreign tax credit (see Schedule 2)	26,093	
Tax reduction (13% of $1,930,900)	251,017	
		302,786
Part I tax payable		$ 264,899

CHAPTER 11

Schedule 1: Non-business foreign tax credit

Lesser of: (a) amount paid .... $ 25,875

(b) $\dfrac{\text{foreign non-business income}}{\substack{\text{Div. B income minus s. 112 ded.} \\ \text{and net capital loss ded.}}} \times \substack{\text{tax otherwise payable} \\ \text{after abatement minus} \\ \text{general tax reduction}}$

$= \dfrac{\$172,500}{\$2,645,000 - (\$517,500 + 0)} \times \$316,668^{(1)}$ .... $ 25,676

Schedule 2: Business foreign tax credit

Least of: (a) amount paid .... $ 36,800

(b) $\dfrac{\text{foreign business income}}{\substack{\text{Div. B income minus s. 112 ded.} \\ \text{and net capital loss ded.}}} \times \substack{\text{tax otherwise payable} \\ \text{before deductions} \\ \text{minus general tax} \\ \text{reduction}}$

$= \dfrac{\$115,000}{\$2,645,000 - (\$517,500 + 0)} \times (\$733,742 - 251,017)$ $ 26,093

(c) $733,742 - $251,017 - $25,676 .... $457,049

— NOTE TO SOLUTION

(1) $733,742 - $166,057 - $251,017

Exercise 11

The total investment tax credit is 15% of $90,000 = $13,500.

Taxable income before qualified current expenditures	$300,000
Less: qualified current expenditures................................	90,000
Taxable income	$210,000
Net federal tax: @ 15% of $210,000	$ 31,500
Less: investment tax credit	$(13,000)
Part I tax payable	$ 18,500

Note that the $13,000 of investment tax credit will be brought into income in the following year.

Exercise 12

(A) Since control of Computer Rental Ltd. (Computer) was acquired on January 1, 2018, by Processing Ltd. (Processing), Computer is subject to a loss restriction event.

- Subsection 249(4), which deems Computer to have a taxation year end on December 31, 2017, will not cause the corporation to have an additional taxation year, because that date is the normal year end of the corporation.

- Therefore, the amounts described as 2017 non-capital and net capital losses are in reality a 2017 business loss and a 2017 allowable capital loss.

The $50,000 accrued capital loss on the marketable securities will be deemed to be an allowable capital loss of $25,000 for the year ended December 31, 2017 [par. 111(4)(d)] and the adjusted cost base of the securities will be reduced to their fair market value [par. 111(4)(c)].

Unless capital gains are generated in the year ending December 31, 2017, the net capital losses and allowable capital losses of $145,000 (i.e., $40,000 + $80,000 + $25,000) will not be available for deduction after December 31, 2017. Computer may elect to realize a capital gain of up to $300,000 on the land and recapture of up to $5,000 on the furniture and fixtures [par. 111(4)(e)].

- If Computer elects on the maximum amount available on the land, it will generate a taxable capital gain of $150,000; this will cause the adjusted cost base of the land to become $450,000 (i.e., $150,000 + $300,000).

- If Computer elects an amount on the furniture and fixtures, recapture will be created that will offset its business loss for the deemed year end. This will cause the UCC of the class to become $165,000; however, Processing does not want this to be done because of the assumption in the required that the non-capital losses can be used in the future.

- Therefore, Computer should elect only on the land and only to the extent that this election generates a taxable capital gain equal to the expiring losses of $145,000.

- The proceeds of disposition necessary to create a capital gain to offset the expiring loss is:

   ACB of the land $150,000 + (2 × $145,000) = $440,000

   - If Computer makes the election, the new ACB for the land will be $440,000.

The UCC of the computers is reduced to $200,000 [ssec.111(5.1)]. The $280,000 reduction (i.e., $480,000 – $200,000) is deducted as CCA in the deemed year end.

— Division B income for 2017

Par. 3(a):	income from non-capital sources (non-negative)			Nil
Par. 3(b):	net taxable capital gains:			
	taxable capital gain elected on land ($\frac{1}{2}$ × ($440,000 – $150,000))		$ 145,000	
	allowable capital losses in 2017	$80,000		
	allowable capital loss on securities deemed realized ($\frac{1}{2}$ × ($120,000 × $70,000))	25,000	(105,000)	$ 40,000
Par. 3(c):	par. 3(a) + par. 3(b)			40,000
Par. 3(d):	losses from non-capital sources:			
	business loss for 2017		$ 90,000	
	loss on computers (deemed)		280,000	
				(370,000)

Division B Net income (technically cannot be negative)	(330,000)
Division C deductions:	
Net capital losses from 2016, limited to net taxable capital gains in par. 3(b)	(40,000)
Non-capital loss for the year ended December 31, 2017	$(370,000)

Computer has non-capital losses of $75,000 + $370,000 = $445,000 at December 31, 2017. This is the same with or without the election under par. 111(4)(e). The advantage of the election is that the ACB of the land is bumped up to $440,000.

(B) Deductibility of non-capital losses in 2018:

- Spar. 111(5)(a)(i) requires that the computer rental business be carried on throughout the year ended December 31, 2018 and with a reasonable expectation of profit.

- Spar. 111(5)(a)(ii) allows a deduction of non-capital losses to the extent of:

Computers income from the computer rental business	$ 25,000
Computers income from the rental of similar properties, i.e., rental of work stations*	40,000
deductible non-capital loss in 2018	$ 65,000
available for carry over to 2019 ($445,000 – $65,000)	$380,000

*Assuming that the rental of work stations is similar to the rental of computers.

CHAPTER 11

— Taxable income for 2018 will be nil:

income from rental operations (Division B income)	$ 65,000
less: non-capital loss	(65,000)
taxable income	Nil

Deductibility of non-capital losses in 2019:

- Since the computer rental operations were discontinued in 2019, the computer rental business was not carried on throughout 2019 and the test in subpar. 111(5)(*a*)(i) is not met.

- Therefore, the $380,000 of non-capital losses cannot be deducted in 2019.

- It is worth noting that if this business is commenced again in a future year and carried on throughout any such year, the losses can then be deducted, subject to the 20-year carryover period being met.

Exercise 13

(A) Permanent Establishments

(i) Ontario:

— The corporation has a fixed place of business including the head office, factory premises, and warehouse which qualify as permanent establishments [Reg. 400(2)].

(ii) Saskatchewan:

— A public warehouse that belongs to another corporation is not a fixed place of business because Canco has no control over such a warehouse.

— The sales representative in Saskatchewan does not operate from a fixed place of business of the corporation.

— He operates from his home, which is not identified to the public as Cancos place of business since the companys name does not appear on the premises.

— The office in the home was operated at the sales representatives own expense — the sales representative does not have general authority to contract, because head office must give credit approval [Reg. 400(2)(*b*)].

— The sales representative does not have a stock of merchandise owned by the corporation from which he regularly fills orders, because head office arranges shipping from a warehouse [Reg. 400(2)(*b*)].

(iii) Other provinces:

— Sales representatives work on the same basis as described for Saskatchewan and, therefore, there is no fixed place of business and no permanent establishment in the other provinces.

(iv) Poughkeepsie, New York:

— The fixed place of business is the office maintained by the sales representative in his home.

— It is identified to the public as the corporations office by the phone book listing.

— The company pays the cost of maintaining the office in his house.

— Furthermore, Reg. 400(2)(*b*) applies because the sales representative has authority to contract by the acceptance of orders.

— As in the case of Saskatchewan, the public warehouse is not a fixed place of business.

(B) Allocation of Taxable Income

	Gross revenue		Salaries & wages		
	Amount	%	Amount	%	Average percentage
Ontario	$ 7,750,000*	77.5	$1,400,000	93.3	½ (77.5 + 93.3) = 85.4
New York	$ 2,250,000*	22.5	100,000	6.7	½ (22.5 + 6.7) = 14.6
	$10,000,000	100.0	$1,500,000	100.0	100.0

Ontario:	85.4% of $300,000 =	$256,200
New York:	14.6% of $300,000 =	43,800
		$300,000

Ssec. 124(1) abatement: 10% of $256,200 = $25,620

Exercise 14

The deemed year end, by virtue of ssec. 249(4) as a result of the loss restriction event, coincides with the normal year end of Childco.

As a result of the loss restriction event, the following losses are restricted on January 1, 2018:

- 2013 net capital loss of $50,000 and 2016 net capital loss of $100,000 expire on December 31, 2017 as a result of the loss restriction event, unless an election is made under par. 111(4)(e) to realize the accrued gain on the land to offset the net capital losses (i.e., $50,000 + $100,000).

- The non-capital losses available under par. 111(1)(a) for carryover on December 31, 2017 are:

2013 non-capital loss	$300,000	
2014 non-capital loss	250,000	
2015 non-capital loss	200,000	
2016 non-capital loss	150,000	
2017 non-capital loss (see below)	230,000	$1,130,000

- The losses from non-capital sources for the 2016 taxation year are:

Business loss	$ 50,000	
Accrued losses — business		
Building	100,000	
Equipment	Nil	
Patent	80,000	$230,000

Par. 111(4)(e) Election

In order to offset the $150,000 of net capital losses that would otherwise expire on the loss restriction event, a minimum total gain of $300,000 must be elected under par. 111(4)(e) on the land. Electing on the land at $1,000,000 will trigger the $300,000 of accrued capital gains resulting in a taxable capital gain of $150,000 and raising the ACB of the land to $1,000,000. The following would result:

Ssec. 3(a): income from non-capital sources	$	Nil
Ssec. 3(b): net TCG		
deemed TCG on land (½ × ($1M - 700K))		150,000
Ssec. 3(c): Ssec. 3(a) + Ssec. 3(b)	$	150,000
Ssec. 3(d): losses from non-capital sources		(230,000)
Division B income (technically cannot be negative)	$	(80,000)

* Florida sale allocated to U.S. establishment [Reg. 402(4)(a)].

CHAPTER 11

Less Division C deductions:

Par.111(1)(*b*) Net Capital losses $150,000

Par.111(1)(*a*) Non-capital losses 0 (150,000)

Non-capital loss for year ended Dec. 31, 2017 .... $(230,000)

Non-capital loss - 2017 Par. 111(8)(*b*) - Proof

Business loss $230,000

+ net capital loss claimed 150,000   363,333

– 3(*c*) .... (150,000)

Non-capital loss .... $ 230,000

Deductibility of restricted non-capital losses

- Conditions of deductibility:

  (i) the loss business must be carried on for a profit or reasonable expectation of profit;

  (ii) loss business must be carried on throughout each year that a non-capital loss is to be deducted.

- Sources of income from which non-CL's from a loss business may be deducted:

  (i) income from the loss business, or

  (ii) income from a business where substantially all of the income is derived from the sale of similar properties or the rendering of similar services.

- Comments on above rules

  — is Childco being operated with a reasonable expectation of profit?

    — losses are declining

    — any other evidence of an attempt to turn Childco around

- The losses are only available in Childco

  — if another source of income is put into Childco (it may be possible to offset Childco's losses against that source of income, as long as that source is from the sale of similar products or services);

  — if Parentco transferred some of its business to Childco (the transferred business would only be considered similar if it were considered vertically integrated with Childco's business (IT-206R - ARCHIVED)).

Chapter 12

Integration for Business and Investment Income of the Private Corporation

Learning Goals

Know

By the end of this chapter you will know:

- How the tax system works to integrate the tax on individual shareholders with the tax on private corporations for business and investment income.

Understand and Explain

By the end of this chapter you will understand and be able to explain:

- How the small business deduction helps to achieve the integration of business income.
- The rules for associated corporations.
- The investment tax credit for scientific research and experimental development.
- How investment income is taxed in a private corporation.

Apply

By the end of this chapter you will be able to apply your knowledge and understanding to:

- Determine if corporations are associated.
- Compute the small business deduction.
- Calculate the investment tax credit.
- Compute tax payable and refundable tax on investment income in a private corporation.
- Assess whether various types of income should be incorporated.

Review Questions
¶12,800 in the Study Guide

Multiple Choice Questions
¶12,825 in the Study Guide

Exercises
¶12,850 in the Study Guide

Assignment Problems
¶12,875 in the Study Guide

CHAPTER 12 — LEARNING CHART

Problem Descriptions

Textbook Example Problems

12-1	Small business deduction
12-2	Specified investment business
12-3	Related groups of companies
12-4	Associated corporations
12-5	Associated corporations
12-6	Associated corporations
12-7	Associated corporations
12-8	M&P profits and small business deduction
12-9	Investment tax credits
12-10	Investment tax credits — indirect costs
12-11	Connected corporations
12-12	Refundable Part I tax
12-13	Refundable dividend tax on hand
12-14	Part I tax, RDTOH dividend refund

Multiple Choice Questions

1	Small business deduction
2	Identify type of income
3	General rate reduction
4	Part IV tax
5	Associated corporations
6	Associated corporations

Exercises

1	Identify type of income
2	Arm's length
3	Associated corporations
4	Sharing small business deduction
5	Associated corporations
6	Calculate Part I tax
7	Calculate Part I tax, RDTOH, dividend refund
8	Type of income, Part IV tax
9	Type of income
10	Investment income — personal vs. corporate
11	Interest income from US subsidiary
12	Association
13	Association
14	Discussion of corporate tax & rates on various types of income earned by a CCPC
15	Association
16	Intercompany payments
17	Part IV Tax; Dividend Refund
18	Intercompany payments

Problem Descriptions

Assignment Problems

1	Corporate tax rates
2	Explain small business deduction
3	Explain dividends
4	Explain investment income
5	Personal services business
6	Corporate tax — public vs. CCPC
7	Part IV tax
8	RDTOH, dividend refund
9	Active business vs. property income
10	Associated corporations
11	Associated corporations
12	Associated corporations
13	Tax payable
14	SR&ED
15	Tax payable
16	Dividend refund
17	Comprehensive
18	Find the errors
19	Comprehensive
20	Identify types of income
21	Identify types of income
22	Incorporating investments
23	Association
24	Calc of TI, Fed tax & Refundable Part I for CCPC
25	Dividend Refund
26	Errors in RDTOH calculation
27	Incorporate or not
28	Share ownership

CHAPTER 12

Study Notes

¶12,800   REVIEW QUESTIONS

(1) Explain the purpose behind the concept of integration.

(2) It has been said that "ideal integration depends on the existence of two factors in the tax system". Briefly explain what they are.

(3) The dividend gross-up and tax credit has been described as the major tool of integration in the Act. Give a brief explanation of how it works in theory.

(4) What is the purpose of the small business deduction?

(5) On July 15 of this year, Mr. Smith bought all the shares of a company which was the Canadian subsidiary of a US parent. There are no losses or ITCs being carried forward by the company. What advice would you have for Mr. Smith with regard to his choice of year end for the acquired corporation?

(6) Give an example of when paragraph 125(1)(*b*) will give a lower limit for the small business deduction than paragraph 125(1)(*a*).

(7) List some tax and non-tax advantages of incorporation.

(8) List some tax and non-tax disadvantages of incorporation.

(9) Mr. Mould has just started up a manufacturing operation to supply parts to the auto industry. Given his need for start-up capital, he is happy that his tax rate is reduced by both the small business deduction of 18% and the general rate reduction of 13%. Comment.

(10) Are there any tax rules that prevent an individual from deferring tax on portfolio dividends by flowing them through a corporation?

(11) What are five tools that are used in the tax laws to integrate the taxation of investment income earned through a corporation?

(12) Theoretically, what does the 16% or 38% gross-up on dividends from taxable Canadian corporations represent?

(13) Theoretically, what does the dividend tax credit represent?

(14) Explain how integration theoretically works if a $1,000 capital gain is realized in a CCPC.

(15) Mr. Orville owns all the shares of Holdco which in turn owns all of the shares of Opco, a CCPC carrying on an active business in Canada. In recent years, Opco has done very well and its income is well in excess of the business limit. Last year Mr. Orville paid a dividend of $150,000 from Opco to Holdco. However, since he needed the cash in Opco to expand, he loaned the money back to Opco and charged 10% interest. The interest charged to Opco amounted to $15,000 in the year. How will this interest income be taxed in Holdco?

(16) A number of years ago a reorganization was undertaken so that now A Ltd. owns voting preferred shares in B Ltd. These preferred shares have only 7% of the votes and are now only worth 7% of the value. The other shares of B Ltd. are owned by the son of the only shareholder of A Ltd. Are A Ltd. and B Ltd. connected?

(17) Under paragraphs 186(1)(*c*) and (*d*), the recipient private corporation may choose to reduce the amount subject to the Part IV tax by applying otherwise available non-capital losses of the year or of a carryover year. Either the non-capital losses can be deducted from dividend income subject to Part IV tax or they can be deducted in the calculation of taxable income subject to Part I tax. What factors should be considered in deciding which option to choose?

¶12,825   MULTIPLE CHOICE QUESTIONS

Question 1

Concept Corp, a CCPC, correctly calculated its taxable income for its year ended December 31, 2018 as follows:

Income from retailing business carried on in Canada	$ 120,000
Loss from retailing business carried on in United States	(20,000)
Interest income from long-term bonds	30,000
Taxable capital gain from sale of a capital asset	5,000
Net income	$ 135,000
Non-capital losses	(3,000)
Taxable income	$ 132,000

Concept Corp and X Ltd. are associated corporations. X Ltd. claimed a 18% small business deduction on $385,000 for 2018. The taxable capital of Concept Corp and X Ltd. is significantly less than $10 million. Which one of the following amounts is the maximum 18% small business deduction for Concept Corp for 2018?

(A) $18,000

(B) $20,700

(C) $21,600

(D) $23,760

Question 2

M Ltd. provides management advisory services to ACC Ltd. and is not involved in any other business. Mr. Mud is the sole shareholder and only employee of M Ltd. Mr. Mud and his son each own 50% of the issued shares of ACC Ltd. Which one of the following statements is TRUE?

(A) If Mr. Mud would reasonably be regarded as an employee of ACC Ltd., but for the existence of M Ltd., then M Ltd. is carrying on a "personal services business".

(B) M Ltd. is carrying on a "personal services business", unless it employs in the business more than five full-time employees throughout the year, which it does not.

(C) M Ltd. is carrying on a "specified investment business".

(D) M Ltd. is carrying on an "active business".

Question 3

B Ltd. is a Canadian-controlled private corporation which distributes plastic bottles. The following information relates to its year ended December 31, 2018.

Active business income earned in Canada	$495,000
Net income, Division B	520,000
Taxable income	520,000

B Ltd. is not associated with any other corporation. B Ltd. did not earn any foreign business income nor any investment income. B Ltd.'s taxable capital is well below $10 million. Which of the following amounts is the maximum general rate reduction for the year ending December 31, 2018:

(A) $2,600

(B) $3,250

(C) $56,017

(D) $67,600

Question 4

A Ltd., a private corporation, received non-eligible dividends from B Ltd. and C Ltd. during its year ended December 31, 2018.

	B Ltd.	C Ltd.
Amount of dividend received by A Ltd.	$120,000	$120,000
Percentage of shares owned by A Ltd. (votes and value)	70%	8%
Dividend refund received by the payer of the dividend	$ 40,000	$400,000

A Ltd. and C Ltd. are not related. All three are taxable Canadian corporations. Which one of the following amounts is the Part IV tax payable by A Ltd.?

(A) $60,000

(B) $73,600

(C) $74,000

(D) $92,000

Question 5

Joanne owns 55% of the common shares of J Co. and Doug (her spouse) owns 55% of the common shares of D Co. Which of the following would *not* make J Co. and D Co. associated?

(A) If Joanne owned 25% of the common shares of D Co.

(B) If Doug owned 25% of the common shares of J Co.

(C) If a trust for their twin two-year-old daughters controls T Co. and no special elections were made.

(D) If J Co. and D Co. each owned 40% of the shares of R Co., a corporation carrying on a retailing business.

Question 6

In which of the following situations are X Ltd. and Y Ltd. NOT associated?

(A) Rod owns 10% of voting shares of X Ltd. and 50% of the voting shares Y Ltd. and Patrick owns 60% of the voting shares of X Ltd. and 10% of the voting shares of Y Ltd. Rod and Patrick are not related.

(B) The adult son of the controlling shareholder of X Ltd. controls Y Ltd. and owns 25% of the voting shares of X Ltd.

(C) A mother controls Company X. Her two adult daughters each own 30% of the voting shares of Y Ltd. Her adult son owns 25% of the voting shares of Y Ltd.

(D) A brother and sister each own 30% of the voting shares of Sibco Inc. A mother and father each own 20% of the shares. The mother and father each own 50% of the voting shares of Parentco Inc.

CHAPTER 12

¶12,850 EXERCISES

Exercise 1

ITA: 125(7)

The taxpayer company carried on the business on a comparatively small scale of lending money on mortgages. The company was operated by two individuals who also owned and managed a number of other companies. All the companies operated out of the same office premises and used more or less the same office staff and equipment. The taxpayer company had no full-time employees. It was listed in the telephone directory but did no direct advertising. No attempt was made to keep track of the amount of time spent by the office staff on the work of each company and no specific charge was made for office space, use of telephones and equipment or staff.

The company made loans to potential borrowers referred to it by independent agents. Its clientele came mainly from those who found it difficult to obtain loans through the normal commercial channels. The agents had a general idea of the sort of loans which might be acceptable, but because those were relatively high-risk loans, the company had to examine them very carefully. Occasionally, an outside appraisal was made, but normally someone from the company would visit the property to examine it. Often considerable negotiations as to terms were involved. Post-dated cheques for five years would be obtained from borrowers and turned over to the bank as collateral for the company's line of credit.

For the year in question, the company held three mortgages involving $11,084. The sale of a small property, interest and other income resulted in total income of $4,609. Net income before taxes was shown as $3,479. The mortgages outstanding and net income of the company increased continuously from the year in question to the present time. During the year in question, the company's line of credit at the bank was estimated at $7,500 to $15,000, but it is now $25,000.

— *REQUIRED*

From the facts provided in the case, determine the type of business that is carried on by the company under the current legislation.

Exercise 2

ITA: 251

(A) By reference to provisions of the *Income Tax Act*, determine which of the following individuals or groups of individuals are not at arm's length with Alpha Corporation Limited:

(i) Mr. Beta, who owns 25% of the shares of Alpha and is not related to any other shareholders.

(ii) Mr. Beta and his brother, who together own 55% of the shares of Alpha and they are not related to any other shareholder.

(iii) Mr. Delta, who has an option to purchase all of the shares held by Mr. Beta and his brother anytime during the next three years.

(iv) Mr. Epsilon, who has an option to purchase all of the shares held by Mr. Beta and his brother from their estates within five years of their death.

(B) By reference to provisions of the *Income Tax Act*, determine under which of the following conditions Tau Corporation Limited and Lambda Corporation Limited do not deal with each other at arm's length:

(i) Tau is controlled by two brothers, A and B, and Lambda is controlled by A.

(ii) Three unrelated individuals together control Tau and one of these individuals controls Lambda.

(iii) Tau is related to Sigma Corporation Limited and Sigma is related to Lambda.

Exercise 3   ITA: 251, 256

Consider each of the following unrelated cases:

(A) Ava owns 55% of the shares of Jay-one Ltd. and 70% of the shares of Jay-two Ltd. Jay-one Ltd. owns 60% of the shares of Jay-three Ltd. The remaining shares in all three corporations are owned by persons unrelated to Ava.

(B) Abigail owns 30% of the common shares of Benco Ltd. and all of the shares of Rayco Ltd. The other 70% of the common shares of Benco Ltd. are owned by Abigail's cousin. However, Abigail's mother owns all of the voting preferred shares of Benco Ltd. and has sufficient votes to elect more than 50% of the Board of Directors of Benco Ltd.

(C) Adam owns 100% of the shares of Adamco Ltd. and 25% of the shares of Kidco Ltd. His daughter and son-in-law each own 20% of the shares of Kidco Ltd. and the remainder of the shares are owned by persons unrelated to all three.

(D) Sister One and Sister Two each own 50% of Sisco Ltd. and 25% of Cousco Ltd. Each sister has a daughter over the age of 18 who owns 25% of Cousco Ltd.

— REQUIRED

In each unrelated case, determine whether the corporations named are associated. Substantiate your answer by reference to specific provisions of subsection 256(1).

Exercise 4   ITA: 125(1), 256(1), 256(2.1)

Alpha and Beta are two sisters living in Halifax. While Alpha controls Taxit Ltd., Beta owns 25% of the shares of the corporation. Beta also owns 100% of the shares of Sibling Ltd. The active business income for Taxit during the current taxation year was $465,000 and for Sibling was $560,000. The taxation years for both corporations end December 31.

— REQUIRED

How much should each company claim as a small business deduction on their active business income for the taxation year?

Exercise 5   ITA: 251, 252, 256

The common shares of Chutzpah Enterprises Limited were owned by the three Chutzpah brothers as follows:

Aleph Chutzpah	40%
Bett Chutzpah	40%
Gimmel Chutzpah	20%

The common shares of Schlock Sales Limited were owned by the following:

Bett Chutzpah	45%
Dallied Chutzpah	45%
Unrelated person	10%

Aleph Chutzpah is married to Dallied Chutzpah.

— REQUIRED

Determine whether the two corporations are associated. Substantiate your answer by reference to specific provisions of subsection 256(1).

Exercise 6

ITA: 123–126

The following data pertains to Moosonee Company Limited, a Canadian-controlled private corporation for its fiscal year ended December 31, 2018:

Canadian-source business income	$110,000
Canadian investment income	7,000
Income under Division B	117,000
Taxable income all of which is earned in Canada	79,700

— REQUIRED

Compute the federal Part I tax payable plus provincial tax at a 5% rate for 2018 if all of the business income is considered to be active. Moosonee Company Limited is not associated with any other corporation.

Exercise 7

ITA: 123–127, 129, 186

Ay Ltd. is a Canadian-controlled private corporation with a December 31, 2018 fiscal year end. The company operates in Alberta. Taxable income for the year is calculated as follows:

Canadian-source business income		$ 90,000
Dividends from CCPCs:		
Non-connected corporations		30,000
Wholly owned corporation which received a dividend refund of $4,000 as a		
result of paying the dividend		20,000
Canadian-source investment income		100,000
Canadian-source taxable capital gains		20,000
Income under Division B		$260,000
Less: donations	$ 40,000	
taxable dividends from CCPCs	50,000	
non-capital losses	20,000	
net capital losses	20,000	130,000
Taxable income		$130,000

The refundable dividend tax on hand account had a nil balance at the end of the previous year. No dividends were paid in the preceding year. Dividends of $70,000 had been paid during the year to the only shareholder, an associated corporation which has only income from investments.

— REQUIRED

(A) Compute the federal Part I tax and provincial tax at a 4% rate (using federal taxable income as the tax base) payable by the company for the 2018 taxation year.

(B) Compute the refundable dividend tax on hand balance at the end of the year and the dividend refund for the taxation year.

Exercise 8

ITA: 125, 129, 186, 256(1)

Sunlight Limited is owned 50% by H Ltd. and 50% by W Ltd. The two holding companies are 100% owned by Mr. Bennett and Mrs. Bennett, respectively. Sunlight Limited derives all of its income from active business carried on in Canada. It rents facilities from H Ltd. to which it pays $120,000 in annual rent, deducting this amount as a business expense. Sunlight also pays dividends to the two holding companies which is the only other income of those corporations.

— REQUIRED

(A) What is the nature of the rental income to H Ltd.?

(B) Is there a Part IV tax liability for the two holding companies on the dividends received from Sunlight Limited?

Exercise 9

ITA: 125, 129, 256

Janna Management Limited owns a building most of which it rents to Rayna Consulting Services Limited which carries on an active business. Janna and Rayna each own 50% of both corporations. Janna Management Limited also provides managerial, administrative and maintenance services to the unincorporated professional practice of Dr. Adam. The result of these transactions is that Janna Management Limited receives 60% of its income from rent and 40% from providing services and has available an excess business limit for the purposes of the small business deduction. The services provided to the professional practice are provided by Janna, Rayna and four other full-time employees.

— REQUIRED

Determine the nature of its income and the deductions from tax available to Janna Management Limited.

Exercise 10

ITA: Part I, IV

Dana Toews lives in a province with a 12% provincial corporate tax rate and owns an investment portfolio that generated the following Canadian-source income during the year:

Interest	$ 7,000
Portfolio dividends from CCPCs	15,000
Capital gains	6,000

Her cash needs require that $15,000 of the corporation's after-tax profits be distributed as a dividend. The corporation will retain and reinvest the remainder. She already has taxable income of $20,000 from other sources. She has federal personal tax credits of $1,951 and provincial tax credits of $1,200.

— REQUIRED

Compare the total personal tax on the income from the portfolio with the total tax if a corporation owned the securities.

Exercise 11

ITA: 123.3, 126, 129(1), 129(6), 256

Johnson & Co Ltd. holds all the issued shares in Johnson & Co (USA) Inc. Two years ago, the Canadian corporation advanced $100,000 in the form of a loan to the US corporation. The US corporation pays Johnson & Co interest at the rate of 5%. This 5% is comparable to the cost of borrowing at a US bank, but is less than the prescribed interest rate under the Canadian Act. Assume that rate is 7%. (Ignore any subsection 17(1) considerations.)

— REQUIRED

Explain the tax obligations of the Canadian corporation relative to this 5% interest.

Exercise 12

In each of the following unrelated situations, determine whether A Ltd. is associated with B Ltd. Provide reasons for your answer.

(a) Joan owns 70% of the voting shares of A Ltd. and 30% of the voting shares of B Ltd. Another 25% of the voting shares of B Ltd. are owned by A Ltd., and the remaining 45% of the shares of B Ltd. are owned by strangers.

(b) John owns 100% of the shares of A Ltd. and Jill owns 100% of the common shares of B Ltd. John owns 100% of the non-voting, redeemable, retractable, 8% preference shares issued by B Ltd. These shares were issued for $80,000 in 1988, when the prescribed rate of interest was 10%. The redemption value of the shares is $80,000. John and Jill are husband and wife.

(c) Joe owns 100% of the shares of A Ltd. and his son, Jack, age 20, owns 100% of the shares of B Ltd. B Ltd. markets the products manufactured by A Ltd. Prior to the incorporation of B Ltd., in 1988, A Ltd. marketed its own products. Jack is currently attending the University of Waterloo and thus, his father carries on the day-to-day operations of B Ltd. and makes the necessary business decisions for Jack.

(d) Jim and Jane are cousins. They each own 50% of the common shares of A Ltd. A Ltd. owns 100% of the common shares of X Ltd. John, Jim's father, owns 100% of the common shares of B Ltd., as well as preferred shares of X Ltd. valued at $50,000. The value of all the shares of X Ltd. is estimated to be $80,000.

CHAPTER 12

Exercise 13

. For each of the following situations, determine whether or not the corporations are associated, and provide references to the *Income Tax Act* to support your conclusions. (Assume each corporation has a December 31 year end.)

(a)

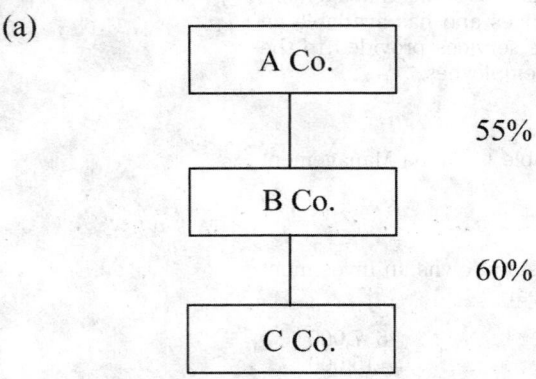

(b)

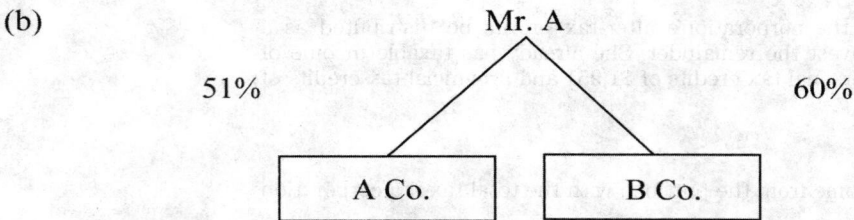

(c)

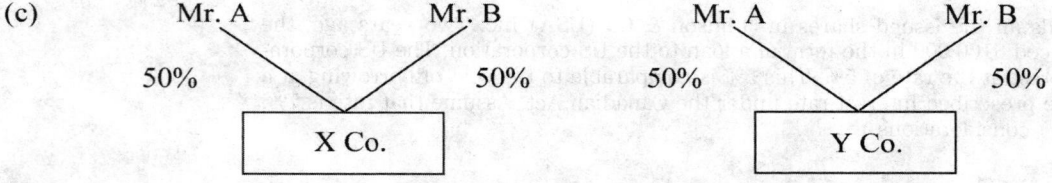

Mr. A is not related to Mr. B

(d)

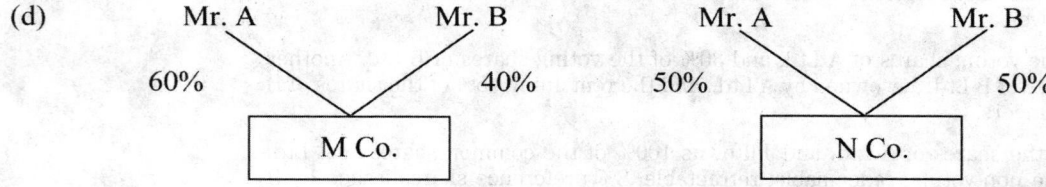

Mr. A is not related to Mr. B

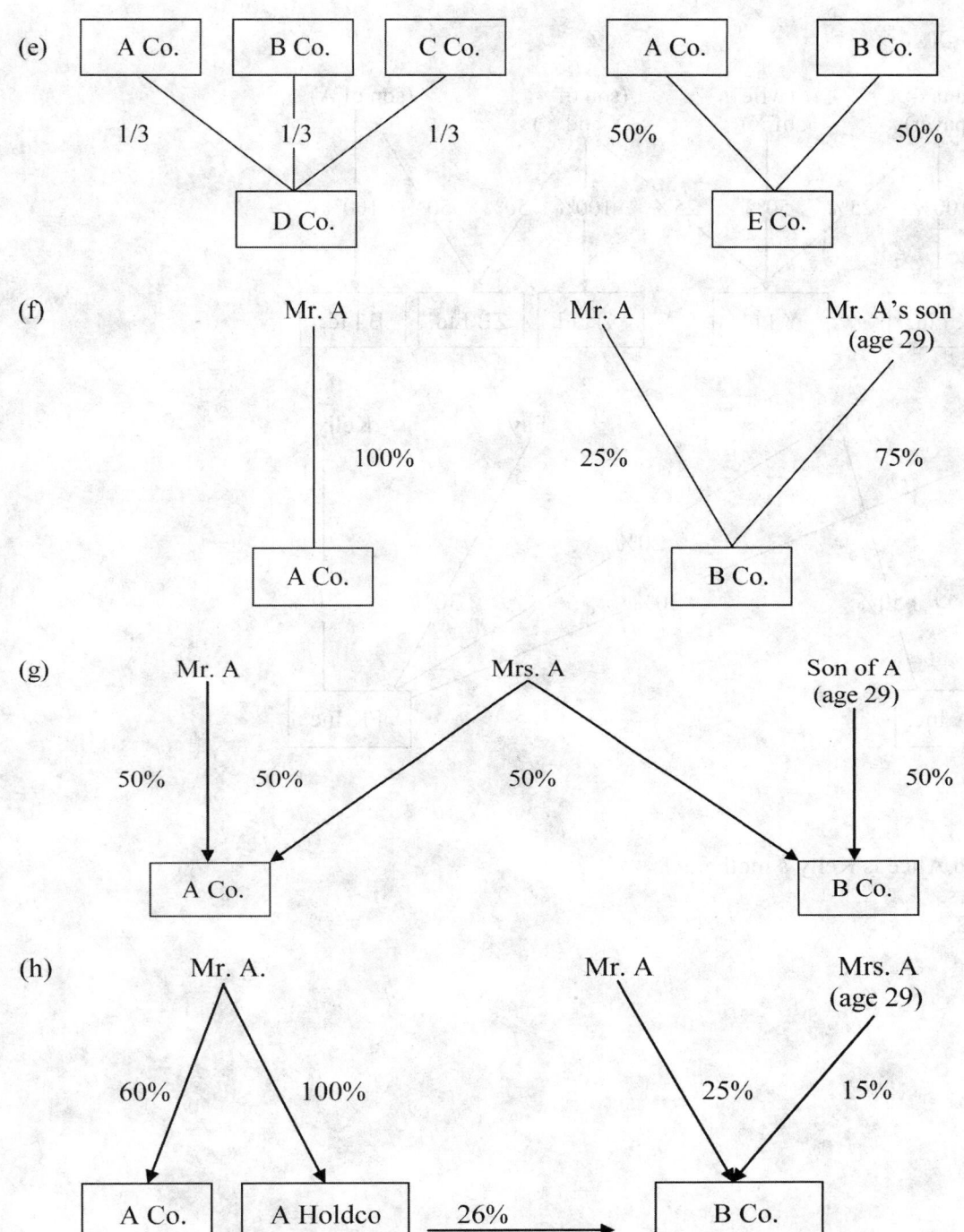

(i) Are A Co. and B Co. associated?

(ii) If the 26% shareholdings in B Co. were held in A Co., would A Co. and B Co. be associated?

(i)

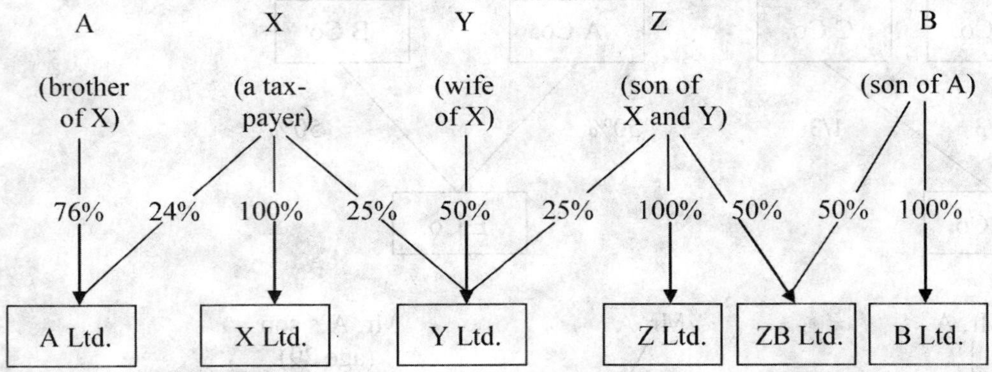

A	X	Y	Z		B
(brother of X)	(a tax-payer)	(wife of X)	(son of X and Y)		(son of A)

A Ltd.	X Ltd.	Y Ltd.	Z Ltd.	ZB Ltd.	B Ltd.

76%   24%   100%   25%   50%   25%   100%   50%   50%   100%

(j)

Ruth   Alice   Fay   Kelly

50%   50%   20%   20%   30%   30%

RA Inc.   FK Inc.

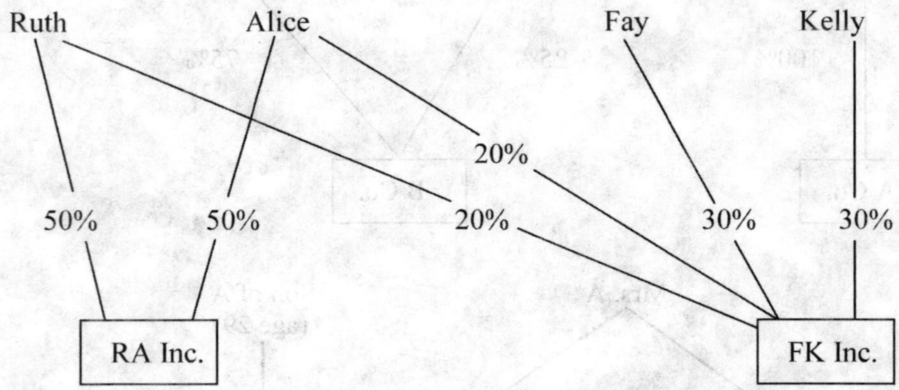

Ruth is Fay's mother and Alice is Kelly's mother.
Ruth and Alice are sisters.
Fay is 17 and Kelly is 22.

(k)

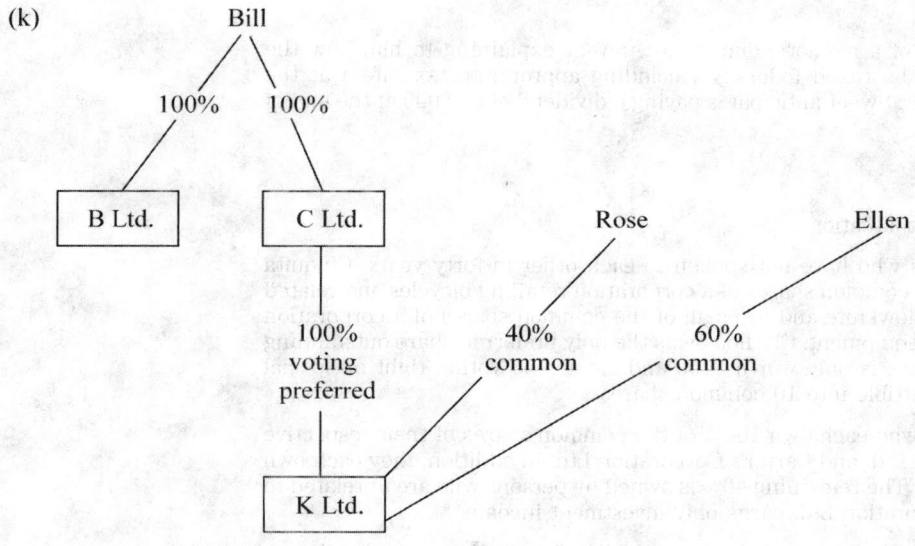

Rose and Ellen are Bill's children and are over 18 years of age.
K Ltd.'s preferred shares have a value of $2 million and the common shares have a value of $150,000.

Exercise 14

Your client, Mr. Sweet, a Canadian resident, has recently transferred all his unincorporated candy manufacturing and retailing businesses to a new corporation controlled by him. Since Mr. Sweet is still very confused over the corporate tax structure, he has requested a written explanation of how the tax system would affect the corporation and his situation in general. Mr. Sweet has provided you with the following data upon which to base your explanation.

Sweet Ltd.
Projected Income for Tax Purposes
By Source
For the Year Ended December 31, 2018

Manufacturing and processing income	$ 50,000
Retailing income — Canada	75,000
Retailing income — New York outlet*	17,500
Bank interest — above Canadian operations	1,000
— US retailing*	500
Canadian treasury bills**	3,000
Canadian bond interest	1,500
Dividends from taxable Canadian corporations — non-connected (Received June 15)	2,500
Recapture of CCA from the sale of certain Canadian equipment	7,500
Rental income — 5% of factory building space***	12,500
— small warehouse (not required for its operations)	3,500
Taxable capital gains:	
Manufacturing equipment	4,500
Securities of public corporations	4,000
Allowable capital losses	(5,500)
Total income for tax purposes	$ 177,500

* This is the only business operation outside of Ontario and these amounts are expressed in Canadian dollars. There has been no withholding tax in the United States on these amounts.

** Seasonal investment of excess cash.

*** Based on five-year lease.

— REQUIRED

Prepare in point form the contents of a memorandum to Mr. Sweet explaining to him how the various amounts described above would be taxed federally (including appropriate tax rates) at the corporate level taking into account that Mr. Sweet anticipates paying a dividend of $50,000 at the end of each year.

Exercise 15

Consider the following unrelated fact situations.

(A) Chiquita and Clorilda are sisters who have not spoken to each other in forty years. Chiquita lives in Dundas and owns all of the common shares of a corporation retailing bicycles and related equipmeprobt. Clorilda lives in Yellowknife and owns all of the common shares of a corporation retailing snowmobiles and related equipment. Clorilda owns the only preferred share outstanding in Chiquita's corporation. This share is only worth $100 and carries no voting right or special dividend privileges, but it is convertible into 10 common shares.

(B) Caspar and Carter are brothers who each own 100% of the common shares of their respective corporations, Caspar's Corporation Ltd. and Carter's Corporation Ltd. In addition, they each own 30% of Ceecombo Corporation Ltd. The remaining 40% is owned by persons who are unrelated to Caspar or Carter. Ceecombo Corporation Ltd. earns only investment income.

(C) Chauncey, Clarabelle, and Clyde are siblings who each own 20% of the voting shares of Xerxes Ltd. Basil, Bertha, and Bambi are the other brother and sisters of Chauncey, Clarabelle, and Clyde. Basil, Bertha, and Bambi each owns 25% of the voting shares of Xylona Ltd. In addition, Chauncey and Clarabelle each owns 12.5% of the voting shares of Xylona Ltd. Unrelated parties own the unspecified amounts of shares in Xerxes Ltd.

(D) Alphonso owns 100% of the voting shares of One Corporation Ltd., which carries on business in Northwestern Ontario. Althea, who is married to Alphonso, owns 100% of the voting shares of Another Corporation Ltd. which carries on business in Manitoba and was formed to provide geographic diversification. The two corporations are in the same business and use the same business name and logo, although they deal with separate clientele. When Another Corporation Ltd. was formed, Althea used money given to her by Alphonso to acquire the shares. In addition, One Corporation Ltd. loaned Another Corporation Ltd. both equipment and funds for operations. Since Althea's experience with business was limited, her corporation was managed by a former employee of One Corporation Ltd. who had moved to Manitoba after a divorce. Each year, salaries and bonuses were set so that net profit for each corporation remained at about $500,000.

(E) The common shares of Yolanda Ltd. are 50% owned by Eunice and 50% owned by Fifi who is not related to Eunice. Eunice owns all of the non-voting preferred shares of Yolanda Ltd., but as a result of this added investment, she has a tie-breaking vote in the event that the two share-holders are opposed in a vote of the common shareholders in a meeting of the Board of Directors. Eunice also owns 55% of the fair market value of all of the issued shares of Zerlinda Ltd., the other shares being owned by unrelated parties.

(F) Edbert owns 60% of the shares of Una Ltd. and 25% of the shares of Velda Ltd. His cousin Filbert owns 50% of the shares of Velda Ltd. Edbert holds an option to acquire all of the shares of Velda Ltd. owned by his cousin if his cousin dies. The unspecified holders of shares in both corporations are unrelated parties.

— REQUIRED

Determine whether the corporations involved in the above independent fact situations are associated. State clearly all of the reasons supporting your opinion and all the appropriate authority in the *Income Tax Act* and/or the cases (if necessary) that apply to this topic.

Exercise 16

Mr. Holder owns 80% of the shares, and is the only employee, of Holdall Investments Ltd., an investment holding company. The other 20% of the shares are owned by his father, who founded Held Manufacturing Ltd., a wholly owned subsidiary of Holdall Investments Ltd. Held Manufacturing carries on a business of manufacturing top quality woodworking tools. Held Manufacturing Ltd. loaned some surplus funds to Holdall Investments Ltd. on the security of a mortgage on an apartment building, which Holdall Investments Ltd. purchased with the borrowed funds. Holdall Investments Ltd. made monthly principal and interest payments on that loan. Holdall Investments Ltd. owns the strictly commercial building used by Held Manufacturing Ltd. and receives rent from the latter company. Ms. Holdette, Mr.

Holder's daughter, owns 100% of the shares of Holdette Management Services Ltd. which provides management services to Held Manufacturing Ltd. in return for a fee. Ms. Holdette, who is the only employee of Holdette Management Services Ltd., was formerly the manufacturing vice-president of Held Manufacturing Ltd. Holdette Management Services Ltd. rents office space from Holdall Investments Ltd. All companies operate only in Ontario where the individuals mentioned are resident.

— REQUIRED

Determine the income tax implications for the corporations described. Provide any advice necessary to improve the situation.

Exercise 17

Mr. Stevens owns 100% of the shares of Stevens Holdings Inc. (SHI) which owns 100% of Fancy Operating Ltd. (FOL). Both SHI and FOL have a December 31 year end.

The following information pertains to the December 31, 2018 year ends: (Neither company paid any dividends in 2017).

Stevens Holdings Inc.

— balance in refundable dividend tax on hand account at December 31, 2017 was $8,000

— received taxable dividend from FOL of $75,000

— received taxable dividend from Canadian Pacific Ltd. of $8,000 on October 31, 2018

— earned interest income of $12,000

— realized a capital gain of $42,000

— paid a capital dividend of $10,500 and a taxable dividend of $50,000 to Mr. Stevens on February 15, 2018

Fancy Operating Ltd.

— balance in refundable dividend tax on hand account at December 31, 2017 was $2,000

— earned active business income of $80,000 and interest income of $7,000

— paid taxable dividends to SHI of $75,000 on July 15, 2018

— REQUIRED

(i) Calculate the dividend refund for FOL for 2018.

(ii) Calculate the Part IV tax for SHI for 2018.

(iii) Calculate the dividend refund for SHI for 2018.

Exercise 18

Mr. C.A. Smith is a Chartered Professional Accountant and is the sole shareholder and employee of C.A. Managem Inc., a corporation that provides administrative services to Public Company Limited (Public). Public formerly employed Mr. C.A. Smith as its Vice-President, Finance. Mr. C.A. Smith also owns all the shares of C.A. Buildem Inc. (Buildem), which has 10 full-time employees. Buildem operates a small construction business. C.A. Buildem Inc. fully owns C.A. Holdem Company Ltd., an investment company that has no employees and earns interest income from a loan to CA Buildem Inc. and other sources, as well as from portfolio dividends from taxable Canadian corporations. C.A. Managem Inc. also provides administrative services to C.A. Buildem Inc. and C.A. Holdem Company Ltd.

— REQUIRED

Indicate, with reasons, the types of income being earned by each corporation. Describe how each type of income will be taxed, including refundable taxes, if any. Ignore any proration of taxes and surtaxes. Assume that the business limit has not been exceeded.

CHAPTER 12

¶12,875 ASSIGNMENT PROBLEMS

Type 1 Problems

Problem 1

You are again working on the firm's tax publications and have been asked to compare the corporate tax rates for active business income earned by the following:

— a Canadian public company,

— a CCPC with income below $500,000 and

— a CCPC with income above $500,000.

Assume a generic provincial tax rate that you can support.

Problem 2

Still working on the publication you have been asked to calculate the small business deduction and then explain how it works.

(1) What is the purpose behind the small business deduction?

(2) Is this deduction a savings or a deferral? Explain

(3) The purpose behind the components of the calculation.

(4) The purpose behind the associated company rules.

(5) If income is over the annual business limit should the company declare a bonus to reduce the income back down to the annual business limit?

Your calculations should use the following assumptions:

— Active business income	$600,000
— Taxable income	300,000
— Business limit	200,000
— Personal marginal tax rate on employment income	50%
— Personal marginal tax rate on eligible dividends	31%
— Personal marginal tax rate on non-eligible dividends	42%
— Corporate tax rate on ABI below $500,000	14%
— Corporate tax rate on SBI above $500,000	27%

Compare the after-tax personal cash from the following:

1. Calculate the amount of bonus needed to reduce taxable income to the point where all of the taxable income is eligible for the small business deduction.

2. Assuming that the bonus is declared and paid, calculate the personal tax on the bonus received by the individual and their after-tax cash.

3. Assuming that the bonus is not declared, then calculate the amount of corporate tax the company will pay on the amount of the bonus identified in step 1. Then calculate the corporate after-tax cash on this bonus amount not paid. Pay this after-tax cash as a dividend and calculate the amount of personal tax on this dividend and their after-tax cash.

Problem 3

Staying with the tax publication, assuming Canadian portfolio dividends received are $100,000:

— Explain how Canadian dividend income is taxed in a public corporation.

— Explain how Canadian dividend income is taxed in a CCPC.

   (1)　Why are dividends deductible under Division C?

   (2)　What is the purpose of Part IV tax? Is it a permanent or temporary tax? To whom does it apply?

   (3)　Why might there be Part IV tax on dividends from connected corporations?

   (4)　What is the purpose behind the Refundable Dividend Tax On Hand (RDTOH)?

   (5)　Why doesn't Part IV tax apply to public companies?

   (6)　How does the Dividend Refund fit in?

Problem 4

Staying with the tax publication, assuming interest income of $10,000 and capital gains of $40,000:

— Explain how investment income, other than dividends, is taxed in a public corporation.

— Explain how investment income, other than dividends, is taxed in a CCPC.

   (1)　What type of income is included in Aggregate Investment Income (AII)?

   (2)　How is AII calculated?

   (3)　What is the purpose behind the Additional Refundable Tax (ART)?

   (4)　What is the purpose behind the Refundable Dividend Tax On Hand (RDTOH)?

   (5)　Why don't ART and RDTOH apply to public companies?

   (6)　How does the Dividend Refund fit in?

Problem 5

Compare the taxation of active business income and personal services business income assuming income of $100,000.

What is the purpose behind taxing "personal services business" income differently?

Compare the calculation of income and tax payable between an individual earning employment income and a corporation earning personal services business income.

Problem 6

First Gear Inc. is a corporation located in Saint John, New Brunswick that distributes automotive parts in the Maritime Provinces. It is owned by John Robinson who lives in Saint John. For the year ended September 30, 2018, its accounting income statement is as follows:　　*CCPC*

Sales	$1,225,000
Cost of sales and other expenses including CCA	(725,000)
Operating profit	500,000
Other net income	208,500
Net income before taxes	708,500
Provision for taxes	(200,725)
Net income after tax	$ 507,775

Inv. Income

CHAPTER 12

Selected Additional Information

(1) Other income includes:

Portfolio dividends from Canadian public corporation	$ 85,000
Canadian interest income on long-term bonds	123,500
	$208,500

John is confused about how income in his corporation is taxed. He wants to understand it so he can make better decisions. He has asked you to explain how the different types of income earned by First Gear are taxed. Then he wants you to calculate the corporate tax liability and provide any advice you think is appropriate related to the refundable tax. Personally, he is in the top tax bracket. Assume the provincial corporate tax rate is 4% on income eligible for the small business deduction and 12% on other income.

You agree that you will:

(A) Assess the situation.

(B) Identify the issues.

(C) Analyze the issues.

(D) Advise/recommend.

Problem 7

ITA: 186

Ex Ltd., a Canadian-controlled private corporation, received a taxable dividend of $90,000 from its Canadian subsidiary Little Ex Ltd. The subsidiary had paid a total dividend of $120,000 and had received a dividend refund of $18,000.

Compute the Part IV tax payable by Ex Ltd.

Problem 8

ITA: 123–127, 129, 186

Why Limited is a Canadian-controlled private corporation operating solely in Newfoundland and Labrador. For its taxation year ended December 31, 2018, the company reported the following income under Division B:

Active business income	$ 85,000
Taxable capital gain	37,500
Canadian-source interest income	45,000
Taxable portfolio dividends from Canadian-resident public corporations	18,750
Income under Division B	$186,250

The corporation is carrying forward the following amounts:	
Non-capital losses	$ 40,000
Net capital losses (arising in 2013)	52,000

The balance in the refundable dividend tax on hand account at December 31, 2017 was nil. On November 30, 2018, the company paid $112,500 in taxable dividends to its shareholders all of whom are individuals. The taxable portfolio dividends of $18,750 were received on November 1, 2018.

(A) Compute the federal Part I tax and provincial tax at a 4% rate payable by the company for 2018.

(B) Compute the refundable dividend tax on hand balance as at December 31, 2018 and compute the dividend refund for 2018.

¶12,875

Problem 9

ITA: 125(7)

The taxpayer company, a private corporation, owned and operated a small shopping centre from which it received rental income. There were seven separate tenants, only one of them being what is sometimes referred to as a "Triple A" tenant, namely, a Canadian bank. The corporation, through its principal officer, negotiated all the leases, took care of all the complaints from the tenants and arranged for the maintenance of the shopping centre. It required some activity by the company almost daily. The rental income of the company was mainly for use of the property, but also, to a much lesser extent, for services and other things supplied by the company such as heat, repairs, etc.

From the facts provided in the case, determine the type of income that the corporation derives from the business that it carries on under the current legislation.

Problem 10

ITA: 256

Consider each of the following unrelated cases, involving the ownership of the common shares of Canadian-controlled private corporations, for taxation years of all corporations ending on December 31:

(A) Leah Ltd. owns 55% of the shares of Elaine Ltd.

(B) Ms. Miriam owns 51% of the shares of Abigail Ltd. and 60% of the shares of Ethan Ltd.

(C) Ms. Irene and Mr. Mordechai each own 50% of the shares of Clare Ltd. In addition, they each own 50% of the shares of Philip Ltd. Ms. Irene and Mr. Mordechai are not related.

(D) Mrs. Lyn owns 60% of the shares of Jay Ltd. and Mrs. Sarah owns the other 40%. Mrs. Lyn and Mrs. Sarah each own 50% of the shares of Alex Ltd. Mrs. Lyn and Mrs. Sarah are not related.

(E) Janna Ltd., Rayna Ltd. and Adam Ltd. each own ⅓ of the shares of Stan Ltd. Janna Ltd. and Rayna Ltd. each own 50% of the shares of Jonathan Ltd.

(F) Ms. Ruth owns all of the shares of Rick Ltd. Ms. Ruth owns 25% of the shares of Daniel Ltd. and Ms. Ruth's daughter, Elana, who is over 18 years old owns the other 75%.

(G) Mr. Joshua owns 100% of the shares of Gord Ltd. and Ms. Dahlia owns 100% of the shares of Rosalyn Ltd. Mr. Joshua and Ms. Dahlia each own 30% of the shares of Rebecca Ltd. The other 40% of the shares of Rebecca Ltd. are owned by Eden, who is not related to any of the others. Mr. Joshua is the brother of Ms. Dahlia's husband.

(H) Mrs. Yael owns 60% of the shares of Benjamin Ltd. and 30% of the shares of Livi Ltd. Another 25% of the shares of Livi Ltd. are owned by Benjamin Ltd. and the remaining 45% of the shares of Livi Ltd. are owned by Joy, who is not related to any of the others.

(I) Ms. Daniella owns 60% of the shares of Elizabeth Ltd. and 25% of the shares of Ava Ltd. Ms. Samara, who is not related to Ms. Daniella, owns the other 75% of the shares of Ava Ltd. Ms. Daniella holds an option to buy all of the shares owned by Ms. Samara at any time in the next 10 years.

(J) Mr. and Mrs. Jonathan each own 50% of Isabelle Ltd. Mr. Jonathan and his two brothers and one sister each own 25% of Maya Ltd.

In each of the above *unrelated* cases determine whether the corporations are associated. Substantiate your answer by reference to the specific conditions in the provisions of section 256, and consider all possible alternatives.

CHAPTER 12

Problem 11

ITA: 256

Consider each of the following unrelated cases, involving the ownership of shares of Canadian-controlled private corporations. Assume all of the issued shares are common shares unless specifically stated otherwise.

(A) Rachel and Monica, friends, each own 50% of the issued shares of A Ltd. In addition, Rachel owns 80% and Monica owns 20% of the issued shares of B Ltd.

(B) Charlie and Claudia are siblings. Charlie owns 80% of A Ltd. which in turn owns 40% of B Ltd. Claudia owns 60% of B Ltd.

(C) Bob, Bill, and Bert are three brothers who share equally the income of a professional partnership. The partnership owns 100% of the shares of A Ltd. Bert owns 100% of the shares of B Ltd.

(D) Anne and Barbara are sisters. They each own 100% of their respective corporations, A Ltd. and B Ltd. A Ltd. and B Ltd. each own 40% of the shares of C Ltd.

(E) Valerie, Brandon, and Claire are strangers. They each own ⅓ of the shares of A Ltd. Brandon owns 40% of the shares of B Ltd. The remaining 60% are owned by Claire. Claire also owns 100% of the shares of C Ltd.

(F) Valerie and her two nieces each own 25% of the shares of A Ltd. Valerie's husband, Dilon, and his nephew each own 50% of the shares of B Ltd. Dilon also owns the remaining 25% of the shares of A Ltd.

(G) Father owns 100% of the shares of F Ltd. His son, Sean, age 17, owns 100% of the common shares of S Ltd. F Ltd. owns 30% of the issued preferred shares of S Ltd. The preferred shares have the following characteristics:

- non-voting,
- dividend rate fixed at 6%,
- redeemable at $1,000 per share, and
- issue price $1,000 per share.

The prescribed rate of interest was 8% at the time the preferred shares were issued.

You have been asked to determine which of the corporations are associated and substantiate your answer by reference to specific provisions of the Act.

Problem 12

ITA: 256

Both corporations in this case were incorporated for the purpose of buying and selling anti-freeze products. Warren Packaging Limited sold its product ("Dual Duty") to wholesalers who serviced and supplied garages and service stations ultimately for the consumers. Its sole shareholder and president was Mr. Warren. Bradford-Penn Oil Inc. sold its product ("Viceroy") to retailers who sold it on a cash and carry basis to its clients. Mr. Warren's wife was the sole shareholder and president of the latter company.

In essence, both companies were directed by the same person in the same premises. They both had the same year end. The product came in bulk from the same supplier and was packed in smaller quantities with the different brand names.

Management of the companies felt that it was too risky to have the same company distribute the anti-freeze product to both the wholesalers and the retailers. There was only one supplier of bulk anti-freeze available to the two corporations and that supplier marketed its own brand and, as a result, was also in competition with Warren Packaging and Bradford-Penn Oil. Maintaining the source of supply at a competitive price made the business risky.

Management also felt that it was necessary to have two companies with two different brand names to cover the wholesale market and the retail market. Experience had shown that if the same brand were supplied to both the wholesalers and the retailers, one or the other of the markets would be lost. Even if the same company name appeared on the package of the two different brands, it would be difficult to maintain both markets because of price differentials from the different outlets to the ultimate consumers.

In his testimony, Mr. Warren testified that he did not remember his counsellor discussing taxation with him when he decided to separately incorporate the two companies. He also testified that he had given a personal guarantee to the bank to obtain a loan for Warren Packaging Limited and he felt it was necessary to have a limited liability in that corporation. He believed that limited liability was accomplished by his wife's sole ownership of the shares of Bradford-Penn Oil Inc.

You have been asked the following:

(A) Would subsection 256(5.1) apply in this case and, if so, what would be the effect of that application?

(B) Assuming that subsection 256(5.1) does not apply, determine whether Warren Packaging Limited and Bradford-Penn Oil Inc. are associated. Provide reasons for your determination by reference to the legislation and to the facts of the case.

Problem 13

ITA: 123–126

The accountant, Ryan Mailling, of Double-D Retailing Ltd. (DRL), a Canadian-controlled private corporation, has requested your assistance with respect to the calculation of the company's Part I tax payable.

Ryan has provided you with the following information.

(1) DRL is not associated with any other corporation.

(2) For DRL's December 31 taxation year end, the corporation correctly reported:

Active business income	$320,000
Investment income	
Canadian	17,000
Charitable donations	9,000
Net capital loss deducted	2,000
Non-capital loss deducted	10,000
Taxable income	316,000

(3) Taxable capital employed in Canada in 2017 was $11.9 million.

Ryan has asked you to calculate the federal Part I tax payable for the taxation year ended December 31, 2018. Show all calculations whether or not relevant to the final answer.

Problem 14

ITA: 37, 127(5)–(11), 127.1

Natalia, a resident of Canada, owns 100% of the shares of New Age Limited (NAL). NAL carries on scientific research and experimental development (SR&ED) activities with respect to finding the ingredients for a cream which will reduce fat and tone muscles when massaged into the skin.

During its fiscal year ended December 31, 2018, NAL incurred the following costs related to its SR&ED activities:

Salaries for research technicians and assistants	$600,000
Materials consumed	200,000
Supplies consumed	40,000
Small equipment purchased for the laboratory	80,000
A special machine purchased to mix the ingredients in a temperature controlled environment	100,000

The machine and the lab equipment will have no value when the research project is completed.

Additional overhead costs were incurred in 2018 because of the SR&ED project. The accounting system was not sophisticated enough to properly allocate these expenses. Overhead expenses for the year totalled $500,000.

NAL paid Natalia a bonus of $40,000 in 2018 in addition to her salary of $80,000. Natalia spent 25% of her time on the SR&ED project in 2018.

NAL does not expect to have any taxable income for 2018. It had taxable income of $100,000 in 2017. Its taxable capital does not exceed $10 million. It is not associated with any other corporation.

You have been asked the following:

(A) Which of the above costs incurred by NAL in 2018 qualify for deduction under subsection 37(1) as qualifying SR&ED expenditures?

(B) Determine the amount of ITCs and refundable ITCs for 2018.

Problem 15

ITA: 110.1–112, 123–126, 127(3)

Neville Ltd. is a Canadian-controlled private corporation which was incorporated in 2002 with a December 31 year end. In 2018, Neville Ltd. earned net income of $250,000 before taxes for accounting purposes. Included in the calculation of that amount were the following items:

Canadian active business income	$159,000
Dividends from taxable Canadian subsidiary corporations	8,000
Other Canadian investment income:	
— rental income	$115,000
— interest income	15,000
— royalty income	1,000
— taxable capital gain	9,000
Income under Division B	$307,000
Donations to registered charities	$ 60,000
The company also has the following balances at January 1, 2018:	
2012 Net capital loss	$ 10,000
Charitable donations carried forward from 2018	10,000

Neville Ltd.'s 100% owned subsidiary has used $350,000 of the business limit for the small business deduction in 2018. Together, Neville Ltd. and its subsidiary have $8 million of taxable capital in Canada.

You have been asked to calculate the federal Part I tax and provincial tax payable by Neville Ltd. for 2018. Show *all* calculations. Assume the provincial tax rates are: 4% for active business income eligible for the small business deduction and 12% for all other income.

Problem 16

ITA: 123–127, 129, 186

The following selected information has been taken from the records of Sharp Ltd., a Canadian-controlled private corporation, for its fiscal year ended December 31, 2018.

(1) Income for tax purposes:

Active business income (retailing)	$160,000
Canadian bond interest	20,000
Taxable dividends received from taxable Canadian corporations	40,000
Taxable capital gains	30,000
Net income under Division B	$260,000

$250,000 [handwritten]

(2) Division C deductions claimed:

Donations	(2,000)
Net capital losses	(5,000)
Non-capital losses	(13,000)
Taxable dividends received from taxable Canadian corporations	(40,000)

(3) Taxable income .... $200,000   *$190,000* [handwritten]

(4) Part I tax payable is $32,267 including additional refundable tax of $4,267. In computing Part I tax, the following deductions were made:

Small business deduction	$28,000

(5) Summary of taxable dividends received from taxable Canadian corporations:

Date received	Payer	% of voting shares owned	Amount of dividend received	Dividend refund received by payer corp.
Aug. 1, 2018	A Ltd.	6%	$20,000	$30,000
Oct. 1, 2018	B Ltd.	80%	20,000	5,000
			$40,000	

Connected [handwritten note under 80%]

(6) Summary of dividends paid by Sharp Ltd.:

Type of dividend	Amount	Date declared	Date paid
Taxable dividend	$60,000	July 15, 2018	Aug. 15, 2018
Tax-free ssec. 83(2) dividend	20,000	Oct. 15, 2018	Nov. 15, 2018
Taxable dividend	24,000	Dec. 15, 2018	Jan. 15, 2019

[handwritten: Only use this taxable & paid in year → Tax free → Paid next year]

(7) The refundable dividend tax on hand balance at December 31, 2017 was $12,000. The dividend refund for 2017 was $4,000.

You have been asked to:

(A) Compute the dividend refund for 2018.

(B) Explain what would change if Sharp Ltd. was a private corporation, and not a CCPC?

CHAPTER 12

Problem 17

ITA: 123–127; 129, 186

Multi Enterprises Ltd. is a Canadian-controlled private corporation whose fiscal period coincides with the calendar year. For the year 2018, the company's taxable income was calculated as follows:

Income from distributing net of CCA		$220,000
Dividends from taxable corporations:		
(a) connected corporation, dividend payment triggering a dividend refund of $2,750 to the wholly owned subsidiary		11,000
(b) non-connected corporation (portfolio dividends)		20,000
AII Taxable capital gain	$29,000	
Allowable capital losses	12,000	17,000
Property Income Royalties		9,000
Recapture of CCA on disposal of sales equipment		4,000
AII Income from rental of an apartment building (no full-time employees and tenants provide virtually all of their own services)		14,000
ABI ~~AII~~ Interest charged on accounts receivable		5,000
Net income for tax purposes		$300,000
Less: net capital losses carried over	$ 7,000	
non-capital losses carried over	10,000	
donations	26,000	
dividends from taxable Canadian corporations	31,000	74,000
Taxable income		$226,000

At December 31, 2017, there was a nil balance in the refundable dividend tax on hand account. The company paid $72,000 in dividends during 2018 to individual shareholders.

It has been agreed that $200,000 of the business limit for small business deduction will be claimed by the parent, Multi Enterprises Ltd., leaving the remainder for the subsidiary.

The company has a permanent establishment in New Brunswick.

You have been asked to:

(A) Compute the federal Part I tax and assumed provincial tax at a 4% rate on active business income eligible for the small business deduction and 12% for all other income. Show in detail the calculation of all deductions in the computation, using a separate schedule for each special deduction. In calculating the small business deduction list all ineligible items of income, if any, and indicate the amount of the business limit available for the subsidiary.

(B) Compute the refundable dividend tax on hand balance as at December 31, 2018, showing, in detail, your calculations and compute the dividend refund for 2018.

Type 2 Problems

Problem 18

ITA: 110.1–112, 123–127

The controller of Tek Enterprises Ltd. provided you with the following information:

Tek Enterprises Ltd.
Income
For the fiscal year ended December 31, 2018

Canadian wholesaling income		$251,500
Canadian retail business income		90,000
Taxable capital gains		4,500
Interest income:		
Canadian long-term bonds	$20,000	
Interest on accounts receivable outstanding for more than 30 days in the Canadian retail business	5,000	25,000
Dividend income:		
From taxable Canadian corporations	$ 9,000	
From foreign corporations (before foreign tax of $1,800) (Tek Enterprises Ltd. owns less than 5% of the shares)	12,000	21,000
Net income		$392,000

Notes:

(1) Tek Enterprises Limited is a CCPC. It is not associated with any corporations.

(2) The following items were deducted in the computation of Canadian wholesaling income above:

SR&ED expenditures (current in nature) $50,000

(3) The taxable capital gain was calculated as follows:

	Marketable securities	Equipment	Total
Proceeds	$15,000	$ 200	$15,200
Cost	3,000	3,200	6,200
Gain (Loss)	$12,000	$ (3,000)	$ 9,000
			× ½
			$ 4,500

(4) The corporation has net capital losses (incurred in 2008) of $13,000.

You assigned a junior staff member to calculate the federal Part I tax payable for Tek Enterprises Ltd. The following is his calculation.

Net income	$392,000
Dividends	(21,000)
Donations	(75,000)
Net capital losses	(13,000)
Taxable income	$283,000

Basic federal tax (40% × $283,000)		$113,200
Abatement: Taxable income	$283,000 × 10%	$ 28,300
		$141,500

Foreign tax credit:
    Lesser of: (a) Foreign tax paid = $1,800

        (b) $\dfrac{\text{Foreign income } \$12,000}{\$283,000 + \$21,000 + \$13,000} \times \$141,500 = \underline{\$5,356}$ (1,800)

Small business deduction:
    18% × the least of: (a) Active business income:

Wholesaling business	$251,500	
Cdn. retail business	90,000	
	$341,500	
(b) $283,000 – 4 × $1,800 =	$275,800	
(c) Business limit:	$500,000	(49,644)

General rate reduction (13% × $283,000) .... (28,300)

Federal Part I tax payable .... $ 61,756

Write a memo in point-form explaining to the junior staff member the errors in his calculation. HINT: Do the calculations correctly and compare your results to the results of the junior staff member. Then explain the errors.

Problem 19   ITA: 123–127, 129, 186

Rob's Shameless Self-Promotion Sales (RSS-PS) Inc. is a Canadian-controlled private corporation located in London, Ontario. For its fiscal year ended December 31, 2018, the corporation had correctly calculated its income for tax purposes under Division B as follows:

Canadian source:

Consulting income	$160,000
Advertising agency loss	(30,000)
Rental income from warehouse fully rented on a five-year lease	20,000
Retailing income	75,000
Interest on outstanding accounts receivable in retailing business	25,000
Recapture of CCA from sale of fixtures used in retailing business	25,000
Interest income from five-year bonds	75,000
Taxable capital gain	70,000
Dividends from non-connected taxable Canadian corporations	12,000
Division B net income for tax purposes	$432,000

Additional information:

RSS-PS Inc. made the following selected payments during the year:

Scientific research and experimental development (current expenses)	$100,000
Charitable donations	14,000
Taxable dividends	120,000

The balances in the tax accounts on December 31, 2017 were:

Charitable donations from 2015	$ 1,000
Non-capital losses from 2014	56,000
Net capital losses from 2014	12,000
Refundable dividend tax on hand	20,000
Dividend refund for 2017	9,000

RSS-PS Inc. allocated $370,000 of its $500,000 business limit to other associated corporations. The only scientific research and experimental development expenditures of the associated group were made by RSS-PS Inc.

Rob has asked you to:

(A) Compute the federal Part I tax and assumed provincial tax at a 4% rate on active business income eligible for the small business deduction and 12% for all other income, and

(B) Compute the dividend refund for 2018 and the amount of any RDTOH to be carried forward.

Problem 20   ITA: 125, 129, 186, 256

Carl owns 100% of the issued shares of Compunet. He incorporated Compunet earlier this year to provide computer consulting services to Vitamins Inc., a retailer of energy-producing vitamins. Prior to the incorporation of Compunet, Carl headed the computer service division of Vitamins Inc. One hundred per cent of the issued shares of Vitamins Inc. are owned by Carl's cousin, Vince.

Carl's daughter, Sulee, received a degree in computer science from the University of Toronto in April and has been employed by Compunet as a computer consultant since then. Sulee and Carl work well together. They are the only employees of Compunet.

Compunet owns a warehouse. One-half of the warehouse is rented to Vitamins Inc. and the remainder is rented to Mindblasters, a wholly owned subsidiary of Compunet. Mindblasters is a successful retailer of computer games.

During the current year, Compunet received taxable dividends from Mindblasters and paid taxable dividends to Carl.

Carl has asked you to determine the type(s) of income being earned by Compunet, the rate of tax for each type and any refunds available.

Problem 21

ITA: 125, 129, 256

Lemon Ltd. provides management services for Toys-4-U Limited (Toys), a retailer of educational toys, and for certain other corporations described below. Les Lemon is the sole shareholder and only employee of Lemon Ltd. Prior to this year, Les had been employed by Toys as vice-president of financial and administrative services.

Les owns all of the common shares of Rental Ltd. (Rental), which is in the business of renting commercial properties. Rental has no employees, except for Les, and subcontracts all maintenance and administrative services. Rental's income for tax purposes can be broken down as follows:

Lemon Ltd.	10%
Cheap Leasing Ltd. (see below)	25%
Arm's length parties	65%
	100%

Les is also involved with Cheap Leasing Limited (Cheap), which is in the business of leasing educational equipment. The ownership of the common shares of Cheap is as follow:

Les Lemon	25 shares
Lucy Lemon, Les' wife	20 shares
Lemon Ltd.	30 shares
Larry Lemon, Les' uncle	10 shares
Arm's length parties	15 shares

Cheap derives approximately 80% of its income from the educational equipment leasing business. The balance of its income is interest from a loan to Toys. Cheap has four employees in addition to Les.

All of the above corporations are Canadian-controlled private corporations and have December 31 year ends.

You have been asked to identify the various sources of income for the above corporations indicating the reasoning behind your conclusions. Also indicate the *federal* tax rate and any refundable taxes applicable to each income source.

Problem 22

ITA: Part I, IV

Mr. Humphries, a resident of a province with a 40% effective combined federal and provincial corporate tax rate (before the additional refundable tax), has just won a lottery prize of $750,000. He is considering the following investment of these funds: $200,000 of bonds yielding 8% and $550,000 of common shares of Growth Unlimited Limited (a CCPC earning active business income less than the business limit), which pay a dividend to yield 5%. Having taken a course in security analysis, Mr. Humphries can predict with great confidence that he will realize a 10.5% capital gain on the shares within the year. Mr. Humphries currently has taxable income of $30,000. He has federal personal tax credits of $2,100, and provincial personal tax credits of $1,400.

Advise Mr. Humphries on whether he should use an investment corporation with a permanent establishment in the province of which he is a resident to hold the securities he proposes to purchase. Include in your analysis the realization of the predicted capital gain. Use 2018 rates. Also, consider any non-quantitative factors that may be relevant to the decision.

Problem 23

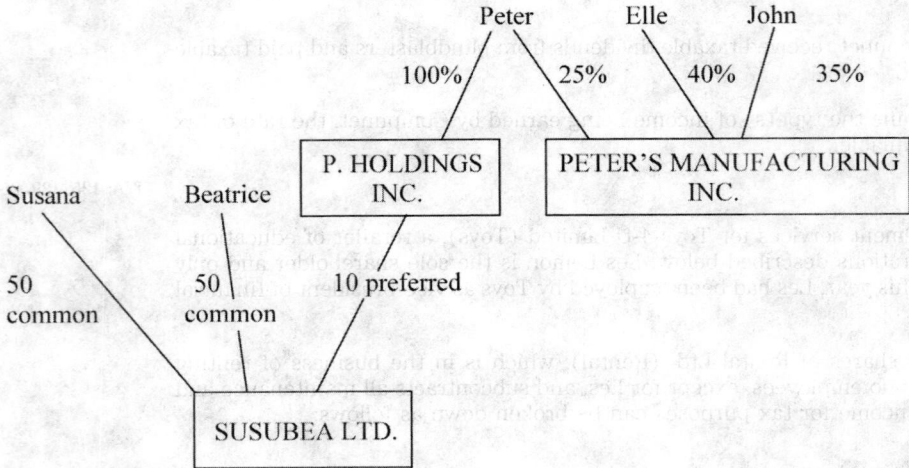

Elle is Peter's wife and John is Peter's brother. Susana and Beatrice are Peter and Elle's daughters, and both are over 18.

Susubea Ltd.'s preferred shares are voting and have a value of $1,500,000 and the common shares held by Susana and Beatrice have a value of $100,000.

— *REQUIRED*

Examine the information in the above diagram and determine whether the corporations involved are associated. Clearly state the reasons supporting your conclusions.

Problem 24

Atlas Manufacturing Ltd. is a Canadian-controlled private corporation located in Digby, Nova Scotia, whose fiscal year end is December 31. The company's income for tax purposes for 2018 was calculated correctly as follows:

Manufacturing income — Note 1	$140,000
Retailing income	200,000
Maintenance service contract loss	(70,000)
Patent income — Note 2	40,000
Rental income — Note 3	30,000
Taxable capital gains net of losses — Note 4	60,000
Recapture of CCA — Note 4	10,000
Interest income on outstanding account receivable on retailing income	14,000
Interest income from a sinking fund trust for replacement of a building	50,000
Foreign business income (gross amount — $Cdn) — Note 5	36,000
Foreign non-business income (gross amount — $Cdn) — Note 5	24,000
Dividends from taxable Canadian Corporations — non-connected	12,000
Profit on sale of excess land — Note 6	100,000
Net income for tax purposes — Division B	$646,000

NOTES:

(1) Manufacturing income was correctly computed according to the provisions of reg. 5200.

(2) The patent income has been determined to be property income.

(3) The rental income was derived from leasing the entire space on a five-year lease in an unused warehouse in a small town in the western part of the province.

(4) The net taxable capital gain and the recapture concerned the disposition of certain specialized maintenance service equipment.

(5) Withholding tax on the non-business income was $3,600 (Cdn). Foreign income tax in the amount of $10,000 (Cdn) was paid on the foreign business income.

(6) The land had been held for approximately five years. It was purchased with the intent of realizing a profit on sale.

Additional Information:

(a)　Atlas made the following selected payments during the year:

Charitable donations	$ 12,000
New equipment — manufacturing	500,000
— retailing	75,000

(b)　The balances in the tax accounts on January 1, 2018 were:

Unused charitable donations	$ 2,000
Investment tax credit	6,000
Unused business foreign tax credit	3,000
Non capital losses	44,000
Net capital losses (arising in 1999)	15,000

(c)　Taxable income earned in Nova Scotia, which is the only Canadian jurisdiction in which Atlas operates, is approximately 90% of the total.

— *REQUIRED*

(a) Calculate the taxable income and federal tax for Atlas Ltd. for the year ended December 31, 2018. (Ignore provincial taxes and dividend refund.)

(b) Compute the refundable portion of Part I tax for 2018.

Problem 25

The following selected and accurate information of its fiscal year ending on December 31, 2018 has been gathered from the books and other records of Vermisht Ltd., a Canadian-controlled private corporation.

Income for Tax Purposes:

Retail operations		
— Canada		$180,000
— United States branch (Note 2)		93,100
Maintenance and service operations		
— Canada		50,000
— United States branch (Note 2)		37,500
Interest income from Canadian sources (Note 3)		58,750
Dividends from taxable Canadian corporations (Note 4)		81,250
Taxable capital gains		25,000
Recapture of CCA (Note 5)		66,250
Rental income from United Kingdom (Note 6)		43,750
Division B income		$635,600
Deductions:		
Donations	$18,750	
Dividends from taxable Canadian corporations	81,250	
Non-capital losses	56,250	
Net capital losses	12,500	168,750
Taxable income		$466,850

Notes and additional information:

(1) The accountant has correctly determined that the Part I tax excluding the additional refundable tax is $85,800 and the small business deduction for 2018 is $52,500.

(2) The United States income above is expressed in Canadian dollars. During 2018, income taxes of $31,250 ($Cdn) were paid to the various levels of US governments and the same amount was correctly deducted under ssec. 126(2) in order to arrive at the Part I tax.

(3) The Canadian interest is from the following sources:

Interest on debt loaned to a Canadian subsidiary, Shmaltz Ltd., of
which Vermisht Ltd. owns 80% of the shares; Shmaltz Ltd. does not
carry on an active business $45,000
Treasury bill interest from seasonal excess cash 10,000
Bank interest on fluctuating cash working capital 3,750
                                                                   $58,750

(4) Dividends:
    Portfolio dividends from non-connected companies received
    March 31 .... $18,750
    Dividends from Shmaltz Ltd., received on July 15 from its subsid-
    iary, which resulted in a total dividend refund of $12,500 to
    Shmaltz Ltd.. 62,500
                                                         $81,250

(5) The recapture arose on the disposal of all of the company's class 10 assets when it discontinued its unprofitable delivery service division.

(6) Rental income of C$43,750 arose from a warehouse in the United Kingdom which had been previously used by the company. The company had discontinued its U.K. operations in 2014. U.K. non-resident withholding tax of C$10,950 was paid during 2017 and the same amount was correctly claimed under ssec. 126(1) in order to arrive at the Part I tax.

(7) The balance in the Refundable Dividend Tax on Hand on December 31, 2017 was $18,750 before the Dividend Refund of $7,500 for the 2017 year.

(8) During 2018, Vermisht Ltd. declared and paid the following taxable cash dividends:

Date Declared	Date Paid	Amount
March 31, 2018	April 15, 2018	$31,250
June 30, 2018	July 15, 2018	$31,250
September 30, 2018	October 15, 2018	$31,250
December 31, 2018	January 15, 2019	$62,500

— *REQUIRED*

Determine the amount of the dividend refund for 2018 for Vermisht Ltd. by clearly presenting all component parts and their calculations.

Do not recalculate the Part I tax and the related tax credits. Assume that they have been computed correctly.

Problem 26

The following calculation of refundable dividend tax on hand (RDTOH), at the end of 2018 has been done incorrectly by a junior staff. You are required to draft a memorandum explaining what was done incorrectly (see required).

Refundable Portion of Part I Tax
(for year ended December 31, 2018)

Aggregate Investment Income (AII)
Net TCG for the year — additional equipment .... $ 8,000
                      — securities .... 13,000 $ 21,000

Property income (Cdn. and foreign)
— Dividends from taxable Cdn. Corporations............... $ 39,000
— Rental income — Note 1 21,000
— Interest — T Bills 7,000
        — bonds of connected, not associated corporations 16,000
— Profit on sale of land not used in business 110,000
— US bond interest net of tax of $1,650 9,350
— ABI from US branch net of tax of $28,000 — Note 2 .... 35,000 237,350
                                                                $258,350

Refundable Portion of Part I Tax

Least of:

1. $30\frac{2}{3}\% \times$ AII $= 30\frac{2}{3}\% \times \$258,350$ $79,227

2. $30\frac{2}{3}\% \times (\$350,000 - 34,486 - 1,650 - 58,000)$ $78,465

3. Part I tax $78,353

Least amount = $78,353

RDTOH, beginning of year .... Nil

RDTOH, end of year $78,353

Notes and Additional Information:

Note 1   Rental income arose from seasonal excess warehousing space of 11%. The warehouse is normally used in the company's active business.

Note 2   Foreign taxes equal the foreign tax credit claimed and foreign funds are in Canadian dollars.

— REQUIRED

Draft a memorandum, in point form, explaining in your own words what was done incorrectly; why it was done incorrectly, and how it should be done correctly.

Do not redo the calculations.

Assume that all input numbers in themselves are correct.

Type 3 Problems

Problem 27

ITA: 123–125, 129, 186

You recently met Susan Taylor at a cocktail party. As a result of your conversation with her, Susan has come to you for tax advice. She wants to know how her income will be taxed. She also wants to know whether she should incorporate and earn the same types of income through a corporation called High Income Limited. She would be the sole shareholder and only employee of that corporation. Susan has received various types of income in 2018. These incomes are as follows:

● Interest income from GIC — $5,000

● Dividend income from a publicly traded corporation — $10,000

● Capital gains from selling public company shares — $20,000

● Susan owns 40% of all the issued and outstanding common shares of Stage Lighting Limited (Stage). Her best friend, Mary, who lives in Ontario, owns the rest of the common shares. The company is in the business of manufacturing customized lighting products. She received $20,000 in dividends (for which Stage *did not* receive any dividend refund) from Stage this year. All income earned by Stage is eligible for the small business deduction.

Susan would like to understand whether she should incorporate a holding company to earn the four different types of income mentioned above.

Susan runs a small fashion store selling high-end handmade scarves. The business is operated as a sole proprietorship. Active operations started four years ago and the business started to make sizable profit last year. The estimated taxable retail income in 2018 is $200,000. Susan would like to know whether she should incorporate this business.

Additional Information and Assumptions

Assume that the effective combined federal and provincial corporate tax rates for 2018 on the following types of income are:

● Active business income (ABI) (eligible for the small business deduction)

38% – 10% – 18% + 5% (net provincial) 15%

- Specified investment business income

38% – 10% + 10⅔% + 14% (provincial) – initially 52⅔%

52⅔% – 30⅔% – ultimately when dividends paid 22%

- Capital gains

Taxed portion is taxed as income from a SIB above

Non-taxed portion 0%

The non-taxed portion of the capital gain is added to the capital dividend account. Dividends can be paid out of the balance of this account with no tax cost to the recipient shareholder.

Assume that, if the ABI increases to the point where it exceeds $500,000 (small business deduction), then the effective federal rate on the ABI in excess of the small business limit will be

- Combined federal and provincial rate:

38% – 10% – 13% (general rate reduction) + 14 (provincial) 29%

Assume that the effective combined federal and provincial personal tax rates for 2018 are:

- The effective combined federal and provincial personal tax rate:

Top marginal rates 33% (federal) + 17% (provincial) 50%

- Effective combined federal and provincial tax rate for dividends from:

Low Rate Income Pool [for dividends paid after 2017] 42.0%

General Rate Income Pool 31.0%

You have agreed with Susan that you will draft a memo analyzing the tax implications of the above situation. Your memo will address and conclude on the following issues:

(A) Based on the theory and a conceptual understanding of incorporation, determine whether Susan can save and/or defer income tax by incorporating a holding company to earn interest income, dividend income from a public company, capital gains from selling public company shares, and dividend income from Stage Lighting Limited.

(B) Based on the theory and a conceptual understanding of incorporation, determine whether Susan can save and/or defer income tax through incorporation of her fashion business.

(C) Discuss some of the general (i.e., not specific to Susan) quantitative and qualitative pros and cons of incorporation.

Problem 28

Mickey and Nicki Waterloo are husband and wife entrepreneurs. Most of the time, when they start a business, they will do so with another person, in order to let that person handle the day-to-day business matters and, also, to provide a potential buyer at some point in the future. Usually this other person will have a shareholding in the operating company, but Mickey and/or Nicki will maintain control. It is, also, usual for each company to have a shareholder agreement with a buy/sell provision that calls for a corporate repurchase on death, disability, bankruptcy, or retirement. Maximizing the use of the small business deduction is also a goal.

At this time, Mickey and Nicki have the following interests, which are all held through a holding company (Holdco) owned 100% by Mickey.

(1) Holdco owns 20% of a company called Sales Co. Inc. The other 80% is owned by Joe Shea, who runs the company. In order to finance the operations, Holdco has invested $100,000 in non-voting preference shares with a redemption value of $100,000 and a dividend rate of 8%.

(2) Holdco and Fred Smith have shared ownership of two companies. Holdco owns 90% of Retail One Inc. and 10% of Retail Two Inc., while Fred owns the other 10% of Retail One Inc. and 90% of Retail Two Inc.

Mickey and Nicki share ownership in two companies. Mickey owns 40% of Ours Inc., Nicki owns 100% of Mine Inc., and Mine Inc. own 60% of Ours Inc. Both Mickey and Nicki are actively involved in these businesses.

On the advice of their lawyer, they set up a discretionary trust for their two children, Dick, who is 12 years old, and Jane, who is 10 years old. This trust borrowed money from the bank (with personal guarantees from Mickey and Nicki) and bought treasury shares from a newly incorporated company, Kids Are Fun Inc. This company sells games through a retail store. It was capitalized with a loan from Nicki.

Advise Mickey and Nicki of the tax implications of the share ownerships outlined above on the small business deduction.

CHAPTER 12 —
DISCUSSION NOTES FOR REVIEW QUESTIONS

(1) The purpose of integration is to avoid the double taxation of income earned through a corporation. Integration should cause the total tax paid by a corporation and its shareholders to be equal to the total tax paid by an individual who carries on the same economic activity directly and not through a corporation. The system should be neutral as to the form of organization used.

(2) Ideal integration depends on:

(a) When the corporation itself pays tax, the shareholder must include in income and pay tax on the full pre-tax income earned by the corporation and then get a full credit for all the income tax paid by the corporation.

(b) All after-tax income would have to be either paid out as dividends in the year earned or taxed in some manner at the shareholder level in that year to avoid the indefinite deferral of tax that might otherwise be available if the corporate rates were lower than individual tax rates. This would equate the position of the shareholder with the position of the proprietor, partner or owner of investments who must pay tax on income from his or her economic activity whether or not it is distributed.

(3) The gross-up is intended to add to the dividend received by the individual shareholder an amount equal to the total income tax paid by the corporation on the income that gave rise to the dividend. Thus, the grossed-up dividend is intended to represent the corporation's pre-tax income. The shareholder will pay tax on the grossed-up dividend at his or her personal rate. The tax credit is intended to give the shareholder credit for the total tax paid by the corporation on the shareholder's behalf. This procedure is intended to equalize the tax paid on the income that is flowed through the corporation to its shareholders with the tax paid on the same income that is earned directly. When the gross-up is 16% and the total (i.e., federal and provincial) corporate tax rate is 13.8%, integration is theoretically perfect. When the gross-up is 38% and the total (i.e., federal and provincial) corporate tax rate is 27.5%, integration is, also, theoretically perfect.

(4) Its purpose is to help small CCPCs retain capital in order to expand their businesses. This is accomplished by using a relatively low corporate tax rate after the small business deduction to defer tax until the income is paid out as a dividend.

(5) There is a deemed year end on July 14 as a result of the acquisition of control and he is deemed to acquire control at the commencement of that day. Mr. Smith can now choose any year end he wants and the company should qualify as a CCPC throughout the year.   ITA: 249(4), 256(9)

(6) Paragraph 125(1)(*a*) deals with Division B income (net of expenses) while paragraph 125(1)(*b*) starts off with taxable income. Therefore, if there are Division C deductions such as donations or loss carryforwards then paragraph 125(1)(*b*) could be lower.

(7) Some advantages of incorporation are:

- limited liability except for personal guarantees;

- tax savings if the combined corporate tax and the personal tax on the dividend is less than the personal tax would be on the same income;

- tax deferral if the corporate tax rate is less than the personal tax rate on that income;

- income splitting with family members as employees or shareholders (beware of the attribution rules and the tax on split income);

- estate freezing;

- availability of registered pension plans to the owner;

- separation of business and personal activities;

- greater flexibility as to the timing and type of income received personally;

- continuity of separate legal entity;

- deferral of accrued capital gains on transfer of shares to a spouse;

- access to financing;

- availability of capital gains exemption on QSBCS; and

- availability of deferral of capital gains on shares of an SBC.

(8) Some disadvantages of incorporation are:

- tax cost if combined corporate tax rate is over 13.8% for income eligible for the small business deduction and 27.5% for other business income;

- a prepayment of tax at lower levels of personal income on business income not eligible for the small business deduction;

- additional legal and accounting costs;

- inability to deduct losses against personal income — this disadvantage may be offset somewhat by the availability of the ABIL; and

- greater difficulty in accessing cash generated by the business for personal use.

(9) He will not be able to get the general rate reduction on income eligible for the small business deduction. In addition, the question does not indicate whether this venture is incorporated. If it is not, then these deductions are not available since they are only available to incorporated businesses.

ITA: 125.1(1)(*a*)

(10) Part IV tax of 38⅓% on portfolio dividends prevents a significant deferral of tax.

(11) (a) Refundable Part I tax;

(b) Part IV tax;

(c) Dividend gross-up and tax credit;

(d) Refundable dividend tax on hand; and

(e) Dividend refund.

(12) The gross-up is intended to place the shareholder in an income position equivalent to that of the corporation before it paid corporate taxes. At an assumed corporate tax rate of 13.8% or 27.5%, the 16% or 38% gross-up, respectively, represents the underlying corporate tax. This is added to the after-tax dividend to tax, theoretically, the pre-tax corporate profits in the hands of the individual shareholder.

(13) The dividend tax credit is intended to give the shareholder credit against his or her taxes for the taxes paid by the corporation on the income from which the dividend was paid. Since the gross-up theoretically takes the dividend up to the pre-tax corporate income level, the dividend tax credit is needed to reduce the individual tax by the theoretical amount of corporate tax already paid on that income. At a corporate tax rate of 13.8%, for example, tax of $13.80 would be paid on corporate income of $100. The gross-up of 16% would take the individual's income on that dividend of $86.20 back up to the $100 of corporate pre-tax income level. Assuming a provincial dividend tax credit of ³/₁₁ of the gross-up, the total dividend tax credit would be 13.8% of the grossed-up dividend or $13.80. Thus the dividend tax credit represents the underlying corporate tax paid on the dividend.

(14) Of the $1,000 capital gain, $500 is not taxable and is allocated to the capital dividend account to be passed out to the shareholders tax-free as a capital dividend. This provides for the tax-free receipt of this $500 whether the capital gain is realized in the corporation or by the individual directly.

ITA: 82(3)

The remaining $500 is theoretically taxed at an approximate initial rate of Part I tax of 40%. An additional refundable tax of 10⅔% is also levied and added to this account. Then,

30⅔% of the income is classified as refundable Part I tax and added to the refundable dividend tax on hand account. Dividend payments result in a return to the corporation of 38⅓% of dividends that are paid. This would leave an effective tax rate in the corporation on taxable capital gains of 20% which is higher than the 13.8% level at which integration works.

(15) Ordinarily the interest would be taxed at the full rate of 40% (38% − 10% + 12% provincial) plus the 10⅔% additional refundable tax under Part I with part of this being classified as refundable Part I tax and added to the refundable dividend tax on hand account. However, since the two companies are associated and the interest is being deducted against the active business income of Opco, the deeming rules will deem the interest income to be active business income and not eligible for the refundable tax treatment.

ITA: 129(6)

(16) While A Ltd. does not have more than 10% of the votes and value of B Ltd., A Ltd. does have control, since A Ltd. and the son of the only shareholder are related and do not deal at arm's length. Thus, over 50% of the voting shares belong to a person with whom A Ltd. does not deal at arm's length.

ITA: 186(2)

(17) The factors to be considered are:

- the same non-capital losses cannot be deducted under both provisions;
- the normal corporate tax rates under Part I are usually higher than the 38⅓% Part IV tax;
- the Part IV tax is a refundable tax and not a permanent tax like Part I tax;
- the non-capital losses would otherwise expire without any value; and
- the corporation is not expected to pay a dividend to claim the refund until years in the future.

CHAPTER 12 — SOLUTIONS TO MULTIPLE CHOICE QUESTIONS

Question 1

(B) $20,700 is correct. It is calculated as follows:

Least of:	(a)	income from an active business carried on in Canada	$120,000
		net of loss from an active business carried on in Canada	0
			$120,000
	(b)	taxable income	$132,000
	(c)	business limit: $500,000 – $385,000	$115,000

The least is (c): $115,000 × 18% = $20,700

(A) $18,000 is incorrect. The foreign business loss of $20,000 has been netted against the $120,000 of Canadian business income.

(C) $21,600 is incorrect. This amount is 18% of the Canadian active business income.

(D) $23,760 is incorrect. This amount is 18% of the taxable income.

Question 2

(D) is correct. M Ltd. is carrying on an active business. The business is not a personal services business as the services are provided to an associated corporation. M Ltd. and ACC Ltd. are associated. M Ltd. is not a specified investment business as the principal purpose is not to derive income from property. Thus, by default, it is carrying on an active business.

ITA: 125(7)
ITA: 256(1)(*d*)

(A) is incorrect. M Ltd. is not carrying on a personal services business for the reasons outlined above.

(B) is incorrect. M Ltd. is not carrying on a personal services business for the reasons outlined above.

(C) is incorrect. M Ltd. is not carrying on a specified investment business as the principal purpose is not to derive income from property.

Question 3

(B) $3,250 is correct. This amount is 13% of taxable income of $520,000 in excess of ABI eligible for the SBD, which is $495,000 (i.e., 13% of $520,000 – $495,000).

(A) $2,600 is incorrect. This amount is 13% of taxable income in excess of $500,000.

(C) $56,017 is incorrect. This amount is 13% × (Canadian ABI minus the SBD of $89,100 (i.e., 18% of $495,000)).

(D) $67,000 is incorrect. This amount is 13% × taxable income.

Question 4

(C) $74,000 is correct.

ITA: 186(1), 186(4)

Dividend received from non-connected corporation, C Ltd.:	
$120,000 × 38⅓%	$46,000
70% of $40,000 dividend refund received by connected	
corporation, B Ltd.	28,000
	$74,000

B Ltd. is connected to A Ltd., because of *de jure* control and because A Ltd. holds more than 10% of   ITA: 186(2), 186(4)
B Ltd.

(A) $60,000 is incorrect. This amount is 70% and 8% of the dividend refunds received by B Ltd.
and C Ltd., respectively.

(B) $73,600 is incorrect. This amount applies the Refundable Part I tax rate on investment income,
30²/₃%, to the total dividends received.

(D) $92,000 is incorrect. This amount is 38¹/₃% × the dividends received and ignores the special
rules for connected corporations.

Question 5

(D) is correct. Neither J Co. nor D Co. is associated with R Co., since neither Joanne nor David own
at least 25% of the shares of R Co. through J Co. and D Co. Their ownership is only 22% (i.e., 55% of   ITA: 256(2)
40%). Hence, J Co. and D Co. cannot be associated through R Co.

(A) and (B) are incorrect because Joanne controls J Co. and her spouse controls D Co. Two corpo-   ITA: 251(6)(b)
rations are associated under paragraph 256(1)(c), if related persons control each corporation and either
person owns at least 25% of the shares of the related persons' corporation. Spouses are related by
marriage.

(C) is incorrect because if a trust for their twin daughters controls a third company, T Co., those   ITA: 256(1.2)(f)(ii),
shares are deemed to be owned by the beneficiaries. In addition, because those beneficiaries are minors,   256(1.3)
their shares are deemed to be owned by each of Joanne and Doug. Therefore, J Co. and T Co. are   ITA: 256(1)(a)
associated because they are deemed to be controlled by the same person (Joanne). The same is true for
D Co. and T Co. (each deemed to be controlled by Doug). The two corporations are associated with each
other unless an election is made and the third corporation (T Co.) is deemed to have a business limit of   ITA: 256(2)
nil.

Question 6

(C) is correct. X Ltd. and Y Ltd. are not associated because although X Ltd. is controlled by a   ITA: 256(1)(d)
person who is related to each member of the various groups of persons (i.e., a pair of the two daughters
and one son or all three) who controls Y Ltd., there is no cross-ownership of at least 25%. Thus, X Ltd.
and Y Ltd. are not associated.

(A) is not correct. X and Y are associated. The same group (Rod and Patrick) controls both   ITA: 256(1)(b)
corporations. This group controls X Ltd., despite the fact that Patrick himself controls X Ltd. It does not   ITA: 256(1.2)(b)(i)
matter that the individuals are not related.

(B) is not correct because X Ltd. and Y Ltd. are associated because they are controlled by related   ITA: 256(1)(c)
persons (a parent and son are related by blood) and one of the persons owns not less than 25% of the   ITA: 251(6)(a)
shares of both companies.

(D) is not correct. Sibco and Parentco are associated. Sibco is controlled by a related group of two,   ITA: 256(1)(e)
three, or four of its shareholders. Parentco is controlled by the related group of the mother and father.
Each member of any related group that controls Sibco is related to each member of the related group
that controls Parentco. The mother and father, together, own at least 25% of the shares of both
corporations.

CHAPTER 12 — SOLUTIONS TO EXERCISES

Exercise 1

[Note: The facts of this case are those of *The Queen v. Rochmore Investments Ltd.* However, the legislation under which the case was decided did not contain a definition of "active business" or "specified investment business".]

76 DTC 6156 (F.C.A.)

Under the current legislation, "active business" is defined to exclude "a specified investment business" in such a way that if a business is not a specified investment business (and is not a personal service business), it is an active business. Note that the definition includes an adventure in the nature of trade and is only applicable in respect of the small business deduction.

ITA: 125(7), 248(1)

In this particular case, the facts indicate that it is carrying on a specified investment business. It would appear that the principal purpose of the corporation's business is to derive income from interest on mortgage loans. It does not appear to be carrying on the business of a credit union and it is not in the business of leasing movable property. If it did, the corporation would be considered to be carrying on an active business. Since the corporation had no full-time employees, it cannot escape the definition of a specified investment business, to be treated as an active business, through paragraph (*a*) of the definition, which requires more than five full-time employees.

ITA: 125(7)

The only possibility for escape is in paragraph (*b*) of the definition of "specified investment business". If the taxpayer company did not have more than five full-time employees because another corporation associated with it provided the services to the taxpayer corporation that would otherwise be performed by its own full-time employees, then the taxpayer corporation could be considered as carrying on an active business. In this case, the two principal operators of the taxpayer corporation own and manage a number of other companies. Further facts are required to determine if any of these other corporations are associated with the taxpayer corporation and if such an associated corporation provides services that would otherwise be provided by more than five full-time employees of the taxpayer corporation. This seems unlikely given the facts outlined in the case.

ITA: 125(7)

The taxpayer corporation, therefore, is likely carrying on a specified investment business. It is not carrying on a personal services business because it is not likely that the principals of the taxpayer corporation would reasonably be regarded as employees of the persons to whom the mortgage loans were made.

Exercise 2

(A) (i) Mr. Beta is at arm's length with the corporation because his 25% ownership does not give him control. However, paragraph 251(1)(*b*) could always apply if the facts indicate that the non-related persons are not dealing at arm's length at a particular moment in time.

ITA: 251(2)(*b*)

(ii) Mr. Beta and his brother are not at arm's length with the corporation. Mr. Beta and his brother form a related group; since they are siblings, each is related by blood.

ITA: 251(2)(*b*)(ii), 251(6)(*a*)

(iii) Mr. Delta is not at arm's length with the corporation because of the share purchase option. This provision deems Mr. Delta to control Alpha Corp. unless the exceptions in this subparagraph are met.

ITA: 251(5)(*b*)(i)

(iv) Mr. Epsilon is at arm's length with the corporation because of the exception, which is contingent on the death of Mr. Beta, unless paragraph 251(1)(*b*) applies, as described in (i), above.

ITA: 251(5)(*b*)(i)

(B) (i) The corporations are not at arm's length. This subparagraph applies where Lambda Corp. is controlled by a person (i.e., A) and Tau Corp. is controlled by a related group (i.e., A and B). A is related to himself for purposes of share ownership and to his brother.

ITA: 251(2)(*c*)(iii), 251(5)(*c*), 251(6)(*a*)

(ii) The corporations are at arm's length because subparagraph 251(2)(*c*)(iv) does not apply where there is an unrelated group of persons controlling one corporation, unless the person controlling the other corporation is related to each member of the unrelated group. For example, if two first cousins control one corporation and their grandfather controls the other, the two corporations would be related. Of course, factual non-arm's length can always apply as described in (A)(i), above.

(iii) The corporations are related and, hence, they are not at arm's length. This provision deems two corporations to be related where each corporation is related to another common corporation.

ITA: 251(3)

Exercise 3

(A) Jay-one Ltd. and Jay-two Ltd. are associated, both being controlled by the same person. Jay-one Ltd. and Jay-three Ltd., are associated. Since Ava has voting control of Jay-one Ltd. and Jay-one Ltd. in turn has voting control of Jay-three Ltd., then Ava controls Jay-three Ltd. Therefore, all three corporations are controlled by the same person. As a result of this application of the association rule in paragraph 256(1)(b), the election under subsection 256(2) is not available to Jay-one Ltd., because Jay-three Ltd. and Jay-two Ltd. are associated without subsection 256(2).

ITA: 251(1)(b), 256(1)(a), 256(1)(b)

(B) Benco Ltd. and Rayco Ltd. are associated. Benco Ltd. is controlled by Abigail's mother and Rayco Ltd. is controlled by Abigail. Abigail and her mother are related. Abigail owns at least 25% of the shares, which are not of a specified class, of both corporations.

ITA: 256(1)(a), 256(1)(c)

(C) Adamco Ltd. and Kidco Ltd. are associated. Adamco Ltd. is controlled by Adam. Kidco Ltd. is controlled by the group consisting of Adam, his daughter and his son-in-law. Adam is related to himself, to his daughter and to his son-in-law. Adam owns at least 25% of the shares which are not of a specified class of Kidco Ltd.

ITA: 252(1)(e), 256(1)(d), 256(1.5), 251(6)(a), 251(6)(b)

(D) Since both corporations are controlled by a group, paragraph 256(1)(e) is the only possibility for association. However, while Sisco Ltd. is controlled by a related group of sisters, Cousco Ltd. is not controlled by a related group. The two sisters as a group do not control Cousco Ltd. One sister and her daughter do not control the company. Finally, cousins and aunts and nieces are not related by the rules. Therefore, the condition in paragraph 256(1)(e) fails and the two corporations are not associated unless subsection 256(5.1) can be used with the argument that control in fact is exercised by Sister One and Sister Two through direct or indirect influence on their daughters or unless subsection 256(2.1) is invoked on the basis that one of the main reasons for the separate existence of the two corporations is to reduce taxes.

ITA: 251(6)(a)

ITA: 251, 252

Exercise 4

Taxit and Sibling are associated:

ITA: 256(1)(c)

— each corporation is controlled by one person;

— the person who controlled one was related to the person who controlled the other;

— one of these persons owned not less than 25% of the shares which are not of a specified class of each corporation.

Since the two corporations are associated, they must share the small business deduction on a maximum of $500,000 of active business income. The Act requires that the corporations file an agreement, in prescribed form, allocating the $500,000 business limit. If an agreement is not filed within the time period indicated in subsection 125(4), that subsection empowers the Minister to make an allocation.

ITA: 125(3)

They could each gain their eligibility for the small business deduction on a full $500,000 by having Beta reduce her holdings in Taxit to below 25% or by having Beta convert her holdings in Taxit to shares of a specified class (i.e., in essence, non-voting preferred shares). However, this strategy would work only as long as there are no factors present of the kind that would enable the deeming provisions to apply.

ITA: 256(2.1)

Exercise 5

Since neither corporation is controlled by one person, and both corporations are not controlled by the same group of persons, the only provision in subsection 256(1) that can potentially apply is paragraph 256(1)(e). That paragraph sets out three conditions, each of which must be met by the facts of the case for association.

(1) Each corporation must be controlled by a related group. — The group of brothers controlling Chutzpah Enterprises Limited is related. The group consisting of Bett and Dalled Chutzpah controlling Schlock Sales Limited are related as brother-in-law and sister-in-law or by paragraph 251(6)(a) and paragraphs 252(2)(b) and (c). Therefore, the condition is met.

ITA: 251(2)(a), 251(6)(a)
ITA: 251(6)(b)

(2) Each of the members of one of the related groups was related to all of the members of the other related group. — Consider the group consisting of Aleph and Bett Chutzpah which is a related group controlling Chutzpah Enterprises Limited and the group Bett and Dalled Chutzpah which is a related group controlling Schlock Sales Limited. Aleph is related to his brother Bett, as discussed above, and to Dalled. Bett is related to himself and his sister-in-law, Dalled, as discussed above. Therefore, the condition is met.

ITA: 251(2)(*a*), 251(6)(*a*), 256(1.5)

(3) One or more members of both related groups must own, either alone or together, not less than 25% of the issued shares of any class, other than a specified class, of shares of the capital stock of the other corporation. — Bett, who is a member of both related groups, owns alone the minimum 25% of the shares necessary to meet this condition. Common shares are not shares of a specified class.

ITA: 256(1.1)

Exercise 6

Part I tax payable

Part I Tax on Taxable Income

Taxable income	$ 79,700
Tax @ 38% on $79,700	$ 30,286
Deduct: Federal tax abatement (10% of $79,700)	7,970
Net	$ 22,316

Additional refundable tax (ART) — 10⅔% × lesser of:

(a) AII	$ 7,000	
(b) TI – SBD income amount (Schedule 1)	Nil	
Total		$ 22,316
Deduct small business deduction (see Schedule 1) ...	14,346	
General reduction (see Schedule 2)	Nil	14,346
Part I federal tax payable		$ 7,970
Provincial tax @ 5% of $79,700		3,985
Total tax payable		$ 11,955

Schedule 1: *Small Business Deduction*

18% of the least of:

Income from an active business	$110,000(I)
Taxable income	$ 79,700(II)
Business limit	$500,000(III)

Small business deduction — 18% of $79,700 = $14,346

Schedule 2: *General Reduction*

Taxable income		$ 79,700
Less: income eligible for the small business deduction	$79,700	
AII	7,000	(86,700)
Net		Nil
13% of Nil		Nil
Total		$ Nil

Exercise 7

(A) *Part I Tax on Taxable Income*

Tax @ 38% of $130,000	$ 49,400
Deduct: federal tax abatement (10% of $130,000)	13,000
Net	$ 36,400

Additional refundable tax (ART) — 10⅔% of lesser of:

(a) AII ($100K + $20K + $50K – $20K – $50K) = $100,000	
(b) TI – SBD income amount ($130K – $90K) = $40,000	4,267

Total		$ 40,667
Deduct: small business deduction (see Schedule 1)	16,200	
general reduction	Nil	16,200
Part I tax payable (federal)		$ 24,467
Provincial tax @ 4% of $130,000		5,200
Total tax		$ 29,667

Schedule 1: *Small Business Deduction*

18% of least of:

Income from active business [$260K – (100K + 20K + 50K)]	$ 90,000(I)
Taxable income	$130,000(II)
Business limit	$500,000(III)
Small business deduction — 18% of $90,000 lesser of (I), (II), and (III)	$ 16,200

(B) *Refundable Portion of Part I Tax*

Note — the solution below is based on the current tax legislation for the refundable portion of Part I tax as the proposed changes are not effective until taxations years beginning after 2018.

Least of:

(a) 30⅔% × aggregate investment income (30⅔% × $100,000)		$ 30,667
(b) Taxable income	$130,000	
Less: amount eligible for SBD	(90,000)	
30⅔% × $40,000 =		$ 12,267
(c) Part I tax		$ 24,467
Refundable portion of Part I tax — The least		$ 12,267

Part IV Tax on Taxable Dividends Received

Taxable dividends subject to Part IV tax:

Non-connected corporations × 38⅓ ($30,000 × 38⅓%)	$ 11,500
Connected corporations to the extent of share of dividend refund to payer	4,000
Total Part IV tax payable	$ 15,500

Refundable Dividend Tax on Hand

RDTOH at end of last year	Nil	
Deduct: Dividend refund for last year	Nil	Nil
Add: Refundable portion of Part I tax		$ 12,267
Part IV tax		15,500
RDTOH at end of year		$ 27,767

Dividend Refund

Taxable dividends paid in year ($70,000 × 38⅓%)	$ 26,833(VI)
RDTOH at end of year	$ 27,767(VII)
Dividend refund — lesser of (VI) and (VII)	$ 26,833

Exercise 8

(A) Sunlight Limited and H Ltd. are associated. H Ltd. is controlled by one person, Mr. Bennett. He is related to each member of the group, H Ltd. and W Ltd. that controls Sunlight Limited, because he is related to H Ltd. which he controls and he is related to W Ltd., which is controlled by his wife. Also, he owns not less than 25% of the shares of Sunlight Limited through his ownership of shares in H Ltd. These shares are not specified shares. By a similar analysis, Sunlight Limited and W Ltd. are associated.

ITA: 256(1)(d)
ITA: 251(2)(b)(i), 251(2)(b)(iii)
ITA: 256(1.2)(d)

Since the rental income would be deductible as an expense from the income of an active business of an associated payer, it will not be income from property of the recipient. It will be deemed to be income from an active business of the recipient, H Ltd. Since H Ltd. has only dividend income it will be eligible for the small business deduction in respect of the rental income as long as it is allocated a part of the business limit of the associated corporations.

ITA: 129(6)(a)(i)

ITA: 129(6)(b)(i)
ITA: 125(1)

(B) Since Sunlight is connected with both holding companies there will be no Part IV tax liability unless Sunlight gets a dividend refund as a result of the dividends it pays. However, Sunlight earns only active business income which is not subject to refundable taxes and dividend refunds.

Exercise 9

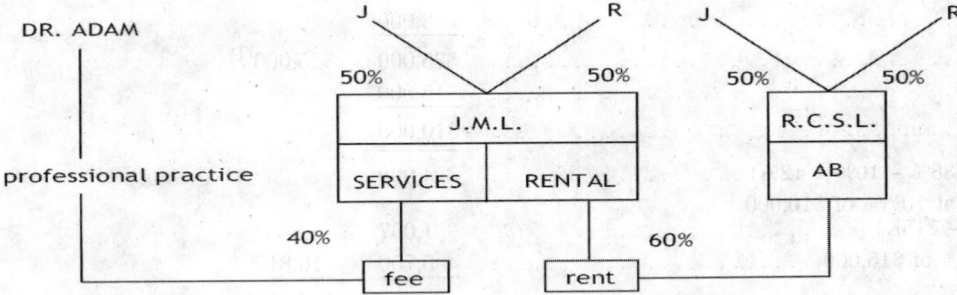

(A) Rent from RCSL:

(i) RCSL is associated with JML;

ITA: 256(1)(b)

(ii) RCSL deducts the rent from its active business.

Therefore, the rent is deemed to be income of JML from an active business, eligible for the small business deduction.

ITA: 125(1), 129(6)(b)(i)

(B) Services fee from Dr. Adam:

(i) JML's income from providing services would be considered income from an active business unless further facts indicate that it is carrying on a personal services business;

(ii) the business of providing services would be a personal services business if one or both of the shareholders of JML, who are specified shareholders (because they own at least 10% of the shares of JML), performed the services and would be regarded as an employee of the professional practice of Dr. Adam, unless those services are provided by more than five full-time employees of J.M.L. and these employees are employed throughout the year.

Therefore, if the services fee is considered income from an active business, it would qualify for the small business deduction.

Exercise 10

Interest income		$ 7,000
Dividends grossed up (1.16 × $15,000)		17,400
Taxable capital gains (½ × $6,000)		3,000
Incremental taxable income		$27,400

Federal tax on total taxable income of $47,400
(i.e., $27,400 incremental + $20,000 other income):

Tax on first $46,605	$ 6,991	
Tax on next $795 @ 20.5%	163	$ 7,154
Less: dividend tax credit ($^8/_{11}$ × 16% of $15,000)	$ 1,745	
other personal tax credits	1,951	(3,696)
Basic federal tax		$ 3,458
Provincial tax		
Tax on first $46,605	$ 4,661	
Tax on next $795 @ 12%	95	4,756
Less: dividend tax credit ($^3/_{11}$ × 16% of $15,000)	$ 655	
other personal tax credits	1,200	(1,855)
Total tax on taxable income of $47,400		$ 6,359

Taxation of Income From Investment Portfolio Through a Corporation

Corporation			Available cash
Interest income		$ 7,000	
Dividends		15,000	
Taxable capital gains		3,000	
Income		$25,000	$25,000[1]
Less: dividends [sec. 112]		15,000	
Taxable income		$10,000	
Tax under Part I @ 40% (38% – 10% + 12%)		$ 4,000	
Additional refundable tax at 10⅔% of $10,000 ($7K + $15K + $3K – $15K)		1,067	
Tax under Part IV @ 38⅓% of $15,000		5,750	10,817
Retained in corporation[1]			$14,183
Refundable tax:			
Part I (30⅔% of ($7K + $15K + $3K – $15K))		$ 3,067	
Part IV (38⅓% × $15,000)		5,750	8,817
Available for distribution to shareholders as taxable dividend			$23,000[2]

Shareholder		
Taxable dividend (per requirements)		$15,000
Gross-up (16% of $15,000)		2,400
Incremental taxable income		$17,400

Federal tax on total taxable income of $37,400
(i.e., $17,400 incremental + $20,000 other income):

Tax @ 15%		$ 5,610

Less: dividend tax credit ($^8/_{11} \times$ 16% of $15,000)	$1,745	
other personal tax credits	1,951	(3,696)
Basic federal tax		$ 1,914
Provincial tax		
Tax @ 10%		$ 3,740
Less: dividend tax credit ($^3/_{11} \times$ 16% of $15,000) .... $ 655		
other personal tax credits 1,200		(1,855)
Total tax on taxable income of $38,400		$ 3,799

Total Taxes Paid

Through corporation:

Corporation after refund on $15,000 of dividends paid ($11,167 − 38⅓% × $15,000)		$ 5,417
Shareholder		3,799
Total		$ 9,216
Received directly		$ 6,359

— *NOTES TO SOLUTION*

(1) Ignores the non-taxable portion of capital gain which can be distributed tax free.

(2) Note that a dividend of $22,650 will result in a dividend refund of only $8,682 (i.e., $22,650 × 38⅓%), not the $8,817 that was added to the RDTOH for the year. This deficiency results from imperfections in the tax rates. A larger dividend of $23,000 (i.e., $8,817/38.33%) would have to be paid, using other sources of funds, to clear the RDTOH.

Exercise 11

The two corporations are considered associated for Canadian tax purposes. Generally, interest income received from an associated corporation that is deductible in computing that corporation's active business income would be considered active business income. However, as the interest is US-sourced, and not from a "source in Canada", and is not deductible in computing active business income in Canada, it will be considered investment income to the Canadian corporation and not income from an active business. Hence, the small business deduction will not apply.

ITA: 256
ITA: 129(6)

The interest will be subject to the full corporate tax rate, including the 10⅔% additional refundable tax on investment income. The addition to RDTOH (30⅔%) will also apply.

ITA: 123.3, 129(1)

Exercise 12

(a) Joan controls A Ltd. Therefore, Joan controls 55% of the votes (30% directly and 25% indirectly) of B Ltd. The companies are associated by par. 256(1)(*b*), as both are controlled by the same person. A Ltd. and B Ltd. are also associated by par. 256(1)(*d*). Joan controls A Ltd. The related group of Joan and A Ltd. control B Ltd. In respect of each corporation, Joan owns at least 25% of the shares.

(b) A Ltd. and B Ltd. are not associated, because the 25% cross-ownership test is not met as the preference shares are "shares of a specified class" as defined in ssec. 256(1.1). That is, they are non-voting shares that have a fixed dividend rate (8%) which does not exceed the prescribed rate in effect at the time the shares were issued (10%), and the amount which can be received on redemption is equal to the consideration paid for the shares.

John may be in a position to control B Ltd. by ownership of the preference shares. If the financing provided by John is critical to B Ltd. and, if B Ltd. is unable to replace it elsewhere, then John would have undue influence since, by exercising his right to retract the shares, he could cripple the business. Thus, John would control B Ltd. by "*de facto* control" (ssec. 256(5.1)). If this is the case, John would control A Ltd. and B Ltd. and they would be associated, (par. 256(1)(*b*)).

(c) It appears that Joe would have "*de facto* control" (ssec. 256(5.1)) of B Ltd. since he controls the day-to-day operations and without the marketing rights to A Ltd.'s product, B Ltd. would have no business.

Even without "*de facto* control", it is likely that the CRA would deem A Ltd. and B Ltd. to be associated by virtue of ssec. 256(2.1), arguing that it may reasonably be considered that one of the main reasons for the separate existence of those corporations is to reduce the amount of taxes that would otherwise be payable.

(d) If the preference shares are "shares of a specified class", then A Ltd. and B Ltd. are not associated.

If the preference shares are not "shares of a specified class", then A Ltd. and B Ltd. are associated by ssec. 256(2), unless X Ltd. elects not to be associated with A Ltd. and B Ltd. A Ltd. controls X Ltd; therefore, A Ltd. and X Ltd. are associated by par. 256(1)(*a*). If the preference shares are not "shares of a specified class", then B Ltd. owns shares of X Ltd. having more than 50% of the FMV of all shares issued by X Ltd. This deems B Ltd. to control X Ltd. by spar. 256(1.2)(*c*)(i). Therefore, B Ltd. and X Ltd. would be associated by par. 256(1)(*a*). Thus, A Ltd. and B Ltd. would be associated with the same corporation, X Ltd., at the same time and, thus, would be deemed to be associated with each other by ssec. 256(2).

Exercise 13

(a) B Co. controls C Co. — 256(1)(*a*): associated

A Co. controls B Co. — 256(1)(*a*): associated

A Co. controls C Co. — 256(1)(*a*): associated

(b) A Co. and B Co. are controlled by the same person — 256(1)(*b*): associated.

(c) Each of the corporations is controlled by the same group — 256(1)(*b*): associated.

(d) Each of the corporations is controlled by the same group — 256(1)(*b*): associated. Subpararaph 256(1.2)(*b*)(i) ensures that a corporation controlled by one person will be considered controlled by the group, notwithstanding that one person in the group (Mr. A.) controls one of the corporations himself (M Co.).

(e) Both D Co. and E Co. are controlled by the same group of persons, i.e., A Co. and B Co. — 256(1)(*b*): associated

(f) Mr. A. is related to his son and Mr. A. owns not less than 25% of B Co. — 256(1)(*c*): associated

(g) Each of the corporations is controlled by a related group. Each member of one of the related groups is related to all members of the other related group. Mrs. A, who is a member of both related groups, owns, in respect of both corporations, not less than 25% of the issued shares of any class, other than a specified class. — par. 256(1)(*e*): associated.

(h) (i)   Mr. A controls A Co. Mr. A is related to each member of a group that controls B Co. Mr. A owns, in respect of both corporations, not less than 25% of the issued shares of any class, other than a specified class. — 256(1)(*d*): associated.

Paragraph 256(1.2)(*d*) deems Mr. A. to own 100% of the 26% of the shares in B Co. owned by A Holdco.

(ii) A Co. and B Co. are associated under par. 256(1)(*b*). Mr. A controls both A Co. and B Co. Mr. A controls A Co. directly through his 60% share ownership. Mr. A controls B Co. through the 26% held "indirectly" via A Co. and the 25% held directly for a total of 51%. Note that Mr. B can be considered to "indirectly" control all 26% of the shares held by A Co. in B Co. because Mr. A has voting control over A Co. and can thus dictate to A Co. how it manages and/or votes its ownership in B Co.

(i) A Ltd. and X Ltd. are not associated, even though one person (X) controls one corporation and is related to the person who controls the other corporation (A, his brother), since neither person owns at least 25% of the other's corporation.

Par. 256(1)(*c*) — not associated

Par. 251(6)(*a*) — related

X Ltd. and Y Ltd. are associated, since the controlling shareholder of X Ltd. is related to each member of a group that controls Y Ltd. (i.e., himself and his spouse), and X owns at least 25% of the shares outstanding in both X Ltd. and Y Ltd.

Par. 256(1)(*d*) — associated

Par. 251(6)(*b*) — related

Y Ltd. and Z Ltd. are associated, since the controlling shareholder of Z Ltd. is related to each member of a group that controls Y Ltd. (i.e., his mother and himself), and Z owns at least 25% of the outstanding shares of both Y Ltd and Z Ltd.

Par. 256(1)(*d*) — associated

Par. 251(6)(*a*) — related

X Ltd. and Z Ltd. are associated, since they share a common association with Y Ltd.

Ssec. 256(2) — associated unless Y Ltd. elects not to be associated with X Ltd. and Z Ltd.

Z Ltd. and B Ltd. with ZB Ltd.:

(1) are not associated. Although both Z Ltd. and B Ltd. are each controlled by one person, Z and B respectively, neither is related to each member of the controlling group of the other corporation (i.e., ZB Ltd.). Z and B are deemed to be related to themselves for purposes of determining control but are not related to each other since they are cousins.

Sec. 251 related

Par. 251(5)(*c*)

(2) although the technical rules above would not associate the corporations, they can be deemed associated under ssec. 256(2.1), if one of the main reasons for the separate existence is to reduce taxes levied under the *Income Tax Act*.

Note: All the above situations in which no association was found would have to be reviewed in light of the concept of de facto control (ssec. 256(5.1)).

(j) The corporations are associated by virtue of paragraph 256(1)(*b*) since RA Inc. and FK Inc. are both controlled by the two sisters, Ruth and Alice.

Ruth owns 50% of RA Inc. and Alice owns 50% of RA Inc. Together, they control RA Inc.

Ruth owns 20% of FK Inc. and is deemed to own the 30% of FK Inc. owned by Fay by virtue of subsection 256(1.3). This results from the fact that Fay is Ruth's daughter, she is under 18 years of age and it is not reasonable to consider that Fay manages the business and affairs of FK Inc. without a significant degree of influence by Ruth. Therefore, Ruth owns 50% and Alice owns 20% of FK Inc. Together they control FK Inc.

(k) B Ltd. and C Ltd. are associated by virtue of par. 256(1)(*b*) as they are both controlled by Bill. C Ltd. and K Ltd. are associated by virtue of par. 256(1)(*a*) since C Ltd. is deemed to control K Ltd. by spar. 256(1.2)(*c*)(i) because C Ltd. owns shares of the capital stock of K Ltd. having a fair market value of more than 50% of the fair market value of all issued and outstanding shares of K Ltd.

Bill is deemed to own the shares of K Ltd. which are owned by C Ltd. by virtue of par. 256(1.2)(*d*). Thus, K Ltd., C Ltd., and B Ltd. are all associated with each other by virtue of par. 256(1)(*b*) as they are all controlled by the same person: Bill.

C Ltd. and K Ltd. are also associated by virtue of par. 256(1)(*c*). C Ltd. is controlled by Bill, and K Ltd. is controlled by Ellen, who is related to Bill. Bill meets the 25% share ownership test in K Ltd. (through the preferred shares) by virtue of paragraph 56(1.2)(*d*). Note that the preferred shares are not specified because they are voting shares.

C Ltd. and K Ltd. are also associated by virtue of paragraph 256(1)(*d*). Bill is related to Rose and Ellen, a related group that controls K Ltd. Paragraph 256(1.2)(*d*) again deems Bill to own 100% of the preferred shares of K Ltd.

Note: Section 256(2) is not applicable, as B Ltd. and K Ltd. are associated by virtue of par. 256(1)(*b*)).

Exercise 14

1. Basic Part I tax rate of 38% is applied to the taxable income. Taxable income is the "net" income minus certain deductions (Division C) such as the $2,500 of dividends from taxable Canadian corporations.

2. From this amount is deducted a series of tax credits:

   (a) federal abatement to provinces is based on 10% of the taxable income earned in a province (in this case Ontario) which is calculated by removing taxable income not attributed to a province (in this case the foreign business income and bank interest earned in New York).

(b) The small business deduction (SBD) of 18% is based on the least of:

   (i)   annual business limit of $500,000

   (ii) taxable income earned in Canada adjusted for income on which the corporation paid foreign taxes

   (iii) active business income (ABI) from a business carried on in Canada:

Manufacturing and processing income	$ 50,000
Retailing	75,000
Bank interest — above operations	1,000
Interest on Canadian treasury bills (incidental ABI)	3,000
Recapture of CCA on certain Canadian equipment	7,500
	$136,500

(c) Manufacturing and processing profits tax credits:

   Subject to certain restrictions, a credit is allowed on manufacturing income in excess of the amount of active business income on which the corporation calculates the SBD. This credit is 13% on such income.

(d) X Ltd. is entitled to a foreign tax credit for taxes paid in the United States. The business income is not subject to withholding; the interest income is normally subject to withholding.

(e) A 13% tax reduction is available on taxable income not eligible for the M&P profits deduction, the small business deduction, nor refundable Part I tax treatment.

3. Other taxes and refunds:

(a) Taxes are paid at the 28% (38% − 10%) rate on Canadian and foreign investment income or specified investment business income.

   This same income is subject to the $10\frac{2}{3}$% additional refundable tax.

   Refundable Part I tax is accumulated, at a rate of $30\frac{2}{3}$% of aggregate investment income, in the RDTOH account.

   Aggregate Investment Income (AII)

Net TCG for the year	$3,000	
less: net capital losses claimed	—	$ 3,000
Property income (Cdn. and foreign)	$20,000[1]	
less: dividends	2,500[2]	17,500
less: losses from property	—	
		$20,500

[1] Canadian bond interest	$1,500
Rental income: small warehouse	3,500[3]
5% of factory building	12,500[3]
Dividends	2,500
	$20,000

[2] Dividends that are deductible under ssec. 112(1) are property income but are subtracted when computing aggregate investment income since they are not ultimately subject to Part I tax.

[3] Rental of warehouse and 5% of factory building appear to be property or specified investment business income since the space is not needed in the business.

(b) Dividends from taxable, non-connected Canadian corporations ($2,500) are not taxable under Part I. Instead, they are taxed under Part IV at the rate of $38\frac{1}{3}$%. Part IV tax is refundable.

(c) The refundable Part I tax in 3(b) and the refundable Part IV tax in 3(c) are returned to the corporation at the rate of $0.383 for every dollar of taxable dividends paid (i.e., $38\frac{1}{3}$% × $50,000 = $19,167). The refund cannot exceed RDTOH, which in this case is $7,245. RDTOH is the sum of the refundable Part I tax on investment income, i.e., $30\frac{2}{3}$% × $20,500 = $6,287 plus the refundable Part IV tax, i.e., $38\frac{1}{3}$% × 2,500 = $958.

(d) If a portion of the $50,000 dividend is paid from the capital dividend account, then that portion of the dividend will be received tax-free by the shareholder. As a tax-free dividend, it does not generate a dividend refund in the corporation. The capital dividend account includes the untaxed portion of capital gains. A valid election must be made under ssec. 83(2) to permit the payment of the capital dividend.

Note to Solution — Sourcing of Income

	ABI Cdn	ABI For'n	PSB	Investment Cdn	Investment For'n	Dividend Conn	Dividend Port
M & P	$ 50.0						
Retail — Canada	75.0						
— N.Y		$17.5					
Bank — Canada	1.0						
— US		0.5					
T Bills	3.0			$ 1.5			
Dividends							$2.5
Recapture	7.5						
Rental				12.5			
Rental				3.5			
TCG				4.5			
TCG				4.0			
ACL				(5.5)			
	$136.5	$18.0	$ —	$20.5	$ —	$ —	$2.5

Exercise 15

(A) — Sisters are related [spar. 251(2)(a)(i) and par. 251(6)(a)].

— All of the conditions for association in paragraph 256(1)(c) are met as follows:

(i) each corporation was controlled by one person through the common shares;

(ii) the person, who controlled one corporation, was related to the person who controlled the other (sisters);

(iii) one of those persons (Clorilda) owns not less than 25% of the shares of any class, other than a specified class (through her preferred share in the bicycle corporation and her common shares in her own corporation) of each corporation;

— the preferred shares are not a specified class because they are convertible [par. 256(1.1)(a)].

(B) — All of the conditions for association between Caspar's corporation and Ceecombo Corporation in par. 256(1)(d) are met as follows:

(i) Caspar's Corporation was controlled by one person;

(ii) Ceecombo Corporation was controlled by a group of persons (Caspar and Carter) and Caspar was related to each member of the group because he is related to his brother [spar. 251(2)(a)(i) and par. 251(6)(a)] and to himself [ssec. 256(1.5)];

(iii) Caspar owns not less than 25% of the shares of any class, other than a specified class, of each corporation.

— Similarly, using the same logic, Carter's Corporation and Ceecombo Corporation are associated [par. 256(1)(d)].

— Since Ceecombo Corporation is associated with Caspar's Corporation and Carter's Corporation is associated with Ceecombo, Caspar's Corporation is associated with Carter's Corporation [ssec. 256(2)].

— However, Ceecombo Corporation should elect annually not to be associated with either Carter's Corporation or Caspar's Corporation, since it cannot use the small business deduction with investment income.

(C) — Paragraph 256(1)(*e*) sets out three conditions each of which must be met for association and all are met as follows:

    (i)   each corporation must be controlled by a related group

        — brothers and sisters are related [spar. 251(2)(*a*)(i) and par. 251(6)(*a*)] and, hence, the condition is met;

    (ii) each member of a related group must be related to all members of the other related group

        — again, all of the brothers and sisters are related as above and, hence, the condition is met;

    (iii) one or more persons who were members of both of the related groups either alone or together, must own not less than 25% of the issued shares of any class other than a specified class

        — Chauncey and Clarabelle are members of both related groups;

        — together, Chauncey and Clarabelle own not less than 25% of the shares of any class of Xylona Ltd. and of Xerxes Ltd.

(D) — The corporations are not associated under the technical rules of sec. 256, unless ssec. 256(5.1) applies, as discussed below.

— They may be deemed to be associated if it may reasonably be considered that one of the main reasons for the separate existence is tax reduction [ssec. 256(2.1)].

— Arguments for the taxpayer (see *Covertite* case (79 DTC 136)):

    (i)   separate existence for geographic diversification,

    (ii) new corporation in a new geographic location,

    (iii) business dealt with separate clientele,

    (iv) key employee in Manitoba corporation.

— Arguments against the taxpayer (see *Alpha Forming* case (83 DTC 5021)):

    (i)   Althea borrowed from Alphonso,

    (ii) Althea had limited experience in the business,

    (iii) use of the same business name and logo,

    (iv) setting of remuneration just under S.B.D. limits,

    (v) only shareholder of each corporation is the spouse of the other.

— The corporations may be associated, if Alphonso is considered to control Another Corporation in fact [par. 256(1)(*b*)]

— this can only be determined on the basis of further facts;

— One Corporation, which is controlled by Alphonso, may be in a position to exercise influence over Another Corporation through the loan arrangements for equipment and funds used to establish Another Corporation;

— Another Corporation is managed by a former employee of One Corporation, and that person may be subject to influence by Alphonso;

— the exception in ssec. 256(5.1) would not apply because Another Corporation and the controller, Alphonso, are not at arm's length;

— a decision either way is possible.

(E) — The two corporations are associated, because they are both controlled by Eunice [par. 256(1)(*b*)]

— Eunice controls Yolanda Ltd. either:

— because she owns more than 50% of the fair market value of all the issued shares [spar. 256(1.2)(*c*)(i)], or

— because of her casting vote [ssec. 256(5.1)].

— Eunice controls Zerlinda Ltd., because she owns more than 50% of the fair market value of all the issued shares [spar. 256(1.2)(*c*)(i)].

(F) — The two corporations are not associated:

— paragraph 256(1)(*b*) does not apply, because the option held by Edbert is not exercisable until the death of his cousin and, hence, par. 256(1.4)(*a*) does not deem Edbert to own the shares he has under option;

— paragraph 256(1)(*d*) does not apply because cousins are not related individuals under ssec. 251(6).

Exercise 16

(A) Association of corporations

— Holdall Investments Ltd. is associated with Held Manufacturing Ltd. [par. 256(1)(*a*)].

— Holdette Management Services Ltd, is not associated with either Holdall Investments Ltd. Or Held Manufacturing Ltd.

— paragraph 256(1)(*c*) does not apply to associate Holdette and Holdall, despite the relationship of Mr. Holder and Ms Holdette because the 25% cross-ownership condition is not met

— subsection 256(2.1) would not likely be invoked for reasons discussed below.

(B) Application of deeming rules [ssec. 129(6)]

— Rental payments by Held Manufacturing Ltd. to Holdall Investments Ltd.

— Holdall Investments Ltd. is carrying on a "specified investment business" in respect of its rental operation by virtue of the definition of that term [ssec. 125(7)]

— condition is met that rent be income from property of Holdall Investments Ltd.; income from property is defined to include income from a specified investment business [par. 129(4)]

— condition is also met that the rent be deducted from income from an active business of an associated payer corporation

— therefore, the rent is not included in income from property of Holdall Investments Ltd., but is deemed to be income of Holdall Investments Ltd. from an active business [spar. 129(6)(*b*)(i)].

— Since the rent is deemed to be income from an active business, it qualifies for the small business deduction [ssec. 125(1)]. Held Manufacturing Ltd. and Holdall Investments Ltd. must allocate the $500,000 business limit between themselves.

— Interest payments by Holdall Investments Ltd. to Held Manufacturing Ltd.

— condition is met that interest would be income from property of Held Manufacturing Ltd.

— the interest is deductible from rental income of the apartment building which is income from property and separate from the commercial rent deemed to be active business income, as discussed above, of Holdall Investments Ltd., the associated payer corporation

— therefore, subsection 129(6) does not apply and the interest is not deemed to be income from an active business carried on by Held Manufacturing Ltd., and, as interest income, is eligible for the refundable Part I tax treatment under section 129.

CHAPTER 12

(C)   Application of "personal services business" definition [ssec. 125(7)] to Holdette Management Services Ltd.

— The exceptions to the application of the definition are not met

— Holdette Management Services Ltd. does not employ throughout the year more than five full-time employees

— the fees paid to Holdette Management Services Ltd. are not received from a corporation with which it was associated.

— Ms Holdette who performs the services is a specified shareholder, as defined [ssec. 248(1)], of Holdette Management Services Ltd.

— furthermore, she could reasonably be regarded as an officer or employee of Held Manufacturing Ltd. because she had been its manufacturing vice-president.

— Therefore, Holdette Management Services Ltd. would not be eligible for the small business deduction or the general rate reduction, and would pay tax at the full corporate rate plus an additional 5% pursuant to s. 123.5

— furthermore, the corporation is denied any deduction other than salary, wages and other benefits paid to Ms Holdette who performs the services [par. 18(1)(p)]

— there could be a deduction for the rent paid to Holdall Investments Ltd., on the assumption that Ms. Holdette negotiates contracts on behalf of the corporation [spar. 18(1)(p)(iii)].

— It is not likely that subsection 256(2.1) would be applied to deem Holdette and Held to be associated so that the personal services business definition would not apply

— while the separate existence of the corporations may have been to carry on business in the most effective manner, one of the main reasons for the separate existence could not have been to reduce taxes, because total taxes are in fact increased due to the personal services business status of Holdette Management Services Ltd.

(D)   Advice for improvement

— Holdette Management Services Ltd. should be wound up, and Ms Holdette should go back to work for the Held Manufacturing Ltd.

— this would avoid the adverse tax effects on the personal services business

— perhaps she could be offered shares in either Holdall Investments Ltd, or Held Manufacturing Ltd. so that her remuneration could consist of salary and/or dividends.

— Alternatively, at least 25% of the shares (of any class other than a specified class) in Holdette Management Service, Ltd. should be issued to Mr. Holder. This would cause Holdette Management Services Ltd. to become associated with Holdall Investments Ltd. [par. 256(1)(c)] and Held Manufacturing Ltd. [ssec. 256(2)]. As a result, Holdette Management Services Ltd.'s management fee would be active business income by virtue of the exception in paragraph (b) of the definition of a "specified investment business" [ssec. 125(7)], the rent to Holdall Investments Ltd. would be deductible and Holdall Investments Ltd. would receive it as active business income [ssec. 129(6)].

Exercise 17

Note — the solution below is based on the current tax legislation for the refundable portion of Part I tax as the proposed changes are not effective until taxations years beginning after 2018.

(i) Dividend refund in FOL

Refundable dividend tax on hand, 31/12/2017	$ 2,000
Refundable portion of Part I tax ($7,000 × 30²/₃%)	2,147
Refundable dividend tax on hand, 31/12/2018	$ 4,147

Lesser of:

(a) 38¹/₃% of taxable dividends paid ($75,000)	$ 28,750
(b) Refundable dividend tax on hand	$ 4,147
FOL's dividend refund	$ 4,147

(ii) Part IV tax for SHI

Canadian Pacific Ltd. dividends ($8,000 × 38¹/₃%)	$ 3,067
FOL dividends — connected	
$4,147 × 100%	4,147
Part IV tax	$ 7,214

(iii) Dividend refund for SHI

Accounting income ($75,000 + $8,000 + $12,000 + $42,000)	$137,000
Less: dividends deductible — sec.112	(83,000)
Non-taxable portion of gain (½)	(21,000)
Taxable income (all investment income) (interest $12,000 + taxable capital gain $21,000)	$ 33,000
Refundable dividend tax on hand, 31/12/2018	$ 8,000
Refundable portion of Part I tax ($33,000 × 30²/₃%)	10,120
Part IV tax payable	7,214
Refundable dividend tax on hand, 31/12/2018	$ 25,334

Lesser of:

(a) 38¹/₃% of taxable dividends paid ($50,000)	$ 19,167
(b) Refundable dividend tax on hand	$ 25,334
SHI's dividend refund	$ 19,167

CHAPTER 12

Exercise 18

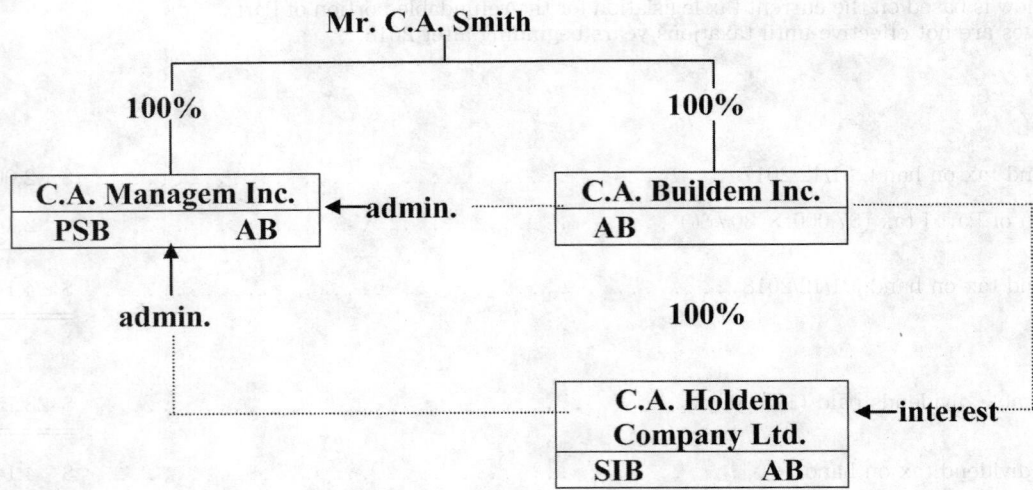

C.A., Managem Inc.

(a) Carrying on a personal services business by virtue of paragraph 125(7) with respect to the income from Public.

    (i) as the sole employee of C.A. Managem Inc., Mr. Smith provides services on behalf of C.A. Managem Inc.,

    (ii) Mr. Smith is a specified shareholder of C.A Managem Inc. by virtue of subsection 248(1), since he owns not less than 10% of the issued share capital.

    (iii) Mr. Smith would reasonably be considered as an employee of Public because he was formerly an employee of that company,

    (iv) C.A. Managem Inc. and Public are not associated corporations.

Taxed at full corporate rates under Part I on personal services business income (not eligible for the small business deduction or general rate reduction), plus an additional 5% tax under s.123.5

    — C.A. Managem Inc. may deduct only salary paid to Mr. Smith, the cost of any benefit or allowance paid to him, amounts expended in connection with selling property or negotiating contracts (as required by subparagraph 18(1)(*p*)(iii)) and legal fees incurred in collecting amounts owing to it on account of services rendered;

(b) Carrying on an active business by virtue of its association with C.A. Buildem Inc. and C.A. Holdem Company Limited by virtue of par. 256(1)(*b*), and since Mr. Smith controls each corporation either directly or indirectly,

    ● consulting income from C.A. Buildem Inc. and C.A. Holdem Company Limited is not personal services business by virtue of the exception in paragraph (*d*) of the definition in subsection 125(7) that the services are rendered to associated corporations; therefore, this income is active business income by virtue of the definition of active business in ssec. 125(7); and

    ● income from associated companies is eligible for the 18% small business deduction under subsection 125(1) to the extent of the amount of the $500,000 business limit allocated to Managem Inc. in the associated group.

C.A. Buildem Inc.

(a) Associated with C.A. Holdem Company Limited by virtue of par. 256(1)(*a*).

(b) Income is from an active business (by reference to the various definitions in subsection 125(7), with 10 full-time employees, any income earned by C.A. Buildem Inc. must be active business income)

    (i) consulting fees deductible from active business income,

    (ii) income is eligible for the 18% small business deduction under subsection 125(1).

(c) If C.A. Buildem Inc. receives dividend income from C.A. Holdem Company Limited, then this dividend can be deducted from Part I taxable income by virtue of subsection 112(1). Since Buildem Inc. owns 100% of C.A Holdem Company Limited, the two companies are connected, as defined in subsection 186(4) since C.A. Buildem, owns more than 10% of the votes and value. Therefore, C.A. Buildem Inc. has a liability for Part IV tax under par. 186(1)(*b*) only if C.A. Holdem Company Limited receives a dividend refund as a result of the dividends paid.

C.A. Holdem Company Limited

(a) Interest income would ordinarily be income from property:

  (i) interest is deductible from active business income of C.A Buildem Inc.,

  (ii) interest is deemed by spar. 129(6)(*b*)(i) to be income of C.A Holdem Company Limited from active business.

  (iii) C.A. Holdem Company Limited is eligible for the 18% small business deduction on its deemed active business income under subsection 125(1), to the extent of the amount of the business limit allocated to C.A. Holdem Company Limited in the associated group.

(b) The remaining income of C.A. Holdem Company Limited is from property or a specified investment business by virtue of par. 125(7)(*e*) since the corporation has no employees and an associated corporation cannot meet the services test:

  (i) interest income is taxed at full corporate rates under Part I plus 10⅔% additional refundable tax and is eligible for refundable tax treatment of 30⅔% on the basis of dividends paid;

  (ii) the dividend income is excluded from Part I taxable income by virtue of ssec. 112(1); however, the dividends would likely be subject to Part IV tax of 38⅓% since C.A. Holdem Company Limited likely has only a portfolio interest (less than 10% voting power) in the companies it invests. These dividends are also eligible for refundable tax treatment as described above.

Chapter 13

Shareholder-Manager Remuneration and Tax Planning for the Owner-Manager

Learning Goals

Know

By the end of this chapter you will know:

- The common elements of compensation for a corporation's shareholder-manager.
- The basic elements of the capital gains exemption.
- The issues related to the general anti-avoidance rule.

Understand and Explain

By the end of this chapter you will understand and be able to explain:

- The issues related to the choice of different types of compensation for a shareholder-manager.
- The benefits of the capital gains exemption.
- The rewards and risks of income splitting using a corporation.
- Why the general anti-avoidance rule is designed the way it is.

Apply

By the end of this chapter you will be able to apply your knowledge and understanding to:

- Choose the compensation plan for a shareholder-manager.
- Determine whether the capital gains exemption applies.
- Calculate the capital gains exemption.
- Calculate the benefits and penalties from income splitting using a corporation.

Review Questions
¶13,800 in the Study Guide

Multiple Choice Questions
¶13,825 in the Study Guide

Exercises
¶13,850 in the Study Guide

Assignment Problems
¶13,875 in the Study Guide

CHAPTER 13 — LEARNING CHART

Problem Descriptions

Textbook Example Problems

13-1	Shareholder benefit
13-2	Shareholder benefit
13-3	Shareholder loan
13-4	Shareholder loan
13-5	Shareholder loan — deemed interest benefit
13-6	Salary vs. dividends
13-7	Salary vs. dividends
13-8	Small business corporation
13-9	QSBC
13-10	QSBC — modified asset test
13-11	Capital gains deduction
13-12	Corporate attribution

Multiple Choice Questions

1	Shareholder loan
2	Shareholder loan
3	Deductibility of bonus
4	GAAR
5	GAAR
6	Corporate attribution
7	Small business corporation

Exercises

1	Bonus payable
2	Shareholder loan
3	Shareholder loan — series of transactions
4	Shareholder loan — car
5	Shareholder loan — car
6	Salary vs. dividend
7	Salary vs. dividend
8	Small business corporation
9	Capital gains deduction
10	Corporate attribution
11	GAAR
12	GAAR
13	Shareholder loans
14	Employment income — stock options, low interest loans, company car, car allowance
15	Shareholder loans & unpaid amounts
16	Capital gains deduction, personal tax credits, donations — charitable & political
17	Owner/Manager Remuneration: Salary vs. Dividends
18	QSBC shares
19	QSBC shares

Problem Descriptions

Assignment Problems

1	Salary vs. Dividends
2	QSBC shares
3	QSBC shares
4	Capital gains deduction
5	Corporate attribution
6	GAAR
7	GAAR
8	Shareholder benefit
9	Shareholder loans
10	Shareholder loans
11	Shareholder loans
12	Incorporation, compensation
13	Incorporation, compensation
14	Salary/dividend planning
15	Owner/manager advice
16	Tax planning, GAAR
17	Purchase of a business, compensation
18	Employment income — stock options, low interest loans, company car, car allowance
19	Shareholder loans, unpaid remuneration & other amounts; attribution

---

CHAPTER 13

Study Notes

¶13,800 REVIEW QUESTIONS

(1) Mr. Smith owns a small manufacturing company that has suddenly become very profitable. This year his accountant has told him to declare a bonus to himself of approximately $150,000 in order to reduce his corporate income to the business limit. His dilemma is that he also needs the money in his business in order to finance expansion. What should he do?

(2) Mr. Jones owns a distributing company that is earning well over $500,000 each year. He has been declaring a bonus to himself each year but is now rethinking this strategy. What items should he consider when deciding whether to pay the bonus or leave the money in the company? Assume that the provincial corporate income tax rate is 12% on their income in excess of the small business deduction limit.

(3) What is the range of fiscal year ends that might be chosen to allow the owner of a company to declare a bonus and be taxed on it personally in either of two calendar years?

(4) What are the five criteria for the deductibility of bonus accruals as decided in the *Totem Disposal* case?

(5) Mr. Chow is the sole shareholder of Chocobar Inc. His wife's brother has just come to him and asked to borrow some money in order to start up his professional accounting practice. Mr. Chow has decided to have Chocobar Inc. lend his wife's brother $20,000 on October 31, 2018, with interest only for the first two years and then principal payments of $10,000 per year starting in the third year. The fiscal year end of the company is December 31. Discuss the tax implications of the loan.

(6) Ms. Jones is the President and sole shareholder of a construction company. She has two vice-presidents who are not related to her. As part of their compensation package she has agreed that all employees of the company are entitled to an interest-free loan from the company of up to $25,000. Ms. Jones herself has taken her $25,000 loan and bought a boat. Comment.

(7) If your province of residence were to declare a tax holiday for all CCPCs, what impact would this have on compensation for your owner-manager clients?

(8) How much personal tax will a single individual pay on $30,000 of non-eligible dividend income if that is his or her only source of income and his or her only non-refundable tax credit is his or her personal credit.

(9) Ms. Simpson owned 10% of the shares of a small business corporation that went out of business. Six months after it ceased business she sold her shares to an arm's length person, Mr. X, for $1. When she went to claim a loss on her investment she did not know how much she could write off. In order to have the loss treated as an ABIL, the company needed to be a small business corporation at the time of sale and at that time it did not have any assets used in an active business. She has not used any of her capital gains exemption before. Can you clarify this situation for her?

(10) What does the phrase "all or substantially all" mean?

(11) A corporation that has had 40% of its assets invested in term deposits for the last two years, and the balance in active business assets, qualifies as a "small business corporation" but not a "qualified small business corporation". Do you agree or disagree? Explain.

(12) Mr. Smith, who is 61 years of age, incorporated his company 20 years ago for $100 of share capital. He has worked full time for the business since then and has prospered. The company now has some excess capital. He has decided to have his wife set up an investment holding company and his company will lend her company $100,000 of cash for her to invest and thereby split income. Will the corporate attribution rules apply?

¶13,825   MULTIPLE CHOICE QUESTIONS

Question 1

Stan owns 100% of the shares of S Ltd. which has a December 31 year end. He is also an employee of S Ltd. On January 1, 2018, S Ltd. loaned Stan $200,000 interest-free to assist him in purchasing a new home. Stan signed a promissory note for the loan. Under the terms of the note, the loan is to be repaid in five equal annual instalments commencing January 1, 2019. Such a loan is not available to other employees. Which *one* of the following statements is *true* under current tax administrative practice?

(A) Stan will have $200,000 included in his income in 2018.

(B) Stan will have $160,000 included in his income in 2018.

(C) An imputed interest benefit will be calculated for 2018 using a rate not in excess of the rate in effect at January 1, 2018, as the loan was used to purchase a home.

(D) The portion of the loan not repaid within one year of the end of the 2018 calendar year, will be included in Stan's income in 2020.

Question 2

In 2018, S Ltd., which has a December 31 year end, made the following loans to shareholders. All of the shareholders are resident in Canada and are not related to S Ltd. or each other. This was the first time that these shareholders had received a loan or had become indebted to S. Ltd. Since S Ltd. was not in the business of lending money, it was very careful, in each case, to ensure that *bona fide* arrangements were made at the time the loan was made for repayment of the loan within a reasonable time. Taking all this into consideration, which one of the following loan principal amounts will be included in the borrower's income in 2018?

(A) A loan to Mrs. A, a vice-president and 20% shareholder. The loan was made to assist Mrs. A in the purchase of newly issued shares of S Ltd. The loan was made on April 1, 2018, and repaid on April 1, 2019. No other employees have received similar loans.

(B) A loan made to B Ltd., a corporation which is a 20% shareholder of S Ltd. The loan was used to help B Ltd. repurchase some of its shares for cancellation and pay off a bank loan.

(C) A loan to Mrs. C, a vice-president and 20% shareholder. The loan was made to assist Mrs. C in the purchase of a home. The loan was made on April 1, 2018, and will be repaid on April 1, 2020. No other employees have received similar loans.

(D) A loan to Mr. D, an S Ltd. vice-president and 5% shareholder. Mr. D deals at arm's length with S Ltd. The loan was made to assist Mr. D in the purchase of a home computer for employment use. Five other employees of the company currently work at home and have received similar loans. None of the other employees are shareholders. Mr. D's loan was made on April 1, 2018, and will be repaid on April 1, 2020.

Question 3

In computing the net income on the financial statement of Fortelli Inc. for its year ended December 31, 2018, bonuses of $300,000 were accrued. On August 15, 2019, $100,000 of the bonus was paid to the owner-manager, and the remaining $200,000 of bonuses were paid to the sales staff on August 31, 2019. Which one of the following statements is *true*?

(A) If the $100,000 bonus, due to a related party, was not paid by December 31, 2020, it would be included in Fortelli Inc.'s income in the year 2021.

(B) The $100,000 bonus is not deductible in 2018, but the $200,000 bonus is deductible.

(C) An election is available to deem the bonus paid and loaned back to the corporation. This election can be used if the bonuses are not going to be paid by the appropriate deadline.

(D) The $300,000 bonus is not deductible in 2018.

Question 4

The Act contains a general anti-avoidance provision often referred to as the GAAR. Which one of the following statements concerning the GAAR is *false*?

(A) The tax benefit that results from an avoidance transaction will be denied.

(B) When the GAAR is applied, a penalty will be assessed, in addition to the tax owing plus interest.

(C) An avoidance transaction is any transaction that results in a tax benefit, unless the transaction can reasonably be considered to have a *bona fide* purpose other than obtaining the tax benefit.

(D) The GAAR applies to transactions that result in a misuse or abuse of the Act read as a whole.

Question 5

The general anti-avoidance provision, GAAR, is most likely to apply to which *one* of the following transactions?

(A) As part of an estate freeze, Bill had a trust for his adult children acquire 80% of the common shares of B Ltd. Until then, Bill had owned all the shares of B Ltd., a successful grocery retail outlet. Each year B Ltd. pays dividends to the trust which are paid to the children all between the ages of 22 and 28. As university students, they have no other income and all work part time for the grocery store during the summer.

(B) Sam transferred his unincorporated pizza business, on tax-deferred basis, to a corporation, for the sole purpose of reducing tax by claiming the small business deduction.

(C) Paul gave his son a gift of $10,000 and the son invested it in dividend-paying shares. His son does not pay tax on the dividend income as he is a 19-year-old student with little other income. Paul will celebrate his 65th birthday two years after his son graduates. It is anticipated that Paul will receive a birthday gift of $10,000 from his son at that time.

(D) Mary owns all the shares of M Ltd., a CCPC that carries on an active business. For M Ltd.'s taxation year ended June 30, 2018, Mary accrued herself a bonus of $700,000 that reduced M Ltd.'s taxable income to $300,000.

Question 6

Mrs. Boehmer, age 50, owns all the Class A common shares of a corporation which has an investment portfolio worth $500,000. The Class A shares were issued to Mrs. B on incorporation. The corporation has no other assets or liabilities and has a December 31 year end. On January 1 of the current year, Mr. Boehmer (Mrs. Boehmer's husband), age 51, subscribed for $1 million Class B non-voting preferred shares of the corporation and paid for them in cash. The purpose of this transaction was to income-split with his wife. The corporation earned $10,000 during the year and paid a $10,000 cash dividend to Mrs. Boehmer. Assuming the prescribed rate is 3% throughout the year, what is the minimum amount of income that Mr. Boehmer must report in the year in respect of his investment in the corporation?

(A) $10,000

(B) $11,600

(C) $15,000

(D) $30,000

Question 7

Ms. Prentice owns P Ltd., a Canadian-controlled private corporation with assets worth $4 million and liabilities amounting to $1 million. Sixty per cent of its assets are used in an active business carried on in Canada by the corporation and 20% are used in an active business carried on in Canada by a corporation controlled by Ms. Prentice's brother. The remaining assets (non-active business assets) earn investment income. Which of the following is the minimum amount of non-active business assets that P Co must sell in order for its shares to qualify as shares of a small business corporation? Assume that the after-tax proceeds on the sale will be used to pay off some of the corporation's liabilities.

(A) None

(B) $400,000

(C) $444,445

(D) $1,333,333

¶13,850   EXERCISES

Exercise 1

ITA: 78

Slipit Ltd. declared a bonus payable of $10,000 to Mr. Schneider, its president and majority share-holder, on September 30, 2018, its fiscal year end. If the bonus is paid it will be subject to withholding tax in the amount of $3,500.

— *REQUIRED*

(A) If the corporation is to get a deduction with no future consequences for the bonus payable, by what date must the bonus be paid?

(B) What are the consequences of not paying the bonus by this date?

(C) Assume that, instead of a bonus, the amount owing to Mr. Schneider is rent, properly included on the cash basis, on the only rental property he owns and rents to the corporation:

   (i) If the corporation is to get a deduction with no future consequences for the rent payable, by what date must the rent be paid?

   (ii) What are the consequences of not paying the rent by this date?

   (iii) How can these consequences be avoided without paying the rent?

Exercise 2

ITA: 15(2), 80.4

Mr. Nesbitt relocated his private business, Leverage-Lovers Limited, to Alberta from Ontario at the end of May 2017. As a result of the move, the corporation made the following loans on June 1, 2018 to Mr. Nesbitt, the president and majority shareholder:

   (a) a $75,000 loan at 2% interest per year with a five-year term but amortized over a 25-year period to purchase a house in the new location;

   (b) a $5,000 loan at 5% interest per year with no definite term to buy furniture for the new house; and

   (c) a $10,000 loan with no interest but with a five-year term to buy previously unissued, fully paid shares from the corporation.

The corporation uses the calendar year as its fiscal year, and by the end of 2019; all the loans described were still outstanding. Any interest required to be paid on the loans at the indicated rates was paid in 2018. Assume that the prescribed rates applicable to shareholder loans during 2018 were: 1st quarter, 4%; 2nd quarter, 3%; 3rd quarter, 4%; and 4th quarter, 4%. Ignore the effects of the leap year, if applicable.

— *REQUIRED*

Discuss the tax consequences in 2018 of the loan described, if Mr. Nesbitt received the loans:

   (A) by virtue of his employment;

   (B) by virtue of his shareholdings.

Exercise 3

ITA: 15(2), 20(1)(*j*)

Mr. Sims is a shareholder of Wonder Ltd. which has a December 31 year end. Consider the following transactions in his shareholder loan account:

Date	Loan (repayment)	Balance
Dec. 31/Year 1	—	Nil
Jan. 31/Year 2	$ 20,000	$ 20,000
Apr. 30/Year 2	25,000	45,000
June 30/Year 3	(15,000)	30,000
Sept. 30/Year 3	(17,000)	13,000
Mar. 31/Year 4	(12,000)	1,000
Nov. 30/Year 4	10,000	11,000
May 31/Year 5	(11,000)	Nil
Nov. 30/Year 5	23,000	23,000
July 31/Year 6	(14,000)	9.000
Dec. 31/Year 6	—	9,000

— REQUIRED

(A) If it is assumed that these transactions result in the conclusion that there is a series of loans and repayments, compute the principal amounts that must be included or the repayments that may be deducted for each of the years indicated according to the guidelines in IT-119R4.

(B) If there has not been a series of loans and repayments, how would the amounts differ from the above? How would you argue there was no series of loans and repayments?

Exercise 4

ITA: 15(2), 80.4; ITR: 4300

Colton Marlach is a major shareholder and senior executive of Burlon Ltd. He was required to use a car about 60% for the duties of his employment. On April 1, under a plan available to the five other senior executives of the corporation, he was granted a car loan of $35,000 at a rate of interest of 1% per annum and agreed to annual payments on the anniversary day of $7,000 for principal and monthly payments of interest at the end of each month. During the year, he faithfully made the monthly interest payments for seven months but neglected to make the interest payments for the last two months of the year.

— REQUIRED

What are the income tax consequences to the taxpayer? Assume that the prescribed rates were as follows:

first quarter	2%	third quarter	2%
second quarter	1%	fourth quarter	3%

Ignore the effects of the leap year, if applicable.

Exercise 5

ITA: 6(1)

Consider the data provided in Exhibit 13-4 in ¶13,100.

— REQUIRED

Analyze the situation if the employment use of the car is 20,000 out of 30,000 km.

Exercise 6

ITA: 82(1), 117, 121, 123–125

Payton Hewitt is the sole shareholder and employee of Conduit Corporation Ltd. which operates a processing business in a province with a 4% corporate rate (i.e., a total corporate rate of 14%) on its income. The corporation has income of $20,000 before salaries and corporate taxes which is eligible for the small business deduction. Mr. Hewitt has no other income and has federal tax credits of $2,000 and provincial tax credits of $1,290. He requires all of the income generated by the business.

— REQUIRED

Consider the following three remuneration alternatives:

(A) all salary,

(B) all dividends, and

(C) $10,000 in salary and the remainder in dividends.

Compare the net cash to Mr. Hewitt for these alternatives ignoring employment income deductions available to an employee.

Exercise 7

ITA: 82(1), 117, 121, 123–125

Aaron Storey is a sole proprietor generating $80,000 in income before taxes from a processing business operating in a province with a 4% corporate rate (i.e., a total corporate rate of 14%). He requires $25,000 before taxes for living expenses and has federal personal tax credits of $2,100 and provincial tax credits of $1,400. He has no other source of income or deductions (except as assumed for (B)(iii), below). The business has a December 31 taxation year end.

¶13,850

— REQUIRED

(A) Compute the tax that would be paid if he continues to operate the business as an unincorporated proprietorship.

(B) Compare your answer in (A) with the total tax that would be paid if he incorporates the business and remunerates himself by the following alternative methods:

(i) $25,000 in salary;

(ii) $25,000 in dividends; and

(iii) $2,085 in salary and $22,915 in dividends.

Ignore deductions available to employees. (Assume that the excess federal or provincial tax credits resulting from this case can be used against tax on other income.)

Exercise 8

ITA: 248(1)

Consider each of the following independent proportions of assets at fair market value. Assume the assets are owned by a Canadian-controlled private corporation. Active business assets refer to assets used principally in an active business carried on primarily in Canada.

	A	B	C	D
Active business assets	85%	50%	—	40%
Marketable securities	15	—	20%	20
Shares of a connected small business corporation	—	50	80	40
	100%	100%	100%	100%

— REQUIRED

Determine whether each of the above proportions meets the test of a small business corporation as defined in the Act.

Exercise 9

ITA: 110.6

Bobby Mills has provided you with the following information:

	2016	2017	2018
Taxable capital gains on sale of qualified small business corporation shares	$75,000	—	$300,000
Business investment loss (before ssec. 39(9) adjustment)	—	—	160,000
Interest income	—	$ 600	1,200
Grossed-up taxable dividends	—	140	—
Net rental income (loss)	—	(1,100)	(220)
Carrying charges	—	1,075	—

The 2016 taxable capital gain was fully offset by a capital gains deduction in that year.

— REQUIRED

Determine Bobby's capital gains deduction for 2018 supported by all the necessary calculations. Assume that there were no other capital transactions before 2016.

Exercise 10

ITA: 74.4

Mrs. Albert, age 45, owns all of the outstanding common shares of a corporation, Prince Albert Inc., which operates a small retail store in Saskatoon. Her husband, age 48, owns the building with a fair market value of $2,000,000, in which the store is located. He is planning to transfer it to Prince Albert Inc. in exchange for $600,000 of cash, a 5% demand note for $200,000 and non-voting preference shares for $1,200,000. The fair market value of the business assets (which are all of the assets excluding cash used to pay for the building) in the company immediately before the transfer is $6,000,000. Of the total space in the building, 20% is used in the retail business. The net rental income that Mr. Albert earned in the previous year was $50,000.

— REQUIRED

Determine the tax consequences, if any, to Mr. Albert for 2018, assuming the prescribed interest rate is a constant 4% and that the sale took place on January 1, 2018. The corporation's year end is September 30. Dividends of $20,000 were paid on the preference shares in 2018.

ITR: 4301(c)

Exercise 11

Gangster Production Ltd., a Canadian-controlled private corporation, paid its shareholder-manager, Herb, a salary of $250,000 which reduced the corporation's income to $499,500 for the taxation year. The amount of the salary is considered to be reasonable.

— REQUIRED

Determine whether the general anti-avoidance rule (GAAR) would apply in this situation.

Exercise 12

Over the past two years, your client, a lawyer in sole practice, has developed several software packages for the preparation of legal contracts. At a recent small-business seminar, your client learned that she could pay her spouse and children a salary. By doing so, your client's total tax paid as a family unit would drop substantially.

— REQUIRED

If tax is avoided, how would the general anti-avoidance rule affect the transactions?

Exercise 13

Grace Ravens is a shareholder and a senior executive of Maximum Marketing Ltd., which has a December 31 year end. On June 1, 2017, the corporation provided her with the following loans under a policy for loans to executives of the corporation:

(i) a $100,000 loan at 2% interest per year with a five-year term, with principal repayments of $10,000 due December 31 each year, to purchase a new house in downtown Toronto which she lives in;

(ii) a $10,000 loan at 5% interest per year with no definite terms of repayment to purchase furniture for her new home; and

(iii) a $20,000 loan at no interest with a three-year term to buy additional, previously unissued shares of Maximum Marketing Ltd. from treasury.

On December 31, 2017, she repaid $10,000 principal on the house loan and $1,000 principal on the furniture loan as well as the interest due on the loans. On December 31, 2018, Grace paid $10,000 principal on the house loan and $1,000 principal on the furniture loan. On January 15, 2019, she paid interest on the house and furniture loans for the year ended December 31, 2018.

In summary, then, the remaining balances at the noted dates are as follows:

	January 1, 2018	January 1, 2019
House loan	$90,000	$80,000
Furniture loan	9,000	8,000
Stock loan	20,000	20,000

Assume the prescribed rates of interest for 2018 were as follows: 1st quarter — 4%; 2nd quarter — 4%; 3rd quarter — 5%; and 4th quarter — 5%. The prescribed rate on June 1, 2017 was 5%.

— REQUIRED

Calculate the tax consequences in 2018 to Grace Ravens of the loans described above.

Exercise 14

Ms. Mover has been offered a new job as vice-president of operations with Shaker Ltd., a Canadian-controlled private corporation. In addition to the basic salary and commissions, a number of benefits have been offered as indicated below:

(a) The remuneration package includes a stock option to purchase 8,000 previously unissued, fully paid, shares of Shaker Ltd. at $12 per share. The current FMV is $20 per share. Ms. Mover would be expected to exercise half of the option immediately to show her confidence in the company.

(b) Under an employee-loan policy, Shaker Ltd. will loan Ms. Mover the $48,000 required to exercise half of the option at no interest, repayable at $8,000 per annum for 6 years and evidenced by a *bona fide* note. Any outstanding balance would be due in full on termination of employment.

(c) Under the employee-loan policy, Shaker Ltd. will also loan Ms. Mover $350,000 at 2% interest to purchase a home in Vancouver where Shaker Ltd. is located. Ms. Mover currently lives in Saskatoon. The interest is payable monthly over 25 years and the principal is repaid annually over 25 years. Assume the prescribed rate is 4% when the loan is granted and immediately drops to but does not fall below 3% for 5 years. Also, assume for purposes of your calculation that no principal was repaid in the first 5 years.

(d) Ms. Mover will be travelling extensively and will be provided with a company car leased by Shaker Ltd. for $900/month including $100 for insurance and all applicable HST. She anticipates 24,000 business kilometres and 6,000 personal kilometres per year. Shaker Ltd. will pay all operating costs, estimated at $300/month, including HST.

(e) In lieu of reimbursing specific minor travelling expenses (e.g., meals), Shaker Ltd. will pay Ms. Mover a monthly allowance of $850. More substantial travelling expenses (e.g., air fares and hotels) will be specifically reimbursed.

— *REQUIRED*

Advise Ms. Mover as to the 2018 income tax implications of the above employment benefits, supported by your calculations on the basis that she is employed for a full calendar year.

Exercise 15

You have been assigned the audit of Revelation Limited, a Canadian-controlled private corporation, for the 2018 taxation year. Its year end is December 31. At the outset of your audit, Mr. Newlight, the company's sole shareholder and president, informed you that he had just finished a correspondence course in taxation and that all the corporate accounting and taxation matters were well in hand.

Your audit (March 2019), however, revealed the following:

Salary paid to Mr. Newlight	$85,000
Salary paid to Mrs. Care, a very old unrelated family friend who is responsible for part-time typing duties on occasional Fridays	25,000
Royalty payable to Mr. Newlight — Accrued in 2017	2,000
— Accrued in 2014	3,000

The royalty expense was deducted in computing the income of the corporation.

In addition, you discovered that the following loans, each secured by a promissory note, had been made during the 2018 taxation year:

● A $200,000, 3% loan, dated July 1, 2018, made to Mr. Newlight in his capacity as President. Other senior employees are eligible for loans on similar terms. The loan was repayable over 10 years in equal instalments of principal payable on the anniversary date, but with interest payable monthly, to enable Mr. Newlight to purchase a new home for his own occupancy.

● A $15,000 non-interest-bearing loan, dated September 1, 2018, made to Mr. Newlight. The loan was repaid on January 31, 2019. Further investigation of prior years revealed that loans in similar amounts had continually been taken out and repaid in subsequent years.

● A $500 non-interest-bearing loan, dated October 1, 2018, made to Mrs. Care for the purpose of enabling her to purchase a ticket for a Caribbean cruise.

Assume that the prescribed interest rate for the first quarter of 2018 was 4%; for the second quarter, it was 3%; for the third quarter, it was 4%; and for the fourth quarter, it was 5%.

— *REQUIRED*

Discuss the tax implications for 2018 of the foregoing information providing any advice to Mr. Newlight that you consider necessary. Support your answer with calculations where appropriate and provide reasons for your conclusions.

Exercise 16

Mrs. Blue sold qualified small business corporation shares in April 2018 for proceeds of $523,000. She inherited the shares in 2003 when her father died. At that time, their value was $138,000. The only other capital gain Mrs. Blue has had was in 2001 when she sold some securities on which she recognized a capital gain of $33,000. She sheltered the $33,000 gain entirely with the capital gains deduction. She has not claimed any net capital losses, since 1988. She had the following items of investment income in 2017 and 2018:

	2017	2018
Non-eligible dividends (cash amount)	$6,000	$ 5,000
Interest expense to purchase investment portfolio	9,000	13,000
Rental income	2,000	2,500

— REQUIRED

Calculate the maximum capital gains deduction available to be claimed by Mrs. Blue when preparing her 2018 tax return.

Exercise 17

Mr. Ink is the sole shareholder and manager of Ink Inc., a Canadian-controlled private corporation. Ink Inc. distributes fountain pens in the $75 to $250 range. The corporation is expecting unusually high profits for the current year, around $580,000. Mr. Ink is wondering if the corporation should pay him salary and/or dividends for the current year.

— REQUIRED

What are some of the considerations that should be taken into account in advising Mr. Ink as to whether he should be paid salary and/or dividends for the current year?

Exercise 18

Determine which of the following CCPCs are "small business corporations" and state the reason for your conclusion.

	A Co.	B Co.	C Co.	D Co.
Assets (@ FMV)				
Term deposits	$ 0	$ 0	$15,000	$ 0
Land	50,000	0	0	40,000
Building	35,000	0	0	60,000
Equipment	0	80,000	0	0
Shares of X Ltd.	0	20,000	0	0
Shares of Y Ltd.	15,000	0	15,000	0
Liabilities (@ FMV)				
Accounts payable	10,000	2,000	0	0
Bank loan	10,000	0	0	0

Additional Information

(a) In each of the above situations, the land, building and equipment are used by the owner in an active business carried on in Canada with the exception of D Co. In the case of D, the land and building are leased to Spouse Co., a CCPC, and are used by Spouse Co. in its active business, which it carries on in Canada. D Co. is owned 100% by the spouse of the sole shareholder of Spouse Co.

(b) X Ltd. is a public company.

(c) Y Ltd. is a small business corporation. A Co. and C Co. each own 50% of Y Ltd.

Exercise 19

For each of (a), (b), (c), and (d), determine whether Holdco would meet the 24 month "asset test" as it relates to qualified small business corporations. The assets of Holdco and Subco, as shown below, are started at their fair market value. The assets and their values have remained constant for the past three years.

	Assets Used in an Active Business*	Investment in Subco	Other Assets	Total
(a) Holdco	$60,000	$25,000	$15,000	$100,000
Subco	20,000	0	80,000	100,000
(b) Holdco	30,000	50,000	20,000	100,000
Subco	95,000	0	5,000	100,000
(c) Holdco	45,000	15,000	40,000	100,000
Subco	70,000	0	30,000	100,000
(d) Holdco	0	75,000	25,000	100,000
Subco	92,000	0	8,000	100,000

*In each case, the active business is carried on in Canada.

CHAPTER 13

¶13,875   ASSIGNMENT PROBLEMS

Type 1 Problems

Problem 1

A. You have just incorporated and started your business. Your corporate pre-tax profit is $30,000. This is your only source of income. Would you prefer to receive your compensation as $30,000 of salary or a dividend of the after-tax profit?

B. Now your company is making $600,000 after your salary of $220,000. Should you:

(1) Declare a bonus of $100,000 to reduce income to the business limit?

(2) Pay a dividend equal to the amount needed to bring the corporate cash to corporate cash available under the $100,000 bonus option in (1) above?

(3) Do nothing?

The first thing you should do is consider what comparison you are going to make to decide between the compensation options. This will help you organize your calculations.

Please ignore the CPP payroll costs in your analysis.

The provincial corporate tax rate on active business income is 4% if it is eligible for the small business deduction and 12% if it is not.

(A) Assess the situation.

(B) Identify the issues.

(C) Analyze the issues.

(D) Advise/recommend.

Problem 2

Karen, a resident of White Rock B.C., owns all the common shares of Cyber Corp. which was incorporated in 2002. Karen invested $1,000 into the share capital of Cyber Corp.

Cyber Corp is located in White Rock and distributes computer equipment and games to retail stores in southern B.C. The following is the balance sheet.

Cyber Corp.
Balance Sheet
as at December 31, 2018

Assets				FMV
Cash	$	4,500	$	4,500
Marketable securities		300,000		700,000
Accounts receivable		800,000		780,000
Inventory		920,000		920,000
Prepaid expenses		1,000		1,000
Investment in Cyber Sub Inc.		1,000		100,000
Fixed assets		140,000		150,000
Goodwill — Class 14.1		—		200,000
		$2,166,500		$2,855,500

Liabilities & Shareholders' Equity		
Accounts payable and accrued liabilities	$	600,000
Loans payable		400,000
Future income taxes		100,000
Share capital		1,000
Retained earnings		1,065,500
		$2,166,500

The investment in Cyber Sub Inc., a CCPC, was made two years ago to distribute a new line of games. It is 25% owned by Cyber Corp and uses all of its assets in a Canadian active business.

The relative values of Cyber Corp's assets have remained stable over the past three years. The marketable securities comprise Cyber Corp's investment portfolio which is not held as part of the corporation's business activities. The estimated value of the goodwill of the business is $200,000.

Karen was recently offered $1,800,000 for the shares of Cyber Corp.

Karen would like to know whether, if she sold her shares of Cyber Corp, she would be able to claim the capital gains exemption on the sale. If they do not qualify for the CGE then she wants to know if there is anything that can be done to qualify.

For the next meeting you agree that you will:

    (A) Assess the situation.

    (B) Identify the issues.

    (C) Analyze the issues.

    (D) Advise/recommend.

Problem 3   ITA: 110.6

Rogo Dan owns all of the common shares of Julie Inc. which in turn owns all of the shares of two other companies, Opco Inc. and RE Inc. Opco Inc. carries on an active business in Sudbury. RE Inc. owns real estate, of which 100% is used by Opco Inc. in its business. All three corporations are CCPCs. The following are further details:

Julie Inc. assets:	
Shares of Opco Inc. at FMV	$850,000
Shares of RE Inc. at FMV	800,000
Portfolio investments at FMV	75,000
Opco Inc. assets and liabilities:	
Active business assets at FMV	$900,000
Term deposits	50,000
Liabilities	100,000
RE Inc. assets and liabilities:	
Land and building at FMV	$800,000
Portfolio investments at FMV	200,000
Mortgage	200,000

[handwritten margin note: No AB asset of own]

The proportion of assets in each of the companies has been constant over the past three years. Rogo has owned the shares of Julie Inc. for the past five years.

Rogo would like your advice on the following:

(A) Does Julie Inc. meet each of the three tests necessary for its shares to be qualifying small business corporation shares?

(B) If the shares of Julie Inc. are not QSBC shares, then suggest ways of purifying Julie Inc. and indicate the tax consequences of your recommendations.

Problem 4   ITA: 110.6

Phil Zamboni realized taxable capital gains of $12,000 in 2002. This gain was offset by a capital gains deduction of $12,000 in that year.

In 2016, Zamboni received interest income of $825 and grossed-up taxable dividends of $200. He also incurred a net rental loss of $15,000 and carrying charges totalling $1,475 in 2016.

In 2017, Zamboni earned investment income of $200. He had a rental loss that year in the amount of $13,000 and carrying charges of $2,000. He also realized a business investment loss of $26,000 in December 2017.

In 2018, Zamboni sold the shares of Maps Unlimited Ltd., a qualified small business corporation, for a capital gain of $185,000 and he realized a capital loss of $21,000 on the sale of public company shares. He also received $1,650 in interest and incurred a net rental loss of $1,000 in 2018.

Zamboni had no other previous capital transactions, investment income, or investment expenses.

Phil has asked you to calculate his capital gains deduction for 2018 supported by all the necessary calculations.

Problem 5

Bob Smith, age 50, incorporated Smith Inc. 20 years ago when he purchased all of the 100 shares from the company for $100. Smith Inc. is a "small business corporation" which carries on an active business in Victoria, B.C. Bob works full time in the business.

Thirteen years ago, Bob felt that he would like to involve his wife Betty in the share ownership and, on the advice of his accountant, Holdco Inc. was incorporated with Bob and Betty each owning 50 common shares which they bought for $1 each with their own funds. Bob then transferred his common shares of Smith Inc., which were worth $600,000, to Holdco Inc. and elected under s. 85 to defer the tax. As consideration for the transfer, Bob received preference shares with a non-cumulative dividend rate of up to 6% and a fair market value of $600,000. Betty has had no involvement in the Smith Inc. business.

On July 1, 2018, Smith Inc. sold some property that was used in the active business for net proceeds of $150,000. This amount was then paid as a dividend from Smith Inc. to Holdco Inc. on the same day. Bob and Betty plan to have the corporation invest this amount and use it as capital for their retirement. After the sale of the property and the payment of the dividend to Holdco Inc., Smith Inc. has a fair market value of $800,000 and is still a "small business corporation". Bob received $6,000 in dividends on his preferred shares of Holdco Inc. in December 2018.

Assume that the prescribed rate for 2018 was 4%. Bob is in the top tax bracket. Betty has a part-time retail sales job and no other source of income.

Bob and Betty have just emailed you about this transaction and immediately a concern about the corporate attribution rules comes to your mind.

Before you meet with Bob and Betty you decide to:

    (A) Assess the situation.

    (B) Identify the issues.

    (C) Analyze the issues.

    (D) Advise/recommend.

ITR: 4301(*c*)

ITA: 245

Problem 6

Consider each of the following independent fact situations.

(1) Adam Aref has contributed the maximum amount to an RRSP on the first business day of each year in respect of the previous year and shortly thereafter has withdrawn the funds.

(2) Bill Sheridan loaned his wife $1,000,000 five years ago through a non-interest bearing promissory note. His wife invested the funds in GICs and earned $80,000 of interest income which was properly attributed to him, except for any compound interest. Bill gave his wife another cash amount to cover the income tax on the compound interest.

(3) Wells Ltd. is owned 100% by Mrs. Hogart. Stieb Ltd. is owned by Mrs. Hogart's husband and minor children. Wells Ltd. made an interest-free loan out of its taxable surplus to Stieb Ltd. such that the corporate attribution rule does not apply. Stieb Ltd. used the proceeds of the loan to earn property income.

(4) Traub has $200,000 of investments and a mortgage on his personal home for a similar amount. Traub sold the investments, paid off the mortgage, and reborrowed to acquire the investments.

(5) Andy made a loan to his adult child's corporation, Vancouver Hockey Puck Ltd., in order to avoid attribution, since the corporation used the funds to earn property income.

Discuss whether the general anti-avoidance rule (GAAR) applies to the above situations.

Problem 7

ITA: 245; IC 88-2

Consider each of the following independent fact situations:

(1) An individual transfers his or her unincorporated business to a corporation primarily to obtain the benefit of the small business deduction.

(2) An individual provides services to a corporation with which he or she does not deal at arm's length. The company does not pay a salary to the individual because payment of a salary would increase the amount of a loss that the company will incur in the year.

(3) A taxable Canadian corporation, which is profitable, has a wholly owned taxable Canadian corporation that is sustaining losses and needs additional capital to carry on its business. The subsidiary could borrow the monies from its bank but the subsidiary could not obtain any tax saving in the current year by deducting the interest expense. Therefore, the parent corporation borrows the money from its bank and subscribes for additional common shares of the subsidiary and reduces its net income by deducting the interest from its business.

(4) Profitco and Lossco are taxable Canadian corporations. Lossco is a wholly owned subsidiary of Profitco. Lossco has non-capital losses that would be deductible if Lossco had income. In order to generate income in Lossco from which its non-capital losses may be deducted, Profitco borrows from its bank and uses the monies to subscribe for common shares of Lossco. Lossco lends these monies to Profitco at a commercial rate of interest. Profitco repays the bank. The amount of share subscription is not in excess of the amount of monies that Lossco could reasonably be expected to be able to borrow for use in its business on the basis solely of its credit from an arm's length lender.

(5) Each of two private corporations owns less than 10% of the common shares of a payer corporation that is to pay a substantial taxable dividend. The payer corporation will not be entitled to a dividend refund on the payment of the dividend. None of the corporations is related to any of the others. The private corporations form a corporation, Newco, transfer their shares of the payer corporation to Newco in exchange for common shares of Newco, and elect under subsection 85(1) (assume that this is done correctly to avoid tax on the transfer) in respect of the transfer. Following the transfer of the payer corporation's shares to Newco, Newco will be connected with the payer corporation. The payer corporation pays the dividend to Newco, free of Part IV tax. Newco pays the same amount to the private corporations as a dividend, free of Part IV tax. The primary purpose of the transfer of the shares is to avoid the Part IV tax which would be payable if the dividend were received directly by the private corporations.

(6) The owner of land inventory has agreed to sell the property to an arm's length purchaser. The purchaser wants to buy the property for cash, but the owner does not want to have the profits recognized in the year of sale. The owner sells the land inventory to an intermediary company deferring receipt of the proceeds of disposition of the land for several years after the date of sale. In this way, a reserve can be claimed under paragraph 20(1)(*n*). The intermediary sells the land to the third party for cash. The owner receives interest from the intermediary in respect of the monies received by the intermediary from the third party.

For each of these fact situations, advise whether the part of the general anti-avoidance rule (GAAR) that asks the question "can it reasonably be considered that the transaction would not result, directly or indirectly, in a misuse of the provisions of the Act or an abuse having regard to the provisions of the Act read as a whole" applies.

Type 2 Problems

Problem 8

ITA: 15(1), 18(1)

Mia Gibbons is president of Pump You Up Ltd., a private corporation she started and owns. Mia has recently signed a lease for an upscale downtown condominium which she intends to move into next month. Mia has arranged for Pump You Up Ltd. to pay the $2,000 monthly rental for the condominium. No other employees have their rent paid by the company.

Mia has asked you to explain the income tax consequences of this arrangement to Mia and to Pump You Up Ltd.

For the next meeting you agree that you will:

(A) Assess the situation.

(B) Identify the issues.

(C) Analyze the issues.

(D) Advise/recommend.

Problem 9

Kristie owns 35% of Big City Developments Inc. (BCD), which has a December 31 year end. She is also an employee of the company. On March 31, Year 1, she purchased her shares of BCD from treasury for $150,000. BCD lent her all the funds for the share purchase at an interest rate of 2%. She is required to repay the loan at the rate of $25,000 each January 1.

On May 15, Year 1, BCD loaned Kristie $75,000 to purchase a new motor home and boat. Since she is a significant shareholder, she was not required to repay any of the loan in Year 1 or Year 2. At the end of Year 3, Kristie repaid $25,000 of the loan.

You have agreed to calculate the income tax implications to Kristie as a result of receiving these loans for Years 1, 2, and 3, assuming the prescribed rate of interest for shareholder loans was 3% throughout all the years. (Ignore the effects of a leap year, if applicable.) Assume that the loans are received because of Kristie's employment and not because of her shareholdings (i.e., other employees have received or are eligible to receive similar loans).

Problem 10

It is February 2019 and, as the auditor for Skies Limited, you have discovered several items in your 2018 year-end audit that require further consideration.

Skies Limited is a manufacturer located in Stratford, Ontario. Mr. Scott is an 80% shareholder and president of the company which has a December 31 fiscal year end. His son Joe, who is vice-president, owns the other 20% of the shares. They both live in Stratford.

Harry is the VP-Sales. He is neither related to Mr. Scott nor is he a shareholder. A significant portion of his income is made up of commissions.

Shareholder Loans

The records showed that the corporation has made several loans to Mr. Scott and his son, Joe, who is also an employee of the corporation.

Each of the following was evidenced by a separate promissory note, duly signed and approved by the Board of Directors:

(a) A $180,000 non-interest bearing loan to Joe to finance the purchase of previously unissued, fully-paid shares from the corporation at their fair market value. The note is dated August 1, 2018 and the loan is repayable in $18,000 annual instalments.

(b) A $270,000 1% loan to Mr. Scott to finance the purchase a new home, a few blocks from his old home. The note is dated June 1, 2018 and the loan is repayable over 15 years in equal instalments of principal payable on the anniversary date; interest is payable monthly.

(c) A $24,000 0% loan to Harry to finance the purchase a car to be used in his employment. The note is dated June 1, 2018; it requires principal to be paid annually, on May 31st, over five years.

Any interest required to be paid on the loans at the indicated rates was paid in 2018. Assume the prescribed rates for 2018 are 2% for the first and second quarters, and 3% for the third and fourth quarters.

Mr. Scott would like to understand the tax implications of these loans to him, Joe, Harry, and Skies Ltd.

You know that you have to decide whether they received the loans by virtue of employment or shareholding. Mr. Scott told you that these are the only employees to receive a loan.

For the next meeting you agree that you will:

    (A) Assess the situation.

    (B) Identify the issues.

    (C) Analyze the issues.

    (D) Advise/recommend.

Problem 11

ITA: 15(2), 15(2.3), 15(2.4), 15(2.6), 20(1)(*j*), 80.4; ITR: 4300(7)

In 2018, Sunshine Publishing Ltd., a book publishing company with a fiscal year end on December 31, made a loan of $100,000 to Stuart Sunshine, the president and majority shareholder. Both Stuart and Sunshine Publishing Limited are Canadian residents.

This is the first loan that Stuart ever received from the company, and it helped him finance the purchase of a new home which was built just outside Toronto, 10 kilometres farther from the corporate headquarters than Stuart's previous home. The loan was made on May 1, 2018, and a mortgage agreement was signed on that date. This agreement requires that the $100,000 owing be repaid over five years in equal instalments of $20,000 on each anniversary date, starting on May 1, 2020, without interest. Early prepayments of principal are allowed.

Assume that the prescribed rates applicable to taxable benefits are: 1% for the first quarter of 2018, 2% for the second quarter, 3% for the third quarter, 2% for the fourth quarter, and 1% for all of 2019. (Ignore the effects of a leap year, if applicable.)

Stuart has asked you for the following advice:

(A) It is now December 2018 and Stuart has asked you to advise him on the tax consequences of the loan. It is not a company policy to make housing loans to employees and no other loans have been made to employees on similar conditions. What are the income tax consequences of this loan to Stuart in 2018 and 2019?

(B) If it was a company policy to make such loans to employees and other loans had been made to employees on similar terms and conditions, how would this change your answer to Part (A)?

(C) Assume the following facts: it was a company policy to make such loans to employees; other loans had been made to employees on similar terms and conditions; Stuart was a 9.5% shareholder rather than a majority shareholder; he was not related to any shareholders of the company; and the loan was to buy a rental property rather than a home. How would this change your answer to Part (B)?

Problem 12

ITA: 82(1), 117, 121, 123–125

Nancy Ball presently operates a retailing proprietorship with a December 31, year end and makes $150,000 of net income for tax purposes annually. She is thinking of incorporating her business and has asked for your advice. She lives in a province where the provincial corporate tax rate is 4% of this type of federal taxable income. She has $2,100 of federal personal tax credits, $1,400 of provincial personal tax credits, and no other income.

You have agreed that you will do the following:

(A) Estimate the personal taxes that Nancy would pay currently on $150,000 of business income compared with the amount of corporate and personal taxes that would be paid if she incorporated her business and only took out a salary of $50,000. Ignore all payroll taxes (e.g., Canada Pension Plan premiums) when making your estimates.

(B) Based on your calculations in (A), estimate the amount of personal tax that Nancy defers by keeping the remaining after-tax retained earnings in her company this year. [Hint: compute the additional personal tax that she would pay on a dividend equal to the corporation's after-tax retained earnings.]

Problem 13

Mrs. Edwards, age 49, presently operates a retailing proprietorship with a December 31 fiscal year end. She expects income for tax purposes of $210,000 from the business. Since the business currently requires considerable amounts of working capital, she can only afford to withdraw $50,000 annually to meet her family's needs. Mrs. Edwards has combined federal and provincial personal credits of $4,600 and has no other income.

She is considering the incorporation of her business. If she does so, she has been advised that if she makes all withdrawals from the business in the form of $50,000 in salary, she will end up with enough after-tax cash to meet her family's needs.

She has come to you for advice on whether she should incorporate her business or not. She lives in a province where the provincial corporate tax rate is 4% of federal taxable income eligible for the small business deduction. Ignore any Canada Pension Plan premiums payable on the income.

You have agreed to do the following:

(A) Calculate the total tax that Mrs. Edwards would pay in 2018 on the $210,000 earned personally. Then, calculate the total tax that would be paid, by the company and her personally, if she incorporated her business and only took out a salary of $50,000. Compare the two options.

(B) Determine how much personal tax Mrs. Edwards will defer each year by keeping the after-tax retained earnings (after paying the $50,000 salary) in her company. Do this by computing the additional personal tax that she would pay on a dividend equal to the corporation's after-tax retained earnings.

(C) What is the absolute income tax cost or savings for Mrs. Edwards if she incorporates?

Compare:

(a) The personal tax incurred when the income is earned directly by Mrs. Edwards with

(b) The total income tax incurred at the personal and corporate level by using a corporation to earn the income. Consider the corporate tax plus the personal tax on the salary and personal tax on the dividend paid out of after-tax retained earnings.

(D) Mrs. Edwards has a husband, Mr. Edwards, age 50, who currently does not work, and two children, one in high-school who is 16 years old and another who is in university and is 19 years old. Assuming Mrs. Edwards chooses to incorporate, suggest ways of income splitting with her family members.

Problem 14

ITA: 82(1), 117, 121, 123–125.1

Iris Kroneman approaches you with the following information:

(a) She resides in a province with a 3% corporate tax rate (i.e., a total tax rate of 13%) where she owns and operates an incorporated business which generates income in the amount of $125,000 before taxes.

(b) She has federal personal tax credits of $2,100 and provincial personal tax credits of $1,400 including, among others, the marital status tax credit.

(c) She requires $65,000 before taxes for living expenses each year.

(d) She wants to maximize her Canada Pension Plan contributions each year. The CPP calculations are as follows:

Pensionable earnings (salary)	$55,900
Basic exemption	(3,500)
Maximum contributory earnings	$52,400
Employee rate	4.95%
Maximum contribution	$ 2,594

(e) She wants to make the maximum RRSP contribution based on the earned income you determine she should have. Assume that her earned income for 2017 is the same as for 2018.

You have agreed to determine the tax consequences of the salary/dividend combination for Ms. Kroneman that will achieve her goals.

Type 3 Problems

Problem 15

Herb Smith, the tax partner, has just talked to you about one of his clients, John Barwell. John has owned his retail store, Aurora Collectibles, for the past four years. Despite a recession, he has been able to do very well with the store by offering customers decorating advice along with the antiques and other unusual items that he sells. Last year, his store earned net income of $125,000.

When he first started the business, he set it up as a proprietorship and financed it with a loan of $100,000 from his wife, Alison, and a $75,000 bank operating loan. Currently, both of the loans remain unpaid, since both John and Alison enjoy a lifestyle that uses up all of their cash flow. Both John and Alison agree that they are going to improve their spending habits. They want John to pay off the bank operating loan from the business earnings. Once this is done, any excess cash will be used by John to invest in some property that they will eventually move the store into. Alison isn't involved in the retail store business.

Herb wants you to identify the tax issues and tell him what analysis you propose to do to help John and Alison. He doesn't want you to get into the numbers yet.

Problem 16

Charles Wong, the vice-president of Arctic Oil Corporation, loves to minimize his income taxes. He spends much of his time hiring tax professionals to seek loopholes in the *Income Tax Act*. One loophole that he discovered was as follows.

Since Arctic Oil Corporation is in a loss position this year, he has found a way to defer much of his employment income to the next year. It won't cost the firm any money at all and his corporation is even willing to loan him funds (interest free) to live on.

Arrangements like this lead to legislation of rules for "salary deferral arrangements" and provisions for the taxation of benefits received as low-interest loans. However, the business-purpose and the substance-over-form concepts were enacted in the general anti-avoidance rule to place a broad restriction on taxpayer behaviour. Charles is having less and less success in his pursuit of loopholes in the tax system.

You have realized that Charles needs to have a better understanding of the difference between tax minimization and effective tax planning. Charles may have to change his objective of tax minimization. In your opinion, a better understanding of the concept of substance over form may help him to avoid being caught under the general anti-avoidance rule. As his tax adviser, help Charles to understand this by explaining:

● the difference between tax minimization and effective tax planning;

● why he should change his tax minimization objective; and

● how he can avoid the application of the GAAR.

Problem 17

On September 9, 2018, Wayne Dunkel, a tax partner with BDO Canada LLP in Waterloo, Ontario, came out of a meeting with Samantha Greene, a client who wants to purchase a dental practice. Wayne has to make a recommendation on whether Samantha should buy the practice personally or through a corporation, how she should structure the purchase and her compensation.

Samantha Greene

Dr. Samantha Greene is a dentist who, on graduation from the Schulich School of Medicine and Dentistry at Western University in 2013, worked for a dentist in London, Ontario. This year she is purchasing a dental practice in Waterloo.

Samantha is married to Roger and they have two children, Scott (2) and Kelly (4). Roger works for a local high-tech company where he earns a salary of $180,000. His company does not have a pension plan.

Samantha has been wondering lately if she should be contributing to the Canada Pension Plan and an RRSP as a way to save money. Recently, she and Roger have found that it is too easy to spend all of their income on current consumption and they would like to make sure they set money aside for the future. In fact, they would like to see if they could live off of Roger's income and set Samantha's aside to make extra payments on the mortgage on their home and for savings. Assume that Samantha had enough earned income in 2017 to maximize her 2018 RRSP contribution.

Dental Practice

Samantha has made an offer to a retiring dentist to purchase his dental practice for $1.0 million. She is buying the assets since the previous dentist was not incorporated. The purchase price covers the purchase of the equipment, leasehold improvements and the goodwill associated with the practice. It is 100% financed through a loan from the bank with an interest rate of 6% and a personal guarantee from Samantha and Roger. The loan is repayable over ten years with principal payments of $100,000 on October 31 of each year, starting in 2019. Additional principal payments can be made on this loan annually on October 31. The closing date for the purchase is November 1, 2018.

Neither Samantha nor Roger like the idea of having a personal guarantee and would like to eliminate this as soon as possible by repaying the loan. They have both agreed that Samantha would own the practice and that they do not want to plan for income splitting.

Samantha expects the practice to earn $400,000 after expenses but before income tax and any compensation to her. In the future, Samantha anticipates that she will need to reinvest significantly in the practice to upgrade the leasehold improvements and equipment.

Samantha would like your advice on how to structure the purchase of the practice. Assume the provincial corporate tax rate applicable to income eligible for the small business deduction is 4% and 12% for income in excess of the small business deduction limit.

Next Meeting

Before the next meeting with Samantha, Wayne knows he needs to:

(A) Assess the situation.

(B) Identify the issues.

(C) Analyze the issues.

(D) Advise/recommend.

Problem 18

Ms. Mogul has been offered a new job as Vice-President of Marketing with Ganz Ltd., a Canadian-controlled private corporation. In addition to the basic salary and commissions, a number of benefits have been offered as indicated below.

(a) The remuneration package includes a stock option to purchase 10,000 previously unissued fully paid shares of Ganz Ltd. at $10 per share. The current FMV is $25 per share. Ms. Mogul would be expected to exercise half of the option immediately to show her confidence in the company, which plans to go public in the near future.

(b) Under a corporate policy applicable to senior executives, Ganz Ltd. will loan Ms. Mogul the $50,000 required to exercise half of the option at no interest, repayable at $10,000 per annum for 5 years and evidenced by a *bona fide* note. Any outstanding balance would be due in full on termination of employment.

(c) Under a corporate policy applicable to senior executives, Ganz Ltd. will also loan Ms. Mogul $250,000 at 3% interest to purchase a home in Toronto where Ganz Ltd. is located. Ms. Mogul currently lives in Winnipeg. The interest is repayable monthly over 25 years and the principal is repaid annually over 25 years. Assume the prescribed rate was 5% when the loan was granted and does not fall below 5% for 5 years. Also, assume for purposes of your calculation that no principal was repaid in the first 5 years.

(d) Ms. Mogul will be travelling extensively and will be provided with a company car leased by Ganz Ltd. for $900/month including $100/month for insurance. She anticipates 45,000 business kilometres and 5,000 personal kilometres per year. Ganz Ltd. will pay all operating costs, estimated at $300/month. All amounts given include HST.

(e) In lieu of reimbursing specific minor travelling expenses (e.g., meals), Ganz Ltd. will pay Ms. Mogul a monthly allowance of $750. More substantial travelling expenses (e.g., airfares and hotels) will be specifically reimbursed.

— REQUIRED

Advise Ms. Mogul as to the current year's tax implications of the above employment benefits, supported by your calculations on the basis that she is employed for a full calendar year.

Problem 19

You have been assigned to the audit of Allmine Ltd., a Canadian-controlled private corporation, for the 2018 taxation year. Its year end is December 31. At the beginning of the audit, Mr. Ego, the company's sole shareholder and president, informed you that he has always had a keen interest in taxation and, thus, he has kept the corporate taxation matters well in hand.

During the audit which occurred in April 2019, the following items were noted:

(a) Allmine Ltd. declared a bonus of $150,000 payable to Mr. Ego on December 31, 2018. At the time of the audit, the bonus had not been paid. Mr. Ego indicated to you that the bonus will not be paid to him until January 2020 to give him the optimum deferral of tax as he does not have an immediate need for the funds.

(b) On January 1, 2018, Mr. Ego and his son received the following loans from Allmine Ltd. by virtue of Mr. Ego's shareholding therein:

— a $30,000 loan was received by Mr. Ego to enable him to purchase a fishing boat. The loan agreement which was signed January 1, 2018 stated that the loan was to bear interest at 4% per annum. The interest is payable annually on each anniversary date of the loan. The principal is repayable December 31, 2020. At the time of the audit, Mr. Ego had not repaid any principal nor had he paid any interest.

— a $20,000 interest-free loan was received by Mr. Ego's 25-year old son to enable him to purchase previously unissued fully paid shares of Allmine Ltd. from Allmine Ltd. Mr. Ego's son is an employee of Allmine Ltd. A promissory note was signed for the loan. The note indicated that the principal would be repaid on the fifth anniversary of the loan.

(c) On December 31, 2017, Mr. Ego's wife received a loan from Allmine Ltd. by virtue of her husband's shareholding therein. The loan was in the amount of $60,000 and was non-interest bearing. Mrs. Ego used the funds to redecorate the family home. She repaid the loan on December 31, 2018.

(d) Mr. Ego's wealthy brother, Bob, guaranteed a $1,000,000 loan to Allmine Ltd. on January 1, 2015, when the company originally started operations. The loan guarantee fee is 0.8% annually. No fee has ever been paid on the guarantee, although the company has accrued the fee annually. The fee expense has been deducted in computing the income of the company for each of 2015, 2016, 2017, and 2018.

(e) Mr. Ego's wife owns all the shares in Hair Inc., which owns and operates a hair styling salon. All the assets of Hair Inc. are used in an active business carried on in Canada. Mr. Ego loaned Hair Inc. $10,000 interest-free on January 1, 2018. No repayments have been made on the loan as at the date of the audit.

(f) Mr. Ego wishes for his wife and his two sons to each have a $1,000 compound-interest Canada Savings Bond. He currently has three such bonds. He thinks that by his wife and children owning the bonds, less income tax will be paid on interest. His two children are currently 16 and 20 years of age. He is considering getting the bonds into their hands by one of the following methods:

   (i) giving the bonds to them without receiving any financial consideration in return; or

   (ii) loaning them the funds, interest-free, to enable them to purchase similar bonds.

— *REQUIRED*

Discuss the income tax implications of the foregoing information, providing any advice to Mr. Ego that you consider necessary. Support your answer with calculations where appropriate. Ignore the effects of leap year.

Note: assume the prescribed interest rates for 2018 were:

1st quarter	3%
2nd quarter . . .	2%
3rd quarter	5%
4th quarter	5%

CHAPTER 13 —
DISCUSSION NOTES FOR REVIEW QUESTIONS

(1) Mr. Smith can pay the bonus within the 179-day limit and loan the net after-tax amount back to the company. The bonus will provide Mr. Smith with RRSP room, which he could use to reduce taxes in a future period. If he does loan the funds back to the corporations, he should consider charging interest to the company in order to reduce payroll taxes by converting future salary payments into interest income. He should also consider securing the loan. Another option is to leave the money in the corporation and pay tax at 27%. Leaving the funds in the corporation will allow him to take advantage of a tax deferral benefit of the difference between his personal tax rate and the 27% corporate tax rate. ITA: 78(4)

(2) (a) If he leaves the money in the company, the income over $500,000 will not be eligible for the small business deduction, but it will be eligible for the general rate reduction. The corporate marginal tax rate will be 27% (i.e., 38% – 10% – 13% + 12%), which is less than all but the lowest personal tax rate (federal and provincial combined).

(b) If he declares and pays the bonus the personal marginal tax rate will be 50% (i.e., 33% + 17%) (see ¶10,250 for provincial rates for study guide purposes).

(c) He can defer approximately 22.7% (see calculation below) of tax by leaving the income in the company to be taxed.

(d) If he leaves the income in the company to be taxed, he will have to pay tax on the dividend when he eventually pays it out. The combined tax rate at that point, assuming the 38% dividend tax credit, will be approximately 49.7% slightly below the 50% personal tax cost of paying out the bonus now, a small tax savings.

(e) Calculation:

Corporate income	$1,000
Corporate tax @ 27%	(270)
After-tax income	$ 730
Dividend paid	$ 730
Gross-up (38%)	277
Taxable dividend	$1,007
Tax @ 50%	$ 504
Dividend tax credit	(277)
Net personal tax	$ 227
Net cash after tax	$ 503
Total tax ($270 + $227)	$ 497

(3) If he or she chooses a fiscal year end on or after July 6, but no later than December 31, then the bonus can be paid within the 179 days in either this calendar year or on January 1 of the next calendar year. ITA: 78(4)

(4) The following are the five criteria for the deductibility of bonus accruals as decided in the *Totem Disposal* case:

- reasonableness of the bonus in relation to profit and services rendered;

- payment for real and identifiable service;

- some justification for expecting a bonus over regular salary (e.g., a company policy);

- reasonableness of the time between determining profit and establishing the bonus; and

- a legal obligation to pay the accrued bonus.

(5) Mr. Chow is related to his brother-in-law. Therefore, they are deemed not to deal with each other at arm's length and the brother-in-law is connected with Mr. Chow. As a result, the conditions in the shareholder loan rule are met and none of the exceptions are met. Therefore, the brother-in-law will be required to take the full amount of the loan into income in 2018 since none of it was repaid by December 31, 2019. In 2020 and 2021, the brother-in-law will be able to deduct the principal repayments. The imputed interest benefit included in his 2018 tax return can be removed through an amended return to eliminate the benefit.

ITA: 15(2.1), 251(2)
ITA: 15(2), 15(2.4)
ITA: 20(1)(*j*)

ITA: 80.4(3)(*b*)

(6) Since Ms. Jones is a shareholder and received a loan, the shareholder loan rules apply. Although Ms. Jones is an employee, the boat does not fit into one of the exceptions. Therefore, Ms. Jones will have to take the $25,000 into income unless she repays it within one year from the end of the taxation year in which she received the loan. If she has to include the principal in income then the imputed interest rules will not apply. When she repays the loan, she will be entitled to a deduction.

ITA: 15(2)
ITA: 15(2.4)(*b*)–(*d*), 15(2.6)
ITA: 80.4, 80.4(3)(*b*)

(7) This provincial tax holiday would bring the combined corporate tax rate on income eligible for the small business deduction down to 10% (38% − 10% − 18%), which is below the 13.8% rate of perfect integration. This would provide a tax incentive (saving) to flowing active business income through a corporation, paying corporate tax and then paying dividends. There would then be an advantage to paying dividends instead of salary to the owner due to the fact that the dividend tax credit is greater than the underlying corporate tax. There would also be a significant tax deferral benefit to leaving funds in the corporation.

(8) With the 16% dividend gross-up his taxable income would be $34,800. The federal tax would be $5,220 less the dividend tax credit of $3,491 (i.e., $8/11 \times $4,800$) and the personal credit of $1,771 (in 2018) leaving basic federal tax of nil. Provincial tax on $34,800 would be $3,480, less the provincial dividend tax credit of $1,309 (i.e., $3/11 \times $4,800$) and the provincial personal tax credit of $1,181 (i.e., $11,809 \times 0.10$), leaving provincial tax of $990.

(9) It is true that in order to claim an ABIL the shares need to be shares in a small business corporation. However, the definition of small business corporation allows the status as a small business corporation to continue for 12 months for purposes of the ABIL provisions. Since she sold the shares within six months she should be able to claim the loss as an ABIL.

ITA: 248(1)
ITA: 39(1)(*c*)

(10) In several Income Tax Folios and Interpretation Bulletins, the CRA states that the phrase means at least 90%. It should be noted that this phrase has not been specifically determined by the courts and it is unclear whether the courts would allow 85% or require 95% as the percentage necessary to meet this test. Practitioners generally use 90%.

(11) This corporation is neither, since in order to meet the definition of "small business corporation" it has to meet the 90% test at the determination time. Since the corporation does not meet this test it is neither an SBC nor a QSBC.

(12) The preamble to the corporate attribution rule refers only to situations where "individuals have transferred or loaned property." In this case his corporation has loaned the funds to her corporation. It could not even be said that he did it indirectly since he has not loaned or transferred any money to his own corporation. Therefore, even though her corporation is not an SBC, the corporate attribution rules should not apply. However, GAAR should be considered.

ITA: 74.4(2)

The December 13, 2017 draft legislation related to income sprinkling needs to be considered. Dividend income earned by the spouse from her corporation that is derived from a related business would be subject to tax on split income (TOSI). A related business is a business carried on by a corporation in which a related person (Mr. Smith) is either:

- actively engaged on a regular basis in its activities, or

- in which he owns 10% of the fair market value of the shares.

Mr. Smith meets both of these conditions. As a result, TOSI would apply to dividends received by his spouse unless they are considered "excluded amounts".

CHAPTER 13

Dividend income on "excluded shares" are not subject to TOSI. For the spouse's shares in her company to be considered "excluded shares", 90% or more of the income of the corporation must be derived from sources other than a related business. This would not be the case as the invested funds in Mrs. Smith's corporation would be derived from Mr. Smith's business through the $100,000 loan. Once Mr. Smith reaches the age of 65, it would be possible to split dividend income with Mrs. Smith as the dividends would be deemed to be an excluded amount under the "reasonable return" exception.

CHAPTER 13 — SOLUTIONS TO MULTIPLE CHOICE QUESTIONS

Question 1

(B) is correct under administrative practice outlined in the text. If $40,000 of the loan is repaid within one year of the end of the year of S Ltd. in which the loan was made, then $160,000 must be included in the year of the loan. Subsequent repayments are deductible in the year of the repayment.

ITA: 15(2)
ITA: 15(2.6)
ITA: 15(2.4)

(A) is incorrect under administrative practice. Only the part of the loan ($160,000) that was not paid before the one-year limit will be included in Stan's income in 2018, the year he received the loan. The limit is one year after the end of the taxation year of the lender in which the loan was made. He does not meet the other criteria for exclusion. Since such a loan is not available to other employees, it is not reasonable to conclude that he received the loan because of his employment.

(C) is incorrect. There is no imputed interest benefit when the loan is included in income. If there was an imputed interest benefit the prescribed rate protection rule would not apply as the loan was not received because of his employment.

ITA: 80.4(1), 80.4(3)(*b*), 80.4(4)

(D) is incorrect. One year after the end of the calendar year in which the loan is received has no significance. The shareholder loan rule includes the loan in income in the year it is *received* (i.e., 2018) unless it is repaid by one year after the end of the taxation year of the *lender* in which the loan was made, or the loan meets one of the specific exclusions.

ITA: 15(2)

Question 2

(C) is the correct answer. The shareholder loan rule would include the principal amount of the loan in Mrs. C's income in 2018 because none of the exception tests are met.

ITA: 15(2.2), 15(2.3), 15(2.4), 15(2.6)

(1) The exception test in subsection 15(2.2) does not apply because Mrs. C is resident in Canada.

(2) The exception in subsection 15(2.3) does not apply since the money is not lent in the ordinary course of money lending business.

(3) None of the exceptions for employees in subsection 15(2.4) are met, because it is not reasonable to conclude that the loan is received because of employment since no other employees have received similar loans.

(4) The exception in subsection 15(2.6) does not apply since the debt was repaid on April 1, 2020, which is more than one year from the end of S Ltd.'s December 31, 2018 fiscal year.

The loan in (A) would not be included in Mrs. A's income because the one-year repayment exception test applies: the debt is repaid on April 1, 2019, which is within one year from the end of S Ltd.'s December 31, 2018 fiscal year. Note, however, that the imputed interest benefit rule would apply to compute a deemed interest benefit on the loan.

ITA: 15(2.6)

ITA: 80.4(2)

The loan in (B) would not be included in B Ltd's income because the shareholder loan rule does not apply to corporate shareholders resident in Canada.

ITA: 15(2)

The loan in (D) would not be included in Mr. D's income because one of the exceptions for employees is met: Mr. D is not a specified employee and it is reasonable to conclude that the loan is received because of employment, since the computer is for employment use and other employees currently working at home have received similar loans. Since Mr. D is not a specified employee, the loan does not have to be for any specified purpose. A specified employee is an employee who is either a specified shareholder (i.e., generally, a person who owns at least 10% of the shares of any class of the corporation) or a person who does not deal at arm's length with the corporation. Since Mr. D owns only 5% of the shares of S Ltd. and deals at arm's length with the corporation, he is not a specified employee.

ITA: 15(2.4), 248(1)

Question 3

(D) is correct. Since the $300,000 bonus is unpaid on the 180th day after the end of the taxation year of Fortelli Inc. in which the expense was incurred, it is not deductible until 2019, the taxation year in which it is actually paid.

ITA: 78(4)

(A) is incorrect. This amount refers to the rules in subsection 78(1) for unpaid amounts due to related persons, other than pension benefits, retiring allowances, salary, wages, or other remuneration.

(B) is incorrect. Subsection 78(4) does not distinguish between amounts owed to related and unrelated persons.

(C) is incorrect for the same reason as (A).

Question 4

The correct answer is (B). There is no penalty. The tax benefit that would otherwise have been enjoyed is denied.

ITA: 245(2)

(A) is incorrect as it is true in accordance with subsection 245(2).

(C) is incorrect as it is true in accordance with subsection 245(3).

(D) is incorrect as it is true in accordance with subsection 245(4).

Question 5

(C) is correct. The purpose of the transaction seems to be the reduction or avoidance of tax on the income earned on the $10,000 gift. This transaction goes against the spirit of the Act, read as a whole, and falls within the definition of an avoidance transaction. Note that an attribution rule would apply if it was a loan instead of a gift.

ITA: 245(3)
ITA: 56(4.1)

(A) is incorrect. The transaction is an estate freeze that can reasonably be considered to have been undertaken for *bona fide* purposes other than to obtain the tax benefit. This transaction does not result in a misuse or abuse of the Act, read as a whole. Note that the December 13, 2017 draft legislation related to income sprinkling will apply to dividends received by the children. The dividends will be derived from a "related business". A related business is a business carried on by a related corporation in which the related person owns shares worth 10% of the value of the corporation. Bill owns 20% of the corporation. TOSI applies unless the income can be considered an "excluded amount". The dividends are excluded if derived from an

IC 88-2, par. 10

"excluded business". The children do not work in the business 20 hours per week throughout the year and, therefore, would not be considered to be actively engaged in the business during the year. Further, the children have not contributed property to the operating company and could not meet either of the "safe harbor capital return" or "reasonable return exception". Starting in 2018, Bill should stop paying dividends from the trust to the children.

(B) is incorrect. The incorporation of a business and the claiming of a small business deduction by a CCPC is specifically provided for in the Act. This transaction does not result in a misuse or abuse of the Act, read as a whole.

IC 88-2, par. 11

(D) is incorrect. The Act will deny the deduction of the bonus to the extent it is in excess of a reasonable amount. To the extent the transaction is reasonable, it does not result in a benefit. Corporate tax will be reduced by the accrual, but Mary will pay tax on the income personally.

ITA: 67; IC 88-2, par. 18

Question 6

(D) is correct. All the conditions for corporate attribution are met. As a result, Mr. Boehmer is deemed to have income of 3% × $1,000,000 = $30,000. Note that this amount would be reduced by taxable dividends subject to TOSI under the December 13, 2017 draft legislation related to income sprinkling. However, TOSI would not apply to the dividends received by Mrs. Boehmer. The dividends are not derived from a "related business" and are income on "excluded shares". The Class A common shares provide Mrs. Boehmer with 10% or more of the votes and value of the corporation and meet the definition of an "excluded share".

ITA: 74.4

Note also that dividends paid to Mr. Boehmer would also not be subject to TOSI as long as they were considered to be a reasonable return on his $1,000,000 contribution of property to the corporation.

Taxable dividends paid to Mr. Boehmer would reduce the deemed income inclusion under the corporate attribution provision.

(A) incorrectly attributes the cash dividend received by Mrs. Boehmer to Mr. Boehmer: $10,000.

(B) incorrectly attributes the grossed up dividend received by Mrs. Boehmer to Mr. Boehmer: $11,600 [using the 16% gross-up].

(C) incorrectly computes the attributed amount to Mr. Boehmer based on $500,000: 3% × $500,000 = $15,000.

ITA: 74.4

Question 7

(C) is correct. In order to be a small business corporation, the percentage of assets used in an active business by the corporation and the corporation controlled by Ms. Prentice's brother must be at least 90%. It is now 80% (60% + 20%) or $3,200,000.

ITA: 248(1) "small business corporation"

Therefore, total assets must be $3,200,000/90% or $3,555,555.

Therefore, $444,445 ($4,000,000 – $3,555,555) of the non-active business assets must be sold and the after-tax proceeds used to pay off the company's liabilities.

(A) is incorrect because the corporation does not currently meet the 90% test.

(B) incorrectly assumes that 10% of the assets must be sold: 10% × 4,000,000 = $400,000.

(D) incorrectly ignores the assets used by the related corporation and calculates that since active business assets are $2,400,000 (60% × $4,000,000), total assets must be $2,400,000/90% or $2,666,666 to meet the 90% test. As a result, $1,333,333 ($4,000,000 – $2,666,666) of the non-active business assets must be sold.

CHAPTER 13 — SOLUTIONS TO EXERCISES

Exercise 1

(A) The bonus must be paid on or before 179 days from the end of the year in which it was deducted. In this case, it must be paid on or before March 28, 2019. (Administrative practice would allow payment on the 180th day.)   IT-109R2, par. 10

(B) If the bonus is not paid on or before March 28, 2019, the corporation may not deduct the bonus in its 2018 taxation year. The bonus may only be deducted when it is paid.

(C) (i) The rent must be paid within two years from the end of the year in which it was deducted. In this case, it must be paid by September 30, 2020.

(ii) If the rent is not paid by September 30, 2020, the corporation must add the $10,000 to its income for its 2021 taxation year beginning October 1, 2020. This does not cancel the payable, such that if the rent is ever paid, the shareholder will declare the rental income, but there will be no deduction for the corporation.

(iii) An election can be filed before the date on which the corporation must file its tax return for 2021. In this case, that date is March 31, 2022. If such an election is filed, Mr. Schneider will be deemed to have income of $10,000 and to have loaned that amount back to the corporation on October 1, 2020. When the loan is repaid to Mr. Schneider, there are no tax consequences since the amount of the loan has already been taxed. The election can be filed late. However, $2,500 (effectively, a late-filing penalty) will be added back to the income of the corporation for its 2021 fiscal year. Mr. Schneider's tax position is not affected by this late-filed election.   ITA: 78(1)(b)   ITA: 78(3)

Exercise 2

(A) *Employee*

Principal Amount

— Note that the shareholder loan rule applies in this case because he is a shareholder.   ITA: 15(2)

(a) House Loan

The Act would exempt the principal amount of this loan from income since Mr. Nesbitt received the loan in his capacity as an employee (i.e., by virtue of his employment), the purpose of the loan was to purchase a house and *bona fide* arrangements were made for repayment of the loan within a reasonable time;   ITA: 15(2.4)(b)

— however, an interest benefit on a "home purchase loan" would be included in income as shown in the calculation below.   ITA: 80.4

(b) Furniture Loan

There is no exemption from income for this loan because it was not repaid within one year of the 2018 taxation year of the corporation;   ITA: 15(2.3), 15(2.4), 15(2.6)

— since the loan is included in income in 2018, there is an exception for the purposes of the imputed interest benefit and, hence, there is no interest benefit.   ITA: 15(2), 80.4(3)(b)

(c) Share Purchase Loan

This loan is exempt from income because Mr. Nesbitt received the loan in his capacity as an employee and *bona fide* arrangements were made to repay the loan within a reasonable time;   ITA: 15(2.4)(c)

— no exception to the imputed interest rules, there is an interest benefit as shown in the calculation below.   ITA: 80.4

Interest Benefit

(a) interest on "home purchase loan" made to an officer or employee computed, at lesser of: (i) the prescribed rate in effect during the period in the year that the loan was outstanding, and (ii) the prescribed rate in effect at the time the loan was made. This "lesser of" choice can be made on a quarter-by-quarter comparison of tax rates. In this case, the 3% prescribed rate in June 2018, when the loan was received, is less than the rate for the other two quarters of 2018 in which the loan was outstanding. Therefore, the benefit would be based on the following calculation: ITA: 80.4(1)(*a*), 80.4(4)

June–Dec. 2018: 3% of $75,000 × $^{214}/_{365}$ $1,319

(b) interest on share purchase loan computed at prescribed rates in effect during the period in the year that the loan was outstanding ITA: 80.4(1)(*a*)

June 2018: 3% of $10,000 × 30/365 = $ 25

July–Sept. 2018: 4% of $10,000 × 92/365 = 101

Oct.–Dec. 2018: 4% of $10,000 × 92/365 = 101   227

Subtotal $1,546

(c) Less: interest paid on above loans (2% of $75,000 × 214/365) 879

Benefit calculated under ssec. 80.4(1) and included in employment income . . . $ 667 ITA: 61(1)(*a*), 6(9)

Less: deduction for imputed interest on loan to buy shares . . . . 227 ITA: 20(1)(*c*), 80.5

Net benefit under Division B . . . . $ 440

(B) *Shareholder*

If Mr. Nesbitt received the loans by virtue of being a shareholder, then all the loans would be included in income in the year that the loans were received, unless the loans were repaid by the end of the fiscal year in which the loans were made. Where a loan is outstanding in the year in which the loan was made, there would be an imputed interest inclusion. However, the inclusion would be reversed on the filing of the amended return for the loan inclusion. ITA: 80.4(2)
ITA: 15(2)

For imputed interest, the main difference is that the benefit on the loan to purchase the house would be based only on the prescribed rate in effect during the period in the year that the loan was outstanding and reduced by the amount of interest paid on the loan by the shareholder in the period not later than 30 days after the corporation's year end. This is because the calculation of the imputed interest benefit by virtue of shareholdings does not take into account the special rules for a "home purchase loan". ITA: 80.4(2), 80.4(7), 248(1)
ITA: 110(1)(*j*)

Exercise 3

(A) The CRA indicates that it examines the balance in the account at the end of each year of the lender considering a net increase as a loan to be included in the income of the borrower and a net decrease as a repayment to be deducted from the income of the borrower. This approach would result in the following:

IT-119R4, par. 34-35

Lender's year end	Change from previous year	Income [ssec. 15(2.6)] or repayment [par. 20(1)(j)]
Year 2	$45,000	income
Year 3	(32,000)	repayment
Year 4	(2,000)	repayment
Year 5	12,000	income
Year 6	(14,000)	repayment

(B) If there is no series of loans and repayments, then repayments are considered to apply first to the oldest loan outstanding unless the facts clearly indicate otherwise. Applying this approach would result in the following:

IT-119R4, par. 27

Lender's year end	Net inclusion (or deduction)	Explanation
Year 2	$25,000	— only the $20,000 borrowed in year 2 is repaid within one year of year 2; the $25,000 loan was not fully repaid within one year, so it must be taken into income in year 2
Year 3	(12,000)	— repayment of $12,000 of the $25,000 year 2 loan previously included
Year 4	(12,000)	— repayment of part of balance of year 2 loan
	Nil	— Nov. 30/year 4 loan repaid within one year of year 4
Year 5	(1,000)	— repayment of remainder of April 30/year 2 loan
	23,000	— full amount of Nov. 30/year 5 loan, since not fully repaid within one year of year 5
Year 6	(14,000)	— repayment of $14,000 of year 5 loan

Note that these methods of calculation are based on administrative practice and are not stipulated by the Act. Note that based on these methods, while total inclusions net of deductions over the period amount to $9,000 under each alternative, the time pattern of net inclusion is more favourable in this case if there is no series of loans and repayments considered.

If the loans are all part of a single running loan account, they are likely a series of loans and repayments. However, if the loans are for separate purposes, with differing repayment or other terms, and the repayments relate to specific loans, the facts might suggest there was no series of loans and repayments.

Exercise 4

Since he is a shareholder of the corporation, the shareholder loan rule applies and the loan that was received by the taxpayer should be included in income. However, the Act provides an exclusion for the $35,000 principal amount of the loan because:

ITA: 15(2)
ITA: 15(2.4)(d)

— the taxpayer is an employee of the lender;

— the loan is to enable him to acquire a motor vehicle to be used by him in the performance of his employment duties;

— the taxpayer received the loan because of his employment, not because of his shareholdings, since other employees were eligible for a loan; and

— *bona fide* arrangements were made, at the time the loan was made, for repayment within a reasonable time.

CHAPTER 13

Since the loan is a low-interest loan, the imputed interest benefit rule applies to impute an interest benefit calculated as follows:

ITA: 80.4(1)

April 1 to June 30: $^{91}/_{365} \times 1\%$ of $35,000 =		$ 87
July 1 to Sept. 30: $^{92}/_{365} \times 2\%$ of $35,000 =		176
Oct. 1 to Dec. 31: $^{92}/_{365} \times 3\%$ of $35,000 =		265
Total		$ 528
Less: interest *paid* (not payable) ($^{214}/_{365} \times 1\%$ of $35,000)		205
Net interest benefit		$ 323

The Act deems the imputed interest benefit of $323 to have been paid in the year. As a result, a part of the interest will qualify as a deduction of interest *paid* limited as follows:

ITA: 80.5
ITA: 8(1)(*j*), 67.2

Lesser of:

(a) interest deemed paid	$323	
interest *paid* ($^{214}/_{365} \times 1\%$ of $35,000)	205	$ 528
(b) $\dfrac{\$300}{30} \times 214$ days of interest paid		$2,140
Lesser amount $\times$ 60% business usage (60% of $528)		$ 317

Exercise 5

Shareholder-Manager Pays Tax on Benefit

Benefit from use of car:		
standby charge[1] (10,000 km/20,004 km $\times$ $^2/_3 \times$ $6,000)	2,000	
value of operating costs of personal use[2]	1,000	ITA: 6(1)(*e*)
Incremental taxable income	$ 3,000	
Tax @ 50% on $3,000 of incremental taxable income	$ 1,500	

Shareholder-Manager Leases Car Personally

Incremental taxable income ($2,880 + $6,000)	$ 8,880
Less: deduction for business use of car [66⅔% of ($6,000 + $2,880)]	(5,920)
Add: HST rebate (13/113 $\times$ $5,920)[3]	681
Incremental taxable income	$ 3,641
Tax @ 50% on $3,641 of incremental taxable income	$ 1,821
Tax net of HST rebate ($1,821 – $681)	$ 1,140

Notice that the second alternative is the better by $360.

— NOTES TO SOLUTION

[1] This calculation assumes that business usage of 66⅔% meets the test that the primary distance travelled was for business. Generally, the term "primarily" has been interpreted by the CRA to mean more than 50%.

ITA: 6(2)

[2] The election includes a benefit of 50% of the standby charge of $2,000 (i.e., $1,000) which is less than 25¢ $\times$ 10,000 km or $2,500.

ITA: 6(1)(*k*)

[3] In reality, the HST rebate would have to be taken into income in the following year. Note that the present value considerations on the rebate have been ignored. Also, ignored is the effect of the input tax credit (ITC) received by the corporation if it incurs the annual lease and operating costs. If the corporation pays additional salary equal to its net costs for these items after ITC and, hence, if the shareholder manager must pay the HST from other sources, it can be shown that the shareholder-manager's after-tax retention is reduced by the after-tax equivalent of the HST costs. This would reduce the advantage of the second alternative.

Exercise 6

Corporation	*Remuneration alternatives*		
	Salary	*Dividends*	*Combination*
Income before salary and taxes	$ 20,000	$20,000	$ 20,000
Salary	(20,000)	—	(10,000)
Taxable income	Nil	$20,000	$ 10,000
Tax @ 14% (i.e., 38% – 10% – 18% + 4%)	—	(2,800)	(1,400)
Available for dividends	Nil	$17,200	$ 8,600
Shareholder			
Employment income (ssec. 8(1) deductions not considered)	$ 20,000	—	$ 10,000
Grossed-up dividends (1.16 × dividend)	—	$19,952	9,976
Taxable income	$ 20,000	$19,952	$ 19,976
Federal tax before dividend tax credit . . .	$ 3,000	$ 2,993	$ 2,996
Dividend tax credit (8/11 of gross-up)	—	(2,001)	(1,001)
Personal tax credits	(2,000)	(2,000)	(2,000)
Basic federal tax*	$ 1,000	$ 1	$ Nil
Provincial tax	2,000	1,995	1,998
Provincial dividend tax credit (3/11 of gross-up)	—	(751)	(375)
Provincial personal tax credits	(1,290)	(1,290)	(1,290)
Total tax*	$ 1,710	Nil	$ 333
Summary			
Income before salary and taxes	$ 20,000	$20,000	$ 20,000
Less: tax paid by corporation	Nil	(2,800)	(1,400)
tax paid by shareholder	(1,710)	(1)	(333)
Net cash to shareholder	$ 18,290	$17,199	$ 18,267
Excess federal dividend and personal tax credits			
($2,993 – $2,001 – $2,000)		$ 1,008	
($2,996 – $1,001 – $2,000)			$ 5
Excess federal dividend and personal tax credits			
($1,995 – $751 – $1,290)		$ 46	

* Cannot be negative.

There is almost perfect integration at a corporate tax rate of 14% (perfect integration results at a corporate rate of 13.8%) as long as all of the dividend tax credit is used. The full dividend tax credit is not used in either Alternative B or C. As a result, the best alternative is A. Alternative C, the combination option, ensures use of all but $5 of the dividend tax credit and, therefore, is better than Alternative B. The unused dividend tax credit of $5 combined with a small tax cost to paying dividends at a rate of 14% results in Alternative C being worse than Alternative A.

Exercise 7

(A)

Taxation of Income from Sole Proprietorship

Income from business and taxable income		$80,000
Federal tax		
Tax on first $46,605	$ 6,991	
Tax on next $33,395 @ 20.5%	6,846	$13,837
Personal tax credits		(2,100)
Basic federal tax		$11,737
Provincial tax (12% of ($80,000 – $46,605) + $4,661)		8,668
Provincial personal tax credits		(1,400)
Total tax paid		$19,005

(B)

Taxation of Income through a Corporation

	All salary	All dividends	Combination
Corporation			
Income before salary and taxes	$ 80,000	$ 80,000	$ 80,000
Salary	(25,000)	—	(2,085)[3]
Taxable income	$ 55,000	$ 80,000	$ 77,915
Tax @ 14% (i.e., 38% – 10% – 18% + 4%)	(7,700)	(11,200)	(10,908)
Available for dividend	$ 47,300	$ 68,800	$ 67,007
Shareholder			
Salary[1] .... (A)	$ 25,000	—	$ 2,085
Dividend .... (B)	—	$ 25,000	22,915
Gross-up @ 16% of dividend	—	4,000	3,666
Income	$ 25,000	$ 29,000	$ 28,666
Federal tax	$ 3,750	$ 4,350	$ 4,300
Dividend tax credit ($^8/_{11}$ × gross-up) ...	—	(2,909)	(2,666)
Personal tax credits	(2,100)	(2,100)	(2,100)
Basic federal tax	$ 1,650	(659)	(466)
Provincial tax	2,500	2,900	2,867
Provincial dividend tax credit ($^3/_{11}$ × gross-up)	Nil	(1,091)	(1,000)
Provincial personal tax credits	(1,400)	(1,400)	(1,400)
Total tax .... (C)	$ 2,750	$ (250)	Nil
Disposable income (A + B – C)	$ 22,250	$ 25,250	$ 25,000
Total Taxes paid			
Through corporation:			
Corporation	$ 7,700	$ 11,200	$ 10,908
Shareholder	2,750	(250)	Nil
Total	$ 10,450	$ 10,950	$ 10,908
Paid directly by proprietor	$ 19,005	$ 19,005	$ 19,005
Tax Saving (maximum[2])	$ 8,555	$ 8,055	$ 8,097

At these rates, all salary results in the biggest overall tax savings because of the deduction in the corporation for the salary paid (assuming that dividends will be distributed when the owner-manager's income will be such that there will be no tax on the dividends). However, the $25,000 salary will not provide the shareholder with sufficient funds to cover his living expenses. He will be $2,750 short because of the personal tax he will pay on the salary. Both dividend options provide him with the $25,000 of funds he needs for his living expenses because personal tax will not apply to dividends received because of the dividend tax credit. The tax cost of the combination option is the lower of the two options and results in a $458 cost relative to the $25,000 salary option.

—NOTES TO SOLUTION

[1] Assumes no deductions available to employee.

[2] Assumes amount retained in the corporation can be distributed in the future as taxable dividends in amounts that will not attract tax after personal tax credits.

[3] Negative allowed only due to assumption in the required.

Exercise 8

In each of the cases, the test to be applied to the facts is whether all or substantially all (i.e., at least 90%) of the fair market value of the assets are:

(a) used principally in an active business carried on primarily in Canada by the corporation (or a related corporation);

(b) shares or debt of a connected SBC; or

(c) a combination of (a) and (b).

(A) This situation depends on whether the marketable securities are used in the active business or are passive investments not necessary to the active business. If the marketable securities are used in the active business, then the 90% test is met. This would be the case, for example, if the marketable securities represented a short-term investment of cash surpluses, awaiting the purchase of inventory for the next season.

(B) In this situation, the 90% test is met with a combination of active business assets and shares in a connected SBC.

(C) In this case, the marketable securities cannot be considered to be used in an active business, because the corporation has no other active business assets to carry on such a business. Since the shares of a connected SBC represent only 80% of the total fair market value of the corporation's assets, the 90% test is not met.

(D) Again, this case fits the definition of an SBC if the marketable securities are considered to be used in an active business. If the facts of this case so indicate, then the 90% test is met by a combination of active business assets (including the marketable securities) and the shares of a connected SBC.

Exercise 9

(A) Unused lifetime deduction in 2018:

Lifetime cumulative deduction limit		$ 424,126
Less: prior years' deductions:		
Capital gains deduction claimed in 2016		75,000
Capital gains deduction available for 2018		$ 349,126

(B) Annual gains limit for 2018:

Net taxable capital gains for 2018[1]		$ 225,000
Minus:		
Net capital losses deducted in 2018	Nil	
ABILs realized in 2018[1]	5,000	5,000
Annual gains limit for 2018		$ 220,000

(C) Cumulative gains limit for 2018:

Cumulative net taxable capital gains ($75,000 + $225,000)			$ 300,000
Minus:			
Cumulative net capital losses deducted		Nil	
Cumulative ABILs realized		$ 5,000	
Cumulative capital gains deductions		75,000	
Cumulative net investment loss:			
Investment expenses —			
Cumulative carrying charges	$ 1,075		
Cumulative net rental losses			
($1,100 + $220)	1,320		
	$ 2,395		
Investment income —			
Cumulative interest income			
($600 + $1,200)	(1,800)		
Cumulative grossed-up dividends	(140)	455	80,455
Cumulative gains limit for 2018			$ 219,545

(D) Least of (A), (B), (C) .... $ 219,545

—*NOTE TO SOLUTION*

[1] Allowable business investment loss (ABIL):

BIL before ssec. 39(9) reduction		$ 160,000
Disallowed portion — Lesser of:		
(a) BIL	$ 160,000	

(b) Adjustment factor × cumulative
CG deductions of previous
years (2 × $75,000) $150,000
Minus: Cumulative disallowed
BIL of prior years . . . .   Nil $ 150,000

Lesser of (a) and (b)		(150,000)
BIL after adjustment		$ 10,000
ABIL (½ × $10,000)		$ 5,000
Allowable capital loss (ACL):		
Disallowed portion of BIL		$ 150,000
ACL (½ × $150,000)		$ 75,000
Net TCG for 2018:		
TCG		$ 300,000
Less: ACL		75,000
Net TCG		$ 225,000

Exercise 10

The disposition of the real estate is a transfer for tax purposes in 2018. The facts do not provide enough details on the cost base to determine the tax effect of the disposition.

In this case it can likely be established that one of the main purposes of the transfer of the building may reasonably be considered to be to reduce the income of Mr. Albert and to benefit Mrs. Albert who is a designated person and a specified shareholder. Had Mr. Albert kept the building himself he would have earned $50,000 of rental income on which he would have been taxable. Instead, he will receive $10,000 of interest and $20,000 of dividends. Mrs. Albert benefited from the rental income since this will accrue to the common shares of the corporation. Therefore, it may be argued that the purpose test will have been met.

Furthermore, the corporation will no longer be a "small business corporation", since the fair market value of the assets of the corporation will be as follows: ITA: 248(1)

Retail assets, 75%	$6,000,000
Building, 25%	2,000,000
Total	$8,000,000

Even if 20% of the building (FMV $400,000) is classified as an active business asset, the corporation will still not be a small business corporation since all or substantially all of the fair market value of the assets are not used principally in an active business carried on primarily in Canada.

Mr. Albert's attributed amount	
FMV of the building transferred	$2,000,000
Less: cash received	(600,000)
Outstanding amount	$1,400,000
Interest imputed at 4%	$56,000
Less: interest received (5% of $200,000)	(10,000)
1.16 × dividends received	(23,200)
Attributed amount	$22,800
Mr. Albert would also have	
Interest income	10,000
Taxable dividends ($2,000 × 1.16)	23,200
Total income	$56,000

Note that the December 13, 2017 draft legislation related to income sprinkling should be considered in regard to the interest income and taxable dividends received by Mr. Albert. The income and dividends are derived from a related business because a related person, Mrs. Albert, owns 10% of the fair market value of the shares of the corporation through her common share ownership and could be subject to TOSI if the amounts do not meet the exceptions available. It appears that Mr. Albert is not actively engaged in the corporation's business and the income would not be considered to be from an "excluded business". Further, his shares do not provide 10% of the votes and value of the corporation and thus are not "excluded shares". However, if the interest and dividends represent a "reasonable return" in regard to the property Mr. Albert contributed to the corporation, i.e., the building, the income and dividends would be excluded amounts and as such would not be subject to TOSI.

Exercise 11

The following comments are based on the application of the logic presented in Exhibit 13-11 to the facts of this situation.

(1) Does any other provision of the Act or other rule of law apply to stop the taxpayer from achieving the intended advantage? No, the amount paid is considered to be reasonable and, hence, is not prohibited. Remuneration is considered to be an expense incurred to produce income from business and, thus, is not prohibited.

ITA: 67

ITA: 18(1)(*a*)

(2) Does the transaction result, directly or indirectly, in a tax benefit, i.e., a reduction, avoidance or deferral of tax or an increase in a refund? On the one hand, corporate tax is reduced, but on the other hand the individual receives income subject to tax at a higher rate. However, the reduction of income to the corporation reduces the potential for double taxation on income taxed at more than a 27.5% rate in the corporation which may be considered to be a tax benefit. If it is concluded that there is no tax benefit, GAAR should not apply.

ITA: 245(1)

(3) Is the transaction part of a series of transactions, which would result, directly or indirectly, in a tax benefit? If the answer to question 2 is yes, then proceed directly to question 4.

(4) Can the transaction reasonably be considered to have been undertaken or arranged primarily for *bona fide* purposes other than to obtain the tax benefit? No, a tax reduction for the corporation was probably the primary purpose. On the other hand, it might be argued that, since the amount paid was reasonable, it is necessary remuneration.

(5) Can it reasonably be considered that the transaction would result directly or indirectly in a misuse of the provisions of the Act or an abuse having regard to the provisions of the Act read as a whole? No, "the Act recognizes the deductibility of reasonable business expenses".

IC 88-2, par. 18

Exercise 12

The general anti-avoidance rule allows for transactions or a series of transactions to be disregarded if they are without a *bona fide* purpose. If your client's spouse and children are not providing any services to her business, it is obvious that the transactions were arranged primarily to obtain a tax benefit with no *bona fide* purpose, and they will be disregarded by the CRA. Any tax benefit derived from the transactions will be eliminated. If there is some service being provided to justify a salary, the amount of salary must be reasonable in the circumstance or the deduction by your client can be disallowed without the need to apply the GAAR. In fact, if the unreasonable salaries are still taxed in the hands of the spouse and children, after the expense is disallowed, the result is worse than the application of the GAAR that disregards the payment.

Exercise 13

This question deals with subsection 15(2) and sections 80.4 and 80.5 of the Act. *The effects of leap year are ignored.*

Tax consequences to Grace Ravens for 2018:

(i) House loan

Paragraph 15(2.4)(*b*) would exempt the principal amount of this loan from income since Grace Ravens is also an employee, the purpose of the loan was to purchase a house for her occupation, she received the loan in her capacity as an employee (under corporate policy) and bona fide arrangements were made for repayment of the loan within a reasonable time. Section 80.4 would include an interest benefit on an employee loan for 2018 as shown in the calculation below. Since Grace Ravens received the loan by virtue of being an employee, the calculation of the imputed interest benefit would be made under ssec. 80.4(1) at the prescribed rate of interest in effect throughout the year. Subsection 80.4(4), the prescribed rate protection rule, also applies to benefits calculated under ssec. 80.4(1). However, the 5% rate to be applied would result in a larger benefit.

January 1 to June 30	$90,000 × 4% × 181/365 =	$1,785
July 1 to December 31	$90,000 × 5% × 184/365 =	2,268
Gross interest benefit on house loan		$4,053
Less: interest paid on house loan ($90,000 × 2%)		(1,800)
Benefit calculated under ssec. 80.4(1) and included in income		$2,253

(ii) Furniture loan

There is no exemption from income for this loan in ssecs. 15(2.2) to (2.5), and the loan is not exempt by ssec. 15(2.6), because it was not repaid within one year of the 2017 taxation year of the corporation. For 2017, a net amount of $9,000 [$10,000 — included under ssec. 15(2) less $1,000 repaid and deducted under par. 20(1)(*j*)] is included in her income. For 2018, she can deduct the $1,000 repaid in the year under ssec. 20(1)(*j*).

(iii) Share purchase loan

This loan is exempt from income by virtue of par. 15(2.4)(*c*) because the proceeds were used to acquire previously unissued shares, she received the loan in her capacity as an employee and *bona fide* arrangements were made to repay the loan within a reasonable amount of time. There is an interest benefit for 2018 as shown in the calculation below.

January 1 to June 30	$20,000 × 4% × 181/365 =	$ 397
July 1 to December 31	$20,000 × 5% × 184/365 =	504
Interest benefit on share purchase loan		$ 901

Section 80.5 would deem this imputed interest benefit to also be interest paid.

Paragraph 20(1)(*c*) would allow a deduction for the interest paid since the loan was used to buy shares.

Summary

Total interest benefit [$2,253 + $901]	$3,154
Repayment of principal on furniture loan	(1,000)
Deductible interest on share purchase loan	(901)
Net income inclusion for 2018	$1,253

Exercise 14

(a) As a CCPC, Shaker Ltd. can grant a stock option to an arm's length employee and the employee will qualify under ssec. 7(1.1) for a deferral of the stock option benefit until the taxation year in which the shares are disposed (8,000 × ($20 – $12)) = $64,000). Therefore, there will not be an immediate employment income inclusion under ssec. 7(1) when one-half of the option is exercised and 4,000 shares are acquired. Provided Ms. Mover does not dispose of the shares (other than as a consequence of her death) for two years, there will be an offsetting deduction equal to ½ of the employment benefit, available under par. 110(1)(*d.1*).

The ACB of Ms. Mover's shares would be $20 per share. Any proceeds of disposition in excess of $20 per share would represent a capital gain, possibly eligible for the capital gains deduction if Shaker Ltd. is a qualified small business corporation at the time of the sale.

If Ms. Mover does not hold the share for two years, she is not entitled to a deduction for ½ of the stock option benefit under par. 110(1)(*d.1*). She also would not be entitled to the deduction under par. 110(1)(*d*) as the option exercise price was less than the FMV of the shares at the time the option was granted.

When Ms. Mover exercises the remainder of the option and acquires another 4,000 shares, the tax consequences will be the same, (subject to the FMV of the shares at the date of exercise).

There are no tax implications if Ms. Mover does not exercise the option for the remaining 4,000 shares.

(b) Subsection 15(2) will include the full amount of the loan in the shareholder's income. However, a loan to an employee to purchase previously unissued, fully paid shares from the corporation is exempt (par. 15(2.4)(*c*)) provided the loan was made to her in her capacity as an employee (e.g., "under an employee loan policy") and *bona fide* arrangements were made for repayment within a reasonable time. Six years would likely be reasonable in these circumstances.

Subsection 80.4(1) deems the employee to receive a benefit equal to the amount of the loan multiplied by the prescribed rate of interest, which varies quarterly, minus any interest paid (which is NIL in this case).

Section 80.5 deems the interest benefit to be interest paid in the year. Since the loan was incurred to buy shares of Shaker Ltd., which have the potential of earning dividend income, Ms. Mover will have an interest expense deduction equal to the taxable benefit under ssec. 80.4(1).

The loan to purchase a house will also qualify for exemption under par. 15(2.4)(*b*).

The loan qualifies as a "home purchase loan".

Subsection 80.4(4) provides that, in calculating the interest benefit on a home purchase loan, the rate used to calculate the benefit shall not exceed the prescribed rate at the time the loan was made (and a new loan is deemed to be made every five years).

Provided the 2% interest on the loan is paid by Ms. Mover within 30 days of the end of each year, the taxable benefit calculated under subsection 80.4(1) for the first year would be:
$$(\$350,000 \times 0.03) - (\$350,000 \times 0.02) = \qquad \$3,500$$

(c) Ssec. 6(2) standby charge:

$$\frac{6,000}{20,004} \times (\$900 - \$100) \times 12 \times \tfrac{2}{3} = \qquad \$1,920$$

Par. 6(1)(*k*) operating costs:

lesser of: (i) $0.25 × 6,000 km = $1,500

       (ii) election*:
          ½ × $1,920   = $960   960

Total employment inclusion $2,880

* this election requires that the employer be notified in writing before the end of the taxation year that the operating benefit is to be calculated in accordance with spar. 6(1)(*k*)(iv).

(d) As V.P. Operation, Ms. Mover would likely be negotiating contracts and, thus, qualify under spar. 6(1)(*b*)(v). As such, a reasonable travelling allowance would not be included in income. If the allowance is not reasonable, Ms. Mover would include the allowance in income and would deduct her travel expenses under par. 8(1)(*h*). She could also deduct these under 8(1)(*f*), limited to commission income. This would be advantageous if the allowance is not enough to cover the actual expenses. The reimbursement of business expenses (e.g., air fares and hotels) would not be taxable to Ms. Mover.

Exercise 15

(A) Salary to Mr. Newlight ..... Section 67 should not apply, as Mr. Newlight is the president and sole shareholder. As well, the amount of the salary will be of little concern to the CRA as it places Mr. Newlight in a high personal tax bracket.

(B) Salary to Mrs. Care .... Section 67 may apply given nature and extent of duties performed. Decision of Gabco ((Ex. Ct.) 68 DTC 5210).

(C) $2,000 royalty payable to Mr. Newlight .... [Subsection 78(1)] If not paid in 2019, added to the corporation's income in 2019. Recommend to pay if possible; otherwise, file joint agreement within six months of 2020 year end, i.e., June 30, 2021; deemed received and loaned back in 2020.

(D) $3,000 royalty payable to Mr. Newlight . . . . Would be added to the corporation's 2017 income unless joint agreement filed by June 30, 2018 (six months after year end of third succeeding year). If no agreement filed, can late file (and should recommend to file) joint agreement. Result of late filing is that 25% of $3,000 would be added back to corporation's income in 2017 but 100% is treated as having been paid to Mr. Newlight and loaned back to corporation on January 1, 2017.

(E) $200,000 loan . . . . Principal amount exempt [par. 15(2.4)(b)] since it is a housing loan for his habitation and bona fide repayment terms exist [par. 15(2.4)(f)]; also, the loan was made in his capacity as an employee [par. 15(2.4)(e)]. Imputed interest for 2018 is calculated as follows:

Subsection 80.4(1) applies since the loan was made by virtue of his office.

Lesser of (computed on a quarter-by-quarter basis):

(a) interest at prescribed rate in effect during period in 2018 that loan was outstanding; and

(b) interest at prescribed rate in effect at time loan made on July 1, 2018 [ssec. 80.4(4)].

Since the prescribed rate on July 1, 2018 (the date the loan was granted) is less than or equal to the prescribed rates in each of the quarters during the year that the loan was outstanding, the lesser amount will be based on the 4% rate in effect on July 1, 2017 and the imputed income is computed as follows:

$$\frac{184}{365} \times 0.04 \times \$200,000 = \underline{\underline{\$4,033}}$$

Imputed interest $4,033

Less: interest paid for the year

$$\frac{184^*}{365} \times 0.03 \times \$200,000 =$$
$3,025

Net benefit $1,008

---

*184 days = interest payments made at month-end July through December 2018. The effects of leap year are ignored.

Note: Interest on the $200,000 loan is not deductible since the purpose is not to produce income [par. 20(1)(c)].

(F) $15,000 loan . . . . Principal amount is included in income in 2018 [ssec. 15(2)]; ssec 15(2.6) will not apply since the repayment is part of series of loans and repayments.

No imputed interest, since principal amount included in income [ssec. 80.4(3)]; par. 20(1)(j) will not apply since the repayment is part of series of loans.

(G) $500 loan . . . . Not included in either income of Mr. Newlight or Mrs. Care; ssec. 15(2) will not apply as not a loan to shareholder or person connected to shareholder. Section 80.4 and subsection 6(9) will levy an imputed interest benefit as follows:

$$\frac{92}{365} \times 0.05 \times \$500 = \underline{\underline{\$6}}$$

Exercise 16

Capital Gains Deduction

(a) Unused lifetime deduction:

Lifetime cumulative deduction limit	$424,126
Less: prior year's deductions ($33,000 × ½)	(16,500)
	$407,626

(b) Annual gains limit:

Net taxable capital gains this year:

Proceeds	$523,000	
ACB (par. 69(1)(c))	(138,000)	
	$385,000 × ½	$192,500
Less: net capital loss claimed		0
		$192,500

(c) Cumulative gains limit:

Cumulative net taxable capital gains

($33,000 × ½ + $192,500)		$209,000
Minus:		
Cumulative net capital losses claimed		(0)
Cumulative ABILs claimed		(0)
Cumulative capital gains deduction claimed		(16,500)
CNIL:		
investment expense ($9,000 + $13,000)	$(22,000)	
dividends (1.16 × ($6,000 + $5,000))	12,760	
rent ($2,000 + $2,500)	4,500	(4,740)
		$187,760

The maximum capital gains deduction available is the lesser of (a), (b), and (c), above, $187,760.

Exercise 17

Considerations include the following:

- Mr. Ink's cash requirements;
- Mr. Ink's other sources of income;
- Mr. Ink's personal effective tax rate;
- The corporation's effective tax rate on income:

  - Does it qualify for the small business deduction ("SBD")?

  - Tax deferral benefit is significant for income eligible for the SBD. Funds should be retained in the corporation.

  - Tax deferral benefit also exists for income above the SBD limit depending on Mr. Ink's personal tax bracket.

- If he doesn't require funds, it would be better to keep the funds in the corporation to take advantage of the tax deferral benefit (consider the impact on the SBC status of the corporation).

- If he needs funds, consider the tax cost/savings of dividends taking into account the combined corporate tax rate and Mr. Ink's personal tax rate for income eligible for the small business deduction and income above the small business deduction limit.

  - If a bonus is determined to be tax effective, the amount must be reasonable and a legal obligation to pay the bonus must exist if paid after year end.

- Does the corporation qualify for investment tax credits? If it does, this is another incentive to pay a bonus to reduce the corporations' income to $500,000.

- Is the corporation eligible for quarterly tax instalments? If income is above the small business deduction limit, this would require the corporation to make monthly tax instalment payments.

- Mr. Ink may want a salary to be eligible for CPP and RRSP contributions.

- Does Mr. Ink have a CNIL balance for which he needs to receive a dividend in order to enable him to claim the capital gains deduction in the current year? and

- RDTOH — to recover the RDTOH, the payment of a taxable dividend is required. If the corporation has a GRIP balance, there would be minimal tax cost to paying eligible dividends after taking into account the dividend refund to the corporation. [Note that starting for tax years that begin after 2018, eligible dividends will only result in a refund of Part IV tax in eligible RDTOH. As a result, the advantage of paying eligible dividends to obtain a refund of refundable Part IV tax will no longer exist for dividends paid after December 31, 2018.]

Exercise 18

A Co. is a small business corporation. 100% of the FMV of its assets are used in an active business carried on by it in Canada or invested in a connected small business corporation, Y Ltd.

B Co. is not a small business corporation. Only 80% of the FMV of its assets are used in an active business. Therefore, it does not meet the "all" or "substantially all" test, interpreted to be 90% by the CRA.

C Co. is not a small business corporation. Only 50% of the FMV of its assets are qualifying assets, being shares of a connected small business corporation.

D Co. is a small business corporation. 100% of its assets are used in an active business carried on in Canada by a corporation *related* to it (Spouse Co.).

Exercise 19

To meet the "asset test", the corporation must:

at all times in the previous 24 months, where the corporation existed, be a Canadian-controlled private corporation with more than 50% of the value of its assets being:

(i) assets used in an active business carried on primarily in Canada,

(ii) shares of connected "small business corporations", or

(iii) a combination of (i) and (ii).

Alternatively, the "asset test" will be met if:

at all times in the previous 24 months, where the corporation existed, the CCPC had more than 90% of the value of its assets being:

(i) assets used in an active business carried on primarily in Canada,

(ii) assets used in an active business carried on primarily in Canada, or

(iii) a combination of (i) and (ii).

(a) In this case, more than 50% of the FMV of the assets of Holdco are invested in assets used in an active business. Therefore, Holdco will meet the asset test.

(b) In this case, Holdco has more than 50% of the FMV of its assets invested in a combination of (i) assets used in an active business carried on in Canada and (ii) shares of a connected corporation with more than 90% of the FMV of its assets used in an active business carried on in Canada. Therefore, Holdco will meet the asset test.

(c) In this case, Holdco does not have more than 50% of the FMV of its assets invested in active business assets and shares of connected small business corporations. Holdco also does not have 90% (but does have greater than 50%) of its assets used in an active business, invested in shares of connected companies which meet the 50% test, or a combination thereof. Since Holdco cannot meet the 50% test on assets used in an active business and cannot meet the 90% test on a combination of business assets and investments in Subco, the connected company, Subco, must meet a 90% test based on its own assets so that it can be included in Holdco's 50% test. In this case, Subco does not meet this test. Therefore, Holdco will not meet the asset test.

(d) In this case, Holdco does not have any assets used in an active business. However, Subco meets the 90% test based on its own assets and, therefore, can qualify for inclusion in Holdco's 50% test. Thus, Holdco has more than 50% of the FMV of its assets invested in shares of a connected corporation with more than 90% of the FMV of its assets used in an active business carried on in Canada. Therefore, Holdco will meet the asset test.

Chapter 14

Rights and Obligations Under the Income Tax Act

Learning Goals

Know

By the end of this chapter you will know:

- The basic rules related to tax compliance.
  - Filing deadlines
  - Payment deadlines
  - Instalment payments
  - Appeal deadlines
- The tax issues related to death of a taxpayer.

Understand and Explain

By the end of this chapter you will understand and be able to explain:

- The basic rules related to tax compliance.
- How a deceased taxpayer is taxed.

Apply

By the end of this chapter you will be able to apply your knowledge and understanding to:

- Calculate instalments payable.
- Calculate penalties.
- Calculate the taxable income and tax payable for a deceased taxpayer.

Review Questions
¶14,800 in the Study Guide

Multiple Choice Questions
¶14,825 in the Study Guide

Exercises
¶14,850 in the Study Guide

Assignment Problems
¶14,875 in the Study Guide

CHAPTER 14 — LEARNING CHART

Problem Descriptions

Textbook Example Problems

14-1	Reporting tax information
14-2	Installments — corporation
14-3	Penalties and interest
14-4	Net worth assessment
14-5	Obligation to withhold
14-6	Obligation to withhold

Multiple Choice Questions

1	Late filing penalty
2	Normal reassessment period — corporation
3	Notice of objection — individual
4	Final return due date
5	Installments — CCPC
6	Installments — individual

Exercises

1	Withholding tax requirements
2	Windfalls
3	Installments — individual
4	Installments — CCPC
5	Penalties — late filing
6	Notice of reassessment
7	Compare interest paid to and by CRA
8	Preparer penalties
9	Appeal procedure
10	Rents earned by non-resident
11	Interest on tax refunds
12	Death of a taxpayer
13	Death of a taxpayer
14	Instalments — corporation
15	Penalties
16	Filing due date; Bal due date; Instalments
17	Taxation of non-resident; Filing due dates
18	Taxation of non-resident; Filing due dates
19	Deceased taxpayer

Assignment Problems

1	Filing deadlines
2	Deadlines for Notice of Reassessment
3	Notice of Objection
4	Back dating
5	Personal instalments
6	Corporate instalments
7	Notice of Reassessment
8	Preparer penalties
9	Withholding tax on rent

Problem Descriptions

10	Withholding tax on compensation
11	GST/HST
12	Comprehensive
13	Death of a taxpayer

Study Notes

¶14,800 REVIEW QUESTIONS

(1) In each of the following situations indicate whether the answer is true or false and give a reference to the Act.

(a) The taxable income of Unco Inc., a corporation resident in Canada, was nil for the year. As a result, it did not have to file a corporate tax return.

(b) Mr. Austen sold his shares in a qualified small business corporation and realized a $200,000 capital gain. The full amount of the gain was eligible for the capital gains exemption leaving his taxable income at nil. He does have to file a tax return for the year.

(c) Instalments for individuals are due on the 30th of March, June, September, and December.

(2) Mr. Smith paid his first instalment on time but was unable to pay his second one on time. He paid both the second and the third instalments on September 15. Is there any way he can avoid the interest that was charged to him for the late payment on the second instalment?

(3) Bearings Inc. has been quite profitable, but this year the corporation realized a business loss that it is going to carry back to the third preceding year. They are also hoping to collect interest from the date they filed the return for that third preceding year. What do you think?

(4) Ms. Taylor received a Notice of Reassessment from the CRA to disallow certain expenses that she had claimed. She contacted her accountant who sent a letter to the CRA outlining the basis for the deduction. Both Ms. Taylor and her accountant feel that the deduction will be allowed. Should she also file a Notice of Objection?

(5) Murray Corp. has had a bad year. The corporation lost money for the first time in its history and some of its key employees have left. Because of all this confusion Murray Corp. was late in getting its financial records in shape and it did not file its corporate tax returns until seven months after the end of the year. Murray Corp. still needs the cash so it is waiting anxiously for the tax refund from the loss being carried back to the third preceding year. Do you think Murray Corp. will be disappointed?

(6) Describe the different tax returns that can be filed for a deceased individual.

¶14,825   MULTIPLE CHOICE QUESTIONS

Question 1

Jane filed her tax return for the 2017 taxation year on September 15, 2018. She enclosed with the return a cheque for $10,000, the balance of tax owing. Neither Jane nor her husband carried on business in 2017. Jane will be assessed a late filing penalty of:

(A) $500

(B) $900

(C) $950

(D) $1,000

Question 2

A Canadian-controlled private corporation received a notice of assessment for its taxation year ended December 31, 2017. The date of mailing on the notice of assessment was August 15, 2018. The normal reassessment period for the corporation's 2017 taxation year ends:

(A) December 31, 2020

(B) August 15, 2021

(C) December 31, 2021

(D) August 15, 2022

Question 3

Darol disagrees with the notice of assessment he received for his 2017 tax return. The date of mailing on the notice of assessment was October 16, 2018. The tax return was filed on June 15, 2018 as Darol carried on a business in 2017. The notice of objection must be filed by:

(A) December 31, 2018

(B) January 14, 2019

(C) April 30, 2019

(D) June 15, 2019

Question 4

Bill was a lawyer with a very successful law practice. He died March 31, 2018. Which *one* of the following is the due date for his 2017 tax return?

(A) April 30, 2018

(B) June 15, 2018

(C) June 30, 2018

(D) September 30, 2018

Question 5

The controller of X Ltd., a Canadian-controlled private corporation, estimates that the company's taxes payable for its year ended December 31, 2018, will be $200,000. Taxes payable for each of the previous three years was as follows:

2015 — $212,000

2016 — $180,000

2017 — $140,000 (taxable income was $600,000)

What is the minimum monthly instalment that X Ltd., which is not an eligible small CCPC, must pay in the 2018 taxation year and the due date for the final balance of tax?

(A) The minimum monthly instalment is $11,667 and the due date for the final balance of tax is February 28, 2019.

(B) The minimum monthly instalment is $16,667 and the due date for the final balance of tax is February 28, 2019.

(C) The minimum monthly instalment is $16,667 and the due date for the final balance of tax is March 31, 2019.

(D) The minimum monthly instalment is $15,000 and the due date for the final balance of tax is February 28, 2019.

Question 6

Ms. Jones is a retired partner in a law firm and has taxable income of $70,000 each year from the partnership, her RRIF and her investments. She expects to pay $25,000 in tax in respect of 2018. She paid $16,400 in tax in respect of 2017 and $15,300 in respect of 2016. No tax is withheld on any of this income.

Which of the following is the minimum amount that Ms. Jones should pay for her 2018 quarterly income tax instalments, in order to avoid any unnecessary interest costs?

(A) 4 payments of $6,250

(B) 2 payments of $4,100 and 2 payments of $6,250

(C) 2 payments of $3,825 and 2 payments of $4,100

(D) 2 payments of $3,825 and 2 payments of $4,375

CHAPTER 14

¶14,850   EXERCISES

Exercise 1

ITA: 153(1)

List five payments from which the payer must withhold tax.

Exercise 2

Give two examples of a windfall that would reduce an estimate of income in a net worth assessment.

Exercise 3

ITA: 156(1)

In 2018, Mr. Owens projects his income to be $40,000 consisting of employment income of $25,000 and income from a small business, operated as a sideline, of $15,000. He expects that his tax liability will be $6,000 on the business income. During 2016 and 2017 he paid $3,000 and $4,000, respectively, in tax on the business income. Is he required to make instalments for 2018? If so, how much must he pay in instalments during 2018 so that he does not incur interest and when must each instalment be paid?

Exercise 4

ITA: 157(1)

A corporation that is not an eligible small CCPC uses the calendar year for its taxation year. In 2016, it paid tax of $158,400. By the end of March 2018, it had computed its tax for 2017 at $237,600. It estimates that it will have to pay $356,400 in tax for 2018. Is the corporation required to make instalments for 2018. If so, how much must it pay in instalments during 2018 and when must each be paid?

Exercise 5

ITA: 150(1), 162(1), 238(1)

X, Y, and Z filed their personal tax returns on May 5, 2018, for the 2017 year. X and Y are employees and Z is a proprietorship business owner. X determined that he owed $4,700 in tax on that date and enclosed a cheque for the $4,700; Y computed a refund of $2,000; and Z included a cheque for $3,500 relating to his balance of tax. What penalties and offences might each be liable for?

Exercise 6

ITA: 152(4), 163, 220(3.1); IC 00-1R

Mr. DeHaan has approached you, on July 12, 2018, for some advice considering a reassessment notice for the 2015 year that he has received. Mr. DeHaan has misplaced the reassessment notice but assures you that it was dated June 15, 2018. In your conversation with Mr. DeHaan, he reveals that he has had considerable difficulty with the CRA in the past, and has had to pay penalties under the Act. Mr. DeHaan is positive that he has complied with the law in this situation and wishes to dispute the assessment.

ITA: 162, 163

— *REQUIRED*

(A) Determine what additional information you require from Mr. DeHaan before discussing the relative merits of the particular disputed items.

(B) Assuming you accept the engagement, what steps would you immediately take?

(C) Explain to Mr. DeHaan the penalty under section 163.

Exercise 7

ITA: 161, 164

Compare the calculation and tax treatment of interest paid on amounts owing to the CRA and interest paid on refunds by the CRA.

Exercise 8

ITA: 163.2; IC 01-1

You have been engaged by Sid Fisher, a self-employed new client, to prepare an income statement and his tax return. Sid has instructed you to prepare these based on a figure for his total revenue and a list of his business expenditures, which he has provided to you. Based on your quick review of these data, you concluded that the expenditures were consistent with Sid's type of business and the amounts appeared to be reasonable. You prepared the income tax return, showing $100,000 of total revenue and $70,000 of expenses.

Subsequently, Sid's return was selected for audit. The CRA determined that many of the expenses deducted in the return could not be substantiated by adequate records. The CRA concluded that some of these expenditures may not have been made. The CRA, also, discovered that only 65% of the actual revenues of the business had been reported.

— REQUIRED

Determine whether you are at risk of being assessed under the civil penalties provisions of the Act.   ITA: 163.2

Exercise 9

ITA: 165(1), 169, 172, 180

Outline briefly the full appeal procedure indicating the time allowed between steps in the procedure.

Exercise 10

ITA: 216, 220(3)

A non-resident individual owns a rental property in Canada and has paid non-resident withholding tax on the gross rental revenue since 2013. He has heard that he may be able to recover some of this withholding tax if he files Canadian income tax returns for those years. What would you advise him?

Exercise 11

ITA: 161

Mr. Steve Parrott's only source of income is from his dry cleaning business. In March and June of 2017, he paid instalments of $2,000 each in respect of his 2017 taxes. By September, he realized things were not going well and he would likely have a loss for the year. He, therefore, paid no further instalments.

On June 15, 2018, Steve filed his 2017 tax return claiming a loss and a refund of his $4,000 instalments. He also filed a T1A carrying the loss back to 2016. He expects a tax refund of $5,000 from the carryback.

— REQUIRED

What interest can Steve expect to receive on his tax refunds?

Exercise 12

ITA: 70, 104, 111

Sam Elder died on September 10, 2018. Discuss how the following are to be reported:

(A) $200, accrued but unpaid, interest on his bank account.

(B) $100 dividend declared on September 15, 2018 and paid on September 30 (the previous dividend was paid on March 30).

(C) CPP of $600 for August 2018, received on September 3 and $200 for the period September 1 to 10, received on October 4.

(D) Charitable donations for the period January 1 to September 10, 2018.

(E) Capital losses incurred in 2017 of $4,000, of which no amount was deducted in 2017.

(F) Income of $900 from a trust established on his wife's death, of which Sam was a beneficiary, for the year ended December 31, 2017.

(G) $50,000 in life insurance payable on Sam's death.

CHAPTER 14

Exercise 13

ITA: 70, 150

After the 2017 personal tax season, the brother (Mr. Kaye) of one of your clients (Ms. Kaye) contacted you with respect to his sister. He indicated that his sister had passed away on May 2, 2018, at the age of 50.

Mr. Kaye indicated that his sister, who was not married, had the following income from January 1 to May 2, 2018:

(a) Salary — $22,000, of which $2,000 was vacation pay that had not been paid at the time of her death.

(b) Bond interest payable of $950 that had not been received at the time of death.

(c) Interest in her savings/chequing account of $150.

(d) Interest of $140 on a 60-day GIC that matured on May 15, 2018.

(e) Grossed-up dividend income of $1,380 on 100 Flying High shares, payable on April 30, 2018, but had not been paid at the time of her death.

(f) The fair market value of Flying High shares on May 2, 2018, was $25/share. These shares had been purchased for $10/share in 2011.

(g) Her RRSP had a value of $34,000 at the date of her death. In March 2018, Ms. Kaye made an RRSP contribution, in respect of 2018, of $9,000. Her earned income for 2017 was $80,000.

— *REQUIRED*

Discuss the tax implications and filing requirements as a consequence of Ms. Kaye's death.

Exercise 14

Mr. Black owns all the shares in Black Inc. Black Inc. is not associated with any other corporations and claims a deduction under subsection 125(1) every year.

Mr. Black is aware that you recently attended an excellent tax course and has approached you for advice regarding the following problem. Exactly one year has gone by since Black Inc.'s December 31, 2017 year end and a corporate tax return has not yet been filed. Further, on the advice of his brother-in-law, the controller, no instalments were made on account of 2017 or 2018. Whenever Mr. Black's brother-in-law is asked about the situation, he simply replies, "Don't worry". Mr. Black couldn't stop worrying, so on April 1, 2018 he sent a cheque on behalf of the corporation for $5,000 to the CRA on account of 2017 taxes.

Black Inc.'s actual/estimated income tax liabilities in respect of 2016 through 2018 are as follows:

Actual 2016	$ 6,000
Estimated 2017	12,000
Estimated 2018	14,000

— *REQUIRED*

(A) Calculate the payment schedule that should have been followed for 2018 under each alternative available under subsection 157(1), assuming the above estimates of tax prove accurate.

(B) Calculate the amount of any penalties that may be assessed against Black Inc. for failing to file the 2017 corporate return by the required date. (Assume the return is filed and tax liability for the year is paid on January 15, 2019.)

(C) Assuming no instalments have been made in respect of 2019, determine the minimum instalment amount that should be remitted by January 31, 2019.

Exercise 15

Bogin Wite is the president of Cal Antiques Inc., a company in the business of fabricating original antiques and then selling them across Canada and the United States. The company has been family-owned since April 2005 at which time Bogin was appointed president. Bogin and Cal Antiques Inc. have not prepared and filed tax returns since 2010. On July 14, 2018 Bogin received a notice from the CRA demanding the filing of all personal and corporate tax returns. He did not comply with the notice and on October 6, 2018, a CRA auditor visited the company's office in Waterloo, Ontario. After spending five days reviewing corporate and personal records, the auditor prepared a report detailing her findings which included the following information:

Personal and corporate bank loans . . . . Nil
Estimate of personal net worth . . . . $ 2,000,000
Loans taken by Bogin from the company (ignore section 15 effects) 1,500,000

Prior to leaving, the auditor told Bogin very politely that the CRA would be contacting him in the near future. Bogin's concern over the situation caused him to arrange a meeting with his lawyer and a professional accountant (who was recommended to him by a friend) in order that he might understand his circumstances and plan his course of action.

— *REQUIRED*

Prepare, in point form, your report to Bogin which will answer the following questions:

(A) What could the CRA's position be regarding penalties and offences?

(B) What course of action could Bogin take on receipt of any assessment if he disagrees with its contents?

(C) What is a "net worth assessment" and why could it be applied in Bogin's situation?

Exercise 16

1. By what date must the tax returns be filed for:

   (i) corporations?

   (ii) individuals (other than deceased individuals)?

2. Jean filed her tax return for the 2018 taxation year on March 31, 2019. She received a notice of assessment on May 28, 2019, disallowing her RRSP deduction. The notice of assessment was dated on May 24, 2019.

   By what date must Jean file a notice of objection if she wishes to dispute the assessment?

3. Mr. Pan expects income of $65,000 in 2018, consisting entirely of income from a consulting business. He expects to pay $17,000 in tax in 2018. He paid $11,000 in tax on his 2017 business income and $9,000 in tax on his 2016 business income.

   How much must Mr. Pan pay in instalments during 2018, and when must each be paid?

4. Taxed Ltd., a CCPC, has a December 31 year end and is not associated with any other corporation. Its federal income tax liability for 2016 was $20,000, and for 2017 it was $26,000. It estimates that it will have to pay $44,000 in federal income tax for 2018.

   (i) How much must Taxed Ltd. pay in instalments for 2018 and when must each be paid? Assume that Taxed Ltd. paid all of its 2017 instalments on time and in sufficient amount.

   (ii) When must the final balance of federal income tax for 2018 be paid?

Exercise 17

Mo Moves was born and lived all his life in Canada until February 1, 2014, when he moved to the United States. On November 1, 2018, he returned to Canada permanently. In each of calendar years 2014 through 2018, he earned $40,000 of interest income from funds on deposit with the U.S. Savings & Loans bank. In 2016, he received employment income from Canada for services performed in the United States. In 2017, he earned interest from a GIC in Canada and had a capital gain of $100,000 on the disposition of his cottage property located in Canada. During 2015, he spent 192 days in Canada vacationing and visiting his sick mother. In 2018, he spent 170 days visiting in Canada between January 1 and November 1.

— *REQUIRED*

(a) For each of the years, 2014 through 2018, which sources of income are subject to tax in Canada? Explain.

(b) For which of the years, 2014 through 2018, is he required to file a Canadian tax return? Explain.

(c) For the years he is required to file a return, which years, after 2015, is he entitled to claim personal tax credits? Indicate whether he is entitled to the full amount or a prorated amount.

Exercise 18

What is the filing deadline for each of the following:

(a) annual tax return for an individual resident in Canada;

(b) tax return filed by a non-resident individual reporting Canadian rental income in accordance with sec. 216;

(c) unfiled returns for deceased taxpayers;

(d) returns for corporations;

(e) trust returns;

(f) notices of objection for a corporation;

(g) section 85 elections; and

(h) elections with respect to unpaid amounts.

Exercise 19

Mr. James has just found out that he is the executor of the estate of his late aunt, Ms. Ray. Ms. Ray died on July 15, 2018. Mr. James would like to know the tax treatment that results in the least tax to the estate for the following items:

(a) A rental property which was left to Ms. Ray's daughter:

	Land	Building
Original cost in 1994	$ 38,000	$ 65,000
UCC — December 31, 2017	N/A	35,000
FMV — July 15, 2018	118,000	165,000

(b) Net rental income before CCA of $5,200 earned from January 1, 2018 to July 15, 2018.

(c) 1,000 shares purchased in 2009 for $17,000, which have a fair market value of $38,000 on July 15, 2018 and were left to Ms. Ray's husband.

(d) Non-eligible dividend income:

Amount	Declared	Paid
$300	January 3, 2018	January 31, 2018
$325	April 6, 2018	April 30, 2018
$325	July 5, 2018	July 31, 2018

(e) Net income from Ms. Ray's legal practice which had a December 31 year end:

January 1, 2018 to July 15, 2018 .... $63,000

(f) Term life insurance of $100,000, which was paid to Ms. Ray's estate on her death.

(g) RRSP's with a fair market value of $72,000 payable to her estate.

(h) Ms. Ray was a beneficiary of a testamentary trust established on the death of her father. Ms. Ray's income from the trust was:

January 1, 2018 to July 15, 2018 .... $ 5,000

¶14,875 ASSIGNMENT PROBLEMS

Type 1 Problems

Problem 1

ITA: 150(1)

When must the tax returns for the following be filed: (a) a corporation, (b) a deceased person (terminal return only), (c) a trust, and (d) an individual?

Problem 2

ITA: 152(4)

An individual filed her 2017 tax return on April 30, 2018. The CRA responded with a notice of assessment mailed on May 27, 2018. If the CRA wishes to make an additional assessment of tax for 2017, by what date must it issue a notice of reassessment?

Problem 3

ITA: 165, 169

Rachel, a new client, requested some assistance with her personal income tax assessment. The CRA is claiming that her car expenses are not deductible because they were incurred to earn employment income. Rachel argues that the expenses were incurred to earn commission income in accordance with her employment contract and the *Income Tax Act*.

Outline the legal rights that Rachel has with respect to her assessment and the steps she should undertake with the CRA.

Problem 4

ITA: 163(2), 163.2

Mr. Turner visited his accountant Ms. Blackford, on March 31, 2018, to discuss the tax consequences of a recent transaction. On January 10, 2018, Mr. Turner received a dividend of $100,000 from Dot.com Ltd., a company he owns 100%.

Ms. Blackford explained that if he had transferred his shares of Dot.com Ltd. to a holding corporation on December 31, 2017, he could have deferred personal tax of $36,000 on the dividend until it was paid out of the holding corporation to him personally.

Ms. Blackford indicated that the documentation with respect to the transfer of the shares to the holding corporation and the payment of the dividend to the holding corporation can be back-dated to achieve the result desired.

What are the tax consequences of back-dating the documentation with respect to the transfer of the securities?

Problem 5

ITA: 156, 156.1, 161, 163.1

Bert Logan's daughter Amanda is an accounting student. After a brief review of Bert's previous tax returns she advised him that he would likely have to begin making income tax instalments for 2018; however, she was uncertain about how these instalments were to be calculated and the consequences of making inadequate instalments. Amanda called one of the tax specialists at her employer firm, First and Partners, for assistance.

Amanda provided the following information:

(a) 2016 actual tax liability was $8,750;

(b) 2017 actual tax liability was $7,640; and

(c) 2018 estimated tax liability is $5,520.

You have been asked to write a memo, in point form, for partner review explaining the options available to calculate instalment payments for Bert Logan and the consequences if incorrect instalments are made.

Problem 6

ITA: 157, 162, 163, 163.1

Ruffle Limited, a public company, specializes in the games business. For their fiscal year ended October 31, 2016, the company's tax liability was $54,024. Due to the success of the board game, Run About, the company's bottom line has increased significantly, resulting in a tax liability of $69,036 for the fiscal period ended October 31, 2017.

Ruffle Limited's climb to success came to a halt in the next fiscal year. Due to increased competition, profits are expected to decline significantly and the controller of Ruffle Limited estimates the tax payable for the fiscal period ending October 31, 2018 to be $45,000.

In addition, the controller informed you that, due to cash flow problems, the actual instalments for June, July, and August 2018 were $1,050 less than the amount required. The controller also indicated that in order to compensate for this shortfall an instalment payment of $4,500 was made in October 2018 and that the remaining outstanding balance would be included in the December remittance.

The controller has asked you, his tax accountant, to provide him with required instalments for the 2018 taxation year.

Problem 7

ITA: 161, 162, 163.1; IC 00-1R

On September 1, 2018, you started in your new position as manager of taxation for Malic Corporation, a large public company with a December 31 year end. On the second day into the job, Maureen Smythe, the VP Finance, comes into your office with a folder entitled "Outstanding Items". She tells you that the folder was found in the bottom drawer of your desk when the office was cleaned up after the previous manager of taxation left. She is concerned about the following items found in the file:

(a) Paper-clipped to the corporation's notice of assessment for the 2012 taxation year (dated September 30, 2013), is a reassessment, dated April 30, 2018, that states that the corporation has been assessed additional tax for the 2012 taxation year in the amount of $722,500.

(b) A memo to the tax files from the previous manager stating that for the 2017 taxation year minimum instalments were made for January to October, no instalment was made in November, and an instalment of $1.45 million was made in December.

(c) A partially completed tax return for the 2017 taxation year indicating taxes payable of $10.76 million. The return had not been filed.

(d) A schedule of information from previous tax returns showing the tax liabilities for the 2014 to 2016 taxation years were $7.5 million, $5.4 million, and $9.2 million, respectively.

After reviewing the files Ms. Smythe leaves with you, you determine that you need to do the following:

(A) Comment on the validity of the CRA reassessment.

(B) Determine whether there is tax owing for the 2017 taxation year, calculate any late filing penalties, if any, and comment on any late installment penalties, if any.

(C) Discuss the interest charges applicable.

Problem 8

ITA: 163.2; IC 01-1

Bill, an accountant, lives in an exclusive neighbourhood where house prices are in excess of $1,000,000. He has recently become friendly with a new neighbour and in March the neighbour hired Bill to prepare his personal tax return. The neighbour gave Bill a T4 reporting $60,000 of income. Thinking that the income was on the low side, Bill asked if this was all the income he had and the neighbour replied that it was. Bill did not ask any further questions but prepared the tax return. When the neighbour's tax return was audited by the CRA, it was discovered that he had in excess of $300,000 in income for the year.

Advise Bill as to whether he is at risk of being assessed under the civil penalty provisions in the Act.

ITA: 163.2

Problem 9

ITA: 212(1), 215(3), 215(6), 216(1); IC 77-16R4

After several years of visiting Florida, Mr. Singh moved from Toronto to Florida on December 31, 2017, and became a non-resident of Canada. Mr. Singh decided to rent his house in Canada for the next few years. Mr. Singh has arranged with a relocation agency, Gone-Today-Here-Tomorrow, to collect the rent, pay all expenses and remit the balance to him quarterly. During 2018, the house was rented for $1,950 for January to June, and $2,150 for July to December. Expenses amounted to $1,550 per month.

You have been asked to discuss withholding tax and other tax implications concerning Mr. Singh's rental property.

Problem 10

ITA: 153

A Canadian university hires a well-known American lecturer to lecture on American history. The work will take approximately six weeks and she is to be paid $20,000.

You have been asked to determine whether there is a requirement to withhold Canadian tax on the $20,000.

Problem 11

ETA: 169(4), 169(5), 223; 225(1)–(4), 228(1)–(3), 237(1), 238(1), 238.1, 239(1), 243, 244(1), 245(2), 246(1), 248, 286(1)

Authors' Note: The following problem includes GST/HST implications. Students should review Chapter 20 of the textbook, "Goods and Services Tax (GST)/Harmonized Sales Tax (HST)", before attempting this problem.

Mr. E. Evans has decided to open a small car detailing company. The individual at the name registration office suggested that Mr. Evans walk down to the CRA office and pick up the information package with respect to tax filing, etc.

Mr. Evans had anticipated that the package of information obtained at the CRA office would include information on the harmonized sales tax ("HST"). Unfortunately, this information was not included in the package obtained. Mr. Evans approached you to explain the obligations of a registrant under the *Excise Tax Act*.

Provide the appropriate explanations.

Type 2 Problems

Problem 12

ITA: 153, 162(1), 162(2), 212(1)(d), 233.3; ITR: 108(1.11); IC 77-16R4

On January 10, 2018, you started your new job as controller for Bordessa Corporation, a Canadian-controlled private corporation with a December 31 year end. On your first day, the president and owner-manager of the company has asked you to follow up on some personal and corporate tax concerns that he has.

(1) The company is the exclusive Canadian manufacturer and distributor of menswear designed by a famous U.S. designer and pays the designer a royalty equal to 10% of sales each quarter. Royalty payments are due one month after each quarter end (i.e., on April 30, July 31, October 31, and January 31). The company's financial statements show a 2017 royalty expense of $60,000. The financial statements also show the amount of royalties payable at the company's December 31, 2017 year end to be $20,000 (the comparable number for December 31, 2016 is $10,000). According to the company's 2017 cheque register, however, only $45,000 has been paid to the menswear designer and only $5,000 has been paid to the CRA. The president wants to know how much the company should remit when it makes its January 31, 2018 payment to make up for unpaid royalties and withholding taxes it owes in respect of 2017.

(2) The company accrued a $100,000 bonus payable to the President on its financial statements. This bonus was declared by way of a director's resolution at the company's Board of Directors' last 2017 meeting. The president understands that his bonus must be paid within 180 days after the year end in order for it to be deductible in 2017 and you have verified that this is correct. This is the first time the company has accrued such a bonus and the president wants to know the deadline for the remittance of payroll deductions on the bonus. You do a quick review of payroll remittances for 2016 and 2017 and find that they amounted to about $120,000 in each year.

ITA: 78(3)

(3) The president tells you that he filed his 2016, 2015, and 2014 tax returns yesterday (January 9, 2018) after receiving a demand to file these returns in December 2017. He is expecting a net refund of $5,490 (see the schedule below). He wants to know whether he will be assessed any penalties for late filing and what the amount of the penalties will be. He tells you that his wife is a self-employed medical doctor.

	Balance due (Refund $)
2014	(20,500)
2015	10,000
2016	5,010
Net refund expected	(5,490)

(4) During 2017, the president of the company inherited U.S. stock from a distant relative who lived in the U.S. The value of the stock at the date of the relative's death was C$120,000. The president has asked you if he has to report this on his 2017 tax return. The stock is held in safekeeping at a stockbroker's office in Toronto.

Report your findings to the president.

Problem 13

ITA: 60, 70, 118.93; IT-210R2, IT-212R3, IT-326R3

In early March, you were preparing your client list with respect to the personal tax return preparation season. When you came across Mr. Ricky's name you remembered that Mrs. Ricky had called you regarding her husband's death. Mr. Ricky had passed away March 1, 2018, at age 62. Mrs. Ricky is the executrix.

Mr. Ricky owned and operated a Canadian-controlled private corporation, Shining Ltd. Mr. Ricky's 100 shares had an adjusted cost base and paid-up capital of $55,000. The fair market value of the shares at the date of death was $5,750,000.

Mr. Ricky earned $12,000 per month in salary, which was paid by direct deposit on the last day of the month. A non-periodic bonus of $50,000 had been declared on February 15, 2018, but had not yet been paid at the time of his death. CPP of $2,594 has been, or will be, withheld on this income. He is not eligible for EI.

In addition to his shares, Mr. Ricky owned bonds with accrued interest of $917 in 2018 to the date of his death. Further, Mr. Ricky had owned two rental properties. Net rental income before capital cost allowance was $4,000 for each of the months of January and February 2018.

Other Information:

(1) All assets of Shining Ltd. have been used in the active business of the corporation.

(2) The shares of Shining Ltd. have been owned by Mr. Ricky since 2000.

(3) Mr. Ricky had earned income in 2017 of $95,000. He contributed to his RRSP the maximum amount allowed as a deduction in 2017 but did not make the 2018 contribution. His RRSP was worth $295,000 at the time of his death. Mrs. Ricky is the designated beneficiary of his RRSP.

(4) His 2017 personal tax return was prepared but not filed at the time of his death.

(5) Mr. Ricky had not used any of his capital gains exemption.

(6) All of Mr. Ricky's assets have been left to his wife, except for the two rental properties that are bequeathed to his 20-year-old daughter.

(7) The rental properties had the following details:

	Unit #1 Land	Unit #1 Building	Unit #2 Land	Unit #2 Building
Fair market value	$100,000	$100,000	$120,000	$80,000
Capital cost	90,000	72,000	110,000	83,000
UCC		50,000		52,000

The partner has asked you to prepare a memo to the tax file explaining the tax implications of the above information, the filing requirements for Mr. Ricky's tax returns and any planning opportunities available.

Before you meet with the partner you want to:

¶14,875

(A) Assess the situation.

(B) Identify the issues.

(C) Analyze the issues.

(D) Advise/recommend.

CHAPTER 14

CHAPTER 14 —
DISCUSSION NOTES FOR REVIEW QUESTIONS

(1) (a) False. All corporations resident in Canada have to file tax returns within six months of the end of the year.

ITA: 150(1)(a)

(b) True. An individual is required to file a tax return if he or she "has disposed of a capital property". Even if there is no taxable income or tax liability a return must be filed. In addition, Mr. Austen may lose his capital gains deduction in respect of this transaction, if he does not file the return.

ITA: 110.6(6), 150(1)

(c) False. Instalments must be paid on the 15th of each of those months.

ITA: 156(1)

(2) An instalment interest offset is available on prepaid or overpaid instalments. However, this credit offset can only be applied against instalment interest owing; it is not refundable and may not be applied against any other debt. To benefit, he would have to pay the December 15 instalment on September 15 which would offset the fact that the June 15 instalment was three months late. In addition, the prescribed interest rate for the last quarter would have to be equal to or greater than the prescribed interest rate for the second quarter.

ITA: 161(2.2)

(3) They will not be able to collect interest for the last three years. Interest will not be received for the period prior to the filing of the tax return for the year in which the request is made to carry the loss back.

ITA: 164(5)

(4) Since the accountant sent a letter to the CRA, it may take some time before a reply is received. If the reply is received late and there is disagreement, it may be too late to file a Notice of Objection. Therefore, it may be prudent to file the Notice of Objection in the first place unless the matter is a minor one.

ITA: 165(1)

(5) In order to amend the tax returns for the third preceding year the company would have had to file form T2A by the time the corporate tax returns are due for the loss year which is six months after the fiscal year end. However, Murray Corp. did not meet this deadline since it did not file until seven months after the year end. Therefore, the CRA will not have to let the corporation carry the loss back at all. However, the loss will still be available to be carried forward.

ITA: 152(6)

(6) The following are the returns that can be filed:

(a) Terminal return — This return reports the income for the period in the year before the date of death and includes any gain or loss on the deemed disposition on death. Full personal credits may be claimed.

ITA: 70(1)

(b) Rights or things — "Rights or things" can be reported on a separate return to take advantage of the lower marginal tax brackets. Also, the full personal tax credits allowed can be claimed again.

ITA: 70(2), 118(1), 118(2)

(c) A separate return for income earned from a graduated rate estate for the period from the last year end of the estate to the date of death.

ITA: 104(23)

CHAPTER 14 — SOLUTIONS TO MULTIPLE CHOICE QUESTIONS

Question 1

(B) is correct. The penalty is $900. The initial penalty rate of 5% is increased by 1% for each *complete* month after April 30, 2018, that the return was not filed to a maximum penalty of 5% + 4% = 9%.   ITA: 162(1)

(A) is incorrect as it includes only the initial penalty of 5% of the unpaid tax.

(C) is incorrect as it includes ½% for the half month of September. Only complete months should be counted for purposes of the penalty.

(D) is incorrect as it includes 1% for the month of September. Only complete months should be counted for purposes of the penalty.

Question 2

(B) August 15, 2021, is correct. The normal reassessment period for a CCPC ends three years after the day of mailing of a notice of assessment for the year.   ITA: 152(3.1)

(A) December 31, 2020, three years after the end of the taxation year, is incorrect. The three-year period commences with the date of mailing of the notice of assessment, not the last day of the fiscal year.

(C) December 31, 2021, four years after the end of the taxation year, is incorrect.

(D) August 15, 2022, four years after the day of mailing of a notice of assessment for the year, is incorrect. It would be correct if the taxpayer were a corporation other than a CCPC.   ITA: 152(3.1)

Question 3

(D) June 15, 2019, is correct. The notice of objection filing due date is one year after Darol's filing-due date for 2017.   ITA: 165(1)

(A) December 31, 2018, being one year after the end of the taxation year, is incorrect.

(B) January 14, 2019, being 90 days after the date of mailing of the notice of assessment, is incorrect in this case. For an individual and a graduated rate estate, the due date is the later of this date and one year after the filing-due date for the tax return.

(C) April 30, 2019, being one year after the filing-due date for 2017 for an individual *not* carrying on a business, is incorrect. Darol's filing-due date for 2017 was June 15, 2018, as he carried on business in 2017.

Question 4

The correct answer is (D) September 30, 2018, being six months after the date of death.   ITA: 150(1)(*b*)

(A) is incorrect. It is the most common due date for 2017 personal tax returns. This date is not correct for two reasons: first, he has income from carrying on business, and second, he has at least six months from the date of death.   ITA: 150(1)(*a*)(i)

(B) is incorrect. It is the date the return would have been due if he had not died.   ITA: 150(1)(*a*)(ii)

(C) is incorrect as it is six months after the end of the year for which the return is being filed.

Question 5

(A) is correct. The minimum monthly instalment is the least of:

− $\frac{1}{12}$ of the estimated taxes payable: $\frac{1}{12} \times \$200,000 = \$16,667$

− $\frac{1}{12}$ of the prior year's taxes payable: $\frac{1}{12}$ of $140,000 = \$11,667$

− $\frac{1}{12}$ of the second prior year's taxable payable ($\frac{1}{12}$ of $180,000 = \$15,000$) for two months and 10 payments of $11,000 ($\frac{1}{10} \times [\$140,000 − 2 \times \$15,000]$).

The least of these is either the prior year method or the second prior year method. Only the prior year method ($11,667 per month) is listed as a choice in this question. Because X Ltd. had taxable income in the prior year of more than the small business deduction limit, it must pay its final balance due within two months of year end (February 28, 2019).

(B) and (C) incorrectly base the instalments on estimated taxes payable. (B) has the correct final due date. (C) incorrectly uses the balance-due day that is three months after the end of the year which is applicable only for Canadian-controlled private corporations that have taxable income that is less than the small business deduction limit in the prior year.

(D) incorrectly uses the amount for the first two payments of the second prior year method for all 12 payments but has the correct final due date for the balance due. (D) would have been a correct answer had it indicated that the payments for the last 10 months would be $11,000 per month.

Question 6

(D) is correct (two payments of $3,825 and two payments of $4,375). The minimum quarterly instalment is the least of:

– ¼ of the estimated taxes payable: ¼ × $25,000 = $6,250

– ¼ of the prior year's taxes payable: ¼ of $16,400 = $4,100

– ¼ of the second prior year's taxable payable (¼ of $15,300 = $3,825) for two months and two payments of $4,375 (½ × [$16,400 – 2 × $3,825]).

(A) is incorrect because four payments of $6,250 is not the minimum payment.

(B) is incorrect because two payments of $4,100 and two payments of $6,250 is not the minimum amount. Four payments of $4,100 would result in the minimum amount.

(C) is incorrect because two payments of $3,825 and two payments of $4,100 is not the minimum amount. If the first two payments are $3,825, the last two payments must be $4,375. Alternatively, four payments of $4,100 can be made.

CHAPTER 14 — SOLUTIONS TO EXERCISES

Exercise 1

Subsection 153(1):

(a) salary or wages or other remuneration, including stock option benefits, from employment;

(b) a superannuation or pension benefit;

(c) a retiring allowance;

(d) a death benefit for long service from an employer;

(e) an Employment Insurance benefit;

(f) a benefit under a supplementary unemployment benefit plan;

(g) an annuity payment;

(h) a benefit from a deferred profit sharing plan;

(i) fees, commissions and other amounts for services;

(j) a payment under a registered retirement savings plan;

(k) certain amounts resulting from an income averaging annuity;

(l) a payment from a registered retirement income fund.

Exercise 2

Inheritance, gambling winnings, lottery prize, etc.

Exercise 3

As his net tax owing in the current year and one of the two preceding years is in excess of $3,000, he is required to make instalments.

Instalments of $750 ($\frac{1}{4} \times$ $3,000) must be paid by March 15 and June 15 and instalments of $1,250 (i.e., ($4,000 – 2 $\times$ $750) $\times$ $\frac{1}{2}$) must be paid by September 15 and December 15. The balance of the tax liability must be remitted by the balance-due date of April 30, 2019.

Exercise 4

As the corporation's estimated taxes payable for the current year and the taxes paid for the preceding year exceed $3,000, instalments are required.

The Act would allow the following: ITA: 157(1)(*a*)(iii)

January 31 and February 28, 2018 — $\frac{1}{12}$ of $158,400 or $13,200;

Last day of March to December 2018 — $\frac{1}{10}$ of ($237,600 – 2 $\times$ $13,200) or $21,120;

Balance on the last day of the third month after the taxation year end, where a small business deduction was taken by virtue of section 125 in the current or preceding year and the corporation and associated corporations' aggregate taxable incomes for the preceding year did not exceed the small business deduction limit, or, in this particular case, the last day of February 2019, as applicable to any other case.

Exercise 5

Subsection 150(1):

Y and Z will incur no penalties; furthermore, Y is not required to file since no tax is payable, unless he disposed of capital property.

Subsection 162(1):

Failure to file when required — 5% of unpaid tax plus 1% of unpaid tax per complete month past due for a first offence:

X — 5% of $4,700 or $235 plus 1% of $4,700 $\times$ nil = $235.

Y — 5% of nil or nil.

Z — no penalty as the return is not due until June 15. Interest charges on the unpaid tax from April 30 will, however, apply.

Subsection 238(1):

Failure to file as or when required — liable on summary conviction to a fine of $1,000 to $25,000 or a fine and imprisonment for up to 12 months;

— Y could be fined if there has been a demand to file under subsection 150(2).

Exercise 6

(A) Facts to be determined:

(i) Date of mailing of 2015 original assessment in order to determine the three-year limit (i.e., the   ITA: 152(4)
normal reassessment period for an individual).

(ii) Obtain date of mailing of notice of reassessment.

(B) Steps to be taken:

(i) Procure an engagement letter or a signed consent form which gives permission to discuss   Form T1013
Mr. DeHaan's case with officials of the CRA.

(ii) Start discussions with the CRA.

(iii) File a Notice of Objection prior to the expiry of the 90-day period based upon the date of
mailing determined above (i.e., September 12, 2018, if mailed on June 15, 2018).

(iv) Warn Mr. DeHaan that certain second-time offences may carry heavier penalties than the
first-time offence.

(C) A penalty of 10% of unreported income could be imposed on Mr. DeHaan, if the current   ITA: 163(1), IC 00-1R
reassessment is his second offence within three years of the first offence. Under the CRA's voluntary
disclosure program, a valid voluntary disclosure may result in a waiver of penalties.

Exercise 7

The Act computes interest at a basic prescribed rate plus 4% on amounts owing to the CRA from   ITA: 161
the earliest date the amount was due until the date it was paid:

— the interest is not tax deductible.

Interest is computed at the same basic prescribed rate plus 2% on refunds by the CRA to non-   ITA: 164(3)
corporate taxpayers and at the basic prescribed rate to corporate taxpayers:

— the interest is taxable;

— if the interest relates to instalments, an interest offset is computed using the 4% addition,   ITA: 161(2.2)
against interest owing on late instalments for interest earned on early instalments.

Both interest calculations are based on daily compounding.

Interest on the overpayment of taxes for individuals will start to accrue 30 days after the later of the
balance due day for the return (i.e., April 30, 2019 for 2018 returns) or the date the return is filed.

An individual's refund interest accruing over a period can be offset by any arrears interest that
accrues over the same period, to which the refund interest relates. Hence, only the excess refund
interest is taxed to the individual.

Exercise 8

The CRA has commented on this type of situation. The conclusion is that the good faith defence is available, since the income statement reveals nothing that would lead you to question the validity of the information provided to you. As a result, the preparer penalty would not apply in your situation.

IC 01-1

Use of the flowchart presented in the chapter may be helpful in analyzing this situation and reaching this conclusion.

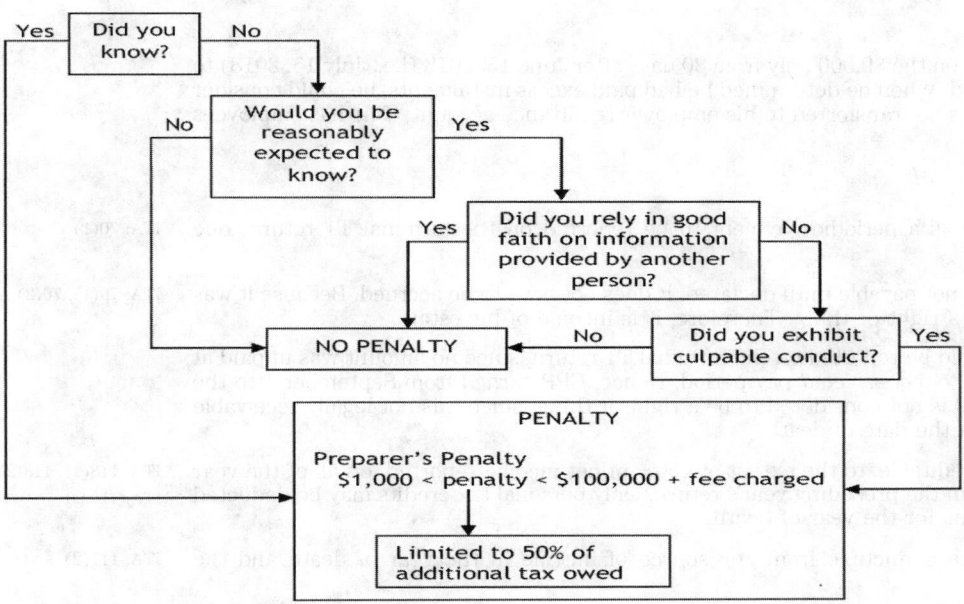

Exercise 9

(a) Notice of objection:

ITA: 165(1)

— to be filed by *individual* taxpayers and graduated rate estates by the later of:

   (i) one year after the filing-due date, which is normally April 30 or June 15 except for graduated rate estates and deceased persons, and

ITA: 248(1)

   (ii) the 90th day after the mailing date of the notice of assessment;

— to be filed within 90 days of mailing of notice of assessment for all other taxpayers;

— a prescribed form is not required.

(b) Appeal to the Tax Court of Canada:

ITA: 169

— after 90 days of date of decision on notice of objection or 90 days after the mailing of the notice of objection if there has been no response to it;

— may be able to elect informal procedure under subsection 18(1) of the *Tax Court of Canada Act*.

(c) Appeal to the Federal Court of Appeal (section 17.6 of the *Tax Court of Canada Act*):

— within 30 days from date of mailing of decision of the Tax Court of Canada only if that taxpayer chose the general procedure in the Tax Court of Canada.

(d) Appeal to Supreme Court of Canada:

— on recommendation of Federal Court of Appeal;

— with permission of Supreme Court of Canada.

Exercise 10

A tax return may be filed by a non-resident within two years after the end of the year that rents were paid. In that return, rental income for the year, net of expenses, would be reported and any withholding tax paid in the year in respect of rental revenue would be considered taxes paid for the year.

ITA: 216

This individual is eligible to file this return for 2016, 2017, and 2018. The 2013, 2014, and 2015 rents do not fall into the eligible filing period. However, the Minister may extend the time for filing a return. The individual may consider requesting such an extension.

ITA: 216
ITA: 220(3.2)

Exercise 11

Steve will receive interest on the $9,000 only from 30 days after June 15, 2018 (i.e., July 15, 2018) to the date the cheque was mailed. When he determined he had paid excess instalments, he could consider requesting that the instalments be transferred to his employer remittance account, if he has employees from whom he withholds tax.

Exercise 12

(A) The accrued interest is a periodic payment to be reported on the terminal T1 return, due April 30, 2019.

ITA: 70(1)

(B) Since the dividend is not payable until declared, it does not have to be accrued. Because it was declared after death, it is not a right or thing. Therefore, it is income of his estate.

ITA: 70(1), 70(2)

(C) The $800 of CPP would be reported on the terminal T1 return, since no amount was unpaid at the date of death that related to a *completed* pay period. Hence, CPP earned from September 1 to the date of death on September 10 is not considered to be a right or thing, since it is not legally receivable for a completed pay period on the date of death.

(D) The donations are creditable, to the extent of 100% of net income reported, on all of the year of death returns combined or in the preceding year's return. Only personal tax credits may be deducted on each of the separate returns for the year of death.

ITA: 118(1), 118(2)
ITA: 118.93

(E) Net capital losses are deductible from any source of income in the year of death and the preceding year.

ITA: 111(2)

(F) Trust income of $900 for the year ended December 31, 2017 must be reported on the terminal return. An election is permitted to report the trust income payable to Sam for the stub period, January 11, 2018 to September 10, 2018 on a separate return, also due April 30, 2019. The personal tax credits can be deducted on this return.

ITA: 104(23)(d)

ITA: 118(1), 118(2)

(G) Life insurance proceeds received on death are not taxable.

Exercise 13

Ms. Kaye's 2018 terminal personal tax return is required to be filed by April 30, 2019. In Ms. Kaye's 2018 return all accrued income earned on a periodic basis during the period January 1 to May 1, 2018 should be included. In addition, all capital property (such as her Flying High shares) is deemed to have been disposed of at the fair market value. A claim for the full personal tax credits can be made on the terminal return even though Ms. Kaye died on May 2, 2018. The RRSP contribution of $9,000 is deductible on her 2018 terminal return, since it is less than the maximum amount (i.e., lesser of $26,230 and 18% of $80,000).

ITA: 150(1)(d)
ITA: 70(1)
ITA: 70(5)

Ms. Kaye's 2018 terminal return will include the following:

Salary	$22,000
Bond interest	950
Savings account interest	150
GIC interest	140
Dividend income	1,380
Taxable capital gain [½ ($25 − $10) × 100]	750
RRSP accumulation	34,000
RRSP contribution	(9,000)
Taxable income	$50,370

Ms. Kaye's legal representative can report amounts which were receivable but not received at the date of death, on a separate tax return, called a "rights or things" return, instead of on the terminal return.   ITA: 70(2)

The unpaid vacation pay of $2,000, interest payable of $950 and $1,380 of grossed-up dividend income would qualify as income from "rights or things." Personal tax credits equal to the amounts claimed in the terminal return may be claimed again on the "rights or things" return. This return is due on the date that is the later of one year after death and 90 days after assessment of any return for the year of death.

Alternatively, the legal representative can assign the income from "rights or things" to a particular   ITA: 70(3)
beneficiary.

Exercise 14

Part (A)

Since Black Inc. did not pay the instalments that it owed for 2017, it did not meet the conditions to be an eligible CCPC for purposes of its 2018 instalment payments. Therefore, monthly instalments were required for 2018.

	Instalments		Balance
	Jan./Feb.	*Mar. — Dec.*	*Total*
Par. 157(1)(*a*) (i)	$1,167	$1,167	$14,000
(ii)	1,000	1,000	12,000
(iii)	500	1,100	12,000

The instalment base for alternatives (ii) and (iii) is defined [Reg. 5301].

Part (B)

Par. 162(1)(*a*) 5% × ($12,000 – $5,000) $350

(*b*) 1% × 6 × ($12,000 –
$5,000)   420 $770

— subsection 162(1) is applicable as above for a first occurrence; the penalty is doubled for a repeated occurrence within three taxation years [ssec. 162(2)].

Sec. 163.1: penalty for late or deficient instalments

— 50% of interest payable under sec. 161 in excess of the greater of $1,000 and 25% of interest payable under sec. 161 if no instalments paid.

Ssec. 238(1) On summary conviction:

(a) a fine of not less than $1,000 and not exceeding $25,000;

(b) imprisonment for a term not exceeding 12 months; or

(c) both a fine and imprisonment.

Part (C) Monthly instalments will be required for 2019 since the required instalments were not paid for 2018 and, therefore, Black Inc. does not meet all of the conditions to be an eligible CCPC for 2019. The minimum instalment required by January 31, 2019 in this case is the taxes payable for the second preceding taxation year [2017] divided by 12 = $12,000/12 = $1,000. [Spar. 157(1)(*a*)(iii)]

Exercise 15

(A) Penalties:

— Subsection 162(1): failure to file as and when required, based on unpaid tax (5% plus 1% per month for a first occurrence).

— Subsection 162(2): repeated assessment of penalties within three taxation years.

— Penalty of 10% of unpaid tax plus 2% of unpaid tax per month, not exceeding 20 months.

— Interest will also be payable [sec. 161].

— Section 163.1: penalty for late or deficient instalments penalty of 50% of interest payable under sec 161 in excess of the greater of $1,000 and 25% of interest payable under sec. 161 if no instalments paid.

    Offences:

— Subsection 238(1): failure to file as and when required (fine of $1,000 to $25,000 and/or up to 12 months imprisonment on summary conviction).

    — In addition to penalties under section 162, unless proceedings under section 238 come first, in which case the penalty under section 162 cannot be added later [ssec. 238(3)].

— Paragraph 239(1)(*d*): wilful evasion (fine of 50% to 200% of tax evaded or fine plus up to 2 years in prison on summary conviction).

    — If proceedings by indictment, the minimum fine would be 100% of tax evaded, and the period of imprisonment can be up to five years. Both a fine and imprisonment are possible [ssec. 239(2)].

    — In addition to penalties under section 162 or 163, unless section 239 proceedings come first [ssec. 239(3)].

(B) Appeal procedure:

— File Notice of Objection within 90 days of mailing a Notice of Assessment for the corporation and the later of one year after the filing-due date for the year and 90 days after the mailing of the Notice of Assessment for the individual.

    — Notice of Assessment has not been mailed yet, so watch for date.

— Might try informal discussion before Notice of Objection.

— Burden of proof that assessment is wrong is on the taxpayer.

(C) Net worth assessment:

— Method of estimating income and, hence, tax for a period when no returns filed.

    — Closing net worth less opening net worth less windfalls plus personal or living expenses.

    — Based on estimates.

— Arguments based on estimates of assets and liabilities at the beginning and the end of the period as well as estimates of windfalls and personal or living expenses.

Exercise 16

1. (i) A corporation must file tax returns within six months after the end of the its taxation year (par. 150(1)(*a*)).

  (ii) Individuals must file tax returns on or before April 30 of the following calendar year, or on or before June 15 if they (or their spouse or common-law partner) are carrying on business (par. 150(1)(*d*)).

2. A notice of objection must be filed by the later of

  (i) 90 days of the mailing of the notice of assessment to which the objection is being made — in this case by August 22, 2019; and

  (ii) one year after the original due date of the tax return, i.e., April 30, 2020 (ssec. 165(1)).

3. Mr. Pan must pay quarterly instalments as follows in 2018:

March 15	$ 2,250
June 15	2,250
September 15	3,250
December 15	3,250
Taxable income	$11,000

Any remaining balance of tax must be paid by April 30, 2019 (ssec. 156(1)).

4. Taxed Ltd. should pay the following instalments in 2018:

● One instalment on March 31 of $5,000, and

● Three instalments, one each on June 30, September 30 and December 31, respectively, of $\frac{1}{3} \times [\$26,000 - \$5,000] = \$7,000$ each

The balance of tax is due on the last day of March 2019 where a small business deduction is taken and taxable income for 2018 did not exceed $500,000. Otherwise, the balance is due on the last day of February 2019 (ssec. 157(1)).

Exercise 17

(a) In 2014, he is a non-resident of Canada from February 1 through December 31, and is resident in Canada from January 1 through January 31. He will be taxable in Canada on his worldwide income for the month of January. For the balance of the year he has no Canadian-source income and, thus, is not required to report any income on his Canadian tax return.

In 2015, Mo is deemed to be resident in Canada for the full year as he sojourned in Canada for 183 days or more (par. 250(1)(a)). Therefore, he will be taxable in Canada on the $40,000 of U.S. interest income.

In 2016, he is a non-resident of Canada and he will not be taxable in Canada on any of his income. The employment income is not taxable in Canada as it was earned outside of Canada.

In 2017, he is a non-resident of Canada. He will be taxable in Canada on the capital gain from the disposition of taxable Canadian property (ssec.2(3)) and subject to withholding tax on the interest income.

In 2018, he is a non-resident of Canada from January 1 through October 31, and is resident in Canada from November 1 through December 31. He will be taxable in Canada on the U.S. bank interest earned during the months of November and December.

(b) In 2014, he is required to file a tax return as he is resident in Canada for part of the year. He is required to file a tax return for 2015 as he is deemed resident in Canada and had tax payable. In 2017, he is required to file a tax return as he disposed of a capital property. In 2018, he is required to file a tax return as he is resident in Canada for part of the year and has tax payable with respect to the U.S. interest income (ssec. 150(1)).

(c) In 2016 and 2017, he is not entitled to personal tax credits. In 2018, he is entitled to personal tax credits, prorated for the number of days he is resident in Canada.

Exercise 18

Filing deadlines:

(a) Individuals — on or before April 30 of the following calendar year.

(b) Sec. 216 return — within two years from the end of the calendar year in which the rental income was earned.

(c) Unfiled returns for deceased taxpayer — the later of April 30 of the calendar year following the year in which the income was earned or six months from the date of death.

(d) Corporations — within six months after the corporation's year end.

(e) Trust returns — within 90 days from the end of the year.

(f) Notices of objection — within 90 days of the date of mailing of the Notice of Assessment or Reassessment for which the objection is being filed.

(g) Section 85 elections — on or before the earliest day any taxpayer making the election is required to file a return for the taxation year in which the transaction to which the election relates occurred (ssec. 85(6)).

(h) Elections with respect to unpaid amounts — on or before the day the taxpayer who deducted the expense is required to file his tax return for the third taxation year following the year the amount was expensed (ssec. 78(1)).

Exercise 19

(a) By virtue of par. 70(5)(a), the land will be deemed disposed of at fair market value at the time of Ms. Ray's death. A taxable capital gain on the land of $40,000 [($118,000 − $38,000) × ½] will be included in Ms. Ray's terminal return.

By virtue of par. 70(5)(b), Ms. Ray's daughter will be deemed to have acquired the land at its fair market value and, therefore, she will have an adjusted cost base of $118,000.

By virtue of par. 70(5)(*a*), the building will be deemed disposed of at fair market value. The proceeds will be $165,000 and, therefore, a taxable capital gain on the building of $50,000 [($165,000 − $65,000) × ½] and recapture of $30,000 ($65,000 − $35,000) will be included in Ms. Ray's terminal return.

Ms. Ray's daughter will be deemed to have acquired the building at a cost equal to the deemed proceeds of $165,000.

(b) The net rental income of $5,200 will be included in Ms. Ray's terminal return. No CCA can be claimed as the rental property was deemed disposed of immediately before her death.

(c) By virtue of par. 70(6)(*a*), the shares will be deemed disposed of at their adjusted cost base of $17,000 and no capital gain will be realized. Ms. Ray's husband will be deemed to have acquired the shares for $17,000. Unless she had net capital losses to offset, there would be no benefit in electing the transfer to be at FMV by ssec. 70(6.2).

(d) The dividends paid on January 31, 2018 and April 30, 2018 will be included in Ms. Ray's terminal return. The taxable amount would be $725 [($300 + $325) × 1.16].

The dividend declared on July 5, 2018, before Ms. Ray's death, but not paid until July 31, 2018, after her death, may be included on a separate rights or things return by virtue of ssec. 70(2) with an additional personal credit.

(e) The income of Ms. Ray's legal practice of $63,000 must be included in Ms. Ray's terminal return. If this amount is a right to a share of income of a partnership at the time of death, it could instead be included on a rights and things return.

(f) The life insurance is not taxable on Ms. Ray's terminal return or to the estate.

(g) The full amount of Ms. Ray's RRSPs must be included in her terminal return by virtue of ssec. 146(8.8). Ms. Ray's estate and her spouse can jointly elect to include the RRSP proceeds in Mr. Ray's income under ssec. 146(8.91). Mr. Ray can then transfer these funds to his RRSP and claim a deduction under ssec. 60(1).

(h) The income from the testamentary trust from January 1, 2018 to the date of death of $5,000 must be included in Ms. Ray's terminal return.

Chapter 15

Corporate Distributions, Windings-Up, and Sales

Learning Goals

Know

By the end of this chapter you will know:

- The basic provisions of corporate surplus and the implication of its distribution.

Understand and Explain

By the end of this chapter you will understand and be able to explain:

- The tax paid or tax-free components of corporate surplus.
- The process for analyzing the tax consequences of selling the assets or shares of a corporation.

Apply

By the end of this chapter you will be able to apply your knowledge and understanding to:

- Calculate the corporate surplus components and the tax consequences of its distribution.
- Calculate whether the shareholders should sell shares or assets of a corporation.

Review Questions
¶15,800 in the Study Guide

Multiple Choice Questions
¶15,825 in the Study Guide

Exercises
¶15,850 in the Study Guide

Assignment Problems
¶15,875 in the Study Guide

CHAPTER 15 — LEARNING CHART

Problem Descriptions

Textbook Example Problems

15-1	Capital dividend account
15-2	Share attributes — tax consequences
15-3	Capital dividend
15-4	Wind-up calculations
15-5	Assets vs. shares

Multiple Choice Questions

1	Capital dividend
2	Redemption of shares
3	Winding-up consequences
4	Winding-up — available for distribution
5	Paid-up capital
6	Sale of goodwill — tax consequences

Exercises

1	Capital dividend account
2	Capital dividend account
3	Withdrawing cash from a corporation
4	Stock dividend
5	Independent situations — tax consequences
6	Winding-up
7	Winding-up
8	Winding-up
9	Capital dividend account

Assignment Problems

1	Capital dividend account
2	Capital dividend account
3	Deemed dividends
4	Redeem vs. sell shares
5	Withdrawing funds from investment corporation
6	Wind up of a corporation
7	Sale of assets with wind-up
8	Sale of assets with wind-up
9	Corporate distribution
10	Assets vs. shares
11	Purchase of asses vs. shares
12	Refundable dividend tax on hand; capital dividend account

Study Notes

¶15,800　REVIEW QUESTIONS

(1) Assuming that you are working in a province in which only par value shares can be issued, what journal entry would you use to record the issuance of 100 common shares, which had a par value of $100 each, for $30,000?

(2) In jurisdictions without par value shares, how is the paid-up capital determined?

(3) What are "high-low" shares?

(4) What are the four basic components of the capital dividend account?

(5) Calculate the effect on the capital dividend account as a result of the sale of unrecorded goodwill this year for $100,000. The only other transaction in Class 14.1 took place three years ago when a customer list was purchased for $10,000. The balance in the CEC account is now approximately $6,000.

(6) Smith Co. has total PUC of $10,000. It decided to make a distribution of capital in the amount of $9,000, but when it actually paid out the $9,000, the PUC was only reduced by $8,000. What are the tax consequences?

(7) What are the three components of a distribution on the winding-up of a corporation where the only shareholder is an individual?

(8) Glee Co. is a CCPC that is in the process of being wound up under the general winding-up rule. ITA: 88(2) One of its assets is a building that has an accrued terminal loss. The lawyer has suggested that subsection 13(21.2) will apply to deny the terminal loss to the corporation on winding-up. What do you think?

(9) Technically, on the winding-up of a corporation under the general winding-up rule, how are the ITA: 88(2) proceeds of disposition of the shares calculated?

¶15,825   MULTIPLE CHOICE QUESTIONS

Question 1

Which one of the following statements is FALSE?

(A) A capital dividend is usually received tax-free.

(B) A corporation must elect to pay a capital dividend, not later than the day the dividend is paid.

(C) If a private corporation has had more capital gains than capital losses, it will probably have a balance in its capital dividend account.

(D) The payment of a capital dividend by a private corporation will trigger a dividend refund.

Question 2

Mr. Andrews owned Class A special shares of Atlantis Ltd. with the following characteristics:

Fair market value	$60,000
Cost	20,000
Paid-up capital	10,000

These shares were redeemed. Which one of the following best describes the tax consequences of the redemption to Mr. Andrews?

(A) A capital gain of $40,000

(B) A dividend of $40,000

(C) A dividend of $50,000 and a capital gain of $40,000

(D) A dividend of $50,000 and a capital loss of $10,000

Question 3

X Ltd. had $40,000 available for distribution to its sole shareholder, Xavier, on winding-up. The balances in the tax accounts of X Ltd. were as follows:

Share capital (paid-up capital)	$ 2,000
RDTOH	Nil
Capital dividend account	8,000
Other surplus (LRIP taxed at low CCPC rate)	30,000
	$40,000

Xavier paid $1,000 for the shares of X Ltd. when he purchased them two years ago. Which one of the following statements is TRUE?

(A) The winding-up can occur on a tax-deferred basis. Xavier will be able to defer the recognition of any income for tax purposes.

(B) Xavier will have dividend income of $30,000 which will be grossed-up to $34,800 for tax purposes. In addition, he will have a capital gain of $1,000.

(C) Xavier will have dividend income of $30,000 which will be grossed-up to $34,800 for tax purposes. In addition, he will have a capital gain of $9,000.

(D) Xavier will have a capital gain of $39,000 on the winding-up of X Ltd.

Question 4

Art, the sole shareholder of Art's Variety Inc. with a November 30 year end, has decided to wind up the corporation, effective December 1. The balance sheet as at that date is anticipated to be as set out below.

Assets

Cash	$ 45,000
Refundable dividend tax on hand	30,000
Land, at cost (FMV, $850,000)	250,000
Building, at UCC (FMV, $780,000; cost, $380,000)	180,000
	$505,000

Liabilities & Equity

Liabilities	$ 20,000
Paid-up capital	5,000
Capital dividend account	10,000
Other surplus	470,000
	$505,000

Art's Variety Inc. is a Canadian-controlled private corporation. It pays tax at a combined federal and provincial rate of 14% on business income in the winding-up period and 50⅔% including the additional refundable tax on investment income.

The amount available for distribution to Art on the windup will be:

(A) $1,655,000

(B) $1,373,667

(C) $1,557,000

(D) $1,858,333

Question 5

At the beginning of its first taxation year, Newco Ltd., a newly incorporated company, issued 100 common shares to Mr. A for $10,000. On June 1 of the same year, Newco issued an additional 100 common shares to Mr. B for $15,000 (which is the fair value of the shares on that date). On December 30 of the same year, Mr. C acquired all of Mr. A's common shares for $20,000. At the end of this year (December 31), which of the following statements is true?

(A) The total paid-up capital of the common shares is $25,000, ½ of which is attributable to each of Mr. C and Mr. B.

(B) The total paid-up capital of the common shares is $35,000, ½ of which is attributable to each of Mr. C and Mr. B.

(C) The total paid-up capital of the common shares is $25,000, $10,000 of which is attributable to Mr. C and $15,000 of which is attributable to Mr. B.

(D) The total paid-up capital of the common shares is $35,000, $20,000 of which is attributable to Mr. C and $15,000 of which is attributable to Mr. B.

Question 6

C Co. is a Canadian controlled private corporation with a December 31 year end. During the year it sold all its assets including goodwill. The goodwill was sold for fair market value: $1 million. The cost of the goodwill and the company's Class 14.1 UCC balance was Nil. Which of the following is a correct statement?

(A) C Co. will report a taxable capital gain of $500,000 and its capital dividend account will increase by $500,000.

(B) C Co. will report active business income of $500,000 and its capital dividend account will increase by $500,000.

(C) C Co. will report active business income of $750,000 and its capital dividend account will increase by $250,000.

(D) C Co. will report a taxable capital gain of $750,000 and its refundable dividend tax on hand account will increase by $230,000.

¶15,850 EXERCISES

Exercise 1

ITA: 89(1)

The following capital properties have been sold by a Canadian-controlled private corporation during the year ended December 31:

	A	B	C
Proceeds of disposition	$4,000	$1,000	$2,000
Cost	2,000	2,000	2,000
Selling expenses	400	100	200

— *REQUIRED*

Compute the effects of the dispositions on the capital dividend account.

Exercise 2

ITA: 89(1)

Action Ltd., a Canadian-controlled private corporation, sold the following two capital properties during the fiscal year ending December 31:

	Cost	Proceeds	Selling costs
Property 1	$75,000	$110,000	$11,000
Property 2	40,000	11,000	5,500

— *REQUIRED*

Compute the effects of these sales on:

(A) the net income for tax purposes, and

(B) the balance in the capital dividend account.

Exercise 3

ITA: 83, 84

Mr. Duong, the sole shareholder of Investment Limited, a Canadian-controlled private corporation, requires some cash for other personal investment transactions. Investment Limited's share capital is composed of 100 common shares with an ACB and PUC of $1 per share and 1,000 6% preferred shares with an ACB and PUC per share of $15 and a retractable value of $75 per share. Mr. Duong is considering the following alternatives:

(a) Mr. Duong would cause Investment Limited to redeem 800 preferred shares at $75 per share.

(b) Mr. Duong would cause Investment Limited to pay a cash dividend of $60,000 on the common shares. Investment Limited has a capital dividend account of $75,000.

(c) Mr. Duong would cause Investment Limited to make a non-dividend cash distribution of $60,000 on the preferred shares.

— *REQUIRED*

Discuss the tax implication of the above transactions.

Exercise 4

ITA: 54, 84(3), 248(1)

A Canadian-controlled private corporation with no GRIP balance has paid a dividend this year in the form of 10 first preference shares each having a redemption value of $1,000 and a paid-up capital value of $1.00.

— *REQUIRED*

(A) What are the tax consequences of the receipt of the dividend by an individual shareholder?

(B) What are the tax consequences to the corporation?

(C) What are the tax consequences to the individual shareholder of a sale at their fair market value of the shares received?

(D) What are the tax consequences to the individual shareholder of a redemption of the shares received?

Exercise 5

ITA: 53(1)(*b*), 53(2)(*a*), 84(1), 84(3), 84(4)

The following situations deal with Canadian-controlled private corporations and their non-arm's length shareholders. However, each transaction, described below, is separate and distinct from the other transactions unless the contrary is stated.

(a) X Ltd. issued to the daughter of its only shareholder retractable special shares (preferred shares) with a PUC of $150 and a redemption value of $1,000 for $100 cash.

(b) A, the sole shareholder of A Ltd., gave the corporation land with an FMV of $150,000.

(c) Y, the controlling shareholder of Y Ltd., converted debt of $20,000 for preferred shares with a PUC and redemption value of $2,000 plus cash of $20,000.

(d) Z, the sole common shareholder of Z Ltd., is considering causing the corporation to make a payment as a return of capital (PUC). The shares have an FMV of $50,000, PUC of $10,000 and ACB of $20,000:

(i) payment is for $5,000;

(ii) payment is for $18,000.

— *REQUIRED*

Discuss the tax consequences of the above transactions.

Exercise 6

ITA: 54, 83(2), 84(2), 88(2), 89(1)

Flare Limited is a Canadian-controlled private corporation, founded 20 years ago by Mr. Siewert who holds all of the outstanding shares. The following balance sheet reflects the position of the corporation after selling all assets and paying all liabilities:

Flare Limited

BALANCE SHEET

as at December 31, 2018

Cash	$ 950,000		Capital stock (PUC)	$ 625,000
RDTOH	50,000		Capital dividend	
			account	150,000
			Other surplus	225,000
				$1,000,000
Total assets	$1,000,000			

— *REQUIRED*

(A) Determine the components of the distribution to Mr. Siewert.

(B) Compute the taxable capital gain or allowable capital loss on the disposition of Mr. Siewert's shares on January 1, 2019, assuming that their adjusted cost base was $350,000.

¶15,850

Exercise 7

ITA: 54, 83(2), 84(2), 88(2), 89(1)

Twilight Ltd., a CCPC with no GRIP balance, has been wound up this year and its only shareholder has surrendered her shares. She received $30,000 in total from the corporation for her shares which had a cost to her equal to their paid-up capital of $2,000. The company had elected a capital dividend on a dividend of $2,000. All business income of the CCPC has been taxed only at the low rate.

— REQUIRED

What are the tax consequences to the shareholder if she will be taxed on any income from the winding-up at a combined (33%) federal and (17%) provincial marginal rate of 50%?

Exercise 8

ITA: 54, 83(2), 84(2), 88(2), 89(1)

Authors' Note: The following question includes GST/HST implications. Students should review Chapter 20 of the textbook, "Goods and Services Tax (GST)/Harmonized Sales Tax (HST)", before attempting this problem.

Dwight Limited is a Canadian-controlled private corporation which will be wound up by its only shareholder, Mr. Warren, who bought the shares at their paid-up capital value of $2,000. As at December 31, 2018, its balance sheet appears as follows:

Dwight Limited

BALANCE SHEET

as at December 31, 2018

Assets			*Liabilities*		
Cash	$ 20,000		Bank loan	$ 47,000	
RDTOH	10,000		Wages payable	3,000	
Inventories at cost			Total	$ 50,000	
(FMV: $220,000)	200,000		*Shareholder's Equity*		
Land at cost					
(FMV: $70,000)	40,000		Paid-up capital	$ 2,000	
Buildings at UCC			Surplus	318,000	
(cost: $200,000;			Total	$370,000	
FMV: $300,000)	60,000				
Equipment at UCC					
(Cost: $100,000;					
FMV: $80,000)	40,000				
Total	$370,000				

The balance in the corporation's capital dividend account was nil as at the above balance sheet date. The assets are to be liquidated, the liabilities paid and the net proceeds distributed to Mr. Warren effective January 1, 2019.

— REQUIRED

(A) Compute the amount available for distribution to the shareholder assuming the corporation pays corporate tax at the rate of 14% on the first $500,000 of active business income, 27% on active business income not eligible for the small business deduction, and 40% initially on any other income, plus the additional refundable tax on investment income, from the winding-up. The balance in the corporation's GRIP is nil.

(B) Determine the components of the distribution to the shareholder.

(C) Compute the taxable capital gain or allowable capital loss on the disposition of Mr. Warren's shares assuming that their adjusted cost base was $1,000.

(D) Discuss the HST implications on the wind-up of Dwight Limited.

Exercise 9

The following non-depreciable capital properties have been sold late in the year by a Canadian-controlled private corporation during the taxation year ended December 31, 2018:

Property	Cost	Proceeds of Disposition	Selling Costs
1	$ 4,000	$ 8,000	$ 700
2	$ 4,000	$ 2,000	$ 100
3	$ 4,000	$ 4,000	$ 300

— *REQUIRED*

Compute the effects of the dispositions on the capital dividend account.

¶15,875 ASSIGNMENT PROBLEMS

Type 1 Problems

Problem 1

ITA: 89(1)

Sabres Limited, a Canadian-controlled private corporation whose fiscal year end is December 31, provides you with the following data concerning its tax accounts and capital transactions for 2018. The balance in its capital dividend account was nil on January 1, 2018. Ms. Tsakiris, a Canadian resident, is the sole shareholder.

Sabres Limited is considering winding up the corporation and wishes to determine the impact of the sale of all its capital assets on its tax surplus accounts. The following capital assets are recorded in the books of account:

Assets	Cost	UCC	Estimated proceeds	Estimated selling costs
Investments	$60,000		$ 22,000	$ 500
Land	40,000		200,000	10,000
Building	70,000	$ 45,000	125,000	6,000
Equipment	35,000	Nil	8,000	400
Customer lists (Class 14.1) (Note 1)	40,000	16,000	60,000	—

Notes:

(1) The balance in Class 14.1 reflects the purchase of the customer lists in 2008 for $40,000 less the tax write-offs for 2008 to 2017, inclusive.

(2) In addition to the above assets, there is $35,000 of goodwill which will also be sold.

You have been asked to determine the effect on income and the capital dividend account balance immediately after the above transactions.

Problem 2

ITA: 89(1)

Bob Stein is a friend of yours who owns all the shares of Stein Ltd., a Canadian-controlled private corporation incorporated in 2002. He has heard recently about something called the capital dividend account and he is wondering if his company might have one. He would like you to explain to him what a capital dividend account is, advise him on whether his company qualifies for one and determine if Stein Ltd. has a CDA balance. Bob lives in Vancouver where the company is located.

Use the following format for your analysis:

Date	Transaction	Untaxed CG/CL	Capital Dividend Received	Untaxed ECP	Life Insurance	Capital Dividend Paid	Balance

Bob has provided you with the following additional information:

You have reviewed the tax returns of the corporation for the period January 1, 2002 to December 31, 2018, and made the following notes:

2004 Disposed of bonds resulting in a capital gain of $10,000.

2005 Received taxable dividend of $2,000 and capital dividend of $5,000.

2006 Disposed of shares resulting in a capital loss of $4,000.

2009 Disposed of equipment resulting in a capital gain of $6,000 and recapture of $3,000.

2010 A customer list was purchased for $40,000.

2011 Sold vacant land and reported capital gain of $100,000.

2012   2011 capital gain on sale of vacant land was reassessed by the CRA as income. Stein Ltd. did not fight the reassessment.

2013   Sold shares resulting in a capital gain of $20,000.

2014   Received life insurance proceeds of $100,000 on a life insurance policy on the life of the company president purchased in 2008 by the corporation. As at January 1, 2014, the company's interest in the policy had an adjusted cost basis of $20,000.

2015   Paid capital dividends of $50,000.

2018   Sold a customer list for $100,000. The company's Class 14.1 balance at the time of the sale was $25,000.   ITA: 89(1)

2018   Sold shares resulting in a capital gain of $37,500.

(A) Assess the situation.

(B) Identify the issues.

(C) Analyze the issues.

(D) Advise/recommend.

Type 2 Problems

Problem 3   ITA: 53(1)(b), 84

The following situations deal with a Canadian-controlled private corporation and its shareholders. Each transaction described below is separate and distinct from the other transactions.

(a) Capital Inc. issued 135 preferred shares with PUC equal to $110 each for $11,050 cash and assets with an FMV of $2,800.

(b) Plastics Ltd. has shares with an FMV of $35,000 and a PUC of $5,500. Plastics Ltd. is considering making the following paid-up capital reductions on these shares. The sole shareholder has an ACB of $16,000 on her shares:

(i) Payment of $4,000; and

(ii) Payment of $8,000.

(c) Festivals Ltd. has 4,500 common shares with a PUC of $22,500. In March of this year the corporation declared and distributed a 15% stock dividend in common shares with a PUC of $3,375.

(d)(i) The sole shareholder of Baker Corp. Ltd. contributed assets worth $38,400 to the corporation in return for cash of $15,400 and preferred shares with a PUC of $23,000 (redemption value of $23,000).

(ii) A year later, the sole shareholder redeemed the preferred shares.

Explain paid-up capital and how it is calculated.

Discuss the tax consequences for deemed dividends for each of the above transactions.   ITA: 84

Problem 4   ITA: 54, 84(3), 84(6)

Ms. Chiu owns the following shares of four different CCPCs:

	Corp A Class A	Corp B Class B	Corp C Class C	Corp D Class D
# of shares	1,000	1,000	1,000	1,000
FMV	$50,000	$50,000	$50,000	$50,000
ACB	20,000	40,000	20,000	80,000
PUC	20,000	20,000	40,000	100,000

Assume:

(1) Ms. Chiu does not own any other shares of these corporations.

(2) She is not related to any of the other shareholders.

(3) She is in the top marginal tax bracket.

(4) The shares are not QSBC shares.

(5) None of the companies have a GRIP balance.

Ms. Chiu has asked you to explain the tax consequences if her shares in each of the companies are redeemed by the companies for their fair market value or she sells her shares in each of the companies for their fair market value.

(A) Assess the situation.

(B) Identify the issues.

(C) Analyze the issues.

(D) Advise/recommend.

Problem 5

It is October 2018 and you have just come out of a meeting with your tax partner, Ashley, and her clients, Mark and Hilary Miller. Ashley has asked you to assess the situation to identify the issues and develop a research plan. She would then like to meet with you to review your work. After that meeting she wants you to analyze the major issues, reach a conclusion and propose the advice she should give to Mark and Hilary.

Facts:

Mark and Hilary have been married for 35 years. They have lived in Wellesley, Ontario for many years and work in the technology sector in Waterloo. They have two children who are both married and living in Waterloo. Both Mark and Hilary plan to retire in about five years and expect to have retirement income of $130,000 each at that time.

They set up Hilmar Investments Inc. ("HII") 15 years ago to manage their investment capital. The company earns Canadian interest income, realizes capital gains and losses and earns dividend income from publicly-traded companies. Based on their salaries, they are both in the top marginal tax bracket and expect to remain there until they retire. Since they have enough personal cash from their salaries they have left any income earned by HII in the corporation. Since the company earns dividends from publicly-traded companies it has a GRIP balance of $60,000 as at August 31, 2018.

At this point in their lives they would like your advice on how much money they can take out of the corporation without paying any corporate or personal tax. Then they would like to know if it makes sense for them to take more money out of the corporation as salary or dividend. Hilary would also like advice on the $40,000 she borrowed from HII given that she will repay it in October. They both agree that they want to minimize their risk of reassessment by the CRA.

The following is the balance sheet of HII.

Hilmar Investments Inc.
BALANCE SHEET
Year ended August 31, 2018

		Notes:
Current Assets		
Cash	$ 20,000	
Term deposits	155,000	(1)
Due from shareholder	40,000	(2)
	215,000	
Long-term Investments		
Investments (at cost)	400,000	(3)
RDTOH	25,000	
	$640,000	
Current Liabilities		
Income tax payable	$ 8,000	
	8,000	
Shareholders' Equity		
Share capital	100,000	(4)
Retained earnings	532,000	(5)
	$640,000	

Notes:

(1) The term deposits are due on October 6, 2018.

(2) The loan to the shareholder represents $40,000 borrowed by Hilary on July 1, 2017 to buy a car. She signed a note payable at the time she borrowed the money. The note does not specify any repayment terms or interest rate. Hilary plans to repay the loan in October when she receives her bonus at work.

(3) The long-term investments have a fair market value of $760,000.

(4) Hilary and Mark each paid $50,000 for 50 common shares of the company on incorporation 15 years ago.

(5) Included in the retained earnings is a capital dividend account balance of $30,000, which all relates to prior year net capital gains. In addition, the company has a net capital loss carry forward balance of $10,000.

(6) The provincial corporate tax rates for income eligible for the small business deduction and income above the small business limit are 4% and 12% respectively.

(A) Assess the situation.

(B) Identify the issues.

(C) Analyze the issues.

(D) Advise/recommend.

Problem 6

ITA: 54, 83(2), 84(2), 88(2)

J. Tilkenhurst Limited (JTL) is a Canadian-controlled private corporation which was started 10 years ago by Mr. Santosh Prasad with an initial investment in common shares of $18,000. Mr. Prasad has decided that it's time to retire and move to his retirement home in Saskatoon, Saskatchewan. Therefore, in January 2019 Mr. Prasad wishes to have JTL sell the assets to a corporate purchaser at their fair market value and then wind up JTL. He would like your advice on how much capital he would have to invest if he wound up JTL, and he would like your advice on whether he should not wind up JTL but keep it.

The following is a projected tax balance sheet prior to the sale of the assets and the distribution of the resulting net cash as at the intended date of the winding-up:

J. Tilkenhurst Limited
BALANCE SHEET
as at December 31, 2018

Cash		$ 15,000
RDTOH		6,000
Accounts receivable	$60,000	
Less: reserve for doubtful accounts	5,000	55,000
Inventory		110,000
Marketable securities		26,000
Land		85,000
Building — UCC		23,000
Equipment — UCC		10,000
Customer list — UCC		20,600
		$350,600
Liabilities		$ 45,000
Future income taxes		41,000
Common shares (PUC)		18,000
Capital dividend account (no unabsorbed negative amounts)		12,000
Other surplus		234,600
		$350,600

Additional Information

(1)

Assets	Cost	FMV
Accounts receivable	$ 60,000	$ 52,000
Inventory	$110,000	$127,000
Marketable securities	$ 26,000	$ 26,000
Land	$ 85,000	$150,000
Building	$ 66,000	$ 97,000
Equipment	$ 30,000	$ 6,000
Customer lists	$ 42,453	$ 70,000

The books of account do not reflect unrecorded goodwill with an estimated fair market value of $60,000. This is in addition to the customer lists.

The accounts receivable are to be sold to a factoring company.

Santosh is in the top personal tax bracket in 2018 and expects to be in that bracket in 2019 as well. After that he expects his retirement income to be approximately $100,000 per year.

The customer lists were purchased in 2013.

The provincial corporate tax rate for income eligible for the small business deduction is 4% and 12% for income above the small business deduction limit.

For the next meeting you agree that you will:

(A) Assess the situation.

(B) Identify the issues.

(C) Analyze the issues.

(D) Advise/recommend.

Problem 7

ITA: 54, 83(2), 84(2),
84(2.1), 89(1)

Ms. Bast owns all the common shares of Batterup Ltd., a Canadian-controlled private corporation, which started operations in 2005. Batterup Ltd. has been quite profitable in recent years. As a result, Three-Strikes Ltd., a Canadian public corporation, has offered Ms. Bast $252,500 for the assets, excluding cash, as at December 31, 2018. The offer price reflects unrecorded goodwill of $47,500. Ms. Bast wants to wind up the company after the sale of the assets.

The *pro forma* balance sheet of Batterup Ltd. as at December 31, 2018, is as follows:

Assets	Cost	UCC	FMV
Cash........................	$ 2,500		
Accounts receivable (net)	8,750		$ 7,500
Inventory	22,250		15,500
Land	11,000	—	45,000
Building	35,000	$ 7,500	95,000
Equipment	45,000	22,000	10,000
Marketable securities	14,250	—	32,000
	$138,750		$205,000
Liabilities			
Current liabilities	$ 54,000		
Future income taxes	5,000		
Shareholder's Equity			
Paid-up capital	10,000		
Capital dividend account........	4,000		
Retained earnings	65,750		
Total liabilities and equity........	$138,750		

Additional Information:

(1) Batterup Ltd. pays corporate tax at the overall rate of 14% on active business income eligible for the small business deduction, 27% on active business income not eligible for the small business deduction, and an initial 40% rate for investment income, plus the 10⅔% additional refundable tax on investment income. The corporation has a GRIP balance of nil.

(2) The reserve for doubtful accounts at December 31, 2018 was $1,500.

(3) Batterup Ltd. and Three-Strikes Ltd. elected under section 22.

You have agreed to do the following for Ms. Bast:

(A) Compute the amount available for distribution to the shareholder.

(B) Determine the components of the distribution to the shareholder.

¶15,875

(C) Compute the taxable capital gain or allowable capital loss on the disposition of Ms. Bast's shares on the winding-up. (Assume the adjusted cost base of Ms. Bast's common shares is $10,000.)

(D) Explain the conditions for and advantages of using a section 22 election.

Problem 8

ITA: 54, 83(2), 84(2), 88(2), 89(1)

You have been approached by Mr. Sidney Chow, a Canadian resident, for advice on the sale of his business. He would like to know whether he should keep his corporation after the sale. He wants to understand how much tax he will pay on the sale and how much he would have available to invest after the sale of the business.

He is considering an offer from a corporate purchaser who will buy the business assets from Chow Enterprises Ltd. (CEL) and continue the business. The purchase will take place on December 31 and the selling price of the assets will be their fair market value at that time (see information below).

Mr. Chow purchased all the common shares of CEL from the company on incorporation in 2005.

The following information on Chow Enterprises Ltd. has been prepared:

Chow Enterprises Ltd.
BALANCE SHEET
as at December 31, 2018

	Tax Value	FMV	Cost
Cash	$ 10,000	$ 10,000	
RDTOH	5,000	5,000	
Accounts receivable . . . . $ 30,000		18,000	
Less: reserve for doubtful debts . . . . (5,000)	25,000		
Land	55,000	150,000	$ 55,000
Building (Class 1) — UCC	95,000	320,000	170,000
Equipment (Class 8) — UCC	12,000	3,000	30,000
Goodwill (Class 14.1) — UCC	15,150	120,000	50,000
	$217,150	$626,000	
Liabilities	$ 35,000		
Future income taxes	12,000		
Common shares — PUC	20,000		
Capital dividend account	8,000		
Other surplus	142,150		
	$217,150		

Additional Information

(1) Goodwill was acquired in 2008 in connection with a similar business which was purchased that year. The fair market value reflects the goodwill for the combined businesses.

(2) The corporation has a GRIP balance of nil.

(3) Sidney is in the top personal tax bracket. Sidney is wondering if he should instead sell the shares of the corporation and wants to know what share price he should sell the shares for.

(4) The corporate tax rate for income eligible for the small business deduction is 4%. For income in excess of the small business limit the provincial tax rate is 12%.

For the next meeting you agree that you will:

(A) Assess the situation.

(B) Identify the issues.

(C) Analyze the issues.

(D) Advise/recommend.

Problem 9

ITA: 14, 38, 82, 83(2), 117, 121, 123, 124, 129

Mr. Waseem incorporated Luck Unlimited Limited in 2018 taking one share with a paid-up capital value of $1 and a note representing a loan to the company of $499,999. The company operates in a province with a 14% corporate tax rate on active business income eligible for the small business deduction, a 27% total corporate tax rate on other active business income, an initial 40% corporate tax rate on investment income before the 10⅔% additional refundable tax. Mr. Waseem has a 50% combined personal tax rate (including a 17% personal provincial tax on income rate). The company purchased the assets of a business in the same year for $500,000. The purchase price was allocated to the land and building of the business in the amount of $400,000 and to goodwill in the amount of $100,000. However, before the business had commenced, the company sold the assets of the business for $700,000, including $170,000 for goodwill.

Mr. Waseem has asked you to determine how much of the $700,000 received in the corporation he would retain if he removed all of this amount from the corporation. Assume that the sale of land and building was considered to result in a *capital gain*.

Problem 10

ITA: 54, 83(2), 84(2), 84(2.1), 89(1)

Ms. Debbie, the sole shareholder and president of Shining Limited, a CCPC, has been considering selling her common shares to Let's-Make-a-Deal Ltd., a CCPC. However, Ms. Debbie recalls reading somewhere that one should compare a share sale with an asset sale to determine which would result in higher after-tax cash flow.

Ms. Debbie provides you with the following information:

(1) The cost of Ms. Debbie's common shares in Shining Limited was $120,000.

(2) Shining Limited pays tax at the overall rate of 14% on the first $500,000 of active business income, 27% on additional active business income, and 40% on all other income, plus the 10⅔% additional refundable tax on investment income. The corporation has a GRIP balance of nil.

(3) Ms. Debbie's combined federal and provincial personal tax rate is 50%, including a personal provincial tax on income rate of 17%. The provincial dividend tax credit is ³/₁₁ of the 16% gross-up on dividends from the LRIP and ⁵/₁₁ of the gross-up on dividends from the GRIP.

(4) Financial information concerning Shining Limited on December 31, 2018 is as follows:

Assets	Book cost	UCC	FMV
Cash (required as working capital)	$ 23,000		
Marketable securities (required as working capital)	58,000		$ 54,000
Inventory	41,000		50,000
Land	154,000		210,000
Building (Note)	213,700	$195,000	440,000
Goodwill	Nil		85,000
	$489,700		$839,000

Liabilities	
Current liabilities	$ 43,000
Future income taxes	4,800
Paid-up capital	120,000
Capital dividend account	48,000
Retained earnings	273,900
	$489,700

(5) Shining Limited earned active business income of $50,000 during the year.

NOTE: The original cost of the building in Class 1 was $410,000. Book cost of $213,700 is net book value after accumulated amortization.

You have agreed to do the following analysis:

(A) If Ms. Debbie sells all of the assets, except cash, to Let's-Make-a-Deal Ltd., pays the outstanding liabilities, and then winds up Shining Limited, determine the net amount available for distribution to her, showing all computations.

(B) Determine the components of the distribution to Ms. Debbie.

(C) Determine the amount, including principal, Ms. Debbie would retain from this distribution.

(D) Determine a selling price for the Shining Limited shares that results in the same after-tax net cash retained as the net cash from sale of assets followed by a wind-up, as determined in Part (C). You will consider the payment of a capital dividend before the sale of shares. Also, assuming that the shares of Shining Limited are QSBCS at the time of their sale, you will consider the use of Ms. Debbie's capital gains deduction, none of which she has used before.

(E) Based on the indicated fair market value of the net assets, you will determine the maximum price a Canadian-controlled private corporation should be willing to pay for the shares of Shining Limited. You will assume that the CCPC pays tax at the low rate of 14% on all of its business income, that it uses an after-tax discount rate of 5%, and that it does not expect to sell the fixed assets of Shining Limited for a very long time. Also, you will assume that if the purchaser bought the assets, it would have to invest $23,000 in cash to meet working capital requirements.

Type 3 Problems

Problem 11

Glenda is considering the purchase of a family-run catering business, called Palace Catering Ltd. The corporation specializes in the planning, preparation, and hosting of professional dinners, parties, and activities. Although Glenda is qualified for operating and managing the business, there is a high probability that profits from operating this business will not begin for a couple of years. She is wondering if she should purchase the net assets from the corporation or 100% of the shares presently held by the vendor family. The corporation had a proven record of profits until two years ago, when the death of the chef, along with the retirement of two employees resulted in a loss of business. The accumulated non-capital loss carryforward is $84,000.

Glenda's plan for the new business is to carry on catering. She is also toying with the idea of producing dessert cakes for sale to hotels and restaurants. Over the next two years she expects she could make profits on the sale of cakes of $4,000 and then $18,000. Thereafter, she estimates profit from the cakes of about $25,000 annually.

Glenda plans to use an 8% small business loan to purchase the business. If there are any further operating losses she will use the proceeds from her bond investment to finance the business over the next few years. From January 1 to August 31 of the current year, Glenda earned $38,000 as senior hostess at the Professional Club in Saskatoon, and $12,000 in interest income.

Glenda would like your advice on what should be considered in deciding on a share purchase or an asset purchase.

Problem 12

It is now December 31, 2018. Recently, Mr. X received an offer from a U.S. multi-national to purchase his company, XYZ Limited. It is planned that the sale will close on March 1, 2019, the day after the corporation's normal year end. XYZ Limited is 100% owned by Mr. X and is a CCPC.

Prior to the sale, Mr. X would like to pay himself the maximum available capital dividend. The corporation previously paid out a capital dividend in the amount of $50,000 on March 31, 2015, after receiving a capital dividend of the same amount from a related corporation.

On February 1, 2018, it sold a licence with an unlimited life for $300,000. There was no cost associated with this licence.

The company has disposed of the following capital assets since its inception:

Date	Description	Cost	Proceeds
January 31, 2015	Land	$115,000	$ 175,000
February 14, 2015	Equipment	$ 15,000	$ 4,500
February 28, 2018	Securities	$ 31,500	$ 22,500

XYZ Limited has also accepted an offer to sell vacant land for $290,000. The transaction is expected to close on January 31, 2019. The original cost of the land was $485,000. The land is capital property.

Mr. X would like to ensure that the company pays out a taxable dividend sufficient to clear the balance in the company's refundable dividend tax on hand (RDTOH) account. During the tax year, XYZ Limited received $10,000 in dividends from taxable Canadian corporations (not connected corporations) and $15,500 in interest income. Mr. X is suspicious of foreign banks and, therefore, invested all of the company's surplus funds in Canada. XYZ Limited has always maintained a policy of declaring a bonus to reduce active business income to the small business deduction limit — $500,000 for 2018. Mr. X has determined Part I tax payable for the year to be $77,853.

— *REQUIRED*

Part A

Calculate the balance expected to be in the company's capital dividend account on February 28, 2019. Show all calculations. On what date should the company pay out the capital dividend? Explain.

Part B

Calculate XYZ Limited's RDTOH balance at the end of the year. (Assume the opening RDTOH balance is zero.) What is the taxable dividend that should be paid in order to reduce the RDTOH balance to nil?

CHAPTER 15 —
DISCUSSION NOTES FOR REVIEW QUESTIONS

(1) Debit: Cash $30,000
    Credit: Share capital $10,000
    Credit: Contributed surplus $20,000

(2) In these jurisdictions, the paid-up capital is the "stated capital" as determined by the directors of the corporation under corporations law. Generally, this stated capital will be the fair market value of the consideration for which the shares were issued. However, these statutes provide that, in connection with certain non-arm's length transactions, the corporation may establish an amount which is less than the consideration for which the shares were issued as the stated capital and such amount as so determined will then be the amount of PUC for tax purposes.

(3) In no par value jurisdictions, in certain non-arm's length situations, the stated capital (PUC) can be set at less than the fair market value of the consideration received by the corporation. In these situations, the PUC may be kept low to avoid certain penalty provisions of the Act. This will result in the redemption value of the shares being high to represent the value of the assets transferred and the PUC being low to avoid tax penalties or to benefit from a deemed dividend on redemption rather than a capital gain, if the tax on dividends is lower than the tax on an equal amount of capital gain. This ignores the capital gains exemption.

(4) The four basic components of the capital dividend account are:

(a) the non-taxable portion of net capital gains;

(b) capital dividends received from other corporations;

(c) proceeds from life insurance policies net of their adjusted cost base; and

(d) capital dividends paid, which reduce the account.

(5)

UCC balance (Class 14.1)	$6,000
LCP	(10,000)
Recapture	$(4,000)
Adjustment 25% of LCP (for eligible capital property acquired before 2017)	$2,500
Recapture	$(1,500)
Capital gain ($100,000 – $10,000)	90,000
Taxable capital gain	$45,000
Capital dividend account	$45,000

The $45,000 added to the CDA is one-half of the economic gain of $90,000 (i.e., ½($100,000 – $10,000)).

Class 14.1 includes goodwill. Property that was eligible capital property owned by the taxpayer on January 1, 2017, i.e., the customer list was transferred into Class 14.1 on that date.

(6) The $8,000 reduction in capital will not cause a deemed dividend. However, the extra $1,000 of payment will be a deemed dividend since it is considered to be a distribution out of taxable surplus.

ITA: 84(4)

(7) The three components of a distribution are:

(a) paid-up capital which is returned tax-free;

(b) a capital dividend to the extent of the capital dividend account and the election of a capital dividend; and

(c) a taxable dividend to the extent of the balance.

(8) On the winding-up of the corporation, subsection 13(21.2) does not apply. Therefore, the terminal loss will be allowed as a deduction to the corporation.

(9) The Act provides the definition of "proceeds of disposition" for purposes of the calculation of capital gain or loss. The proceeds do not include the deemed dividend on the winding-up distribution. Therefore, the proceeds are calculated as the amount distributed less the deemed dividend.

ITA: 88(2)

ITA: 83(2)

ITA: 69(5)(*d*)

ITA: 54
ITA: 84(2)

CHAPTER 15 — SOLUTIONS TO MULTIPLE CHOICE QUESTIONS

Question 1

(D) is false. Only taxable dividends paid are included in the computation of dividend refunds. ITA: 129(1)

(A) is true. ITA: 83(2)(b)

(B) is true. ITA: 83(2)

(C) is true. ITA: 89(1) "capital dividend account" (a)

Question 2

(D) is correct.

Redemption amount	$ 60,000
PUC	(10,000)
Dividend	$ 50,000

ITA: 84(3)

Redemption amount	$ 60,000
Dividend	(50,000)
Proceeds of disposition	$ 10,000
ACB	(20,000)
Capital loss	$(10,000)

ITA: 54

(A) is incorrect. This amount ignores the redemption deemed dividend. ITA: 84(3)

(B) is incorrect. This amount calculates the dividend using the cost as opposed to the PUC.

(C) is incorrect. The dividend has not been subtracted from the redemption amount to arrive at the proceeds of disposition.

Question 3

(B) is correct.

Funds available for distribution	$ 40,000
PUC	(2,000)
Deemed dividend	$ 38,000
Elected amount of capital dividend	(8,000)
Taxable dividend	$ 30,000

ITA: 84(3)

Funds available for distribution	$ 40,000
Deemed dividend	(38,000)
Proceeds of disposition	$ 2,000
ACB	(1,000)
Capital gain	$ 1,000

ITA: 54

(A) is incorrect. Only subsidiaries in which the parent company owns at least 90% of the shares can wind up on a tax-deferred basis.

(C) is incorrect. The capital dividend has been subtracted from the deemed dividend in the calculation of the proceeds.

(D) is incorrect. The ACB has been subtracted from the funds available to arrive at a $39,000 capital gain. The general winding-up rule and the deemed dividend on winding-up have been ignored. ITA: 84(2), 88(2)

Question 4

(C) $1,557,000 is correct.

	Deemed proceeds	Business income	Investment income	CDA	RDTOH
Opening balance		Nil	Nil	$ 10,000	$ 30,000
Cash	$ 45,000				
Land	850,000		$300,000	300,000	
Building	780,000	$200,000	200,000	200,000	
	$1,675,000		$500,000	$510,000	
Liabilities	$ (20,000)	× 14%	× 50⅔%		
Tax	(281,333)	$ 28,000	$253,333		$153,333
RDTOH	183,333				$183,333
	$1,557,000				

(A) $1,655,000 is incorrect. The tax and RDTOH have not been accounted for. Only the liabilities were deducted.

(B) $1,373,667 is incorrect. The RDTOH has been omitted.

(D) $1,858,333 is incorrect. The liabilities and the income tax have not been deducted in the computation of the amount available for distribution.

Question 5

(A) is correct. The total paid-up capital of the common shares is $25,000, ½ of which is attributable to Mr. C and ½ is attributable to Mr. B. The total paid-up capital of the common shares is

100 common shares issued to Mr. A $10,000
100 common shares issued to Mr. B 15,000

$25,000

(B) and (D) are incorrect. The total paid-up capital of the common shares is not $35,000. The sale by Mr. A to Mr. C for $20,000 does not affect the paid-up capital of the shares.

(C) is incorrect because the $25,000 total paid-up capital of the common shares is split equally among the shares and is not based on the issue price of the shares.

Question 6

(A) is correct. There will be a capital gain equal to the $1 million proceeds of disposition less an adjusted cost base of nil. This will result in a taxable capital gain of $500,000, an addition to the RDTOH of $153,335 and the non-taxable portion of the gain of $500,000 will be added to the capital dividend account.

ITA: 89(1) "capital dividend account" (c.2)

(B) and (C) are incorrect. The disposition of goodwill no longer results in business income unless there is recaptured depreciation in Class 14.1.

(D) is incorrect. The capital gains inclusion rate is 50%, not 75%.

CHAPTER 15

CHAPTER 15 — SOLUTIONS TO EXERCISES

Exercise 1

	A	B	C
Proceeds of disposition	$ 4,000	$ 1,000	$ 2,000
Less: adjusted cost base	(2,000)	(2,000)	(2,000)
selling expenses	(400)	(100)	(200)
Capital gain (loss)	$ 1,600	$(1,100)	$ (200)
Adjustment to CDA (½ × capital gain (loss))	$ 800	$ (550)	$ (100)

Exercise 2

(A) Net income for tax purposes	Property 1		Property 2	
Proceeds of disposition		$110,000		$ 11,000
Less: ACB	$75,000		$40,000	
selling costs	11,000	86,000	5,500	45,500
Capital gain (loss)		$ 24,000		$(34,500)
Taxable capital gain (allowable capital loss)		$ 12,000		$(17,250)
(B) Adjustment to CDA (½ × capital gain (loss))		$ 12,000		$(17,250)

Exercise 3

(A) Where Investment Limited redeems the preferred shares, Mr. Duong will have a deemed dividend equal to: ITA: 84(3)

Redemption amount	$60,000
Less: PUC (800 × $15)	12,000
Deemed dividend	$48,000 ITA: 84(3)

Mr. Duong will not have a capital gain on the transactions because the adjusted proceeds of disposition equals the ACB of shares as demonstrated below:

Proceeds of disposition	$60,000	
Less: Deemed dividend	48,000	ITA: 84(3)
Adjusted proceeds of disposition	$12,000	ITA: 54 "proceeds of disposition" (j)
Less: ACB (800 shares × $15)	12,000	
Capital gain	Nil	

(B) The dividend payment of $60,000 will be a taxable dividend unless Investment Limited makes an election to treat the cash dividend as a distribution from the capital dividend account. Where this election is made, the dividend will be tax-free to Mr. Duong.   ITA: 83(2)

(C) A non-dividend distribution to Mr. Duong in excess of the PUC of the preferred shares will result in a deemed dividend of $45,000 (i.e., $60,000 – $15,000). The ACB of the shares will be reduced by the non-taxed portion of the payment of $15,000. The PUC of the shares must be reduced by the $15,000 in this case to reflect the tax-free distribution of PUC If PUC is not reduced by $15,000 in this transaction, an additional $15,000 will be treated as a deemed dividend.   ITA: 84(4) ITA: 53(2)(a)(ii) ITA: 84(4)(a)

Exercise 4

(A) The amount of the stock dividend is $1.00 per share and must be grossed up and included in income of the shareholder. Thus, income would total $11.60 (1.16 × $1.00 × 10 shares). The dividend tax credit would be available on the $1.00 amount of the stock dividend or about $0.16 total (including provincial tax effect) per share. The adjusted cost base of the shares on the acquisition date would be $10.00 in total (i.e., $1.00 per share).

(B) The corporation will be deemed to have paid a dividend of $10.00 for determining its dividend refund and other amounts dependent on dividends paid.

(C)	Proceeds of disposition (10 shares @ $1,000 FMV)	$10,000	
	ACB (see (A), above)	(10)	
	Capital gain	$ 9,990	
	Taxable capital gain (eligible for capital gains deduction)	$ 4,995	
(D) (i)	Redemption amount (10 shares @ $1,000)	$10,000	
	PUC (10 shares @ $1.00)	(10)	
	Deemed dividend on redemption	$ 9,990	ITA: 84(3)
(ii)	Proceeds of disposition (above)	$10,000	
	Less: deemed dividend	(9,990)	ITA: 54 "proceeds of disposition" (*j*)
	Adjusted proceeds of disposition	$ 10	
	ACB	(10)	
	Capital gain	Nil	

Exercise 5

(a) This transaction would cause an immediate deemed dividend of $50 since the daughter could immediately retract the shares and receive $150 tax free whereas the price paid for the shares was only $100.   ITA: 84(1)

Deemed dividend		ITA: 84(1)
PUC increase	$150	
PUC decrease	(Nil)	
	$150	
Increase in net assets	(100)	
Deemed dividend	$ 50	ITA: 84(1)

This $50 deemed dividend would be added to the ACB of the preferred shares acquired by the daughter.

In addition, there would be a subsection 84(3) deemed dividend on the ultimate redemption of the preferred shares as calculated below:

Redemption of shares			
Redemption amount		$1,000	
PUC — Special share		(150)	
Deemed dividend on redemption		$ 850	ITA: 84(3)
Proceeds of disposition		$1,000	
Less: deemed dividend		850	ITA: 54 "proceeds of disposition" (*j*)
Adjusted P of D		$ 150	
ACB			
— original cost	$100		
— ssec. 84(1) deemed dividend	50	(150)	ITA: 53(1)(*b*)
Capital gain		Nil	
Economic consequences			
Redemption amount		$1,000	
Actual price paid		(100)	
Economic gain on redemption		$ 900	

Tax results:

Deemed dividend	$ 50	ITA: 84(1)
Deemed dividend	850	ITA: 84(3)
Total gain taxed ($1,000 – $100)	$ 900	

(b) As long as there is no capital gain or loss triggered on the transfer, the gift of land to the corporation should have no other immediate tax consequences. The accounting and tax records would show an increased balance in the contributed surplus account. However, the withdrawal of this contributed surplus can only be in the form of taxable dividend subject to the gross-up and tax credit mechanism. However, the Act permits the capitalization of the contributed surplus into PUC as long as the amount did not arise under one of the corporate tax-free rollover provisions, discussed in the next few chapters.

ITA: 84(1)(*c*.3)

(c) Y has received $2,000 more in consideration than the cancelled debt (i.e., $2,000 + $20,000 versus $20,000); therefore, Y will have an income inclusion of:

PUC increase	$2,000	
Net asset increase ($20,000 – $20,000)	Nil	
Deemed dividend	$2,000	ITA: 84(1)

The cost of the shares is nil since the $20,000 cash cancelled the debt; however, there will be an increase in ACB equal to the deemed dividend of $2,000.

ITA: 53(1)(*b*)

(d) (i) Since the payment of $5,000 is less than the PUC of the outstanding share(s) (i.e., $10,000), there are no immediate tax consequences because this payment is a return of the original investment in the corporation with tax-paid funds. However, the adjusted cost base of the shares is reduced to $15,000 (i.e., $20,000 – $5,000) by the amount of the return of capital which would result in a potential higher capital gain on the ultimate disposition of the shares.

ITA: 53(2)(*a*)(ii)

Deemed dividend		ITA: 84(1)
PUC before distribution	$10,000	
PUC after distribution	(5,000)	
PUC decrease (not an increase)	$ 5,000	
Adjusted cost base		
ACB prior to distribution	$20,000	
Distribution amount	(5,000)	
New ACB	$15,000	

(ii) Since the payment of $18,000 exceeds the PUC of the outstanding share(s), there will be a deemed dividend of $8,000. However, the ACB of the share(s) will only be reduced by the non-taxed portion of the payment to $10,000.

ITA: 84(4)

Exercise 6

(A)	Funds available for distribution to shareholder	$1,000,000	
	Less: paid-up capital	(625,000)	
	Deemed dividend on winding-up	$ 375,000	ITA: 84(2)
	Less: capital dividend elected	(150,000)	ITA: 83(2), 88(2)(*b*)(i)
	Taxable dividend (sufficient to clear RDTOH)	$ 225,000	
(B)	Taxable capital gain (allowable capital loss) to Mr. Siewert:		
	Proceeds on winding-up	$1,000,000	
	Less: deemed dividend	(375,000)	ITA: 54 "proceeds of disposition" (*j*)
	Proceeds of disposition	$ 625,000	
	ACB	(350,000)	
	Capital gain	$ 275,000	
	Taxable capital gain (½)	$ 137,500	

Exercise 7

Funds available for distribution	$30,000	
Less: paid-up capital	(2,000)	
Deemed dividend or winding-up	$28,000	ITA: 84(2)
Less: capital dividend elected	(2,000)	ITA: 83(2), 88(2)(b)(i)
Deemed taxable dividend	$26,000	

Capital gain or loss on disposition of shares:

Actual proceeds from distribution	$30,000	
Less: deemed dividend	(28,000)	ITA: 54 "proceeds of disposition" (j)
Proceeds of disposition	$ 2,000	
Cost	(2,000)	
Capital gain (loss)	Nil	
Taxable capital gain	Nil	

Net cash retained:

Funds distributed		$30,000
Tax on incremental income from distribution:		
Deemed taxable dividend	$26,000	
Gross-up (16% × $26,000)	4,160	
Taxable capital gain	Nil	
Incremental taxable income	$30,160	
Combined federal and provincial tax @ 50%	$15,080	
Less: combined dividend tax credit in province @ (⁸/₁₁ + ³/₁₁) × .16 × $26,000	(4,160)	10,920
Net cash retained		$19,080

Exercise 8

(A)

	Proceeds	Income Bus.	Income Invest.	C.D. a/c	RDTOH
Opening balances		Nil	Nil	Nil	$ 10,000
Cash	$ 20,000	Nil	Nil		
Inventories	220,000	$ 20,000	Nil		
Land[(1)]	70,000	Nil	$ 15,000	$15,000	
Buildings[(2)]	300,000	140,000	50,000	50,000	
Equipment[(3)]	80,000	40,000	Nil		
Liabilities	(50,000)				
Income taxes[(5)]	(60,933)	$200,000[(4)]	$ 65,000		19,933
RDTOH[(6)]	29,933				$ 29,933
	$605,000			$65,000	

CHAPTER 15

(B) Funds available for distribution to shareholder $605,000

Less: paid-up capital 2,000

Deemed dividend on winding-up . . . . $603,000   ITA: 84(2)

Less: capital dividend elected 65,000   ITA: 83(2)

Deemed taxable dividend (clears RDTOH) $538,000

(C) Taxable capital gain to Mr. Warren

Actual proceeds on winding-up $605,000

Less: deemed dividend 603,000

Proceeds of disposition . . . . $ 2,000

Cost . . . . (1,000)

Capital gain . . . . $ 1,000

Taxable capital gain (½ × $1,000) . . . . $ 500

(D) Where a corporation is wound up and the general winding-up rules of the Act apply, the supply of property on the wind-up is subject to HST. HST is payable on any taxable supplies of property. However, an election may be available, in which case the payment of HST is not required. In order to qualify, a registrant must have sold or transferred all or substantially all of the assets used in a commercial activity that is part of a business carried on. Since Dwight Ltd. is being wound up by Mr. Warren it would qualify for this election.   ITA: 88(2)   ETA: 167(1)

— *NOTES TO SOLUTION*

(1) Proceeds on sale of land . . . . $ 70,000

Cost . . . . (40,000)

Capital gain . . . . $ 30,000

Taxable capital gain (½ × $30K) (investment income) . . . . $ 15,000

Capital dividend account (½ × $30K) . . . . $ 15,000

(2) Actual proceeds on sale of building $300,000

UCC . . . . (60,000)

Gain $240,000

Recapture ($200K – $60K) (business income) $140,000

Taxable capital gain (½ × ($300K – $200K)) (investment income) . . . . . . $ 50,000

Capital dividend account (½ × ($300K – $200K)) . . . . $ 50,000

(3) Actual proceeds on sale of equipment . . . . $ 80,000

UCC . . . . (40,000)

Gain . . . . $ 40,000

Recapture ($80K – $40K) — fully accounts for gain (business income) . . . . $ 40,000

(4) The $500,000 business limit for the small business deduction must be prorated for the number of days in the taxation year. Since the winding-up may take some time to complete, this solution assumes that the corporation maintains its eligibility for the small business deduction in the year in which the sale of assets occurs. In this case, there would be no need to bonus down to the business limit for the small business deduction, given active business income of $200,000.   IT-73R6, par. 9

(5) Income taxes

14% × ABI ($200,000) $28,000

50⅔% × investment income ($65,000) . . . . 32,933 $ 60,933

RDTOH (30⅔% of $65,000) . . . . $ 19,933

(6) Assumes a minimum $78,087 (i.e., 29,933/38⅓%) is to be distributed as a taxable dividend to produce a refund of the full RDTOH.

Exercise 9

Capital dividend account:

	1	2	3
P of D	$ 8,000	$ 2,000	$ 4,000
Less: ACB	$(4,000)	$(4,000)	$(4,000)
Selling costs	$ (700)	$ (100)	$ (300)
Capital gain (loss)	$ 3,300	$(2,100)	$ (300)
Adjustment to capital dividend account ($\frac{1}{2} \times$ capital gain (loss))	$ 1,650	$(1,050)	$ (150)

Chapter 16

Income Deferral: Rollover on Transfers to a Corporation and Pitfalls

Learning Goals

Know

By the end of this chapter you will know:

- The basic provisions of the *Income Tax Act* that relate to the transfer of property to a corporation on a tax-deferred basis.

- The basic provisions of the *Income Tax Act* that relate to the transfer of shares of a corporation in both non-arm's length and arm's length transactions.

Understand and Explain

By the end of this chapter you will understand and be able to explain:

- The basic tax consequences of the transfer of property to a corporation by a shareholder on a rollover basis.

- The means that a corporation can use to pay for the property transferred.

- Potential traps or pitfalls on the transfer of shares to a corporation.

Apply

By the end of this chapter you will be able to apply your knowledge and understanding to:

- Calculate the tax consequences of the transfer of property to a corporation on a rollover basis.

- Use the rollover tools to accomplish a taxpayer's objectives.

Review Questions
¶16,800 in the Study Guide

Multiple Choice Questions
¶16,825 in the Study Guide

Exercises
¶16,850 in the Study Guide

Assignment Problems
¶16,875 in the Study Guide

CHAPTER 16 — LEARNING CHART

Problem Descriptions

Textbook Example Problems

16-1	Elected amounts — 85(1)
16-2	Consideration received — 85(1)
16-3	PUC of shares received — 85(1)
16-4	Comprehensive — 85(1)
16-5	Non-arm's length sale of shares

Multiple Choice Questions

1	Sale of depreciable asset to a corporation
2	Non-share consideration
3	Capital cost of asset to corporation
4	ACB of share consideration
5	Section 22
6	Non-share consideration

Exercises

1	Elected amount, income, non-share consideration
2	Cost and PUC of consideration
3	Comprehensive 85(1)
4	Gifting
5	Transfer of depreciable property
6	Comprehensive 85(1)
7	Transfer of depreciable property
8	Non-arm's length sale of shares
9	Non-arm's length sale of shares
10	Sale of shares by a corporation
11	Section 85: Transfer of land and building to a corp.
12	Section 85: Transfer of a business to a corp.
13	Section 84.1
14	Section 55(2)
15	Section 84.1
16	Section 55(2)

Assignment Problems

1	Section 85 elected amounts
2	Transfer of assets to a corporation
3	Transfer of assets to a corporation
4	Transfer of assets to a corporation, sale or redeem shares
5	Transfer of assets to a corporation
6	Transfer of assets to a corporation, gifting
7	Transfer of assets to a corporation
8	Estate freeze
9	Sale of shares by corporation

Study Notes

¶16,800   REVIEW QUESTIONS

(1) In tax terms, what does the word "rollover" mean and how does it impact on both the transferor and the transferee?

(2) Della Inc. is a corporation that was incorporated in Delaware, U.S.A., in 1965 and has been resident in Canada since 1974 when its sole shareholder, Mr. Della, moved to Canada. During this year, Mr. Della wanted to transfer some land and a building, that was capital property to him, to Della Inc. for use in the business. He did transfer the property to the corporation and used section 85 to defer the accrued gain. Comment on whether there is any technicality that would not allow him to use section 85.

(3) When using section 85, the elected price is very important since it is used in the determination of four things that arise on the transfer. What are they?

(4) Since the tax value and the fair market value are usually fixed, what is the one decision variable that you can use that will have an effect on the limits of the elected transfer price range?

(5) When using section 85, what is the maximum amount of boot that should be taken in order to maximize the deferral?

(6) Ms. Smith heard at a party last night that she can avoid the "half-year rule" for CCA by first purchasing the equipment personally and then selling it shortly thereafter to her corporation and electing under section 85. She thinks that the corporation will then be able to claim the full CCA in the first year instead of only one half. What do you think and why?   ITR: 1100(2)

(7) How is the cost of the consideration taken back by the transferor in a section 85 transfer determined?

(8) Bar Ltd., a CCPC, owns shares in Lite Ltd., a small business corporation, that have gone down in value. Bar Ltd.'s problem is that it cannot sell the shares because there is no market. Bar Ltd. then decides that it will sell the shares to a company owned by the wife of the sole shareholder of Bar Ltd., called Spouse Ltd., claim an ABIL and at least be able to withdraw from Spouse Ltd. the fair market value of the shares of Lite Ltd. Bar Ltd. does not own any shares in Spouse Ltd. Since there is no gain to defer, they will not elect under section 85. Comment on this strategy.

(9) Using section 85, what is the amount that determines how much the transferor can withdraw from the company on a tax-free basis?

(10) Ms. Smith has decided to transfer some portfolio shares to her wholly owned company in exchange for more shares of the company. The shares have a cost of $5,000 and a fair market value of $8,000. She plans to elect at $8,000 and take back shares with a PUC and redemption amount of $10,000. What are the tax consequences to Ms. Smith and her company?

(11) If the optimal value of the boot is equal to the tax value of the property transferred under section 85, what will the ACB and PUC of the shares taken back be?

(12) Given that FMV is often not easily arrived at when transferring assets under section 85, what protection can you use to avoid a one-sided adjustment by the CRA if their value is different than yours?

(13) What is the purpose behind section 84.1?

(14) Mr. Blythe got a good deal a few years ago on the shares of a company that he just bought. He paid $10,000 for the shares even though the PUC of the shares is $100,000. Today the company is worth $100,000 again thanks to his hard work. Mr. Blythe has never used his QSBC share capital gains exemption. How can he get money out of the company without paying any personal tax?

¶16,825   MULTIPLE CHOICE QUESTIONS

Question 1

Pauline plans to sell a depreciable asset to a corporation owned by her husband. The characteristics of the assets are as follows:

FMV	$3,000
Capital cost	2,200
UCC	800

Which *one* of the following statements is *true*?

(A) The gain will be deferred due to the spousal rollover since the corporation is owned by Pauline's husband.

(B) Pauline should file a section 85 election and elect at $2,200 to defer the tax on the sale.

(C) Pauline should file a section 85 election and elect at $800 to defer the tax on the sale.

(D) If a section 85 election is not made, the capital cost and UCC of the asset to the corporation will be $3,000.

Question 2

Steve plans to sell a non-depreciable asset that has a mortgage of $15,000 to S Ltd. S Ltd. is a taxable Canadian corporation. Steve owns all the shares. Steve and S Ltd. will file an election under section 85. S Ltd. will assume the mortgage. For proceeds, Steve would like to receive a non-interest bearing note for the maximum amount possible without incurring adverse tax consequences. The balance of the consideration will be in shares of S Ltd. Steve considers any tax incurred an adverse consequence. The asset has the following characteristics:

FMV	$100,000
ACB	40,000

What is the maximum amount of the note that Steve should take?

(A) $100,000

(B) $85,000

(C) $40,000

(D) $25,000

Question 3

Susan sold a Class 1 depreciable asset to a corporation that she controls in exchange for a non-interest bearing demand loan of $100,000 and preferred shares redeemable for $80,000 in total. Susan and the corporation filed a section 85 election electing for the transfer to take place at $120,000. The characteristics of the asset were as follows:

FMV	$180,000
Capital cost	100,000
ACB	100,000
UCC	75,000

The capital cost of the asset to the corporation is:

(A) $120,000

(B) $110,000

(C) $90,000

(D) $75,000

CHAPTER 16

Question 4

Sylvia is the sole shareholder of Strained Ltd., a taxable Canadian corporation. Sylvia transferred a non-depreciable capital property having an adjusted cost base of $40,000 and a fair market value of $50,000 to Strained Ltd. in exchange for the following package of consideration.

Cash	$ 3,000
Debt	2,000
Preferred shares (FMV and legal stated capital)	15,000
Common shares (FMV and legal stated capital)	30,000
	$50,000

Sylvia and Strained Ltd. made a joint election under section 85, electing a transfer price of $40,000.

The cost to Sylvia of the common shares received as consideration is:

(A) $35,000

(B) $23,000

(C) $23,333

(D) $20,000

Question 5

Which one of the following is an advantage for a vendor and purchaser using a section 22 election to transfer accounts receivable rather than electing under section 85?

(A) The vendor will realize a loss that may be a superficial loss.

(B) The vendor will realize a loss that is a capital loss.

(C) The vendor will not be required to add the prior year's doubtful debts reserve to income.

(D) The purchaser will be able to take a doubtful debts reserve on the accounts receivable.

Question 6

Rebecca transfers land to R Co and makes a joint election with R Co under section 85 of the *Income Tax Act* in the amount of $50,000. The land has a cost of $50,000 and a fair market of $210,000. Rebecca takes back a demand promissory note of $60,000 and redeemable, retractable preference shares worth $150,000 in value. The tax consequences of this transaction are that:

(A) Rebecca is deemed to dispose of the land for proceeds of $50,000.

(B) R Co.'s cost of the land is $50,000.

(C) Rebecca's cost of the preference shares is $150,000.

(D) R Co.'s cost of the land is $60,000.

¶16,850   EXERCISES

Exercise 1

ITA: 85(1), 85(5.1)

Consider the following cases involving the transfer of capital assets to a corporation for consideration including both common shares and boot.

	A	B	C	D	E	F	G
Fair market value	$120	$100	$ 80	$100	$110	$100	$ 80
Adjusted cost base	N/A	75	N/A	75	N/A	75	N/A
Capital cost	100	N/A	100	N/A	100	N/A	100
UCC of class	200	N/A	50	N/A	150	N/A	50
FMV of class	170	N/A	110	N/A	140	N/A	110
Boot	150	200	80	50	80	90	20

— REQUIRED

(A) Compute the minimum elected amount possible given these data.

(B) Compute the effects on income given these data.

(C) Indicate the maximum boot that should be taken in each case to maximize the deferral of taxation.

Exercise 2

ITA: 85(1), 85(2.1)

Dee transferred capital property to Dee Ltd. The capital property had an adjusted cost base of $5,000 and a fair market value of $10,000. Dee could receive any of the following packages of consideration:

	A	B	C
Notes at fair market value	$5,000	$2,500	$4,000
Preferred shares at fair market value and LSC	4,500	7,500	—
Common shares (LSC)	500	—	6,000

— REQUIRED

(A) Given an elected amount of $5,000, what would be the cost of each item of consideration under each possible package of consideration?

(B) What will be the PUC for tax purposes under each possible package of consideration?

Exercise 3

ITA: 13(7)(*e*), 84(3), 85(1), 85(2.1), 110.6

Last year Mr. Good, age 50, purchased a business location including land for $150,000 and a brick building for $436,224. He operated the business as a sole proprietorship for a year taking maximum capital cost allowance on the building. On your advice, this year he incorporated the business using section 85 to transfer the land and building to the corporation without triggering any of the gain that had accrued on these assets during the year. The following is a summary of the transfer under section 85.

	Tax value	Appraised FMV	Elected amount	Consideration Assumed mortgage	New debt	Common shares
Land	$150,000	$375,000	$150,000	$150,000	—	$225,000
Building (UCC)	427,500	525,000	427,500	97,500	$330,000	97,500
	$577,500	$900,000	$577,500	$247,500	$330,000	$322,500

CHAPTER 16

— *REQUIRED*

(A) What are the tax consequences of electing a transfer price of $577,500 as indicated?

(B) (i) Compute the cost of the consideration received from the corporation.

   (ii) Compute the PUC for tax purposes of the common shares.

(C) (i) What are the tax consequences to Mr. Good if the corporation redeems the debt issued by the corporation for $330,000 and he sells his shares in the corporation for $425,000?

   (ii) What are the tax consequences to Mr. Good if the corporation redeems the common shares for $425,000?

Exercise 4

ITA: 85(1)(*e*.2), 85(2.1)

Mother owned some debt securities which she transferred to a corporation in which Daughter (age 29) owns all of the common shares. These securities cost Mother $100,000 and had a fair market value at the time of transfer of $125,000. Section 85 was used to transfer the securities at an elected amount of $100,000. As consideration for the securities transferred, Mother received a note having a value of $100,000 and a preferred share having a fair market value and an LSC of $1,000.

— *REQUIRED*

What are the tax consequences of this transaction and how could they have been avoided?

Exercise 5

ITA: 85(1)(*e*.1), 85(2.1)

Ron Roberts, who owns 100% of Rollover Ltd., has come to you concerning transferring some additional assets to the corporation. The following facts relate to the transfer:

Asset #1
Capital cost $10,000
Undepreciated capital cost   5,000
Fair market value   20,000
Asset #2
Adjusted cost base . . . . $ 8,000
Fair market value   14,000

Ron wishes to take back one no par value common share and $18,000 cash.

— *REQUIRED*

Discuss the tax implications of the proposed transaction.

Exercise 6

ITA: 22, 85

Mrs. Designer has provided you with the following balance sheet and additional information relative to her unincorporated ladies' fashion business.

Mrs. Designer

(A Proprietorship)

BALANCE SHEET

May 31, 2018

Cash		$ 4,000	Accounts payable		$ 14,000
Short-term investments		10,000	Mortgage payable		
Accounts receivable	$ 12,000		(current maturity) . . .		6,000
Allowance for doubtful					$ 20,000
accounts	(2,000)	10,000			
Inventory		5,000			
Prepaid insurance		500			
		$ 29,500			
Building cost	$ 80,000		Mortgage payable	$ 60,000	
Accumulated			Current portion	(6,000)	$ 54,000
depreciation	(18,000)	$ 62,000	Proprietor's equity		47,500
Land, cost		30,000			$101,500
		$ 92,000			$121,500
		$121,500			

¶16,850

Additional Information

(1) Income for tax and financial accounting purposes have always been the same.

(2) The UCC of the building is equal to the net book value of $62,000.

(3) The proprietorship began to carry on business about seven years ago.

(4) The May 31, 2018 fair market value of various assets owned by the proprietorship are:

Short-term investments	$ 5,000
Accounts receivable	9,000
Inventory	25,000
Prepaid insurance	400
Building	60,000
Land	26,500
Goodwill	44,000

Effective June 1, 2018, Mrs. Designer wants to transfer her business assets to a corporation (Hi-Fashion Co. Ltd.) in which her husband owns 100% of the common shares.

She has indicated that, provided the company assumes the business debts, she would receive the balance in debt and preferred shares (stated value $100) as full consideration.

— REQUIRED

(A) Determine which assets should not be transferred to the corporation under section 85 and those that should not be transferred at all and give reasons.

(B) Determine the amounts to be elected on the various assets to avoid any taxes.

(C) Determine the consideration to be received without any tax consequences.

(D) Determine the adjusted cost base of the consideration in part (C), above.

(E) Determine the tax PUC of the preferred shares received.

(F) Determine the cost/capital cost of the transferred assets for the corporation, Hi-Fashion Co. Ltd.

Exercise 7

ITA: 13(7)(*e*), 85(1), 85(2.1), 110.6

In 2018, Ms. Kvetch transferred a depreciable capital property (the only one in its class) to a corporation which she controls. The property had an undepreciated capital cost of $27,000, a capital cost of $30,000 and a fair market value of $100,000. She elected to transfer the property under section 85 at $80,000 in order to offset the resultant taxable capital gain with a net capital loss of $25,000. As consideration for the property, she received a note for $80,000 and common shares with a stated value of $20,000.

— REQUIRED

What are the income tax implications of this transaction?

CHAPTER 16

Exercise 8

ITA: 84(3), 84.1, 85

Mr. Newberry, age 45 and a Canadian resident, owned all of the common shares with a paid-up capital value and cost of $75,000 in an operating company, Opco Ltd. Mr. Newberry started Opco Ltd. in 1999 and has been actively involved in operating the business since inception. He transferred these shares under section 85 to a company, Broco Ltd., owned by his brother at a time when the value of the Opco Ltd. shares was $800,000. As consideration for the shares transferred he received a note with a principal amount of $500,000 and non-voting preferred shares with a paid-up capital and fair market value of $300,000 such that an elected amount of $500,000 was possible under section 85. Mr. Newberry offset all of the resultant $425,000 of capital gain with his available QSBC share capital gains exemption. Both Opco Ltd. and Broco Ltd. are Canadian-controlled private corporations.

— *REQUIRED*

(A) What are the tax consequences of the transfer to Mr. Newberry?

(B) What are the tax consequences if the preferred shares received from his brother's corporation are redeemed by that corporation for their fair market value?

(C) What are the tax consequences if the preferred shares are sold in an arm's length transaction for their fair market value?

Exercise 9

ITA: 54, 84(3), 84.1

Ms. Erin, age 30, owns all of the common shares of Davpet Ltd. She has owned the shares since she incorporated the business in 2014. The shares have a PUC and cost of $1,000. Their current fair market value is $300,000. The shares are qualified small business corporation shares and she is anxious to crystallize her capital gains exemption on the accrued gain in these shares. Her father owns all of the common shares of Lenmeag Ltd., a Canadian-controlled private corporation, and is willing to use that corporation to assist her in her plans.

— *REQUIRED*

(A) Determine the immediate tax consequences, if Ms. Erin sells her common shares in Davpet Ltd. to Lenmeag Ltd. for their fair market value, receiving a $300,000 note from Lenmeag Ltd. which will ultimately be repaid in cash. Her father will allow her to continue to manage Davpet Ltd. and she will ultimately inherit the shares of Lenmeag Ltd. to reacquire control of Davpet Ltd.

(B) Determine the tax consequences, alternatively, if she sells her shares of Davpet Ltd. to Lenmeag Ltd. for their fair market value of $300,000, receiving $300,000 of the common shares of Lenmeag Ltd. No section 85 election is made.

Exercise 10

ITA: 55(1)–(6)

Vendco Ltd. owns all of the shares of Preyco Ltd. The shares of Preyco have a total adjusted cost base of $100,000 and a fair market value of $1,000,000. Since its incorporation in 1994, Preyco has realized and retained $700,000 of income and has no refundable taxes.

Vendco wishes to sell its shares in Preyco to Purchco. It causes Preyco to borrow $900,000 from the bank and to pay a dividend on its shares of $900,000. This reduces the fair market value of Preyco's shares to $100,000 and Purchco buys the shares for this amount.

— *REQUIRED*

What are the tax consequences of these transactions?

Exercise 11

Mr. Kelly, a resident of Canada, has come to you for advice concerning the transfer of assets to a newly incorporated corporation, to be wholly owned by him.

The transfer took place on October 31, 2018. The assets transferred were as follows:

(i) land purchased by him in 2005 for $240,000 which had appreciated in value to $370,000 as at October 31, 2018, and

(ii) a building purchased by him in 2005 for $190,000, which was worth $280,000 as at October 1, 2018. The undepreciated capital cost of the building as at October 31, 2018 was $160,000.

Mr. Kelly and the corporation filed a joint election pursuant to s. 85 of the *Income Tax Act*, electing to transfer the land at $340,000 and the building at $160,000. The election form indicated that the consideration received by Mr. Kelly consisted of common shares that provide Mr. Kelly with control of the corporation and with a fair market value of $150,000 and $500,000 cash.

— *REQUIRED*

(a) What are the income tax consequences of electing at the transfer prices indicated for the land and the building?

(b) Compute the cost for income tax purposes of the shares received from the corporation.

(c) Compute the PUC for income tax purposes of the shares received.

(d) What are the income tax consequences to Mr. Kelly if:

(i) the corporation redeems the shares for $150,000?

(ii) Mr. Kelly sells the shares for $150,000?

Exercise 12

Beamen Laiken Retail Emporium has been operated as a sole proprietorship since 1975. The following are the balance sheet items for the retailing operations as at August 31, 2018, its fiscal year end:

	Tax value	Fair market value
Cash	$ 4,000	$ 4,000
Marketable securities	23,000	15,000
Accounts receivable (net of $5,000 reserve)	32,000	35,000
Inventory	75,000	72,000
Prepaid expenses	2,000	2,000
Land at cost	60,000	135,000
Building, at UCC (capital cost: $150,000)	90,000	180,000
Fixtures, at UCC (capital cost: $113,000)	68,000	30,000
Intangible assets (Class 14.1) (cost: $25,000)	6,000	24,000
	360,000	497,000

Beamen wishes to incorporate this business and have the corporation assume $65,000 in liabilities of the business. He will be the only shareholder of the corporation.

— *REQUIRED*

(a) Indicate, with a brief explanation:

(i) which assets cannot or should not be transferred to the corporation under ssec. 85(1), and

(ii) which assets should not be transferred at all to the corporation.

(b) Determine the amounts to be elected on the various assets to avoid any taxes.

(c) Determine the consideration (rounded to the nearest $100) to be received without any tax consequences.

(d) Determine the adjusted cost base of the consideration received.

(e) Determine the tax PUC of the shares received.

Exercise 13

Ms. Hollymar, age 55, owned common shares in an operating company, Hollymar Ltd. The shares had a cost and paid-up capital value of $1,000 in 2007 when she incorporated the company. At the present time they are valued at $65,000. In order to crystallize $50,000 of her capital gains exemption, she incorporated a holding company, MH Holdings Ltd., and transferred her common shares in Hollymar Ltd. to MH Holdings Ltd., electing at $51,000 under s. 85(1). As consideration, Ms. Hollymar received a note for $51,000 and common shares valued at $14,000 from MH Holdings Ltd. The shares of Hollymar Ltd. are QSBC shares.

— *REQUIRED*

Determine the immediate tax consequences of the transfer.

Exercise 14

Sell Ltd., a CCPC, owns 100% of the shares of Target Ltd. (a CCPC). The shares of Target Ltd. have appreciated greatly in value since Target Ltd. was incorporated by Sell Ltd. A large part of the share appreciation is attributed to land that has tripled in value since Target Ltd. acquired it.

An arm's length company, Acquisition Corporation, has offered to purchase 100% of the shares of Target Ltd. from Sell Ltd. for a purchase price equal to fair market value.

In the course of these acquisition discussions, Sell Ltd. causes Target Ltd. to pay Sell Ltd. a dividend equal to the accrued capital gain on Target Ltd.'s shares.

Acquisition Ltd. then buys 100% of the Target Ltd. shares for a price equal to Sell Ltd.'s adjusted cost base of the Target Ltd. shares.

— *REQUIRED*

Part A   What tax advantage was Sell Ltd. attempting to realize by causing Target Ltd. to pay the dividend?

Part B   Explain how ss. 55(2) could act to minimize the tax advantages of the above transactions and what additional information you would require to determine the tax consequences to Sell Ltd. resulting from the above series of transactions?

Exercise 15

Mr. Expandit, age 60, is a retailer who incorporated his business in 1981 under the name of Expandit Ltd. The common shares of Expandit Ltd., held by Mr. Expandit, have a paid-up capital value and cost of $2,500 and were issued to Mr. Expandit on incorporation in 1988. The present fair market value of the shares is $4,000,000.

Mr. Expandit wishes to incorporate a holding company, Holdexpanditco Ltd., for estate planning purposes. His daughter, age 34, will invest $45,000 of her own money in 500 common shares with a total stated value of $10. His wife will invest $12,500 of her own money in 7% voting preferred shares with a total stated value of $100. He will take back as partial consideration for his shares of Expandit Ltd. 3,500 voting, retractable 6% preferred shares with a total stated value of $100 and a total retraction value of $3,500,000. In addition, he will take back $500,000 in cash. He will elect with the corporation to transfer his shares of Expandit Ltd. at $500,000 to use up the remainder of his capital gains exemption.

— *REQUIRED*

(A) Outline the tax consequences of Mr. Expandits plan supported by your computations assuming:

    (i) an ultimate redemption of the 6% preferred shares at their fair market value; and

    (ii) an arm's length sale of the 6% preferred shares.

(B) Indicate briefly your recommendations as to how Mr. Expandit might rearrange his plan to avoid any problems arising from the plan presented.

Exercise 16

Flogit Ltd. is a Canadian-controlled private corporation that owns all of the shares of Unloaded Ltd., another Canadian-controlled private corporation. The following data pertain to the shares and surpluses of Unloaded Ltd:

PUC of shares	$ 60,000
ACB of shares to Flogit Ltd.	85,000
FMV of shares	875,000
Retained income earned after 1971	225,000

— *REQUIRED*

Determine the tax consequences in each of the following situations:

(A) Unloaded Ltd. pays a dividend of $225,000 to Flogit Ltd., which in turn sells the shares, then valued at $650,000, to Buyem Ltd.

(B) Unloaded Ltd. pays a dividend of $790,000 to Flogit Ltd., which in turn sells the shares, then valued at $85,000, to Buyem Ltd.

(C) Buyem Ltd. subscribes for all of a newly created class of shares in Unloaded Ltd. for $875,000. Unloaded Ltd. then redeems the old shares owned by Flogit Ltd. for their fair market value of $875,000.

¶16,875 ASSIGNMENT PROBLEMS

Type 2 Problems

Problem 1   ITA: 85(1)

The following assets are to be transferred under section 85 for consideration including common shares plus boot as indicated below.

	Fair market value	*ACB/ Capital cost*	*UCC*
Land	$ 75,000	$60,000	—
Marketable securities	65,000	55,000	—
Building*	95,000	85,000	$70,000
Equipment	50,000	65,000	40,000
Furniture and fixtures	10,000	15,000	7,000
Licence**	100,000	82,500	60,000

* Only asset in class.

** Indefinite life.

For each of the assets transferred:

A. Assess whether they qualify for transfer under section 85.

B. Determine the minimum possible elected amounts.

C. Compute the effects on income.

D. Indicate the maximum non-share consideration (boot) that can be taken and not create any income.

E. Determine what would happen if the non-share consideration on the land was $70,000 and on the equipment was $45,000.

Use the following format:

				Consideration		
Asset	Tax Value	FMV	Elected Amt	New Debt	Pref Shares	Income

Problem 2

ITA: 85(1)

Elijah Pitts operates a simple but profitable business as a proprietorship. Given the level of profits he is attaining, he would like to incorporate. The latest balance sheet of his proprietorship follows.

Elijah Pitts Enterprises
Balance Sheet (condensed version)
(Tax value basis)
December 31, 2018

Assets	
Cash	$ 5,000
Accounts receivable (trade)	15,000
Office equipment (UCC)	10,000
	$30,000

Liabilities	
Bank loan (operating)	$ 4,000
Accounts payable	5,000
	9,000
Proprietorship Equity	$21,000
	$30,000

He advises you that the current value of the office equipment is $12,000, that he fully expects to collect all of the receivables, and that the value of the goodwill is $20,000. If he does incorporate, he prefers to minimize any tax liability that incorporation might bring.

Design in detail what you believe to be the optimum plan for transferring the assets to the corporation, including any section 85 rollover. Indicate the tax values of the assets owned by the corporation.

Problem 3

ITA: 85(1)

Peter Handy is a Canadian resident who owns all the shares of The Handyman Shop Inc. (Handyman). He has been operating successfully for the past ten years but is finding that increasingly there are more lawsuits against retailers for injuries sustained by hobbyists, particularly for the tools that Handyman develops internally. While they do have product liability insurance to cover claims, Peter is concerned that, as the amount of the awards increase, a lawsuit might threaten the equity he has built up in the assets, particularly the land and building, and may even put him out of business.

A friend told him that he should transfer the business assets and liabilities, other than the land, building and mortgage, to a new subsidiary corporation, Tool Man Inc. (Tool Man), and then use Handyman as a holding company to accumulate assets. Peter would like your advice on this proposal or other ideas you might have.

Handyman has the following assets and liabilities:

	Book Value	Tax Value	Fair Market Value
Cash	$220,000	$220,000	$ 220,000
Inventory	440,000	395,000	395,000
Furniture and fixtures	120,000	60,000	80,000
Building	750,000	450,000	1,550,000
Land	80,000	80,000	1,300,000
Goodwill	nil	nil	800,000
Accounts payable	(250,000)		
Bank loan	(300,000)		
Mortgage payable	(180,000)		

CHAPTER 16

¶16,875

Before your next meeting with Peter you want to:

(A) Assess the situation.

(B) Identify the issues.

(C) Analyze the issues.

(D) Advise/recommend.

Problem 4

ITA: 84(3), 85

Ms. Hart, age 45, has just met with you to talk about incorporating her business and having her husband participate in its future growth in value.

She is a Canadian resident and has provided you with the balance sheet and additional information concerning her unincorporated active retail clothing business.

She has picked November 10, 2018 as the date when she wishes to transfer all of her business assets and liabilities to a corporation (Hart Ltd.) in which her husband owns 100% of the common shares. She wants your advice on how to do this with the minimum amount of personal tax. Mr. Hart is also a Canadian resident.

The following financial information concerning the business as of November 10, 2018, has been provided:

	Tax value	Fair market value
Shares in public companies (note 1)	$ 11,000	$ 6,000
Accounts receivable (net allowance) (note 2)	13,000	10,000
Inventory	8,000	9,000
Land (held as inventory)	100,000	220,000
Prepaid property insurance	600	600
Building (Class 1, cost $90,000)	70,000	150,000
Land (capital property)	140,000	160,000
Goodwill	nil	80,000

Additional Information:

1. The shares are capital property to Ms. Hart. She owns less than 1% of each public company.

2. The tax reserve for doubtful debts taken in the previous year was $1,000. The original cost of the accounts receivable before deducting the reserve was $14,000.

3. The unincorporated business has liabilities of $60,000 which are to be assumed by Hart Ltd.

Ms. Hart has specifically asked you to provide her with a tax-effective plan to achieve her objectives.

She has heard that she will have to receive some preference shares as consideration so she wants to know the tax consequences if she sells these shares or has the company buy them back at a later date.

For the next meeting you agree that you will:

(A) Assess the situation.

(B) Identify the issues.

(C) Analyze the issues.

(D) Advise/recommend.

Problem 5

ITA: 85

Tse Enterprises Ltd. (TEL) has carried on a retail business for about 20 years. Joe Tse, age 55, acquired all 100 common shares of TEL on incorporation and paid $1 each for these shares.

On November 30th Joe intends to have TEL transfer its business assets and liabilities to a new corporation, Tse Inc. (Tse), in which he wants to have control.

Three of his four children, all in their 20s, are active in the business and have each already subscribed for 100 common shares of Tse at $1 per share.

Joe wants to make sure he can still earn income for his retirement, even if the business doesn't prosper under the management of his children. In particular, he wants to keep the land and building in TEL so he can earn rental income and reduce the amount that Tse owes TEL.

TEL has $3,000 of net capital losses that he would like to use on the transfer.

The following are the projected balance sheet of TEL and certain additional information:

Assets	Projected Balance Sheet Nov 30, 2018	Projected Fair Market Value Nov 30, 2018
Cash	$ 12,000	$ 12,000
Accounts receivable (Net of $10,000 allowance)	110,000	102,000
Inventories	90,000	100,000
Shares of Supplyco Ltd.[1]	36,000	40,000
Land	96,000	103,000
Buildings[2]	48,000	144,000
Equipment[2]	72,000	60,000
Goodwill	—	90,000
	$464,000	$651,000

Liabilities[3]		
Bank loan	$ 30,000	
Accounts payable	31,000	
Accrued liabilities	6,000	
Mortgage on land and building	84,000	
	$151,000	
Common Shares	100	
Retained Earnings	312,900	
	$464,000	

Notes to Balance Sheet

[1] These shares represent a 2% ownership in the common shares of Supplyco Ltd. which is a small business corporation.

[2] Fixed assets are recorded at original cost less accumulated financial accounting depreciation. No single piece of equipment is worth more than its cost. Tax data follow:

	Original cost	UCC
Buildings	$ 95,000	$42,000
Equipment	110,000	57,000

[3] Liabilities are to be assumed by the corporation. In addition, TEL will receive as consideration for the transfer of assets the maximum in notes payable that it can receive without negative tax consequences plus voting retractable preferred shares.

Joe would like your advice on the transfer of the assets of TEL to Tse, including the consideration he should receive. His controller also wants to know what the tax values of the assets will be in Tse.

CHAPTER 16

¶16,875

Before you meet with Joe you want to:

(A) Assess the situation.

(B) Identify the issues.

(C) Analyze the issues.

(D) Advise/recommend.

Problem 6

ITA: 85

Mr. Schminkie, age 45, the sole proprietor of a small manufacturing business wishes to have his wife involved in the business on an equal basis. Mr. Schminkie's barber advised him that this is possible by incorporating a company and having Mr. and Mrs. Schminkie, age 44, subscribe for all the common shares equally. Then, Mr. Schminkie could transfer all the assets of the business to the newly formed company, taking back Class A and Class B non-voting preference shares as consideration. Mr. Schminkie thought this was a wonderful idea and proceeded with incorporating the company.

The assets and liabilities of the proprietorship and certain additional information are provided as follows:

Assets	Balance sheet Dec. 31/17	Fair market value Dec. 31/17
Cash	$ 20,000	$ 20,000
Accounts receivable[1]	90,000	85,000
Inventories	86,000	86,000
Shares in Public Co.	50,000	20,000
Land — Parcel I[3]	200,000	339,000
Building[2]	15,000	75,000
Land — Parcel II[4]	20,000	45,000
Equipment[2]	35,000	5,000
Auto[2]	10,000	12,000
Goodwill	—	60,000
	$526,000	

Liabilities[5]	
Bank loan	$169,000
Accounts payable	43,000
Mortgage on building	30,000
	$242,000
Proprietor's equity	284,000
	$526,000

Notes to Balance Sheet

[1] The accounts receivable are net of a $6,000 reserve for doubtful accounts which represents the closing reserve for the previous fiscal period.

[2] Fixed assets are recorded at original cost less accumulated financial accounting depreciation. Tax data is as follows:

	Original cost	*UCC*
Building	$60,000	$15,000
Equipment	80,000	35,000
Auto	16,000	11,000

[3] Parcel I of land is the property upon which the building used in the business is situated.

[4] Parcel II of land was acquired in 2017. Mr. Schminkie purchased it with the intention to sell as soon as the fair market value exceeded $50,000. Mr. Schminkie speculates this will occur by April 19, 2018, at which point he will sell for the quick profit.

[5] Liabilities are to be assumed by the corporation.

You have been asked to do the following:

(A) Indicate which assets should not be transferred to the corporation at all.

(B) Indicate which assets should be transferred to the corporation, but cannot or should not be transferred under section 85 and briefly explain why.

(C) For the assets which can be transferred under section 85 to the corporation, indicate the maximum amount of debt in addition to the shares that can be taken as consideration to defer all possible capital gains, losses, other income and other available adverse tax consequences given the consideration to be taken. The corporation will issue a maximum of $200,000 Class A retractable non-voting preference shares with a dividend rate of 5% and the remainder of the share consideration will be Class B retractable, non-voting preference shares with no dividend entitlement.

(D) Determine Mr. Schminkie's cost of the consideration and the PUC for tax purposes of the preferred shares that he receives for the transfer of assets.

(E) Compute the tax consequences of a redemption of the preferred shares of the corporation at their fair market value after the transfer of assets to the corporation.

(F) Advise on what could be done to avoid a benefit problem, if the Class B consideration is limited to an authorized share capital amount of only $50,000 and the Class A consideration remains the same.

Problem 7

ITA: 84.1, 85(1)

Mrs. Andrews, a Canadian resident, has just told you about a proposed transaction she is planning to undertake shortly. She would like your advice on her plan.

She recently set up Von Trapp Holdings Limited (Holdings) with 100 common shares, which she owns and are worth $1 each. The plan is for her to sell her shares in Plummer Enterprises Inc. (Plummer) to Holdings in order to crystallize her capital gains exemption and for her to have a holding company to accumulate capital away from the risks of the business. She has never claimed the capital gains exemption in the past.

Mrs. Andrews currently owns 100% of the outstanding common shares of Plummer. Plummer is a small business corporation and meets all the tests for the shares to be qualified small business corporation shares. Plummer and Holdings are both Canadian resident corporations. She purchased the Plummer shares ten years ago from an unrelated third party for their then fair market value of $200,000. *ACB* The fair market value of the Plummer shares today is $4 million. The paid-up capital of these shares is $1,000. *PUC* *FMV*

Mrs. Andrews plans to transfer her shares of Plummer to Holdings on December 3rd and has been advised by someone else to jointly elect under section 85 with Holdings and take back the following consideration:

(a) Non-interest bearing note for $200,000, and

(b) Voting preference shares that are retractable for $3.8 million and have a dividend rate of 6%.

You realize early in the discussion that you will need to consider, among other things, the impact of s. 84.1 on this transaction.

Before you meet with Mrs. Andrews you want to:

(A) Assess the situation.

(B) Identify the issues.

(C) Analyze the issues.

(D) Advise/recommend.

Problem 8

ITA: 84(3), 84.1, 85

Mrs. Domm owns all 100 common shares of Low-Cal Caterers Inc. (Low-Cal), a Canadian-controlled private corporation with a December 31 year end. Low-Cal was incorporated in 1999 when Mrs. Domm invested $250,000 in common shares with a paid-up capital of the same amount. The Low-Cal shares are now valued at $2,000,000. She has already used up $300,000 of her capital gains exemption on other shares.

Mrs. Domm would like to freeze the present value of Low-Cal so that any future increase in value would accrue to her 20-year-old son, Sam. She proposes that Sam incorporate a new corporation, Sam Pickings Holdings Ltd. (Sam Pickings), with $100 of his own money by acquiring all the common shares of the new corporation.

Mrs. Domm would then transfer her common shares in Low-Cal to Sam Pickings using a section 85 election in order to defer the inherent gain on these shares. Mrs. Domm would like to receive as consideration a non-interest-bearing note for $798,252 and the balance of the fair market value for 1,000 6% non-cumulative, voting preference shares with a retraction value, fair market value, and paid-up capital of $1,201,748. Since she would also like to use all of her remaining capital gains exemption (of $548,252 for QSBC shares), she proposes that the elected amount under section 85 be $798,252. You have determined that both Low-Cal and Sam Pickings are small business corporations at the present time and that Low-Cal meets all the conditions for QSBC shares.

You have agreed to do the following:

(A) Describe the tax consequences to Mrs. Domm of the proposed section 85 transfer of the Low-Cal common shares to Sam Pickings.

(B) Advise on how you would change the above proposed consideration package so that Mrs. Domm achieves her objectives as stated above.

(C) Describe the tax consequences if Mrs. Domm sold to Sam Pickings for cash or debt just enough of the 100 common shares of Low-Cal common shares to realize a capital gain of $548,252 in order to utilize her capital gains exemption as described above.

(D) Indicate the tax consequences for parts (A) and (B) if Mrs. Domm:

 (i) redeems all the preference shares in Sam Pickings for their fair market value; or

 (ii) sells all the preference shares in Sam Pickings to an arm's length party for their fair market value.

Problem 9

ITA: 55(1)–(6)

Holden Limited has received an offer from an unrelated corporation, Corporate Raider Inc., to purchase all of Holden's common shares in a wholly owned subsidiary, Profits Galore Ltd. All three corporations are Canadian-controlled private corporations and have December 31 year ends.

The common shares of Profits Galore Ltd. have an adjusted cost base and paid-up capital of $500,000 and a fair market value of $2.4 million. Profits Galore Ltd. has realized and retained income for tax purposes of $900,000 since its incorporation in 2001. All of this realized income was derived from active business assets.

Holden Limited has come to you for your comments on two acquisition alternatives proposed by Corporate Raider Inc.

Plan A would first have Profits Galore Ltd. borrow from the bank $1.9 million and, then, immediately pay a dividend to its parent corporation, Holden Limited, for the same amount. Corporate Raider Inc. would then purchase the common shares of Profits Galore Ltd. from Holden Limited for the residual fair market value of $500,000. Then, Corporate Raider would inject $1.9 million into Profits Galore Ltd. through a common share subscription so that the bank loan could be repaid.

Plan B would have Holden Limited transfer its common shares in Profits Galore Inc. to Corporate Raider Inc. on a tax-free basis by jointly electing under section 85 at a transfer price of $500,000. Holden Limited would accept as consideration only special shares of Corporate Raider Inc. with a paid-up capital of $500,000 and a redemption/retraction value of $2.4 million. These shares would represent 15% of all the voting rights and fair market value of Corporate Raider Inc. Holden Limited would, then, retract the special shares which it holds in Corporate Raider.

Holden Limited has asked you to describe the tax implications of the above acquisition alternatives supported by any relevant calculations.

CHAPTER 16 —
DISCUSSION NOTES FOR REVIEW QUESTIONS

(1) In general, a rollover allows for a partial or complete deferral of the recognition of income on the transfer of property from one person to another. The transferor, in return for the property transferred, should receive a package of consideration, the total fair market value of which should be equal to the fair market value of the property transferred. The transferor is the one who is deferring the recognition of income. The transferee usually steps into the position of the transferor in terms of the tax value of the asset received. Therefore, on the ultimate disposition of the asset by the transferee, the income will be recognized. Examples of rollovers include subsections 73(1), 85(1), 88(1) and sections 51 and 86.

(2) In order to use section 85, the corporation must be a "taxable Canadian corpora- ITA: 85(1.1)
tion", which is defined to be a "Canadian corporation" that is not exempt from tax. A ITA: 89(1)
"Canadian corporation" is defined to include a company that is resident in Canada and was
either incorporated in Canada or resident in Canada since before June 18, 1971. In this case,
Della Inc. has been resident in Canada only since 1974 and, therefore, is not a Canadian
corporation and not a taxable Canadian corporation. Although the real estate is capital
property to Mr. Della and, thus, it is "eligible property", this property cannot be transferred
using section 85 since the transferee is not a taxable Canadian corporation.

(3) The following are the four uses of the elected price:

(a) it is the proceeds of disposition to the transferor;

(b) it is the cost of the property to the corporation;

(c) it is used to determine the ACB of the package of consideration taken by the transferor from the corporation in return for the assets transferred to the corporation; and

(d) it is used to calculate the paid-up capital of the shares taken as consideration by the transferor from the corporation.

(4) On the transfer, the only decision variable you have is the non-share consideration or ITA: 85(1)(b), 85(1)(c)
boot. If the boot is higher than the tax cost (lower limit) for the particular asset transferred,
then the elected amount is increased. The boot cannot, however, raise the elected amount
above fair market value.

(5) The maximum "boot" that should be taken in order to maximize the deferral is the tax value of the asset transferred. If, however, the asset being transferred is shares and section 84.1 applies, the maximum boot should be the greater of the PUC and the modified ACB (removing any CGE element) of the shares transferred.

(6) She may have heard about a regulation which allows the transferee to avoid the half- ITR: 1100(2), 1100(2.2)
year rule as long as the transferor was not dealing at arm's length with the corporation at the
time of the transfer (which is true in this situation) and the property was owned continuously
by the transferor (Ms. Smith) for the period from a day that was at least 364 days before the
end of the taxation year of the corporation in which the asset was acquired to the date the
property was transferred to the corporation. For example, if the transfer happened April 1st
and the taxation year end of the corporation was December 31st, Ms. Smith would have to
have owned the property continuously from January 1st of that year through to April 1st.

(7) The elected transfer price is equal to the total cost of the consideration taken back. This elected amount is allocated among the different types of consideration in the following manner:

First: to non-share consideration (boot) up to the FMV of that property as long as that ITA: 85(1)(f)
          FMV does not exceed the FMV of the assets transferred to the corporation;

Second: to preferred shares up to the FMV of those shares after the transfer but only to ITA: 85(1)(g)
          the extent that there is a balance left after the boot has been deducted from
          the elected amount; and

Third: to common shares to the extent that the elected amount exceeds the FMV of the boot and the cost allocated to the preferred shares.

ITA: 85(1)(*h*)

(8) Normally, the sale of shares in an SBC would allow Bar Ltd. to claim the loss as a business investment loss. However, the ABIL is denied, since it must sell to an arm's length person. Bar Ltd. and Spouse Ltd. do not deal at arm's length since they are related. Therefore, the loss would be an ordinary capital loss.

ITA: 39(1)(*c*)
ITA: 251

However, in this case, Bar Ltd. is transferring the shares to a corporation controlled by the sole shareholder's wife, an affiliated person; therefore, the superficial loss will be denied to Bar Ltd. However, Spouse Ltd. can take advantage of the ability to add the loss to the cost base of the Lite Ltd. shares now owned by Spouse Ltd. The rule applies whenever a taxpayer disposes of capital property to an affiliated person, including a corporation that was controlled, directly or indirectly in any manner whatever, by the taxpayer, by the spouse of the taxpayer or by other affiliated persons. Section 84.1 will not apply as a corporation (not an individual); Bar Ltd is transferring the shares to a non-arm's length corporation.

ITA: 53(1)(*f*), 54, 251.1
ITA: 40(2)(*g*), 54 "superficial loss"
ITA: 85(1)(*e.2*)

(9) The "elected amount" determines how much can be withdrawn tax-free since this is the starting point for determining the ACB and the PUC of the shares. In addition, it is the amount that is used to determine how much boot to take back on the transaction to fully defer the accrued income (except when 84.1 applies).

(10) The elected amount is correct since the upper limit is the FMV of $8,000. Ms. Smith will realize a capital gain of $3,000. The company will have a cost in the portfolio shares of $8,000 which is the elected amount. There will be a paid-up capital reduction to reduce the PUC to $8,000. Thus, on redemption, she will have a deemed dividend for $2,000 (i.e., $10,000 of redemption value – $8,000 of PUC).

ITA: 85(1)(*b*)
ITA: 85(2.1)

(11) If boot is equal to the elected amount and equal to the tax value of the property being transferred, then the ACB and PUC of the shares will be nil.

(12) Price adjustment clauses are often used to provide for an adjustment to the consideration taken back in the event that the assessed value is different than what was originally used. The courts have determined that the price adjustment clause will only be recognized if the parties have reasonably and in good faith attempted to determine fair market value. The CRA's position on them is outlined in an Income Tax Folio.

Income Tax Folio
S4-F3-C1

(13) The provision is designed to prevent an individual from stripping the fair market value in excess of the greater of his or her modified ACB or the PUC out of the company by selling the shares to a non-arm's length corporation.

(14) He can reduce the PUC of the shares by $100,000. This will cause his ACB in the shares to become negative $90,000 which will give rise to an immediate capital gain. Alternatively, he can transfer his shares to a holding company under section 85 and take back a note for $100,000 and one share with a nominal value of, say, one cent. Section 84.1 will not give rise to a deemed dividend, since the boot does not exceed the greater of the modified ACB and the PUC. In either case, he can use his capital gains exemption to shelter the gain if the shares are QSBC shares.

ITA: 40(3), 53(2)(*a*)(ii), 84(4)

CHAPTER 16

CHAPTER 16 — SOLUTIONS TO MULTIPLE CHOICE QUESTIONS

Question 1

(C) is correct. Electing at $800, the UCC of the transferred asset, will defer recapture as well as the capital gain.   ITA: 85(1)(e)

(A) is incorrect. The spousal rollover applies to transfers to a spouse or a spousal trust, but never to a corporation.   ITA: 73(1)

(B) is incorrect. Electing at $2,200 will defer the capital gain, but recapture of $1,400 will be incurred.

(D) is incorrect. Since the corporation will have acquired the depreciable asset from a non-arm's length individual, $2,600 (i.e., $2,200 + ½ ($3,000 − $2,200) is the maximum amount that the capital cost could be.   ITA: 13(7)(e)

Question 2

(D) $25,000 is correct. In order to defer the gain, Steve will elect at $40,000, the ACB of the asset. The elected amount cannot be less than the non-share consideration. Since S Ltd. assumed the mortgage of $15,000, an additional $25,000 of non-share consideration is the maximum that can be taken.   ITA: 85(1)

(A) $100,000 is incorrect. This amount would result in a capital gain of $60,000 as well as a shareholder benefit of $15,000.   ITA: 15(1)

(B) $85,000 is incorrect. This amount would result in a capital gain of $60,000.

(C) $40,000 is incorrect. This amount would result in a capital gain of $15,000.

Question 3

(B) $110,000 is correct. Since the corporation has acquired the depreciable property from a non-arm's length individual, the capital cost is limited to the transferor's capital cost, $100,000 plus the taxable capital gain on the transfer, $10,000. This totals $110,000.   ITA: 13(7)(e)

(A) $120,000, the elected transfer price, is incorrect for the same reason that (B) is correct.

(C) $90,000, the transferor's UCC plus the taxable capital gain on the transfer, is incorrect. The starting point is the transferor's capital cost, not UCC.   ITA: 13(7)(e)

(D) $75,000, the transferor's UCC, is incorrect for the same reason that (B) is correct.

Question 4

(D) $20,000 is correct.

Elected transfer price		$40,000
Allocated to non-share consideration:		
Cash	$3,000	
Debt	2,000	$ 5,000
Allocated to the preferred shares, up to their FMV		15,000
Allocated to the common shares, remainder		20,000
		$40,000

ITA: 85(1)(g)
ITA: 85(1)(h)

(A) $35,000 is incorrect. The elected amount, in excess of the non-share consideration, has all been allocated to the common shares.

(B) $23,000 is incorrect. None of the elected amount has been allocated to the cash.

(C) $23,333 is incorrect. The allocation between the preferred and common shares has been done based on proportionate values.

Question 5

(D) is correct because a section 22 election ensures that the purchaser will be able to take a doubtful debts reserve on the accounts receivable.

(A) and (B) are incorrect because a section 22 election ensures that the loss to the vendor is a business loss rather than a capital loss or superficial loss. If no section 22 election is made, the vendor will realize a loss that is a capital loss. Further, if the vendor and purchaser are affiliated persons, the loss will be denied and will be a superficial loss.   ITA: 54

(C) is incorrect because the vendor is always required to add the prior year's doubtful debts reserve to income. It does not matter whether or not a section 22 election is made.   ITA: 12(1)(*d*)

Question 6

(D) is correct. Because the promissory note is $60,000, the elected amount is deemed to be $60,000. The elected amount determines the proceeds of disposition to Rebecca, R Co.'s cost of the land, the cost of the consideration to Rebecca, and the paid-up capital of the shares issued as consideration after the paid-up capital reduction.   ITA: 85(2.1)

(A) is incorrect because the proceeds to Rebecca are deemed to be $60,000 not $50,000 as discussed above.

(B) is incorrect because R Co.'s cost of the land is deemed to be $60,000, not $50,000 as discussed above.

(C) is incorrect because Rebecca's cost of the preference shares is zero. It is calculated as the elected amount minus the boot ($60,000 – $60,000 demand note).   ITA: 85(1)(*g*)

CHAPTER 16 — SOLUTIONS TO EXERCISES

Exercise 1

	A	B	C	D	E	F	G
(A) Minimum elected amount or deemed proceeds	$120	$100	$ 80	$ 75	$100	$ 90	$ 50
(B) Proceeds	$120	$100	$ 80	$ 75	$100	$ 90	$ 50
Cost	100	75	100	75	100	75	100
Capital gain	$ 20	$ 25	Nil*	Nil	Nil	$ 15	Nil
Taxable capital gain (½)	$ 10	$ 13	Nil	Nil	Nil	$ 8	Nil
Lesser of cost or proceeds	$100		$ 80		$100		$ 50
UCC of class	200		50		150		50
Recapture	Nil		$ 30		Nil		Nil
Income from shareholder benefit	$ 30	$100	Nil	Nil	Nil	Nil	Nil
(C) Maximum "boot"	$100	$ 75	$ 50	$ 75	$100	$ 75	$ 50

ITA: 15(1)

---

* No capital loss on depreciable property.

Exercise 2

(A) Cost of consideration received:	A	B	C
Elected transfer price	$5,000	$5,000	$5,000
Allocated to note up to FMV	5,000	2,500	4,000
Allocated to preferred up to FMV	Nil	$2,500	Nil
Allocated to common shares	Nil	Nil	$1,000

(B)

	A	B	C
LSC before reduction	$5,000	$7,500	$6,000
Reduction in PUC			
(a) Increase in LSC of all shares	$5,000 (A)	$7,500 (A)	$6,000 (A)
(b) Elected amount	$5,000	$5,000	$5,000
Less: boot	5,000	2,500	4,000
Excess, if any	Nil (B)	$2,500 (B)	$1,000 (B)
Total reduction in PUC (A – B)	$5,000	$5,000	$5,000

ITA: 85(2.1)

— REQUIRED

(a) What are the income tax consequences of electing at the transfer prices indicated for the land and the building?

(b) Compute the cost for income tax purposes of the shares received from the corporation.

(c) Compute the PUC for income tax purposes of the shares received.

(d) What are the income tax consequences to Mr. Kelly if:

  (i) the corporation redeems the shares for $150,000?

  (ii) Mr. Kelly sells the shares for $150,000?

Exercise 12

Beamen Laiken Retail Emporium has been operated as a sole proprietorship since 1975. The following are the balance sheet items for the retailing operations as at August 31, 2018, its fiscal year end:

	Tax value	Fair market value
Cash	$ 4,000	$ 4,000
Marketable securities	23,000	15,000
Accounts receivable (net of $5,000 reserve)	32,000	35,000
Inventory	75,000	72,000
Prepaid expenses	2,000	2,000
Land at cost	60,000	135,000
Building, at UCC (capital cost: $150,000)	90,000	180,000
Fixtures, at UCC (capital cost: $113,000)	68,000	30,000
Intangible assets (Class 14.1) (cost: $25,000)	6,000	24,000
	360,000	497,000

Beamen wishes to incorporate this business and have the corporation assume $65,000 in liabilities of the business. He will be the only shareholder of the corporation.

— REQUIRED

(a) Indicate, with a brief explanation:

  (i) which assets cannot or should not be transferred to the corporation under ssec. 85(1), and

  (ii) which assets should not be transferred at all to the corporation.

(b) Determine the amounts to be elected on the various assets to avoid any taxes.

(c) Determine the consideration (rounded to the nearest $100) to be received without any tax consequences.

(d) Determine the adjusted cost base of the consideration received.

(e) Determine the tax PUC of the shares received.

Exercise 13

Ms. Hollymar, age 55, owned common shares in an operating company, Hollymar Ltd. The shares had a cost and paid-up capital value of $1,000 in 2007 when she incorporated the company. At the present time they are valued at $65,000. In order to crystallize $50,000 of her capital gains exemption, she incorporated a holding company, MH Holdings Ltd., and transferred her common shares in Hollymar Ltd. to MH Holdings Ltd., electing at $51,000 under s. 85(1). As consideration, Ms. Hollymar received a note for $51,000 and common shares valued at $14,000 from MH Holdings Ltd. The shares of Hollymar Ltd. are QSBC shares.

— REQUIRED

Determine the immediate tax consequences of the transfer.

CHAPTER 16

Exercise 14

Sell Ltd., a CCPC, owns 100% of the shares of Target Ltd. (a CCPC). The shares of Target Ltd. have appreciated greatly in value since Target Ltd. was incorporated by Sell Ltd. A large part of the share appreciation is attributed to land that has tripled in value since Target Ltd. acquired it.

An arm's length company, Acquisition Corporation, has offered to purchase 100% of the shares of Target Ltd. from Sell Ltd. for a purchase price equal to fair market value.

In the course of these acquisition discussions, Sell Ltd. causes Target Ltd. to pay Sell Ltd. a dividend equal to the accrued capital gain on Target Ltd.'s shares.

Acquisition Ltd. then buys 100% of the Target Ltd. shares for a price equal to Sell Ltd.'s adjusted cost base of the Target Ltd. shares.

— *REQUIRED*

Part A   What tax advantage was Sell Ltd. attempting to realize by causing Target Ltd. to pay the dividend?

Part B   Explain how ss. 55(2) could act to minimize the tax advantages of the above transactions and what additional information you would require to determine the tax consequences to Sell Ltd. resulting from the above series of transactions?

Exercise 15

Mr. Expandit, age 60, is a retailer who incorporated his business in 1981 under the name of Expandit Ltd. The common shares of Expandit Ltd., held by Mr. Expandit, have a paid-up capital value and cost of $2,500 and were issued to Mr. Expandit on incorporation in 1988. The present fair market value of the shares is $4,000,000.

Mr. Expandit wishes to incorporate a holding company, Holdexpanditco Ltd., for estate planning purposes. His daughter, age 34, will invest $45,000 of her own money in 500 common shares with a total stated value of $10. His wife will invest $12,500 of her own money in 7% voting preferred shares with a total stated value of $100. He will take back as partial consideration for his shares of Expandit Ltd. 3,500 voting, retractable 6% preferred shares with a total stated value of $100 and a total retraction value of $3,500,000. In addition, he will take back $500,000 in cash. He will elect with the corporation to transfer his shares of Expandit Ltd. at $500,000 to use up the remainder of his capital gains exemption.

— *REQUIRED*

(A) Outline the tax consequences of Mr. Expandits plan supported by your computations assuming:

    (i) an ultimate redemption of the 6% preferred shares at their fair market value; and

    (ii) an arm's length sale of the 6% preferred shares.

(B) Indicate briefly your recommendations as to how Mr. Expandit might rearrange his plan to avoid any problems arising from the plan presented.

Exercise 16

Flogit Ltd. is a Canadian-controlled private corporation that owns all of the shares of Unloaded Ltd., another Canadian-controlled private corporation. The following data pertain to the shares and surpluses of Unloaded Ltd:

PUC of shares	$ 60,000
ACB of shares to Flogit Ltd.	85,000
FMV of shares	875,000
Retained income earned after 1971	225,000

¶16,850

	A	B	C
(c) Allocation of reduction to different classes:			
Preferred shares			

$$\$5,000 \ \times \ \frac{\$4,500}{\$5,000} = \underline{\$4,500}$$

Common shares

$$\$5,000 \ \times \ \frac{\$500}{\$5,000} = \underline{\$\ \ 500}$$

Tax PUC

	A	B	C
Preferred shares	Nil	$2,500	
Common shares	Nil		$1,000

Note how the PUC after reduction is equal to the amount of the $5,000 ACB of the original capital property that has not been recovered through the notes received as consideration.

Exercise 3

(A) The elected amount becomes the proceeds of disposition of the assets transferred by Mr. Good. Since his adjusted cost base on the land and his undepreciated capital cost on the building are equal to these proceeds, there will be no capital gain on that land and no recapture on the building. The corporation is deemed to acquire these assets at a cost equal to the elected amount. On the building, the corporation is deemed to have a capital cost of $436,224 and to have taken capital cost allowance of $8,724 making it liable for future recapture and for a potential future capital gain if ultimate proceeds exceed $436,224. This places the corporation in the same position as Mr. Good was in with respect to the building prior to the transfer.

(B) (i) The cost of the debt and shares taken as consideration would be computed as follows:

Elected transfer price		$577,500
Allocated to debt:		
— mortgage assumed	$247,500	
— new debt issued	330,000	577,500
Allocated to shares		Nil

(ii) LSC before reduction		$322,500
Reduction in PUC		ITA: 85(2.1)
(1) Increase in LSC of all shares	$322,500 (A)	
(2) Elected amount	$577,500	
less: boot ($247,500 + $330,000)	577,500	
Excess, if any		Nil (B)
Total PUC reduction (A – B)		(322,500)
Tax PUC after reduction		Nil

(C) (i) If the new debt is redeemed for $330,000, given its adjusted cost base in Mr. Good's hands of $330,000, there would be no gain or loss. However, on the disposition of the shares, the following would result:

Proceeds of disposition	$425,000
Adjusted cost base	Nil
Capital gain	$425,000

CHAPTER 16

Taxable capital gain	$212,500	

(ii)	Redemption amount	$425,000	
	Less: PUC	Nil	
	Deemed dividend	$425,000	ITA: 84(3)
	Redemption amount	$425,000	
	Less: deemed dividend	425,000	
	Proceeds of disposition	Nil	ITA: 54 "proceeds of disposition" (j)
	Less: adjusted cost base	Nil	
	Capital gain	Nil	

Draft legislation released December 13, 2017 extends the TOSI rules to include taxable capital gains from the disposition of shares of a private corporation in split income. Split income also includes taxable dividends from a private corporation (including a deemed dividend on a redemption of shares). In (i) above, as long as the taxable capital gain is on a QSBC share, the TOSI will not apply. As well, income on excluded shares is not included in split income. The common shares will be excluded shares because the shares provide Mr. Good with 10% of the votes and value of the corporation and the other conditions found in the definition of excluded shares will be met.

Exercise 4

The benefit rule would apply. The amount of the benefit would be equal to:

ITA: 85(1)(e.2)

Fair market value of property transferred			$125,000
Less greater of:			
(a) fair market value of all consideration received	$101,000	101,000	
(b) elected amount	$100,000		
Benefit			$ 24,000

The proceeds of disposition of the securities to Mother would be increased by the amount of the benefit, $24,000, to $124,000 resulting in a capital gain of $24,000 on the transfer. The cost of the property to the corporation would also be increased by $24,000 to $124,000. However, the cost of the consideration received would be as follows:

Elected amount	$100,000
Allocated to note (up to FMV)	100,000
Allocated to preferred share	Nil

Thus, the cost of the consideration received or of the shares owned by Daughter, which would increase in value by $24,000, is not increased by the amount of the benefit resulting in potential double taxation.

The $1,000 LSC of the preferred share would not be reduced and would equal tax PUC.

Reduction in PUC   ITA: 85(2.1)

    (a) Increase in LSC . . . . $ 1,000 (A)

    (b) Elected amount (as increased by benefit) $124,000

         Less: boot   100,000

         Excess, if any . . . .   24,000 (B)

            Total PUC reduction (A – B) . . . .   Nil   ITA: 257

To avoid the problem of the $24,000 benefit being potentially taxed twice, Mother should have taken more share consideration in the amount of $24,000 such that the fair market value of all   ITA: 85(2.1) consideration received was equal to the fair market value of the property transferred. The PUC of these shares will be reduced to nil by the above formula, but this will not have any immediate tax consequences.

Exercise 5

Elected amount	*Range*
Asset #1	$5,000–$20,000
Asset #2	$8,000–$14,000

However, the Act forces the minimum elected amount to be $18,000 because of the non-share   ITA: 85(1)(*b*) consideration taken in that amount.

Assign the elected amount as follows:

Asset #1	$ 5,000
Asset #2	13,000
	$18,000

Note that the minimum amount is assigned to the depreciable asset to avoid recapture being fully taxed.

Income

Asset #1	P of D	$ 5,000
	ACB	10,000
	CL	Nil
Asset #2	P of D	$13,000
	ACB	8,000
	CG	$ 5,000
	TCG	$ 2,500

Under corporate law[(1)], the paid-up capital of the one common share would be equal to the net fair market value of the assets transferred to the corporation. In this case, the PUC would be $16,000 (i.e., $20,000 + $14,000 – $18,000). However, the Act will reduce the PUC as follows: ITA: 85(2.1)

    (a) Increase in legal PUC of all shares on the transfer to the
         corporation . . . . $16,000 (I)

    (b) Elected amount $18,000

         Less: non-share consideration ("boot")   18,000

Excess, if any	Nil (II)
Total PUC reduction (I – II)	$16,000

Since there is only one class of shares issued, there is no prorating of this reduction. As a result, the PUC of the share will be reduced to nil (i.e., $16,000 – $16,000) for tax purposes. The PUC is reduced to nil, because all of the tax-paid cost in UCC of $5,000 and ACB of $8,000 has been recovered through cash.

— NOTE TO SOLUTION

[1] Where the transferor and the corporation do not deal at arm's length, the legal stated capital (the initial PUC) can be less than the fair market value of the transferred assets at the discretion of the corporate directors.

Exercise 6

(A) Items not transferred under subsection 85(1):

Cash	$ 4,000	(not capital property and therefore not eligible property)
Short-term investments	5,000	(capital loss denied)
Accounts receivable	9,000	(use section 22[1])
Prepaid insurance	400	(business loss of $100)(not capital property and therefore not eligible property)
Building	60,000	(terminal loss of $2,000 denied)
Land	26,500	(capital loss denied)
Total	$104,900	(assume proprietorship debt of $74,000 and take back new debt for the balance of $30,900)

The building may not be transferred using the rules in section 85 because of the unrealized terminal loss. A stop-loss rule applies to deny the loss. Mrs. Designer can continue to claim CCA on the $2,000 terminal loss on her return until the building is disposed of by Hi Fashion Co. Ltd to an arm's length person.

ITA: 13(21.2)

If the short-term investments are considered assets used in the active business of the corporation, they can be transferred to the corporation for use in the business. Section 85 need not be used where there is no unrealized gain to defer. The capital loss will be considered to be a superficial loss because the corporation is affiliated with the transferor, Mrs. Designer. Therefore, a stop-loss rule will deny the loss to Mrs. Designer.

ITA: 54

ITA: 40(2)(*g*), 53(1)(*f*)

Section 85 need not be used when there is no accrued income to defer. If the short-term investments cannot be considered as assets used in an active business, then they should not be transferred to the corporation, because it will seriously jeopardize the qualification of the shares of the corporation as QSBCSs.

The land need not be transferred under section 85 for the same reasons as the short-term investments, because of the unrealized capital loss. The loss will be denied to Mrs. Designer.

(B) and (C) Items transferred under subsection 85(1) and consideration:

				Consideration			
	Tax value	FMV	Elected amount	Assumed debt[2]	New debt	Pref. shs.	Income
Inventory	$ 5,000	$25,000	$ 5,000	Nil	$ 5,000	$20,000	Nil
Goodwill	Nil	44,000	1	Nil	Nil	44,000	$0.50
	$ 5,000	$69,000	$ 5,001	Nil	$ 5,000	$64,000	

Since the corporation will qualify as a small business corporation, the Act will not apply to attribute income or capital gains back to Mrs. Designer.   ITA: 74.4, 248(1)

(D) Elected transfer price . . . . $ 5,001

    Allocated to debt consideration:

        debt assumed . . . .   Nil

        new debt 5,000   5,000

    Allocated to ACB of preferred shares . . . . $ 1

(E) LSC before reduction $64,000

    Reduction in PUC   ITA: 85(2.1)

        (i) Increase in LSC of all shares . . . . $64,000 (A)

        (ii) Elected amount . . . . $ 5,001

            Less: boot 5,000

            Excess, if any . . . .   1 (B)

            Total PUC reduction (A – B) . . . . (63,999)

    Tax PUC after reduction . . . . $ 1

The $1 of PUC after the reduction represents the amount of tax-paid cost that has not been recovered through boot received from the corporation. The $1 of income resulting from the transfer of the goodwill is a tax-paid cost. A total of $5,000 of total tax-paid cost was recovered through boot.

(F) For those assets *not* transferred under subsection 85(1) and not subject to the specific provisions discussed below, the cost amount for tax purposes to the corporation would be equal to the fair market value of the consideration:

    Cash . . . . $ 4,000

    Prepaid insurance   400

    Building (UCC to trans-

    feree) 60,000

    $64,400 = debt consideration

Under section 22, the purchaser, Hi-Fashion, would record the accounts receivable at their face value of $12,000 which would be their adjusted cost base for tax purposes. Under the conditions of section 22, the corporation must include in its income the business loss of $3,000 recognized by the transferor (i.e., difference between the face value ($12,000) and the fair market value ($9,000)). Hi-Fashion is now entitled to set up a reserve to offset any potential doubtful debts (i.e., $3,000), plus an amount equal to any further decline in value. In addition, the corporation is now eligible to write off any realized bad debts since it has included an amount in income in respect of these receivables.

The ACB of the short-term investments and the land to the corporation will be their fair market value plus the denied superficial loss. Therefore, the ACB of the short-term investments will be $10,000 ($5,000 FMV + $5,000 denied loss) and that of the land will be $30,000 ($26,500 FMV + $3,500 denied loss). This puts the corporation in the same tax position on these assets as Mrs. Designer was in before the transfer. Note that the corporation will hold investments with an ACB of $10,000 and land with an ACB of $30,000. The transferee will have received debt consideration of $5,000 and $26,500 respectively for the properties.

The capital cost and, therefore, the ACB of the building in the corporation is $80,000 for purposes   ITA 13(21.2)
of calculating future recapture and capital gains on the disposition of the property.

For the inventory that has been transferred under subsection 85(1), the cost base would be the elected amount (i.e., inventory — $5,000). The goodwill, which is a Class 14.1 property, would have a cost base equal to the elected amount of $1 (capital cost/ACB and UCC).

CHAPTER 16

— NOTES TO SOLUTION

(1) Reserve of $2,000 from last year must be brought into income this year. There will be a full business loss of $3,000 (i.e., face value of $12,000 less fair market value of $9,000) using section 22.

(2) The $104,900 of debt consideration for the assets not transferred under subsection 85(1) could include all assumed liabilities of $74,000, leaving none to be assumed in the subsection 85(1) transfer.

Exercise 7

An elected transfer price of $80,000 will result in the following: ITA: 85(1)

Recapture ($27,000 – $30,000)	$ 3,000
Taxable capital gain [½ ($80,000 – $30,000)]	25,000
Income.	$28,000
Less: net capital loss	25,000
Incremental taxable income	$ 3,000

ACB of consideration received:

Note	$80,000
Common shares	Nil

PUC of common shares: ITA: 85(2.1)

LSC of shares issued		$20,000
Less: PUC reduction			ITA: 85(2.1)
(a) increase in LSC	$20,000 (A)	
(b) elected amount	$80,000	
boot	80,000	
excess, if any	Nil (B)	
(A – B)	$20,000	
PUC for tax purposes	Nil	

Capital cost of transferred property to corporation for CCA and recapture purposes is equal to the aggregate of:

(a) capital cost to transferor		$30,000
(b) proceeds of disposition to transferor	$80,000	
less: capital cost of property transferred	30,000	
excess, if any	$50,000	
½ of excess		25,000
Deemed capital cost to corporation		$55,000

ITA: 13(7)(e)(i)

The capital cost used for future CCA write-offs, which shield business income from full tax, will be increased by the taxable capital gain triggered, but not, in effect, the untaxed portion of the capital gain.

Capital cost and adjusted cost base of the depreciable property for future *capital gains* purposes (equal to elected amount) is $80,000.

Exercise 8

Part (A)

Section 84.1 applies because Mr. Newberry is a Canadian resident and is not at arm's length with his brother who controls the corporation to which the Opco shares were transferred. Therefore, Mr. Newberry is not at arm's length with Broco Ltd. In addition, Opco Ltd. is connected with Broco Ltd., since Broco owns all of its outstanding common shares.

ITA: 251(2)(b)(iii)
ITA: 186(2)
ITA: 84.1(1)(a)

PUC reduction:

(a) Increase in LSC of brother's corporation		$ 300,000	(A)
Less:			
(b) Greater of:			
(i) PUC of operating company shares	$75,000		
(ii) Modified ACB* of operating company shares	$75,000	$ 75,000	
Less: FMV of boot		500,000	
Excess, if any		Nil	(B)
PUC reduction (A – B)		$ 300,000	
PUC after reduction		Nil	

The PUC after reduction is nil because all of the $75,000 hard cost in the operating company shares has been recovered in boot from the brother's corporation.

Deemed dividend:

ITA: 84.1(1)(b)

Sum of:			
(a) Increase in LSC of brother's corporation		$ 300,000	(A)
(b) FMV of boot		500,000	(D)
(A + D)		$ 800,000	
Less sum of:			
(c) Greater of:			
(i) PUC of operating company shares	$ 75,000		
(ii) Modified ACB* of operating company shares	$ 75,000	$ 75,000	(E)
(d) PUC reduction	300,000	(F)	
(E + F)		375,000	
Deemed dividend (A + D) – (E + F)		$ 425,000	

ITA: 84.1(1)(a)

* Adjusted actual cost.

This deemed dividend is equal to the excess of the $500,000 in boot received from the brother's corporation over the $75,000 of hard cost in the operating company shares transferred.

Draft legislation released December 13, 2017 dealing with TOSI indicates that split income includes taxable dividends from a private corporation (including deemed dividends) unless the income meets the definition of an excluded amount. An excluded amount includes income from a property to the extent that the amount is (where the individual has attained the age of 17) derived directly or indirectly from an excluded business of the individual. As it appears that Mr. Newberry was actively engaged on a regular, continuous and substantial basis in the activities of the business in any five prior years of Opco, the deemed dividend would be arguably derived from an excluded business of Mr. Newberry and TOSI would not apply.

Capital gain or loss on disposition of Opco Ltd. shares:		
Elected amount and proceeds of disposition for operating company shares	$ 500,000	ITA: 85(1)
Less: deemed dividend	425,000	ITA: 54 "proceeds of disposition" (*k*)
Adjusted proceeds of disposition for operating company shares	$ 75,000	
Less: ACB of operating company shares	75,000	
Capital gain (loss) if any, (not denied*)	Nil	ITA: 40(2)(*g*)
ACB of Broco Ltd. shares received:		
Cost of shares of Broco Ltd. after allocation of $500,000 elected amount to "boot"	Nil	ITA: 85(1)(*g*)

---

* He is not affiliated with Broco Ltd. by the definition of "affiliated person" in section 251.1, since he does not control, directly or indirectly, Broco Ltd.

Part (B)

Ultimate redemption of shares of brother's corporation		
Redemption amount	$ 300,000	
Less: PUC	Nil	
Deemed dividend on redemption	$ 300,000	ITA: 84(3)
Proceeds of disposition	$ 300,000	
Less: deemed dividend on redemption	300,000	ITA: 84(3)
Adjusted proceeds of disposition	Nil	ITA: 54 "proceeds of disposition" (*j*)
Less: adjusted cost base	Nil	
Capital gain (loss)	Nil	

Summary of income effects:		
Sec. 84.1 deemed dividend	$ 425,000	
Redemption deemed dividend	300,000	ITA: 84(3)
Capital gain (loss) on transfer	Nil	ITA: 85(1)
Capital gain (loss) on redemption	Nil	
Net economic effect	$ 725,000	

Note that $725,000 represents the accrued gain on the Opco Ltd. shares at the time of the transfer.

Part (C)

Ultimate arm's length sale of shares of brother's corporation	
Proceeds of disposition	$ 300,000
Less: adjusted cost base	Nil
Capital gain	$ 300,000

Summary of income effects:		
Sec. 84.1 deemed dividend	$ 425,000	
Capital loss on transfer	Nil	ITA: 85(1)
Capital gain on arm's length sale	300,000	
Net economic effect	725,000	

Again, the $725,000 represents the accrued gain in the Opco Ltd. shares at the time of the transfer.

Draft legislation released December 13, 2017 extends the TOSI rules to include taxable capital gains from the disposition of shares of a private corporation in split income. Split income also includes taxable dividends from a private corporation (including a deemed dividend on a redemption of shares). In (B) above, the deemed dividend on redemption under 84(3) would be split income as it is deemed to be a dividend received by an individual in respect of shares of the capital stock of a private corporation. As the preferred shares are non-voting shares, they would not meet the definition of an excluded share. However, as Mr. Newberry has been actively engaged in Opco Ltd.'s business, the income could be considered to be derived directly or indirectly from an excluded business of Mr. Newberry. The Opco Ltd. business would be an excluded business as Mr. Newberry would have been actively engaged on a regular, continuous and substantial basis in any five prior tax years.

In (C) above, as long as the taxable capital gain is on a QSBC share, TOSI will not apply. As well, although the shares will not be excluded shares, the taxable capital gain on the disposition of the shares is derived directly or indirectly from an excluded business of Mr. Newberry.

Exercise 9

For either alternative involving the sale of the Davpet Ltd. shares, the conditions of section 84.1 are met. Davpet Ltd. is a corporation resident in Canada and its shares are held as capital property by Ms. Erin, a Canadian resident. These shares are sold to a non-arm's length corporation, Lenmeag Ltd., since Ms. Erin is related to her father who controls Lenmeag Ltd. The two corporations are connected, since all of the shares of Davpet Ltd. are owned by Lenmeag Ltd. after the sale.

(A) Since no new shares of Lenmeag Ltd. were issued in this alternative, there is no PUC reduction. However, there will be an immediate deemed dividend computed as follows:

Deemed dividend: ITA: 84.1(1)(b)

    Sum of:

(a) Increase in LSC of Lenmeag Ltd. shares		Nil	(A)
(b) FMV of "boot"		$300,000	(D)
(A + D)		$300,000	

    Less sum of:

(c) Greater of:

(i) PUC of Davpet Ltd. shares	$1,000	
		$1,000 (E)
(ii) Modified ACB of Davpet Ltd. shares	$1,000	

(d) PUC reduction		Nil (F)	ITA: 84.1(1)(a)
(E + F)		1,000	
Deemed dividend (A + D) − (E + F)		$299,000	

This deemed dividend represents the excess of the $300,000 in boot received from Lenmeag Ltd. over the $1,000 in PUC of the Davpet Ltd. shares.

CHAPTER 16

Proceeds of disposition for the Davpet Ltd. shares will be reduced so that there will be no capital gain against which to offset the QSBC share capital gains deduction, as follows:

ITA: 54 "proceeds of disposition" (k)

Proceeds (Consideration in debt received on sale)	$300,000
Less: sec. 84.1 deemed dividend	299,000
Adjusted proceeds of disposition	$ 1,000
ACB of Davpet Ltd. shares	(1,000)
Capital gain	Nil

ITA: 54 "proceeds of disposition"(k)

When the $300,000 debt is repaid by Lenmeag Ltd., there will be no further tax consequences. However, the plan is ineffective, because Ms. Erin will have to pay tax on a deemed dividend of $299,000 at the time of the sale of her shares instead of the intended capital gains.

Draft legislation released December 13, 2017 dealing with TOSI indicates that split income includes taxable dividends from a private corporation (including deemed dividends) unless the income meets the definition of an excluded amount. An excluded amount includes income from a property to the extent that the amount is (where the individual has attained the age of 17) derived directly or indirectly from an excluded business of the individual. It appears that Ms. Erin is actively engaged on a regular, continuous and substantial basis in the activities of the business in either the taxation year of the transfer or any five prior years of Davpet Ltd. (including any years before incorporation that the business was operating as a sole proprietorship). In such case the deemed dividend would be arguably derived from an excluded business and the deemed dividend would not be subject to TOSI.

(B) In this alternative, there will be a PUC reduction, computed as follows:

PUC reduction:

ITA: 84.1(1)(a)

(a) Increase in LSC of Lenmeag Ltd.		$300,000 (A)
Less:		
(b) Greater of:		
(i) PUC of Davpet Ltd. shares	$1,000	
		$ 1,000
(ii) Modified ACB of Davpet Ltd. shares . . .	$1,000	
Less: FMV of "boot"	Nil	
Excess, if any		1,000 (B)
PUC reduction (A – B)		$299,000
PUC of new Lenmeag Ltd. shares after reduction ($300,000 – $299,000)		$ 1,000

The PUC of $1,000 after reduction represents the $1,000 of hard cost in the Davpet Ltd. shares transferred. None of that $1,000 of cost was recovered through boot on this transfer.

Since no "boot" was received, there will be no deemed dividend. As a result, proceeds of disposition for the Davpet Ltd. shares are equal to the $300,000 common share consideration received from Lenmeag Ltd. The result is the following:

Proceeds of disposition for Davpet Ltd. shares..................	$300,000
ACB	1,000
Capital gain	$299,000
Taxable capital gain (½ × $299,000)	$149,500
Less: Capital gains deduction for QSBCS	149,500
Effect on taxable income of Ms. Erin.........................	Nil

The ACB of the Lenmeag Ltd. shares acquired by Ms. Erin will be equal to the $300,000 fair market value of the shares in Davpet Ltd. given up. As a result, when the shares of Lenmeag Ltd. are either sold or redeemed the $300,000 ACB of the shares will shield an equal amount from being taxed as a capital gain and the objective of crystallizing the QSBC share capital gains exemption will be accomplished without an immediate capital gain or deemed dividend on the sale of the Davpet Ltd. shares.

Exercise 10

Of the $900,000 dividend received by Vendco, $700,000 can be attributed to post-1971 earnings of Preyco and, therefore, can be received by Vendco without tax consequences under Part I and Part IV of the Act. The other $200,000 of the total dividend received will be deemed to be a gain of the dividend recipient.

These results are equivalent to Vendco's receiving a dividend from Preyco, of $700,000 without tax consequences and then selling the shares of Preyco to Purchco for their fair market value of $300,000 (i.e., $1,000,000 – $700,000). With an adjusted cost base of $100,000 for the shares, a capital gain of $200,000 would result.

Exercise 11

(a) The ranges for making a sec. 85 election are as follows:

	Lower	Upper
Land (ACB/FMV)	$240,000	$370,000
Building (UCC/FMV)	160,000	280,000

The elected amounts of $340,000 and $160,000 for the land and building respectively, are in these ranges. In addition, the non-share consideration of $500,000 does not exceed the combined elected amounts. The elected amount becomes the proceeds of disposition of the assets transferred by Mr. Kelly. Since his adjusted cost base on the land is $240,000, he will have a capital gain of $100,000. Since the elected proceeds for the building are equal to the UCC of the building, there will be no recapture on the building.

The corporation is deemed to acquire the assets at a cost equal to the elected amount. Therefore, the cost of the land to the corporation is $340,000. On the building, the corporation is deemed to have a capital cost of $190,000 and to have taken capital cost allowance of $30,000 (ssec. 85(5)).

(b) The cost of the shares taken as consideration is as follows:

Elected transfer price	$500,000
Allocated to cash	500,000
	$0

(c)   Legal PUC before reduction

      Ssec. 85(2.1) reduction in PUC: $150,000

      (i) Increase in legal PUC of all shares . . . . $150,000 (A)

      (ii) Elected amount $500,000

          Less boot (cash)   500,000

          Excess, if any . . . .   0 (B)

                  PUC reduction (A-B)   150,000

      Tax PUC after reduction $0

(d) (i) Redemption:

          Proceeds on redemption $150,000

          Less: PUC   0

          Deemed dividend (ssec. 84(3)) $150,000

          Proceeds on redemption $150,000

          Less: deemed dividend   150,000

          Proceeds of disposition (sec. 54)   0

          Less: adjusted cost base of shares   0

          Capital gain $0

      (ii) Sale:

          Proceeds of disposition $150,000

          Adjusted cost base of shares   0

          Capital gain $150,000

Draft legislation released December 13, 2017 extends the TOSI rules to include taxable capital gains from the disposition of shares of a private corporation in split income. Split income also includes taxable dividends from a private corporation (including a deemed dividend on a redemption of shares). In (i) above, the deemed dividend on redemption under 84(3) would be split income as it is deemed to be a dividend received by an individual in respect of shares of the capital stock of a private corporation. The common shares would provide Mr. Kelly with 10% of the votes and value of the corporation and, therefore, meet the definition of an excluded share. As a result, the deemed dividend would not be subject to TOSI.

In (ii) above, as long as the taxable capital gain is on a QSBC share, TOSI will not apply. As well, the shares are excluded shares because the shares provide 10% of the votes and value of the corporation to Mr. Kelly.

Exercise 12

(a) (i)　Items not transferred under S. 85(1):

Cash	$ 4,000	(not eligible)
Accounts receivable	35,000	(use S. 22 election*)
Inventory	72,000	(no gain to defer — $3,000 business loss)
Prepaid expenses	2,000	(not eligible)
Fixtures	30,000	(no gain to defer — terminal loss denied by S. 13(21.2))*
Liabilities assumed	(65,000)	
FMV of debt consideration	$78,000	

Treatment of Accounts Receivable with a Section 22 election:

Proprietor		Corporation	
Reserve	$ 5,000	A/R	$37,000
Income	$ 5,000	Consideration	$35,000
		Income (S. 22)	2,000
Consideration	35,000		
Business loss	2,000	— can claim reserve at year end	
A/R	37,000	— can write off bad debts	

* Beamen will maintain the denied terminal loss of $38,000 in Class 8 (F&F). He can continue to claim CCA on this balance until the company disposes of the assets or ceases to use them in the business. The company will set up a balance of $30,000 in its Class 8.

(ii)　Items not transferred at all to the corporation:

Marketable securities should be held personally. If they are transferred to the corporation, the accrued capital loss of $8,000 will be denied as a superficial loss whether or not an election is made under S. 85(1). A denied loss is added to the cost of the securities in the corporation. If the securities are held personally, the loss can be realized on an arm's length sale when the corporation needs additional funds. After the sale, the cash can be transferred to the corporation for debt consideration. In addition, these are active business assets and may cause the corporation to cease being a small business corporation for purposes of the capital gains exemption.

(b)　　Items transferred under S. 85(1) and

(c)　　Consideration:

	Tax Value	FMV	Elected Amount	Assumed Debt	Debt	Shares	Income
Land	$ 60,000	$135,000	$ 60,000	$Nil	$ 60,000	$ 75,000	$Nil
Building	90,000	180,000	90,000	Nil	90,000	90,000	Nil
Intangible	6,000	24,000	6,000	Nil	6,000	18,000	Nil
	$156,000	$339,000	$156,000	$Nil	$156,000	$183,000	

(d)   ACB of consideration received:

           Elected amount $156,000

           Allocated to debt consideration:

                 Assumed debt . . . . $ Nil

                 New debt   156,000   156,000

           Allocated to ACB of shares . . . .   Nil

(e)   Tax PUC of shares:

           Increase in legal PUC of corporation on transfer $183,000

           Reduced by (S. 85(2.1)):

           (A) Increase in legal PUC $183,000

           (B) Elected amount $156,000

                 FMV of boot   156,000

                 Excess, if any . . . .   Nil

           (A - B) $183,000

           Tax PUC of shares . . . .   Nil

Exercise 13

Since the conditions for S. 84.1 to apply are met, the following would result:

PUC reduction (S. 84.1(1)(*a*)):

(1) increase in legal PUC of MH Holdings Ltd. . . . . . . $14,000   (A)

less

(2) greater of:

     (a)   PUC of Hollymar Ltd. shares $1,000

                                                             $ 1,000

     (b)   Modified ACB of Hollymar Ltd. shares $1,000

         less: FMV of boot   51,000

         excess, if any . . . .   Nil   (B)

PUC reduction (A - B) $14,000

PUC of MH Holdings Ltd. after the reduction ($14,000 - 14,000) . . . .   Nil

Deemed dividend (S.84.1(1)(*b*)):

Sum of:

(1) increase in legal PUC of MH Holdings Ltd. shares	$14,000 (A)	
(2) FMV of boot	51,000 (D)	
(A + D)	$65,000	

Less sum of:

(3) greater of:

(a) PUC of Hollymar Ltd. shares	$1,000	
		$ 1,000 (E)
(b) Modified ACB of Hollymar shares	$1,000	
(4) PUC reduction under S.84.1(1)(*a*)	14,000 (F)	
(E + F)		15,000
Deemed dividend (A + D) - (E + F)		$50,000

Draft legislation released December 13, 2017 dealing with TOSI indicates that split income includes taxable dividends from a private corporation (including deemed dividends) unless the income meets the definition of an excluded amount. An excluded amount includes income from a property to the extent that the amount is (where the individual has attained the age of 17) derived directly or indirectly from an excluded business of the individual. It appears that Ms. Hollymar is actively engaged on a regular, continuous and substantial basis in the activities of the business in either the taxation year of the transfer or any five prior years of Hollymar Ltd. In such case, the deemed dividend would be arguably derived from an excluded business and the deemed dividend would not be subject to TOSI.

Capital gain on transfer of Hollymar Ltd. shares:

Elected amount	$51,000
Less: S. 54(*k*) exclusion from proceeds for deemed dividend	50,000
Proceeds of disposition	$ 1,000
ACB	(1,000)
Capital gain	Nil

Exercise 14

Part A

Tax advantage Sell Ltd. was attempting to realize:

- Avoiding taxable capital gain
- Receiving a tax-free intercorporate dividend

Part B

Impact of S. 55(2):

- The dividend, or a portion thereof, will be deemed to be proceeds of disposition
- A capital gain will result

Additional information required:

- The portion of the dividend received by Sell Ltd. that was subject to Part IV tax in Sell Ltd.; and
- The post-71 income ("safe income") of Target Ltd.

Exercise 15

(A) PUC reduction [par. 84.1(1)(*a*)]

    (i) Increase in legal stated capital (LSC) of shares received from the purchaser corporation in respect of the subject shares . . . . $ 100 (A)

    Less

    (ii) greater of:

        (1) PUC of subject corporation shares . . . . $ 2,500 ⎤

                                                     ⎬ $ 2,500

        (2) modified ACB of subject shares $ 2,500 ⎦

        Less: FMV of non-share consideration received 500,000

    Excess, if any . . . . Nil (B)

    PUC reduction (A - B) . . . . $ 100

    PUC after reduction ($100 - $100) . . . . Nil

Deemed dividend [par. 84.1(1)(b):]

Sum of:

    (a) Increase in LSC of shares received from the purchaser corporation in respect of the subject shares . . . . $ 100 (A)

    (b) FMV of non-share consideration received . . . . 500,000 (D)

        (A + D) $ 500,100

Less sum of:

    (c) Greater of:

        (i) PUC of subject corporation shares . . . . $ 2,500 ⎤

                                                     ⎬ $ 2,500 (E)

        (ii) modified ACB of subject shares (above) . . . . $ 2,500 ⎦

    (d) PUC reduction under par. 84.1(1)(a)   100 (F)

        (E + F) 2,600

Deemed dividend (A + D) - (E + F) $ 497,500

Draft legislation released December 13, 2017 dealing with TOSI indicates that split income includes taxable dividends from a private corporation (including deemed dividends) unless the income meets the definition of an excluded amount. An excluded amount includes income from a property to the extent that the amount is (where the individual has attained the age of 17) derived directly or indirectly from an excluded business of the individual. It appears that Mr. Expandit is actively engaged on a regular, continuous and substantial basis in the activities of the business in either the taxation year of the transfer or any five prior years of Expandit Ltd. In such case, the deemed dividend would be arguably derived from an excluded business and the deemed dividend would not be subject to TOSI.

    Ssec. 85(1) election on transfer of subject corporation shares:

    Elected amount . . . . $ 500,000

    Less: par. (*k*) of def. "proceeds of disposition" in sec. 54 exclusion from proceeds of sec. 84.1 deemed dividends 497,500

    Adjusted proceeds of disposition of transferred shares . . . . $ 2,500

ACB of transferred shares	(2,500)
Capital gain (loss)	Nil

ACB of purchaser corporation shares received as consideration:

Elected amount	$ 500,000
Less: FMV of non-share consideration received	500,000
ACB	Nil

(i) Hypothetical redemption of purchaser corporation shares for FMV:

Deemed dividend on redemption:

Redemption amount	$3,500,000
Less: PUC after par. 84.1(1)(a)	Nil
Deemed dividend on redemption [ssec. 84(3)]	$3,500,000

Capital loss on redemption

Redemption amount	$3,500,000
Less: deemed dividend on redemption [ssec. 84(3)]	3,500,000
Adjusted proceeds of disposition [sec. 54]	Nil
ACB	Nil
Capital gain (loss) (loss would not be denied; no longer controlled by Mr. Expandit)	Nil

Summary of income effects

Sec. 84.1 deemed dividend	$ 497,500
Ssec. 84(3) deemed dividend	3,500,000
Capital loss on redemption	Nil
Ultimate capital gain (loss) to the corporation	Nil
Net economic effect (equal to gain: $4,000,000 - $2,500)	$3,997,500

(ii) Arm's length sale of purchaser corporation shares for FMV

Proceeds of disposition	$3,500,000
ACB	Nil
Capital gain	$3,500,000

Summary of income effects

Sec. 84.1 deemed dividend	$ 497,500
Capital gain	3,500,000
Ultimate capital gain (loss) to the corporation	Nil
Net economic effect (equal to gain: $4,000,000 - $2,500)	$3,997,500

Draft legislation released December 13, 2017 extends the TOSI rules to include taxable capital gains from the disposition of shares of a private corporation in split income. Split income also includes taxable dividends from a private corporation (including a deemed dividend on a redemption of shares). In (i) above, the deemed dividend on redemption under 84(3) would be split income as it is deemed to be a dividend received by an individual in respect of shares of the capital stock of a private corporation. As long as the preferred shares would provide Mr. Expandit with 10% of the votes and value of the corporation, the shares would meet the definition of an excluded share. As a result, the deemed dividend would not be subject to TOSI.

In (ii) above, as long as the taxable capital gain is on a QSBC share, TOSI will not apply. As well, the shares are excluded shares because the shares provide 10% of the votes and value of the corporation to Mr. Expandit.

(B) — Take non-share consideration up to $2,500 to avoid paragraph 84.1(1)(*b*) deemed dividend

— Consider section 86 internal freeze, but the fair market value of the boot plus the PUC of the new shares cannot exceed the PUC of the old shares to avoid triggering adverse tax consequences. Section 86 cannot be used if crystallization of the capital gains exemption is an objective.

Exercise 16

(A) The $225,000 dividend would be received by Flogit Ltd. tax free:

— no Part I tax [ssec. 112(1)]

— no Part IV tax as long as Unloaded does not receive a dividend refund on the payment of the dividend

— since the dividend is attributable to post-1971 earnings, subsection 55(2) would not apply and a capital gain would be computed as:

P of D	$650,000
ACB	(85,000)
Capital gain	$565,000

(B)

Dividend received		$790,000
Less: dividend attributable to post-1971 income	$225,000	
dividend subject to Part IV tax	Nil	225,000
Deemed proceeds of disposition [par. 55(2)(*b*)]		$565,000
Add: actual proceeds of disposition		85,000
Total proceeds of disposition		$650,000
Less: adjusted cost base		85,000
Capital gain		$565,000

(C) Deemed dividend on redemption:

Redemption amount paid		$875,000
Less: PUC		60,000
Deemed dividend on redemption [ssec. 84(3)]		$815,000
Less: part of dividend designated as a separate dividend attributable to post-1971 income [par. 55(5)(*f*)]	$225,000	225,000
Other part of dividend deemed not to be a dividend		$590,000

Proceeds of disposition of shares redeemed

Redemption amount paid	$875,000
Less: designated deemed dividend	225,000
Proceeds of disposition	$650,000

Capital gain or loss on disposition of shares

P of D	$650,000
ACB	(85,000)
Capital gain	$565,000

Chapter 17

Income Deferral: Other Rollovers and Use of Rollovers in Estate Planning

Learning Goals

Know

By the end of this chapter you will know:

- The basic provisions of the *Income Tax Act* pertaining to corporate rollovers that are useful in many planning situations.

Understand and Explain

By the end of this chapter you will understand and be able to explain:

- The tax consequences of the various rollovers discussed and their uses in various planning situations.

- The use of rollovers to execute an estate freeze.

Apply

By the end of this chapter you will be able to apply your knowledge and understanding to:

- Determine the tax consequences of a wind-up or an amalgamation.

- Determine the tax consequences of a basic estate freeze.

- Determine whether an estate freeze achieves a client's goals.

Review Questions
¶17,800 in the Study Guide

Multiple Choice Questions
¶17,825 in the Study Guide

Exercises
¶17,850 in the Study Guide

Assignment Problems
¶17,875 in the Study Guide

CHAPTER 17 — LEARNING CHART

Problem Descriptions

Textbook Example Problems

17-1   Share-for-share exchange
17-2   Reorganization of capital
17-3   Reorganization of capital
17-4   Reorganization of capital

Multiple Choice Questions

1   Amalgamation, wind-up
2   Wind-up
3   Reorganization of capital
4   Share-for-share exchange
5   Estate freeze
6   Estate freeze

Exercises

1   Share-for-share exchange
2   Reorganization of capital
3   Reorganization of capital
4   Amalgamation, wind-up
5   Convertible property
6   Section 85.1
7   Section 86 Reorganization of capital

Assignment Problems

1   Sections 85 and 85.1
2   Capital reorganization
3   Capital reorganization, gifting
4   Amalgamation vs. wind-up
5   Corporate structure
6   Sections 85, 86, 84.1
7   Extension of Problem 6
8   Estate planning
9   Estate planning

Study Notes

¶17,800   REVIEW QUESTIONS

(1) What legal documents need to be filed in order to accomplish a reorganization of capital rollover?   ITA: 86

(2) What are some of the occasions in which a reorganization of capital rollover might be used?   ITA: 86

(3) What adjustments are there as a result of a deemed dividend that arises on a reorganization of capital rollover?   ITA: 86

(4) Legally, what happens to two corporations that are amalgamated?

(5) At the time of amalgamation there is a deemed year end for tax purposes. What are some of the other tax rules that are impacted by this deemed year end?   ITA: 87(2)(*a*)

(6) Acme Co. is a CCPC with a January 31 year end. The owners want to change the year end of the company to July 31 to allow bonuses to be paid either in this year or the next. It is now July and they do not have time to receive clearance from the CRA so they incorporate another company and amalgamate it with Acme on July 31 to create a new year end. Do you have any problems with this tactic?

(7) In order for the subsidiary wind-up rollover to apply, what ownership criteria need to be met?   ITA: 88(1)

(8) Ms. Sweeney purchased 1,000 convertible preferred shares at a total cost of $10,000. These shares gave her the right to convert each preferred share into two common shares. She exercised her conversion right at a time when the common shares were trading at $10 each. What is the ACB of her new common shares?

(9) What is the primary purpose of estate freezing?

(10) What might be some of the secondary objectives of an estate freeze?

(11) What are the three principal methods of freezing the value of growth assets?

(12) What are the basic steps involved in doing a Holdco freeze?

(13) When doing an estate freeze on the shares of a small business corporation in favour of a spouse, what is one of the biggest dangers? Assume that the freeze was done correctly.

(14) Describe when a "reverse or asset freeze" would be used and the steps you would take to accomplish it.

¶17,825   MULTIPLE CHOICE QUESTIONS

Question 1

P Ltd. is a profitable taxable Canadian corporation with a December 31 fiscal year end. It has a wholly owned subsidiary, L Ltd., with a June 30 fiscal year end. L Ltd. has a significant 2013 non-capital loss balance. Therefore, consideration is being given to either amalgamating P Ltd. and L Ltd. or winding up L Ltd. into P Ltd. in order to utilize the loss. The amalgamation or the winding-up will take place on November 1, 2018. Which *one* of the following statements is *true*?

(A) The newly amalgamated corporation can utilize the non-capital loss in its deemed year ended October 31, 2018.

(B) The newly amalgamated corporation cannot utilize the non-capital loss until its taxation year commencing one year after the amalgamation.

(C) If a winding-up takes place, P Ltd. can utilize the non-capital loss in its taxation year commencing January 1, 2019.

(D) If a winding-up takes place, P Ltd. can utilize the non-capital loss in its taxation year ended December 31, 2018.

Question 2

On September 1, 2015, X Ltd. acquired all the shares of Y Ltd. for $500,000. At that time, Y Ltd. had land with a fair market value of $130,000 and a cost of $100,000. On September 1, 2018, a winding-up of Y Ltd. into X Ltd. took place. At the time of the winding-up, the tax values of Y Ltd.'s assets totalled $420,000. The fair market value of the land at this time was $300,000. X Ltd. received $15,000 of dividends from Y Ltd. between September 1, 2015 and September 1, 2018. The adjusted cost base of the land after the winding-up cannot exceed:

(A) $100,000

(B) $130,000

(C) $165,000

(D) $180,000

Question 3

In the course of the reorganization of the capital of A Ltd., Chris exchanged all his common shares of A Ltd. (which are capital property to him) for the package of consideration outlined below.

Cash.	$ 135
Preferred shares (50 shares redeemable at $100 each)	5,000
	$5,135

At the time of the exchange, Chris' common shares had an ACB of $2,000 and a FMV of $5,135. Which one of the following best describes the tax consequences to Chris as a result of the exchange?

(A) Chris will have no capital gain on the disposition of his common shares and the ACB of his preferred shares is $2,000.

(B) Chris will have no capital gain on the disposition of his common shares and the ACB of his preferred shares is $1,865.

(C) Chris will have a capital gain of $3,135 on the disposition of his common shares and the ACB of his preferred shares is $5,135.

(D) Chris will have a capital gain of $135 on the disposition of his common shares and the ACB of his preferred shares is $2,135.

Question 4

Shelly exchanged her shares of Abigail Inc., a public corporation, for shares of Clare Ltd., another public corporation, when Abigail Inc. was taken over by Clare Ltd. Her shares of Abigail Inc. had the following characteristics:

FMV $12,000

ACB   7,000

PUC   5,000

Section 85.1 is often used in take-over situations. Which one of the following statements with respect to the rollover in this case is FALSE?

(A) When there are many diverse shareholders, a share-for-share exchange rollover is easier to accomplish than a subsection 85(1) rollover because there is no need for each shareholder to file an election.   ITA: 85.1

(B) The ACB of Shelly's shares of Clare Ltd. is $7,000.

(C) The ACB of the Abigail Inc. shares acquired by Clare Ltd. from Shelly is $5,000.

(D) Non-share consideration, up to the PUC of the exchanged shares, $5,000, could have been received by Shelly without any adverse tax consequences to her.

Question 5

Mr. Winters owns 100% of the shares of ABC Co., a small business corporation. He would like to freeze the value of this company for tax purposes at today's value and transfer future growth to his children without giving up control over the company. He does not want to pay tax any sooner than he has to. His will currently leaves everything to his wife. Which of the following plans will achieve his objectives?

(A) His children should subscribe to common shares of a holding company and he should transfer his shares of ABC to this holding company, electing under section 85 at tax cost and taking back voting redeemable retractable preferred shares as consideration.

(B) He should change his will to leave his shares of ABC to his children rather than his wife.

(C) He should gift the ABC shares to his children during his lifetime.

(D) He should sell the ABC shares to his children at fair market value, taking back debt as consideration.

Question 6

Which of the following techniques will allow Mr. Singh to use up his $848,252 capital gains exemption on the accrued gain on shares of a qualified small business corporation? The shares were issued to him 20 years ago for $1 and are worth $1 million now.

(A) A reverse asset freeze.

(B) An internal freeze, using section 86.

(C) A holdco freeze, taking back boot of $1.

(D) A holdco freeze, taking back boot of $848,253.

¶17,850   EXERCISES

Exercise 1

ITA: 85.1

Magnamous Publico Ltd., a widely-held public corporation, has offered to exchange its common shares, currently trading on a designated stock exchange at $14.70 per share, for the common shares of Targetco Ltd., another widely-held public corporation. The shares of Targetco Ltd. trade currently on the same stock exchange in the range of $12 to $12.25 each. Magnamous Publico Ltd. has offered to exchange one of its common shares for every two common shares tendered by shareholders of Targetco Ltd.

Mr. Stewart owns 1,000 shares of Targetco Ltd. which he bought several years ago for $11.25 each. Their paid-up capital value is $11 per share. On the announcement of the exchange offer their value on the market rose to $12.35. Mr. Stewart is interested in the exchange offer, but does not wish to realize any of the accrued gain on his shares of Targetco Ltd. Upon taking up the exchange offer, Mr. Stewart indicates that he will never own more than 10% of the shares of Magnamous Publico Ltd.

— *REQUIRED*

What are the tax consequences to Mr. Stewart and to Magnamous Publico Ltd. of taking up the exchange offer?

Exercise 2

ITA: 86

Aaron Chui owned some Class A preferred shares of a corporation that reorganized its capital structure. He exchanged all these shares which had an adjusted cost base and paid-up capital of $20,000 and a fair market value of $30,000 for the following consideration:

Cash.	$6,750
Fair market value of Class B preferred shares (LSC: $10,000)	17,550
Fair market value of common shares (LSC: $3,250)	5,700

— *REQUIRED*

What are the tax consequences to Mr. Chui as a result of this exchange?

Exercise 3

ITA: 86(2)

Mrs. Janna, age 50 and her daughter Rayna, age 28, respectively, own 75% and 25% of the 100 common shares of Adam Ltd. Adam Ltd. operates a commercial bakery business. The total fair market value of all the shares of the corporation is $600,000. The shares were acquired by both individuals at a total cost of $1,000 on incorporation about 18 years ago.

Mrs. Janna is now prepared to freeze the future growth of her ownership in the corporation, so that the future growth will be passed on to her daughter. Mrs. Janna will give up all of her common shares for preferred shares of Adam Ltd. having a legal stated capital of $750 and a fair market value of $350,000. As a result, Rayna will own all of the common shares.

— *REQUIRED*

What are the tax consequences under section 86 to Mrs. Janna on the proposed transaction?

Exercise 4

ITA: 87, 88(1)

M&M Limited owns all of the shares of Acme Limited. The cost of the shares to M&M was $750,000 and they now have a fair market value of $1,000,000. Acme's only asset is land which cost it $500,000. The land had a fair market value of $900,000 when the shares of Acme were purchased by M&M (at a bargain price!) and the land now has a fair market value of $1,000,000.

— *REQUIRED*

Determine the income tax consequences to M&M Limited and Acme Limited of using either an amalgamation or a winding-up of a subsidiary to combine.

ITA: 87, 88

Exercise 5

ITA: 51

Charlie owns $10,000 of debentures of Charlie's Cars Ltd. They were purchased several years ago at their face value and are convertible into 16 common shares of the corporation for each $100 of debentures owned at the option of the holder. When the common shares traded on the market at $100 each, Charlie exercised the conversion privilege.

— *REQUIRED*

What are the tax consequences of this conversion?

Exercise 6

Mr. Scotch, age 35, owns all 100 issued class A shares of Tape Inc., located in Toronto, Ontario. Tape Inc. manufactures florescent tape for gift wrapping. He acquired these shares in 2002. A widely held public company, Threem Inc., is interested in acquiring Tape Inc. Mr. Scotch is considering a proposal to sell his class A shares of Tape Inc. to Threem Inc. in exchange for common shares of Threem Inc.

— REQUIRED

(i) Will sec. 85.1 apply to this transaction? Why or why not?

(ii) Assuming sec. 85.1 applies, what are the tax consequences to Mr. Scotch and to Threem Inc. if Mr. Scotch's shares had the following attributes:

Paid-up capital	$100,000
ACB	$300,000
Current FMV	$700,000

(iii) Mr. Scotch has a net capital loss carryforward available of $300,000 from the disposal of some portfolio securities in 1999. He would like to be able to apply this against the gain on the exchange of his class A shares. Is this possible?

(iv) Could sec. 84.1 apply to this transaction if the paid-up capital of the shares Mr. Scotch receives from Threem Inc. in exchange for his class A shares of Tape Inc. exceeds the paid-up capital of the class A shares of Tape Inc.?

Exercise 7

Ichbin Verblonget owns the common shares of Verblonget Ltd. The shares have a PUC and adjusted cost base of $1,000 and a fair market value of $10,000. Mr. Verblonget wants to effect a reduction in the value of the common shares and has caused the corporation to undertake a capital reorganization. The corporation will exchange the common shares for the following package of consideration:

Cash (at FMV)	$ 100
Preferred shares (at FMV)	5,900
Common shares (at FMV)	4,000
Total	$10,000

— REQUIRED

Determine the tax consequences to Ichbin Verblonget as a result of the capital reorganization.

¶17,875   ASSIGNMENT PROBLEMS

Type 1 Problems

Problem 1

85.1
85(1)

ITA: 85, 85.1

Jason purchased all of the common shares of Quality Appliances Ltd., a Canadian-controlled private corporation, about 20 years ago, for $500,000. The paid-up capital of the shares was $25,000. These shares have recently been valued at $1,250,000.

Big Distributors Ltd., a Canadian, arm's length corporation, has offered to buy all of Jason's shares. The following alternatives have been presented to Jason:

Boot

(a) $250,000 in cash and $1,000,000 of FMV in common shares of Big Distributors Ltd.

(b) $1,250,000 of FMV in Big Distributors Ltd.'s common shares.

Jason is at arm's length with Big Distributors Ltd. and, after acquiring its shares, will neither control Big Distributors Ltd. nor own more than 50% of the FMV of its shares.

Jason has asked you to advise him on:

(A) The tax consequences to him if these transactions are conducted using the provisions of section 85.1.

(B) The tax consequences to him if these transactions are conducted using the provisions of section 85.

Problem 2

86

Matt, a resident of Toronto, owns all the common shares of Beam Inc. The adjusted cost base and paid-up capital of these common shares is $300,000 and the FMV is $900,000. In the course of a reorganization of capital in Beam Inc., the following two packages of consideration have been offered to Matt by Beam Inc. in exchange for his common shares:

Package (a)

Cash	$ 10,000
Bond	80,000
FMV and LSC of Class A preferred shares	810,000
– Redeemable and retractable at FMV	

Package (b)

Cash	$500,000
FMV and LSC of Class A preferred shares	400,000
– Redeemable and retractable at FMV	

Matt would like your advice on which option is better for him and whether there is a better option.

Before you meet with Matt you want to:

(A) Assess the situation.

(B) Identify the issues.

(C) Analyze the issues.

(D) Advise/recommend.

Problem 3

ITA: 86(2)

Mr. Fresser, age 67, owns 80% of the common shares of Fresser Ltd., a CCPC. The other 20% is owned by his daughter, Elana, who has worked in the business with Mr. Fresser for the past 22 years.

When the business was incorporated and capitalized, the 1,000 common shares were issued to Mr. Fresser and his daughter for $62,500 in total. They now have a fair market value of $625,000. Mr. Fresser proposes a capital reorganization in which he would give up his common shares in return for $90,000 in cash and $300,000 in retractable voting preferred shares with a legal stated capital of $300,000 which he could redeem at his convenience. As a result, Elana could own all of the outstanding common shares.

CHAPTER 17

Advise Mr. Fresser on:

(A) The tax consequences to him of section 86 on the proposed transaction.

(B) The tax consequences to him of subsequently redeeming the preferred shares for their fair market value.

Type 2 Problems

Problem 4

ITA: 87, 88(1)

Norm Bass has just met with you to ask your advice on the possible merger of his two companies. Norm, a Canadian resident, owns 100% of Normpar Inc. which in turn owns 100% of Jonsub Inc. Both are Canadian companies located in Saskatchewan and both have December 31st year ends.

Normpar purchased the shares of Jonsub in 2013 at a cost of $4.0 million. The first few years were profitable and in 2015 Jonsub paid a dividend of $500,000 to Normpar. But the last two years have not been good as Jonsub has realized non- and net capital losses. It is unlikely that Jonsub will generate sufficient income to absorb the losses in the foreseeable future. However, Normpar expects to generate sufficient business income and taxable capital gains to absorb all of Jonsub's losses.

Norm has heard that he could amalgamate the two companies or wind up Jonsub into Normpar so Normpar could offset its income with the losses.

Norm would like your advice on when Normpar can gain access to the losses of Jonsub if the two companies merge on June 30, 2018, either by amalgamating or by winding up Jonsub into Normpar. After the transaction they want to retain the December 31st year end. Norm is also concerned about what will happen to the $4.0 million ACB that Normpar has in the shares of Jonsub after an amalgamation or wind-up.

The balance sheet of Jonsub Ltd. immediately before the merger is as follows:

Assets:		FMV
Cash	$ 80,000	
Accounts receivable (net of $30,000 reserve)	800,000	
Inventory at cost	920,000	$ 920,000
Land at cost	1,200,000	2,000,000
Building at UCC	300,000	500,000
Equipment at UCC	200,000	150,000
Goodwill (FMV $500,000)		500,000
Total current assets	$3,500,000	
Liabilities and shareholder's equity:		
Accounts payable and accrued liabilities	709,000	
Loans payable	700,000	
Share capital	1,000	
Retained earnings	2,090,000	
	$3,500,000	

Other Information

(1) The fair market value of the land and building at the time Normpar Ltd. acquired control were $1.9 million and $400,000, respectively.

(2) The fair market value of goodwill developed by Jonsub Ltd. (i.e., not purchased) was $300,000 at the time Normpar Ltd. acquired control.

(3) Jonsub has the following losses:

Taxation year of loss	Non-capital loss	Net capital loss
2017	$43,000	$14,000
2016	7,000	10,000

Before you meet with them you want to:

(A) Assess the situation.

(B) Identify the issues.

(C) Analyze the issues.

(D) Advise/recommend.

Problem 5

Heather is excited about the future but she has come to you concerned that her corporate structure is not what it should be for her situation. She would like you to propose a structure that you think will work for her.

Background

Heather lives in Saskatoon and she started her operating company, Heath Inc., sixteen years ago and it is performing very well. On incorporation she paid $100 for 100 common shares. Heath Inc. is currently generating an after-tax operating profit of $300,000 and Heather expects the business to continue to grow over the foreseeable future. Out of the after-tax profit, $100,000 is needed for reinvestment in the business and the remaining $200,000 is available to be reinvested elsewhere. She would like to get this $200,000 out of the company to provide some creditor protection. Her advisors have estimated the current value of the company at $2.0 million.

Last year she had an opportunity she could not refuse. Land and building offered for sale at $1.2 million were perfect for her business, so she incorporated a company, Real Inc., to buy the property. She did this to protect the real estate from any creditor issues that may arise in the future in Heath Inc. Heather paid $100 for 100 common shares. She then loaned Real Inc. $400,000 of personal capital, at an interest rate of 5%, and Real Inc. took out a mortgage for a further $800,000 to buy the property. Real Inc. is charging Heath Inc. market rent to cover the interest and operating expenses, although Real Inc. is still operating at a loss. The value of the real estate has not increased since it was purchased.

This year she had an idea for a new business that she thinks is a sure winner. Again, Heather incorporated a company, New Inc., with her investment of $100 for 100 common shares. This new business will need capital to get started. Her problem is that she does not have any free capital personally but there is extra cash flow in Heath Inc. that she could use.

Also, she is the President of all three companies and is being paid from each. This results in Canada Pension Plan premiums being paid in all three companies and general confusion for her controller. Heather would like to simplify this and, if possible, only be paid from one company.

Heather is in the top personal tax bracket and has never used her capital gains exemption.

Before your next meeting with Heather you want to:

(A) Assess the situation.

(B) Identify the issues:

    (a) Propose an efficient structure for the corporations.

(C) Analyze the issues:

    (a) Develop the details needed to support the steps taken to implement the proposed structure.

(D) Advise/recommend.

Problem 6

Alison owns all of the common shares of Knight Manufacturing Limited (KML) which operates an active business in Belleville, Ontario. Over the past few months she has been thinking about doing an estate freeze on her shares of KML in anticipation of her retirement in a few years.

She has received a proposed plan from an adviser and she would like your thoughts on whether it will accomplish what she wants in a tax-efficient manner.

The following is information provided in the proposed plan:

(1) Alison is 55 years old and a widow. She is a Canadian citizen and resident.

(2) She acquired the shares of KML 20 years ago from an arm's-length person for $400,000. The KML shares have a paid-up capital of $100,000.

(3) She has three children. Sandra (32) works in a big bank in Toronto. Tom (30) is a CPA working for one of the large accounting firms in Vancouver. Helen (28) is an engineer with an MBA and she works in KML with Alison.

(4) KML has a current fair market value of $2.7 million and it is expected that this value will continue to grow rapidly, particularly with Helen's energy and skill leading the way.

(5) Alison is concerned about the issue of control of KML after a freeze. Since Helen is showing significant skills and is rapidly taking over the leadership of the company, Alison wants her to have operating control in the long term. However, she wants to maintain control of KML while she has a significant investment in the company.

(6) Alison is delighted with Helen's role in KML, since she would like to retire in three to five years and travel. She has been too busy with the business over the last 10 years to travel as much as she would like.

(7) Alison would like to freeze the value of KML and have her adult children benefit from the current value that she has built up over the years.

(8) Since Helen is responsible for building the increase in value of the business she would like Helen to benefit from the future growth in value.

(9) She does not want to do anything that would lead to conflict among her children over the business in future years. She has heard too many stories where the children fight over control of the business after the parent is gone, especially where they are not all active in the business.

(10) Alison does not have significant assets outside of KML so she will be relying on her interest in KML for her retirement.

(11) Alison has not used any of her capital gains exemption to date.

(12) All of KML's assets are used in a Canadian active business and have been since incorporation.

(13) Alison does not have a cumulative net investment loss and has never claimed an ABIL.

(14) Alison does not want her children involved in her financial affairs while she is alive.

Proposed plan

The following is the plan proposed by Alison's advisor:

Alison will complete a Holdco Freeze with her children owning the common shares of Holdco.

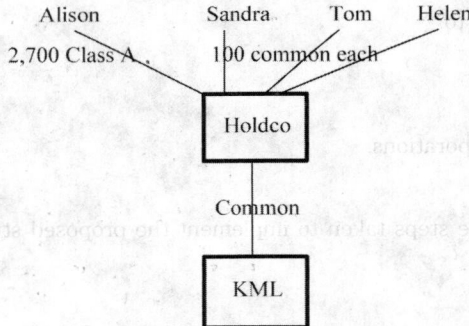

Proposed Sequence of Transactions

(1) The three children will incorporate Holdco Inc. (Holdco) by paying $1 per share for the common shares. Each child would purchase 100 shares from Holdco using money they have earned themselves.

(2) Holdco will have two classes of shares authorized:

(a) Common shares that are fully participating and voting.

(b) Class A preference shares that are voting as well as redeemable and retractable for $1,000 each. They have a non-cumulative dividend of 6% annually.

(3) The common shares of KML owned by Alison should qualify as QSBC shares since the three tests are met:

    (a) KML is a small business corporation.

    (b) She has held the shares for more than two years.

    (c) The asset mix has not changed in the past five years .

(4) Alison will sell her common shares of KML to Holdco in exchange for 2,700 Class A preference shares valued at $2,700,000. She will elect under s. 85 as follows:

	TV	FMV	EA	Debt	Pref	Income	
KML common	$400,000	$2,700,000	$1,248,252		$2,700,000	$848,252	CG

Under s. 85 the elected amount would be $1,248,252, which is enough to trigger a capital gain equal to the available exemption of $848,252.

ACB of Holdco Class A preferred shares

Elected amount	$1,248,252
Allocated to debt	nil
Cost of preferred shares (Holdco)	$1,248,252

Paid-up capital of Holdco preferred shares

PUC reduction [par. 84.1(1)(*a*)]:

(a) increase in LSC of holding company (Holdco) . . . . $2,700,000 (A)

less:

(b) greater of:

    (i) PUC of KML shares $100,000

                                                      $400,000

    (ii) modified ACB of KML shares $400,000

    less: FMV of boot . . . .   nil

    excess, if any . . . .   (400,000) (B)

PUC reduction . . . .   (A – B) $2,300,000

PUC of Holdco shares after reduction $400,000

84.1 Deemed dividend [par. 84.1(1)(*b*)]:

Sum of:

(a) increase in LSC of holding company (Holdco) . . . . $2,700,000 (A)

(b) FMV of boot . . . .   nil (D)

                                                 (A + D) $2,700,000

less sum of:

(c) greater of:

    (i) PUC of KML shares $100,000

                                         $ 400,000 (E)

    (ii) modified ACB of KML shares $400,000

(d) PUC reduction [par. 84.1(1)(*a*)] . . . .   2,300,000 (F)

                                              (E + F) 2,700,000

Deemed dividend   (A + D) – (E + F) $ nil

Capital gain/loss:

Elected amount under ssec. 85(1) for KML shares $1,248,252

Less: sec. 54 exclusion for par. 84.1(1)(b) deemed dividend . . . .   nil

Proceeds of disposition for KML shares $1,248,252

Less: adjusted cost base   400,000

Capital gain/loss . . . .   **$ 848,252**

Stated Results

Alison has frozen the value of her common shares in KML.

As Holdco increases in value this incremental value will accrue to the common shares held by the children.

Alison has used up her $848,252 capital gains exemption.

As Alison needs money in retirement she can:

– Have some or all of the preference shares redeemed.

– Have KML pay a dividend to Holdco with Holdco then declaring a dividend on the preference shares.

You have agreed with Alison that you will evaluate the proposed plan on its technical merit and whether it accomplishes her goals.

Before you meet with her you want to:

(A) Assess the situation.

(B) Identify the issues.

(C) Analyze the issues.

(D) Advise/recommend.

Problem 7

The following alternative structure has been suggested to accomplish Alison's objectives.

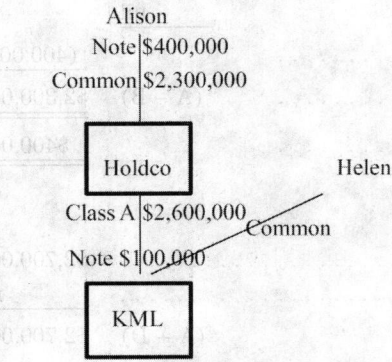

The Class A shares have the following characteristics:

(1) Redeemable and retractable for $2.6 million;

(2) Voting;

(3) Dividend rate of up to 6% per annum.

You have agreed with Alison that you will:

(1) Assess whether this structure can achieve her objectives.

(2) Propose the technical steps needed to move from the current ownership structure to this one.

CHAPTER 17

Type 3 Problems

Problem 8

Georgette is the president and sole shareholder of Vitality Plus Canada Ltd., a wholesale make-up and vitamin distributor. Twenty years ago, after the birth of her third child, Georgette invested $20,000 into the corporation and worked out of her home. Her corporation presently has the Canadian distribution rights for Vitality Plus, a European make-up line that continues to grow in popularity each year.

The company's net income (pre-tax) is approximately $320,000 per year, and Georgette's $100,000 salary is more than sufficient for her needs. The company shares have a current fair market value of approximately –$680,000.

Candice, Georgette's eldest daughter, is 26 years of age and currently works full-time for the business. Since Candice lives at home, Georgette pays her a small salary of $22,000 per year. Candice would eventually like to take over the business but Georgette is not quite ready to retire and still wonders if her other two daughters, aged 20 and 22, would be interested in joining the company. At the same time, Georgette would like to slow down and spend more time with her fiancé, whom she will soon marry.

Georgette, a single mother for several years, has a portfolio of Canadian public utility shares worth about $250,000. The unrealized capital gain on those shares is $120,000. She also has a self-directed RRSP valued at approximately $490,000.

Georgette would like you to prepare a report outlining how she could plan for her new marriage and retirement over the next few years. Consider the options for estate planning arrangements that will assist Georgette in transferring her business to other family members.

Problem 9

Gil and Ruth George have been friends of yours for many years. They have come to you for advice on their estate plan since they want a second opinion to make sure it is going to do what they hope.

Orillia Resorts Inc. (Resorts) is a company purchased by Gil about 20 years ago to operate a tourist resort. Gil originally paid $200,000 for all of the 1,000 common shares of the company, which is now worth $2.4 million as a result of the increase in the value of lakefront property. The common shares have a paid-up capital of $1,000.

They have found that they are no longer able to look after the resort, now that they are both 68 years old. Also, they feel that they would like to spend their summers travelling, instead of working 14 hours a day. They have had discussions with their lawyer and, on her recommendation, are now in the process of transferring the business to their only child, their daughter, Gale, who has been working in the business and is ready to take over.

Gil has never used his capital gains exemption. The only assets in Resorts are the property and equipment used in the business. They have not accumulated any investments personally so they will still be relying on the business for their retirement income. As a result, they would like to keep voting control as long as they have an investment in the company.

The plan proposed by their lawyer has the following steps.

(1) Gil will exchange his common shares of Resorts for 2,400 voting Class A preference shares. Then Gale will purchase 1,000 common shares from the company for $1 per share. The preference shares are redeemable and retractable at $1,000 each with a non-cumulative dividend rate of up to 7%.

(2) Gil will then transfer the preference shares of Resorts to a holding company (Holdco) in exchange for 13,518 Class B preference shares of Holdco plus a note for $1,048,200. On this transfer, he will elect under section 85 at a value of $1,048,252 to use up his capital gain exemption. The preference shares are redeemable and retractable at $100 each with a non-cumulative dividend rate of up to 7%.

(3) Ruth will pay $1,000 for 1,000 common shares of Holdco so she can receive dividends in their retirement years.

The plan is that Resorts will pay a 7% dividend each year to Holdco and then Gil and Ruth will decide how much they will take out of Holdco to live on. This will give them some investment assets outside of the business to provide some security for them in retirement.

Gil and Ruth would like your advice on the following issues:

(1) Does the freeze work technically?

(2) How will they continue to receive income from the business in their retirement?

(3) What are the tax consequence of the proposed plan to both Gil's and Ruth's estates and to Gale as the beneficiary. Assume that Gil dies first and leaves his estate to Ruth. Then assume Ruth dies and leaves everything to Gale.

(4) Is there a better plan?

Before you meet with them you want to:

(A) Assess the situation.

(B) Identify the issues.

(C) Analyze the issues.

(D) Advise/recommend.

CHAPTER 17 —
DISCUSSION NOTES FOR REVIEW QUESTIONS

(1) Either articles of amendment or supplementary letters patent need to be filed with the incorporating jurisdiction in order to reorganize the capital of the corporation. Nothing needs to be filed with the CRA.

(2) Some of the uses of a reorganization of capital rollover include:
    ITA: 86

(a) an estate freeze to allow the children to benefit from future capital appreciation;

(b) a reduction in the value of the common shares to allow a purchaser to buy common shares for a nominal amount; and

(c) a reduction in the value of the common shares to allow employees to buy shares at a reduced value.

(3) A deemed dividend may arise under the reorganization of capital rollover where the redemption proceeds (the reduced PUC of the new shares plus the non-share consideration) exceeds the paid-up capital of the old shares. The deemed dividend results in an adjustment to the proceeds of disposition. As a result, the proceeds will be reduced by any deemed dividend.
    ITA: 54 "proceeds of disposition" (*j*), 84(3), 86
ITA: 84(3)
ITA: 84(3), 86(1)(*c*)

(4) For corporate law purposes, the two predecessor corporations are deemed to continue to exist as an amalgamated corporation. The amalgamated corporation is deemed to have existed previously as the predecessor corporations. Property owned by the predecessor corporations continues to be the property of the new amalgamated corporation. Liabilities enforceable against the predecessor corporations are now enforceable against the new amalgamated corporation.

(5) The deemed year end as a result of an amalgamation has an impact on:

(a) unpaid amounts — the deemed year end will count for purposes of section 78;

(b) CCA will have to be prorated;
    ITR: 1100(3)

(c) the small business deduction business limit ($500,000) will have to be prorated for a short taxation year; and
    ITA: 125(5)

(d) the short taxation year will count as one of the carryforward years available.
    ITA: 111

(6) The CRA has indicated that, if an amalgamation is undertaken with a shell corporation solely to effect a year-end change, the GAAR would be applied. Therefore, this is considered to be an offensive transaction as far as the CRA is concerned.
    IC 88-2
ITA: 245

(7) In order for the rollover on winding up a subsidiary to apply, not less than 90% of the issued shares of each class of the capital stock of the subsidiary need to be owned by the parent, which is a taxable Canadian corporation, and all of the shares of the subsidiary that were not owned by the parent immediately before the winding-up were owned at that time by persons with whom the parent was dealing at arm's length.
    ITA: 88(1)

(8) Her new ACB is the total ACB she had on her preferred shares divided by the total number of new common shares. In this case her new ACB on the common shares would be $10,000 divided by 2,000 or $5 per share.
    ITA: 51

(9) The primary purpose of estate freezing is to freeze all or part of the value of growing assets at their current fair market value in preferred shares held by a taxpayer. Future growth in these assets accrues to someone else, usually the next generation of family members through ownership of common shares. The result will be that this future growth will not be taxed in the hands of the taxpayer on a disposition or at his or her death.

(10) Some secondary objectives of an estate freeze would be to:

(a) defer any immediate tax cost on the freeze transaction and establish the amount of the tax liability on death;

(b) maintain control over the asset that has been frozen;

(c) maintain a source of income from the asset being frozen;

(d) split income with low tax-rate family members (considering TOSI); and

(e) use up the QSBC share capital gains exemption on the asset being frozen, if possible.

(11) The three principal methods of freezing the value of growth assets are:

(a) holdco freeze;   ITA: 85

(b) internal freeze; and   ITA: 86

(c) reverse or asset freeze between corporations.   ITA: 85

Refer to the text for details of these methods.

(12) The basic steps involved in a Holdco freeze are:

(a) incorporate the holding company;

(b) transfer the shares of an operating corporation to the holding corporation using section 85 to avoid incurring an immediate tax cost; and

(c) have the transferor take back, as consideration for the growth asset, debt and preferred shares of the holding company. The preferred shares will have certain characteristics to achieve the freezor's objectives including a fixed retraction value which will freeze the value. Other features would revolve around desired voting control, income and security.

(13) One of the biggest dangers of doing an estate freeze on the shares of an SBC in   ITA: 74.4(2)
favour of a spouse or minor children is that the corporation will subsequently lose its SBC
status and the corporate attribution rules will apply to deem an interest benefit on the
transferor. Remember that the corporation only has to accumulate over approximately 10% of
the FMV of its assets in non-active business assets in order to fall offside. This may be done
easily if the company is generating excess cash and invests it. Keep in mind that the   ITA: 74.4(2)
corporate attribution rules only apply if "one of the main purposes of the transfer or loan may
reasonably be considered to be to reduce the income of the individual and to benefit, either
directly or indirectly, by means of a trust or by any other means whatever, a person who is a
designated person in respect of the individual". Thus, before the corporate attribution rule
applies, this purpose test must be met.

(14) A "reverse or asset freeze" would be used to transfer some or all of the growth
assets of a corporation in which the taxpayer owns common shares to a new corporation
owned by family members who will benefit from the future growth through their ownership of
the new corporation's common shares. The consideration taken back on the transfer will
usually consist of non-growth assets such as debt and preferred shares with a fixed retraction
value. For example, an operating company owns land and building that are used in the
business and the present shareholders want the increase in value of the land and building to
go to their adult children.

The steps that would be taken are as follows:

(a) a new company would be incorporated with the adult children subscribing for the common shares usually for a nominal amount;

(b) the existing corporation would then transfer the growth assets to the new corporation using section 85 to defer any tax; and

(c) the transferor corporation will take back, as consideration for the growth assets, debt and preferred shares of the new corporation. The preferred shares will have certain characteristics to achieve the freezor's objectives including a fixed retraction value which will freeze the value. Other features would revolve around desired voting control, income and security.

CHAPTER 17 — SOLUTIONS TO MULTIPLE CHOICE QUESTIONS

Question 1

(C) is correct. On winding-up, the losses of the subsidiary are not available to the parent, until the parent's taxation year commencing after the commencement of the winding-up. Thus, the losses of L Ltd. would first be available to P Ltd. in its taxation year commencing January 1, 2019.   ITA: 88(1.1)

(A) is incorrect. The predecessor corporations are deemed to have a year end immediately before the amalgamation, October 31, 2018. The amalgamated corporation first exists on November 1, 2018.

(B) is incorrect. The amalgamated corporation can utilize the losses in its first taxation year commencing November 1, 2018.   ITA: 87(2.1)

(D) is incorrect for the reasons (C) is correct.

Question 2

(B) is correct.

X Ltd's adjusted cost base of the shares of Y Ltd.	$500,000
Less: Cost amount of Y Ltd.'s assets	(420,000)
Dividends paid to X Ltd.	(15,000)
Potential bump	$ 65,000

ITA: 88(1)(*d*)

The ACB of the land can be bumped by $30,000, up to its FMV at the time X Ltd. acquired control of Y Ltd., $130,000.   ITA: 88(1)(*d*)

(A) is incorrect. The bump available on a winding-up has not been applied.   ITA: 88(1)(*d*)

(C) is incorrect. The full amount of the bump available has been allocated to the land. The ACB of the land cannot be bumped above the FMV of the land when X Ltd. acquired control of Y Ltd.   ITA: 88(1)(*d*)

(D) is incorrect for the same reason as (C). In addition, the potential bump has not been reduced by the dividends received from X Ltd.

Question 3

(B) is correct. Since Chris exchanged all his common shares as part of a reorganization of capital, the rollover applies automatically. The cost of the preferred shares is equal to the cost of his common shares, less the non-share consideration: $2,000 – $135 = $1,865. For purposes of calculating the capital gain on the disposal of the common shares, proceeds are defined as the cost of the new shares, plus non-share consideration received: $1,865 + $135 = $2,000. As the proceeds equal his ACB, there is no capital gain.   ITA: 86(1)(*b*)   ITA: 86(1)(*c*)

(A) is incorrect. The ACB of the preferred shares has not been reduced by the non-share consideration received.

(C) is incorrect. The tax-deferral provisions have been ignored.

(D) is incorrect. A capital gain equal to the non-share consideration has been recognized.

Question 4

(D) is correct as it is false. The provision specifically states that subsection 85.1(1) does not apply where consideration other than shares of the particular class of the purchaser was received by the vendor. Therefore, in the absence of any other election being made, Shelly would have a capital gain of $5,000 on the exchange if she received any non-share consideration.   ITA: 85.1(2)

(A) is incorrect as it is true. Section 85.1 is automatic; no election is required.

(B) is incorrect as it is true.   ITA: 85.1(1)(*a*)

(C) is incorrect as it is true.   ITA: 85.1(1)(*b*)

Question 5

(A) is the correct answer because this plan will freeze the value of his interest in ABC for tax purposes (since preferred shares don't grow in value) and transfer future growth to his children (because common shares do grow in value) without giving up control (because the preferred shares are voting). There will be no tax on the transfer since he will be electing at tax cost.

(B) is incorrect because changing his will to leave his shares of ABC to his children does not achieve his objective of freezing the value of his interest and having no tax on the transfer.

(C) is incorrect because gifting the ABC shares to his children results in the loss of control and immediate tax on the accrued capital gain because the gift results in a deemed disposition at fair market value.

ITA: 69

(D) is incorrect because, although a sale at fair market value taking back debt as consideration will defer tax somewhat because of the capital gains reserve, there will be tax on the accrued gain payable over the 5-year period and there is a loss of control.

ITA: 40

Question 6

(C) is correct, assuming an election is made at $848,253. The boot must be limited to $1 because the Act will cause any boot in excess of this amount to be a deemed dividend not a capital gain. That is why (D) is incorrect.

ITA: 84.1(1)

(A) is incorrect because a reverse asset freeze involves a transfer by a company rather than an individual. Hence, the $848,252 capital gains exemption cannot be used.

(B) is incorrect because an internal freeze using section 86 involves an automatic rollover. Hence, the $848,252 capital gains exemption cannot be used. While it is possible to accomplish an internal freeze with the crystallization of his capital gains exemption using section 85 as discussed in the textbook, that was not a choice offered in this question.

ITA: 86

CHAPTER 17 — SOLUTIONS TO EXERCISES

Exercise 1

Section 85.1 applies because shares of a Canadian corporation (Magnanimous, the purchaser) are being issued to a taxpayer (Mr. Stewart, the vendor) in exchange for capital property (shares of Targetco) of Mr. Stewart. Since Mr. Stewart wishes to fully defer the accrued gains in his shares he should not include any amount in his income on the disposition of his Targetco shares as a result of the exchange. Mr. Stewart and Magnanimous are at arm's length before the exchange. Furthermore, Mr. Stewart will neither control nor own more than 50% of the fair market value of all of the outstanding shares of Magnanimous after the exchange.

The tax consequences to Mr. Stewart will be as follows:

Proceeds of disposition for Targetco shares ($11.25 × 1,000)	$11,250
ACB of Targetco shares	(11,250)
Capital gain	Nil
ACB of Magnanimous shares received by Mr. Stewart in exchange	$11,250

As a result, the ACB of the 1,000 shares of Targetco given up by Mr. Stewart becomes the ACB of the 500 shares acquired in the exchange and the accrued capital gain on the Targetco shares is deferred. The ACB per share of the Magnanimous shares held by Mr. Stewart will be $22.50 (i.e., $11,250/500).

Magnanimous will have acquired the 1,000 Targetco shares from Mr. Stewart at an ACB equal to the lesser of:

FMV of Targetco shares before exchange (1,000 × $12.35)	$12,350
PUC of Targetco shares before exchange (1,000 × $11.00)	$11,000

The provision will apply to limit the addition to the PUC of Magnanimous shares on their issue in exchange to the amount of the PUC of the Targetco shares received (i.e., $11.00 per share). **ITA: 85.1(2.1)**

Exercise 2

There is no deemed dividend, because the redemption amount paid, consisting of cash for $6,750 and total reduced PUC of the new shares for $13,250, does not exceed the PUC of the old shares of $20,000. **ITA: 84(3)**

Issuance of New Shares

(1) Reduced PUC: **ITA: 86(2.1)(a)**

LSC increase for all new shares		$13,250
Less: PUC of old class A preferred shares	$20,000	
Less: boot	6,750	13,250
PUC reduction		Nil
Total reduced PUC (class B preferreds, $10,000; commons, $3,250)		$13,250

(2) Cost of class B preferred and common shares received:

Adjusted cost base of old shares	$20,000
Less: fair market value of non-share consideration	6,750
Cost of Class B preferred and common shares received	$13,250
Cost of non-share consideration (boot) received (equal to FMV)	$ 6,750

ITA: 86(1)(c)

Allocation of cost of new shares:

Class B preferred shares:

$$\frac{\text{FMV of class B preferred shares}}{\text{FMV of all shares}} \times \text{cost of new shares}$$

$$= \frac{\$17,550}{\$17,550 + \$5,700} \times \$13,250 = \underline{\$10,000}$$

Common shares:

$$\frac{\text{FMV of common shares}}{\text{FMV of all shares}} \times \text{cost of new shares}$$

$$= \frac{\$5,700}{\$17,550 + \$5,700} \times \$13,250 = \underline{\$3,250}$$

Redemption of Old Shares

(1)	Proceeds on redemption of old shares:		ITA: 84(5)(*d*)
	Boot or non-share consideration	$ 6,750	
	Reduced PUC of the new shares — see above	13,250	ITA: 84(5)(*d*)
	Redemption proceeds	$20,000	
	Deemed dividend on redemption:		ITA: 84(3)
	Redemption proceeds	$20,000	
	Less: PUC of old shares	20,000	
	Deemed dividend on redemption	Nil	ITA: 84(3)

(2)	Proceeds of disposition of old shares:			ITA: 86(1)(*c*)
	Cost of all new shares (above)	$13,250		
	Plus: cost of all non-share consideration (equal to FMV)	6,750	$20,000	
	Less: deemed dividend		Nil	ITA: 84(3)
	Proceeds of disposition of old shares		$20,000	
	Capital gain or loss on disposition of old shares:			
	Proceeds of disposition of old shares		$20,000	
	Adjusted cost base of old shares		20,000	
	Capital gain (loss)[(1)]		Nil	

Net economic effect:				
Deemed dividends on redemption			Nil	ITA: 84(3)
Capital gain (loss) on disposition of old shares			Nil	
Accrued capital gain on new shares:				
FMV ($17,550 + $5,700)		$23,250		
ACB		(13,250)	$10,000	
Net economic effect			$10,000	

This $10,000 reflects the accrued gain (i.e., $30,000 – $20,000) on the old shares before the reorganization.

— NOTE TO SOLUTION

[(1)] Capital losses on a redemption are denied where the corporation is still affiliated with the shareholder (e.g., where the shareholder or the shareholder's spouse still controls the corporation after the exchange). ITA: 40(3.6)

Exercise 3

The benefit rule will apply in this case because the FMV of Mrs. Janna's common shares ($450,000, i.e., 75% of $600,000) is greater than the FMV of the preferred shares received on the reorganization ($350,000) and it is reasonable to regard the $100,000 excess as a benefit that Mrs. Janna desired to have conferred on a related person, her daughter.

ITA: 86(2)

There is no deemed dividend, as shown by the following:

ITA: 84(3)

Issuance of New Shares

(1) Reduced PUC:

ITA: 86(2.1)(a)

LSC increase for new preferred shares		$750
Less: PUC of old common shares	$750	
Less: boot	Nil	750
PUC reduction		Nil
Reduced PUC ($750 – Nil)		$750

(2) The cost of the preferred shares received will be equal to:

ITA: 86(2)(e)

ACB of common shares		$ 750
Less: cost of non-share consideration	Nil	
benefit	$100,000	100,000
Cost of preferred shares		Nil

Since no boot was taken back on the exchange the final PUC of the preferred shares will be $750.

Redemption of Old Shares

(1) Redemption amount:

Non-share consideration	Nil	
PUC of preferred shares received	$ 750	$ 750
Less: PUC of common shares given up		(750)
Deemed dividend on redemption		Nil

ITA: 84(3)

(2) The deemed proceeds of disposition of Mrs. Janna's common shares will be equal to the lesser of:

ITA: 86(2)(c)

(a) Cost (equal to FMV) of non-share consideration	Nil
Plus: benefit	$100,000
	$100,000
(b) FMV of common shares given up	$450,000

There will be a capital gain on the disposition by Mrs. Janna of her common shares equal to:

Deemed proceeds of disposition (lesser of (a) and (b), above)	$100,000
ACB of common shares (75% of $1,000)	(750)
Capital gain	$ 99,250

The following net economic effect can be aggregated from the foregoing:

Deemed dividend on redemption		Nil
Capital gain on disposition of common shares		$ 99,250
Accrued capital gain on preferred shares:		
FMV	$350,000	
ACB	Nil	350,000
Net economic effect		$449,250

ITA: 84(3)

This $449,250 reflects the accrued gain (i.e., 75% of ($600,000 – $1,000)) on the common shares held by Mrs. Janna, before the reorganization. Note how $99,250 is realized immediately on the reorganization and the remainder will be realized on the disposition of the preferred shares.

Furthermore, Mrs. Janna has lost the ability to recover $100,000 in tax-paid cost, because the cost of the preferred shares is nil, having been reduced by the benefit. The $100,000 is tax-paid cost because it reflects the $750 of cost in the common shares, plus $99,250 of capital gain realized on the disposition of those shares and included in income. At the same time, Rayna has had the benefit of a $100,000 increase in the value of her shares without any increase in their adjusted cost base. Therefore, the $100,000 of gain will be taxable in her hands on the disposition of her common shares.

Draft legislation released December 13, 2017 extends the TOSI rules to include in split income taxable capital gains from the disposition of shares of a private corporation. As long as the $99,250 capital gain is on a QSBC share, the TOSI will not apply. As well, taxable capital gains on excluded shares is not included in split income. The common shares will be excluded shares because the shares provided Mrs. Janna with 10% of the votes and value of the corporation and the other conditions found in the definition of excluded shares will be met. [Less than 90% of the business income of the corporation is from services and it is not a professional corporation].

Exercise 4

If either section 87 or subsection 88(1) is used:

(A) Acme Limited will be deemed to have proceeds of disposition on the land of $500,000, so the capital gain will be deferred.

(B) M&M will be able to "bump" the cost base of the land on its books

— the "bump" would be computed as follows:		
M&M's ACB of Acme's shares		$750,000
Less the sum of:		
(I) cost amount of Acme's assets	$500,000	
(II) dividends paid by Acme to M&M	Nil	500,000
Increase in ACB of land		$250,000

ITA: 88(1)(*d*)

— this "bump" cannot exceed:		
fair market value of the land at the time control was acquired		$900,000
less: ACB of the land		500,000
maximum "bump"		$400,000

— therefore, the ACB of the land to M&M will be $750,000 after a "bump" of $250,000.

Exercise 5

Adjusted cost base of common shares equal to adjusted cost base of the debentures at the time of conversion $10,000

Adjusted cost base of each common share:

Number of shares received on conversion ($\frac{\$10,000}{\$100} \times 16$)   1,600

ACB of each share ($10,000/1,600) . . . . $ 6.25

Exercise 6

(i)   Sec. 85.1 of the Act applies to a transaction where shares of any particular class of the capital stock of a Canadian corporation ("purchaser", being Threem Inc.) have been acquired by a taxpayer ("vendor", being Mr. Scotch) from the purchaser in exchange for capital property of the vendor that is shares of any particular class of the capital stock of another corporation ("acquired corporation", being Tape Inc.).

Sec. 85.1 does not apply if any of the following conditions are present:

(a)   the vendor and purchaser were, immediately before the exchange, not dealing with each other at arm's length;

(b)   the vendor or person with whom he did not deal at arm's length, or the vendor together with persons with whom he did not deal at arm's length (i) controlled the purchaser, or (ii) beneficially owned shares of the capital stock of the purchaser having a fair market value of more than 50% of the fair market value of all of the outstanding shares of the capital stock of the purchaser immediately after the exchange;

(c)   the vendor and the purchaser have filed an election under ssec. 85(1) or (2) with respect to the exchanged shares; or

(d)   consideration other than shares of the particular class of the capital stock of the purchaser was received by the vendor for the exchanged shares, notwithstanding that the vendor may have disposed of shares of the capital stock of the acquired corporation (other than the exchanged shares) to the purchaser for consideration other than shares of one class of the capital stock of the purchaser.

The Tape Inc. shares owned by Mr. Scotch constitute capital property in his hands and Threem Inc. is a Canadian corporation (ssec. 89(1)). Accordingly, the rules of sec. 85.1 apply to the proposed share exchange assuming none of the conditions set out in the preceding paragraph exist.

(ii)   Tax consequences to Mr. Scotch:

Mr. Scotch is deemed to have disposed of his shares of Tape Inc. for proceeds equal to the ACB of the shares, being $300,000 (spar. 85.1(1)(*a*)(i)). Thus, he incurs no capital gain or loss on the exchange. The ACB of the shares of Threem which he acquired is deemed to be $300,000 (spar. 85.1(1)(*a*)(ii)).

Tax consequences to Threem Inc.:

The cost to Threem Inc. of the Tape Inc. shares is deemed to be $100,000, being the lesser of FMV of $700,000 and PUC of $100,000 (spar. 85.1(1)(*b*)).

(iii)   If Mr. Scotch includes in his income any portion of the gain on the exchange, the provisions of sec. 85.1 will not apply (spar. 85.1(1)(*a*)). Thus, in the absence of making any other tax deferred election, Mr. Scotch will have a taxable capital gain of ½ ($700,000 – $300,000) included in his income and can claim a net capital loss of $200,000*. As net capital losses can be carried forward indefinitely, Mr. Scotch should be cautioned against recognizing the gain just to use his net capital loss carryforward.

* Adjustment to 2016 inclusion rate of (i.e., ½ / ¾ × $300,000).

Draft legislation released December 13, 2017 extends the TOSI rules to include in split income taxable capital gains from the disposition of shares of a private corporation. As long as the $400,000 capital gain is on QSBC shares, the TOSI will not apply. As well, taxable capital gains on excluded shares are not included in split income. The common shares will be excluded shares because the shares provided Mr. Scotch with 10% of the votes and value of the corporation and the other conditions found in the definition of excluded shares will be met. [Less than 90% of the business income of the corporation is from services and it is not a professional corporation].

(iv) Sec. 84.1 will not apply as Mr. Scotch is not disposing of his Tape Inc. shares to a corporation with which he is not dealing at arm's length.

Exercise 7

Tax Consequences of Section 86 Reorganization of Capital

(1) Issuance of New Shares

    (a) Reduced PUC

LSC increase for all new shares		$9,900
Less: PUC of old shares	$1,000	
Less: boot	(100)	900
PUC reduction in total		$9,000

Proration of PUC reduction:

(a) preferred shares: $9,000 × $5,900/$9,900 = $5,364

(b) common shares: $9,000 × $4,000/$9,900 = $3,636

	Preferred Shares	Common Shares
LSC increase by class of share	$5,900	$4,000
Less: PUC reduction by class of share	(5,364)	(3,636)
Reduced PUC	$ 536	$ 364

    (b) Cost of new shares

ACB of old shares	$1,000
– cost of boot	(100)
Cost of new	$ 900

Allocation based on FMV

    900 × 5,900/9,900 = 536   Pref

    900 × 4,000/9,900 = 364   Common

(2) Redemption of Old Shares

    (a) 84(3) on Redemption of Old Shares

        Proceeds

PUC of new shares 84(5)(*d*)	$ 900
FMV of boot	100
	1,000
– PUC of old	(1,000)
84(3) dividend	Nil

(no deemed dividend since new PUC + boot is not greater than old PUC)

86(2) Gifting: None since consideration received equals value transferred.

    (b) CG (CL) on Old Shares

        Proceeds

Cost of new (above)	$ 900
+ boot	100
– 84(3) dividend	(—)
Proceeds	1,000
ACB	(1,000)
CG (CL)	Nil

CHAPTER 17

Chapter 18

Partnerships and Trusts

Learning Goals

Know

By the end of this chapter you will know:

• The basic provisions of the *Income Tax Act* that relate to partnerships and trusts.

Understand and Explain

By the end of this chapter you will understand and be able to explain:

• How a partnership and a trust are established.

• How income earned within a partnership is computed.

• How income of a partnership is taxed.

Apply

By the end of this chapter you will be able to apply your knowledge and understanding to:

• Calculate the income of a partner from a partnership.

• Calculate income of a partnership.

• Calculate taxable income and tax payable of a trust.

Review Questions
¶18,800 in the Study Guide

Multiple Choice Questions
¶18,825 in the Study Guide

Exercises
¶18,850 in the Study Guide

Assignment Problems
¶18,875 in the Study Guide

CHAPTER 18 — LEARNING CHART

Problem Descriptions

Textbook Example Problems

18-1	Partnership income allocation
18-2	Partnership income flow through
18-3	Transfer of partnership property to a corporation
18-4	Transfer of property to a partnership
18-5	Taxable income of trust and beneficiary
18-6	Attribution

Multiple Choice Questions

1	Partnership income flow through
2	ACB of a partnership interest
3	Trust
4	Testamentary trust
5	Types of trusts
6	Testamentary trust

Exercises

1	Partnership income flow through
2	Disposal of partnership interest
3	Taxable income of trust and beneficiary
4	Partnerships
5	Trusts
6	Testamentary trust
7	Trusts & attribution

Assignment Problems

1	Partnership income, ACB
2	Incorporation of partnership interest
3	Partnerships
4	Partnership income, ACB, disposition
5	Partnership income, incorporation
6	Transfer of assets to a partnership
7	Trusts
8	Establish a trust, income allocation, personal tax
9	Estate freeze
10	Merging two businesses
11	Advice on estate plan

Study Notes

¶18,800   REVIEW QUESTIONS

(1) What does the term "partnership" mean and where would you find the definition?

(2) A limited partner can deduct in full losses allocated to that partner by the partnership. True or false? Explain.

(3) An older man, Dadd, and his son, Ladd, wish to carry on a business as a partnership. Dadd is going to contribute land, building and equipment and cash while Ladd is going to contribute energy. They have agreed that they will split the profit from the business on a 50/50 basis; however, they would allocate any capital gain on the land and building fully to Dadd. In addition, any losses in the first five years are to be allocated fully to Dadd. What are your comments on the allocation of the gains and losses?

(4) Assume that you are a partner in a partnership and you are entitled to 25% of the income. How would your income allocation and adjusted cost base be affected by a $1,200 capital gain realized by the partnership?

(5) Assume that you are a partner in a partnership and you are entitled to 25% of the income. How would your income allocation and adjusted cost base be affected by a $100,000 receipt from a life insurance policy on the death of one of your partners?

(6) Ms. Jones is about to become a partner in a partnership and she wants to contribute some property on a rollover basis. There are 13 other partners involved although one of them has just moved to the United States for a four-year assignment. Should Ms. Jones have any concerns about the availability of the rollover?   ITA: 97(2)

(7) What is a trust?

(8) Comment on this statement: "Trusts are taxed in much the same way as partnerships; they are both conduits of income and neither is liable to pay tax".

(9) How is a testamentary and an *inter vivos* trust created?

(10) What is a discretionary trust and how does it work?

(11) One method of transferring the tax liability from the trust to the beneficiary is to either pay out the income or make it payable to the beneficiaries. What types of income retain their source for purposes of calculating the taxable income and tax payable of the beneficiary?   ITA: 104(6)

(12) Ms. Betty is the sole beneficiary of a trust that arose on the death of her father. He died on March 15, 2017. When does the trust file its first tax return? When does Ms. Betty report the income that is allocated to her by the trust in its first tax year end?

¶18,825   MULTIPLE CHOICE QUESTIONS

Question 1

Bert & Ernie
Partnership Income Statement
For the year ended December 31, 2018

Income:

Consulting fees		$300,000
Dividends received from low-rate income of a CCPC		40,000
Gain of sale of shares of taxable Canadian corporations		120,000
		$460,000

Expenses:

Salaries to staff	$50,000	
Capital cost allowance on equipment	15,000	
Office rent	10,000	
Charitable donations	20,000	$ 95,000
Net income		$365,000

The dividends were received from a CCPC whose income was eligible for the small business deduction.

Bert and Ernie each took drawings of $30,000 in the year.

Bert and Ernie share income from the partnership equally. Bert has no other source of income in 2018. Bert will have taxable income in 2018 of:

(A) $185,700

(B) $182,500

(C) $170,100

(D) $165,700

Question 2

On January 1, 2018, Ann and Bob formed a partnership to provide window cleaning services. The partners each contributed $5,000 and agreed that all income and losses would be shared equally. For the fiscal period January 1 to December 31, 2018, the following information is available.

(1) The partnership earned income for tax purposes of $200,000. Included in this amount is a taxable capital gain of $40,000.

(2) The partnership made charitable donations of $12,000.

(3) Ann took draws totaling $70,000.

(4) Ann contributed additional capital of $14,000 to the partnership.

The adjusted cost base of Ann's partnership interest at January 1, 2019, is:

(A) $23,000

(B) $43,000

(C) $63,000

(D) $69,000

Question 3

Al Smith settled a trust in favour of his two children on May 1, 2018. He settled the trust with marketable securities worth $50,000. His adjusted cost base for the marketable securities was $20,000. Al, his wife, and a family friend were named as trustees. His two children are ages five and six. Which one of the following statements is FALSE?

(A) The tax return for the first year of the trust is due March 31, 2019.

(B) The trust is entitled to a deduction in computing its income for amounts paid to the children during the year.

(C) Income in the trust will be subject to a 33% federal rate of tax.

(D) Al can defer the recognition of the capital gain on the transfer of the securities to the trust.

Question 4

The James Stewart family trust was created on and as a consequence of the death of James Stewart on May 1, 2018. Which one of the following statements with respect to the trust is TRUE?

(A) The trust must have a December 31 year end.

(B) The income in the trust will be subject to the same graduated rates of tax applicable to individuals.

(C) The trust return is due six months after the year end of the trust.

(D) The trust is not entitled to claim a dividend tax credit for dividends received and retained in the trust.

Question 5

Which of the following types of trusts has a deemed disposition of all its assets at fair market value on the settlor's death?

(A) An *inter vivos* trust

(B) A joint partner trust

(C) An alter ego trust

(D) A discretionary trust

Question 6

Which of the following is **not** an advantage of providing for testamentary trusts in your will for each of your children with a giftover to your grandchildren on each child's death?

(A) Income-splitting through discretionary income distributions to lower income beneficiaries.   ITA: 104(13.1), 104(13.2)

(B) Avoiding a deemed disposition of assets at fair market value on the child's death that would result if the assets were left directly to the child.

(C) Avoiding the deemed disposition of assets at fair market value on the transfer of assets to the trust on death.

(D) Providing your children with beneficial ownership over their inheritances, but giving control over their inheritances to the trustees of each trust.

¶18,850 EXERCISES

Exercise 1

ITA: 96, 110.1, 118.1, 121

The following income statement was prepared for Bob and Stan Tax Services, a partnership of two individuals who share income equally:

Bob and Stan Tax Services
INCOME STATEMENT
for the year ended December 31, 2018

Gross revenue from operations		$400,000
Less: Amortization on office furniture	$ 3,750	
Donations to charities	5,500	
Dues to Canadian Tax Foundation	550	
Employees' salaries	67,220	
Fringe benefits for employees	11,500	
Heat, light and water	2,400	
Interest expense	725	
Membership in fitness club	1,250	
Office rent	9,000	
Office supplies	2,250	
Repairs and maintenance	575	104,720
		$295,280
Dividends received from a CCPC that has no GRIP balance		4,000
Capital gain		5,000
Net income		$304,280

Additional Information

(1) Maximum capital cost allowance on the furniture for the year is $4,300.

(2) The partners each took drawings of $54,000 in the year.

(3) The dividends were received from a CCPC, all of whose income was eligible for the small business deduction.

— REQUIRED

Bob is your client. He has received personal investment income consisting of $3,500 in dividends from Canadian public companies and $1,200 in interest income. Determine his taxable income for 2018 and analyze the nature of his income.

Exercise 2

ITA: 53(1)(*e*), 53(2)(*c*)

Five years ago, a partnership was formed between David and Katie to carry on a professional accounting practice. Both partners made an initial contribution of $50,000 at that time agreeing to make equal drawings and to share equally in the profits and losses of the practice. The following data pertain to the partnership business during the period from its inception to the end of 2017:

Income of the partnership during the period	$450,000
Losses of the partnership during the period	15,000
Net taxable capital gains included in the above income	20,000
Drawings by the partners in the period	176,000
Capital dividends received by the partnership	4,000
Charitable donations made by the partnership	27,000
In 2018, Katie will retire from the partnership and will receive in full settlement of her partnership interest	250,000

— REQUIRED

Assuming Katie retires on January 1, 2018, what are the tax consequences to Katie of the disposition of her partnership interest in 2018?

Exercise 3

ITA: 104

On January 1, 2018, Mr. Ruester settled a trust for the benefit of his two children, Rebecca and Robert, both over the age of 18, neither of whom has other income. Robert attends, for eight months a year, a university in Canada where tuition is $3,500 per year. All tuition for 2018 was paid in respect of that year. Under the terms of the trust, the trustees have complete discretion to allocate the accumulated income to the beneficiaries in any manner they wish. The trust earned income from cash transferred to the trust by Mr. Ruester. For the 2018 taxation year, the trust received the following income:

Interest	$11,500
Dividends from public corporations	9,000
Capital gain	9,000

The trustees paid the income, and made the appropriate designations as follows:

	Interest	Dividend	Capital gain
Rebecca	$5,500	$3,000	$3,000
Robert	1,500	3,000	3,000
Total paid	$7,000	$6,000	$6,000
Total income accumulated in trust	$4,500	$3,000	$3,000

— *REQUIRED*

Compute the taxable income and the federal taxes payable of the trust and each beneficiary.

Exercise 4

Two of your university friends, who became lawyers, left the firms where they were employed and set up their own practice on January 1, 2018. They started the practice by contributing $10,000 working capital each and decided to split the profits equally and pay themselves equal salaries. They have chosen a December 31 year end for the practice. Their bookkeeper has prepared the following financial statements:

Friends Forever Law Practice
Balance Sheet
As at December 31, 2018

Cash	$ 2,000
Accounts receivable	30,000
Work in progress	25,000
Computer hardware, at cost	10,000
Computer software, at cost	8,000
	$75,000
Accounts payable	$15,000
Initial Partner Capital	20,000
Income for the period	40,000
	$75,000

Friends Forever Law Practice
Income Statement
For the Period Ending December 31, 2018

Income	$230,000
Meals and entertainment	6,000
Office supplies	4,000
Partner's salaries	130,000
Rent	24,000
Secretary's salary	26,000
	190,000
Income for the period	$ 40,000

The work in progress represents work done by the lawyers at their standard charge rate that has not been billed to clients at this time.

— REQUIRED

Part A	Your friends have come to you to determine the amount that they must include in their 2018 tax returns from the practice.
Part B	They would also like to know if there are any partnership-related expenses which they may have incurred personally which they may be able to deduct on their 2018 tax return.
Part C	Compute the adjusted cost base of each partner's partnership interest at January 1, 2019.

Exercise 5

Several years ago, Mr. Snider established an *inter vivos* trust for his daughter, who is now 20 years old. The terms of the trust provided that the trustees had complete discretion to distribute any portion of the annual income of the trust to the beneficiary.

The following income was earned in the trust for its taxation year ended December 31, 2018:

Interest	$15,000
Cash dividends from taxable Canadian public corporation	21,000
Capital gain	16,000
Rental income (after deduction of $1,500 of CCA)	5,000
Total	$57,000

In 2018, 75% of each type of income was paid to the beneficiary and the other 25% was retained by the trust. The daughter had no other source of income in 2018 and has used all of her capital gains exemption. She paid tuition fees of $1,500 in the year for eight months of full-time attendance at university.

— REQUIRED

Compute the taxable income and the basic federal tax payable of the trust and the daughter.

Exercise 6

The Estate of Mr. Frank Wellsay is a graduated rate estate with a November 6 year end. The beneficiaries of the estate are Mr. Wellsay's two grandchildren, Keith Wellsay and Karen Wellsay, and his niece, Marie Barr. This is the second year of the estate. It is now November 1 and the executors of the estate have told you that the estate has earned the following income:

Cash dividends received from Canadian public corporations	$15,000
Interest income	6,000
Capital gains	4,000
Foreign income (in Canadian dollars)	1,300
(Foreign tax withheld — Cdn $195)	
Business income	1,000

The terms of the will indicate that the executors can distribute the income of the estate to the beneficiaries at their discretion (timing and amounts to each beneficiary). The executors are required to distribute the capital of the estate equally to the beneficiaries.

— REQUIRED

Discuss how this income can be taxed (no calculations are required) and when the trust return must be filed.

Exercise 7

On July 1, 2018, Russell created a trust for the benefit of his two children who are 12 and 22 years of age. Russell gifted 500 shares of X Ltd., a taxable Canadian public corporation, to the trust. At the time of the gift, the 500 shares were valued at $240,000. Russell had purchased the shares in 2004 for $90,000. Russell also loaned $100,000 to the trust, interest-free.

During the period July 1, 2018 to December 31, 2018, the trust earned interest income of $6,000 and received $8,000 dividends on the X Ltd. shares. The trust earned exactly the same income during the period January 1, 2019 to June 30, 2019. In addition, the trust sold the 500 shares of X Ltd. on July 15, 2019 for $360,000.

Under the terms of the trust, the trustees, at their discretion, can accumulate the income earned in the trust or pay it out annually to the beneficiaries.

— *REQUIRED*

Part A	What are the tax consequences to Russell of the gift of the shares of X Ltd. to the trust?
Part B	What date should be the day of the first taxation year end of the trust? Briefly explain the reason for the date you select.
Part C	Based on the year end you selected in Part B, what is the due date for the tax return of the trust?
Part D	If all of the income is taxed in the trust, calculate the taxable income for the trust for its first taxation year and calculate the federal taxpayable for the trust.
Part E	Describe the tax implications to the trust and to the beneficiaries if all the income of the trust was paid equally to the two beneficiaries prior to the year end of the trust.

¶18,875   ASSIGNMENT PROBLEMS

Type 2 Problems

Problem 1

ITA: 53(1)(*e*), 53(2)(*c*)

Mr. Clancy has come to you with a question about his interest in the partnership Ludlum, Clancy, Follet & Associates. He has provided you with the following information:

Ludlum, Clancy, Follet & Associates

PROJECTED INCOME STATEMENT

for the year ended December 31, 2018

Gross revenue		$880,250
Expenses:		
Professional staff employee salaries	$229,000	
Office salaries	74,000	
Rent	42,000	
Office supplies	17,000	
Client entertainment	5,075	
Capital cost allowance	16,222	
Donations to charities	25,000	408,297
		$471,953
Dividends from Canadian public companies		25,000
		$496,953

Mr. Clancy has come prepared with some additional information. The adjusted cost base of his partnership interest was $45,792 at the beginning of 2018. His drawings for the year were $77,500. Mr. Clancy is one of four equal partners in the partnership.

On a more personal note, Mr. Clancy is not married and does not have any children. He is 31 years old. His only income is from the partnership. Both he and the partnership are located in Saskatoon, Saskatchewan.

Mr. Clancy is wondering if he should incorporate his partnership interest, but before you consider that, he wants to know what his tax position is, based on the current structure.

You have agreed to do the following :

(A) Compute the partnership income for the year, the income to be allocated to Mr. Clancy, and the nature of the income.

(B) Compute his taxable income and tax payable for 2018 assuming this is his only income. Ignore CPP.

(C) Compute the adjusted cost base of his partnership interest on January 1, 2019.

(D) Compute his after-tax personal cash.

(E) Discuss the CPP and EI implications.

Problem 2

Refer back to Problem 1.

Mr. Clancy wonders whether it would be to his advantage to incorporate his partnership interest. He has asked you to advise him on the following:

1. How the partnership income would be taxed if his partnership interest was owned by a corporation that he personally owned.

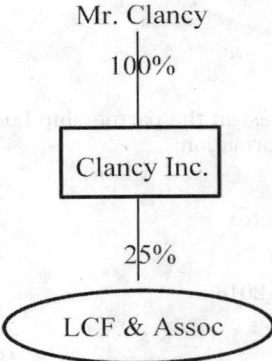

Mr. Clancy

100%

Clancy Inc.

25%

LCF & Assoc

2. Whether he should incorporate his partnership income. If he incorporates, assume that he pays his drawings out as a salary. Ignore CPP.

The provincial corporate tax rate is 4% on active business income eligible for the small business deduction and 12% on any other income.

For the next meeting you agree that you will:

(A) Assess the situation.

(B) Identify the issues.

(C) Analyze the issues.

(D) Advise/recommend.

Problem 3

Jim, Bob, and Stan formed the "Taxman Associates" partnership on February 1, 2016. Each partner contributed $30,000 in return for an equal share of the profits of the partnership. At the end of the 2018 fiscal year of the partnership on December 31, Bob retired and received $240,000 for his partnership interest on January 1, 2019.

The following income statement was prepared for Taxman Associates:

TAXMAN ASSOCIATES
INCOME STATEMENT
For the Year Ended December 31, 2018

Gross revenue		$878,210
Less: Office salaries	$ 85,500	
Rent	40,500	
Office supplies	17,500	
Capital cost allowance	20,060	
Donations	247,500	(411,110)
Capital gain on sale of land (capital property)	$135,000	
Dividend income:		
Non-eligible dividends	36,000	
Capital dividends	14,400	185,400
Net income		$652,000

The financial statements of the partnership revealed the following for the first two fiscal years ended December 31:

	2016	2017
Income (loss) before capital gains (below)	$121,500	$(67,500)
Capital gains on partnership property (November)	Nil	19,800
Charitable donations of partnership	1,350	Nil
Partners' drawings:		
Jim	28,800	14,400
Bob	28,800	18,000
Stan	28,800	14,400

Additional Information

(1) Each partner drew $120,000 from the partnership in fiscal 2018.

(2) The following data pertains to Bob:

(a) he has no other income for 2018;

(b) he is entitled to personal tax credits of $2,000 federally; and

(c) he has a net capital loss of $150,000 (arising in 1999) that is available to be carried forward.

— *REQUIRED*

(A) Compute Bob's income for tax purposes for 2018 as a result of his participation in the partnership.

(B) Compute Bob's taxable income for 2018.

(C) Compute Bob's capital gain on the disposition of the partnership interest.

Problem 4

ITA: 53(1)(*e*), 53(2)(*c*)

40%   20%   20%   20%

About five years ago, Isabelle, Eden, Samara, and Joy formed a partnership to carry on a snow removal and landscape business. All the partners, except Isabelle, made an initial contribution of $40,000. Isabelle made an initial contribution of $80,000. Each agreed to share in the profits and losses of the business based on their initial capital contribution. At the end of the 2018 fiscal year of the partnership, Isabelle and Samara decided to go their separate ways. Samara received $125,000 for her partnership interest, while Isabelle received $250,000 on January 1, 2019. The tax records for the five years ended December 31, 2017 reflected the following cumulative amounts: → Sold partnership   Received Proceeds of Disposition

Income (before capital gains) from operations for tax purposes	$750,000
Losses	80,000
Capital gains (to 2017)	10,000
Drawings by the partners	730,000*
Charitable donations (added back to Division B income for tax purposes)	15,000

* Isabelle, $170,000; Eden, $150,000; Samara, $250,000; and Joy, $160,000.

Financial results for the year ended December 31, 2018, are as follows:

Net income per financial statements	$60,000
Charitable donations (deducted from accounting income)	2,000
Drawings:	
Isabelle	10,000
Samara	5,000
Eden	5,000
Joy	4,000

Other Information

(1) Isabelle is single, and has interest income of $2,500 for the year 2018.

(2) Samara has interest income [*3a*] of $6,600, and has made an RRSP contribution in 2018 of $2,700 (her 2017 earned income was $15,000). *No CG in 2018, sold interest in 2019*

You have agreed to do the following:

(1) Compute the partnership income for the year ended December 31, 2018, and the income to be allocated to the partners.

(2) Advise on the tax consequences to Samara and Isabelle as a result of the disposition of their partnership interests in 2019. Compute Samara's and Isabelle's capital gain on the disposition of their partnership interests on January 1, 2019. *Need to Calculate ACB*

(3) Compute Samara's and Isabelle's taxable income and tax payable for 2018 using the hypothetical provincial tax rate table presented in Chapter 10, ¶10,250.

Problem 5

Brenda and Sasha are equal partners in an interior decorating business in Kenora, Ontario. Their income statement for the year ended December 31 shows:

S&B Interior Decorators
INCOME STATEMENT
December 31, 2018

Revenue	$320,000
Expenses	200,000
Income before gain on asset sale	$120,000
Gain on asset sale	35,000
Net income	$155,000

They have each asked you to prepare their personal income tax return, and to that end have provided you with the following additional information.

- Brenda was paid a salary of $6,000 and it is included in the expenses. *Add it back not deductible expense*

- A $1,000 donation to a registered charity is included in the expenses. *Add it back*

- The asset sold was a piece of land they had purchased in hopes of having their own building from which to operate their business; those plans fell through when the bank wouldn't advance the necessary loans. The $35,000 represents the net gain after real estate broker and legal fees of $5,000. *Purpose was to hold the asset, hold it → Capital Property → Capital Gain*

- Each partner uses (and personally pays for) his/her own car in the business. Brenda's auto expenses for business use are $1,500 and Sasha's is $3,500. *Will get deduction in personal tax*

- The business was originally started by Brenda. Sasha bought in several years later. He borrowed $35,000 from the bank to purchase his partnership interest and has paid $1,800 in interest on the bank loan.

- Included in revenue is $1,000 in interest earned on a GIC.

- Sasha's son is employed in the business and his wages of $2,000 are included in the expenses. He cleans up the store on weekends and does odd jobs. The $2,000 is considered reasonable, no T4 slip has been issued to him by the business.

- S&B's December 31 balance sheet shows that Brenda had drawings of $42,000 and Sasha had drawings of $35,000.

You have agreed to do the following:

(a) Identify the amount of any income, including the types of income, that each of Brenda and Sasha will include in their income tax returns. Identify any other items that will be included in their income tax returns.

(b) Brenda and Sasha are considering incorporating their partnership. What is the most significant property that needs to be considered on a section 85 rollover of their business? *Intangibles*

Problem 6

ITA: 22, 97(2)

Adam and Amit formed a partnership this year to operate a retail store specializing in gag gifts. Adam, who has been in the business for about 13 years as a sole proprietor, owns the following assets:

	Cost amount	Fair market value
Accounts receivable	$17,500	$ 17,000
Inventory	22,000	22,000
Store fixtures (cost: $17,500)	16,000	19,500
Leasehold improvements (cost: $37,500)	33,500	35,000
Goodwill	—	40,000
	$89,000	$133,500

Adam will transfer these assets to the partnership on November 1, 2018, in exchange for a 60% partnership interest. Amit will contribute $59,000 in cash and marketable securities with a fair market value of $30,000 in return for a 40% interest. The marketable securities were purchased about 12 years ago at a cost of $25,000.

You have agreed to advise Adam and Amit on the following:

(A) How can Adam's and Amit's assets be transferred to the partnership with the minimum amount of tax? What is the cost to the partnership of the assets?

(B) What is the maximum non-partnership consideration that Adam and Amit can receive without adverse tax consequences?

(C) What is the adjusted cost base of the partnership interest to each of Adam and Amit, assuming that the only consideration received for the transferred assets is a partnership interest?

Problem 7

Part A

For each of the following trusts settled by Mrs. A explain:

– The tax consequences of the transfer of property by Mrs. A to the trust;

– The rate of tax payable by the trust;

– The tax consequences of the transfer of property from the trust to the beneficiary

(a) On June 1, 2018, Mrs. A settled a painting on her daughters, B and C, in trust for her grandchildren. The painting has a cost to Mrs. A of $500 and a fair market value of $7,000.

(b) Mrs. A provides in her will that her shares of ABC Co. are to be held in trust for her grandchildren. These shares have a cost to Mrs. A of $10,000 and a fair market value of $35,000.

Part B

Mr. B died on March 15, 2018. Mr. B's will provides that the residue of his estate is to be transferred to a trust for the benefit of his wife, Mrs. B, a resident of Canada. The will provides that the income of the trust is to be paid to Mrs. B. The will also allows the executors to pay out capital for the benefit of Mrs. B. On Mrs. B's death, the trust's assets are to be distributed to the Bs' children. Mr. B's assets include shares of XYZ Inc., a public company, which were purchased about 25 years ago for $1,000 and have a fair market value at his death of $100,000.

You have agreed to advise the executor as follows:

(A) Explain the tax consequences to Mr. B arising out of the transfer of the ABC Inc. shares to the trust for Mrs. B.

(B) Explain the tax consequences to the trust of holding the shares and earning dividend income.

(C) Explain the tax consequences if the shares are transferred to Mrs. B.

(D) Explain the tax consequences if the shares are still held by the trust at the time Mrs. B dies.

(E) Explain how your answer to (A) would be different if Mr. B's will provided the trustees with the power to encroach on capital for the benefit of the Bs' children.

Part C

Ms. C, a lawyer, died on June 1, 2018. Ms. C was divorced at the time of her death. Under the terms of her will, her estate is to be distributed equally to her 2 adult children. At the time of death, Ms. C owned investments in publicly traded securities, RRSPs, a house and cottage, artwork and personal properties as well as an interest in her professional partnership. The executor of her estate is her long-time partner Ms J.

You have agreed to advise the executor as follows:

(A) Explain the tax consequences to Ms. C at the time of her death related to the properties she owned at that time.

(B) Explain the tax treatment of the estate arising on Ms. C's death.

(C) Explain the tax consequences of the distribution of properties from Ms. C's estate to her children.

Problem 8

ITA: 104

On January 1, 2017, Mr. Bilodeau settled a trust for his daughter Jane, who became age 17 in 2017. The trust was documented by a written agreement. There are three trustees, Mr. Bilodeau, Mrs. Bilodeau, and a long-time family friend. The trust provided that the trustees had complete discretion to distribute any portion of the capital or annual income of the trust to the beneficiary. *Inter vivos*

Mr. Bilodeau transferred the following assets into the trust on January 1, 2017:

(a) $250,000 cash; and *No Gain*

(b) 1,500 shares of Successful Retailers Ltd. (Retailers), a corporation that is incorporated in Canada and is a CCPC with no GRIP balance. The original cost of the shares about 23 years ago when they were purchased by Mr. Bilodeau was $17 per share. At the date of transfer the fair market value was $500 per share.

The trust immediately purchased a 6% bond with the $250,000 cash. Interest of $15,000 is payable on December 31.

The amount of dividends paid on the Retailers shares for each of 2017 and 2018 is $30,000. The dividends were received only from income eligible for the small business deduction. *Non-eligible*

In each year, the trust is to "accumulate" 60% of the income earned and pay out the remainder to the beneficiary to meet her financial needs. *40% Paid out to the beneficiary*

Mr. Bilodeau is in the top tax bracket. Jane does not have any income other than from the trust.

The trustees would like your advice on the tax consequences of the above transactions and the reporting of the income.

Before you meet with the trustees you want to:

(A) Assess the situation.

(B) Identify the issues.

(C) Analyze the issues.

(D) Advise/recommend.

Problem 9

ITA: 84(1), 85, 86, 104, 129(6)

Gordon Willows is 60 years old. He is the president and sole shareholder of Amazing Results Inc. ("Amazing"). Amazing was incorporated about 25 years ago. At the time of incorporation, Gordon subscribed for 100 common shares without par value for subscription proceeds of $100. These are still the only shares that are issued and outstanding.

Amazing has been involved in the lobbying business and achieves results for its clients which are considered to be simply amazing. Amazing has just been involved in a very successful high-profile lobbying effort and business is booming. Four years ago his daughter Wendy joined the company and has learned the business very well. She has taken on significant responsibility and has proven leadership ability. Amazing has been a very profitable company. It is estimated that the fair market value of the shares is $8 million today. Gordon believes that, under Wendy's leadership, there is a reasonable chance that the value of the shares of Amazing will increase over the next five years to between $9 million and $13 million. This will require a lot of work from Wendy since Gordon plans to cut back on his work activity.

Gordon is divorced with three children.

– Wendy is 35 years old and very active in the business. Her intention is to make a career out of Amazing.

– Wayne, who is 32 years old, is an artist with no interest in Amazing.

– Winona, who is 28 years old, is in a PhD program in accounting. She has stated her intention is to become a researcher at a top university.

Gordon would like to retire from active involvement in Amazing within the next 10 years. He estimates that he will continue to require an income of $200,000 per year thereafter. He wants to take action now so that, in the event of his death, he will not be taxed on the growth of Amazing beyond its current value.

You have looked at Amazing recently and determined that the shares do meet the qualifications to be QSBC shares.

Gordon has decided that a plan should be implemented to ensure that the future growth in value of Amazing will accrue to Wendy. He wants to maintain sufficient voting control over Amazing during his life in the event that Wendy does not fulfil his expectations of her involvement in the business. He has never claimed the capital gains exemption.

He wants you to determine the amount of tax that would be payable in his estate on his death and suggest where the cash come from to pay the tax. On his death Gordon wants to leave his assets equally among his three children.

The tax partner has suggested the following structure.

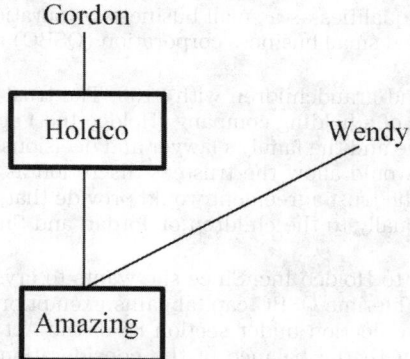

Before your next meeting with Gordon you have been asked to:

(A) Assess the situation.

(B) Identify the issues:

   (a) Determine the high-level technical steps needed to achieve the structure.

   (b) Determine if the proposed structure meets Gordon's goals.

(C) Analyze the issues:

   (a) Complete the technical details.

(D) Advise/recommend.

Type 3 Problems

Problem 10

Kay Sega is a pharmacist and owner of a well-established and unincorporated pharmacy in a Saskatoon mall. Lamia Savitz is a nutritionist and owner of an unincorporated health food store that is located in the same neighbourhood shopping mall. Kay and Lamia both realize that they share many of the same products and customers. They are currently considering combining the two stores to not only save on costs but also to provide opportunities for growth and tax deferral. Kay heard, at a local investment seminar, that tax rates for corporations are much lower than for partnerships. Last year, each earned the following:

- Pharmacy net income from a business $160,000

- Health food store net income from a business $110,000

Advise Kay and Lamia on the alternative methods that would permit the merger to take place. Which alternative will attract the least tax, over time?

Problem 11

Cora Dusk owns 100% of the common shares of a corporation, Cee Ltd. These shares have an original cost of $1,000, a paid-up capital of $1,000 and a fair market value of $1.8 million. At the current time, the common shares are the only shares of Cee Ltd. that are issued and outstanding.

Cora is a Canadian resident, 70 years old and a recent widow. She wants to freeze the value of her common shares of Cee Ltd. in favour of a trust for her children and grandchildren. Cora has a 40-year-old daughter, Jordan, and a 35-year-old daughter, Susanne. All of Cora's grandchildren are under the age of 10. Her current will leaves these shares equally to Jordan and Susanne.

Cee Ltd. carries on a real estate rental business and has nine full-time employees throughout the year, including Cora, Jordan and Susanne. The company qualifies as a small business corporation and the shares which Cora owns meet all the tests to be qualified small business corporation (QSBC) shares.

Cora's plan is to settle one trust for her daughters and grandchildren with $100. The trust would use the $100 to subscribe and pay for 100 common shares of a holding company (Holdco Inc.) at a cost of $1 each. The trustees of the trust will be Jordan, Susanne and the family's lawyer and decisions would be made by a majority of trustees. The trust agreement would allow the trustees discretion as to the allocation of income to beneficiaries on an annual basis. The trust agreement would provide that, at the end of 21 years, the trust capital would be distributed equally to the children of Jordan and Susanne.

Cora would then sell her common shares of Cee Ltd. to Holdco Inc. Since she wants to crystallize the $400,000 remainder in 2018 (after indexation) of her lifetime QSBC capital gains exemption when she freezes the value of her shares, she plans to make an election under section 85 of the Act in the amount of $401,000. She will receive $401,000 of debt, with the balance of the consideration being Holdco Inc. shares with a fair market value and legal stated capital of $1,399,000 from Holdco Inc. in return for her common shares of Cee Ltd.

Cora currently pays tax at the top marginal rate, but Jordan and Susanne do not because of child care expenses, RRSP contributions and other deductions and tax credits.

Cora has asked you for your comments on her stated plans and whether you have any ideas for improvement or alternatives for her to consider.

CHAPTER 18 —
DISCUSSION NOTES FOR REVIEW QUESTIONS

(1) The term "partnership" is not defined in the *Income Tax Act*. The term "partnership" is defined in the provincial Partnership Acts. The Ontario *Partnership Act*, for example, provides that a "partnership is a relationship that subsists between persons carrying on a business in common with a view to profit."

(2) False. The amount of losses a limited partner can deduct in computing income in respect of losses allocated by the limited partnership is limited. The losses can only be deducted to the extent of the limited partner's "at-risk amount" as defined. Generally, the losses may be deducted by a limited partner only to the extent that the total of his or her investment in the partnership plus his or her share of the partnership profit exceeds any amount owing to the partnership by him or her and so on. To the extent that limited partnership losses are restricted, they can be carried forward indefinitely and deducted, but only against income from the limited partnership that gave rise to the loss.

ITA: 96(2.1)
ITA: 96(2.2)

ITA: 111(1)(*e*)

(3) Because Dadd and Ladd do not deal at arm's length, the anti-avoidance rule must be considered. The issue is whether the allocation is reasonable in the circumstances having regard to the capital invested in or work performed for the partnership by the members thereof, or such other factors as may be relevant. For example, the allocation of the capital gain to Dadd may be reasonable given that it was his property in the first place. Since Dadd is the only one with capital and cash invested in the partnership, any losses may be his losses, as the losses impair his capital in the partnership. Arguments can be made that the allocation is reasonable in the circumstances.

ITA: 103(1.1)

Because the decision has been made to allocate income on a 50/50 basis but to allocate all of the losses to Dadd, reference should also be made to another anti-avoidance rule. There should be no problem with this allocation on the basis that the principal reason for the allocation cannot reasonably be considered to be the reduction or postponement of the tax otherwise payable under the Act.

ITA: 103(1)

(4) Income is calculated at the partnership level and then allocated to the partners. A $600 taxable capital gain would be included in the income of the partnership, of which your share is $150 (25% × $600). Your adjusted cost base will be increased by $300, being your share of the taxable capital gain of $150 and your share of the non-taxable portion of $150.

ITA: 53(1)(*e*)

(5) Income is calculated at the partnership level and then allocated to the partners. A $100,000 receipt would not be included in the partnership's income, since life insurance proceeds are not taxable. The adjusted cost base of your partnership interest will be increased by your share or $25,000.

ITA: 53(1)(*e*)

(6) A rollover is available only on a transfer to a Canadian partnership. This is defined to include only those partnerships where all the members are resident in Canada at the particular time. In this case, Ms. Jones will need to determine whether the partner in the United States is still considered a resident of Canada for purposes of the Act. If not, the rollover will not be available.

ITA: 97(2)
ITA: 102

(7) A trust is a relationship whereby a person (who is called a trustee) is bound to deal with property (which is called the trust property) over which he or she has control for the benefit of persons (who are called the beneficiaries) any of whom may enforce the obligation according to the terms of the trust document. A trust is created when a person (called the settlor) transfers property to a trustee.

(8) While it is true that trusts are conduits by allowing certain types of income to flow through to the beneficiaries and retain their character for tax purposes (for example, dividends, capital gains, foreign income), the income of a trust may be subject to tax. Trusts are taxed as an individual on any income that is not paid or payable to the beneficiaries. The rate of tax paid depends on whether the trust is an *inter vivos* trust or a testamentary trust.

ITA: 104(2), 104(6)

CHAPTER 18

(9) A testamentary trust is created as a consequence of the death of an individual. An *inter vivos* trust is one that is created during the lifetime of an individual. An *inter vivos* trust may also be created for tax purposes where a person other than the deceased has contributed property to a testamentary trust.

(10) A discretionary trust is a trust where the trustee is given the power of choice. The trustee may be given the power to determine the date of distribution of trust property, whether income or capital is to be paid to a beneficiary, how much is to be paid to a beneficiary and in what proportions among a group of beneficiaries it is to be paid. This feature gives the trust a great deal of flexibility and is a very useful planning tool for income splitting (subject to TOSI) and estate equalization purposes.

(11) The special treatment applies to the following types of income:

(a) taxable dividends from a Canadian corporation which allows the beneficiary to use the dividend gross-up and tax credit;   ITA: 104(19)

(b) net taxable capital gains which are eligible for the capital gains deduction available in respect of qualified shares of a small business corporation and qualified farm property (note that net capital losses do not flow through to the beneficiary);   ITA: 104(21)–(21.3)

(c) non-taxable dividends which are excluded from the computation of taxable income;   ITA: 104(20)

(d) foreign income and related foreign tax paid to allow the beneficiary to claim the foreign tax credit; and   ITA: 104(22)

(e) superannuation and pension benefits.   ITA: 104(27), 104(28)

(12) The trust would file a tax return for the fiscal period ending on December 31, 2017 on or before March 31, 2018 (that is, 90 days after the end of the trust's year). She would report the income allocated to her for the December 31, 2017 taxation year on her 2017 personal tax return, i.e., the calendar year in which the fiscal year end of the trust fell. A testamentary trust that is created by will is not an "estate" and so cannot be a graduated rate estate with an off calendar year end.   ITA: 104(13), 104(14)

CHAPTER 18 — SOLUTIONS TO MULTIPLE CHOICE QUESTIONS

Question 1

(D) $165,700 is correct.

Net income per financial statement		$ 365,000
Add: Donations		20,000
Sale of shares — Taxable capital gain	$ 60,000	
— Accounting gain	(120,000)	(60,000)
		$ 325,000
Bert's share		× ½
		$ 162,500
Dividend gross-up: $20,000 × 16%		3,200
Taxable income		$ 165,700

(A) $185,700 is incorrect. The only adjustment that was made was for the dividend gross-up.

(B) $182,500 is incorrect. All of the adjustments have been ignored: donations, net accounting/tax gain, and the dividend gross-up.

(C) $170,100 is incorrect. All adjustments were made except for the dividend gross-up, which, at 38%, was incorrect on dividends from a CCPC out of its LRIP.

Question 2

(C) $63,000 is correct.

Contributions — initial		$ 5,000
— additional		14,000
Share of profit		100,000
Share of non-taxable portion of capital gain		20,000
Share of charitable donations		(6,000)
Drawings		(70,000)
ACB		$ 63,000

(A) $23,000 is incorrect. The capital gain has been excluded completely.

(B) $43,000 is incorrect. The non-taxable portion of the capital gain has not been included.

(D) $69,000 is incorrect. The ACB has not been reduced by Ann's share of the charitable donations.

Question 3

(A) is true. The tax return is due 90 days after the year end of the trust. *Inter vivos* trusts are taxed on a calendar year basis.   ITA: 150(1)(*c*), 249(1)(*b*)

(B) is true. The trust is entitled to the deduction.   ITA: 104(6)

(C) is true. The tax rate is 33%.   ITA: 122(1)

(D) is false. Al is deemed to have received proceeds equal to the fair market value of the marketable securities transferred to the trust. Therefore, Al is required to recognize the $30,000 capital gain.   ITA: 69(1)(*b*)

CHAPTER 18

Question 4

(A) is true. The taxation year of a testamentary trust that is not a graduated rate estate must have a   ITA: 104(2), 122(1)
calendar year end.

(B) is false. Only a graduated rate estate is taxed as an individual and only for the first 36 months   ITA: 104(23)
from the date of death. A testamentary trust that is created by will is not an "estate" and cannot be a
graduated rate estate.

(C) is false. The trust return is due 90 days after the end of the fiscal period of the trust.   ITA: 150(1)(*c*)

(D) is false. The trust is entitled to claim a dividend tax credit for dividends received from taxable   ITA: 104(2), 121
Canadian corporations.

Question 5

(C) is correct. An *alter ego* trust has a deemed disposition on the settlor's death.   ITA: 248(1)

(A) is incorrect. An *inter vivos* trust generally has a deemed disposition at fair market value at the
end of 21 years, unless it is a joint partner trust (described in (B)), in which case the deemed
disposition takes place on the partner (i.e., spouse or common-law partner) beneficiary's death.

(B) is incorrect. A joint partner trust has a deemed disposition on the death of the partner (i.e.,
spouse or common-law partner).

(D) is incorrect. A discretionary trust would always have a deemed disposition at fair market value
at the end of 21 years, since it cannot be a joint partner trust (which, by definition, must pay the income
out to the beneficiary and, therefore, cannot be discretionary).

Question 6

(C) is correct. Avoiding the deemed disposition is not an advantage. You cannot avoid the deemed   ITA: 104(4)
disposition at FMV if the beneficiaries of the testamentary trust are your children.

(A) is incorrect because income-splitting through distributions to beneficiaries is an advantage.
(TOSI does not apply to dividends or taxable capital gains on property inherited on the death of a parent
where the child is under the age of 25.)

(B) is incorrect, because avoiding the deemed disposition on the child's death is an advantage.

(D) is incorrect, because providing your children with beneficial ownership but not control over
their inheritance is an advantage.

CHAPTER 18 — SOLUTIONS TO EXERCISES

Exercise 1

Partnership's net income for financial accounting purposes		$304,280
Deduct: Capital gain		5,000
		$299,280
Add: Amortization on office furniture	$ 3,750	
Donations	5,500	
Membership in fitness club	1,250	
Taxable capital gain ($\frac{1}{2} \times$ $5,000)	2,500	13,000
		$312,280
Deduct: Capital cost allowance		4,300
Income to be allocated (Division B)		$307,980
Bob's share of income from partnership		$153,990
Add: Gross-up of Bob's share of partnership dividends		
(16% $\times$ $4,000 $\times$ $\frac{1}{2}$)	$ 320	
Grossed-up personal dividends ($3,500 $\times$ 1.38) . . .	4,830	
Personal interest income	1,200	6,350
Bob's net income (Division B) and taxable income		$160,340

Analysis of Bob's income:

	Personal	*Partnership*	*Total*
Grossed-up dividends	$4,830	$ 2,320	$ 7,150
Interest	1,200	—	1,200
Taxable capital gains	—	1,250	1,250
Business income		150,740	150,740
Total	$6,030	$154,310*	$160,340

* $153,990 + $320 gross-up

— NOTE TO SOLUTION

(1) Drawings taken by the members of a partnership do not constitute a business expense but are a method of distributing partnership income to members of the partnership.

(2) Charitable donations are not deductions in computing the income of a partnership but are used as the basis for computing the charitable donations tax credit for an individual partner.

(3) Fees paid to a fitness club are non-deductible expenses.   ITA: 18(1)(*l*)

(4) Bob will be eligible for the following federal dividend tax credit:

— on share of partnership dividends ($\frac{8}{11} \times$ $320)	$	233
— on personal dividends ($\frac{6}{11} \times$ $1,330)		725
Total	$	958

Exercise 2

Adjusted cost base of Katie's partnership interest:

Contributions			$ 50,000
Add:	Share of profits excluding taxable capital gain (½ × ($450,000 – $20,000))	$215,000	
	Share of full capital gain (½ × $20,000 × ²⁄₁)	20,000	
	Share of capital dividends (½ × $4,000)	2,000	237,000
			$287,000
Deduct:	Share of losses (½ × $15,000)	$ 7,500	
	Drawings (½ × $176,000)	88,000	
	Share of donations (½ × $27,000)	13,500	109,000
ACB of partnership interest January 1, 2018			$178,000

Capital gain on disposition of partnership interest:

Proceeds of disposition	$250,000
ACB	178,000
Capital gain	$ 72,000
Taxable capital gain (½ of $72,000)	$ 36,000

Exercise 3

	Trust	Rebecca	Robert
Income			
Interest	$ 4,500	$ 5,500	$ 1,500
Taxable capital gain	1,500	1,500	1,500
Taxable dividends	4,140	4,140	4,140
Net income/taxable income	$10,140	$11,140	$ 7,140
Federal tax (@ 33% for trust and 15% for individuals)	$ 3,346	$ 1,671	$ 1,071
Personal tax credit @ 15% of $11,809	—	(1,771)	(1,771)
Tuition credit and education credit	Nil	Nil	Nil
Dividend tax credit @ ⁶⁄₁₁ of $3,000 × 0.38	(622)	(622)	(622)
Total tax	$ 2,724	$ Nil	Nil

Note: None of the tuition tax credit was claimed by Robert. Federal tuition tax credits of $525[1] are transferable to a parent, or the unused amount less any amount transferred to a supporting person may be carried forward. The definition of tax payable and the ordering rules require that the personal, tuition and education tax credits be deducted before the dividend tax credit which is lost in this case.

ITA: 118.9(1)
ITA: 118.61
ITA: 118.81, 118.92

— NOTE TO SOLUTION

[1] Lesser of:

(a) $750 (federal) = $750	⎫	
	⎬	$ 525
(b) (15% × $3,500) = $525	⎭	
Minus ($1,071 – $1,771)		Nil
Net amount transferred to parent		$ 525

Exercise 4

Part A

Partnership income for tax purposes:

Income for the period				$ 40,000
Add:	Partners' salaries			130,000
	Meals and entertainment (50%)			3,000
Deduct:	Work in progress (sec. 34) — if an election made			(25,000)
	Capital cost allowance:			
	Class 50 $10,000 × 55% × ½	$2,750		
	Class 12 $8,000 × 100% × ½	4,000		(6,750)
Taxable income of the partnership				$141,250

Therefore, each partner must include $70,625 of income from the partnership in their 2018 tax return.

Part B

They may also be able to deduct the following expenses which they may have incurred personally:

– any interest expense on the capital contribution of $10,000;

– the business portion of any car expenses;

– any promotion expenses;

– expenses for any office in the home (to a maximum of business income before the deduction), if the work space is used exclusively for business purposes and it is used on a regular and continuous basis for meeting clients (s. 18(12)).

Part C

Adjusted cost base of partnership January 1, 2019:

Capital contribution	$ 10,000
Share of partnership income*	70,625
Draws ($130,000 divided by 2)	(65,000)
Adjusted cost base	15,625

* only added to partnership ACB on January 1, 2019

Exercise 5

	Trust	Daughter	Total
Income:			
Interest	$ 3,750	$11,250	$15,000
Grossed-up dividend (1.38 × $21,000)	7,245	21,735	28,980
Taxable capital gain (½ × $16,000)	2,000	6,000	8,000
Rental income (before CCA)	1,625	4,875	6,500
CCA	(1,500)		
Division B income	$13,120	$43,860	
Capital gains deduction	Nil	Nil	
Taxable income	$13,120	$43,860	
Federal tax (trust @ 33%)	$ 4,330		
(dtr — $43,860 at 15%)		$ 6,579	
Less: personal tax credit	Nil	(1,771)	
tuition credit (15% of $1,500)	Nil	(225)	
dividend tax credit (6/11 of gross up)	(1,088)	(3,265)	
Basic federal tax	$ 3,242	$ 1,318	

Exercise 6

(1)   The income can be taxed either in the trust or in the incomes of any one of or combination of the beneficiaries in any proportion. The trust is discretionary; therefore, income can be paid out or not to any beneficiary.

(2)   Income is computed in the trust as an individual, then the graduated rates of tax for individuals is applied to the taxable income of the trust for no more than 36 months after death, after which the estate becomes a testamentary trust subject to the highest personal rate of taxation.

(3)   If amounts are paid or made payable to the beneficiaries from the trust, then these amounts are deducted from the taxable income of the trust.

(4)   The income deducted from the trust's net income is taxed in the hands of the beneficiary as income from property unless it falls within certain categories specified in the *Income Tax Act*, in which case it retains its source for the purposes of calculating the taxable income and tax payable of the beneficiary.

(5)   Dividends retained in the trust are grossed up and qualify for the dividend tax credit.

(6)   If dividends are actually paid, this income retains its nature. The amounts will be taxed on the beneficiaries' returns as taxable dividends from Canadian corporation. This enables the beneficiary to use his or her dividend tax credit.

(7)   If the capital gains are taxed in the trust, then 50% of the capital gain is taxable.

(8)   The trust does not get a capital gain exemption.

(9)   Capital gains designated to beneficiaries retain their nature.

(10)   Net taxable capital gains on QSBC shares (or qualified farm property) of a trust that are allocated to individual beneficiaries and designated by the trust are eligible for the capital gains deduction subject to the trust's annual gains limit and cumulative gains limit. In order to qualify, the trust must be resident in Canada throughout the year.

(11)   Foreign income and its related foreign tax paid retain its nature when paid or deemed to have been paid to a beneficiary.

(12)   Interest income would be treated as property income if allocated to a beneficiary.

(13)   Business income would be treated as property income if allocated to a beneficiary.

(14)   Amounts that are paid/deemed paid to beneficiaries are included in their income in the calendar year in which the trust's year ends (i.e., if amounts are paid out of the trust in the period November 7, 2017 to November 6, 2018, then the beneficiary includes the amounts received in his or her 2018 tax return.

(15)   The trust return must be filed within 90 days of the year end, which is November 6. Therefore, the due date would be February 4.

Exercise 7

Part A

Russell is deemed to have a disposition at fair market value on gifting the shares to the trust. Thus, he will have a taxable capital gain of $75,000 to report in 2018 ($\frac{1}{2} \times$ ($240,000 − $90,000)).

Part B

December 31, 2018. *Inter vivos* trusts are taxed on a calendar basis.

Part C

March 30, 2019. The tax return must be filed within 90 days after the trust's taxation year end.

Part D

Trust income

Interest	$ 6,000
Dividends ($8,000 × 1.38)	11,040
	$17,040
Federal tax ($17,040 × 33%)	$ 5,623
Dividend tax credit [6/11 × gross-up]	(1,658)
Federal tax	$ 3,965

Part E

The trust is entitled to a deduction for the income paid to the beneficiaries in computing net income.

The interest and dividend income paid to the 12-year-old will be subject to attribution and will be included in Russell's income for tax purposes for 2018. The interest and dividend income paid to the 22-year-old will also be subject to attribution if it can reasonably be considered that one of the main reasons for Russell making the loan was to reduce tax.

The dividend income will retain its character and thus be subject to the gross-up and dividend tax credit provision.

The 2019 capital gains realized by the trust on the sale of the shares, if paid to the beneficiaries, will not be subject to attribution. The capital gains retain their character.

Chapter 19

International Taxation in Canada

Learning Goals

Know

By the end of this chapter you will know:

- The basics of Canadian taxation of non-residents.
- The Canadian tax law applicable to cross-border transactions.
- Canadian taxation of residents with foreign investments.

Understand and Explain

By the end of this chapter you will understand and be able to explain:

- The taxation of non-residents with Canadian investments or business dealings.
- The tax treatment of cross-border transactions between Canadian residents and foreign persons.
- The taxation of Canadian residents earning income from foreign investments.
- The basic application of tax treaties.

Apply

By the end of this chapter, you will be able to apply:

- Your knowledge and understanding of the key provisions applicable to non-residents, cross-border transactions, and foreign income earned by Canadian residents.
- Your knowledge and understanding of the impact of a tax treaty on the taxation of various sources of income earned by non-residents in Canada.
- The provisions of the *Income Tax Act* applicable to cross-border loans and transactions.
- Your knowledge and understanding of foreign investment by Canadian residents.

Review Questions
¶19,800 in the Study Guide

Multiple Choice Questions
¶19,825 in the Study Guide

Exercises
¶19,850 in the Study Guide

Assignment Problems
¶19,875 in the Study Guide

CHAPTER 19 — LEARNING CHART

Problem Descriptions

Textbook Example Problems

19-1	Taxation in Canada of U.S. corporation
19-2	Branch tax
19-3	Sale of shares of CCPC
19-4	Going non-resident — RRSP
19-5	Canadian rent paid to non-resident
19-6	Part-year resident
19-7	Deemed acquisition on becoming resident
19-8	Deemed disposition of becoming non-resident
19-9	Transfer pricing
19-10	Thin capitalization
19-11	Cross-border shareholder loans
19-12	Low-interest cross-border loans
19-13	Low-interest cross-border loans
19-14	Dividends from non-foreign affiliates
19-15	Dividends from foreign affiliates
19-16	Investment income in foreign corporation

Multiple Choice Questions

1	Disposal of Canadian real estate
2	Income in year of immigration
3	Foreign partnership income
4	RRSP on emigration
5	Dividend from foreign subsidiary
6	Individual owns U.S. condo
7	Investment income in foreign corporation

Exercises

1	Deemed disposition on becoming non-resident
2	Foreign tax credit
3	Income earned in Canada by non-resident
4	Low-interest cross-border loans
5	Immigration — moving expenses
6	Dividends from foreign corporation
7	Rental property owned by non-residents

Assignment Problems

1	Canadian income of non-resident individual
2	Sale of property by non-resident individual
3	Canadian income of non-resident corporation
4	Canadian income of non-resident individual
5	Individual becoming a non-resident
6	Transfer pricing

CHAPTER 19

Problem Descriptions

Study Notes

¶19,800   REVIEW QUESTIONS

(1) Describe two objectives that international tax treaties strive to achieve.

(2) Distinguish between a part-year resident and a non-resident.

(3) Briefly explain the intention behind the "transfer pricing" legislation.

(4) Briefly explain the "thin capitalization rules" and what they are designed to prevent.

(5) Is a non-resident who owns shares in a Canadian corporation taxable on the disposition of those shares? Does the purchaser have a withholding requirement?

(6) Can a part-year resident claim the full amount of personal tax credits in the year of arrival/departure?

(7) How would you calculate the gain on the disposition of a rental property that an immigrant to Canada owned in the country he/she emigrated from for five years prior to coming to Canada and is disposing after his or her move? If the rental property was located in Canada how would your answer change?

(8) When is a non-resident employer required to withhold and remit Canadian tax from an employee's employment income?

(9) What withholding tax rate applies to dividends from a Canadian corporation to a shareholder resident in the United States?

(10) When is it best for a non-resident to make a section 217 election for Canadian RRSP benefits received?

(11) Would a non-interest-bearing loan by a Canadian corporation to its non-resident parent company result in a Canadian tax liability?

(12) What is the purpose of deeming that an immigrant has disposed of and reacquired all of his or her capital property on entering Canada?

(13) Under what circumstances might a non-resident be entitled to the same or similar total personal tax credits that are allowed to a resident?

(14) When and how much of a foreign tax credit can be claimed by a Canadian resident for withholding taxes paid to a foreign jurisdiction on dividend income?

(15) What is the purpose of the FAPI rules related to foreign passive income?

(16) How would you describe exempt surplus and its treatment for Canadian tax purposes?

(17) What is the purpose of filing an election under subsection 93(1) when a Canadian corporation disposes of shares of a foreign affiliate?

¶19,825   MULTIPLE CHOICE QUESTIONS

Question 1

Jari Kitsopolous is a resident of Greece. Last year, he disposed of real estate located in Saskatchewan for a gain. Jari will pay Canadian income taxes at which of the following rates?

(A) Federal tax based on the tax rate schedule plus Saskatchewan taxes.

(B) Federal tax based on the tax rate schedule plus an additional federal tax.

(C) Withholding tax only at 25%.

(D) Withholding tax only at 33⅓%.

Question 2

Prior to immigrating to Canada, Mai Kim had money on deposit in a Canadian bank and earned $1,000 interest. After taking up Canadian residence, she immediately used that deposit towards a down payment on a home. Which of the following is the correct tax treatment of the $1,000 interest earned in the year of immigration?

(A) She pays a 25% non-resident tax and the interest is excluded from the Canadian tax return for the period of residency.

(B) She does not pay any Canadian tax in relation to the interest.

(C) The income is included in her Canadian tax return for the period of residency, but she receives a foreign tax credit for any taxes paid in her previous country of residence.

(D) The income is included in her Canadian tax return for the period of residency based on a proration calculated as the number of days resident divided by 365 days.

Question 3

Antonio Sperilli immigrated to Canada from Brazil last year, but continues to be a partner in a Brazilian business. What is the correct tax treatment of any income earned from the partnership?

(A) It is subject to tax only in Brazil.

(B) It is included in Antonio's Canadian income tax return, but any Brazilian taxes are deductible from the partnership income.

(C) It is included in Antonio's Canadian income tax return, but a foreign tax credit may be claimed in Antonio's Brazilian tax return for any Canadian income taxes paid.

(D) It is included in Antonio's Canadian income tax return, and a foreign tax credit may be claimed for any Brazilian taxes paid.

Question 4

Betty Albright emigrated from Canada to the United States last year. At the time that she gave up her Canadian residence, she held an RRSP with a fair market value of $100,000. Which of the following statements is true?

(A) The RRSP is taxable Canadian property and Betty will have to file a Canadian non-resident tax return when she disposes of the RRSP.

(B) There is a deemed disposition of the RRSP at fair market value on emigration.

(C) There will be a withholding tax at the time Betty terminates the RRSP and has it paid to her.

(D) Non-resident withholding tax should be paid, at 25%, from the income earned in the RRSP after emigration.

Question 5

Maxwell Rock Ltd. is a Canadian incorporated entity with a December 31 year end. The corporation has a gravel pit operation owned and operated in Collingwood, Ontario. The company expanded operations into the United States this year through a January 15, 2018 100% acquisition of a U.S. incorporated company with gravel pits operating in Michigan. The U.S. corporation also has a mining operation in Paraguay. In the U.S. corporation's first November 30, 2018 taxation year end since acquisition, it earned C$100,000 after-tax business income from its Michigan operation and C$200,000 after-tax business income in Paraguay. On December 15, 2018, the U.S. company paid a dividend to Maxwell Rock Ltd. of C$150,000. Which of the following statements is true?

(A) Maxwell will include the C$150,000 dividend in taxable income for the year in which the dividend was received. A foreign tax credit can be claimed for the withholding tax paid to the U.S. government on the dividend.

(B) Maxwell will include the C$150,000 dividend in Division B income for the year in which the dividend was received. An offsetting deduction of C$100,000 will be available for the portion of the dividend paid from exempt surplus.

(C) Maxwell will include the C$150,000 dividend in Division B income for the year in which the dividend was received. An offsetting deduction will be available in computing taxable income for C$150,000 because the dividend was from exempt surplus.

(D) Maxwell will include the C$150,000 dividend in Division B income for the year in which the dividend was received. A deduction will be available in computing taxable income for the underlying tax paid by the U.S. company on the business income earned in the United States and Paraguay.

Question 6

Bob Smith is a Canadian resident and owns a condominium in Arizona that he and his family use during their winter holidays. The property is left vacant the rest of the year. What is Bob's filing obligations regarding this property?

(A) Bob is required to file Form T1135 reporting foreign property ownership.

(B) Bob is exempt from filing a Form T1135 as the property is personal-use property.

(C) Bob is required to file a Form T1135 only if the property has a cost of over $100,000.

(D) Bob needs to file a U.S. Form 1040NR (non-resident income tax return) and declare the ownership of the property to the U.S. Internal Revenue Service.

Question 7

Jane Alison, a resident of Canada, sold $100,000 of her Canadian mutual funds and invested the funds in common shares of a newly incorporated U.S. corporation. Jane's friend, Tori, also a Canadian resident, invested $500,000, and a third friend, a U.S. resident, invested $400,000 in common shares of the corporation. The $1 million was invested in fixed income securities with future plans to invest in U.S. stock markets. Which statement is correct regarding the interest income on the investments?

(A) It will not be taxed in Canada until dividends are paid to the shareholders. A foreign tax credit will be available for the U.S. withholding tax.

(B) It will not be taxed in Canada until dividends are paid to the shareholders. An offsetting deduction will be available under Division C because the dividend will be paid from taxable surplus.

(C) It will not be taxed in Canada until dividends are paid to the shareholders. An offsetting deduction will be available under Division C because the dividend will be paid from exempt surplus.

(D) It will be included in income of the Canadian shareholders annually because the company is a controlled foreign affiliate.

¶19,850   EXERCISES

Exercise 1

Alan Croupier is moving to Venezuela on August 1. In anticipation of this move, he has sold all of his assets except for 1,000 common shares in Tell Canada (a TSX listed company). The shares have a value of $40,000 and his adjusted cost base is $28,000. What is Alan's tax position on these shares should they remain unsold at the time of his departure?

— REQUIRED

Are there any alternatives available to Alan in respect to the Tell Canada shares in the year of departure?

Exercise 2

A non-resident is liable for Canadian taxes where they are employed in Canada, carry on business in Canada, or dispose of taxable Canadian property. In most countries, the non-resident will also be subject to tax in his or her country of residence on this same income. Tax treaties will alleviate the double taxation burden by allowing for foreign tax credits.

— REQUIRED

As the income will be taxed in two countries, does the taxpayer claim a foreign tax credit in both countries? If not, in which country is a foreign tax credit claimed?

Exercise 3

Sam-son Industries Inc. is a small American company located in Minneapolis, Minnesota. Sam-son sells various items by mail-order, mostly advertising trinkets such as pens, telephone diaries, post-it notes, and similar items, to Canadian businesses. Last year was the first year the company did this and profits on its Canadian sales amounted to $76,000. The company did not have sales representatives enter Canada during the year. The principals of Sam-son are worried about their liability for Canadian income tax and have come to you for advice.

— REQUIRED

Advise Sam-son on their Canadian tax liability. Include an explanation of your rationale.

Exercise 4

Johnson & Co Ltd., a Canadian-controlled private corporation, holds all the issued shares in Johnson & Co (USA) Inc. Two years ago, the Canadian corporation advanced $100,000 in the form of a loan to the U.S. corporation. The U.S. corporation pays Johnson & Co interest at the rate of 1%. This 1% is comparable to the cost of borrowing at a U.S. bank, but is less than the prescribed interest rate under the Canadian Act. Assume the prescribed rate is 2%.

— REQUIRED

Describe the tax obligations of the Canadian corporation relative to this 1% interest.

Exercise 5

Mary Jane is a Canadian citizen and has been living and working in Singapore for the past 11 years. Mary Jane moved back to Canada on October 13, 2018 and incurred $8,000 in moving expenses. Mary Jane paid her own moving expenses and did not receive a reimbursement from her new employer. She earned $35,000 in employment income from October 13 to December 31, 2018.

— REQUIRED

Advise Mary Jane if she is entitled to claim her moving expenses.

Exercise 6

Canco is a Canadian incorporated manufacturer and wholly owned subsidiary of a U.S. incorporated company. In 2016, Canco invested C$500,000 of excess cash in a newly incorporated Dutch company (Dutchco) and received an 80% common share interest in the entity. The U.S. parent invested C$125,000 for the remaining 20% interest. All except C$200,000 was used to acquire a distribution business. The distribution business will distribute products manufactured in Canada and the United States to European customers. For its December 31, 2017 year end, Dutchco earned C$30,000 from the distribution business and C$12,000 in interest on a money market account holding the C$200,000 of excess cash. For its December 31, 2018 year end, Dutchco earned C$50,000 from the distribution business and C$12,000 in interest. The company paid a C$50,000 dividend to its shareholders in February 2018. Dutchco paid corporate tax of 20% on its income each year. Withholding tax of 5% applied to the dividend paid to Canco.

— *REQUIRED*

Determine the Canadian tax consequences of the investment in Dutchco and the dividend received in 2018.

Exercise 7

Mr. and Ms. Doe are citizens and residents of China. They purchased a condominium in their names in Waterloo, Ontario, for their son, Joe. Joe moved to Waterloo in August 2018 to attend university and rented two rooms to his friends, Sam and Harry, who are both Canadian residents. Joe will live in Canada for at least four years while attending school. Sam and Harry each pay rent of $400 per month to Joe, who deposits the funds into his parents' Canadian bank account. Joe pays the mortgage, utilities, and property taxes for the property from this account. His parents will occasionally withdraw excess funds from the account.

— *REQUIRED*

(A) Discuss the Canadian tax implications associated with the rental of the property and any options available to the non-residents.

(B) What will happen if the condominium is sold in the future?

(C) Would it have been better for Joe's parents to give or lend Joe funds to purchase the condominium in his name?

¶19,875   ASSIGNMENT PROBLEMS

Type 2 Problems

Problem 1

Andrew English has agreed to play professional soccer with the Toronto Metros of the Canadian Soccer League starting March 1, 2019. Andrew lives in England and will live in Canada temporarily for the five months of the soccer season. His three-year contract calls for an annual salary of $95,000. At the time of signing this contract in England in the fall of 2018, the Metros gave Andrew a signing bonus of $25,000. Andrew's agent was paid $5,000 to represent him in negotiating the contract. Andrew will earn C$100,000 playing soccer in England during the other seven months.

Determine Andrew's Canadian income tax obligations. What deductions/credits may he claim against Canadian income?

Problem 2

Kresna Dubchuk lives in Kenya and is in the process of selling her Canadian real property, situated in New Brunswick, which has been rented to various tenants over the last 10 years. The selling price of the property is $100,000 and her ACB is $35,000. She will incur $6,500 in real estate commissions and $500 in legal fees in connection with the sale.

A few days after complying with the requirements concerning the proposed disposition of the property, Kresna receives a copy of a proposed assessment from the CRA from the agent collecting the rent on her behalf in Canada. The assessment is for income taxes, plus penalties and interest for the past three taxation years.

(A) Describe and detail Kresna's Canadian tax obligations arising on the sale of this property.

(B) What is the probable cause of the proposed assessment? Can you offer Kresna and her agent any professional assistance with regard to the proposed assessment? If so, detail what you might advise her.

Problem 3

A corporation resident in the United States (USCO) recently expanded its sales activities in Canada. Up until two years ago, the company had been selling small amounts of product directly to Canadian customers. The Canadian sales resulted from U.S. tradeshows, industry magazines, and the company's website. USCO did not have a sales force in Canada or a direct advertising program. Starting last year, USCO hired three sales employees to work from an office rented by USCO in Toronto. The company uses an independent wholesaler and bonded warehouse in Mississauga to keep a supply of its products on hand. Shipping instructions are faxed to the warehouse. Invoicing is done in Dallas and payments are remitted to the U.S. head office. All purchase orders are subject to approval and acceptance by USCO's home office.

The Canadian balance sheet and income statement for USCO's second year of operations ending December 31 was as follows:

Balance Sheet (000s)

Assets		Liabilities/Equity	
Cash (Cdn currency)	$ 50	Accounts payable	$ 400
Accounts receivable	150	Bank loan (used to purchase fixed assets)	150
Inventory	400	Tax liability	104
Fixed assets (UCC)	200	Home office account	146
Total assets	**$800**	**Total liabilities/equity**	**$800**

Income Statement (000s)		
Sales		$ 500
Expenses		
Sales expenses . . .	$ 120	
Office expenses	30	
Advertising	90	
Total expenses		240
Pre-tax profit		260
Tax provision		104
After tax profit . . .		**$ 156**

For its first year of operations ending December 31, the Canadian operations incurred a taxable loss of $4,000 and had an investment allowance, as defined in the Regulations, of $2,000.   ITR: 808

The aggregate FMV of the assets is $820,000 (Cash — $50,000, A/R — $150,000, Inventory — $410,000, Fixed Assets — $210,000). The $50,000 cash balance was the lowest balance outstanding for the year.

Assume an Ontario income tax rate of 12%.

(A) How will USCO be taxed under Canadian domestic tax law?

(B) Without considering the Canada–U.S. Tax Convention, calculate USCO's total federal and provincial Canadian tax liability under Parts I and XIV of the Act. Assume that pre-tax profit represents taxable income.

(C) Would USCO be considered to have a permanent establishment under paragraphs 1, 2, or 5 of Article V of the Canada–U.S. Tax Convention? How does paragraph 6, Article X of the Canada–U.S. Tax Convention impact the Canadian tax return for the company? Perform calculations to reflect the impact.

Problem 4

Sally Juarez is retired and lives in Mexico, but virtually all of her investment assets, and her income, are Canadian. In 2018, Sally realized the following income (all Canadian except as identified):

Dividends on shares in Canadian Public Co Ltd.	$ 5,000
Interest on deposit in bank	8,000
Gain on sale of raw land (assume business income)	60,000
Gain on sale of Public Co Ltd. shares	15,000
Gain on sale of real estate	30,000
Share of income from business partnership	7,000
Mexican pension income	20,000

Sally has paid $7,500 in Canadian withholding tax on the property gains.

Without considering the implications of the Canada–Mexico Tax Convention, calculate Sally's taxable income earned in Canada and tax owing (refund). Identify any other Canadian tax requirements. Assume any business income was earned in a province where the personal tax rates are the hypothetical rates shown in ¶10,250 of Chapter 10. Ignore any CPP/QPP implications.

Problem 5

Cal Murphy is emigrating from Canada to take up residence in Jakarta, Indonesia. At the time of his departure, Cal will have the following Canadian assets:

	FMV	Cost
Principal residence	$450,000	$335,000
RRSP	75,000	N/A
20% interest in CCPC (active)	145,000	1,000
GIC at TrustCo	15,000	15,000

Cal has not been impressed by the capital appreciation he has made on his residence, so he intends to keep it and rent it out for $2,500 monthly. He intends to sell it at some future opportune time but believes this will be many years from now. The expected expenses for the mortgage, taxes, repairs, insurance, and sundry for the house are expected to be about $2,200 a month. Cal's brother, Joseph, will be collecting the rents for him and depositing them to Cal's Canadian bank. This money will be kept at the bank in a savings account in case of any unanticipated expenses.

His 20% shareholding in the CCPC is not easily liquidated, and so he is retaining it, for now, to earn about $5,000 in annual dividend income. He is anxious to dispose of the shares, but has not yet found a prospective purchaser, despite a fairly exhaustive attempt to do so. The $145,000 fair market value was determined by a chartered business valuator.

Cal is not at all sure what to do with the RRSP. He can liquidate it either before or after his planned departure date. Cal intends to renew the GIC when it matures as he is uncertain as to the Indonesian banking system, and won't transfer the money to an Indonesian bank until he's done some research.

Cal and his wife separated last year, and Cal has custody of their only child, who will be moving to Indonesia with Cal. Cal receives $500 in monthly child support and Mrs. Murphy will continue to pay the support to Cal in Indonesia.

Cal has engaged you to advise him of his current (year of departure) and any future Canadian tax obligations.

Identify and advise Cal of his current and future Canadian tax position. Ignore the Canada–Indonesia Tax Convention in your analysis. Include any options or alternatives he may have available and any planning advice you think appropriate.

Problem 6

Samsystems Inc. (SI) is a Canadian-controlled private corporation and a leading edge developer and manufacturer of furniture components with subsidiaries worldwide. You are the tax manager for SI. The controller of the corporation is very concerned that the corporation's intercompany transactions do not meet the transfer pricing requirements of the Act. In a recent meeting, the controller provided you with the following information concerning the company's transactions with foreign corporations.   ITA: 247

Transactions with Samsystems Netherlands Inc. (SNI)

SI sells metal drawer slides to its newly acquired, wholly owned subsidiary and Netherlands resident, SNI. SNI was acquired by SI in July and has two divisions: a manufacturing division that manufactures ergonomically designed furniture components, and a distribution division that distributes curtain rod products purchased from Thailand and now drawer slides purchased from SI, as well. All products purchased by the distribution division are sold to arm's length European distributors.

Until the purchase of SNI, SI was selling drawer slides directly to European distributors for all European sales. Now all European sales are through SNI. Over the next two years, SNI plans to replace the use of distributors in the European market and sell SI's slides directly to original equipment manufacturers. SNI does not own any trademarks related to the sale of SI products. SNI is responsible for collection of receivables from European distributors. However, SI is responsible for all warranty costs associated with the sale of its products by SNI. All patents for Canadian-manufactured products are owned by SI.

For Canadian sales, SI sells drawer slides to arm's length distributors in Canada. All international sales of the slides are sold by subsidiaries of SI (including SNI) in various countries.

A subsidiary of SI, U.S. resident Samsystems United States Inc. (SUSI) (see below), manufactures a similar drawer slide to SI's. These slides are sold by the U.S. company to arm's length distributors in the U.S. market.

For its taxation year ending December 31, SNI's distributor division earned a gross margin of 30% and an operating profit of 5% of sales for its sales of SI product. For sales of curtain rods, the division earned a gross margin percentage of 35% and an operating profit of 8% of sales.

CHAPTER 19

Transactions with SUSI

SUSI was acquired by SI through a share purchase in July. For several years prior to the acquisition, SUSI had purchased ergonomic furniture components from SI for distribution to original equipment manufacturers in the U.S. After the acquisition of SUSI, SI continued to sell these products to the company. SUSI does not own any trademarks for the sale of SI's product and does not distribute products for any other entity. SI sells its ergonomic products in Canada through arm's length Canadian distribution companies.

Advise the controller on the possible transfer pricing methodologies that could be applied to the above transactions under section 247. Indicate why discarded methodologies would not be appropriate. Describe how you would apply these methodologies and indicate what additional information you will need from the client to help you determine the appropriate methodology.

Problem 7

Ergold Ltd. is a Canadian subsidiary of a Swedish company. The company is a distributor of automated milking machines to dairy farmers in Canada. Its sole supplier is the Swedish parent company. The current transfer pricing policy between Ergold Ltd. and its parent company has resulted in losses in Canada for its years of operation since incorporation as follows:

Year Ended December 31	Taxable Loss	Gross Revenue
2016....	$ 200,000	$ 3,000,000
2017....	$ 400,000	$ 6,500,000
2018....	$ 850,000	$ 9,500,000

The company does not appear to have any internal or external uncontrolled comparable transactions that would allow you to apply a traditional transaction method. In discussions with some of your colleagues in your Toronto office transfer pricing group, you have discovered that recent transfer pricing studies have concluded, using the transactional net margin method, that similar distributors operating in Canada earn an operating margin percentage of 5% of sales. You mention this to the controller. He indicates that he does not believe that there is much of a concern as he has heard that because of the company's small size there would not be any penalties applicable if the CRA were to audit. Ergold's effective tax rate is approximately 27%.

How would you respond to the controller? How can you convince the controller that he should consider having your firm prepare a transfer pricing report to provide it with documentation to support its transfer pricing?

Problem 8

Witmold Ltd., a subsidiary of a U.S. corporation, received a loan from the U.S. parent company of $6 million on December 2, 2017 to purchase manufacturing equipment. The company started making loan payments of $72,500 per month on January 2, 2018. On July 15, due to a problem collecting from its major customer, the company borrowed an additional $600,000 from the U.S. parent. This loan was a 2% loan and was repaid 14 days after receipt when the customer paid the accounts receivable.

Because of the above problem, the company did not make its August to October payments on the loan but began making payments again in November. Witmold Ltd. plans to catch up and make its August to October payments sometime in 2019. The total interest expense booked to the financial statements for 2018 was $458,808 for both loans.

In November 2018, Witmold's controller realized that, due to thin capitalization restrictions, the interest deduction on the loan for tax purposes would be limited. As a result, on November 30, 2018, $500,000 of the loan balance was converted to paid-up capital of the common shares held by the U.S. parent company. There were no other share capital transactions during the year. Witmold's comparative balance sheet for its December 31, 2018 taxation year was as follows:

	2018	2017
Assets		
Cash	$ 250,000	$ 6,200,000
A/R	300,000	500,000
Inventory	1,200,000	800,000
Fixed assets	6,600,000	400,000
Total assets	**$ 8,350,000**	**$ 7,900,000**

Liabilities

Accounts payable	. . . .	$	450,000	$ 300,000
Loan to parent	. . . .		5,345,300	6,039,452

Equity

Retained earnings	. . . .		1,754,700	1,260,548
Common stock	. . . .		800,000	300,000
Total liabilities & equity	. . .		**$ 8,350,000**	**$ 7,900,000**

The details of the loan balance after each payment for 2018 was as follows:

Date	Loan Balance
02-Dec-16	$6,000,000
02-Jan-17	5,966,952
02-Feb-17	5,933,687
02-Mar-17	5,900,203
02-Apr-17	5,866,499
02-May-17	5,832,573
02-Jun-17	5,798,424
02-Jul-17	5,764,051
02-Aug-17	5,801,951
02-Sep-17	5,840,101
02-Oct-17	5,878,502
02-Nov-17	5,844,655
30-Nov-17	5,380,524
02-Dec-17	5,310,382
02-Jan-18	5,272,800

Compute the amount of interest that the company will be able to deduct for tax purposes for its December 31, 2018 taxation year end.

Problem 9

Ronal Canada Ltd. is a Canadian subsidiary of Ronal Inc., a U.S. multinational public corporation. You are the tax manager responsible for reviewing the corporate tax return and tax provision for the Canadian company for its December 31, 2018 taxation year end. During your review, you ask for a detailed summary of the intercompany receivable balance of $6.5 million on the company's financial statements. The controller has provided you with the following information:

Receivable from Ronal Argentina Ltd.	$4,100,000
Receivable from Ronal Germany Ltd. . . .	540,000
Receivable from Ronal Switzerland Ltd.	1,860,000
Total intercompany receivable	$6,500,000

The receivable from Ronal Argentina Ltd. relates to a 1% loan made by Ronal Canada Ltd. to Ronal Argentina Ltd. October 1, 2015. The loan was repaid in January 2019. Ronal Argentina Ltd. is a wholly owned subsidiary of Ronal Inc.

The receivable from Ronal Germany Ltd. is a trade receivable related to the sale of goods by Ronal Canada Ltd. to Ronal Germany Ltd. in November 2018. Ronal Germany Ltd. usually pays its trade payable within 90 days of receiving an invoice. Ronal Canada Ltd. sells goods to related companies under the same terms as sales to its regular customers. Ronal Germany Ltd. is a wholly owned subsidiary of Ronal Inc.

The receivable from Ronal Switzerland Ltd. relates to a sale of a piece of equipment to Ronal Switzerland Ltd. December 1, 2017 to be used in its ongoing manufacturing operations in Zurich. Ronal Switzerland is not required to pay interest on the payable to Ronal Canada Ltd. Ronal Switzerland Ltd. is a wholly owned subsidiary of Ronal Canada Ltd.

The controller indicated that, on January 15, 2017, Ronal Canada Ltd. had used excess cash of $5 million to invest in common shares of a subsidiary of Ronal Inc., Ronal Luxembourg Ltd. Ronal Luxembourg used the funds to make a non-interest-bearing loan to Ronal Germany Ltd. on that same day.

(a) Does subsection 15(2) and/or subsection 80.4(2) apply to the receivable from Ronal Argentina? If so, how will this impact Ronal Canada Ltd.'s tax provision? Consider the application of subsection 227(6.1) in your response.

(b) Does subsection 17(1) or 17.1(1) apply to the receivable from Ronal Argentina? If so, how will this impact Ronal Ltd.'s tax provision?

(c) Does subsection 15(2) and/or subsection 80.4(2) apply to the receivable from Ronal Germany Ltd.? Does subsection 17(1) or 17.1(1) apply to this loan? If so, how will this impact Ronal Ltd.'s tax provision?

(d) Does subsection 15(2) and/or subsection 80.4(2) apply to the receivable from Ronal Switzerland Ltd.? Does subsection 17(1) or 17.1(1) apply to this loan? Does 212.3(2) apply to this loan? If so, how will this impact Ronal Ltd.'s tax provision?

(e) Does subsection 17(1) or 17.1(1) apply to the investment in Ronal Luxembourg? Does 90(6) apply to the loan to Ronal Germany? Does 212.3(2) apply to the investment in Ronal Luxembourg? If so, what advice could you provide to the client?

Problem 10

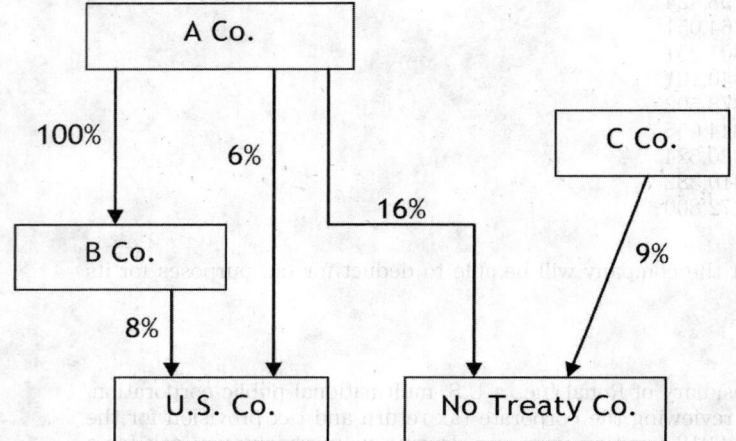

A Co., B Co., and C Co. are Canadian resident corporations. C Co. is not related to either A Co. or B Co. B Co.'s share capital consists of 1,000 common shares. The companies have a December 31 year end.

A Co. and B Co. received dividends of C$36,000 and C$48,000, respectively, out of a total dividend of C$600,000 paid by U.S. Co. on December 31, 2018. U.S. Co.'s taxation year end is October 31.

U.S. Co. was incorporated in the United States in 2016, issuing 100 common shares to its shareholders. The share structure of the corporation has not changed since incorporation. The company is operated and managed from the U.S. The company's only business is the manufacturing of auto parts supplied to various customers, including A Co. U.S. Co. earned net income from its operations of C$900,000 from the time of incorporation up to its October 31, 2018 taxation year end. U.S. Co. paid U.S. federal and state tax of C$180,000 on those earnings. U.S. Co. has not paid any dividends and has not incurred capital gains or losses in previous years. The company does not own shares in any other company.

No Treaty Co. is a cut-and-sew sweatshop incorporated in a country with which Canada does not have a treaty or a TIEA. For its first taxation year ending December 31, 2018, the company earned C$500,000 net income from its operations. On this net income, the company paid a 20% tax to the government of the foreign country. The company does not own shares in any other company and did not incur any capital gains or losses in the year.

No Treaty Co. paid a dividend to shareholders of C$222,000 on January 31, 2019; this is the first dividend payment made by the company. A Co. and C Co. received dividends of C$35,520 and C$19,980, respectively. A dividend withholding tax of 3% applied to the dividends.

Part A

Determine whether the corporation paying the dividend is a foreign affiliate of the Canadian company receiving the dividend.   ITA: 95(1)

Part B

Depending on your response in Part A, determine whether a Division C deduction is available to the   ITA: 113(1)
Canadian corporation in respect of the dividend. If not, how will the dividend be treated for tax   ITA: 126(1)
purposes?

Part C

If a Division C deduction is available, follow these steps to calculate the deduction:

(1) Compute the relevant surplus balances for the company showing all components.   ITR: 5907

(2) Compute the portion of the full amount of the dividend (whole dividend) paid out of each   ITR: 5901
surplus balance.

(3) Compute the portion of the dividend received by the Canadian shareholder out of each   ITR: 5900
surplus balance.

(4) If needed, compute the foreign tax applicable to the portion of the dividend received by the   ITR: 5900(1)(*d*)
Canadian shareholder out of taxable surplus. (Refer to the definition of "underlying foreign tax").   ITR: 5907

(5) Calculate the Division C deductions.   ITA: 113(1)

Part D

What is the rationale for the double taxation elimination mechanism applied under Parts B and C?

Part E

How would the dividends be treated if they were paid to Canadian resident individuals instead of corporations?

Ignore foreign exchange differences in your solution.

Problem 11

Mallot Co. is a Canadian-resident corporation owning 60% of the common shares of Trotter Inc., a U.S.-incorporated company operating and managed out of Chicago. Mallot Co. owns 60 common shares of the company that were issued to it for a capital contribution of US$60,000 at the time of incorporation.

The other 40% of Trotter Inc. is owned by Mr. Tellus, a Canadian resident. Trotter Inc. has been operating a medical supplies business since its incorporation on January 1, 2011 and has an October 31 year end. Mr. Tellus owns 40 common shares of the company that were issued to him for a capital contribution of US$40,000.

You are filing the December 31, 2018 tax return for Mallot Co. and have been provided with the following information:

(1) Trotter Inc. had earnings (losses) from its active business operations in the United States and related tax liabilities (refunds) since incorporation as follows:

Taxation Year End	Earnings (Loss) (US$)	Tax Paid (Refunded) (US$)
October 31, 2014	$200,000	$50,000
October 31, 2015	$100,000	$25,000
October 31, 2016	$100,000	$25,000
October 31, 2017	($200,000)	($50,000)
October 31, 2018	$50,000	$12,500

(2) In the October 31, 2015 taxation year end, Trotter Inc. sold some equipment used in its operations incurring a capital gain of US$100,000 on which it paid a tax of US$20,000. It also paid a dividend of US$100,000 to shareholders that year.

(3) On October 31, 2016, Trotter Inc. received a dividend for US$200,000 from a wholly owned subsidiary, N, located in a country that is not a designated treaty country. N has a December 31 year end and was acquired in an arm's length transaction in 2016 for US$50,000. You have been told

that the dividend represented all of N's active business income for 2016 and that no underlying income tax on the income and no withholding tax on the dividend was paid to the government on that income. U.S. domestic tax of US$50,000 was paid by Trotter Inc. on the dividend.

(4) On September 1, 2018, Trotter Inc. disposed of 100% of its shares in N to the controlling Canadian shareholder of Mallot Inc. and incurred a capital gain on the sale of US$150,000 on which it paid tax of US$15,000. You have been told that all of the assets of N were used in its active business operations. N earned active business income of US$50,000 in 2017 and US$50,000 to the date of disposition in 2018.

Assume that the Canadian dollar is on par with the US dollar.

Compute the surplus balances for Trotter Inc. as of December 31, 2018.

Problem 12

Ragyun Co. (Ragyun) is incorporated and operates in Hungary. The structure of the corporation is as follows:

All unrelated Canadian residents:

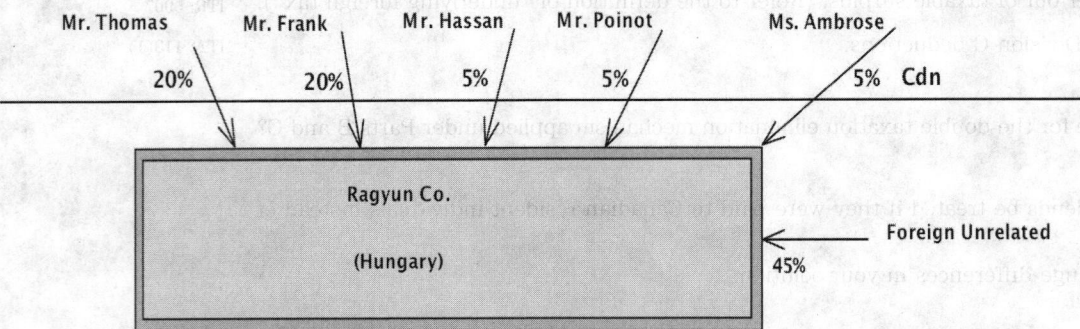

Ragyun was formed on January 1, 2018 and has an October 31 year end. The company was formed to hold a patented technology that the Canadian shareholders developed in Canada and transferred to the corporation at the time of incorporation. The technology was valued at $55,000 at the time of transfer. The foreign unrelated shareholders contributed cash of $45,000 at the time of incorporation for common shares. The company holds the patented technology, a small amount of cash, and investment properties.

Ragyun's income for 2018 included a $20,000 gain on the sale of shares in another foreign entity, Maya Inc. Ragyun owned 1% of the shares of Maya Inc. as a speculative investment. Also included in income was a $10,000 gain on the sale of shares of Tech Inc., a corporation that Ragyun owned in Hungary. Tech Inc. is an engineering firm (whose activities and assets relate only to the engineering business) that provided services to Ragyun in the final development phase of the technology. Because of a dispute with the firm, Ragyun sold the 60% share interest to another shareholder of Tech Inc. Ragyun's income also included $5,000 of dividend and interest income from investments in mutual funds, and $25,000 in royalties from licensing the technology to unrelated foreign corporations.

Ragyun has two employees. One is responsible for administration and accounting for the company, and the other is responsible for marketing and arranging licence agreements.

Ragyun paid tax of $7,200 on its income to the Hungarian taxing authorities for the 2018 taxation year end. On January 31, 2019, Ragyun paid a dividend of $52,800 to its shareholders. A 15% withholding tax applied to dividends paid to the Canadian shareholders.

Part A

Is Ragyun a foreign affiliate or controlled foreign affiliate (CFA) of Ms. Ambrose?

Part B

Is Ragyun a foreign affiliate or controlled foreign affiliate (CFA) of Mr. Frank?

Part C

Calculate foreign accrual property income (FAPI) for Ragyun for 2018. Calculate the impact of the FAPI on Mr. Frank's taxable income for 2018 and the adjusted cost base of his shares.

Part D

How will the January 31, 2019 dividend affect Mr. Frank's taxable income for 2019 and the adjusted cost base of his shares?

Part E

How will the January 31, 2019 dividend affect Ms. Ambrose's taxable income for 2019?

Part F

How would your response to C and D above change if Mr. Frank were Frank Corporation, a Canadian resident corporation with a December 31 year end?

CHAPTER 19

CHAPTER 19 —
DISCUSSION NOTES FOR REVIEW QUESTIONS

(1) One objective of international tax treaties is to eliminate double taxation. This is accomplished by ensuring that income is not taxed in more than one country or by providing a foreign tax credit for the taxes paid in the other country. The second objective of the treaties is to prevent tax evasion. This is accomplished through "sharing of information" provisions in the treaties. Treaties facilitate information exchange and promote resolution of disputes related to domestic tax laws of the two countries.

(2) A part-year resident is a taxpayer who either becomes a permanent resident of Canada or relinquishes permanent resident status at some point in the year. This taxpayer is taxable in Canada on worldwide income only during the period of residency. Non-Canadian source income is not taxable in Canada for the period during the year that the taxpayer is not a resident of Canada. A non-resident is a person who is resident somewhere other than Canada and is taxable in Canada only on Canadian employment or business income, or taxable capital gains on taxable Canadian property. Part XIII withholding tax may apply to certain other types (passive sources) of Canadian-source income earned by a non-resident.
ITA: 2(3)
ITA: 114

(3) The transfer pricing rules are intended to ensure that transactions between Canadian taxpayers or partnerships and non-arm's length non-resident persons occur at an arm's length price, i.e., the price that would be used between unrelated persons. In that way, profits cannot be exported beyond the Canadian tax authorities.
ITA: 247(1)

(4) The thin capitalization rules are designed to prevent the erosion of Canada's tax base through deductible interest payments on loans to Canadian corporations by non-residents. By under-capitalizing a Canadian subsidiary, a foreign parent could receive deductible interest that would otherwise be profits of the subsidiary that are taxable in Canada instead of the subsidiary repatriating the profits through non-deductible dividends.
ITA: 18(4)

(5) A non-resident is taxable on the disposition of taxable Canadian property (TCP). TCP is defined in the Act and includes shares of an unlisted corporation resident in Canada, if more than 50% of the fair market value of the shares is derived from real or immovable property situated in Canada, or Canadian or timber resource properties at any time in the prior five years. Listed shares of a Canadian resident corporation are TCP only if, at any time in the prior five years, the non-resident and non-arm's length persons owned not less than 25% of the shares of the corporation and more than 50% of the fair market value of the shares were derived from real or immovable property situated in Canada, or Canadian or timber resource properties. The relevant tax treaty would need to be considered to determine whether a treaty article overrides the domestic law. Unless the shares are treaty-protected property, the purchaser of the shares is required to withhold and remit 25% of the purchase price unless the non-resident obtains a certificate of compliance and remits a tax payment of 25% of the gain on the property to the CRA no later than 10 days after the disposition.
ITA: 248(1)
ITA: 116(1)

(6) Some personal tax credits are prorated for the portion of the year the individual is resident in Canada, for example, the basic personal tax credit, age credit, etc. Other credits can be claimed in full, for example, the donation credit, medical expense credit, etc.

(7) If the rental property were located in the country from which the individual was emigrating, the individual would be taxable only on the taxable capital gain resulting from the appreciation in value from the time he or she moved to Canada. The cost base used to calculate the gain would be the fair market value of the property at the date of the move to Canada. If the property were a rental property located in Canada, the property would be taxable Canadian property and would be exempt from the deemed disposition rules when the individual immigrated to Canada. As a result, on disposition of the property, the individual would be taxable on the taxable capital gain calculated using the original purchase price of the property as the adjusted cost base.
ITA: 128.1(1)(c)

(8) A non-resident employer is required to withhold and remit tax from **remuneration** paid to an employee related to duties performed in Canada. The employee will file a Canadian tax return to include the Canadian employment income less any income exempt from tax under the relevant Canadian tax treaty. The tax withholdings will be applied against any taxes payable on the return. Employers resident in countries that have a tax treaty with Canada which exempts the employment income from Canadian tax can apply for a withholding tax waiver. The exemption to the income tax withholding requirement for non-resident employers applies to a qualifying non-resident employer for qualifying non-resident employees. A qualifying non-resident employer must be resident in a treaty country and needs to obtain certification to be eligible for the waiver. A qualifying non-resident employee is an employee who is resident in a treaty country, is exempt from Canadian tax under the treaty on the employment income and works in Canada for less than 45 days in the calendar year or is present in Canada for less than 90 days in any 12-month period during which the salary is paid.

> ITA: 153(1), (6), (7); ITR: 102

(9) The withholding tax rate is 25%. However, under the Canada–U.S. Income Tax Convention this rate is reduced to 5% if the shareholder owns at least 10% of the voting stock of the corporation and is reduced to 15% in all other cases.

> ITA: 212(1)
> Article X Canada–U.S. Tax Convention

(10) There would only be a benefit to a section 217 election where the individual's tax calculated under Part I on those benefits would be less than the 25% withholding tax rate (or the reduced rate under the relevant tax treaty).

> ITA: 212(1)(*l*), 217

(11) If the loan is not repaid within one year of the end of the taxation year in which the loan was made, Part XIII tax will apply to a deemed dividend to the shareholder equal to the loan balance. Subsection 17(1) will not apply where Part XIII tax is paid (and not refunded on a repayment of the balance). A refund of the Part XIII tax may be requested within two years of the calendar year in which a repayment of the balance occurs (in which case, subsection 17(1) could apply).

> ITA: 15(2), 214(3)(*a*)

It would be possible for the non-resident and the Canadian-resident corporation (CRIC) to file an election to treat the loan as a "pertinent loan or indebtedness". In such case, subsection 15(2) and section 17 would not apply to the loan. Instead, the amount included in computing income of the Canadian corporation each year is the greater of the interest computed on the balance at a high prescribed rate (5%) and all amounts of interest payable by the Canadian corporation for a debt obligation owing by the Canadian corporation that was used to fund the loan.

> ITA 17.1(1); ITR 4301(*b*.1)

(12) The purpose of the deemed disposition/acquisition rule is to provide a tax cost base from which future income/gains are determined for Canadian income tax purposes. Properties that are taxable in Canada irrespective of the residency status of the owner are exempt from the deemed disposition/acquisition rule, e.g., real property situated in Canada.

> ITA: 128.1(1)

(13) Non-residents who are filing a Canadian income tax return for employment income, business income, or because they have disposed of taxable Canadian property, are entitled to claim the same personal tax credits available to a resident where their Canadian-source income represents 90% or more of their world income.

> ITA: 118.94

(14) A Canadian resident individual may reduce Part I taxes payable by a foreign tax credit for tax withholdings up to a rate of 15%. Withholding taxes in excess of 15% are deductible in computing Division B income. A Canadian resident corporation may claim a foreign tax credit for withholdings unless the dividends are received from a foreign affiliate, in which case Division C deductions apply.

> ITA: 113(1), 126(1)
> ITA: 20(11)

(15) The FAPI rules prevent a Canadian resident from deferring tax on investment income by holding investments offshore in controlled foreign affiliates. The rules require the Canadian investor to pay tax on the foreign investment income as it is earned each year instead of when it is received as a dividend.

> ITA: 91(1)

CHAPTER 19

(16) Exempt surplus of a foreign affiliate represents income or gains for which Canada relinquishes its right to tax. Active business income earned in countries with which Canada has a treaty or tax information exchange agreement as well as the non-taxable portion of capital gains become exempt surplus of a foreign affiliate [other than the non-taxable portion of gains included in hybrid surplus for dispositions of shares in foreign affiliates that are excluded property]. The taxable portion of gains on the disposition of properties used principally to gain or produce active business income in a designated treaty country is also included in exempt surplus.

ITR: 5907, "exempt earnings"

(17) A subsection 93(1) election allows a Canadian corporation to access the surplus accounts of the foreign affiliate being sold without having to pay dividends on the shares of the foreign affiliate in advance of the sale. If the foreign affiliate has exempt surplus, the exempt surplus can be deemed to have been paid as a dividend to the Canadian corporation and received tax free. The dividend will also reduce the proceeds of disposition and thus the capital gain on the disposition of the shares of the affiliate.

CHAPTER 19 — SOLUTIONS TO MULTIPLE CHOICE QUESTIONS

Question 1

(B) is correct. Jari is taxed as a non-resident on the disposition of taxable Canadian property. The tax is federal tax on the graduated rate schedule plus 48% of tax otherwise payable. The Canada–Greece tax treaty does not override Canada's right to tax the taxable capital gain.

ITA: 2(3), 115, 120(1)

(A) is not correct. Income earned in a particular province for a non-resident includes only employment income and income from carrying on business.

ITR: 2602(1)

(C) and (D) are not correct. Non-residents are taxable on gains from the disposition of taxable Canadian property under Part I of the ITA. Withholding tax is exigible under Part XIII. Jari will need to pay 25% of the actual or estimated gain on filing a notice either prior to or within 10 days of the sale. If the notice is not filed, the purchaser must withhold and remit 25% of the purchase price of the property within 30 days of the end of the month of purchase.

ITA: 2(3), 115(1)

Question 2

(B) is correct. The interest was earned while Mai was a non-resident, before she became a resident of Canada. Withholding tax does not apply to interest paid by a Canadian resident bank to unrelated non-residents.

ITA: 2(3), 212(1)(*b*)

(A) is incorrect. Only interest that is not fully exempt interest paid to a non-arm's length person and participating debt interest is subject to 25% withholding tax.

ITA: 212(1)(*b*)

(C) and (D) are incorrect. The interest was not earned during her period of residency.

Question 3

(D) is correct. As a resident of Canada, Antonio is taxed in Canada on his worldwide income. Canada provides a foreign tax credit to alleviate potential double taxation of the income.

ITA: 126(2)

(A) is incorrect. As a resident of Canada, Antonio is subject to tax on his worldwide income.

(B) is incorrect. Deductions for business foreign tax credits are not available in Division B of the ITA.

(C) is incorrect. Business income is sourced to the country in which the business activities are carried on (or where a permanent establishment is located under treaty). Brazil has jurisdiction to tax the income, and Canada provides a foreign tax credit for the Brazilian tax.

Question 4

(C) is correct. There are no tax consequences until Betty receives payments from her RRSP/RRIF, at which time, the payer will withhold tax on each payment. The withholding tax rate is 25%, but is reduced to 15% under treaty for annuity payments if the RRSP is matured and converted to an annuity.

212(1)(*l*)
Article XVIII

(A) is not correct. Taxable Canadian property, as defined, does not include RRSPs.

ITA: 248(1)

(B) is not correct. Excluded rights or interests are exempt from deemed disposition at the time of emigration.

ITA: 128.1(10)

(D) is not correct. Only payments out of an RRSP are subject to withholding tax.

ITA: 212(1)(*l*)

Question 5

(B) is correct. The exempt surplus balance of Maxwell Rock Ltd. will be $100,000 at the end of the year. The business income earned in Michigan is the net earnings for the year from an active business carried on by it in a designated treaty country and would be exempt surplus of the U.S. company. The business income earned in Paraguay is included in taxable surplus because the income is being earned in a country that is not a designated treaty country. Of the $150,000 dividend paid to Maxwell, $100,000 will be considered to have been paid from exempt surplus and $50,000 will be considered to have been paid from taxable surplus. The exempt surplus portion of the dividend is fully deductible in computing taxable income.

ITR: 5901
ITA: 113(1)(*a*)

(A) is incorrect. Dividends received by a corporation from a foreign affiliate are not eligible for a foreign tax credit.   ITA: 126(1)

(C) is incorrect. Only $100,000 of the dividend is paid from exempt surplus.

(D) is incorrect. A deduction will be available in computing taxable income for the underlying tax paid associated with the dividend paid by the U.S. company from business income earned in Paraguay but not from business income earned in the United States. The business income earned in the United States is exempt surplus and is fully exempt from tax in Canada when paid as a dividend.   ITA: 113(1)(b)

Question 6

(B) is correct, for the reason stated in the question.

(A) and (C) are incorrect for the reason stated in (B).

(D) is incorrect. Bob would only need to file a U.S. form 1040NR in relation to an income producing property.

Question 7

(D) is correct. The company will be a controlled foreign affiliate of each of the Canadian shareholders because (i) it is a foreign affiliate (each Canadian shareholder owns not less than 1% of the shares and not less than 10% of the shares with related persons) of the company, and (ii) it is a controlled foreign affiliate because it is controlled by less than five unrelated Canadian residents (Jane and Tori). The income of the corporation will be FAPI because it will be considered income from property. The shareholder's participating percentage of the income as of the end of the affiliate's taxation year will be included in Division B income. A deduction for the related U.S. tax paid on the income calculated using the relevant tax factor will also be available.   ITA: 95(1)

ITA: 91(1)

ITA: 91(4)

(A) is incorrect. The income will be taxed annually. Dividends paid to the Canadian shareholders will be included in Division B income. Foreign tax credits will be available against Part I tax for U.S. tax withholdings. An offsetting deduction will be available for the lesser of the amount of the dividend and the cumulative total of prior year's net income inclusions for FAPI.   ITA: 12(1)

ITA: 126(1)

ITA: 91(5)

(B) is incorrect. The income will be taxed annually. An offsetting deduction for a dividend is not available under Division C because the dividend is not received by a corporation. Division C deductions are only available to Canadian resident corporations.   ITA: 113(1)

(C) is incorrect. The income will be taxed annually. An offsetting deduction for a dividend is not available under Division C because the dividend is not received by a corporation.   ITA: 113(1)

CHAPTER 19 — SOLUTIONS TO EXERCISES

Exercise 1

Alan is deemed to have disposed of the shares on emigration at their fair market value of $40,000. Given his ACB of $28,000, he will have a capital gain of $12,000, and a taxable capital gain of $6,000.

Alan can elect to defer paying the tax that results from the deemed disposition rule. The election must be made on or before the balance due date for the year in which emigration takes place. If the election is made, the payment of the tax can be deferred without interest until the properties are actually sold. Since security is not required for up to $100,000 of capital gains resulting from the deemed disposition rule, Alan will not be required to post security with the CRA.

ITA: 220(4.5), (4.51)

Exercise 2

No, a foreign tax credit is not claimed in both countries. To do so would eliminate the taxes on the income altogether. The country (the source country) where the income is sourced has the first right of taxation and consequently, a foreign tax credit is allowed only in the other country (the residence country).

A non-resident will pay the Canadian income taxes on income from duties of office and employment performed in Canada, income from business carried on in Canada, and on taxable capital gains on taxable Canadian property. These taxes will then be used as a foreign tax credit in the country of residence. Note that some countries will recognize CPP/QPP contributions as taxes, in addition to any income taxes paid to Canada. Note that treaties can limit or eliminate a country's jurisdiction to tax source income. The country of residence will provide a tax credit only if taxes are paid.

ITA: 2(3)

Exercise 3

Canada levies tax on non-residents who carry on business in Canada. Carrying on business in Canada is distinguishable from carrying on business with Canada. While Sam-son solicits sales from Canadians, it does not solicit sales in Canada through an agent or servant. Given these facts, Sam-son is not carrying on business in Canada and is not liable for Canadian income taxes on the $76,000 profit originating from within Canada.

ITA: 2(3), 253

Exercise 4

The interest is U.S. sourced and will be considered investment income to the Canadian corporation.

The interest will be subject to the full corporate tax rate, including the $10^{2/3}$% additional refundable tax on investment income. The addition to RDTOH ($30^{2/3}$%) will also apply.

Subsection 17(1) requires an interest income inclusion equal to interest computed using the prescribed rate less the actual interest included in income on the loan. If the interest paid is considered to be computed at a reasonable rate, an income inclusion is not required. Imputed income will not arise if the 1% rate being paid is comparable to the U.S. borrowing rate.

The foreign affiliate dumping provision does not apply because Johnson & Co. Ltd. is not controlled by a non-resident corporation.

ITA: 212.3(1)

Exercise 5

The Act defines "moving expenses" as including any expenses incurred as, or on account of, travel costs in the course of moving the taxpayer from the old residence to the new residence, cost of transporting or storing household effects, cost of meals and lodging, etc. It appears Mary Jane's expenses would qualify under this definition; however, the move must be an eligible relocation as defined by the Act. The definition of "eligible relocation" only includes relocations that are both from and to a residence in Canada unless the person is a student or person absent from but a resident of Canada.

ITA: 62(3)

ITA: 62(1); 248(1)
ITA: 62(2)

Exercise 6

Dutchco is a foreign affiliate of Canco as Canco owns not less than 10% of the shares of the company. Dutchco is a controlled foreign affiliate of Canco as it is controlled by a Canadian resident.

Dutchco is earning income from an active business in a country with which Canada has a tax convention. This income would be treated as exempt surplus. The company is also earning income from property. This income would be treated as FAPI and would become part of Dutchco's taxable surplus.

For 2017 and 2018, Canco must include, in respect of each share it owns in Dutchco, the share's participating percentage of FAPI less a deduction for the foreign accrual tax applicable to the FAPI income inclusion.

Income Inclusion	$ 9,600	80% of $12,000	ITA: 91(1)
Deduction	$(7,680)	20% of $9,600 multiplied by the relevant tax factor of 1/(38% − 13%)	ITA: 91(4)
2017 Income Inclusion	$ 1,920		

The net income inclusion is added to the adjusted cost base of the shares of Dutchco held by Canco, i.e., $500,000 + $1,920 = $501,920.

Income Inclusion	$ 9,600	80% of $12,000	ITA: 91(1)
Deduction	$(7,680)	20% of $9,600 multiplied by the relevant tax factor of 1/(38% − 13%)	ITA: 91(4)
2018 Income Inclusion	$ 1,920		

The net income inclusion is added to the adjusted cost base of the shares of Dutchco held by Canco, i.e., $501,920 + $1,920 = $503,840.

When the dividend is paid in 2018, it will be included in Canco's Division B income. A deduction is available for the portion of the dividend prescribed to have been paid from exempt surplus. Exempt surplus includes exempt earnings for any taxation year ending in the period that starts with the first day of the taxation year in which Dutchco became a foreign affiliate and ends at the time the dividend is paid. FAPI is included in taxable surplus in a similar manner. The exempt surplus and taxable surplus balances of Dutchco at the time of the dividend would be as follows: **ITA: 12(1), 90(1)**

	Exempt Surplus	Taxable Surplus	
Income for December 31, 2017 taxation year end of the affiliate	$30,000	$12,000	ITR: 5907(1)
Income/profits tax paid to Netherlands tax authorities	($ 6,000)	($ 2,400)	
Balance February 2017	$24,000	$ 9,600	

Surplus balances are not impacted by 2018 income amounts because the dividend was paid within the first 90 days of 2018. **ITR: 5901(2)(a)**

The portion of the whole dividend of $50,000 deemed to have been paid out of exempt surplus would be $24,000. The portion of the whole dividend deemed to have been paid out of taxable surplus would be $9,600. The remainder, of $16,400, would be considered to have been paid from pre-acquisition surplus.

The 2018 income inclusions less deductions for Canco related to the dividend would be as follows:

Dividend Income	$ 40,000	$50,000 × 80%	ITA: 12(1), 90(1)
Deduction (Note 1)	$(19,200)	$24,000 × 80%	ITA: 113(1)(a)
Deduction (Note 2)	$ (5,760)	Lesser of: (1) $5,760 [$2,400 × 80% × (1/(38% − 13%) − 1)], and (2) $7,680 [$9,600 × 80%]	ITA: 113(1)(b)
Deduction (Note 2)	$ (1,536)	Lesser of: (1) $1,536 [$9,600 × 80% × 5% × 1/(38% − 13%)], and (2) $1,920 [$9,600 × 80% less: paragraph 113(1)(b) deduction of $5,760]	ITA: 113(1)(c)
Deduction (Note 3)	$ (1,920)	Lesser of: (1) $1,920 [$9,600 × 80% less: paragraph 113(1)(b) deduction of $5,760], and (2) 2017 net FAPI inclusion of $1,920 added to the ACB of the shares	ITA: 91(5)
Deduction (Note 1)	$(13,120)	$16,400 × 80%	ITA: 113(1)(d)
Net Inclusion (Deduction)	$ (1,536)		

The subsection 91(5) deduction reduces the adjusted cost base of the shares of Dutchco held by Canco. The adjusted cost base of shares after the February 2018 dividend and FAPI inclusions/adjustments for 2018 is $501,920.

Note 1 — The portion of the dividend paid from exempt surplus, i.e., $19,200, and pre-acquisition surplus, i.e., $13,120, is not taxed in Canada.

Note 2 — The portion of the dividend paid from FAPI, i.e., $7,680 ($40,000 – $19,200 – $13,120), is taxed in Canada after taking a deduction for $5,760 related to the underlying foreign tax on the income from which this portion of the dividend was paid and a deduction of $1,536 related to the withholding tax on that portion of the dividend.

Note 3 — There is a further deduction of $1,920 to reverse the prior year's FAPI inclusion. This deduction prevents the double taxation of the passive income earned in the CFA by ensuring that the FAPI is not taxed a second time when the dividend is paid out. This deduction is limited to $1,920, which is calculated as the total amount of the taxable surplus dividend, i.e., $7,680 net of the deduction of $5,760 related to the underlying tax on the income from which this portion of the dividend was paid.

Exercise 7

(A) The rents paid by Sam and Harry to Joe's parents are subject to a 25% withholding tax. Joe is acting as an agent for his parents in collecting the rents and would be required to deduct and withhold the tax from the rents received and submit it to the Receiver General. Failure to withhold can result in interest charges and a penalty of 10% to 20% of unremitted withholdings.

ITA: 212(1)(d), 215(3), 227(8), 227(8.3)

Joe's parents can file a Canadian tax return within two years of the end of the year to obtain a refund of any Part XIII tax paid in excess of the Part I tax payable (using graduated tax rates) on the net rental income (rents less mortgage interest, CCA, utilities, and property taxes).

ITA: 216(1)

Alternatively, an undertaking (NR6) to file an income tax return can be filed prior to the first rental payment for the year indicating Joe's parents' intent to file a Canadian tax return within six months of the end of the year. In that case, withholding tax can be reduced to 25% of the net rents received (i.e., rents less mortgage interest, utilities, and property taxes). The return must be filed within six months of the end of the year or Joe will become liable for the excess of 25% of the rents received less the withholdings remitted to CRA.

ITA: 216(4)

(B) If the condominium is sold in the future, Joe's parents will have disposed of taxable Canadian property. They will be required to file a personal tax return to report the taxable capital gain on the disposition of the property. They will also be required to file a separate personal tax return to report any recapture on the disposition of the property. The Canada–China Tax Convention would need to be reviewed to determine if the taxable capital gain on the disposition of the property is treaty exempt. Assuming not, the purchaser would be required to withhold 25% of the proceeds paid for the land and 50% of the proceeds paid for the building within 30 days of the end of the month of the purchase, unless Mr. and Mrs. Doe have obtained a clearance certificate and paid 25% of the estimated (or actual) capital gain on the disposition of the property plus an estimate of the tax on the recapture related to the disposition of the property.

ITA: 248(1)

ITA: 116(1), (5)

(C) Assuming Joe will become a resident of Canada under common law, he will be taxed on his worldwide income. He would need to report the rental income net of deductions on his personal tax return each year. The rents paid to him by the roommates would not be subject to withholding tax. If Joe were to own the condominium in his name, it may be possible for him to treat the property as his principal residence on its sale. He would need to be able to argue that the income-producing use is ancillary to the main use of the property as a principal residence, and he would not be able to claim CCA on the property in order to do so. If Joe's parents were to loan him the funds to purchase the property, the attribution rules would not apply, as the rules only apply to individuals who are residents of Canada. Any interest Joe were to pay on loans from his parents would be subject to withholding tax, as the interest would be paid to a non-arm's length person. The Canada–China Tax Convention may reduce the rate to 10%.

ITA: 212(1)(b)

CHAPTER 19

Comprehensive Section

Learning Goals

Apply

By the end of this section you will be able to apply your knowledge and understanding to:

- Develop a comprehensive response, qualitative and/or quantitative, dealing with multiple subject matters.

- Advise and recommend on the tax implications related to the facts presented.

- Advise and recommend on tax planning techniques to maximize deductions and minimize overall tax.

Comprehensive Case Problems
¶20,850 in the Study Guide

COMPREHENSIVE SECTION — LEARNING CHART

Problem Coverage and Chapter References

Problem	Coverage	Chapters
1	Income from business for tax purposes	4, 5, 6, 7, 8
2	Division B income of an individual from various sources	3, 4, 5, 6, 7, 8
3	Income from business for tax purposes	4, 5, 7, 8
4	Individual taxes payable	3, 4, 6, 7, 9, 10
5	Employment income	3, 9, 10
6	Income, taxable income, taxes payable for an individual	3, 6, 7, 9, 10
7	Income, taxable income, taxes payable for an individual	3, 6, 7, 9, 10
8	Taxable income of an individual	3, 6, 7, 8, 9, 10, 13
9	Taxable income of an individual; adjusted taxable income for AMT	3, 6, 7, 9, 10
10	Division B income and taxable income of a corporation	4, 5, 6, 7, 8, 11
11	Division B income and taxable income of a corporation	4, 5, 6, 7, 8, 11
12	Taxable income (corporate)	4, 5, 6, 7, 8, 11
13	CCPC — T2S(1) & comprehensive federal tax payable calculation	4, 5, 7, 8, 11, 12
14	Integration & investment income	6, 7, 10, 11, 12, 13
15	Individual Division B income calculation	3, 6, 7, 9, 10
16	Comprehensive personal tax calculation	3, 6, 7, 9, 10
17	Sale of assets vs. shares	7, 8, 11, 12, 15
18	Business income reconciliation; corp. tax calculation; CDA	4, 5, 6, 7, 8, 11, 12
19	Corporate distribution	11, 12, 13, 15, 17
20	Integration of business income; s. 85 transfer of business to corp.	6, 9, 10, 11, 12, 13, 15
21	Income from business for tax purposes; taxable income of a corporation; tax-deferred winding-up	4, 5, 6, 7, 11
22	Acquisition of control; amalgamation; windup	7, 8, 11, 17
23	Case	7

Study Notes

¶20,850 COMPREHENSIVE CASE PROBLEMS

Problem 1

The income statement for Holly Industries Limited for its 2018 year ended December 31 shows the following:

Holly Industries Limited
Statement of Income
Year ended December 31, 2018

Sales	$4,782,170
Cost of sales	$3,556,478
	$1,225,692
Expenses	
Selling	$ 394,924
General and administrative	$ 305,148
Amortization	$ 230,000
Interest on long-term debt	$ 37,427
Other interest	$ 55,460
	$1,022,959
Other income	
Profit on sale of fixed assets	$ 100,000
Equity in income of associated company	$ 92,096
Income from other investments	$ 17,329
Gain on sale of land	$ 189,800
Loss on sale of portfolio investments	$ (52,400)
	$ 346,825
Income before income taxes	$ 549,558
Income taxes	
Current	$ 166,700
Deferred	$ 8,000
	$ 174,700
Net Income	$ 374,858

An analysis of various accounts revealed the following information:

Note 1

Included in the cost of sales:

(A)

	Dec. 31/17	Dec. 31/18
Inventories:		
Raw materials	$ 210,000	$ 295,000
Work-in-process	$ 370,000	$ 565,000
Finished goods	$ 595,000	$ 715,000
	$1,175,000	$1,575,000

(B) The Dec. 31, 2018 finished goods ending inventory is stated net of a reserve for a possible decline in market price of $57,000.

Note 2

Included in general and administrative expenses are the following transactions:

(A) Connection of a gas line on conversion of furnace	$ 17,000
(B) Cost associated with the valuation of land sold	$ 2,800

(C) Donations consisting of $64,000 to registered charities . . . . $ 64,000
(D) Premium for term life insurance policy on the president in which the company is the beneficiary and the policy is used as collateral for a bank operating line of credit . . . . $ 22,200
(E) Advertising targeted at the Canadian readers of an exclusive foreign magazine distributed in Canada . . . . $ 13,375
(F) Membership in private clubs for senior executives . . . . $ 3,200
(G) Cost of reorganizing the company's share capital . . . . $ 16,000
(H) Meals and entertainment with clients (incurred in equal monthly amounts) $ 12,000
(I) Cost of employee training seminar to teach employees about new provincial workplace safety laws . . . . $ 7,200
(J) Cost of Christmas party to which all employees were invited . . . . $ 17,700

Note 3

Included in interest on long-term debt and other interest are the following transactions:

(A) Bond interest paid to November 30, 2018 . . . . $ 10,000
  Bond interest accrued to December 31, 2018 . . . . $ 950
  Amortization of bond premium . . . . $ 375
(B) Interest on deficient provincial tax instalments . . . . $ 1,200
  Interest on late municipal property taxes . . . . $ 500

Note 4

Included in other income are the following transactions:

(A) Sale of capital property:

	Cost	Proceeds	Book Value
Land	$ 65,000	$202,800	$13,000
Truck	$ 80,000	$ 25,000	$10,000
Equipment - Class 8	$300,000	$ 75,000	$20,000
Building - Class 3*	$ 50,000	$ 60,000	$15,000
Portfolio Investments	$ 60,000	$ 7,600	$60,000
Equipment - Class 39**	$ 50,000	$ 7,500	$22,500

  * There are still other buildings in Class 3.

  ** This was the last asset in the class.

(B) Income from other investments includes receipt of a ssec. 83(2) dividend of $5,000 and a cash dividend of $7,500 from an associated company.

Additional Information:

The company had the following balances in its tax accounts on January 1, 2018:

Depreciable Property:
Class 3 . . . . $225,000
Class 8 . . . . $ 55,000
Class 10 . . . . $354,000
Class 39 . . . . $ 10,000
Class 43 . . . . $190,000

There were no asset additions during the year.

— REQUIRED

Prepare a reconciliation between net income per the income statement and net income for tax purposes under Division B, with supporting calculations. Briefly explain why any of the above items were omitted from the reconciliation.

Problem 2

Mr. Rich is president of a large public corporation located in Toronto. He has provided you with the following selected data concerning his 2018 revenue and expenses.

(a) Employment income information:

Gross salary	$ 350,000
- Membership in a Toronto social club*	$ 2,500
- a 2% 10-year loan advanced on November 1, 2018 to acquire a home to be repaid in equal annual instalments both principal and interest on the anniversary date. (Assume that the prescribed rate for the last quarter of 2018 is 5%)	$ 500,000
- a company car available for the whole year and leased at an annual cost of $15,000 including $1,000 for insurance, and HST @ 13%	$ 15,000
- the operating costs of the above car which is used 20% for business (total kilometres driven - 20,000), including HST	$ 3,000
- contributions to a registered pension plan by the company only	$ 10,000
- medical premiums	
- Ontario health tax levy	$ 500
- Dental plan premium	$ 200

(b) Rental income (losses) from two condominiums:

Property 1	$ 3,000
Property 2	$ (16,000)

For property 2 only, 50% of the loss is attributed to the maximum capital cost allowance claimed. Property 1 was sold during 2018 for $200,000. The real estate commission was $10,000. The capital cost and undepreciated cost at the date of sale were $70,000 and $60,000, respectively.

(c) Investment portfolio:

Dividends received from taxable public Canadian corporations	$8,000	
Dividends received from U.S. corporations net of withholding tax of 15%	$3,400 (Cdn)	$ 11,400

* Mr. Rich uses the membership at the Toronto social club for networking with current and future clients.

The above amounts do not include interest income of his family on funds given to them by Mr. Rich.

Wife	$20,000
Son - 21	$ 3,000
Son - 18	$ 3,000
Son - 16	$ 3,000

During 2018 he sold 100 shares of X Ltd., a Canadian public company for $10,000. The brokerage costs were $300. The following data relates to the cost of these shares:

2010	Acquired 200 shares for $8,000
2011	Received a stock dividend of 10% which increased the corporation paid-up capital by $10 per share
2013	Acquired 500 shares for $11,400
2015	Acquired 1,200 shares for $24,000
2018	Received a stock dividend of 10% which increased the corporation's paid-up capital by $10 per share

Also during 2018, he sold 1,000 shares (500 to his wife and 500 to his oldest son) of Y Ltd., a taxable Canadian public corporation, for $10 each when the fair market value was really $15. Mr. Rich's adjusted cost base was $5. Both his wife and son received $1,500 of dividends during the year. No elections were filed on the sale of the shares to his wife.

(d) Disposition of personal assets:

Mr. X sold the following personal assets during 2018:

	Year of Purchase	Cost	Proceeds
Antique Table	2001	$ 1,200	$ 500
Antique Clock	2007	$ 350	$ 800
Jewellery	2009	$ 1,000	$ 1,600
Sailboat	2010	$25,000	$32,000

Mr. X took back a promissory note of $20,000, due in one year, in respect of the sale of the sailboat.

Calculate Mr. Rich's income for 2018 from the following sources:

(i) employment,

(ii) property, and

(iii) net taxable capital gains.

Ignore the effects of a leap year in your answer.

Problem 3

The following is a condensed 2018 Income Statement for Thingamajig Manufacturing Ltd. for its fiscal year end on December 31. The company was incorporated in Ontario in 1994 and has been continuously in the same business since that date.

Sales	$ 1,750,000
Cost of manufacturing (see note (1), below)	$(1,050,000)
Gross margin	$ 700,000
General and administrative expenses (see note (2), below)	$ (294,000)
	$ 406,000
Extraordinary income and expenses (see note (3), below)	$ (77,000)
Net income	$ 329,000
Provision for income taxes	$ (91,000)
Net income after taxes	$ 238,000

Note 1

Included in the cost of manufacturing:

(a) Inventories:	Dec. 31, 2017	Dec. 31, 2018
Raw materials	$ 70,000	$ 94,500
Work-in-process	$ 52,500	$ 45,500
Finished goods	$140,000	$175,000
	$262,500	$315,000

(b) The finished goods opening inventory is stated net of a reserve for a possible decline in market price of $35,000.

(c) The raw material inventories above have been stated on a LIFO basis. The equivalent amounts on a FIFO basis would be:

December 31, 2017 — $115,500

December 31, 2018 — $157,500

Note 2

Included in the general and administrative expenses are the following selected transactions:

(a) Damages paid to a competitor in an out-of-court settlement concerning a trademark infringement which resulted in a loss of the competitor's profits equal to the damages paid of $14,000.

(b) Contributions made in January 2019 and allocated by the accountant to 2018 deferred income plans for senior executives:

	Money-purchase Registered pension plan*	Employment compensation
Executive A	$ 8,350	$130,000
Executive B	$ 6,400	$ 70,000
Executive C	$ 5,300	$ 50,000

* Contributions matched by employees

(c) Costs related to the acquisition of new machinery and equipment other than the direct laid-down costs:

Costs in issuing bonds to finance new machinery and equipment

— accounting and legal	$ 3,500
— printing	$ 550
— commission paid	$ 850
Bond interest paid to October 31, 2018	$ 4,550
Accrued bond interest to December 31, 2018	$ 1,450
Amortization of bond discount	$ 700

(d) An analysis of the promotion account revealed the following selected expenditures:

Membership in several private clubs for senior executives	$ 2,800
Magazine advertising paid in 2018:	
— ads in magazines distributed only in South America	$ 21,000
— ads in Canadian periodical to be run early in 2019	$ 17,500
Charitable donations	11,200

Note 3

Included in the extraordinary income and expenses are the following selected amounts:

(a) Sale of certain capital property:

	Cost	Proceeds	Book value
Marketable securities	$ 10,500	$ 7,000	$10,500
Equipment — Class 43	$ 42,000	$11,200	$15,000
Patent — Class 14	$ 45,000	$70,000	$ 3,500
Government licence — Class 14.1	$ 8,000	$35,000	$ 700
Trucks*	$ 19,600	$ 1,300	$ 4,200

* The company has decided to lease its trucks in the future and, therefore, disposed of all of its trucks, the only assets in this class.

(b) Write-down of investments in a wholly owned subsidiary:

Loss incurred for 2018 .... $52,500

(c) Receipt of a ssec. 83(2) dividend of $10,000 and a cash dividend of $45,000 from wholly owned subsidiary.

(d) Cost of reorganizing the company's share capital $12,600.

Additional Information:

(1) The company has claimed $55,000 for depreciation in the books of account.

(2) The company had the following balances in its tax accounts on January 1, 2018.
Depreciable property:

Class 3	$ 49,000
Class 8	$ 8,400
Class 10 (two-seat delivery van)	$ 1,500
Class 14	$ 35,900
Class 14.1	$ 29,650
Class 43	$ 35,000

(3) The company made the following capital purchases during the year:

Used building to be used 100% for manufacturing activities	$315,000
Manufacturing machinery	$ 87,000
Tools (costing under $500 each and not including electronic communications equipment)	$ 16,000

(4) During the year, the company made an improvement costing $7,000 to a leased warehouse. The 15-year lease commenced 10 years ago and has two successive options to renew of 5 years and 3 years, respectively.

Prepare a reconciliation between net income per the condensed income statement and income for tax purposes under Division B, with supporting schedules. Briefly explain why any of the above items were omitted from the reconciliation.

Problem 4

Mr. Debit, age 66, who resides in Toronto, has provided you with the following information concerning his 2018 tax return:

Employment income for tax purposes	$100,000
Business income for tax purposes	8,900
Property income (loss) for tax purposes:	
Rental loss (not due to CCA)	(11,000)
Canadian interest income	1,350
Taxable dividends, in cash, received from:	
— taxable Canadian public corporations	560
— U.S. corporations — before withholding of 15% tax	(Cdn.) 1,500
Less: carrying charges on bank loan to purchase Canadian securities which yield the above dividends	(200)

Taxable capital gains (allowable capital losses):

Shares of X Ltd., a Canadian public company	$(6,000)	
Shares of ABC Ltd., a Canadian-controlled private corporation, all of whose assets are employed in earning active business income in Canada	(3,000)	
Shares of Y Ltd., a Canadian public company	500	
Listed personal property	3,000	
Personal-use property	1,000	(4,500)

Other income for tax purposes:	
Old Age Security benefits	7,040
Pension annuity received	490
Deduction:	
Capital portion of above annuity	(200)

Additional Information:

(1) During the year Mr. Debit married Ms. Credit, age 48, a widow who received the following income in 2018:

	Before marriage	After marriage
Employment insurance	$2,000	$ 700
Annual pension from her deceased husband's estate	3,000	—
Interest — Canadian	200	150
Dividends from taxable Canadian public corporations	—	300
	$5,200	$1,150

(2) Ms. Credit moved into Mr. Debit's home immediately after the marriage along with her 72-year-old mother, whose only income is the Old Age Security Pension of $6,942.

(3) Mr. Debit supported the following persons, in his home, during 2018:

(a) Ms. Credit.

(b) Ms. Credit's mother (physically infirm, certified as impaired by a medical doctor, lives with Mr. and Mrs. Credit).

(c) Donald, age 19, a second-year McGill University student, had the following sources of funds and selected expenses for 2018:

Employment income for tax purposes	
— Montreal	$ 150
— Toronto	6,000
Canadian bank interest income	200
Scholarship	3,100

Student loan		2,000
Tuition fees — allowable for tax purposes for eight months full time attendance at university		3,000
Eligible moving expenses to Toronto	$300	
to McGill	300	600

(d) Debra, age 19 at the start of the year, who was unemployed for most of the year and whose total income for tax purposes was only $1,200.

(e) David, age 15, who is a paraplegic and has been confined to bed or wheelchair since early childhood. He has been certified by a medical doctor as impaired. David has no income for tax purposes.

(f) Donna, Mr. Debit's 50-year-old sister, is mentally infirm as certified by a medical doctor and requires the services of a full-time attendant, which cost Mr. Debit $8,000 in 2018. Donna has no income for tax purposes.

(4) Mr. Debit made the following selected payments during 2018:

Charitable donations (consistent with prior years)		$1,000
Political donations to Federal Political Party		500
Medical insurance premiums		
Liberty Mutual — Extended Health Care		200
Sun Life — Drug Plan		180

(5)   Mr. Debit paid $1,500 for surgery (essential, not cosmetic) for Donald, not reimbursed by provincial plan   1,500

(6)   Mr. Debit has the following loss carryovers from 2017:

Capital loss from sale of LPP, not claimable in 2017	$2,000
Net capital losses, arising in 1999	6,000

(7) Maximum Employment Insurance premiums and CPP contributions were withheld from Mr. Debit's employment income.

(8) Mr. Debit did not claim a capital gains deduction or net capital losses in the period 1985 to 2017, inclusive, since he did not have any capital gains in that period.

— *REQUIRED*

(A) Compute Mr. Debit's Division B income, according to the rules in section 3, and his taxable income, according to the rules in section 111.1.

(B) Determine his federal tax using his optimum personal tax credits in accordance with the ordering rules in section 118.92.

Also, set out clearly any alternative answers and the reason for your position supported by any necessary calculations.

Problem 5

Ms. Janrayad was appointed as president of Massive Ltd., a public corporation, on January 1, 2018. She provides you with the following information concerning her receipts, taxable benefits, and expenditures:

Gross salary		$100,000
Income taxes withheld	$30,000	
CPP contribution (max. amount)	2,594	
EI contribution (max. amount)	858	33,452
Net salary		$ 66,548

Massive Ltd. pays the following amounts on behalf of Ms. Janrayad:

(a) Fringe benefits:

(i)	Dental Plan — Sun Life group plan	$ 175
(ii)	Registered Pension Plan (6% defined benefit plan)	$ 6,000
(iii)	Membership fees in Businessperson's Private Dining Club	$ 1,100

(b)   Massive Ltd. provides Ms. Janrayad with a car to be used in connection with the duties of her employment. Ms. Janrayad uses the car 70% for business and 30% for pleasure based on total kilometres for 2018 of 25,000. Insurance costs of $2,000 and gas and oil costs of $3,000 were paid by Ms. Janrayad.

The company paid the following automobile expenses directly to third parties, including HST where applicable:

    (i)   Repairs and maintenance . . . . $ 2,000

    (ii)   Lease costs . . . . $ 7,700

(c)   Massive Ltd. pays the following allowances:

    (i)   Ms. Janrayad receives 20 cents per business kilometre as an allowance.

    (ii)   Ms. Janrayad, who travels regularly away from her employer's place of business to negotiate contracts, receives a monthly allowance of $450 to cover her accommodation and meals while travelling. She is, however, required by her contract to pay for these expenses directly. Her actual expenses were $3,500 for meals (incurred in equal monthly amounts) and $6,000 for accommodation, all of which were reasonable in the circumstances.

(d)   Ms. Janrayad moved from Halifax to London on January 1, 2018 to accept the position at Massive Ltd. Massive Ltd. paid her a moving allowance of $17,000. Ms. Janrayad incurred the following expenses:

Air fare for family . . . . $ 1,750

Moving cost of furniture   1,400

Costs of disposing of Halifax home

  — legal fees   800

  — real estate commission   15,500

One day in London

  — meals   80

  — accommodation   175

Costs of purchasing London home

  — prepaid realty taxes   550

  — legal fees   1,100

  — land transfer tax   450

(e)   Ms. Janrayad had the option to purchase up to 6,000 previously unissued common shares from the company at $11 per share. The fair market value of the shares at the time of granting the right on January 1, 2018 was $11.

On October 1, 2018, Ms. Janrayad decided to exercise part of her right and purchased 3,600 shares with a fair market value of $17 per share as at that date.

(f)   Massive Ltd. has lent Ms. Janrayad the following:

    (i)   a $35,000 loan on October 1, 2018 at 2% interest per year with a five-year term. Ms. Janrayad used this loan to exercise her stock option in October. Ms. Janrayad pays interest on the loan at the end of each quarter;

    (ii)   a $150,000 loan on January 1, 2018 at 3% interest per year with a five-year term but amortized over a 25-year period to purchase a house in London. On January 1, 2019, Ms. Janrayad repaid $15,000 in principal in addition to the interest for the year.

Assume that the prescribed rates for the year were:

1st quarter — 4%	3rd quarter — 5%
2nd quarter — 4%	4th quarter — 5%

— *REQUIRED*

    (A) Calculate Ms. Janrayad's employment income for tax purposes (as determined by Subdivision a of Division B of the Income Tax Act) supported by all necessary calculations and explanations where there are alternative methods.

    (B) Explain why any amounts were excluded from the calculation in Part A of the required.

    (C) Explain any other tax consequences of the amounts included in Part A.

Problem 6

The following information concerns a client, Mr. White, who brought you this information for preparation of his tax return.

Gross salary		$ 60,000
Less: Canada Pension Plan (CPP) premium		(2,594)
Employment Insurance (EI) premium		(858)
Registered Pension Plan (RPP) contribution (employer contributes an equal amount)		(800)
Income taxes withheld		(15,000)
Net Pay		$ 40,800
Pension income received on a periodic basis		6,000
Rental property loss excluding capital cost allowance		(10,000)
Investment income		
Dividends from taxable Canadian public corporations (grossed up)	9,000	
Canadian bank interest	6,000	15,000
Capital gains and capital losses		
X Ltd — a Canadian-controlled private corporation (CCPC) that qualifies as a "small business corporation"	(28,000)	
Y Ltd — a public company	11,250	
Personal-use property	4,500	
Listed personal property	6,000	(6,250)
		$ 45,498

Additional Information:

(a)   The following selected payments were made during the year:

Brokerage fee on the acquisition of some shares	$	200
Legal fees in respect of an appeal of income taxes paid	$	1,000
Contribution to a Registered Retirement Savings Plan (RRSP)	$	8,500
Charitable donations (consistent with prior years)	$	1,000
Federal political donation	$	100

(b)   Mr. White has the following carryovers as at January 1, 2018:

Charitable donations	$	500
Listed personal property losses	$	8,000
Net capital loss balance (from 1999)	$	12,000

(c)   Mr. White utilized a capital gains exemption of $11,250 in 1987.

(d)   The cumulative disallowed portion of business investment losses in previous years is nil.

(e)   In 2017, Mr. White had, essentially, the same income except that his salary was $55,000 and RPP contribution was $700. His pension adjustment for 2017 was $1,600.

— *REQUIRED*

(A)   Determine Mr. White's 2018 taxable income, demonstrating clearly the ordering rules found in Division B and Division C, supported by any necessary calculations.

(B)   Explain the tax implications of any amount or any part thereof which was not included in your answer in Part A.

Problem 7

Buck Shot, age 59, has asked you for some assistance in preparing his 2018 tax return. He is married and has three children, ages 21, 19, and 15.

(a) Net salary from employment

Gross salary and taxable benefits.		$90,000
Less: Income tax withheld	$28,425	
Registered pension plan contributions (required contributions to a defined benefit plan)	3,600	
Contribution to United Way	500	
CPP	2,584	
EI	858	35,967
Net salary		$54,033

(b) Buck Shot has the following other sources of income:

Taxable capital gains (allowable capital losses)

— Winchester Rifles Ltd. (public company)	$18,000
— Artwork (a painting)	600
— Shares of Bell Canada (public company)	(1,000)
Monthly pension of $1,500 from previous employer	18,000

(c) His wife, age 48, has the following property income:

Dividends from Bell Canada (public company), cash amount	$	600
Interest on Canada Savings Bonds given to her by Buck Shot		600
Canadian Bank Interest		300
Interest on loan to her brother		250
Dividends from U.S. corporations*		3,600

---

* Mrs. Shot paid $1,540 in bank interest to purchase these shares.

Buck Shot has heard that it is possible for him to include on his tax return the dividends from taxable Canadian corporations received by his wife. He is unaware of whether this is of advantage to him. He is also aware of the fact that he can split up to 50% of his pension income with his wife if it is to his advantage from a tax perspective.

(d) Agnes, the 21-year-old, attended Ryerson Polytechnic University for eight months as a full-time student during the year and has income for tax purposes of $2,500. She paid tuition fees of $6,000.

(e) Robert, age 19, and Charles, age 15, are attending high school and have no income except for $300 of interest from GICs, given to them by Buck Shot. Charles attends a special school for the disabled and is confined to a wheelchair. Buck Shot paid $4,000 in tuition fees in respect of this school for 2018.

(f) The following disbursements were made by Buck Shot in 2018:

Donation to Lakehead University	$150
Premiums for private health insurance	320
Donation to provincial political party	150

(g) Buck Shot has a net capital loss balance of $25,770 which arose in 1999.

— *REQUIRED*

(A) Prepare a statement of income, taxable income and basic federal tax according to the ordering rules for Division B, Division C, and Division E of the Federal Income Tax Act. Utilize any elections with respect to Buck Shot's wife's dividends or his pension income. Explain your decisions and show your calculations.

(B) Give an explanation for each item omitted from your answer in Part A.

Problem 8

Marilyn is a marketing representative for a Canadian-controlled private corporation, Tax Books Inc. She has worked for this company since January 1, 2016. She is married to Jorge, who is working full-time on his Masters of Sociology degree. Marilyn and Jose have two children, ages 4 and 7. Marilyn has asked you to look at her 2018 tax information.

Marilyn provides you with the following information:

1. Marilyn received a salary of $70,000, a performance bonus of $15,000 and commissions of $5,000 (based on sales she generated). Her employer withheld the following amounts from her pay:

Income tax	$30,000
CPP and EI	3,452
RRSP contributions	3,000

   (Marilyn's employer matches her RRSP contributions)

   [The contributions of both parties were made equally throughout each month of 2018. The January and February 2018 contributions were used on Marilyn's 2017 tax return.]

Group disability insurance premium	150

   ($25 per month; Marilyn pays half and the employer pays half)

Donations to United Way (she has been doing this for several years)	300

2. Her employer provides her with the following:

   (a) An automobile which cost $20,000 plus HST @ 13%. The car was available to Marilyn for the entire year and she used the car 40% for business during 2018. She put approximately 30,000 kilometres on the car during 2018. Tax Books Inc. also pays for all of the operating costs of the car.

Gas, oil changes and repairs	$2,000 (including applicable HST)
Insurance	$1,200

   (b) Annual membership fee of $700 in a local golf club so that she can meet potential clients.

   (c) Personal tax preparation costs, $400, including HST, in 2018 to have her 2017 tax return prepared.

3. Marilyn was given a trip to St. Lucia worth $900 by one of Tax Books Inc.'s suppliers who appreciated the work done by Marilyn. She bought another ticket for Jorge and they went during December of 2018.

4. Marilyn owns 50% of the shares of Microcosm of Life Limited, a Canadian-controlled private corporation. In 2017, she had $15,000 included in her income for loans made to her by the company. During 2018, she repaid $10,000 of this loan.

5. Marilyn is a director for Taxed-to-the-Hilt Public Company, and this company paid her $500 in director's fees for 2018.

6. In February of 2018 Marilyn gave Jorge 200 shares of Looney Canadian Public Co., which she had bought three years ago for a total of $1,000. In May 2018, the shares paid dividends for the first time of $6 per share. He sold all 200 shares in November 2018 for net proceeds of $10,000.

7. Marilyn's father runs a retail business. Marilyn has owned the real estate out of which the business operates for five years. In February 2018, she sold the land and building. There was no gain on the land. The selling price allocated to the land was equal to the original cost. The details on the building are as follows:

Sale price	$250,000
Legal fees including HST	1,000
Cost of building	160,000
Net rental income to Marilyn for January and February	1,400
Cash received	100,000
Mortgage receivable from the purchaser	150,000

   At the time of the sale, Marilyn did not have a mortgage payable on the property and capital cost allowance of $2,300 had been claimed on the building since she had purchased it. The mortgage receivable from the purchaser was being amortized over 25 years and is due in three years. She received interest of $3,000 on the mortgage during 2018. The balance of the mortgage outstanding at the end of 2018 was $145,000.

8. In January 2018, Marilyn contributed $7,000 to her RRSP and $2,000 to a spousal RRSP for Jorge. She did not report these contributions on her 2017 income tax return.

9. Marilyn showed you the carryforward information from her 2017 tax return. Her earned income for 2017 was $80,000. She had unused RRSP deduction room of $100 at the end of 2017. Marilyn's cumulative net investment income balance was $2,000 at the end of 2018. She has a net capital loss carry forward from 1999 of $1,500. She received both Notices of Assessment for 2016 and 2017 tax returns during 2018. She paid $450 for interest and penalties for her 2016 return in 2018. Also, in 2018, she received $200 refund interest on her 2017 refund.

10. The two children received interest income in 2018:

    — $200 generated by deposits of previously received child tax benefits cheques; and

    — $400 from corporate bonds purchased by Marilyn during 2017

11. In January of 2018, Marilyn's employer stopped the RRSP matching plan, so Marilyn stopped having RRSP contributions deducted from her pay.

12. From October to December of 2018, Marilyn was off work and receiving disability insurance. She received $4,000 per month and did not have to pay any premiums during this time.

— *REQUIRED*

Determine Marilyn's taxable income for 2018. Show all your calculations. Briefly explain why you omitted any of the above information from your calculations. Calculate the effect of the disability insurance receipts on Marilyn's 2018 tax situation.

Problem 9

On September 1, 2018, Stan moved 530 km from Ottawa, Ontario to Toronto, Ontario, to start a new job with Bullet Investors Group as a commissioned salesman. From January 1, 2018 to August 31, 2018, he was unemployed.

Before he moved, he sold an antique table and painting for $800 and $1,500, respectively. They were purchased in 2007 for $1,100 and $700, respectively.

Stan paid for the following moving expenses, which were then reimbursed by Bullet Investors Group:

Packing and moving furniture and other personal items	$2,000
Three days receipted meals and accommodation in Toronto, waiting for the painting of the Toronto home to be finished (meals $200, accommodation $300)	500
Cancellation of lease on the apartment he lived in until he moved on September 1	400
	$2,900

Stan received gross salary of $34,000, including commission income of $10,000 from Bullet Investors Group in 2018. His payroll deductions consisted of the following:

CPP contributions	$1,510
EI contributions	564
Union dues	210
RPP employee contribution	1,300
Income tax	5,700

His T4 slip indicated that his pension adjustment was $3,000 for 2018.

Sundry amounts received by Stan during 2018:

Interest on savings account	$ 925
Dividends from taxable Canadian public corporations	8,000
Dividends from a U.S. corporation, net of $300 tax withheld ($Cdn)	1,700
HST Rebate with respect to 2017 employment expenses, excluding CCA	250
Lottery winnings..	300
Employment insurance benefits	9,000
Retiring allowance	35,000
	$55,175

The retiring allowance was received from Simple Ltd., his previous employer. He had worked for Simple Ltd. from February 1, 1987 to December 31, 2017, during which time he was always a member of the pension plan and all contributions to that RPP vested immediately.

On March 20, 2018, Stan sold shares of Simple Ltd. for $70,000. These shares represented a minority arm's length interest in his former employer, a Canadian-controlled private corporation. He paid $10,000 for the shares, which were purchased pursuant to the company's stock option plan. The values of the shares were: at the time the option was granted in 2007, $15,000, and at the time he exercised the option in 2009, $25,000.

His stock market transactions for 2018 were as follows:

February 2	purchased 500 shares of X Ltd. for $2 each
February 28 ...	purchased 1,000 shares of X Ltd. for $10 each
March 15	sold 500 shares of X Ltd. for $5 each

Stan made the following sundry payments during 2018:

TFSA administration fee paid outside the TFSA	$ 100
Interest expense for the purchase of the marketable securities	500
Legal fees to contest income tax assessment	600
Donations to registered charities (consistent with prior years)	700
RRSP contributions:	
January–February 2018 (all of which was deducted on his 2017 tax return)	2,500
March–December 2018	6,000
January–February 2019	40,000
	$50,400

The pension adjustment reported on Stan's 2017 T4 slip was $1,400. His earned income for 2017, as calculated under ssec. 146(1), was $70,000. His unused RRSP deduction room at the end of 2017 was $800.

Stan has net capital losses of $4,000 and listed personal property losses of $200, both incurred in 2009. He has used his entire capital gains deduction entitlement as of the end of 2017.

Stan has to repay $2,700 of employment insurance benefits received during 2018 due to his high income level for 2018.

— REQUIRED

Determine Stan's taxable income for 2018. Show all your calculations. Briefly explain why you omitted any of the above information from your calculations. Reconcile Stan's taxable income to "adjusted taxable income" for minimum tax purposes.

Problem 10

You have been asked to reconcile accounting income to taxable income for your client, Leonard Hockey Stick Manufacturing Corporation. The income statement for the year ended December 31, 2018 is shown below:

Leonard Hockey Stick Manufacturing Corporation
Statement of Income
For the Year Ended December 31, 2018

Sales	$2,300,000
Cost of Goods Sold	1,180,000
Gross Profit	$1,120,000
Operating Expenses	470,000
Administrative Expenses	450,000
Income from Operations	$ 200,000
Other Income and Expenses	10,000
Income Before Taxes	$ 210,000
Income Taxes — Current	45,700
— Future	3,500
Net Income for the Year	$ 160,800

During your review of the working paper file and last year's tax return, you have made the following notes to yourself because you think that there might be tax implications associated with these items.

1. Leonard Hockey Stick Manufacturing Corporation is a Canadian corporation owned 50% by Chrisa and 50% by her husband, Neil. Chrisa and Neil are both residents of Canada for income tax purposes. The company manufactures hockey sticks in Mississauga, Ontario.

2. The opening allowance for doubtful accounts at January 1, 2018 was $12,000. The closing allowance for doubtful accounts was $18,000. The net increase has been reflected as bad debt expense for accounting purpose. The allowance is determined by identifying specific accounts where collection is unlikely.

3. The "Other Income" includes the following items:

Capital dividend received from 80% owned small business corporation, David Hockey Pucks	$12,000
Dividend received from 100% owned subsidiary company, Peter Wood Products Limited	$ 7,000
Dividend received from 1% owned Lori Ice Machine Canadian Public Corp.	$ 500
Dividend from 1% foreign investment in Miriam Duffle Bags Inc. (in Canadian dollars)	$ 200
Increase in cash surrender value of life insurance	$ 1,520
A loss from investment in shares of Mark Goal Nets Inc. which was a small business corporation owned 99% by a neighbour of Chrisa and 1% by Leonard Hockey Stick Manufacturing Corporation. Unfortunately, the manufacturing company went bankrupt in November 2018 and Leonard Hockey Stick Manufacturing Corporation lost its original investment of $6,000	$ (6,000)
The company has a long-term investment in the shares of Miriam Duffle Bags Inc., but there was a gain on foreign exchange from 2017 to 2018 from converting the shares from US to Canadian dollars	$ 1,500
Gain on disposition of the expensive car driven by Chrisa and Neil for business purposes (difference between net book value and proceeds received)	$ 1,000

4. During the year, the company's purchases and dispositions of fixed assets were as follows:

January 1, 2018	Purchased a new automobile for company use — cost (including HST @ 13%) . . . . (The appropriate HST was recovered as in input tax credit)	$36,160
August 1, 2018	Sold the expensive car driven by Chrisa and Neil that the company had purchased in 2013 — proceeds (less HST) . . . . (Purchase price of the car in 2013 was $36,000 before HST)	$27,000
January 15, 2018	Purchased specialized computer software for the company's accounting department	$ 6,000

5. The closing Undepreciated Capital Cost balances for December 31, 2017 were as follows:

Class 3	$102,000
Class	$ 50,000
Class 10	$ 30,000 (delivery van)
Class 10.1	$ 10,000
Class 43	$ 80,000

6. The schedule for interest expense showed the following items:

(a)	Interest on long-term debt used to purchase building and manufacturing equipment	$31,000
(b)	Interest on loan used to purchase the new automobile this year	$ 4,200
(c)	Financing fee charged by bank to purchase new automobile	$ 300
(d)	Interest on late corporate income tax instalments	$ 300
(e)	Interest on loan obtained in October 2018 used to purchase vacant land on which the company plans to build a driving range in the future	$ 6,000

7. Operating and Administrative Expenses include the following amounts:

Landscaping expenses	$ 15,000
Amortization expense	$ 48,000
Donations to registered charities	$ 5,000
Premiums on life insurance policies on Chrisa and Neil — these policies are not required by the bank for any outstanding loans	$ 2,000
Meals and entertainment expenses (incurred in equal monthly amounts)	$ 3,440
Curling club memberships for Chrisa and Neil and Janna, the vice-president of marketing	$ 6,000
Reserve for future warranty expense for hockey sticks (actual expenses paid in the year to honour warranties were $1,200)	$ 1,500
Management bonuses accrued - all paid by June 28, 2018	$370,000

— *REQUIRED*

Reconcile net income for financial statement purposes to taxable income for Part I federal tax purposes.

Problem 11

The following reconciliation between net income per the income statement and taxable income for the year ending December 31, 2018 was prepared by the bookkeeper of your client, Bupkeh Manufacturing Ltd., a Canadian-controlled private corporation. The engagement partner has asked you to identify those items which were handled incorrectly.

Net income per the financial statements — (Note 1)		$ 560,000
Add:		
Reserve for warranties — (Note 2)	$ 85,000	
Excess registered pension plan payments — (Note 3)	35,000	
Unpaid bonuses — (Note 4)	140,000	
Charitable donations — (Note 5)	60,000	
Taxable capital gains — (Note 6)		
Land	330,000	
Building	55,000	
Depreciation	40,000	745,000
		1,305,000
Deduct:		
Book profit — land — (Note 6)	$440,000	
— building — (Note 6)	230,000	
Inventory reserve — (Note 7)	8,500	(678,500)
Income for tax purposes		626,500
Charitable donations — (Note 5)	$ 60,000	
Non-capital losses — (Note 8)	160,000	
Net capital losses — (Note 8)	280,000	
Dividends from taxable Canadian corporations — (Note 9)	11,700	(511,700)
Taxable income		$ 114,800

Note 1

The net income per the financial statements includes a deduction for income taxes payable for the year of $71,000 and deferred taxes of $14,000. This amount also reflects certain extraordinary items as reflected in subsequent notes.

Note 2

The reserve for warranties was computed as follows:

Warranty reserve — January 1, 2018	$ 55,000
Provision for future warranties	85,000
	140,000
Actual warranty expenditures	50,000
Warranty reserve — December 31, 2018	$ 90,000

Note 3

The company and employees contribute equal amounts each (6% of gross salary) to a registered pension fund which is a defined contribution (money purchase) plan. The $35,000 represents the company contributions in respect of 2018 made on January 31, 2019.

Note 4

Because of cash-flow restrictions, payment of bonuses to certain key employees has been deferred although there is a bona fide obligation to pay them by May 2019.

2018	Unpaid bonuses	$140,000 (accrued in 2018)
2017	Unpaid bonuses	$115,000 (accrued in 2017)

Note 5

Charitable donations for 2018 included the following amounts:

University scholarships paid directly to children of employees	$ 20,000
Assistance to the spouse of employee who recently died	6,000
Donation to registered charities	25,000
Building fund of several universities	9,000
	$ 60,000

Note 6

On July 1, 2018, the corporation sold a warehouse and the related land. The company does not intend to replace the building and has entered into a long-term lease arrangement for similar space.

Sale of land and building

Land	— cost	125,000
	— selling price	565,000
Building	— cost	$180,000
	— book value	110,000
	— UCC class 3	140,000
	— selling price	340,000

Other: (1) the company paid a real estate commission of 10% and an appraisal fee of $2,500 in respect of this sale. These amounts were expensed.

(2) the company took back as part of the consideration a 10-year 11% mortgage of $675,000 with interest and principal payment due on the anniversary date. Interest is included in income when received.

Long-term lease

The company entered into a 10-year lease with two successive options of five years each, on July 1, 2018. The annual rent is $30,000. In order to secure the lease, the company had to pay the owner the first and the last year's rent in advance plus $35,000 for leasehold improvements. The last year's rent and leasehold improvements were not expensed but are in a balance sheet account labelled "prepaid costs".

Note 7

A reserve of $8,500 for an estimated decline in values was applied to the closing inventory.

Note 8

The non-capital losses represent the balance remaining from a 2016 loss of $25,000 and the full amount of the 2017 loss of $135,000. The net capital loss originated in 2002.

Note 9

These dividends were received from a wholly-owned subsidiary on June 15, 2018, and a grossed-up amount of 1.17 × the dividends received was included in income. Of the actual amount received, the subsidiary had elected that $2,000 be paid from its capital dividend account.

—REQUIRED

Prepare a draft memorandum for the client explaining the incorrect treatment of the items in the reconciliation (or omitted items) so that the bookkeeper can prepare the reconciliation correctly in the future.

Problem 12

Griffin Rock owns 100% of a Canadian corporation, Snowblowers Plus, Inc. The company's year end is December 31. You are the audit senior and must prepare the tax return for the company. The income statement and additional information obtained from the audit are summarized below.

Snowblowers Plus, Inc.
Income Statement
For the year ended December 31, 2018

Sales		$5,500,000
Cost of goods sold		
Opening inventory	$ 300,000	
Amortization on equipment	20,000	
Labour	2,700,000	
Materials	900,000	
Ending inventory	(400,000)	(3,520,000)
Gross profit		1,980,000
Administrative expenses		
Amortization of capital assets	15,000	
Employee benefits	28,000	
Insurance	15,000	
Interest expense	20,000	
Management salaries	380,000	
Office salaries	90,000	
Utilities	35,000	(583,000)
Sales expenses		
Advertising and marketing	100,000	
Promotion	14,000	
Sales commissions and salaries	374,000	
Travel	45,000	(533,000)
Operating income		864,000
Other		
Gain on sale of land	130,000	
Dividend income	11,000	
Interest income	10,000	151,000
Net income before taxes		1,015,000
Income taxes		
Current	426,600	
Deferred	20,000	(446,600)
Net income		$ 568,400

Additional information that was noted for the purposes of preparing the client's tax returns.

1. Opening UCC balances as at January 1, 2018:

Class 1	$83,000
Class 8	60,000
Class 10	40,000

    During the year, the company undertook the following transactions with respect to fixed assets. All costs are exclusive of HST @ 13% where applicable.

    (a) The existing administrative building was demolished. A new administrative building was constructed on the same land at a cost of $200,000. The original building was purchased in 2003 at a cost of $45,000. There is still a manufacturing plant and warehouse included in Class 1.

    (b) Two new cars were purchased to be used by the president and the vice-president for business purposes. The cars each cost $35,000.

    (c) The company sold three of its computers to employees at a fair market value of $200 each. The computers had originally cost the company $1,000 each.

    (d) New manufacturing equipment was purchased during 2018 costing $90,000. Machinery which had originally cost $10,000 and had been set up in Class 29 many years ago, was scrapped during the year.

    (e) New office furniture was purchased during the year at a cost of $20,000.

    (f) The company sold a piece of land that it was holding, for the expansion of its business operations, for $150,000. The land had been purchased in 2011 for $20,000. On the sale of the property, a mortgage of $50,000 was taken back. The purchasers had repaid $27,500 by Snowblowers Plus, Inc.'s year end. The balance of the mortgage was not due until 2019.

2. Ten thousand marketing brochures were purchased during 2018 costing $5,000. Only 1,000 brochures were used at December 31, 2018. The company did not set up a prepaid expense as the amount was immaterial for accounting purposes.

3. Promotion expense contains the following items:

Meals for salespeople who travel outside the city	$3,000
Meals for entertaining business clients or potential clients	4,300
Season tickets to Toronto Maple Leaf hockey games	800
Staff Christmas party	900
Golf club membership for the president and vice-president	5,000
	$14,000

4. Management salaries include a bonus to the shareholder of $90,000. This amount was paid on August 31, 2019 and all source deductions (income tax, CPP) were remitted by the company on September 15, 2019.

5. Dividend income consists of the following amounts:

Deemed dividend on redemption of 250 preferred shares of ABC Canadian Ltd. (before the redemption, the company owned 9% of the shares; now it owns 7% of the shares)	$2,500
Taxable dividend from XYZ Inc., a CCPC in which the company owns 50 of 200 shares	3,000
Taxable dividend from a US corporation, Ex-why-zee Corp., net of 15% withholding tax. The company owns less than 1% of Ex-why-zee's shares. The dividends are stated in Canadian dollars	1,700
Capital dividend from Y Not Ltd., a Canadian corporation in which the company has a 50% interest	3,800
	$11,000

6. During 2018, the sole shareholder transferred, to the company, a warehouse that he had purchased in 2001. The transfer was done by way of a tax-free rollover under section 85 of the Income Tax Act. The details on the transferred property at the date of the transfer are as follows.

Cost	$100,000
UCC	95,000

Fair market value	200,000
Elected transfer price	190,000
Consideration	
Note to shareholder	190,000
10,000 preferred shares	10,000

The shareholder reported the disposition on his 2018 personal tax return. His return reported $5,000 recapture and $90,000 capital gain. The shareholder utilized his capital losses carried forward to eliminate the gain elected.

7. In 1999, the company sustained a capital loss of $12,000. To date, this loss had not been used.

8. In order to finance the new building addition, the company had to obtain new financing. The company incurred $600 in obtaining the new financing. The amount was claimed as an expense on the financial statements.

9. The company is registered for HST.

— REQUIRED

Determine the taxable income for the December 31, 2018 tax return of Snowblowers Plus, Inc. Show all your calculations.

Problem 13

The CA in your office who has completed the file for your client, Make-it and Save-it Inc., has left for a well-deserved two-week vacation. Before leaving, she asked you to prepare Schedule 1 of the T2 Corporate Tax Return and calculate federal Part I and Part IV tax for the year ended December 31, 2018.

The CA has provided you with financial statements, which have been prepared for tax purposes, and notes on selected items in the financial statements (Appendix I).

— REQUIRED

Calculate net income, taxable income, and federal Part I and Part IV tax for Make-it and Save-it Inc. for the year ended December 31, 2018.

APPENDIX I
Make-it and Save-it Inc.
Balance Sheet
December 31, 2018

Assets

Current

Cash	$ 210,000	
Accounts receivable	935,000	
Prepaid expenses	35,000	
Inventory	1,025,000	
		2,205,000
Capital assets, net of amortization		1,322,000
Investments		790,000
		$4,317,000

Liabilities

Current

Accounts payable	$ 360,000	
Income taxes payable	280,000	
		640,000
Long-term debt		1,000,000
Due to shareholder		1,353,000
		2,993,000

Shareholder's Equity

Share capital	150,000
Retained earnings	1,174,000
	1,324,000
	$4,317,000

Sales	$6,665,000
Cost of goods sold, Schedule A	5,878,000
Gross profit	787,000

Expenses

Advertising	152,000
Amortization of capital assets	12,000
Automotive expenses	58,000
Bad debts	138,000
Charitable donations	2,000
Interest on long-term debt	80,000
Management salaries	200,000
Moving expense	25,000
Office expense	118,000
Professional fees	36,000
Promotion	63,000
Salaries and benefits	
Administrative	205,000
Sales	410,000
	1,499,000

Loss from manufacturing operations	(712,000)

Other income (deductions)

Dividend income	55,000
Gain on disposition of Plant #1	1,300,000
Loss on disposition of equipment	(9,000)
Income from Make-it and Save-it (Alberta) Inc.	100,000
Interest	7,500
Rental, Schedule B	30,400
Restructuring cost	(50,000)
Write-down of investments	(25,000)
	1,408,900

Income before income taxes	696,900
Income taxes	200,000
Net income for the year	496,900
Retained earnings, beginning of year	977,100
Dividends (paid October 15, 2018)	(300,000)
Retained earnings, end of year	$1,174,000

APPENDIX I (continued)

Schedule A

Make-it and Save-it Inc.
Cost of Goods Sold
For the Year Ended December 31, 2018

Opening inventory	$1,675,000
Material cost	4,020,000
Direct labour	720,000
Amortization	128,000
Overhead	360,000
	6,903,000
Closing inventory	1,025,000
Cost of Goods Sold	$5,878,000

Schedule B

Make-it and Save-it Inc.
Statement of Rental Income and Expenses
For the Year Ended December 31, 2018

Rent		$ 40,000
Expenses		
Amortization of capital assets	3,000	
Property taxes	4,000	
Repairs and maintenance	1,800	
Utilities	800	
		9,600
Net Rental Income		$ 30,400

Make-it and Save-it Inc.
Additional Notes

1. Make-it and Save-it Inc. (MSI) is a Canadian-controlled private corporation. The company is a manufacturer of office furniture. It also has marketable securities, some interest-bearing investments and a rental property. MSI has a wholly-owned subsidiary, Make-it-Rich Investments Ltd. and owns 37.5% of Make-it and Save-it (Alberta) Inc.

2. The inventory is valued at cost which is determined on a standard cost basis. The cost of the inventory exceeds fair market value by $10,000. The write-down was not recorded for financial statement purposes since it was not considered material.

3. Capital assets, net of amortization

		December 31, 2017		December 31, 2018	
		Cost	Accumulated Amortization	Cost	Accumulated Amortization
Land	— Plant #1	$ 187,500	$ —	$ —	$ —
	— Plant #2	—	—	300,000	—
	— Warehouse	50,000	—	50,000	—
	— Rental property	80,000	—	80,000	—
Building	— Plant #1	280,000	180,000	—	—
	— Plant #2	—	—	500,000	20,000
	— Warehouse	100,000	40,000	100,000	43,000
	— Rental property	120,000	60,000	120,000	63,000
Manufacturing equipment		655,000	370,000	725,000	455,000
Office equipment		50,000	30,000	50,000	36,000
Computer equipment		30,000	10,000	30,000	16,000
		$1,552,500	$ 690,000	$1,955,000	$ 633,000

Cost, net of accumulated amortization	$862,500	$1,322,000

Due to significant advancements in just-in-time inventory control, the company was able to significantly reduce its space requirements for its manufacturing plant. As a consequence, the company sold its Plant #1 for $1,850,000 ($918,750 for the land and $931,250 for the building) and purchased Plant #2 during the year.

The company purchased two new pieces of manufacturing equipment in 2018: one machine was traded-in for a new machine for a net price of $37,000 in July 2018 and one (without a trade-in) for $62,000 in November 2018. The new machine purchased in July 2018 had a list price of $43,000. The old piece of equipment had an original cost of $35,000 and has been depreciated to a net book value of $15,000.

There were no other additions or disposition of capital assets during the year.

The closing UCC's at December 31, 2017 were:

Class 3 — plant and warehouse	$160,000
Class 3 — rental property	60,000
Class 8	20,000
Class 10	20,000
Class 43	200,000

4.   The investment in Make-it-Rich Investments Ltd. is accounted for using the cost method and the investment in Make-it and Save-it (Alberta) Inc. is accounted for using the equity method.

	2017	2018
Make-it and Save-it (Alberta) Inc.		
Opening	$280,000	$300,000
Share of income	60,000	100,000
Dividend	(40,000)	(60,000)
Closing	300,000	340,000
Make-it-Rich Investments Ltd.	200,000	200,000
Term deposits	100,000	150,000
Marketable securities		
Cost	125,000	125,000
Write-down to market value	—	(25,000)
	$725,000	$790,000

The dividend paid by Make-it and Save-it (Alberta) Inc. on January 31, 2018 resulted in a dividend refund of $23,000.

5. Accounts payable at December 31, 2018 includes bonuses payable to employees of $40,000 and bonuses payable to the shareholder of $110,000. The bonuses are considered reasonable and are expected to be paid in September 2019.

6. The promotion account has been analyzed and includes the following items which were incurred evenly throughout the year:

Concert tickets given to customers	$ 1,000
Meals and entertainment incurred by salespeople	22,000
Meals and entertainment incurred by management	8,000
Staff Christmas party	32,000
	$63,000

7. After the move was complete, management completed an operational review of the company and determined that there was a number of excess staff. Management has determined that $50,000 will be required in severance payments to staff and has recorded the expense accordingly. The staff was terminated during January 2019.

8. Dividend income

Marketable securities — received evenly throughout the year	$ 5,000
Make-it-Rich Investments Ltd. — received August 1, 2018	50,000
	$55,000

    The dividend paid by Make-it-Rich Investments Ltd. resulted in a dividend refund of $19,167.

Problem 14

Ryan Taylor lives in a province with a combined federal and provincial corporate tax rate of 40% on CCPC investment income, before applying any refundable tax on CCPCs investment income. He owns the following investments and anticipates the following Canadian-source income for future years.

	Value at Dec. 31, 2018	Type of Income in 2019	Income Anticipated
ABC Company Bonds	$100,000	Interest	$11,000
XYZ Canada Co. shares	400,000	Dividends	20,000
Ace Technology shares	50,000	Capital gains	15,000
Safe Bank of Canada shares	50,000	Dividends	4,000
		Capital gains	3,000
	$600,000		$53,000

In addition to the above investment income, Ryan expects to earn approximately $80,000 employment income. The total adjusted cost base for the above investments is $450,000. The above-named companies are all public companies.

— REQUIRED

Ryan asks you whether it is financially more attractive for him to own his investments through a corporation or to own them directly, as he currently does. Assume that he and his investments will generate the anticipated amounts mentioned above. In addition to his $80,000 employment income, his cash needs require that $14,000 of the corporation's after-tax profits be distributed to him. Assume federal personal tax credits of $2,450 and provincial personal tax credits of $1,550.

Use hypothetical provincial personal tax rates as set out in chapter 10 of the text.

Problem 15

Your client, Maven Public Co. Ltd., which is listed on the Toronto Stock Exchange, has asked you to give some tax advice to their new vice-president, Morris Minor, age 50, who will be responsible for the marketing of the company's products starting next January. This position will require extensive travelling across Canada. In particular, Morris will have direct responsibility in renewing the contracts for several chain-store private brand products.

In your first interview with Morris, the following facts and background information were brought to your attention. Morris is presently employed by Action Properties Ltd., a family-owned company (a CCPC) operating out of Moose Jaw. Morris is not related to the controlling group of shareholders. The company had no pension plan but did have a generous stock option plan in which Morris actively participated. Morris had acquired his shares at an option price of $15 on January 1, of the following years:

2015 — 200 shares	2017 — 300 shares
2016 — 100 shares	2018 — 400 shares

Morris can still acquire an additional 1,000 shares at an option price of $15 before he leaves his present employer on December 31. However, when Morris terminates this employment contract he must sell all of the shares obtained under the stock option to the controlling family at the fair market value based on an independent party's assessment (approximately $100 each). This value has remained the same throughout the period over which shares were purchased. Since Morris does not have any spare cash, he plans to borrow the required funds from the bank in order to purchase the additional 1,000 shares.

Your client, Maven Public Co. Ltd., has made the following offer to Morris, which is a standard package available for all the senior executives, plus an annual salary of $150,000:

— A moving allowance of $15,000 plus a reimbursement of an actual loss on the disposition of the family home up to a maximum of $50,000.

— A monthly travel allowance of $1,500.

— Membership in two clubs of his choice.

— Premiums or other payment of the following medically related plans:

  — Liberty Mutual Extended Health Care: $250

  — Sun Life — Drug Plan: $200

  — Sun Life — Income Protection While Ill: $800

  Participation in a contributory defined benefit pension plan of 2% of his gross salary which would result in a pension income of $1,715 for each year of service plus a retiring allowance of one year's salary.

— An annual security option, granted on January 1 each year, to purchase 5,000 shares of the company. The first option will be granted January 1, 2019. Options can be exercised after a one-year period has expired from the date of grant. The first option will be exercisable at 80% of the market value at the time of grant (January 1, 2019 — estimated market value $10 per share). Assume the fair market value at the date of exercise is $20 per share.

— Group term life insurance of $400,000 paid by the company at an approximate cost of $2 per $1,000 of coverage.

— 2% loans available January 1, 2019:

  — to acquire a home up to a maximum of $250,000, evidenced by a 25-year mortgage.

  — to acquire an automobile up to a maximum of $15,000 with no definite repayment period.

(Assume that the prescribed rate for 2019 will be 5% for all quarters)

— *REQUIRED*

Prepare a draft memorandum to Mr. Minor explaining the tax implications of the events arising from the proposed departure from his present employer and the proposed compensation package offered by Maven Public Co. Ltd.

Problem 16

Mr. Grocer is a fellow member of a service club. You have known each other since December 2017 when he joined your service club after moving from Saskatoon to Dundas, Ontario, to become the local supermarket manager. It is early January 2019 and Mr. Grocer knows that you have a Master of Taxation degree and has asked you to look at his 2018 tax situation for him. He provides you with the following information:

1. Mr. Grocer is 40 years old. His wife is 38 years old. They have two children, Bran, who is eight, and Muffin, who is five. After a five-year absence, Mrs. Grocer decided to re-enter the work force to continue her career as an electrical engineer in September of 2018.

2. Mr. Grocer has never been part of a pension plan and in 2015 started contributing to RRSPs for himself and Mrs. Grocer since neither had done so previously. In June 2018 he contributed $8,000 to his own RRSP and $6,000 to Mrs. Grocer's RRSP. His total employment income in 2017 was $65,000. Based on his 2017 Notice of Assessment, Mr. Grocer had no unused RRSP contribution room.

3. He earns a gross salary of $70,000 (deductions of income tax, CPP and EI of $20,000, $2,594 and $858, respectively) and has the following fringe benefits from the supermarket in Dundas:

   – For all of 2018 he has had the use of a car purchased by his employer on January 2, 2018 for $16,000 plus $2,080 HST. During 2018, he drove the car 30,000 kilometres of which 19,500 kilometres were for business purposes.

   – The supermarket paid for all of the operating expenses of the car.

	Net	HST	Total
Gas	$ 3,097	$ 403	$ 3,500
Oil changes	266	34	300
Repairs	531	69	600
Insurance	1,200	–	1,200

   – He received a $60,000 loan from the supermarket on December 1, 2017 in order to purchase a house in Dundas. The loan is interest-free and is repayable in five equal instalments on the anniversary date of the loan.

4. He paid $8,000 of eligible expenses in December 2017, to move from Saskatoon to Dundas. He was able to deduct $5,400 of this in 2017.

5. In January of 2018, he sold 5,000 shares in Outasite Corp. which are qualified small business corporation shares. He felt that he had done well selling them for $26,000 as had purchased them in 2015 for only $5,000. The shares of Outasite Corp. had provided him with cash, non-eligible dividends of $300 in 2015, $300 in 2016 and $200 in 2017. These dividends were his only investment income and he thought that the gain and the $800 dividends over the past four years were a pretty good deal. Mr. Grocer has not used any of his capital gain exemption yet.

6. Mr. Grocer owns a rental property in Saskatoon which he purchased in 2017. In 2017, there was a rental loss of $3,000. However, in 2018 the property generated a loss of only $1,000. These losses do not include CCA; the CCA is disallowed since it would increase the rental loss.

7. Bran and Muffin have no income other than $200 interest each from bonds purchased by Mr. Grocer on December 30, 2017.

8. Mrs. Grocer has no income other than $2,000, which she withdrew from her spousal RRSP in August 2018, and her employment income of $23,000 from September to December 2018.

   Note: The prescribed rates are as follows:

4th quarter 2017	3%
1st quarter 2018	2%
2nd quarter 2018	1%
3rd quarter 2018	1%
4th quarter 2018	1%

— *REQUIRED*

Compute Mr. Grocer's federal income tax payable for 2018 showing all necessary calculations.

Problem 17

Scrum Limited is a Canadian-controlled private corporation started by Lach Forward with an investment in common shares equal to their paid-up capital of $150,000. Lach is the only shareholder of the company and would like to retire from the business and travel to the South Pacific. He is considering several alternatives for the disposition of the business.

The corporation is taxable at a total corporate rate of 20% on its active business income eligible for the small business deduction and 50⅔% initially on its investment income (including the 10⅔% refundable tax on CCPC's investment income). Lach has never had any capital gains or losses personally.

The following is a projected balance sheet with estimated fair market values at the expected date of disposition.

Scrum Limited

Balance Sheet

as at December 31, 2018

Assets

Current assets

Cash	$	47,000
Marketable securities at cost (FMV: $35,000)		65,000
RDTOH		10,000
Inventory at cost (FMV: $82,000)		114,000
	$	236,000

Fixed assets

Land at cost (FMV: $460,000)		220,000
Building at UCC (FMV: $1,600,000; Cost: $1,300,000)		1,120,000
		$ 1,576,000

Liabilities and Shareholder's Equity

Liabilities	$	134,000
Shareholder's equity		
Paid-up capital		150,000
Capital dividend account		85,000
Other surplus		1,207,000
		$ 1,576,000

— *REQUIRED*

(A) If Lach sells the assets on the open market and winds up the corporation in late 2018, what would be the net amount available for distribution to him after paying all liabilities? Assume that the company is not associated with any other corporations and assume that all of the corporation's income has been taxed at the low corporate rates over the years. Show all computations.

(B) If these funds are distributed to Lach, determine the nature of the distribution to him for tax purposes and its components.

(C) Determine the amount that Lach would retain from this distribution after tax. Assume that Lach's marginal tax rate on income from this transaction is 44% (including Provincial Tax).

(D) How would this retention after taxes compare with the retention from a sale of the shares of the company for $2,000,000?

Problem 18

Fine Foods Inc. is a Canadian company owned 60% by Dom Delicious and 40% by his friends and relatives. All shareholders are Canadian residents. The company is a retailer of specialty foods.

You are the auditor for Fine Foods Inc. and have been given the following income statement which has been prepared for financial accounting purposes for the fiscal year ended December 31, 2018.

Fine Foods Inc.

Income Statement

for the Year Ended December 31, 2018

Sales	$ 2,850,000
Cost of sales	1,200,000
Gross profit	$ 1,650,000
Administrative expenses	780,000
Operating income	870,000
Other income	210,648
Net income before taxes	$ 1,080,648

Additional Information:

1. Administrative expenses include the following items:

   (a) depreciation of $26,050;

   (b) landscaping of grounds, $8,000;

   (c) payments of $9,500 made to the company's lawyer and bank in respect of obtaining a three-year second mortgage on the company's head office building. The company used the funds for its business operations; and

   (d) racquet club memberships totalling $9,500 for both Dom and the Vice-President, Marketing

2. Other income includes the following items:

   (a) taxable dividends of $60,000 (received evenly throughout the year) from sundry portfolio investments in Canadian companies and a capital dividend of $5,000 from Good Grub Corp., a Canadian company of which Fine Foods Inc. owns 1%;

   (b) gain on sale of land, building and equipment of $96,000. One of the sales branches operated out of this building until it was sold;

   (c) interest income of $12,000 received from an associated corporation, Fine Wine Corp., which deducts the interest payments in computing its income from an active business carried on by it in Canada;

   (d) interest of $5,000 on a two-year guaranteed investment certificate; and

   (e) net rental income of $22,000 earned from renting out 10% of the company's warehouse for the annual three-month slow period.

3. The refundable dividend tax on hand account balance at December 31, 2017 was $25,000. The dividend refund for 2017 was $5,000. The capital dividend account balance as at December 31, 2017 was $4,000.

4. UCC of depreciable assets at December 31, 2017

Class 1	$ 99,000
Class 3	$210,000
Class 8	$ 2,000

5. The proceeds from the land, building, and equipment were $50,000, $80,000, and $2,500, respectively. These were the only assets disposed of during the year. The land, building, and equipment cost $20,000, $50,000, and $3,000, respectively. The land and building are an old property that was acquired in 1986 and as a result the building is included in Class 3 for CCA purposes.

6. On December 15, 2018, Fine Foods Inc. purchased a new $40,000 automobile. The automobile is to be used by Dom who negotiates contracts for the company. This was the only asset acquired by the company during the year.

7. The company paid its shareholders taxable dividends totalling $30,000 on January 31, 2018.

8. The business limit allocated to Fine Foods Inc. is $150,000.

— *REQUIRED*

    (A) Compute the federal Part I tax payable by the company for the 2018 taxation year.

    (B) Compute the refundable dividend tax on hand balance at the end of the year and the dividend refund for the taxation year.

    (C) Compute the maximum capital dividend that can be paid to the shareholders.

Problem 19

Ottawa Associates Inc. is a business that was set up 25 years ago by Grant Carter to provide consulting services to the federal government. When the economy was good, the company was able to generate substantial profits and, even now, with a slow economy, the profits are approximately $550,000 before tax. Grant now feels that the company is worth $1,200,000 based on the income it is generating.

Grant is 50 years old this year. When he started the business, another shareholder, John Price, owned the other 50% of the shares. Each had put $10,000 of cash into the corporation as share capital. Initially, their working relationship had been excellent, but John had wanted to branch out into other areas of consulting, while Grant wanted to concentrate on government consulting. Fifteen years ago, they had agreed to go their own separate ways and Grant had bought John's shares from him for $30,000.

Grant's wife, Betty, does not work in the business directly. However, she does receive a salary for her work as secretary-treasurer of the corporation and for the time she spends on charitable activities, which is sometimes of benefit to Grant in his business. Grant would like to involve Betty in the ownership of the business, unless there are any problems with this.

Grant and Betty's two children, Scott and Kelly, are 21 and 16 years old, respectively. Scott is in university at Queen's and Kelly is in high school in Ottawa. At this point, it is not certain whether Scott and Kelly will join Grant in the business, but both are open to the possibility. Both work in the business during the summer holidays and are paid enough to cover their schooling costs.

Grant and Betty are now planning to build the cottage they have always wanted. They feel they need a place to unwind on the weekends and, also, they want a place for the children to come back to once they have left home. They see the cottage as a family gathering place. The land and construction costs are going to be approximately $200,000. Although they have that much extra cash in the corporation, they do not want to pay tax on the dividends to get the cash out. As a result, they plan to take out a mortgage to finance the cottage and pay it off over 10 years from Grant's bonus cheques.

Please provide your recommendations. Assume a total corporate tax rate on income not eligible for the small business deduction of 27% (i.e., 15% federal and 12% provincial). Assume that Grant is in the 50% marginal tax bracket.

Problem 20

Mr. Soul Proprietor has come to you asking your advice on incorporating his second-hand book business, which he began in 2005. Soul has three bookstores under the name Slightly-Dirty Books and is considering further expansion in the future. Soul provides you with the following financial statements.

SLIGHTLY-DIRTY BOOKS

BALANCE SHEET

as at December 31, 2018

Assets

Cash		$ 2,000
Accounts receivable (net of $100 reserve)		500
Inventory — at cost		40,000
Land — at cost		80,000
Buildings (Note (1))	$360,000	
Less: accumulated depreciation	191,000	169,000
Office equipment (Note (1))	$ 20,000	
Less: accumulated depreciation	12,000	8,000
Goodwill (Note (2))		7,500
		$307,000

Liabilities and Capital

Liabilities

Current		
Accounts payable	$ 7,500	
Bank loan	5,000	
Accrued liabilities	1,200	
Current portion of long-term debt	8,000	$ 21,700
Long-term		
Mortgages on building at 10½%	$150,000	
Less: current portion	8,000	142,000
		$163,700
Capital — S. Proprietor		143,300
		$307,000

INCOME STATEMENT

for the year ended December 31, 2018

Sales:		
— used books	$230,000	
— magazines	40,000	
— tobacco and sundries	80,000	$350,000
Cost of sales:		
— opening inventory	$ 23,000	
— purchases — net	260,000	
	$283,000	
— closing inventory	40,000	243,000
		$107,000

Selling costs:

— Wages (Note (3))	$ 35,000	
— Property taxes	5,000	
— Utilities and heat	3,000	
— Insurance	1,000	
— Others	3,000	47,000
Net income		60,000

Notes to Financial Statements:

(1) The buildings and equipment were in Classes 3 and 8, respectively. The book value is equal to undepreciated capital cost and depreciation expense has equalled capital cost allowance in each year.

(2) The goodwill was purchased when Soul bought out another bookstore this year. The balance sheet amount reflects the UCC.

(3) The wages expense includes $10,000 paid to Mrs. Proprietor and $5,000 paid to his two children, ages 19 and 16, who work on a part-time basis at the store.

Additional Information:

(1) Soul has withdrawn approximately $35,000 each year from the business. He has personal federal tax credits of $2,100 and provincial tax credits of $1,200.

(2) Soul has contributed the maximum amount to an RRSP annually. Assume that Soul's earned income for 2017 was $35,000. The RRSP is registered in his wife's name.

(3) Soul has a net capital loss of $25,000 that arose in December 2017.

(4) Soul is considering further expansion of his business and expects additional net income of $12,000 for each store that he adds.

(5) The fair market values of the assets shown on the balance sheet are as follows:

Accounts receivable	$ 500
Inventory	40,000
Land	140,000
Buildings	360,000
Equipment	3,000
Goodwill	20,000

— REQUIRED

Prepare a memo outlining the tax implications of the impending incorporation in a province with a 5.5% corporate tax rate, including:

— taxation of income in a proprietorship vs. a corporation;

— transfer of business assets and liabilities to a corporation;

— other considerations.

Ignore CPP and personal surtax effects. Assume the personal tax rates are as set out in Chapter 10 of the textbook.

Problem 21

Ever EZ Ltd. is a CCPC which carries on business in Canada. All of the issued shares are owned by Mr. EZ. The income statement for the year ended December 31, 2018 is as follows:

Ever EZ Ltd.
Income Statement
For the Year Ended December 31, 2018

Sales	$3,000,000
Cost of sales	800,000
Gross profit	2,200,000
Selling and administrative expenses	1,200,000
Operating income	1,000,000
Other income and expenses	56,000
Income before income taxes	$ 944,000

During the audit of Ever EZ Ltd., which takes place in April 2019, the following information is obtained:

1. Selling and administrative expenses include the following:

Salesperson bonuses based on 2018 sales, not paid as at the time of the audit		$ 200,000
Management bonuses, not paid as at the time of the audit:		
Mr. EZ	$ 300,000	
Mr. Jack, the controller, not related to Mr. EZ	100,000	400,000
Club membership fees and dues:		
Golf club annual dues for Mr. EZ	$ 2,000	
Golf club annual dues for the sales manager	1,500	
Community service club membership for the sales manager	200	
Fitness club membership for the controller	800	4,500
Travel expenses for which the salesmen were reimbursed:		
Meals	$ 8,000	
Accommodation	6,000	
Air fare	13,000	27,000
Entertainment expenses for which the salesmen were reimbursed:		
Cocktails	$ 2,000	
Lunches and dinners	800	
Tickets to baseball games	2,400	5,200
Automobile allowances for the salesmen		15,960
Advertising:		
Advertising space in the June 2018 issue of a foreign magazine aimed at the Canadian market	$ 8,000	
Advertising space in the November 2018 and February 2019 issues of a Canadian magazine	13,000	21,000
Donations to registered charities		66,000
Amortization		180,000

Accounting fees:

For the audit of the financial statements	$ 12,000	
For a five-year projection required by the bank to approve long-term financing for the new warehouse	4,000	16,000
Premium on term insurance on the life of Mr. EZ with the company as the beneficiary. The life insurance policy was required as collateral for the mortgage on the warehouse		2,600

Interest expense:

January to April 30 on loans to cover materials and labour for the new warehouse during the period of construction	$ 28,000	
May 1 to December 31, mortgage interest on the new warehouse	42,000	
July 1 to December 31 for the purchase of a new automobile	2,000	$ 72,000

2. EZ Ltd. employs four salesmen. Each salesman drove 7,000 kilometres for employment purposes in 2018. As the allowance was based on a per km rate of $0.57 and was considered reasonable, it was not reported as a taxable benefit.

3. EZ Ltd. always claims the maximum CCA possible under the *Income Tax Act*. The controller calculated the CCA for 2018 to be $200,000. In calculating the $200,000, the controller forgot to calculate CCA on the following items:

   (a) Ever EZ Ltd. spent $30,000 in 2017 on improvements to the office building, which it leases. The lease is a three-year lease commencing March 1, 2017 with two three-year renewal options.

   (b) Ever EZ Ltd. purchased land for $80,000 and built a new warehouse costing $700,000 on it in 2018. It was completed April 30, 2018. The land and building have been included on the balance sheet at cost. The cost of the building was calculated as follows:

Materials	$316,000
Labour	320,000
Utilities service connection	14,000
Landscaping	50,000
	$700,000

4. Included in the caption "other income and expenses" was a gain of $100,000 on the sale of shares of a long-term investment. Ever EZ Ltd. had paid $20,000 for the shares when purchased in 2008. It sold them for $120,000 in 2018. Ever EZ Ltd. received a down payment of $30,000 on the sale. The remainder of the proceeds are due in $18,000 instalments on January 31, each year, commencing January 31, 2019.

5. Also included in the caption "other income and expenses" were the following dividends:

Dividends received from taxable Canadian corporations (less than 5% of the issued shares owned by Ever EZ Ltd.)	$ 12,000
Dividends received from taxable Canadian corporations (25% of issued shares owned by Ever EZ Ltd.)	43,000
Dividends received from foreign corporations (less than 5% of the issued shares owned by Ever EZ Ltd.)	5,000
	$ 60,000

6. Ever EZ Ltd. wound-up its wholly-owned subsidiary, "Sub Ltd." on March 31, 2017. At that time, Sub Ltd. had the following unused losses:

	Non-capital	Net Capital
Fiscal year ended December 31, 2016	$200,000	—
Fiscal year ended December 31, 2006		$ 27,500

7. In 2017, Ever EZ Ltd. incurred Scientific Research and Experimental Development (SR&ED) expenditures of a current nature of $500,000. Only $200,000 of this expenditure was deducted for tax purposes in 2017. Investment tax credits of $175,000 related to the $500,000 expenditures were claimed on the 2017 tax return. No further SR&ED expenditures were made in 2018.

— *REQUIRED*

(A) Reconcile the income, as stated in the income statement, to net income for income tax purposes on the assumption the corporation wishes to minimize both net income and taxable income. Show all your calculations.

(B) Reconcile net income, as calculated in Part A, to taxable income.

Problem 22

Fred Famished has just telephoned you to ask you about an opportunity he has to acquire another business. Fred is the president of Tasty Foods Inc. (Tasty), an extremely successful company which owns a chain of fast food restaurants across Canada.

Fred has been concerned with the rising cost of food supplies for his restaurants. In your conversation, he told you that he was considering purchasing all of the shares of Yummy Supplies Ltd. (Yummy), a restaurant supply business, which supplies many of Tasty's restaurants.

Yummy has recently incurred losses from its operations. Fred feels that this was due to poor management of the business; with the right people in charge of the company, Fred feels that it could be restored to profitability.

Fred has just faxed you the following information about Yummy:

Taxation Year Ended	Net Capital Losses	Non-Capital Losses
December 31, 2017	$20,000	$250,000
December 31, 2016	$55,000	$450,000

Fred proposes that Tasty buy the shares of Yummy on July 16, 2018. It is estimated that Yummy has incurred additional business losses of $120,000 in the period January 1, 2018 to July 15, 2018.

The following information about Yummy's fixed assets as at July 15, 2018 was also included in the fax:

Assets	Cost	UCC/CEC	FMV
Land.	$200,000	N/A	$500,000
Class 3	$400,000	$350,000	$450,000
Class 8	$ 80,000	$ 50,000	$ 60,000
Class 10	$ 90,000	$ 80,000	$ 20,000
Inventory	$200,000	N/A	$100,000
Marketable Securities	$ 12,000	N/A	$ 8,000

Fred is very excited about the acquisition of Yummy. In particular, he feels the losses of the company will be helpful in the future to save income taxes.

— *REQUIRED*

(A) Fred has asked you about the income tax implications to Yummy with respect to Tasty's acquisition of the shares of Yummy. Discuss these implications, supporting your answer with calculations where necessary.

(B) Fred is interested in using the losses of Yummy to reduce taxes on the profits of Tasty. Advise him if this is possible and, if so, how he could use these losses.

Problem 23

Belleville Furniture Inc. ("Belleville") is a manufacturer of high-quality dining room furniture. This is the second generation of the Parker family that has owned the company, and the founder's son, Dave Parker, is having some problems since foreign imports are being brought into Ontario and sold at a price lower than Belleville's cost. Dave is certainly concerned about the short term, but feels that within the next eight to twelve months Belleville can adjust its sourcing of raw materials and the manufacturing process in order to reduce its costs to the point where its can be competitive, not only in the local market, but also in the Northeastern United States.

Dave's immediate problem is that when he asked the bank to increase Belleville's operating line of credit enough to cover Belleville's operational problems for the next eight to twelve months, the bank became concerned since its sole security for the operating loan is the inventory and the under 90-day accounts receivables. To maintain the existing line of credit, and to even consider the increase, the bank wants personal guarantees from both of Dave and his wife, Nancy, as well as a collateral mortgage on the company's building. As a result, Dave has you working on cash flow projections to support the loan, his lawyer is preparing the collateral mortgage, and an appraiser is preparing a valuation of the property. Dave feels that his chances of being approved are good.

Dave has agreed that he will sell the 20% interest that he personally owns in a company that operates a lumber mill that supplies Belleville. Dave bought the shares from the company on incorporation five years ago for $50,000 to help the arm's length supplier start the lumber mill. The other 75% of the company is owned by the supplier who has agreed to have his holding company buy the shares from Dave for $40,000 in cash. Dave had borrowed all the money for this investment through an interest-only demand loan with the bank. The bank has agreed to leave the full amount of the loan outstanding as long as Dave contributes the full $40,000 of proceeds into Belleville.

To prepare for its entry into the U.S. market, Belleville will set up a U.S. dollar bank account at its local bank for deposits from U.S. customers.

Dave would like your advice on the tax implications of his situation.

CHAPTER 20 — SOLUTIONS TO COMPREHENSIVE CASE PROBLEMS

Problem 1

Net income per income statement			$ 374,858
Add			
Provision for income tax — current			
— current		$ 166,700	
— deferred		$ 8,000	
Amortization		$ 230,000	
Loss on sale of portfolio investments		$ 52,400	
Reserve — decline in market price on inventory		$ 57,000	
Cost associated with valuation of land sold		$ 2,800	
Donations		$ 64,000	
Advertising in a foreign magazine		$ 13,375	
Membership in private clubs		$ 3,200	
Cost of reorganization		$ 16,000	
Non-deductible portion of meals and entertainment ($12,000 × 50%)		$ 6,000	
Interest on deficient tax instalments (Note 7)		$ 1,200	
Taxable capital gain on land (202,800 – 65,000 – 2,800) × ½		$ 67,500	
Recapture CCA Class 8		$ 20,000	
Amortization of bond premium		$ 375	
Taxable capital gain on building		$ 5,000	$ 713,550
			$1,088,408
Deduct			
Profit on sale of fixed assets		$ 100,000	
Equity in income of associated company		$ 92,096	
Gain on sale of land		$ 189,800	
Ssec. 83(2) dividend		$ 5,000	
Capital cost allowance (Note 8)		$ 164,850	
Terminal loss on Class 39		$ 2,500	
Allowable capital loss — portfolio investments [($7,600 – $60,000) × ½]		$ 26,200	$ 580,446
Division B Income			$ 507,962

Items not included:

(1) Connection of gas line — deductible under par. 20(1)(*ee*).

(2) Premium for life term insurance policy on president — deductible because it is used as collateral.

(3) Bond interest paid/accrued for 2018 is deductible per par. 20(1)(*c*). Interest on municipal property taxes — deductible if used as alternative financing.

(4) Dividends are included in Division B income.

(5) Employee training seminar expenses — deductible as a cost of doing business.

(6) Cost of Christmas party to which all employees were invited — deductible as a cost of doing business and not limited under sec. 67.1.

(7) Since this interest is on provincial tax instalments (not addressed under par. 18(1)(t)), an argument could be made supporting its deductibility as alternative financing.

	Cl. 3: 5%	Cl. 8: 20%	Cl. 10: 30%	Cl 14.1 — 5%	Cl. 39: 25%	Cl. 43: 30%	Total
UCC, Jan.1, 2017	$225,000	$ 55,000	$354,000	$ 0	$10,000	$190,000	
Additions				$16,000			
Dispositions							
Truck...............			$(25,000)				
Equip. Cl. 8		$ (75,000)					
Building	$(50,000)						
Equip. Cl. 39					$(7,500)		
Less ½ net addition				$(8,000)			
UCC, Dec. 31, 2018	$175,000	$ (20,000)	$329,000	$ 8,000	$ 2,500	$190,000	
CCA	$ (8,750)		$(98,700)	$ (400)		$(57,000)	$164,850
Recapture..............		$ 20,000					
Terminal loss					$(2,500)		
Add back ½ of net additions				$ 8,000			
UCC, Jan. 1, 2019	$166,250	Nil	$230,300	$15,600	Nil	$133,000	

Problem 2

(i)   Employment income ....

        Salary.. $ 350,000

        Toronto social club membership (assumed for benefit of company) ...... Nil

        Imputed interest [$500,000 × 5% × $^{61}/_{365}$[1]] .... $ 4,178

        Standby charge ⅔ × ($15,000 – $1,000) .... $ 9,333

        Operating costs ($0.26 × 80% of 20,000 km)[2] .... $ 4,160

        Registered pension plan and medical plans .... Nil

                                  $ 367,671

(ii)   Property income: ....

        Rental — property 1 .... $ 3,000

             — property 2 (loss prior to claiming CCA) .... $ (8,000)

        Recapture....................................... $ 10,000

                             $ 5,000

        CCA limited to rental income (max: $8,000 on property 2) .... $ (5,000)

                             Nil

        Dividends from taxable public Canadian corporations ($8,000 × 1.38) .... $ 11,040

        Dividends - U.S. corporations (gross) .... $ 4,000

        Stock dividend - X Ltd. Shares ($1,920 × 1.38) .... $ 2,650

        Attributed interest — wife....................................... $ 20,000

             — son (16)[3].. $ 3,000

        Attributed dividend - wife ($1,500 × 1.38) (property sold for less than FMV) .... $ 2,070

                             $ 42,760

(iii) Net taxable capital gains:

Rental property ($200,000 – ($70,000 + $10,000)) × ½................	$ 60,000
Antique table - ($1,000 – $1,200)	Nil
Antique clock - ($1,000 – $1,000)	Nil
Jewellery - ($1,600 – $1,000 = $600) × ½.......................	$ 300
Sailboat - 2,625* × ½..	$ 1,313
Shares - X Ltd. ($10,000 – $2,155** – $300) × ½.................	$ 3,773
Shares - Y Ltd. — wife ($5 – $5)***	Nil
— wife ($15 – $5)**** × ½.....................	$ 2,500
Net taxable capital gain	$ 67,886

* Sailboat

P of D	$ 32,000
ACB...	$ 25,000
Gain..	$ 7,000

Reserve - lesser of

$(1)^{4/5} × \$7,000 = \$5,600$

$(2)^{20/32} × \$7,000 = \$4,375$ .... $ (4,375)

Capital Gain	$ 2,625

** ACB of X Ltd. Shares

2010 200 shares (purchased)	$ 8,000
2011 20 shares (st. div)	$ 200[4]
2013 500 shares (purchase)	$ 11,400
2015 1200 shares	$ 24,000
2018 <u>192</u> shares (st. div)	1,920[4]
	$ 45,520

ACB of shares: $45,520 ÷ 2,112 shares × 100 shares = $2,155

***Mr. Rich did not elect out of the rollover in ssec. 73(1).

****Section 69 applies to deem proceeds to be equal to the fair market value of the property.

(1) No interest paid in 2018.

(2) As business use of the vehicle is less than 50%, Mr. Rich may not elect to include 50% of the standby charge (assuming it were more beneficial to do so) in lieu of the operating cost benefit determined by the $0.26 per km alternative.

(3) Note that if Mr. Rich had *loaned* the funds to his adult children (instead of *giving* them the funds), interest income would be attributed to Mr. Rich under ssec. 56(4.1).

(4) A stock dividend received has an ACB equal to the increase in paid-up capital on the issue.

Problem 3

Net income after taxes, per income statement				$238,000
Add:				
Par. 18(1)(a)	Provision for income taxes		$ 91,000	
Sec. 10	Excess of FIFO over LIFO (Dec. 31, 2018)		$ 63,000	
Par. 18(1)(b)	Amortization of bond discount		$ 700	
Par. 18(1)(l)	Membership in private clubs		$ 2,800	
Ssec. 18(9)	Prepaid advertising		$ 17,500	
Par. 18(1)(a)	Charitable donations		$ 11,200	
Sec. 3	Book loss — securities (10.5K - 7K)		$ 3,500	
Sec. 3	— equip. (15K - 11.2K)		$ 3,800	
Sec. 3	— trucks (4.2K - 1.3K)		$ 2,900	
Sec. 38	Taxable capital gain — patent [½ × ($70,000 – $45,000)]		$ 12,500	
Sec. 38	Taxable capital gain — Government license (Sched. 2)		$ 13,500	
Ssec. 13(1)	Recapture — patent (45K – 35.9K)		$ 9,100	
Ssec. 9(3)	Loss on wholly owned subsidiary		$ 52,500	
Par. 18(1)(b)	Cost of reorganization		$ 12,600	
Par. 18(1)(b)	Depreciation		$ 55,000	
Ssec. 147.2(1)	Disallowed RPP deduction (Sched. 1)		$ 1,800	
Par. 20(1)(e)	80% of issue costs of $4,900		$ 3,920	$357,320
				$595,320
Deduct:				
Par. 18(1)(e)	Reserve — decline in market prices on inventory		$ 35,000	
Sec. 10	Excess of FIFO over LIFO (Dec. 31, 2017)		$ 45,500	
Sec. 38	ACL — securities (7K - 10.5K) × ½		$ 1,750	
Sec. 3	Book gain — patent (70K – 3.5K)		$ 66,500	
	— govt. lic. (35K – .7K)		$ 34,300	
	Ssec. 83(2) dividend		$ 10,000	
Par. 20(1)(a)	CCA (Sched. 2)		$ 57,268	
Ssec. 20(16)	Terminal loss — trucks (Sched. 2)		$ 200	$250,518
Division B income				$344,802

Schedule 1

	A	B	C	Total
RPP deductible contribution — least of:				
Total of employee and employer Contributions	$16,700	$12,800	$ 10,600	
18% of employment compensation	$23,400	$12,600	$ 9,000	
Dollar limit	$26,230	$26,230	$ 26,230	
Non-deductible employer contributions	Nil	$200	$ 1,600	$ 1,800

Schedule 2

	Cl. 1: 4%	Cl. 3: 5%	Cl. 8: 20%	Cl. 10: 30%	Cl. 12: 100%
Jan. 1/18 UCC	Nil	$49,000	$ 8,400	$ 1,500	Nil
Purchases	$315,000	-	-	-	$16,000
Disposals	-	-	-	$(1,300)	-
Dec. 31, 2018 UCC	$315,000	$49,000	$ 8,400	$ 200	$16,000
½ net amount	(157,500)	-	-	-	N/A
UCC	$157,500	$49,000	$ 8,400	$ 200	$16,000
CCA for 2018 = $57,268	(6,300)	(2,450)	(1,680)	-	(16,000)
Terminal loss	-	-	-	(200)	-
Recapture	-	-	-	-	-
½ net amount	$157,500	-	-	-	-
Jan. 1, 2019 UCC	$308,700	$46,550	$ 6,720	Nil	Nil

	Cl. 13: S.L.	Cl. 14: S.L.	Cl. 14.1: 5%	Cl. 43: 30%	Cl. 53: 50%
Jan. 1/18 UCC	Nil	$35,900	$29,650	$35,000	Nil
Purchases	$ 7,000	-	12,600	-	$87,000
Disposals	-	(45,000)	(8,000)*	(11,200)	-
Dec. 31, 2018 UCC	$ 7,000	(9,100)	$34,250	$23,800	$87,000
½ net amount	N/A	Nil	(2,300)	Nil	(43,500)
UCC	$ 7,000	$(9,100)	$31,950	$23,800	$43,500
CCA for 2018 = $57,268	-	(350)[1]	-	(1,598)	(7,140)	(21,750)
Terminal loss	-	-	-	-	-
Recapture	-	$ 9,100	-	-	-
½ net amount	-	-	$ 2,300	Nil	$43,500
Jan. 1, 2019 UCC	$ 6,650	Nil	$32,652	$16,660	$65,250

Note: The building must be new to receive the 10% CCA rate for manufacturing buildings and the building purchased in 2018 is previously used.

* The government licence was sold in the current year for $35,000. The original cost was $8,000; therefore, we would remove the proceeds from the pool. The sale of government licence would also create a capital gain of $13,500 [50% × (35,000 – 8,000)].

Other Items

— damages paid as part of a normal risk of doing business

— only 20% of costs of issuing bonds deductible [par. 20(1)(*e*)]; remainder deductible over next four years

— bond interest paid is deductible [par. 20(1)(*c*)]

— accrued bond interest is deductible [par. 20(1)(*c*)]

— ads in South American magazine not prohibited because not directed to a Canadian market [ssec. 19(1)]

— cash dividend included in Division B income [par. 12(1)(*j*)]

— charitable donations deductible under Division C not Division B.

— NOTES TO SOLUTION

(1) Lesser of: (a) $\frac{1}{5} \times \$7,000$ .... $\$ 1,400$

                        $\$700 \times \frac{1}{2} = \$350$

            (b) $\$7,000/(5 + 5) = \$700$ .... $\$ 1,250$

Problem 4

Part (A)

Par. 3(*a*)	Income — employment		$100,000
	— business		8,900
	— property[1]		3,423
	— other ($490 + $7,040)		7,530
Par. 3(b)	Y Ltd.	$ 500	
	LPP ($3,000 × 2 for full capital gain) $6,000		
	Less: carry forward (full capital loss) 2,000		
	$4,000 × ½	2,000	
	PUP	1,000	
		$ 3,500	
	X Ltd.	(6,000)	Nil
			$ 119,853
Par. 3(c)	Capital portion of annuity	$ 200	
	Old Age Security benefits subject to clawback[2]	4,461	
			$ (4,611)
			$ 115,192
Par. 3(d)	ABIL — ABC Ltd. (no disallowed portion of BIL)	$ 3,000	
	Rental loss	11,000	(14,000)
	Income under Division B		$ 101,192
Division C deductions:			
	Par. 111(1)(b) Net capital loss of $6,000 (limited to par. 3(b) net TCG)		Nil
	Taxable income		$ 101,192

Part (B)

Federal tax on first	$ 93,209	....	$ 16,545
on next	7,983 @ 26%	....	2,076
	$101,192	....	$ 18,621

Less: Federal tax credits:

Basic personal	(1,771)
Equivalent-to-married — David[3]	(1,771)
Caregiver amount — Ms. Credit's mother[4]	(1,048)
Dependants — David (infirm but not over 18)	(327)
— Donna (infirm — Canada caregiver tax credit eligible) . . .	(1,048)
Age	Nil[5]
Canada employment credit	(179)
Employment Insurance premiums (15% of $858)	(129)
CPP contributions (15% of $2,594)	(389)
Pension [15% of $490 – $200]	(44)
Disability transfer — David [$1,235 basic + $721 supplement for <18 yrs old]	(1,956)
— Ms. Credit's mother [IT-519R, par. 7]	(1,235)
— Donna	(1,235)

Transfer of tuition fees and education credits:[6]

Lesser of:		
(a) $750		
(b) student's credit — $450	450	
Less: Part I tax after personal tax credit	Nil	(450)

Transfer from spouse[7]	(300)

Medical expenses on behalf of Mr. Debit:

Premium — private plan	380 (B)	
Less the lesser of:		
(a) $2,302	(2,302) (C)	
(b) 3% of Division B income		
(3% of $101,192) = $3,036	Nil	
15% of $nil: 15% × (B — C)	Nil	

Medical expenses incurred on behalf of Donald	$1,500		
Less 3% of Donald's net income (3% × $5,900)	(177)		
Excess, if any	$1,323		
15% × $1,323		198	
Medical expenses incurred on behalf of Donna	$8,000		
Less 3% of Donna's net income	(Nil)		
Excess, if any	$8,000		
15% × $8,000	$1,200		(1,398)

Charitable gifts

15% of $200	$ 30	
29% of ($1,000 – $200)	232	(262)

Dividend tax credit (6/11 of $213 i.e. gross up))		(116)
Basic federal tax		$ 4,963

Less: federal foreign tax credits

Lesser of:

(a) $225

(b) $\dfrac{\$1,500}{\$101,192}$ × ($5,079) = $75 See note   (75)

federal political contributions tax credit[8]	(350)
Net federal tax	4,538
Repayment of Old Age Security benefits[2]	4,461
Total federal tax	$8,999

The unused foreign taxes paid of $225 – $75 = $150 can be claimed on a provincial tax return subject to a similar formula to the federal formula above and any balance still not claimed can potentially be claimed under ss. 20(11) as a deduction in computing income.

—NOTES TO SOLUTION

(1) Subsection 82(3) is not considered because Mr. Debit gets a higher overall credit by using the equivalent-to-married credit this year. Therefore, the property income of Mr. Debit is as follows:

Canadian interest income		$ 1,350
Taxable dividends		
Canadian ($560 × 1.38)	$ 773	
U.S	1,500	2,273
		$ 3,623
Less interest expense		(200)
		$ 3,423

(2) Lesser of:

(a) Old Age Security benefits			$ 7,040
(b) Income under Division B (excluding par. 60(w) deduction)			
($101,192 + $4,461)		$105,653	
Less:		75,910	
Excess, if any		$ 29,743	
15% of excess			$ 4,461

(3) Note that David is eligible for the equivalent to spouse credit; however, Debra is too old as she was 18 at the start of the year

(4) David qualifies for the $2,182 Canada Caregiver credit while Donna and Mrs. Debit's mother qualify for the $6,986 credit.

(5) Age tax credit base .... $ 7,333

Less: base reduction of lesser of:

(a) $7,333			
(b) Division B income	$101,192		
Less: threshold	(36,976)		
Excess, if any	$ 64,216 × 0.15	$ 9,632	
Lesser amount			(7,333)
Net base			Nil

(6) Donald

Employment income — Montreal		$ 150	
— Toronto		6,000	$6,150
Canadian bank interest		200	
Scholarship (non-taxable)		Nil	200
			$6,350
Moving expense ($300 + $150*)			(450)
Division B income and taxable income			$5,900
Federal tax @15% of $5,900			885
Less: basic personal tax credit			1,771
Net federal tax			Nil

Credits available for transfer to Mr. Debit:

Tuition fees (15% of $3,000)	450
Total	$ 450

---

* Limited to the income earned in Montreal, plus any taxable scholarship income [scholarship is not taxable in this case].

(7) Transfer of pension credit to Mr. Debit:

Ms Credit's income ($5,200 + $1,150)	$6,350
Dividend gross-up (38% × $300)	114
Division B income and taxable income	$6,464
Federal tax @15% of $6,464	970
Less: basic personal tax credit	(1,771)
Federal tax after tax credits	Nil

Less: pension tax credit utilized	Nil
Net federal tax	Nil
Pension credit available (15% of $2,000: max.)	300
Less: Part I tax after personal tax credit	Nil
Pension credit available for transfer	300

(8) $300 + 50% of ($500 − $400)

Problem 5

A.

Ms. Janrayad
Employment Income

Reference

Sec. 5(1)	Salary	$100,000	
Sec. 6(1)(k)	Operating benefit — car (election)	963	Note 1
Sec. 6(1)(e)	Standby charge	1,925	Note 2
Sec. 6(1)(b)(v)	Travel allowance	5,400	Note 3
Sec. 6(1)(b)	Moving allowance......................................	17,000	
Sec. 6(9)	Interest on debt	1,765	Note 4
Sec. 7(1)	Stock option exercised	21,600	Note 5
		148,653	
	Less:		
Sec. 8(1)(h)	Travel expenses	7,750	Note 3
	Employment income — Subdivision a	$140,903	Note 6

Calculations and other explanations:

(1) The operating costs using the elective method under subsection par. 6(1)(k) would result in a lower income inclusion.

($1,950 ($0.26 × 7,500 km) vs. $963 (50% × $1,925)).

(2) The standby charge will be computed as:

$$\frac{7,500 \text{ km}}{20,004 \text{ km}} \times (2/3 \times \$7,700) = \$1,925$$

Ms. Janrayad is entitled to the standby charge reduction, since she uses the car for business greater than 50% of the total kilometres.

(3) Allowances are dealt with in par. 6(1)(b), which includes all allowances in income with specified exceptions. Subparagraph 6(1)(b)(v) applies to persons who negotiate contracts such as Ms. Janrayad. The allowance must be reasonable in order for it not to be taxable.

Ms. Janrayad received the following allowances for travel expenses during 2018:

70% × 25,000 kms × 20¢ =	$3,500	
$450 × 12	5,400	
	$8,900	

The 20¢ per kilometre is based solely on kilometres driven (spar. 6(1)(b)(x)) and it is reasonable (spar. 6(1)(b)(v)) compared with actual expenses (70% of ($2,000 + $3,000) = $3,500).

Her other actual travel expenses were $9,500 (i.e., $3,500 for meals, $6,000 for accommodation).

Since her other actual travel expenses, which were reasonable, exceeded her $450 monthly allowance, this allowance was not a reasonable amount. Therefore, the allowance is included in income and she can claim her actual expenses under 8(1)(h). However, the maximum amount deductible in respect of meals is the 50% fractional amount. Therefore, she can deduct the following:

Meals (50% × $3,500)	$1,750
Accommodation	6,000
	$7,750

No amount is deductible under paragraph 8(1)(*h*.1) in respect of motor vehicle expenses (i.e., insurance and gas and oil), because she was in receipt of an excluded allowance of 20¢ per kilometre.

(4) The subsection 6(9) benefit as calculated under section 80.4 would be the sum of:

(a) share loan — prescribed rate

4th quarter 5% × $35,000 × 92/365 = ... $ 441

(b) home relocation loan

Lesser of the prescribed rate at the time of the loan (i.e., 4%) and the prescribed quarterly rate while the loan is outstanding in the year compared on a quarter-by-quarter basis

The resulting calculation is:

4% × $150,000 × 365/365 = ...		6,000
		$6,441
Less amounts paid:		
(a) 2% × $35,000 × 92/365	$ 176	
(b) 3% × $150,000	4,500	4,676
		$1,765

(5) There is no tax effect when Ms. Janrayad is granted the right to purchase shares through the stock option plan.

When Ms. Janrayad exercises the stock option in respect of 3,600 shares in 2018, she must take into employment income the difference between the fair market value and the option price.

3,600 shares × ($17 — $11) = $21,600

(6) An HST rebate would be available based on 2018 deductible expenses, calculated as:

13/113 of $7,750 (meals and accommodation) $892

Paragraph 6(8)(*a*) would require the inclusion of the $892 rebate in 2019 employment income.

B. Items excluded from computation of employment income in A:

(1) Income tax is not deductible.

(2) CPP contributions and EI premiums are eligible for non-refundable tax credits.

(3) Massive Ltd.'s contribution to the dental plan is not a taxable benefit under par. 6(1)(*a*).

(4) Registered pension plan contributions are exempted under par. 6(1)(*a*).

(5) Membership fees paid by the employer for social clubs will not be included in the income of the employee if the advantage is primarily the employer's not the employee's (Income Tax Folio S2-F3-C2: Employees Fringe Benefits).

(6) Moving expenses are not deductible in computing employment income, but are deductible against all sources of income under subdivision e.

C. Other tax consequences:

(1) Allowable moving expense deduction

Par. 62(3)(*a*) Travelling cost — air fare	$ 1,750	
Par. 62(3)(*b*) Household effects — transporting	1,400	
Par. 62(3)(*c*) Meals and lodging near the new residence		
— meals (100% deductible per s. 67.1(1))*	80	
— lodging	175	
Par. 62(3)(*e*) Selling costs of Halifax residence		
— legal fees	800	
— real estate commission	15,500	

Par. 62(3)(f) Allowable purchase cost of London residence

— legal fees 1,100
— land transfer tax 450
                                                                                $ 21,255

Prepaid realty taxes not deductible under ssec. 62(3).

---

* If no receipts are provided, the CRA permits a deduction of $17 per meal to a maximum of $51 per person per day for 2017. The 2018 rates will be available on the CRA website in 2019.

(2) There will be a deduction under paragraph 110(1)(d) in 2018, since the option price ($11) is equal to the fair market value at the date the option was granted and on the assumption that Ms. Janrayad will be dealing with the corporation at arm's length after the transaction. The par. 110(1)(d) deduction is equal to ½ of the ssec. 7(1) inclusion or $10,800.

(3) Ms. Janrayad can deduct imputed interest of $265 (i.e., $441 − 176) as an expense by virtue of sec. 80.5 and par. 20(1)(c), plus the $176 interest paid on her loan to buy shares by virtue of par. 20(1)(c).

Problem 6

Part A

Income — Division B

Par. 3(a) Employment Income

Gross salary	$60,000	
RPP	(800)	
	59,200	
Property Income:		
Dividends	$9,000	
Interest	6,000	15,000
Pension	6,000	$80,200

Par. 3(b) Capital Gains

Y Ltd. ($11,250 × ½)	$5,625	
PUP ($4,500 × ½)	2,250	$ 7,875
Less: disallowed ABIL on X Ltd. shares		
(2 × $11,250) × ½	11,250	Nil
LPP	$ 6,000	
Less: LPP carryover (max.)	(6,000)	Nil
		80,200

Par. 3(c) Subdivision (e) deductions:

Legal fees	$ 1,000	
RRSP - lesser of:		
1) $26,230		
2) 18% × $45,000 (2017 earned income*) = $8,100		
Lesser is	$ 8,100	(7,500)
Less prior year pension adjustment	(1,600)	6,500
		72,700

Par. 3(d) Rental loss			$(10,000)
BIL on X Ltd.			
BIL		$ 28,000	
Less: Disallowed portion			
(S. 39(9)) – 2 × CG ded.		(22,500)	
		$ 5,500	
1/2 Allowable		(2,750)	(12,750)
Division B income			$ 59,950
Division C deductions			
Par. 111(1)(b) Net capital losses			Nil**
Taxable Income			$ 59,950

* Earned income for 2017: Par. 146(1)(c)		
Employment income before RPP deduction		$ 55,000
Rental loss		(10,000)
		$ 45,000

** Net capital losses (Ssec. 111(1.1))

lesser of		
(i) Net TCG in 2018		Nil
(ii) Adjusted net capital losses claimed ($12,000 × ½ ÷ ¾)		$ 8,000
lesser amount		Nil

Part B

(i)   Income taxes are not deductible in arriving at income or taxable income.

(ii)   Brokerage fees are added to adjusted cost base of the acquired share.

(iii)   The excess RRSP contribution of $1,000 in 2018 will not be subject to a penalty of 1% per month for each month it remains in the plan, since the amount contributed in excess of the amount deductible is not greater than $2,000. However, unless the excess is deducted under the available contribution room of a subsequent year or withdrawn within one year it will eventually be included in income and taxed again.

(iv)   Federal political donations are not deductible under division B or C but a tax credit would be given of $75.

(v)   LPP loss can be carried forward for a maximum of seven years.

(vi)   Net capital losses can be carried forward indefinitely.

(vii)   The disallowed portion of BIL under par. 39(9)(b) is twice the cumulative capital gains deduction. i.e., 2 × $11,250 for a capital gains deduction claimed prior to 1988.

(viii)   The net capital loss balance at December 31, 2018 is: 1999 — $12,000
2018 — $3,375

The 2018 net capital loss is the portion of disallowed ABIL not utilized against taxable capital gains in 2018 [$11,250 – $7,875]

(ix)   CPP and EI premiums and charitable donations provide tax credits under Division E.

Problem 7

Part A

3(a) Employment Income

Gross income	....	$90,000	
Less: RPP (pars. 8(1)(m) and 147.2(4)(a))	....	(3,600)	$ 86,400
Pension Income	....		18,000
Property Income:			
Attributed from — wife	....	600	
— Charles	....	300	900
			105,300

3(b) Net taxable Capital Gains

($18,000 + $600 − $1,000)	....		17,600

3(c) Subtotal $122,900

Less: Subdivision e deductions — split pension income . . . . (9,000)

Division B Income 113,900

Division C Deductions (sec. 111.1 ordering)

111(1)(b) Net capital loss carryover ($25,770 × ½ / ¾) . . . . (17,180)

Taxable Income . . . . $ 96,720

Split Pension Income Decision

The maximum split pension is $18,000 × ½ = $9,000.

Tax savings to Buck Shot ($9,000 × 26%)		$ 2,340
Loss of married credit:		
Before split 15% × [$11,809 − (600 × 1.38 + 300 + 250 + 3,600)]		(1,025)
After split 15% × [$11,809 − (600 × 1.38 + 300 + 250 + 3,600 + 9,000)]		0
Tax payable by Mrs. Buck Shot on split pension (see below)		(26)
Net savings from splitting pension income		$ 1,289

Tax paid by Mrs. Buck Shot:		
Division B Income ($600 × 1.38 + 300 + 250 + 3,600 + 9,000)		$13,978
Federal tax @ 15%	$ 2,097	
Less: basic amount	(1,771)	
Less: pension amount	(300)	
Net tax payable	$ 26	

Due to the decision to split pension, it doesn't make sense to include Mrs. Buck Shot's dividends in Mr. Buck Shot's income, because he won't gain any additional married credit but will pay tax at a rate of approximately 20% on the dividend.

Basic Federal tax:

Taxable income		$96,720
Federal tax on first $93,209	$16,545	
on next $3,511 @ 26%	913	$17,458

Less tax credits:

Basic personal	$1,771	
Married (see Note above)	Nil	
Canada caregiver (Charles)	327	
Canada employment credit	179	
EI (15% of $858)...................................	129	
CPP (15% of $2,594)	389	
Pension credit (15% of $2,000)	300	
Transfer of Charles' impairment credit [$1,235 + 721]	1,956	
Transfer of Agnes' tuition and education credit sec. 118.9		
Lesser of: (i) $750		
(ii) 15% of $6,000 = $900	750	
Medical tax credit (15% of ([$4,000 + 320] less lesser of [$2,302 and 3% of $113,900])	0	
Charitable donation tax credit (15% of $200 + 29% of ($500 + 150 − 200))	161	
		(5,962)
Basic and total federal tax		$11,496

Part B

(i) Income taxes withheld from employment income are not deductible.

(ii) The $300 of interest income from the GIC given to Robert is taxable to Robert because he is 18 or older in 2018.

(iii) Provincial political party donation not deductible (par. 18(1)(n)). A provincial tax credit may be available in computing provincial taxes payable, not taxable income.

(iv) The impairment credit for Charles includes both the basic amount of $1,236 and the additional amount of $721 available to individuals under the age of 18. [ssec. 118.3(2)]

Problem 8

Taxable Income Calculation

Inclusions:

Salary	$ 70,000
Performance bonus	15,000
Commissions	5,000
RRSP contributions made by employer, par. 6(1)(a)....................	3,000
Automobile standby charge, Note 1	5,424
Automobile operating benefit (0.26 × 60% × 30,000 km)...............	4,680
Payment by employer for tax return preparation, par. 6(1)(b)	400
Trip to St. Lucia, received by virtue of employment, par. 6(1)(a)	900
Director's fees, par. 6(1)(c)	500
Disability income, Note 4	11,587
Taxable dividends attributed to Marilyn ($6 × 200 shares × 1.38)	1,656
Interest income on mortgage receivable	3,000
Net rental income	1,400

Recapture on rental building	2,300	
Income tax refund interest.	200	
Taxable capital gains, Note 2	23,190	
Interest income attributed from children	400	$148,637

Deductions:

RRSP deduction, Note 3	14,000	
Repayment of shareholder loan, par. 20(1)(*j*)	10,000	(24,000)
Net capital loss utilized in the year ($1,500 × ½ / ¾)	1,000	(1,000)
Taxable income		$123,637

Items not included in the above calculation:

(a) Income taxes withheld are not deductible in computing income for tax purposes.

(b) CPP and EI premiums paid by an employee are not deductible in computing income for tax purposes, but are eligible for non-refundable tax credits.

(c) There is no taxable benefit for group disability insurance premiums paid by the employer [par. 6(1)(*a*)]. There is no deduction for group disability premiums paid by an employee.

(d) Donations to United Way are not deductible in computing income for tax purposes, but are eligible for non-refundable tax credits.

(e) Membership in the golf club appears to be primarily to the employers advantage and is, therefore, not a taxable benefit.

(f) There is no capital gain/loss to Marilyn on the transfer of the shares of Looney to Jorge because the transfer is deemed to occur at the ACB of the shares [ss. 73(1)]. Jorges ACB for the shares will be $1,000 (equal to Marilyn's ACB at the time of the transfer) [ss. 73(1)].

(g) Payments of interest and penalties for income taxes are not deductible for tax purposes.

(h) Interest income on child tax benefits invested for children is not attributable to Marilyn.

Note 1: Automobile Standby Charge Benefit

Automobile Standby Charge Benefit, par. 6(1)(*e*) and ssec. 6(2)

($20,000 + $2,600) × 2% per month × 12 months = $5,424

There is no reduction available in computing the standby charge because the automobile was driven less than 50% for employment purposes in 2018.

Note 2: Calculation of Taxable Capital Gains

1. Gains are attributed to Marilyn from Jorge on sale of shares of Looney Canadian Public Co.

Proceeds of disposition	$ 10,000
Adjusted cost base	(1,000)
Capital gain	$ 9,000

2. Sale of building

Proceeds of disposition	$ 250,000
Adjusted cost base	(160,000)
	90,000
Less: Cost of sales — legal fees	(1,000)
Capital gain	$ 89,000

2018 reserve per spar. 40(1)(a)(iii)
Lesser of:

(i) $\dfrac{\text{Mortgage receivable of \$145,000} \times \$89,000}{\text{Total proceeds of \$250,000}} =$ $ 51,620

and

(ii) $^4/_5 \times \$89,000 =$ $71,200

Gain on shares	$ 9,000
Gain on building	89,000
Less: reserve	(51,620)
Capital gains	46,380
Multiply by taxable portion	½
Taxable capital gains	$ 23,190

Note 3: RRSP Deduction Calculation

Contributions deducted from pay		$ 3,000
Contributions made by employer		3,000
Contribution to own plan		7,000
Contribution to spousal plan		2,000
Less: amounts used on 2017 return ($6,000/12 months × 2 months)		(1,000)
Total contributions available for 2018		$ 14,000
2017 earned income	$80,000	
	× 18%	
	$14,400	
or 2018 limit of	$26,010	$ 14,400
Plus: 2017 carry forward room		100
		$ 14,500
RRSP deduction for 2018		$ 14,000

Note 4: 2018 Disability Benefits

Marilyn must include the disability benefits in income per par. 6(1)(*f*)

3 months of disability benefit received		$ 12,000
Less:		
Disability insurance premiums paid since January 1, 2016		
($25/month × 1/2 × 33[1] months for 2016 – 2017)		413
Amounts to be included on 2018 return		$ 11,587

1 Marilyn did not pay premiums for October to December 2018 when she was off work.

Problem 9

Employment income:

S. 5	Salary and commission	$34,000	
S. 6(8)	HST Rebate	250	
S. 7(1.1)	Stock option benefit $25,000 – $10,000 = $15,000	15,000	
S. 8(1)(*i*)	Union dues	(210)	
S. 8(1)(*m*)	RPP	(1,300)	
Employment income			47,740

Property income:

S. 12(1)(*c*)	Interest	$ 925	
S. 12(1)(*j*)	Dividends from taxable Canadian corporations $8,000 × 1.38	11,040	
S. 12(1)(*k*)	Dividends from a U.S. corporation [no gross up]	2,000	
S. 20(1)(*c*)	Interest expense re marketable securities	(500)	13,465

S. 38	Taxable capital gain:		
	Simple Ltd. shares $70,000 – $25,000 =	$45,000	
	Table: $1,000 – $1,100 = (100) [PUP loss denied]	0	
	Painting: $1,500 – $1,000 = $ 500		
	Less 2008 LPP loss (200)	300	

X Ltd.

Proceeds	$ 2,500
ACB	(3,667)
	(1,167)
Superficial loss	1,167
	0

	Shares	ACB	ACB/sh
Feb. 2 purchase	500	$ 1,000	
Feb. 28 purchase	1,000	10,000	
	1,500	11,000	$ 7.33
Mar. 15 sale	(500)	(3,667)	
Superficial loss		1,167	
	1,000	8,500	$ 8.50

	45,300	
	× ½	22,650

Other income:

S. 56	Retiring allowance	35,000	
	Employment insurance	9,000	44,000

Other deductions:

S. 60(*i*) RRSP [S. 146(5)]

least of (a) undeducted premiums paid on
or before 60 days after 2018
$6,000 + $40,000 = $46,000

(b) lesser of (1) $26,230

(2) 18% of 2017 earned income
18% × $70,000 = $12,600

minus 2017 PA	(1,400)	
	11,200	
plus unused deduction room	800	(12,000)

S. 60(*j*.1)	Least of (i) retiring allowance received $35,000	
	(ii) contributions $46,000 – $12,000 = $34,000	
	(iii) $2,000 × 9 years (pre-1996) = $18,000	(18,000)
S. 60(*o*)	Legal Fees to Contest tax assessment	(600)
		97,255
S. 60(*v*.1)	Employment Insurance repaid	(2,700)

Net income under Division B		94,555
S. 110(1)(*d*)	Stock option deduction ½ × $15,000 =	(7,500)
S. 111	Net capital loss carry over	(4,000)
Taxable income		$83,055

Adjusted taxable income:

Taxable income		$ 84,388
Add:	30% (i.e., 80% – 50%) of capital gain 1.3 × $45,300	13,590
	Stock option deduction	7,500
		105,478
Less:	Dividend gross-up	(3,040)
	30% of net capital loss (0.3 × $2,667)	(800)
Adjusted taxable income		$101,638

Information omitted from calculations:

Stan is not entitled to a deduction for moving expenses as he was reimbursed by this employer for all moving expenses incurred.

CPP, EI, and income tax withheld are not deductible for tax purposes ssec. 8(2).

Lottery winnings are not taxable.

Donations are not deductible.

Foreign tax paid on dividend not deductible since it is better to claim an FTC.

TFSA administrative fee is not deductible.

Problem 10

Net income per financial statements		$160,800
Add:		
	Current income taxes .... $ 45,700	
	Deferred income taxes 3,500	
	Life insurance premiums 2,000	
	Loss on investment in Mark Goal Nets Inc. (MGNI) 6,000	
	Reserve for future warranty costs 1,500	
	Non-deductible interest on car loan [$4,200 − (365 × 300/30)] 550	
	Cost of financing 300	
	Curling club memberships 6,000	
	Non-deductible interest on income taxes 300	
	Non-deductible interest on vacant land (Note 1) 6,000	
	Non-deductible cost of meals and entertainment (50% of $3,440) 1,720	
	Depreciation 48,000	
	Donations 5,000	
		126,570
		$287,370

Less:		
	Capital dividend .... $ 12,000	
	Increase in cash surrender value of life insurance 1,520	
	Allowable business investment loss in MGNI (6,000 × ½) 3,000	
	Gain on disposition of car 1,000	
	Unrealized gain on foreign exchange 1,500	
	CCA (Note 1) 57,100	
	20(1)(e) [1/5 × 300 cost of financing × 365/365] 60	
	Actual warranty expenses 1,200	(77,380)
Net income for tax purposes		$209,990
Less:		
	Donations .... $ 5,000	
	Dividend from Peter Wood Products 7,000	
	Dividend from Lori Ice Machine Canadian Public Corp. 500	(12,500)
Taxable income for Part I tax		$197,490

Note 1 — Calculation of CCA

	Opening UCC	Additions	Lesser of Cost and Proceeds	CCA Rate	CCA for the Year
Class 3	$102,000	—	—	5%	$ 5,100
Class 8	50,000	—	—	20%	10,000
Class 10	30,000	—	—	30%	9,000
Class 10.1	10,000	—	— [2]	30%	1,500
Class 10.1	—	$ 30,000[1]	—	30%	4,500
Class 12	—	6,000	—	100%	3,000
Class 43	80,000	—	—	30%	24,000
					$57,100

(1) Maximum amount is $30,000

(2) ½ of CCA is allowed in year of disposition — no recapture. UCC at the end of the year would be nil.

Interest on vacant land added to cost of property — can only claim CCA once available for use / substantially complete

Problem 11

Reconciliation Errors

1. Income taxes payable of $71,000 and deferred taxes of $14,000 must be added to income for financial statement purposes, since they are not incurred to earn income.

2. A reserve for future warranties is not an allowable deduction unless the special conditions of par. 20(1)(*m*.1) are met, so the $85,000 addback in the reconciliation is correct. However, the actual expenditure of $50,000 should be deducted.

3. The $35,000 of RPP contributions may be deductible in 2018 or 2019 as long as they were made in accordance with the plan as registered (par. 147.2(1)(*a*)). In this case, the overall limit of employer and employee contributions is $26,230 for 2018 and the amount for 2019 is yet to be calculated based on appropriate indexing. Contributions to a registered pension plan can be made up to 120 days after the end of the year to which the contributions apply and still be deductible. [sec.147.2(1)]

4. The 2018 bonus is deductible in 2018, if it is paid on or before June 30, 2019. The 2017 bonus should have been added back to 2017 income when the return was filed. If it was not, then an amended return for 2017 should be filed as soon as possible to reduce interest charges. The 2017 bonus will be deductible when it is paid in 2019.

5. (a) The scholarships would be a deductible expense of the corporation, as part of employee remuneration under par. 18(1)(*a*).

   (b) The assistance to the spouse of an employee would be deductible from the income (Division B) of the corporation as an expense of doing business, in the form of a death benefit as defined in sec. 248.

6. (a) The real estate commission and the appraisal fee are expenses of disposition which would be deducted with adjusted cost base from proceeds of disposition in the calculation of a taxable capital gain. Therefore, these amounts must be added back in the reconciliation and the taxable capital gains figures must be adjusted. Both expenditures should be pro-rated to the land and the building.

   (b) The capital gain inclusion rate is ½.

   (c) Recapture on the building must be added in the reconciliation.

   (d) A capital gains reserve in respect of the land and building is deductible. It would be calculated as the lesser of:

   (i) $\dfrac{\$675,000}{\$565,000 + 340,000} \times$ capital gain on the land and building (as corrected)

   (ii) ⅘ × capital gain on the land and building (as corrected)

   A reserve deducted in 2018 must be brought into income as a capital gain in 2019 and a new reserve can be deducted in 2019 and the following four years.

   (e) Interest for six months at 11% of $675,000 would have to be accrued and added to the reconciliation (ssec.12(3)).

   (f) Since the lease began July 1, 2018 and a payment of the first year's rent was made, six month's rent or $15,000 is a prepaid expense at December 31, 2018 and should not be deducted, i.e., it should be added back in the reconciliation. Leasehold improvements are class 13 depreciable property eligible for capital cost allowance on a straight-line basis. The CCA in 2018 would be one-half of $35,000/(10 + 5) or $1,167.

7. The reserve for decline in value of inventory must be added back to closing inventory in the calculation of cost of goods sold resulting in an addition to income in 2018.

8. Capital cost allowance should be deducted in arriving at net income for the year.

9. The net capital loss deducted in 2018 cannot exceed the taxable capital gains for the year.

10. (a) The capital dividends received are not taxable and should be deducted in arriving at income for tax purposes. Furthermore, no deduction under Division C may be taken for these dividends.

    (b) Taxable dividends received by a corporation are not subject to the gross-up rule. Therefore, the actual dividend of $8,000 (i.e., ($11,700/1.17) – 2,000)) should be all that is included in the calculation of income under Division and deducted in the calculation of taxable income.

Problem 12

Net income per financial statements		$568,400
Add:		
Income tax provision	$446,600	
Depreciation [$20,000 + 15,000]	35,000	
Taxable capital gain on sale of land (Note 2)	55,250	
Prepaid expenses expensed for accounting [9,000/10,000 × $5,000]	4,500	
Meals and entertainment (Note 3)	4,050	
Club dues, par. 18(1)(*l*)	5,000	
Management bonus not paid within 179 days after the year end [ssec. 78(4)]	90,000	
Financing costs (par. 20(1)(*e*) – ⅘ × $600)	480	
Foreign taxes withheld, netted from accounting income (Note 4)	300	
		641,180
		1,209,580
Less:		
CCA (Note 1)	63,440	
Gain on sale of land	130,000	
Capital dividend not taxable	3,800	(197,240)
Net income for federal tax purposes		1,012,340
Less:		
Dividends from taxable Canadian corporations [S.112]		
Deemed dividend on preferred shares	2,500	
Dividend from XYZ Inc.	3,000	(5,500)
Net capital losses from capital loss of previous years [$12,000 / ¾ × ½]*		(8,000)
Taxable income		$998,840

* The inclusion rate for capital gains in 1999 was ¾ and, therefore, the net capital loss needs to be adjusted to the 2018 inclusion rate before being applied.

Note 1 — Capital Cost Allowance

	Class 1	Class 1b	Class 8	Class 10
Opening balance	$ 83,000	$ Nil	$ 60,000	$ 40,000
Additions	145,000(c)	200,000(b)	20,000	0
Lesser of cost and proceeds				(600)
Half-net		(100,000)	(10,000)	0
	228,000	$100,000	70,000	39,400
Rate	4%	6%	20%	30%
CCA	$ 9,120	$ 6,000	$ 14,000	$ 11,820

	Class 10.1	Class 10.1	Class 43
Opening balance	$ 0	$ 0	$ Nil
Additions	30,000(a)	30,000(a)	90,000
Lesser of cost and proceeds			
Half-net	(15,000)	(15,000)	(45,000)
	15,000	15,000	45,000
Rate	30%	30%	30%
CCA	$ 4,500	$ 4,500	$ 13,500

Total CCA = $63,440

(a) A separate class is required for each automobile costing greater than $30,000. The addition to the CCA class is limited to $30,000 since the company would have received an HST input tax credit on $30,000 for each car.

(b) The new administrative building is eligible for a 6% CCA rate, provided that it is put into a separate class 1b from the existing buildings.

(c) The warehouse transferred from the sole shareholder using section 85, is added to Class 1. Since the shareholder and the corporation are related, the capital cost is limited to the shareholder's capital cost ($100,000) plus the taxed portion of the capital gain realized by the shareholder on the transfer (½ × $190,000 – $100,000 = $45,000). Therefore, the total addition to Class 1 is $145,000. The ½ year rule does not apply for 2018 since the property was owned by a related party for more than 365 days before the 2018 year end of the corporation.

Note 2 — Gain on Disposition of Land

Proceeds of disposition	$150,000
Less: adjusted cost base	(20,000)
Gain	130,000
Less: reserve [par. 40(1)(a)(iii)]	(19,500)
Capital gain	110,500
Inclusion rate	½
Taxable capital gain	$ 55,250

Reserve calculation
Lesser of:

(i) $\frac{4}{5} \times$ gain of $130,000 ..... $104,000

and

(ii) $\dfrac{\text{mortgage receivable, end of year}}{\text{total proceeds}} \times \text{capital gain}$

$\dfrac{\$ 22,500}{\$150,000} \times \$130,000$ ..... $ 19,500

Note 3 — Meals and Entertainment

Meals for salespeople	$ 3,000
Meals for entertaining clients	4,300
Seasons tickets	800
	8,100
Rate disallowed	50%
Disallowed portion	$ 4,050

Note 4 — Foreign Dividends

$1,700 is net of withholding tax of 15%. Therefore, withholding tax must be $1,700/(1 – 0.15) × 15% = $300.

Problem 13

Schedule 1

New income for the year			$ 496,900
Add:	Income taxes	$200,000	
	Amorization – cost of sales	128,000	
	– rental	3,000	
	– other	12,000	
	Charitable donations	2,000	
	Meals and entertainment (note 1)	15,500	
	Unpaid bonuses – employee	40,000	
	– shareholder	110,000	
	Restructuring cost (a reserve)	50,000	
	Write-down of investments	25,000	
	Loss of disposition of equipment	9,000	
	Dividend – Make-it and Save-it (Alberta) Inc.	60,000	654,500
			1,151,400
Deduct:	Inventory write-down	10,000	
	Capital cost allowance (note 2)		
	– Cl. 1	8,000	
	– Cl. 3	3,000	
	– Cl. 8	4,000	
	– Cl. 10	6,000	
	– Cl. 43	58,200	
	Gain on disposition of Plant #1	1,300,000	
	Income from Make-it and Save-it (Alberta) Inc.	100,000	(1,505,850)
			(354,450)
	Taxable capital gains (note 3)		525,000
Net Income			170,550
	Dividends (note 4)		(115,000)
	Donations		(2,000)
Taxable income			$ 53,550

Income Analysis

			Dividends		
	ABI	AII	Connected	Portfolio	Total
Securities				$ 5,000	$ 5,000
Make-it-Rich			$ 50,000		50,000
Make-it-and-Save-it			60,000		60,000
Rental		$ 30,400			30,400
TCG		525,000			525,000
Interest		7,500			7,500
ABI (Balance)	$ (507,350)				(507,350)
	$ (516,950)	$562,900	$110,000	$ 5,000	$160,950

Part I Tax

Federal tax 38% @$53,550	$ 20,349
Federal tax abatement 10% @$53,550	(5,355)
Small business deduction (note 5)	Nil
Tax reductions (ABI nil; AII > taxable income)	Nil
Additional refundable tax (note 7)	5,712
Part I tax	20,706
Less Dividend refund (note 6)	$ (6,131)
Net Part I tax (refund)	(25,425)

Part IV Tax

Dividend income subject to Part IV tax

Marketable securities — not connected ($5,000 × 38⅓%)	$ 1,917
Make-it-and Save-it (Alberta) Inc. — connected ($23,000 × 37.5%)	8,625
Make-it_Rich Investments Ltd. — connected ($19,167 × 100%)	19,167
Part IV tax	$ 29,709

Notes to Solution

1.   Meals and Entertainment

Concert tickets given to customers	$ 1,000
Meals and entertainment incurred by salespeople	22,000
Meals and entertainment incurred by management	8,000
	31,000
	× 50%
	$ 15,500

2.   Capital Cost Allowance

	Cl. 1	**Cl. 3**	**Cl. 3**	**Cl. 8**
Opening	$ —	$ 160,000	$60,000	$20,000
Additions	280,000[c]	—	—	—
Disposals	(120,000)[b]	(160,000)[a]	—	—
Net 1/2	(80,000)	—	—	—
	80,000	—	60,000	20,000
Rate	10%	5%	5%	20%
CCA	$ 8,000	$ —	$ 3,000	$ 4,000

Replacement property — elect on former business property

[a]   S. 13(4)(c) reduction of UCC

Lesser of:

(i) proceeds	$931,250	
(ii) capital cost	280,000	$280,000

Less:

Lesser of:

(i) excess of $280,000 (determined above) over UCC ($160,000)	$120,000	
(ii) cost of replacement property	500,000	(120,000)
		$160,000

[b]   Deemed proceeds of disposition under S. 13(4)(d) (equal to reduction calculated under S. 13(4)(c) above) $120,000

[c]   Building

Cost or replacement	$500,000
S. 44(1)(f) reduction for deferred gains (see note 3)	(220,000)
	$280,000

	Cl. 10	**Class 43**
Opening	$ 20,000	$ 200,000
Additions	—	105,000
Disposals	—	(6,000)
Net ½	—	(49,500)
	20,000	249,500
Rate	30%	30%
CCA	$ 6,000	$ 74,850

3. Taxable Capital Gains
   Replacement property
   Capital gain
   Land — Lessor of

   (1) Proceeds of dispostion $ 918,750
         ACB   (187,500)
             731,250

   (2) Proceeds of dispostion $ 918,750
         Replacement cost   (300,000)
             $ 618,750 $618,750

   Building — Lesser of

   (1) Proceeds of dispostion $ 931,250
         ACB   (280,000)
             $ 651,250

   (2) Proceeds of dispostion $ 931,250
         Replacement cost   (500,000)
             $ 431,250   431,250
                             1,050,000
                                     1/2
                             $525,000

4. Dividends
   Sec. 112 deduction

Marketable securities	5,000
Make-it and Save-it (Alberta) Inc.	60,000
Make-it-Rick Investments Ltd.	50,000
	$ 115,000

5. Small business deduction
   Active business income (loss) $(516,950)
   See Income Analysis
   Lesser of:

Active business income	$ Nil	
Annual business limit	$ 500,000	$ Nil
		× 17.5%
		$ Nil

6. Dividend Refund
   Lesser of   (1) 38⅓% × 300,000 = $ 115,000
              (ii) RDTOH =   46,131

7.   Additional Refundable Tax (ART)
       $10^2/3\%$ × lesser of:

       1. All = $562,900

       2. Taxable income – SBD amount = $ 53,550
         $53,550 – Nil =

ART = $10^2/3\%$ × $53,550 $ 5,712

Aggregate Investment Income (AII)

Net TCG for the year	$ 525,000	
less: net capital losses claimed	—	$525,000
Property income (Cdn. and Foreign)		
– Dividends	$ 115,000	
– Rental	30,400	
– Interest	7,500	
less: dividends deducted under Division C	(115,000)	$ 37,900
less: losses from property		—
		$562,900

Refundable Portion of Part I Tax
Least of:

1. $30^2/3\%$ × AII = $30^2/3\%$ × $562,900 $172, 623
   Less: NBFTC – 8% × FII =   Nil $172,623

2. $30^2/3\%$ × (TI – SBD amount – $100/38^2/3\%$ ×
   NBFTC – 4 × BFTC) = $30^2/3\%$ × (53,550 –
   Nil – Nil – Nil) $ 16,422

3. Part I tax = $20,706 $ 20,706

Lease amount = $16,422
Refundable Dividend Tax On Hand

Opening balance		$ Nil
Refundable Part I tax		16,422
Part IV tax		29,709
RDTOH at Dec. 31, 2018		$ 46,131

Problem 14

Note: *There are several alternative ways to approach this question. The following is an example of one approach.*

	Investments Owned by a Corporation	
In the Corporation		
Interest income	$11,000	
Dividends	24,000	
Capital gains—taxable portion	9,000	
Net income	44,000	
Dividends (sec. 112)	(24,000)	
Taxable income subject to Part I tax	$20,000	
Dividend income subject to Part IV tax	$24,000	
Aggregate investment income		
Interest	$11,000	
Taxable capital gains	9,000	
	$20,000	
Part I tax @ 50.67% of $20,000 (40.00% + 10.67%)	$ 10,133	
Part IV @ 38⅓% of $24,000	9,200	
Net tax before tax refund potentially available	19,333	19,333
Tax refund potentially available:		
Investment income × 30⅔% $ 6,133		
Part IV tax 9,200		
$15,333		
Dividend refund if $40,000 taxable dividend paid	(15,333)	
Dividend refund if $5,000 taxable dividend paid		
(i.e., $14,000 required - $9,000 capital dividend)		(1,917)
Total corporate tax	$ 4,000	$17,416

	Investments Owned by Ryan	Investments Owned by a Corporation	
In Ryan's Hands			
Employment income	$ 80,000	$ 80,000	$ 80,000
Interest income	11,000	0	0
Dividend (eligible)	24,000	24,000	5,000
Dividend (non-eligible)		16,000	
Add dividend gross-up (eligible)	9,120	9,120	1,900
Add dividend gross-up (non-eligible)		2,560	
Capital gains — taxable portion	9,000	0	0
Taxable income	$133,120	$131,680	$ 86,900
Federal Tax on $46,605 @ 15%	$ 6,991	$ 6,991	$ 6,991
on next $46,603 @ 20.5%	9,554	9,554	8,260
on balance @ 26%	10,377	10,003	
	$ 26,922	$ 26,548	$ 15,251
Personal tax credits	(2,450)	(2,450)	(2,450)
Dividend tax credit (eligible)	(4,975)	(4,975)	(1,036)
Dividend tax credit (non-eligible)		(1,862)	
Basic federal tax	$ 19,497	17,262	11,765
Provincial tax *	16,240	16,024	9,496
Provincial personal tax credits	(1,550)	(1,550)	(1,550)
Provincial dividend tax credit **	(4,145)	(4,844)	(864)
Total personal tax	$ 30,042	$ 26,892	$ 18,847
Total tax paid (corporate and personal)	$ 30,042	$ 30,892	$ 36,263

* The provincial personal tax has been calculated using provincial rates as set out in chapter 10 paragraph 10,250.

** Provincial dividend tax credits on eligible dividends assumed to be 5/11 of the gross up $4,145 ($9,120 × 5/11); on non-eligible dividends assumed to be 3/11 of the gross up $698 (2,560 × 3/11).

There is nominal tax cost related to the use of the corporation if the corporation pays out all of the corporation's after-tax earnngs to Ryan each year. However, if Ryan only pays $14,000 of dividends from the corporation, $9,000 of which the corporation can elect to pay to Ryan as a tax-free capital dividend, Ryan will incur a pre-payment of $5,372 of tax ($36,263 – $30,892) if the investments are held through a corporation. This is because the effective corporate tax rate on the retained income exceeds Ryan's personal marginal tax rate.

Therefore, there are no tax advantages to incorporating this investment income.

Note:

The gross-up for Ryan personally on $24,000 of public company dividends is 38%. The federal dividend tax credit is 6/11 of the gross-up and the provincial dividend tax credit is assumed to be 5/11 of the gross-up.

If Ryan's corporation receives $24,000 of dividends from public corporations, this amount can be added to the General Rate Income Pool (GRIP) of the corporation. Thus when the entire after-tax earnings of the corporation of $40,000 [$44,000 income less $4,000 corporate tax] is paid to Ryan as a dividend, $24,000 can be elected to be paid out of GRIP and the remaining $16,000 is considered paid out of LRIP. Therefore, a dividend up to $24,000 is subject to the 38% gross-up and related dividend tax credit and a dividend in excess of this amount is subject to a 16% gross-up and related dividend tax credit.

Other considerations:

1. The assets could be transferred to the corporation without incurring a tax liability on the accrued gains by making a proper election under section 85 of the *Income Tax Act.*

2. The corporation would provide greater flexibility in the timing of the receipts of income subject to personal tax.

3. The corportation provides a vehicle for estate planning.

4. There would be additional administrative costs in maintaining the corporation (i.e., legal, accounting, capital tax, etc.)

5. The potention for double taxation exists wheen the corporation is used. The accrual gain on the assets will be taxed in the corporation when the assets are sold. This same accrued gain would be reflected in the shares of the corporation and would be taxed on their disposal.

Problem 15

Old Employer's Stock Option

- Can acquire 1,000 shares and dispose of all 2,000 shares prior to December 31, 2018.

- There will be an employment income inclusion in 2018:

  2,000 shares × ($100 − $15) = $170,000

- 300 of the shares will qualify for the par. 110(1)(*d*.1) deduction, due to their holding period in excess of two years:

  300 shares × ($100 − $15) × ½ = $12,750

- Interest on bank loan may not be deductible since the loan is for the purpose of acquiring shares for a quick resale and the only income that could result is a capital gain, since there will be too little time in the holding period to receive dividends. This interest expense would still be denied since it was not incurred to earn income from business or property.

Public Co. Compensation Package

- Moving allowance is taxable under par. 6(1)(*b*) since it is not one of excepted allowances.

- Only certain moving expenses are deductible under sec. 62 and, hence, there may be a net taxable amount, (i.e., house hunting expenses).

- One-half of a reimbursement of an actual loss in excess of $15,000 on the disposition of the family home upon a change of employment location is a taxable benefit (ssec. 6(22)).

- Capital loss on family home is nil since it is personal-use property.

- Monthly travel allowance is taxable unless it is reasonable in the circumstances (spar. 6(1)(*b*)(v) for taxpayers involved in negotiating contracts).

- If his reasonable travel expenses exceed his allowance, he may deduct them under par. 8(1)(*h*) and (*h*.1), provided that he is required to pay them according to the terms of his contract; of course, in order to deduct travel expenses, the travel allowance must be included in his income on the basis that it is not reasonable.

- A club membership paid by an employer will not be considered to be a taxable benefit under par. 6(1)(*a*) by administrative practice (IT-470R — ARCHIVED) as long as the membership is principally for the employer's advantage.

- Premiums on medically-related plans:
    - Liberty Mutual Extended Health Care and Sun Life-Drug plan are specifically exempted as a taxable benefit under par. 6(1)(*a*) as these are private health insurance premiums.
    - Sun Life income protection is not taxable as employment income per par. 6(1)(*a*), but any benefits received from said plan are taxable under par. 6(1)(*f*), since the employer paid all or any part of the premium.

- Pension plan:
    - Would have a deduction under paragraph par. 8(1)(*m*) of $3,000 (2% × $150,000) for his premiums paid into the plan;

- He would still have a potential RRSP contribution to his or his spouse's plan which will depend on the dollar limit for the year, his prior year's earned income, and his pension adjustment for the prior year.

- Stock option:

  - Employment inclusion of $12 per share in 2019 (year of exercise) ($20 – $8).

  - ACB of shares increased by a similar amount ($12) so that it equals the FMV at time of acquisition ($20).

  - Since the option price ($8) is less than or equal to the FMV at the grant date ($10) no deduction is available in Division C [par 110(1)(*d*)].

- Group term life insurance premium is a taxable benefit. Hence there is a taxable benefit of $800.

Loans

- Would not be a shareholder at the time of the loan, so ssec. 15(2) not relevant.

- Subsection 80.4(1) (by virtue of employment) would impute — a benefit on the

  (a) housing loan at the lesser of:

  1. prescribed rate in force at the time the loan was made (5%)

  2. the changing prescribed rate in force during the year the loan is outstanding (5%)

  plus

  (b) car loan at the changing prescribed rate per quarter during the year the loan is outstanding (5%)

  minus

  2% provided paid by January 30 of 2019 on both loans

  The housing loan rate at the time the loan was made is changed on each fifth anniversary of the loan.

  The interest on the car loan (paid in the year plus imputed benefit) would be deductible under par. 8(1)(*j*) because the imputed interest benefit is deemed to be interest paid in the year (sec. 80.5) to the extent (based on kilometres) the car was actually used in course of his employment.

Problem 16

Inclusions in Income

Employment income		
Salary	$ 70,000	
Car — Operating benefit, Note 1	1,139	
Car — Standly charge, Note 2	2,278	
Housing loan benefit, Note 3	738	
Total employment income		$ 74,155
RRSP income attributed from spousal plan		2,000
Interest income attributed from children ($00 × 2)		400
Rental loss		(1,000)
Taxable capital gain (Note 5)		10,500
		86,055

Deductions from Income

Less:

Moving expenses remaining from 2017 ($8,000 – $5,400) to extent of employment income in 2018 of $75,187		$ 2,600	
RRSP contribution deductible, Note 4		11,160	
			(13,760)
Net income			72,295
Less:			
Capital gains deduction, Note 7			(7,886)
Taxable income			$ 64,409

Federal Tax Payable

Tax on $46,605 @ 15%	$ 6,991	
Tax on $17,804 @ 20.5%	3,650	
$64,409	$ 10,641	
Non-refundable tax credits		
Basic	$ 11,809	
CPP	2,594	
EI	858	
	$ 15,261	
	× 15%	(2,289)
Federal tax payable		$ 8,352

Notes:

1. **6(1)(e) Standby Charge Benefit**

    Mr. Grocer is allowed the standby charge reduction since the car is used greater than 50% for business.

    $$\frac{10,500}{20,004} \times 2\% \times 12 \text{ months} \times (\$16,000 + 2,080) = \underline{\$2,278}$$

2. **6(1)(k) Benefit on Operating Costs Calculation**

    Lesser of:

(i) Total kilometres	30,000	
Less: business use kilometers	19,500	
Personal use kilometers	10,500 × $0.26 = $2,730	

    (ii) ½ × $2,278 = $1,139

    Lesser is $1,139.

    Mr. Grocer qualifies for the alternative method of determining a benefit derived from employer paid automobile operating costs under par. 6(1)(k), since he drove the automobile greater than 50% for employment purposes in the year and assuming that he notified his employer before December 31, 2018. The operating benefit under the alternative method results in a decreased income inclusion.

3. **Loan Benefit Calculation**

    The loan would qualify as a home purchase loan and home relocation loan.

    Remember,

$60,000	received December 1, 2017
$12,000	($60,000/5) repaid December 1, 2018
$48,000	outstanding from December 1 to December 31, 2018

    Benefit is calculated using the

    Lesser of:

    (a) prescribed rate in effect at the time the loan was made (3%); and

    (b) prescribed rates in effect during the year while the loan was outstanding.

Calculation (the effect if leap year is ignored):

01/01/18 to 31/03/18	2% × 90/365 × $60,000 =	$296
01/04/18 to 01/12/18	1% × 245/365 × $60,000 =	403
02/12/18 to 31/12/18	1% × 30/365 × $48,000 =	39
		$738

4. <u>Deductive RRSP Contribution</u>
Least of:
(a) 2017 earned income × 18%

Employment income	$65,000
Rental loss	(3,000)
Earned income	$62,000
	× 18%
	$11,160

(b) Amounts contributed

Self	$ 8,000
Spousal	$ 6,000
	$14,000

(c) limit for 2018 — $26,230

5. <u>Capital Gain</u>

Proceeds	$26,000
Less: adjusted cost base	5,000
Capital gain	$21,000
Taxable capital gain ($^1/_2$)	$10,500

6. <u>Cumulative Investment Loss Calculation</u>

2015 Income — dividends	$300 × 1.25	$ 375
2016 Income — dividends	$300 × 1.25	375
2017 Income — dividends	$300 × 1.18	236
2017 Expenses — rental loss		(3,000)
2018 Income — interest from children		400
2018 Expenses — rental loss		(1,000)
CNIL account		$(2,614)

7. <u>Capital Gains Deduction</u>

Taxable capital gains	$10,500
Less: CNIL, Note 6	(2,614)
Capital gain deduction	$ 7,886

Comprehensive Section

Problem 17

(A)

	Proceeds	Business Income	Investment Income	Capital Dividend	RDTOH
Opening balance				$ 85,000	$10,000
Cash	$ 47,000				
Marketable securities, Note 1	35,000		$(15,000)	(15,000)	
Inventory	82,000	$(32,000)			
Land, Note 2	460,000		120,000	120,000	
Building, Note 3	1,600,000	180,000	150,000	150,000	
Liabilities	(134,000)				
Income tax, Note 4	(158,800)	$148,000	$255,000		78,200
RDTOH, Note 5	88,200				$88,200
	$ 2,019,400			$340,000	

(B) Funds available for distribution $ 2,019,400
Less: paid-up capital (150,000)

Deemed dividend on winding-up (s. 84(2)) $ 1,869,400
Less: capital dividend elected under s. 83(2) (s. 88(2)(b)(i)) (340,000)

Deemed taxable dividend (sufficient to clear RDTOH) $ 1,529,400

(C) Calculation of taxable capital gain on the disposition of shares on the winding-up:

Actual proceeds from distribution		$ 2,019,400
Less: deemed dividend		(1,869,400)
Proceeds on disposition (s. 54)		$ 150,000
Cost		(150,000)
Capital gain		$ Nil
Taxable capital gain		$ Nil

Net cash retained after sale of assets and subsequent winding-up:

Funds distributed on wind-up		$ 2,019,400
Tax on incremental income from distribution:		
Deemed taxable dividend	$ 1,529,400	
Gross-up (16%)	244,704	
Grossed-up dividend	$ 1,774,104	
Taxable capital gain	—	
Capital gains exemption (Note 6)	—	
Incremental taxable income	$ 1,774,104	
Combined tax rate of 44%	780,606	
Less: approximate combined dividend tax credit = gross-up	(244,704)	(535,902)
Net cash retained		$ 1,483,498

(D)   Sale of shares for $2,000,000

Proceeds of disposition	$ 2,000.000
Adjusted cost base	150,000
Capital gain	$ 1,850,000
Taxable capital gain ($\frac{1}{2} \times$ $1,850,000)	$ 925,000
Capital gains exemption assuming Scrum Limited is a qualifying small business corporation ($\frac{1}{2} \times$ $848,252)	424,126
Taxable income	$ 500,874
Tax thereon at 44%	$ 220,385
Net proceeds ($2,000,000 − $220,874)	$ 1,779,615

Conclusion: Wind-up and distribution will provide Lach with $296,117 less than a straight sale of shares ($1,483,498 vs. $1,779,615).

However, if on the sale of assets, the cash is retained in the corporation and the wind-up does not occur, personal tax of $535,902 is deferred indefinitely. The corporation will have cash of $2,019,400 − RDTOH $88,200 = $1,931,200 to invest.

Notes:

(1)   Marketable Securities

Proceeds of disposition	$ 35,000
Cost	(65,000)
Capital loss	$ (30,000)
Allowable capital loss ($\frac{1}{2} \times$ $30,000)	$ (15,000)
	$ (30,000)
Capital dividend account ($\frac{1}{2} \times$ $30,000)	$ (15,000)

(2)   Land

Proceeds of disposition	$ 460,000
ACB	(220,000)
Capital gain	$ 240,000
Taxable capital gain ($\frac{1}{2} \times$ $240,000)	$ 120,000
Capital dividend account ($\frac{1}{2} \times$ $240,000)	$ 120,000

(3)   Buiding

Proceeds of disposition	$ 1,600,000
Capital cost	1,300,000
Capital gain	$ 300,000
Taxable capital gain ($\frac{1}{2} \times$ $300,000)	$ 150,000
Capital dividend account ($\frac{1}{2} \times$ $300,000)	$ 150,000
UCC	$ 1,120,000
Lesser of cost and proceeds	(1,300,000)
Recapture	$180,000

(4)　Income Taxes

Active business income

Inventory	$ (32,000)
Building recapture	180,000
	$ 148,000

Tax @ 20% on $148,000		$ 29,600
Investment income		
Marketable securities, allowable capital loss	(15,000)	
Land, taxable capital gain	120,000	
Building, taxable capital gain	150,000	
	$ 255,000	
Tax @ 50⅔%		129,200
Part I tax		$ 158,800

(5)　RDTOH

Opening balance	$ 10,000
30⅔% of investment income $255,000)	$ 78,200
	$ 88,200

A distribution of $230,087 (i.e., $88,200 / 38⅓%) in taxable dividends will be required to receive a dividend refund of $88,200, which clears the RDTOH account.

(6)　CGE

At the time the company is wound up and the disposition of shares takes place, the only asset in the company is cash, which is not used in an active business. Therefore, immediately before the determination time the company is not an SBC and therefore cannot be a QSBC.

Problem 18

(a)

Computation of the federal Part I tax payable by Fine Foods Inc. for the December 31, 2017 taxation year:

Net income before taxes		$ 1,080,648
Add:		
Depreciation per financial statements	$ 26,050	
Financing expenses (Note 2)	7,600	
Racquet club memberships (par. 18(1)(*l*))	9,500	
Taxable capital gains (Note 4)	30,000	73,150
		$ 1,153,798
Deduct:		
Gain on sale of fixed assets	$ 96,000	
Capital dividend received (par. 83(2)(*b*))	5,000	
CCA (Note 3)	15,960	116,960
Net income for federal tax purposes		1,036,838
Less: taxable dividends received (sec. 112)		60,000
Taxable income		$ 976,838

Part I Tax

Tax at 38% on $976,838 of taxable income		$ 371,198
Federal tax abatement ($976,838 × 10%)		(97,684)
		273,514
Additional refundable tax (Note 8)		3,733
Less: Small business deduction (Note 6)		(27,000)
Tax reduction (Note 7)		(102,939)
Part I tax payable		$ 147,308

Notes:

(1) The amount paid for landscaping of grounds is specifically allowed as a deduction (par. 20(1)(*aa*)).

(2) Fine Foods Inc. can deduct only 20% of the financing costs incurred during the year (par. 20(1)(*e*)) (20% × $9,500). Therefore, $7,600 (being $9,500 – $1,900) must be added back to income for tax purposes.

(3) CCA:

Class	Opening Balance	Additions	Lower of cost and proceeds	CCA	Ending Balance
1	$ 99,000	—	—	$ 3,960	$ 95,040
3	210,000	—	$50,000	8,000	152,000
8	2,000	—	2,500	(500)	—
10.1	—	$30,000*	—	4,500	25,500
				$15,960	

* 30,000 is the maximum addition to CCA class assuming the company is registered for HST.

(4)   <u>Sale of Assets:</u>

Land	Proceeds of disposition		$ 50,000	
	ACB		20,000	
	Capital gain			$ 30,000
Building	Proceeds of disposition		$ 80,000	
	ACB		50,000	
	Capital gain			$ 30,000
	Capital gains			$ 60,000
	Taxable portion			× 1/2
	Taxable capital gains			$ 30,000

(5)   <u>Income:</u>

	Active Business Income	Investment Income	Dividend Income	Total
Dividend income			$60,000	$ 60,000
Interest income from GIC		$ 5,000		5,000
Rental income — ancillary	$ 22,000			22,000
Interest income (s. 129(6))	12,000			12,000
Taxble capital gains		30,000		30,000
Business income	907,838			907,838
Division B income	$941,838	$35,000	$60,000	$ 1,036,838

(6)   <u>Small Business Deduction:</u>
18% of the least of:

(a) active business income (Note 5)	$941,838	
(b) taxable income (no foreign tax credits)	$976,838	
(c) business limit	$150,000	$ 27,000

(7)   <u>Tax reduction:</u>

Taxable income		$ 976,838
Less: 100/13 × M&P profit deduction	Nil	
100/18 × small business deduction	150,000	
AII	35,000	(185,000)
Net		$ 791,838
13% of $791,838		$ 102,939

(8)   <u>Additional refundable tax:</u>
$10\frac{2}{3}\%$ × lesser of:
1. AI = $35,000
2. TI − SBD amount = $976,838 − 150,000 = $826,838
$10\frac{2}{3}\%$ × 35,000 = $3,733

(b)

Computation of the refundable dividend tax on had balance at the end of the year and the dividend refund for the taxation year.

RDTOH:

Refundable portion of Part I tax:

(a) $30\frac{2}{3}\% \times \text{AII} = 30\frac{2}{3}\% \times 35,000 = 10,733$

Less: NBFTC – 8% × FI   – $ 10,733

(b) $30\frac{2}{3}\% \times (\text{TI} - \text{SBD amt} - 100/38\frac{2}{3} \times \text{NBFTC} - 4 \times \text{BFTC}) = 30\frac{2}{3}\% \times \$826,838$ $253,564

Part I tax payable	$148,058
Refundable portion of Part I tax	
Lease of amounts	$ 10,733
Part IV tax payable ($60,000 × 38⅓%)	$ 23,000

Refundable Dividend Tax On Hand (RDTOH)

RDTOH at end of preceding tax year	$ 25,000
Deduct: Dividend refund for preceding tax year	(5,000)
	$ 20,000
Add: Refundable portion of Part I tax	10,733
Part IV tax payable	23,000
RDTOH at end of taxation year	$ 53,733

Dividend Refund

Taxable dividend paid in the year ($30,000 × 38⅓%)	$ 11,500(A)
RDTOH at end of the taxation year	$ 53,733(B)
Dividend refund – the lesser of amounts (A) and (B)	$ 11,500

(c)

Computation of the maximum capital dividend that can be paid to the shareholders (par. 89(1)(b)).

Capital dividend account balance, beginning of year	$ 4,000
Add: Capital dividends received from Good Grub Corp.	5,000
Non-taxable portion of capital gains ($60,000 – 30,000)	30,000
Capital dividend account balance, end of year	$ 39,000

Problem 19

The main issues in this case relate to:

- compensation, and

- how to get cash out of a corporation.

1. Compensation

(a) Bonus

- The pre-tax profit in the corporation is $550,000, so he could pay himself a bonus of $50,000 on which he would pay about 50% tax, leaving $25,000 after tax.

- Alternatively, the corporation could retain the income and pay tax at 28% (15% federal and 13% provincial) leaving about 72%, or $36,000, after tax.

- The tax deferral is (50% − 28%) × $50,000 = $11,000.

- If the funds are kept in the corporation, then the $36,000 could be paid out later as a dividend from GRIP with personal tax of approximately 31% (after the 38% gross-up and tax credit) on this dividend, leaving about $24,840 after tax.

- If a bonus is not paid, then:

  — corporate tax instalment options will be based on this higher tax liability;

  — the final tax instalment will be due at the end of the second month instead of at the end of the third month following year end;

  — some tax is deferred with a little double tax on payment of the dividend.

- If a bonus is declared, then:

  — Was there a valid liability at December 31?

  — Is it reasonable?

  — Will it be paid before 180 days after the year end?

  — Some double tax will be avoided; in fact, a slight tax savings will be realized.

(b) Salary to Betty

- Is the salary reasonable in relation to the work performed?

- Especially important since she is not dealing at arm's length.

- What is reasonable to pay a secretary-treasurer for the activities she performs?

- Was this expense incurred to earn income, since her activity was to be involved with local charities?

- If disallowed, then double tax; no deduction in the company but income to the recipient.

(c) Salaries to children

- What is a reasonable amount to pay Scott and Kelly?

- Was this expense incurred to earn income?

- If disallowed, then double tax; no deduction in the company but income to the recipient.

(d) Reorganization to involve Betty in share ownership and provide her with dividend income

- Given the excess cash it is holding, the corporation may not be a small business corporation (SBC) (may not meet the 90% test).

- Grant cannot crystallize to use up his capital gain exemption if the company does not qualify as an SBC.

- He might consider purifying the company by paying out the PUC, paying off liabilities, or paying a dividend, etc.

- The corporate attribution rules in subsection 74.4(2) may apply to deem an interest benefit on the full value of the shares received as consideration less any interest received and 5/4 times any dividend received.

2. Methods of Receiving Cash from the Company

   (a) Paid-up capital reduction

   - The paid-up capital of the corporation appears to be $20,000.

   - Now that Grant owns all the shares, he can reduce the paid-up capital of the company by $20,000 and there will be no deemed dividend under subsection 84(4).

   - A PUC reduction will cause a corresponding reduction in his ACB, but since his ACB is $40,000 before the reduction this will only reduce his ACB to $20,000.

   (b) Arm's length ACB

   - Grant can transfer his shares to a holding company under subsection 85(1), elect at whatever value he chooses between his ACB and FMV, and take back cash equal to his arm's length ACB without triggering a subsection 84.1 deemed dividend.

   - This is one way of getting some extra cash out of the corporation tax free, i.e., the $20,000 by which his ACB exceeds the PUC.

   (c) Company Loan for the Cottage [T-119R3]]

   - Interest paid on a mortgage taken out to buy a cottage personally will not be deductible.

   - They can borrow from the company but need to assess subsections 15(2), 80.4(1), and 80.4(2).

   - Who should borrow the money, Grant or Betty?

   - This withdrawal of cash will probably not cause the corporation to become a SBC, since the cash has been replaced with an investment.

3. Other Issues

   (a) Valuation

   - Is the company really worth $1,200,000, or is most of that value personal goodwill of Grant?

   (b) Holding company

   - Consider setting up a holding company to separate the excess cash from the business liabilities.

   - After the holding company has been established, pay a dividend.

   - On the transfer to the holding company, the capital gain exemption can be crystallized by electing under subsection 85(1).

   - Betty could be included in the ownership, but corporate attribution [c. 74.4(2)] needs to be considered.

   - He can receive cash on the transfer equal to the ACB without triggering a deemed dividend under section 84.1.

Problem 20

(A) Comparison of taxes of proprietorship vs. corporation

Proprietorship

Net income per income statement	$ 60,000
Less: RRSP contribution (18% of $35,000)	6,300
Taxable income	$ 53,700
Tax on first $46,605 @ 25%	$ 11,651
Tax on next $7,095 @ 32.5%	2,306
Total	$ 13,957
Personal tax credits	(3,300)
Net tax	$ 10,657

Corporation

Income for tax purposes	$ 60,000
Less: salary to Soul	35,000
Taxable income	$ 25,000
Tax @ 15.5% (38% – 10% – 18% + 5.5%)	(3,875)
Retained in the corporation available for distribution	$ 21,125

Shareholder

Employment income		$ 35,000
Dividend income ($21,125 x 1.16%)		24,505
Less: RRSP (18% of $35,000)		(6,300)
Taxable income		$ 53,205
Tax on first $46,605 @ 25%	$ 11,651	
Tax on next $6,600 @ 32.5%	2,145	
Total		$ 13,796
Personal tax credits		(3,300)
Dividend tax credit (assumed equal to gross up on dividend above)		(3,380)
Net tax		$ 7,116

Comparison of taxes

Taxes on proprietorship income		$ 10,657
Taxes through corporation:		
Corporate tax	$ 3,875	
Personal tax	7,116	10,991
Tax savings (cost) of corporation		(334)[1]

Other considerations

— there is a tax cost/disadvantage to the corporation

— however, there may be other advantages of the corporate form

   — the possibility of deferring tax, if funds are retained in the corporation

   — potential limited liability

   — family income splitting using a "small business corporation" engaged in active business in Canada

— the children could own shares (minor child's shares should be held in trust) to allow for the payment of dividends from profits of future expansion at a low or no tax cost. However, the rules related to tax on split income and the related requirements for involvement in the business of children at various ages would need to be taken into consideration before incurring any costs to set up a structure that allows for this

— similarly, wife could own shares for the same purpose, but again, the rules related to tax on split income would need to be reviewed in light of the spouse's involvement in the business

— potential estate freeze of the business assets

— separation of business and personal activities

— availability of RPP to the owner-manager and family members as well as other fringe benefits that can be provided to such employees at a low or no after-tax cost (e.g., loans, car, insurance, and private medical coverage)

— stabilization of income to individual and timing flexibility

— availability of $848,252 capital gains exemption to each individual shareholder, if shares are of a small business corporation and meet certain other conditions

— continuity of separate legal entity

— disadvantages of incorporation

— cost of incorporation

— cost of compliance with laws

— loss of availability of business and capital losses to offset personal income

— capital gains deduction not available to a corporation

(B) Tax implications of transferring assets to a corporation

Items not transferred under ssec. 85(1) (transfer at FMV for debt consideration)

	Tax value	FMV	Transfer	Debt	Shares	Income
Cash	$ 2,000	$ 2,000	$ 2,000	$ 2,000	Nil	Nil
Equipment	8,000	3,000	3,000	3,000	Nil	Nil[2]
A/R (use sec. 22)	500	500	500	500	Nil	Nil[3]
Inventory	40,000	40,000	40,000	40,000	Nil	Nil[4]
	$ 50,500	$ 45,500	$ 45,500	$ 45,500	Nil	Nil

Items transferred under ssec. 85(1)

	Tax value	FMV	Elected amount	Consideration Debt	Pref. shs.[5]	Income
Land	$ 80,000	$140,000	$130,000	$ 130,000	$ 10,000	$ 25,000*
Building	169,000	360,000	169,000	169,000	191,000	Nil
Goodwill	7,500	20,000	7,500	7,500	12,500	Nil
	$ 256,500	$520,000	$306,500	$ 306,500	$ 213,500	
Liabilities assumed				163,700		
New debt issued . . .				$ 142,800		

* Taxable capital gain to offset net capital losses of $25,000. Add the full capital gain ($25,000 x 1/2 = $50,000) to the ACB of the land.

Cost of consideration received

Elected amount		$306,500
Allocated to debt consideration:		
Debt assumed.	$163,700	
New debt issued	142,800	306,500
Cost of preferred shares		Nil

PUC of preferred shares

Legal stated capital (LSC) of preferred shares			$213,500
Less: Ssec. 85(2.1) reduction in PUC			
(i) increase in LSC of all shares on transfer	$ 213,500(A)		
(ii) corporation's cost of property under ssec. 85(1) (i.e., elected amount)	$306,500		
FMV of non-share consideration	306,500		
Excess, if any		Nil (B)	
PUC reduction	(A – B)		213,500
PUC for tax purposes.			Nil

— NOTES TO SOLUTION

(1) Due to imperfections in tax rates preventing perfect integration.

(2) The terminal loss is denied. The capital cost addition to UCC to the corporation will be $3,000. Soul will hold a notional asset in Class 8 with a value of $5,000 in the class.

(3) Add back the $100 reserve and deduct a $100 business loss, due to the election under section 22. The result is net income of nil.

(4) It is not necessary to transfer the inventory, in this case, by electing under subsection 85(1), because there is no income to defer.

(5) Shares should be taken such that fair market value of total consideration from the corporation equals the fair market value of assets transferred. This will avoid any problem with the benefit rule which would arise if the wife and/or children own shares in the corporation.

Problem 21

Part A

Income per the financial statements		$ 944,000
Add: items not deductible for tax purposes:		
Bonuses unpaid 180 days after the end of the tax year		
($200,000 + $400,000)		600,000
Non-deductible club dues ($4,500 – $200)		4,300
Non-deductible portion of meals and entertainment expenses		
$13,200 × 50%		6,600
Non-deductible portion of automobile allowances		
Allowance	$ 15,960	
Deductible portion ($0.55 × 5,000 + $0.49 × 2,000) × 4	14,920	1,040
Advertising in a foreign magazine aimed at the Canadian market	8,000	
Prepaid advertising in the Canadian magazine		
($13,000 × ½)	6,500	14,500
Donations		66,000
Amortization		180,000
Accounting fee for arranging financing ($4,000 × 80%)		3,200
Interest during period of construction and relating to the construction		28,000
Taxable capital gain on the sale of shares		
$120,000 – $20,000	$ 100,000	
less capital gains reserve		
lesser of		
(1) $100,000 × ⅘ = $80,000		
(2) $100,000 × $90,000/$120,000 = $75,000	(75,000)	
	25,000 × ½	$ 12,500
Deduct: items deductible for tax purposes:		
Gain on the sale of the shares		(100,000)
SR&ED expenditures $500,000 – $200,000	$ 300,000	
ITC claimed	(175,000)	(125,000)
Landscaping		(50,000)

CCA: Class 13, Leasehold improvements

Lessor of: (a) ⅕ × $30,000 = $6,000

(b) $30,000/(3 + 3) = $5,000 × ½ $ 2,500

Class 1 warehouse:

Material	$316,000	
Labour	320,000	
Interest during construction	28,000	
Utilities service connection . . .	14,000*	
	678,000	
	× 6% × ½	20,340
Other	200,000	(222,840)
Net income for tax purposes		$1,362,300

    * This solution assumes the utilities service connection cost was incurred during the construction period and thus the cost has not been expensed but instead has been added to the cost of the building in accordance with ssec. 18(3.1). If the utilities service connection was done outside the construction period, it is fully deductible.

Part B

Division C deductions

Net income for tax purposes (Part A)	$1,362,300
Donations to registered charities, not to exceed $1,362,300 × 75% = $1,021,725	$ (66,000)
Dividends from taxable Canadian corporations ($12,000 + $43,000)	$ (55,000)
Net capital losses (limited to taxable capital gains)*	(12,500)
Non-capital losses**	(200,000)
Taxable income	$1,028,800

    * Available $27,500

    ** These non-capital losses (as well as the net capital losses) became losses of Ever EZ when Sub Ltd was wound up in 2017. The losses are available to use starting the year after the winding-up, which is the 2018 taxation year.

Problem 22

Part A

Tax Implications of Acquisition

Deemed Taxation Year-End

On July 16, 2018, Tasty will acquire control of Yummy, and Yummy is subject to a loss restriction event. The rules in the *Income Tax Act* (ssec. 249(4)) deem Yummy to have a taxation year end immediately prior to the loss restriction event. Therefore, Yummy will have a taxation year ending July 15, 2018, which will cover the period January 1, 2018 to July 15, 2018.

Consequences of a taxation year end include:

- Corporate tax returns must be filed for Yummy within six months of this deemed year end (by January 15, 2019).

- Any CCA claimed in this deemed year end must be prorated for a short taxation year ($^{196}/_{365}$).

Accrued Losses at July 15, 2018

The *Income Tax Act* requires certain unrealized losses to be realized for tax purposes when there has been a loss restriction event. Therefore, the non-capital loss for the taxation period ended July 31, 2018 should be calculated.

Adjustments to the loss include:

1. Ssec. 111(5.1) requires inherent terminal losses on each CCA class to be realized for tax purposes on a class by class basis. For Yummy, the losses that are realized by virtue of ssec. 111(5.1) are as follows:

    Class 10 $60,000 (FMV of $20,000 – UCC of $80,000)

2. Ssec. 10(1) requires that inventory be valued at the lower of cost and FMV. Therefore, the inherent loss in Yummy's inventory of $100,000 must also be realized on the acquisition of control.

Therefore, the non-capital loss of Yummy for the taxation period ending July 15, 2018 should recalculated to be:

Loss as per question	$120,000
Loss per S.111(5.1)	60,000
Loss per S.10(1)	100,000
	$280,000

Yummy can choose to recognize accrued recapture by making a designation under par. 111(4)(*e*). The effect of this designation on classes with accrued recapture would be to reduce the non-capital loss of Yummy for the period ending July 15, 2018. Elections can be done on the following assets:

Maximum Designation

Class 3	$ 50,000	(cost of $400,000 – UCC of $350,000)
Class 8	10,000	(FMV of $60,000 – UCC of $50,000)
	$ 60,000	

The minimum designations are $400,000 and $60,000, respectively, and the maximum designation for each class is the FMV.

If the designation is made under par. 111(4)(*e*) for both classes, the non-capital loss for the taxation period ending July 15, 2018 becomes $228,750. While the designation under par. 111(4)(*e*) is available, it may not be best to do it as the objective may be to maximize non-capital losses carried forward as it is expected that Yummy will be profitable very soon.

Net Capital Losses

At the time of the loss restriction event Yummy's net capital losses carried forward of $75,000 are lost by virtue of par. 111(4)(*a*). They will not be available after the deemed taxation year end ending July 15, 2018.

Also, the inherent capital loss in the marketable securities of $4,000 is triggered at the time of the loss restriction event (par. 111(4)(*d*)). Therefore, Yummy will have a net capital loss of $2,000 in its taxation year ending July 15, 2018 which will also be lost at the time of the loss restriction event. The ACB of the marketable securities is reduced to $8,000 (par. 111(4)(*c*)).

An election can be made (par. 111(4)(*e*)) to recognize accrued capital gains immediately before the loss restriction event to use up any net capital losses that exist. The deemed proceeds can be any amount between the ACB and the FMV of the elected asset.

The net capital losses that exist at July 15, 2018 are $77,000 ($75,000 + $2,000). This reflects gross capital losses of $154,000. Both the land (gain of $300,000) and the building ($50,000) have accrued capital gains as at July 15, 2018, which total $350,000.

If the land is elected on, a gross gain of $154,000 can be generated which will offset the capital losses that would otherwise be lost. The new ACB of the land after the election would be $354,000 ($200,000 + $154,000). Alternatively, Yummy could elect to recognize a $50,000 capital gain on the building and elect on the land to realize a capital gain of $104,000.

The full capital gain of $350,000 could be triggered, resulting in a taxable capital gain of $175,000. Of this gain, $77,000 would be offset by net capital losses with the remaining taxable capital gain of $98,000 reducing the non-capital loss for the taxation period ending July 15, 2018 to $190,750 ($288,750 – $98,000). However, triggering the entire gain may not be wise as Fred expects to turn Yummy around and make it profitable in the near future. He would likely want to have non-capital losses carried forward maximized in order to reduce taxable income in the future.

The loss for the taxation year ended July 15, 2018 will be as follows:

Sec. 3(a)	Business and property income		Nil
Sec. 3(b)	Taxable capital gain	$ 77,000	
	Allowable capital loss	(2,000)	75,000
Sec. 3(c)			75,000
Sec. 3(d)	Business loss		(288,750)
Division B income (technically cannot be negative)			(213,750)
Division C deductions:			
Net capital losses			(75,000)
Non-capital losses			0
Non-capital loss for the deemed year ended July 15, 2018			(288,750)
Non-capital loss balance December 31, 2017			(700,000)
Non-capital loss balance at July 16, 2018			$ (988,750)

Part B

Availability of Non-Capital Losses After the Loss Restriction Event

Ssec. 111(5) states that non-capital losses will be available for deduction after a loss restriction event only if the following conditions are satisfied:

1. The business of Yummy (restaurant supply business) must be carried on for profit, or with a reasonable expectation of profit throughout the year the losses are to be used (spar. 111(5)(a)(i)).

2. The losses can only be deducted to the extent of income from the restaurant supply business or from a business selling similar products or providing similar services (spar. 111(5)(a)(ii)).

Methods in Which Tasty Can Utilize Losses of Yummy

After the shares of Yummy have been acquired, Tasty could get access to these losses by using the following techniques:

1. **Amalgamate Tasty and Yummy** — By virtue of section 87 of the Income Tax Act, an amalgamation could take place on a tax-deferred basis. The losses of Yummy would be available to the amalgamated company by virtue of s. 87(2.1). Note that both Tasty and Yummy would have deemed year ends immediately before the amalgamation.

2. **Wind-up Yummy into Tasty** — By virtue of section 88 of the *Income Tax Act*, a wind-up of a parent and its wholly-owned subsidiary could take place on a tax-deferred basis. The losses of Yummy would be available to Tasty by virtue of ssec. 88(1.1). Note that the losses would be available for use in the first taxation year of Tasty that commences after the wind-up and in subsequent years.

3. **Transfer profitable assets from Tasty to Yummy under a tax-deferring basis using s. 85** — These assets would generate profits in Yummy — the losses of Yummy could then be applied against these profits.

4. **Run the business profitably** — Change financing structure.

5. **Increase prices to Tasty, if possible.**

For the losses to be available against the taxable income of Tasty, however, the business of Tasty must be a restaurant supply business or a business providing similar services or similar products. It will have to be determined as to whether the fast food restaurant business is providing similar products or similar services as the restaurant supply business. If it is not, the non-capital losses of Yummy will only be available to be used against income generated from the restaurant supply business.

Problem 23

The main tax issues in this case relate to:

- inventory valuation,
- liability for U.S. tax,
- the refinancing of the business, and
- foreign exchange.

(1) Inventory valuation

- Lower of cost or market or all at market are acceptable methods of valuing inventory for tax purposes (ssec. 10(1); Reg. 1800).
- Reserves for decline in the value of inventory are not allowed as a deduction for tax purposes (par. 18(1)(e)).
- A deduction is allowed if the decline is real and measurable as at year end.

(2) Sales in the United States

- It needs to be determined whether the company has a permanent establishment in the U.S.
    - If they do, then this will result in it having to file a U.S. tax return and pay tax in the U.S. on the profits of that permanent establishment.
- A business foreign tax credit would be available for any tax paid in the U.S. (ssec. 126(2)).
- The 10% federal abatement is not available for profits earned by a Canadian company carrying on business in the U.S.

(3) Refinancing Issues

(a) Personal guarantees

- Tax treatment of losses resulting from contributions made to the company as a result of a personal guarantee being called (IT-239R2).
    - These losses may be BILs if the company is a small business corporation and if the money was loaned to earn income from business or property (par. 39(1)(c)).
- Interest expense deductible if borrowing to meet obligation under personal guarantee (IT-445).
- Guarantee fees could be charged to show that the guarantees were made to earn income.

(b) Professional fees for the financing

- Legal fees for collateral mortgage, accounting fees for cash flows and the appraisers fees for the real estate appraisal can be deducted straight-line over five years (par. 20(1)(e)).

(c) Sale of shares

- Since the suppliers company is probably a SBC, the ABIL is available, since he deals at arm's length with the supplier (sec. 251, par. 39(1)(c); IT-219).

(d) Interest expense

- After the sale of the shares, interest on the full $50,000 loan will be deductible (ssec. 20.1(1)).
- He should secure the loan that he makes to the company.

(4) US dollar bank account

- Foreign exchange gains and losses on the money in this account would probably be income in nature, given that the bank account is for the collection of accounts receivable (IT-95R).